Ⓢ1885202

shakespearean criticism

"Thou art a Monument without a tomb,
And art alive still while thy Book doth
 live
And we have wits to read and praise to
give."

*Ben Jonson, from the preface
to the First Folio, 1623.*

Mr. WILLIAM SHAKESPEARES

COMEDIES, HISTORIES, & TRAGEDIES.

Published according to the True Originall Copies.

LONDON
Printed by Isaac Iaggard, and Ed. Blount. 1623.

Frontispiece to the First Folio (1623). By permission of the Folger Shakespeare Library.

shakespearean criticism

Excerpts from the Criticism of
William Shakespeare's Plays and Poetry,
from the First Published Appraisals
to Current Evaluations

Michelle Lee
Editor

GALE GROUP
THOMSON LEARNING

Detroit • New York • San Diego • San Francisco
Boston • New Haven, Conn. • Waterville, Maine
London • Munich

STAFF

Janet Witalec, Lynn M. Zott, *Managing Editors, Literature Product*
Kathy D. Darrow, Ellen McGeagh, *Content-Product Liaisons*
Michelle Lee, *Editor*
Mark W. Scott, *Publisher, Literature Product*

Jessica Menzo, Madeline S. Harris, *Associate Editors*
Jenny Cromie, *Technical Training Specialist*
Deborah J. Baker, Joyce Nakamura, Kathleen Lopez Nolan, *Managing Editors, Literature Content*
Susan M. Trosky, *Director, Literature Content*

Maria L. Franklin, *Permissions Manager*
Kim Davis, Debra Freitas, *Permissions Associates*

Victoria B. Cariappa, *Research Manager*
Sarah Genik, *Project Coordinator*
Tamara C. Nott, Tracie A. Richardson, *Research Associates*

Dorothy Maki, *Manufacturing Manager*
Stacy L. Melson, *Buyer*

Mary Beth Trimper, *Manager, Composition and Prepress*
Gary Leach, *Composition Specialist*

Barbara J. Yarrow, *Manager, Imaging and Multimedia Content*
Robyn V. Young, *Project Manager, Imaging and Multimedia Content*
Dean Dauphinais, *Senior Editor, Imaging and Multimedia Content*
Kelly A. Quin, *Editor, Imaging and Multimedia Content*
Leitha Etheridge-Sims, Mary K. Grimes, David G. Oblender, *Image Catalogers*
Lezlie Light, *Imaging Coordinator*
Randy Bassett, *Imaging Supervisor*
Robert Duncan, *Senior Imaging Specialist*
Dan Newell, Luke Rademacher, *Imaging Specialists*
Christine O'Bryan, *Graphic Specialist*

Since this page cannot legibly accommodate all copyright notices, the acknowledgments constitute an extension of the copyright notice.

While every effort has been made to secure permission to reprint material and to ensure the reliability of the information presented in this publication, the Gale Group neither guarantees the accuracy of the data contained herein nor assumes any responsibility for errors, omissions or discrepancies. Gale accepts no payment for listing; and inclusion in the publication of any organization, agency, institution, publication, service, or individual does not imply endorsement of the editors or publisher. Errors brought to the attention of the publisher and verified to the satisfaction of the publisher will be corrected in future editions.

This publication is a creative work fully protected by all applicable copyright laws, as well as by misappropriation, trade secret, unfair competition, and other applicable laws. The authors and editors of this work have added value to the underlying factual material herein through one or more of the following: unique and original selection, coordination, expression, arrangement, and classification of the information.

All rights to this publication will be vigorously defended.

Copyright © 2002 Gale Group, Inc.
27500 Drake Road
Farmington Hills, MI 48331-3535

All rights reserved, including the right of reproduction in whole or in part in any form.

Gale Group and Design is a trademark used herein under license.

Library of Congress Catalog Card Number 86-645085
ISBN 0-7876-5844-8
ISSN 0883-9123
Printed in the United States of America

10 9 8 7 6 5 4 3 2 1

Contents

Preface vii

Acknowledgments ix

List of Plays and Poems Covered in *SC* xi

Literary Criticism Series Advisory Board xv

The Comedy of Errors 1
   Introduction.. 1
   Overviews and General Studies 1
   Character Studies 17
   Production Reviews 27
   Themes 30
   Further Reading 57

The Merchant of Venice 58
   Introduction... 58
   Overviews and General Studies 59
   Character Studies 87
   Production Reviews 123
   Themes 127
   Further Reading 184

Pericles 186
   Introduction... 186
   Overviews and General Studies 186
   Character Studies 190
   Production Reviews 215
   Themes 219
   Further Reading 246

Religion and Theology 248
   Introduction... 248
   Overviews and General Studies 249
   Themes 256
   Further Reading 345

Cumulative Character Index 349

Cumulative Topic Index 361

Cumulative Topic Index, by Play 383

Preface

Shakespearean Criticism (*SC*) provides students, educators, theatergoers, and other interested readers with valuable insight into Shakespeare's drama and poetry. A multiplicity of viewpoints documenting the critical reaction of scholars and commentators from the seventeenth century to the present day derives from hundreds of periodicals and books excerpted for the series. Students and teachers at all levels of study will benefit from *SC,* whether they seek information for class discussions and written assignments, new perspectives on traditional issues, or the most noteworthy of analyses of Shakespeare's artistry.

Scope of the Series

Volumes 1 through 10 of the series present a unique historical overview of the critical response to each Shakespearean work, representing a broad range of interpretations.

Volumes 11 through 26 recount the performance history of Shakespeare's plays on the stage and screen through eyewitness reviews and retrospective evaluations of individual productions, comparisons of major interpretations, and discussions of staging issues.

Volumes 27 through 56 in the series focus on criticism published after 1960, with a view to providing the reader with the most significant modern critical approaches. Each volume is ordered around a theme that is central to the study of Shakespeare, such as politics, religion, or sexuality. The topic entry that introduces each volume is comprised of general essays that discuss this theme with reference to all of Shakespeare's works. Following the topic entry are several entries devoted to individual works.

Beginning with volume 57 in the series, *SC* provides a works-based approach; each of the four entries contained in a regular volume focuses on a specific Shakespearean play or poem. The entries will include the most recent criticism available on the works, as well as earlier criticism not previously included in *SC*. Select volumes contain topic entries comprised of essays that analyze various topics, or themes, found in Shakespeare's works. Past topic entries have covered such subjects as Honor, Jealousy, War and Warfare, and Elizabethan Politics.

Until volume 48, published in October 1999, *SC* compiled an annual volume of the most noteworthy essays published on Shakespeare during the previous year. The essays, reprinted in their entirety, were recommended to Gale by an international panel of distinguished scholars.

Organization of the Book

An *SC* entry consists of the following elements:

- The **Introduction** contains background information that introduces the reader to the work or topic that is the subject of the entry and outlines modern interpretations of individual Shakespearean topic, plays, and poems.

- Reprinted **Criticism** for each entry consists of essays arranged chronologically under a variety of subheadings to facilitate the study of different aspects of the play, poem, or topic. This provides an overview of the major areas of concern in the analysis of Shakespeare's works, as well as a useful perspective on changes in critical evaluation over recent decades. The critic's name and the date of composition or publication of the critical work are given at the beginning of each piece of criticism. Unsigned criticism is preceded by the title of the source in which it appeared. Footnotes are reprinted at the end of each essay or excerpt. In the case of excerpted criticism, only those footnotes that pertain to the excerpted texts are included.

- A complete **Bibliographical Citation** of the original essay or book precedes each piece of criticism.

- Critical essays are prefaced by **Explanatory Notes** as an aid to students using *SC*. The explanatory notes summarize the criticism that follows.

- Each volume includes such **Illustrations** as reproductions of images from the Shakespearean period, paintings and sketches of eighteenth- and nineteenth-century performers, photographs of modern productions, and stills from film adaptations.

- An annotated bibliography of **Further Reading** appears at the end of each entry and suggests resources for additional study. In some cases, significant essays for which the editors could not obtain reprint rights are included here.

Indexes

A **Cumulative Character Index** identifies the principal characters of discussion in the criticism of each play and nondramatic poem.

A **Cumulative Topic Index** identifies the principal topics in the criticism and stage history of each work. The topics are arranged alphabetically, by topic.

A **Cumulative Topic Index, by Play** identifies the principal topics in the criticism and stage history of each work. The topics are arranged alphabetically, by play.

Citing *Shakespearean Criticism*

When writing papers, students who quote directly from any volume in the Literary Criticism Series may use the following general format to footnote reprinted criticism. The first example pertains to material drawn from periodicals, the second to material reprinted from books.

> Tetsuya Motohashi. "Body Politic and Political Body in *Coriolanus*," in *Forum for Modern Language Studies* XXX, no. 2 (April 1994): 97-112; reprinted in *Shakespearean Criticism,* vol. 50, ed. Kathy D. Darrow (Farmington Hills, Mich.: The Gale Group, 2000), 119-128.

> Mary Hamer. "Authority and Violence," in *William Shakespeare: Julius Caesar* (Northcote House, 1998), 12-20; reprinted in *Shakespearean Criticism,* vol. 50, ed. Kathy D. Darrow (Farmington Hills, Mich.: The Gale Group, 2000), 230-34.

Suggestions are Welcome

Readers who wish to suggest new features, topics, or authors to appear in future volumes, or who have other suggestions or comments are cordially invited to call, write, or fax the Managing Editor:

Managing Editor, Literary Criticism Series
The Gale Group
27500 Drake Road
Farmington Hills, MI 48331-3535
1-800-347-4253 (GALE)
Fax: 248-699-8054

Acknowledgments

The editors wish to thank the copyright holders of the excerpted criticism included in this volume and the permissions managers of many book and magazine publishing companies for assisting us in securing reproduction rights. We are also grateful to the staffs of the Detroit Public Library, the Library of Congress, the University of Detroit Mercy Library, Wayne State University Purdy/Kresge Library Complex, and the University of Michigan Libraries for making their resources available to us. Following is a list of the copyright holders who have granted us permission to reproduce material in this volume of *SC*. Every effort has been made to trace copyright, but if omissions have been made, please let us know.

COPYRIGHTED EXCERPTS IN *SC*, VOLUME 66, WERE REPRODUCED FROM THE FOLLOWING PERIODICALS:

Cardozo Studies in Law and Literature, v. 5, Spring, 1993. Reproduced by permission.—*CLA Journal,* v. 37, 1993. Reproduced by permission.—*Commentary,* v. 96, 1993 for "Who Is Shylock?" by Robert Alter. Copyright © 1993 by the American Jewish Committee. All rights reserved. Reproduced by permission of the publisher and the author.—*Early Modern Literary Studies,* v. 2, 1996. Reproduced by permission.—*International Journal of Psycho-Analysis,* v. 36, March-April, 1955. Copyright © Institute of Psychoanalysis. Reproduced by permission of the publisher and author.—*Mediaevalia: A Journal of Medieval Studies,* v. 16, 1993. Reproduced by permission.—*The New York Times,* May 19, 2001. Copyright © 2001 by the New York Times Co. Reproduced by permission.—*Pacific Coast Philology,* v. 12, October, 1977. Reproduced by permission.—*Philosophy and Literature,* v. 21, October, 1997. Reproduced by permission.—*Renascence,* v. 51, Summer, 1999. Reproduced by permission.—*Representations,* v. 57, Winter, 1997 for "Othello Circumcised: Shakespeare and the Pauline Discourse of Nations" by Julia Reinhard Lupton. Copyright © 1997 by The Regents of the University of California. Reproduced by permission of the publisher and the author.—*The Sewanee Review,* v. 105, Winter, 1997. Copyright © 1997 by David Solway. Reproduced by permission of the editor.—*Shakespeare Newsletter,* v. 48, Summer, 1998. Reproduced by permission.—*Shakespeare Quarterly,* v. 4, April, 1953; v. 26, Winter, 1975; v. 50, Spring, 1999; v. 51, Fall, 2000. Reproduced by permission of Johns Hopkins University Press.—*Shakespeare Studies,* v. 4, 1969; v. 12, 1979; v. 17, 1985; v. 18, 1986. Reproduced by permission.—*Shakespeare Survey,* v. 33, 1980; v. 50, 1997; v. 52, 1999. Reproduced by permission of Cambridge University Press.—*Soundings,* v. 70, Spring/Summer, 1987. Reproduced by permission.—*Studies in English Literature, 1500-1900,* v. 30, Spring, 1990. Reproduced by permission.—*Studies in the Humanities,* v. 17, June, 1990. Reproduced by permission.—*TCI,* v. 32, January, 1998. Copyright © 2002, PRIMEDIA Business Magazine & Media Inc. All rights reserved. Reproduced by permission.—*Textual Practice,* v. 5, Spring, 1991. Reproduced by permission of the publisher and the author. www.tandf.co.uk/journals.—*Variety,* v. 375, August 2, 1999; v. 378, April 3-9, 2000. Reproduced by permission.

COPYRIGHTED EXCERPTS IN *SC*, VOLUME 66, WERE REPRODUCED FROM THE FOLLOWING BOOKS:

Abrams, Richard. From "The Gaping Pig—and Worse: Shylock's Christian Ducats," in *Afterimages: A Festschrift in Honor of Irving Massey.* Shuffaloff, 1996. Copyright © 1996 by Shuffaloff. All rights reserved. Reproduced by permission.—Battenhouse, Roy. From "Introduction: An Overview of Christian Interpretation," in *Shakespeare's Christian Dimension.* Indiana University Press, 1994. Copyright © 1994 by Indiana University Press. All rights reserved. Reproduced by permission.—Berley, Marc. From "Jessica's Belmont Blues: Music and Merriment in *The Merchant of Venice*," in *Opening the Borders: Inclusivity in Early Modern Studies.* Associated University Presses, 1999. Copyright © 1999 by Associated University Presses. All rights reserved. Reproduced by permission.—Bloom, Harold. From "*Pericles,*" in *Shakespeare: The Invention of the Human.* Riverhead Books, 1998. Copyright © 1998 by Riverhead Books. All rights reserved. Reproduced by permission of Riverhead Books, a division of Penguin Putnam, Inc.—Bryant, James C. From "Shakespeare's Use of Religious Controversy in *King John*," in *Tudor Drama and Religious Controversy.* Mercer University Press, 1984. Copyright © 1984 by Mercer University Press. All rights reserved. Reproduced by permission.—Delvecchio, Doreen and Antony Hammond. From the Introduction to *Pericles, Prince of Tyre.* Cambridge University Press, 1998. Copyright © 1998 by Cambridge University Press. All rights reserved. Reproduced by permission of Cambridge University Press.—Hall, Jonathan. From "Mercantilism and Desire in *The Comedy of Errors*," in *Anxious Pleasures: Shakespearean Comedy and the Nation-State.* Fairleigh Dickinson University, 1995. Copyright © 1995 by Fairleigh Dickinson University Press. All rights reserved. Reproduced by permission.—Hunter, Robert G. From "Shakespeare's Comic Sense as It Strikes Us Today: Falstaff and the Protestant Ethic," in **Shakespeare: Pattern of Excelling Nature.** University of Delaware Press, 1978. Copyright © 1978 by University of Delaware Press. All rights reserved. Reproduced by permission.—Kleinberg, Seymour. From "*The Merchant of Venice*: The Homosexual as Anti-Semite in Nascent Capitalism," in **Literary Visions of Homosexuality.** Haworth Press, 1983. Copyright © 1983 by Haworth Press. All rights reserved. Reproduced by permission.—Lewis, Cynthia. From "'A Foolish Consistency': Antonio and Alienation in *The Merchant of Venice*," in **Particular Saints: Shakespeare's Four Antonios, Their Contexts, and Their Plays.** Associated University Presses, 1997. Copyright © 1997 by Associated University Presses. All rights reserved. Reproduced by permission.—MacCary, W. Thomas. From "The Early Comedies: *The Comedy of Errors*," in **Friends and Lovers: The Phenomenology of Desire in Shakespearean Comedy.** Columbia University Press, 1985. Copyright © 1985 by Columbia University Press. All rights reserved. Reproduced by permission.—McDonald, Russ. From "Fear of Farce," in **"Bad" Shakespeare: Revaluations of the Shakespearean Canon.** Fairleigh Dickinson University, 1988. Copyright © 1988 by Fairleigh Dickinson University Press. All rights reserved. Reproduced by permission.—Rosen, Alan. From "The Rhetoric of Exclusion: Jew, Moor, and the Boundaries of Discourse in *The Merchant of Venice*," in **Race, Ethnicity, and Power in the Renaissance.** Associated University Presses, 1997. Copyright © 1997 by Associated University Presses. All rights reserved. Reproduced by permission.—Tanner, Tony From "Which is the Merchant Here? And Which the Jew?: The Venice of Shakespeare's *The Merchant of Venice*," in **Venetian Views, Venetian Blinds: English Fantasies of Venice.** Rodopi, 1999. Copyright © 1999 by Rodopi. All rights reserved. Reproduced by permission.—Tippins, Darryl. From "'Can you make no use of nothing?&rsquo: Nihilism and Meaning in *King Lear* and *The Madness of King George*," in **Performance for a Lifetime.** Loyola University New Orleans, 1997. Copyright © 1997 by Loyola University New Orleans. All rights reserved. Reproduced by permission.—Weisberg, Richard H. From "Antonio's Legalistic Cruelty: Interdisciplinarity and *The Merchant of Venice*," in **Un-Disciplining Literature: Literature, Law, and Culture.** Peter Lang, 1999. Copyright © 1999 by Peter Lang. All rights reserved. Reproduced by permission.—Whitworth, Charles. From "Rectifying Shakespeare's Errors: Romance and Farce in Bardeditry," in **The Comedy of Errors: Critical Essays.** Garland Publishing, Inc., 1997. Copyright © 1997 by Garland Publishing, Inc. All rights reserved. Reproduced by permission of Routledge, Inc., part of The Taylor & Francis Group, and the author.—Yaffe, Martin D. From "The Mistreatment of Shakespeare's Shylock," in **Shylock and the Jewish Question.** Johns Hopkins University Press, 1997. Copyright © 1997 by Johns Hopkins University Press. All rights reserved. Reproduced by permission.—Zuckert, Michael. From "The New Medea: On Portia's Comic Triumph in *The Merchant of Venice*," in **Shakespeare's Political Pageant: Essays in Literature and Politics.** Rowman & Littlefield, 1996. Copyright © 1996 by Rowman & Littlefield. All rights reserved. Reproduced by permission.

PHOTOGRAPHS APPEARING IN *SC*, VOLUME 66, WERE RECEIVED FROM THE FOLLOWING SOURCES:

Act II, scene ii of William Shakespeare's *The Comedy of Errors,* photograph. The Folger Shakespeare Library. Reproduced by permission of The Folger Shakespeare Library.—Act IV, scene iv of William Shakespeare's *The Comedy of Errors,* photograph. The Folger Shakespeare Library. Reproduced by permission of The Folger Shakespeare Library.—Act V, scene i of William Shakespeare's *The Comedy of Errors,* photograph. The Folger Shakespeare Library. Reproduced by permission of The Folger Shakespeare Library.—Brook, Pamela as Marina, Pat Bentley-Fisher, Trudy Cameron, and Joan Gaskill as Whores, and Amelia Hall as Bawd in Act IV, scene ii of the 1973 Stratford Festival production of William Shakespeare's *Pericles,* directed by Jean Gascon, photograph by Robert C. Ragsdale. Reproduced by permission of the Stratford Festival Archives.—Canada, Ron as Iago and Patrick Stewart as Othello in a 1997 theatrical production of William Shakespeare's *Othello,* photograph. AP/Wide World Photos. Reproduced by permission.—Forrest, Edwin as King Lear, photograph. The Library of Congress.—Garrick, David as Hamlet, photograph. The Library of Congress.—Gielgud, John as Shylock in a production of William Shakespeare's *The Merchant of Venice,* photograph. Hulton/Archive Photos. Reproduced by permission.—Henry, Martha as Thaisa, Nicholas Pennell as Pericles, and Edward Atienza as Gower in Act II, scene iii of the 1974 Stratford Festival production of William Shakespeare's *Pericles,* directed by Jean Gascon, photograph by Robert C. Ragsdale. Reproduced by permission of the Stratford Festival Archives.—O'Neill, Raymond as Antiochus Lord, Nicholas Pennell as Pericles, Joan Gaskell as Antiochus Woman, Nachum Buchman as Antioch, Judith Cockman as Antiochus Woman, and Jack Wetherall as Antiochus Lord in Act I, scene i of the 1973 Stratford Festival production of William Shakespeare's *Pericles,* directed by Jean Gascon, photograph by Robert C. Ragsdale. Reproduced by permission of the Stratford Festival Archives.—Powys, Thomas as Cerimon, Scot Denton as Fisherman, Martha Henry as Thaisa, and Richard Monette and Daniel Buccos as Fishermen in Act III, scene ii of the 1973 Stratford Festival production of William Shakespeare's *Pericles,* directed by Jean Gascon, photograph by Robert C. Ragsdale. Reproduced by permission of the Stratford Festival Archives.—Scene from William Shakespeare's *The Comedy of Errors,* photgraph. Copyright © Robbie Jack/Corbis. Reproduced by permission.—Scenes from William Shakespeare's *Henry V,* photograph. The University of Michigan Library. Reproduced by permission.—Scene from William Shakespeare's *Merchant of Venice,* photograph. The University of Michigan Library. Reproduced by permission.—Scenes from William Shakespeare's *The Merchant of Venice,* photograph. The University of Michigan Library. Reproduced by permission.—Wreford, Roger as Shylock, photograph. Getty Images. Reproduced by permission.

List of Plays and Poems Covered in *SC*

Vol. 1
The Comedy of Errors
Hamlet
Henry IV, Parts 1 and 2
Timon of Athens
Twelfth Night

Vol. 2
Henry VIII
King Lear
Love's Labour's Lost
Measure for Measure
Pericles

Vol. 3
Henry VI, Parts 1, 2, and 3
Macbeth
A Midsummer Night's Dream
Troilus and Cressida

Vol. 4
Cymbeline
The Merchant of Venice
Othello
Titus Andronicus

Vol. 5
As You Like It
Henry V
The Merry Wives of Windsor
Romeo and Juliet

Vol. 6
Antony and Cleopatra
Richard II
The Two Gentlemen of Verona

Vol. 7
All's Well That Ends Well
Julius Caesar
The Winter's Tale

Vol. 8
Much Ado about Nothing
Richard III
The Tempest

Vol. 9
Coriolanus
King John
The Taming of the Shrew
The Two Noble Kinsmen

Vol. 10
The Phoenix and Turtle
The Rape of Lucrece
Sonnets
Venus and Adonis

Vol. 11
King Lear
Othello
Romeo and Juliet

Vol. 12
The Merchant of Venice
A Midsummer Night's Dream
The Taming of the Shrew
The Two Gentlemen of Verona

Vol. 13
1989 Yearbook

Vol. 14
Henry IV, Parts 1 and 2
Henry V
Richard III

Vol. 15
Cymbeline
Pericles
The Tempest
The Winter's Tale

Vol. 16
1990 Yearbook

Vol. 17
Antony and Cleopatra
Coriolanus
Julius Caesar
Titus Andronicus

Vol. 18
The Merry Wives of Windsor
Much Ado about Nothing
Troilus and Cressida

Vol. 19
1991 Yearbook

Vol. 20
Macbeth
Timon of Athens

Vol. 21
Hamlet

Vol. 22
1992 Yearbook

Vol. 23
As You Like It
Love's Labour's Lost
Measure for Measure

Vol. 24
Henry VI, Parts 1, 2, and 3
Henry VIII
King John
Richard II

Vol. 25
1993 Yearbook

Vol. 26
All's Well That Ends Well
The Comedy of Errors
Twelfth Night

Vol. 27
Shakespeare and Classical Civilization
Antony and Cleopatra
Timon of Athens
Titus Andronicus
Troilus and Cressida

Vol. 28
1994 Yearbook

Vol. 29
Magic and the Supernatural
Macbeth
A Midsummer Night's Dream
The Tempest

Vol. 30
Politics
Coriolanus
Henry V
Julius Caesar

Vol. 31
Shakespeare's Representation of Women
Much Ado about Nothing
King Lear
The Taming of the Shrew

Vol. 32
1995 Yearbook

Vol. 33
Sexuality in Shakespeare
Measure for Measure
The Rape of Lucrece
Romeo and Juliet
Venus and Adonis

Vol. 34
Appearance versus Reality
The Comedy of Errors
Twelfth Night
As You Like It

Vol. 35
Madness
Hamlet
Othello

Vol. 36
Fathers and Daughters
Cymbeline
Pericles
The Winter's Tale

Vol. 37
1996 Yearbook

Vol. 38
Desire
All's Well That Ends Well
Love's Labour's Lost
The Merry Wives of Windsor
The Phoenix and Turtle

Vol. 39
Kingship
Henry IV Parts 1 and 2
Henry VI Parts 1, 2, and 3
Richard II
Richard III

Vol. 40
Gender Identity
The Merchant of Venice
Sonnets
The Two Gentlemen of Verona

Vol. 41
Authorship Controversy
Henry VIII
King John
The Two Noble Kinsmen

Vol. 42
1997 Yearbook

Vol. 43
Violence
The Rape of Lucrece
Titus Andronicus
Troilus and Cressida

Vol. 44
Psychoanalytic Criticism
Hamlet
Macbeth

Vol. 45
Dreams
A Midsummer Night's Dream
The Tempest
The Winter's Tale

Vol. 46
Clowns and Fools
As You Like It
King Lear
Twelfth Night

Vol. 47
Deception
Antony and Cleopatra
Cymbeline
The Merry Wives of Windsor

Vol. 48
1998 Yearbook

Vol. 49
Law and Justice
Henry IV, 1 and 2
Henry V
Measure for Measure

Vol. 50
Social Class
Coriolanus
Julius Caesar
The Two Noble Kinsmen

Vol. 51
Love and Romance
Pericles
The Phoenix and Turtle
Romeo and Juliet
Sonnets
Venus and Adonis

Vol. 52
Morality
Richard II
Richard III
Timon of Athens

Vol. 53
Race
Othello
The Merchant of Venice

Vol. 54
Beginnings and Endings
The Comedy of Errors
Love's Labour's Lost
The Two Gentlemen of Verona

Vol. 55
Feminist Criticism
All's Well That Ends Well
Much Ado about Nothing
The Taming of the Shrew

Vol. 56
Historical Revision
Henry VI, Parts 1, 2 and 3
Henry VIII
King John

Vol. 57
As You Like It
Henry IV, Parts 1 and 2
Macbeth
The Winter's Tale

Vol. 58
Antony and Cleopatra
A Midsummer Night's Dream
Richard II
The Two Noble Kinsmen

Vol. 59
Hamlet
The Merry Wives of Windsor
The Rape of Lucrece
Troilus and Cressida

Vol. 60
Topics Volume
Death
Homosexuality
Myth
Succession

Vol. 61
Cymbeline
Henry VIII
King Lear
The Tempest

Vol. 62
Richard III
Sonnets
Titus Andronicus
Twelfth Night

Vol. 63
All's Well That Ends Well
Henry VI, Parts 1, 2, and 3
Julius Caesar
The Two Gentlemen of Verona

Vol. 64
Coriolanus
Love's Labour's Lost

The Phoenix and Turtle
The Taming of the Shrew

Vol. 65
Measure for Measure
Romeo and Juliet
Time

Vol. 66
The Comedy of Errors
Pericles
The Merchant of Venice
Religion

Future Volumes

Vol. 67
Henry V
Timon of Athens
Much Ado about Nothing
Venus and Adonis

Vol. 68
King John
Much Ado about Nothing
Othello
Revenge
Venus and Adonis
The Winter's Tale

Literary Criticism Series Advisory Board

The members of the Gale Group Literary Criticism Series Advisory Board—reference librarians and subject specialists from public, academic, and school library systems—represent a cross-section of our customer base and offer a variety of informed perspectives on both the presentation and content of our literature criticism products. Advisory board members assess and define such quality issues as the relevance, currency, and usefulness of the author coverage, critical content, and literary topics included in our series; evaluate the layout, presentation, and general quality of our printed volumes; provide feedback on the criteria used for selecting authors and topics covered in our series; provide suggestions for potential enhancements to our series; identify any gaps in our coverage of authors or literary topics, recommending authors or topics for inclusion; analyze the appropriateness of our content and presentation for various user audiences, such as high school students, undergraduates, graduate students, librarians, and educators; and offer feedback on any proposed changes/ enhancements to our series. We wish to thank the following advisors for their advice throughout the year.

Dr. Toby Burrows
Principal Librarian
The Scholars' Centre
University of Western Australia Library

David M. Durant
Joyner Library
East Carolina University

Steven R. Harris
English Literature Librarian
University of Tennessee

Mary Jane Marden
Literature and General Reference Librarian
St. Petersburg Junior College

Mark Schumacher
Jackson Library
University of North Carolina at Greensboro

Gwen Scott-Miller
Fiction Department Manager
Seattle Public Library

The Comedy of Errors

For further information on the critical and stage history of *The Comedy of Errors,* see *SC,* Volumes 1, 26, 34, and 54.

INTRODUCTION

Critics agree that *The Comedy of Errors,* Shakespeare's shortest play, is one of his earliest comedies. The play relies heavily on elements of farce, deriving its humor from a twisted and improbable plot and the chaos that ensues when two sets of identical twins find themselves in the same city. With characters who have been seen as one-dimensional and the play's reliance on slapstick humor, *The Comedy of Errors* has often been derided as an immature effort. Some modern critics, however, defend the play against such attacks, maintaining that it has been unfairly undervalued due to its farcical elements. Popular areas of modern critical analyses include the play's romantic features, the Antipholus brothers's search for self, and the play's exploration of mercantilism. In production, reviewers have noted how easily the deeper issues of the play can get lost within the chaotic and farcical plot, and have praised productions in which such issues remain accessible.

The twin brothers, Antipholus of Syracuse and Antipholus of Ephesus, have been viewed as two halves, each searching for unity. A. Bronson Feldman (1955) takes a psychoanalytic approach to the play, maintaining that the brothers are in fact divided aspects of Shakespeare's self—Antipholus of Ephesus as ego, and Antipholus of Syracuse as alter ego. Other critics, including W. Thomas MacCary (1985), find that through the brothers Shakespeare explored the search for selfhood. In MacCary's analysis, Antipholus of Syracuse is searching for himself, while Antipholus of Ephesus represents the ideal ego of his brother. Jonathan Hall (1995) observes that Antipholus of Ephesus is going through a crisis of identity, and stresses that this crisis is related to his inability to honor his pledge as a merchant.

Questions regarding the play's genre have also generated criticism. Russ McDonald (1988) uses his examination of *The Comedy of Errors* to highlight Shakespeare's effort to construct meaning in farce and to demonstrate Shakespeare's affinity for this genre. Maintaining that *The Comedy of Errors* is a mix of two genres, farce and romance, Charles Whitworth (1991) focuses on the play's romantic elements. Whitworth asserts that Egeon's narrative, which frames the play, contains many romantic features, including a shipwreck, as well as separation, rescue, loss, and reunion. Furthermore, the stylized, formulaic language of this narrative is also characteristic of the romance genre, states Whitworth, who concludes that at the play's end, romance and farce merge.

The way the play's serious, romantic, and farcical elements are treated in production varies dramatically. In his review of the 1996 Royal Shakespeare Company's production, directed by Tim Supple, Robert Smallwood (1997) praises the way the production balanced the play's humor with its deeper issues. Smallwood also lauds individual performances as well as the unobtrusiveness of the production's musical accompaniment. Dennis Harvey (2000) discusses the Aurora Theater's 2000 production of the play, directed by Danny Scheie. Harvey notes that the director's decision to use seven actors to play sixteen roles intensified the gender issues in the play and the chaos of mistaken identity. Under Scheie's direction, according to Harvey, the seven players provided a comic "rambunctious" that was perfect for a staging of *The Comedy of Errors.* Wilborn Hampton (2001) reviews a radically different version of the play, a musical version by Trevor Nunn and Guy Woolfenden, directed by John Rando. Hampton comments that while some liberties were taken with the text, such as the incorporation of cliches from the culture of the 1960s and 1970s, the production was faithful to the "spirit" of the original.

OVERVIEWS AND GENERAL STUDIES

A. Bronson Feldman (essay date 1955)

SOURCE: Feldman, A. Bronson. "Shakespeare's Early Errors." *International Journal of Psycho-Analysis* 36, no. 2 (March-April 1955): 114-33.

[*In the essay below, Feldman presents a psychological biography of Shakespeare based on a detailed analysis of the plot and characters of* The Comedy of Errors.]

Veterem atque antiquam rem novam ad vos proferam

1

If we could understand the motives that impelled William Shakespeare to the writing of plays, what were the reasons for his giving a whole life of wealthy imagination to the theatre, we might come into possession of the main keys to the psychology of the stage itself, of plays, the players, and their public. In the hope of contributing toward this achievement I have undertaken an intensive analysis of a play by the paramount dramatist which most historians regard as one of the earliest—if not the very first—of his creative efforts in theatre: *The Comedy of Errors*. Because of the crude frivolity, the juvenile character of this drama, scholars have not paid it serious attention. The eyes of psycho-analysis turn the more readily to it precisely because of this juvenile character. We know how the childishness of an artist will betray the deepest secrets of his mind, the unconscious origin of the passions of his life. If it is true that the *Errors* stands the nearest of Shakespeare's works to his infancy, we may expect to discover in it the primary springs of his fantasy, the driving forces of all his dramatic work.

Analysis of the comedy is not an easy task, for Shakespeare bequeathed it to us in a palimpsest form. There is plenty of evidence that he revised this product of his youth several times, and it did not reach the press until he had been in his grave many years. We need not be dismayed by the rapid shifts in quality of its stagecraft and the abrupt variations of the style. The changes in the drama will mystify us only when we lose sight of its substance, the farcical plot, which throws over all the sophistications of Shakespeare's mature art the unmistakable shadow of his novice mind. Scarcely any of his other plays exhibits so hearty an interest in plot as the *Errors*. The plot is the thing in which we shall catch the conscience of the poet. Shakespeare apprehended this fact and therefore laboured to fill the fabric of the comedy with snares and delusions, ever hopeful of escape from knowledge. With extreme cunning he wrote and rewrote the drama, turning it into a net of Gordian knots which nowhere present a single loose end to enable us to unravel the purport of the play. At whatever point we select to begin our analysis we are bound to use a sharpness without subtlety, to cut the fabric so that it can be untied with the loving patience it deserves.

Suppose we begin the investigation of Shakespeare's *Errors* with the obvious motive of the farce. Manifestly its purpose is to provoke laughter, extravagant, strenuous, far-fetched laughter, not without tears. The poet means to be merry, like his hero in the middle of the drama, 'in despite of mirth' (III, i). With its wild, unbelievable story and dreamlike duplication of characters, the comedy aims at delirium. The prime emotion appears to be one of hysteria, as if the author produced it from a desperate want of hilarity, feeling that he must have merriment or run mad. He does not leave us in doubt about the source of this manic humour. It functioned for him in the same way that the clown Dromio of Syracuse serves his curious master. 'When I am dull with care and melancholy,' the master remarks, Dromio 'Lightens my humour with his merry jests' (I, ii). Again and again Shakespeare stresses relief from a devouring sorrow as sufficient excuse for his jokes, no matter how ribald or fierce. He seems to have put such gaiety on the plane of athletic sports, considering it precious recreation:

> Sweet recreation barr'd, what doth ensue
> But moody moping, and dull melancholy,
> Kinsman to grim and comfortless despair . . . ?
>
> (V)

Below the surface motive of the comedy, then, we can plainly see the motive of evading melancholiac depression.

The intensity of the poet's depression on the threshold of his *Errors* may be estimated by the fact that he altered the raw Roman material of the play in order to give it a groundwork of tragedy. For the sake of its sorrowful opening scene Shakespeare sacrificed elements from his Latin source which would have made the plot more plausible.

In the *Menaechmi* of his beloved Plautus the twins around whom the comedy revolves are separated by a commonplace event. The father takes one to a distant market town and the boy is lost in a crowd. A merchant finds the little Menaechmus and carries him away across the Adriatic Sea to Epidamnus. The lad's father dies of grief. Back in their native Syracuse the grandfather, learning of the double loss, and anxious to preserve the memory of the lost boy, who was named after him, changes the name of the remaining twin from Sosicles to Menaechmus. The new Menaechmus grows up and travels across the Adriatic hoping to find out what happened to his dear brother. Shakespeare desired more sensational reasons for the parting of the twins. He invented a tempest and a shipwreck to account for it. He refused to let the father die of grief, but increased the old man's torments by parting him from the second son. This boy leaves his father to go in search of a brother whom he has never known. And old Aegeon is compelled, years later, to sail in search of both his sons, across the Mediterranean Sea to Ephesus. Shakespeare completes his disruption of the family by having brutal seamen separate the mother from the child she saved in the wreck. In the midst of this welter of narrative we are disappointed to observe that he names the twins Antipholus and fails to explain why they have identical names. To augment the mystification he bestows on their twin servants the single name Dromio. We know that he got the idea for his two sets of twins from another comedy by Plautus, *Amphitruo,* but the Latin dramatist adequately accounted for his twins here by making one of each pair a god masquerading to delude mortals.

Plautus opens his *Amphitruo* with the statement, from the mouth of the god Mercury, that the play commences as a tragedy. Shakespeare may have been encouraged by this to start the *Errors* in the same manner. But the Roman playwright shows us nothing piteous and terrible, like the first scene of Shakespeare's play. Plautus's excuse for the tragic element in his work is that 'it is not right to make a play where kings and gods talk entirely comedy'. The tragic element in Shakespeare's work concerns no god or king, only the poor old merchant Aegeon, who has no parallel in Plautus.

What could have driven Shakespeare to make these drastic alterations in his material? Why did he discard the simple disappearance of a twin in a crowd for the barely credible separation at sea? The tempest must have had a special meaning to the dramatist. The central image of Aegeon's tragic tale, the splitting of his ship, must have exerted an irresistible fascination on Shakespeare's mind. He lavished so much imagination on the disaster that he neglected to make clear the reason for calling both of Aegeon's sons Antipholus. The reckless omission of this important detail gives us a glimpse of the hysterical haste with which the poet went to work on the comedy. His reason appears to have been overwhelmed by the images of the storm and the wreck.

He makes the old man speak of his misfortune as 'this unjust divorce' (I, i). Now, matrimony has often been compared to a sea, and divorce to shipwreck. How conscious of these metaphors the dramatist may have been, we cannot say. It is incontestable, however, that the thought of divorce was running in his mind when he composed *The Comedy of Errors*. Its central events occur in consequence of an estrangement between the hero, Antipholus of Ephesus, and his wife. And the two Latin comedies from which Shakespeare derived the raw stuff of his farce obtain their effects of fun from breaches of marriage.

So far as I am aware, only one of Shakespeare's critics, Frank Harris, has recognized that the poet's own alienation from his wife was a stimulus to the writing of the *Errors* (1). Unfortunately Harris's interpretation of the play raised more riddles than he solved, obscuring the merit of his discovery. He erred in attempting to sift details from the drama to fit his imaginary biography of the poet. In this essay I intend to steer clear of questions of biography, relying for argument exclusively on the text of the play and its literary analogues.

The 'unjust divorce' of Aegeon and his Aemilia is the work of wind, water, and stone, or the caprice of the goddess Fortune, as the venerable traveller insists. The alienation of Antipholus and his Adriana, on the other hand, is portrayed as an error, the climax of a series of errors. The marriage of this couple, Shakespeare seems to say, is nothing but a comedy of errors, indeed a mistake from the start. Adriana's sister suspects that Antipholus married her for her riches (III, ii). He grew cold to her, if not cruel. Before the action of the play commences, he was in the habit of keeping late hours away from his house. 'His company must do his minions grace', Adriana complains, 'Whilst I at home starve for a merry look' (II, i). She accuses him of unkindness and he charges her with shrewish behaviour. Both are right. Yet until the confusions of the comedy begin, we are led to believe, their temperaments have never exploded in hate. For only a week (prior to the day of the drama), Adriana declares near the end, her husband had been behaving strangely.

> This week he hath been heavy, sour, sad,
> And much different from the man he was;
> But till this afternoon his passion
> Ne'er brake into extremity of rage.

From the lips of Luciana and Aemilia the poet casts the blame for the estrangement on the wife. They rebuke her for 'self-harming jealousy', for breaking the peace of her household with wicked thoughts of her husband wandering abroad in pursuit of unlawful love. According to the judgement of these women, her conduct toward Antipholus is enough to explain his melancholy and the 'unjust divorce' of their souls.

The dramatist's compassion for the melancholy Antipholus bears witness for our conviction that Shakespeare identified himself with the outraged husband. He had broken away from his own wife and felt a strong impulse to justify the act on the stage. It could not be shown straightforwardly, of course. In the first place the poet was too blind with tears of self-pity to see the naked truth. Moreover he sensed that his wife did not hold a monopoly of the guilt in their disgrace. He had the intelligence and the courage to admit that he had contributed wrongs and miseries to the marriage; but his courage took the peculiar path of confessing his sins under the mask of comedy. Adopting the counsel of his Luciana, 'Be not thy tongue thy own shame's orator' (III, ii), he showed the world his shame by means of a variety of tongues. He discloses his guilt with a mirthy grimace while protesting, in an agony of remorse, that he is innocent. The core of the whole play is an apology for Shakespeare's errors in matrimony. He is not to blame, the drama pleads in its grotesque fashion: nor should the woman in the case be condemned, though discerning persons of her sex might decide that she was responsible. The fact of the matter, Shakespeare wishes us to think, is that the marriage had been wrecked because the bride and the groom did not really know the individuals they wedded. It was a case of mistaken identity.

In some such way, I imagine, the ego of the poet defended itself against his conscience or superego in the supreme court of his unconscious mind. I and my woman, the dramatist inwardly contended, have done nothing more damnable than entertain strangers as lovers.—She took me in, like Alcmena in *Amphitruo*, thinking that a hero was going to sleep by her side, and in happy ignorance she united with a god. Alas, poor god! He took in holy wedlock what he thought was an angel, and she turned out to be a termagant, at any rate a woman of torturing whims. Nevertheless, as Plautus says, 'The god will not allow his sin and fault to fall upon a mortal's head.' In our pitiable and ridiculous way we are trying to correct our mistakes. Anyhow, I am.—Thus seeking balm for hurt vanity, and excuses for his marital follies and cruelties, the dramatist contrived his *Comedy of Errors*.

The dramatic process in his unconscious took the shape of a dreamlike confusion of identities. He pictured himself as two persons, the husband Antipholus and his double, the unmarried twin, Antipholus of Syracuse, who is taken for the husband by his unhappy Adriana. There is nothing here to prove a split in the dramatist's personality. On the contrary, he has retained his ego entire and dealt himself the luxury of an alter ego. He demonstrates the sort of esteem for himself which makes people say of certain gentlemen that they are too brilliant, they should have been born twins.

The resemblance between the brothers Antipholus is more than skin-deep. The Duke of Ephesus indicates their true relationship when he exclaims.

> One of these men is genius to the other.
> . . . Which is the natural man,
> And which the spirit? Who deciphers them?
>
> (V.)

On the first appearance of the brother from Syracuse he reveals himself as a victim of the same unexplained melancholy that the brother of Ephesus suffers from:

> He that commends me to mine own content
> Commends me to the thing I cannot get.
>
> (I, ii.)

The Syracusan may well be described as the 'genius' or spiritual double of the husband. He is more lyrical in speech, and briefly manifests a tendency to speculative thought. On his arrival in Ephesus, weary from a long voyage, he delays his dinner to gratify a desire to look on the town, 'Peruse the traders, gaze upon the buildings. . . .' His enthusiasm for sights and insights leads him to bewilderment and hazard, but nothing can diminish it. He vows that he will 'in this mist at all adventures go' (II, ii). The Syracusan's intellectual faculties are never so vivid as his carnal ones. He is almost as brutal as his brother. Both of them are quick to beat their servants' skulls for similar audacities. They cherish in common a profound and unfunny antagonism to the woman Adriana. After making her acquaintance for an hour or two the Syracusan twin confesses,

> She that doth call me husband, even my soul
> Doth for a wife abhor.
>
> (III, ii.)

The Ephesian bursts into a fury against his wife for barring him mysteriously from their house. He orders a rope's end to be brought with a view to punishing her (IV, i). He even threatens to pluck out her eyes (IV, iv)! In short, his soul abhors her too. It is not the spirit of virtue in the twins that shrinks from the shrill lady. Shakespeare does not depict them as patterns of chastity. The Ephesian pays a bold homage to the harlot who runs the Porpentine inn. His brother makes love to Luciana shortly after their first sight of each other, and plans to leave her city the same day. The egoism of this fellow is oddly displayed by Shakespeare in his pretext for abandoning Luciana. Her charms, he says, 'almost made me traitor to myself'.

> But lest myself be guilty to self-wrong,
> I'll stop mine ears against the mermaid's song.
>
> (III, ii.)

His scruples do not prevent him from accepting the wifely services of her sister; he lets Adriana labour under the impression that she is doing her duty to her mate. The promptitude of the twins in embracing female hospitality is nearly equalled by their good-will to men, especially men of their station in society. To these singular features we should add their mode of showing anxiety as soon as they experience a loss of money. All these touches of nature make them more than kin. The creator wisely relinquished his attempt (traces of which survive in three old stage directions) to mark the twins apart by styling the Syracusan 'Erotes'—the amorous—and his brother 'Sereptus'—the stealthy.

Incidentally, the poet gives two different statements of their age. In the first scene we learn that the Syracusan journeyed at eighteen in quest of the other. Since then, Aegeon remarks, five summers have passed, or, to be exact, as he is in the final scene, 'seven short years'. To the father, then, the twins are twenty-five years old. The mother dates their birthday earlier. 'Thirty-three years,' she declares, 'have I but gone in travail Of you, my sons' (V). We are sorry to miss the evidence of those she calls 'the calendars of their nativity'. The two Antipholi are presented as men of 'gravity' and 'serious hours', but demeanour is no index to age. Adriana in chagrin asserts that her mate is 'deformed, crooked, old and sere' (IV, ii). But can we trust her testimony in the face of the romance of his twin and her sister Luciana? We cannot even be sure that Dromio of Ephesus tells the truth when he says, examining Dromio of Syracuse, 'I see by you I am a sweet-fac'd youth' (V). The cause of the poet's discrepant chronology lies, I feel sure, in his revision of the play at different stages of his career, and may be of use to biographers.

I have been unable to locate in Latin or Greek literature the name that Shakespeare chose for his ego surrogates. There was a famous artist, a painter, named Antiphilus in the era of Alexander the Great. Possibly he was remembered by the dramatist when he cloaked his unconscious self as Greek for *The Comedy of Errors*. The principle of determinism in the choice of names still challenges us to elucidate Shakespeare's designation for his doubles. It strikes me that the spelling 'Antipholus' was intended characteristically for a pun. We know how fond the poet was of trifling with words; he could truly be called a pun-addict. Also well know is his conviction that by means of wit and drama he could purge the stupidities, the intellectual diseases of the world (2). In the light of these facts I suggest that the name of his heroes may be translated into English as *anti-follies*. Otherwise the appellation is just Greek to me. If I am right in this surmise it would help to explain Shakespeare's failure to record the reason for the twins bearing the same name. The humane development, the culture of his psyche would not permit him free rein in self-righteousness. As a fool of Fortune in marriage he must have felt uneasy in his posture of justice above the fools of the world. In the conflict between righteous vanity and the woe and shame of his 'unjust divorce' the memory of the latter would suffice to make him oblivious of the motive for naming his protagonists Antipholus.

There is no difficulty in accounting for the name of the twin servants, Dromio. It is simply an Italian variation of the name the Roman playwright Terence bestowed on slaves in his first comedy, *The Woman from Andros,* in *The Self-Tormentor,* and *The Brothers.* Shakespeare unquestionably had Italian buffoons in mind when he created the brothers Dromio. A drum, by the way, was a typical property of clowns in his time.

As twin slaves of the Antipholi, one a bachelor like his master, all of precisely the same age, the Dromios could be viewed as simply burlesques of the aristocratic twins. They share certain qualities of their respective employers. The married Dromio, for example, expresses with his scullion Luce the lechery which his master has subdued and refined. The unmarried servant shows less carnality than his brother, and more religion and imagination. His spiritual attributes form a remarkable contrast of Shakespeare's dramatic method with that of Plautus, since the English artist modelled his Syracusan clown on the role that the god Mercury plays in *Amphitruo* as the double of the slave Sosia. The English poet transformed the divine Sosia into a human being with a rare talent for superstition, just as he changed the Jupiter who usurps Amphitryon's bed into a mortal proud of his chastity, with a rare talent for metaphysics. Between Plautus and Shakespeare, clearly, there was a progress of reason in theology, ensuing in the wake of a tremendous restriction of libido. The Syracusan twins, with all their fleshly frailty, are unquestionably superior in morals to the Roman gods. If the Roman dramatist has any advantage over Shakespeare in ethics, I would say that it consists of his superior passion for liberty. Plautus never lets pass an opportunity to express his sadness and hatred at the sight of humanity in chains. To Shakespeare's eyes the bondage of a Dromio was too light to be taken seriously. He seems to have enjoyed a feudal sense of intimacy between lord and labourer. Antipholus depicts the feudal idea when he warns Dromio not to let 'Your sauciness jest upon my love' because 'I familiarly sometimes Do use you for my fool, and chat with you' (II, ii). Their relation might be defined as even more intimate, anagogically. It is possible that Dromio incarnates the 'earthy-gross conceit' which Antipholus deplores in himself (III, ii), that is the vulgar and servile qualities of the genius who created them both.

The Comedy of Errors contains another set of mental twins, who have eluded the scrutiny of Shakespearean experts and critics. It is conceivable that the dramatist himself was not aware of their identity. Their likeness is drawn with so much dexterity and painstaking cleverness that I am inclined to think he meant them to be equals and opposites. He struggled cordially to discriminate them, and the opinion of generations of scholars on their portraits is proof that he was too successful. The cost of this success, in my opinion, is the defeat of the dramatist's honest intention, and injustice to the woman whom he sketched twice as the wife Adriana and her sister. There are good reasons for thinking that when Shakespeare outlined their characters he proposed, perhaps unconsciously, to limn two aspects or phases of the same lady, his own wife. Luciana would then represent the girl he made his bride, beautiful, tender, and gleaming with extraordinary wisdom; and Adriana would stand for the woman she became, or rather the creature Shakespeare fancied lay potential in his bride. In changing her image to the two distinct heroines he surpassed the metamorphoses of his favourite poet, Ovid, whose mythic transformations he constantly held in the 'quick forge and workinghouse' of unconscious thought.

The essential identity of the sisters emerges when we compare their characters in detail. The outstanding trait of Adriana is her shrewishness. Antipholus of Syracuse contrasts her with Luciana primarily on account of the unmarried sister's kind and courteous manner, her 'gentle sovereign grace' (III, ii). Next to this quality he adores her 'discourse', or adroitness in conversation. Now Luciana herself, though critical of her sister's headstrong attitude to Antipholus, testifies that

> She never reprehended him but mildly,
> When he demean'd himself rough, rude, and wildly.
>
> (V.)

Shakespeare presents the shrew as a model of tenderness in the scene where she humours her husband, believing him almost insane—'poor distressed soul' (IV, iv). She exhibits her devotion to him in worry over his arrest for debt, which she hastens to pay off despite his torrent of insults. As for Adriana's 'discourse', we have every reason to believe her when she affirms that her conversation has been dulled and her wit turned barren by the chill hostility of her husband. 'If voluble and sharp discourse be marr'd,' says she, 'Unkindness blunts it more than marble hard' (II, i). There is no sign that Antipholus ever acted toward her with generosity, except before their wedding, when she was certainly Luciana-like. The unmarried sister, however, is by no means exempt from Adriana's defects. She too can pour a swift shrillness of epithets on people who offend her (II, ii). Her volubility on occasions can be bluntly evil (III, ii). We may trust the judgement of Adriana when she states that her sister will want to 'bear some sway' after she weds, and upbraid her husband if he strays from home to linger in sirens' taverns. Apart from temper and talent in talk the girls are supposed to be distinguished by their looks. Adriana speaks as if 'homely age' had deprived her of virgin loveliness, but a moment later she declares that a 'sunny look' from her husband would quickly restore her beauty: 'he hath wasted it' (II, i). If he had never led her to the nuptial altar she would have glittered precisely as alluring as her sister and the hostess of the Porpentine, whom Antipholus praises as 'Pretty and witty, wild, and yet, too, gentle' (III, i). Shakespeare does not tell how old she and Luciana are. If there is any difference in their ages, it is not enough to cleave their souls asunder. They too are one.

In the names of the two girls, I suspect, the dramatist has informed us, in his paradoxical way, that they are twins. If we take Luciana to mean 'the bright one', by the facile substitution (in accordance with Grimm's law) of a *t* for the *d* in Adriana, we could translate her name as 'the dark one'. It may also signify the lucent or luscious one gone dry. (For my purpose it is unnecessary to render the last syllables of their names more concretely. To the reader who wishes to take them as meaning simply Anna, I answer: As you like it.)

It is not unlikely that Shakespeare designed these 'witches', as Antipholus of Syracuse calls them (III, ii), to stand for the great moon goddess of their city, Diana. Another name for the moon divinity, in the religion of ancient Rome, was Lucina. The Syracusan worships Luciana as 'more than earth divine', hails her 'Fair sun', and speaks of her sister as 'night'. In the writer's unconscious, according to my surmise, the feminine 'sun' was nothing but the shining face of the moon. He symbolized her sister by the dark side of Diana. The name of this goddess might be interpreted, without stretching the patience of philology, as meaning 'the double one'. Frazer has observed that Diana appears in ancient myth like a partner of Janus, the two-faced god of Rome (3). The idea of the twofold deity could have provided our poet with the inspiration to change the setting of the *Errors* from Plautus's Epidamnus to Ephesus. Presumably he was tempted to keep the scene in Epidamnus, since the name appealed to his passion for puns and devilry. He made that town the birthplace of the Antipholi (I, i), and the Syracusan brother is told to pretend that he voyaged from there to Ephesus. When he plans to abandon Luciana his servant buys him passage on a vessel bound for Epidamnus. At all events Shakespeare made Ephesus serve his dramatic aims as a city of the damned. The Epidamnus of Plautus is a town of swindling, sponging, and seduction. Shakespeare's Ephesus is a town of deeds more dreadful, infernal crafts, 'And many such-like liberties of sin' (I, i). Its wenches, according to Dromio of Syracuse, are accustomed to cry, 'God damn me', which he says is equivalent to the prayer, 'God make me a light wench'. These girls are therefore worthy to function as ministrants of the moon. Dromio argues that their heavenly bodies are hellish: 'It is written, they appear to men like angels of light: light is an effect of fire, and fire will burn; ergo, light wenches will burn' (IV, iii). But Dromio, like his master, is an enemy of all things pagan, when these confront them in the flesh. For the literate Antipholus the cult of Diana would surely have poetic charms, with its visions of wildwood nymphs and vestals entranced or dancing by her silver flame. Outside poetry, however, he would agree with the illiterate Dromio that her religion was witchcraft or else sheer lunacy. Both master and slave are devout Christians—actually Roman Catholics—and according to Christian tradition the sylvan retinue of Diana eventually turned into ghosts and monsters, like the 'goblins, owls, and elvish sprites' whom Dromio sees everywhere in Ephesus (II, ii). In the period of Shakespeare a host of scholars were convinced that warlocks and beldames of hell worshipped her: 'in the night-times,' it is written, 'they ride abroad with Diana, the goddess of the Pagans' (4). The divinity receives no worship in Shakespeare's play because he converted Ephesus to a Christian town. Nevertheless we can glimpse her 'sovereign grace', divided among the women of the comedy, performing its magic in the afternoon and dusk. She exercises her spells not only through the dextrous Luciana and the sinister Adriana, but also through the unnamed inn-keeper whom Dromio fancies might be 'Mistress Satan' (IV, iii).

By the supernal power of sex which Diana represents the characters are all flung into craziness. True, this does not occur until the hero Antipholus of Syracuse sets foot in the city. Shakespeare toiled hard to impress us with the notion that Antipholus is ever on guard against the power of sex. How could he act as the prime mover of its madness in the comedy? My answer is that, despite his piety, he is the evil 'genius' of the *Errors*. To each of the women in it his apparition radiates a satanic magnetism, of which he is blissfully unaware. His Dromio seems to comprehend this. When Antipholus warns the hostess of the Porpentine, 'Avaunt, thou witch!' Dromio dryly remarks: 'Fly pride, says the peacock' (IV, iii). Apropos of the peacock, we recall that the bird was a companion of the goddess Juno, in whom Frazer has discerned a twin of Diana (5). So the Syracusan may rightly be regarded as a minion of the moon. Wherever he walks it looks as if lunacy prevails; no wonder he must ask himself,

> Am I in earth, in heaven, or in hell?
> Sleeping or waking? mad or well-advis'd?
>
> (II, ii.)

He might well speak of his experience in the words of another of Shakespeare's heroes:

> It is the very error of the moon;
> She comes more near the earth than she was wont,
> And makes men mad.
>
> (*Othello*, V, ii.)

The adventures of Antipholus prove to be 'well-advised'. He manages to enjoy himself among the Ephesians, and unites with Luciana in the end.

The omission of the moon-goddess from Shakespeare's *Errors* was probably dictated by discretion more than religious propriety. The educated subjects of Elizabeth were accustomed to hearing the Virgin Queen extolled as the English Diana, and literary allusions to the divinity of the moon were frequently assumed to imply an opinion of her Majesty (6). Shakespeare apparently endeavoured to banish all thought of Elizabeth from the minds attending to his farce. Perhaps he remembered the penalty inflicted on his forerunner Richard Edwards when that comic dramatist referred to classic Greek personalities in language that was construed as criticism of some Tudor courtiers (7). Shakespeare could not afford to have any wit of the royal court construe the function of Diana in his comedy as a joke on the Queen. He described the city of Ephesus, remember, as a hotbed of black magic, swarming with

> Dark-working sorcerers that change the mind,
> Soul-killing witches that deform the body.
>
> (I, ii.)

If he had introduced the goddess of these magicians in the play he would have risked damnation as one who hinted that Elizabeth was the mistress of mountebanks and hell-hags. Insofar as her Majesty is glanced at in the *Errors* it is through the glare of the authority of Solinus, the 'sweet prince' of Ephesus. The Duke is barely more than an abstraction, law and order incarnate. The first syllable of his name, Sol, would serve to ward off suspicion that the poet delineated him as a deputy of Diana, the antagonist of the sun. Solinus will not stand for nonsense and moonshine; he is emblematic of system, a foe of anarchy, indeed a deputy of the superego in us all.

So Shakespeare expelled the magnificent moon-woman from *The Comedy of Errors*. A quick look at a concordance tells us that the moon is not mentioned even once. Yet the shadow of the goddess is perceptible in every scene. She glows above the heads of the women in their excitement or serenity and broods tenebrously over the men. When the young Shakespeare wrote the comedy, in the darkness of his unconscious, he must have offered a mocking reverence to her 'whom all Asia and the world worshippeth', and echoed the cry of the silversmiths against the apostle Paul: 'Great is Diana of the Ephesians!' (*Acts of the Apostles,* xxix, 28).

To the learned of Shakespeare's period Diana was the goddess of virginity. Luciana would therefore seem to be a truer embodiment of the Diana ideal than Adriana. Let us not be deceived by this seeming. The emphasis of the poet on the 'unviolated honour' of the wife, her horror of the licentious (II, ii), her lack of offspring, and the gestures of frigid purity that drove her husband to the Porpentine inn, prove her deserving of a vestal's glory.

Shall we assent to the proof? Is it not also seeming, a tissue of ostensible truth? We have seen Luciana portrayed as a temptress, a siren luring the bachelor Antipholus to 'self-wrong'. Shakespeare in fact makes her an advocate of hypocrisy. In the belief that Antipholus is her brother-in-law, she instructs him to execute his lust by stealth: 'Teach sin the carriage of a holy saint; Be secret-false' (III, ii). The purity of her sister is no less illusory. Some may reject the accusations of her husband—'Dissembling harlot!' 'O most unhappy strumpet!' (IV, iv)—as products of fallacy, brought on by the revelation that she welcomes an unknown man in his absence. Those who think so should try to explain the slip of her servant Dromio's tongue when, early in the play, he talks of her husband's delay in coming home: 'Why, mistress', he blurts, 'sure my master is horn-mad.' She responds at once to the indictment of adultery. 'Horn-mad, thou villain!' He hastens to correct himself, 'I mean not cuckoldmad' (II, i). From the psychopathology of such mistakes we can deduce a hint of veracity in Dromio's slip. Apparently his master has behaved like a man stung by fancies of his wife's adultery long before her afternoon's entertainment. Is it conceivable that the headstrong Adriana had done absolutely nothing to promote those fancies? Hours before he calls her strumpet she weeping brands herself with the stigma. She calls herself a 'stale' of Antipholus. Later, in fantasy of his own sins, she announces:

> I am possess'd with an adulterate blot;
> My blood is mingled with the crime of lust.
>
> (II, ii.)

Her basis for this self-accusation is a mere metaphor of marriage, that she and her mate are in wedlock one. Under the tones of uxorious indignation we can detect the voice of repressed sensuality, just as under the chambers of Adriana we find dwelling the kitchen-wench Nell, or Dowsabel, whose lascivious advances frighten Dromio of Syracuse. The acuteness of Shakespeare's unconscious satire on the virginal sisters may be perceived in the third name he invented for the obscene kitchen-wench. He also calls her Luce, as if to invite comparison with the chaste yet hypocritic Luciana.

The truth is that the sisters, like the brothers, are impure in heart. Among the paradoxes of the comedy the confidence they display in their virginity and virtue is perhaps the most absurd. They are all sinners, all fools—what you will: 'Smother'd in errors, feeble, shallow, weak' (III, ii).

2

Our investigation of the *Errors* thus far leads to the conclusion that the comedy was precipitated out of the poet's unconscious by marital troubles and disaster. We have still to elucidate the riddle, what made a gentleman of his courage and intelligence prone to sexual conflict and disaster? How did he ever come to entertain strangers as lovers? His marriage could not have been the first enterprise of this sort. Before he married he must have committed other erotic errors more or less like those he has caricatured in his play. In all his affairs of the heart, we may be sure, the blind god Cupid led him blind, quelling his intelligence and making his courage flare up. In the mist of passion he would go at all adventures, no matter what tortures and remorse might follow. The Narcissus in him could usually single out somebody to blame for his stumbling and sprawls. If not, there was always fortune to be cursed, or his birth stars.

The answer to our riddle must lie in the nature of this Narcissus in Shakespeare, the colossal self-love which could project itself into the twin heroes of the comedy and have enough energy left to make their twin clowns and other characters ruddily vital and radiant. From the Narcissus pool of his soul he drew the power—and 'will in overplus'—to surmount the tragic defeats and comic humiliations of his life. From mysterious fountains in the same pool his ego also drank sweet poison, mistaking jets of self-pity for the elixir of self-love, and so steeping itself in a melancholy that not seldom resembled madness. It was in flight from the peril of utter unreason that Shakespeare wrote *The Comedy of Errors*. For the play not only endeavours to explain the struggle of the poet's conscience with an event; it struggles to explain the poet, to assist the understanding of the stranger he felt was himself. To love oneself and win self-knowledge: is the feat possible?

So far as Shakespeare had the strength, when he composed the *Errors,* to venture the feat—handicapped by his terror of baring himself to taunts and mental rapine—he did it in meditation and development of his 'personae', the two Antipholi. Naturally he endowed them with his admirable traits—his dignity, his noble charity and generosity, his affection for the arts of peace, his grace to women and goodwill to men. Dignity or honour obliged him to add his less attractive traits—his impulses to jealousy and revenge, his severely controlled lust and ferocity, and the will to lie, steal, mutilate, or kill. We have already noticed how the Ephesian, on being locked out of his house, commands the purchase of a rope's end to lash his wife, and later, when she brings a doctor for his distraction, threatens with his own nails to pluck out her 'false eyes' (IV, iv). In a parallel scene of the *Menaechmi* the slave Messenio threatens to gouge out the eyes of some men who are trying to drag his master off as a lunatic. The memory of this probably lurked in Shakespeare's mind when he pictured the half-crazed husband menacing his wife. Antipholus vents his sadistic wrath on Dr. Pinch instead, applying fire to his beard, extinguishing it with pails of puddled mire, while his servant nicks the doctor with scissors (V). Meanwhile his brother turns thief with the golden chain that the Ephesian wished to give a courtesan to spite his wife. The theft ensues on the dinner which the Syracusan has obtained from Adriana by turning cheat. Afterward he and his Dromio scare off the two sisters and the courtesan with naked swords (IV, iv). These little larcenies and bestialities recompense the twins for their grand refusal to tread the path of unholy dalliance and adultery.

It is curious to see how the bachelor brother treats the house of Adriana like an inn, and makes love to one of the hostesses, immediately before the espoused one determines to dine at the inn whose mistress Shakespeare merely names Courtesan. In neither episode does the house become a brothel, like the home of Erotium in Plautus, where Menaechmus the newcomer dines with the prostitute at his brother's expense. The wish, which George Meredith styles sentimental, to get pleasure unpaid for is obviously behind the comic conception of both playwrights. But Shakespeare's horror of indulging the wish deprives his play of much humour. He presents Antipholus of Ephesus as a paragon of idealism in morals. 'How dearly,' says his wife, 'would it touch thee to the quick, Shouldst thou but hear I were licentious.' She conjures a vision of him tearing the wedding ring from her finger to 'break it with a deep divorcing vow' (II, ii). Less than two hours later her husband gives the hostess of the Porpentine the chain he had promised Adriana, and takes or snatches a ring from the courtesan (IV, iii). It is likely that Shakespeare considered this a token of second wedlock, a marriage made in hell.

In the poet's self-portraiture his attitude to matrimony reveals a profound and painful ambivalence. Luciana lectures her sister on the divine rights of the male in wedlock and the necessity of obedience in wives. The essence of this sermon runs veritably through all of Shakespeare's dramas, apparently integral to his dogmas of church and state. At the same time he preaches the doctrine that male and female are incorporated at the wedding altar into one. By this ritual the wife partakes in the godlike rights of her mate, and therefore can limit or confine them. She can demand obedience from him. Shakespeare recognized the privilege, the sovereignty of the wife, yet could not bring himself to admit it frankly. Instead he tossed in childlike anguish between the horns of his dilemma.

The heroines of Plautus exhibit a pride of sex, or sense of feminine dignity, unknown to the women of *The Comedy of Errors.* Alcmena refuses to endure her husband's charges of unchastity. She demands her goods and slaves from him and prepares for divorce. The wife of Menaechmus, lacking her solitary strength, still castigates her husband for his thieving, and summons her father to protect her from outrage. Erotium is stronger: she storms at her double-crossing lover and drives him out of her house. The men in the *Menaechmi* and *Amphitruo* are forced to appease, cajole, and act subservient to their women.

Except in the case of Aemilia, Shakespeare commands his ladies to act subservient to their men. Even that grand dame mainly functions as a guardian of her men, and condemns the woman who troubles their voluptuous peace. The freedom that Aemilia enjoys from sexual bondage is the outcome of her holiness. She is a governess of nuns. For women who did not covet the virgin's gloriole, and set their hearts on independence, the poet seldom had anything but anger, mockery, and tears.

At the root of his agony seems to burn the irresistible urge to embrace strangers as lovers. His ego, as I conceive it, constantly hunted for objects on whom to shower the surplus of his libido, and invariably learned that the objects were doomed to be foreigners. Again and again he must have tried to join an alien soul to his own and waked from the dream of friendship or the honeymoon aghast and bewildered by the discovery that he was once more alone with the unknown, marvelling like his Antipholus:

> What! was I married to her in my dream?
> Or sleep I now and think I hear all this?
>
> (II, ii.)

The plot of *The Comedy of Errors,* if we interpret it truly, will provide us with clues to the mystery of the poet's tendencies in love.

Ordinarily when one hears the popular phrase, a man's better half, one thinks it refers to his wife. Sir Philip Sidney employed it in his *Arcadia* as equivalent to true-love. When Shakespeare uses it—or a variant—we cannot tell what he means. Sidney's usage appears to be intended when Antipholus of Syracuse appeals to the stranger Luci-

Antipholus of Syracuse, Dromio of Syracuse, Adriana, and Luciana in Act II, scene ii of William Shakespeare's The Comedy of Errors.

ana as 'mine own self's better part' (III, ii). Earlier in the comedy we find the phrase aimed differently. Adriana, reproaching the man she fancies is her husband, exalts herself as 'better than thy dear self's better part' (II, ii). If we take this as a boast of superiority to the woman of his heart, we are confronted with an enigma. Who could this rival woman be? Judging by Adriana's jealousy, we might guess it is her husband's courtesan, though the wife gives no sign of having information about the temptress of the inn. Adriana simply suspects that his eye offers 'homage' somewhere (II, i). It is surprising to hear her, suddenly definite about his alleged sin, allude to the rival with the phrase of respect. Presumably Shakespeare designed it here for irony. The rest of Adriana's speech, however, is so earnest and tragic that we feel it imperative to search for a deeper design.

She pleads for compassion to the frostily intellectual Antipholus of Syracuse:

> How comes it now, my husband, O! how comes it,
> That thou art thus estranged from thyself?

> Thyself I call it, being strange to me,
> That, undividable, incorporate,
> Am better than thy dear self's better part.
> Ah, do not tear away thyself from me,
> For know, my love, as easy mayst thou fall
> A drop of water in the breaking gulf,
> And take unmingled thence that drop again,
> Without addition or diminishing,
> As take from me thyself and not me too.

Thus Adriana sees her husband's inner existence as a structure of three parts: himself, a 'better part', and herself, the best, the only one she calls estranged.

With the probe of psycho-analysis we are able to explore the identity of the second person of this trinity, and determine the moment of her mingling with the hero's self. Shakespeare has betrayed her unaware.

The simile Adriana employs for her spouse's original ego—a drop of water—is familiar to Antipholus, since he has employed it in soliloquy for himself. In one of his first utterances in the play he muses:

> I to the world am like a drop of water,
> That in the ocean seeks another drop;
> Who, falling there to find his fellow forth,
> Unseen, inquisitive, confounds himself.
>
> (I, ii.)

The 'breaking gulf' of Adriana's speech recalls the comparison of matrimony to a sea. The ocean of Antipholus he himself compares to the world. It strikes me as a less extensive vastness. Long before Edward Carpenter consciously thought of sex as oceanic, poets and other visionaries had established the likeness in their dreams, and written rapturously about the ocean unaware of its sexual analogy. The real meaning of Antipholus's ocean springs to view in the lines of his soliloquy that follow the mournful image. In these verses the 'fellow' he seeks becomes twofold:

> So I, to find a mother and a brother,
> In quest of them, unhappy, lose myself.

The emergence of the mother in the goal of his search may perplex us after reading the reference to his fellow, especially when we remember that Aegeon had not mentioned the mother as an object of his boy's voyages. No such motive appears in the *Menaechmi,* where the twins' mother, Teuximarcha, is named once and conveniently forgotten. In *The Comedy of Errors* the mother Aemilia plays a majestic and strategic part. Until the last scene, only her Syracusan son manifests a faith that she is still alive, but he manifests it only in these two lines. Shakespeare obviously found the subject too venerable or extremely touchy. My readers may seize this occasion to protest that the brother of Antipholus could not be sanely regarded as an object in the ocean of sex. Granting they are right, at the hazard of their tolerance, I am tempted to suggest that the 'fellow' whom Antipholus yearns to find is in a potent sense feminine. In view of my belief that the Syracusan is a 'genius' or demon double, it is logical (by the laws of folklore) to assume that he is seeking a body, a material form. Insofar as the Ephesian is earthier and more matter-of-fact he performs this material function. Since earth and matter are from ancient times symbolic of the maternal, I am led to wonder if the 'water' Antipholus longs for is not—more than just feminine—motherly?

In consequence of this reasoning we have to translate the quest of Antipholus for reunion with his mother as a dream-journey of desire for rebirth. In dreams, and in dramas too, 'Birth is almost invariably represented by some reference to water: either we are falling into water or clambering out of it, saving someone from it or being saved by them, i.e. the relation between mother and child is symbolized' (8). Shakespeare in fact nearly stripped away the last web of glamour between our scientific insight and his poetically concealed sperm-drop endeavouring to reach the womb. It will be noted that Adriana speaks of a drop of water falling in and then being taken from 'the breaking gulf'. To the woman there is hope of ultimate redemption for the 'drop'. To the malcontent Antipholus the falling drop is fated to devastation, to 'confound himself'. Nevertheless he travels on, 'unseen, inquisitive'.

Just as he fancies himself confounded and lost in the ocean of the world, he looks with fascination on the city of Ephesus and resolves to wander through its labyrinth of streets: 'I will go lose myself' (I, ii). Shakespeare was well acquainted with the poetic practice of hailing cities as foster-mothers. His fellow-playwrights (for diverse examples, Thomas Watson and Thomas Dekker) fondly alluded to their birthplace London as a mother. To Shakespeare the metropolis must have seemed a stepmother, with all the charms and criminal appetites of stepmothers in fairy tales; for many years London let him starve for love.

At this point the sceptical reader will have ripened for me a cluster of pungent questions. Among the foremost perhaps is this: Will the venerable Aemilia fit into the equation which Adriana proposes for her distressed mate's ego? In other words, Is the mother his dear self's better part?

From the text of the comedy I have extricated but one piece of proof that Aemilia is the true rival of the wife in the heart of her son. In the final act Antipholus of Syracuse, flying from the wife and her compatriots, escapes into the sanctuary over which the long lost Aemilia rules. She and the Syracusan are of course ignorant of each other's identity. Adriana, frustrated, demands from Solinus protection of her marital rights, not knowing the relation of Aemilia to her man: 'Justice, most sacred duke, against the abbess!' Her grievance plainly sounds as if the abbess had stolen her beloved. Unconsciously, so to say, Adriana has fathomed the abyss of the Antipholus mind. Old customs of matrimony ordain that a man shall hold his wife above his mother in the scale of his values. The spouse is generally judged more valuable in political economy. So the miserable girl is justified in claiming that she is better than her husband's 'better part'. Love, notwithstanding, laughs at her priority. Safe in the bosom of the priory church the 'genius' Antipholus can defy both wife and duke. The genuine Antipholus, by the dictates of Shakespeare's reality principle, stays outside the sacred refuge and faces the music of political economy. On his ego wounds the abbess cannot perform the miracles which her 'wholesome syrups, drugs, and holy prayers' promise the spirit from Syracuse. With the confidence of maternal power she expects 'To make of him (the fugitive) a formal man again'. But she is powerless to make a healthy head of a family out of the profane or 'natural' son.

A sequel question we have to meet is—How could Aemilia be the 'better part' of the twins when one of them extols Luciana as his better part? The evidence for my answer is scanty and fragmentary, but it is the best we could hope to obtain from the poet at the stage of his self-knowledge and self-revelation where he wrote his *Errors*. My answer is twofold. When the Syracusan makes love to Luciana the poet revels in the illusion that the mother's image in this interval is demoted in his heart. And in that interval he is eager to entertain a stranger as a lover. The poet's unconscious remains undeceived by the gesture of demotion and goes ardently ahead with its drive for the assimilation of Luciana to the image of Aemilia. Whatever real person he had in view when he conceived the younger character vanished while the erotic scene was plotted; or rather her memory dissolved into the familiar and permanent memory of his mother. Luciana could become the 'better part' of Antipholus solely by metamorphosis into Aemilia.

At once the vigilant reader will inquire, Does this mean that Aemilia is a simulacrum of the goddess Diana? I think, no. Diana in the drama—insofar as she is visible—is actually a simulacrum of Aemilia. She has been converted from pagan goddess to Christian abbess, from a queen of vestals to a governess of nuns. That is why the influence of the Ephesian moon-woman is felt throughout the play. The influence of the mother assumes the mythical radiance. She is the goal of the Syracusan's journey and therefore the driving force of Shakespeare's plot. In the love song of Antipholus to Luciana I find a faint proof of her immanence in the moonshine of the dramatist's soul. He imagines her sister weeping continually till she creates a 'flood of tears'. Then he begs Luciana not to drown him in the flood—not to unite him to Adriana out of pity—since he wants her alone for his love:

> Sing, siren, for thyself, and I will dote:
> Spread o'er the silver waves thy golden hairs,
> And as a bed I'll take them and there lie.
>
> (III, ii.)

The waves are silver, we know, because the moon beams on them. By what magic could the golden locks of Luciana fall on her sister's silver tears? Only by identification of the two. This becomes possible to fantasy if we translate them into phases or aspects of a personification of the moon. But Antipholus does not dream of reclining on the moon; he visions himself on a white-crested sea. In the language of homely reality, he wishes to lie on his mother's breast and suck her milk. We can now understand why the two sisters, the bright and the dark, may claim to possess parts of the hero's self. Having convinced his ego of their semblance to his mother, they gained admission to her fane in himself and in turn enjoyed his idolatry. In exchange for this reverence they had to give up his love. Loving them signified to him 'self-wrong' and internal treason, i.e. betraying the maternal deity erected by his ego in childhood. Since the goddess belonged to none but himself, worshipped without prospect or hope of sexual intercourse, she could reign in his unconscious both as mother and as virgin. This psychic contradiction has its mythic parallel in the cult of Diana, who was revered for her strict and frosty chastity and adored for her warm sympathy with women giving birth. In the sanctuary of Diana at Rome her statue displayed many breasts, as if she herself had known the bliss of maternity (9). The Roman women, delivering their babies, invoked the assistance of Lucina, the moon.

Aemilia's children are restored to her at the end of the comedy, and Shakespeare down-rightly indicates her stature in their twin minds. He denies the daughter-in-law an apology for Antipholus's truculence or a pardon for her faults. For the sake of popular romance he bestowed on Luciana three lines of reassurance of the other brother's love. There is no mistaking the significance of the happy ending. It is joy over the return of the twins to the supreme love of their life. For the sake of this overwhelming attraction one Antipholus is cruel to her rivals, and the other hardens his heart to the allurements of girls. Under the mask of the abbess we discover the secret cause of her son's unjust divorce. From some abysmal temple in his brain her moon-coloured idol governs his sexual tides. She is a jealous goddess, and will have no other mistresses before her. Union with another is iniquity to her, and she is never slow to revenge the sin. In retaliation for her child's efforts toward liberty, to hunt for a new love elsewhere, she flogs his ego from her stronghold in his head, with silver cords.

The wish for maternal pillow and milk brings to the surface of the dramatist's mind the idea of death. In the 'glorious supposition' that Adriana's tears and Luciana's hair have been made a bed for Antipholus, he is ready to believe 'He gains by death that hath such means to die'. In the midst of his ecstasy the thought of extinction becomes sweet to him. Why? The sole reply that occurs to me is that the mother in the dramatist's mind must be dead. Whether the woman in whose image he fashioned his goddess was really in her grave is a question beyond our present interest. Our business is to explain the connexion in Shakespeare's drama of the thoughts of mother and death. The apparition of Aemilia near the final curtain, like a *dea ex machina,* leaves me with an inkling that she is a holy ghost. Her sacredness is stressed to a degree unworthy of mortals, summoning to mind the observation that humans must perish before they turn angelic or divine. We can glimpse the phantom character of the abbess more plainly when a minor individual of the play defines in her presence the background of her home:

> . . . the melancholy vale,
> The place of death and sorry execution,
> Behind the ditches of the abbey here.
>
> (V.)

The odour of tombs and hecatombs hangs over the happiness of the comedy's last scene. Could such things be close to the mother of the poet's doubles if death was not irrevocably close to the poet's own mother in his thoughts?

Alert readers of the play will note the curious fact that Shakespeare designates the home of Aemilia an abbey and also a priory. She herself is always called abbess. In view of the poet's passion for paronomasia we may wonder whether he sensed a likeness between the spirit of the abbess and the abyss, the 'vale', behind her house? The airs of both are sublime and malignant, capable of blasting mortal happiness. If our assumption of their likeness is correct we can proceed to unravel some of the most tenacious knots in the drama. The flourishing of the metaphor in the poet's head would mean that he regarded the matrix not just as a fountain of life—Adriana's 'breaking gulf'— but as a desert of death too. This ambivalence of his concepts of the womb and vagina would account for the antithetical nature of his two heroines, the lucid and cool yet golden Luciana and her arid and hot yet night-hued sister, each an embodiment of the divine mother in the dramatist's brain. When he regarded females as distinct personalities (aliens) his endopsychic mother acted as their prototype, the pattern of all beauty and wit. When he regarded them as creatures entwined in his destiny (lovers) she acted as their severest critic, an implacable competitor of the whole sex. In her activity as the model of loveliness she fomented tempests in his libido; in polar opposition she obstructed it, lifting before his mind's eye the rock on which the loves of his life were wrecked.

The rock in the sexual sea on which Aegeon's family-ship was split is specifically a symbol of the male organ which children often believe the mother possesses within her vagina (10). The infant mind, detecting the absence of the penis in infant females, commonly concludes that they have lost it, that the instrument of virility was mysteriously excised. The idea that stronger, elder females may have retained it persists, and mothers who evoke dread in their sons by exhibiting masculine qualities frequently appear in their dreams with the organ in full view; or else the nightmares show them brandishing emblems of it. By the poetic mechanism of displacement people shift their sentiments of dread from the clitoral zone to the mother's or vampire-woman's 'hard heart'. When the stony bosom surprises her children by abruptly yielding milk or kindness, folklore pays tribute to the sublime woman by picturing her as a rock which miraculously lavishes a reviving liquid when struck by a magic wand. In the *Errors* Shakespeare paid tribute to the sublime woman of his dreams by picturing her as an abbess, which may well be englished as *she-father*. It was the assertion of her masculinity in his unconscious that obstructed his endeavours to love other women. Whenever he engaged in sexual union he became acutely aware of the void in the vagina, and suffered the fear of losing his penis. Fantasies of his own castration blazed in his mind. Under the agony of such thoughts his ego prostrated itself before the maternal image and begged for mercy, repudiating the pursuit of happiness everywhere else. In short, he spiritually castrated himself. Having made himself a eunuch for the goddess's sake, he could approach her bosom with confidence and nestle down to delectable oblivion. We witness a theatrical mimicry of the act in the entrance of Antipholus to his mother's abbey. Cut off from his living family, the hero approaches the rock of the church and it opens to admit him, with the promise of 'wholesome syrups' and holy whispers for his peace. Secure within the rock, lulled by his illusion of Catholic death, he could smile defiantly at remembrance of marital or political economy. Not the legion of hell nor the populace of Ephesus could prevail against the maternal stone. Nevertheless the ideas of castration and death were always associated in the poet's head with pangs of cuts and mutilations, sights and smells of blood, visions of skeletons and severed skulls. Even in the final felicity of his play the horrible recollection of such things sticks to his poetry.

Shakespeare was probably persuaded to let the last act take place among these ghastly adumbrations by reasons of dramatic economy. He wanted to disclose the brothers' identity and restore them to their parents on the same street where Aegeon was being led to execution for violating the law of Ephesus.

This entrance of Aegeon reminds us that we have yet to reckon his part in the ego of the dramatist. Surely, if the abbess is the image of Shakespeare's mother, the tragic merchant must somehow stand for his father. Judging by the play we would imagine that the dramatist did not live in awe of his mother's husband. Aegeon does not glow for us with the flame of ideality. He warms us with embers of a singular humbleness, the emotion of a man who knows how little history he is able to make. Shakespeare spends no moonrays of theopathy on him. He seems to have felt for the ineffectual old man a filial pity, bordering on disdain. Since he often felt similarly toward himself, experiencing failure after failure, the poet unconsciously installed his father close to the centre of himself, opposite but intimate.

So intimate was their psychic valence that it might be considered identification. There are moments in the speeches of Aegeon when the voice of the poet can be clearly heard. For instance, in the father's narrative of the calamity that divided his family. He states that when the tempest menaced his ship not far from Epidamnum the sky conveyed to his thought 'A doubtful warrant of immediate death', which he himself 'would gladly have embrac'd'. We are granted no reason for this gladness in the face of the danger to his wife and babes. It makes sense only if we recall that the sea is a symbol for sex and drowning, to Shakespeare's unconscious, a mode of reunion with the mother. The poet is thinking of his own wife and off-spring when Aegeon reports that the incessant weepings of his wife and the 'piteous plainings' of the infants forced him to hunt for means of rescue. Aemilia does not impress us as a lady capable of incessant weepings, but Adriana is almost perpetually in tears. Finally, at the end of Aegeon's tale, it is the son, brooding over the central tragedy of his life, the loss of maternal love, who sighs:

> Thus have you heard me sever'd from my bliss,
> That by misfortune was my life prolong'd,
> To tell sad stories of my own mishaps.

The misery and impotence of the son provide us with a mirror of the woeful and ineffectual life of the sire, a mirror which emits the virtues of the father and the genius of his boy. Barring these features, our verdict is bound to be that Shakespeare's personality was precisely what we should expect from the flesh of the heir to his father's natural shocks and outrageous fortune.

Naturally the paternal position in the dramatist's mind was not a static one. During remembrance of the father's fulfilments of claims to the mother's labour and love, the radius between Shakespeare's ego nucleus and the paternal image would certainly widen, and sparks of hate shoot across it. To the boy's way of thinking, the mother belonged to nobody but him. Intruders on their sacred privacy merited all extreme penalties known to savage and child. The father's intrusions were especially resented, because the world and the mother sanctioned them as good or just. Nobody but the boy seemed to object to the divorce of his mother and himself. On such occasions he could contemplate the thought of the father's extinction with a stern joy, the joy of justice done. Doubtless he exhausted his fancy in devising perfect punishments for the old man, according to the law of talion.

The memory of a particular paternal intrusion may have burnt in the poet's unconscious when he invented the legend of Aegeon. He sentenced the old man to death for having dared to enter the precincts of the holy city of Ephesus. Mercantile enmity—so runs the legend—incited the city of Diana and Syracuse to proclaim a state of hatred between them. They decreed a halt of their traffic and intercourse, and resolved, as Duke Solinus puts it,

> . . . if any, born at Ephesus,
> Be seen at Syracusan marts and fairs;
> Again, if any Syracusan born
> Come to the bay of Ephesus, he dies.
>
> (I, i.)

Aegeon is doomed to decapitation for dropping his anchor in the bay of Ephesus. He can be forgiven only when his sons regain the mother.

Here I will chance the suggestion that the name Syracuse may be interpreted as a pun. Since the dramatist altered the location of his comedy from Epidamnus to Ephesus, but preserved the home of his hero in Syracuse, I felt it necessary to examine the name for a possible motive for keeping it. Since it is pronounced Syracusa throughout the play, construing it as *Sire-accuser* did not strike me as too fantastic.

It has probably occurred to the alert reader that the name Ephesus may also be a pun. As a city of enchantment and witchcraft it may well have appealed to the poet as a region which *effaces* the true identities of men and women and puts in their places moon-animated *effigies*.

If an accusation of Shakespeare's sire prompted the invention of the framework of his plot, another accusation provided the substance of its middle event.

The first scene of Act III, perhaps the oldest portion of our palimpsest, communicates through its metrical antiquity a major trauma of the poet's childhood. Antipholus approaches his wife's door and finds himself locked out. His Dromio calls for servant-girls (all having English names) to open the door. The other Dromio, snug inside, inquires,

> Dost thou conjure for wenches, that thou call'st for such store,
> When one is one too many? Go, get thee from the door.

The persons in the house are eating a commonplace meal. With these words of Dromio the dramatist conjures up a different feast. The clown is informed that the 'master' stands outside; he pretends to be touched:

> Let him walk from whence he came, lest he catch cold on's feet.

Now psycho-analysis conjures up a vision of the child Shakespeare straining at the door of his parents' chamber and clamouring to get in. Possibly his humorous father responded in the Dromio way. Antipholus knocks at the barrier hard and listens to Luce the kitchen-girl deride him: 'Let him knock till it ache'. He rages, 'You'll cry for this, minion, if I beat the door down.' The droll inside remarks that the town is 'troubled with unruly boys'. Adriana orders the newcomer to go away. Injured and perplexed he lingers there, unable to comprehend how his woman could be so frozen-hearted when he stood in need of her warmth. In the autumnal gloom of his heart he murmurs, 'There is something in the wind, that we cannot get in.' His slave replies, 'You would say so, master, if your garments were thin. Your cake here is warm within; you stand here in the cold.' The forlorn master wishes he had an iron crow to wrench his way in.

Obscene notions raced through the dramatist's brain as he wrote the scene. He recalled the passage in Plautus where Amphitryon, knowing that his wife is entertaining a stranger and unable to gain entrance to her quarters, cries out that he will break in the door, and swears to destroy whomever he sees in his path, wife, father, anyone. No sooner does he raise his arm to execute his oath than Jupiter's thunder breaks from the heavens to arrest him. Amphitryon falls flat before the sound of the god. The piety of the Latin poet seems to have stirred Shakespeare to derision of the divine thunder. In the corresponding scene of his comedy the memory of the celestial admonition is evoked by a mere reference to the breaking of wind. The connexion between the anal and the heavenly thunder was long ago pointed out by psycho-analysis (11). That Shakespeare associated paternal efforts at dictatorship with flatulence may properly be disputed. We cannot doubt that he associated paternity with wind. The symbolism of the pompous epithet he invented for the sea, in the first scene of his play, cannot be comprehended otherwise. He calls it 'the always-wind-obeying deep'. The resistance of the real sea to air-force counted for nothing in his mind when he thought of the sexual sea, in particular his amorous mother, and her submission to father-force.

The memory of his banishment from the mother's room excited ideas of libidinal rancour and amorphous fears. Death-wishes against her and his father, too, must have surged in his head at the time of the trauma, and colliding with pulses of incest produced an unvanquishable terror, a terror he never overcame (12).

A friend, Balthazar, dissuades Antipholus from attacking the door, assuring him that the honour of his wife is unviolated:

> —your long experience of her wisdom,
> Her sober virtue, years, and modesty,
> Plead on her part some cause to you unknown;
> And doubt not, sir, but she will well excuse
> Why at this time the doors are made against you.

The friend warns him that violent entrance would bring down on his head 'vulgar comment', mob ridicule and calumny,

> That may with foul intrusion enter in
> And dwell upon your grave when you are dead;
> For slander lives upon succession,
> For ever housed where it gets possession.

Antipholus calms down, and determines to visit the wild hostess of the Porpentine inn,

> Since mine own doors refuse to entertain me,
> I'll knock elsewhere to see if they'll disdain me.

And so the scene ends.

What little master Shakespeare did when he departed from the forbidden chamber, we can reasonably surmise. Unruly boys of genius are as prone as the dullest lads to the frenzy and torpor of masturbation. When he grew up he wreaked a vicarious vengeance on his parents. He contrived in imagination to get his 'spirit' inside the coveted dwelling, with all its cakes and ale at his disposal, while his carnal self (in empathy with the father as husband) stayed outside with fever and chills.

Shakespeare never lost the conviction that slander was a family heritage, like a curse among the ancient Greeks. It is my conviction that he unconsciously proved it true, by rehearsing again and again, in young manhood and old age, in various disguises, the fatal scene of his infancy, thus inflicting on his children the iniquity of his parents. This repetition compulsion traverses and threads together all his dramatic works.

The sadism of the fantasies Antipholus indulges in after his exclusion reminds me that my summary of Aegeon's death sentence omitted a detail of grave importance psychologically. He is formally condemned because of his inability to pay an exorbitant fine, a thousand marks. The Duke grants him a day in which to collect the money among the Ephesians. By the lucky discovery of his rich sons the old man comes within reach of it, but Solinus releases him from the fine. Money and its worries are never remote from the dramatist's mind. His Syracusan double, in the first act, is fearful that he may lose a thousand marks of his own. In the next act he is portrayed as obsessed with the idea of his gold. In the third he gets the chain his brother had requested and comments on the acquisition with pleasure:

> I see a man here needs not live by shifts,
> When in the streets he meets such golden gifts.

Later the Ephesian double is arrested for debt to the goldsmith, and the money for his freedom is given to his twin. We are not told the metal of the courtesan's ring, but there is no need to know. The poet's obsession on the yellow treasure is manifest without it. We note that he manifests it, not in ordinary conditions of trade, but luxuriously or anxiously. It glitters for him as gift, fine, or debt. One would think that he suffered from the craving to obtain it free and the dread of losing it. These emotions generally run high in the syndrome of the melancholiac. Psychoanalysis has linked his terror of poverty with the peculiar mode of sexuality known as anal erotic, which frequently explodes in demonstrations of sadism (13). In melancholy the passion for excrement characteristic of this kind of sexuality appears torn out of its normal context of absorbing interest in by-products, commodities, stock-piles, profit and thrift. The anal-erotic mood of melancholy serves as regression under the spur of anxiety to the state of mind where bowel movements signified gifts or obligations to the mother. If the child at this stage of libidinal development does not deliver the ordure on demand, or squanders it in caprice, he hazards the loss of maternal love. Conversely, in the unconscious of the chronically sad, the belief that they have lost maternal love may spur their intellects backward to infantile concern for their ordure, as something wantonly spent or else owed. Under the frown of the maternal divinity in their conscience, their egos writhe in guilt and look forward to doing penance for their financial faults. The result is the dread of penury which we find so active in the melancholiac, and which afflicted Shakespeare most of his life.

The first idea that comes to the abbess's mind when she hears of Antipholus's daily gloom is the likelihood that he has lost money: 'Hath he not lost much wealth by wrack of sea?' It is perfectly natural for the mother to worry over the disposal of his gold.

We must not let ourselves be fooled by Shakespeare's costuming of his heroes as merchants. His skull did not carry comfortably the cap of commerce; and he would not have masked his doubles as money-men if he had not been an apprentice in drama emulating Plautus, while steeped in sorrow in a period of financial distress. The Roman dramatist was not bothered by the morals and manners of the market-place. He worked for an audience of buyers and sellers, who rejoiced in the worship of Mercury, god of merchants and thieves. Shakespeare, on the contrary, worked for an audience of spenders and lenders, above all the courtiers of his Queen. Consequently he could not rest content with a hero like Plautus's Menaechmus, who was raised by an Epidamnian trader and inherited his cheap principles as well as his fortune. Antipholus of Ephesus is a soldier rather than a salesman. He was brought to the city by 'that most famous warrior, Duke Menaphon', the uncle of Solinus, and earned the latter's gratitude by serving him in battle, taking deep scars to save his life (V). In this conception of Antipholus as a warrior I sense one of those infant inventions which Freud named 'the family romances'. (14). Nobody understood better than Shakespeare how to spin these daydreams in which children strive to liberate themselves from disappointing and domineering parents by creating imaginary fathers and mothers of nobler blood and more generous hearts. In these fantasies they become the foster sons and daughters of monarchs, or else they are changelings, exiled or stolen from royal cradles and raised by poor but honest wretches who bear a strange resemblance to their real fathers and mothers. Shakespeare's transfer of the lost Antipholus to the care of the martial Duke Menaphon, instead of another merchant like father Aegeon, sounds like a 'family romance', and expresses a mild contempt for the old man's occupation.

It is difficult to see how the poet could have dealt with the paternal figure in a manner so supercilious and icy if the old fellow was still alive. The hypothesis that the father was dead has no cult to support it. If my interpretation of his personality is correct, the stately but futile old man could never mount in his son's mind to the pedestal of a god. After death he would stay a ghost. When Antipholus of Syracuse greets his father he asks, 'Aegeon art thou not? or else his ghost?' The query may be taken as a conventional phrase of amazement on meeting an acquaintance long unseen or lost. There are features in Aegeon which give the word a lurid precision. He pictures his face as hidden

> In sap-consuming winter's drizzled snow,
> And all the conduits of my blood froze up.

(V.)

His last words in the play are addressed to Aemilia; they contain not one quaver of affection or anticipation of happiness and peace. Instead he is pallidly conscientious, almost accusing, requiring her to tell the fate of the son she carried with her from the unspeakable rock. This duty done, he is mute.

3

The double Antipholus regains the divine Aemilia. 'After so long grief, such festivity!' she cries before departing with her family into the abbey. The felicity of the author, the actors, and the spectators, in the last episode of the *Errors* is so cordial and uncontrolled that one is reluctant to survey it from the standpoint of criticism. Yet the combination of childish and ghoulish elements in the scene needs to be illumined if we are ever to grasp the psychology of Shakespeare, and eventually the psychology of the stage. Is it necessary for the comedy to conclude in environs redolent of bloody graves? What have these to do with the dominant theme of mistaken identity, the entertainment of aliens as lovers?

The replies to these problems, to which our analysis inevitably leads, can perhaps be presented best in the form of a synopsis briefly reviewing what might have happened to Shakespeare before he could compose *The Comedy of Errors*. Whether the tale I shall unfold corresponds to the facts of the poet's life is a question for future biography to decide. It will suffice for me to point out that no other hypothesis on the play arranges its details in a coherent and rational structure, casting light on all its parts. What once appeared to be discrete and random inspirations, figures of speech, epigrams and exclamations—poetry scattered from a cornucopia without concord or intrinsic sense—now emerges in a network everywhere meaningful, reflecting real movements of life. By the Freudian dialectic we are able to discern the method in the dramatist's seeming madness.

First, there was a tempestuous period which culminated in the wreck of Shakespeare's family. During an absence from home, in a strange city, he had violated his marriage oath; he entertained a stranger as a lover. He did it in absolute ignorance of the real lusts that impelled him. The woman of the adventure had unconsciously reminded him of the dark and marvellous stranger who had been his mother. After the adventure he felt that he had committed a loathsome sin. He thought it was adultery. It was imaginary incest: in a kind of dream he had ascended to his father's place by his mother's breast. The paternal image within him grieved and grew angry. As a child Shakespeare had reverenced his father's might: as a boy he had loved him for his athletic prowess and companionship. Always he had feared and hated him as the man whom his mother obeyed. The permanent residue of these emotions in the poet's brain, circling round the memory of his father, agitated him as self-condemnation. Weakness of paternal authority in his youth, the stealthy disdain he felt for the old man, left him secretly glad that he had done the deed.

But the mental image of his mother felt polluted and betrayed. He dreaded her more than any other power in the universe, because she could shut him out from love and leave him eternally alone. To escape these punishments he would happily submit to her whips. The permanent residue of these terrors and the beatitude of their union in erotic pain, circling round the memory of his mother, tortured him exquisitely as self-damnation. With the father's ghost he felt as if he was in purgatory; now he had plunged into hell. He suffered from extreme masochism, and his narcissistic ego refused to bear it. Hunting for avenues of relief, he heard a rumour that his wife was false to him. The proofs were preposterous, but too opportune for his conceit to resist. He wanted an excuse to vent the sadism of his conscience; with barely suppressed exultation he accused his wife of his own crime, without daring to face her with the witnesses or evidence. He fled from her and her offspring, outraged and sorrowing over his exclusion from her love. Consciously he feared that if he faced her he might do something frightful. Unconsciously he flamed with a lust for destruction, which his ego habitually directed on the internal images or external effigies of his parents, because of the scars and frustrations they had imposed on his infant vanity. Sadist thoughts evoked unconscious remembrance of his anal malice to the mother, the way he scattered bowel-gold to her disgust and ire, or refused to pay it forth till she became peremptory. This remembrance was sharpened by the fact that the time of his fury against his wife was also a time of pecuniary distress. Still he lavished money on inns and individuals who enjoyed his flow of talk. Observing that these luxuries only increased his misery, he retreated to a solitude where his main expenses were sweetly sour thoughts, tears, and poetry. He may also have been saddened by the funeral of a friend, for his mind dwelt fondly on graves and effigies of the dead. The urge to self-slaughter kindled memories of his passions of guilt and pangs of outcast love at the time his imagination first confronted the tombs of his father and mother. His heart felt eaten by remorse; the nerves of his maternal temple drained vitality from his Narcissus pool, just as he had once drained life-liquid from her breast.

The poet consciously defined the causes of his melancholy as he knew them in the questions that the abbess asks Adriana concerning the fugitive Antipholus:

> Hath he not lost much wealth by wrack of sea?
> Buried some dear friend? Hath not else his eye
> Stray'd his affection in unlawful love?
> A sin prevailing much in youthful men,
> Who give their eyes the liberty of gazing.

After the unjust divorce of his wife, in his refuge of tranquil contemplation and poetry, he remembered two comedies by Plautus which appealed to him as works of art full of semblances and lessons of his wicked experience. Turning over the ancient Latin leaves he discharged a heartful of pity and terror with laughter over their lusty gods, jealous husbands, and noble but stubborn wives. The infinitely funny intrigues struck him like a mixture of his own wishes and accomplishments. Possibly, with the aid of alcohol, he fell asleep on his copy of Plautus. Through the laughter and the sleep he replenished the libido in his Narcissus pool, and energetically renewed the ego struggle to control the drives of the id. The source of this new strength is the essence of Shakespeare's genius, and like all genius remains a sphinx to psycho-analysis. The physiology of narcissism may some day solve the riddle. Meanwhile we have our hands full with the problem of the devices by which the genius's ego manages the id. Shakespeare's ego not only declined to give the pulses of his id the outright ecstasies of sex and destruction they craved. He exposed them to the ridicule of the world, twisted, transmuted, and 'dolled' or puppeted up. Thus they got the sole outlet his conscience and commonsense could afford.

The basic design for the exposure, the plot, occurred to him in a dream. He crossed in fantasy the four twins of the *Amphitruo,* with its celestial cuckoldry, and the two twins of the *Menaechmi,* with its domestic quarrelling, cheating of prostitutes, and final satisfaction of restored brotherhood. The outcome was a farce about himself, on the surface displaying the will to believe that the source of his troubles was erroneous marriage, the mistaken union of strangers. He stated his plea of innocence according to his habit of paronomasia: 'Not mad, but mated; how I do not know.' He, put these words in the mouth of Antipholus, courting Luciana (III, ii), and showed their personal significance by repeating the idea from the mouth of Duke Solinus: 'I think you are all mated or stark mad' (V). Shakespeare was afraid to find out why mating checkmated him. To be mated, in the English of his lifetime, meant not only to be married; a single man mated was a man confounded, rendered impotent. Shakespeare's impotence resulted from incest-guilt after mating with a facsimile of his maternal idol. No sooner was he free of one facsimile than, like Antipholus's drop of water, he drifted wildly about 'to find his fellow forth', that is to mate again. Like that waterdrop he was destined to be confounded and lost ('mated'), forever looking for a mother from whom he was forever in flight. The dream which *The Comedy of Errors* ensued displaced the passion of his quest, making its object a brother, a fellow-male, the dramatist's material self. Finding him gave the dreamer the pacific illusion that he was no longer estranged from himself. Latent in the dream was an odyssey of a motherless child, who accused his sire of separating him from the beloved, and sailed alone across a sexual sea to a maternal territory, in which, by the contrary lights of a lunar mother he reached at last the goddess of his desire, the mother-in-death.

By the inner dramatic method which Freud designates the dream-work, Shakespeare saw the fiercest of his unconscious wishes fulfilled. He wanted to rise to his father's place by his mother's breast. He performed the incest in fantasy in a variety of ways. (i) He divided himself into doubles, one of whom floats away with the mother when the father's ship is split. (ii) His doubles end their vicissitudes in the bosom of the mother's church, itself a symbol of maternity. (iii) By identifying himself with father Aegeon he also attained his heart's wish: (*a*) he sailed the sea of sex as captain of a family vessel, 'giving honour unto the wife, as unto the weaker vessel' (I Peter, iii, 7); (*b*) he guided his mast into the forbidden harbour of Ephesus, the town of the great mother-goddess Diana. (iv) By identifying Ephesus with the mother, the poet presented his double from Syracuse with a chance to lose himself in her midst. (v) In a regression to infantile rivalry with the father over food, he tricked the wife into serving him a meal while the hungry husband fretted outside. The poet puts emphasis on the sweetness of the meal, comparing it to a cake, an emblem of motherly labour. (vi) He at least made a gesture of sexual promise to the romantic facsimile of his mother whom he named Luciana.—It will be remarked that for each of these incestuous scenes, except the last, the dreamer provided a condign and cruel chastisement, bordering on bloodshed. (i) For floating off with the mother, one double endured not only the hardships of storm and wreck but also suffered a kidnapping by rude fishermen. (ii) For joining the mother in the bosom of her church, the doubles have to bear the sights and smells of its charnel background, a place of capital retribution. (iii) For riding the matrix-boat, the son-incorporating Aegeon is wrecked at sea, and for trespassing on the waters of Ephesus, he is menaced with a hangman's axe, a symbolic castration. (iv) For losing a twin-self in the city of Ephesus, the poet had to pay with the spectacle of the city loosing itself on the twin, hounding him—with his drawn sword—to 'melancholy vale' and monastery (a house of symbolic castration, of 'eunuchs for the kingdom of heaven's sake'—Matthew, xix, 12). (v) For tricking the mistress of the hero's home, his 'natural' self must stand in impotent wrath and cold, an exile from her breast, or her larder. By these brutal exactions the poet mentally redeemed his soul from guilt. At the same time, in the theatre of his mind's night, he gratified his lust for falling together with his father and mother to destruction, or rather to sanguine chaos and the brink of death. The coalescence of both these lusts of sex and destruction took place in the fantasy of returning to the womb of the mother in her tomb.

Having accomplished his heart's desires in dream, he woke refreshed, and broke the long fast of his sadness with gusto and glee. Then, after some earnest reflection on raw material and art, he sat down to write *The Comedy of Errors*. In the affectionate endeavour to justify himself on the stage, he multiplied reasons for the conduct of his puppets, employing a technique analogous to the secondary elaboration of dreams. Next he carried out a tertiary elaboration: he issued his drama-work in a texture to satisfy actors and critics, fulfilling requirements of the contemporary theatre. He garnished the play with coeval allusions ('modern instances'), indicated erudition delicately, sprinkled the scenes with extra dirty jokes for the groundlings, 'wise saws' and singable lines for students and gentry, and crowned the concoction with passages that bright particular 'stars' could sink their histrionic teeth into joyously. Despite rubs and botches, contradiction and extravagance, he knew he had produced a gem comparable to the *Menaechmi* of Plautus, which was said to be that master's earliest drama. Would the world ever realize what it cost him? what bleeding fragments of his life he carved and morselled before he could set forth this dish fit for the lords?

Scripsi et salvavi animam meam.

References

(1) Harris, Frank. *The Man Shakespeare* (1909), bk. II, ch. 1.

(2) Cf. Jaques's speech on the liberty of motley in *As You Like It,* II, vii; Hamlet's lines on the purpose of playing (*Hamlet,* III, i).

(3) Frazer, Sir James. *The Golden Bough,* abridged edition (1942), 165.

(4) Scot, Reginald. *Discoverie of Witchcraft* (1584), bk. 12, ch. iii.

(5) Frazer. *Op. cit.,* 165.

(6) Wilson, E. C. *England's Eliza* (1939), ch. v, 'Diana'. Cf. also ch. vii, 'Cynthia, the Ladie of the Sea'.

(7) Edwards, Richard. Prologue to *Damon and Pythias* (1587), quoted by E. K. Chambers, *The Elizabethan Stage* (1923), IV, 193.

(8) Freud, Sigmund. *A General Introduction to Psychoanalysis* (1935), 137.

(9) Frazer. *Op. cit.,* 3, 141.

(10) Freud. 'On the Sexual Theories of Children', *Collected Papers* (1924), II, 65f.

(11) Jones, Ernest. 'The Madonna's Conception Through the Ear', *Essays in Applied Psycho-Analysis* (1923), 274f.

(12) Cf. Sharp, Ella Freeman. 'From *King Lear* to *The Tempest*', *Int. J. Psycho-Anal.,* 27, (1946), 19f.

(13) Freud. 'Mourning and Melancholia', *Collected Papers,* IV, 163.

(14) ———. 'Family Romances', *Collected Papers,* V, 74.

CHARACTER STUDIES

W. Thomas MacCary (essay date 1985)

SOURCE: MacCary, W. Thomas. "*The Comedy of Errors.*" In *Friends and Lovers: The Phenomenology of Desire in Shakespearean Comedy,* pp. 81-90. New York: Columbia University Press, 1985.

[*In the essay below, MacCary maintains that Antipholus of Syracuse is the primary focus of* The Comedy of Errors, *noting that his search for his brother may be viewed as a search for himself.*]

A common structural aspect of the early comedies is delayed marriage; this fact emphasizes the importance to these plays of the young male's trepidation at committing himself physically and emotionally to a woman. In three of these plays the alternative of identification with other males is first tried, and then, only with regret, dismissed as inadequate. In *The Two Gentlemen of Verona* and *Love's Labor's Lost* the other males are friends, but in *The Comedy of Errors* the protagonist seeks his twin brother, whom he speaks of as "myself." It is in this play that we are closest, then, to the narcissistic pattern of object-choice. We do not find in Antipholus of Syracuse the sensational aspects of the love life of pathological narcissists as defined by Kernberg—polymorphous perversity and sexual promiscuity; rather social isolation is his characterizing feature. We might rather choose to use the Elizabethan term melancholy for this, and associate him with Antonio, *The Merchant of Venice,* and Jaques in *As You Like It,* those outsiders who know not how to love.

Before defining this trait further with an examination of the "drop of water" speeches, and before pressing the contention that it is from Antipholus of Syracuse's point of view that we see the action of the play, I think it would be helpful to show that this kind of investigation does not raise new problems, but responds to those raised by other critics, namely, that the play is strangely without an end in marriage, and thus seems not to fit the romantic pattern of comedy. Legatt observes of the final scene and of the relation between Antipholus of Ephesus and his wife Andriana: "The director may contrive a forgiving embrace, but nothing in the text requires it. . . . For the critic, with only the text before him, the final state of the marriage must remain an open question."[1]

Palmer and Bradbury, in their preface to the collection of essays *Shakespearean Comedy,* explain why this play is not included in their discussion:

> Of the ten comedies which belong to the first half of Shakespeare's career, only *The Comedy of Errors, The Taming of the Shrew* and *The Merry Wives of Windsor* are not given detailed consideration here: an omission which reflects less on their merits than on the volume's prevailing interest in the more "romantic" plays.[2]

I have argued elsewhere that the comic tradition prejudices us against *The Comedy of Errors,* and this might account for its low estimation by critics in the Shakespearean corpus.[3] We have been accustomed by Menander, Plautus, and Terence, and their successors, to expect marriage to be not only the end of comedy, but its goal, i.e., that the genre's teleology is marriage and the immersion of the individual in society that marriage symbolizes. Frye, Barber, and Salangar, as we have seen, epitomize the criticism propounding this romantic tradition in comedy. There is, however, a different kind of comedy, represented for us by Aristophanes, some Plautus, some Shakespeare, Molière, and a few later comic poets, in which desires are fulfilled, but not for the male in the female. Rather, this tradition focuses on the male's search for and expression of himself, and this is figured with twins, doubles, friends, and other mirroring devices. I call this kind of comedy narcissistic, and in Aristophanes, at least, I find the polymorphous perversity and sexual promiscuity which Kernberg places at one extreme of his continuum of configurations.

J. R. Brown says that "the audience of Shakespearean comedy is not led towards an intimate knowledge of a single character,"[4] and that the doubling of pairs of lovers in Shakespearean comedy is a means of "dispersing our interest, and giving us range rather than concentration."[5] This seems to me again a function of the socialized view we have been encouraged, at least since Barber, to impose on the comedies. In *The Comedy of Errors* we are introduced to Antipholus of Syracuse by his father, and from this beginning we know that the driving force behind him is his search for his lost twin brother, which we soon come to realize, through language and incident, is a search for himself. Egeon tells us:

> My youngest boy, and yet my eldest care,
> At eighteen years became inquisitive
> After his brother, and importun'd me
> That his attendant, so his case was like,
> Reft of his brother, but retain'd his name,
> Might bear him company in the quest of him;
> Whom whilst I labour'd of a love to see,
> I hazarded the loss of whom I lov'd.
>
> (I.i.124-31)

Then, immediately, we meet Antipholus of Syracuse, and almost his first lines create an image of his self-concern; he meditates in an aside on a local merchant's valediction, "Sir, I commend you to your own content":

> He that commends me to mine own content
> Commends me to the thing I cannot get.
> I to the world am like a drop of water
> That in the ocean seeks another drop,
> Who, falling there to find his fellow forth,
> (Unseen, inquisitive) confounds himself.
> So I, to find a mother and a brother,
> In quest of them, unhappy, lose myself.
>
> (I.ii.33-40)

Rhetoric is overripe in parts of the play, but this is not one of them; here the paradox is a function of the psychological condition described, not of the language used to describe it. The whole content of the play is figured in "content": he cannot find "contentment" until he finds his "content," his brother, his external self. The drop of water image flows then naturally from this notion of the lost object as the whole of the subject. In order to assure himself of his own existence Antipholus of Syracuse sets out to find his brother (and mother), but in that search he loses the image of himself in the world which teems with others. The project in the stage of primary narcissism is for the subject to introject the image of himself which first his mother and then others project to him. Until that task is accomplished the choice of objects different from the self (both unlike and distinct from the self) is impossible. Indeed, first the mother and then the entire world are seen as a threatening, engulfing void.

Kernberg describes the overcoming of these feelings, and, with reference to an image first used by Freud himself, speaks directly to the dilemma of Antipholus of Syracuse:

> Sexual passion assumes the capacity for continued empathy with—but not merger into—a primitive state of symbiotic fusion (the "oceanic feeling" of earlier psychoanalytic literature), the excited reunion or closeness with mother at a stage of self-object differentiation, and the gratification of oedipal longings in the context of overcoming feelings of inferiority, fear and guilt regarding sexual longings.[6]

It is, of course, these oedipal feelings that Wheeler concentrates on; indeed he sees the great comic problem (especially in the "problem comedies") as overcoming the guilt oedipally associated with sexuality because of the incestuous pattern which is the origin of its longings. But I stress the anxiety which is a consequence of pre-oedipal fragmentation in the sense of self: the child is still shoring up fragments of his object-relations against the ruins of his symbiosis with his mother. Kernberg always insists that ego boundaries must be maintained in a happy love relationship, just as he insists that ego boundaries must be securely drawn before mature love is possible; hence his distinction between "empathy" and "merger." It is about merger that Antipholus of Syracuse fantasizes, and not as an experience of love, but rather as a consequence of having failed to integrate his ego through a normal sequence of object-relations beginning with his mother, but focused on his brother.

I am not constructing a psychobiography for Antipholus of Syracuse; I am not treating the separation from his mother, almost at birth, as the traumatic genesis of recurrent pathology. Rather I am suggesting that Antipholus of Syracuse is the focus of attention in *The Comedy of Errors* because we readily identify with him, and we readily identify with him because we have all passed through the phase of primary narcissism—more or less successfully. The less successful we have been, the more compulsive we become at recapitulating its pattern, and thus we understand what Antipholus of Syracuse tells us about his sense of deprivation. He raises to consciousness in us memory traces of our own psychic development—not because we have all had twins and lost them, but because we have all struggled to find in our early environment ("the precursor of the mirror is the mother's eyes") an image of ourselves we can assimilate towards, or, rather, introject as ourselves. In this way, by a very complicated (here completely abridged) argument, we can claim that Antipholus of Ephesus represents the ideal ego of Antipholus of Syracuse, and that, ontogenetically speaking, the ideal ego preexists the ego.

Just as Antipholus of Syracuse was introduced to us by his father, and we hear first from another that the young man seeks his twin and then hear from his own lips that this is his sole concern; so we first hear of Antipholus of Ephesus from his wife and his sister. Next we meet not him, but Antipholus of Syracuse again, confused by them for him. From all of them we learn of two different attitudes toward marriage: should the wife restrain, inhibit, and bind her husband to her, claiming he is a part of her, or should she allow him his free movement in the world, waiting patiently at home, never presuming to question or complain? The two Antipholi move in different directions: Antipholus of Syracuse seeks his mother and his brother, and in the process loses himself, while Antipholus of Ephesus flees his wife to find himself. Adriana and Luciana, the dark, binding wife and the bright, liberal wife-to-be, clearly polarize the sexual argument that runs through all the early comedies: the man's sphere is outside, the woman's inside; the man acts and the woman obeys. Though we might find the strongest statement of the first proposition in *The Two Gentlemen of Verona*, and of the second in *The Taming of the Shrew*, it is in *The Comedy of Errors* that the overriding theme of male and female identity is clearest: women define themselves by their relations to men, but men define themselves in their own terms. Adriana hauntingly recapitulates the drop of water imagery of Antipholus of Syracuse's opening speech, and, thinking she is speaking to her husband, speaks to a stranger and so drives him mad, as later her husband will appear.

> How comes it now, my husband, O, how comes it,
> That thou art then estranged from thyself?—
> Thyself I call it, being strange to me,
> That undividable, incorporate,
> Am better than thy dear self's better part.
> Ah, do not tear away thyself from me;
> For know, my love, as easy mayst thou fall
> A drop of water in the breaking gulf,
> And take unmingled thence that drop again
> Without addition or diminishing,
> As take from me thyself, and not me too.
>
> (II.ii.119-29)

The dominant point of view in the play is that of Antipholus of Syracuse, and hence the male's. Here we have a strong statement by the woman of what she requires from the man, but it is negated by another woman, that man's mother, at the conclusion of the play.

> And thereof came it that the man was mad.
> The venom clamours of a jealous woman
> Poisons more deadly than a mad dog's tooth.
>
> (V.i.68-70)

The extraordinary thing that Shakespeare accomplishes in all this is, of course, first the expropriation of Antipholus of Syracuse's own image by Adriana, a threatening, demanding, inhibiting woman. I mean to play on the two meanings of image: she speaks of him as a drop of water just as he had spoken of himself as a drop of water earlier, and in that drop of water we see, of course, his mirror image, his twin brother, his ideal ego, his external soul—but certainly not his wife. Then the reunion of the twins occurs under the mother's auspices: she is the woman who matters most, and she effaces herself.

The situations and language of the play so specifically equate individual psychological needs with socially imposed sexual roles that we are encouraged to add, from later comedies, the physical distinction of the sexes as an explanation. Adriana and Luciana debate the nature and convention of sexual difference:

ADR.

> Why should their liberty than ours be more?

LUC.

> Because their business still lies out o' door.
>
> (II.i.10-11)

Shakespeare follows the social convention of domesticating women: they stay at home. When they go out into the world, they are dressed as men, equipped with swords, and their tongues are sharpened to a rapier wit. Julia and Portia will debate their wearing of codpieces, the addition to their lack. Clearly Shakespeare encourages us to see for these women an identification between the house and the body: while they are women they stay inside, hidden, like their genitals; but when they become men, they go outside, and wear their genitals openly, even accentuated, in the male fashion of the day. Adriana is usurping male prerogatives, so that she frightens the man she thinks is her husband to madness, and locks him up inside; she is corrected in this behavior by her sister and by the mother of both that man and her husband. Portia and Rosalind are threatening to males in their transvestism; Julia, Viola, and Imogen are not. We shall consider their difference. Now we need only appreciate that Shakespeare, playing upon men's fears, figures women as expansive, absorbing, engulfing creatures whose roles and natures must be defined by walls and social conventions.

The second drop of water speech, in which Adriana pleads conjunction with her husband—the first half of which was quoted above—continues with a suggestion of venereal disease:

> How dearly would it touch thee to the quick,
> Shouldst thou but hear I were licentious?
> And that this body, consecrate to thee,
> By ruffian lust should be contaminate?
> Wouldst thou not spit at me, and spurn at me,
> And hurl the name of husband in my face,
> And tear the stain'd skin off my harlot brow,
> And from my false hand cut the wedding-ring,
> And break it with a deep-divorcing vow?
> I know thou canst; and therefore, see thou do it!
> I am possess'd with an adulterate blot,
> My blood is mingled with the crime of lust;
> For if we two be one, and thou play false,
> I do digest the poison of thy flesh,

Being strumpeted by thy contagion.

(II.ii. 130-44)

One need only compare Sonnet 129 to appreciate what Antipholus of Syracuse would hear in all this:

> The expense of Spirit in a waste of shame
> Is lust in action, and till action, lust
> Is perjured, murderous, bloody, full of blame,
>
> . . . . .
>
> All this the world well knows, yet none knows well
> To shun the Heaven that leads men to this Hell.

From the male perspective the sin of fornication and the threat of disease are both in the woman, in that waist of shame, that Hell, to which is compared the Heaven of the Poet's union with the Fair Youth, and Antipholus of Syracuse's reunion with his lost brother.

The basis of Shakespeare's male characters' fear of the females who would marry them is derived from their fear of reincorporation by the pre-oedipal mother. Water we know to be the most frequent dream-symbol for the birth process.[7] In his drop of water speech Antipholus of Syracuse acknowledges his origin from the mother but, deprived of some image of himself in another drop of water (his twin brother, but also his ideal ego), he fears reversal of the birth process. Of course, this is the latent content of this dreamlike speech; the manifest content (though it, too, is unconscious, so only we, the audience, having just heard the family history, can appreciate it) is the separation of child from mother by shipwreck. The sea is actually prominent in several other plays where reintegration of the nuclear family is a goal: *Twelfth Night, The Tempest, Pericles*. This fear of the overwhelming mother is, then, articulated by Antipholus of Syracuse, and reenforced by Adriana, who would lock him up, and indeed does lock up her own husband, claiming he is mad, the state to which she has almost driven Antipholus of Syracuse. The whole situation can be corrected only by the real mother Emilia, who appears at the end and says, essentially, everything is going to be all right: "You two boys have found each other and me—your father is here, too, but he is not so important in this pre-oedipal struggle for identity which you are recapitulating—and now you can even think about marriage."[8] Shakespeare develops the theme of madness then in the framework of the nuclear family: madness is being two of the same or nothing at all. The twins are confused for each other, so they each think there is an other of them in the world, which is maddening, but they also fear the loss of self entirely, so that two became none, all being absorbed by the sea, the threatening mother and her representations.

Kernberg points out that male fears of close relations with women are derived originally from memories of the pre-oedipal mother, that because men know themselves to have been originally dependent on an all-powerful being different from themselves, they resist such attachments in maturity.[9] Women obviously have a different perspective. I think it is best argued that Shakespeare's perspective is always that of the male, though his so-called bisexuality is often hailed as the hallmark of his genius. Adriana is a male's nightmare image of the overwhelming mother; the chaste Emilia is its correction. Luciana also presents herself as a correction of Adriana's threatening persona. Psychoanalytic critics have pointed out that the names are significant: Adriana is the "dark lady" *(ater)* and Luciana the "bright lady" *(lux)*. Antipholus of Syracuse spontaneously responds to this heavenly creature, and the play on love and reflected light, on self and other occurs, which also dominates *The Two Gentlemen of Verona* and *Love's Labor's Lost*:

Luc.

What, are you mad that you do reason so?

Syr. Ant.

Not mad, but mated, how I do not know.

Luc.

It is a fault that springeth from your eye.

Syr. Ant.

For gazing on your beams, fair sun, being by.

Luc.

Gaze where you should, and that will clear your sight.

Syr. Ant.

As good to wink, sweet love, as look on night.

Luc.

Why call you me love? Call my sister so.

Syr. Ant.

Thy sister's sister.

Luc.

That's my sister.

Syr. Ant.

No,
It is thyself, mine own self's better part,
Mine eye's clear eye, my dear heart's dearer heart,
My food, my fortune, and my sweet hope's aim,
My sole earth's heaven, and my heaven's claim.

(III.ii. 53-64)

This is the Neoplatonic figure of the man defining himself by reference to the woman: he sees himself in her eyes, thinks indeed that he is but a reflection of her light. There is also play on the names: Luciana is light; Adriana is night. We shall see that in *The Two Gentlemen of Verona* Silvia will be a moon goddess, and first Valentine, then Proteus will play Endymion to her. Here, in *The Comedy of Errors*, the figure is not developed, but implied in the extravagance of Antipholus of Syracuse's language is the

Act IV, scene iv of the 1996 Open Air Theatre production of The Comedy of Errors.

distinction between self and Self which Zweig traces from the earliest Christian literature through Shakespeare and beyond. What Narcissus gazes *at* is only a deceptive image of himself (the imitation of an imitation), but the true Christian, or the true Neoplatonic lover, sees *in* himself a manifestation of God's grace, as the world of physical objects participates in *(methexis)* the Forms. This gives a metaphysical model for love which is generally contradicted in Shakespeare; indeed the extravagance of the language here suggests parody.

Having questioned whether Shakespeare ever centers desire or the universe in Truth or Being, having found instead that both erotically and philosophically he sees a tension of opposites mutually defining each other, we offer the following hypothesis: the Neoplatonic worship of the woman represents oedipal orientation of desire; the search for the self in a twin or friend represents primary narcissism; the fear of the overwhelming mother can be read as either oedipal or pre-oedipal, depending on the imagery of its expression. The "oceanic feeling" suggests those pre-oedipal anxieties which come with the recognition that the mother is separate and independent, i.e., anxieties occurring at the end of the symbiotic phase. The sexualized imagery of binding, of locking in or out of the house, suggests oedipal anxieties, i.e., fears of sexual incompetence. That there is no strong father figure, but only strong women in the play, tilts the argument to the pre-oedipal side. Emilia is awesome; Dromio's kitchen wench is disgusting; Adriana is threatening; Luciana is benevolent but colorless. We do not yet see that assimilation between self-images and images of the desired female which, beginning with *The Two Gentlemen of Verona*, becomes Shakespeare's major comic concern.

Notes

1. A. Legatt, *Shakespeare's Comedy of Love* (London: Methuen, 1974), p. 9.

2. D. Palmer and M. Bradbury, *Shakespearean Comedy* (New York: Crane, Russak, 1972), pp. 7-8.

3. W. T. MacCary, "*The Comedy of Errors:* A Different Kind of Comedy," *New Literary History* (1978), 9:525-36.

4. J. R. Brown, "The Presentation of Comedy: The First Ten Plays," in D. Palmer and M. Bradbury, eds. *Shakespearean Comedy* (New York: Crane, Russak, 1972), p. 9.

5. *Ibid.*, p. 10.

6. O. Kernberg, "Boundaries and Structures in Love Relations," *Journal of the American Psychoanalytic Association* (1977), 25:99. The reference to Freud is to the opening of *Civilization and Its Discontents*.

7. S. Freud, *The Interpretation of Dreams*, in J. Strachey, ed. and tr., *The Standard Edition of the Complete Psychological Works of Sigmund Freud* (London: Hogarth Press, 1953-74), 5:399-401.

8. Antipholus of Syracuse was only eighteen when he began his search (I.i.125), and is twenty-three when the action of the play takes place (I.i.132). The twins should then be played as young men, and not middle-aged, as they often are. In Plautus' *Menaechmi* they are technically termed *adulescentes;* of course, comedy notoriously polarizes its male characters between *adulescens* and *senex* to accentuate the difference in the effects of love upon them.

9. Kernberg, "Boundaries and Structure," p. 108.

Robert Viking O'Brien (essay date 1996)

SOURCE: O'Brien, Robert Viking. "The Madness of Syracusan Antipholus." In *Early Modern Literary Studies* 2, no. 1 (April 1996): 3.1-26.

[*In the following essay, O'Brien asserts that Shakespeare exploited his Elizabethan audience's emotional response to* The Comedy of Errors *by suggesting that Antipholus of Syracuse is truly in danger of succumbing to madness.*]

Many readers of *The Comedy of Errors* notice that Egeon's possible execution provides a dark frame around what appears to be one of Shakespeare's most light-hearted comedies. Yet the threat of death that hangs over Egeon in the frame plot also hangs, in the main plot, over his Syracusan son. This threat results from Antipholus' Syracusan origins, of course, but also—less obviously and more significantly—from the possibility that Syracusan Antipholus is losing his mind. The Elizabethans believed that, without correction, insanity usually led to death; for Shakespeare's audience, the deaths of Lear and Ophelia probably seemed inevitable as soon as the characters went mad. I shall argue in this essay that, in *The Comedy of Errors*, Shakespeare uses the possibility that Syracusan Antipholus is genuinely threatened by madness, and therefore death, to manipulate his audience's anxieties. I shall also show how, despite the play's dependence on a classical source, Syracusan Antipholus' descriptions of his "transformed" mind draw on specific, Elizabethan ideas about both supernatural and natural causes of madness.

The character's first appearance on stage, as a wanderer newly disembarked from a ship, draws on strong cultural associations between wandering, water, and insanity. Michel Foucault explores these associations in *Madness and Civilization* when he investigates a reality behind the imaginary Ship of Fools. Boats of mad people did in fact ply European rivers, for boatmen were often charged with removing the insane to the countryside or to another city.[1] Foucault sees these mad boats both as a practical solution to the social threat posed by the insane, and as a ritual laden with significance. The water over which the mad are carried purifies them at the same time it excludes and confines them (7-12). He relates this ritual to older cultural material relating madness and sea-borne passengers.[2]

When Syracusan Antipholus arrives in Ephesus "stiff and weary" from his long journey over the sea, he gives his money to his servant and sends the servant away. He says that he plans to wander the town and look at its buildings and inhabitants. When the only other person in Ephesus who knows his identity leaves, Syracusan Antipholus is in the position of a lunatic released from one of the ships of fools described by Foucault. Antipholus soon discovers that he is incapable of interpreting what is said to him, and the city's inhabitants see him as mad.

His situation is the same as the parallel character's in Plautus' *Menaechmi,* Shakespeare's primary source. If the resemblance between Syracusan Antipholus and Foucault's released madmen stopped there, it would be difficult to claim that features of the scene resemble the cultural pattern described by Foucault. Antipholus' first soliloquy reinforces that pattern, however, by using water as its central metaphor:

> He that commends me to mine own content
> Commends me to the thing I cannot get.
> I to the world am like a drop of water
> That in the ocean seeks another drop,
> Who, falling there to find his fellow forth,
> (Unseen, inquisitive) confounds himself.
>
> (1.2.33-38)[3]

We find the metaphor of water dissolving into water elsewhere in Shakespeare as an expression of "losing one's self." It appears, for example, in *Richard II*'s deposition scene, when Richard describes himself as melting "away in water drops!" (4.1.263), in Hamlet's famous soliloquy, "O that this too too sallied flesh would melt, / Thaw, and resolve itself into a dew!" (1.2.129-30), and in *Antony and Cleopatra,* when Antony describes himself as being like the shapes one sees in the clouds: "That which is now a horse, even with a thought / The rack dislimns, and makes it indistinct / As water is in water" (4.14.9-11).[4] If these characters associate their own unsettled identities or extreme melancholy with water, the great mad characters immerse themselves in it. Lear tears off his clothes in the driving rain and asks for the land to be submerged: "You cataracts and hurricanoes, spout / Till you have drench'd our steeples, drown'd the cocks!" (3.2.3-4). Ophelia enters the water of the weeping brook "like a creature native and indued / Unto that element" (4.7.179-80). The connection between water and madness does not, of course, originate with Shakespeare. According to Foucault, it either begins with the ritual of the mad ships, or the ships themselves reflect an older cultural pattern: "One thing at least is certain, water and madness have long been linked in the dreams of European man" (12).

Wandering and madness are similarly linked. Foucault outlines how the wandering madmen of pre- and early-modern Europe typify this connection, which reflects a reality similar to that found in the late twentieth-century United States. In Elizabethan England, mentally-disturbed vagrants were a "ubiquitous presence" (Rosen 153) represented in ballads by the figure of Tom o'Bedlam, who wanders in search of his "stragling sences" (Lindsay 35). Edgar's soliloquy in *King Lear* reflects this presence as well:

> The country gives me proof and president
> Of Bedlam beggars, who, with roaring voices,
> Strike in their numb'd and mortified arms
> Pins, wooden pricks, nails, sprigs of rosemary;
> And with this horrible object, from low farms,
> Poor pelting villages, sheep-cotes, and mills,
> Sometimes with lunatic bans, sometime with prayers,
> Enforce their charity.
>
> (2.3.13-20)

Syracusan Antipholus also connects mental confusion and wandering when he bids farewell to the merchant in the second scene: "I will go lose myself, / And wander" (1.2.30-31). "Lose myself" and "wander" mean much the same thing here, but the first phrase hints at a loss of identity, an unsettling of the psyche that is more explicitly described in Antipholus' first soliloquy. Significantly, this soliloquy ends by describing the effect of Antipholus' wanderings: "So I, to find a mother and a brother, / In quest of them, unhappy lose myself" (1.2.39-40).

Wandering defines Syracusan Antipholus' character. Indeed, the first Folio uses Syracusan Antipholus' status as a wanderer to distinguish him from his twin. The Folio's stage directions call him "Antipholis Erotes" (1.2.S.D.), while his brother is called "Antipholis Sereptus" (2.1.S.D.). *Surreptus*, or "stolen away," was a common Renaissance epithet for Plautus' town-dwelling twin. *Erotes,* on the other hand, appears only in Shakespeare's play. Textual scholars have suggested several meanings for the name, but most see it as a corruption of *Erraticus*, formed from the verb *errare*, to wander (Foakes, xxvi-vii). The epithet fits the Syracusan twin, who, like his father, has presumably traveled "in farthest Greece, / Roaming clean through the bounds of Asia" (1.1.132-33). Ephesian Antipholus, on the other hand, has had a settled life.

If we take "wandering" as a mental rather than physical state, the distinction applies to the play's present action as well. Ephesian Antipholus' wife may believe that he is wandering mentally, but despite this diagnosis and his treatment by Dr. Pinch, the Ephesian twin remains "settled" in his sense of reality. His situation is thus safely in the realm of error as "mistaking." Just as various characters mistake him for his twin, his wife and Dr. Pinch mistake him for a madman. He knows they are wrong. The Syracusan twin's situation is altogether different. The state of mind described in the first soliloquy becomes more unsettled in the confusing confrontations that follow. Syracusan Antipholus never thinks the characters he meets are mistaken or mad—instead, he doubts his own sense of reality. When confronted by the raging, jealous Adriana, for example, Syracusan Antipholus wonders if he married her and was unaware of it, or if he is now dreaming: "What, was I married to her in my dream? / Or sleep I now, and think I hear all this?" (2.2.181-82). This kind of questioning continues to the very end of the play: even after most of the problems of mistaken identity have been cleared up, Syracusan Antipholus alludes to the possibility that he is still dreaming (5.1.376).

These are the questions of a madman, for as Robert Burton, citing Avicenna, says, madmen "wake as others dream" (335). The wandering twin in the *Menaechmi* does not ask such questions. Unlike Shakespeare's Syracusan Antipholus, Plautus' Syracusan Menaechmus never doubts his own sense of reality. He pretends to be insane, *"adsimulem insanire"* (831), rather than thinking he is insane. Unlike Hamlet's "antic disposition," this pretence is never ambiguous: Plautus continually shows us the character's sanity. When confronted with someone's inexplicable words or behavior, Menaechmus assumes that the other character, not he, is mad.

A comparison of the confused-identity scenes in the *Menaechmi* and *The Comedy of Errors* reveals the difference. In the *Menaechmi,* the humor in these scenes often results from arguments over who is insane. For example, in the first such scene, a cook mistakes the wandering twin for the settled one. Syracusan Menaechmus immediately decides that the man is insane—*"certe hic insanust homo"* (283)—and when the cook insists that he knows Menaechmus well, Menaechmus gives him money to be purified by a priest, *"nam equidem insanum esse te certo scio"* (292). An argument follows over who is sane. Neither character doubts his own sanity for a moment.

In Shakespeare's play, scenes involving the settled twin provide similar humor, as do some scenes involving the wandering one. Yet when Syracusan Antipholus is mistaken for his brother, he is bewildered in a way that Syracusan Menaechmus never is. Shakespeare's wandering twin rarely argues with characters who confuse him with his brother, and even when he does argue, the exchange has an unsettling quality not found in Plautus. In *The Comedy of Errors'* first scene of mistaken identity, for example, Syracusan Antipholus meets his servant's twin and asks how he has completed his errand so quickly:

> How chance thou art return'd so soon?
>
> EPH. DRO.
>
> Returned so soon? Rather approached too late. . . .
>
> (1.2.42-43)

The exchange is the first in a series of unsettling disruptions of Antipholus' sense of time. The period's "faculty psychology," which derives ultimately from Aristotle's *De Anima,* associates such disruptions with the decay of the sensitive soul's perceptive faculties, a decay that, like the decay of the intellective soul, signals the onset of madness (Park 465-73).

G. R. Elliot describes how disrupted time gives the play a feeling of "weirdness" absent in Plautus (95-106). While Elliot explores this feeling as a feature of the *Comedy*'s atmosphere, more recent scholars have seen the play's strangeness as a representation of psychological states. For example, in an essay on the relation of the frame plot to the interior plot of mistaken identity, Barbara Freedman asks what it means to be recognized as someone else. She sees Syracusan Antipholus' situation as representing "a present persona confused with a past, denied persona—a part of the self with which [one] no longer identifies" (367). In Freedman's reading, the play's mistaken identities realize repressed parts of the psyche. This realization can be frightening, and Freedman sees the play as a kind of nightmare. That the play does not have what Harry Berger calls a "green world" (3-40) makes it all the more terrifying: "By not removing the play's action to a magical island or forest, Shakespeare stresses the essence of nightmare: the imagined fulfilment of repressed fears and desires in everyday reality" (Freedman 363).

The threat of death hangs over this "farce," as does the threat of madness that appears again in *Hamlet* and *King Lear.* Syracusan Antipholus struggles with this threat throughout the play. When the first confusions arise, he tries to determine their nature and includes the possibility that he has lost his senses: "Am I in earth, in heaven, or in hell? / Sleeping or waking, mad or well advis'd?" (2.2.212-13). In the third act, he decides he is on earth and that witches are twisting his mind (3.2.155). He generally adheres to this explanation for the rest of the play. When he falls in love with Luciana, he believes he is surrendering his mind to a witch's power (3.2.161-63). In the fourth act, he attributes various confusing offstage encounters to "Lapland sorcerers" (4.3.11).

Antipholus has been prepared for this explanation by stories he has heard about Ephesus, which is said to be inhabited by "Dark-working sorcerers that change the mind" and "Soul-killing witches that deform the body" (1.2.99-100). Significantly, no such association exists in the *Menaechmi.* Like Shakespeare's Ephesus, which "is full of cozenage, / As nimble jugglers that deceive the eye, / . . . Disguised cheaters, prating mountebanks" (1.2.97-98, 101), Plautus' Epidamnum is filled with tricksters of various kinds (260-61). None of these is said to be practicing black magic, however, and scholars have suggested that Shakespeare changed the play's setting to allow for the possibility of such magic (Foakes xxix).

For Shakespeare's audience, the city would have been most familiar as a center of pagan worship. In Acts, devotees of Diana drive Paul from the city. Before his expulsion, however, Paul performs a number of exorcisms. When these exorcisms are unsuccessfully imitated by "vagabond Jews," the failed exorcists are attacked by a possessed madman: "the man in whom the evil spirit was leaped on them, and overcame them, and prevailed against them, so that they fled out of that house naked and wounded" (19.16). This failure and Paul's successes lead to conversions and the burning of magic books: "Many of them also which used curious arts brought their books together, and burned them before all men" (19.19). In the Bible, Ephesus is associated with magic—"curious arts"—and with madness caused by possession.

Both in the first-century Near East and in Elizabethan England, people commonly attributed madness to possession that in turn was often attributed to black magic. In both places, people tried to exorcise madness-inducing demons with different degrees of success, and the successes were often conscious frauds. Shakespeare uses an account of such frauds to create Edgar's pretended madness in *King Lear:* the names of Poor Tom's demons come from Samuel Harsnett's *Declaration of egregous Popish Impostures, to withdraw the harts of her maiesties Subiects from their allegiance, and from the truth of Christian Religioun professed in England, vnder the pretence of casting out devils* (1603).[5] If, in *King Lear,* Shakespeare used pretended exorcisms to create pretended madness, in *Twelfth Night* he had one of his characters use pretended exorcism to harass another character. Feste's exorcism of Malvolio—"Out hyperbolical fiend! how vexest thou this man!" (4.2.25-6)—remains comic as long as the audience feels certain that Malvolio is sane: the scene's sinister undertone results from a vague fear that he may lose his sanity. The parallel scene in *The Comedy of Errors* lacks this undertone because, as mentioned earlier, Ephesian Antipholus' sanity is never in doubt. The audience is free to laugh at what might otherwise be a frightening exorcism:

> I charge thee, Satan, hous'd within this man,
> To yield possession to my holy prayers
> And to thy state of darkness hie thee straight;
> I conjure thee by all the saints in heaven.
>
> (4.4.52-53)

This passage may allude to the fraudulent exorcisms described later in Harsnett's *Declaration.* The earliest dates given for *The Comedy of Errors*' composition, 1584-89 (Foakes xvii), would make those exorcisms contemporary events; the latest would make them recent history. Even if Shakespeare is not alluding to fraudulent exorcisms, his audience probably saw Doctor Pinch much as Ephesian Antipholus does, as "a mountebank, / A threadbare juggler and a fortune-teller" (5.1.239-40). We should note, however, that although Shakespeare's audience may have regarded Pinch as a fraud or a quack, they would have seen nothing unusual in his treatment of Ephesian Antipholus' supposed madness: "They fell upon me, bound me, bore me thence, / And in a dark and dankish vault at home / There left me" (5.1.247-49). The "dark-room treatment," which also appears in *Twelfth Night* (4.2), was "one of the chief methods for the treatment of the insane in both Elizabethan and seventeenth-century England" (Reed 11). Shakespeare's audience probably took its efficacy for granted. The problem with this treatment in *The Comedy of Errors* results from the sanity of the patient and the (possible) fraudulence of the practitioner. The same is true of Pinch's attempted exorcism. Its ridiculousness should not lead us to conclude that Shakespeare and his audience did not believe in genuine exorcisms or in madness caused by possession. Even a thinker as relentlessly skeptical as Thomas Hobbes, writing in the middle of the next century, felt compelled to take possession-induced madness seriously, if only to dispute it (142-46). Before Hobbes, supernatural causes for mental illness were taken for granted, even by those who favoured explanations based on physical humours. In *The Anatomy of Melancholy*, for instance, Robert Burton departs from his description of humor-induced melancholy for a lengthy "Digression of the nature of Spirits, bad Angels, or Devils, and how they cause Melancholy" (157-79).

As the preceding example shows, belief in supernatural causes for mental illness was not limited to the illiterate, who were less familiar with "physical" explanations based on the theory of humours. The learned explanation for madness was in fact more likely to be supernatural than natural (Porter 30). Even medical doctors who ordinarily pointed to "natural" causes would, in extreme cases, point to supernatural ones (Rosen 146). For the Elizabethans, these causal categories were not contradictory. The Bible lent authority to supernatural interpretations; the classics lent authority to natural *and* supernatural interpretations: in the *Phaedrus*, for example, Plato describes both kinds of madness (265A). Throughout the Middle Ages, the idea of natural causes coexisted with that of supernatural intervention (Clarke 82). By the late sixteenth century, learned discussions of madness often focused on distinguishing between the two explanations (Kocher 297-305).

In his struggle to understand what is happening to him, Syracusan Antipholus wavers between the two explanations. Generally, he provides a supernatural explanation, but this explanation is itself bound up with the physical, for the play continually connects mental transformations to physical ones. Syracusan Antipholus' initial description of the inhabitants of Ephesus—"Dark-working sorcerers that change the mind, / Soul-killing witches that deform the body" (1.2.99-100)—makes this connection, as does the following exchange between Syracusan Antipholus and Dromio:

SYR. DRO.

    I am transformed, master, am I not?

SYR. ANT.

    I think thou art in mind, and so am I.

SYR. DRO.

    Nay, master, both in mind and in my shape.

SYR. ANT.

    Thou hast thine own form.

SYR. DRO.

    No, I am an ape.

(2.2.204)

Dromio's words foreshadow his later questioning of Syracusan Antipholus: "Do you know me sir? Am I Dromio? Am I your man? Am I myself?" (3.2.72). In this scene, Dromio's fear of transformation results from his encounter with his twin's lover, the hideous kitchen wench who knows various "privy marks" on his body, so "that I, amazed, ran from her as a witch. / And I think if my breast had not been made of faith, and my heart of steel, / She had transformed me to a curtal dog" (3.2.143-45). Dromio's description of this comically terrifying encounter immediately follows Antipholus' wooing of Luciana. Like Dromio's encounter, this wooing also involves transformation, but what Dromio feared, Antipholus desires: "Are you a god? would you create me new? / Transform me then, and to your power I'll yield" (3.2.39-40).

Antipholus repudiates this wish after he hears Dromio's story. He realizes that his desire is leading him toward madness and suicide, so "lest myself be guilty to self-wrong, / I'll stop mine ears against the mermaid's song" (3.2.161-63). Antipholus here wards off the enchantments of a woman he believes to be a witch (3.2.155). At the same time, he resists the love-induced madness that could lead him to commit the sin of self-murder.

Madness brought on by love appears so frequently in the period's literature that we tend to think of it as a convention—something Cervantes could mock, for example, by having Don Quixote, in the Sierra Morena, imitate Orlando Furioso (197-203). Yet these literary madnesses reflected a reality. In *The Anatomy of Melancholy*, Robert Burton supplies a long list of mad, suicidal lovers from literature and then tells his readers to

> Go to Bedlam for examples. It is so well known in every village, how many have either died for love, or voluntarily made away themselves, that I need not much labour to prove it; Death is the common catastrophe to such persons.
>
> (763-64)

Burton, who devotes almost a third of his *Anatomy* to love melancholy (see Reed 106), provides what may strike us as a strangely physical description of how such love is engendered: the beloved infects the lover through the eyes, for "rays, . . . sent from the eyes, carry certain spiritual vapours with them, and so infect the other party" (681). Once the infection has occurred, Burton says, the passion lodges in lower regions of the psyche, from whence it rises to distort the lover's senses, and, in extreme cases, drive him or her mad.

A similarly physical idea of madness appears in *The Comedy of Errors*. After Syracusan Antipholus' confusing encounter with Adriana, he asks "What error drives our eyes and ears amiss?" (2.2.184). On one level, his question suggests a possibility not thought of by other characters in the play: mistaken identity is responsible for their confusion. On another level, Antipholus' question suggests an actual disordering of the senses. Shakespeare is playing on a meaning of "error" largely lost to us, that of "fury" or "extravagance of passion" (*OED*). As in Burton's *Anatomy of Melancholy,* in Elizabethan physical psychology, extreme passion—an upsurge from the lower regions of the psyche—destroys the higher faculties (DePorte 115-18). Timothy Bright's *Treatise of Melancholy* (1586), for example, describes how "vehement contemplations" disorder the senses (35).

Bright says this disordering can "cause horrible and fearfull apparitions" (131). If not corrected, it leads to madness and death. Indeed, Elizabethan parish records often list, as causes of death, mental states like "frenzy" and "thought" (Forbes 117-18). Shakespeare's drama reflects the idea that uncorrected madness is ultimately fatal; as Foucault notes in *Madness and Civilization,* "In Shakespeare . . . madness . . . occupies an extreme place, in that it is beyond appeal. Nothing ever restores it either to truth or reason. It leads only to laceration and thence to death" (31-32).

The Comedy of Errors is not *King Lear.* Nevertheless, as I have argued here, this seeming farce touches upon what would have been a genuine anxiety for the Elizabethan audience. Syracusan Antipholus is struggling for his mind and his life when he cries out, near the end of the play,

> The fellow is distract, and so am I,
> And here we wander in illusions—
> Some blessed power deliver us from hence!
>
> (4.3.40-43)

Such outcries are comic because the audience is aware of the cause of Syracusan Antipholus' confusion. But however faint, the anxiety produced by fear of madness remains, darkening the play's entertaining confusions.

Notes

1. For the transportation of the insane during the Middle Ages, see also Rosen 140-41.

2. Foucault believes that the relationship had special significance for Europeans "on the horizon of the Renaissance" (18), when madness to some extent replaced death as a theme for meditation (13-15). Foucault briefly traces the literary use of madness from Erasmus' *Praise of Folly* to Cervantes and Shakespeare (12-17, 27-32). Curiously, Foucault's description of this development has been blamed for the relative lack of new work on madness in Tudor and Stuart England. Carol Thomas Neely claims that, in *Madness and Civilization,* Foucault's "Renaissance" has few distinguishing characteristics: it is merely a continuation of his "Middle Ages" (779). This has led younger scholars to focus on the late seventeenth and eighteenth centuries, the period of Foucault's "great confinement," when the older view of madness is replaced by one continuous with the present view. It seems to me that Foucault does distinguish between notions of madness before the late seventeenth century. In any event, we can hardly blame him for inadequately describing those differences: as its subtitle indicates, *Madness and Civilization* focuses on "Insanity in the Age of Reason," not earlier periods.

3. Quotations from *The Comedy of Errors* come from the New Arden edition. All other Shakespeare quotations come from *The Riverside Shakespeare.*

4. See Foakes' note on 1.2.33-38 in the New Arden edition of *The Comedy of Errors.* In his list of water-into-water metaphors, Foakes also includes the Duke's comment in *The Two Gentlemen of Verona* that "love is as a figure / Trenched in ice, which with an hour's heat / Dissolves to water, and doth lose his form" (3.2.6-8).

5. In *Shakespearean Negotiations,* Stephen Greenblatt explores the political and cultural implications of Shakespeare's use of Harsnett (94-128). For a different reading of those implications, see Murphy.

Works Cited

Aristotle. *Aristotle's De Anima, Books II and III*. Trans. D. W. Hamlyn. Oxford: Oxford UP, 1968.

Berger, Harry, Jr. *Second World and Green World: Studies in Renaissance Fiction-Making.* Berkeley: U of California P, 1988.

Bright, Timothie. *A Treatise of Melancholie. Containing the causes thereof, & reasons of the strange effects it worketh in our minds and bodies: with the physic cure, ad spirituall consolation for such as have thereto adjoined an afflicted conscience.* London: Thomas Vautrolier, 1586. Facsimile. The English Experience 212. Amsterdam: Da Capo P, 1969.

Burton, Robert. *The Anatomy of Melancholy.* Ed. Floyd Dell and Paul Jordan-Smith. New York: Tudor Publishing Company, 1927.

Cervantes Saavedra, Miguel de. *The Ingenious Gentleman Don Quixote de la Mancha.* Trans. Samuel Putnam. 2 vols. New York: Viking P, 1949.

Clarke, Basil. *Mental Disorder in Earlier Britain: Exploratory Studies.* Cardiff: U of Wales P, 1975.

DePorte, Michael V. *Nightmares and Hobbyhorses: Swift, Sterne, and Augustan Ideas of Madness.* San Marino: Huntington Library, 1974.

Elliott, G. R. "Weirdness in *The Comedy of Errors.*" *University of Toronto Quarterly* 60 (1939): 95-106.

Foakes, R. A. Introduction. *The Comedy of Errors.* William Shakespeare. London: Methuen, 1962. xi-lv.

Forbes, Thomas Rogers. *Chronicle from Adgate: Life and Death in Shakespeare's London.* New Haven: Yale UP, 1971.

Foucault, Michel. *Madness and Civilization: A History of Insanity in the Age of Reason.* Trans. Richard Howard. New York: Vintage Books, 1973.

Freedman, Barbara. "Egeon's Debt: Self-Division and Self-Redemption in *The Comedy of Errors.*" *English Literary Renaissance* 10 (1980): 360-83.

Greenblatt, Stephen. *Shakespearean Negotiations: The Circulation of Social Energy in Renaissance England.* Berkeley: U of California P, 1988.

Hobbes, Thomas. *Leviathan.* Ed. C. B. Macpherson. Harmondsworth, Middlesex: Penguin, 1951.

Kocher, Paul H. *Science and Religion in Elizabethan England.* New York: Octagon Books, 1969.

Lindsay, Jack, ed. *Loving Mad Tom: Bedlamite Verses of the XVI and XVII Centuries.* New York: Augustus M. Kelley, 1970.

Murphy, John L. *Darkness and Devils: Exorcism and "King Lear".* Athens: Ohio UP, 1984.

Neely, Carol Thomas. "Recent Work in Renaissance Studies: Did Madness Have a Renaissance?" *Renaissance Quarterly* 44:4 (Winter 1991): 776-91.

Park, Katharine. "The Organic Soul." *The Cambridge History of Renaissance Philosophy.* Eds. Eckhard Kessler, Charles B. Schmitt, Quentin Skinner. Cambridge: Cambridge UP, 1988. 464-84.

Plato. *The Dialogues of Plato.* Trans. B. Jowett. 4 vols. Oxford: Oxford UP, 1953.

Plautus. *Menaechmi.* In *Plautus,* 2: 364-487. Loeb Classical Library. London: William Heinemann, 1917.

Porter, Roy. *Mind-Forg'd Manacles: A History of Madness in England from the Restoration to the Regency.* Cambridge: Harvard UP, 1987.

Reed, Robert Rentoul, Jr. *Bedlam on the Jacobean Stage.* Cambridge: Harvard UP, 1952.

Rosen, George. *Madness in Society: Chapters in the Historical Sociology of Mental Illness.* Chicago: U of Chicago P, 1968.

Shakespeare, William. *The Comedy of Errors.* Ed. R. A. Foakes. Arden Shakespeare 4. London: Methuen, 1962.

———. *The Riverside Shakespeare.* Ed. G. Blakemore Evans. Boston: Houghton Mifflin, 1974.

PRODUCTION REVIEWS

Robert Smallwood (review date 1997)

SOURCE: Smallwood, Robert. "Shakespeare Performances in England, 1996." *Shakespeare Survey* 50 (1997): pp. 201-24.

[*In the excerpt below, Smallwood applauds Tim Supple's 1996 production of* The Comedy of Errors, *maintaining that it was straightforward and "attentive" to Shakespeare's language. Smallwood additionally praises the performances of the actors as well as the effectiveness of the musical accompaniment.*]

Tim Supple's version of *The Comedy of Errors,* which opened (prior to a national and international tour) at The Other Place in Stratford in June came from a world of Shakespeare production altogether different from Ian Judge's. Curious, therefore, that this was the first time the RSC had offered the play since Judge's own main-stage production in 1990, when one actor played both Antipholuses and one both Dromios, creating an evening of slick and brilliant theatrical razzmatazz in which the romance of the play's ending was entirely destroyed by the need to resolve (through the use of doppelgängers) the technical problems created by the doubling. Supple's reading of the piece was infinitely simpler. It presented the play in an unchanging set (designed by Robert Innes Hopkins) of a brick floor backed by a wall with central double doors, a window with a grille, and a bell in a niche above—the simplest of suggestions of a sunlit square in Greece or Turkey. As one entered the theatre one encountered an elderly man dressed in a dirty, ragged cloak and chained to a grid in the centre of the floor, alternately slumped in despair or pacing in anguish and frustration to the limit of his chain. The sound of breaking waves could be heard in the distance, and as 7.30 approached the music that would accompany the production began faintly, hauntingly on that Turkish equivalent of the lute, the *'ud;* then the bell rang sharply, the old man stood up, and, accompanied by a gaoler carrying a great sword and a blindfold, in strode Leo Wringer's crisply dapper Solinus, a black man in a white, high-buttoned military suit, a whiff of Caribbean dictatorship about him, to order, not without a touch of contempt, 'Merchant of Syracusa, plead no more.'

The opening dialogue made clear the principles upon which the rest of the production would be based. It was straightforward, sharply focused, and attentive to the language, and it neither sought, nor needed, to extract from Aegeon's narrative any cheap laughter at the succession of unhappy coincidences that had befallen him. The power of the story was conveyed to us partly by the simplicity with which Christopher Saul's Aegeon told it, but more by the intensity of the listening from Solinus, who was transfixed by what he heard, his attitude changing from the terse and official to the personal and committed as the account progressed. There was no padding, no pantomime pauses and double-takes, just a grief-worn old man telling of his journeyings to despair, punctuated by sad and sympathetic sounds from the little collection of middle eastern instruments—*'ud, zarb, balafan, sitar,* with a violin and female singer—that brought a quality of eeriness, of strangeness and mystery, to the play. The use of music to underscore Shakespearian dialogue so often has the depressing effect of putting a generalized emotional wash over everything that the success of Adrian Lee's accompaniment here is worth remark. It derived partly from its spareness, and from the unfamiliar quality of instrumental sounds, but chiefly from the fact that musicians and actors had rehearsed together from the start, language and sound growing into organic unity. Only once, at the end, did the music intrude. The intensity of the play's conclusion was so fully conveyed to the audience that we needed to make our contribution to the event, to make the play and the space ours, through applause, long before the singer had concluded her valedictory vocalizing. It was an odd failure of judgement on the part of a director who otherwise conveyed his respect and affection for the play with unstinted tact.

He costumed the production in modern dress, the Antipholuses in pale linen suits and suede shoes, their similarity carried most tellingly in identical curly brown hair-styles and jutting little beards. Their Dromios both wore baggy black shorts and t-shirts, but it was Duke Vincentio's formula for blurring identity, shaven heads, that most effectively persuaded us into believing in the confusions. Adriana, in an elegant modern suit with a boldly slit skirt, contrasted sharply with her sister Luciana, modest to the point of austerity (if not dowdiness) in long-skirted grey. And for once the Courtesan (Maeve Larkin) and Dr Pinch (Leo Wringer) remained within the realms of credibility, her red high-heeled shoes being the principal, rather innocently transparent, signal of her professional status, while he, in shiny black tight-fitting suit and black hat, and brandishing a Bible (or book of spells), combined a sense of the evangelical preacher from the southern United States with a hint of the voodoo magician in a way that was both witty and disturbing.

There have, no doubt, been productions of *The Comedy of Errors* in which the central scenes of mistaken identity were more boisterously farcical. Not that the big set pieces—the visiting Antipholus's bewildered response to Adriana's recriminatory tirade, his Dromio's fear of sexual possession by the kitchen maid, the increasing pace and panic of the final arrest and asylum sequence—were not splendidly funny. But they were played against a strong sense of the deeper issues being explored in the play. The complaints of Sarah Cameron's brittle, ill-at-ease Adriana derived from genuine and painful bewilderment and hurt at the loss of her husband's love. Thusitha Jayasundera brought to Luciana a quiet, self-contained intelligence, an apparently knowing caution about emotional commitment and the 'troubles of the marriage-bed' (2.1.27), that gave the role a stillness and depth that contrasted tellingly with the rawness of her sister's anxieties and vulnerabilities. To her brother-in-law's ardent wooing she responded with a firm and dignified, though wistful, rejection. His hopeful eagerness for a kiss, which she seemed about to allow but at the last moment rejected, left her with tears in her eyes—for her sister, but also for herself and for him. Even at the end, the impediments gone, she remained cautious and thoughtful, the feminist conscience of the play, uncertain about commitment. Robert Bowman's Antipholus of Syracuse responded to the blandishments of Ephesus with a beautifully poised mixture of innocent delight and wary bafflement. His distrust (aided by the plaintive, otherworldly music, reinforcing his suspicions of magic and witchcraft) could be seen gradually developing into frightened uncertainty about the stability of his own identity ('If everyone knows us and we know none . . .' (3.2.160)), forcing him into close alliance with his Dromio (Dan Milne) in a relationship that was always, and quite rightly, more trusting, and fonder, than that of their twins. His voice, lighter than his Ephesian brother's and with a faint crack to it, gave him a gentle, hesitant, slightly fey quality, very different from his twin's solid, four-square bass. Simon Coates's Antipholus of Ephesus found all the harshness of the part, his resentments fierce, his anger towards his wife bitter and self-righteous, his rage with his Dromio (Eric Mallett) hard and unamused. Funny noises from the band's percussion more or less persuaded us to laugh at his brother's slapstick attacks on *his* Dromio, but the energy with which the Ephesian Antipholus hit his servant made that impossible, the audience's mounting distaste on several occasions seeming to shame the band into silence as the blows rained down.

The production, then, treated the play with deep respect and with a thoughtful, affectionate delight in the story it had to tell. The effect of all this was most marked, and most welcome, at the play's ending. Aemilia—who last time at Stratford, in a hat like a double lampshade, had been the last in a succession of absurd caricatures—was here, in Ursula Jones's performance, a figure of quiet dignity and gentle authority, costumed simply in a nun's habit. The revelations that accompanied her arrival had a feeling of the miraculous about them, giving to the reunions something of a sacred quality. From here, it was clear, the route to the restoration of Sebastian to Viola, of Marina to Pericles, of Hermione to Leontes, was straight and direct. The ending was not, however, all unalloyed joy—any more than it is in those later plays. The wonder and delight had a touch of muted uncertainty, of hesitation about daring to believe, that gave them a profound seriousness. Much was still to be understood, much to be forgiven. Precisely what had happened between brother and sister-in-law at Adriana's dinner? He had certainly appeared after it in a state of bemused exhaustion and now, at the end, its memory cast its little shadow over the long-yearned-for reunion with his brother. And how much did Adriana deserve the Abbess's energetic telling off that left her publicly humiliated, the Courtesan sniggering in the background? Precisely how culpable was the Ephesian Antipholus's friendship with the Courtesan? Adriana winced and glared at him as he thanked her rival for his 'good cheer'; he registered his wife's pain and revealed his own embarrassment and shame. Theirs had been the first embrace in the reunion sequence, the long stare of uncertain wonder between the brothers broken by Antipholus of Ephesus's energetic 'No, I say nay to that' (5.1.372) as Adriana was about to repeat her dinnertime confusion between them. He held her in his arms tentatively, awkwardly; these two, one knew, had a lot of bridges to mend. The two pairs of brothers finally achieved their embraces after Aegeon's unfastened chains had clattered to the floor, an event that followed hard upon the Goldsmith's last little moment of fuss about *his* chain. Then, and most movingly, those two elegantly dressed young men in turn took their ragged, exhausted father, just rescued from death's door, in their arms and Aemilia began her final speech of blessing, receiving the embraces of her sons as she declared her heavy burden finally delivered. The verbal benedictions done, she blessed everyone manually as they knelt in front of her before making their exits to the gossips' feast: the Duke, benevolent and eager; Aegeon returning her long, hesitant gaze before going in, without an embrace—thirty-three years of separation, and a nun's habit, clearly requiring a great deal more thought on both sides; Adriana compelled, in spite of protest, to accompany the Courtesan; Luciana, silent through the scene, once moving close to Antipholus of Syracuse but forced away again by the pressure of the scene's events and now departing alone; an unwilling Balthazar, his financial obsessions and sartorial vulgarity strongly suggesting that abbeys are unfamiliar territory; and Aegeon's erstwhile guard, respectfully removing his cap and leaving his sword at the door—an exquisitely detailed and thoughtful sequence of exits. The two pairs of twins were thus left to face the future, Antipholus of Ephesus much less certain that he regarded it with enthusiasm than his brother—for he'd not been searching for anyone, anywhere, and life for him had been just fine until this appalling day. He watched his brother kiss his servant Dromio on the lips, a kiss that rendered thanks for loyalty and patience and friendship through years of wandering, but also marked the end of all that; for, now that it was no longer to be just the two of them, things would never be quite the same again. The Ephesian Dromio watched that kiss too and seemed to will his master to perceive the need for symmetry. His Antipholus did, indeed, think about the possibility for a moment or two; but there was no way that he could change so quickly—or that this director would be tempted along so sentimental a road. Perceiving the unkissed Dromio's disappointment, Antipholus of Syracuse rescued the situation by instructing his servant to 'Embrace thy brother there', a piece of sensitivity to the text that was typical of so much in the production. And so the two shaven-headed, bare-kneed sufferers of the play's blows and buffets, real and metaphorical, were left alone to discover from each other, with poignant hopefulness, that after all they were sweet-faced youths, and to scurry off, hand in hand, after the rest. And it was all done in precisely two hours, without fuss and without self-indulgence, by constant alertness and sensitivity to the play's language and delight in the wonders of the story it has to tell. A pity we weren't allowed to applaud it quite as soon as we wanted to.

Dennis Harvey (review date 2000)

SOURCE: Harvey, Dennis. Review of *The Comedy of Errors*. *Variety* 378, no. 7 (3-9 April 2000): 58.

[*In the following review, Harvey offers high praise for the Aurora Theater's production of* The Comedy of Errors, *finding it to be "entirely error-free."*]

> Solinus/Courtesan: Brian Yates Sharber
> Egeon/Angelo/Dr. Pinch: Joan Mankin
> Antipholus of Ephesus/of Syracuse: Susannah Schulman
> Dromio of Ephesus/of Syracuse: Brad DePlanche
> Balthasar/First & Second Merchant/Maid/Emilia: Adam Gavzer
> Adriana: Susan Marie Brecht
> Luciana: Johanna Falls
> Musician/Constable: Scrumbly Koldwyn

There's something about "The Comedy of Errors"' "generic Shakespeare" nature that gives directors leave to treat it as a near-blank page—one on which virtually any stylistic or conceptual fillip can be imposed. Under almost every circumstance, the play bounces back, frivolous yet hardy as a Neff ball. It's become a signature piece for idiosyncratic Bay Area director Danny Scheie, who first staged his ingenious vest-pocket version as a college thesis project in 1985, then scored a hit at Shakespeare Santa Cruz three years later, reprising the production in the first annum of his brief SSC artistic directorship in '93.

Substantially reworked each time, the show's latest incarnation is packing the high-polish but determinedly small-scale Aurora Theater Co.'s minuscule Berkeley City Club space and might well run all year if not for their re-lysked commitments. (Scheie opens yet another "Comedy" for Seattle Shakespeare Fest on April 13.) An unalloyed delight, overflowing with comic inspiration, this rambunctious yet flawless little staging cries for a commercial transfer.

Always fascinated by the mistaken-identity and gender-blur elements that drive many of the Bard's comedies, Scheie heightens those aspects here by using just seven actors to play all 16 roles. (Onstage pianist Scrumbly Koldwyn chips in with a few line readings as well.)

Plot's patent contrivance is underlined by their frequent crossdressing, and pushed to breaking point when some thesps eventually have to switch characters within a single scene.

Thus well-born Antipholuses (Susannah Schulmann, whose Southerngent Ephesean edition is particularly inspired) and their twin slaveys Dromio (a maniacally inventive Brad DePlanche) are double-cast, while other performers take as many as five roles apiece. Sole exceptions are Syracusean businessman Antipholus' wife Adriana (Susan Marie Brecht, wringing infinite variations on spousal exasperation) and her sister Luciana (an airheaded-flapper Johanna Falls). Letter is flattered if nonplused when her supposed in-law, A. of Epheseus, becomes a smitten suitor, while politely evading his "wife."

Setting the piece in a vague early-20th century NYC, Scheie lifts ideas from the prior century's stage melodramas, vaudeville, even the Three Stooges and "Gone With the Wind." A red curtain at one end of the small, unelevated playspace is sole "set"; gags include the aristocratic twins' death-sentenced father Solinus (Joan Mankin) illustrating his tragic family separation 33 years ago via classroom transparency-projector.

But humor is mostly dependent on the terrific cast's game slapstick, broad albeit precise physical characterizations, and spot-on timing.

Scheie's anything-goes approach might lead one to expect a gimmicky skim across the text. Yet his great strength as a Shakespearean director is the cogent emphasis placed on every line, rendering this "Comedy" a constant source of laughs big and small, rather than one hinged on flashy set pieces.

Ensemble is rounded out by nimble contribs from Adam Gavzer (lending his parts a giddy multinationality) and Brian Yates Sharber (especially outrageous as an indignant lady of the evening). At barely over two hours, including intermission, this "Comedy" is one of the fastest-paced in memory, as well as one entirely error-free.

Wilborn Hampton (review date 2001)

SOURCE: Hampton, Wilborn. "A Little Shakespearean Traveling Music." *The New York Times* (19 May 2001): B10.

[*In the review below, Hampton discusses a staging of Trevor Nunn and Guy Woolfenden's musical version of* The Comedy of Errors, *directed by John Rando, contending that the production honored the spirit of the original play.*]

When Ben Jonson eulogized Shakespeare as being not of an age but for all time, he had no way of knowing about the 1960's. But it has been the proof of Jonson's tribute that Shakespeare's plays have survived transportation to just about every decade since, although admittedly some travel better than others.

"The Comedy of Errors," an early play that is about the closest Shakespeare came to pure farce, is one that travels especially light, and a campy and brash staging of Trevor Nunn and Guy Woolfenden's musical version by the director John Rando and the Acting Company offers a diverting evening, depending on how one might enjoy a night at a Hippie theme park.

The adaptation was first produced by the Royal Shakespeare Company in 1976. Mr. Nunn, who was then artistic director at the R.S.C. and soon to make his fame in America by directing "Nicholas Nickleby," "Les Miserables" and "Cats," wrote lyrics cued by lines from Shakespeare's text to music set by Mr. Woolfenden.

In the Acting Company revival the irreverent tone is set in the opening scene and incorporates a grab bag of cultural cliches from the 1960's and 70's that takes several liberties with Shakespeare's text but keeps to the spirit of the play.

As the Duke of Ephesus, strutting like a cartoon Central American dictator complete with droopy mustache and reflector sunglasses, expounds the background, the entire cast hisses every time he mentions the word "Syracuse." It gets progressively more rowdy as Mr. Rando and his energetic cast pull out all stops for laughs.

There are sight gags, pratfalls, costuming and lighting gimmicks, silly walks, tumbling tricks. One character reads Cosmopolitan magazine, another uses a can of hair spray, yet another takes a snapshot. The scene in which Antipholus of Ephesus argues with Dromio of Syracuse through a door is played over an intercom. Characters exchange high-fives and Dr. Pinch shows up in an Afro and tie-dyed robe with a voodoo doll around his neck. There is a running gag with a cat from an old James Bond movie; some business with a whip and gun is borrowed from "Raiders of the Lost Ark," and there is a long chase scene that Mack Sennett would have loved.

Needless to say, a lot of this has nothing to do with Shakespeare, and it occasionally veers close to being a sophomoric parody. But like Moonwork Theater's recent musical version of "Twelfth Night," which was set in a 1940's nightclub and struck a similar vein, the cumulative effect is humorously contagious. The songs are mostly amusing ditties, but a couple of them aim at full production numbers reminiscent of rock musicals of the era.

The members of the Acting Company cast are clearly enjoying themselves and the performances are by and large good. Todd Cerveris and Michael Thomas Holmes as flower children versions of Dromio E. and Dromio S. take top honors, closely followed by Evan Robertson and Corey Behnke, each of whom could double as an androgynous rock star, as Antipholus E. and Antipholus S.

Michele Tauber, looking like Mama Cass in a tentlike blue paisley dress, is convincing as Adriana, and Beth Bartley, who could stand in for Sally Field in her hippie days, is credible as Luciana. Some smaller turns are especially good. Royden Mills is a delight as Angelo the goldsmith, a "cool dude" if ever there was one, and Gregory Jackson is deadpan funny playing the Second Merchant as a cross between a refugee from "Get Smart" and Inspector Clouseau.

THEMES

Russ McDonald (essay date 1988)

SOURCE: McDonald, Russ. "Fear of Farce." In *"Bad" Shakespeare: Revaluations of the Shakespearean Canon,* edited by Maurice Charney, pp. 77-90. Rutherford, N.J.: Farleigh Dickinson University Press, 1988.

[*In the essay that follows, McDonald uses his examination of* The Comedy of Errors *to highlight Shakespeare's effort to construct meaning in farce and to demonstrate Shakespeare's affinity for this genre.*]

Zeus's sexual lapses notwithstanding, gods are not supposed to be indecorous, and a characteristic of modern Bardolatry has been its insistence on Shakespeare's artistic dignity, particularly his attachment to the approved dramatic forms. The popular image of Shakespeare as the embodiment of high culture, the author of *Hamlet* and certain other tragedies, as well as a very few weighty comedies, is merely a version of a bias that also, if less obviously, afflicts the academy. What I am talking about is a hierarchy of modes, or, to put it another way, genre snobbery. That tragedy is more profound and significant than comedy is a prejudice that manifests itself in and out of the Shakespeare Establishment: in the impatience of undergraduates who, taking their first class in Shakespeare, regard the comedies and histories as mere appetizers to the main course, the tragedies; in Christopher Sly's equation of "a commonty" with "a Christmas gambol or a tumbling trick"; in the disdain of the tourist at the Barbican box office who, finding *Othello* sold out, refuses a ticket to *The Merry Wives of Windsor;* in the decision of that Athenian student to preserve his notes from Aristotle's lecture on tragedy but not to bother with the one on comedy.

If there is a hierarchy of modes, there is also a hierarchy within modes: *de casibus* tragedy is less exalted than Greek, for example. So it is with the kinds of comedy, and the play to which I shall address myself, *The Comedy of Errors,* rests safely in the lowest rank. Farce is at the bottom of everyone's list of forms, and yet Shakespeare is at the top of everyone's list of authors. Thus, the problem I mean to examine is generated by competing hierarchies. Most literary critics have little occasion to think about farce, and those who concern themselves chiefly with the creator of texts such as *Macbeth* and *Coriolanus* do their best to avoid the form. For many years the earliest comedies were treated unapologetically as farces and Shakespeare was praised, if mildly, for his skill at contriving such brilliant and pleasing trifles. But the need to preserve his association with higher things has led in the last three or four decades to a revision of this opinion. It seems inappropriate that the cultural monument known as Shakespeare should have anything to do with a popular entertainment that we connect with the likes of the Marx brothers (Groucho and Harpo, not Karl and Moritz). Criticism resists a Shakespeare capable of wasting his time on such a trivial form.

My purpose is to suggest that Shakespeare could be "bad," but my definition differs somewhat from those of most of the other contributors to this volume. Rather than reexamine texts that may have been overvalued or seek to locate weaknesses in dramatic technique, I shall argue that Shakespeare's taste was not invariably elevated and that certain plays are less "significant" than others (or at least that they signify different things in different ways). By addressing myself to what is and is not considered "Shakespearean," I claim an interest in one of the fundamental issues of this collection: canonicity. A work like *The Comedy of Errors* must be deformed if it is to conform to that category known as Shakespearean comedy—as a farce it is noncanonical—and such misrepresentation demands a rejoinder.

The first part of this essay surveys the evasions that critics have devised for treating Shakespeare's efforts in farce, with concentration on the dodges applied to *Errors*. The remainder, a straightforward study of that play's theatrical action, proposes to identify the playwright's strategies for the production of meaning in farce. In light of the concerns of this volume, to contend that *Errors* succeeds not as an early version of a romantic comedy or as an allegory of marriage but as an out-and-out farce is risky, for such an argument looks like yet another defense of the artistic experiments of a novice and thus seems to exemplify the very Bardolatry that many of these essays vigorously dispute. In fact, however, my aim is to establish Shakespeare's delight in and commitment to a dramatic form that has become infra dig. To recognize such a bent is to augment our sense of Shakespeare's actual range. We whitewash our subject by refusing to admit his attraction to farce and declining to explore his talent for it.

I

Suspicion of farce has fostered two main critical maneuvers, here summarized by Barbara Freedman: "The first is represented by that group of critics who know that Shakespeare never wrote anything solely to make us laugh and so argue that Shakespeare never wrote farce at all. . . . The more popular critical approach, however, is to agree that Shakespeare wrote farce, but to consider *Errors* (as well as Shakespeare's other predominantly farcical plays) to be nonsensical *insofar* as they are farce."[1] To begin with the first group, its members are undaunted by Shakespeare's demonstrable choice of classical or Italian farces for source material: in such cases he may be seen "transcending the farce which a lesser writer might have been satisfied to make,"[2] and thus the form is mentioned so that it can be dismissed.

The most familiar and pernicious tactic of those who would dissociate Shakespeare from the vulgar category is to discuss the early plays as precursors of the mature style, as seedbeds, that is, for ideas and methods that will flower in the later comedies and even in the tragedies. (In fact, hothouses would make a better simile, since the ideas and methods are found blooming in the early play itself by the time the critic finishes.) A. C. Hamilton, for example, asserts that *The Comedy of Errors* provides a foundation for the later comedies by revealing "their basis in the idea that life upon the order of nature has been disturbed and must be restored and renewed through the action of the play."[3]

Hamilton's reticence to detect inchoate forms of particular dramatic themes from later works is not shared by Peter G. Phialas, who identifies "certain features of structure and theme, and even tone, which anticipate significant elements of Shakespeare's romantic comedies." Specifically, *"The Comedy of Errors,* though in the main concerned with the farcical mistakings of identity, touches briefly a theme of far greater significance, the ideal relationship of man and woman."[4] This anticipatory practice amounts to reading the career backward: a play is conditioned by what follows it, and its distinctive qualities may be underrated or deformed. The prophetic approach tends to manifest itself in and to merge with the second defensive strategy.

Put simply, this way of thinking involves deepening the farces, exposing their profundity. It has become the preferred means of protecting Shakespeare against his own immature tastes or the vulgar demands of his audience,[5] and it has attracted some eloquent and powerful advocates. Derek Traversi, for example, unites the two critical defenses, seeing *Errors* as both serious in itself and important in its tonal prefiguration of the later work. He emphasizes "the deliberate seriousness of the story of Aegeon, which gives the entire action a new setting of gravity, a sense of tragic overtones which, elementary though it may be in expression, is yet not without some intimation of later and finer effects."[6] In other words, the play is profound but not too profound.

That the dignifiers succeeded some time ago in making this serious position canonical is apparent in the following passage from R. A. Foakes's Introduction to the New Arden edition, published in 1962:

> These general considerations may help to illustrate the particular quality of *The Comedy of Errors.* The play has farcical comedy, and it has fantasy, but it does more than merely provoke laughter, or release us temporarily from inhibitions and custom into a world free as a child's, affording delight and freshening us up. It also invites compassion, a measure of sympathy, and a deeper response to the disruption of social and family relationships which the action brings about. Our concern for the Antipholus twins, for Adriana and Luciana, and our sense of disorder are deepened in the context of suffering provided by the enveloping action. The comedy proves, after all, to be more than a temporary and hilarious abrogation of normality; it is, at the same time, a process in which the main characters are in some sense purged, before harmony and the responsibility of normal relationships are restored at the end. Adriana learns to overcome her jealousy, and accepts the reproof of the Abbess; her husband is punished for his anger and potential brutality by Doctor Pinch's drastic treatment; and Antipholus of Syracuse is cured of his prejudices about Ephesus. Behind them stands Egeon, a prototype of the noble sufferer or victim in later plays by Shakespeare, of Antonio in *The Merchant of Venice,* and of Pericles, central figure in a play which uses more profoundly the story on which Egeon's adventures are based.[7]

A variation of this argument is found in Harold Brooks's much-cited essay, which associates *Errors* not with a farce such as *Supposes* but with a recognition play such as the *Ion* or *The Confidential Clerk.*[8]

Those who see Shakespeare as "transcending" farce must consent to a divorce between the "serious" issues that they elect to stress and the main business of the play.[9] In other words, the critics analyze delicate sentiments while the characters knock heads. The discovery of gravity requires great emphasis on the frame story of Egeon, or Adriana's matrimonial laments, or the wooing of Luciana. Brooks candidly declares the incongruity between his emphasis and Shakespeare's: "The *Comedy* appeals first and foremost to laughter, as is obvious at any performance. I have dwelt on its serious themes and strands of romance because it is these that student and producer are prone to discount."[10] One might respond that student and producer would in this case be taking their cue from the author, who was himself prone to discount the serious themes and strands of romance at this stage of his career. We should question critical means that seek to convert the early comedies into something other than they are.

The Comedy of Errors is a superlative example of dramatic farce, a simple form of comedy designed chiefly to make an audience laugh. Freedman points out that farces are almost always characterized by an "insistence on their own meaninglessness, an insistence which by no means should be accepted at face value."[11] In other words, to regard the play as a highly developed form of farce is not to outlaw ideas. Mistaken identity is at the heart of *The Comedy of Errors,* as Antipholus of Syracuse explains in the final moments: "I see we still did meet each other's man, / And I was ta'en for him, and he for me, / And thereupon these errors have arose" (5.1.388-90).[12] This basic formula is the source of pleasure and of meaning in the farcical comedy. My goal is to increase, if only slightly, our sense of how meaning comes about in farce, and my method for doing so is to concentrate on what an audience sees and hears in the main action.[13] It seems reasonable to conclude—and worth pointing out, given the critical history of the text in question—that dramatic significance ought to proceed as much from the essential as from the ancillary features of a text.

II

To err is human, and one way of describing the imperfect condition of our experience is to say that we inhabit a state of division, of disunity, of separation from God, from nature, from one another. Lest this seem too portentous a beginning for a discussion of a farcical comedy, let me hasten to say that splitting (of ships, of families, of other human relations) is one of the most important of the play's patterns of action. In one sense, of course, the plot of *The Comedy of Errors* is founded on the natural division of twinship, for nature has split a single appearance into two persons. In the source play, Plautus exploits the confusion inherent in this division by geographically separating the

Menaechmus brothers, and Shakespeare has increased the complexity of the original plot, as everyone knows, by doubling the twins.[14] What is less familiar is his tactic of making the normal avenues of reconciliation into obstacle courses laid with traps and dead ends. Virtually all comedy represents characters' attempts to overcome their isolation through marriage or reconciliation, with farce throwing the emphasis on the amusing difficulties involved in such efforts. Marriage, systems of law, commerce, language—all these are forms of communion or institutions through which people seek or give satisfaction, social instruments and (implicitly) comic means for joining human beings in a happy and fruitful relation.

And yet, for all their value, these means are naturally imperfect and likely to collapse under various pressures, either of accident or human will or their own liability to misinterpretation. When they break down, the confusion that frustrates the characters delights the audience. To a great extent, the comedy of *Errors* arises from the number of barriers Shakespeare has erected and the ingenuity with which he has done so. The greatest obstacles arise in the principal characters' relations with their servants, in the arena of commerce, and in the realm of speech itself. Shakespeare generates amusing conflict by exaggerating the forces that separate people and by weakening the media that connect them.

The presence of four men in two costumes leads first to the attenuation of the normal bonds between servant and master and between husband and wife. From the twin Sosias in Plautus's *Amphitruo,* Shakespeare creates in the Dromios a pair of agents, go-betweens who link husband to wife or customer to merchant. They are extensions of their masters' wills, instruments by which each of the Antipholuses conducts business or gets what he wants. In the farcical world of the play, however, the will is inevitably frustrated as these servants become barriers, sources of confusion, gaps in a chain of communication. For Antipholus of Syracuse, lost in a strange, forbidden seaport, his one sure connection, his "bondman," seems to fail him. This treatment of the twin servants, moreover, is representative of Shakespeare's method with other characters, including Adriana, Luciana, and the Courtesan. Although the females are often said to contribute to the play's Pauline analysis of proper marriage, their primary value is as comic troublemakers. Adriana's eloquence and Luciana's charm make the two women memorable, to be sure, but they are hardly complex. Adriana's main function is to doubt her husband, to rail against his neglect, to chase him in the streets, to enlist a conjurer to minister to him; Luciana's role is to attract Antipholus of Syracuse and thereby to fuel her sister's rage.

The disintegration of personal bonds is accompanied by the weakening of the multiple commercial connections. Although the thematic importance of debts is familiar enough,[15] it is also relevant that many of the play's amusing confrontations are grounded in thwarted commercial exchanges. Ignoring the maxim that it is best to eliminate the middleman, Shakespeare has added a host of them. Angelo the Goldsmith, Balthazar, and the First and Second Merchants are all Shakespearean inventions—businessmen, literal agents who exist to get in the way. Each functions as an additional barrier separating the twin Antipholuses, as another hedge in the maze at the center of the comedy. The Second Merchant, for instance, appears only twice and exists for no other reason than to make demands and increase the comic pressure: he has been patient since Pentecost and now needs guilders for a journey; he presses Angelo to repay the sum; Angelo must seek payment from Antipholus of Ephesus who, not having received the chain for which the money is demanded, refuses to accommodate him. In short, this importunate stranger is unnecessary: Angelo might have pursued compensation on his own initiative.

In the critical rush to find "meaning" or "tonal variety" in the addition of Luciana, Egeon, and Emilia, the structural value of the lesser auxiliary figures may be overlooked. Their untimely or mistaken demands for payment increase the confusion on the stage and damage the ties that connect them to their fellow citizens. Adriana joins the line of claimants when she tries forcibly to collect the love owed her by her husband, and her vocabulary indicates that Shakespeare has established an analogy between marital responsibilities and the cash nexus.

The setting of the comedy, as the occupations of the secondary figures remind us, is mostly the street, or "the mart," and from the beginning we observe that the business of the street is business. Most of the confrontations between characters and much of the dialogue concern the physical exchange of money or property, and other personal dealings are figured in financial terms. Egeon is a Syracusan trader unable to make the necessary financial exchange—a thousand marks for his freedom—and this fine or debt seems to have resulted from a protracted trade war. Many years before, after a period in which his "wealth increas'd / By prosperous voyages," Egeon had found himself separated from his wife by his "factor's death, / And the great care of goods at random left" (1.1.41-42). Now without family or funds, the insolvent businessman leaves the stage, whereupon Antipholus of Syracuse enters with an Ephesian merchant who tells him of the stranger's plight—"not being able to buy out his life"—and warns the young traveler to conceal his identity "lest that your goods too soon be confiscate." The citizen then returns Antipholus's bag of gold and pleads the need to pay a business call: "I am invited, sir, to certain merchants, / Of whom I hope to make much benefit" (1.2.24-25). He leaves Antipholus to his "own content, . . . the thing [he] cannot get."

This endearing soliloquy is usually said to prefigure the theme of self-understanding in the later comedies, but what is less often said is that Antipholus analyzes his dilemma in terms of self-possession: he fears that in seeking to recover his family he will "lose" himself. At the end of the same scene he frets about the loss of his treasure, worrying that Dromio "is o'er-raught of all [Antipholus's] money" and recalling the city's reputation for "cozenage," "cheaters," and "mountebanks."

The bag of gold that Antipholus gives to Dromio to deliver to the inn is the first in a list of theatrical properties that provoke farcical contention. The initial dispute occurs with the entrance of Dromio of Ephesus, to whom "the money" demanded can only be the "sixpence that I had o' Wednesday last, / To pay the saddler for my mistress' crupper"; the "charge" is not a bag of gold but a command "to fetch you from the mart"; the "thousand marks" are not coins but bruises administered by master and mistress. As Antipholus of Syracuse worries about fraud, Dromio of Ephesus reports the misunderstanding to his mistress in a speech whose opposing clauses suggest the nature of the impasse: "''Tis dinner time,' quoth I; 'my gold,' quoth he." The metal becomes a metaphor at the end of the first scene of act 2, when Adriana speaks of reputation as a piece of enameled gold (2.1.109-15), and thus Shakespeare uses it to link the end of the scene with the beginning of the next: Antipholus of Syracuse enters puzzling over the bag of money, apparently not lost at all, whereupon his own Dromio enters, denies any knowledge of the recent dispute over the gold, and earns a beating. The pattern of confusion thus established with the thousand marks is repeated in squabbles over control of a chain, a ring, a dinner, a house, a spouse, a bag of ducats, a name, a prisoner, and a pair of strangers seeking sanctuary.

The vocabulary of these disputes is almost invariably the parlance of the marketplace: Antipholus of Ephesus and his business cronies politely debate the relative value of a warm welcome and a good meal ("I hold your dainties cheap, sir, and your welcome dear"); Nell "lays claim" to the Syracusan Dromio; to the Courtesan, "forty ducats is too much to lose"; the Officer cannot release Antipholus of Ephesus for fear that "the debt he owes will be required of me"; Antipholus of Ephesus is known to be "of very reverend reputation, . . . / Of credit infinite"; Dromio of Ephesus, declared mad and tied up, describes himself as "entered in bond" for Antipholus; and when the Abbess sees Egeon in act 5, she offers to "loose his bonds, / And gain a husband by his liberty." The great scene before Antipholus's house (3.1) becomes a dispute not just over property but over ownership of names and identity. In their efforts to get paid or to pay others back for wrongs suffered, characters often speak of "answering" each other:

EPH. ANT.

I answer you? Why should I answer you?

ANGELO.

The money that you owe me for the chain.

(4.1.62-63)

The merchants become enraged when their customers refuse to answer them with payment; Adriana is furious that her husband will not return a favorable answer to her

Lady Abbess, Duke of Ephesus, Antipholus of Syracuse, Dromio of Syracuse, Adriana, Luciana, and others in Act V, scene i of William Shakespeare's The Comedy of Errors.

requests that he come home to dinner; Antipholus of Ephesus will make his household answer for the insult of locking him out; and neither Antipholus is able to get a straight answer from either of the Dromios. This financial use of "answer" links cash to language, the most complicated and potentially ambiguous medium of all.

Exploiting the pun as the linguistic equivalent of twinship, Shakespeare creates a series of verbal equivalents for the visual duplications of the action. Initially, it seems to me, his practice is to please the audience with repeated words and images: most obviously, he develops the conflicts by ingeniously employing the language of commerce. The normal give-and-take of business activity and family life is impaired by the mistakings of the action, and when the members of the household take Antipholus of Ephesus for a troublemaker in the street, his Dromio describes him as having been "bought and sold." The "loss" of one's good name or "estimation" is risky in this world of commerce, as Balthazar explains: "For slander lives upon succession, / For ever housed where it gets possession" (3.1.105-6). Adriana's anger at her husband leads Luciana to charge her with possessiveness, and then when Antipholus of Syracuse confesses that Luciana,

> *Possessed* with such a gentle sovereign grace,
> Of such *enchanting* presence and discourse,
> Hath almost made me *traitor* to myself,
>
> (3.2.158-60; italics mine)

the diction of ownership ("possessions") is cleverly modulated into that of witchcraft and madness ("possession"). This ambiguity pays its most amusing dividends when Doctor Pinch attempts to exorcise the demons from Antipholus of Ephesus:

> I charge thee, Satan, hous'd within this man,
> To yield possession to my holy prayers,
> And to thy state of darkness hie thee straight;
>
> (4.4.52-54)

The problems of confused identity and the loss of self-control are soon compounded by the question of freedom of action. The Dromios' lives are not their own, as they reiterate in complaining that, as slaves, they are not adequately rewarded for service. These various senses of bondage—to service, to customers, to wives, to the law, to business commitments (the Second Merchant is "bound to Persia"), to a rope—reinforce each other, especially in the last two acts, as the lines of action intersect:

EGEON.

> Most might duke, vouchsafe me speak a word.
> Haply I see a friend will save my life,
> And pay the sum that may deliver me.

DUKE.

> Speak freely, Syracusian, what thou wilt.

EGEON.

> Is not your name, sir, called Antipholus?
> And is not that your bondman Dromio?

EPH. DRO.

> Within this hour I was his bondman, sir;
> But he, I thank him, gnawed in two my cords.
> Now I am Dromio, and his man, unbound.
>
> (5.1.283-91)

Egeon, expecting to be set at liberty, is mistaken, bound by the limitations of his senses. And here Dromio, the "freedman," steals from his master the privilege of response. As mistakes are exposed and corrected, Shakespeare relies upon the commercial vocabulary that has served him from the beginning: Antipholus of Syracuse wishes "to make good" his promises to Luciana; when Antipholus of Ephesus offers to pay his father's fine, the Duke pardons Egeon and restores his freedom and self-control ("It shall not need; thy father hath his life"); and the Abbess offers to "make full satisfaction" to the assembled company in recompense for the confusion of the day.

Words offer a way of resolving the divisions that the play explores, but at the same time they entail enormous possibilities for error. Given the present critical climate, some remarks about the unreliability of language are to be expected, but if words are included among the other media of exchange that Shakespeare has chosen to twist and complicate, then such a conclusion seems less fashionable than useful. Shakespeare almost from the beginning expands the wrangling over who owns what to include a series of battles over words and their significance. The two Dromios again offer the sharpest illustrations of such cross-purposes, usually in their interchanges with their masters. In the first meeting of Antipholus of Syracuse with Dromio of Ephesus, the shifts in meaning of "charge" and "marks" I have already cited represent the struggle for control of meaning that underlies the farcical action. Both servants are adept at shifting from the metaphorical to the literal:

ADR.

> Say, is your tardy master now at hand?

EPH. DRO.

> Nay, he's at two hands with me, and that my two
>   ears can witness.
>
> (2.1.44-46)

When Antipholus of Syracuse threatens Dromio of Syracuse, "I will beat this method in your sconce," the servant resorts to linguistic subversion: "Sconce call you it? so you would leave battering, I had rather have it a head; and you use these blows long, I must get a sconce for my head, and insconce it too, or else I shall seek my wit in my shoulders" (2.2.34-39).

Yet the servants can speak highly figurative language as well: both describe the arresting officer in metaphors so elaborate that they baffle the auditors (4.2.32-40 and 4.3.12-30). Some of the verbal excursions resemble vaudeville turns, particularly the banter between the two Syracusans on baldness, and such jests represent verbal forms of what happens dramatically in the main action. In showing that "there is no time for all things," Dromio of Syracuse jestingly disproves an indisputable axiom, just as the errors of the main plot raise a challenge to the reality that everyone has accepted until now. This is more than what Brooks deprecatingly calls "elaborations of comic rhetoric."[16]

The struggle over what words signify quickens as the characters sense that reality is slipping away from them. The locking-out scene (3.1) depends for its hilarity on the stichomythic exchanges between those outside (Dromio and Antipholus of Ephesus) and those inside (Dromio of Syracuse and Luce, and later Adriana). The contestants, particularly those in the security of the house, manipulate meanings and even rhyme and other sounds as they taunt the pair trying to enter, for possession of the house is apparently an advantage in the battle of words. The Dromios' attitudes toward language are almost always playful and subversive, so that even at their masters' most frustrated moments, the servants take pleasure in twisting sound and sense, as in Dromio of Ephesus's puns on "crow" ("crow without a feather?"; "pluck a crow together"; and "iron crow").

The trickiness of language can cause characters to lose the direction of the dialogue:

ADR.

>Why, man, what is the matter?

SYR. DRO.

>I do not know the matter; he is 'rested on the case.

ADR.

>What, is he arrested? tell me at whose suit?

SYR. DRO.

>I know not at whose suit he is arrested well;
>But is in a suit of buff which 'rested him, that can I tell.
>Will you send him, mistress, redemption, the money in his desk?

ADR.

>Go, fetch it, sister; this I wonder at,
>   *Exit* Luciana.
>That he unknown to me should be in debt.
>Tell me, was he arrested on a band?

SYR. DRO.

>Not on a band, but on a stronger thing;
>A chain, a chain, do you not hear it ring?

ADR.

>What, the chain?

SYR. DRO.

>No, no, the bell, 'tis time that I were gone,
>It was two ere I left him, and now the clock strikes one.

(4.2.41-54)

Rhetorically, the key to this passage is antanaclasis: Dromio wrests a word from Adriana's meaning into another of its senses, as with "matter" (*trouble* and *substance*), "case" and "suit" (both meaning *case in law* and *suit of clothes*), "band" (*bond* and *ruff*). The ambiguous pronoun reference in "hear it ring" illustrates the power of words to entrap: Adriana and the audience need a moment to adjust as Dromio abruptly shifts the focus from his narrative to the present.

Just as words are apt to slip out of their familiar senses, customers or husbands or servants seem to change from moment to moment. Dialogue and stage action illustrate the limits of human control as characters try to react to these confusing turns of phrase or of event. Antipholus of Syracuse, offered a wife and a dinner, can be flexible: "I'll say as they say" (2.2.214). But words may conflict with other words and realities with other realities, as the Duke discovers in seeking the undivided truth: "You say he dined at home; the goldsmith here / Denies that saying. Sirrah, what say you?" (5.1.274-75). Conflicts of personal identity, of contracts, of words, of stories, all make the truth seem elusive and uncertain.

Shakespeare's strategy of breaking the integuments that bind human beings to one another accounts for much of the mirth in *Errors* and for much of the significance as well. By interfering with familiar and normally reliable systems of relation—master to servant, wife to husband, customer to merchant, speaker to auditor—the dramatist achieves the dislocation felt by the characters and the "spirit of weird fun" enjoyed by the audience.[17] There is, moreover, an additional verbal medium that Shakespeare has twisted to his own use, that of the play itself. The ironic bond between playwright and spectator, that relation which Shakespeare inherited from Plautus and cultivated throughout the first four acts and by which he assures us that we know more than the characters know, is suddenly abrogated when the Abbess declares her identity at the end of the fifth act: we have thought ourselves superior to the errors and assumptions of the ignorant characters, but we too have been deceived. Emilia's reunion with her husband and sons completes the comic movement of the action. This is farce, so the emphasis throughout is on the delights of disjunction; but this is also comedy, so the drama moves toward a restoration of human ties and the formation of new ones. Sentiment asserts itself in the final moments, of course, but Shakespeare does not overstate it, and the shift from pleasure in chaos to pleasure in order need not jar. The confusion must end somewhere, and it is standard practice for the farceur to relax the comic tension by devising a mellow ending to a period of frenzy.[18]

Shakespeare attempted to write farce in *The Comedy of Errors,* and he succeeded. Certain effects and values are missing from this kind of drama: there is no thorough examination of characters, no great variety of tones, no profound treatment of ideas, no deep emotional engagement. But farce gives us what other dramatic forms may lack: the production of ideas through rowdy action, the pleasures of "non-significant" wordplay, freedom from the limits of credibility, mental exercise induced by the rapid tempo of the action, unrestricted laughter—the satisfactions of various kinds of extravagance.[19] Indeed, farce may be considered the most elemental kind of theater, since the audience is encouraged to lose itself in play. This is bad Shakespeare in the sense that the young dramatist was content with an inherently limited mode; the play is not *Twelfth Night.* Its value is in its theatrical complexity. And yet the boisterous action does generate thematic issues. To admit that Shakespeare willingly devoted himself to farce is to acknowledge a side of his career too often neglected or misrepresented. That the author of *King Lear* was capable of writing *The Comedy of Errors* should be a source of wonder, not embarrassment.

Notes

1. Barbara Freedman, "Errors in Comedy: A Psychoanalytic Theory of Farce," in *Shakespearean Comedy*, ed. Maurice Charney, *New York Literary Forum*, 5-6 (1980): 233-34.

2. R. A. Foakes, Introduction to *The Comedy of Errors*, New Arden Shakespeare (1962; reprint, London: Methuen, 1963), li.

3. A. C. Hamilton, *The Early Shakespeare* (San Marino, Cal.: Huntington Library, 1967), 107.

4. Peter G. Phialas, *Shakespeare's Romantic Comedies* (Chapel Hill: University of North Carolina Press, 1966), 3, 16. Compare the remarks of Sir Arthur Quiller-Couch in his Introduction to *The Comedy of Errors* (Cambridge: Cambridge University Press, 1922), p. xxii: "Sundry passages, even in its farcical episodes, show us the born poet, the born romancer, itching to be at his trade."

5. It would be easy enough to make merry with some of these attempts: a title such as Gwyn Williams's "*The Comedy of Errors* Rescued from Tragedy," *Review of English Literature* 5 (1964): 63-71 furnishes a sense of how far some commentators have been willing to go.

6. Derek Traversi, *Shakespeare: The Early Comedies*, Writers and Their Work 129 (London: Longmans, Green, 1960), 12.

7. Foakes, Introduction, l-li.

8. Harold Brooks, "Theme and Structure in *The Comedy of Errors*," in *Early Shakespeare*, ed. John Russell Brown and Bernard Harris (London: Edward Arnold, 1961; New York: Schocken Books, 1966), 69. Although I shall dispute the arguments of Foakes and Brooks and their less persuasive followers, I should acknowledge that this approach can be useful. In the first place, it can cast light into neglected corners of the texts. Moreover, it usually proceeds from laudable motives. Foakes, for example, recognizing the condescension often directed at comedy generally, deliberately attempts to mitigate it by underscoring the serious aspects of the work: he intends his analysis as a rejoinder to the "tradition of regarding comedy in general as inferior to 'serious' plays, and Shakespeare's comedies in particular as entertainments, plays of escape into a careless world" (p. xl).

9. The latest manifestation of this argument is Karen Newman's discussion of Antipholus of Syracuse's "inner life and realistic development" (*Shakespeare's Rhetoric of Comic Character* [London: Methuen, 1985], 84).

10. Brooks, "Theme and Structure," 69.

11. Freedman, "Errors in Comedy," 234.

12. This and all subsequent citations to *The Comedy of Errors* are to the New Arden edition. Parenthetical text references are to act, scene, and line.

13. Robert Y. Turner, *Shakespeare's Apprenticeship* (Chicago: University of Chicago Press, 1974), writes about *Errors* and its mode in a way that describes my approach: "Rather than separate the 'comic intrigue' and 'comic rhetoric' from the themes, we should ask how it is that themes, quite serious in other contexts, become the stuff of farce" (p. 167). Others who look at Shakespeare's early work in this way include G. R. Elliott, "Weirdness in *The Comedy of Errors*," *University of Toronto Quarterly* 9 (1939): 95-106, reprinted in *Shakespeare's Comedies: An Anthology of Modern Criticism,* ed. Laurence Lerner (Harmondsworth, Eng.: Penguin, 1967), 19-31, and Paul A. Jorgensen, in his Introduction to the play in *The Complete Pelican Shakespeare* (Baltimore: Penguin, 1969), 55-58. Barbara Freedman's extremely stimulating essay should be required reading for anyone interested in the play or in farce generally.

14. Two exhaustive articles by Erma Gill cover this topic: "A Comparison of the Characters in *The Comedy of Errors* with Those in the *Menaechmi*," *University of Texas Studies in English* 5 (1925): 79-95; and "The Plot-Structure of *The Comedy of Errors* in Relation to Its Source," *University of Texas Studies in English* 10 (1930): 13-65.

15. See John Russell Brown, *Shakespeare and his Comedies* (London: Methuen, 1957), 54-57, and Freedman's "Errors in Comedy," 239-40.

16. Brooks, "Theme and Structure," 69.

17. Elliott, "Weirdness," 30.

18. Francis Fergusson offers an extremely enlightening discussion of the play's ending: "All who successfully devise farce for the theatre feel the need of this final change of mood. I used to notice that the old burlesque shows at Minsky's recognized it instinctively. The travelling salesmen would be guffawing all evening at slapstick, broad jokes, and chorines with but three crucial rhinestones; but at the end the lights would soften, the music would slide from the hot, through the blue, to the frankly old-timy, and a grey-haired mamma or 'mom' would take the centre of the stage to gaze thoughtfully into the electric moonlight. So the patrons received the whole treatment, gently eased at last out of their farcical mood into something warmer, damper, and homier." Fergusson's essay is brief but satisfying: "Two Comedies: *The Comedy of Errors* and *Much Ado About Nothing*," *Sewanee Review* 62 (1954): 24-37; reprinted in Lerner, *Shakespeare's Comedies,* 32-43. The quotation is found on p. 35 of Lerner.

19. See Turner on what farce can do that other modes cannot: "Farce affords its distinctive pleasures that arise from its very limitations. It has the power to make us laugh at cuckolds, shrews, beaten servants, unpaid goldsmiths, unjust laws, even potential incest" (*Shakespeare's Apprenticeship,* 167).

Charles Whitworth (essay date 1991)

SOURCE: Whitworth, Charles. "Rectifying Shakespeare's *Errors:* Romance and Farce in Bardeditry." In *The Comedy of Errors: Critical Essays,* edited by Robert S. Miola, pp. 227-60. New York: Garland Publishing, Inc., 1997.

[*In the essay below, originally published in 1991, Whitworth studies the romantic elements of* The Comedy of Errors, *urging that the play be recognized as romance in its form and in much of its substance. Whitworth focuses in particular on the structure, content, and language of the framing tale of Egeon of Syracuse.*]

What in the world can/should/does an editor do to the text of a Shakespeare play?[1] We are reminded by a growing host of performance critics but also, and more significantly, by textual scholars and editors, that play texts are both potential, to be realized in performance, rather than ends in themselves, and, as things in themselves, unstable. We are enjoined to privilege those early texts of Shakespeare—where there exist more than one—which appear to embody his theatrical practice or that of his colleagues, rather than those which represent his first thoughts or a scribe's transcription, and, generally, to have the *play* in mind as we edit the *text*.[2] What then is the role of the textual editor *vis à vis* a Shakespeare play? How can whatever he does make any real difference? He works perforce only with the printed signs of Quartos and Folios. The director and actors of the play may start from the text he or another editor prepares, but they can and do deviate from it, cut it, rewrite it, rearrange it, re-edit it at will, even throw it away, as the actor Richard McCabe—or was it Puck?—did with a copy of the New Penguin edition of *A Midsummer Night's Dream* in the RSC's 1989 production. Some directors go back to the original printed texts, circumventing all subsequent editions. But the vaunted indefiniteness of the dramatic text is not for the editor. He must make choices and fix them in print, however he may equivocate and canvass alternatives in his notes. He must fix that which must remain unfixed, fluid, open, ambiguous, always at the mercy, inspired or banal, of producers.[3] But if that very production, or the totality of all productions, past, present, and future, is the essence of the play, is he not in some quixotic, perverse way engaged in denying that essence? Is not his enterprise both subsidiary and paradoxical, at the same time both prior to and parasitic upon the living business of the theatre? He works for years to produce a printed text, agonizing over accidentals, solving and resolving cruxes, emending, guessing, inventing, admitting defeat, and delivers his text to be printed, bound, and read.

But reading is not the activity for which that play was written. Performing is. And his text, over which he sweated for so long, will never be performed as he edited it. It will be reproduced, transformed, literally, in the sweat of rehearsal and performance: Brook's *Dream,* Hall's *Hamlet,* Nunn's *Macbeth,* Warner's *Titus,* not his, the editor's. The edition used as script is rarely even mentioned in the theatre programme.[4] "A poem should not mean but be," said MacLeish. An editor's text cannot mean. Can it be? Certainly there can be no *play* on the editor's carefully constructed page. The editor of a novel or a poem or a treatise has no such anxiety. His text goes to its ultimate consumer, the reader, as he has prepared it, unmediated in its essentials. The play editor's text never goes to its ultimate consumer, the play-goer, as he has prepared it, especially in its essentials.

The editor's quest for his text is, from one perspective, a romantic one. He encounters obstacles, fights giants, dodges between Scylla and Charybdis (who shall remain nameless), comes upon ancient strongholds, smoking ruins, signs of skirmishes, dry bones, dust, the landscape of the editorial history of his text. When it is a Shakespeare play, that landscape is vast, the terrain complicated, with traps for the unwary and the challenges of predecessors, the illustrious and the silly, the flamboyant and the hapless, with many of whom he must pause to do battle. But the quest itself is absurd: he can never succeed. He will think he has it, but like Sir Calidore's Blatant Beast, it will escape again, never be finally pinned down, penned in, tamed. What is worse, all productions of his play will repeatedly release it, in virtually infinite mutations, all of them the play, none of them his play. (Even if he convinces himself that he has got the text, he may have lost, or slain, the play.)

To what or whom is the editor of a dramatic text responsible? To the author? He, in Shakespeare's case, is long dead, and besides, we do not, cannot, know what exactly he wrote or wanted. He is, in a crucial sense, irrelevant. To the reader? To the director, to the actor, all of whom are also readers, but who read to different ends than do the student, the teacher, the literary critic, the "mere" reader? And those to whom the ultimate, infinite re-creations of the play belong, theatre practitioners, amateur and professional, great and small, have no responsibility to any *editor's* text, They may rely upon a single edition, which they will still cut and rearrange as it suits them, or they may work from several, picking and choosing, referring to earlier printed texts, even preferring less reliable texts to more reliable ones.[5] Their responsibilities are various: to that chimera, "the play," in the objectivity of which they sometimes display a touching faith, to the audience, society, the box office, sponsors.

The two activities, reading a printed text and seeing/hearing a performance, are, obviously, radically different.[6] The one thing you cannot do as you read the book is really see and hear a performance (imagination is something else); at a performance, you see, hear, even smell sometimes (as in the 1980 RSC production of *As You Like It* when the most delicious aroma of roast chicken wafted over the stalls as the banished duke and his men sat down to their feast in Act II, scene vii), but you cannot read the printed text of the play, the book simultaneously. To the reader, the medium is print; to the spectator-auditor, the media are many, but print is not normally one of them. The editor provides for the one activity, the director, actors, designer, composer, and others for the other. The editor may hope fervently that his edition is adopted by some director and that his cherished readings will be spoken and thus achieve a fleeting immortality. But he knows that even if that happens, his *text,* what he edited, will be only part of the *play.* He cannot provide for those other essential parts, including the way each phrase and line of his text is delivered. The actor *gives* meaning to words, can indeed give different meanings to the same words, meanings which the editor cannot entertain or even imagine.[7] His text is thus at an even further remove from final or definitive meaning. Whether blueprint or skeleton (or some other, always inadequate, metaphor), his text will be the merest starting-point for the performance, that text which was the goal of his long arduous quest. Not only is it destined to be rehandled in the very act of being realized, it is doomed, even as allegedly fixed, permanent, printed, preserved artifact, to be superseded. The beast breaks out as it is being apprehended.[8]

On the other hand, is it really as hopeless as all that? The writing of a play is an act of literary composition. The editor deals with a literary artifact, written, printed, as any literary work is. Written words are the medium, as they are for a novel or a poem. We cannot edit what is not there, that third dimension: the performance. (Nor should the editor, however much he may yearn to do so, stage the play on the page; to do so is to limit the text's potentiality.) We can only edit that text which is different in its structure and layout—speech prefixes, stage directions, act and scene divisions, and so on, rather than authorial voices, paragraphs, quotation marks, chapters, and so on—but similar in its medium: words. The editor of a dramatic text will always have divided, irreconcilable loyalties: to the written text he works from, the material cause (in Aristotelian terms) of what he aims to make, and to the performed play, the final cause.

These and other related questions have occurred to me, a moderately experienced editor of Renaissance dramatic texts but a relative novice as a Shakespeare editor, as I have worked on an edition of *The Comedy of Errors* for the Oxford Shakespeare. They are, some of them, simple matters, but they are also, I am convinced, fundamental matters. They are theoretical, or rather philosophical, questions about the nature of the editing enterprise where dramatic texts are concerned, and about the nature of those texts themselves. I do not wish to belabour the obvious, nor to over-dramatize harmless drudgery, but I do wish to pose such questions, even the more naive-sounding ones, and to worry, and encourage my fellow-editors to worry, about what we do. This concern has not sprung *ex nihilo,* but neither is there yet any articulated theory of dramatic textual editing that addresses these and related questions. Greg's famous theory of copy-text and the guidelines for editors that were derived from it went unchallenged for a surprisingly long time, such were Greg's stature and authority.[9] But even as editors, the great majority of whom have not considered themselves textual theorists *per se,* have worked, they have recognized the limitations and contradictions in Greg's impressive rationale. Its shortcomings are more clearly seen as the peculiar extra-literary nature of early play-texts, the differences between playwriting and authoring, and the primacy of performance over mere reading emerge and are articulated. I am one of that majority, just an editor, not a bibliographer or textual critic *tout court,* and the questions and sceptical reflections which have arisen in the course of the workaday business of editing a Shakespeare play-text (scepticism has not yet induced paralysis) have led, not to a new theory, but to a preoccupation with the peculiarity of that business.

With these queries pending, or looming, I propose to engage in a sort of quizzical intermittent trialogue with recent Shakespearean textual theory, specifically as enunciated by the editors of the Oxford *Complete Works* and related publications, and by other textual critics, all on one side, and "my" play/text, *The Comedy of Errors,* on the other.[10] On this side too is some limited experience of testing editorial solutions in the arena of performance when I had the opportunity to advise the director Phyllida Lloyd on textual matters as she prepared and rehearsed a production of *The Comedy of Errors* for the Bristol Old Vic.[11] Like Antipholus of Syracuse, I am "smothered in *Errors.*" I can only hope that my efforts do not prove me, as he claims to be in the second half of that line, "feeble, shallow, weak" (II.ii.35).

The Comedy of Errors is not a particularly difficult text, compared with others in the Shakespeare canon. It does not raise the "two-text" issue since the Folio of 1623 contains the only early version of the play, and it is not radically corrupt, incomplete, or otherwise maimed. It has its own peculiarities, to some of which I shall return later: a small handful of cruxes, some confusion over characters' names, an occasional vagueness in stage directions, as well as the usual misprints, verse-prose transpositions, unmetrical lines, lacunae, and the like. It is a uniquely Shakespearean amalgam of disparate genres, romance and farce, an early comedy that has more in common with *Twelfth Night* and *Pericles* than with the other plays more nearly contemporary to it, and little of the comedy of young love so prominent in most of Shakespeare's first ten comedies.

I want to discuss here some of the problems and puzzles, critical and editorial, it poses, within the framework of the theoretical and procedural issues adumbrated above. The romance and the farce of editing Shakespeare's plays will, I hope, be both evoked and illustrated in this context, the particular surprises and misprisions, double-takes and double thinking involved in doing the mundane job of editing this text framed, as it were, by the larger questions, as the immediate, hectic business of the farcical comedy is framed and overarched by the mythical, romance motifs of erring, losing, seeking, and finding. The harmless, hopeful drudge sets forth, in the giant shadows of his predecessors, equipped with the tools of the trade, instinct, and some notion of what the achieved thing should be like. He should not deceive himself that he has a perfect idea of the thing-in-itself. Romance versus farce; editing texts for readers versus performing plays for theatre audiences; the editor's need to choose, to set something and not something else down in print, but with space for glosses, collations, explanations versus the performer's need to say one thing and not another, despite the "openness" of the text, with no place for verbal glosses or commentary, but virtually unlimited scope for glossing by gesture, expression, inflection; telling, in narrative and in introductions and commentaries on the page versus showing, in performance, with sets, costumes, and music on the stage; diegesis versus mimesis—these complementary, often contradictory sets of conventions, requirements, and procedures seem to me to be reflected in the play, *The Comedy of Errors*.

Romance is essentially a narrative genre, not a dramatic one. I take it that there are fundamental differences between those two modes, which are more or less identical to Plato's diegesis and mimesis.[12] Drama, as theatre, occurs in the present, is immediate, visual as well as aural; narrative is usually in the past tense, is mediated by a narrator who may or may not be the "author," and nowadays is experienced silently and privately, by reading, though it used more commonly to be experienced aurally and with others. Romance depends upon discursive passages of description, scene-setting, and mood-making, and upon the omniscient narrator's mediation, guidance, information, suspense-building, reassurance, and so on. The time scale is, or can be, vast: "Once upon a time, long ago" is not the dramatist's opening gambit, but it is the essence of the romancer's. Consider Shakespeare's various ploys to overcome that initial obstacle. He uses prologues and epilogues, choruses, frames (themselves either narrative or dramatic), lumps of narrative within the plays (for example, Prospero, Orlando, the Third Gentleman in *The Winter's Tale*, or Egeon at the beginning of *Errors*), even a real historical poet, Gower, who appears in *Pericles* to tell the story that we are unlikely to credit without his assurances as to its authenticity. Only after forty lines, with references to his book, does Gower hand us over to "the judgement of [our] eye"; not content, he presents dumb-shows, refers often to his sources, and in all, appears seven times throughout the play, speaking some 300 lines, including an epilogue, all in order to mediate the romance narrative to a theatre audience, to turn telling into showing. Shakespeare's practice in many of his plays amounts to an inversion, or turning inside out, of Plato's and Aristotle's "mixed mode" (a narrative with some direct dialogue): he writes drama, with a lot of narrative, external and internal, to account for that which is beyond the dramatist's and his audience's reach. An Elizabethan paradigm of this kind of mode-switching is George Peele's marvellous little fantasy, *The Old Wife's Tale*, which announces itself as "tale" but is a play, but a play in which a tale being told turns into a play being performed for an audience which includes the tale-teller herself and her auditors, a play in which several characters tell romance-like tales of travel, hardship, and enchantment.[13] In the vogue of performance studies, we must acknowledge that there are limits to the dramatist's art, even as we claim that his written text is not fully realized until it is performed. Shakespeare's and others' metadrama is a recognition of those limits; it is also a challenge to them, pushing out the circumscribing walls of the wooden O's and concrete caverns in which the performance is confined. There are things the dramatist cannot do, *qua* dramatist, when it comes to story-telling, that the romance narrator can do. But in the theatre the theatrical naturally prevails.

To come to cases: in the theatre, will comedy and its vigorous stepchild, farce, where they are present, inevitably overwhelm, if not subvert, romance? Does romance have a chance where farce pops in its zany face (or arse)? Is *The Comedy of Errors*, romance in its form and in much of its matter, doomed to live *on stage* in a single dimension, that of farce? Is the romance to be left to readers only, while theatre audiences get farce(d): two works living under one title? Farce is a viewerly, spectator-friendly genre; romance is a readerly, imagination-friendly one. Romance requires imagination, farce leaves nothing to it. As readers of romance, we have to create our own Arcadias and Faerylands, Illyrias, Bohemias, and Ardens (or Ardennes if we are reading the Oxford Shakespeare). Romance is not visual; it is, "to speak metaphorically, a *speaking* picture." Farce has to be seen to be (dis)believed.[14] Is it wrong for directors, designers, and actors to take the farce and let the romance go (or worse, send it up)? Or do the improbabilities of romance pushed further, treated comically on stage, necessarily *become* farcical? That is, is the difference I am talking about one of degree and not of kind? But if so, why isn't *Cymbeline*, of all the outrageously improbable plays, called a farce, or *Twelfth Night*? What is the point of Shakespeare's having encased his "farce"—if that is what it is—in a romance, a story which, on its own, has all the sentiment, pathos, and wonder of *Pericles*? Will we even agree that *The Comedy of Errors*, in its larger dimension, *is* romance? For we are told and have been told for a long time that the play is *a farce*, and theatre practitioners have, it seems, always treated it so.

In 1819, Frederick Reynolds turned the play into an operatic farce. He added songs from other Shakespeare plays, with musical settings by various composers, including Mozart. A reviewer for the *European Magazine* found Reynolds's enormities just the remedy for a silly, incredible play:

> It was attended by the most crowded house since the beginning of the season, and the audience were throughout in a unanimous temper to applaud. . . . No illusion of the stage can give probability to the perpetual mutations of four persons, paired in such perfect similitude that the servant mistakes his master, and the master his servant; the wife her husband, and

the husband his wife. All this so strongly contradicts common experience, that it repels us even in description; but on the stage, with the necessary dissimilarity of countenance, voice, manner, and movement, that occurs between the actors, however disguised by dress, the improbability becomes almost offensive.[15]

The anonymous reviewer is carried away by his own rhetoric: no husband mistakes his wife, because there are no twin women.[16] Even the farce, let alone what was left of the romance, failed to work for this dyspeptic critic, but whether audiences liked the play or not, farce it was and farce it remained. C. E. Flower, in his preface to the play in the Memorial Theatre acting edition, makes much of the text of the "Comedy, or as we should now call it Farce" being fully restored in the 1881 Stratford production.

Many of us would concur in Dr. Johnson's opinion that "Shakespeare's plays are not in the rigorous and critical sense either tragedies or comedies, but compositions of a distinct kind," accurately reflecting "the real state of sublunary nature" with its "chaos of mingled purposes and casualties."[17] It is well known that Shakespeare drew upon Plautus' comedy, *The Menaechmi,* about twin brothers from Syracuse, accidentally separated in childhood, one of whom journeys in search of the other. It is also clear that in Act III, scene i, he had in mind the first scene of Plautus' *Amphitruo,* in which Jupiter and Mercury impersonate Amphitruo and Sosia, master and servant.[18] But the ingredient that Plautus did not provide was the plot which frames, overarches, and ultimately subsumes the comedy of twins mistook, servants beaten, masters maddened, and merchants thwarted. That plot, which sets *The Comedy of Errors* in another mode altogether, belongs to a different tradition, one which also went back to antiquity, which Shakespeare knew well and turned to again and again, in which he seems to have been more at home than ever he was in the strictly-structured, rule-governed school of classical comedy. Dr. Johnson, keeping to the Folio's tripartite division of the plays into comedies, histories, and tragedies, opined of Shakespeare that "in comedy he seems to repose, or to luxuriate, as in a mode of thinking congenial to his nature . . . His tragedy seems to be skill, his comedy to be instinct."[19] I would refine Johnson's distinction and suggest that it was particularly *romance* and the dramatic genre that approximates it that were most congenial, even instinctive, to Shakespeare throughout his career. He manifests a peculiar fondness for romance, for old, hoary, much-told tales of wonder and wandering, of storms, shipwrecks, pirates, mistaken identity, oracles and mysteries, treachery and betrayal, bravery and devotion, of parents and children, husbands and wives, brothers and sisters torn asunder and tossed by Fate, but brought together at last against all odds. All of his comedies and tragicomedies contain such elements, some are essentially of that kind.

Just such a tale, of course, is that of old Egeon of Syracuse, his wife, and twin sons and twin servants, shipwrecked, separated, rescued, lost, finally reunited after years of despair and searching, but not before further trials, danger, and anguish. *The Comedy of Errors* begins with it and ends with it, and its dominant moods and motives run right through the farcical comedy, tempering it and transforming it into a new kind of whole which cannot, without distortion, even denaturing, be described or performed simply as "farce." That long discursive opening scene, in which the actors, especially the one who plays Egeon, must grip the audience's attention and imagination with pure tale-telling, holds the cruel promise of execution for the sad, worn-out old man.[20] The comedy which follows must be coloured by it. Johnson may have had in mind that scene, among others, when he complained of the tediousness of Shakespeare's passages of narration:

> He affects a wearisome train of circumlocution and tells the incident imperfectly in many words which might have been more plainly delivered in few. Narration in dramatic poetry is naturally tedious, as it is unanimated and inactive and obstructs the progress of the action; it should therefore always be rapid and enlivened by frequent interruption. Shakespeare found it an encumbrance. . . .[21]

Well, maybe, but he repeatedly brought it upon himself by his choice of romance material. The language of Egeon's narrative is stylized, formulaic, the language of romance: "Once upon a time, long ago . . ." is the mode; and Egeon's story begins a long time ago, at the beginning of his life, in fact: "In Syracusa was I born. . . ."

Within a few lines of the start of the next scene, we see that the two plots, Plautine comedy and Hellenistic romance, are related, that the promise of doom will not be kept because the elements necessary to avert disaster and to bring about the happy dénouement begin immediately to assemble. Scene ii begins, in sharp contrast to the deliberate narrative tempo of Scene i, dramatically in mid-conversation, in mid-sentence with a friendly local merchant warning the newly-arrived Syracusans of their danger as proscribed foreigners in Ephesus, and pointing the warning with news of another Syracusan who is to be executed that very afternoon. The "wearisome train of circumlocution," the narrative, ends, and the brisk, immediate action of drama begins: *in medias res* takes over from "Once upon a time. . . ." The frequent reminders of the time of day in the play—in eight of its eleven scenes—keep Egeon and his impending fate constantly in mind while he is absent from the stage, in tension with the expectation raised by the romance conventions of the first scene that it will be averted. Shakespeare's observation of the unity of time, here as nowhere else before *The Tempest,* heightens that effect. The theme was rendered visually by the clock in Theodor Komisarjevsky's 1938 Stratford production: its hands moved as the hours ticked away, and sometimes ran to catch up. Reference to Egeon (not by name, of course) in the second scene links his plot to that of Antipholus and Dromio of Syracuse: father, son, and servant, unknown to each other, are in the same place at the same time, aliens all three, despairing seekers for each other and the rest of their family.

Furthermore, the two stories are linked immediately and explicitly by references in both to money. Egeon desperately needs money to save his life; barely half-a-dozen lines after he goes off, "hopeless and helpless," to seek it, Antipholus receives back from the merchant the money he had held in safe-keeping, the very sum, we are soon told (I.ii.81), that Egeon requires. And the place where all of them are, the alien town of Ephesus, is established as one where money counts, and where the making of profit has priority over the taking of pleasure: the merchant excuses himself from accompanying Antipholus on a sight-seeing tour because he has an appointment with "certain merchants / Of whom [he] hope[s] to make much benefit" (I.ii.24-5).[22] Shakespeare's changing of Plautus' Epidamnus to Ephesus was no doubt suggested by the primary source for his Egeon plot, the famous story of Apollonius of Tyre in Gower's *Confessio Amantis*. It was in Ephesus, where his long-lost wife had been restored to life after shipwreck and become a priestess in the temple of Diana, that Apollonius was reunited with her at last. Egeon finds his long-lost Emilia in Ephesus. Thus, years before he dramatized the story in its entirety in *Pericles,* he seized upon it as the unlikely frame-plot for his most classical comedy. The alteration of Diana's temple to a Christian priory and Diana's priestess to a Christian Abbess are probably due to the prominence of Ephesus and its affairs in St. Paul's New Testament writings, in Acts and the Epistle to the Ephesians, although Gower supplied a hint by referring to Apollonius' wife as an "Abbess." From Paul, Shakespeare would certainly have known about the reputation of Ephesus for strange goings-on, with evil spirits, sorcerers, exorcists, and others who practised "curious arts," as well as its artisans and merchants. Perhaps Demetrius the silversmith in Acts XIX who makes idols for the devotees of Diana suggested Angelo the goldsmith who purveys trinkets for the servants of Venus. Plautus' Epidamnus survives, however, in no fewer than seven references in the play.[23] In his choice of Ephesus, whatever the origin of that choice may have been, Shakespeare gave himself both the strangeness, the menace, and the surreal atmosphere of the typical romance setting, and the urban, mercantile, domestic scene of Roman comedy. The very setting embodies the two primary modes that he fused in this play.

Egeon's story of separation at sea introduces *that* central motif, and sea imagery recurs frequently. Metamorphosis and loss of identity are introduced in the second scene, expressed in the sea image in Antipholus' first soliloquy:

> I to the world am like a drop of water
> That in the ocean seeks another drop,
> Who, failing there to find his fellow forth,
> Unseen, inquisitive, confounds himself,
> So I, to find a mother and a brother,
> In quest of them unhappy, lose myself.
>
> (I.ii.35-40)[24]

Adriana uses the same image later when, ironically, she is pleading with this Antipholus, the wrong one, not to tear himself away from her (II.ii.128-32). Transformation, dissolution, loss of oneself—this related group of states and their various images form a major theme, or super-motif.

In Act II, Adriana wonders if age is diminishing her beauty, causing her husband to seek his pleasure in the company of other women; in Act V, when his own son does not recognize him, Egeon exclaims that grief and time must have altered him beyond recognition (both characters use the rare word *defeatures,* its only two occurrences in Shakespeare). Time's ravages, added reminders of the immediate, real time that is passing in the play's day, and related to the transformation and dissolution motif, become the subject of two comic exchanges (II.ii.;IV.ii.). Metamorphosis is mentioned repeatedly, sometimes humorously, sometimes fearfully. The workaday city of Ephesus itself is curiously animate: its very buildings are called "Centaur," "Phoenix," "Tiger," and "Porcupine."

Enchantment continues to work upon Antipholus: someone hands him a gold chain, Dromio brings him a bag of gold. Convinced they are bewitched, he calls upon divine aid—"Some blessed power deliver us from hence"—whereupon a courtesan appears (IV.iii.44) (in Adrian Noble's 1983 RSC production, she rose spectacularly from beneath the floor, scantily clad in red and black). Antipholus and Dromio behold not a heavenly rescuer, but Satan herself. Divine aid will come, and in female form, when the Abbess appears and gives them sanctuary, but not just yet. (Parenthetically, we may notice that Antipholus of Syracuse falls under the spells, as he believes, of a series of enchantresses: Adriana in II.ii., Luciana in III.ii., the courtesan in IV.iii., finally the Abbess in V.i.—one enchantress per act, a neat distribution—with, as prelude, the soliloquy in I.ii. in which he voices his fears of sorcerers, witches, and the like. This underlines his vulnerability and impressionability, and is reminiscent of the case of a famous hero of chivalric romance, Sir Percival, one of the Grail knights of Arthurian legend, whose experiences with women during his quest, including his mother, his sister, and the fiend in female guise several times, similarly underline his susceptibility to error and his innocence. In contrast, Antipholus of Ephesus is always accompanied by men only—his servant, friends, business acquaintances, creditors, the officer who arrests him—until IV.iv., the conjuring scene, when at last he is surrounded by women, who insist that he is mad; his brother thinks *himself* mad, the victim of witches. Another way in which Shakespeare differentiates the brothers, making the Syracusan the romance protagonist while the Ephesian retains the role of the thwarted and irate husband of domestic comedy, is by giving the former no fewer than six soliloquies and asides, totalling fifty lines, while his brother has none.)

A new order, that of genuine divine authority, not Dr. Pinch's sham, intervenes in the person of the Abbess. Her claim to be able to heal the supposedly mad Antipholus and Dromio is the claim of a power superior to those of mere magic, sorcery, even the devil. Now the Duke returns, leading old Egeon to execution. At its height of frenzy, the comical-farcical action, which, as we have seen, is far from being only that, is interrupted by the resumption of the tragicomic one. But its progress is halted too, literally, physically, by the prostrate Adriana, imploring the Duke to intercede with the Abbess and get her husband restored to her. Farce impedes romance temporarily. At this moment, the two plots merge, under the auspices, as it were, of both spiritual and temporal authority, both benign, the Abbess and the Duke. Romance resumes, and subsumes farce. To be sure, the unravelling will take some 300 more lines and there will be further supposes and surprises, even pathos, along the way.

Time, which Dromio claimed had gone back an hour, has now gone back years, to when the family was whole, before the events narrated by Egeon a few hours earlier took place. The boys were infants then, new-born. It is, fittingly, the Abbess, the holy mother, who gives explicit utterance to the metaphor of rebirth, describing this moment as one of nativity, repeating the word (if the Folio is right) for emphasis:

> Thirty-three years have I but gone in travail
> Of you, my sons, and till this present hour
> My heavy burden ne'er deliverèd.
> The Duke, my husband, and my children both,
> And you the calendars of their nativity,
> Go to a gossip's feast, and joy with me.
> After so long grief, such [nativity].
>
> (V.i.403-9)

Both *Pericles* and *Cymbeline* use similar language when they are reunited with children whom they had believed long dead.[25] The imminent death with which the play began is transfigured into birth: then we met with things dying, now with things, as it were, new-born. That same death-dealing Duke becomes the life-giving lord: "It shall not need. Thy father hath his life." Patron already to one Antipholus, the Duke becomes godfather to both at their re-christening. Even the little coda, with its comic business between the pairs of twins, not yet entirely free from error though beyond its more baleful effects, ends on that note. The Dromios resolve that since they do not know which is elder, but came into the world "like brother and brother," they will now go hand in hand, not one before another, a visual image of recognition and reunion, the joining, not the confounding, of water drops, and a verbal reminder of birth and rebirth. Komisarjevsky's clock should by now have been running furiously backward, whirling away the years, for in the biggest and best of the comedy's errors, Time has indeed gone back, all the way from death to birth, from the intense dramatic final moment to the expansive narrative "Once upon a time," from the end of the play to the beginning of the story. But that, essentially, is what happens in romance.

The editor in his quest may face anything from minor, uncontentious emendations to hopeless cruxes, from mere commas and full stops to be distributed judiciously, to gaping blanks where text should be, and to heaps of text where less, or none, should be. He will be grateful, in the present case, for the relative brevity and relative cleanness of the Folio text of *The Comedy of Errors,* and that there is only the Folio text to contend with, no two- or three-headed monsters. *Errors* is the fifth play in the Folio, following *The Tempest, The Two Gentlemen of Verona, The Merry Wives of Windsor,* and *Measure for Measure,* all of which were set by the compositors from transcripts made by Ralph Crane. The four plays which follow *Errors*—*Much Ado About Nothing, Love's Labour's Lost, A Midsummer Night's Dream, The Merchant of Venice*—are all reprints of Quartos.[26] *Errors* stands alone among the first nine plays in the Folio in having apparently been set from Shakespeare's foul papers, a genesis it shares with only seven others in the volume. This orthodox view, held by Chambers, McKerrow, Greg, and nearly everyone since, of the nature of the printer's copy for *Errors* has recently been challenged by Paul Werstine.[27] His argument that authorial foul papers might have been used in the theatre, and thus that the standard "foul papers versus prompt copy" dichotomy may not be so rigid after all, is rebutted by Wells and Taylor.[28] Some of the confusions in the text are of the sort usually attributed to unperfected authorial copy: descriptive or narrative stage directions, imprecise distinctions between characters, uncertain or alternate names for characters, missing or imprecise entrances and exits, and so on. All of these require editorial emendation but not all are necessarily problematic for performers.

Take the names, for example. No editor is likely to hesitate before emending *"Iuliana"* and *"Iulia"* in the stage direction and first speech prefix at III.ii. The character in question is clearly Luciana, Adriana's sister, who has already appeared and been named at II.i.3. But the misnamings occur in column *a* of gathering H4, probably the first column of this play set by Compositor C; meanwhile, C's partner, Compositor D, was getting it right seven times—*Luc.*—in column *b* of the same page (this is not to suggest that they were necessarily setting the page simultaneously, side by side). Surely Shakespeare, writing his play seriatim and not by formes, did not forget his character's name between the end of II.ii, where she has the last line, and the beginning of III.ii. Did he on the spur of the moment decide to change her name to "Juliana" to avoid confusion with Luce, who had just made her one and only appearance barely eighty lines before, then revert to "Luciana," the aberration preserved in the foul papers? Compositor D was in no doubt, nor was B, the third *Errors* compositor, and C himself conformed subsequently, though he vacillated between *Luc.* and *Luci.* on three other pages. Such speculation need not trouble even an editor intent on establishing a consistent text; he emends whether it was Shakespeare the composer or C the compositor who erred. A director may never know if he has not seen the Folio text or an apparatus that records such things.

But Luce is a different, more substantial matter. This character, later identified as the kitchen-maid, appears in III.i. and engages in a slanging match with Dromio and Antipholus of Ephesus, who vainly seek entry to their own house, while their twins are inside, enjoying their usurped places. In the Folio, Luce is named once in a stage direction, seven times in speech prefixes, and three times in the dialogue. This is her only scene, though in many productions she returns in the general mêlées in IV.iv. and V.i. (usually taking the small part of the messenger in V.i., which justifies her presence on stage), and to be reunited with the right Dromio as her master and mistress are reunited. John Dover Wilson, in his first Cambridge Shakespeare edition of the play (1922), listed the character as "Luce, or Nell" and he has been followed by many editors since. A few imply that there are two characters, one of whom does not appear. Only the new Oxford edition goes so far as to change the character's name to "Nell," and to give only that in Dramatis Personae, stage directions, speech prefixes, and dialogue. Luce is expunged.

The basis for this emendation is Dromio of Syracuse's reference to the woman in question as "Nell" in his comic set-piece duologue with Antipholus of Syracuse in III.ii. There is no reason to identify Luce, who appears in III.i., with Nell the kitchen-maid described as globular in shape by Dromio in III.ii. But the person who stood behind the door and "reviled" Antipholus of Ephesus, that is, Luce, is identified as the kitchen-maid at IV.iv.75-6. So did Shakespeare begin with a maid called "Luce," then change her name to "Nell," perhaps to avoid confusion with Luciana, or did he originally plan a second maidservant for the second Dromio? If the latter, then he changed his mind before the end where Dromio of Syracuse gratefully relinquishes any claim in the kitchen-maid to his brother (V.i.417-19). In any case, as the text stands in the Folio, the name "Nell" occurs only once, in a set-piece, where Dromio is desperately inventing witty replies to straight-man Antipholus' questions. The scene, with Dromio's (geo)graphic anatomizing of spherical Nell, is the comical counterpart in prose to Antipholus' lyrical wooing of Luciana in rhyming verse in the immediately preceding seventy lines of the same scene; we witness the first wooing, Dromio reports the other, with grotesque embellishment. "Nell" is an *ad hoc* invention by Dromio; it allows him (and Shakespeare) their harmless necessary pun on "ell": "What's her name?" "Nell, sir. But her name and three-quarters—that's an ell and three-quarters—will not measure her from hip to hip" (III.ii.110-13). He even spells it out to be sure we get it, as bad punsters usually do. The actor might pause momentarily before replying "Nell, sir," as if inventing the name and lining up his gross pun on the spot. This single occurrence of the name in this highly artificial context hardly warrants changing "Luce" to "Nell" eleven times.[29] No editor, to my knowledge, has bothered to mention the name "Dowsabell," let alone proposed that Luce be called that. Yet this same Dromio calls this same woman "Dowsabell" at IV.i.110.

Nevertheless, a director may choose to call the character "Nell," as Phyllida Lloyd did in her 1989 Bristol Old Vic production. She read and was persuaded by the Oxford editors' argument, liked the jingle of "If thy name be called Nell, Nell thou hast answered him well" (III.i.53), and thought the name suited the actress playing the role. My arguments for retaining "Luce" did not prevail; the director simply chose to do otherwise as she was free to do, citing a recent major edition of the play, and no one could protest that the text was grievously violated or directorial whim irresponsibly indulged. The Oxford editors print "Nell," I would print "Luce," and both of us will have done as we did for good reasons. Who will be right? What are the criteria for deciding that question? Shakespeare's intentions? Whatever they were, we cannot recover them, and they may anyway have been one thing at one time, another at another. The beast has not been slain or caught, greasy Nell is forever loose.

Other names and other creatures are less troublesome. The place-name "Epidamium" occurs seven times in the Folio, three on pages set by Compositor C, four on pages set by B. Though minim error is a distinct possibility, the agreement of two compositors makes it more likely that they set what they were reading in their copy. But there was no such place.[30] May an editor rectify Shakespeare's errors? Some would not: the Riverside Shakespeare and David Bevington, in both his last revision of Hardin Craig's edition (1980) and his new Bantam (1988), read "Epidamium." Most editors, however, including the Oxford, follow Pope in emending to "Epidamnum." But the place in question is Epidamnus, the setting of Plautus' *Menaechmi*. Why the classicist Pope should have chosen the accusative form of the noun (which occurs in various declined forms in *Menaechmi*) is mildly puzzling. Feeling slightly giddy at venturing where no fool editor has ever rushed before, I would propose "Epidamnus," the correct Latin name for the city Shakespeare apparently had in mind. But does it matter? In performance, not a whit. A fictitious place, a mere name on two romance characters' Mediterranean itineraries, that is all it is. But for the editor, it must matter, however insignificant it is: something must be printed and justified against the contending alternatives. In performance, almost anything can be said and no one will blink.

The Courtesan's house is called the Porpentine. This is an archaic spelling of "porcupine," so a modernizing editor should prefer the modern form. Shakespeare used only "porpentine" though "porcupine" was already current; it occurs eight times in his works, five times in *Errors*. But it is a proper name here. Is that then an argument for retaining its archaic form? No. That is to opt for quaintness, a practice that mars the otherwise splendid Riverside edition. A quaintness quotient has no place in a scholarly modernizing editor's set of guidelines. We modernize other spellings, so why not this? Curiously, it has been relatively modern editors, starting with Aldis Wright in the famous nineteenth-century Cambridge Shakespeare, who have reverted to "Porpentine," while Rowe modernized the spelling and was followed by editors until Wright. The Oxford, like eighteenth-century editions, has "Porcupine" (and thus obviates the need for a gloss). No editor, I believe, has retained the Folio spelling "Tyger," another house-name, at III.i.96, nor "Centaure" for the inn where Antipholus of Syracuse lodges at I.ii.9. And in the context of those other recognizable beastnames which abound in the play, "Porpentine" sounds odd in performance as well as looking odd on the page.

Another problem facing editors, but which causes little or no difficulty in the theatre, is the unmetrical line, whether short or long. The New Cambridge editor of *Errors* rhetorically asks *à propos* of one such, "Need we be worried by a line which is metrically short?"[31] Editors, *pace* Dorsch, usually are, assuming that Shakespeare always wrote regular iambic pentameter and that verse lines which contain fewer or more than the standard number of syllables (excluding feminine endings) must be faulty. But perhaps Dorsch is right and the assumption needs reexamining; Shakespeare, like Homer, must have nodded now and then. Metrifying Shakespeare is harder when a syllable or a word is missing than when there are too many; adding something requires that we invent or reconstruct Shakespeare. The line "A meane woman was deliuered" (I.i.54) has been regularized by most editors, usually by adding F2's "poor" before "mean," though some recent editors, from Peter Alexander (1951) to Bevington, leave the line as it stands in F. In performance it is easy and natural for an actor to pause a beat before saying "mean" or to emphasize it to mark the difference between this woman and Egeon's own wife, about whom he has just been speaking, and thus fill out the line. The same holds for many other such lines, short by a mere syllable. A good actor will not chant verse or mark the metre obtrusively anyway (nor will he reduce it to prose), and a missing syllable here and there, provided the sense is clear and the surrounding flow of the verse is maintained, is hardly going to be disastrous. But again, an editor, producing a printed text, may feel the lack more keenly and will probably at least consider whether to supply it, even if he finally decides not to, or writes a note asking whether we need be worried by it.

Gary Taylor's eloquent advocacy of invention by editors must be endorsed with caution and caveat (note 10 above). It will seem to many chillingly like an unrestricted licence. The naturally conservative editor and the naturally, or supernaturally, inventive poet seldom cohabit in one mind, and Taylor is right when he observes: "It is because those who have the facility seldom possess the judgement to restrain their inclination that those with a gift for emendation . . . invariably indulge in it too often" ("Inventing," p. 43). Though no harm may be done by adding a word to fill out a line of verse, will enough be gained to warrant the in(ter)vention? Taylor's own "mean-born" in the line under discussion seems to me to be a scant improvement over F2's redundant "poor mean." The condition of *her* birth is not relevant, and to refer to it here points away from the birth that is relevant, that of her "burden, male twins" (I.i.55). The point is that she is now "mean," that is poor, of low estate, and so is willing to sell her twin sons to Egeon to be servants to his. If the compulsion to metrify proves too strong, I would favour "A mean young woman was deliverèd," but, like many editors, most actors, and any audience, I can live with the Folio's mere nine syllables. In general, editors seem less troubled by F's long "Vnwilling I agreed, alas, too soone / wee came aboard" (I.i.60), which some retain, or the very short one resulting from breaking it up into two: "Unwilling I agreed. Alas, too soon / We came aboard" (following Pope).[32] Sometimes when the latter choice is made, a note solemnly remarks on the rhetorical effect of such a short line at this decisive moment in Egeon's narrative. Such "effect" has been imported by the editor, of course, in breaking up the long line, and an actor can impart rhetorical effect in his delivery by pausing, sighing, whatever, if such an effect seems appropriate at this point, whether or not the line is printed as one or as two in his script.

The inventing editor will find somewhat more fertile ground in Dromio of Syracuse's frantic outburst at II.ii.192-3: "This is the Fairie land, oh spight of spights, / We talke with Goblins, Owles and Sprights." Here is another short line, lacking two syllables this time. The Second Folio, that anonymous first edited text of the First Folio, recognizes the problem, but does not get it right somehow, reading "and Elves Sprights." Pope changed "Elves" to the unmistakably bisyllabic "elvish." Theobald transformed "owls" to "ouphs." Most modern editors, however, have stuck with F's three unmetrical monsters. Even the Oxford retains an octosyllabic line, but modernizes Theobald's "ouphs" to "oafs," a lexically legitimate move all right, but one that creates a misleading and therefore undesirable secondary meaning for modern readers and audiences (as any modernization may run the risk of doing). The short line invites expansion. Is it not plausible that, by haplography, Compositor D conflated "oules and elues and" in his copy to "Owles and"? "We talk with goblins, owls, and elves, and sprites" seems appropriate to Dromio's terrified state, his fevered brain coining monsters pellmell.[33] But, of course, the actor has even more reason here to pause, engage in business, break the line up, and hence stretch it that extra foot, than was the case with Egeon's line in the first scene discussed earlier. If in performance, where and only where his text can become a play, it does not matter if a word is missing, is the editor justified in indulging the inventing itch? Of course, we edit for *readers,* who can interrupt their reading of the text, who indeed are invited to do so, to jump to the fine print at the bottom of the page where we discuss the options and defend our decisions, as theatre-goers at a performance cannot. For the play editor's peace of mind, the ideal reader of his edition will be a literary reader and not a theatrically-minded one, and will read it as he or she reads a novel, a poem, Johnson's *Dictionary,* or Lawrence's letters. When Shakespeare was but the prince of poets, happy drudges lost less sleep.

Lacunae of a whole line or more, even in a rhyming verse passage where it seems clear that something is missing, are dealt with in performance, while the editor sweats and strains and, maybe, invents iambic pentameter. A case in point occurs in *Errors* III.i., at the height of the furious row between those inside the Phoenix and the rightful occupants and guests outside. In a long rhymed passage, immediately following the line in which Luce's name appears twice, the Folio reads as follows:

ANTI[PHOLUS OF EPHESUS].

Doe you heare you minion, you'll let vs in I hope?

LUCE.

    I thought to haue askt you.

S. DRO.

    And you said no.

E. DRO.

    So come helpe, well strooke, there was blow for blow.

Theobald emended "hope" to "trow" in the first line, producing a triple rhyme, of which there are four others in the passage: lines 19-21, 64-6, 67-9, 76-8. But he produced no more sense. Some modern editors have followed him, including Cuningham, Foakes (new Arden), Wells (New Penguin), Levin (Signet), and Dorsch; the last is peremptory in dismissing Malone's conjecture that a line rhyming with "hope," perhaps ending with "rope," had dropped out (p. 68 n.). Just as many, however, have preferred to retain F's "hope," usually citing Malone's conjecture: Wilson (1922 and 1961), Alexander, Jorgensen (Pelican), Riverside, Bevington, Tetzeli. Only the Oxford, though, both retains "hope" and leaves a space in brackets to indicate that a line is missing before "Do you hear . . . I hope?" Gary Taylor admits ("Inventing," p. 43) to not having the temerity to insert his own line into Shakespeare's text in another play, but says further that he would feel no compunction about marking a lacuna and mentioning the conjecture in a note. This he did in the present case, recording "*E. Dro.* Thou wouldst answer well to hanging, if I had a rope." This supplies the rhyme, but leaves Luce's (in the Oxford text, Nell's) "I thought to have asked you" still unattached. What did she think to have asked whom? Bevington thinks the missing line should follow rather than precede the "hope" line, but does not conjecture.[34]

As textual adviser to the Bristol Old Vic production of *Errors* in 1989, I discussed the lacuna with the director, who, while using the Arden edition as her script, studied the text very carefully, consulting several other editions. Prior to one rehearsal, I composed several alternative lines, one of which she might choose to insert in the gap. Alas for my inventions, I arrived to find that she had decided to ignore the lacuna, keep the Arden's "trow," and try to make sense of what was there. The actors had invented business to that end. Nell's and Dromio of Syracuse's half-lines were a resumption of a hypothetical previous conversation, a further sally in the former's attempt to seduce the latter. A little personal drama was simmering away indoors even as the larger, more public drama boiled over outdoors. The large Nell spread-eagled the small Dromio against the door. In the fever of the moment, it worked. Dromio's "And you said—no?" became a plea for mercy. No one gave a further thought to the dread lacuna, which in any case was filled from outside when the other Dromio, in mime, thrust a privy member through the letter slot, and the outraged, frustrated Nell inside applied a vacuum cleaner to it. The audience roared its amusement at the mayhem which ensued, and the rejected inventing editor had, willy-nilly, to join in. An emboldened editor may invent, but if he cannot insert his invention in his text, and performers who know about it do not want or need it, it can only survive as a conjecture, buried in a note. What then is its status or point? Inventing Shakespeare only to lose him in the apparatus seems an unprofitable expense of spirit. Yet Taylor's plea is a powerful one, and it enhances that task of helpful drudgery to which editors earnestly commit themselves. It urges the editor to recreate as well as to recover, to become Shakespeare in some sort, momentarily. That his invention, which may not become text, will *be* only if it is spoken in performance and if it is, will *be* only for an instant, are the absurd odds against which he plays. Taylor's description of such inventive emendation as game is reminiscent of the late Philip Brockbank's advocacy of "festive scholarship." Ludic editing serves Shakespeare, the play, and the reader, not just the black signs on the white pages of F. *Ludus*—the medieval Latin word meant *game* and *play,* as students of medieval drama well know. But games have rules and boundaries, as Taylor reminds us. Because he cannot cheat and write his invention into Shakespeare, the gaming editor offers it and hides it wistfully, playfully, at the same time. It may be in print all right, but it is out of bounds, off stage, below the line. A director like John Barton may write hundreds of lines of "Shakespeare" in his adaptation and they get spoken at every performance. The inspired editor invents, and directs furiously in his head.

May an editor adopt a reading recorded only in acting editions? If we mean what we say about the primacy of performance, why not? A crux or a confusion may be clarified by an actor or director who *has* to get or make sense out of it, and that reading may be passed down in playhouse tradition, unknown to scholarly editors who collate those dozens of other scholarly editions. In *Errors* I.ii., Antipholus of Syracuse speaks his first soliloquy, quoted earlier (p. 238). In the Hull adaptation of the late eighteenth century, revised by John Philip Kemble in 1811, the Folio's "falling" in line 37 is emended to "failing." Thus the parallel drawn by Antipholus between the water drop and himself is exact: it seeks its fellow in the vast ocean, and failing to find it, loses (confounds) itself; he, seeking his family in the wide world, unhappy (unsuccessful) in his quest, loses himself. When this emendation was suggested to Owen Teale who played Antipholus in the Bristol production, he grasped it immediately, perceiving the logic and clarity it achieved. An eighteenth-century theatrical emendation lived again in performance 200 years later. It is a tiny change, to be sure, an *i* for an *l,* and the improvement in sense is slight if real. But should we continue to resist or ignore it in modern editions because an actor not an editor first invented it, and when a simple explanation, compositorial misreading of *i* for *l,* is available anyway? Which reading would Shakespeare have opted for, the actor's, the compositor's, or the editor's? His own—but that begs a few questions.

We have, it would seem, come almost full circle, from making a text by remaking another text which never was, and never will be, what it is meant to be, unless it is performed, and then will be something else quite, to realizing that performance not only makes the play, but can, and often does, make the text itself. Of course, the example just given is a very small one, one word, one letter, in an entire play. We do not edit performance, or base our scholarly editions solely or mainly on texts derived from performance—at least, we do not *say* that we are doing so. But what of those Shakespeare revisions preserved in the Folio? A modern edition of *Hamlet* based on the Folio text may, it would seem, be said to be derived from a performance text. But we as editors unmake and remake that particular early text upon which we base our editions, wherever it emanated from, by modernizing its spelling and punctuation, correcting its obvious misprints, spelling out speech prefixes, adding and expanding stage directions, even reconstructing, as the Oxford editors reconstructed the *Pericles* Quarto, and by emending cruxes, mending lacunae, inventing Shakespeare. In each repeated effort to fix *our* text, pin it down, get it right, we make *the* text more, not less, unstable. For each edition is another text, different from all others, be it by no more than a few commas (it is of course always more than that), as each production is a new text, in that larger sense of the word, as well as enunciating a new text in the narrower sense. Every edition is, and is not, definitive. And each performance of a single production has its peculiarities of rhythm, mood, tempo, "feel," as performers are always telling us.

Actors and directors talk readily about remaking Shakespeare when they do a new production. Indeed, most believe that is what the theatre is about.[35] Editors are more reluctant to acknowledge that they too remake Shakespeare, even when they are engaged in producing diplomatic texts or facsimiles. This implies—and this is no earth-shaking discovery of mine—that that TEXT of Shakespeare which we believed, avowedly or tacitly, it was a duty to attempt to recover *in toto* and exactly, not only is not there to be recovered, that that concept itself is faulty, but that if it were it could never be "restored" in our editions, old- or modern-spelling, diplomatic or inventive. Editors of multi-text plays such as *Hamlet* and *King Lear* have come to realize that, if they have the courage of their convictions, they cannot have all the *Hamlet* or *Lear* that Shakespeare may have written in their edited texts. They cannot print the complete words of *Hamlet* and call it Shakespeare's play. To print all the *Hamlet* that Shakespeare wrote at different times, on first, second and subsequent thoughts, even if one is convinced that he did write all of it, is to produce something under Shakespeare's name that he never invented.[36] We can only edit texts, finally, not plays, not authors. Once we accept that our control-text, be it Folio *Hamlet* or *Errors*, Quarto *Lear* or *Pericles*, is itself only a version, and perhaps a partial one, of Shakespeare's own total *Hamlet, Errors, Lear*, or *Pericles*, and that the very existence of that entity is doubtful and unprovable, we may find ourselves freed from the old idolatry. And if we further accept that all our texts are remakes of versions of uncertain provenance, well, we

Antipholus of Ephesus, Adriana, and others in Act IV, scene iv of William Shakespeare's The Comedy of Errors.

shall be in no worse company than that of the poets banished by Plato from the commonwealth for making counterfeit copies of imitations of the Forms.

This freedom should in turn help us to overcome the "inhibition of seriousness," as Taylor calls it, the po'-facedness of scientistic textual scholarship which has prevented editors from realizing the playful truth that the object of the quest is given much of its substance and shape by the quester himself. The editor does not return with the captured TEXT in hand, but emerges at the other end of the labyrinthine way with the text that he has found, *trouvé*.[37] Such a concept of the editor's art, partway between setting out to find and retrieve a determinate object that is known to exist *a priori* out there, and the free, frivolous invention, the parlour-game that Taylor, as he predicts, will be accused of encouraging, seems to me a fruitful one. What I find will, of course, be partly determined by what I look for, and it is no game of blind man's buff that I play, or random hunt I set out upon. Not just any treasure trove will do; ghastly roadside warnings like *The Other Shakespeare* and the deformed corpses of

A. L. Rowse's brood litter the way. But what I cannot come back with, however I may "struggle for the vision fair," is the one and only *Comedy of Errors* by Shakespeare.

I might have multiplied the examples of textual puzzles and problems in *The Comedy of Errors,* and proposed or speculated about them at length. I have avoided the most notorious crux in the play, Adriana's speech beginning "I see the jewel best enamelléd" (II.i.108-12). Whatever an editor decides to print in these lines is bound not to be right. The actress Rosie Rowell managed to make the passage sound quite meaningful as it stands in most modern editions when she played Adriana in Bristol in 1989. Editing inevitably complicates such cruxes, while performance, also inevitably, simplifies them: it must. As Stanley Wells suggests, "For some reason—perhaps because an edition can be annotated—one is more willing to confront a reader than a playgoer with nonsense" (*Re-editing,* p. 49). But often, what is nonsense on the page is given sense on the stage, or at least an audience is easily persuaded that it makes sense. The moment comes and goes in seconds, and an audience which is not going to worry whether it is "Epidamium" or "Epidamnum" or "Epidamnus," or fret over Luce or Nell, will be swayed by the gist of what Adriana says as she grieves at her husband's supposed desertion. They will not see the collations and commentaries, or the whole articles devoted to emending and explaining the five lines spoken in fifteen seconds in performance.[38] To return to one of the issues raised at the beginning, it is because he must print this or that but not both that the editor has to resolve cruxes, but he sets about it knowing that he can canvass, collate, comment, and explain also, while the actor has to say it, play it, and be done. Shakespeare, of all people, knew that reading a speech and playing it were worlds apart, that obscurity can evaporate in the action of the stage. May it be that some of the famous cruxes are our own inventions, as readers, critics, and editors? Shakespeare did not count on us getting in the way.

I am not yet sure whether to stick to the Folio's double nativity" in the Abbess's final speech (V.i.403-9, quoted above, pp. 240-1). Double nativity at the end of a play about two pairs of twins lost at sea, separated, then reborn, in the words of their new-found mother, is fitting. Besides the play was performed, probably for the first time, at Christmas 1594. Nativity was seasonal. Johnson proposed "festivity" in the final line, Dyce adopted it and was followed by the Oxford edition, but Hanmer's "felicity" fits the line and sums up the tragicomic action best: "After so long grief, such felicity." Whichever word is spoken in performance, the joy, the felicity, the festivity of comic dénouement and romance rebirth are ambient. Editors will make various decisions; performance will variously fix that particular word at that moment, but will unfix and remake the very text it speaks, playing and showing nativity, festivity, felicity, and more, where the edition can read one of them, collate others, comment on all, but convey none. Text and performance merge, and the printed word, apparently always the same but, as a famous son of ancient Ephesus, Heraclitus, would have known, always in flux, is confounded by the act that gives it being but is itself evanescent, rushing headlong to its own closure, the final curtain.

Romance and farce merge at the end of *The Comedy of Errors,* I have argued. The local absurdities, cruxes, and confusions of the latter are confounded in the eternal improbabilities and incredibilities of the former. Both genres flaunt unlikelihood, the one calling us to witness with our own eyes that it is true, the other telling us even as it shows us that it cannot possibly be true. To attempt to create a coherent whole out of such unlikely components seems doubly unlikely, ludicrous. But Shakespeare brazenly pulled it off. Setting out yet again to edit a Shakespeare play-text may appear an unlikely, quixotic venture, but we do it all the time, put our names to it, package it and sell it—Wilson's, Foakes's, Wells's, Bevington's, Dorsch's, Whitworth's *Errors*—claiming, or at least acquiescing in publishers' claims, that we've got it, the play, right here. Performance too is risky, volatile, ephemeral, over as soon as it is done, and just as brazen, each new show—the Lord Chamberlain's Men's, Kemble's, Komisarjevsky's, Nunn's, Noble's, Lloyd's *Errors*—implying each time that for that time, this one is it, the play, Shakespeare's *Comedy of Errors*.[39] Rectify Shakespeare's *Errors*? Perform Shakespeare's, the whole of Shakespeare's, and nothing but Shakespeare's *Errors*? Not very likely. Yet on and off we and they go, doing it because it must be done, repeatedly. None of the products of these efforts, the myriad performances, the endless editions, though they stretch out to the crack of doom, can be Shakespeare's *Errors*. All of them, hypothetical and actual, future, present, and past, not one before another, may be so called.

Notes

1. A prior question, in the poststructuralist era, might be to do with how "text" in such a context should be construed. I shall use the term in a conventional sense, to denote the written or printed pages which collectively make up a single work of dramatic literature, a play as it is read in book form. The differences between a play text as edited and read, and a play as performed and seen/heard are crucial to this discussion.

2. Among the fuller arguments for this general case is Stanley Wells's *Reediting Shakespeare for the Modern Reader* (Oxford, 1984); one of the most recent and vigorous is T. H. Howard-Hill's "Modern Textual Theories and the Editing of Plays," *Library,* Sixth Series, II (1989), 89-115. Especially pertinent to the concerns of this essay is Howard-Hill's "Playwrights' Intentions and the Editing of Plays," *TEXT,* 4 (1988), 269-78, in which testimony is adduced from an unexpected quarter: C. S. Lewis, half a century ago, anticipated central issues in the current text-performance debate.

3. I do not mean that an editor should interpret in the text itself. An example of editorial overfixing is the

Oxford Shakespeare's "understand" in the speech of Dromio of Ephesus at *Comedy of Errors,* II.i.51-3 (all references will be to the Oxford *Complete Works,* in modern spelling, ed. Stanley Wells and Gary Taylor (Oxford, 1986), unless otherwise indicated). In modern as in Elizabethan English, *understand* is not hyphenated. To hyphenate it is to interpret reductively, to accord priority, with a nudge and a wink, to the secondary meaning, "stand up under his blows." An editor as annotator may of course do that in his commentary, if he judges it necessary; it is an actor's job to do so in delivering the line, if he judges it necessary.

4. The New Penguin Shakespeare is the RSC's "house" edition and is frequently mentioned in programme credits. Directors there often use others as well or instead; the Arden is a favourite because of its copious annotation, which, however, actors often admit, can be either an encumbrance or irrelevant to their work. Antony Sher writes that the company used both New Penguin and Arden editions when rehearsing *Richard III* in 1984: "and when there are discrepancies we'll choose whichever is more useful for our purposes" (*Year of the King* [London, 1985], p. 156).

5. In his 1988/9 production of *Hamlet* for the RSC, director Ron Daniels transposed a scene in accordance with the "bad" Quarto of 1603. He also cut 900 lines from the New Penguin text, itself based on the "good" Quarto of 1604/5, with liberal helpings from the Folio.

6. On hearing versus seeing a play in Shakespeare's time, see Andrew Gurr, *Playgoing in Shakespeare's London* (Cambridge, 1987), pp. 85-97.

7. A good example of this occurred in Deborah Warner's 1988 production of *King John,* when Salisbury (Edward Harbour), as he spoke the lines "My arm shall give thee help to bear thee hence, / For I do see the cruel pangs of death / Right in thine eye" (V.iv.58-60), to the mortally wounded Count of Melun, reached behind his back to receive a misericord from his companion Pembroke, with which he put Melun out of his agony. The stage business not only conferred a novel meaning upon "My arm shall give thee help to bear thee hence," but was appropriate in the context, a soldierly act of mercy to a dying, noble enemy who had done the English lords a good turn by warning them of treachery.

8. At least three noteworthy editions of *The Comedy of Errors* have appeared since I undertook my own in 1985: that in the Oxford *Complete Works,* T. S. Dorsch's New Cambridge (1988), and David Bevington's Bantam (1988). There was a bilingual German-English edition by Kurt Tetzeli von Rosador in 1982, and the script used in the BBC television production was published in 1984. Meanwhile, a variorum edition is in progress in the United States, and the Arden is being revised, etc.

9. The classic essay "The Rationale of Copy-Text" is reprinted in Greg's *Collected Papers,* ed. J. C. Maxwell (Oxford, 1966), pp. 374-91. Howard-Hill challenges the rationale and the editorial tradition since Greg in the first article cited in n. 2 above.

10. Besides works already referred to, I would include in this body of recent work in the immediate light of which my (and others') current editing of Shakespeare is being conducted: Stanley Wells and Gary Taylor, *Modernizing Shakespeare's Spelling, with Three Studies in the Text of "Henry V"* (Oxford, 1979); the same authors' (with John Jowett and William Montgomery) *William Shakespeare: A Textual Companion* (Oxford, 1987); Wells, *Shakespeare and Revision,* Hilda Hulme Memorial Lecture, University of London, 3 December 1987 (London, 1988); Gary Taylor and Michael Warren (eds.), *The Division of the Kingdoms: Shakespeare's Two Versions of "King Lear"* (Oxford, 1983), and several articles written in response to this volume; Gary Taylor, "Inventing Shakespeare," *Jahrbuch 1986* (Bochum, 1986), 26-44; Taylor, "Revising Shakespeare," *TEXT,* 3 (1987), 285-304; Taylor, other articles by Taylor and the other members of the Oxford team, and reviews of their books and edition. To these could be added a host of articles, both theoretical and on specific matters relating to the Shakespeare text, such as Folio and Quarto printers and compositors, published in the last decade by such scholars as Fredson Bowers, G. Thomas Tanselle, D. F. McKenzie, Paul Werstine, Howard-Hill, and many others. Among all of these, the Oxford *Textual Companion* is the one for a desert island, or for the editor-errant travelling (moderately) lightly. It is a monumental work of scholarship, and while editions continue to bloom and fade, it will fertilize them and fodder their editors and critics for generations to come.

11. Preliminary consultations on the text were held in November and December 1988, when Miss Lloyd was Sir Barry Jackson Fellow in the School of Performing Arts, University of Birmingham, with practical work on text and performance with drama students. Several such sessions also took place with the Bristol Old Vic company during rehearsals of the production, which ran from 16 February to 11 March 1989 at the Theatre Royal, Bristol.

12. Aristotle, typically, complicated this straightforward distinction: for him, in drama, the poet's agents, the actors, imitate for him by taking on the characters of the persons; thus drama is in one sense a mediated form (*Poetics,* 1450a-b). But since for Aristotle action is more important than character, the immediacy of the representation or imitation gives the dramatic genre, tragedy, its superiority over the narrative one, epic (1462a-b). Conversely, Homer is a good narrative poet to the extent that he speaks little in his own person and a great deal in the (assumed) persons of his characters. Another Aristotelian tangent worth pursuing would be the consequences for the subse-

quent study of drama as *poetry* of Aristotle's relegation of the elements of *performance*—spectacle, music, etc.—to positions of minor importance.

13. This dimension of Peele's play is discussed more fully in the introduction to my New Mermaids edition (London and New York, 1996), pp. xxvi-xxvii.

14. I realize that I have oversimplified both romance and farce for the sake of my argument. There can be more to farce than buffets and pratfalls. But critics who label *The Comedy of Errors* "farce" also oversimplify the genre in focussing on those elements, and thus fail to do justice to the play.

15. Reprinted in Gāmini Salgādo, *Eyewitnesses of Shakespeare* (New York, 1975), pp. 68-9.

16. But this is as nothing compared with the hash made of the play by one reviewer of the 1989 Bristol Old Vic production. Among other things, he names the wrong actor in the part of Angelo, refers to Adriana's entrance in a swimming pool when it was Luciana who appeared thus, says that the Abbess comes out leading the Ephesian Antipholus, and that Shakespeare unforgivably marries off the Abbess and Egeus (a double howler); that Egeus (again) is "bailed" at the end when, of course, he is pardoned and released unconditionally. Finally, he says, we shall never know which Dromio ends up with Nell (as that production called Luce), when it is perfectly clear a few lines from the end that the Syracusan resigns her with relief to his Ephesian twin (*Financial Times*, 21 February 1989).

17. Preface to Johnson's edition of *The Plays of William Shakespeare* (1765), reprinted in W. K. Wimsatt (ed.), *Dr. Johnson on Shakespeare* (Harmondsworth, 1969), p. 62.

18. The fullest, often irksomely exhaustive treatment of sources for the play is T. W. Baldwin's *On the Compositional Genetics of "The Comedy of Errors"* (Urbana, Illinois, 1965).

19. *Johnson on Shakespeare*, p. 64.

20. Phyllida Lloyd, in her 1989 Bristol Old Vic production, had the courage, as most modern directors have not, to put Egeon alone on stage with the Duke for the first scene. Egeon was lit by a single white spot. Some of the Duke's questions were given to recorded voices off, as of a crowd or press corps, but the theatre audience were not distracted, as so often, by a stage audience busily listening and reacting.

21. *Johnson on Shakespeare*, p. 67.

22. The word "money" occurs twenty-six times in *Errors*, more than in any other play in the canon. *Marks* and *mart* also occur more times than in any other play. *Gold/golden* are found more times only in *Timon of Athens; ducats* and *merchant(s)* more times only in *The Merchant of Venice*.

23. Plautus, incidentally, set one of his plays, *Miles Gloriosus,* in Ephesus, and another, *Curculio,* in Epidaurus, mentioned in Egeon's narrative; most are set in Athens. Epidamnus was in Illyria.

24. On the reading "failing" for F's "falling," see above, pp. 250-1. Antipholus' lines about seeking and failing to find his mother and brother are an abbreviated romance narrative on the same theme as Egeon's: another link between the plots. The inner plot, the farcical comedy itself, sounds a romance chord. In *Menaechmi*, the romance story is told briefly in the Prologue, outside the play.

25. *Pericles,* xxi. 183-5; *Cymbeline* V.vi.369-71.

26. Wells, Taylor, *et al., William Shakespeare: A Textual Companion,* p. 39.

27. "'Papers' and 'Prompt Books': Printer's Copy for Shakespeare's *Comedy of Errors,*" *Studies in Bibliography,* 41 (1988), 232-46.

28. *Textual Companion,* p. 266.

29. But see the note in its defence (*Textual Companion,* p. 267).

30. Compositor C also set "Epidarus" at another place on the same page where "Epidamium" appears twice. F2 corrected the former to "Epidaurus." But Shakespeare might have gone back and changed it if he had revised his foul papers, because Emilia later says that she and the children with her had been picked up by men of "Epidamium," not Epidaurus (V.i.357).

31. T.S. Dorsch (ed.), *The Comedy of Errors* (Cambridge, 1988), p. 64 (n. to II.ii.181).

32. Henry Cuningham (old Arden) thought "We came aboard . . ." an incomplete line and proposed to complete it thus: ". . . and put to sea, but scarce," an intelligent conjecture, if one accepts the short-line hypothesis.

33. Gareth Roberts has strengthened the case for "owls" and against replacing it with "elves," arguing that it is quite plausible for Dromio to fear being sucked black and blue by a *strix,* a screechowl's body housing a witch or other malign spirit ("*The Comedy of Errors* II.ii.190: 'Owls' or 'Elves'?," *Notes & Queries,* N.S. 34 (1987), 202-4).

34. *The Comedy of Errors* (New York, 1988), p. 29n.

35. Though the kind of informed, sensitive inventiveness that Gary Taylor urges editors to exercise is sometimes in the theatre, unfortunately, usurped by directorial arrogance, duncicality, or perversity.

36. *Ergo,* we cannot edit *Hamlet,* but either the bad Quarto or the good Quarto or the Folio of *Hamlet.* If *Hamlet* is an eclectic edition, Shakespeare did not write it. If Shakespeare wrote different versions at different times, which survive as Quartos and Folio, eclectic editions are amalgamations and adaptations,

misleadingly labelled. A comparable case-history from Elizabethan nondramatic literature is that of Sidney's *Arcadia*(s). He may have written all of the "old" *Arcadia* and all of the incomplete "new" *Arcadia* which breaks off in mid-sentence in Book III, but he did not write the composite *Arcadia* published in 1593. That was constructed after Sidney's death by his literary executors, who also rewrote some of the "old" *Arcadia* used to piece out the "new," and, with a link passage by yet another author, Alexander, was the version read for more than 300 years: the Countess of Pembroke's *Arcadia* more than her brother's, in a significant sense. Yet even after the discovery and publication of the complete "old" *Arcadia* early this century, some editors (e.g. Maurice Evans) and critics (e.g. C. S. Lewis, Walter R. Davis) have edited and written about the composite version, insisting, in some cases, on its primacy (see Lewis, *English Literature in the Sixteenth Century* (Oxford, 1954), pp. 331-3).

37. As in Provençal *trobar*—find, make, invent, compose, as the *troubadours* did.

38. The latest and most detailed discussion, of many, is Gary Taylor's "Textual and Sexual Criticism: A Crux in *The Comedy of Errors*," *Renaissance Drama*, N.S. 19 (1988), 195-225. My use of masculine pronouns throughout this essay when referring to Shakespeare editors reflects the fact observed by Taylor at the beginning of his, namely, the virtual absence of women from the field.

39. I have deliberately excluded film and television from this discussion. They are quite different media from the stage, and Shakespeare's plays were not written for them. Film is a cool medium, its message frozen.

Jonathan Hall (essay date 1995)

SOURCE: Hall, Jonathan. "Mercantilism and Desire in *The Comedy of Errors*." In *Anxious Pleasures: Shakespearean Comedy and the Nation-State*, pp. 239-52. Madison, N.J.: Farleigh Dickinson University Press, 1995.

[*In the essay below, Hall stresses that the crisis of identity experienced by Antipholus of Ephesus is related to his inability to honor his pledge as a merchant, and that through Antipholus of Syracuse, the mercantile, "venturing hero," Shakespeare explored anxieties concerning eroticism.*]

The advent of mercantile capitalism should not be understood as a purely "economic" transition, if by that term we mean the severely delimited and specialized set of theories and practices characteristic of the epoch of bourgeois hegemony. The later "science" of political economy tends (naturally, as it now seems to us) to obscure its own basis in an alienation of the practices of monetary power and rationalized administration from all other social interrelations and cultural practices. It is constituted as an impersonal science precisely through a "forgetting" of its nonetheless persistent and real connections with the politics of the everyday, that is interpersonal relations of every sort and, consequently, the organization of even supposedly private desire. But this economic scientism, so familiar to us as to appear almost unquestionable (except occasionally on moral grounds), is a late development of bourgeois culture, and in our epoch of monopoly capitalism it sits rather awkwardly with the culture of individual enterprise. Capitalist "adventure," with its sense of personal risk, still has its practitioners, however few and far between, but it is now inescapably marked out as the glamorous myth of an inglorious practice. This is not a moral issue alone, for imperial "adventurers" always had their critics; it arises rather from the sense of there being an already established world market, in which some win and some lose, but neither outcome makes any real difference to general social conditions. In short, nothing collective is any longer at stake in the individual "adventure." And yet, as Marx remarked à propos of post-revolutionary bourgeois culture in general, such a prosaic state of affairs nevertheless had heroic beginnings.[1] One could make the same point about early capitalist "adventure" itself, which borrowed quite a lot of its imaginative self-representations from feudal quest narratives. As Michael Nerlich points out in his *Ideology of Adventure,* the earlier "quête de l'aventure," whereby a knight sought to define himself as a true knight, is taken over by the despised "borjois" with the necessary modifications of the ideal.[2]

I will start my enquiry into Shakespeare's dramatic and poetic participation in the construction of the new modalities of mercantile desire with a comparison between Shakespeare's first merchant comedy, *The Comedy of Errors,* and its Plautine models, *Menaechmi* (and to a lesser extent *Rudens*), not to study influences but to explore the radically different universes of discourse in which both authors construct their heroes' desires. It is no doubt true to say that both plays draw on the ancient device of the comic double which throws identity into doubt, and that their pleasures arise from dealing with the anxiety which this entails.[3] My approach, however, will not be to pursue what is historically constant in Shakespeare's comedy and its ancient sources, but, on the contrary, to address the difference in the two plays' negotiation of that crisis of identity. I will argue that the historical specificity of Shakespeare's rewriting of the crisis has important reverberations in the representation of desire and the unconscious in his play. Shakespeare's manic plot does not merely "out-Plautus Plautus," as Theodore Weiss observes,[4] but sets up a relationship of anxiety and decentering completely alien to Plautus's universe of discourse.

In Plautus's play, names and property go astray, and in the last resort, it must be said, wife and mistress are close to being considered as forms of property, whose alienation does not greatly disturb the owner. Indeed, the play ends with the wife being auctioned off along with the other household effects. This comic auction, which provides the closure of the play, is the ultimate affirmation of ownership, and ownership is understood as the right to consume or enjoy. The twin double appears as a rival consumer of the sexual favors of Menaechmus's mistress, and of the meals prepared by his wife. There is another minor rival, who is comic because of his impotent parasite status. That is Peniculus, whose name is usually translated in the secondary literature as "little brush" or "table-sweeper." But, of course, it also means "little penis." Both wife and mistress are metonymically linked to the meals that they serve to male appetite throughout the play, which tends to underline the link between ownership and consumption.

The identification of the Menaechmi as a family of maritime merchants seems curiously perfunctory when the play is viewed retrospectively, back across the Renaissance when the merchant is seen as a more complex, and even heroic figure. In Plautus, the merchant is represented merely as owner and consumer, and the greatest threat to Menaechmus through the appearance of his twin concerns the comic interruption of his rights to consume. Insofar as there is a utopian or festive ending, it consists in the restoration of those rights, and in the expansion of the circle of consumers to include the twin brother, Sosicles, and the freed slave Messenio. The social identity of the merchant that is disturbed and then restored in Plautus's play, is the identity of a consumer within a stable world momentarily interrupted. The ending is a restoration of the "familia" as a stable social unit.

Plautus's play has within it a formal potential which Shakespeare develops much later, but in a way which transforms the whole discourse. The contrasts between land and sea, between safety and danger, between fixed property and mercantile movement, are represented in the difference between the established, propertied, and initially satisfied twin and his traveling alter ego. The threat to the propertied self comes from this uncertain other, who is also part of the merchant's own self. But there is no suggestion in Plautus that the mobile twin is the representative of a different form of desire, a desire which might seek to perpetuate its own motion even at the expense of fixed property and the satisfactions of consumption. In other words, Plautus's play is about merchants within a landed, agrarian society. Their confirmation as owners and consumers in the final celebration is the achievement of their desires within a utopian overcoming of rivalry. In Shakespeare's play, by contrast, whatever the formal closures at the end, the desiring (male) self seeks a perpetuation of its mobility. My argument, then will be that Shakespeare reexplores the ancient topos of the loss of the self within a newly "monetarized" world, and this has large implications for his representation of the male erotic drives. In Shakespeare's play, identity is constructed within a totally different social and political order, although the word "constructed" does not sufficiently suggest the precarious and provisional nature of the construction. In Ephesus, identity is equivalent to reputation, which is supported by the ability to pay cash at a specified time. Angelo expresses the normality of the belief that, as some still say, a gentleman's word is his bond, when he gives the golden chain to a baffled Antipholus of Syracuse on the mistaken grounds that the latter has "bespoken" it:

SYR. ANT.

Made it for me, sir? I bespoke it not.

ANGELO.

Not once, nor twice, but twenty times you have.
   Go home with it, and please your wife withal,
And soon at supper-time I'll visit you,
And then receive my money for my chain.

SYR. ANT.

I pray you, sir, receive the money now,
For fear you ne'er see chain nor money more.

ANGELO.

You are a merry man, sir; fare you well. [Exit]
                    (*The Comedy of Errors*, 3.2.170ff.)[5]

The assumption is that the public name should ensure that the spoken word corresponds to an ability to provide cash at the agreed time, without the slowing and (literally) deadening recourse to law, written bonds or contracts, and the force of the state. That is why there is also a residual aristocratic sense that a name carries value in itself. Only a nobleman's utterance would command sufficient trust. L. C. Knights points, very pertinently, to the insistence in England at the time on the difference between the noble trader in overseas commerce and the ignoble domestic retailer.[6] In Elizabethan society, the hybrid social identity of the merchant as nobleman permits the mobility of that political economy, in which the socially guaranteed identity of the nobleman itself functions as credit. And it is precisely this precarious identity that is disrupted, in Shakespeare's play, when the name goes astray. The crisis is not a metaphysical affair but an economic and semiotic one, culminating in Antipholus of Ephesus' apparent failure to honor his pledge (*4.1.1*ff). The crisis of identity is a failure of *credit* (etymologically derived from "belief," but, from 1542, denoting the delivery of goods in the belief in a future ability to pay [*OED*]). The failure of credit brings about an immediate threat of violent "reterritorialization."

The failure of this identity is a social crisis entailing a general arrest in both senses of the word. As Angelo, the goldsmith is arrested, he in turn arrests Antipholus of Ephesus for a failure to back up a verbal promise with money. Credit enables exchange, being a system of generalized belief, no longer held without anxiety, that the mere sign (which is what name or reputation has now become) should correspond to a "real" value (gold). Reputation, and its potential ruin, is not an individual matter, nor is it any longer a purely feudal family matter of honor, where the nobleman defends and defines his name with his body and blood if necessary. If identity fails, in the specific social form of mercantile reputation, then there must be a recourse to the law. It is ultimately the law, and not persons themselves, which underwrites the system of mutual trust, and it is only the law which guarantees that the value of a promise will inhere in a real body. Thus the law is the last resort of the system, the violence whose existence is necessary, but whose emergence into visibility is itself a sign of crisis. Its violence is the guarantor of stability at the center of a system of circulation and deferral, but its emergence brings about the death of the system that it guarantees.

For capitalism, as we know, "time is money," and time in this play becomes an organizing principle in the plot in a way entirely absent from Plautus. The golden chain must be paid for by five o'clock, or the law will ineluctably swing into action. Meanwhile, Egeus must also find money to redeem himself from the law within twenty-four hours, or the law will inevitably exchange his blood for the amount due. This father figure escapes from the dangers of the sea only to be more deeply engulfed in those of the market. Furthermore, as this monetarized time becomes more active in the structuring of plot, it too contributes to the surreptitious subversion of the solidity of identity. Not only is it no longer a question of who you are and whether you can pay (which will re-establish who you are), but correlatively whether you can pay by a stipulated time. This makes identity (reputation) dependent upon external factors over which even the nominally powerful have no control. Just as the system of circulation is permanently liable to sudden arrest, so is the individual, and his arrest can take the form of a complete stop. The monetarization of both time and the bourgeois individual involves this perpetual danger.

The judicial violence, represented unwillingly by the duke, is the necessary precondition for all the social mobility in the play, although it is also its absolute antithesis. That mobility depends on "credit," which is the understanding that the name stands in for golden coinage (just as the "names" which underwrite Lloyds of London still do). When the violence emerges into visibility, it arrests the very movement that it is supposed to guarantee. This has in fact already happened, in a serious register, before the main action. In this sense the main action repeats in a comic register the sociopolitical scenario that has condemned the merchant father, Egeon, to death at the very outset. The duke states clearly the reasons for the law's exaction:

> The enmity and discord which of late
> Sprung from the rancorous outrage of your Duke
> To merchants, our well-dealing countrymen,
> Who, wanting guilders to redeem their lives,
> Have sealed his rigorous statutes with their bloods,
> Excludes all pity from our threat'ning looks.
>
> (*1.1.5*ff.)

The duke himself makes no claim for abstract or universal principles of right here. He is not talking within the terms of Roman law, but from within the constraints of a mercantilist polity. The system is no longer centered on the duke himself, and does not even coincide geographically with his territory. The madness of proliferating doubles is not limited to the Antipholus and Dromio couples in this play, for the duke of Ephesus is also the double of the duke of Syracuse. In other words, there is a decentering of power; the constraints upon the duke come from outside his realm and point to a loss of sovereignty in the nominal sovereign himself. That is why the duke shares the patriarchal impotence of Egeon, with whom he sympathizes. At the same time, this decentering of power must be negated by the exercise of judicial violence. The statutes must be sealed in blood. As blood must replace ink, the body must replace the abstract word, and power must be seen to reside in territoriality and the duke's own person. However, this violence is not really *identical* with personal rule because personal rule implies a sovereign decision on whether to use violence or mercy, and the duke is not so free. He is constrained to negate by reterritorializing violence the half-acknowledged truth of his loss of sovereignty.

This division in power entails a psychologization of the nominal powerholder, and the duke becomes a figure of split desires. When, like the sultan in *1001 Nights,* he commands the reluctant Egeon to tell his tale and postpone his death for twenty-four hours, it is he who desires to "procrastinate" the death which he must pronounce, not Egeon. And this desire for the story is the agent of deferral which enables the play to take place. In other words, although he continues to talk of himself as the embodiment of the law, he in fact behaves as its reluctant and constrained representative, putting himself in the position of the audience and seeking the deferral of the sentence through the narrative of the play itself. This noncoincidence of even the ruler's desires with his "own" discourse is a significant effect of the decentering of power which haunts this comedy.

The duke talks from within the language of contemporary political imperatives, which are actually the guarantees of overseas trade. But those same imperatives, when credit fails, freeze trade and life itself. Then the body of the debtor is answerable to the law. In important ways the issues of *The Merchant of Venice* are prefigured here. The reason why the duke in this early comedy is helpless before the law (given that he no longer embodies but represents it), is that his (i.e., *its*) power, authority, and "honor" are indeed at stake, as he says (*1.1.142*ff.). To restore them requires that he impose death. In the main action of the play, when gold and jewels are restored to their owners, ownership is not the most important aspect of the restoration, as it is in Plautus. What is more important is the avoidance of the last resort of the law.

At a simple level, of course, the audience is gratified because the destruction of bodies is avoided, but this is dependent upon another subtler gratification: namely that spoken words re-acquire value without the resort to the systemic violence that both underwrites and destroys credit. Circulation becomes possible again. Time can become productive instead of being death-bound. The ship for Persia can depart, and the loving address from Antipholus of Syracuse to Luciana becomes permissible (*5.1377*ff.). The duke is released from his reterritorializing obligation by this resolution of the plot. But, although his sovereignty is restored, this restoration can never be absolute, since the plot has also revealed its contingent quality. Critics have often noted an alleged inconsistency (whether psychological or compositional) in the way that the duke no longer requires the guilders in payment for Egeon's life as soon as they are in fact available. The real point would seem to be that the duke only reacquires the sovereign power to act mercifully when the system of credit is restored. Then the actual surrender of gold coinage to the state is neither necessary nor desirable. The main issue is its return to circulation. Properly speaking, too, the crisis of identity is not resolved in Shakespeare's play, but postponed. The postponement only looks like resolution, because what is restored is a polity that requires a permanent deferral of its last resort of power in order to function at all. Stability is deferred, because in this polity the only stability is death. This is rather like saying that the system requires a permanent crisis of identity in order to function at all. So it is to this question of the psychological counterpart of monetarization that we must now turn.

It is not only the power of the sovereign that is decentered in the process of mercantilist "deterritorialization," but the discourse of (male) desire itself. It is often noted that the town of Ephesus appears to be governed by witchcraft, and that the duke's exclamation near the end, "I think you have all drunk from Circe's cup" (*5.1.271*), sums up a great deal, particularly with regard to sexual identity. It is significant that the town of Ephesus is also governed by another magic, which is even more deceptive than that of Circe's isle. This magic, which also dissolves the self, is the market, and it operates as the silent condition of possibility for the metaphoric equivalence of self and money (which, as we have said, is the basis of credit). When Antipholus of Syracuse thinks that he has been robbed, he exclaims:

> Upon my life, by some device or other
> The villain is o'eraught of all my money.
> They say this town is full of cozenage,
> As nimble jugglers that deceive the eye,
> Dark-working sorcerers that change the mind,
> Soul-killing witches that deform the body,
> Disguised cheaters, prating mountebanks,
> And many such-like liberties of sin:
> If it prove so, I will be gone the sooner.
> I'll to the Centaur to go seek this slave;
> I greatly fear my money is not safe.
>
> (*1.2.95*ff.)

Through Antipholus of Syracuse's extended metaphor, the normal or commonplace fear for the loss of money is translated into a demonization of the everyday deceptions of the marketplace. This speech is factually erroneous in its misapprehension of the plot situation, but its governing metaphor articulates a psychic truth. In other words, it functions to convert an "error," which is a factual matter to be resolved by clarification, into psychic truths of desire. These can never be resolved. For the most striking power of the market is that it has *already* worked its own particular magic upon Antipholus' speech. The magic power is already there in the way in which Antipholus accepts the metaphoric equivalence of himself and his money. This governing metaphor blurs a distinction between clear factual "error" and the psychic disposition which produces it and unwittingly displays itself. So, even as Antipholus produces a comically inappropriate demonic version of its power, for the amusement of the audience who see it as an "error," he confirms that demonic power in a way that makes it less certain for them that it *is* simply an "error."

In general, the fears of Antipholus and Dromio of Syracuse, who are the mercantile "venturing" pair, provide more of the disturbing comedy in the play than the pair resident in Ephesus, because of the way in which they mentally transform errors into sorcery, and the women whom they encounter, into fearful witches and sirens. The inappropriateness of this response provides a comedy of "errors," but Shakespeare's use of the comic goes much further than this. Shakespeare's dramatic discourse explores, through the metaphors, the anxieties which sustain both the comedy and the eroticism of his venturing hero. For him, the market and the town are like a fair, in which all the familiar forms of seduction and deception are present, but they are also a scene in which deception is indistinguishable from magic, and the self is therefore at risk. And there is fascination in the fear, which implies a strong desire for the loss of self that is feared.

The psychological possibilities of reading which emerge here, in marked contrast with the Plautine models, should not be understood in terms of Shakespeare's revelation of the timeless truths of the psyche, however. What happens is more interesting. Shakespeare constructs the very possibility of modern psychologistic readings by reworking the Plautine versions of what Bakhtin calls the "involuntary adventure" of the classical narrative:

> It goes without saying that in this type of time, an individual can be nothing other than completely *passive,* completely *unchanging.* . . . to such an individual things can merely *happen.* He himself is deprived of any initiative. He is merely the physical subject of the action.
>
> [emphases in original text][7]

Bakhtin is concerned with what he terms "chronotopes," namely the narrative modes of constructing a hero within certain pregiven conditions of space and temporality together with the limiting possibilities of action which they imply. But Michael Nerlich's comment, which provides the point of departure for his own *Ideology of Adventure,* makes a very telling point:

> What Bakhtin overlooks, strangely enough, is the fact that the passive, suffering, unchanging human being to

whom things happen is the absolute opposite of the modern view of adventure or the adventurer.[8]

Nerlich's overall argument, in a nutshell, is that the feudal "quête de l'aventure," later appropriated by the mercantile bourgeoisie, posited "adventure" as active desire, not as unsought and unwelcome event. Here, I would argue, is the historical issue in Shakespeare's transformation of the quest narrative of romance into metaphors of desire in this play. This refers us back to the dominant maritime metaphors.

Unlike the storms in Plautus's *Menaechmi* and *Rudens*, the storm in this play is psychologized into revealing metaphors of desires in the male self.[9] The storm which has separated the whole family from each other, sets up a desire for reintegration, which is *partly* gratified at the level of family and state, by the end of the play. But if we focus on Antipholus of Syracuse, who is in search of his brother and mother, the storm at sea which separated him from both his mirror image (his twin) and his nurturing mother, is also what has constituted him as a desiring subject, precisely through that primal separation. Thus what he is seeking is his own annihilation as separate individual, and the sea which threatens to engulf him is also the goal of his desire. As he says early in the scene, at the level of his desires he is not a separate entity but is constituted by a loss and a regressive desire to return to the engulfing sea:

> He that commends me to mine own content
> Commends me to the thing I cannot get.
> I to the world am like a drop of water
> That in the ocean seeks another drop,
> Who, falling there to find his fellow forth,
> Unseen, inquisitive, confounds himself.
> So I, to find a mother and a brother,
> In quest of them, unhappy, lose myself.
>
> (*1.1.33*ff.)

The quest for the mother and brother involves the loss of isolated self-hood. He is not only seeking "to find his fellow forth" (the identical brother), but also the mother who is identified with the ocean. So we have in the metaphor of the ocean and the two drops, a search for a separate male identity in the twin brother, and less avowedly, a search for fusion with a mother figure which overthrows identity by engulfment. It might appear farfetched to say that this constitutes an erotic drive, if it were not demonstrable that Adriana unknowingly returns his metaphor to him, but reaccentuated so that the merging of male into female is an image of fulfillment and not of loss:

> How comes it now, my husband, O how comes it
> That thou art then estranged from thyself?—
> Thy "self" I call it, being strange to me
> That, undividable, incorporate,
> Am better than thy dear self's better part.
> Ah, do not tear away thyself from me;
> For know, my love, as easy mayst thou fall
> A drop of water in the breaking gulf,
> And take unmingled thence that drop again
> Without addition or diminishing,
> As take from me thyself, and not me too.
>
> (2.2.122ff.)

The comedy of "errors," or mistaken identities, at this point permits an extraordinary effect: Antipholus' metaphor of desire, strongly marked by a "death wish," is returned to him as a metaphor of completion. What he fears is also what he seeks. To put it another way, his quest is already aimed at a loss of selfhood, although at the same time that loss is what he fears. Within the situational "error" and its attendant amusement, Adriana confronts him, and the audience, with a disturbing truth of desire, that its fulfillment would be the "confounding" of the self that it seeks and fears.

By psychologizing the external storm, previously the agent of Fate or Fortune, Shakespeare transforms that purely narrative event into a strange collaboration with the subjective desire of the mercantile "adventurer." This does not mean that such events simply discard their external or "accidental" quality. They certainly retain that unwilled quality, but they also become ambiguously doubled with subjective desire. What happens in these narratives of adventure capitalism is extremely ambiguous. The adventurer has a conscious goal shadowed by an unconscious self-destructive one. This contradictory desire, which requires an "adventure" narrative, is a new construction of the (male) self, and it is explored through the principal metaphors of this comedy. This fear of the loss of self, which is also the secret truth of desire persists in the comic situation of mistaken identity when Antipholus of Syracuse tries to declare his love to Luciana, and she rejects it because she takes him for Adriana's husband. At the situational level, the "error" is clear to the audience. They can see the honest intention in the duplicity of Luciana's discourse when, thinking that she is talking to a deceiving husband, she urges him to be even more deceitful in order to spare her sister's feelings:

> If you did wed my sister for her wealth,
> Then for her wealth's sake use her with more kindness;
> Or if you like elsewhere, do it by stealth,
> Muffle your false love with some show of blindness.
> Let not my sister read it in your eye;
> Be not thy tongue thy own shame's orator;
> Look sweet, speak fair, become disloyalty;
> Apparel vice like virtue's harbinger;
> Bear a fair presence, though your heart be tainted;
> Teach sin the carriage of a holy saint,
> Be secret false; what need she be acquainted.
>
> (3.2.5)

Although she then turns to talk of women as the victims of deceit, this speech begins to cast a lot of doubt on the speaker's known "honesty," for how could honesty be so eloquent about the strategems of duplicity? Despite her honesty, her words are the site of psychic mobility, because what happens here is that Luciana speaks from an assumed position of dialogue with a hypocrisy that she attributes to Antipholus. An utterance is conditioned by its addressee even when that "other" is imagined. An audience which saw the joke here must also feel a disquiet, because even honest language is no longer an expression of a self.

It is, of course, an impenetrable problem to Antipholus of Syracuse, who is attempting to declare his love in accordance with neo-Platonic conventions, which hold that love is the language of truth. He perceives that her words are deceitful, not just in the sense that she is enjoining deceit, but also in the sense (lethal for neo-Platonism) that they are not expressive of the being that inspires love in him. This disastrous disruption—and let us not forget that it is funny—leads him on to the idea that her words are an attempt by her to separate his soul from its truth (i.e., that they are a soul-changing enchantment, Circe-like, close to witchcraft). Although this is actually an erroneous interpretation of her intentions, *it is not untrue about her words' effect upon him*. Once again, then, the "error" of situation goes on to disclose a truth of his desire: his self-abandonment to the destructive magic which he fears (earlier he has said "I'll entertain the offer'd fallacy"; *2.2.185*) is the truth of *his* discourse of desire:

> Teach me, dear creature, how to think and speak;
> Lay open to my earthly gross conceit,
> Smother'd in errors, feeble, shallow, weak,
> The folded meaning of your words' deceit.
> Against my soul's pure truth, why labour you
> To make it wander in an unknown field?
> Are you a god? would you create me anew?
> Transform me then, and to your power I'll yield.
>
> *(3.2.333ff.)*

This perplexed, but enthusiastic lover transforms her first into a masculine god that will recreate him (above), and then into a mermaid and siren whose love will kill him:

> O, train me not, sweet mermaid, with thy note
> To drown me in thy sister's flood of tears;
> Sing, siren, for thyself, and I will dote;
> Spread o'er the silver waves thy golden hairs,
> And as a bed I'll take thee, and there lie,
> And in that glorious supposition think
> He gains by death that hath such means to die;
> Let love, being light, be drowned if she sink.
>
> *(3.2.45ff.)*

Theodore Weiss calls this "love as the great school, the enlightenment of a young man by a beautiful young woman."[10] But if there is "enlightenment" here, it is in a fearful destructiveness, because the truth of *his* desire emerges in these metaphors of love and death, namely that he *would* hand himself over, body and soul, to what he fears. This, then, is Shakespeare's use of plot of the mistaken identities. The "errors" provide the occasion for the metaphorical utterance of normally unstated truths. The scene ends when Antipholus of Syracuse, (who has been informed of his Dromio's flight from Nell, the engulfing "mountain of mad flesh" which claims to be his wife), responds to this with the same fear of the siren's song:

> There's none but witches do inhabit here,
> And therefore 'tis high time that I were hence;
> She that doth call me husband, even my soul
> Doth for a wife abhor. But her fair sister,
> Possess'd with such a gentle sovereign grace,
> Of such enchanting presence and discourse,
> Hath almost made me traitor to myself;
> But lest myself be guilty to self-wrong,
> I'll stop my ears against the mermaid's song.
>
> *(3.2.155)*

The goddess who enchants is also the mermaid or witch who threatens. But this is not an accurate statement about Luciana as a character, as though she were represented dramatically by Shakespeare as half-witch, half-goddess. It is no longer a simple "error." Such images are the product of Antipholus's surrender to what he fears; in short, they are metaphors of his desire, not representations of Luciana's inward being. Although Antipholus of Syracuse succumbs to the disturbing charms of witchcraft, this is not exactly the same as surrendering to Luciana. He surrenders to a false representation of her, but to a truth of his own desire, in which enchantment and fear are contributory. The "madness" of the plot, which disturbs and frightens him, also promises him the gratifications of the loss of self for which the market and the sea are joint metaphors. All this has very little to do with representation of the women through their own speech, which is also part of the plot.

The entirely nonmagic quality of the women, in marked contrast to the power which they acquire over Antipholus, is part of the comic effect. Neither Adriana nor Luciana bear any resemblance to Circe or to mermaid figures. Like Miranda later, Luciana could well protest: "No wonder, sir, but certainly a maid" (*The Tempest, 1.2.430-31*). The magic arises from the way in which the plot provides an opportunity for the play of male fantasies. Its comic quality arises from its non-coincidence with the representation of the women outside those fantasies. The melancholy "death wish" which promises its own gratifications has nothing to do with Shakespeare's representation of women, but everything to do with his exploration of the new discourse of desire.

Notes

1. "Wholly absorbed in the production of wealth and in the peaceful struggle of competition, it no longer comprehended that the ghosts of Roman times had watched over its cradle. But unheroic as bourgeois society is, it nevertheless took heroism, sacrifice, terror, civil war and the battles of nations to bring it into being. And in the classically austere traditions of the Roman republic its gladiators found the ideals and the art forms, the self-deceptions that they needed in order to conceal from themselves the bourgeois limitations of the content of their struggles and to keep their zeal on the high plane of the great

1. historical tragedy." Karl Marx, *The Eighteenth Brumaire of Louis Bonaparte* (Peking: Foreign Languages Press, 1978), 11; (originally, New York: *Die Revolution,* 1852).

2. Michael Nerlich, *Ideology of Adventure: Studies in Modern Consciousness 1100-1750,* volume 1 (Minneapolis: University of Minnesota Press, 1987), 51-64.

3. There is a recurrent association of twins and doubles with death. See, for example, Otto Rank, *The Double: a Psychoanalytic Study,* trans. and ed. Harry Tucker Jr. (New York: Meridian, 1979).

4. Theodore Weiss, *The Breath of Clowns and Kings: Shakespeare's Early Comedies and Histories* (London: Chatto and Windus, 1971), 25.

5. All references to Shakespeare's plays in this book are to the Arden editions.

6. L. C. Knights, *Drama and Society in the Age of Jonson* (London: Chatto and Windus, 1937), 51ff. The domestic grocer is still a figure of contempt in British culture. Margaret Thatcher's father marked her off from the patrician wing of the Tory party.

7. M. M. Bakhtin, "Forms of Time and of the Chronotope in the Novel," *The Dialogic Imagination,* trans. Caryl Emerson and Michael Holquist (Austin and London: University of Texas Press, 1981), 105.

8. Nerlich, *Ideology of Adventure,* 4.

9. See Coppélia Kahn, *Man's Estate: Masculine Identity in Shakespeare* (Berkeley: University of California Press, 1981), 199ff. My argument is a location of this psychological reading in a historical discourse.

10. Weiss, *Breath of Clowns and Kings,* 22.

FURTHER READING

Criticism

Christensen, Ann C. "'Because Their Business Still Lies Out a' door': Resisting the Separation of the Spheres in Shakespeare's *The Comedy of Errors.*" *Literature and History* 5, no. 1 (spring 1996): 19-37.

Contends that in *The Comedy of Errors* Shakespeare examined Elizabethan concerns about the increasing separation between the public/commercial and private/domestic spheres.

Freedman, Barbara. "Errors in Comedy: A Psychoanalytic Theory of Farce." In *Shakespearean Comedy,* edited by Maurice Charney, pp. 233-43. New York: New York Literary Forum, 1980.

Contends that the genre of farce in general, and *The Comedy of Errors* in particular, deliberately denies and displaces meaning, a practice necessary for ordinarily unacceptable aggression to be accepted in a humorous manner.

Hennings, Thomas P. "The Anglican Doctrine of the Affectionate Marriage in *The Comedy of Errors.*" *Modern Language Quarterly* 47, no. 2 (June 1986): 91-107.

Argues that unlike its Plautine source, *The Comedy of Errors* ultimately celebrates Christian society, family, and marriage.

Maguire, Laurie. "The Girls from Ephesus." *The Comedy of Errors: Critical Essays,* edited by Robert S. Miola, pp. 355-92. New York: Garland Publishing, Inc., 1997.

Argues that *The Comedy of Errors* offers two distinct models for female behavior through the characters of Adriana and Luciana.

Marcotte, Paul J. "Eros in *The Comedy of Errors.*" *Revue de l'Universite d'Ottawa* 38, no. 4 (October-December 1968): 642-67.

Explores how Shakespeare's concept of love influenced *The Comedy of Errors.*

Salgādo, Gāmini. "'Time's Deformed Hand': Sequence, Consequence, and Inconsequence in *The Comedy of Errors.*" *Shakespeare Survey* 25 (1972): 81-91.

Demonstrates the way in which *The Comedy of Errors* uses its form, language, and plot to manipulate the audience's understanding of temporal sequence.

The Merchant of Venice

For further information on the critical and stage history of *The Merchant of Venice,* see *SC,* Volumes 4, 12, 40, and 53.

INTRODUCTION

Among Shakespeare's most popular dramas, *The Merchant of Venice* remains a contentious piece to critics, who generally categorize it as a "problem play." Its plot centers on the merchants Antonio and Shylock, a Jewish moneylender. Finding Antonio unable to repay his loan, Shylock demands a pound of the Christian's flesh, as stipulated in his contract. Portia, the drama's heroine, arrives disguised as a male law clerk at the ensuing trial, and overturns the agreement. While essentially a romantic comedy concerning Antonio, Portia and the Venetian gentleman Bassanio (whom Portia eventually marries), the drama nevertheless depicts a number of troubling aspects chiefly related to the harsh punishment of Shylock, including his forced conversion to Christianity. Additionally, the ambiguous qualities of the three major figures in the drama have led to numerous conflicting interpretations of the characters. Such varying interpretations tend to be born out by modern productions of *The Merchant of Venice,* as directors privilege either Portia's comic triumph or Shylock's tragic defeat. Furthermore, contemporary critics have continued to explore the play's extensive themes, including conflicts of ethnicity, religion, and social exclusion, as well as the fundamental tensions it depicts between love, money, law, and mercy.

Over the course of its critical history, scholars have focused on the play's three principal figures—Antonio, Portia, and Shylock. Antonio, despite his status as the Venetian merchant of the work's title, has only infrequently been considered its most significant character. Cynthia Lewis confronts this exclusionary tradition in her 1997 study, which views Antonio as the locus of equivocation and contradiction in a play rife with ambivalence. More often, Antonio's character has been discussed in conjunction with Portia by commentators who emphasize the generic status of *The Merchant of Venice* as a romantic comedy. Characterizing Antonio and Portia as competitors for the love of Bassanio, Michael Zuckert (1996) sees this comic rivalry as providing the fundamental structure of the drama. Accordingly, Zuckert deems the bond between Antonio and Shylock as secondary to Portia's triumph. Such observations, however, are balanced by those of commentators who, captivated by the figure of Shylock, make an interpretation of the Jewish moneylender vitally important to the work. Robert Alter (1993) represents a number of critics who place Shylock at the center of *The Merchant of Venice.* Alter examines the range of interpretations elicited by his character: from comic villain to sympathetic and even tragic figure, vilified as an outsider for his religion and profession. Martin D. Yaffe (1997) offers an alternative to the traditional view that Shylock's depiction in *The Merchant of Venice* is anti-Semitic. Instead, Yaffe acknowledges perceptions of both positive and negative qualities in this complex character. Charles Edelman (1999) takes a somewhat revisionist position in regard to Shylock, contending that Elizabethan audiences would not necessarily have viewed his character as a stereotypical object of derision or a stock, comic stage villain.

The array of possible character interpretations offered by *The Merchant of Venice* has certainly contributed to the drama's continued theatrical popularity. In his review of Richard Olivier's 1998 staging of the play at the New Globe Theatre, John W. Mahon (1998) notes the centrality of Portia to the performance as well as its harsh portrayal of early modern anti-Semitism. Lois Potter's (1999) observations on the same Globe season include comments on Portia's asides to the audience and on the overall carnivalesque quality of the production. Director Trevor Nunn's interpretations of character for his 1999 staging of *The Merchant of Venice* at the Royal National Theatre, in contrast, were viewed as considerably less light-hearted than Olivier's. In his assessment, Hal Jensen (see Further Reading) remarks on Nunn's effective treatment of the darker elements of the play, including his nuanced exploration of character psychology and Shylock's Jewishness. Reviewer Matt Wolf observes the politicized quality of Nunn's staging in its depiction of the brutality inflicted on Shylock. For her 1998 Royal Shakespeare Company production, Barbara Gaines created an urban, American atmosphere evocative of the Roaring Twenties, a geographic and temporal location that reviewer Davi Napolean (1998) observes could be considered analogous to one Elizabethan audiences might have associated with Renaissance Venice.

Thematic criticism of *The Merchant of Venice* has touched on a wide range of subjects. Keith Geary's analysis (see Further Reading) treats the play's theme of love versus friendship, as Portia dons the clothing of a young man in order to both rescue Antonio and displace him as the principal object of Bassanio's affections. Seymour Kleinberg (1983) provides a similar, if somewhat more radical, interpretation of the relationship between Antonio and Bassanio, regarding the merchant as a homosexual whose love for his friend is again displaced, but in this reading by the social norms of heterosexual love and marriage. The dynamics of social exclusion figure prominently in a number of recent critical discussions of the drama. Susan Oldrieve (1993) notes the marginalization of Portia and Shylock as, respectively, a woman and a Jew, in a society dominated by patriarchal and Christian tradition. Alan Rosen (1997) presents a complementary analysis based on language, in which the Jewish Shylock and the Moorish Prince of Morocco are presented as outsiders in the play, both in terms of their ethnic differences and of their unique modes of expression, which vary sharply from standard Venetian discourse. Richard H. Wiesberg (1999) represents judicial appraisals of *The Merchant of Venice* by arguing for an ironic interpretation of the drama that eschews simple associations of Christianity with compassion and Judaism with strict or unfeeling legality. Updating critical interest in the setting of the play, Tony Tanner (1999) concentrates on tensions between the dramatic worlds of mercantile Venice, Shylock's Jewish ghetto, and the fairy-tale enchantment of Belmont.

OVERVIEWS AND GENERAL STUDIES

Cary B. Graham (essay date 1953)

SOURCE: Graham, Cary B. "Standards of Value in *The Merchant of Venice.*" *Shakespeare Quarterly* 4, no. 2 (April 1953): 145-51.

[*In the following essay, Graham maintains that shifting standards of moral, economic, and social value in* The Merchant of Venice *provide a fundamental insight into the variety of interpretations and responses the drama has elicited.*]

Recently Professor E. E. Stoll remarked, ". . . nearly everything certain in Shakespeare scholarship has in some quarters been disputed, as nearly everything uncertain has been affirmed."[1] Although the statement was not applied especially to *The Merchant of Venice,* it is obvious that this play is a fruitful source of disagreement. It may be called either comedy or tragedy. Shylock may be regarded as a villain, a comic figure, or a martyr. Bassanio may be either an idealized Renaissance lover or a wastrel who recoups a squandered fortune by risking the life of a dear friend who in turn may be either a good businessman or a fool. Jessica is a charming young Jewess who is justified in leaving an unhappy home to elope with a handsome Christian lover, or she is an ungrateful wench who robs a provident father and who proves a traitor to her own religion. Indeed, as the reader will be reminded in the pages which follow, all of these varied conclusions have been reached.[2] But comparatively little attention has been paid to Shakespeare's use of standards of value in *The Merchant of Venice.*[3] A glance at the values employed, their relationships within the play, and their connection with the intellectual background of the Renaissance may explain in part the technique of Shakespeare in appealing to an audience and may help to show why interpretations have varied so widely.

In the bond story, the first value to be established is that of friendship. Antonio, offering his purse, his person, his extremest means, values the friendship of Bassanio far more highly than material wealth. When Antonio says to Shylock,

> If thou wilt lend this money, lend it not
> As to thy friends, for when did friendship take
> A breed for barren metal of his friend?
> But lend it rather to thine enemy,
> Who, if he break, thou mayst with better face
> Exact the penalty
>
> (I. iii. 133-138)

the comparative worth of money and friendship has been used to suggest a penalty, an extreme form of which is proposed by Shylock a moment later. Again, in II. viii, Salanio and Salarino emphasize the friendship of Bassanio and Antonio in contrast with the mercenary values endorsed by Shylock. Later, in the trial scene when Antonio appears doomed, he comments first upon the kindness of Fortune, which is about to cut him off from the misery of an old age in poverty, and then upon the superior value of Bassanio's friendship.

In the same story appears another value which was a familiar topic in Renaissance literature and which Shakespeare himself employed in other plays—that of appearance as compared or contrasted with reality.[4] When Antonio agrees to the bond, appearance and reality should be the same, but they are not. "I like not fair terms and a villain's mind," says Bassanio. At the opening of the trial scene, the converse is true: appearance and reality are the same, but they should not be, as the Duke points out:

> Shylock, the world thinks, and I think so too,
> That thou but lead'st this fashion of thy malice
> To the last hour of act; and then 'tis thought
> Thou'lt show thy mercy and remorse more strange
> Than is thy strange apparent cruelty.
>
> (IV. i. 17-21)

Meaningful though the values of friendship and of appearance and reality may be, even more significant and certainly more complex is the problem of the value of money as an interest-bearing commodity. What Shylock calls interest, or thrift, Antonio regards as usury, or excess; and, as he says, "I do never use it." As Professor John W. Draper has pointed out, the conflict of values in Shylock and Antonio, based partly upon religion but even more upon mercantile ideals, would be especially significant to Elizabethans, who were caught in the midst of the change from the medieval economic system to the modern capitalistic system.[5] A specific treatment of this conflict of values appears in the Jacob-and-Laban story, with which Shylock responds to Antonio's reluctant offer once to break a custom and pay interest. The complexity of this apparently simple story is indicated in such varying interpretations as the following: the story conceals the workings of Shylock's mind as he tries to concoct a bond that will allow him to "collect interest without taking interest";[6] the story is a "sophistical and specious defense of what to an Elizabethan was manifestly wrong";[7] the story exposes the fallacy of "the formal principles underlying the Christian condemnation of usury."[8] But the analogy serves not merely to emphasize opposing values; it is also a fitting preliminary to the pound-of-flesh penalty and to Shylock's direct attack after Bassanio has objected to the bond.

> O father Abram, what these Christians are
> Whose own hard dealings teaches them suspect
> The thoughts of others! Pray you, tell me this:
> If he should break his day, what should I gain
> By the exaction of the forfeiture?
> A pound of man's flesh taken from a man
> Is not so estimable, profitable neither,
> As flesh of muttons, beefs, or goats.
>
> (I. iii. 161-168)

This speech serves as a forceful reminder that, although Antonio earlier had offered to pay interest, in the final arrangement it is Shylock who has foregone his own values by lending money without charging interest. "This is kind I offer." Note at this point, too, the opposed conclusions: either Shylock the money-lender has met Antonio the merchant on his own ground—friendship, not profit in the form of interest—or he has deliberately trapped Antonio into a possibly fatal agreement.

Despite conflicting interpretations, Shylock's renouncing of his values, for whatever reason, sets the precedent for later shifts in value needed to motivate his actions. In II. viii, Salanio reports the lament of Shylock for the loss of ducats and daughter. In addition to suggesting that here Shylock's sense of values is confused, Salanio predicts that Shylock will transfer his resentment to Antonio, who was in no way responsible for the elopement.

> Let good Antonio look he keep his day
> Or he shall pay for this.
>
> (II. viii. 25-26)

In III. i, the report is verified and the prediction is fulfilled: Shylock concludes by vowing to cut out the heart of Antonio. But the shifting of values which leads to this conclusion is by no means one-sided in its implications. The taunting words of Salanio and Salarino about the flight of Jessica and about the loss of Antonio's ships lead Shylock to utter the "Hath not a Jew eyes" speech, and this may be interpreted as a plea for tolerance. However, as various critics have noted, the speech in its entirety is a plea not for charity but for revenge.[9] Now the flesh of Antonio does have a greater value than that of "muttons, beefs, or goats." But even if revenge is rejected on principle, it is difficult to ignore Shylock's charge that revenge is a Christian practice. There is enough truth in the statement to emphasize a balancing of values not entirely complimentary to the good Antonio and the handsome Bassanio. The ensuing dialogue between Tubal and Shylock stresses alternately the financial losses of Shylock and those of Antonio. As a result Shylock is driven to the point of valuing revenge above everything else. III. iii, reveals Shylock in exactly the same state of mind (note the reiteration of "I'll have my bond"), and the way is clear for the battle of values in the trial scene. Here Shylock defends his claim to Antonio's flesh by forcefully reminding the Christians that they own slaves. Just as in his plea for revenge, there is sufficient truth in the analogy to make it dramatically effective. The next value in the scene is that of mercy as compared with strict justice, developed in Portia's speech; and this value, together with that of Shylock's revenge and the Antonio-Bassanio friendship, is used to build up to the surprise reversal, where Shylock's own words—"A Daniel come to judgment, etc."—are echoed by Gratiano. Obviously Shylock, valuing his revenge above all else, shows no mercy for Antonio. But do the Christians, valuing so highly the "quality of mercy," exhibit no revenge toward Shylock? Conflicting opinions on this point are responsible, at least in part, for the question of whether or not Shakespeare himself was anti-Semitic. Dr. S. A. Tannenbaum, recalling uncomplimentary references to Jews in *Macbeth, The Two Gentlemen of Verona, Much Ado About Nothing, Love's Labour's Lost,* and *1 Henry IV,* says, "Shakespeare's anti-Semitic prejudice is clearly shown in *The Merchant of Venice,*"[10] Professor H. B. Charlton calls Shylock's punishment a callous one which shows Shakespeare's antipathy.[11] Opposed to this opinion is that of Professor T. M. Parrott, who finds "no tinge of race-hatred" in Shakespeare and who believes that the audience would consider the enforced conversion of Shylock a means of salvation for him.[12] Professors William A. Neilson and Charles J. Hill believe ". . . it is impossible to accuse Shakespeare . . . of anti-Semitism."[13] Professor Norman Nathan sees no evidence of anti-Semitism in Shylock's punishment, and reminds us that according to law he would have lost both his money and his life.[14] Others maintain that, whether or not Shakespeare himself was prejudiced, he sharply criticised both Jew and Christian. This is the conclusion of Sir Arthur Quiller-Couch, who finds the intended victims "as heartless as Shylock without any of Shylock's passionate excuse,"[15] and of John Palmer, who says that when the bond story is concluded, both Christian and Jew have charged each other with "an inhumanity which is common to both parties."[16]

In the casket story the comparative values of appearance and reality are fundamental. The choice of the right casket is far from a mere gamble; it is a test of the suitor's ability to evaluate appearance. In each case the procedure is the same: the candidate explains carefully that appearance may not reflect reality, he tries to apply the principle in the casket situation, and his failure or success is emphasized in the scroll found in the casket he has chosen. Morocco correctly argues that the outward appearance of his complexion should not obscure the inward reality of his bravery, but in choosing the gold casket he violates the principle that the apparent value may not coincide with the real value. Arragon rejects the lead casket because it does not look fair enough; he rejects the gold casket with a caustic reference to "the fool multitude, that judge by show"; then, quite unaware that the basis of his first rejection places him in the group he has scorned in the second, he selects the silver casket whose inscription promises him as much as he deserves. Both Morocco and Arragon are misled by apparent values: Morocco fails because he wrongly evaluates the caskets; Arragon, because he wrongly evaluates himself. The decision of Bassanio is somewhat more involved. Portia has clearly indicated her preference for him (III. ii. 1-24), and some critics believe that by means of the song, which contains words rhyming with *lead* and which warns the hearer against fancy, Portia gives Bassanio the clue to the proper choice.[17] However, the acceptance of this conclusion does not preclude the emphasis upon values.[18] Bassanio discourses at length upon the theme,

> So may the outward shows be least themselves;
> The world is still deceived with ornament
>
> (III. ii. 73-74)

as it applies in law, in religion, in morality, and in beauty—in short, the subjects to which the values of the play are closely related. His thoughts point logically to his choice of the lead casket. Of the three suitors only Bassanio, as Professor Thomas M. Parrott has remarked, employs "the understanding which pierces below the surface and fastens upon reality."[19] At the same time, just as in the bond story, the values in the casket scenes have formed the basis of conflicting estimates of character. The English critic John Palmer looks upon Bassanio merely as a young man whose quest of beauty and fortune forms one of the "ingredients in a tall story."[20] Sir Arthur Quiller-Couch considers him a fortune-hunter whose lofty speeches are not in keeping with his nature.[21] Professor Charles Read Baskervill, tracing the background of the casket scenes in the Renaissance conception of Platonic idealism,[22] sees Bassanio as an ideal lover whose standards of value are exalted by contrast with those of Morocco and Arragon. At this point in the play (III. ii), Shakespeare shifts the emphasis from appearance and reality to the comparative values of love, wealth, and friendship. Portia, learning of Antonio's danger, unhesitatingly sends away her newly acquired husband and some of her newly acquired wealth:

> Pay him six thousand, and deface the bond;
> Double six thousand, and then treble that,
> Before a friend of this description
> Shall lose a hair through Bassanio's fault.
> . . . . .
> For never shall you lie by Portia's side
> With an unquiet soul.
>
> (III. ii. 302-308)

As the casket story ends, both dialogue and action connect the values of this story with those previously employed in the bond story. Money, love, friendship—the greatest of these, in true Renaissance tradition, is friendship.

As noted previously, the elopement episode is mainly responsible for the shifting of Shylock's standards so that revenge alone has any value for him. But Shakespeare has shown also that in the home life of Shylock and Jessica there is little harmony. Jessica's values are not those of Shylock, and it is not merely financial standards that separate them. Jessica's suggestion of tediousness and unhappiness is substantiated by the Shylock who goes to dinner in "hate, to feed upon the prodigal Christian," who releases Launcelot to help impoverish Bassanio, who scorns music and merriment, who instructs Jessica to "Let not the sound of shallow foppery enter my sober house," and who leaves his daughter behind locked doors with the threat that perhaps he will return immediately. Shylock's reaction to the elopement and the robbery, as reported in II. viii, by Salanio, emphasizes about equally the father's loss of his daughter and his loss of ducats and jewels; and Salanio is prejudiced against Shylock. However, in III. i, the very scene in which appears Shylock's so-called plea for tolerance, Shylock himself emphasizes mainly his financial loss. Of the approximately seventy-five lines spoken by Shylock in this scene, only ten refer to Jessica; and even these lines express Shylock's bitterness and rage rather than love for his daughter. In the remaining scenes he speaks of her only once—to express the wish that she had been married to any of the stock of Barrabas rather than to a Christian. Indeed, there is not one line in the entire play in which Shylock directly expresses affection for his daughter. Thus the picture of Shylock at home and the revelation of his changing values after the robbery tend to balance, in the eyes of reader or audience, the fact that Jessica is a thief and an apostate. However, once more conflicting standards of value have led to opposed estimates of character. For example, Sir Walter Raleigh, who sees Shylock as a tragic figure, says that his heart "is stirred with tender memories in the midst of his lament over the stolen ducats";[23] Professor Harold R. Walley, who considers Shylock the villain in a romantic comedy, says that he "laments loudest the gold that has gone with her [Jessica] and anxiously computes the cost of recovery."[24]

The ring episode, which concludes the play, is primarily a comic treatment of the comparative values of appearance and reality and those of love and friendship, especially the latter. The mock quarrel involving both pairs of lovers is carefully prefaced first by the dialogue of Jessica and Lorenzo which turns upon fidelity in love and upon other values,[25] next by Portia's comments about the nature of true value, and finally by her vow of faith, all of which are ironically effective preliminaries. As the quarrel proceeds, it becomes evident that the ring story is an ingenious combination of parallels and reversals, based upon values previously employed in the bond story and the casket story, and made amusing by the device of dramatic irony. In the bond story the value of friendship leads Antonio, at the request of Bassanio, to risk and apparently to lose everything in helping his friend to win Portia. In the ring story the value of friendship leads Bassanio first to leave his bride and then, at the urging of Antonio, apparently to lose her. In the bond story Antonio himself suggests a penalty and thus leads Shylock to propose the pound-of-flesh forfeit. In the ring story Bassanio insists upon the civil doctor's accepting some remembrance, and thus leads Portia to ask for the ring. Even the threatened loss of Antonio's flesh in the bond story is recalled by the rueful remark of Bassanio:

> Why, I were best to cut my left hand off
> And swear I lost the ring defending it.
>
> (V.i.177-178)

Finally, the exposure of disguise which resolves the ring story also reveals to Bassanio that his successful judging of appearance and reality in the casket story has been balanced by his failure in the ring story: Portia's request was not what it appeared to be. Thus, the play ends with comic emphasis upon values introduced earlier in the play for serious purposes.

Probably no one would contend that Shakespeare was interested merely in dramatizing values. However, his use of them is surely one of the important elements in this play. As is apparent from the connections mentioned, the pattern of related values helps to unify the effect of four stories probably drawn from at least three different sources. These values are employed for both serious and comic effects, for both adventure and romance. They are fundamental in almost every scene of the play. They involve every major character and most of the minor figures—even Launcelot Gobbo offers a somewhat dubious evaluation of the standards represented by Shylock, Bassanio, and Jessica. They help to indicate the significance of the play in its own age by reflecting the Renaissance interest in such topics as the proper value of material wealth, the comparative worth of love and friendship, and the problem of judging reality by appearance. Finally, the extent, the variety, and the complex relationships of these values provide at least a partial explanation for the fact that thoughtful readers, sensitive actors, and responsive audiences—themselves influenced in turn by the standards of their own environment—have arrived at widely different conclusions about the central figures in the play.

Notes

1. "A German Producer's *Hamlet*," SQ [*Shakespeare Quarterly*], I (1950), 38.
2. Adapted from a paper read at the May 1950 meeting of the Indiana College English Association. All textual quotations are from *The Complete Plays and Poems of Shakespeare*, ed. William A. Neilson and Charles J. Hill (Cambridge, 1942).
3. Alfred Harbage, *As They Liked It* (New York, 1947), and Donald A. Stauffer, *Shakespeare's World of Images* (New York, 1950), have discussed moral values in Shakespeare, but neither of them has given detailed treatment of the values in this play.
4. Shakespeare's use of this idea has been pointed out by Theodore Spencer, *Shakespeare and the Nature of Man* (New York, 1942), pp. 84-85, *et passim.*
5. "Usury in *The Merchant of Venice*," MP [*Modern Philology*], XXXIII (1935), 38, 46-47.
6. Leah W. Wilkins, "Shylock's Pound of Flesh and Laban's Sheep," *MLN,* LXII (1947), 28.
7. Harold R. Walley, "Shakespeare's Portrayal of Shylock," *Essays in Dramatic Literature,* ed. Hardin Craig (Princeton, 1935), p. 237.
8. H. B. Charlton, *Shakespearian Comedy* (New York, 1940), p. 141.
9. For example, John Palmer, *Comic Characters of Shakespeare* (London, 1947), p. 79, and E. E. Stoll, *Shakespeare Studies* (New York, 1927—reprinted, 1942), p. 268.
10. "Shakespeare an Anti-Semite?" SAB, XIX (1944), 47-48.
11. Charlton, p. 128. For a brief list of others who hold similar opinions, see Norman Nathan, "Three Notes on *The Merchant of Venice*," SAB, XXIII (1948), 160-161.
12. *Shakespeare: Twenty-three Plays and the Sonnets* (New York, 1938), p. 212.
13. Neilson and Hill, p. 116.
14. Nathan, p. 155.
15. *Shakespeare's Workmanship* (New York, 1931), p. 75.
16. Palmer, p. 87.
17. For example, John E. Hannigan says that Portia "had loaded the dice in violation of her father's will," ("Shylock and Portia," SAB, XIV, 1939, p. 173), and Hardin Craig says that the song contains "a plain indication of the nature of the choice" (*The Complete Works of Shakespeare,* New York, 1951, p. 504).
18. Thomas M. Parrott doubts that the song was intended to guide Bassanio's choice, and he suggests that, even so, it was Bassanio's "quick intelligence that caught the clue" (*Shakespearean Comedy,* New York, 1949, p. 141).
19. *Shakespeare: Twenty-three Plays and the Sonnets* (New York, 1938), p. 211.
20. Palmer, p. 63.
21. Quiller-Couch, p. 75.
22. "Bassanio as an Ideal Lover," *Manly Anniversary Studies* (Chicago, 1923), pp. 90-103.
23. *Shakespeare* (London, 1907), p. 150.
24. Walley, p. 240.
25. Harbage, pp. 188-189.

Michael Zuckert (essay date 1996)

SOURCE: Zuckert, Michael. "The New Medea: On Portia's Comic Triumph in *The Merchant of Venice*." In *Shakespeare's Political Pageant: Essays in Literature and Politics*, edited by Joseph Alulis and Vickie Sullivan, pp. 3-36. London: Rowman & Littlefield, 1996.

[*In the following essay, Zuckert views* The Merchant of Venice *as a highly unified work that depicts Antonio and Portia as rivals for the love of Bassanio, a competition in which Portia is victorious.*]

Partly because of its clever plot, striking characterizations, and moments of beautiful poetry, *The Merchant of Venice* has remained one of Shakespeare's best known, most often performed, and most discussed plays. It is also one of his most troubling plays. It is troubling in form because it presents a series of actions that are difficult to integrate into a coherent and unified whole.[1] It is troubling in substance because it presents a Christian society in the ugliness of its anti-Semitism, and while Shakespeare clearly has a broader view than his Venetians, his presentation of the Jew nonetheless appears to draw from the same unsavory and stereotypical prejudices that move the Christian Venetians. Moreover, among the comic resolutions of the play, the "setting to rights" of all the disruptions that have impelled the play's action, are the forced conversion of Shylock to Christianity, and the desertion by Shylock's daughter, Jessica, of both her father and her ancestral religion. Hers is a voluntary conversion to be sure, but it seems to carry the same point as Shylock's coerced conversion: Jews and Judaism are not worth the respect of Christian men and women.[2]

The focus on Shylock is not merely a product of our post-holocaust sensibilities, but seems to have been part of the reception of the play from the outset.[3] Perhaps it is the lure of the exotic, or perhaps it is a reaction to the character who seems to suffer most and to show the strongest and most complex passions, but it is in some ways a puzzling focus, for the play's title directs us not to Shylock, but to the merchant of Venice, that is to say, to Antonio. The focus on Shylock also contributes to the formal puzzles the play has provided, for if the play is taken to revolve centrally around Shylock and the pound of flesh pledge, then aspects of the play like the courting of Portia and the casket test seem extraneous, or at least very difficult to relate to the main story.[4]

If we follow Shakespeare's indications, we see that the focus on Shylock is largely misplaced, and the puzzlement over the formal unity of the play mistaken. Indeed, *The Merchant of Venice* is a marvel of formal coherence, and once we grasp that, we can come to a better understanding of the substantively troubling elements of this play as well. As is frequently the case in Shakespeare's dramas, he uses the opening scenes to set the problem the main action of the play attempts to resolve.[5] The problem is this: both Antonio and Portia love Bassanio; Antonio and Portia are rivals for the love of Bassanio. The play gives us the contest between the two for Bassanio. The winner of that contest, of course, is Portia, but judging from Shakespeare's title if nothing else, there is something about the losing contender that particularly requires attention. The various major events in the play are phases of the contest between Antonio and Portia. She triumphs in three stages: first, in the trial of the caskets, where Bassanio, with her help, selects the right casket and thus "wins" her; or rather, is won by her. Then in the legal trial of Antonio where Portia saves Antonio from Shylock and thereby saves Bassanio from an overwhelming and unending debt to Antonio; had Antonio lost his case to Shylock, he would therein have triumphed over Portia.[6] Finally, in the ring episode, Portia triumphs for the third and final time, achieving at last Antonio's concession of defeat.[7] Such is the story of *The Merchant of Venice*; of course the story of Shylock, the elopement of Jessica, and all the rest must find a place in this story, but this is the story in which they must find their place.[8]

With an economy suited to the chief site of the play Shakespeare quickly, if a bit subtly, establishes the problem of *The Merchant* in the opening words of each of the first two scenes. Antonio, the merchant of Venice, and therefore the central figure in Venice, the mercantile city, begins in *medias res*, in answer to a question he has just been posed: "In sooth I know not why I am so sad" (1.1.1).[9] Portia, the beautiful mistress of the "beautiful mountain," opens in a way remarkably close to Antonio's: "By my troth, Nerissa, my little body is aweary of this great world" (1.2.1-2). Despite the great difference between Venice and Belmont, the two worlds of the play, the central figures in each of these worlds are seized by the same deep sadness.

The opening laments by Antonio and Portia set in motion the chief actions of the two opening scenes—the quest for the source of the sadness of each. Antonio's sadness is something very recent and not some abiding quality of his. Solanio has just now asked about it, and even complained of it. As Antonio tells us: "you say it wearies you" (1.1.2).[10] Gratiano soon after reinforces our impression of Antonio's sudden seizure by melancholy: "Believe me, you are marvelously changed" (1.1.76).

Antonio's sadness is apparently as mysterious as it is sudden. Antonio professes himself such a "want-wit" on its account that he cannot say how he "caught it, found it, or came by it." As he concludes, "I have much ado to know myself" (1.1.3-7). Nonetheless, he thinks he knows himself well enough to reject out of hand his friends' repeated suggestions that his melancholy derives from anxiety over his mercantile ventures, a natural enough state of mind in venturesome Venice.[11] Almost like the birds of the air, or the lilies of the field, Antonio is not anxious over his worldly affairs; he has taken such care of them that he need not fear fortune (1.1.8-45, 73-75).[12] He parries his friends' other suggestions so they too come to accept the mystery of it (1.1.47-48).

The search to plumb Antonio's sadness ends when he is left alone with his friend Bassanio; here we indirectly discover the sudden source of his sadness when we discover what Antonio has been looking forward to, or rather dreading, all that day:

> Well, tell me now, what lady is the same
> To whom you swore a secret pilgrimage
> That you today promised to tell me of?
>
> (1.1.119-21)

Bassanio, a younger and "noble kinsman," is especially dear to Antonio; the older man has been a regular benefactor to the younger and both speak of the love Antonio has shown toward Bassanio (1.1.57, 130-55). As is said later in the play, "I think he [Antonio] only loves the world for him [Bassanio]" (2.8.50). The expectation that his friend wishes to court a lady, a wish he must understand to be both rightful and inevitable, leads him to see his situation as fated, scripted, as it were, by the broader patterns and laws of life.[13] "I hold the world but as the world, Gratiano—/ A stage, where every man must play a part, / And mine a sad one" (1.1.76-78).[14]

Portia's opening scene is much the same as Antonio's—the same world-weary sadness, the same effort by her companion to plumb her sadness. Yet there is an important difference, too: Portia is perfectly aware of the causes of her world-weariness; from the outset she is much more self-knowing than her Venetian counterpart. Her sadness derives from her father's will, according to which she may marry only the man who successfully passes the test of the caskets. Like Antonio, she feels her fate lies in the hands of external forces (1.2.22-25). Nerissa, her servant, has more confidence in the dead father's judgment than Portia does. Only "one who you shall rightly love" will choose rightly among the caskets. It is, Nerissa thinks, good protection for a very rich heiress against the wrong sort of gold-digger.[15] Portia resents her lack of autonomy, and perhaps the lack of confidence in her judgment, but it appears she also does not wish so much protection against gold-diggers. Part of her uncommon self-knowledge consists in her awareness of the conflict within herself between what we might call her head and her heart. "I can easier teach twenty what were good to be done, than to be one of the twenty to follow mine own teaching. The brain may devise laws for the blood, but a hot temper leaps o'er a cold decree" (1.2.15-19). Portia, it appears, resents the constriction, or rather nullification of her right of choice not only in the abstract, for she has her eye on someone in particular. It is none of the six suitors already come to Belmont from all over Europe (1.2.108-9). Yet there is one whom she fancies, as even Nerissa well knows: Bassanio, who, both women agree, is "best deserving a fair lady" (1.2.117-18; cf. 2.9.100).

Antonio mopes because Bassanio wishes to court Portia. Portia mopes because the casket test may keep her from Bassanio. It is unclear at this point whether she fears that another will succeed before Bassanio can, or whether she fears he will be unwilling to take or unable to pass the test himself. Antonio and Portia both suffer for Bassanio, both want Bassanio. Although neither knows the other, they are rivals for Bassanio.

I

"'Shall I then betray my father's throne . . . ?'"[16]

In that rivalry Antonio has the first move. At first glance his move is surprising. To Bassanio's request for aid Antonio is all cooperation, all generosity. At second glance, his reaction is perhaps not so surprising. It is, after all, his habitual way to be generous, especially to Bassanio, who prefaces his request with a reminder of how much Antonio has given him in the past. As Allan Bloom observes, "Antonio . . . bases his whole life on generosity. . . . Antonio has money; it is, however, not for his own enjoyment, but rather for his friends." Along the same lines, David Beauregard identifies Antonio as the very embodiment of the Aristotelian virtue of liberality or generosity, the proper mean between prodigality and avarice, represented within the play respectively by Bassanio and Shylock.[17]

Nonetheless, the depiction of Antonio's generosity falls somewhat short of Aristotle's description of that virtue, the possessor of which "will give to the right persons the right amounts at the right times." On this criterion, Antonio must be judged deficient in virtue, for he gives to a self-professed prodigal, one who has wasted and, for all Antonio has reason to believe, will continue to waste. "He who gives to those he should not . . . is not generous but may be given another name," pronounces Aristotle.[18] The genuine virtue of generosity benefits the recipient where the pseudo-virtue does not. Antonio and Bassanio illustrate Aristotle's concern, for Antonio's repeated aid does not help Bassanio become a more responsible and self-sufficient, that is to say, virtuous, individual, but instead contributes to his lack of self-control with regard to spending and appearances, and encourages in him a tendency to view others as means toward satisfying his own pressing needs.

If Antonio's aid cannot be understood as a manifestation of the virtue of liberality, his response to Bassanio's request must be examined more carefully. Although Antonio fears Bassanio rushes to make a "secret pilgrimage" to a lady, that is to say, that Bassanio wishes to journey to the lady as to a shrine, as to one he adores or reverences, Bassanio assures him that his "chief care is to come off fairly from [his] great debts," the "most" of which are owed to Antonio. Although Bassanio speaks of Portia's beauty and virtues, he does not speak of his love for her—in marked contrast to his frequent references to the love he owes Antonio and has received from (but not given to?) Antonio (1.1.130-31, 146-47; cf. 161-76). Bassanio presents his case almost entirely as an investment opportunity for Antonio.[19] He is especially concerned to convince Antonio that further supplies would not amount to throwing good money after bad: by shooting a second arrow after the lost first arrow both men might hope to recoup what has already been lost. Bassanio has reason for hope: Portia is "richly left," and has sent him "fair speechless messages . . . from her eyes" (1.1.161, 163-64). Bassanio guessed Portia's feelings just as Nerissa did; he is adept at discerning, and quick to take advantage of, the love others have for him.

Antonio reacts not so much to the promise of repayment—no doubt he has heard such talk before—but he seems to be set much at ease by Bassanio's general approach to Portia: he is going a-courting not for the sake of his love for the lady, but for the sake of his obligation of money and love to Antonio. Antonio's feeling of relief is increased when Bassanio substitutes for the older man's image of a pilgrimage the new image of a "quest." She is not a quasi-deity but the "golden fleece," and he will become one of the "many Jasons come in quest of her" (1.1.170-72, cf. 3.2.241).[20] Bassanio, the new Jason, wishes to outfit an expedition like that to Colchis. He needs money, servants and finery, not a troop of heroes, but this, after all, is Christian, mercantile Venice, not pre-Trojan War Greece.

Under the circumstances of the quest, Antonio's reply to Bassanio's request is not surprising at all. Rather than a threat to their bond of friendship, as a marriage of love might be, it is an expression of Bassanio's deep sense of the continuing power and obligation of that bond. For Antonio to respond with his wonted generosity, moreover, is to bind anew in the very moment and in the very deed by which Bassanio attempts to discharge (some of) the bond already in place.[21]

Portia's first move is not against Antonio—she has no idea he is part of the story—but is, or seems to her to be against her father. To the new Jason, Portia is the golden fleece, but in her feelings and actions she is Medea, the daughter of King Aeëtes, the possessor of the fleece. Like Portia, Medea too falls in love with the Jason who visited her father's court.

> . . . the daughter of King Aeëtes conceived an overpowering passion . . . and when by reason she could not rid her of her madness she cried: . . . "I wonder if this is not what is called love, or at best something like this."

Like Portia, Medea sees in herself the old conflict between head and heart:

> "Come, thrust from your maiden breast these flames that you feel, if you can, unhappy girl. . . . But some strange power draws on against my will. Desire persuades me one way, reason another."

Indeed Portia even comes very close to stealing some of her lines from Medea's:

> "I see the better and approve it, but I follow the worse."

Like Portia's father, Medea's sets a formidable test between the questers and the object of their quest. Like Portia, Medea decries her father's test:

> "For why do the mandates of my father seem too harsh? They certainly are too harsh."[22]

Medea does not merely lament her situation, however. She "gave [Jason] the magic herbs, gave him instruction / In how to use them," helped him to yoke the "bronze-footed bulls, fire breathers," and to sow the serpent's teeth, and to resist the armed men who spring from the teeth, and finally, to put to sleep the dragon who guarded the golden fleece itself. All this she did for love and in exchange for a promise of marriage.[23]

But does Portia follow Medea's love-struck lead and help her new Jason overcome the barrier set up by her father? In the literature on the play this is surely one of the two or three most controverted questions. One of the strongest pieces of evidence against her acting the part of Medea to this extent is Portia's explicit vow to do no such thing: "I could teach you / How to choose right, but then I am forsworn. / So will I never be" (3.2.10-12). Yet there is some ambiguity in what she says here. Just what does it mean to "teach him how to choose right": she surely does not come right out and give the correct answer, and thus under a literalist interpretation of her oath (and we see later that Portia is quite capable of giving and taking advantage of literalist interpretations) she can avoid being "forsworn" even if, as I (and many other readers) believe, she gives Bassanio a good deal of help.[24]

Her denial is too ambiguous to settle the question whether she follows Medea this far, and thus we must consider both the casket scene and its context with greater care.[25] In marked contrast to the treatment the other suitors get, Portia does not rush Bassanio to undergo the test: "I pray you tarry; pause a day or two / Before you hazard" (2.7.1-3; 2.9.1; 3.2.1-2). As she thinks further on it, she would have him tarry even more: "I would detain you here some month or two / Before you venture for me" (3.2.9-10).

As eager as she is to be rid of the first two, she is welcoming of the company of her Venetian swain. Yet her desire for delay bespeaks even more than her fondness for Bassanio. She wishes him to wait, "for in choosing wrong / I lose your company. Therefore forbear a while" (3.2.2-3).

Portia here finally answers a question she left us with in her opening appearance in the play: she dreads the casket test not so much because she fears it will give her to another, but because she fears it will not give her to the one she favors. In a few moments Portia will project a new image for herself and Bassanio—not Medea and Jason, but Hesione and Heracles. Hesione was daughter of Laomedon, king of Troy in the generation before the Trojan War. In order to expiate the anger of the gods and the demands of his subjects, Laomedon chained Hesione to a rock on the Trojan shore as a "virgin tribute . . . / To the sea monster" (3.2.53-60).[26] Portia's new metaphor redefines the situation considerably; the casket is not something set up by a loving and wise father for her benefit, as Nerissa had urged, but is, to say the least, hostile to her best interests. It is easy enough to see how Portia can understand it so.[27] She might well envisage the intention, not just the likely effect of the casket test to be to exclude Bassanio as a suitor. The Venetian, after all, visited Belmont while the father still lived, and had he known and approved of Portia's liking, then the whole rigmarole of the caskets would make no sense. Nerissa (and Bassanio, too) knew of Portia's feelings and perhaps, she suspects, the father did, too.

Even if he did not know that Portia's affections turned in Bassanio's direction, the young Venetian seems the very sort of chap from whom he must have been attempting to guard his daughter. The wealthy heiress is a natural target for young men who are deeply in debt and without the means to continue in the style of life to which they have been accustomed. To see the application to Bassanio, we need only recall the circumstances of his quest, and his image of Portia as the golden fleece: Bassanio seeks to cut a figure in the world, or in nautical Venice, to "show a more swelling port" than he can afford (1.1.124). Marriages to such young men, a father might reason, do not promise well for young heiresses; they are anything but love matches.[28] Thus the father set the winning casket as the one about giving, not about getting, as the one that did not promise outward wealth.

So Portia-Hesione is threatened with the denial of her heart's desire by her father-Laomedon via exposure to the casket test-sea monster. Her sadness goes as deep as it does because she knows, or at least intensely fears that her father's ploy will succeed, as directly or indirectly intended, in eliminating Bassanio. Her doubts about Bassanio pop through the surface of things when he responds to her awkward but clearly heartfelt request for delay with an ultraconventional lover's image: "Let me choose, / For as I am, I live upon the rack." To which she retorts: "Upon the rack, Bassanio? Then confess / What treason there is mingled with your love" (3.2.24-27).

She speaks better than she knows, for she has not heard the earlier negotiations between Bassanio and Antonio nor has she yet experienced Bassanio's treason of the ring. She knows her man . . . and yet. . . . When Bassanio returns with another stock profession of love she again opens her troubled mind: "Ay, but I fear you speak upon the rack, / where men enforced, do speak anything" (3.2.32-33). It is all so playful, and yet she speaks her real doubts here; justifiable ones at that if we recall the "force" under which Bassanio is (at least in part) acting. He is, in Belmont, as part of his "plots and purposes . . . to get clear of all the debts" he owes. These, not the rack, are his "necessity."

The next exchange is the pivot of the whole scene, and we must therefore attend to its nuances with some care.

BASSANIO:

    Promise me life, and I'll confess the truth.

PORTIA:

    Well then, confess and live.

BASSANIO:

    Confess and love
    Had been the very sum of my confession!

    (3.2.34-36)

As many critics have noticed, Bassanio's "confession" is pretty lame: no soaring love poetry (or even love prose) here. Among the striking features of the exchange, however, is Portia's straining to allay her own doubts about Bassanio, her own suspicions about his loyalties and his sincerity. "Confess and live," she says; perhaps against her better judgment she commits herself in advance to being satisfied with the merest gesture of an answer—which is pretty much all she gets, too, as Bassanio punningly echoes back to her promise (cf. also 3.2.54). Because he builds his answer on her answer Bassanio completes the rack image by almost reversing it: "O happy torment, when my torturer / Doth teach me answers for my deliverance" (3.2.37-38). She "taught" him the answer that freed him from the rack, where she had earlier refused to teach him the answer to the casket test. But let us note how she taught him; she gave him a clue, a word ("live"), which he is able to translate into the required profession of love. Bassanio has shown her how she can "teach" him "answers for deliverance" without telling him them directly, and therefore without being foresworn.[29]

Bassanio is the third to try his wits at the caskets, and as in most fairy tales, the third time is a charm. Some critics go so far as to suggest that because he is third, he is the inevitable victor, and therefore has no need for Portia's help. This is surely a foolish argument. Even if there is something formally foreordained for Bassanio in coming third, this does not settle the issue of how or what makes him successful. That is an entirely separate matter. That Goldilocks finds that the porridge, chair, and bed are "just right" consistently on her third try does not imply, after all, that there is no significance to the fact that it was, consistently, the one that was the mean that was "just right."

As has been noticed by many previous readers, Portia's hints, if there are such, come in the form of the song she sings as Bassanio ponders the alternatives. She prefaces her song, however, with an indispensable clue: "If you do love me, you will find me out" (3.2.41). To the other contestants she gave no such guidance. Just as Bassanio had taken her comment about love as a hint in the preliminary banter that was the playful foreshadowing of the casket test itself, this hint about love proves invaluable to Bassanio.

Portia's statement about love is so important because it helps set the contrast between that and "fancy." She sings of fancy, but, she has made clear, the casket test is about something else, about love. Love is the unspoken but implicit contrast to the point she makes in her song: fancy is born in the eyes, not in the heart or head. Its birth is in the sphere of appearance, and so fragile is it that it fails to survive its infancy. Fine appearance, external promise—gold and silver—engender not love, but only its poor surrogate fancy. This is enough to tell the attentive Bassanio what he must do, but just in case he or some of the critics fail to get the point Portia opens her song with her oft-noted triple rhyme: "bred," "head," and "nourished."[30]

Not to worry, however, for Bassanio proves himself an exceedingly apt pupil. He picks up her thought exactly: "So may the outward shows be least themselves; / The world is still deceived with ornament" (3.2.73-74). After a longish survey of the many cases where fair, but false, exteriors conceal corrupt interiors, Bassanio draws just the point:

> Therefore then, thou gaudy gold,
> Hard food for Midas, I will none of thee;
> Nor none of thee, thou pale and common drudge
> 'Tween man and man. But thou, thou meager lead,
> Which rather threaten'st than dost promise aught,
> Thy paleness moves me more than eloquence;
> And here choose I.
>
> (3.2.101-7)

If Bassanio has not been cued by Portia, then this chain of reasoning must be his own. But is that plausible? Is Bassanio the man to voice those sentiments? Does Bassanio really reject Midas's "hard food"? Does Bassanio turn away from external appearance and show?[31]

Bassanio's reflections are not only remarkably unlike himself, but they are altogether unlike the reasonings of the other suitors. Both Morocco and Aragon produced long speeches to justify their choices, and both reasoned entirely in terms of the legends on the caskets. Bassanio says nothing at all relating to the legends; his speech picks up entirely from Portia's song about fancy and appearance. In selecting the lead he shows neither understanding nor acceptance of the teaching about love its legend proclaims.[32]

Portia, we must conclude, extends her Medea-like behavior to helping her Jason overcome the trial established by her father to protect his treasure from adventurers like Jason. This is relatively easy for her to do because she sees herself as Hesione, the victim of her father, and not as the beneficiary of a wise and provident plan. Nonetheless, both images, Medea and Hesione, promise poorly for her. The one won by Jason, the other by Heracles, both were deserted by their respective heroes. Both images foreshadow Portia's almost fate.

II

> And when Medea saw this, Medea unsheathed her knife
> and cut the old man's throat; then, letting the old blood
> all run out, she filled his veins with her brew.[33]

The second phase of the contest for Bassanio culminates in the play's most famous scene, the trial in Venice over Antonio's forfeit of his bond. This incident is thematically important, moreover, for in it the broader significance of the love contest between Antonio and Portia begins to become clear: the struggle between Antonio and Portia is concealed here beneath a struggle between Antonio and Shylock, whose struggle in turn brings in the competing visions of the Old and New Testaments.[34]

It is not, perhaps, immediately apparent that the trial is part of the contest over Bassanio, because the antagonists are not Antonio and Portia, but rather Antonio and Shylock, with Portia as the judge who ultimately sides with Antonio. The news of the impending trial intrudes itself suddenly and violently on the scene of love; hardly have the lovers exchanged vows and rings, hardly have Nerissa and Gratiano joined the love fest than the emissaries from Venice arrive with Antonio's letter and the announcement of his default to Shylock. The letter distresses Bassanio and well it might. His friend and benefactor is to die on account of the debt Antonio incurred on his behalf. Portia notes his distress immediately.

But Bassanio's grief is not merely the grief a friend suffers at the misfortune of a friend; it is misery multiplied by guilt. As he confesses to Portia: "I have engaged myself to a dear friend, / Engaged my friend to his mere enemy / To feed my means" (3.2.261-63).

Bassanio's natural and creditable feelings are thus strong as it is, but Antonio has a knack for saying the very things that will heighten both Bassanio's misery and his guilt. Antonio's letter not only reports his situation, but refers directly to the bond of debt and guilt between them: "all debts are cleared between you and I if I might but see you at my death" (3.2.318-20). Surely there is something ironic in Antonio's wish: how can Bassanio and he be quits if Antonio goes "the last full measure" for Bassanio by dying for him? And how can Bassanio ever *feel* free of this debt if he is there to see this death for which, Antonio reminds him, he is responsible?[35] All these questions prove more than justified when we look ahead to discover what Antonio wishes Bassanio to see and, more importantly, to hear in his last moments. When it looks as though the trial will surely go against him Antonio delivers what appears to be a prepared statement. He responds to Portia's invitation to address the court as a whole, but his words are to and for Bassanio alone. He opens and closes his speech the same way: "Give me your hand Bassanio; fare you well. / Grieve not that I am fall'n to this *for you* . . ." And at the end: "Repent but you that you shall lose your friend, / And he repents not that he repays *your debt*" (4.1.264-65; 277-78).[36] Just in case Bassanio does not feel sufficiently responsible, and thus not sufficiently grateful, Antonio reminds him at this awful moment for whose sake he undergoes this fate—and how willingly at that.

He reserves the chief point of these, his dying words as he thinks, for the middle of his speech, however.

> Commend me to your honorable wife.
> Tell her the process of Antonio's end,

> Say how I loved you, speak me fair in death;
> And when the tale is told, bid her to be judge
> Whether Bassanio had not once a love.
>
> (4.1.272-76)

This speech makes perfectly clear what Antonio is doing: why does he, after all, drag Bassanio's "honorable wife" into it? Why does he insist that Bassanio recount his death to her, and wring from her a confession that indeed Antonio loved Bassanio . . . better than she or any ordinary lover could do. Who can match, who will match Antonio's gesture of love? As Solanio once said, Antonio "only loves the world" for Bassanio. He so loves Bassanio that facing the threat of the loss of Bassanio he will lose the world, or, better yet, to prevent the loss of Bassanio, he will sacrifice the world. In the contest with Portia, Antonio has raised the stakes, infinitely, and then has played the ultimate trump card.[37]

It may seem a desperate and hopeless ploy, but in fact it succeeds, for Bassanio answers Antonio with the very declaration Antonio is seeking:

> Antonio, I am married to a wife
> Which is as dear to me as life itself;
> But life itself, my wife, and all the world
> Are not with me esteemed above thy life.
> I would lose all, ay sacrifice them all
> Here to this devil, to deliver you.
>
> (4.1.281-86)

Antonio is not given a reply, but this must be very gratifying to him. Where earlier on Bassanio spoke much of the debts of love he owed, he never spoke of the love he felt; now, this light young man has offered to sacrifice his own life for his friend, and, it must not be overlooked, the life of his wife as well. At least for the moment Bassanio is so overwhelmed with gratitude and guilt that he renders Antonio all the esteem and attachment the older man has sought, and declares him victor in the contest for his affection between Antonio and Portia.[38] Antonio has gained all by "giving and hazarding all he hath." Antonio is the true and proper winner of the casket test.[39]

Nonetheless, the audience can see more clearly than Bassanio and probably than Antonio himself the paradoxical, if not self-contradictory, character of Antonio's self-sacrificing love. He gives up all—to get all. His selflessness is only a more subtle form of selfishness, for he wishes not merely to possess the object of his love, but to establish himself as the most lovable human being, as the one most worthy of love and thus as the one whose love supplants all others and lasts indefinitely.[40]

The only character in the play who seems clear-eyed about Antonio is Portia. From the moment that she observes Bassanio's reaction to Antonio's letter, she knows she does not have the full devotion of her husband. Portia shows the same wisdom in the face of Bassanio's feelings toward Antonio as Antonio showed when Bassanio resolved to court Portia. She does not in any way attempt to thwart Bassanio in his efforts to aid his friend. Indeed, her first words once she understands the situation is her offer to pay the debt, to pay double or more so that Antonio will be free from Shylock. We must see her offer in terms of her self-interest as well as her generosity. To keep her husband, or rather, to win from him the kind of loving attachment she seeks, she must save Antonio.[41] Before they can consummate this marriage, Portia insists, Bassanio must go to Antonio; the matter of Antonio must be taken care of before the marriage of Bassanio and Portia can be properly fulfilled (3.2.303-6).

Instead of paying off the debt Portia will have to preside over a trial where Shylock prosecutes Antonio to receive legal satisfaction on his contract. As most readers of the play have noticed, this trial concerns not only the two parties to it, but their respective religions and religious laws. That is to say, in the midst of this play about the rivalry between Portia and Antonio arises this most serious and far-reaching consideration of the meaning and relative merits of the two elements of what we have come to call the Judeo-Christian tradition.

We can understand the appearance of this apparently extraneous set of themes as follows. Antonio, as has often been noted, acts upon a model of human existence rooted in Christianity. He not only engages in the acts of charity prescribed by Christian precept, but, in his willingness to undergo sacrifice of his life for the sake of his love he engages in a particularly powerful form of the imitation of Christ. Antonio's justification and explanation are to be found in Christianity.[42] As Jesus says in order to explain his upcoming passion to his followers: "greater love hath no man than this, that a man lay down his life for his friends." This self-sacrificing love is not merely the extraordinary act of the extraordinary god-man, but is the model for all humanity: "'This is my commandment, that you love one another as I have loved you.'"[43]

The New Testament authors, however, understand the life, death, and teaching of Jesus in terms of their relation to the older Jewish law, as both the completion and rejection of the old Jewish law. The defense and justification of Christianity originally appears in the form of a critique and attack on Judaism. Portia must defeat Antonio, but, strangely enough, she can do this only if Antonio can defeat Shylock; that is to say, only if Christianity can defeat or appear to defeat Judaism.

Antonio not only adheres to Christian doctrine, but, as Barbara Lewalski emphasizes, he imitates or even plays the part of Christ at various important moments in the drama. "Antonio, who assumes the debts of others . . . reflects on occasion the role of Christ satisfying the claim of Divine Justice by assuming the sins of mankind."[44] The trial is one such occasion: Antonio-Christ is once again put on trial, accused by the Jew, who seeks his life. Portia too has her part in this emblematic episode—in this case not as Medea or Hesione—but as Pontius Pilate. But she is a Pilate who prevents the passion of Christ. She is a

John Gielgud as Shylock in the 1938 Stratford production of The Merchant of Venice.

new or reverse Pilate and thereby she will ultimately prove a new or nontragic Medea.

The tension between Antonio and Shylock obviously predates the action of the play and enters it from almost the very moment Shylock does. Upon first catching sight of Antonio, Shylock announces, "I hate him" (1.3.39). The feeling is, apparently, mutual, for Shylock complains of Antonio's extraordinarily uncivil treatment. "You that did void your rheum upon my beard / And foot me as you spurn a stranger cur / Over your threshold!" (1.3.114-16). The feelings of extreme enmity are related in both cases to the religion of the other: "I hate him for he is a Christian," says Shylock; Antonio abuses Shylock in turn as a "misbeliever" (1.3.39, 108).

Shylock mentions two other reasons, reasons that have led some critics to discount the importance of the religious issue. In addition to hating him as a Christian, Shylock also says: "But more, for that in low simplicity / He lends out money gratis, and brings down / The rate of usance here with us in Venice" (1.3.40-42). Many readers conclude from these lines that Shylock's real complaint is the economic harm Antonio does to him. However, this is to read Shylock's "But more" as though he means "a greater reason for my hatred"; a better reading, given the list of reasons Shylock is presenting, is to take "more" as "in addition." These additional points are all related: "He hates our sacred nation, and he rails, / . . . On me, my bargains, and my well-won thrift, / Which he calls interest" (1.3.45-48). Shylock attributes Antonio's practice of lending money gratis to "low simplicity," that is to say, to a base motive; he almost certainly means to accuse Antonio of acting out of enmity to Jews, specifically to harm them by decreasing their earning power (also cf. 3.1.45-47).

Shylock is thus not impressed by Antonio's pretenses to virtue and high principle. This appears to be Shylock's general perspective on the Christians and particularly on Antonio. Two issues in the play specifically divide Shylock from the Christians. They refrain from taking interest, which the Jews do not, while the Jews refrain from eating pork, which the Christians do not. The dietary laws of the Jews prompt Shylock to respond harshly to Bassanio's dinner invitation: "I will buy with you, sell with you, talk with you, walk with you, and so following; but I will not eat with you, drink with you, nor pray with you" (1.3.33-35). It is most telling that Shylock conjoins eating and drinking with praying: the dietary restraints are part of the holiness of the holy people. Those who do not keep to the dietary laws are unclean, that is to say, unfit to approach God. Shylock believes he even has the testimony of Jesus on his side, for he refers to a biblical story in which "your prophet the Nazarite conjured the devil into" a herd of swine (1.3.31-33).[45] Even Jesus understood the uncleanliness of pork, yet his so-called followers fail to.

At the same time, the Christians refrain from taking interest; yet, as Shylock makes clear, the Venetians—and especially Antonio—have no hesitation about engaging in high-flying commerce aimed at economic gain. Shylock rehearses Antonio's various ventures, argosies bound for Tripoli, the Indies, Mexico, England—all directions of the compass, all continents—all with the intention of enriching himself. The Christian attitude toward money and gain is, in a word, hypocritical. Gain from lending money is in principle no different from gain for other kinds of economic activity, and, Shylock believes, the story of Jacob the patriarch testifies to the divine favoring of enterprise and the legitimacy of gain (1.3.86-87).[46] Usury is merely a way of thriving, and all thriving is legitimate, if it is not done unjustly. Such is Shylock's view.

Antonio more than returns Shylock's feelings, and sees the latter's hateful qualities as rooted in his Jewishness. Antonio's most comprehensive statement occurs at the end of the scene: "The Hebrew will turn Christian; he grows kind" (1.3.175). Antonio is unkind to Shylock because Shylock, as a Jew, is himself unkind. The greatest evidence or manifestation of that unkindness is Shylock's practice of taking interest on the loans he makes to the Christian merchants of Venice. Contrary to Shylock's theory, Antonio does not oppose usury merely to vex and harm the Jewish money-lenders, but rather he despises the money-lenders because they take interest. As he understands it, the different practices he and Shylock stand for stem from their respective faiths. Antonio seems to understand well the Jewish law regarding usury: "'You shall not lend upon interest to your brother. . . . To a foreigner you may lend upon interest, but to your brother you shall not lend upon interest.'"[47] Antonio makes direct reference to this law in his negotiation with Shylock:

> If thou wilt lend this money, lend it not
> As to thy friends—for when did friendship take
> A breed for barren metal of his friend?—
> But lend it rather to thine enemy . . .
>
> (1.3.129-32)

Antonio translates the law's "brother" into "friend" and "foreigner" into "enemy," but he brings out a central thought in the Jewish law nonetheless. By forbidding usury within the people, the law recognizes the evil of usury. By allowing an evil toward the "foreigner," the Jewish law indeed treats them as "enemies."

The evil in charging interest to friends remains obscure so long as attention remains exclusively focused on the essentialist issue centering on the "barren" and "non-breeding" character of metal. That is relevant only indirectly; if money "bred," that is, increased naturally, then it would not be unreasonable or unjust for the owner of the money to be able to reap the natural increase. But because money does not increase in this way, it is "unjust," because there is an "inequality" in the transaction "which is contrary to justice." The lender receives more than he gave.[48] The one who pays usury does not restore (a part of) natural increase, nor does he act voluntarily (as Shylock implies), but rather he acts "under a certain necessity insofar as he needs to borrow money which the owner is unwilling to lend without usury."[49] No wonder Antonio (and Bassanio too) treats it largely as a matter of "kindness"; the usurer is unkind, for he takes advantage of the pressing necessities of his debtor.[50] In the exchange among Antonio, Shylock, and Bassanio this last aspect is much emphasized (1.3.60, 111, 152).

Thomas Aquinas expresses Antonio's understanding with great lucidity in his discussion of the "sin of usury."

> The Jews were forbidden to take usury from their brethren, i.e., from other Jews. By this we (Christians) are given to understand that to take usury from any man is evil simply, because we ought to treat every man as our neighbor and brother.[51]

Antonio understands Christianity to involve both a broadening and a deepening of the Jewish law. It is broader because it is universal—injunctions to treat the other as neighbor or brother are not limited to one's own narrow nation. It is deeper in that the benevolence human beings owe to one another has no calculating quality to it; it is selfless. It is more sublime in that, as becomes clear later, the ultimate expression of Christian love is not merely disinterested benevolence, but self-sacrifice. Antonio is thus an apostle of Christian love, who uses Shylock and the Jews as a foil against which to define his moral vision, and uses the issue of usury as a vehicle for that moral vision.[52]

This is the abiding view each has of the other as the play opens. Yet almost immediately a new dynamic is introduced by Antonio's application to Shylock for a loan to aid his beloved friend. The Jew and the Christian agree to a loan with no interest, but with the pound of flesh pledge for collateral. This "deal" has led to one of the greatest controversies about the play: just what is Shylock up to in proposing these terms? Whatever Shylock's motives, after the elopement of Jessica, he is resolved to take advantage of Antonio's forfeiture of his bond.

Shylock and Antonio, Jew and Christian—just when it looks as though Shakespeare is setting up a contest between these two versions of the biblical religion, the terms of the relationship change. Most importantly, Shylock falls away from his status as paradigmatic Jew; the confrontation between the two in Portia's court in Venice is thus an aborted moment of judgment between those two great religions.

Shylock had raised two criteria to distinguish Jew and Christian. The Jews as the holy people, as the people of the law, are especially concerned with the clean and the unclean, sanctifying all their lives to God under the law.[53] That means, in particular, that the Jews must keep their special dietary laws; they do not eat in friendship and intimacy with other men of other nations; they are the nation set apart.[54] Shylock at first prided himself on his observance of the distinction between the clean and the unclean, the permitted and the forbidden. Yet suddenly and with little explanation, Shylock admits that he has agreed to dine with the Christians (2.5.11). We must understand this in relation to his bargain with Antonio. He has, as Antonio implied, in effect become a Christian. Just as he violates the dietary laws, so he violates the law respecting usury. True, the Jewish law legitimates interest taken from non-Jews, but it forbids what Shylock has potentially done in the "merry bond" and actually does in his resolve to collect his debt after Jessica runs off with Lorenzo: one may not indirectly, and thus a fortiori directly take what amounts to the life of another as a pledge in loan.[55] The Jewish law recognizes (at least some) moral claims of human beings as such. Shylock has done what the Law explicitly forbids. And this is to say nothing of the commandment, "you shall not kill," a closely related provision of the law.[56] Shylock reveals himself to be a bad human being, a devil incarnate, not because he is a Jew, but because and insofar as he falls away from the Jewish law.

Portia's courtroom triumph over Antonio—that is to say, Antonio's triumph over Shylock—cannot be a triumph of Christianity over Judaism, for Shylock no longer represents Judaism, as is made perfectly clear in his most famous speech.

> Hath not a Jew eyes? Hath not a Jew hands, organs, dimensions, senses, affections, passions?—fed with the

same food, hurt with the same weapons . . . ? If you prick us, do we not bleed? . . . And if you wrong us, shall we not revenge?

(3.1.55-63)

This angry and moving speech must be contrasted with Shylock's earlier claim to Antonio: "sufferance is the badge of all our tribe" (1.3.107). So far as that is true, Shylock's speech about revenge, and his resolve to exact fully Antonio's pledge indicates a break with this forbearing attitude. Moreover, Shylock here speaks not as a Jew, nor even as a quasi-Christian; the standard is a purely human standard: "If a Jew wrong a Christian, what is his humility? Revenge! If a Christian wrong a Jew, what should his sufferance be by Christian example? Why revenge!" (3.1.65-68). Despite the ways or teachings or precepts of the two biblical religions, the human way is revenge. Shylock no longer even pretends to take his bearings and find his justification in the law.[57] He has, in his own way, become a political philosopher, discerning a harsh and universal nature beneath the varying laws of the nations.

The judgment Shylock undergoes at the hands of Portia is thus not a judgment on him as a Jew, or on Judaism as such. This is not to say there is no such judgment in the play—his loss of his daughter fulfills that role. Jessica enters a forbidden relation and forsakes her family, people and God (cf. 3.1.30, 32, 80-85). Her initial situation is rather like that of so many tragic lovers—Romeo and Juliet, Pyramus and Thisbe—forbidden her love by her parents or her people, yet not Jessica the lover, but Shylock the parent suffers the tragic fate in this case. Jessica lives in a community where her love is to be controlled by the laws. She is to marry inside the community and defer to her parents in choice of mate. Yet her love escapes these restraints; love cannot be so readily bidden. Like Shylock himself in his revenge, she learns and teaches something of the universality of nature in her love. The Jewish notion of a holy people, a people set apart, gives too little notice to nature, both in its higher manifestations like love, and in its lower, like revenge. No people can be simply holy; no people can be simply set apart. This is Shakespeare's judgment on Shylock. The perspective of that judgment shares something important with the Pauline Christian condemnation of Judaism as particularistic, but it is not necessarily the same as that perspective and surely not the same as Antonio's virulent anti-Jewish pronouncements.

Shylock is a Jew who violates his own law, the observance of which would at least have saved him from the inhumanity to which he sinks in his hatred for Antonio. Likewise, just as Shylock's defeat cannot stand for the defeat of the Jewish way, so Antonio's triumph does not represent a triumph of Christian principles. Although the disguised Portia delivers a lovely speech on mercy, the outcome of the trial does not in fact depend upon mercy, Christian or otherwise. Shylock's suit fails in two respects, on two legal technicalities. Both of these derive from the Jewish law, whence Portia has imported them into Venetian law. She first grants Shylock the right to his pound of flesh, but "in the cutting of it" he is allowed not "one drop of Christian blood" (4.1.305-9). Now this literalism is frequently decried as contrary to the reasonable meaning of the law: if Shylock has a right to the flesh, he must have a right to any necessary appurtenances of the flesh. Yet this fine-honed distinction is not of Portia's making; it derives instead from the Jewish dietary laws: "'However, you may slaughter and eat flesh . . . Only you shall not eat the blood.'"[58] If the distinction between the flesh and the blood is valid, as the Jewish law insists that it is, then the conclusion Portia draws is valid as well. No wonder Shylock cries out "Is that the law?" (4.1.313).

The second part of Portia's verdict comes when she turns the tables on Shylock: an alien may not directly or indirectly attempt the life of a citizen. Shylock has quite openly done that very thing, and thus must pay the penalty for it. But as we have noted above, this law, especially as applied to the circumstances at hand is part of the Jewish law as well: one may not take "'a life in pledge.'"[59] One may supply various theological interpretations of Portia's legal maneuverings—interpreting her as attempting to illustrate, for example, the Pauline principle that righteousness under the law is not possible for sinful man. Although that interpretation resonates with Portia's speech on mercy, it does not fit so well the way the scene develops: the insistence that the Jewish law is perfectly sufficient to produce the just—and merciful—outcome.

One must instead view the trial as a reenactment of the trial of Jesus, with Antonio in the title role, Shylock in place of the Jews prosecuting Jesus, and Portia taking the part of Pontius Pilate.[60] Shylock insists on the law ("I stand here for the law") under which Antonio must pay the penalty of his default, i.e., must die; his predecessors urged much the same: "The Jews answered [Pilate], 'We have a law, and by that law he ought to die . . .'"[61] In the trial of Antonio Portia urges Shylock to recognize that if he presses his claim, "this strict [code] of Venice / Must needs give sentence 'gainst the merchant there," to which Shylock replies, "My deeds upon my head" (4.1.203-5). Wittingly or unwittingly, he thus echoes the very thought of his predecessors, who responded to Pilate's resolve to "wash his hands" of the matter, "'His [Jesus'] blood be on us and on our children.'"[62]

Antonio casts himself as decisively in the role of Jesus as Shylock does in the role of Jesus' Jewish accusers. From his opening lines in the scene until the moment when Portia's verdict goes against Shylock, Antonio takes the part of one who suffers a fated martyrdom, a martyrdom, as we have seen, of self-sacrifice motivated by love.

> I do oppose [says Antonio]
> My patience to his fury, and am armed
> To suffer with a quietness of spirit
> The very tyranny and rage of his.

(4.1.10-13, cf. 83)

He calls himself "the tainted wether of the flock, / Meetest for death," like the scapegoat on whom the community heaps its sins, and which is an image of Jesus' redemptive mission (4.1.114-15).

Yet the trial of Antonio does not end as did the trial of Jesus, because Pontius-Portia plays her part differently. Two things are particularly striking in the behavior of the original Pontius Pilate. First, he repeatedly proclaims his conviction of Jesus' innocence. "And Pilate said to the chief priests and the multitudes, 'I find no crime in this man,'" a conclusion he repeats twice more after further inquiry.[63] Judging Jesus under the relevant law, the Jewish law, Pilate found no grounds to condemn him. Yet he gave in to the repeated urgings of the Jews: "But they were urgent, demanding with loud cries that he should be crucified. And their voices prevailed. So Pilate gave sentence that their demand should be granted. . . . Jesus he delivered up to their will."[64]

Portia, the new Pilate, breaks with her predecessor on one central point: unlike Pilate, who sacrificed his judgment of the law to fear of the mob or concern for politics, she sticks to the law, the Jewish-become-Venetian law.[65] Under that law Antonio is free from Shylock's bond. Portia gives Antonio a victory of sorts, although it is also a most telling defeat, by sticking to the letter and spirit of the old law. She thus doubly thwarts the new Jesus: she neither vouchsafes him his longed-for martyrdom, nor does she appeal to specifically Christian principle to do so.

III

> I am abandoned; I have lost my throne, my native soil, my home, my husband—who alone for me took the place of all![66]

The trial is a great triumph for Portia, and yet she is never closer to suffering the tragic fate of Medea—abandonment by the one she loves, by one who has sworn eternal and complete devotion to her. Despite the fact that she has prevented Antonio from rendering that "last full measure" of his devotion to his beloved, Bassanio has yet been deeply affected by Antonio's gesture. He confesses to esteeming Antonio more highly than her and would sacrifice her life (and his own) in order to save Antonio's. Bassanio apparently has taken to heart the injunction to love as Antonio has loved him.[67] Although Portia has defeated Antonio, it yet might appear that he has gotten all he could have hoped for from the episode. He has won Bassanio's love with his offer to sacrifice his life, without needing to carry through on his offer.[68]

Feeling victorious, Antonio provokes the third round in his contest against Portia by intervening in the post-trial exchange between Bassanio and the disguised Portia over the ring Portia has requested from Bassanio as a reward or remembrance for her service to the two friends. Bassanio is most reluctant to part with the ring:

> Good sir, this ring was given me by my wife,
> And when she put it on she made me vow
> That I should neither sell nor give nor lose it.
>
> (4.1.440-43)

Should he do any of these things, Portia had meaningfully observed earlier, "Let it presage the ruin of your love . . ." (3.2.171-73). As soon as he hears the reason for Bassanio's refusal to surrender the ring Antonio enters the discussion in order to loosen his friend's resolve.

> My lord Bassanio, let him have the ring.
> Let his deservings, and my love withal,
> Be valued 'gainst your wife's commandment.
>
> (4.1.448-50)

A more calculating move can hardly be imagined. Both to register the implications of Bassanio's declaration at the trial and to reinforce his supreme position Antonio prods Bassanio to do the thing that most concretely symbolizes his triumph. He makes the point perfectly explicit: his "love" is to be weighed against Portia's "commandment."[69] In accord with his declaration Bassanio accedes. What Bassanio said at the trial was thus not idle talk—he is more devoted to Antonio than to his wife.

Here then is Portia's greatest moment of crisis. She must act decisively in order to restore her love, a need with which the audience are in full sympathy, for we cannot willingly accept an Antonian victory in this contest.[70] Portia has our sympathies because we have seen the less attractive underside to Antonio's love. The claim he raises is the claim of sacrifice and selflessness, yet we see this to be largely fraudulent; beneath the selflessness is a deep and potent self-seeking. The deficient character of Antonio's love is visible in at least two of its effects. First is his "spoiling" of Bassanio: he seeks to render Bassanio dependent rather than good. His "selfless" love is selfish in that it does not produce the good of the beloved, but of the lover.[71] Secondly, we see, perhaps with surprise, the virulence of his hatred for Shylock. While Shylock is not entirely attractive either, his most vicious acts are the consequences of the attitudes of the Antonios of the world. Antonio is a genuine anti-Semite, a genuine hater. He displays what Machiavelli had earlier denounced as "pious cruelty." His philosophy of love ironically issues in acts of hatred.

Portia returns from Venice to Belmont in a darkly melancholy mood. Her melancholy is foreshadowed in a remarkable dialogue between Jessica and Lorenzo, in which these two newlyweds celebrate the night and their love by recounting the tales of ill-fated lovers of note from the past. These reminders of failed and betrayed loves reflect both on their own love and on the unfolding betrayal of Portia by Bassanio. It is probably no coincidence that the central item in this exchange concerns Medea: "In such a night / Medea gathered the enchanted herbs / That did renew the old Aeson" (5.1.12-14). Aeson was Jason's father, a very old and dying man to whom Medea brought new youth and salvation through her magic. Nonetheless, Jason's gratitude did not prevent his subsequent abandonment of Medea. The parallel to Portia and Bassanio is clear: as Medea saved Aeson, so Portia saved Antonio.

"In such a night as this . . . ," a moonlit night, a night for lovers, and yet a night that reveals the unsteadiness, the evanescence, the unreliability of love. A night for recalling disloyal lovers. Even Lorenzo's famous and quite lovely rapture on the music of the spheres fits the mood. Even though: "There's not the smallest orb which thou behold'st / But in his motion like an angel sings," nonetheless this heavenly

> Harmony is [only] in immortal souls,
> [And] whilst this muddy vesture of decay
> Doth grossly close it in, we cannot hear it.
>
> (5.1.60-65)

Perhaps it is Jessica's keen appreciation of how far earthly love falls below Lorenzo's heavenly harmonies that leads her to confess, "I am never merry when I hear sweet music" (5.1.69). In this comic celebration of love, Shakespeare comes to the very brink of exposing love in its lunar, that is, false and fleeting, cold and changing character.

By the time Portia arrives, the brightness of the moon, which so impressed Lorenzo and Jessica, is shown for what it is—unsteady and unreliable. Not the moon, but a "little candle" from her own hall, is all she can see now. By her yet lesser light, Portia stands much deeper in her despair of love than Lorenzo and Jessica.

> That light we see is burning in my hall;
> How far that little candle throws his beams!
> So shines a good deed in a naughty world.
>
> (5.1.89-91)

Can there be any doubt that she is the "little candle"—Portia reduced to a little candle!—casting little light, having little good effect in herself and yet shining brightly by contrast with the "naughty world," the betrayers, the self-promoters, adventurers and hypocrites—the Jasons and Antonios—around her. Despair gnaws at her heart; all the world empties itself of meaning and goodness. "Nothing is good, I see, without respect" (5.1.99), that is, but by contrast. The good is merely what appears better by contrast to something worse or less.[72]

Despair gnaws at Portia, yet she does not give way to it. On hearing of the approach of her husband, she resolves, "Let me give light."[73] In this now dark night, the moon obscured, "the sun . . . hid," Portia will attempt to bring the world back to light. But this requires something of her as well: "Let me give light, but let me not be light" (5.1.129). Portia requires a certain weightiness, a moral seriousness, in order to bring the world back into light. One is tempted to say that she must repent her earlier lightness, that lightness that did not, for example, take sufficiently seriously her father's warnings and her father's efforts to help her find a suitable husband. Both she and Bassanio must grow beyond where they were at the opening of the play in order to be worthy of love—solar rather than lunar love, let us say. She must grow to transcend her alter-ego Medea; Medea the enchantress, associated with the moon, must give way to Portia, the Sun, source of illumination.[74] Portia resolves to be the light by being weighty; not Antonio, but she, is to be "the true light."[75]

From the moment Portia greets Bassanio on his arrival at Belmont, the delicate negotiation between them commences. Bassanio once again signals how things stand with his curt return of Portia's greeting ("I thank you, madam") and his far more expansive introduction of Antonio: "This is the man, this is Antonio, / To whom I am so infinitely bound" (5.1.133-35).[76]

Portia, however, quietly corrects him: "You should be . . . much bound," but not apparently, "infinitely bound" (5.1.136). If Bassanio is infinitely bound to Antonio, then, of course, he has no bond left for Portia. She is less forthcoming to Antonio, however, than Bassanio would apparently have her be: she "scants this breathing courtesy," that is, elaborate words of welcome. How welcome he is "must appear in other ways than words," in part because he is welcome in order to be part of the final showdown over Bassanio, and in part because just how welcome he is will depend on subsequent events (5.1.139-41).

Before Portia even mentions Bassanio's infidelity, Nerissa and Gratiano erupt into an argument over their parallel situation. This proves most useful to Portia (did she preconcert it with her maid?), for it allows her to accuse Bassanio, indirectly at first in the guise of accusing Gratiano, of the great violation of trust he has committed.

> You were to blame—I must be plain with you—
> To part so slightly with your wife's first gift,
> A thing stuck on with oaths upon your finger,
> And so riveted with faith unto your flesh.
>
> (5.1.166-69)

Her lines echo earlier images of the almost crucified Antonio, but it is Bassanio she casts now as the central actor in the moral drama. It is he who is "riveted"; it is he who receives "faith." Bassanio needs to see himself as a serious moral agent in a serious moral relationship with Portia. Before the trial he was little given to this kind of moral seriousness in any form, because of the general levity of his character. In the wake of Antonio's gesture, Bassanio is equally little given to the kind of moral agency Portia calls forth, for he sees Antonio as the center and himself as the merely reflected image, infinitely bound to the original.

Bassanio at first inclines to defend himself in terms that reflect the very Antonio-centeredness she must overcome.

> Sweet Portia
> If you did know to whom I gave the ring, . . .
> And would conceive for what I gave the ring . . .
> You would abate the strength of your displeasure.
>
> (5.1.192-98)

Although many critics are entirely appeased by this defense—indeed some see it as a sign of Bassanio's understanding and acceptance of the burden of love—Portia is not in the least satisfied—and rightly not.

> If you had known the virtue of the ring,
> Or half her worthiness that gave the ring,
> Or your own honor to contain the ring,
> You would not then have parted with the ring.
>
> (5.1.199-202)

In giving it away, Bassanio has undervalued the ring itself and what it means—"a thing held as a ceremony," a symbol of their love and its hoped-for abidingness. As such a thing, no reasonable person would demand it and no service can be commensurable with it. It was, of course, Antonio, who prevailed on him to present the ring to Balthazar/Portia, precisely to get Bassanio to make the point Portia now blames him for. Thus Bassanio also undervalued Portia relative to Antonio in giving up the ring, whereas, she implies, she is more worthy than Antonio. Bassanio is guilty of disloyalty, but also of poor judgment; he does not see through the character of Antonio's "selfless" love, but is flattered by the appearances he does discern. He thereby misses the true source of human value. Accordingly, she also accuses him of undervaluing himself by so lightly setting aside his own oath; a man's oath and his resolve to keep it are tokens of his true dignity as a moral agent. To be bound by one's own word is to legislate for oneself and to commit oneself to being the kind of human being that can determine itself to its own commitments, to its vision of its own future. But in the shadow of Antonio Bassanio takes himself as little seriously as he took his love or the character of his wife.[77]

Bassanio takes up only part of the immediate challenge posed by Portia's accusation: it was not a smirch upon his honor to give away the ring but a requirement of it (5.1.218-19). So much was this a demand of his honor that had Portia, who now claims to speak on behalf of his honor, "been there [he] thinks [she] would have begged / The ring of [him] to give the worthy doctor" (5.1.221-22). He replies to her charge about his honor, but she no doubt notices that he has said not a word about the other two points of her accusation, that he slighted both their love as symbolized by the ring, and herself. She is therefore not in the least appeased by his defense.

If he will stand on his honor as a thing apart from their marriage, then she will threaten his honor in a way that will remind him that his honor is now at least in part in her keeping:

> Let not that doctor e'er come near my house.
> . . . . I will become as liberal as you;
> I'll not deny him anything I have,
> No, not my body nor my husband's bed.
>
> (5.1.223-28)

This is not merely a threat to his honor, but an expression of hers: "Now by mine honor, which is yet mine own, / I'll have that doctor for mine bedfellow" (5.1.232-34). If Bassanio attempts to treat his honor as his own, that is, independent of her and their marriage, then she can treat her honor in the same way. But, of course, the premise of her speech is precisely the opposite, that both their honors are now inseparably bound up with the other's; her first need is to get Bassanio to see and understand at least this much. By standing up for her own honor, she at the same time attempts to make him see and understand something of her undervalued worth.

Before Bassanio can reply, Nerissa, Gratiano, and Antonio intervene. Antonio's brief interjection—"I am th' unhappy subject of these quarrels"—is especially important, because the discussion between Portia and Bassanio has been moving in the direction of the recognition of Antonio's role in the incident. At first Bassanio defended himself for giving the ring away "unwillingly," constrained by the "civil doctor's" unwillingness to accept anything but the ring (5.1.196, 210). After Portia reminds him of the unreasonableness of such a gift, Bassanio subtly shifts ground. In his next speech he refers to the "enforced" character of his gift, but no longer is the doctor implied to be the source of the compulsion. It is left at the vague admission, "I was enforced to send it after him" (5.1.216). But the audience knows and Portia knows or suspects that the compulsion came from Antonio. This is just what Portia is attempting to make Bassanio see and to truly understand. She can free Bassanio from the bond of Antonio's love only by exposing its grasping underside.

As in the casket scene, Bassanio proves a remarkably apt pupil of Portia's subtle instruction. She brings him to the self-knowledge he has thus far almost completely lacked: "I swear to thee, ever by thine own fair eyes, / Wherein I see myself" (5.1.242-43). He sees himself and his situation in her eyes, that is to say, he sees himself as she does; as Portia puts it, he sees himself as a double-dealer: "In both my eyes he doubly sees himself, / In each eye one" (5.1.244-45). Because of this newly acquired self-knowledge, he capitulates completely. He no longer protests that Portia would have willed he do as he did, but twice within ten lines he asks her pardon. The first time he continues to speak of it as an "enforced" deed, but he now calls it a "wrong." The second time he drops all reference to compulsion, and calls it not merely wrong, but a "fault" (5.1.240, 247).

Bassanio at one and the same moment has broken Antonio's spell and become a man, responsible for himself and the moral character of his actions. He has finally become worthy of Portia, who has herself become worthy of the love of another mature adult by facing her own errors and despair. By this last scene she is no longer the talented, beautiful, wealthy but spoiled heiress of the opening of the play and the casket scene, just as he is no longer the fortune-hunting adventurer. Neither Medea nor Jason, Portia and Bassanio become fit heroes of a comic world where love thrives.[78]

In order to recognize his deed as a "fault," Bassanio must see in Portia's eyes not only himself, but his susceptibility to Antonio and the character of Antonio's love game. She helps him to see both by making him relive and ponder deeply his own and Antonio's deeds, but also by making him look into himself and reconsider the nature of love. He discovers not only the underlying will to power in Antonio's professed selfless love, but he discovers a core of selfishness in love itself.[79] The lover seeks an exclusive possession—sexual, but more than sexual—of the beloved. Love is of and for the other, but it is of and for the self, as well. This was true even of Antonio's love, but only illicitly so. By becoming more self-consciously selfish in his understanding of love, Bassanio also becomes more genuinely loving. He gives up not only Antonio, but that pride that prevented him from admitting fault and asking pardon. To paraphrase a much less insightful, more modern statement, Bassanio discovers that love is learning to say you're sorry. Bassanio comes to understand the kind of risk and hazard that, according to the lead casket, love entails.

Contrary to first impression, Antonio's kind of love does that much less well. Bassanio and Portia learn that love has an indissolubly exclusive character. It can never be the foundation for society as a whole. Human beings cannot build their lives on the purely selfless or sacrificial love which Jesus and Christianity command. In the final analysis, *The Merchant of Venice,* while not overtly a political play, has deep political implications. Those implications are emblematized most of all in the outcome of the trial: the law provides a solider basis for just and decent social life than the replacement of the law with love can do. A humanely just society is far more the achievement of good laws than of love.[80]

The promise of *The Merchant of Venice* nonetheless is the promise of love, through which pleasure, duty, and honor can find harmonious reconciliation. In love and the responsibility it breeds lies the good of the soul and whatever of eternity human beings can attain.[81] The culminating moment of the decisive scene is Bassanio's final apology and acceptance of the meaning of his marriage. "Pardon this fault, and by my soul I swear / I never more will break an oath with thee" (5.1.248-49). In that "never more" lies the real moral of this lovely tale of love and marriage: and they lived happily ever after.

Notes

1. David N. Beauregard, "Sidney, Aristotle, and *The Merchant of Venice*: Shakespeare's Triadic Image of Liberty and Justice" *Shakespeare Studies* 20 (1988): 33, 48; John Lyon, *The Merchant of Venice* (Boston: Twayne, 1988), xi, xv, 1-17, 95-96; Barbara K. Lewalski, "Biblical Allusion and Allegory in *The Merchant of Venice,*" *Shakespeare Quarterly* 13 (1962): 328; Joan Ozark Holmer, "Loving Wisely and the Casket Test: Symbolic and Structural Unity in *The Merchant of Venice,*" *Shakespeare Studies* 11 (1978): 53; Herbert S. Donow, "Shakespeare's Caskets: Unity in the *Merchant of Venice,*" *Shakespeare Studies* 4 (1968): 86.

2. On *The Merchant of Venice* as "the most scandalously problematic of Shakespeare's plays," and "the only one of Shakespeare's plays . . . which a sizable body of sane people might consider unfit to be seen or read," see Lawrence Danson, *The Harmonies of The Merchant of Venice* (New Haven: Yale University Press, 1978), 2-3; Derek Cohen, *Shakespeare's Motives* (London: Macmillan, 1988), 104-18; Lewalski, "Biblical Allusion," 333-34; Lynda E. Boose, "The Comic Contract and Portia's Golden Ring," *Shakespeare Studies* 20 (1988): 241.

3. On the stage history, and Shylock's role in it, see Lyon, *Merchant,* xiv-xvi, and more generally, ibid., 43; on Shylock as "the play's strongest and most discussed piece of characterization," see 106. Marion D. Perret, "Shakespeare's Jew: Preconception and Performance," *Shakespeare Studies* 20 (1988): 263-64.

4. See, e.g., Harley Granville-Barker, "*The Merchant of Venice,*" in *Prefaces to Shakespeare* (Princeton: Princeton University Press, 1947), ii, 89, 91.

5. *Contra* Lyon, *Merchant,* 31.

6. Barbara Tovey, "The Golden Casket: An Interpretation of *The Merchant of Venice,*" in *Shakespeare as Political Thinker,* ed. John Alvis and Thomas West (Durham, N.C.: Carolina Academic Press, 1981), 228; Donow, "Shakespeare's Caskets," 87.

7. Thus Lyon is quite mistaken to say that the ring incident represents "a new and independent plot [that gets] fully underway only in [the] last act" (*Merchant,* 117); or to call it "the tangential ring plot" (118).

8. The clearest account heretofore of the structure is in Lawrence Hyman, "The Rival Lovers in *The Merchant of Venice,*" *Shakespearean Quarterly* 21 (1970), 109-10.

9. Quotations are from the Signet edition, ed. Kenneth Myrick (New York: Penguin Books, 1965).

10. *Contra* Allan Bloom, *Shakespeare's Politics* (New York: Basic Books, 1964), 19: "Antonio is sad, and life does not mean much to him" because of his Christianity. Also *contra* Danson, who associates Antonio's sadness with the "moral failure" of his treatment of Shylock (*Harmonies,* 32). Neither Bloom nor Danson account for the sudden onset of Antonio's sadness. (Also *contra* Thomas Fujimara, "Mode and Structure in *The Merchant of Venice,*" *PMLA* [*Publications of the Modern Language Associations of America*] 81 [1966]: 509.)

11. Though cf. Lars Engle, "Thrift Is Blessing: Exchange and Explanation in *The Merchant of Venice*" *Shakespearean Quarterly* 37 (1986): 21-22 and Allan Haladay, "Antonio and the Allegory of Salvation," *Shakespeare Studies* 4 (1968): 111.

12. Cf. Lewalski, "Biblical Allusion," 328-29.

13. Cf. Lewalski, "Biblical Allusion," 329; Thomas Cartelli, "Shakespeare's *Merchant,* Marlowe's *Jew*: The Problem of Cultural Difference," *Shakespeare Studies* 20 (1988): 257-58.

14. Danson rejects the conception that Antonio's love for Bassanio underpins his melancholy because this is "not coherent with the play's overall shape and tone" (*Harmonies,* 36, 38, 40). This is, of course, a circular argument. Lyon, *Merchant,* 47, accepts Antonio's love for Bassanio as the cause of sadness, however, as does Keith Geary, "The Nature of Portia's Victory: Turning to Men in *The Merchant of Venice,*" *Shakespeare Survey* 37 (1984): 58-59.

15. See Holmer, "Loving Wisely," 54.

16. Ovid *Metamorphoses* 7.38; Frank Justus Miller, trans., Loeb Classical Library, 345.

17. Beauregard, "Sidney, Aristotle, and *The Merchant of Venice,*" 33-39, 47-48; Bloom, *Shakespeare's Politics,* 19; Danson, *Harmonies,* 51-55; Lyon, *Merchant,* 45; Geary, "Nature of Portia's Victory," 60.

18. Aristotle, *Nicomachean Ethics,* ed. and trans. Hippocrates G. Apostle (Grinnell, Iowa: The Peripatetic Press, 1975), 1120, 1126-130.

19. Cf. Geary, "The Nature of Portia's Victory," 59: "Bassanio . . . describes his projected journey to Belmont less in terms of intended marriage than as if it were a business venture . . ."; also Engle, "Exchange and Explanation," 25.

20. Boose, "Comic Contract," 248.

21. Tovey, "Golden Casket," 221, 223; cf. Geary's statement: "The scene is tense with an unspoken loosening of ties" ("Nature of Portia's Victory," 59).

22. Ovid *Metamorphoses* 7.9-21, Loeb Classical Library, 343.

23. On the comparison of Portia and Medea, see Donow, "Shakespeare's Caskets," 87-88.

24. Danson rejects in the strongest terms the notion that Portia can have hinted at the right answer: "The imputation . . . that Portia through the most blatant trick makes her . . . father's dying inspiration nugatory—is one which . . . would make the rest of the play inexplicable." In other words, it conflicts with Danson's sense of the larger patterns and meanings in the whole (*Harmonies,* 117-18). This is a perfectly reasonable approach, but its circularity must again be noted. The position Danson merely takes for granted is that there is no plausible construal of the whole consistent with this "imputation." That, I believe, is false, and indeed, to go further, it is Danson, I will suggest, who ignores many elements of the play that are not only consistent with this imputation, but insistently point toward it. A more balanced approach to the question is in Lyon (*Merchant,* 92-97). Lyon also contains a good discussion of the scholarly to and fro on the issue.

25. *Contra* Geary, "Nature of Portia's Victory," 62.

26. On the story of Heracles and Hesione, see Robert Graves, *The Greek Myths* (Harmondsworth, Middlesex: Penguin Books, 1966), 2:168-73.

27. So far as I know, Lewalski is the critic to pay the most attention to the Hesione image, but she does not much analyze what this implies about Portia's stance toward the casket test ("Biblical Allusion," 336).

28. Cf. Geary, "Nature of Portia's Victory," 62. Bassanio is a "fortune-hunter."

29. Cf. Olivia Delgado de Torres, "Reflection on Patriarchy and the Rebellion of Daughters in Shakespeare's *The Merchant of Venice* and *Othello,*" *Interpretation* 21 (Spring 1994): 343; Bloom, *Shakespeare's Politics,* 24-27.

30. Tovey, "The Golden Casket," 217.

31. *Contra* Holmer: "Only Bassanio, his wisdom revealed in his soliloquy over the caskets, is capable of loving wisely, and therefore his character guarantees the right choice . . ." ("Loving Wisely," 59); and Donow, "Shakespeare's Caskets," 91.

32. Cf. the contrary reading in Lewalski, "Biblical Allusion," 335. She does not note Bassanio's complete failure to attend to the legends or to show any signs of absorbing their point. Also *contra* Hyman, "Rival Lovers," 114.

33. Ovid *Metamorphoses* 7.285-87, Loeb Classical Library, 363.

34. Cf. Tovey, "Golden Casket," 229.

35. Cf. Tovey: "Such a letter is calculated to make Bassanio spend the rest of his life in remorseful remembrance" ("Golden Casket," 225).

36. Emphasis added.

37. Hyman, "Rival Lovers," 112; Geary, "Nature of Portia's Victory," 63, 65.

38. Cf. Tovey: "Bassanio's preference for Antonio could hardly be stated in starker terms" ("Golden Casket," 229).

39. Holmer, "Loving Wisely," 60.

40. In his portrayal of Antonio, Shakespeare has come very close to Nietzsche's understanding of self-denying love in 1.13 of *The Gay Science*: "Even if we offer our lives, as martyrs do for their church, this is a sacrifice that is offered for *our* desire for power or for the purpose of preserving our feeling of power" (trans. Walter Kaufmann [New York: Random House, Vintage Books, 1974], 87); also cf. 1.14. Cf. Tovey, "Golden Casket," 224-225, 233; Bloom, *Shakespeare's Politics,* 19-21; Geary, "Nature of Portia's Victory," 64.

41. Cf. Tovey: "As soon as she hears of Antonio's predicament, Portia clearly recognizes the threat that his imminent martyrdom poses to her married life." ("Golden Casket," 228); cf. Bloom, *Shakespeare's Politics,* 29; Delgado de Torres, "Reflections on Patriarchy," 343; Geary, "Nature of Portia's Victory," 64; Boose, "Comic Contract," 250.

42. See Lewalski, "Biblical Allusion," 329, 338.

43. John 15.12 RSV. Martin Luther, *The Freedom of a Christian,* in *Three Treatises,* trans. W. A. Lambert, revised by Harold J. Grimm (Philadelphia: Fortress Press, 1960), 302-9.

44. Lewalski, "Biblical Allusion," 334, cf. 339; Tovey, "Golden Casket," 227.

45. Cf. Mark 5.1-13.

46. On Shylock's use of the story of Jacob, see Engle, "Exchange and Explanation," 32.

47. Deut. 23.19-20; cf. Deut. 28.12. Note that Deut. 23 joins the very two issues that Shylock joins—usury and uncleanness.

48. Thomas Aquinas *Summa Theologica* 2-2 Q. 78, A1 Resp.

49. *Ibid.* A1, ad obj. 7.

50. On Shylock, see 1.3.110; on Bassanio, see 1.3.140; cf. 139, 150, 165, 175.

51. *Aquinas* 2-2 Q. 78 A1 ob. 2.

52. On Antonio's Christian vision see St. Paul, *Letter to the Galatians,* who sees Christianity as a counter-movement to Judaism along three dimensions:

    Jewish
    Particularistic
    Worldly Prosperity (Flesh)
    Law

    Christian
    Universalistic (cf. esp. Gal. 3.28)
    Spiritual Prosperity
    Faith-Love (cf. Gal. 3.13; 5.13-14)

    According to Antonio's lights at least, Shylock embodies all three of the Jewish traits, and he the Pauline triad.

53. Cf. Deut. 14.

54. Cf. Deut. 14.2, 21, 28-29.

55. Deut. 24.6.

56. Deut. 5.17 RSV.

57. *Contra* Bloom, *Shakespeare's Politics,* 23-24, 27.

58. Deut. 12.15-16 RSV.

59. Deut., 24.6 RSV.

60. See Tovey, "Golden Casket," 232.

61. John 19.7 RSV.

62. Matt. 27.24-25 RSV.

63. Luke 23.4, 14, 22 RSV; cf. John 19.6.

64. Luke 23.23-25; cf. John 19.12-16 RSV.

65. *Contra* Tovey, "Golden Casket," 237.

66. Ovid *Heroides* 12.161-63; Grant Showerman, trans., Loeb Classical Library, 155.

67. Cf. esp. 5.1.47: Bassanio's "horn full of good news."

68. Thus Tovey considerably understates the situation when she says all that remains for Portia is a "chastising" of her unfaithful husband ("Golden Casket," 230). Cf. Hyman: "The climax of the play, Portia's turning the tables on Shylock, is also the high point of Portia's victory over Antonio" ("Rival Lovers," 112).

69. Cf. Hyman, "Rival Lovers," 112.

70. This is quite independent of any suggestion of a homoerotic character of Antonio's feelings for Bassanio. Given the echoes of Christianity in the play, I do not believe this is the point Shakespeare is attempting to explore. Cf. Hyman, "Rival Lovers," 110; Geary, "Nature of Portia's Victory," 59-60, 66. Note that even though Antonio is denied his Christlike sacrifice, he continues to cast the situation in Christian (love) vs. Jewish (commandment) terms.

71. Cf. Plato *Symposium* 177-185; Tovey, "Golden Casket," 233.

72. Boose misses Portia's near despair and near failure in her presentation of Portia as the source of "the castrating manipulations of the benefactress who has strategically orchestrated all such acquisitions" ("Comic Contract," 249).

73. Cf. Gen. 1.3 RSV.

74. Robert Graves, *Greek Myths,* 1:335, 2:253, 258; but cf. Ovid *Metamorphoses* 12.208-9.

75. Cf. John 1.9 RSV.

76. Cf. John 19.5 RSV.

77. Thus Holmer seems to miss almost entirely what has happened in the ring episode when she says that in giving away the ring "Bassanio is as firmly devoted to Portia as ever; . . . the bond is still intact" ("Loving Wisely," 71).

78. See Donow, "Shakespeare's Caskets," 92.

79. Consider Hyman, "Rival Lovers," 115; in his otherwise fine treatment of the play, Geary misses the real dynamic of this episode when he puts its weight on the revelation of Balthazar's identity ("Nature of Portia's Victory," 66). The decisive things have happened before that revelation occurs. Also see Aristotle *Ethics* 1170b30-1171a21.

80. *Contra* Boose, who sees the ending of the play as showing "an anxiously defensive hostility directed against . . . the social bond itself" ("Comic Contract," 251).

81. *Contra* Tovey's identification of Belmont and Portia with Platonic philosophy. At this point this otherwise excellent essay loses touch with the play, as in the judgment that Portia acts "to emancipate the potential philosopher [Bassanio!] from the religion of his city" ("Golden Casket," 234-37).

Tony Tanner (essay date 1999)

SOURCE: Tanner, Tony. "Which Is the Merchant Here? And Which the Jew?: The Venice of Shakespeare's *The Merchant of Venice*." In *Venetian Views, Venetian Blinds: English Fantasies of Venice,* edited by Manfred Pfister and Barbara Schaff, pp. 45-62. Amsterdam: Rodopi, 1999.

[*In the following essay, Tanner analyzes the three crucial locations in* The Merchant of Venice—*Antonio's Rialto Venice, Shylock's Venetian ghetto, and harmonious Belmont—and discusses the troubling elements of this romantic comedy that arise through the juxtaposition of these settings.*]

> see how yond justice rails upon yond simple thief. Hark in thine ear: change places, and handy-dandy, which is the justice, which is the thief?
>
> (*King Lear* IV.vi.151-4)

When Portia, disguised as Balthasar, "a young and learned doctor", enters the Court of Justice in *The Merchant of Venice,* her first, business-like, question is "Which is the merchant here? And which the Jew?" (IV.i.173) It is an astonishing question. We know that Shylock would have been dressed in a "gaberdine", because, we are told, Antonio habitually spits on it. This was a long garment of hard cloth habitually worn by Jews who, since 1412, had been obliged to wear a distinctive robe extending down to the feet. Shylock would have been, literally, a 'marked' man (in a previous century he would have had to wear a yellow hat). Antonio, a rich merchant who, we are again told, habitually comes "so smug upon the mart" (where 'smug' means sleek and well-groomed, as well as our sense of complacently self-satisifed), is more likely to have been dressed in some of the 'silk' in which he trades (look at the sumptuously dressed Venetian merchants in Carpaccio's paintings to get some idea). It would have been unmissably obvious which was the merchant and which was the Jew. So, is that opening question just disingenuousness on Portia/Balthasar's part—or what?

The first act is composed of three scenes set in the three (relatively) discrete places, or areas, each of which has its distinct voices, values, and concerns. Together, they make up the world of the play. I will call these—Rialto Venice; Belmont (Portia's house, some indeterminate distance from Venice; probably best thought of as being like one of those lovely Renaissance palaces still to be seen in the Veneto); and Ghetto Venice (Shylock's realm: the word 'ghetto' never appears in the play, and, as John Gross has pointed out, Shakespeare makes no mention of it. But the name *Ghetto Nuovo* (meaning New Foundry) was the name of the island in Venice on which the Jews were, effectively, sequestered (and from which the generic use of 'ghetto' derives); and, clearly, Shylock lives in a very different Venice from the Venice enjoyed by the confident Christian merchants. Hence my metaphoric use of the name for what, in Shakespeare, is simply designated as 'a public place'). The opening lines of the three scenes are, in sequence:

> In sooth I know not why I am so sad.
> It wearies me, you say it wearies you . . .
>
> By my troth, Nerissa, my little body is aweary of this great world.
>
> Three thousand ducats—well.

Sadness and weariness on the Rialto and in Belmont; money matters in the Ghetto. Is there any inter-connection? Can anything be done?

Antonio speaks first, which is quite appropriate since *he* is the 'Merchant' of the title—not, as some think, Shylock. Had Shakespeare wanted Shylock signalled in his title, he could well have called his play *The Jew of Venice,* in appropriate emulation of Marlowe's *The Jew of Malta* (1589), which was playing in London in 1596 when Shakespeare (almost certainly) started his own play, and which he (most certainly) knew and, indeed, deliberately echoed at certain key points (of which, more by and by). But Shylock is a very different figure from Barabas, who degenerates into a grotesque Machiavellian monster. In fact, Shylock only appears in five of the twenty scenes of the play; though he is, overwhelmingly, the figure who leaves the deepest mark—'incision' perhaps (see later)—on the memory. He shuffles off, broken, beaten, and ill—sadder and wearier than anyone else in Venice or Belmont—at the end of Act Four, never to return. But, while the triumph and victory belong unequivocally to Portia, it is the Jew's play.

However, Antonio is our merchant, and very Hamlet-ish he is, too. He sounds an opening note of inexplicable melancholy:

> But how I caught it, found it, or came by it,
> What stuff 'tis made of, whereof it is born, I am to learn . . .
>
> (I,i,3-5)

We might later have a guess at at least some of the 'stuff' it is made of, but for now Salerio and Solanio (another of those effectively indistinguishable Rosencrantz-and-Guildenstern couples Shakespeare delights in—it offers another 'which-is-which?' puzzle in a lighter key), try to commiserate with him and cheer him up. And in their two speeches, Shakespeare—breathtakingly—manages to convey a whole sense of mercantile Renaissance Venice. Of course, they say, you are understandably worried—"your mind is tossing on the ocean"—about your "argosies" (a very recent English word for large merchant ships, coming from the Venetian Adriatic port of Ragusa—and also used in Marlowe's play). Salerio, packing all the pride and confident arrogance of imperial, incomparable Venice into his lines, imagines those ships as "rich burghers on the flood", or "pageants [magnificent floats in festival and carnival parades] of the sea", which

> Do overpeer the petty traffickers
> That cursy [curtsy] to them, do them reverence,
> As they fly by them with their woven wings.
>
> (I,i,12-14)

Other sea-faring traders are "petty traffickers": Venetian merchants, attracting and exacting world-wide admiration and deference, are something quite superbly else. Solanio chimes in, evoking a merchant's necessary anxieties about winds, maps, ports, piers, and everything that, he says, "might make me fear / Misfortune to my ventures"—'ventures' is a word to watch. Salerio develops the theme, imagining how everything he saw on land would somehow remind him of shipwrecks:

> Should I go to church
> And see the holy edifice of stone
> And not bethink me straight of dangerous rocks,
> Which touching but my gentle vessel's side
> Would scatter all her spices on the stream,
> Enrobe the roaring waters with my silks—
> And in a word, but even now worth this,
> And now worth nothing?
>
> (I,i,29-36)

"But now a king, now thus", says Salisbury when he watches King John die, pondering the awesome mortality of kings (*King John* V,vii,60). In this Venice, there is much the same feeling about the loss of one of their argosies, monarchs (or burghers—it was a republic) of the sea as they were. And what a sense of riches is compacted into the lines imagining spices scattered on the stream, and waves robed in silk—an image of spilt magnificence if ever there was one.

It is important to note Salerio's reference to "church . . . the holy edifice of stone". In one of those contrasts dear to artists, the stillness and fixity of the holy edifice of stone is to be seen behind the flying ships on the tossing oceans and flowing streams—the eternal values of the church conjoined with, and in some way legitimating, the worldly wealth-gathering of the sea-venturing, transient merchants; the spiritual ideals sustaining the material practices. For Venice was a holy city (the Crusades left from there), as well as the centre of a glorious worldly empire. It was an object of awe and fascination to the Elizabethans. Indeed, as Philip Brockbank suggested, Venice was for Renaissance writers what Tyre was for the prophet Isaiah—"the crowning city, whose merchants are princes, whose traffickers are the honourable of the earth" (*Isaiah* 23:8). But Tyre was also a "harlot" who made "sweet music", and Isaiah prophesies that it "shall commit fornication with all the kingdoms of the world" (Venice was also famed, or notorious, for its alleged sensualities—in Elizabethan London there was a brothel simply named 'Venice'). But, also this about Tyre:

> And her merchandise and her hire shall be holiness to the Lord: for it shall not be treasured nor laid up; for her merchandise shall be for them that dwell before the Lord, to eat sufficiently, and for durable clothing.
>
> (23:18)

Traditionally, religion is ascetic and preaches a rejection of worldly goods. But here we see religion and the 'use of riches' creatively reconciled—and by spending, not hoarding. As Tyre, so Venice. But there is, in *Isaiah,* an apocalyptic warning—that God will turn the whole city "upside down" and "scatter" the inhabitants—

> And it shall be, as with the people, so with the priest . . . as with the buyer, so with the seller; as with the lender, so with the borrower; as with the taker of usury, so with the giver of usury to him. The land shall be utterly emptied, and utterly spoiled: for the Lord hath spoken this word.
>
> (24:2,3)

Ruskin would say that that was effectively what *did* happen to Venice. But that is another story. The point for us here is that the Venetian setting of his play allowed Shakespeare to pursue his exploratory interest in (I quote Brockbank)

> the relationship between the values of empire and those of the aspiring affections, human and divine; those of the City of Man and those of the City of God . . . between the values we are encouraged to cultivate in a mercantile, moneyed and martial society, and those which are looked for in Christian community and fellowship; between those who believe in the gospel teachings of poverty, humility and passivity, and those who (as the creative hypocrisy requires) pretend to.

Returning to the play, Solanio says that if Antontio is not sad on account of his "merchandise", then he must be in love. Antonio turns away the suggestion with a "Fie, fie!". As it happens, I think this is close to the mark, but we will come to that. Here Solanio gives up on trying to find a reason for Antonio's gloom—

> Then let us say you are sad
> Because you are not merry; and 'twere as easy
> For you to laugh and leap, and say you are merry.
>
> (I,i,47-9)

And he leaves with Salerio, who says to Antonio—"I would have stayed till I had made you merry". 'Merry' is a lovely word from old English, suggesting pleasing, amusing, agreeable, full of lively enjoyment. "To be merry best becomes you," says Don Pedro to the vivacious Beatrice "for out o' question, you were born in a merry hour" (*Much Ado* II,i,313-4)—and we feel he has chosen just the right word. The princely merchants of Venice favour the word, for, in their aristocratic way, they believe in 'merriment'. It is an unequivocally positive word; it has no dark side, and carries no shadow. Yet in this play, Shakespeare makes it become ominous. When Shylock suggests to Antonio that he pledges a pound of his flesh as surety for the three thousand ducat loan, he refers to it as a "merry bond", signed in a spirit of "merry sport" (I,iii,170,142). The word has lost its innocence and is becoming sinister. The last time we hear it is from Shylock's daughter, Jessica in Belmont—"I am never merry when I hear sweet music" (V,i,69). After her private duet with Lorenzo, nobody speaks to Jessica in Belmont and these are, indeed, her last words in the play. It is hard to feel that she will be happily assimilated into the Belmont world. Something has happened to 'merry-ness', and although Belmont is, distinctly, an abode of "sweet music", a note of un-merry sadness lingers in the air.

When Bassanio enters with Gratiano, he says to the departing Salerio and Solanio, as if reproachfully, "You grow exceeding strange; must it be so?" (I,i,67) It is a word which recurs in a variety of contexts, and it reminds us that there is 'strangeness' in Venice, centring on Shylock, whose "strange apparent cruelty" (IV,i,21) is some sort of reflection of, response to, the fact that he is treated like "a stranger cur" (I,iii,115) in Venice. And he is, by law, an alien in the city—the stranger within. Gratiano then has a go at Antonio—"You look not well, Signior Antonio" ("I am not well", says Shylock, as he leaves the play—IV,i,395: now the merchant, now the Jew. Sickness circulates in Venice, along with all the other 'trafficking').

> You have too much respect upon the world;
> They lose it that do buy it with much care.
> Believe me, you are marvelously changed.
>
> (I,i,74-6)

His scripture is a little awry here: what people lose who gain the whole world is the *soul,* not the world. A *mondain* Venetian's slip, perhaps. But we are more likely to be alerted by the phrase 'marvelously changed'. Shakespearian comedy is full of marvellous changes, and we may be considering what transformations, marvellous or otherwise, occur in this play. In the event, the 'changes' turn out to be far from unambiguous 'conversions'. Somewhere behind all these conversions is the absolutely basic phenomenon whereby material is converted into 'merchandise' which is then converted into money—which, as Marx said, can then convert, or 'transform' just about anything into just about anything else. It is perhaps worth remembering that Marx praised Shakespeare, in particular, for showing that money had the power of a god, while it behaved like a whore.

Jessica willingly converts to Christianity, hoping for salvation, at least from her father's house, but it hardly seems to bring, or promise, any notable felicity or grace. Shylock is forced to convert to Christianity—which, however construed by the Christians (he would thereby be 'saved'), is registered as a final humiliation and the stripping away of the last shred of his identity. When Portia gives herself to Bassanio, she says:

> Myself, and what is mine, to you and yours
> Is now converted.
>
> (III,ii,166-7)

and this is to be felt as a willing conversion, a positive transformation—just as she will, like a number of other heroines, 'change' herself into a man to effect some genuine salvation. Sad Antonio, it has to be said, is not much changed at all at the end—though his life has been saved, and his ships have come sailing in. Venice itself, as represented, is hardly changed; not, that is, renewed or redeemed—though it is a good deal more at ease with itself for having got rid of Shylock. If that is what it *has* done. One hardly feels that, as it were, the realm has been purged, and that the malcontent threatening the joy of the festive conclusion has been happily exorcised. The play does not really end quite so 'well' as that. It is not a 'metamorphic' celebration.

It is Bassanio's plea for financial help from Antonio that concludes the first scene, and the way in which he does so is crucial to an appreciation of what follows. He admits that he has "disabled mine estate" by showing "a more swelling port" than he could afford. 'Swelling port' is 'impressively lavish life-style', but I think we will remember the 'portly sail' of the Venetian argosies just referred to, also, no doubt, 'swollen' by the winds (cf the 'big-bellied sails' in *A Midsummer Night's Dream*). The Venetian princely way of life is both pregnant and distended—fecund and excessive. As Bassanio is, however inadvertently, recognising by using a key word: he is worried about his 'great debts'

> Wherein my time, something too prodigal,
> Hath left me gaged.
>
> (I,ii,1490-50)

Shylock calls Antonio a "prodigal Christian", and it was always a fine point to decide to what extent 'prodigality' was compatible with Christianity (think of the parables of the Prodigal Son, and the Unjust Steward), and to what extent it contravened it. It is one of those words which look two ways, pointing in one direction to the magnanimous bounty of an Antony, and in the other to the ruinous squandering of a Timon. Clearly, the munificent prodigality of Antonio is in every way preferable to the obsessive meanness and parsimony of Shylock. But there is a crucial speech on this subject, tucked away, as was sometimes Shakespeare's wont, where you might least expect it. Salerio and Gratiano are whiling away the time in front of Shylock's house, waiting to help Lorenzo in the abduction of Jessica. Salerio is saying that lovers are much more eager to consummate the marriage than they are to remain faithful ('keep obliged faith') subsequently. "That ever holds" says Gratiano:

> All things that are
> Are with more spirit chased than enjoyed.
> How like a younger or a prodigal
> The scarfed bark puts from her native bay,
> Hugged and embraced by the strumpet wind!
> How like the prodigal doth she return,
> With over-weathered ribs and ragged sails,
> Lean, rent, and beggared by the strumpet wind.
>
> (II,vi,12-19)

An apt enough extended metaphor in a mercantile society, and the Venetians must have seen many ship sail out 'scarfed' (decorated with flags and streamers) and limp back 'rent'. It may be added that Gratiano is something of a cynical young blade. But the speech stands as a vivid reminder of one possible fate of 'prodigality', *and* of marriage. Ultimately of Venice too, perhaps.

Bassanio, whatever else he is (scholar, courtier) is a 'prodigal', and he wants to clear his 'debts'. Antonio immediately says that "my purse, my person" (a nice near pun, given the close inter-involvement of money and body in this play) "lie all unlocked to your occasions" (I,i,139). This open liberality might be remembered when we later hear the frantically retentive and self-protective Shylock (a name not found outside this play) repeatedly warning Jessica to "look to my house . . . lock up my doors . . . shut doors after you" (II,v,16,29,52). The difference is clear enough, and need not be laboured. Antonio also positively invites Bassanio to "make waste of all I have" (I,i,157)—insouciantly negligent aristocrats like to practise what Yeats called 'the wasteful virtues'. The contrast with 'thrifty' Shylock, again, does not need underlining.

But Bassanio has another possible solution to his money problems; one which depends on 'adventuring' and 'hazard'.

> In Belmont is a lady richly left;
> And she is fair and, fairer than that word,
> Of wondrous virtues . . .
> Nor is the wide world ignorant of her worth,
> For the four winds blow in from every coast
> Renowned suitors, and her sunny locks
> Hang on her temples like a golden fleece,
> Which makes her seat of Belmont Colchos' strand,
> And many Jasons come in quest of her.
> O my Antonio, had I but the means
> To hold a rival place with one of them,
> I have a mind presages me such thrift
> That I should questionless be fortunate!
>
> (I,i,161-176)

Antonio, all his wealth at sea, at the moment has neither "money, nor commodity"; but he will use his "credit" to get "the means". He will borrow the *money* from Shylock to finance Bassanio's quest of a second *golden* fleece. So it is that the seemingly discrete worlds of the Ghetto, the Rialto, and Belmont are, from the beginning, indeed, inter-involved.

Venice, as we have seen it and will see it, is overwhelmingly a man's world of public life; it is conservative, dominated by law, bound together by contracts, underpinned by money—and closed. Belmont is run by women living the private life; it is liberal, animated by love, harmonised by music and poetry ('fancy'), sustained by gold—and open. However cynical one wants to be, it will not do to see Belmont as "only Venice come into a windfall" (Ruth Nevo). It is better to see it as in a line of civilised, gracious retreats, stretching from Horace's Sabine farm, through Sidney's Penshurst, Jane Austen's Mansfield Park, up to Yeats's Coole Park. As Brockbank said, such places ideally offered "the prospect of a protected life reconciling plenitude, exuberance, simplicity and order." It was Sidney who said that "our world is brazen, the poets only deliver a golden", and you might see Belmont as a kind of 'golden' world which has been 'delivered' from the 'brazen' world of trade and money. Yes, somewhere back along the line, it is all grounded in ducats; but you must think of the churches, palaces, art works and monuments of the Renaissance, made possible by varying forms of patronage, and appreciate that the "courtiers, merchants and bankers of the Renaissance found ways of transmuting worldly goods into spiritual treasure" (Brockbank). Belmont is a privileged retreat from Venice; but, as Portia will show, it can also fruitfully engage with it.

In scene two, we are in Belmont, and Portia is weary. Partly surely, because she must be bored stiff with the suitors who have come hopefully buzzing round the honey-pot—the silent Englishman, the mean Scotsman, the vain Frenchman, the drunken German, and so on, as she and Nerissa amuse themselves discussing their different intolerabilities. But, more importantly, because she is under the heavy restraint of a paternal interdiction (familiar enough in comedy, though this one comes from beyond the grave). She has been deprived of *choice*—and she wants a mate. Then we learn from Nerissa about the lottery of the casquets, which she thinks was the "good inspiration" of a "virtuous" and "holy" man. We shall see. But we note that, in this, Belmont (in the form of Portia) is as much under the rule of (male) law as Venice. There are "laws for the blood" in both places, and they may by no means be "leaped" or "skipped" over (I,ii,17ff.). In other comedies, we see inflexible, intractable, unmitigatable law magically, mysteriously melt away or be annulled. Not in this play. Here, the law is followed, or pushed, to the limit—and beyond. Indeed, you might say that Belmont has to come to Venice to help discover this 'beyond' of the law.

And now, in scene three, we are in Shylock's Venice; and we hear, for the first time, what will become an unmistakable voice—addressing, as it were, the bottom line in Venice: "three thousand ducats—well". Shylock speaks in—unforgettable—prose, and this marks something of a crucial departure for Shakespeare. Hitherto, he had reserved prose for, effectively, exclusively comic (usually 'low') characters. With Shylock, this all changes. For Shylock is *not* a comic character. He has a power, a pain, a passion, a dignity—and, yes, a savagery, and a suffering—which, whatever they are, are not comic.

On his first appearance, Shylock establishes his 'Jewishness' by, among other things, revealing his adherence to Jewish dietary rules—"I will not eat with you, drink with you, nor pray with you" (I,iii,34-5). But when Antonio appears, Shylock reveals a darker side of his nature in an 'aside':

> I hate him for he is a Christian;
> But more, for that in low simplicity
> He lends out money gratis, and brings down
> The rate of usance here with us in Venice.
> . . . . .
> He hates our sacred nation, and he rails,
> Even there where merchants most do congregate,
> On me, my bargains, and my well-won thrift,
> Which he calls interest. Cursed be my tribe
> If I forgive him.
>
> (I,iii,39-49)

Shylock gives three good reasons for his hating of Antonio—insofar as one can have *good* reasons for hatred: personal, professional, tribal. This is interesting in view of his response during the trial scene, when he is asked why he would not prefer to have ducats rather than Antonio's flesh:

> So can I give no reason, nor I will not,
> More than a lodged hate and a certain loathing
> I bear Antonio . . .
>
> (IV,i,59-61)

His opening exchange with Antonio really defines the central concern of the play, and is crucial. He has already mentioned 'usance' ('a more cleanly name for usury'), 'thrift' (which means both prosperity and frugality—'thrift, Horatio, thrift'), and 'interest'. And 'usury', of course, is the heart of the matter. Any edition of the play will tell you that the law against lending money at interest was lifted in 1571, and a rate of 10% was made legal. Queen Elizabeth depended on money borrowed at interest, so did most agriculture, industry, and foreign trade by the end of the sixteenth century (according to R H Tawney). So, indeed, did Shakespeare's own Globe Theatre. Plenty of Christians lent money at interest (including Shakespeare's own father); and Bacon, writing "Of Usury" in 1625, said "to speak of the abolishing of usury is idle". Antonio, scattering his interest-free loans around Venice, is certainly an 'idealised' picture of the merchant, just as Shylock sharpening his knife to claim his debt, is a 'demonised' one. But Aristotle and Christianity had spoken against usury, and there was undoubtedly a good deal of residual unease and ambivalence about it. Ruthless usurers were thus especially hated and abused, and since Jews were identified as quintessential usurious money-lenders, (and, of course, had killed Christ), they were available for instant and constant execration. This must certainly be viewed as a collective hypocrisy—one of those 'projections' by which society tries to deal with a bad conscience (not that Shakespeare would have seen many Jews in London; it is estimated that there were less than two hundred at the time). Shakespeare was not addressing a contemporary problem; rather, he was exploring some of the ambivalences and hypocrises, the value clashes and requisite doublenesses, which inhere in, and attend upon, all commerce.

The play is full of commercial and financial terms: 'moneys', 'usances', 'bargains', 'credit', 'excess' and 'advantage' (both used of usury and profit), 'trust', 'bond' (which occurs vastly more often than in any other play: curiously 'contract' is *not* used—Shakespeare wants us to focus on 'bond'), 'commodity' and 'thrift'. Launcelot Gobbo is "an unthrifty knave", while Jessica flees from her father's house with "an unthrift love". This last serves as a reminder that both here and elsewhere in Shakespeare the language of finance and usury could be used as a paradoxical image of love (happiness accrues and passion grows by a form of *natural* interest). You will hear it in Belmont as well as on the Rialto. When Portia gives herself to Bassanio, she, as it were, breaks the bank:

> I would he trebled twenty times myself,
> A thousand times more fair, ten thousand times more rich,
> That only to stand high in your account,
> I might in virtues, beauties, livings, friends,
> Exceed account.
>
> (III,ii, 153-7)

Rich place, Belmont; generous lover, Portia!

The absolutely central exchange occurs when Antonio and Shylock discuss 'interest', or 'borrowing upon advantage'. "I do never use it" declares Antonio (what is the relationship between 'use' and 'usury'? Another consideration.) Shylock replies, seemingly rather inconsequentially: "When Jacob grazed his uncle Laban's sheep. . . ." Antonio brings him to the point. "And what of him? Did he take interest?" Shylock seems to prevaricate: "No, not take interest—not as you would say / Directly int'rest" and then recounts the story from Genesis. This tells how Jacob tricked—but is that the right word?—his exploitative uncle, Laban: they agreed that, for his hire, Jacob should be entitled to any lambs, in the flocks he was tending, that were born "streaked and pied". Following the primitive belief that what a mother sees during conception has an effect on the offspring, Jacob stripped some "wands" (twigs or branches), so that some were light while others were dark, and "stuck them up before the fulsome ewes" as the rams were impregnating them. In the subsequent event, a large number of "parti-coloured lambs" were born, which of course went to Jacob. Nice work; but was it also sharp practice? Or was it both, and so much the better? Or, does it matter? Not as far as Shylock is concerned:

> This was a way to thrive, and he was blest;
> And thrift is blessing if men steal it not.
>
> (I,iii,86f.)

'Ewes' may be a pun on 'use'; and for Shylock, it is as legitimate to use ewes in the field as it is to use usury on the 'mart'. Not so for Antonio:

> This was a venture, sir, that Jacob served for,
> A thing not in his power to bring to pass,
> But swayed and fashioned by the hand of heaven.
> Was this inserted to make interest good?
> Or is your gold and silver ewes and lambs?
>
> (88-92)

And Shylock:

> I cannot tell; I make it breed as fast.
>
> (88-93)

Antonio's last line effectively poses *the* question of the play. It was a line often quoted, (or more often, slightly misquoted), by Ezra Pound in his increasingly unbalanced vituperations against usury and Jews. The root feeling behind it is that it is somehow *unnatural* for inorganic matter (gold, silver, money) to reproduce itself in a way at least analogous to the natural reproductions in the organic realm ("they say it is against nature for *Money* to beget *Money*", says Bacon, quoting Aristotle). This enables Antonio to reject Shylock's self-justifying analogy: Jacob's story does *not* "make interest good", because he was having, or making, a "venture", and the result was, inevitably, "swayed and fashioned" by—heaven? nature? some power not his own. This, revealingly, was how Christian commentators of the time justified Jacob's slightly devious behaviour (as Frank Kermode pointed out)—he was making a *venture*. Antonio's ships are 'ventures', and Bassanio is on a venture when he 'adventures forth' to Belmont. It seems that the element of 'risk' (= to run into danger) and 'hazard' purifies or justifies the act. As 'hazard' was originally an Arabian word for a gaming die, this would seem to enable gambling to pass moral muster as well. Perhaps it does. Whatever, there is seemingly *no* risk, as well as no nature, in usury. Shylock's answer, that he makes his money "breed as fast", is thought to tell totally against him; and Bassanio's subsequent remark, "for when did friendship take / A breed for barren metal of his friend?" (I,iii,130-1), is taken to orient our sympathies, and values, correctly. But this won't quite do.

Because, like it or not, money most certainly *does* 'breed'. It may not literally copulate, but there is no way round the metaphor. Sigurd Burckhardt is the only commentator I have read who has seen this clearly, and he wrote: "metal ['converted' into money] is not barren, it does breed, is pregnant with consequences, and capable of transformation into life and art". For a start, it gets Bassanio to Belmont, and the obtaining of Portia and the Golden Fleece (or Portia *as* a golden fleece). And, as if to signal his awareness of the proximity, even similitude, of the two types of 'breeding', with the lightest of touches: when Gratiano announces he is to marry Nerissa at the same time as Bassanio marries Portia, Shakespeare has him add—"We'll play with them the first boy for a thousand ducats" (III,ii,214). You 'play' for babies, and you 'play' for ducats. Which also means that when Shylock runs through the streets crying "O my ducats! O my daughter!", (echoing Marlowe's Barabas who cries out "oh, my girl, my gold", but when his daughter *restores* his wealth to him), we should not be quite so quick to mock him as the little Venetian urchins. He may not use his money to such life-enhancing and generous ends as some of the more princely Venetians; but he has been doubly bereaved (which literally means—robbed, *reaved,* on all sides, *be-*).

Having mentioned that robbery, I will just make one point about the Jessica and Lorenzo sub-plot. However sorry we may feel for Jessica, living in a 'hell' of a house with her father; the behaviour of the two lovers is only to be deprecated. Burckhardt is absolutely right again: "their love is lawless, financed by theft and engineered by a gross breach of trust". Jessica "gilds" herself with ducats, and throws a casket of her father's wealth down to Lorenzo ("Here, catch this casket; it is worth the pains" II,vi,33—another echo-with-a-difference of Marlowe's play, in which Abigail throws down her father's wealth from a window, to her *father*). This is an anticipatory parody, travesty rather, of Portia, the Golden (not 'gilded') Fleece, waiting to see if Bassanio will pass the test of *her* father's caskets (containing wisdom, rather than simple ducats). He 'hazards' all; this couple risk nothing. They squander eighty ducats in a night—folly, not bounty. Jessica exchanges the ring her mother gave her father as a love-pledge, for—a monkey! They really do make a monkey out of marriage—I will come to their famous love duet in due course. Their's is the reverse, or inverse, of a true love match. It must be intended to contrast with the marriage made by Bassanio and Portia. This marriage also, admittedly, involves wealth—as it does paternal caskets; but, and the difference is vital, wealth *not gained or used in the same way.*

Those caskets! Shakespeare took nearly everything that he wanted for his plot (including settings, characters, even the ring business in Act V) from a tale in *Il Pecorone* (The Dunce), a collection of stories assembled by Giovanni Fiorentino, published in Italy in 1558—everything except the trial of the caskets. In the Italian story, to win the lady, the hero has to demonstrate to her certain powers of sexual performance and endurance. Clearly, this was not quite the thing for a Shakespearean heroine. So Shakespeare took the trial-by-caskets from a tale in the thirteenth-century *Gesta Romanorum,* which had been translated into English. Here, a young woman has to choose between three vessels—gold, silver, lead—to discover whether she is worthy to be the wife of the Emperor's son. All we need note about it is one significant change that Shakespeare made in the inscriptions on the vessels/caskets. Those on the gold and silver ones are effectively the same in each case—roughly, "Who chooseth me shall gain/get what he desires/ deserves". But in the mediaeval tale, the lead casket bears the inscription *"Thei that chese me, shulle fynde [in] me that God hath disposid".* Now, since the young woman is a good Christian, she could hardly have been told more clearly that this was the one to go for. It is, we may say, no test at all. Shakespeare changes the inscription to "Who chooseth me must give and hazard all he hath" (II,vii,9). This is a very different matter. Instead of being promised a placid and predictable demonstration of piety rewarded, we are in that dangerous world of risk and hazard which, at various levels, constitutes the mercantile world of the play. And to the prevailing lexicon of 'get' and 'gain' has been added the even more important word—'give'. One of the concerns of the play is the conjoining of *giving* and *gaining* in the most appropriate way, so that they may 'frutify' together (if I may borrow Launcelot Gobbo's inspired malapropism). "I come by note, *to give* and *to receive*", Bassanio announces to Portia (III,ii,140—my italics). Which is no less than honesty.

While she is anxiously waiting as Bassanio inspects the caskets, Portia says:

> Now he goes,
> With no less presence, but with much more love,
> Than young Alcides [Hercules], when he did redeem
> The virgin tribute paid by howling Troy
> To the sea monster. I stand for sacrifice;
> The rest aloof are the Dardanian wives,
> With bleared visages come forth to view
> The issue of th' exploit. Go, Hercules!
>
> (lII,ii,53-60)

The "virgin tribute" was Hesione, and her rescue by Hercules is described in Book XI of Ovid's *Metamorphoses* (where it is preceded by stories concerning Orpheus, who turned everything to music, and Midas, who turned everything to gold—they are both referred to in the play, and are hovering mythic presences behind it). Portia's arresting claim—"I stand for sacrifice"—resonates through the play; to be darkly echoed by Shylock in court—"I stand for judgment . . . I stand here for law" (IV,i,103,142). When she says "stand for", does she mean 'represent', or 'embody'; or does she imply that she is in danger of being 'sacrificed' to the law of her father, unless rescued by right-choosing Hercules-Bassanio? Or is it just that women are always, in effect, 'sacrificed' to men in marriage, hence the "bleared visages" of those "Dardanian wives"? Something of all of these, perhaps. In the event, it is Portia herself who, effectively rescues, or—her word—'redeems', not Troy, but Venice. Bassanio (courtier, scholar, *and* fortune-seeker) is, as we have seen, if not more, then as much Jason as Hercules. The point is, I think, that he has to be *both* as cunning as the one *and* as bold as the other. The 'both-ness' is important.

This is how Bassanio thinks his way to the choice of the correct casket:

> So may the outward shows be least themselves;
> The world is still deceived with ornament.
> In law, what pleas so tainted and corrupt,
> But being seasoned with a gracious voice,
> Obscures the show of evil?
>
> (III,ii,73-7)

This, *mutatis mutandis,* is a theme in Shakespeare from first to last—"all that glitters is not gold", and so on (II,vii,65). Bassanio is on very sure grounds in rejecting the gold and silver and opting for lead, *in the context of the test.* But—'ornament': from *ornare*—to equip, to adorn. Now, if ever there was an equipped and adorned city, it was Venice. It is aware of dangerous seas and treacherous shores, of course; but it is *also* a city of beauteous scarves, and silks and species—and what are they but 'ornaments' for the body and for food? Bassanio is an inhabitant and creation of an ornamented world, and is himself, as we say, an 'ornament' to it. So why does he win by *going through a show* of rejecting it? He wins, because he realises that he has to subscribe to the unadorned modesty of lead, *even while* going for the ravishing glory of gold. *That* was the sort of complex intelligence Portia's father had in mind for his daughter. Is it hypocrisy? Then we must follow Brockbank and call it "creative hypocrisy". It recognises the compromising, and willing-to-compromise, doubleness of values on which a worldly society (a society in the world) necessarily rests, and by which it is sustained. The leaden virtues, and the golden pleasures. Bothness.

Such is the reconciling potency of Belmont; and Portia seals the happy marriage with a ring. But, meanwhile, Shylock is waiting back in Venice for his pound of flesh, and he *must* be satisfied. Must—because he has the law on his side, and Venice lives by law; its wealth and reputation depend on honouring contracts and bonds—as Shylock is the first to point out: "If you deny [my bond], let danger light / Upon your charter and your city's freedom". Portia, as lawyer Balthasar, agrees: "There is no power in Venice / Can alter a decree established" (IV,i,38-9,220-1). "I stay here on my bond" (IV,i,241)—if he says the word 'bond' once, he says it a dozen times (it occurs over thirty times in this play—never more than six times in other plays). We are in a world of law where 'bonds' are absolutely binding. Portia's beautiful speech exhorting to 'mercy' is justly famous; but, as Burckhardt remarked, it is impotent and useless in this 'court of justice', a realm which is under the rule of the unalterable letter of the law. Her sweet and humane lyricism founders against harsh legal literalism. The tedious, tolling reiteration of the word 'bond' has an effect which musicians know as 'devaluation through repetition'. The word becomes emptier and emptier of meaning, though still having its deadening effect. It is as if they are all in the grip of a mindless mechanism, which brings them to a helpless, dumb, *impasse*; with Shylock's dagger quite legally poised to strike. Shylock, it is said, is adhering to the old Hebraic notion of the law—an eye for an eye. He has not been influenced by the Christian saying of St Paul: "The letter killeth but the spirit giveth life." For Shylock, the spirit *is* the letter; and Antonio can only be saved *by* the letter. It is as though Portia will have to find resources in literalism which the law didn't know it had.

> Tarry a little; there is something else.
> The bond doth give thee here no jot of blood;
> The words *expressly* are "a pound of flesh."
> Take then thy bond . . .

Shed thou no blood, nor cut thou less nor more
But just a pound of flesh.

(IV,i,304-7, 324-5; my italics)

Ex-press: to press out. Portia squeezes new life and salvation out of the dead and deadly law—and not by extenuation or circumvention or equivocation. "How every fool can play upon the word!", says Lorenzo, in response to Launcelot's quibbles. But you can't 'play' your way out of the Venetian law courts. Any solution must be found within the precincts of stern, rigorous law. "The Jew shall have all justice . . . He shall have merely justice and his bond". (IV,i,320,338) And, to Shylock: "Thou shalt have justice more than thou desir'st". (315) Portia makes literalism yield a life-saving further reach. Truly, the beyond of law.

Life-saving for Antonio—and for Venice itself, we may say. But not, of course, for Shylock. He simply crumples; broken by his own bond, destroyed by the law he "craved". But prior to this, his speeches have an undeniable power, and a strangely compelling sincerity. Necessarily unaristocratic, and closer to the streets (and the ghetto life back there somewhere), his speech in general has a force, and at times a passionate directness, which makes the more 'ornamented' speech of some of the more genteel Christians sound positively effete. Though his defeat is both necessary and gratifying—the cruel hunter caught with his own device—there is something terrible in the spectacle of his breaking. "I pray you give me leave to go from hence. I am not well." (IV,i,394-5) And Gratiano's cruel, jeering ridicule, with which he taunts and lacerates Shylock through the successive blows of his defeat, does Christianity, does humanity, no credit. Like the malcontent or kill-joy in any comedy, Shylock has to be extruded by the regrouping, revitalised community, and he is duly chastised, humiliated, stripped, and despatched—presumably back to the Ghetto. He is never seen again; but it is possible to feel him as a dark, suffering absence throughout the final Act in Belmont. And in fact, he does make one last, indirect 'appearance'. When Portia brings the news that Shylock has been forced to leave all his wealth to Jessica and Lorenzo, the response is—"Fair ladies, you drop manna in the way / Of starved people." (V,i,293-4) 'Manna' was, of course, what fell from heaven and fed the children of Israel in the wilderness. This is the only time Shakespeare uses the word; and, just for a second, its deployment here—at the height of the joy in Christian Belmont—reminds us of the long archaic biblical past stretching back behind Shylock—who also, just for a second, briefly figures, no matter how unwillingly, as a version of the Old Testament God, providing miraculous sustenance for *his* 'children' (a point made by John Gross).

But why did not Shakespeare end his play with the climactic defeat of Shylock—why a whole extra Act with that ring business? Had he done so, it would have left Venice unequivocally triumphant, which perhaps he didn't quite want. This is the last aspect of the play I wish to address, and I must do so somewhat circuitously. Perhaps Shylock's most memorable claim is:

I am a Jew. Hath not a Jew eyes? Hath not a Jew hands, organs, dimensions, senses, affections, passion?—fed with the same food, hurt with the same weapons, subject to the same diseases, healed by the same means, warmed and cooled by the same winter and summer as a Christian is? If you prick us, do we not bleed?

(III,i,55-61)

That last question, seemingly rhetorical (of course you do), but eventually crucial (Shylock seems to have overlooked the fact that if he pricks Antonio, *he* will bleed too), is prepared for, in an admittedly small way, by the first suitor to attempt the challenge of the caskets. The Prince of Morocco starts by defending the "shadowed livery" of his "complexion", as against "the fairest creature northward born":

And let us make incision for your love
To prove whose blood is reddest, his or mine.

(II,i,6-7)

So, a black and a Jew claiming an equality with white Venetian gentle/gentiles (another word exposed to examination in the course of the play), which I have not the slightest doubt Shakespeare fully accorded them (the princely Morocco, in fact, comes off rather better than the silvery French aristocrat who follows him). And Morocco's hypothetical 'incision' anticipates the literal incision which Shylock seeks to make in Antonio. When Bassanio realises that Portia is going to ask to see her ring, which he has given away, he says in an aside:

Why, I were best cut my left hand off
And swear I lost the ring defending it.

(V,i,177-8)

So, there may be 'incisions' made 'for love', from hate, and out of guilt. Portia describes the wedding ring as

A thing stuck on with oaths upon your finger,
And so riveted with faith unto your flesh.

(V,i,168-9)

'Rivetting on' is, I suppose, the opposite of Shylock's intended cutting out; but, taken together, there is a recurrent linking of law (oaths, bonds, rings)—and flesh. The play could be said to hinge on *two* contracts or bonds, in which, or by which, the law envisions, permits, requires, ordains, the exposing of a part of the body of one party to the legitimate penetration (incision) by the other party to the bond. If that party is Shylock, the penetration/incision would be done out of hate—and would prove fatal; if that other party is Bassanio it should be done out of love—and give new life. Shylock swears by his 'bond'; Portia works through her 'ring'.

It should be noted that, in the last Act, when Bassanio is caught out with having given Portia's ring away to Balthasar, he stands before Portia as guilty and helpless as Antonio stood before Shylock. And, like Shylock, she insists on the letter of the pledge, and will hear no excuses and is not interested in mercy. Like Shylock too, she promises her own form of 'fleshly' punishment (absence from Bassanio's bed, and promiscuous infidelity with others). As with the word 'bond' in the court scene, so with the word 'ring' in this last scene. It occurs twenty-one times, and at times is repeated so often that it risks suffering the semantic depletion which seemed to numb 'bond' into emptiness. *Both* the word 'bond' and the word 'ring'—and all they represent in terms of binding/bonding—are endangered in this play. But the law stands—and continues to stand; bonds must be honoured or society collapses: there is nothing Bassanio can do. Then, just as Portia-as-Balthasar found a way through the Venetian *impasse,* so Portia-as-Portia has the life-giving power to enable Bassanio to *renew* his bond—she gives him, mysteriously and to him inexplicably, the same ring, for a second time. (She has mysterious, inexplicable good news for Antonio, too, about the sudden safe arrival of his ships.) A touch of woman's magic. For Portia is one of what Brockbank called Shakespeare's "creative manipulators" (of whom Prospero is the last). Like Vincentio (in *Measure for Measure*), she uses "craft against vice". She can be a skilful man in Venice (a veritable Jacob), and a tricky, resourceful, ultimately loving and healing woman in Belmont (a good Medea with something of the art of Orpheus—both figures invoked in the scene). She can gracefully operate in, and move between, both worlds. Because she is, as it were, a man-woman, as good a lawyer as she is a wife—more 'both-ness'; she figures a way in which law and love, law and blood, need not be mutually exclusive and opposed forces. She shows how they, too, can 'frutify' together.

The person who both persuades Bassanio to give away his ring, and intercedes for him with Portia ("I dare be bound again") is Antonio. He is solitary and sad at the beginning, and is left alone at the end. He expresses his love for Bassanio in an extravagant, at times tearful way. It is a love which seems to be reciprocated. In the court scene, Bassanio protests to Antonio that

> life itself, my wife, and all the world
> Are not with me esteemed above thy life.
> I would lose all, ay sacrifice them all
> Here to this devil to deliver you.

Portia, (she certainly does "stand for sacrifice"!), permits herself an understandably dry comment:

> Your wife would give you little thanks for that
> If she were by to hear you make the offer.
>
> (IV,i,283-8)

Perhaps this is why she decides to put Bassanio to the test with the ring. I do, of course, recognise the honourable tradition of strong male friendship, operative at the time. I also know that 'homosexuality', as such, was not invented until the late nineteenth century. I am also totally disinclined to seek out imagined sexualities which are nothing to the point. But Antonio is so moistly, mooningly in love with Bassanio (and so conspicuously uninvolved with, and unattracted to, any woman), that I think that his nameless sadness, and seemingly foredoomed solitariness, may fairly be attributed to a homosexual passion, which must now be frustrated since Bassanio is set on marriage. (Antonio's message to Bassanio's wife is: "bid her be judge / Whether Bassanio had not once a love", which implies 'lover' as much as 'friend'; revealingly, Antonio's one remaining desire is that Bassanio should witness the fatal sacrifice he is to make for him.) Even then, we might say that that is neither here nor there. Except for one fact. Buggery and usury were *very* closely associated or connected in the contemporary mind as unnatural acts. Shylock is undoubtedly a usurer, who becomes unwell; but if Antonio is, not to put too fine a point on it, a buggerer, who is also unwell, well. . . .

Perhaps some will find the suggestion offensively irrelevant; and perhaps it is. But the atmosphere in Venice-Belmont, is not unalloyedly pure. The famous love duet between Lorenzo and Jessica which starts Act Five, inaugurating the happy post-Shylock era—"In such a night . . ."—is hardly an auspicious one, invoking as it does a faithless woman (Cressid), one who committed suicide (Thisbe), an abandoned woman (Dido), and a sorceress (Medea whose spells involved physical mutilation), before moving on to a contemporary female thief—Jessica herself. I hardly think that she and Lorenzo will bear any mythological 'ornamenting'. And that theft has become part of the texture of the Belmont world. It is a place of beautiful music and poetry—and love; but with perhaps just a residual something-not-quite-right lingering from the transactions and 'usages' of Ghetto-Rialto Venice. (The very last word of the play is a punningly obscene use of 'ring' by Gratiano, the most scabrous and cynical voice in Venice—again, a slightly off-key note.) There is moonlight and candle-light for the nocturnal conclusion of the play, but it doesn't 'glimmer' as beautifully as it did at the end of *A Midsummer Night's Dream*. Portia says:

> This night methinks is but the daylight sick;
> It looks a little paler. 'Tis a day
> Such as the day when the sun is hid.
>
> (V,i,124-6)

A little of the circulating sickness has reached Belmont. The play is a comedy; but Shakespeare has here touched on deeper and more potentially complex and troubling matters than he had hitherto explored, and the result is a comedy with a difference. And, of course, it is primarily Shylock who makes that difference.

Now, let's go back to the beginning. "Which is the merchant here? And which the Jew?" It turns out to be a good question.

Bibliography

Brockbank, Philip: "Shakespeare and the Fashion of These Times". *Shakespeare Survey* 16 (1963).

Burckhardt, Sigurd: "The Merchant of Venice: The Gentle Bond". *Journal of English Literary History* 29 (1962).

Gross, John: *Shylock. Four Hundred Years in the Life of a Legend.* London 1992.

Kermode, Frank: "The Mature Comedies". In: Brown, J. R. / B. Harris (eds.): *Early Shakespeare.* Stratford-upon-Avons Studies, 3. London 1961.

Nevo, Ruth: *Comic Transformations in Shakespeare.* London 1980.

Tawney, R. H.: *Religion and the Rise of Capitalism.* London 1926.

CHARACTER STUDIES

Robert Alter (essay date 1993)

SOURCE: Alter, Robert. "Who Is Shylock?" *Commentary* 96, no. 1 (1993): 29-34.

[*In the following essay, Alter focuses on Shylock as the central figure of* The Merchant of Venice, *contending that the source of the play's enduring popularity can be found in the variety of theatrical interpretations of Shylock's character.*]

The Merchant of Venice has inspired a certain ambivalence through much of its four-century history, and that ambivalence is sharply inscribed in the changing interpretations of the play. What is more surprising is that it has been one of Shakespeare's two most popular plays (the second being *Hamlet*), as the English literary critic John Gross shows through careful documentation in his highly instructive new study, *Shylock: A Legend and Its Legacy.* Why this should be so is something of a puzzle.

An account of the plan of John Gross's book might make it sound like one of those tedious chronological surveys of the "reception history" of a familiar literary work. In fact, Gross handles his subject with such urbane intelligence and wit, such fine alertness to the telling detail and anecdote, such a nice balance of both aesthetic and moral judgment, that his survey becomes a deeply interesting case-study of the ambiguous relations between literature and historical reality.

Shylock is divided into three roughly equal sections. The first deals with the play itself and its original contexts; the second mainly with stage productions from the 17th century to the present; and the third with the archetype of Shylock and critical, fictional, and dramaturgical interpretations of it. There is a certain Germanic thoroughness to all this—as supposed literary specialists within universities increasingly limit their reading to the same dozen or so texts of Continental theory, the crown of scholarship may well be passing to literary journalists like Gross—but it is carried out with an engaging English lightness of touch.

Thus, we learn all the pertinent facts about Shakespeare's sources; the actual condition of Jews in England (what few there were) and in Venice in the 16th century; Shakespeare's own possible involvement in lending money for interest and venture capitalism. The middle section patiently reconstructs from the available sources the principal English and American productions of the play and their critical reception, and some attention is also accorded to German and French stage interpretations. The final section casts its net wide enough to include various fictional extrapolations from Shakespeare's story; a discussion of Jews in Proust; the psychoanalyst Theodore Reik's free associations, triggered by the play, about his relationship with his daughter; and the British critic M. C. Bradbrook's dumbfounding proposition that "The concentration camps of Nazi Germany bred many heroes and martyrs but also a few Shylocks." Throughout, Gross has a gift for bringing out the absurd and the outrageous through tersely acerbic understatement, though there are a few points (as in his pillorying of Jonathan Miller's 1970 National Theater production) where his sense of moral and aesthetic seemliness leads him to vigorously explicit judgments.

In broad terms, one can speak of two underlying versions of Shylock between which stage productions have oscillated over the centuries. The first, which dominated productions throughout the 18th century, conceived the Jew demanding his pound of flesh as an embodiment of "savage fierceness, a deadly spirit of revenge," in the words of Nicholas Rowe's 1709 essay on Shakespeare. That conception was memorably realized in the middle of the century in the treatment of the role by the famous Irish actor Charles Macklin. "There was such an iron-visaged look," a contemporary of Macklin's observed, "such a relentless, savage cast of manners, that the audience seemed to shrink from the character."

But in 1814, a hitherto unknown actor in his early twenties named Edmund Kean effected a revolution in the stage interpretation of Shylock by casting off the traditional red wig that had linked the Jew with the devil of the medieval mystery plays and endowing him (in Gross's words) "with a large measure of dignity and humanity." William Hazlitt, present at the performance as a reviewer, was thunderstruck with admiration. Another contemporary, Douglas Jerrold, said that Kean's sympathetic interpretation of the Jew seemed to the audience "like a chapter of Genesis."

Later in the century, the actor Henry Irving picked up a cue from Hazlitt in proclaiming, "I look upon Shylock as the type of a persecuted race; almost the only gentleman in the play, and the most ill-used." Irving's forceful playing of the role became the interpretation that dominated the latter part of the Victorian age. Gross associates this philo-Semitic Shylock with the growth of liberalism in

19th-century England, accompanied by a reflex of conscience about earlier ill-treatment of the Jews and an increasing acceptance of Jews in social and political life. One might add to these plausible reasons a certain imaginative sympathy on the part of the Romantics with the outsider, the figure of the cursed or hunted man, the image of suffering humanity entrammeled in the demonic.

The more or less neat swing from antipathy to sympathy between the 18th and 19th centuries disappears in our own century amid a welter of critical and stage interpretations. At least since the 1920's, there has been no preponderant version of Shylock. Sundry variations on the old diabolic conception alternate indiscriminately with new efforts to render the long-suffering human dignity of the Jew, and there have even been occasional reversions to the oldest stage notion of Shylock as a grotesque figure of fun.

The curious thing about all this, as Gross has occasion to note at several points, is that critics and directors in our time have very often been entirely unaffected by what happened to the real Jews of Venice and Berlin and Warsaw in the terrible middle decades of the century. Shakespeare of course did not write his comedy with an eye to possible future catastrophes of European history, and the play as he framed it certainly has its own thematic and dramaturgical integrity. Gross cites a delicate case in point in the comments on the play, written in 1939, by the eminent American critic Mark Van Doren.

Shylock's voice, Van Doren observed, however differently it might sound in another universe, must, in the world of the play, be "nothing but a snarl, an animal cry sounding outrageously among the flute and recorder voices of persons whose very names, unlike his own, are flowing musical phrases." This is beautifully and precisely put (Shylock in fact expresses a petulant distaste for music; his speech-rhythms are abrupt, emphatic, and unmusical; Belmont in the play is a realm of enchanting song; and so forth). Nevertheless, Gross is troubled that Van Doren—an admirably humane critic and personally sympathetic toward Jews—could say all this in 1939 without the least gesture of regret for what the Christian habit of thinking of Jews in bestial terms had led to. Literature may be a realm apart, governed by its own subtle laws of imaginative coherence, and Gross grants the virtue of studying those laws in a spirit of detachment. But literature also issues from, and feeds back into, the realm of history and politics, and in view of this, Gross finds a moral flaw in Van Doren's exquisitely disinterested account in 1939 of Shakespeare's Jew.

If *The Merchant of Venice* is a play likely to elicit an uneasy conflict of perceptions about its moral center in critics, directors, actors, and audiences, this ambiguity has in no way diminished its perennial popularity. In 19th-century New York alone, there were more than 100 productions, or an average of at least one a year. In a smaller time frame, from 1918 to 1939, there were nine different productions of the play in Stratford-on-Avon, and ten each in the West End of London and at the Old Vic. It was a perennial favorite for English school performances; and in American high schools in the last two decades of the 19th century it was, together with *Julius Caesar,* the literary text most frequently studied.

Beyond the Anglo-American sphere, the play has also had an uncanny appeal for far-flung audiences. It was the first drama of Shakespeare's to be performed in Armenian, the first to be performed in its entirety in Chinese, and the first in Japanese (by a kabuki troupe). In Belgium, up to 1950, there were more than twice as many Flemish-language productions of *The Merchant* as of any other Shakespeare play.

The extraordinary magnetism exerted by this play on audiences and directors is hard to explain in intrinsic literary terms. If one assumes that the work bracketed with *Hamlet* at the center of the Shakespeare canon would have to be a comedy (the histories and the late romances being perhaps too hybrid in form to win all-time popularity contests), more compelling candidates readily come to mind. *The Taming of the Shrew* and *Much Ado About Nothing* are livelier and more witty by far. *A Midsummer Night's Dream* is a more splendidly extravagant deployment of the fairy-tale elements in which *The Merchant* is supposed to excel, just as both *Twelfth Night* and *As You Like It* outstrip it in the rich celebration of a world of song, play, and love's fulfillment. And for the sheer funniness of boisterous farce, *The Merry Wives of Windsor* makes *The Merchant*'s efforts at stage humor look stale and unprofitable.

There are, of course, magnificent moments in *The Merchant of Venice*: Shylock's famous speeches, Portia's courtroom address, and Lorenzo's magical evocation of the harmony of the heavens near the end of the play (the speech beginning "How sweet the moonlight sleeps upon this bank!"). But in between, much of the poetry is no more than serviceable, and the comic byplay is often labored and unfunny—dreadful, drearily repeated puns on words like "Moor" and "more," mechanically insistent malapropisms, crude jeering like Gratiano's taunt to Shylock that he will have to hang himself at the state's expense because the court has not left him the value of a cord. Then the double plot of the creditor's pound of flesh and the fair lady's three caskets is a compounding of contrivance with contrivance. Either one must say, as many critics have done, that folk-tale fantasy makes good theater, or one has to conclude that the mixed marriage of genres here strains even the loose boundaries of comic plausibility.

The Merchant of Venice, then, has its artistic as well as its moral problems. Nevertheless, there must be something about its plot and its central figure that has a powerful hold on the imagination and that accounts for its perdurable popularity. When I refer to the play's central figure I mean Shylock, even though it is Antonio who is the merchant of the title and Bassanio who is the romantic lead, and even though the Jew is only intermittently on stage, entirely excluded by the fifth act. But Gross's history—which provides a starting point for the reflections that follow—offers ample evidence that it was Shylock who was the constant lodestar for actors and audiences: all the great male performers wanted to play him; most critical accounts are, above all, responses to this compelling figure.

The one explanation which I think can be dismissed out of hand is that the play's appeal derives from its exploitation of anti-Semitic fantasy, here tapped into by the greatest dramatic poet in the language. This will not wash because, as Gross shows, many of the most spectacular successes of the play from 1814 onward were passionately philo-Semitic productions. Nor, surely, can anti-Semitism account for the popularity of the play in cultures quite unfamiliar with Jews, or in adaptations that have effaced the Jewish identity of the villain.

With regard to the surprising exportability of *The Merchant of Venice* to exotic regions, Gross suggests that the fairy-tale elements of the story may explain its universal appeal. (I shall have more to say below about the intertwining of different generic strands in the play.) Still, if the play works its magic for some of the same reasons in kabuki as at the Old Vic, it must also in other respects have a distinctive freight of meaning for the Christian West. Among the frequent reminders Gross provides of that fact, perhaps the most sobering is his report of the spate of productions in Nazi Germany—though with some directorial squirming at the miscegenation allowed by the nonracist anti-Semitism of the plot.

The ultimate power of *The Merchant* resides in Shylock; and Shylock, as the history of the play's interpretation indicates, is an explosively unstable figure, both as comic villain and as Jew. Let me propose that there is at once a poor fit and a synergy between Shylock's dramatically archetypal role as ill-spirited obstacle in the comic plot—the old man, *senex*, of Roman comedy who tries to withhold his fair daughter as well as his wealth from her destined lover—and his ethnically archetypal role as bloodsucking Jewish moneylender. There is, I suspect, something about the transgression of boundaries in the ambiguous dynamic between those two roles that gives the play its peculiar fascination.

The catalogue of negative attributes exhibited by Shakespeare's Jew is, alas, what could be expected almost anywhere in Christendom from the First Crusade to the Enlightenment. Shylock is, from his first appearance, the sullenly obdurate outsider ("I will buy with you, sell with you, talk with you, walk with you, and so following; but I will not eat with you, drink with you, nor pray with you"). So far, so good, at least in regard to the historical record: resentment against the Jew as stubborn alien belongs to what the historian Gavin Langmuir has called "anti-Judaic" feeling, in contradistinction to anti-Semitic animus which instead of reacting to the real condition of Jews projects lurid fantasies on to them.

Such fantasies, however, soon abound in the play. The Jew is demonic—"the very devil incarnation," his servant Launcelot Gobbo announces, with considerable corroboration from the plot; his house is represented as a kind of hell, the antipodes of the aristocratic *paradiso* of Portia's Belmont. He is also repeatedly referred to in bestial terms, as a cur or wolf (Van Doren's "snarl" is quite to the point). In the algebra of archetypes, the combination of beast of prey and devil yields vampire, an identity Shylock is prepared to claim for himself in his first speech to Jessica—"I'll go in hate, to feed upon / The prodigal Christian."

Usury itself, the play suggests (in historical bad faith, for it was widespread among Christians by the late 16th century), is a kind of vampirism, and Shylock's implacable demand for his pound of flesh is a horrific literal translation of that metaphor. In turn, Gross plausibly suggests that Shylock's murderous bond is a proposal "to commit ritual murder at one remove." Portia's courtroom denial to Shylock of any drop of blood thus goes to the very core of the anti-Semitic nightmare image. The fantasy of the Jew battening on Christian blood is interfused in the tale of the pound of flesh with the hostile stereotype of the Jew as usurer—as it would continue to be in a wide variety of texts, from Marx's notorious essay on the Jews to Nazi and Communist propaganda.

Beyond this cluster of repellent traits that are drawn from age-old anti-Semitic imaginings, Shylock exhibits one salient characteristic more closely associated with comic villains than with Jews: he is a dour hater of the revels that are at the heart of the comic world. He is mistrustful of the masked carnival figures surging through the Venetian streets; he despises music ("the vile squealing of the wry neck'd fife") and is suspicious of metaphor, with an odd little tic of literally "translating" the ones he uses himself; and he sternly disapproves of all forms of risk-taking, whether in business or in games of chance. Finally, and perhaps most crucially, he is a man with a rigidly fixed identity who abhors disguises and exchanged identities. Hence his hostility to the Venetian masks, and hence the poetic justice of his being foiled in justice by a woman got up as a man. The ultimate pain of his forced conversion at the end of Act IV may be the violation not of his creed but rather of his hard-set sense of self. Shylock is the man who insists on being one thing alone in a comic world that celebrates multifariousness and a playful conjuring with appearances.

Now, to all this it is essential to add the dimension of Shylock that has been so abundantly noted by critics since Hazlitt and by actors since Kean—that Shakespeare, with his unrivaled gift for endowing his characters with life, bestowed more touching humanity on Shylock than the prejudices of his culture might have allowed. The most frequently cited prooftext is of course the great "Hath not a Jew eyes" speech, and though that ends in justifying vengeance, Shylock also observes that he has learned the code of vengeance from the Christians—by no means a historically implausible claim in the 16th century.

A more succinct, almost startling, instance in which Shylock's humanity suddenly shines through is when he is told that Jessica, after eloping with much of the family treasure, has traded a particular turquoise ring for a monkey: "It was my turquoise," he cries out in distinctly uncomic anguish. "I had it of Leah when I was a bachelor. I would not have given it for a wilderness of monkeys." This is no villain who speaks here but a man who truly loved, and was loved by, a wife he still mourns in his long condition as widower, who left him this only daughter, now become his heartless betrayer.

We will remember the ring given Shylock as a pledge of love later on, when Portia and her companion Nerissa give rings to their betrothed lovers, making them solemnly vow that nothing will lead them to part with the rings; the two women then cunningly extract these very tokens of love when they appear in men's disguise in the trial scene. At the very end, with amorous rebukes and teasing sexual puns, the women restore the rings to their bridegrooms and forgive their trespass—but in comparison with Shylock's naked pain over the loss of his dead wife's token of love, there remains a lingering sense of gratuitous monkey business in Belmont. This is a detail in no way required by the comic plot or the larger thematic design, but which Shakespeare's humane genius drew him into imagining.

The character of Shylock, then, bursts through the conventional limits of the comic *senex* in two opposite directions—in the representation of the suffering of a much-wronged outsider (the "tragic" Shylock, as some critics would have it) and in the demonization of what in other comedies would be the figure of fun (the mythic Shylock). It is hard to think of another comedy that pushes so powerfully against the boundaries of genre in these two opposite ways. Before the fact, one might imagine that such a contradictory conception of character could not work; but in the incandescence of Shakespeare's imagination, the alternating tragic and mythic Shylock comes vividly to life, and perhaps the contradiction at the core of the character explains the power of this strange figure.

But I have been speaking of the play as though the genres and archetypes of literature evolved in a vacuum, without any relation to history. My account so far may say something about the fascination with *The Merchant* experienced by audiences in Tokyo and Beijing, but for theatergoers in mid-18th-century London or in New York after the Civil War, not to mention Berlin of the 1930's, there were obviously other potent considerations involved. Jews, too, would come to be fascinated with *The Merchant of Venice*—John Gross offers some piquant anecdotes, for example, about Yiddish productions—but the history of the reception of the play is above all a history of responses by a culturally and often creedally Christian audience.

In this regard, I would argue that there is a deep if somewhat murky correlation between the transgression of the limits of comedy in the play and its intermittent transgression of the boundaries between self and reviled other, insider and outsider. Those contradictory excesses in the characterization of Shylock remind us that comedy's world, where all tigers turn paper, and all obstacles to sweet fulfillment are in the end gracefully overleaped, is only make-believe. In the real world that comedy displaces, there are nightmarish terrors that cannot be dispelled, and pleasure is all too often bought at the price of someone else's pain. Shakespeare in this fashion plays a kind of dangerous game with the genre in which he is working while he nevertheless affirms its logic, rounding out the play with the moonlit postlude of the fifth act in which the figure of Shylock has been entirely exorcised and love sounds its bantering lute song on the threshold of consummation.

Something roughly equivalent occurs in the play's treatment of the cultural conventions of anti-Semitism. It was clearly not part of Shakespeare's conscious design to question the received wisdom of Christian hostility toward the Jews. Living in a country from which they had been banished for four centuries, he had little or no opportunity for firsthand acquaintance with them, and so what he "knew" about Jews was what his culture knew—that they were rapacious, greedy, cunning, and inhumanly cruel. All this is Shylock. There is nothing new about the hostile stereotypes, but, as Gross soberly observes, Shylock the Jewish villain, imbued with the force of Shakespeare's intrinsic poetic power and subsequent prestige, "helped to spread [the stereotypes] and to keep them vigorously alive. He belongs, inescapably, to the history of anti-Semitism."

If this bleak truth were the whole truth, one might sympathize with the protesters who have emerged from some modern Jewish communities in response to productions of *The Merchant of Venice*. But Gross is quick to remind us of Shakespeare's inclination, as a playwright who disliked one-sided conflicts, to "build up" Shylock. He could not resist trying to imagine what it might be like to be a Jew, and "dramatic imagination, when it is pitched at the Shakespearean level, becomes a moral quality, a form of humanism." The disparity between the antipathetic and the empathetic representation of Shylock leaves, in Gross's view, a lingering hint of nastiness in the play. Portia, Antonio, Bassanio, Lorenzo embody the comic virtues of grace, playfulness, intelligence, and loving friendship, but they are also utterly cold, callous, and exasperatingly blithe in seeing the Jew as no more than a vile cur to be driven off with cudgels. It is hardly a prejudice that can have a claim to historical innocence.

Yet it could well be that this peculiar dissonance between the anti-Semitic conception of Shylock and the moments of incipient or genuine empathy is precisely what has excited the imagination of audiences over the centuries. One must remember that it was the Jew who was constantly the archetypal alien in the mind of Christian Europe. There were, to be sure, other candidates: the Muslims, who were actual imperial adversaries; the Orientals, of inscrutable repute; and still more exotic, purportedly savage, types, like black Africans and American Indians. But all these stood on the other side of a distant cultural horizon.

The Jew alone was in the midst of Christendom, speaking Christian languages, conducting trade with Christians, often looking and acting far more "Christian" than the stereotypes of prejudice were willing to admit. And it was thus the Jew, stubborn in his particularism, despised by Christians, who raised disturbing questions about the boundaries of Christian collective identity. Hence a certain persistent edginess about the Jewish other, which could generate anything from a simple perception of difference, or similarity in difference, to genteel discrimination, active persecution, forced conversion, even mass murder.

What happens in *The Merchant of Venice* is that the accepted definition of self by way of contradistinction to the excluded other is buoyantly sustained, as one might expect in a comedy, while the two-sided representation of Shylock flashes an intermittent, stroboscopic light on a radically antithetical possibility of identity. Perhaps there might be hidden affinities between self and other; perhaps the very otherness of the other is largely a cultural construct.

The intimations of such a possibility in Shakespeare's treatment of Shylock are quite unsentimental. If there are moments when he provides insight into Shylock's very human anguish as an outsider, this invitation to identify with the Jewish villain may also suggest that the predatory aspects of the character, his unbending cruelty, are not to be so patly identified as the exclusive property of the hated alien, but may comfortably nest as well in the Christian heart. If in Shylock the diabolic is made human, perhaps what the culture assumes definitionally to be human may have its own dark part in the diabolic. It is not mere coincidence that the first sympathetic portrayals of Shylock in criticism and on the stage came at the very moment that the blighted Byronic hero was dominating the English literary imagination.

The plot of the comedy, of course, keeps Christian community and Jewish outsider perfectly distinct. In Belmont, far above the mire of Venetian trade with its shady Jewish practitioners, the circle of melodiously named heroes and heroines is happily drawn tight. No Jewish foot is allowed to profane these precincts, except for that of the lovely Jessica, cleansed by baptismal waters. But down in the savage give-and-take of the commercial world of Venice, the barriers between insider and outsider are not always impermeable, and there are fleeting hints that the savagery exists on both sides.

Thus, in Act III, Scene III, Shylock visits Antonio in jail to warn him that on the morrow he will have his pound of flesh. Antonio, ever the perfect gentleman, addresses his Jewish adversary courteously as "good Shylock," hoping he will persuade the moneylender to show compassion. The Jew, in an ecstasy of triumphant vengefulness, scarcely lets him get a word in edgewise, repeatedly insisting, "I will have my bond." Antonio quickly abandons the attempt to address Shylock, and with a kind of shrug, explains to his friend Solanio that the Jew hates him because he, Antonio, has given loans without interest.

In all these respects, the scene is entirely an anti-Semitic set-up: Christian nobility, reasonableness, and charity over against "Old Testament" vengeance; pre-capitalist Christian lending as a kind of philanthropy over against Jewish usury. But even when he is playing with loaded dice, Shakespeare cannot refrain from giving Shylock one quick fair throw. "Thou call'dst me dog before thou hadst a cause, / But since I am a dog, beware my fangs." It is a very small gesture in a scene designed to expose Shylock's inhumanity, but it is nonetheless astonishing. For the fact of the matter is that every Christian in the play, given half a chance, is happy to call Shylock dog, and would clearly do so even without the excuse of his insistence on his terrible bond.

The plot revolving around the pound of flesh preserves the simple and pernicious cultural opposition between bestial Jew and human Christian, or, in theological terms, between the old dispensation of implacable law and the new dispensation governed by the quality of mercy which is not strained. Mercy, however, as exercised by the Christian characters, is conspicuous for *not* dropping as the gentle rain from heaven on any Jewish head. Shylock, treated like a beast of prey as a matter of Christian cultural practice, defiantly tells Antonio that this, then, is what he will become.

The Merchant of Venice, not through Shakespeare's intention but through his uncanny dramatic intuition, invites Christian audiences to a kind of out-of-self experience. If the looming, sinister other embodies all the hateful qualities that Christian culture would like to think are alien to it, there are also brief but powerful intimations that the other may be the moral and psychological consequence of treatment by the self; that the self may harbor the fearsome attributes it habitually projects on the other; and that both participate profoundly in a vulnerable human condition which the self is usually predisposed to see as its own private property.

Actual productions of *The Merchant of Venice* have generally opted either for the humane, suffering Shylock or for the diabolic one. But it seems plausible that the magnetism of the work is generated by the interplay between the two perspectives, with all the freight of historical and psychological ambiguities that I have tried to describe. This is by no means Shakespeare's most satisfying play, but the ultimate source of its strange appeal, so finely traced by John Gross, may perhaps be found in the very tensions and disjunctions of its underlying conception.

Cynthia Lewis (essay date 1997)

SOURCE: Lewis, Cynthia. "'A Foolish Consistency': Antonio and Alienation in *The Merchant of Venice.*" In *Particular Saints: Shakespeare's Four Antonios, Their Contexts, and Their Plays,* pp. 51-87. Cranbury, N.J.: Associated University Presses, 1997.

[*In the following excerpt, Lewis regards* The Merchant of Venice *as an ironic tragicomedy, concentrating on Antonio*

I

Antonio opens the play by speaking three times in seven lines of how little he understands himself:

> In sooth, *I know not why I am so sad;*
> It wearies me, you say it wearies you;
> But how I caught it, found it, or came by it,
> What stuff 'tis made of, whereof it is born,
> *I am to learn;*
> And such a want-wit sadness makes of me,
> That *I have much ado to know myself.*
>
> (1.1.1-7; emphasis added)

Thus, he immediately establishes the play's keen interest, which runs throughout, in the inadequacy of human knowledge. As readers and audiences, our first impulse is to provide the reason for Antonio's sadness—in most cases (cases too numerous to mention individually), the cause advanced is Bassanio's imminent departure. To assume so, however, is to remain deaf to Antonio's emphasis and to the dynamic of the entire first scene, which points to the absence of adequate explanations for Antonio's melancholy.[1] In the first part of the scene, Salerio, Solanio, and Gratiano all repeatedly guess at what is ailing Antonio. Clearly, none of them wholly succeeds. In rejecting their theories, Antonio reaffirms his self-estrangement: he does not know himself.

Nor does he appear to know the world in which his ships traffic. Salerio's speech about the perils of the sea (22-40), although familiar to the point of cliché, is nevertheless compelling. What's more, it is readily accessible, indebted as it is to the popular conceit of the sea as fortune and built on two simple metaphorical vehicles, "broth" and "church" (22, 29). A rhetorical *tour de force*, it speaks true: earthly life and goods, "even now worth this, / And now worth nothing," are at the mercy of earthly change (1.1.35-36). Yet, Salerio's persuasive speech does not move Antonio, who, although manifestly steeped in what Lyon calls an "ordinary and 'worldly' world" (31), is nonetheless out of step with that world. He is imprudently confident of his "fortune" (41):

> My ventures are not in one bottom trusted,
> Nor to one place; nor is my whole estate
> Upon the fortune of this present year:
> Therefore my merchandise makes me not sad.
>
> (42-45)

Two scenes later, with like oblivion, he impawns his flesh to Shylock.

Antonio's unskillful maneuvering in a world fraught with danger is pronounced but hardly unique. If he is, as his friends assert, a "strange fellow" and "marvellously chang'd" (51, 76), then he reflects the alienation and unpredictability portended even by the well-adjusted Bassanio as he greets his friends: "Good signiors both, when shall we laugh? say, when? / You grow exceeding strange. Must it be so?" (66-67). All human attachments, the play demonstrates from the start, are precarious. Nor does Venetian Christian culture fully protect its members from social alienation. For, although to themselves they are all natives, to an Elizabethan audience they would have been considered "merchant-strangers," the term applied by Londoners from midcentury on to "foreign or alien traders."[2] The concepts of native and foreign are relative, dependent upon perspective. Whatever sense of their impregnability may be afforded to the Venetians by their luxury, leisure, and power, it is continually undermined and exposed as contingent.

The effect of such undermining is dramatic irony, the tone that, in turn, dominates the play. In the particular case of the opening scene, the audience is being prepared for the crucial irony to follow, when the Venetians, themselves "strangers" in a variety of senses, treat the Jewish usurer increasingly as a foreigner, naming him "Jew" (passim), then "stranger" (3.3.27), finally "alien" (4.1.349).[3] Moreover, one of the chief purposes of such dramatic irony is to expose ostensible binaries in *Merchant*—like Christian versus Jew, or Venice versus Belmont—as suspicious, perhaps artificial. The more an audience probes the characterization of the Christian Italians in act 1, which Shakespeare takes obvious pains to elaborate at length before introducing Shylock at all, the more they resemble their Jewish counterpart.

Take, for example, the conversation in 1.3 where Bassanio, approaching Shylock in Antonio's behalf, misunderstands Shylock's remark, "Antonio is a good man," by replying, "Have you heard any imputation to the contrary?" (12-14). Almost universally, critics have cited this passage to show the difference between Jew and Christian, who, as Shylock's retort to Bassanio implies, do not even speak the same language: "Ho, no, no, no, no! my meaning in saying he is a good man is to have you understand me that he is sufficient" (15-17). Shylock's orientation is financial, we read repeatedly in the criticism on *Merchant,* whereas Bassanio's is moral. But this interpretation is misleading because it ignores Bassanio's attitudes and language as early as 1.1. There, in fact, Bassanio's request to Antonio and his description of Portia appear every bit as mercenary as are Shylock's ruminations over Antonio's suitability as a borrower. Only Bassanio's language is dressier. It is the language of spiritual venturing put to the service of obscuring his motive, which is to gain financial independence from Antonio by attaching himself to "a lady richly left" (161). Read closely, Bassanio's plans to woo Portia through Antonio's renewed generosity are couched in metaphors that are misleadingly high-minded and big-hearted: he wants to "get clear of all [his] debts" to Antonio by "hazard[ing]" another loan from Antonio (134, 151); his object is a woman of "worth" (167); and his "thrift" promises to render him "fortunate" (175-76). Not coincidentally, *thrift* is Shylock's word for "usury," as the audience is about to hear in 1.3 (50, 90).[4]

In effect, Bassanio and Shylock do not speak differently but share the same vocabulary, which Bassanio seems better at manipulating to blur his intent. He may well be attracted to Portia's "fair" looks and "wondrous virtues"—additional elements of her "worth"—as well as to her inheritance (1.1.162-63, 167). Yet, his language of financial speculation in 1.1 fits his professed love for Antonio and Portia only uncomfortably, if at all.

The immediate purpose of the dramatic irony that such implicit comparison between Jew and Christian creates is to puncture any character's pretensions to being essentially different from any other. Such claims to distinctiveness are often made in earnest—for instance, by the duke of Venice, as he pronounces Shylock's sentence at the trial: "That thou shalt see the difference of our spirit, / I pardon thee thy life before thou ask it" (4.1.368-69). They are also parodied by Launcelot Gobbo in 3.5. According to the clown, the conversion from Jew to Christian is of no more consequence than an increase in the price of pork (21-26). In the same scene, moreover, Launcelot is revealed to have easily crossed racial boundaries himself by impregnating the Moor (37-42). In no case are the actual similarities between apparently disparate characters more extensive, however, than in that of Shylock and Antonio, who are far less divided by cultural barriers than bound naturally by their strangeness and estrangement. The one is alienated from Christian society, the other from this world altogether.

Antonio's discomfort in this world has its positive associations with ideal charity, like that of Saint Anthony, and, generally, unlike Shylock's miserliness. The merchant's willingness to dispense interest-free loans is legendary in Venice (1.2.43-45), and his devotion to Bassanio is widely recognized within his social sphere (2.8.35-50). Indeed, a large part of the point about Antonio's willingness to practice hypocrisy in borrowing from Shylock in the first place is that his high regard for Bassanio compels him to. In this sense, he is a conventional wise fool, ruled by irrational love.[5] At the same time, however, his is an obsessive attachment to Bassanio; as Solanio says, Antonio "only loves the world for" his friend (2.8.50). Such recklessness proves at least as harmful to some other characters—Shylock and Portia especially—as Shylock's overt hostility. And perhaps not all of Antonio's indiscretions can be attributed to his heedlessness; some seem every bit as calculated as Shylock's aggressions.

Antonio's affinity with Shylock is first evinced in 1.3, where his nature is disclosed through his open hypocrisies. He will "neither lend nor borrow / By taking nor by giving of excess"—that is, unless he needs to (61-64). He will also borrow from a man he has publicly abused, both verbally and physically, and will likely mistreat again (106-31). He will, in other words, practice the usury he reviles. Presumably, he satisfies his conscience by rationalizing the interest he will owe Shylock as adequate payment for his persecution of the Jew:

> If thou wilt lend this money, lend it not
> As to thy friends, for when did friendship take
> A breed for barren metal of his friend?
> But lend it rather to thine enemy,
> Who if he break, thou mayst with better face
> Exact the penalty.
>
> (132-37)

Antonio thus justifies the contemptuous "face" with which he uses Shylock's money. Worth noting here is Shylock's unwillingness to practice hypocrisy of his own until this point. He has refused Bassanio's hollow invitation to dinner and drawn a telling comparison between himself and the prototypical trickster Jacob, alerting the careful listener to his attitude toward his would-be clients (33-38, 71-90).[6] In addition, he confronts Antonio's hypocrisy directly (106-29). Only after Antonio insists on contracting with Shylock despite his loathing does Shylock assume his own mask of "kindness" (143):

> Why, look you how you storm!
> I would be friends with you, and have your love,
> Forget the shames that you have stain'd me with,
> Supply your present wants, and take no doit
> Of usance for my moneys, and you'll not hear me.
>
> (137-41)

Shylock can match Antonio move for move, ever deepening his resemblance to him.

In fact, Shylock's shift in attitude toward the bond—from "merry sport" to earnest—hinges on another Christian hypocrisy, the central one in Shakespeare's plot (1.3.145). Having finally consented to dine with the Christians in the spirit of "hate" (2.5.14), Shylock discovers too late just how much they have "flatter[ed]" him with their invitation (2.5.13). The dinner turns out to have been a subterfuge to expedite Jessica's elopement, as Shylock bemoans to Salerio and Solanio upon entering after she has fled: "You knew, none so well, none so well as you, of my daughter's flight" (3.1.24-25). Significantly, at no time hereafter is this hoodwinking of Shylock addressed. Even though it is, in the best light, a morally questionable ruse, the Christians are never held in the least bit accountable for it. Only Shylock is reproached in subsequent scenes for his violent, vengeful reaction to it. What might have happened to Shylock's "stony" heart if a Christian or two in the trial scene had apologized for participating in the earlier scheme against him (4.1.4)? Shylock's public humiliation of Antonio—and the firm control over his nemesis that it requires—are partly, as the usurer maintains, "villainy" that the Christians "teach" him (3.1.71).

I am not excusing Shylock's vengeance, which he clearly harbors from the very beginning: he "hates" Antonio "for he is a Christian; / But more, for that . . . / He lends out money gratis" (1.3.42-44). Nor do I intend to vilify Antonio and his Christian company. Neither do I mean to ignore conventional sixteenth-century depictions of Jews as monstrous or to pass over or minimize genuine cultural differences in any society, including Shakespeare's Venice.[7] They do exist. Yet, differing cultural practices may be

Scene from The Merchant of Venice.

mistaken as human differences. I am trying to show that many of the supposed distinctions in *Merchant,* which attach themselves to categories like Christian and Jew, or victim and villain, are just such mistaken disparities. They are relatively superficial, and they invite disproof. For all the acrimony they arouse among the characters and the disagreement they elicit in audience members, attempts to validate them turn quickly into vain exercises in hairsplitting and, worse yet, detours from recognizing the dramatic irony at hand and the uses to which it is put. The profound correspondences among the characters in *Merchant* ultimately redirect the audience's attention from a cultural dilemma to a universally human one.[8] It is the larger problem of feeling at home in the inhospitable world of the flesh, beginning with the body, which, as Shylock's unpleasant analogy to his vengeful humor indicates, may easily betray and "shame" us: "Some men there are . . . / . . . when the bagpipe sings i' th' nose, / Cannot contain their urine" (4.1.47-50). The worldly world of *Merchant* imposes such severe difficulties as to encourage withdrawal from it.

Put another way, Shylock's social alienation—in some ways caused by himself as much as by others—leads him to a madness much like Antonio's folly.[9] Both become increasingly isolated, even imprisoned. As Shylock becomes enslaved to vengeance, his passion finds bizarre reflection in Antonio's passive resignation to it:

> The Duke cannot deny the course of law;
> For the commodity that strangers have
> With us in Venice, if it be denied,
> Will much impeach the justice of the state,
> Since that the trade and profit of the city
> Consisteth of all nations.
>
> (3.3.26-31)

The essential truth of these lines notwithstanding, Antonio's specific explanation as to why Shylock must take his pound of flesh, rendered nearly impenetrable by his tortuous language, provides further evidence of his maladjustment to the material world. Yes, he must be shaken here by Shylock's carnivorous presence in the scene, but his contorted syntax owes to more than his present situation. For instance, is the subject of "will impeach" the "denial of commodity" or "the denial of the course of law"? The construction is muddled. Furthermore, the reason that the court might be "impeached" for a decision against Shylock is not, exactly, that Venice relies on "all nations" for trade; more specifically, it is because Venice must protect the foreigners who have relocated in Venice and who contribute to Venetian wealth and security, as Antonio means, but only vaguely relates.[10] His wording mirrors his malaise, seen especially in his consistent impulse to deal half-heartedly with the complexities of his existence by evasion, if not altogether removing himself. His readiness to die at Shylock's hands in the trial scene is expressed in the terms of Pauline wise folly: "I am a tainted wether of the flock, / Meetest for death; the weakest kind of fruit / Drops earliest to the ground, and so let me" (4.1.114-16). As numerous sequels to this speech demonstrate, however, Antonio's self-negation is not wholly sincere: "You cannot better be employ'd, Bassanio, / Than to live still and write mine epitaph" (4.1.117-18). Antonio still has an ego; in this case, he channels it toward raising himself in others' opinions.

What Antonio projects as his wisely foolish abandonment of self-interest is actually a truly foolish sacrifice of self-protection. He would rather die self-righteous than engage with Shylock, the law, and other worldly concerns, saving whatever face he can by manipulating Bassanio's public display of gratitude toward him. Likewise, the Shylock of acts 3 and 4 foolishly forfeits whatever standing he does enjoy in Venice to satisfy his loathing, as Stephen Greenblatt writes, "against all reason and self-interest."[11] In 1.3, Shylock has appeared attuned to and adept at dealing with life's perils, enumerating the reasons that contracting with Antonio would be unwise (17-25), while Antonio blithely ignores the dangers to his ships and to himself. But by act 4, both men have lost their heads. They are equally at odds with, adrift in, this world.

Their unease, merely an extreme version of that visiting all the major characters, also emerges in Belmont. There it is handled more lightly and yet is enough in evidence to erode the apparent dissimilarities between the play's two settings. Portia's first line echoes Antonio's—both are "weary," predisposed by their fatigue in "this great world" to retreat from it (1.2.2). As reasonable as are Nerissa's objections to Portia's complaints (1.2.3-9, 27-35), we may well sense, as Portia rehearses the relentless list of suitors to whom she has extended entertainment, that her world-weariness is deserved (1.2.39-111). Being stuck in a country house with a pack of unattractive suitors (one of whom just might choose the right casket) is no one's idea of fulfillment. Yet it is one of the play's many metaphors—others including the Venetian law—for the constrictions that accompany this life. No wonder, in a sense, that Antonio is so ready to leave it.

Still, Portia seems gently mocked for traces of the same characteristics that eventually render Antonio ineffectual in the world. Foremost is her tendency to rush headlong into judgments based on shallow differences, especially race and culture. That Bassanio, a Christian Italian, eventually chooses successfully among the caskets should not be misread as the play's complicity in Portia's xenophobia (3.2). For indeed, as Sinead Cusack has written of her own challenges in performing 1.2, the script leaves little opportunity to rescue Portia from close-mindedness:

> For Portia [the problem] is to escape the effect of a spoilt brat maliciously destroying her suitors. Both in rehearsal and in performance this scene [1.2] caused me more trouble than any other. I think we finally made it work, although it was at the price of cutting out the Scotsman, and perhaps one or two others.[12]

Those "others" are all Others—foreigners who, although they may fail the casket test and make miserable husbands, are deemed "strangers" in Portia's household not on those grounds but for reasons more trivial, like, "He hears merry tales and smiles not" (1.2.123). Portia's crush on Bassanio is also implicitly derided when Nerissa omits his name, citing him as the companion of the Marquis of Montferrat (1.2.114)—an "evocative family name," writes Moelwyn Merchant, for its associations with a powerful but financially drained Italian aristocracy.[13] Marquis Boniface of Montferrat had accumulated quite a debt of his own, at the turn of the thirteenth century, while participating in the Crusades; he eventually paid what he owed Venice by scheming with King Philip of Swabia, pocketing in the process "considerable personal gain" (all in the name of Christ, of course).[14]

The dramatic irony at work in scenes where Antonio and Shylock judge each other, then, is also operating in 1.2. Portia, too, falls back on false or incomplete assumptions about what constitutes genuine difference from one person to the next and about how much difference is acceptable. Through involving her in the problem of feeling alienated in the world, Shakespeare adds a new element to the equation. Not only is she wistful by virtue of her immersion in the world, and not only does she long to skirt the difficulties of navigating this life that tire her—difficulties implicit in her father's will. But also, like Antonio and Shylock, she copes with the daunting complexities, dangers, and pain of her situation with oversimplifications: all suitors are worthless but Bassanio, who is flawless. Such a response to the complicated challenge of enlightened courtship is particularly characteristic of youths, who, as Portia herself says, "skip o'er the meshes of good counsel the cripple" (1.2.20-21). In addition, her next line implies that it is a mannerism that she will outgrow, cooling her "hot temper" and accepting responsibility for herself: "But this reasoning is not in the fashion to choose me a husband" (1.2.21-22).

The extent to which Portia does manifest growth in discernment over the play's course is a question set in motion by her first scene. Whatever the final answer to it, Shakespeare has illustrated many times over, in act 1 and beyond, that, when faced with confusion, the human inclination is to impose an order that can only fail to contain the confusion. The unruly world defies the characters' strategies for ordering it. The ultimate effect of the dramatic irony in *Merchant* is perhaps to alienate the audience from the characters enough to confuse and delay its judgment of them, lest that judgment, too, decay quickly into false appearance.

II

Shakespeare's dominant metaphor in *Merchant* for artificial constructs that appear to promise stability is the theater. The stage metaphor recurs throughout the first scene, persistently calling attention to the affectation about Venetian manners. First, Salerio fashions an image of Antonio's argosies as the "pageants of the sea," playing "signiors and rich burghers" to the "petty traffickers," or smaller ships (10-12). That tableau of courtliness and control, however, instantly gives way to Solanio's reminder that Antonio's ships are indeed vulnerable (15-22), whereupon Salerio abandons his initial scenario and pursues another (22-40), this one more in tune with "[w]hat harm a wind too great might do at sea" (24).

Only a few lines later, Antonio makes his own comparison between the world and the stage: "I hold the world but as the world, . . . / A stage where every man must play a part, / And mine a sad one" (77-79). Like Salerio's first description of Antonio's argosies, and like Jaques's celebrated "All the world's a stage . . . ," Antonio's analogy too is reductive.[15] Through casting himself in a "sad" "part" (78-79), he believes he has satisfied curiosity as to his melancholy and cleared his future of mystery. Gratiano's reply, fittingly, is to try to break down Antonio's reserve by enacting the part of the "fool"; he also accuses his friend of playing another role than he admits to, that of "sir Oracle," a man whose "wisdom, gravity, profound conceit" are merely feigned, through his deceptively august silence, in order to cloak his ignorance (92-93). When Gratiano concludes his lecture by advising Antonio to "fish not with this melancholy bait / For this fool gudgeon"—that is, for an inflated "opinion" of his sagacity—he assumes that Antonio has a choice and is not necessarily so scripted as he maintains into a certain way of life (101-2).

Bassanio follows on the heels of this speech with his own categorization of Gratiano, who, he says, "speaks an infinite deal of nothing." This is a tag that critics have, to my knowledge, never questioned but that seems dubious (114). Gratiano's depiction of Antonio appears on target. Bassanio is about to ask Antonio for money, however, and would thus hasten to smooth any feathers that Gratiano had ruffled. What's more, Bassanio, as we have seen, is himself largely performing here, play-acting, as Gratiano has just described Antonio. He would naturally want to write off the perceptiveness of Gratiano's speech. As Bassanio unfolds his plans to Antonio for wooing Portia, he sets up his characterization for the rest of the play as someone who is always, in part, putting on a show and around whom theatrical language hovers. When he later welcomes Launcelot Gobbo into service by giving him a new "livery," it is with flair purchased by Antonio's loan, which also, presumably, underwrites his final Venetian "feast" for his "best esteem'd acquaintance" (2.2.154, 171-72). In 2.9, he is said to be approaching Belmont with "(besides commends and courteous breath), / Gifts of rich value," which he cannot afford, and arriving like a "day in April . . . / To show how costly summer" is approaching (90-91, 94-95). Such are the "fair ostents of love" (2.8.44)—Antonio's words for the production he has subsidized—that later embarrass Bassanio when, having won Portia's hand and learning of Antonio's distress in Venice, he must own up to his role-playing:

> dear lady,
> Rating myself at nothing, you shall see
> How much I was a braggart: when I told you
> My state was nothing, I should then have told you
> That I was worse than nothing.
>
> (3.2.256-60)

To argue that Bassanio chooses the lead casket because he knows firsthand that "outward shows [may] be least themselves" is too cynical (3.2.73). Clearly, his character is delineated to illustrate how even the best of men—including one worthy of Portia's love—may easily be tempted to lie rather than risk rejection. He at least eventually tells her the truth about owning "nothing." And that he continues, even after his confession of his indebtedness, to deal with his discomfort through "outward shows" serves at least one positive purpose: it presents Portia with repeated perceptual tests and lessons through which she can gain experience (3.2.73). Having discovered the element of play-acting in his financial situation (3.2), she is then privy during the trial to his reneging on his vow of love to her (4.1.282-87), and after that to his forfeiting her ring for love of Antonio and for gratitude to Balthazar (4.1.450-51). These instances can only temper her earlier, girlish conviction in Bassanio's perfections, which, just before he makes his choice of caskets, she likens to those of Hercules.[16]

But, even more than providing a catalyst for both Bassanio's and Portia's maturation, Bassanio's continual reliance on theatrics to make his way in the intimidating world forms part of a much larger web in *Merchant,* where action is usually acting. I have discussed already the pressures on both the Christians and Shylock in 1.3 to alternate between honesty and hypocrisy as they formulate the bond. Other instances abound. Jessica elopes disguised, while the Christians, "with varnish'd faces," plan to put on a masque (2.5.33). Portia's father's lottery serves as a skeletal script: it repeatedly prompts suitors to write their own lines within a narrowly defined formula, and it deposits Portia within similar legal confines, which are represented by the casket that encases her picture.[17] Portia's own attempt to swindle her ring from Bassanio is a consciously staged event (4.1). But the theatrical extravaganza in *Merchant* is, of course, the trial, which Portia, with Bellario's help, carefully orchestrates.

The specifics of Portia's conduct in the trial scene temporarily set aside, we should not miss several of the episode's general traits as calculated performance. Much like the final scene in *Measure for Measure,* where Duke Vincentio secretly directs his subjects' reactions to his gestures, 4.1 of *Merchant* is also a virtual play-within-a-play. It thus necessarily reminds the audience that the larger work is also fiction, thereby inviting inspection of the characters' various uses of theatrics. In the trial scene, Portia's advance knowledge of how to overturn the bond not only buys her the time to try coaxing Shylock out of his vengeance; it also rigs the other characters' responses to the court's proceedings—or, at least, severely limits the possibilities of their responses. Shylock, for example, never truly has a chance to persuade his "second Daniel" of his cause. But even more to the point, Portia's control over the trial's outcome, artistic in its breadth and resourcefulness, alerts us to how provisional—illusory, really—are all the constructs that are relied upon to stave off social and personal disorder.[18] Countless details of the scene—from Shylock's pathetically blind trust in the law's letter to the deliberate instruction with which Portia calls upon first the duke, then Antonio, to sentence Shylock—point up how easily the verdict, but for Portia's firm hand, might have gone the other way. Having done her homework and prepared for the worst, she has guarded against loss; her strategy, akin to that of the contract or bond, is meant to minimize risk.

So is, I would argue, the love for Bassanio that Antonio flaunts in the courtroom, which is of suspicious mettle, if only because of its proximity to so many other examples of feigning, like Portia's role-playing. But Antonio himself offers more grounds for doubting his professions of liberality in love because his words and actions hint of the role-playing he has discussed with Gratiano as the play began. Furthermore, in styling himself a saint, ready to sacrifice his life for friendship, he employs the sort of absolute and ideal terms that, like Salerio's metaphor of "pageants" for "argosies" (1.1.11, 9), suggest a pose. No one can be that virtuous—not in the menacing waters of this world, vividly portrayed in *Merchant.* Like Antonio's casting of himself in the role of a sad man and like Portia's close direction of the trial, Antonio's playing the martyr seems devised to eliminate risk—the risk of not having his love returned. Significantly, this lack of risk was the factor that made Christian moralists deem usury corrupt.[19] Once again, for all of Antonio's labors to distance himself from such worldly imperfections, he appears far more like than unlike Shylock. At the same time, cultural stereotypes receive another lick: Christian liberality, hazarding in love, and perhaps even mercy, versus Jewish miserliness, legalism, and revenge seem more than ever like so many theatrical props. As for Antonio, unless the image of himself that he projects is truer than it seems, it will sooner or later crack. In this case, it is sooner, and the exposure of the man behind the staged type shows much about how the rest of *Merchant* is played out.

III

The height of Antonio's role-playing coincides with the point where he most manipulates Bassanio's emotions—that is, when his letter, horrendously timed, intrudes upon the betrothal of Bassanio and Portia, usurping center stage. As Bassanio reads the letter aloud, he may as well be reading a part from a script—in this case, a revision of his life's course:

> Sweet Bassanio, my ships have all miscarried, my creditors grow cruel, my estate is very low, my bond to the Jew is forfeit; and since in paying it, it is impossible I should live, all debts are clear'd between you and I, if I might but see you at my death. Notwithstanding, use your pleasure; if your love do not persuade you to come, let not my letter.
>
> (3.2.315-22)

The letter shows Antonio's love to be conditional. His Christian "kind[ness]," trumpeted by his loyal supporters Salerio and Solanio (2.8.35), craves Bassanio's gratitude in return. It thus represents what Thomas Wilson's *Discourse Upon Usury* refers to as "*Mentalis usura,* an usurie of the mynde, when one hopeth for gayne although no contracte be made," gain not in money but in "thankfull recompense."[20] Antonio's protestations of charity, although they surely embrace some truth about his esteem for Bassanio, also reveal, as Geary puts it, "a desperate attempt to hold on to Bassanio"[21] and thereby raise himself in Bassanio's esteem. Such angling may be read as self-interest disguised as selflessness. It compares to his statement in the next scene, 3.3, that he has "oft deliver'd from [Shylock's] forfeitures / Many that have at times made moan to me" (22-23)—a line that appropriates the religious language of salvation ("deliver'd"), that stresses the abundance of his benevolence ("oft," "Many," "at times"), and that, therefore, sets himself up to appear a kind of Christ. But Antonio's self-consciousness mars his charity.

Throughout the trial scene, Antonio continues to display what Lyon calls his "talent for the . . . self-advertising whine."[22] His demeanor of long suffering is undercut by his repeated plays for Bassanio's affection, as well as by startling reminders of how ill at ease he feels in the world. His melodramatic puns, which Portia's verbal adroitness throws into relief, again betray his distress at the prospect of not belonging:

> Most *heartily* I do beseech the court
> To give the judgment.
>
> For if the Jew do cut but deep enough,
> I'll pay it instantly *with all my heart.*
>
> (4.1.243-44, 280-81; emphasis added)

Such painful awkwardness portrays Antonio at his most foolish, unable to feel or to express a love that entails true risk—unconditional love—and unable to trust that he could be loved without manipulating Bassanio into it.

Antonio's masquerade as a man of infinite patience, toleration, and charity is loaded with implication in a scene that takes up the "quality of mercy" at its center. How much of what passes for Christian kindness in 4.1, the audience might well ask upon witnessing Antonio's exhibition, is the real thing? That question is urged by no character's attitude in the scene more than by Gratiano's. With a name connoting grace itself, Gratiano is the enemy of Antonio's pretensions to love, echoing Shylock's denigration of Antonio's false humility as the fraudulence of a "fawning publican" (1.3.41). Gratiano, in fact, is the entire play's enemy to theatrical spectacle. Shakespeare's alteration of *Il Pecorone,* wherein the Antonio figure (Ansaldo) marries the lady's maid, tempts an audience to think of Gratiano as a branching off of Antonio's character, a kind of twin. Both characters, indeed, expose the play-acting in *Merchant* for what it is—the one, through pretense; the other, through brutal honesty.

I believe that Gratiano has yet to be explored satisfactorily in criticism, though his behavior, especially during the trial, bears significantly upon Antonio's characterization. Gratiano is almost unfailingly regarded as, at best, a Jew-baiting boor and, at worst, proof that Christians can hate as violently as Jews. In either case, he is seen as socially coarse and strident. But depictions of him that stop here take their cue, as implied above, from Bassanio's curt dismissal of Gratiano's observations as "chaff" (1.1.116). In reality, however, not only do Gratiano's statements in 1.1 hit home, but, later, he also speaks the most eloquent lines in *Merchant.* Significantly, that same speech encapsulates most faithfully the play's constant concern with the desolation that results in a world of change and instability:

> All things that are,
> Are with more spirit chased than enjoy'd.
> How like a younger or a prodigal
> The scarfed bark puts from her native bay,
> Hugg'd and embraced by the strumpet wind!
> How like the prodigal doth she return,
> With over-weather'd ribs and ragged sails,
> Lean, rent, and beggar'd by the strumpet wind!
>
> (2.6.12-19)

In addition to prophesying the fate of Antonio's argosies, Gratiano discloses the kernel of truth in *Merchant* that perhaps comes closest to being unimpeachable: that as worldly conditions change, so do human appetites.

This gift of Gratiano's for tapping into the essence of things looks forward to another such unlikely truth-teller in Shakespeare's canon: Lucio, the "fantastic" who dogs the friar/duke throughout *Measure for Measure.* Many differences attain between the two—most especially, that Lucio receives a stiff comeuppance for slandering Duke Vincentio, while Gratiano is never judged for what he says. Yet, much as Lucio has an odd way of speaking factually about the duke (or seeming to)—even as, in ignorance of the duke, he manufactures lies about him—so Gratiano remains mysteriously incapable of forgery. And, like Lucio, he sometimes appears to mirror the truth without trying or meaning to.[23] In 2.6, for instance, just after Jessica exits to "gild" herself with "some moe ducats," Gratiano muses, "Now by my hood, a gentle, and no Jew" (49-51). Although he intends to compliment Jessica, he inadvertently characterizes Gentiles as "gilded," preoccupied with the material wealth that Jessica is now adding both to her costume and to Christian coffers.

Gratiano's irrepressible honesty, again like Lucio's, adheres where it is least wanted, though possibly where it is most needed. Duke Vincentio tries in vain to shake off this "bur," who will nevertheless "stick" (4.3.179), and although reprehensible for slurring the duke, Lucio is still valuable for what he can teach the duke about how his subjects really see him. In a sense, Lucio unveils the duke verbally and does so quite literally in 5.1, when he physically lifts the friar's hood, discovering the real duke beneath his theatrical disguise. Such, I think, is also Gratiano's dramatic function: to resist attempts to suppress truth under a veneer of civility. Bassanio suggests as much when he cautions Gratiano about being himself in Belmont and advises him to play a part instead:

> But hear thee, Gratiano:
> Thou art too wild, too rude, and bold of voice—
> Parts that become thee happily enough,
> And in such eyes as ours appear not faults,
> But where thou art not known, why, there they show
> Something too liberal. Pray thee take pain,
> To allay with some cold drops of modesty
> Thy skipping spirit, lest through thy wild behavior
> I be misconst'red in the place I go to,
> And lose my hopes.
>
> (2.2.180-89)

This is all eerily familiar. Wild? Rude? Bold of voice? Thus far, Gratiano has not born out Bassanio's adjectives, although he will fulfill all such epithets during the trial; Bassanio has reason to exaggerate here because, as a nervous suitor, he wants his "show" to be just so (185). Otherwise, he stands to lose his "hopes" (189)—yet another perfectly ambiguous word for what he could gain, financially or spiritually, through marriage to Portia. And the cost to Gratiano of dispelling Bassanio's illusion of suitability? Life as a social outcast, cut off from Portia's fortune and the conduit of Bassanio's friendship. Naturally, he agrees to "put on a sober habit," to role-play along with his benefactors (2.2.190).

Yet, ironically, Gratiano seems to have less to hide than anyone. Never mind that, until the trial scene, he appears, objectively, to be the most socially well adjusted character in Venice; never mind that Gratiano sails into marriage, which eludes Antonio. He is *persona non grata.* His very presence is seen to imperil the charades that promise wealth, stability, and prosperity amidst the flux. In the end, however, Gratiano proves unable to don a socially acceptable façade, such that his character comes to embody a principle that pervades the play—the habit of truth to assert itself. His impulse to be himself and to utter the realities that other characters may intuit, but would rather suppress, calls to mind Launcelot's words to Old Gobbo in 2.2, as he attempts, finally, to reveal himself to his father: "truth will come to light; . . . in the end truth will out" (79-80). Whatever particular truth Gratiano may impart in a given scene, he always somehow displays the darker forces at work behind the cloak of order, normalcy, and reason. Ultimately, Gratiano's truth is the same truth that spoils the masquers' play when, Antonio announces, "the wind is come about" (2.6.64)—the truth that human artifice can exert precious little control over nature's vagaries.

This trait of Gratiano's does not surface fully until 4.1, where he becomes obstreperous: "O, be thou damn'd, inexecrable dog!" (128). On the face of things, the abrupt switch in his characterization may seem puzzling: the only overt link between the Gratiano of the first three acts and that of act 4 are Bassanio's depictions, which, we have seen, do not square with the actual Gratiano on the page, who initially appears well-meaning, perceptive, and even capable of poetry.[24] How appropriate if the play's chief mouthpiece for discontinuity were himself Janus-faced, composed of irreducible and inexplicable contradictions. That possibility notwithstanding, at least one common thread does unite the earlier and later Gratianos, however sensible or vicious they may be. As in the first three acts, Gratiano can still be counted on in one way or another to demystify what he, along with the audience, sees, thereby uncovering certain truths. Once he and Bassanio have become engaged in Belmont, for instance, Gratiano does not hesitate to use the candid terms of material gain for their "success": "We are the Jasons, we have won the fleece" (3.2.240-41). In the trial scene, Gratiano is likely unaware of how effectively he continues to disrupt illusion. Yet he does so by giving frank, passionate voice to the hostility and racism that the trial as play-within-a-play and Antonio as spurious saint are concealing. Gratiano's aspersions may be vile, but, like Shylock's malicious attack on Antonio, they have the virtue of honesty. In this, Gratiano strangely, paradoxically, lives up to his name. "Mercy is not itself, that oft looks so"; Gratiano's inability to pretend is, in some sense, grace indeed. Recalling the socially repugnant fool in book 1 of *Utopia,* who blurts out the proposition that churchmen ought to minister to the needy rather than to their own desires,[25] Gratiano may well be the character in *Merchant* who most closely approximates the Pauline wise fool. In this he is a foil to the folly-fall'n Antonio.

Yet this is not to say that Gratiano's insults toward Shylock speak equally accurately for all the characters' feelings at the trial or that whatever mercy surfaces during the trial is purely sham. The perspective lent by Gratiano on the multiple, complex occurrences in 4.1 is but a wedge of the entire circle, albeit a sizable wedge. It invites examination of the court proceedings as to their real, versus their ostensible, fairness. How do we understand more precisely the degree to which Shylock's treatment under first Portia, then Antonio, translates into either justice or travesty? The letter from Bellario that introduces Balthazar to the court—another disguised script, juxtaposed against Antonio's letter to Bassanio (3.2)—not only commends the young judge's precocious achievement. It also suggests that the youth's judgment is still being tested: "I leave him to your gracious acceptance, whose trial shall better publish his commendation," writes Bellario to the duke (4.1.164-66). The pun on "trial" enables the word to refer to both the trial over which Portia will preside and the scrutiny with which the audience is urged to evaluate her judgments by virtue of participating in 4.1 as audience-accomplices.

Measuring Portia's success at dispensing authentic justice, as opposed to fakery, requires further explanation of what, exactly, she aims to accomplish in court. Foremost, as indicated at the close of 3.2, she seeks to release her husband's friend from Shylock's tyranny, as much to benefit Antonio (3.4.10-21) as to comfort Bassanio (3.2.305-6). Although her primary goal is private, however, she also clearly takes care while pursuing her own ends to preserve the law's integrity, as when she denies Bassanio's request to bypass the contract entirely and "[w]rest once the law to [her] authority" (4.1.215). Already, then, even before she enters the courtroom, she is at pains to balance private against public concerns. Once the trial is underway, she quickly confronts another, similar challenge—the summons to arbitrate between the letter and the spirit of the law, an objective all the more vexed by the demands on her from both private and public spheres.

At merely a cursory glance, Portia's predicament, caught as she is between opposing and equally valid claims, registers as difficult. Indeed, it epitomizes the situation in which all the characters in *Merchant* repeatedly find themselves: that of making impossible choices. At every turn, various characters face one impasse or another. Jessica must choose between restrictive loyalty to her father or a carefree life with a Christian, a dilemma recapitulated in Portia's deciding whether or not to abide by her father's will. Portia's line in that context—"O me, the word choose!" (1.2.22-23)—expresses her dismay at lacking, rather than having, free choice. But she will soon covet the structured choice afforded her by her father's lottery, since she will freely turn to Bellario, her father reincarnated as uncle, for preinstructions about handling the intricacies of the trial. Choice between seemingly irreconcilable options also presses upon Bassanio, dividing his loyalties between Portia and Antonio. That dilemma is more playfully refigured later, in Bassanio's double desire to keep his word to Portia and yet still reward Balthazar, who are, doubly perplexingly, one and the same (4.1, 2). Furthermore, as 3.2 begins, Bassanio, in what can only be construed as the play's near self-parody, must even choose whether and when to choose. Finally, he would rather know his fate than delay it: "Let me choose, / For as I am, I live upon the rack" (24-25). The trial scene, then, is a culmination of this pattern of impossible choice.

Launcelot Gobbo, further fulfilling his dramatic function in *Merchant* as the mirror of crucial themes, takes the parody of feeling deadlocked to new heights as he struggles with whether to exchange masters:[26]

> The fiend is at mine elbow and tempts me, saying to me, "Gobbo, Launcelot Gobbo, good Launcelot," or "good Gobbo," or "good Launcelot Gobbo, use your legs, take the start, run away." My conscience says, "No; take heed, honest Launcelot, take heed, honest Gobbo, . . . do not run, scorn running with thy heels." . . . "Bouge," says the fiend. "Bouge not," says my conscience. "Conscience," say I, "you counsel well." "Fiend," say I, "you counsel well."
>
> (2.2.2-9, 19-22)

The terms of this parody are those of the old morality drama, Launcelot the Everyman being torn between heavenly and hellish alternatives. The point of the parody is how much more troublesome is the problem of choice in the new drama, which more faithfully renders the world's complexities than do the clear-cut absolutes of moral allegory. In his own rudimentary way, Launcelot suggests the overwhelming confusion that choice entails when he scrambles his moral categories: he aligns the "fiend" with the decision to abandon Shylock, who himself is called "devil" and whose house is "hell" (1.3.98, 2.3.2). "Confusions" continue to reign in 2.2 once Old Gobbo enters and Launcelot plays the role of a befuddling God to his father's blind humankind (37). Launcelot's game of ventriloquizing his own shifting identity in his father's mind cleverly mimics all the characters' sense of dislocation as they fade in and out of apprehension, as well as the audience's continual feeling that reliable knowledge of the characters eludes them (33-101). The punch line that resolves this episode of mistaken identity in 2.2 underscores the very fluidity of identity; Old Gobbo exclaims, on feeling Launcelot's beard: "Lord, how art thou chang'd!" (99).

However humorous is Launcelot's rendition of the quandaries that human judgment visits on the other characters, the problem of choice in *Merchant* is no laughing matter. It is the plight that, perhaps more than any other condition of being human, most binds the characters together as human, underlying and belying their more superficial differences. It is, in other words, the truth behind the mask of racial, cultural, and sexual distinctions that, in this treacherous world of deceptive exteriors, transience, and myopia, to boot, everyone must not only choose but choose between two cherished possibilities, letting one go forever, and also make such choice in a mist. This is the hard, tragic fact at the core of human existence in *Merchant*. The cruel necessity of choosing blindly and with finality informs every character's experience equally and, totally without discrimination, alienates them all from their world and from one another. "Joy" is sometimes the "consequence" of judgment, as in Bassanio's happy choice of caskets (3.2.107). One false move, however, and his history would play out like Shylock's, which illustrates how easily a decisive stance, like complete faith in a bond's legality, may bring loss and sorrow. In *Merchant*, choice persistently entails the possibility of lost and irretrievable opportunity. At its most cynical, the play can even imply that neither of two choices will prove gratifying. Launcelot, again, offers a light handling of a dark notion when he tells Jessica that she is damned whether she claims kinship to Scylla, her father, or to Charybdis, her mother (3.5.15-18). Maneuvering through such narrow straits leaves a wide margin for error.

A comic vision, in which extremes are shown to be reconcilable, is not entirely alien to *Merchant*. Under a comic star, two opposites give enough to produce cosmic or social harmony, as Portia is attempting to do in the trial scene: she works to negotiate a slender pass between the Scylla of Shylock's fury, lack of pity, and adherence to an unjust law, and the Charybdis of Antonio's peculiar passivity, the Christians' readiness to dispense with the law, and her own private bias in the defendants' favor. In striving to mediate between the letter and the spirit of the law, she is hoping to vindicate Antonio through strictly legal means and, perhaps, add Shylock's education in flexibility to the bargain: she does, after all, give him plenty of time to withdraw his claim voluntarily before she subjects him to his own legalese.[27]

But what is so remarkable about Portia in the trial scene is her very willingness to take on such a formidable task, especially since, no matter how well, or comically, she satisfies the various, contrary demands upon her judgment, she will likely fall short of the mark. Her partial inadequacy is virtually guaranteed. Whatever comic impulse may inform Portia's skill at judgment or her inclination to effect peace, it will remain at odds with the tragic discontent sown in the play's first lines and cultivated thereafter. For, in addition to whatever personal failings may inhibit Portia's clearer judgment, she has been placed here, as judge, in an untenable position. If the quibble on "blood" that she plays close to her vest stacks the deck against Shylock, then Portia herself has been no less finessed. Any decision she handed down to the court would be hard-pressed to elude the circumstances handed down to her by the play: namely, the unlikelihood that any choice can fully resolve antipathy or thoroughly erase a sense of bereavement.

Put another way, Portia's judgment, no matter how wise, is bound to savor of some theatrical artificiality because she cannot hope to reach an ideal ruling—that is, a thoroughly convincing resolution. She is not so foolhardy as Antonio, whose display of spirituality is at least partly counterfeit. Her performance in court is far more substantial and credible. Indeed, her appearance at the trial exhibits genuine self-sacrifice, as opposed to Antonio's hollow shows of generosity; she has forfeited her wedding night and now risks considerable damage to everyone by taking the responsibility for Antonio that he refuses to take for himself.[28] This substitution, truly Christian in spirit, evinces her noble recognition that, come what may, someone must step up, settle the contest between Antonio and Shylock, and save Antonio's life. But the conditions of her choice—which are largely out of her control—stipulate that, in some measure, her verdict be implicated as mere pretension to truth, pretension signaled even by her theatrical costume. That disguise brings into incisive focus the bind in which Portia finds herself: she must lean on the power of fiction to perform her office and yet can never shake free of the element of fiction—of untruthfulness to the ideal of justice—in her arbitration.

Judgment in *Merchant,* particularly in the trial scene, most resembles theatrical illusion in this way, in its failure to contain all desires, to embrace all aspects of truth, to satisfy from all points of view. To be sure, some strategies minimize error and narrow-mindedness: slow and patient deliberation, mature awareness of life's impermanence, adopting the widest possible angle from which to perceive. Executed with even the best of intentions and with optimal tactics, however, human judgment is merely relative in quality. So must be, then, the quality of mercy. For this imperfection the audience is prone to hold Portia and her fellow Christians wholly responsible. Yet, if the audience, too, is invested in making the best possible judgment of the proceedings, it may benefit from carefully sorting out the factors for which the characters can be held accountable from those for which they cannot. Finally, the "poor rude world" stakes its claim on Portia as forcibly as it does on Antonio, and human nature, hers included, tends to deny the unpleasant realities of that world through substituting a fiction for them. At the same time, those realities persist, gnawing away at the fragile fictions. Although Portia's shortcomings as an individual and as a member of her culture are conspicuous, her human weaknesses encourage sympathy. If, for the former, she remains a foolish fool, then, for the latter, she becomes a wise one, undertaking a largely thankless job at considerable personal expense and at high risk of the censure that Antonio abhors.

IV

Portia's development as a character over the course of the play traces, in essence, her growing familiarity with and ease in the "poor rude world." At her youngest, in 1.2, her lack of sophistication is implied by Nerissa's more extensive worldly experience ("for aught I see," [5]) and intuition about the advantages to Portia of her father's will (27-33).[29] Even here, however, Portia's appreciation of human limitations is realistic beyond her years: "If to do were as easy as to know what were good to do, chapels had been churches and poor men's cottages princes' palaces" (12-14). Yet her awareness that human inadequacy requires compassion comes and goes. Intolerant of her suitors' gullibility, for instance, she fires off a comment to Arragon that not only puts him down but also runs counter to her own convictions: "To offend and judge are distinct offices, / And of opposed natures" (2.9.61-62). If such were the case, then human sympathy would never be able to temper rigid judgment, as Portia strenuously argues it should when promoting mercy in 4.1 (for example, 184-205). Then again, Portia's suitors, intent as they are on idealizing her into a "mortal breathing saint," do little to discourage her curt dismissals (2.7.40). For Portia, as for Morocco and Arragon, the other is not fully human.

Not until Bassanio enters in 3.2 does Portia noticeably begin to bend, growing more accepting of another's weaknesses and more modest toward her own. Without any cooling of ardor for Bassanio, she acknowledges that he stands to choose the wrong casket (1-24), and she readily forgives him his indiscretion on learning of his indebtedness (299-314). Likewise, she offers herself to Bassanio acknowledging both her merits—"the full sum of me / Is sum of something"—and her shortcomings: she is "unlesson'd . . . , unschool'd, unpracticed," though "she can learn" (157-59, 162). Such concessions to imperfection are intermixed with Portia's increased willingness to accommodate the demands on her of living in a flawed society and an unpredictable world. During Bassanio's choice of caskets, she first pronounces the warning to "tarry," to "pause"—that is, to approach choice as the perceptual challenge it is (1). She will later, of course, reprise this sound advice in the courtroom: "Tarry a little," "Soft, no haste," "Tarry" (4.1.305, 321, 346). In 3.2 she confides to the audience her attempt to heed her own counsel by curbing her "joy" at Bassanio's success:

> [*Aside.*] O love, be moderate, allay thy ecstasy,
> In measure rain thy joy, scant this excess!
> I feel too much thy blessing; make it less,
> For fear I surfeit.
>
> (111-14)

These are the words of a budding realist. Still inclined toward fantasies of Bassanio as a Herculean hero (53-62), she has nevertheless undertaken to mature from and learn through experience, as she promises Bassanio she will (149-65).

And indeed, even in 3.2, which is a prelude to the trial scene, Portia's fortitude of mind and character are clearly superior when measured against her peers'. The other characters surrounding her at the scene's end, all of whom have their own attractions, cannot compete with her impressiveness. Bassanio appears more mature when, earlier in the scene, he chooses "substance"—the real and imperfect Portia—over her effigy, a poor "counterfeit" in which she is drawn as a "demigod" (115-30). But having thus rejected mere "show" at last, his former theatrics ambush him when he is forced to confess his debt to Antonio and is once again brought low in the audience's opinion (256-63). Bassanio's good judgment has somehow outstripped his practical behavior, leaving his actual experience to catch up; he is destined now to learn through trial and error what his choice of truth over "ostent" means pragmatically. At the same juncture in the scene, Jessica has just entered with her Lorenzo (219), the couple presenting a portrait of stolen love next to the earned love of Portia and Bassanio, who seem their elders. Add to this company Antonio, who even *in absentia* makes his presence felt through his cloying letter (315-22). In a telling gesture, Portia asks to hear the letter read aloud (314). She probably craves to know what she is up against. Here again, she sets herself apart in this group of seemers, all of whom seek out ways to skirt the practical difficulties and responsibilities, the complexities of human life. Never again is the specific contrast between Portia and Antonio more lucid than at the close of 3.2: for, while Antonio can conceive of realizing his devotion to Bassanio only through sacrificing his existence, Portia intends to enlist her "little body" in the service of saving Antonio's, toward the ultimate end of physically consummating her marriage with a tranquil husband.[30]

Portia's characterization as one who braves the hard vicissitudes of life in order to enjoy its rewards reaches a turning point in 3.4. Easily deceiving Lorenzo and Jessica, she proposes to "abide" in a "monast'ry two miles off," where she may "live in prayer and contemplation" (26-32). In context, her choice to do just the opposite is crucial. Given the play's larger contention between the active life, which requires risk and flexibility, and the passive life, wherein contemplation breeds dangerous idealism, the monastery is richly symbolic. It represents the literal origins of Antonio's martyrdom, implicitly connecting his saintly behavior with the likes of Saint Anthony, and it suggests the figurative roots of his maladjustment to the material life in which he is engaged. By rejecting the monastic, contemplative life in the guise of embracing it, Portia rejects much about Antonio's values without denying his feelings their validity. She separates the man from his conduct, explicitly extolling his "spirit" (3.4.11-21), though implicitly condemning his destructive behavior by electing to participate in the life he shuns. Affirming her attachment to that life, as well as her self-conception as a servant in it, she borrows as her pseudonym the real name of her man Balthazar.

Such signs bode well. In particular, the suggestions in Portia's choices of reconciling extremes—withdrawal and engagement, censure and approval, master and servant, even male and female—adumbrate an official verdict at the trial that just might avoid the pitfall of all other judgments in the play: that of choosing one option at the exclusion of another. If Portia is indeed trying to achieve private ends without doing damage to public structures, if her deliberations are directed toward serving both the law's spirit and letter and toward bringing Jew and Christian closer to mutual understanding, then earlier scenes would seem to allow her a fighting chance to make some progress on those fronts. Her first substantive statement in the trial scene, which is actually a question, also appears to uphold the characterization of Portia/Balthazar as impartial and poised to recognize the legitimacy in each of two opposing perspectives: "Which is the merchant here? and which the Jew?" (174). What less biased opening could she employ than this one, which denies outward appearance as a factor in her arbitration? Her question indicates her readiness to look beyond misleading racial and cultural distinctions and into the pith of the arguments before her.

Yet I would argue, first, that Portia's question is far more complicated in its significance than I have just said and, second, that the question's tonal ambiguity speaks accurately for that, running throughout the scene, toward Portia's approach to judgment. For not only does her question imply her disinterestedness, but it also exemplifies her theatricality, which continually flirts with false sincerity. In fact, the most obvious point to make about her initial question is that it is a gag—and at Shylock's expense: in late sixteenth-century performance, Shylock's gaberdine and accompanying stage-Jew costuming would have stood out in a crowd of Gentiles.[31] Operating simultaneously on a more serious level, however, Portia's apparently innocent question even more subtly raises suspicions about her neutrality, since her terms for Antonio and Shylock—that is, "merchant" and "Jew"—are not comparable, the one referring to a common means of sustenance in Venice and the other to a set of religious and cultural traits that help to alienate Shylock from within Venice. Thus, Portia, from the start, throws the proceedings somewhat athwart the search for justice. She also alerts the audience to the tension, which prevails from here on out, between catering to private interests and heeding the interests of others.

One way to talk about this tension is in terms of how Portia instructs Shylock. Does she, for example, truly attempt to include Shylock's viewpoint in her consideration? Her speech on the "quality of mercy" can be read as such a gesture (184-205), a generous effort to "mitigate" Shylock's severe legal rigor (203). It also contains undeniable elements of tribalism. In a very real sense, before the trial concludes, Shylock "*must* . . . be merciful" (183; emphasis added). He can either volunteer to render mercy as an ideal Christian does, without "strain" (184), or he will be required to give it "by compulsion," legally (183). In any case, his dissent from the "[w]e" who "do pray for mercy" will not be so much as minimally tolerated. Once Portia unhinges Shylock's leverage, depriving him of legal recourse, his forfeiture of his bond and his control of his fortune, are, absolutely, enforced. One could argue that Shylock always has the opportunity, until Portia plays the trump card of her quibble on "blood" (306-7), to relent and soften his cruel demands of Antonio. And many have so argued. But the only authentic opportunity that Shylock has in the trial is to become a Christian—and not the sort of flawed, real Christian represented by other characters in the courtroom but a perfect Christian who lets go of grudges, sprinkles mercy and good will freely, has no property to speak of, and therefore can pose no threat to organized Venetian society. He is also expected to turn the other cheek to those who deceived him in promoting Jessica's elopement and who themselves make no apologies. In effect, Shylock finally has no choice at all and, as a consequence, no audible voice in Venice, no visible role in its fashioning.

All of this reasoning, of course, perverts the audience's direct experience of the scene because it rests on selective evidence. Naturally, we do not want Antonio to die, we do not want Shylock to commit a killing, and we do not want Portia to fail. But what, in our most enlightened moments, we do want instead—the execution of an unbiased justice that validates Shylock's anger as well as Antonio's right to live despite that anger—is not going to happen. Such a resolution of conflict is the stuff of fantasy, not *The Merchant of Venice.* In fact, if Portia is going to rescue

Antonio, she will not—cannot—succeed completely through reconciling him to Shylock. She must resort to hard choices, choices that effectively exclude Shylock, empowering Antonio and his peers to run roughshod over Shylock's feelings of betrayal and desertion and involving Portia's final treatment of the Jew as the "alien" to whom she finally, explicitly, gives the name (349). Many of Portia's statements in 4.1 are capable of being read as judiciously inclusive of Shylock's sentiments; some of those statements may well contradict that ostensible meaning beneath their outward show.

Why Portia must make decisions that exclude and then even misrepresent some of Shylock's identity is the crucial question. Without doubt, she is compelled to her behavior partly by the peculiar weaknesses of her character that have surfaced earlier. To go from despising "all" of Morroco's "complexion" to manipulating Shylock on grounds that he is an "alien" is a fairly small move (2.7.79, 4.1.349). Moreover, Portia's objectivity toward Shylock is surely challenged by the dynamic she witnesses firsthand between Antonio and Bassanio, who needs little coaxing to switch his devotion from his wife to his friend:

> Antonio, I am married to a wife
> Which is as dear to me as life itself,
> But life itself, my wife, and all the world,
> Are not with me esteem'd above thy life.
> I would lose all, ay, sacrifice them all
> Here to this devil, to deliver you.
>
> (282-87)

Not only has Bassanio adopted Antonio's self-sacrificial stance, but he has also absorbed from Antonio the religious language of love—as in "deliver" (257)—that marks the very removal from this world and its stringent responsibilities that have brought Portia to court in the first place. Here Shakespeare seems deliberately to confound Portia's identities as both judge and wife, demonstrating how lightly the rules of either marriage or of civilization can be abandoned once they prove challenging, as they inevitably and quickly do. Bassanio would just as soon "[w]rest once the law" and "sacrifice" his material life than accept what he cannot change (215, 286). Such far-reaching denial exerts no little stress on Portia's judgment, both private and public. Something has to give or go, lest even the mere semblance of domestic and social order evaporate. That something is Shylock's personality.

Portia's capacity for resolving the controversy at all, given its magnitude, thus deserves admiration. But neither will the attentive audience be able to ignore the abundant details of the scene that tarnish the vision of Portia as custodian of law and marriage alike, because during the trial she is revealed to have compromised standards that, as a judge, she purports to defend. When Shylock denounces morally flaccid "Christian husbands" in an aside, for instance, he briefly transports us to a small but valid arena of dissent against Portia's values (295-97). He fleetingly displays how she has gone to all of this trouble for a man who will disappoint her. At moments like these, Shylock's authority weighs in equal to, if not greater than, his opponents'. Hence, when he is later defeated altogether by Portia's trick and then stripped of legal rights as an "alien," the audience perforce senses grievous loss. Venice preserved means Shylock dismissed.

Such is Shakespeare's strategy for characterizing Portia's mixed triumph in 4.1. Refusing to retreat from Shylock's savagery, as Antonio and Bassanio are wont to do, she proceeds to make good on her theatrical portrayal of a judge to a point. That point lies somewhere beyond fulfilling only her private agenda and yet falls short of accommodating the public good, in the widest sense. She may slip across that point here and there throughout the trial, but she plants herself there solidly when she dredges up "yet another hold" of the law on Shylock (347), whereupon, in Lyon's words, her perseverance at the "ceremonial formalities of the trial to the end" and her "humiliating denial of Shylock's dignity" exhibit a certain "sadism."[32] Beyond that point, then, her pose as judge is empty affectation. Yet Shakespeare enlarges on the issue of what motivates Portia's actions in the trial and of how to assess her actions with a second strategy: by implicitly comparing and contrasting them with Antonio's judgments on Shylock. The overall outcome of this additional strategy, overlayering the other, is to enhance the positive perspective on Portia's performance as arbiter. To watch the duke and Antonio follow Portia in delivering verdicts is to be reminded of the perils that confound not just Portia but anyone who presumes to pass judgment. In this context, relative to her rival Antonio, Portia seems unusually bold and competent.

Still, confusion of tone dominates as Antonio assumes judicial power. That Portia should relay it to Antonio in quite the way she does, for example, underscores her sacrifice of justice for expediency's sake: by handing over formal, legitimate control to Antonio, she seems to license Shylock's elimination from Venetian society by the very man who has most despised him. If so, she has dispensed with justice. Since Shakespeare is making up his own Venetian law to suit his purposes, he could have seen to it that Portia was legally bound to collaborate with Antonio, rather than surrender her judicial office to him; he could have written the scene so that Portia was interjecting obviously fair, friendly advice to help shape Antonio's judgments. Instead, he leaves Antonio solely to his own devices and, through Portia's acquiescence to Antonio's sentences on Shylock, portrays her as sanctioning them. Perhaps Shakespeare is generously creating the chance for Antonio to display how much he has learned about kindness through his own suffering, as Holmer and others have argued.[33] At the same time, however, Shakespeare exposes Portia to greater disapproval from her audience than she has already elicited, should that audience recoil from Antonio's responses to Shylock. It probably does.

As for those responses, neither are they clear-cut; they are not unabashedly steeped in the loathing that Antonio formerly paid Shylock or that Shylock has been directing at Antonio. For starters, that Antonio is willing to take an active step of any kind toward Shylock testifies to his renewed spiritual health; even his honest expression of spite would be preferable to utter passivity, since it would plant Antonio firmly in the world that threatens him and perhaps inaugurate a life-altering introspection. Yet the privilege over Shylock that Portia has surrendered to Antonio is absolute, in that Shylock is suddenly and thoroughly in Antonio's debt, under his control. Such conditions do not make for a true test of Antonio's moral growth any more than they justify whatever ruling he settles on Shylock, since he is now free of imperative to treat Shylock humanely. This lack of constraint coats any apparent kindness on Antonio's part with a sheen of magnanimity, as though he "droppeth" mercy "as the gentle rain from heaven / Upon the place beneath" (4.1.185-86). But for all we know, Antonio may again be feigning charity; if Shylock were at liberty to rebel against his pronouncements, Antonio might once again shrink from, rather than deal with, a challenge to his professed kindness. In truth, Antonio is taking no risk in judging Shylock, unless it be that of garnering his peers' disapproval. And since Gratiano is already being the boor, nearly anything Antonio says will seem enlightened by contrast. The only real pressure on Antonio is to keep up appearances, conforming outwardly to the rules of civilized conduct that Gratiano has, conveniently, already blurred through transgressing them himself.

Not surprisingly, then, the substance of Antonio's response to Shylock is enwrapped in equivocation:

> So please my lord the Duke and all the court
> To quit the fine for one half of his goods,
> I am content; so he will let me have
> The other half in use, to render it
> Upon his death unto the gentleman
> That lately stole his daughter.
> Two things provided more, that for this favor
> He presently become a Christian;
> The other, that he do record a gift,
> Here in the court, of all he dies possess'd
> Unto his son Lorenzo and his daughter.
>
> (380-90)

In fact, the very concept of halving that Antonio takes from the law on which he is putting his personal stamp suggests doubleness about his verdict. On the one hand, he hastens to meet Shylock in the middle, as though he can now see his way clear to settling his differences with his enemy by turning the other cheek. Specifically, in as much as he petitions the duke to dismiss Shylock's debt to the state of half of his wealth (380-82), Antonio opens on a note of liberality. He does not have to make this request for Shylock but, by doing so anyway, seems to favor charity over any private vendetta he may harbor. He further cancels his self-interest by turning his attention to Jessica and Lorenzo, for whom he proposes a trust founded on the other half of Shylock's estate (382-85).

Presumably, then, he intends for everyone to win: Shylock will lose little during his lifetime, since he will be sustained by half his fortune and earnings from the other half, and Jessica and Lorenzo will ultimately inherit all (388-90), including the half that Antonio, apparently, assumes he can manage to their financial benefit, despite his own recently problematic investments. This insistence on Shylock's charity not just to his flesh and blood but also to his son-in-law, is of a piece with Antonio's ultimatum that Shylock convert to Christianity (386-87). Both provisions (to borrow Antonio's word in line 386) can be interpreted as newfound broad-mindedness, a genuine attempt on Antonio's part to bridge the gulf that separates him from Shylock. Nothing about Antonio's speech invites this reading more than his choice of the word *use* to define the trust he means to establish for Jessica and Lorenzo (383). By selecting, rather than disparaging, the single word that most identifies Shylock as "alien," he would seem to be supplanting his former vituperation and rejection of Shylock's person and financial practices with a new acceptance. His diction may well indicate both forgiveness and sympathy.

On the other hand, even while Antonio employs the word, he also redefines it, much as he seeks, in effect, to recreate everything about Shylock in his own image, even if doing so entails forcible baptism. To take control over half of Shylock's investments and to demand his religious conversion is to halt his usury altogether and to coerce his conformity with the rest of Venetian society. From this angle, Antonio's conditions for Shylock are not liberal, liberated, or liberating. They are suffocating. They step up Portia's approach to treating Shylock as an "alien" by prohibiting even that meager distinction, which, though not much, is at least Shylock's proper. Withholding even so much as alienation from Shylock, he doubly alienates him; exacting his own figurative pound of flesh, Antonio pushes Shylock into a culture where full participation is, as we have seen, a mixed blessing. Nor does Antonio's vision of Shylock's future at all obligate the existing society to include the newly converted Jew: as Antonio snidely reminds Shylock, Lorenzo "stole" his daughter (385); now he is going to be rewarded for it with everything Shylock can earn until he dies. Some incentive.

In this light, Antonio has not grown in understanding.[34] Were he truly merciful to Shylock, as the whole dramatic situation is set up here to imply he is, he would simply be merciful without meddling in Shylock's personhood. His penchant for doing so, however, recalls his attitude toward Bassanio, to whom he promises unconditional love that, in reality, involves plenty of urgent provisos. In 4.1, as well, Antonio places conditions on his "favor" toward Shylock (386), conditions so restrictive as to bind the other party in virtually total obligation to his terms. Once released from his bond to Shylock and given the chance to act freely, he even takes it upon himself to advise and manipulate the duke's decision about the half of Shylock's goods that are forfeit to the state. Portia has just told the court in no uncertain terms that the half in question is properly "for the state, not for Antonio," although "humbleness" on Shylock's part may induce the duke to lower such a large sum to only a "fine" (373, 372, 371). As though deaf, Antonio immediately presumes to address his first statement not to his own business but to whether the duke should collect all that the state is owed or just the fine (380-82); furthermore, he makes his next judgment, which does concern himself (382-85), contingent upon the duke's enactment of his opening request: thus, between lines 380 and 385 he tells the duke, in so many words, "Please reduce what Shylock owes the state so long as I am permitted to do what I wish with what he owes me." Subtly but surely, Antonio has interposed himself again where he might take over, whether or not he belongs there.

Such bids for control suggest that, even now, Antonio remains subject to his fears of exclusion. He seems threatened, rushing to alienate Shylock first, as if doing so will preclude his own dispossession. In a matter of minutes, he has pivoted from dealing with the world through emotional paralysis and death-wish to reentering the hardships and confusions of this life by stage-managing. Calm as he may outwardly seem in this scene, his inner panic would appear to endure as he dictates once again how Bassanio should demonstrate his love for his friend: "My Lord Bassanio, let [Balthazar] have the ring. / Let his deservings and my love withal / Be valued 'gainst your wive's commandement" (4.1.449-51).

Thus, a definable pattern in Antonio's characterization from beginning to end comes into focus. His eleven lines about Shylock in 4.1 go by quickly and are overly dense for a first-time audience to grasp fully, but, studied carefully, they, too, substantiate his determination to direct the play's events or to die trying. The theatrical metaphor with which he describes himself in 1.1 has become completely apt by the end of 4.1. Whether Antonio is behaving submissively or asserting himself, he is often practicing some form of passive aggression. The only occasion on which he displays his antagonism outright is in 1.3, and even there it is second-hand, glimpsed through the window of Shylock's narration and affirmed by Antonio himself, who almost, but not quite, loses his temper (106-31). Ordinarily, he is not given to confessing his feelings openly, a habit behind his hypocrisies, like professing love for Bassanio, whose wife he discounts. For his lingering social awkwardness, Antonio is pitiable. But for resorting to misleading emotional and moral theatrics, which are nothing akin to the wise folly he pretends, he verges on abusiveness. In his foolish consistency, he is, at least potentially, as dangerous to social cohesiveness as are large rocks to argosies. Here, too, he is an unrecognized version of Shylock, who differs mainly in that he wears his anger on his sleeve.

If Portia both shares in and countenances Antonio's hypocrisy toward Shylock, she does not abide it toward her marriage. Through appending the substance of act 5 to the action of the trial, Shakespeare fleshes out just how much more competent in judgment has been Portia than we may have thought or than Antonio has proved to be. She accomplishes with the ring trick far more nearly the reconciliation of opposites that also occupied her in the trial. Earlier, her choice resulted in the almost tacit exile of Shylock's variety, albeit menace, from the Venetian order. In act 5, where she forms the triple bond among herself, Bassanio, and Antonio, she comes closer to harmonizing antinomies—here, those of marital love and male friendship.[35] The most prominent feature of Portia's judgments, however, as well as all instances of choice in *Merchant,* is their relative failure or success. No single judgment is completely satisfactory. Some are simply more satisfying than others.

V

The whole of act 5 is informed by the notion of relativism. Introduced as it is by the rhapsody between Jessica and Lorenzo (1-24), the scene is designed to subvert confidence in the image of an ideal world or ideal love within it. The tragic note sounded by each reference to mythical lovers—Troilus and Cressida, Pyramis and Thisby, Dido and Aeneas, Medea and Jason—resonates with the misunderstanding that has plagued the characters' relationships prior to this point, as well as with the distrust sown by Antonio between Bassanio and Portia. Much as the sweetness in the rhapsody is qualified, but not subsumed, by the bitter, so is the ensuing music (68), symbolic of universal harmony, tempered by Portia's remark that Lorenzo recognizes her "as the blind man knows the cuckoo, / By the bad voice!" (112-13). Her self-effacing humor, while not thoroughly at odds with Lorenzo's more grandiose references to "the poet," "Orpheus," and the power of music to raise human nature (79-82), nevertheless introduces a realistic element of flawed human nature into Lorenzo's more philosophic (and naive) meditations.

Portia herself values the idealism and romanticism about Lorenzo's vision, if for no other reason than that it supplies a fixed standard of judgment and a goal for human ambition:

> A substitute shines brightly as a king
> Until a king be by, and then his state
> Empties itself, as doth an inland brook
> Into the main of waters. . . .
> Nothing is good, I see, without respect.
>
> (94-97, 99)

Even so, Portia expresses keen awareness that human action is destined to fall short of the ideal. The perspective that she brings to the scene's idealism, a perspective "season'd" by her recent experiences, repeatedly adds an antiromantic, slightly deflating dimension to the higher-flown diction and sentiments of the characters in her midst (107). The moon seems to the less experienced Jessica and Lorenzo to light the sky as though setting the stage for love. To Portia, however, this night, which is "such a night" to the others, seems hardly extraordinary: "This night methinks is but the daylight sick, / It looks a little paler. 'Tis a day, / Such as the day is when the sun is hid" (124-26). Same night, different impressions.

The difference, moreover, amounts to much. Most important, it characterizes Portia as one who can accept imperfections not by ignoring hobgoblins but by flexing standards just enough to make them attainable. For Bassanio, her attitude means a mild chastening and the forgiveness that yields a second chance (199-255). For Antonio, it also means another chance but not a chance to interfere again in her marriage. When Antonio admits, "I am the unhappy subject of these quarrels," Portia does not disagree but lends him hospitality despite his error: "Sir, grieve not you, you are welcome notwithstanding" (239). Portia's graciousness and grace expand further, as far as they will go, while she witnesses Antonio rebind himself in friendship to Bassanio, this time spiritually instead of physically but, more to the point, to safeguard, not spoil, the marriage (249-53).

This is something of a breakthrough for Antonio, since his pledge to uphold Portia's faith in Bassanio requires his own acceptance of imperfection and, at that, a difficult form of imperfection for him to tolerate: his desire to be included is only partly realized, and his dread of being left out thus only partly allayed. Yet the necessary consequence of Portia and Bassanio's choice to wed is Antonio's loss of status. Although not rejected, he must remain second in Bassanio's regard. As if to represent the compromise at hand, Portia announces (through what agency, who knows?) that three of Antonio's original six argosies have come to port (275-79).[36]

In his last line, Antonio would seem to be commemorating not only his final ostracism from the social bonds that continuously elude him but also, for once, his unwillingness to indulge in play-acting: "I am dumb" (279). Not even a sixteenth-century audience, for whom that word had yet to connote witlessness, could be expected to hear the line without a shudder or an uncomfortable laugh. Owing to his peculiar personality and to the conditions urged on him by Portia, Antonio is still somewhat alienated. His situation, like his muteness, is embarrassing. And yet his silence, recalling the harsh choice yoked upon the resigned Shylock in 4.1, also betokens Antonio's moment of greatest happiness and fulfillment. Settling for what he has been given without another word, he finally becomes a wise fool—dumb and dumbfounded, content with his place in a world whose vastness cannot be overestimated and, when it cannot be controlled, must evoke awe. Paradoxically, Antonio now seems more at ease with his alienation.

What Portia's acceptance of such human limitation means for her is the luxury of sleeping at night without an "unquiet soul" (3.2.306). Whether she planned all along to dispose swiftly of Shylock toward expediting the retrieval of her marriage or whether she did her best and still failed to cajole Shylock out of his destructive humour, Portia never looks back. Many of us, of course, do. The aftertaste of gall is the play's most potent reminder to the audience of the fact of choice and all that it intimates—our lost opportunities and our misgivings that the wrong history is being made, inexorably, against our wishes. Perhaps, ideally, Portia could and should have refrained from conspiring to alienate Shylock. Yet she, too, is ultimately an alien, held hostage by a mutable world and the submission of her judgments to fickle standards. If she undertook another judgment in act 6, she might go on evolving, never fully reaching the "right praise and true perfection" that she herself envisions as the crown of experience (5.1.108). Finally, I do not quite think, as Lyon contends, that *Merchant* portrays "different" and incompatible Portias.[37] Rather, the play seems to me to record fictionally, though impressively realistically, a segment of time during which a capable young woman, in contrast to her foil Antonio, makes repeated, active forays into the distressing territory of judgment and, by fits and starts, becomes a bit better at an essentially impossible task. With every trial of her skills, she sees more clearly and speaks more frankly.

To censure Portia for her inadequate choices, in fact, is a form of self-disgust, unfair though understandable. *The Merchant of Venice,* a tragicomedy until the end and even after the end, assaults the audience with the inherent injustice of its own situation, so much like Portia's, in a mercurial world so much like the play's, a world that consistently makes fools of us all. By implying that apparent differences belie deep-seated likenesses, *Merchant* coaches us to think of presumed opposites as a cinch to reconcile. In the same breath, it takes back what it gives, indicating that the material, mortal world will always prove unruly, will always swerve wayward of forms like law, government, choice—even poetry and drama.

Antonio's efforts to remove himself from such frustrating contradictions or to believe his choices can evade or rise above them are, though understandable, a fruitless turn at cheating human life. That sort of arrogant callowness is the object of no little irony, as it is one last time, now in Lorenzo's response to learning of his inheritance: "Fair ladies, you drop manna in the way / Of starved people" (5.1.294-95). This unsettling line betrays the speaker as flagrantly self-absorbed, misapplying sacred terms to his own worldly needs (as has been Bassanio and Antonio's wont) and misadvertising himself as needy at all, coddled as he is at present in the lap of Portia's luxury. Lorenzo's line escapes the explicit retort that it deserves (although Portia might well wince at it). But the play isn't about to let us forget that the self-satisfied speaker is ripe for sobering, if not now, then soon. For the pattern of *Merchant* has been that of disabusing credulity and overturning such self-idealizations as Antonio's saintliness and Lorenzo's fond portrait of himself and Jessica as God's chosen. The closer Portia ventures toward acknowledging the disparity between "what were good" and what actually is, the more trust she earns from her audience and, unavoidably, the more sorrow she elicits for fading illusions. As if to ratify the abiding value of such earthiness, however, the play's last word belongs to Gratiano, who has always been most at home in the "rude world" and who concludes with a final demystification, calling a "ring" a "ring" (5.1.307). His candid reference to Nerissa's anatomy purges the air of any residual delusions about love and securely grounds spiritual faith where it is "riveted"—in the "flesh" (5.1.169).

Notes

1. Moreover, as John Doebler points out, the "melancholy man without cause" was a Renaissance "stock character" (*Shakespeare's Speaking Pictures: Studies in Iconic Imagery* [Albuquerque: University of New Mexico Press, 1974], 41).

   Since John Russell Brown attributed Antonio's melancholy to Bassanio's departure for Belmont (*The Merchant of Venice,* by William Shakespeare, New Arden ed. [Cambridge: Harvard University Press, 1955], xlvi on 1.1.119), many critics have followed, thereby raising the inevitable question about the nature of Antonio's and Bassanio's feelings for each other. Are those feelings friendly or erotic, at least on Antonio's part, if not on Bassanio's? Here is likely an instance where labels are more self-defeating than helpful, as Marjorie Garber has recently argued about the futility of efforts to categorize sexual identity (*Vice Versa: Bisexuality and the Eroticism of Everyday Life* [New York: Simon & Schuster, 1995]). Even so, I must agree with Joseph Pequigney about the absence of any recognizably erotic language in Antonio's and Bassanio's speeches to and about each other ("The Two Antonios and Same Sex Love in *Twelfth Night* and *The Merchant of Venice,*" *English Literary Renaissance* 22 [1992], see especially 210-21). Their relationship seems a friendship. In any case, I am relying on the assumption that the emotional bond between the two men as it conflicts with Bassanio and Portia's marriage bond is of central concern, whatever the specific nature of the male bonding at hand. Shakespeare is perennially interested in how male-female relationships are negotiated with same-sex relationships to form a workable (if neither completely harmonious nor absolutely fixed) social structure—as in, for example, *A Midsummer Night's Dream, Much Ado about Nothing,* and other works, including two more in this study, *Twelfth Night* and *Antony and Cleopatra.* In my opinion this negotiation is both troublesome and troubling in *Merchant*; I disagree with Pequigney's assertion that the resolution brought about in the love relationships here is relatively trouble-free (see "The Two Antonios," especially 218-21). On these relationships see also the essays of Alice N. Benston ("Portia, the Law, and the Tripartite Structure of *The Merchant of Venice,*" *Shakespeare Quarterly* 30 [1979]: 367-85), Geary ("The Nature of Portia's Victory"), and Newman ("Portia's Ring").

2. *The Oxford English Dictionary* (1989).

3. Christopher Spencer shows that the Christians refer to Shylock as "Jew" sixty-one times in *Merchant* and only fifteen times call him by his proper name (*The Genesis of Shakespeare's "Merchant of Venice,"* in *Studies in British Literature,* vol. 3. [Lewiston, N.Y.: Edwin Mellen, 1988], 95).

4. For a reading of Bassanio's motives similar to mine, see Terry Eagleton: "Having improvidently thrown his money around, Bassanio has come to Belmont to buy up the well-heeled Portia with the aid of Antonio's loan, rashly jeopardizing his friend's life in the process" (*William Shakespeare* [Oxford: Basil Blackwell, 1986], 45).

5. David Beauregard has recently read Antonio as an Aristotelian-Thomistic embodiment of the very virtue of liberality. Beauregard adds to the list of Antonio's sacrifices his patient endurance in 4.1 in the face of injustice (*Virtue's Own Feature: Shakespeare and the Virtue Ethics Tradition* [Newark, Del.: University of Delaware Press, 1995], 88, 99).

6. So much has been written about Shylock's appropriation of Jacob and Laban's story that some acknowledgment of the variety in critical opinion is in order. In brief, critics tend to disagree over whether Shylock's apology for usury is in any sense defensible or is, rather, specious; the latter view is adopted more often, most notably by Joan Ozark Holmer in a brief article ("'When Jacob Graz'd His Uncle Laban's Sheep': A New Source for *The Merchant of Venice,*" *Shakespeare Quarterly* 36 [1985]: 64-65). My own sense of Shakespeare's purpose is informed by other parallels in *Merchant* between Shylock and Jacob. In particular, that Shylock's wife was named Leah does not reflect ironically on Shylock but positively (see Gross, *Shylock,* 68-69). All told, neither the association between the two men nor Shylock's narration of the story in 1.3 seems to me to be charged with a particular tone, but, rather, both seem mixed in tone, capable of evoking irony *and* sympathy. Hence my use of the word *trickster* for Jacob and Shylock both: it incorporates several overtones and looks forward to Shylock's defeat by Portia, another trickster.

7. Evidence that Jews were regarded in Elizabethan England as the devil's kin continues to arise, as in Ruth Samson Luborsky's recent note "The Pictorial Image of the Jew in Elizabethan Secular Books" (*Shakespeare Quarterly* 46 [1995]: 449-53).

8. One recent director of the play has observed that it "can be seen as a warning, as a picture of how we allow our religious beliefs to mask our God-given humanity" (quoted in Felicia Hardison Londré, "Confronting Shakespeare's 'Political Incorrectness' in Production: Contemporary American Audiences and the New 'Problem Plays,'" in *Staging Difference: Cultural Pluralism in American Theatre and Drama,* ed. Marc. Maufort, American University Studies, series 26, vol. 25 [New York: Peter Lang Publishing, 1995], 90).

9. Many critics remark on Shylock's role in alienating himself, perhaps most interestingly Mullaney, "Broth-

9. ers and Others," 82. Other critics have also noticed, as I do, Antonio and Shylock's deeper resemblance beneath their enmity—for example, Jan Lawson Hinely: "Antonio, looking at Shylock, sees himself, distorted but still recognizable" ("Bond Priorities in *The Merchant of Venice*," *Studies in English Literature* 20 [1980]: 223).

10. See Brown, *Merchant,* note to 3.3.27. Brown also notes the difficulty of Antonio's language here in notes to 3.3.19, 30-31.

11. Stephen J. Greenblatt, "Marlowe, Marx, and Anti-Semitism" in *Learning to Curse: Essays in Early Modern Culture* (New York: Routledge, 1990), 43. In fairness to Greenblatt, I must admit that I have lifted his words from a context antithetical to mine, where he is arguing that "the Jew seems to embody the abstract principle of *difference* itself" (43).

12. Sinead Cusack, "Portia in *The Merchant of Venice*," in *"The Merchant of Venice": Critical Essays,* ed. Thomas Wheeler (New York: Garland Publishing, 1991), 342-43.

13. W. Moelwyn Merchant, ed., *The Merchant of Venice,* by William Shakespeare (Middlesex: Penguin, 1967), note to 1.2.108.

14. John Julius Norwich, *A History of Venice* (New York: Knopf, 1982), 129-31.

    Most critics who have taken up the matter of Portia's racism have apologized for it, but I think it is pronounced in 1.2 by being repeated through hints in 2.1.1-3 and more overtly in 2.3.79. Furthermore, why would all the suitors except Bassanio be foreigners to Italy unless to present a perceptual problem to Portia comparable to that posed by the casket test (of which she is herself skeptical)? Surely the lesson that appearances can deceive is not confined to young men.

15. *As You Like It*, 2.7.139-66. As Anne Barton has stated so well: "[Jaques's] words are no sooner spoken than Orlando enters bearing old Adam: a man enfeebled by his years, dependent now upon a younger life, but also the living image of all that Jaques has left out of his type picture: loyal, honest, and discriminating" (introduction to *The Merchant of Venice,* by William Shakespeare, in *The Riverside Shakespeare,* ed. G. Blakemore Evans [Boston: Houghton Mifflin, 1974], 367).

16. The dramatic irony of Portia's comparison of Bassanio to the "young Alcides" is subtle but true (3.2.54-57): as the note in *The Riverside Shakespeare* (Boston: Houghton Mifflin, 1974) points out, "Hercules' motive in rescuing the Trojan princess Hesione [the "virgin tribute" of 1. 56] . . . was not love for her but a desire to possess the horses which Laomedon, her father, had promised him as a reward." Here again is the familiar strain of Bassanio's mixed motives (unless, of course, Shakespeare did not know or remember the story faithfully, which is a distinct possibility).

17. Many critics have read Bassanio's casket choice as a complete theatrical performance, contending that Portia drops pregnant hints to her love throughout 3.2, which include her reference to Bassanio's choice as a "hazard," echoing the inscription on the lead casket (2); her admonition to "[b]eshrow your eyes" (14); the rhyme of "lead" with "bred" and "head" in the round sung during Bassanio's apparently sincere deliberations (63-107); and Portia's line, "I stand for sacrifice" (57). Yet I must agree with other critics who believe that Bassanio's decision is relatively free of assistance and that Portia does her best to uphold the letter and spirit of her father's will. For me, the most convincing evidence lies in her having used the word *hazard* in describing the same lottery to both Morocco (2.1.45) and Arragon (2.9.18). Surely she does not intend to coach either one of them.

18. For much of the material in this paragraph, I am indebted to the fine work of Mullaney and Eagleton. Throughout "Brothers and Others, or the Art of Alienation," Mullaney remains intrigued by the confluence of fictions in the *Merchant,* especially that in the staged trial scene and that in the regime of Elizabeth I. He also notices the benighted Shylock's impotence in the face of an opponent, Portia, who only appears impartial (82-84). Eagleton stresses the notion that systems such as language and law are, in *Merchant* as well as in life, always subject to interpretation (*William Shakespeare*).

    The idea that the play's systems are as mutable as are its concepts about issues like individual identity and human existence is refracted in the feminist criticism of Catherine Belsey and Newman. The latter wonders whether certain aspects of the "Elizabethan sex/gender system" are in fact questioned by this play's peculiar version of transvestism (Newman, "Portia's Ring," 32). Belsey speculates that all examples of transvestitism in Shakespearean comedy "can be read as disrupting sexual difference, calling in question that set of relations between terms which proposes as inevitable an antithesis between masculine and feminine, men and women" ("Disrupting Sexual Difference: Meaning and Gender in the Comedies," in *Alternative Shakespeares,* ed. John Drakakis [New York: Methuen, 1985], 167).

19. See, e.g., Joan Ozark Holmer, "The Education of *The Merchant of Venice*" (*Studies in English Literature* 25 [1985]), 312, and Walter Cohen, "*The Merchant of Venice,*" 768. Holmer also calls Antonio's love for Bassanio a kind of "surfeit" (307).

20. Thomas Wilson, *A Discourse Upon Usury,* ed. R. H. Tawney (New York: A. M. Kelley, 1963), 292. Although I have gone straight to Wilson for my reference, I should acknowledge Holmer for the informa-

tion; Holmer herself is actually discussing the views of Hineley (Holmer, "Education," 326-27; Hinely, "Bond Priorities," 229), but expands on her own ideas in *"The Merchant of Venice": Choice, Hazard, and Consequence* (New York: Methuen, 1995), 249-50.

21. Geary, "The Nature of Portia's Victory," 63.

22. Lyon, *"Merchant,"* 48.

23. Evidence of Lucio's uncanny insight into the duke's identity and machinations is scattered throughout the play but concentrated in 3.2.86-184. I have argued elsewhere that Lucio reflects the duke's aloofness from his subjects and his corresponding need to become more directly involved with his subjects; Lucio's lies about the duke, in a profound sense, tell the truth about the duke's weaknesses as governor (see Cynthia Lewis, "'Dark Deeds Darkly Answered': Duke Vincentio and Judgment in *Measure for Measure*," *Shakespeare Quarterly* 34 [1983]: 271-89).

24. Interestingly, in this aspect too Gratiano parallels Lucio, whose apparent split in personality from the beginning of *Measure* to the end makes his characterization seem incoherent. In the first two acts, he is Claudio's friend and Isabella's advocate; later, his character turns much darker as he slanders the duke and is revealed to have fathered a child for whom he intends to take no responsibility.

25. More, *Utopia,* 27-28.

26. Richard Horwich has observed that *"The Merchant of Venice* is filled with difficult choices" ("Riddle and Dilemma in *The Merchant of Venice*," *Studies in English Literature* 17 [1977]: 191), although he builds differently on this point than I do, citing that, "where Belmont is full of riddles, Venice is the natural habitat of dilemmas" (197). He also maintains that, in the case of dilemmas, "the alternatives are equally desirable or . . . undesirable," availing themselves of no solutions (196), while "riddles have single and wholly correct answers, . . . however hard those answers may be to come by" (198). As useful as I find this distinction, I still think that Belmont is not devoid of dilemmas, as I believe my examples testify. Hinely offers yet a different approach to the play's interest in the "problem" of "evaluating the claims of contradictory demands" ("Bond Priorities," 218-19)—that of how this problem influences the presentation of bonds in *Merchant*. Both Horwich and Hinely notice that Launcelot Gobbo's initial speech in 2.2 mimics lightly the difficult decisions, as that between "fiend" and "conscience," forced upon all the characters (Horwich, "Riddle and Dilemma," 197; Hinely, "Bond Priorities," 219).

27. Cusack, "Portia," 349.

28. Holmer, "Education," 328.

29. I do not mean to glide over the implications of the father's lottery as if they were exclusively advantageous to Portia. As Leventen, Newman, and others have shown, the will is an especially enticing metaphor for patriarchy, including the most stifling, repressive confinements thereof. I do believe, however, that the negative and positive connotations of the will are inseparably entangled. For example, perhaps Portia cannot take control of a trial otherwise dominated by patriarchs without having first been immersed in and irritated by a patriarchal structure like the will.

30. Lawrence Normand, in his provocative essay on the body as scripture in *Merchant,* phrases this idea thus: "Were [Antonio] to realize the scenario he projects, his love for Bassanio would be inscribed in his living body, and its truth proved by incisions which would be neither deletable nor reversible. . . . [This] exchange . . . would turn his physical death into social discourse aimed at recording and validating a certain meaning for it" ("Reading the Body in *The Merchant of Venice*," *Textual Practice* 5 [1991]: 67-68). In other words, Antonio is attempting to freeze emotion in a fluid world; the act of preservation, ironically, perverts the feeling.

31. Exactly how to understand this passage dramatically is a bit baffling, since, in its entirety, it suggests that Portia's question—"Which is the merchant here? and which the Jew?" (174)—is offhand and posed before she has taken opportunity to look about the room. Hence, probably, the duke's follow-up order: "Antonio and old Shylock, both stand forth" (175). By the same token, however, she has too much to lose by not speaking deliberately to begin with; her question is no doubt partly calculated to produce one effect or another. Finally, no matter how harmless may be Portia's intent, her question cannot avoid all dramatic irony, since to the audience (at whom Shakespeare aims the joke) Shylock is so very prominent in appearance.

32. Lyon, *"Merchant,"* 110.

33. Holmer, "Education," 316-17.

34. My remarks about Antonio in act 4 are meant in part to address the sanguine conviction of Holmer and others that, when Antonio judges Shylock, "We observe none of Antonio's former vindictiveness" (Holmer, "Education," 317). Cf. Beauregard, who envisions Antonio's "division of [Shylock's] wealth," which jeopardizes Shylock's very "life" (4.1.376), as a just recompense for Shylock's having sought to take Antonio's life (*Virtue's Own Feature,* 100-101).

35. While I see Walter Cohen's point that the "romantic comedy" of act 5 acts to "obliterate the memory of what has preceded" it (*"The Merchant of Venice,"* 777), I also agree with the many critics who see act 5 as integrated thematically and through its action into the whole play. In particular, Lyon senses that the ties between act 5 and the body of the play are even more intricately knit than is often thought—for

instance, by the recapitulation between Bassanio's wedding ring and the ring that Leah once gave Shylock ("*Merchant*," 117).

36. I hesitate to overread this detail, lest I commit the same sort of indiscretion that I have taken to task at the beginning of this chapter. One does wonder, however, whether Shakespeare was conscious of the delicious parallel between this numerical detail and all manner of references to relativism throughout act 5. Why three out of six, only half?

   The name of the rocks on which Antonio's ships wreck is also an intriguing detail in view of any personal growth that may be seen to result for Antonio from his ordeal: the name "Goodwins"—or Goodwin Sands—literally means "good friends" (*The Concise Oxford Dictionary of Place Names* [Oxford: Clarendon Press, 1960]).

37. Lyon, *"Merchant,"* 112.

Martin D. Yaffe (essay date 1997)

SOURCE: Yaffe, Martin D. "The Mistreatment of Shakespeare's Shylock." In *Shylock and the Jewish Question*, pp. 1-23. Baltimore: Johns Hopkins University Press, 1997.

[*In the following excerpt, Yaffe argues against the conventional view that the depiction of Shylock in* The Merchant of Venice *is anti-Jewish.*]

> The figure of Shylock is like some secondary figure in a Rembrandt painting. To look sometimes with absorption at the suffering, aging Jew alone is irresistible. But the more one is aware of what the play's whole design is expressing through Shylock, of the comedy's high seriousness in its concern for the grace of the community, the less one wants to lose the play Shakespeare wrote for one he merely suggested.
>
> —C. L. Barber, *Shakespeare's Festive Comedy*

In this book I analyze the figure of Shylock, the unfortunate Jewish villain in Shakespeare's *Merchant of Venice*. My immediate aim is to challenge the widespread presumption that Shakespeare is, in the last analysis, unfriendly to Jews. In so doing, my larger hope is to rescue Shakespeare's play as a helpful guide for the self-understanding of the modern Jew.

What modern Jewish readers find most unpalatable and upsetting about the dramatic fate of Shylock is his forced conversion to Christianity. Shylock, a wealthy moneylender, is made to convert to Christianity as part of the surprising outcome of his personal lawsuit in retaliation against a Christian merchant, the play's title character. The merchant has been waging a vehement one-man crusade on the Rialto against him for his putatively un-Christian business practices. Shylock's harsh and humiliating punishment might be more merited, one suspects, if the moral and legal circumstances surrounding it were more clearcut. But they do not seem to be. Despite its otherwise happy ending or perhaps because of it, Shakespeare's Venetian comedy leaves us unsettled and perplexed over the place of the Jew in the modern city.

Shylock's offense in the eyes of the city is in the end not just civil or even religious. It is criminal. He has granted the merchant an emergency loan of three thousand ducats, interest free but with a sinister, life-threatening penalty clause for late payment. The penalty, for which Shylock eagerly sues, is a pound of the merchant's flesh. Yet his suit proves in court to be treasonous. It is tantamount to the seeking of a Venetian citizen's life by a resident alien—and is therefore punishable by death and by forfeiture of the offender's estate, half to his intended victim and half to the city. Nor is this all. Although the court mercifully waives the death penalty and offers to reduce the claim on its half of Shylock's estate, it soon withholds the waiver pending Shylock's agreement to a counterproposal by the merchant. The latter recommends extending the court's mercy even further. But he adds three constraints. In return for the city's forgiving all penalties, Shylock must now allow the merchant trusteeship over half his estate so long as Shylock lives, must immediately convert, and must designate the Christian bridegroom of his recently converted and eloped daughter as his sole heir. Even so, questions here arise.

To begin with, why does the court ignore Shylock's repeated subjection to publicly tolerated harassment concerning both his religion and his means of livelihood (personal lending, we might call it; loansharking, as Shakespeare's Venetians seem to regard it)? During the trial, moreover, why do spontaneous Jew-baiting outbursts from one of the merchant's friends go uncensured? And why does the court fail to forewarn Shylock about the imminent likelihood of self-incrimination, into which it eventually entraps him? Finally, why has the merchant, admittedly prominent and well liked in Venice, been allowed the final say to determine Shylock's punishment in accord with his own biblically inspired anti-usuriousness? In short, is not Christian Venice itself party to the abusive conduct of its citizens toward Shylock? Shakespeare's play makes us wonder: why can't the city just let Shylock be?

In order to know from the foregoing circumstances whether Shakespeare's play deserves its anti-Jewish reputation, we must face such questions and try to answer them squarely. Our task first and foremost is therefore to look in a scholarly way at the answers, if any, the play itself provides. In my view, the play's own remarkable answers have not been well understood or appreciated by modern scholars. Although it is reasonable to expect some help from the accumulated scholarly literature about the play, when we turn to it with our questions, we find that it has not succeeded very well in answering or even in facing them. A few recent examples will serve to illustrate.

Harold Bloom, in his introduction to an anthology of critical essays on Shakespeare's Shylock, castigates the playwright severely.[1] He calls the play "both a superb romantic comedy, and a marvelously adequate version of a perfectly Christian, altogether murderous anti-Semitism" (1). He is particularly incensed by Shakespeare's having inflicted on his antagonist a "false conversion," an imposed acceptance of Christianity without any word of defiance or complaint (1f.). He finds Shylock's quiet acquiescence here dramatically implausible, on the grounds that Shylock is a "proud and fierce Jew" for whom conversion is entirely out of character. "We sooner could see Falstaff as a monk, than we can contemplate Shylock as a Christian" (2). Where Shylock's character lacks consistency, Shakespeare's art fails. Bloom the critic therefore turns to *ad hominem* speculation about the playwright's "agonistic context" and infers a "need to compete with and overgo Marlowe's superb villain, Barabas, the Jew of Malta" (5). Shakespeare, we are told, chiefly meant to outdo his literary rival in fashioning a vivid and memorable portrait of (what he took to be) a Jew. Yet in so doing, and especially in succeeding as well as he did, he could not help appealing to the ruling anti-Jewish prejudices of his Christian contemporaries. "In this one play alone," Bloom concludes, "Shakespeare was very much of his age, and not for all time" (6).

Leaving aside the suggestive comparison with Christopher Marlowe's *Jew of Malta* . . . , I limit myself here to noting a significant omission in Bloom's summary description of Shylock as a "proud and fierce Jew." How, we must ask, are we meant to understand Shylock's Jewishness? Neither Bloom in his introduction nor anyone he selects for his anthology has pursued this question very far—though it is central to Shakespeare's play.

Shylock's Jewishness first comes up in act I, scene iii, during his preliminary encounter on the Rialto with Bassanio, the young man for whose sake the merchant, Antonio, needs the emergency loan. When Shylock asks whether he might speak with Antonio directly, Bassanio at once invites him to dinner for that purpose. Evidently the young man does not expect what Bloom would undoubtedly characterize as Shylock's "proud and fierce" reply:

BASSANIO:

If it please you to dine with us.

SHYLOCK:

Yes, to smell pork, to eat of the habitation which your prophet the Nazarite conjured the devil into! I will buy with you, sell with you talk with you, walk with you, and so following; but I will not eat with you, drink with you, nor pray with you.

(I.iii.29-34)[2]

Yet from Shylock's point of view, his insistence that he will do business and otherwise associate with Venice's Christians but will not eat or drink or pray with them implies, in the first instance, not pride and ferocity so much as a strict loyalty to Jewish law, which among other things forbids eating pork (evidently a staple in Shakespeare's Venice)[3] and prescribes the prayers that Jews in particular must recite before eating and drinking. Shakespeare identifies Shylock's Jewishness here with his law-abidingness, that is, with his pious deference to the legal demands of Jewish orthodoxy.[4] Even so, in act II, scene v, when Shylock next appears, we are given occasion to question the steadfastness of Shylock's piety.

Once the terms of the loan have been agreed on and sealed, Shylock returns home to tell his daughter that he has decided to accept an invitation to eat at Bassanio's after all, albeit "in hate" and for an ulterior motive:

I am bid forth to supper, Jessica.
These are my keys. But wherefore should I go?
I am not bid for love; they flatter me.
But yet I'll go in hate, to feed upon
The prodigal Christian.

(II.v.11-15)

Shylock's ulterior motive, "to feed upon / The prodigal Christian," is connected as well with a second reason for having returned home, namely, to announce to his household servant that he will gladly let him switch to the "prodigal" Bassanio's employment:

The patch is kind enough, but a huge feeder,
Snail-slow in profit, and he sleeps by day
More than the wildcat. Drones hive not with me;
Therefore I part with him, and part with him
To one that I would have him help to waste
His borrowed purse.

(II.v.44-49)

Shockingly enough, the motive for which Shylock is prepared to give over his household servant and which is, at least in part, a further extension of that for which he is prepared to suspend his observance of the dietary laws is that of "help[ing] to waste / [Bassanio's] borrowed purse." Shylock's intent to add to Bassanio's overhead in these ways would have the net effect of increasing the likelihood, however slim, of Shylock's extending yet another loan for Bassanio, this time interest bearing, or even under certain conditions (which almost do transpire) of his collecting on his sinister penalty clause with Bassanio's benefactor. At this point, Bloom might well wish to raise the larger question of whether Shakespeare means to imply that Jewish orthodoxy sanctions hatred or revenge against non-Jews; yet as we shall soon see, it is a question the play answers sufficiently clearly in the negative. Meanwhile, contrary to Bloom, we must say that far from simply succumbing to putative Elizabethan stereotypes concerning Jews, Shakespeare evidently understands both Shylock's piety and his departure from it (which appears to begin well before the forced conversion) by the standards of Jewish orthodoxy itself.

But Bloom notwithstanding, whether or not Shakespeare's play is anti-Jewish cannot be decided by a single argument. Controversy over the treatment of Shylock is not confined to questions of character but permeates the entire fabric of the play. With an eye to the considerable range of disagreement about the play among scholarly critics, John Lyon, in his monograph on *The Merchant of Venice* in Twayne's New Critical Introductions to Shakespeare, sounds a timely warning against one-sided readings.[5]

> The play has suffered from the aggressive justifications of its champions no less than the dismissals of its detractors. It seems a rich play where the potential multiplicity of meanings is in excess of any full realization. And to actualize any single interpretation of the play is to stress, and perhaps overstress, one of its parts at the cost of ignoring or doing violence to parts of the play developing in other, equally interesting ways.
>
> (5)

Lyon's book calls attention, in general, to the rich mix of particulars as the playwright meant us to savor them. He is properly averse to scholarly arguments that would, in effect, dissolve those particulars into thick generalities for the sake of some bland unifying gloss that looks good from a distance. At the same time, we are admonished that the particulars of the play themselves solicit our subsequent wonderment and inference: "*The Merchant of Venice* is no piece of theatrical ephemera: the play is of a substance to merit and require the kinds of sustained recollection and speculation which occur subsequent to our enjoyment of the play in the theatre" (105). Lyon therefore proposes to "characterize, rather than resolve, the play's puzzles" and to "raise questions about the limits of plausible interpretation" (5). Proceeding somewhat idiosyncratically, the central chapters of his book may be described as a freewheeling tour of Shakespeare's plot, which sometimes fends off, sometimes embraces the views of scholarly critics, depending on whether they block or widen a scenic path through the play's main contours. Lyon justifies his procedure by the assertion that the play is "not *finished*" (8). He finds its dramatic action unpolished and its philosophical perplexities left unresolved. Hence, he infers, it is best approached tentatively, as a play-in-progress, whose chief merit is to testify to the creative and provocative genius of its author.

The practical result of Lyon's argument, however, would seem to be the opposite of the full openness to the dramatic and philosophical richness of the play which he has intended. Instead of encouraging us to venture wide eyed and alert into the play's "puzzles," guided above all by Shakespeare's many-layered text, Lyon effectively discourages us from making the necessary effort to explore whether any one speculation is better than another so far as an understanding of the play as a whole (at least as we have it) is concerned. By simply denying that the play is a finished whole, he denies to us from the outset any standard for judging which interpretations are good or better or best beyond our private fancies. And yet that same denial scarcely prevents him (or anyone else) from interposing judgments that may well block our view of the richness of what Shakespeare has left us.

A single example must suffice. Lyon rightly disputes the answer offered by Harold C. Goddard to one of the questions I began by raising, about the propriety of the Venetian court's legal entrapment of Shylock—at the hands, moreover, of a surprise amicus curiae (secretly Bassanio's newly wedded wife, Portia, in disguise): why "didn't she invoke immediately the law prescribing a penalty for any alien plotting against the life of any citizen of Venice instead of waiting until she had put those she supposedly loved [namely, Bassanio and, by extension, his benefactor] on the rack?"[6] To Goddard's hastily advanced claim that "the only possible answer is that she wanted a spectacle, a dramatic triumph with herself at the center," Lyon fittingly adds that there may be forensic reasons as well: "With an opponent as legalistically precise as Shylock, Portia needs as much evidence of the reality of Shylock's malevolent intent as he can be brought to give, and it is perhaps only *at* the last moment that the last-moment solution can be safely and effectively revealed" (105).

Nevertheless, faithful to his general caveat that any solution to a given "puzzle" in the play can be only tentative, Lyon immediately expresses his misgivings about what he has just said and meanwhile drops the issue—except to salvage what he takes to be one incontrovertible point. "Certainly," he assures us, "Portia suffers when considered with hindsight" (ibid.). Yet the assurance Lyon offers follows not from the particulars of Portia's actions during the trial but rather from the doubtful premise that he accepts without argument from Goddard, that Portia's actions are largely self-centered. In her admonitory speech to Shylock about the "quality of mercy" (IV.i.182-203), however, Portia emphasizes that her actions are guided not only by the legalities of the case, of which she is evidently the master, but also by justice seasoned with mercy (cf. IV.i.200f.). Contra Goddard, the prospect therefore opens up that Portia's cross-examination of Shylock, while fulfilling the obvious requirements of justice, is at the same time a high-minded act of mercy on the part of someone, indeed the only one in the courtroom, who knows the law. As I argue later, Portia's words give Shylock himself every opportunity to render a spectacular act of mercy so as to render nugatory the law under which she alone knows he stands guilty. Recalling Lyon's previous words (105), we cannot help wondering whether his offhand suppression of this possibility is a consequence of his unsupported insistence that our receptiveness to the play's details and our thinking about them are two separate things—an assumption belied by anyone whose attention is drawn to the thoughtful details of Portia's speech to begin with.

Lyon does not mention the only other full-fledged monograph on the play, Lawrence Danson's, which might have provided him with a direct challenge to the view that *The Merchant of Venice* lacks a dramatic unity.[7] Danson argues for its unity on the basis of "the fact that the play was written by a Christian for a Christian audience, and that it is about Christian issues" (13). According to Danson, Shakespeare's Christianity does not narrow but broadens his understanding of things; it is "an amplifier, not a deadener of conceivable meanings" (15). Nor need we then presume that Shakespeare's thought is a prisoner of (the Christianity of) his time, for as in those plays that consider issues of kingship, "he is drawing upon ideas common to his time. But that is very different from saying that Shakespeare's ideas are common" (16). Against critics who would impute to Shakespeare a Christian teaching that sets itself in opposition to Judaism and seeks to triumph over it, as mercy over justice or the New Law over the Old, he looks instead to the teaching of "*completion* or *fulfillment*" (17f.), that is, of the reconciliation or harmony of souls among themselves and with the divinely ordered cosmos. The main evidence, so far as Portia's aforementioned "quality of mercy" speech is concerned, is that the warrant for her appeal to the need for mercy to temper justice is the Lord's Prayer (66f.), whose theme as she understands it is common to both Jewish and Christian worship, as her words imply:

> *That, in the course of justice, none of us*
> *Should see salvation. We do pray for mercy,*
> *And that same prayer doth teach us all [sic] to render*
> *The deeds of mercy.*
>
> (IV.i.197-200)

Danson's argument has the further merit of indicating why the play cannot end with Shylock's defeat in the trial scene of act IV but must conclude in the pastoral setting of act V, at the wealthy Portia's estate in Belmont. There the three newlywed couples—Portia and Bassanio, Portia's maid, Nerissa, and Bassanio's companion Gratiano, and Shylock's eloped daughter, Jessica, and her poet husband, Lorenzo—each for the moment at odds, soon become reconciled. In a moonlit setting under the stars, Lorenzo woos Jessica with a speech about cosmic harmony that prepares us for that reconciliation:

> *Look how the floor of heaven*
> *Is thick inlaid with patens of bright gold.*
> *There's not the smallest orb which thou behold'st*
> *But in his motion like an angel sings,*
> *Still quiring to the young-eyed cherubins;*
> *Such harmony is in immortal souls;*
> *But whilst this muddy vesture of decay*
> *Doth grossly close it in, we cannot hear it.*
>
> (V.i.58-65)

The Christian overtones of Lorenzo's words are undeniable, as Danson points out (186f.): the stars are "patens" (or communion dishes); the harmonics of their geometrically ordered motions are angels' songs; and the reason we hear only intimations of those sounds is our "fallen" earthly condition.[8]

Nevertheless Danson does not take into account the chief evidence against his view, namely, that the play contains at least as many allusions to classical mythology and philosophy as to Christian doctrine. Lorenzo's speech about the harmony of the stars is a case in point, for the notion in terms of which that speech becomes intelligible—that the stars are embedded in invisible concentric spheres surrounding the earth—is ultimately of pre-Christian, Pythagorean origin. To be sure, Danson might easily reply that those same Pythagorean allusions are also found in certain Christian authors who have appropriated them, such as Boethius, to whom he refers briefly (187f.). Still, to the claim that Shakespeare's Christianity is the play's final word there is a further objection from the play itself.

During the tense moments of the trial, when Shylock's insistence on the letter of the law seems to be holding sway, an outraged and frustrated Gratiano exclaims against what he takes to be Shylock's inhuman inflexibility:

> *O, be thou damn'd, inexecrable dog,*
> *And for thy life let justice be accus'd!*
> *Thou almost mak'st me waver in my faith,*
> *To hold opinion with Pythagoras,*
> *That souls of animals infuse themselves*
> *Into the trunks of men. Thy currish spirit*
> *Govern'd a wolf, who, hang'd for human slaughter,*
> *Even from the gallows did his fell soul fleet,*
> *And, whilst thou layest in thy unhallowed dam,*
> *Infus'd itself in thee; for thy desires*
> *Are wolvish, bloody, starv'd, and ravenous.*
>
> (IV.i.128-38)

It strikes Gratiano that Shylock's "currish spirit" is evidence for the pagan Pythagoras's view of the transmigration of souls between animals (in this case wolves) and humans. Exasperated, he is on the point of "waver[ing] in [his] faith" to accommodate that view. To Gratiano, at least, Christianity and Pythagoreanism are not simply compatible. Indeed, if Lorenzo is Gratiano's erstwhile teacher in these matters, as the play's description of their close companionship suggests (see I.i.69-71, 106ff.), the same may need to be said of Lorenzo's moonlit speech about harmony and perhaps other Christian-sounding speeches as well. Pace Danson, we shall have to explore how Shakespeare faces and seeks to resolve the evident tension between Christianity and philosophy in the play before we can determine to what extent or in what way its teaching may be said to be Christian.

This last would seem in part to be the aim of Edward Andrew, a political scientist, who also reads the play in the light of what he takes to be its implicit Christian teaching, though unlike Danson he finds that teaching one-sided and faulty.[9] It is the teaching of Christian charity, which Andrew understands to mean the doing of acts of kindness or mercy to others with or without their consent. He follows the literary critic Harry Berger Jr., who adduces the term *mercifixion* to describe Shylock's forced conversion insofar as it is meant for his own good.[10] Shakespeare's scriptural precedent here is said to be Luke 14:23: "Go out into the highways and hedges, and compel them to come in, that my house may be filled." Andrew's interpretation is guided by an appeal to the authority of St. Thomas Aquinas, who appears to him to cite this verse in support of the church's position that it is just to compel unbelievers into the Christian communion. Meanwhile, Andrew also notices an opposing view in the play, which he finds spelled out only incompletely. It is the "possessive individualism" personified by Shylock.[11] As usurer, Shylock embodies the "heartless greed" and "limitless acquisitiveness" at the root of modern entrepreneurial capitalism (4). At the same time, in Shylock's attempts to justify his retaliation against his Christian tormentor, he anticipates the philosophical arguments for religious toleration later articulated in Benedict Spinoza's *Theologico-Political Treatise* (1670) and John Locke's *Letter on Toleration* (1689). Throughout, however, Shylock also shares in his own way the old-fashioned charitableness of his Christian persecutors. According to Andrew's admittedly unconventional analysis of the play, Shylock would like nothing better than to marry his daughter Jessica to a nice Jewish husband. Andrew's Shylock is therefore driven at bottom by a charitable wish to befriend the merchant in order to convert him to Judaism for that purpose.

But Andrew's attributing the merchant's own conversion-seeking zeal to traditional Christian teaching is overly hasty and seriously misleading. In the very passage that Andrew cites in support of his contention that Christianity authorizes the compulsory conversion of Jews, Thomas Aquinas emphasizes exactly the opposite. Here are Thomas's words in response to the question, "Whether the faithless are to be compelled to the faith?"

> I respond that it should be said that certain of the faithless are those who have never taken up the faith, such as gentiles [i.e., pagans] and *Jews*. And such people *are in no way to be compelled to the faith,* in order that they might believe for themselves—since believing is a matter of the will. Nevertheless they are to be compelled by the faithful, if the means are there, in order that they not impede the faith, whether by blasphemies or by bad arguments or even by open persecutions. And on this account faithful Christians frequently make war against the faithless, not in order to compel them to believe (since even if they were to conquer them and hold them captive, they would *leave them at their liberty* concerning whether they wished to believe) but in order to compel them not to impede the Christian faith.[12]

According to Thomas, Jews and pagans alike are exempt from forcible conversion at the hands of Christians, though not from acts of force if they impede the Christian faith by means of slanders, dubious propaganda, or overt harassments. Even so, they are to be left "at their liberty" so far as matters of belief are concerned, if only that they might eventually come to Christian belief on their own. Because belief as such is voluntary, Thomas insists, neither Jews nor pagans can be forced into it.

True, immediately following the passage just quoted, Thomas goes on to justify the punishment of heretics and apostates. But these differ from non-Christians by being deviant and lapsed Christians, who have already put themselves under the authority of the church. In any case, Andrew overlooks Thomas's indication that "liberty" or tolerance is in some sense part of traditional Christian teaching. Despite what Andrew suggests, then, tolerance of Jews can hardly be said to receive its first, to say nothing of its best, philosophical treatment in the theologico-political arguments of Spinoza and Locke. Indeed, in looking later on at the speeches of Shylock to which he calls our attention, we shall have occasion to wonder how well such intimations of the case for religious toleration as Andrew rightly discerns in *The Merchant of Venice* can be understood in terms of the political and religious liberalism of those modern thinkers (as instructive as their arguments might otherwise prove to be). As the example of Pythagoras has already indicated, we shall have to weigh in addition the considerable merits of certain premodern philosophical and theological views that Shakespeare has evidently inherited from thinkers such as Thomas.

It is admittedly possible to read *The Merchant of Venice* as a Christian or quasi-Christian play and yet to defend Shakespeare's presentation of Shylock as being not quite so derogatory toward Jews as it might have been in the hands of another at that time—Marlowe, for example. Such is the approach of the literary journalist John Gross.[13] Shakespeare, he writes, "simply tried to imagine, within the confines of his plot, and within the limits that his culture set him, what it would be like to be a Jew" (349). What is chiefly missing from Shakespeare's Shylock is any "hint . . . of an inner faith, or of religion as a way of life, as opposed to a set of rules" (45). In contrast, the Christian characters in the play are said to "have admirable ideals, and on the whole—in their dealings among themselves, as opposed to their dealings with Shylock—they live up to them" (350). However that may be, the result, to Gross at least, is "tragic," inasmuch as the "anti-Semitism" shown by the other characters "coexists with so many admirable or attractive qualities" (351).

Thankfully, Shakespeare's Shylock is cut somewhat larger than his stereotype. Gross makes much of the playwright's investing his Jewish character with unforgettable habits of speech, including the staccato repetitions and symmetrical constructions of the money-lender's angry outburst promising revenge against the merchant:

> *—and what's his reason? I am a Jew. Hath not a Jew eyes? Hath not a Jew hands, organs, dimensions, senses, affections, passions? fed with the same food, hurt with the same weapons, subject to the same diseases, healed by the same means, warmed and cooled by the same winter and summer as a Christian is? If you prick us, do we not bleed? If you tickle us, do we not laugh? If you poison us, do we not die? And if you wrong us, shall we not revenge? If we are like you in the rest, we will resemble you in that.*
>
> (III.i.50-59)

Gross comments: "Where else, in Shakespeare's time, can you find such sentiments?" (66). True, they are uttered in the service of an "inhuman purpose" (67). And they are followed by an ugly conversation with Shylock's own banker and fellow Jew, Tubal, who presses Shylock mercilessly with reports of looming financial disasters stemming from his eloped daughter's free spending and from the merchant's losses at sea. "Yet," Gross insists, "nothing that happens in the rest of the play cancels out 'Hath not a Jew?' The words have been spoken; the stereotype will never be the same again" (ibid).

Unfortunately, the conclusion Gross would have us reach—that Shakespeare perhaps couldn't help being just a bit anti-Jewish—becomes plausible only if we overlook much of the detailed content of the play. Among Gross's dubious factual claims are that Shylock lacks any "inner faith" (here Harold Bloom seems on stronger ground) and that the Christian characters are by comparison meant to be admirable. (I shall have much to say on the latter point about Gratiano in particular, as well as about the merchant himself, later on.)

Most egregious, because most decisive for his argument, appears to be Gross's erroneous assertion that "at no point [in the play] does anyone suggest that there might be a distinction to be drawn between [Shylock's] being a Jew and his being an obnoxious individual" (351). Portia aside, to whom I have already referred, it is enough for the moment to quote the highest ranking authority of the court, the Duke himself, in his introductory plea for Shylock to show mercy to the merchant:

> *Shylock, the world thinks, and I think so too,*
> *That thou but leadest this fashion of thy malice*
> *To the last hour of act; and then 'tis thought*
> *Thou'lt show thy mercy and remorse more strange*
> *Than is thy strange apparent cruelty;*
> *And where thou now exacts the penalty,*
> *Which is a pound of this poor merchant's flesh,*
> *Thou wilt not only loose the forfeiture,*
> *But, touch'd with humane gentleness and love,*
> *Forgive a moiety of the principal,*
> *Glancing an eye of pity on his losses,*
> *That have of late so huddled on his back—*
> *Enow to press a royal merchant down*
> *And pluck commiseration of his state*
> *From brassy bosoms and rough hearts of flint,*
> *From stubborn Turks and Tartars never train'd*
> *To offices of tender courtesy.*
> *We all expect a gentle answer, Jew.*
>
> (IV.i.17-34)

Here Antonio is said to deserve Shylock's "pity" in light of his overwhelming shipping losses, the putative cause of his failure to repay on time. In the circumstances, the Duke adds, Shylock ought to forgive not only Antonio's penalty but some of his principal too.

What are important here are the Duke's announced reasons for expecting some last-minute, out-of-court refinancing from Shylock. First, he says, everyone including himself believes that Shylock is merely stalling so as to make his eventual show of compassion more spectacular. That is, the Duke attributes to Shylock a sense of theatrics. Second, there is also the depressing magnitude of Antonio's reported losses—enough, as he says, to make even hard-boiled, crudely raised observers act compassionately (Turks and Tartars come to the Duke's mind). Hence, he concludes, "We all expect a gentle answer, Jew." The pertinent question is whether the Duke's concluding reminder that Shylock is a Jew means that he manifestly includes Jews among those who are by nature or upbringing ungentle. Two reasons suggest he does, but then again a third seems to override these. First, a pun on "gentle" yields "gentile," implying that the Duke is seeking a gentile or un-Jewish answer from Shylock.[14] Second, the Duke has already confided to Antonio privately that he considers Shylock incorrigible (IV.i.3-6). Still, third, the Duke, whatever his private opinion, cannot admit publicly that Shylock *as Jew* was "never trained" to be gentle that is, by Jewish law, without weakening his earlier argument that Shylock's apparent lack of compassion was a deliberate theatrical delay. The inescapable conclusion, then, is that the Duke is forced to give the public impression to Shylock and everyone else that Jewish law does after all teach moral decency, including compassion, and that Shylock, being uncompassionate, is simply being a bad Jew. Evidently Gross's approach, which (in contrast to, say, Danson's) looks not much further than the putative stereotypes Shakespeare is said to share with his contemporaries, blurs just that point in the Duke's speech which goes contrary to stereotype.

In other words, the Duke makes a public effort to compliment Shylock's Jewishness and pleads with him simply to live up to it. As with Portia's subsequent speeches in court, a possibility here emerges that is entirely different from any that Gross seems willing or able to acknowledge. Perhaps the possibility is best put by way of our denial of a remark made in passing by an articulate but overly sympathetic reviewer of Gross's book: "It was clearly not part of Shakespeare's conscious design," writes Robert Alter, "to question the received wisdom of Christian hostility toward the Jews."[15] But the facts we adduce, and which Gross and others ignore, suggest just the opposite.

Even so, the question remains today to Shakespeare's apparent moral obtuseness, his lack of sensitivity (as we say) about Jews and Judaism, whether we ultimately ascribe to him a reformer's intention or not. Once the most obvious incidents of the play, such as we first take note of them, are seen for what they are morally, it is hard to resist interpreting *The Merchant of Venice* as a whole simply in their terms—that is, moralistically. How could anyone who writes such stuff, we tend to ask, have been very nice to Jews? The play undeniably draws from an appalling legacy of Jew-hatred in England from, say, 1290, when Jews were officially expelled, till at least 1753, when the ill-fated Jew Bill, as it was called, momentarily dropped professing the sacraments as a naturalization requirement and so opened citizenship to Jews, who had begun to be formally readmitted under Cromwell a century earlier. Perhaps the most convenient place to begin to acknowledge the bearing of that legacy here is James Shapiro's recent *Shakespeare and the Jews*.[16] Shapiro draws from abundant references to Jews in chronicles, sermons, stories, plays, legal opinions, political tracts, and the like surrounding what he calls the "cultural moment" of the play's first staging (10). He disclaims any overall interpretation of the play, or of Shakespeare's private intentions, for that matter. Still, his comments on passages seen to dovetail with the historical evidence he adduces suggest much by way of innuendo which is morally damaging. Although the passages he cites are few and far between, they are worth listing, so that one can see both the force of the argument to which he contributes and its limitations.

That Jews sometimes suffered brutal reprisals for alleged ritual murders of Christians around Easter time, for example, serves to explain a report in the play of an ominous predawn nosebleed on "Black Monday," or Easter Monday, by Shylock's clownish ex-servant, Launcelot, in his chatterbox cover-up of an impending elopement of Shylock's daughter, Jessica, and her Christian lover, Lorenzo (II.v.22-26) (258 n. 71). Launcelot's report resonates a few lines later during his coded message to Jessica, "There will come a Christian by / Will be worth a Jewess' eye" (II.v.40-41)—the "worth" here alluding less, Shapiro argues, to "the value of a lover than the revenge exacted upon the Jewish community for its crimes" (109). That Shakespeare's contemporaries were generally aware that there was no strictly female counterpart to male circumcision as the sign of Jews' covenant with God, moreover, explains the relative ease with which Jessica could break that covenant in marrying Lorenzo (120). And yet the short-lived contemporary belief that women's earrings could somehow substitute for ritual circumcision, Shapiro thinks, might explain Jessica's absconding with Shylock's jewels and Shylock's afterward lamenting that he would rather see her dead at his feet with the jewels in her ear (III.i.77-79) (ibid.). In any case, the further suspicion that a Jewess who could easily convert might just as easily revert to the old covenant seems to Shapiro to underlie the disturbing exchange between Jessica and Lorenzo comparing their hasty marriage to several thwarted love affairs of classical antiquity (V.i.1-24) (58f.). Finally, contemporary theological discussion over the meaning of "circumcision of the heart" in Paul's Letter to the Romans leads Shapiro to speculate that Shylock's insistence on a pound of Antonio's flesh might be a metonym for genital circumcision or even castration (114-21).

The historical import of these and other derogatory images of Jews, according to Shapiro, was to cast doubt over whether Jews could ever be trusted as fellow denizens, much less citizens, alongside Englishmen. To the extent that Shakespeare may be said to have given further currency to such images, he also seems to have lent them further credibility as his national stature rose. Or so Shapiro finds when looking at the public debate over the Jew Bill more than a century and a half later (195-224). The same images continued to be invoked by opponents of the bill, Shapiro notes, and led to its repeal barely two years after its passage, despite arguments in its favor drawn from more enlightened thinkers such as John Toland, Daniel Defoe, and John Locke. Shapiro leads us to infer, though he does not put it in so many words, that the bill might have had an easier time of it had Shakespeare thought better than to write *The Merchant of Venice* in the first place. For these and other moral reasons, he has no hesitation about calling the play "anti-Jewish" (216).

Here is where the limitations of Shapiro's argument become apparent. Assuming that the popular images as Shapiro describes them were as decisive politically as he suggests, there seems a further need to explain why Parliament itself was not altogether dazzled by them, at least for a time. Why, in short, did public life become as receptive as it was to the position in favor of tolerance of Jews as articulated by Toland, Defoe, Locke, and others? Here Shapiro is comparatively silent. It is testimony to the difficulty of this question that it would require him to widen the scope of the inquiry, to move from the narrower question of the popular prejudices latent and prevailing at a given hour (what Shapiro calls "cultural history")[17] to the broader question of how responsible statesmanship would have to discern and guide such prejudices on important public issues such as the Jew Bill.

Let us come closer to the point at hand. Given at least the modest success of enlightened statesmanship in 1753 in overcoming the derogatory images of Jews admittedly found in Shakespeare's then popular play, wouldn't we have to ask—as Shapiro does not—whether Shakespeare himself might have had enough statesmanlike insight to be able to anticipate and even encourage these same possibilities, however modestly, in his dramatic presentation of Shylock? The moment this question occurs to us, unless we simply decide to rule out certain answers beforehand, we are forced to look again at the manifestly derogatory things said of and by Jews in Shakespeare's play, to see whether they are indeed the play's last word or whether instead they might also call to mind other, more salutary images of the behavior of Jews—and of Christians—embedded as well in the psyches of his viewing and reading audience. But this last question can be answered one way or the other not by insinuation from evidence outside Shakespeare's play, but only by firsthand examination of the play itself. . . .

Notes

1. Harold Bloom, ed., *Shylock,* Major Literary Characters Series (New York: Chelsea House, 1991). Citations to this work and to those of other critics are given in the text.

2. I follow the text of the play as found in William Shakespeare, *The Merchant of Venice,* 2d ed., ed. George Lyman Kittredge, rev. Irving Ribner, Kittredge Shakespeares (New York: John Wiley & Sons, 1966). All citations are to that edition unless otherwise noted.

3. Cf. III.v.21-23, 30-33; IV.i.47, 54.

4. Cf. also IV.i.204, 221f., 226f., 233ff., 312.

5. John Lyon, *The Merchant of Venice,* Twayne's New Critical Introductions to Shakespeare (Boston: Twayne, 1988).

6. Harold C. Goddard, *The Meaning of Shakespeare*, 2 vols. (Chicago: University of Chicago Press, 1951), 1:109, as quoted in Lyon, *Merchant of Venice*, 105. Goddard's chapter is reproduced in H. Bloom, *Shylock*, 137-70; the sentence quoted is on 163; Goddard alludes in passing to III.i.32. Similarly, M. J. Landa, *The Jew in Drama* (reprint; Port Washington, N.Y.: Kennikat, 1968), 76f. On the other hand, Bernard Grebanier, *The Truth about Shylock* (New York: Random House, 1962), 282ff., correctly sees that Portia shows mercy to Shylock when exhorting him in effect to exculpate himself legally by showing mercy in turn to Antonio; but Grebanier misses the larger theological and political implications. Cf. chap. 3, sec. 5, and chap. 5, sec. 2, below.

7. Lawrence Danson, *The Harmonies of* The Merchant of Venice (New Haven: Yale University Press, 1978). I omit from fuller consideration Grebanier, who defends the play on the too narrow grounds that Shakespeare understands his Shylock as a banker in conflict with a merchant prince rather than as a Jew in conflict with a Christian: "No one expects compassion from a bank" (*Truth about Shylock*, 213; cf. 95). See, however, I.iii.37, 41-43, with IV.i.17-34 and my remarks on Gross, below.

8. Danson here quotes S. K. Henninger, *Touches of Sweet Harmony: Pythagorean Cosmology and Renaissance Poetics* (San Marino, Calif.: Huntington Library, 1974), 5.

9. Edward Andrew, *Shylock's Rights: A Grammar of Lockean Claims* (Toronto: University of Toronto Press, 1988).

10. Harry Berger Jr., "Marriage and Mercifixion in *The Merchant of Venice*: The Casket Scene Revisited," *Shakespeare Quarterly* 32 (1981): 155-62.

11. Andrew acknowledges his debt for the term to C. B. Macpherson, *The Political Theory of Possessive Individualism: Hobbes to Locke* (Oxford: Clarendon Press, 1964).

12. Thomas Aquinas, *Summa Theologiae* II-II.10.8 (my trans.; my italics).

13. John Gross, *Shylock: A Legend and Its Legacy* (New York: Simon & Schuster, 1992).

14. For a useful discussion of Shakespeare's "verbal usury" in the play, that is, his habit of generating added meaning from given words, see Marc Shell, *Money, Language, and Thought: Literary and Philosophical Economics from the Medieval to the Modern Era* (Berkeley: University of California Press, 1982), 47-83.

15. Robert Alter, "Who Is Shylock?" *Commentary* 96, no. 1 (1993): 33.

16. James Shapiro, *Shakespeare and the Jews* (New York: Columbia University Press, 1996). Shapiro's larger argument disputes the suddenness and thoroughness of the expulsion of Jews under Edward II in 1290 and their readmission under Cromwell in 1656, partly because of the absence of hard documentary evidence in either case and partly because of Englishmen's ongoing fascination with, and abuse of, opinions about Jews in the meantime, as a foil for understanding what being English might mean for themselves.

17. Cf. ibid., 43, with 83, 110, 189 ("the play as a cultural safety-valve"), 228 ("*The Merchant*'s capacity to illuminate a culture").

Charles Edelman (essay date 1999)

SOURCE: Edelman, Charles. "Which Is the Jew that Shakespeare Knew?: Shylock on the Elizabethan Stage." *Shakespeare Survey* 52 (1999): 99-106.

[*In the following essay, Edelman reconstructs Elizabethan perceptions and expectations of Jewish theatrical characters, offering evidence that Shakespeare's Shylock was more likely a tragic figure than simply a comic villain.*]

As John Gross remarks in *Shylock: Four Hundred Years in the Life of a Legend*, 'everyone who writes about the stage history of *The Merchant of Venice* is doomed to quote, sooner or later', the couplet supposedly spoken by Alexander Pope upon seeing Charles Macklin's portrayal in 1741:

This is the Jew
That Shakespeare drew.[1]

Pope's comment shows that he considered Macklin's hard and bitterly malevolent interpretation to be a welcome corrective to the Shylock of Thomas Doggett and his successors in George Granville's adaptation, *The Jew of Venice*,[2] a lurid burlesque of the role that had held the stage since 1701. It also shows a yearning, shared by all students of the play, to reconstruct somehow the first Shylock, about whom there is no reliable contemporary information whatsoever—the actor Thomas Jordan's doggerel description,

His beard was red . . .
His habit was a Jewish gown,
That would defend all weather;
His chin turned up, his nose hung down,
And both ends met together

dates from 1664, when the theatre was not, contrary to the view of E. E. Stoll, 'still swayed by the tradition of Alleyn and Burbage'.[3]

Given that any role is going to be significantly altered from its conception in the dramatist's imagination once it is in the hands of an actor and an audience, this essay is not concerned with the Jew that Shakespeare 'drew'—that

Shylock was forever lost the moment the play was performed. My topic is the Jew that Shakespeare 'knew', the Shylock whom he, Francis Meres, and other spectators saw some time before September of 1598, when the role was reinvented by Richard Burbage or another actor of the 'Lord Chamberlaine his Servants'.[4]

In all that has been written about *The Merchant of Venice*, one point has remained virtually constant: however sympathetic the portrayals of Edmund Kean, Henry Irving, Laurence Olivier, or any number of others may have been, the original Shylock would have conformed to the so-called Elizabethan stereotype of the villainous stage Jew. Gross writes

> . . . to an Elizabethan audience, the fiery red wig that he almost certainly wore spelled out his ancestry even more insistently than anything that was actually said. It was the same kind of wig that had been worn by Marlowe's Barabas, and before that by both Judas and Satan in the old mystery plays.[5]

Similarly, Jay L. Halio, in the introduction to his Oxford edition, notes that 'Shakespeare's initial conception of him was essentially a comic villain, most likely adorned with a red wig and bottle nose.' Halio is at pains to point out, however, that 'the evidence for Shylock as a comic villain' is not to be found in the play, but 'partly in the literary and dramatic traditions which Shakespeare followed, that lie behind the character, and partly in certain generic and other considerations'.[6] He then provides a lucid account of the qualities held in common by such fictional Jews as Zadoch and Zachary in Thomas Nashe's *The Unfortunate Traveller*, and Abraham, the Jewish poisoner in Greene's *Selimus* (both 1594), these three characters probably having been influenced by the notoriety of Dr Roderigo Lopez, tried and executed in the same year, and above all by the popularity of Marlowe's extraordinary creation, Barabas, first seen *c.* 1589.

As cogent as the views of Gross and Halio are, there is a troubling premise behind them: a portrayal possible in 1814, when Kean stunned Drury Lane, and obviously possible, even obligatory nowadays, could not have been done four hundred years ago; one would be hard pressed to think of any other Shakespearian character who is thought to have changed so completely as to be unrecognizable from Elizabethan to modern performance. In questioning this premise, I am not arguing for a 'tragic' Shylock as the correct one, or arguing that the play is pro- or anti-Semitic; my sole object is to challenge the *a priori* assumption that Shylock must have conformed to a particular theatrical tradition, or that he must have been played in a certain way to satisfy the expectations of that wonderfully malleable group, who always think and believe whatever we want them to, Shakespeare's audience.

Assuming that the text remains the same (a point I will take up later), what are the variables that might separate the 1590s *Merchant* from those of the nineteenth century onwards? They might be divided into three categories: (1) limitations imposed by literary or theatrical tradition; (2) limitations imposed by audience beliefs, attitudes, or expectations; and (3) theatrical limitations imposed upon the range of performance options by acting style, costume, the shape of the stage, or any of the many other historically discrete theatrical conventions and technical considerations associated with Elizabethan performance practice.

Earlier I referred to the 'so-called' stereotype of the Elizabethan stage Jew, for it is far from certain that there ever was such a thing. When considering Jews in the early modern drama, we are struck first by how few of them there are, and then by how different these few are from each other. In the twelve years leading up to *The Merchant of Venice*, there are exactly three Jews in extant plays: one of them is a tiny part, the aforementioned Abraham in Greene's *Selimus*. The others are, of course, Barabas in *The Jew of Malta*, and Gerontus in Wilson's *Three Ladies of London* (1584).

Barabas' villainous attributes are too well known to require description here, but Gerontus is by far the most honest and admirable, one might even say 'Christian', character in his play. E. E. Stoll, in his oft-cited argument for the 'traditional' Shylock, summarily dismisses Gerontus as 'the single instance in the Elizabethan drama of an honourable Jew',[7] which is easy for Stoll to do since he has already established that 'to get at Shakespeare's intention (after a fashion) is, after all, not hard', and that 'Shakespeare, more than any other poet, reflected the settled prejudices and passions of his race'.[8] But whatever Stoll may think about *Three Ladies of London,* Gerontus shows that single instance or not, even if there was a stereotypical stage Jew, the Elizabethan theatre was capable of accommodating alternative portrayals.

This leads us away from Jews on the stage and in literature to the far more controversial topic of how Jews were seen in Elizabethan England. Is it true, as James C. Bulman writes in his valuable contribution to the *Shakespeare in Performance* series, that 'some knowledge of the history of anti-Semitism in England is critical to an understanding of the stereotype with which Shakespeare appealed to his audience's prejudices'?[9] Here I am indebted to Laurence Lerner, who in his essay 'Wilhelm S and Shylock',[10] suggests in a most engaging way that the perceived anti-Semitism of the play could be more a product of audience appropriation than anything in the text itself. Had the Elizabethans, all of whom were predisposed to think of Jews as devils and ritual murderers, read enough Terence Hawkes to know that the meaning of the play resided not in the author or actors, but entirely in themselves?

If they had, then it is not hard, as so many have done, to construct a picture of the first Shylock as the archetypical villain, for it is all too true that along with the execution of Dr Lopez (although it should be noted that Lopez's religion was hardly mentioned at his trial),[11] there was pamphlet after pamphlet, sermon after sermon, and story after story, from Chaucer's *Prioress' Tale* to Nashe's *Unfortunate Traveller,* encouraging people to see Jews in the worst possible light. If that is the picture we want, though, we have again gone outside *The Merchant of Venice* to see it, since, as Gross reminds us, however ubiquitous stories about Hugh of Lincoln and well-poisoners might have been, none of the traditional charges are alluded to in the play: nothing about Christ-killers, sorcerers, ritual murderers, crucifiers of children, or host-desecrators.[12]

This brings me to one of the central points of my argument: that it is simply not true that everyone in Elizabethan England, and hence everyone on the stage and in the audience at *The Merchant of Venice,* was an anti-Semite. As James Shapiro shows in *Shakespeare and the Jews,* by the late 1590s a significant number of Jews lived in or visited England, exactly how many depending on how one defined the group. Many were, of course, Marranos, Jews who had to some degree converted to Christianity, including Lopez, and there were others who were considered at least in some respects to have retained their Jewish identity, such as the descendants of the Jewish musicians brought to England from Italy by Henry VIII.[13] There were also the many contacts that merchants, ambassadors, and other English travellers had with Jews—Laurence Aldersey's description of a service he attended at the Venice synagogue in 1581 is one of total respect:

> For my further knowledge of these people, I went into their Sinagogue upon a Saturday, which is their Sabbath day: and I found them in their service or prayers, very devoute: they receive the five bookes of Moses, and honour them by carying them about their Church, as the Papists doe their crosse. Their Synagogue is in forme round, and the people sit round about it, and in the midst, there is a place for him that readeth to the rest: as for their apparell, all of them weare a large white lawne over their garments, which reacheth from their head, downe to the ground, The Psalmes they sing as we doe, having no image, nor using any maner of idolatrie: their error is, that they beleeve not in Christ, nor yet receive the New Testament.[14]

Documents such as this one encourage us to conclude that no matter how pervasive anti-Semitic literature may have been, the idea that a universal 'Elizabethan horror of Jews' must have informed the reception of *The Merchant of Venice* is simply one more Tudor myth, similar not only to the supposed Elizabethan horror of rebellion said to have dictated the reception of the history plays, but also, as I will argue, to the equally mythical Elizabethan horror of usury.

Virtually everything, and worse, that was said about Jews in Elizabethan England was said about Moslems, and yet throughout her reign Elizabeth was busy establishing trade relations with whoever would deal with her, from Morocco to Constantinople, buying saltpetre for gunpowder from the Emperor of Morocco and selling him munitions in return, munitions that were used to annihilate the Portuguese and their fellow Christians at the Battle of Alcazar.[15] And, as most editions of *Othello* point out, in 1600 she received an embassy of sixteen Moors, the portrait of their leader now hanging in the Shakespeare Institute, Stratford-upon-Avon.

How could this have been possible if Islam was, in the words of the Reverend Joseph Hall, 'a rude ignorance and a palpable imposture . . . their laws, full of license, full of impiety: in which revenge is encouraged, multitudes of wives allowed, theft tolerated . . . a monster of many seeds, and all accursed'?[16] Whatever one's private feelings might be, the history of international commerce shows that overt prejudice flies out of the window when there is money to be made.

But what if there is money to be lost? If Shylock's religion, in itself, is not enough to give him automatically the attributes of a Herod or a Barabas, there is still the matter of Shylock as usurer to be considered. Even if most, or at least some, Elizabethans did not in fact feel all that strongly about Jews, perhaps they all, along with Philip Stubbes, thought that 'he that killeth a man, riddeth him out of his paines at once, but he that taketh usury is long in butchering his pacient, suffering him by little and little to anguish, and sucking out his hart blood . . . an Usurer is worse than a Jew, for they to this daye, will not take any usurie of their Brethren, according to the lawe of God'.[17]

Stubbes has done us a favour by distinguishing between Christian and Jewish usurers, since there are actually very few Jews amongst the many usurers in early modern drama. As Garry Wills has noted,

> some who discuss this play believe that only Shylock and his coreligionists are the usurers in Venice. There would be no reason for Elizabethans, so familiar with their own Christian usurers, to assume that. In fact, the usurer, a common figure in the drama of Shakespeare's age, is normally a Christian.[18]

Still, Lawrence Danson writes of 'the Elizabethan horror of the idea of taking interest for the loan of money', going on to say that writers, 'depending for their view of economics upon the most venerable of classical and medieval sources, were unanimous in their condemnation of the practice of usury'.[19]

This might be true, but whether or not Shylock is, in fact, a usurer requires far more careful interrogation than has so far been given to the point. The word 'usury' does not occur in *The Merchant of Venice,* while 'usance' is heard three times: Shylock hates Antonio most of all for bringing down the 'rate of usance' (1.3.43) in Venice, and for having 'rated' him for his 'moneys and [his] usances' (1.3.106). In the third and last use of the word, Shylock is prepared to take

> . . . no doit
> Of usance
>
> (1.3.138-9)

for his loan to Antonio. The only person to use the word 'usurer' is, by report, Antonio:

> He was wont to call me usurer: let him look to his bond. He was wont to lend money for a Christian courtesy: let him look to his bond.
>
> (3.1.43-6)

To Shylock, then, 'usance' is a straightforward synonym for 'interest', which Shylock freely admits he takes—Shakespeare's choice of one term or the other in each case could be purely for metrical reasons. 'Usury', however, is an epithet delivered by the same man who called Shylock 'misbeliever' and 'cut-throat, dog' (1.3.110), after he spat on him, and openly states his willingness to do the same again (1.3.128-9).

The way Shakespeare employs the words 'usance' and 'usurer' in *The Merchant of Venice* epitomizes what was a major public debate of Elizabethan England, for although Elizabethan writers were, as Danson says, 'unanimous in their condemnation of the practice of usury'[20] they were anything but unanimous in defining it. As Norman Jones writes in his endlessly fascinating book, *God and the Moneylenders,* 'all good Christians agreed that usury was wrong, but they could not agree on what it was and when it occurred'.[21]

Until 1545, any charging of interest was considered usury, and hence illegal, with the obvious effect of keeping interest rates extremely high. In response, Henry VIII's 1545 statute defined the offence as interest in excess of 10 per cent, although most loans were for periods much shorter than a year, so the nominal annual interest was actually far higher. Enforcement proved very difficult, however, and rates remained high, so the lawmakers did what they always do when they cannot regulate something—they outlaw it again. In 1552 Henry VIII's statute was repealed and replaced by total prohibition, with the same effect as that other well-known prohibition, so in 1571, a year after one John Shakespeare of Stratford was fined 40 shillings for charging an astonishing £20 interest for a *one-month* £80 loan,[22] Elizabeth's parliament, after extensive debate, restored the legal limit at 10%, whatever the term of the loan was. (If there was a *New York Daily News* in those days, it would have reported that 'Johnny Gloves' was busted for nailing his customers on a 'vig' of six points a week.)[23]

In reading *God and the Moneylenders* and Laura Caroline Stevenson's *Praise and Paradox: Merchants and Craftsmen in Elizabethan Popular Literature,* one learns that writers such as Miles Mosse, who saw usury as the charging of any interest, rather than excessive interest, were what we would call today the extreme right wing, or even a 'lunatic fringe'.[24] Still, interest rates, like taxes, are always too high, so we might easily assume that many in Shakespeare's audience would have known the difficulty of repaying a loan, and would have seen Shylock as a usurer. But for every borrower there is a lender, and there were no banks or credit unions then—ordinary people who needed money borrowed from a neighbour or acquaintance, or found an acquaintance to act as broker to negotiate the loan with someone else. Given the diverse social makeup of the Elizabethan theatre-going public, it is quite probable that some in the audience, since they were engaged in the practice themselves, believed that lending money at the going market rate, or receiving a commission for arranging a loan, was a socially useful and even honourable thing to do. *One* member of the original audience at *The Merchant of Venice* would surely have thought so, presuming he was not acting a part on stage—the play's author.

It has been established beyond doubt that like his father, William Shakespeare loaned out, at interest, what were sizable sums of money, and he was prepared to sue when he was not paid back. He also, as the Quiney correspondence shows, acted as a broker on occasion, arranging loans of what would be, as E. A. J. Honigmann notes, 'five-figure' sums today.[25] When Antonio says

> Shylock, albeit I neither lend nor borrow
> By taking nor by giving of excess
>
> (1.3.59-60)

would not the play's author have expected, even wanted, at least someone in the audience, in those very inflationary times, to ask what Antonio was doing with a shirt on his back?

It is ironic that Stubbes is so often cited as speaking on behalf of the Elizabethans and their horror of charging interest, since his eleven pages on the evils of interest are closely followed by ten pages on the evils of plays and playing, a reminder that moral tracts tell us far more about what audience preconceptions were not, rather than what they were. If we are looking for books to tell us about prevailing social values of early modern England, we might consult those containing tables of interest rates, freely available by the early 1600s, rather than *The Anatomy of Abuses* or *The Arraignment and Conviction of Usurie.*[26]

My last category, theatrical limitations imposed upon the range of performance options, requires discussion of another argument that has been offered for the traditionally villainous Shylock—perhaps the most potent argument in that it relies, to a degree, on the text itself rather than things external to it. I refer to Shylock's famous 'aside', labelled as such in every modern edition of the play I have seen:

> How like a fawning publican he looks.
> I hate him for he is a Christian . . .
>
> (1.3.39-40)

In *Understanding Shakespeare's Plays in Performance,* Halio writes that

> omission of this passage is usually a clear indication of how the director has conceived Shylock's role—and

with it, much else in the play. The script is then tailored accordingly, so that Shylock can emerge, as in Henry Irving's famous portrayal, as a tragic hero.[27]

Specifically referring to both Olivier and Irving, he adds that cutting this speech 'is of course essential for this interpretation'.[28]

Unfortunately, neither Irving, nor Kean, nor Booth, cut a single word of the speech—indeed it was the centrepiece of Irving's portrayal, as described by his grandson:

> His anger grew keener and more savage at the beginning of the aside, 'How like a fawning publican he looks . . .' For a moment he recovered his self-control, and then, on the words, 'If I can catch him . . .' his spleen once more got the better of him.[29]

How did these great 'tragic' Shylocks leave the 'aside' intact, and still manage to stun audiences with their sympathetic portrayals? The answer, I believe, is that the speech is not an 'aside' at all, as the word is usually defined by editors and critics. As is well known, the first quarto of *The Jew of Malta* shows many asides, labelled as such, for Barabas, but this stage direction is used indiscriminately for what are actually two separate conventions.[30] When Barabas is feigning distress over Abigail's entry into the convent, the asides are secret 'whispers to her':

> Wilt thou forsake mee too in my distresse,
> Seduced Daughter, *Goe forget [not]*.
>   *aside to her.*
> Becomes it Jewes to be so credulous,
> *To morrow early Il'e be at the doore.*
>   *aside to her.*
> No come not at me, if thou wilt be damn'd,
> Forget me, see me not, and so be gone.
> *Farewell, Remember to morrow morning.*
>   *aside.*
>
> (D1r, lines 18-19, 28-32)

Other asides, however, invite Barabas to speak directly to the audience, conspiring with them, as it were, with a series of 'one-liners' (in both senses of the term) such as:

> I, like enough, why then let every man
> Provide him, and be there for fashion-sake.
> If any thing shall there concerne our state
> Assure your selves I'le looke unto my selfe. *aside*
>
> (B4r lines 6-9)

and

> I must make this villaine away: please you dine
> With me, Sir, & you shal be most hartily poyson'd.
>   *aside*
>
> (H3r lines 28-9)

Must Shylock imitate Barabas and speak directly to the audience in his twelve-line speech? Can he not, in what we would call a soliloquy if he were alone, think aloud to himself? The one-word stage direction 'aside' appears exactly once in the Folio, in *Titus Andronicus*, when Tamora addresses Titus in her imagination while musing,

> Why thus it shall become
> High witted *Tamora* to glose with all: *aside*
> But *Titus*, I haue touch'd thee to the quicke,
> Thy life blood out: If *Aaron* now be wise,
> Then is all safe, the Anchor's in the Port.
>
> (TLN 2027-31)

There are only two such directions in the various Quartos, both within one speech in Pericles Q1, as Simonides addresses Thaisa, the first 'aside' sitting one line below where it should be:

> Yea, Mistris, are you so peremptorie?
> I am glad on't with all my heart,
> Ile tame you; Ile bring you in subjection. *Aside.*
> Will you not, having my consent,
> Bestowe your love and your affections,
> Upon a Stranger? who for ought I know
> May be (nor can I thinke the contrary)
> As great in blood as I my selfe: *Aside.*
>
> (D4v, lines 2-9)

As in *Titus*, the context implies thinking aloud rather than addressing the audience.[31]

While the very word 'soliloquy' indicates that only the speaker is on stage, there are countless examples in Shakespeare, unmarked by any stage direction, of this other convention for which we have no convenient label—thinking aloud while others are present. It is hard to imagine any Claudius saying

> How smart a lash that speech doth give my conscience.
> The harlot's cheek, beautied with plast'ring art,
> Is not more ugly to the thing that helps it
> Than is my deed to my most painted word.
> O heavy burden!
>
> (3.1.52-6)

directly to the audience.

It is all too easy to confuse Shylock with the great Elizabethan villains such as Barabas, Richard III, and Iago by assuming that in the theatre, he, as they almost certainly did, spoke directly to the spectators. While such generalizations about performance practice are admittedly dangerous, I would suggest that one major limitation of the proscenium arch theatre is that the long aside is most difficult to manage. Further to this point, in the nineteenth century direct address to the audience would have carried with it strong associations of that nineteenth-century descendant of Barabas, the stock villain—'curses! foiled again!'—of the melodrama.

For Kean, Booth, or Irving to turn to the audience and secretly whisper his hatred while Bassanio and Antonio sit there feigning conversation would have been most inimical to a sympathetic portrayal, so they changed the aside into a soliloquy by having Bassanio leave the stage before 'How like a fawning publican' was spoken.[32] This, however, would not have been necessary in the far larger, more flexible, and multi-dimensional space of the Shakespearian theatre, where thinking aloud in a serious mode, at some length, while others are on stage, was common.

If Kean, or indeed Olivier, had played Shylock at the Globe, he would have been able, as the Folio text indicates, to have Antonio and Bassanio on stage while he spoke 'How like a fawning publican he looks . . .' without automatic association of villainy. Indeed, the lines denied Olivier at the National could easily have been restored for the television production through the simple device of the voice-over, television's equivalent of this Elizabethan theatrical convention. 'Fawning publican' and all, he might still have been, as I believe Kean might have been, very much like 'the Jew that Shakespeare knew'.

Notes

1. John Gross, *Shylock: Four Hundred Years in the Life of a Legend* (New York, 1994), p. 105.

2. Gross, *Shylock*, 91-105; John Russell Brown, introd., *The Merchant of Venice* (London, 1955), pp. xxxii-xxxiii; M. M. Mahood, introd., *The Merchant of Venice* (Cambridge, 1987), pp. 42-3; Jay L. Halio, introd., *The Merchant of Venice* (Oxford, 1993), pp. 61-5.

3. Jordan's poem and Stoll's comment in E. E. Stoll, *Shakespeare Studies* (New York, 1942), p. 255.

4. Francis Meres, *Palladis Tamia* (entered 7 September 1598), in *The Riverside Shakespeare*, ed. G. Blakemore Evans (Boston, 1974), p. 1844; the title page of Q1 (1600) claims that the play is printed 'as it hath been divers times acted by the Lord Chamberlaine his Servants'.

5. Gross, *Shylock*, pp. 16-17.

6. Halio, *Merchant of Venice*, p. 10.

7. Stoll, *Shakespeare Studies*, p. 273.

8. Ibid., p. 262, 280.

9. James C. Bulman, *Shakespeare in Performance: The Merchant of Venice* (Manchester, 1991), p. 18.

10. Laurence Lerner, 'Wilhelm S and Shylock', *Shakespeare Survey* 48 (1995), 61-8; p. 64.

11. Peter Berek, 'The Jew as Renaissance Man', *Renaissance Quarterly*, 51 (1998), 128-62; p. 151.

12. Gross, *Shylock*, p. 17.

13. James Shapiro, *Shakespeare and the Jews* (New York, Columbia University Press, 1996), pp. 55-88; Roger Prior, 'A second Jewish Community in Tudor London', *Jewish Historical Studies* 31 (1990), 137-52; see also Gross, *Shylock*, p. 23; Berek, 'The Jew', pp. 131-6.

14. 'The first voyage or journey, made by Master Laurence Aldersey, Marchant of London, to the Cities of Jerusalem, and Tripolis, &c. In the yeere 1581. Penned and set downe by himself', in Richard Hakluyt, *The Principal Navigations Voyages, Traffiques, and Discoveries of the English Nation*, vol. 5 (Glasgow, 1903), pp. 204-5. Brown (pp. xxxvii-xxxviii) discounts anti-Semitism as a large part of the Elizabethans' day to day lives.

15. 'The Amassage of M. Edmund Hogan, one of the sworne Esquires of her Majesties person, from her Highnesse to Mully Abdelmelech Emperour of Marocco, and king of Fes and Sus: on the yeere 1577, written by himselfe', in Hakluyt, vol. 6, pp. 285-93; Eldred D. Jones, *The Elizabethan Image of Africa* (Washington, 1971), p. 35.

16. Samuel C. Chew, *The Crescent and the Rose* (New York, Oxford University Press, 1937), p. 445.

17. Philip Stubbes, *Anatomy of Abuses* (London, 1583), sig. K7^r, K8^v.

18. Garry Wills, 'Shylock Without Usury', *New York Review of Books*, 18 January 1990, 22-5; p. 24, citing A. B. Stonex, 'The Usurer in Elizabethan Drama', *PMLA*, 31 (1919), 190-210; p. 191.

19. Lawrence Danson, 'The Problem of Shylock', in Harold Bloom, ed., *Major Literary Characters: Shylock* (New York, 1991), p. 273.

20. Danson, 'The problem of Shylock', p. 273.

21. Norman Jones, *God and the Moneylenders* (London, 1989), p. 24.

22. S. Schoenbaum, *Shakespeare's Lives*, new edn. (Oxford, 1991), 562-3; E. A. J. Honigmann, '"There is a World Elsewhere", William Shakespeare, Businessman', in *Images of Shakespeare: Proceedings of the Third Congress of the International Shakespeare Association, 1986*, ed. Werner Habicht, D. J. Palmer, Roger Pringle (Newark, 1986), p. 40; see also D. L. Thomas and N. E. Evans, 'John Shakespeare in The Exchequer', *Shakespeare Quarterly*, 35 (1984), 314-18.

23. According to the *Wall Street Journal*, as cited in *The New Dictionary of American Slang*, ed. Robert L. Chapman (London, 1986), 'vig' or 'vigorish'—the extortionate interest charged by criminal loan sharks—would be about 180 per cent per year, or 15 per cent per month. John Shakespeare charged double that.

24. Laura Caroline Stevenson, *Praise and Paradox: Merchants and Craftsmen in Elizabethan Popular Literature* (Cambridge, 1984). Mosse's *Arraignment and Conviction of Usurie*, 1595, receives ample discussion in N. Jones, pp. 144 ff.

25. Honigmann, 'World Elsewhere', pp. 41-5; see also his *Shakespeare's Impact on his Contemporaries* (London, 1982), pp. 8-14.

26. N. Jones, *God and the Moneylenders*, p. 78.
27. Halio, *Understanding Shakespeare's Plays in Performance* (Manchester, 1988), p. 12.
28. Halio, *Merchant of Venice*, p. 10.
29. Lawrence Irving, *Henry Irving: the Actor and his World, by his Grandson, Lawrence Irving* (London, 1951), p. 40.
30. On the aside, see Alan Dessen, *Recovering Shakespeare's Theatrical Vocabulary* (Cambridge, 1995), pp. 51 ff.
31. There is also an 'aside' in the 'bad' Quarto of *Merry Wives of Windsor*—see Dessen, *Recovering Shakespeare's Theatrical Vocabulary*, p. 51.
32. Mahood, introd., *Merchant of Venice*, p. 44.

PRODUCTION REVIEWS

Davi Napoleon (review date 1998)

SOURCE: Napoleon, Davi. "The Flapper of Venice." *Twentieth Century Interpretations* 32, no. 1 (January 1998): 6-7.

[*In the following review of Barbara Gaines's 1998 production of* The Merchant of Venice, *Napoleon concentrates exclusively on design elements that contributed to the project's evocation of urban America during the Roaring Twenties.*]

Although Barbara Gaines decided to place the Shakespeare Repertory Theatre's *The Merchant of Venice* in a 1920s American city, she encouraged to adapt period and place to the play. Synthesizing authentic details that suggested the superficiality of the era with anachronistic elements that evoked the Roaring 20s, design stayed true to the feel of a period rather than the time itself.

Costume designer Nan Cibula-Jenkins says the design team brought pictorial research to the table early, and they knew why they deviated from historical accuracy in every instance. "Even though we were manipulating colors and styles, we wanted the audience to think they were watching people in the 20s. [Back then], all the bathing suits would have been navy or black," she says; she used tropical colors to create a lighthearted ambiance for the Belmont scenes. "Navy would have given the piece a different feeling."

Cibula-Jenkins, who built all the women's clothing and rented the majority of men's garments from the Royal Shakespeare Company, didn't use period undergarments in dance scenes; these would have "distracted from the period ideal. Barbara wanted us to grasp the period in its most idealistic form, so the world seemed almost pushed. She said, 'It's like you're at a party, where everyone is forcing themselves to have a good time.'"

Avoiding visual clutter while suggesting a frenzied state, the design team created "a world force to the point that it was almost frenzied. Barbara wanted us to take the audience to the conclusion, to get on the train and go right to the station," says Cibula-Jenkins.

Gaines opened her production at a rooftop party, where Antonio eventually separates himself from dancing revelers to reflect on his contrasting sadness. Seeking colors and textures that would reflect a world out of kilter, Cibula-Jenkins balanced the langourous middle Belmont scenes with forced gaiety in party scenes that framed them at the end as well as its start. . . . Middle Belmont scenes featured pastels and soft flowing silk chiffons, the more relaxed textures echoing the times. Men wore tail coats in many scenes.

The first time in Western history that women discarded corsets, skirts in the 20s were "incredibly short compared to those worn ten years earlier. Women cut their hair off, an amazing idea. They had been quietly painting their lips, but now they came out and wore makeup overtly. It was a huge breakthrough." Cibula-Jenkins notes that women capable of changes in style were also capable of taking matters in their own hands, as Portia and Nerissa do. "As soon as you pick the 20s, you're in an age when anything goes, a new age of liberation."

But while people celebrated the end of the war and what they imagined would be a carefree future, immigrants struggled with harsh conditions, and the racism, anti-Semitism, and anti-Christianity of the times matched those in Shakespeare's Venice.

Because Elizabethan audiences knew Venice as a place of the kind of monetary exchange we associate with present-day Wall Street, and we have romantic visions of the Italian city, Gaines relocated the play spatially as well as temporally. Cibula-Jenkins and set designer Neil Patel exchanged swatches and talked about yellows and blues in Belmont, with cool grays and metallic for city scenes. Patel took his cue from 30s Art Deco, as furniture with hard edges provided the austere look he wanted. His public place resembled a bank lobby, undecorated and cold. Using the same space as the courtroom with minor adjustments, mainly the addition of a few benches, Patel didn't try to hide the public space but allowed it to resonate throughout the climactic scene. The same space functioned as Shylock's home, again by moving a few pieces of furniture.

Patel provided contrast in the Belmont scenes, for which he used a water motif. We meet Portia on a beach, and revelers dance around a reflecting pool during the final party scene. Again, little changed by Robert Christen transformed the space with warm lights.

Instead of asking sound designer Robert Neuhaus to locate period songs, Gaines commissioned an original score from Aleric Jans, who matched the frenzy of the scenography with an over-the-top driven score, consistent with the sound of the times.

Design elements combined to create an effect that is different from any one of them. "Take that music," says Cibula-Jenkins, "and the 30s furniture and my costumes, and it feels like the 1920s."

John W. Mahon (review date 1998)

SOURCE: Mahon, John W. "Richard Olivier Directs *The Merchant of Venice*." *Shakespeare Newsletter* 48, no. 2 (summer 1998): 43.

[*In the following review of Richard Olivier's 1998 production of* The Merchant of Venice, *Mahon comments on the director's "colorblind" casting, decision to make Portia the play's central figure, and efforts to recreate a historically authentic theater-going experience at the New Globe.*]

The son of Laurence Olivier and Joan Plowright, Richard Olivier has worked in the theatre for some years, both in England and in the United States. He directed *Henry V* at Shakespeare's Globe last summer. He has published several books, including the memoir *Shadow of the Stone Heart: A Search for Manhood.* During a conversation with me in his London home on 15 June, Olivier reflected on his approach to directing *Merchant* at the New Globe on Bankside this summer. His remote preparation for the assignment began much earlier and included a trip last winter to the University of Lecce, in the Italian province of Puglia, where he conducted a workshop on the play for drama students. The Italian students provided insight into the energy of Italian character and expressed satisfaction with a dramatic action that moved from carnival toward the "Passion"/Easter of the courtroom scene. Students in Lecce readily perceived Shylock as a villain.

These responses reinforced Olivier's determination to present *The Merchant of Venice* in terms of what the play would have meant in the 1590s, to release the story in the way it was intended to be told, to serve as a storyteller rather than as an interpreter. Such goals complement the Globe's sacred "a-word," authenticity. They also acknowledge the fact that the Globe space is an actors' space, so that the director's task is to empower the actors to do their jobs.

This space also provokes interaction: seeing the play makes viewers confront their own prejudices. The colorblind casting reflects the reality of Venice at the time: it was a multicultural society in which many servants were Armenians. The Globe of 1998 should reflect the cultural "mix" in England now just as the Globe of the 1590s did then.

Asked how his father might have influenced his concept of the play, Richard Olivier responded that Sir Laurence influenced him to the extent that he wanted to avoid a star like his father or Dustin Hoffman in the Shylock role—that immediately emphasizes the character. (In fact, the Globe's Shylock, the German actor Norbert Kentrup, had long been Sam Wanamaker's choice for the role.) Modern productions tend to "over-weight" the Shylock.

It is Portia's play, even in terms of number of scenes. More importantly, the play highlights her effort to change a masculine world, to move the society from an "either/or" stance to a "both/and" one. Most people seem to agree that feminine intuition like Portia's needs to be disguised in order to succeed in a male world. In general, Olivier observed, Shakespeare surely intended audiences to feel ambiguity about the motives of his characters.

Richard Olivier explained that Globe Education offers workshops for students that explore the anti-Semitism of the play, including the problem that the Christians never apologize for their behavior nor retract their treatment of Shylock. Workshops for business people focus on male/female role-playing and its impact on corporate leadership. Cranfield U's School of Management offered a two-day seminar last June at the Globe's Education Centre. Three Cranfield lecturers joined Richard Olivier to present the program, which cost each participant £1,025!

Addressing other aspects of the production, Olivier noted that, on the Globe stage, costumes become the set and music becomes the lighting; music denotes location—bells for Venice, lutes for Belmont. Operating on the assumption that everything behind the back wall is part of a magic space, Olivier deliberately positioned the three caskets in the discovery space, where they probably would have stood in the original production, not visible to some in the audience, now as then.

Finally, Richard Olivier acknowledged that the Globe space promotes the danger of overplaying to the groundlings and neglecting the audience seated in the galleries. Since the text of the play is performed virtually uncut (only about 5% of *Merchant* was cut), too much "business" unduly lengthens the performance time. The performance tends to evolve over the course of the summer; in the case of *Henry V* in 1997, ten minutes of "business" was shaved off over the course of the production.

Lois Potter (review date 1999)

SOURCE: Potter, Lois. "A Stage Where Every Man Must Play a Part?" *Shakespeare Quarterly* 50, no. 1 (spring 1999): 74-81.

[*In the following excerpted review of the 1998 Globe season, featuring Richard Olivier's production of* The Merchant of Venice, *Potter comments on the overall carnivalesque quality of the production, and mentions the exceptional Shylock of Norbert Kentrup.*]

Reviewers of the first two seasons at the Globe in Southwark, whether in the printed and electronic media or in formal and informal talks at the International Shakespeare Conference in Stratford-upon-Avon, focused more on the new theater's audience than on its productions. Advance discussions of the project had suggested that this was likely to be the case. Paul Nelsen, in a well-informed report from one of the conferences of theater scholars which preceded the official opening, cited various speculations that were being floated there. Would Globe audiences act like fans at a sporting event? Should actors try "warming up the crowd before performances"? Perhaps, some feared, "a stadium-like atmosphere might provoke actors to adopt a fustian style."[1] Accurate predictions, self-fulfilling prophecies, or simply fantasies? The discussions I heard and read in the summer of 1998 were an uneasy mix of the anecdotal ("Well, it wasn't like that on the afternoon when I went") and the abstract: a surprising number of people were ready to claim, on the basis of one visit, or indeed none, that the whole enterprise was irretrievably flawed.

In attempting to fill out the picture of the Globe's 1998 season, I shall have to begin where many others have begun (and indeed ended)—with the controversial production of *The Merchant of Venice*. This production was clearly the centerpiece of the season. Three of the four plays in repertory (*The Honest Whore* and *A Mad World, My Masters* being the other two) dealt in part with money and the world of business; James Shapiro's *Shakespeare and the Jews* was prominently displayed in the theater shop; and a series of readings of complementary plays about Jews was offered by the Globe's educational branch. There was, then, the opportunity to compare Antonio and Shylock to dramatic characters ranging from Londoners such as Middleton's Shortrod Harebrain and Sir Bounteous Progress (apparently a retired usurer) to Dekker's supposedly Milanese linen-draper Candido, the Hebrews who suffer the destruction of Jerusalem by Titus and Vespasian in William Heminge's *The Jews' Tragedy,* and the sophisticated anonymous German or Dutch traveler who finally reveals himself to be one of the title characters of G. E. Lessing's remarkable dark comedy *The Jews.* The small Bear Gardens theater was rarely full for these readings, perhaps because of their low-budget publicity. They were very well done but did not throw much light on the subject of Renaissance anti-Semitism: the Heminges play is a longwinded, sub-Fletcherian dramatization of the more sensational parts of Josephus's *History of the Jews,* while Lessing, of course, belongs to a later age. In any case, it was difficult for visiting academics to take full advantage of all the opportunities offered by the Globe and Bear Gardens. The two Shakespeare plays, playing to standing-room-only by the time I arrived in early August, were completely sold out soon thereafter. This may be one reason why few seem to have explored the relationships among the four plays in the main theater, and I should add that no explicit parallels were drawn among them in performance. Nevertheless, recognizing their existence added considerably to the pleasure of my visits to the Globe.

Though none of the plays have written prologues, the opening moments of each performance offered a prologue-like experience. That of *Merchant* was particularly significant. As the audience was assembling, an Italian madrigal group could be heard performing in the musicians' gallery, while down on the forestage a masked carnival character (Marcello Magni) was teaching the audience a ribald popular song. Eventually the madrigal group descended to perform on the stage level, only to be confronted by Magni's rival group encouraging the audience to join in its aggressive raucousness. High and popular culture, initially separated as neatly as in Robert Weimann's *locus* and *platea,* were now competing for the same space and for our attention. It was both funny and embarrassing; we weren't sure whether we really wanted to participate in this attempted sabotage of high art. How were we "meant" to respond?

Richard Olivier's production of *Merchant* comprised a series of variations on that question. By making the audience take part in the battle between Lent and carnival, it seemed to co-opt them into the pro-laughter position that the play's first scene shows Gratiano urging on Antonio. Yet this Antonio (Jack Shepherd) was clearly in a seriously depressive state (he burst into tears as he asked "Is this anything now?"), and this Gratiano (Andrew French) was almost maniacal in his laughter. Laughter continued to be problematized: the play's second scene invited us to laugh at a series of national stereotypes and to share Portia's horror at the prospect of a suitor with "the complexion of a devil"; the third scene introduced Shylock, no more a carnival figure than Antonio, suddenly attempting to turn a business deal into "a merry sport"; the fourth brought the Prince of Morocco onstage as a caricature of the oversexed black man. Moreover, the disruptive carnival character who started all the trouble at the beginning turned out in the next scene to be Launcelot Gobbo, or rather Marcello Magni, a gifted *commedia dell'arte* improviser and movement artist, who was not so much doubling as illustrating the relationship between anarchic stage clown and household servant/fool. As Launcelot he not only asked for a show of hands to help him decide whether to leave his master Shylock but kicked the cane out from under his blind old father. This was surely the epitome of carnivalesque behavior, with its overturning of traditional models of social and familial behavior, and we were supposed to be on the side of the carnivalesque, weren't we? But the text itself is likely to divide audiences: when Launcelot announces his own death in order to laugh at his father's grief, some will find it comically absurd while others will see it as proof of Bergson's view that laughter requires "an anaesthesia of the heart."

The carnivalesque continued during the intermissions, provoking equally mixed reactions. Magni (again!) raided people's backpacks, attacked illegal photographers with a water bottle, and danced with the spectators. The day I was there, he seemed to be pretty good at guessing which spectators would be least likely to object to ice-cream cones in their hair, but I later heard that some victims had suffered anxiety attacks while others had threatened to sue. (Outside the Globe was an equally carnivalesque character: a street vendor urging audiences to come and get their snacks at half the price being charged inside the theater precincts.) *The Merchant of Venice,* even more than most comedies, gets a lot of its laughs from cruelty; whether or not Shakespeare himself was drawing attention to this fact, I have no doubt that Olivier's production was doing so. It might be argued, of course, that, even if I'm right about the intention of the production, the effect in practice was not to contextualize the cruelty but to justify it. There is no real answer to such objections, since performance criticism is based on spectator response, not directorial intention. Some people apparently felt hurt and alienated by the production, to the point of not wanting to discuss it at all; their feelings are real. But so are the feelings of those who were stimulated by it, of whom I was one.

That Norbert Kentrup played Shylock, having learned English especially for the purpose, was apparently the result of a longstanding wish of Sam Wanamaker's, and one could see why: despite his strong German accent, the actor had a magnificent presence and a dry sense of humor that fitted well into the style of the production. Nevertheless, the time lag between his delivery of his lines and the audience's understanding of them often meant that their full effect was lost. Even so, his finely nuanced interpretation gave the character not only dignity but an element of mystery. What this Shylock had in common with his antagonist Antonio was a capacity for human affection as well as for hysterical hatred. What he had in common with his other antagonist, Portia, was a respect for argument. Kentrup, after Portia's "Then *must* the Jew be merciful," asked, "On what compulsion *must* I?" like a teacher politely pointing out a pupil's failure in logic; nevertheless, he listened to, and seemed moved by, the famous speech with which she answered him. One could almost believe that the bond really was just a joke gone wrong. Unlike most Shylocks, this one did not seem terminally ill when he left the courtroom, and it was possible to feel that the story was not yet over.

In the run-up to the trial scene both Antonio and Shylock made their cases directly to the audience, sometimes darting significant glances upward. Kathryn Pogson as Portia also played many lines, literally, to the gallery. (This was one feature of Globe performances that some reviewers criticized, but I couldn't see why. Do we really want to bring back the fourth wall?) Since the gallery auditors are, traditionally, "the gods," the relation between addressing God and addressing the audience was even clearer than usual. For instance, Portia shared with both God and the audience her very real anxiety as the first two suitors deliberated over the caskets. As the old Prince of Aragon droned soporifically on, she started to pray; and when it became apparent that he was going to talk himself into the wrong choice, she didn't forget to glance upward and say a quick "thank you." What put the audience on her side in the courtroom was the fact that she was as isolated as Shylock. Bassanio and Gratiano were furious to learn that an inexperienced youngster was taking the place of the distinguished lawyer they had been expecting, and her notorious "Which is the merchant here, and which the Jew?" gave them immediate proof of incompetence. It was possible to see the moment at which Shylock's "'Nearest his heart'; those are the very *words*" made her look again at the bond, realizing that its precise wording would be the key to the case. The fifth act fully exploited the comic gifts of both Pogson and Mark Rylance (as Bassanio) in a genuinely funny treatment of the ring scene. Though Lilo Baur as Jessica seemed silently troubled in the final moments, the performance ended with the entire cast (including Launcelot and even Jessica herself) happily singing a madrigal in unison. This might have been meant to signify the final coming together of high and low culture, carnival and Lent—but, as at other times, it was not clear whether it was the characters or the actors who were taking part.

Notes

1. Paul Nelsen, "Oaths and Oracles: Will the Globe Spin on an Axis of 'Authenticity'?" *Shakespeare Bulletin* 13.3 (1995): 27-32, esp. 28.

Matt Wolf (review date 1999)

SOURCE: Wolf, Matt. Review of *The Merchant of Venice. Variety* 375, no. 11 (2 August 1999): 40.

[*In the following review of Trevor Nunn's 1999 production of* The Merchant of Venice, *Wolf surveys the effective performances of the major players and notes the centrality of anti-Semitism and its disturbing consequences in Nunn's handling of the drama.*]

Among the many special relationships talked about in England, perhaps it's time to acknowledge the unique theatrical symbiosis between Shakespeare and Trevor Nunn. The Bard seems to breathe more easily when directed by Nunn, as evidenced over the better part of two decades at the Royal Shakespeare Co. and now at the National Theater. Also, as his present staging of *The Merchant of Venice* definably proves, Nunn has the effect on Shakespeare of wiping a time-honored canvas clean, revealing colors whose clarity is sometimes shocking: After all, when was the last time that *Merchant*—for all its abundant mournfulness—was packed so full of high spirits?

The larkiness of the gentile community is one of the unsettling masterstrokes of a production that has followed

Olympia Dukakis in Martin Sherman's "Rose" as the second show in the Cottesloe studio to receive an ovation at a performance attended by this critic. True, there are moments when the casting doesn't deliver the textual insight felt throughout, and one wishes particularly for a stronger Jessica than Gabrielle Jourdan to deliver an effective closing punch here accompanied by some clever tinkering with the text. (As her suitor, Daniel Evans' fey Lorenzo is comparably out of his league.)

Mostly, however, Nunn works not by altering what, in the wake of the Holocaust, remains a problematic source but via absolute fidelity to the shifting moods of a play whose moments of good cheer, as everyone knows, exact an awful price.

Gratiano (Richard Henders), for instance, may possess a "skipping spirit," but that's only as long as he's hanging out with his mates Bassanio (Alexander Hanson), Salerio (Peter de Jersey) and Solanio (Mark Umbers), whose own approach to money is to drink their coffees and run before anyone notices they haven't paid the bill. When these suited anti-Semites confront the Jew Shylock (Henry Goodman), however, they can't go in for the kill fast enough, amid a community that finds even Shylock's servant, Launcelot Gobbo (Andrew French), ready to crack a joke at his master's expense.

As played by Henders, this Gratiano is a sartorially well turned-out thug who thinks with his fists: Significantly, he throws a playful punch to Alex Kelly's Nerissa, newly got up in legal garb as male clerk to Portia (Derbhle Crotty), wearing her own masculine disguise. Portia, by contrast, begins as a slinky siren dressed by designer Hildegard Bechtler in body-hugging black. (Bechtler is responsible, too, for the sparely appointed traverse set.)

But there's something scary about the zealous embrace of "the law" of this one-time minx during a trial scene that debases everyone involved, and one only wishes Crotty communicated radiance as easily as she does a strict reading of the law that cannot but be—to co-opt her own word—"strained."

The style and sound of the show evoke a jazz-flecked 1920s that incorporates a Klimt canvas for the casket scenes and a drunken, louche ambiance by way of "Cabaret."

Against the period specifics, there's a properly timeless feel to Goodman's fierce and hunted yarmulke-wearing Shylock, which errs only in a tendency to build from whisper to roar that begins to resemble a vocal trick. Sharing a Yiddish exchange with Jessica, Shylock is later subjected to nothing less than emotional rape: the moneylender stripped of everything that matters, starting with family and faith. Goodman doesn't shy away from the hardening of a man who ends up surrendering much more than a pound of flesh in the painful closing-off of his heart. The silencing of Shylock—preceded by his ally Tubal (John Nolan) walking out on him in disgust—casts its inevitable chill over the final scene, which doesn't need a roll of thunder to remind us that the lovers' putative cuckoldry pales next to the "Christianity" imposed upon Shylock.

It's Nunn's strength to sustain interest to the finish, and he is helped no end by Hanson, who cuts easily the most complicated Bassanio I have seen—his decency adrift in a Venice of thwarted loyalties and misplaced loves as embodied by Antonio (David Bamber), the lovesick "merchant" of the title apparently milquetoast demeanor is capable of real rage.

Indeed, though the Jew-baiting in *Merchant* is what resounds through the centuries, it's possible to read the play in its entirety as a so-called "comedy" of reconciliation that leaves at least some of its inhabitants a wreck. Shylock is exiled from the amorous milieu with which *The Merchant of Venice* concludes. But his presence lives on in those unexpected final notes floated by a daughter lost to him in a play that on this occasion sings no less troublingly to us today.

THEMES

Seymour Kleinberg (essay date 1983)

SOURCE: Kleinberg, Seymour. "*The Merchant of Venice*: The Homosexual as Anti-Semite in Nascent Capitalism." In *Literary Visions of Homosexuality,* edited by Stuart Kellogg, pp. 113-26. New York: Haworth Press, 1983.

[*In the following essay, Kleinberg claims that* The Merchant of Venice *dramatizes "the triumph of heterosexual marriage" over homoeroticism, the latter represented by Antonio and his love for Bassanio.*]

When I first read *The Merchant of Venice,* I was dismayed by the anti-Semitism and the materialism of the Venetian world. The play held no charm for me, and I decided that it was simply not very available for someone like myself. Twenty years later, in 1978, after a summer as an NEH fellow at Berkeley, researching the subject of sodomy in the Renaissance, I reread the play. I still found it to be about anti-Semitism under mercantile capitalism, but now just as clearly it was also about homosexual eroticism in conflict with heterosexual marriage, about the rivalry of romantic male friendship with the claims of conventional marriage. This paper explores the relationship of these themes—money, ethnic hatred, sexual rivalry—and argues that they are analogous to one another; they are the matter and the feelings that define the merchant of the title.

Literally, that merchant is Antonio, though in the popular mind the title always invokes Shylock. Part of my argument is that the popular response is also the literal one: Shylock is Antonio. They are psychological counterparts. Antonio is a virulently anti-Semitic homosexual and is melancholic to the point of despair because his lover, Bassanio, wishes to marry an immensely rich aristocratic beauty, to leave the diversions of the Rialto to return to his own class and to sexual conventionality. Antonio is also in despair because he despises himself for his homosexuality, which is romantic, obsessive, and exclusive, and fills him with sexual shame.

For decades now, scholars and critics have noted Antonio's peculiarities. Most see an innocent infatuation in a lugubrious melancholiac, a type Shakespeare was fond of exploiting and an infatuation that was time-honored, dating back to the blood brotherhood of the Germanic tribes on one hand and to the classical Greeks on the other.[1] But in the 1950s, literary critics came under the influence of psychoanalytic thought, and the wholesome nature of Antonio's feelings was questioned. His passivity was the hallmark of neurosis, a defensive pose against "strong homosexual inclination."[2] It was further argued that Antonio's latent homosexuality was really a defense of Shakespeare's, as was the anti-Semitism of the play: Antonio and Shylock were two defenses of the poet against the anxiety he had portrayed in the sonnets, where homoeroticism and usury were complicated metaphors for each other.[3]

In the next decade, the reading of the plays and the sonnets as emotional biography was dismissed as naive. But too much discussion had taken place to dismiss Antonio as unimportant to *The Merchant of Venice*. Typically, a scholar decided that "there is, of course, no need to suggest an active homosexuality between the two men."[4] Some critics admitted that perhaps on Antonio's part, but never Bassanio's, the love bordered on the passionate, an "incipient homosexual relationship . . . less innocent than conventional Renaissance friendship."[5]

This is still the dominant reading today: Antonio may be repressed and perverse, but Bassanio is innocent. And it is consistent with contemporary attitudes toward Shylock, which sentimentalize the play by seeing Shylock as the victim rather than the villain. Such distortions enervate all the readings of character and relationship. Antonio and Bassanio are just the dearest friends; Portia is completely noble when she isn't being delightfully playful. Of course, the play then is a failure, a mishmash of contradictions, inconsistent about character and confused in its moral vision.

Despite the discomfort of affirming Shylock's villainy after the fate of European Jewry during World War II, critics are once again insisting on describing him with the accurate harshness he deserves. But once Shylock's unattractiveness is restored, it is possible to reconsider Antonio and, finally, Portia herself. It is possible to play Shylock with sympathy without ruining the play entirely, as Laurence Olivier did some years ago for an English televised version, in which Shylock's final "speech" is off-stage and off-camera, his true response to his enforced conversion to Christianity at the end of the trial scene: a terrifying scream so shocking that the play dissolves into prophecies of Auschwitz. At that moment, even if we do not hate Portia and condemn all of Venice, they are permanently outside our sympathy. That is an interesting play, but not the one Shakespeare wrote. It may even be a better play, more suitable to modern ideas of justice, but I doubt it. It is a less complex drama, simpler, flatter. The play Shakespeare wrote does look to the future rather than back to the work that preceded it, but it is the future ambiguities of *Twelfth Night*, the enigma of *Measure for Measure*, the despair of *Troilus and Cressida*, perhaps even the cynicism of *All's Well That Ends Well*.

If one wishes to see the plays refracted in the sonnets, assuming the lyric poetry is less masked, then the erotic triangle of the sonnets and the ambiguous sexual character of the speaker's feelings for the young man can serve as a mirror of *The Merchant of Venice*.

It is unmistakable that Antonio and Bassanio are "lovers"; a number of characters, especially Lorenzo, say so. The question is whether Lorenzo and the others, including Antonio, are using the word in its rarer sense of intimate but platonic friends, or whether they use it to denote that friendship while slyly suggesting the erotic nature of the true relationship.

In the canon, of the nearly 150 times Shakespeare uses the words *lover, lover's, lovers,* and *lovers'*, only nine of those instances can be argued as sexually innocent, and four of them are in the play under discussion. Three others occur in *Julius Caesar*, one in *Coriolanus*, and one in *Love's Labors Lost*.[6] In these three plays there is no evidence of sexual suggestion. The term carries the meaning given it by Malone when he glossed it in his edition: "In Shakespeare's time this was applied to those of the same sex who had an esteem for each other."[7] Malone cites Ben Jonson's letter to John Donne in which he signs himself, "Your true lover."

The lexicons, however, note that the overwhelming meaning of *lover* is the modern one, and examples of Shakespeare's lack of reticence about homoeroticism are everywhere in the sonnets and the plays. Even the casual line by the fool in *King Lear*, "He's mad that trusts in the tameness of a wolf, a horse's health, a boy's love or a whore's oath" (III, vi, 19),[8] acknowledges the ordinariness of pederastic infatuation in a society that seemed to tolerate homosexuality or bisexuality for men who had already done their service to society and posterity in marriage and paternity.

Until recently, scholars have been so diffident or so evasive about the subject that their speculations often seem senseless. The modern line is articulated by J. W. Lever: intense male friendship at the end of the sixteenth century in England emerged as a major literary theme; the new seriousness about friendship owed much to Italian Platonism, to the idea of a new kind of love marked by an "absence of physical homosexuality," *Amor Razionale*.[9] Platonic homosexuality belonged to an Italianate culture that was casual about bisexuality, but the new love was not a euphemism for erotic homosexuality. This has been the basis for the standard reading of the sonnets: he loves him but sleeps with her; or he loves him but does not want to sleep with him because the beloved's sex is an odd, unlucky accident, so he sleeps with her in frustration or guilt or lust, but without much affection. That is a valid reading of the ambiguity surrounding the bond between the men in the triangle of the sonnets, but the drama tells another story of the triangle of Antonio, Bassanio, and Portia. Here the conflict is between an assertion of sexuality that is shameful or dangerous and the institution of marriage, between the anarchy of sterile romantic passion and the lawfulness of wedlock.

Critics like Lever presume the friendship must be platonic because the penalties for sodomy were so severe that no poet could venture such sentiments as those in Shakespeare's plays and poems without enormous risk unless the behavior of those involved was innocent, regardless of their inclinations. *Sodomy* by the late sixteenth century always meant "buggery," and sometimes the terms were used interchangeably, as in the English Act of 1533, reissued in 1563, whereby sodomy/buggery was again made a capital offense. *Buggery* is a corruption of *bougrerie,* a reference to the Albigensians, whose religious heresies were supposed to have come from Bulgaria. Thus, sodomy as buggery has its roots in heresy. This is why it was held as so abhorrent, worse even than incest, with which it was compared.[10]

How then are we to account for the openness of Marlowe, both in the life and in the drama, no less James's court and Buckingham's career ("Elizabeth was king; now James is queen")?[11] Nor was this exclusively the vice *anglais*. Pope Julius III (1500-55) was notorious, and the story of Henry III of France, who escaped from Poland dressed as a woman to claim the French throne on the death of his brother, was widely known. There is a mysterious schism between the law of the land, with its penalty of burning at the stake (reserved for heretics, witches, and sodomites) and the evidence of pederasty and bisexuality among Elizabethan aristocrats, for example, the circle centering around the Earl of Southampton and the Jacobean court. Southampton, one of the likeliest candidates for the young man of the sonnets and Shakespeare's sometime sponsor, was a patron of homoerotic and pornographic verse as well.[12] Perhaps he and his circle escaped censure and danger because they married. All upper-class men married. Their duties to property, propriety, and posterity demanded an heir. After that, their romantic predilections were less important socially as long as they were reasonably discreet. Even Richard Barnfield (1574-1627), whose life and career span both reigns and who wrote the most blatant pederastic poetry of the period, *The Affectionate Shepherd* (1594), married and retired to the country to rear a family.

It is on this subject that *The Merchant of Venice* begins: the need to marry. The immediate opening involves Antonio and his friends, who are trying to discern the cause of his melancholia, which Antonio confesses even he is bored with. The temperament Shakespeare and the Elizabethans called melancholia we would paraphrase as depression or neurosis. It is suggested that his sadness is caused by love, the conventional cause, and Antonio does not absolutely deny it when he says, "Fie, fie" (I, i, 46).[13] As soon as he is alone with Bassanio, they investigate a plan by which Bassanio can repay his enormous debts, the largest of which he owes Antonio—if only Antonio will lend him still more money. The yoking of money and love is made explicitly and immediately in the first scene; Bassanio says he owes Antonio "the most in money and in love." Antonio, more frankly, replies that "My purse, my person, my extremest means lie all unlocked to your occasions." In the sonnets, such a line with so much innuendo would be the moment of complicated ironies, and of much scholarly comment: for example, of Shakespeare's fondness for using debt and usury as metaphors for sexual longing. Here in the play, the line elicits no comment; its boldness is so literal it may need none. Plainly, everything is available: Antonio's purse and his person are interchangeable.

When the solution to Bassanio's debts is revealed to be Portia, the heiress of Belmont, Bassanio presents her first as wealthy, then as fair and good; he adds casually that she already seems disposed toward him. Tactfully, he does not elaborate, nor does he mention his feelings, if any, for her. He merely states that she rivals the Golden Fleece, and many Jasons, that emblem of constancy, come to woo her. On these conditions, Antonio is satisfied. Bassanio is a proper young aristocrat: spendthrift, flighty, charming, and beautiful, and he must marry sometime. Only merchants like Antonio can afford to remain single.

Antonio is not married, nor is there ever any hint of such a possibility. Knowing how difficult they are to live with, Shakespeare rarely marries off his melancholiacs. Coincidentally, while there is no clear evidence that these melancholiacs share an aversion to women, they are often more comfortable in exclusively male company, preferably that of a beloved friend (see Jacques in *As You Like It,* Antonio in *Twelfth Night,* Hamlet and Horatio).

Antonio's first characteristic is his melancholia and singularity. His second characteristic is that he hates Jews, notably Shylock. True, all of Venice is casually anti-Semitic, as it is racist in *Othello,* but Shylock tells us that Antonio is special, particularly vicious toward him, spitting on him in public while calling him a misbeliever and a cutthroat dog. Indeed, "Jewish dog" is Antonio's favorite curse for Shylock. Even when he is asking for desperately needed money for his beloved Bassanio, he cannot control his contempt for Shylock. Antonio promises him that even with a loan he is just as likely to spit on him, call him names in public, and worse, undercut Shylock's usury by lending money interest-free—when he has it again. He combines bravura and tactlessness.

Roger Wreford as Shylock in a 1955 production of The Merchant of Venice *at Bristol's Theatre Royal.*

This web of money and love, homoeroticism and anti-Semitism, is established as the context of the play before the first scenes are finished. Love exists only on the condition of money, a case made more than once in the play. When Shylock's daughter, Jessica, elopes with her gentile lover, Lorenzo, she not only takes full caskets with her, she jokes as she climbs out her window, "I will . . . gild myself / With some moe ducats, and be with you straight" (II, vi, 49-50), to which Lorenzo replies that he loves her heartily. Later, when Shylock is told of the elopement, his confusion of his love for Jessica and his passion for his money is intended to be comic. We are told, not shown, that he does not know which grieves him more, the loss of the daughter or the ducats. Our reporters, Salerio and Salanio, find such confusion of money and feeling absurd because Shylock is so coarse about it, apparently so vulgar in his failure to make the distinction. Later in the play, when he refuses to translate feelings into cash, when his grief has turned into hatred and no amount of money can buy that from him, he is no longer amusing. Then, depending on one's sentiments, he is nearer to monstrousness or tragedy. Certainly, he is no longer vulgar.

In the third act, when Shylock has his grand moment of rhetoric about Jewish humanity, presumably falling on the deaf ears of the two Jew-baiters he is speaking to, he makes his feelings very clear. All that he has left of his dignity is his hatred of Christians, especially Antonio. This is interesting but not a subject for compassion. When Tubal enters to tell Shylock of Jessica's profligacy, her spending spree in Genoa where she threw money to the winds to celebrate her honeymoon, we also learn of her contempt for her father, her mother, and her past. She swapped a ring for a monkey on a chain. Shylock cries, "Out upon her!—thou torturest me, Tubal!—it was my turquoise, I had it of Leah when I was a bachelor: I would not have given it for a wilderness of monkeys" (III, i, 125-28). More than one reader has agreed that this is Shylock's really redeeming moment of humanity, his memory of himself as a man in love, who solemnized that love in the symbol of a ring.

The next scene is Bassanio and the three caskets; he chooses correctly. Freud's essay on this scene is one of the masterpieces of psychoanalytic criticism. His thesis is that this choice is simply love over death, that in fact death is transformed into love in the universal wish of mankind to find immortality in the denial of mortality.[14] In simpler terms, it is the choice of marriage and generation, which is also the choice of life and is perhaps the only life eternal.

In Venice, gold and silver are currency; but in Belmont, a world of love and music, they seem to have no meaning except as ornament. Yet at the moment Bassanio chooses the lead casket, Portia has an aside in which she prays that her love for him will be moderate, within the bounds of reason and not subject to the passions of jealousy or despair:

> O love be moderate, allay thy ecstasy,
> In measure rain thy joy, scant this excess!
> I feel too much thy blessing. Make it less,
> For fear I forfeit!
>
> (III, ii, 111-114)

This anxiety is odd, since she is in love with Bassanio and helpless to change her situation. Why does she want the ecstasy of love, "this excess," to be *scanted,* a term borrowed from the idiom of usury?

The moment is swept away with the joyous discovery that Bassanio has guessed correctly; he is now engaged and a millionaire. The two swear oaths of loving loyalty symbolized by the exchange of rings. One assumes that the destiny of engagement rings in Belmont will be different from that of turquoises in Venice, but the fate of Leah's ring casts a shadow on this emblem of love exchanged in the presence of Jessica and Lorenzo. Then comes news that Antonio is forfeit to Shylock, and Portia, immersed in her feelings, manages to make an extraordinarily vulgar quip that eclipses Shylock's confounding of daughters and ducats. When she learns the background of Bassanio's debt to Antonio and of the odd security Shylock demanded, Portia tells Bassanio that after they are married he can have all the gold he needs to ransom his friend, even twenty times the original "petty debt" of 3,000 ducats. Then she puns, "Since you are dear bought, I will love you dear." So much for Jewish monopolies on vulgarity or confusions of feelings and money.

As the act ends, we learn that Antonio is helpless because Venetian law must honor all issues connected with money, otherwise the justice of the state will be "impeached." The honor of mercantile capitalism is spelled out: it demands the compulsive adherence to the letter of the law, regardless of how unjust the consequences may be. If money has already been deeply confused with feeling, it has now locked into the issue of honor.

In Bassanio's absence, Lorenzo tries to cheer Portia up, saying that "if you knew to whom you show this honor / How true a gentleman you send relief" (i.e., Antonio), "how dear a lover of my lord your husband," then she'd not mind the separation though it occurred before their wedding night. Again, the pun on *dear* is raised: beloved, expensive, rare. Portia is now inspired; she must save this man himself. She announces that she is going into retreat for a few days, assuring Lorenzo that "this Antonio / Being the bosom lover of my lord, / Must needs be like my lord" (III, iv, 16-18). But she will see for herself. Lorenzo's description of so "dear a lover" resonates with suggestion for her. This triangle is best completed in person. It is not that Portia suspects her husband of sodomy; such suspicion is too vile for the delicate air of Belmont, though Portia is neither naive nor prudish. But she is ignorant; the mysteries of male affection, with its remarkable loyalty and apparent selflessness, are as foreign to her as the mysteries of marriage. She has heard of both and experienced neither.

At the trial scene in Act IV, all the themes of the play are brought together. Antonio reiterates his hatred of Jews in a line that even the most apologetic of Shakespeare's critics cannot ignore. He tells the court it is wasting its time trying to dissuade Shylock: "You may as well do anything most hard / As seek to soften that—than which what's harder?—/ His Jewish heart" (IV, i, 78-80). When Shylock is told by the Duke that he cannot expect mercy in heaven if he renders none here, Shylock replies that he has done nothing that will require mercy. He goes on to argue by analogy: would the Venetians treat their slaves as their children? would they marry them to their heirs? Of course not. And now Shylock "owns" Antonio, to do with as he wishes, for this pound of flesh is "dearly bought"—an eerie, exact echo of Portia's pun and a poetic linking together of Shylock, Antonio, and Portia in some dim emotional bond for which the complications of the plot merely serve as metaphors.

When Bassanio gallantly if meaninglessly offers to lay down his life for his imperiled friend, Antonio answers the gesture with "I am a tainted wether of the flock, / Meetest for death—the weakest kind of fruit / Drops earliest to the ground, and so let me" (IV, i, 114-116). A "wether" is a sterile male sheep. Why has Antonio abandoned his stoicism? Why does he regard himself as sterile and sick, "tainted," weak, deserving of death? Why is he in despair and self-loathing?

His sense that he is sick and therefore deserves death is his confession of sin, of sexual shame, his veiled admission that he deserves to die because he is a sodomite. It is irrelevant what Bassanio and Antonio have actually done under the guise of their publicly admired courtly friendship. It is entirely relevant that Antonio thinks himself disgusting.

Portia saves Antonio by finding the law pertaining to aliens who threaten the lives of Venetian citizens: those aliens automatically forfeit all their wealth and their lives. A law that presumed alien criminals would be wealthy surely had Jews in mind. If Shylock had been a Venetian citizen, nothing could have saved Antonio. But Jews are not citizens. Shylock forgot that he is at best a guest, and none too welcome. As long as he is Jewish, he is alien and vulnerable.

Antonio hates Shylock not because he is a more fervent Christian than others, but because he recognizes his own alter ego in this despised Jew who, because he is a heretic, can never belong to the state. He hates Shylock, rather than himself, in a classic pattern of psychological scapegoating. What Antonio hates in Shylock is not Jewishness, which, like all Venetians he merely holds in contempt. He hates himself in Shylock: the homosexual self that Antonio has come to identify symbolically as the Jew. It is the earliest portrait of the homophobic homosexual. The basis for that identification between Antonio and Shylock is complex. They are both merchants of Venice, both lend money, both are involved with Bassanio, and both indirectly and painfully become involved with Belmont. Most of all, they have in common that they are heretics. Shakespeare equates the sodomite and the Jew symbolically and psychologically, as they were already equated under Elizabethan law, which allotted the common fate of burning to witches, heretics, and sodomites.

But another, older, more crucial connection between sodomites and Jews was available to the Elizabethan mind. Prior to the Renaissance, sodomy had meanings other than buggery; it was once used to include the sin of bestiality, *bestialitas,* which had the same sexual meaning it does in modern usage, but which had special theological meanings as well.[15] There were cases of men tried and burnt for bestiality. In an obscure work of the turn of this century, Professor E. P. Evans in *The Criminal Prosecution and Capital Punishment of Animals* remarks:

> It seems rather odd that the Christian lawgivers should have adopted the Jewish code against sexual intercourse with beasts, and then enlarged it so as to include the Jews themselves. The question was gravely discussed by jurists whether cohabitation of a Christian with a Jewess, or vice versa, constitutes sodomy. Damhouder (Prax., res. crim. c.96 n.48) is of the opinion that it does, and Nicholas Boer (Decis., 136, n.5) cites the case of a certain Johannes Alardus, or Jean Alard, who kept a Jewess in his house in Paris and had several children by her: he was convicted of sodomy on account of this relation and burned, together with his paramour, "since coition with a Jewess is precisely the same as if a man should copulate with a dog (Dope. Theat. ii, p. 157)." Damhouder includes Turks and Saracens in the same category.[16]

Shylock, the Jewish dog, already a heretic, is also symbol for the sodomite; conversely, Antonio the sodomite with his heretical desires is linked to the other alien in Venice, the not quite human Jew.

At the same moment that Antonio confesses his guilt and desire to die, converting his despair into a martyrdom of love, Portia is faced with a struggle for her husband. She must rescue him from this infatuation with Antonio, so steeped in noble sentiment, romanticism, and perhaps erotic power, so that he can be fully free to enter marriage. She listens carefully while Antonio says farewell to Bassanio:

> Commend me to your honorable wife.
> Tell her the process of Antonio's end,
> Say how I loved you, speak me fair in death,
> And when the tale is told, bid her be judge
> Whether Bassanio had not once a love.
>
> (IV, i, 273-77)

Antonio is confident that Portia will be able to judge, since both of them feel alike; he does not say that Bassanio had a friend beyond compare: he had a love beyond compare. Perhaps he puns when he says "honorable" wife, inferring he was the dishonorable one. What is really important is his resurgent bravura, his assurance that she will never be able to do for *their* beloved what he has, despite her fabled wealth. His request to Bassanio demands that all the parties concerned acknowledge that there has indeed been a triangle of emotional power, which only decorum has prevented from being fully understood. It is not Portia, but Antonio who has made Bassanio rich, and therefore happy.

Bassanio is so deeply moved that he offers to sacrifice everything he owns: his fortune, his life. He even throws in his wife's life, "sacrifice them all to this devil to deliver you." Both Shylock and Portia are astonished by this extravagance. Shylock mutters in contempt and aside, "These be the Christian husbands!" thinking of Jessica and her fate; for such as this she betrayed her father, mother, past. Portia, as the young lawyer, interjects, "Your wife would give you little thanks for that / If she were by to hear you make the offer." She came to Venice to find out what was between her husband and his friend, who she suspected may have been "alike"; well, now she knows.

It will be even trickier to rescue Bassanio than it was to free Antonio. Portia is struggling for mastery now, and it is far more than the conventional mastery of reason over passion, the passion she feared would reduce her to the same abject dependence that her father and his will had placed her in before. Is she always to be a chattel? Is she never to be her own mistress? If she must be married without choice or consent, if she must love her beautiful husband even if his past is shadowed in sexual secrecy, she will at least have a husband all her own, one whose loyalty is exclusively hers: he is to remember whose millions he now has access to, and he is to reevaluate that extravagance which would fling everything, her and her money, to the Jews.

In this charged atmosphere of ethnic hatred, sexual mystery and jealousy, self-loathing, and revenge, Portia succumbs. Despite the lovely rhetoric about mercy that is the most famous speech in the play, when Shylock is vanquished, forced to convert to what he has always hated, she adds the most sadistic line in the scene: "Art thou contented, Jew?" She turns her anger at Antonio on Shylock, expressing it as contempt, and expressing it with a cruelty she does not have to mask. In one stroke she confirms for us Shylock's view of Christians and their society: wretched as he is, what should one expect of Jews if Christians behave this way? It is not that Shakespeare is for Shylock; it is that he is contemptuous of all Venice.

When Portia, still in disguise, demands the ring as payment for her lifesaving work, it is no trivial prank. She wants back the ring she gave Bassanio and that he swore would never leave his finger while he was her husband. She also wants him to refuse. She wants the ring because she no longer trusts her happiness to him, but she wants him to refuse it so that she can forget his extravagance, dismiss it as hyperbole. It is her crucial moment. If he refuses to give her the ring, it means he remembers his vow, and that both she and he can enter the institution of marriage in true conformity. If he gives her the ring, his broken vow annuls her own. For a moment Bassanio resists, but he surrenders to Antonio's persuasion in the play's most overt moment of sexual competition: "My lord Bassanio, let him have the ring, / Let his deservings and my lord withal / Be valued 'gainst your wife's commandment" (IV, i, 449-451). Bassanio yields the ring to one "man" at the behest of another, the ring that linked him to the world of women and marriage. His loyalty to Portia is remiss compared to what he feels for Antonio. Bassanio has many assets; he is beautiful and generous and sincere, but he is also shallow. Out of sight, out of mind. When he was at Belmont, he forgot about Antonio until he was arrested. Now he is with Antonio in Venice, and Portia seems very far away.

For Portia, Bassanio's failure is her victory; the terms of the marriage are void. She has lived up to the agreement of her father and society, and until now has agreed to be dispensed as men saw fit. Her husband replaced her father as her legal master, but he has broken faith, her faith in his word. She is free to negotiate for her freedom. In the fifth act, the issue of sexual competition is mirrored in the agon between men and women and in the conspiratorial bonding between men, the real subject of the squabbling. The ring is now more than a symbol; it is a key. Who has the ring is master of the bedroom. Portia makes that plain; she will yield herself only to the man who has the ring. Since she herself has it, she means to yield to no man ever again. Instead, she will show that she is free to bestow herself as she wishes.

When Bassanio and Antonio arrive, Bassanio introduces his lover to his wife: "This is the man, this is Antonio, / To whom I am so infinitely bound" (V, i, 134-135). Portia observes wryly, "You should in all sense be much bound to him, / For (as I hear) he was much bound to you." Emotional loyalty is identified with the money that has passed between Shylock and Antonio. With that money borrowed from one merchant by another, Antonio has given Bassanio away in marriage only to keep him bound to himself as firmly as ever, perhaps even more. Without Shylock, it could never have been accomplished. Bonding, senses, money are punned upon as issues of loyalty and honor, erotic preference, and emotional commitment rise to the surface of the scene.

Portia pretends to quarrel; Antonio ruefully observes it and remarks, "I am the unhappy subject of these quarrels." Portia agrees with him but says, "You are welcome notwithstanding." That is, despite the fact that you are a guest in my house, that you are alive entirely because of my intervention, you have come between a lawful husband and wife: what further claims can you now have? While Bassanio swears that he will never again be careless about his promises to her, submitting entirely to her ("Pardon this fault and by my soul I swear / I never more will break an oath with thee"), she is not satisfied—not until Antonio offers security for Bassanio's promise, as he did once before:

> I once did lend my body for his wealth,
> Which, but for him that had your husband's ring,
> Had quite miscarried. I dare be bound again,
> My soul upon the forfeit, that your lord
> Will never more break faith advisedly.
>
> (V, i, 249-253)

It is what she has been waiting to hear; if he once offered his body to Jews, it is only fair that he now offer his soul.

The happy ending of the play is the triumph of heterosexual marriage and the promise of generation over the romantic but sterile infatuation of homoeroticism. In this competition, Shakespeare as ever is conservative. Portia must rescue her beloved and guarantee that as corrupt as the world is, with its translation of every feeling into cash, at least she and Bassanio will live to perpetuate it. Though Belmont appears to be different from Venice, it is really the same world, but here Jews like Jessica are welcome converts and sodomites like Antonio brief guests.

If *The Merchant of Venice* is filled with mitigated resolutions for its lovers and villains and fools, that is the way of the world. Antonio of Venice is the symbol of the corruption of erotic feeling under nascent mercantile capitalism, a world where melancholia is romance and sexual guilt is translated into ethnic hatred.

What difference does such a reading of this play make? Is it better because it concerns a homosexual Jew-hater, rather than a monstrous Jew who is practically a butcher? (To be sure, either view is more cogent than one that sees the play as being about a pompous young woman who quotes Scripture about Christian mercy and never understands the subject, that is, the conventional reading, which makes the play a sentimental failure, a thematic mess unable to link together the Rialto and the moonlit terraces of Belmont.) Here is a reading without sentiment. The play is filled with ambiguities about sexuality and money, love and hatred. Nothing is simple, least of all who we are or what we are. What links us to both the Rialto and Belmont is our recognition of our painful complexities and our terrible vulnerabilities before the coldness of the world.

Notes

1. M. R. Ridley, *Shakespeare's Plays* (New York: E. P. Dutton and Co., 1938) is typical: "Antonio does little but wander lugubriously across the stage, an embodiment of the humor of melancholy, enjoying poor

health and indulging an enfeebling infatuation for Bassanio" (p. 91). E. K. Chambers in *Shakespeare: A Survey* (London: Sidgwick and Jackson, 1925) hints at a connection between Antonio and the sonnets, an "echo" (p. 117).

For a full scholarly but entirely unpsychological view of the subject of male bonding, two useful works are Laurens J. Mills, *One Soul in Bodies Twain: Friendship in Tudor Literature and Stuart Drama* (Bloomington: Indiana Univ. Press, 1937) and Lu Emily Pearson, *Elizabethan Love Conventions* (Berkeley: Univ. of California Press, 1933). For a discussion of the psychological and social implications of the subject, see C. S. Lewis, *The Allegory of Love* (London: Oxford Univ. Press, 1936): "The deepest of worldly emotions in this period is the love of man for man, the mutual love of warriors who die together fighting against odds, and the affection between vassal and lord" (p. 9). Lewis' discussion refers to *The Song of Roland,* the work that exemplifies the tradition of male bonding. Alistair Sutherland and Patrick Anderson, eds., *Eros: An Anthology of Friendship* (London: Anthony Blond, 1961) define their subject as "any friendship between men strong enough to deserve one of the more serious senses of the word 'love'" (p. 8). Thorkil Vanggaard, *Phallos: A Symbol and Its History in the Male World* (New York: International Universities Press, 1972) has a lengthy and definitive discussion of male bonding in Norse culture, which he claims included "a genital aspect, based on mutuality and equality between the partners" (p. 119), but which precluded buggery. Most recently, John Boswell, *Christianity, Social Tolerance and Homosexuality* (Chicago: Univ. of Chicago Press, 1980) discusses the subject of Platonic love: "only love between persons of the same gender could transcend sex" (p. 27). Boswell adds, however, that there was a definite but not necessarily conscious sexual nature to the many intense male friendships he documents (p. 134).

2. E. E. Krapf, "Shylock and Antonio: A Psychoanalytic Study on Shakespeare and Antisemitism," *The Psychoanalytic Review,* 42 (April 1955), 118. See K. B. Danks, "The Case of Antonio's Melancholy," *N & Q, NS,* 1 (1954), 111. Earlier, Arthur Acheson tried to connect the play and the sonnets with the life of the author in *Shakespeare's Sonnet Story* (London: B. Quaritch, 1933), pp. 342-83. For an early Freudian view of the subject, see T. A. Ross, "A Note on *The Merchant of Venice,*" *British Journal of Medical Psychology,* 14 (1934), 303f.

3. While biographical readings of the sonnets are increasingly unfashionable or uninteresting to scholars and critics, the lyrical poetry and the drama have been used to enlighten each other since the eighteenth century; usually the sonnets are used to discuss the plays. The latest scholarly edition of the sonnets, edited by Stephen Booth (New Haven and London: Yale Univ. Press, 1977), continues to see all of the canon as one continuous work but disdains biographical inquiry as naive.

The use of usury as an elaborate metaphor for sexuality has long been noted. Leslie A. Fiedler, *The Stranger in Shakespeare* (New York: Stein and Day, 1972) was the first to write extensively of usury as both moneylending and copulation in the sonnets and the play. John Boswell has an interesting comment on the mutual unnaturalness of usury, heresy, and sodomy (p. 331). The most articulate and thorough discussion of this subject is Marc Shell, "The Wether and the Ewe: Verbal Usury in *The Merchant of Venice,*" *Kenyon Review,* 1 (1979), 65-92.

4. J. D. Hurrell, "Love and Friendship in *The Merchant of Venice,*" *Texas Studies of Literature and Language,* 3 (1961), 332.

5. Hurrell, p. 340. See also Graham Midgley, "*The Merchant of Venice*: A Reconsideration," *Essays in Criticism,* 10 (1960), 119-33.

6. Alexander Schmidt, *A Shakespeare Lexicon,* 3rd ed., rev. and enl. Gregor Sarrazin (New York: B. Blom, 1968). Also Marvin Spevack, *A Complete and Systematic Concordance to the Works of Shakespeare* (Hildesheim, Germany: Georg Olms, 1970).

7. In William Shakespeare, *Complete Works,* ed. with notes by Malone et al. (London: J. Rivington and Sons, 1790), III, 67n.

8. William Shakespeare, *King Lear,* ed. Kenneth Muir, The Arden Edition of the Works (London: Methuen, 1952).

9. *The Elizabethan Love Sonnet* (London: Methuen, 1956, 1966), p. 204n. Lever seems to understand the issue but is too decorous or timid to pursue it. See the discussion on p. 103 f. and p. 164 f. The subject of erotic friendship was usually referred to as an issue of "bisexuality," first by Lu Emily Pearson, p. 254 f., and later by G. Wilson Knight, *The Mutual Flame* (London: Methuen, 1955), p. 35 f. Fiedler is the first to have taken up the subject succinctly and lucidly. He puts the homosexual Antonio in a context of aliens like Jews and women, and gives a brilliant reading of the play, particularly of the last act. He also notes that there are two homosexual lovers called Antonio in Shakespeare and concludes that the later character in *Twelfth Night* is the same psychological person as the merchant. Fiedler sees the relationship as platonic and Antonio as an "advocate of an austere Uranian love for whose sake the older lover educates to manliness the boy he adores, and in whose name he is prepared to die, though he knows he cannot ask as much in return, since that boy must rather die to him by marriage" (p. 132).

10. Laurence Stone, *The Crisis of the Aristocracy, 1558-1641* (London: Oxford Univ. Press, 1965). p. 491 f. See also Ivan Bloch. *Sexual Life in England, Past*

and Present, tr. William H. Fostern (London: F. Aldor, 1938): Vanggaard, p. 153; Vern L. Bullough, *Homosexuality, A History* (New York: New American Library, 1979), pp. 34-35, 170-71; and Derrick Sherwin Bailey, *Homosexuality and the Western Christian Tradition* (New York: Longmans, Green, 1955).

John Boswell argues that in the thirteenth century *bougrerie* would not have meant "sodomy," though it could have meant "usury" (usurers were cited as "bougres") and may generally have meant "heretic," p. 290.

11. G. P. V. Akrigg, *Jacobean Pageant or The Court of King James I* (New York: Atheneum, 1967). See also Gordon Rattray Taylor, "Historical and Mythological Aspects of Homosexuality," in *Sexual Inversion: The Multiple Roots of Homosexuality*, ed. Judd Marmor (New York: Basic Books, 1965), p. 145.

12. G. P. V. Akrigg, *Shakespeare and the Earl of Southampton* (Cambridge, Mass.: Harvard Univ. Press, 1968). See also H. Montgomery Hyde, *The Other Love: An Historical and Contemporary Survey of Homosexuality in Britain* (London: Mayflower, 1972). A number of writers cite the work of William Lithgow, "Rare Adventures and Painful Peregrinations" (Glasgow, 1906), which was first written between 1609 and 1622 and describes his travels. Lithgow praises the Venetians for their anti-Jewish attitudes and remarks on the "unfortunate rifeness of sodomy" in the city; cited by Taylor, p. 141, and by Sutherland, p. 144. See also John J. McNeill, S.J., *The Church and the Homosexual* (Kansas City, Kan.: Sheed Andrews and McMeel, 1976).

13. William Shakespeare, *The Merchant of Venice*, ed. John Russell Brown, The Arden Edition of the Works (London: Methuen, 1955). All citations are from this edition of the play.

14. Sigmund Freud, "The Theme of the Three Caskets," *Imago* (1913).

15. Montague Summers, *The History of Witchcraft and Demonology* (New York: Alfred Knopf, 1926). I am indebted to the Summers work for the information on Evans that follows.

16. (London: W. Heinemann, 1906), p. 152. Cited in Summers, note 43, Chapter iii, "Demons and Familiars."

Lawrence Normand (essay date 1991)

SOURCE: Normand, Lawrence. "Reading the Body in *The Merchant of Venice*." *Textual Practice* 5, no. 1 (spring 1991): 55-73.

[*In the following essay, Normand contends that the tensions and conflicts of* The Merchant of Venice *are depicted through references to the body and its association with language.*]

When Morocco challenges a hypothetical fair-skinned suitor 'to make incision for [Portia's] love, / To prove whose blood is reddest, his or mine' (II.i.6-7),[1] he invokes the human body as a place where certain disputed questions can be tested and decided: 'What is Morocco's real nature?', 'What is Morocco's real value?' The question who the better man is, the 'fairest creature northward born' (II.i.4) or the '*tawny Moor*' (s.d. II.i), might be settled by cutting their bodies and comparing their blood: Morocco's redder blood will show his greater courage, and prove his personal value despite his devalued skin colour. His challenge is couched in the Petrarchan rhetoric he uses throughout this scene, and the 'body' is merely verbal; yet a fleeting threat to bring his real body into the scene is voiced. Morocco is challenging the prevailing racist depreciation of his 'complexion' by turning to another conventional corporeal sign, redness of blood. The call for incision invokes a figurative body as a means of asserting personal value, and is typical of many moments in the play when a body is invoked.

Stephen Greenblatt has written that Shakespearean comedy 'constantly appeals to the body and in particular to sexuality as the heart of its theatrical magic'.[2] But, he goes on to argue, there 'is no unmediated access to the body', for sexuality 'is itself a network of historically contingent figures that constitute the culture's categorical understanding of erotic experience'.[3] It is through the mediation of a commonplace cultural figure concerning blood that Morocco brings his body into play in order to demonstrate a case about his human value. When Launcelot scrutinizes the palm of his hand (II.ii.150ff.), he reads his destiny through the figure of palmistry inscribed in his body. Greenblatt's notion that the body makes its appearance through the mediation of familiar cultural figures in language is the starting-point for this essay, which is concerned not only with sexuality but also with wider questions of human value and identity. It is a startling exception to this rule of mediation when Portia commands Antonio in the courtroom to 'lay bare your bosom' (IV.i.248), and Antonio's naked human body appears in the actor's person. A concern with the culturally figured body focuses attention on the relation between language and reality, the interactions between verbal bodies and real ones. But language and its relation to reality is clearly problematized in the play, as the plot's depending on the interpretation of difficult words on the caskets and in the bond easily shows. Language is a bar to communication as much as its easy medium, and its manifestations (speaking, writing, and silence) are areas in which conflicts are actualized and resolutions sought.[4] The play's bodily discourse interpenetrates linguistic discourses such as the legal, theological, and amatory, functioning as a supplement to language, or offering an alternative articulation of the struggles of desire and dominance. The entanglements of the action are brought about through a discourse of figured and real bodies; and disentanglement requires a systematic rearticulation of this discourse in order to arrive at a resolution.

I

Portia starts the play with the power to dispose her own property and voice, but not her *body* in a sexual relation of her own choosing. She experiences this subjection in her body: 'By my troth Nerissa, my little body is aweary of this great world' (I.ii.1-2). Language and body interact as her father's will holds her in confinement. Portia is caught within the inscribed word of patriarchal power, 'under the bind of the law, deprived of her will because of her father's will, inscribed in the living force of his dead letter, locked in a leaden casket'.[5] Opposed to the restriction of his 'cold decree' (I.ii.18-19) are pitted the warm desires of her body, her 'blood' and 'hot temper' (I.ii.18). Portia's resistance to these restrictions lies in mocking, subversive wit, what Lacan calls deriding the signifier.[6] She finds a kind of freedom in mocking the doltish suitors and deriding her father's word by punning on 'will' itself: 'I may neither choose who I would, nor refuse who I dislike, so is the will of a living daughter curb'd by the will of a dead father.' (I.ii.22-5). The opposed meanings of 'will' as 'sexual desire' and 'testament', reveal the conflicting desires of a physically active body and a dead father. Portia's mockery of the suitors has no perlocutionary force since it is powerless to change her situation. Like the speech of a Fool, it makes no mark on the world. In her linguistic play Portia protests at her situation without being able to imagine any solution to it:

> he hears merry tales and smiles not, (I fear he will prove the weeping philosopher when he grows old, being so full of unmannerly sadness in his youth), I had rather be married to a death's-head with a bone in his mouth, than to either of these: God defend me from these two.
>
> (I.ii.46-51)

It is Shylock who most consistently draws the body into his discourse. As Portia is subjected by her father's will, so Shylock is subjected by the dominant antisemitic discourse of Venice, which characterizes him as inhuman. To Launcelot 'the Jew is the very devil incarnation' (II.ii.26); and to Solanio he is 'the dog Jew' (II.viii.14) and 'the devil . . . in the likeness of a Jew' (III.i.19-20). Characterization of Shylock as sub-human voices itself in Launcelot's catachresis ('incarnation' for 'incarnate'), which ungrammatically misbodies the idea of the monstrous. In the court scene, Gratiano imagines Shylock's birth as a monstrous fusing of human and animal, as a wolf's soul enters his mother's womb. Shylock becomes Antichrist in this parody of the anomalous human-divine union of the Virgin Birth:

> thy currish spirit
> Governed a wolf, who hang'd for human slaughter—
> Even from the gallows did his fell soul fleet,
> And whilst thou layest in thy unhallowed dam
> Infus'd itself in thee . . .
>
> (IV.i.133-7)

When Shylock comes to defend himself, his counter-definitions entail the body.

Shylock defends his practice of usury to Antonio and Bassanio in I.iii when he is asked to lend money, by arguing that the increase it involves is analogous to the natural processes of animal procreation. Antagonism erupts over the word 'interest' as Shylock and Antonio attempt to arrange a loan, and there is a struggle over the interpretation of certain biblical texts. Shylock's account of the story of Jacob and Laban in Genesis seeks to present a counter-gloss of Antonio's word 'excess' (57) as Shylock's 'thrift' (45). The crux of Shylock's interpretation of Jacob's actions lies in its representation of production as a bodily process.[7] Shylock thinks of Jacob's skill in sticking 'wands' (79) before the sheep while they are mating, which exploits an analogy in nature between 'parti-colour'd lambs' (83) and partly stripped twigs, as demonstrating both human skill in understanding those laws of analogy, and divine approval in Jacob's profiting from the resulting lambs. Shylock's narrative remains open to various interpretations, but his idea of thrift lies in seeing production which takes place through the body, of either sheep or coins, as natural and ultimately part of God's will. Coins are like sheep in that their use may produce profit. For Shylock the body, understood to be the physical substance of something and its powers of generation, is a site of truth, evidencing human and divine nature. The argument over interest ends with neither side winning. Antonio merely stops Shylock from speaking further: 'Mark you this, Bassanio, / The devil can cite Scripture for his purpose.' (92-3).

'Shylock does treat Antonio as if he were from a group of human beings other than his own Jewish one, but Antonio treats Shylock as if he were from a species of animal other than the human one (a dog)'.[8] Shylock is denied a human body, and therefore possession of human rights. At the same time he is denied the right to coherent speech. In III.i, when he enters distraught at news of his daughter's 'flight' and accuses Solanio and Salarino of complicity in it, they attack the integrity of his speech by cruel quibbling:

SHYLOCK:

> You knew, none so well, none so well as you, of my daughter's flight.

SALERIO:

> That's certain,—I (for my part) knew the tailor that made the wings she flew withal.
>
> (III.i.22-5)

As Shylock's words are rendered ineffectual and their coherent sense destroyed, he resorts to the literal meanings of words, in an attempt to make a perlocutionary utterance with the force of assertion:

SHYLOCK:

> She is damn'd for it.

SALERIO:

> That's certain, if the devil may be her judge.

SHYLOCK:

> My own flesh and blood to rebel!

SOLANIO:

> Out upon it old carrion! rebels it at these years?

SHYLOCK:

> I say my daughter is my flesh and my blood.
>
> (III.i.29-33)

Shylock's assertion is the discursive counterweight to the disintegrating attacks being made on his speech and on his body in general by the two Christians, whose replies subvert his discourse and dissipate its emotional and ideological force. In the face of this, Shylock foregrounds the very act of speaking in order to affirm that his daughter partakes of the same physical substance as himself, and so shares the same racial identity. But Salarino denies even the biological relatedness of father and daughter:

> There is more difference between thy flesh and hers, than between jet and ivory, more between your bloods, than there is between red wine and Rhenish . . .
>
> (III.i.34-6)

Shylock's relatedness to his daughter is threatened by Salerio and Solanio's assaults on the integrity first of his speech, then of his figured body. Shylock defends his speech by apparently literal statements, and by presenting family ties as irrefutably corporeal. The attack on the cultural meanings of Shylock's body prompts another defence which again uses his body as evidence, this time of human identity. 'I am a Jew', Shylock states and goes on to claim a human identity with the Christians on the basis of shared parts and functions of the body: 'eyes . . . hands, organs, dimensions, senses, affections, passions' (III.i.53-4). Since the Venetians do not see a Jew as being human, Shylock anatomizes himself, disintegrating his body into separate functionings which are then presented as neutral and innocent of guilt that attaches, in Christian eyes, to a Jewish body. The Jewish *Gestalt*, more than the sum of its parts, is offensive; but bodily parts might seem innocent of the general guilt.[9] But to Christians who do not recognize a Jew as human this argument is unpersuasive, as Stanley Cavell explains: 'one who does not already know that the other's body "is connected with" sentience cannot be convinced by this argument, or rather cannot understand what it is an argument about, the existence of others'.[10] In this scene the struggle for the recognition of one's speech is implicated in the struggle for the recognition of one's body. The violations of Shylock by the Venetians are directed at his physical body ('You that did void your rheum upon my beard, / And foot me as you spurn a stranger cur' (I.iii.112-13)), his speech, and his cultural body. Shylock ends the scene by swerving from a rhetoric seeking empathy for himself as a human body to a declaration of spiritual affinity for Christian revenge: 'If a Christian wrong a Jew, what should his sufferance be by Christian example?—why revenge! The villainy you teach me I will execute, and it shall go hard but I will better the instruction.' (III.i.63-6).

The forfeit Shylock asks, should Antonio default on the loan, is a fragment of his body: 'an equal pound / Of your fair flesh, to be cut off and taken / In what part of your body pleaseth me' (I.iii.145-7). When he suggests this condition, Shylock can have no expectation of ever claiming the forfeit, for Antonio confidently expects his ships to return with handsome profits. For Shylock the bond is a carnivalesque bargain, a form of words which is indeed at the moment he mentions it a 'merry sport', for the terms are self-evidently absurd and unreal. Despite the malice Shylock voices in an aside that he 'will feed fat the ancient grudge' he bears Antonio (I.iii.43), no narrative extension is imaginable between words and flesh, between the condition inscribed in the bond and the real body which might suffer its effect. Yet the terms of the bond spring from the real relations between Shylock and Antonio, for they will return to Shylock the mutilation of the self which he has suffered from Antonio in the past, and suffers again in this scene. As Cavell argues, Shylock's terms for 'A pound of flesh, to be by him cut off / Nearest the merchant's heart' (IV.i.228-9) is the exact counterpart of what he thinks Antonio in particular has done to him. Shylock 'is telling us that he perceives Antonio's refusal of acknowledgement as mutilation—the denial, the destruction, of his intactness.'[11]

Shylock is a subject mutilated by the Venetians' hostile discourse; Antonio is a subject not securely in discourse at all. Shylock counters Venice's denigration of him, by asserting a secure counter-self in the deployment of his cultural body. Antonio is a decentred self who speaks of himself as inscrutable and mysterious: 'In sooth I know not why I am so sad' (I.i.1). He sees himself as an actor whose part is 'a sad one' (I.i.79) and whose true self is therefore at one remove from his role. His mental state at the start of the play is a pre-discursive one, for its origin and nature are not yet articulated: 'But how I caught it, found it, or came by it, / What stuff 'tis made of, whereof it is born, / I am to learn' (I.i.3-5). While Antonio offers no discursive version of himself, his friends give voice to possible selves for him. In a deliberate game of speech-making he is the subject of attempts to account for his being 'marvellously chang'd' (76). The speeches project verbal forms meant to capture the mysterious melancholy, and they are offered as half-serious self-explanations. Gratiano, whose name recalls the comic doctor of *commedia dell'arte*,[12] and who speaks, as he says, like 'the fool' (79), generates diagnostic fantasies on Antonio's self-presentation, the first of which suggests a cause for melancholy in the body's inactivity. His garrulous discommendation of silence warns that a body which is still and silent turns into a funerary statue, as the blood cools and the living form becomes an effigy: 'Why should a man whose blood is warm within, / Sit like his grandsire, cut in alablaster?' (I.i.83-4). Accordingly, Antonio's alienation from Venetian speech threatens a sort of death. Gratiano focuses on Antonio's 'wilfull stillness' (90) and 'saying nothing' (97), and associates silence with sexual impotence, in allusions to a shrivelled penis and an old maid: 'for silence is only commendable / In a neat's tongue dried, and a maid not vendible' (111-12).[13]

The real source of Antonio's sadness, of course, springs from the change in his relation with Bassanio. His identity as Bassanio's friend is put at risk by Bassanio's imminent journey to Belmont to win a wife, for Antonio would thereupon be displaced from first place in Bassanio's affections. Antonio's passionate declaration that 'My purse, my person, my extremest means / Lie all unlock'd to your occasions' (I.i.138-9) represents a way of reaffirming his love for Bassanio and remaining involved in his affairs at the very moment when Bassanio's 'venture' might lead to Antonio's displacement. It is under threat of this displacement that Antonio agrees so recklessly to Shylock's bond. Antonio brushes aside his friends' attempts to put him into words, and offers no discursive version of himself; instead, he responds to his melancholy by putting his body into the bond. The terms of the bond which Shylock suggests implicate Antonio's body into the financial and legal practices of Venetian society:

> Go with me to a notary, seal me there
> Your single bond, and (in a merry sport)
> If you repay me not on such a day
> In such a place, such sum or sums as are
> Express'd in the condition, let the forfeit
> Be nominated for an equal pound
> Of your fair flesh, to be cut off and taken
> In what part of your body pleaseth me.
>
> (I.iii.140-7)

Antonio's promise to commit his flesh for three thousand ducats reaffirms his bond of friendship with Bassanio at the very moment when Bassanio's turning to the lady might well lead to its dissolution. His passionate attachment to Bassanio is now inscribed in the bond, and authenticated by the body with the promise of his corporeal 'person' in exchange for three thousand ducats. Antonio breaks his silence by means of the bond in which his love is invisibly lodged in a displaced discourse, a financial-cum-legal agreement. What Foucault writes of the workings of sixteenth-century language is true of the bond, for 'what it says is enclosed within it like a promise, a bequest to yet another discourse'.[14] The 'condition' (141) writes Antonio's body as a figure which is a joke, whose transformation into reality is unimaginable. As events will show the body latent in the bond becomes manifest and that body itself 'speaks'.

II

Freud thought that the caskets symbolize the body of a woman: 'If we had to do with a dream, it would at once occur to us that caskets are also women, symbols of the essential thing in woman, and therefore of a woman herself.'[15] The caskets not only symbolize what the suitors seek, they also have inscribed on them texts which the suitors must successfully interpret in order to reach their desired object. As in the case of the bond, textuality and the body are overlaid. The caskets are simultaneously the destination of the suitors' desire, as symbols of woman, and the path along which desire must travel to reach its destination. The reward for correct textual interpretation is possession of Portia's body and her wealth.

Portia's picture is hidden in one of the caskets, shielded by the metal and by her father's inscription. The suitors trace a perilous path through language to seek to arrive at the body. They struggle with a complex set of inscriptions which invites definition of the woman as well as themselves, and in which the body is crucially involved. Morocco's unsuccessful negotiation of the casket test results from his ideological orthodoxy, which holds that there should be a correspondence between the fairest lady and the fairest metal, 'never so rich a gem / Was set in worse than gold' (II.vii.54-5). In Petrarchan terms the choice of the gold casket is logical, but Morocco's way of thinking makes him ignore the person herself and re-present her in coded love-language. Portia's physicality disappears and she is re-inscribed as a purely transcendent value: a 'breathing saint', whose 'heavenly picture' Morocco seeks, and 'an angel' (II.vii.40-58). Edmund Spenser uses the image of woman as an angel swathed in gold in *Epithalamion,* published in 1595, the year before *The Merchant of Venice* was probably first produced:

> Some angell had she beene.
> Her long loose yellow locks lyke golden wyre,
> Sprinckled with perle, and perling flowers a tweene,
> Doe lyke a golden mantle her attyre . . .[16]

Spenser inscribes his future wife as a creature of pure spirit, as Morocco does to Portia. But this aristocratic mode of writing is misplaced in the bourgeois world of the play in which money has a precise value. In fact, Morocco specifically rejects comparison of Portia with another kind of angel which is a coin—'They have in England / A coin that bears the figure of an angel / Stamp'd in gold, but that's insculp'd upon' (II.vii.55-7). The comparison is rejected because the angel on the English coin is merely on the surface of the metal, and therefore not truly part of it. In Morocco's trope of the angel inside the casket, the angel is like the soul which lies deep inside the body, as what animates it and is its truest reality.[17] In this way of thinking, the soul is accorded a far greater value than the body, the angel much more than the gold casket. His discourse of love separates spirit and body, and privileges spirit over body. The figure of the monetary angel, which Morocco specifically rejects, stands in fact as a more accurate image for Portia, for the coin has its beauty marked on its surface, and once put into exchange has financial value, just like Portia herself when she marries.

Arragon fixes on the silver casket because its inscription, '"Who chooseth me shall get as much as he deserves"' (II.ix.36), prompts him into enunciating his own worth:

And well said too; for who shall go about
To cozen Fortune, and be honourable
Without the stamp of merit?

(II.ix.37-9)

The metaphor of 'the stamp' refers to the authenticating of a document, and its validation for social use: Arragon thinks of himself as inscribed.[18] In this metaphor of Arragon as a document on which is written the account of his value lies the fantasy that his body has received a 'stamp of merit'. The stamp is irreversible and publicly attested, and Arragon imagines he can invoke his powers as an imaginary document and employ them to win Portia: he can exchange himself for a fortune—'I will assume desert; give me a key for this, / And instantly unlock my fortunes here' (II.ix.51-2).

The suitors all struggle with the same problem of how to arrange the signifying elements arranged before them—caskets of different metals, and inscriptions—into an order which arrives at the 'correct' answer which is already determined by the father. Morocco aims too high, assembling the elements into a discourse of the transcendent, splitting the spiritual from the material. Portia's body is thereby lost in the Petrarchan mode into which she is cast. Arragon's response combines the material and immaterial in an image which represents his body textually as a legal document; but he excludes Portia from his response and mistakes his own social value. Morocco reads the gold casket as being Portia, Arragon reads the silver casket as being himself, but Bassanio reads the lead casket and its inscription as being a comment on the ironic discourse of choosing. Bassanio is in the best position to grasp the ironic meaning of the lead casket's inscription, and of lead itself, because he is the figure 'in whom outside appearance and inside reality are most unlike':[19] 'So may the outward shows be least themselves' (III.ii.73). Bassanio and Portia have already discovered each other by falling in love, demonstrated in the amorous banter which precedes the choice. There is no need, then, to involve 'ornament' in the choice when love has already been discovered and actualized in verbal exchanges:

ornament is but the guiled shore
To a most dangerous sea . . .
    in a word,
The seeming truth which cunning times put on
To entrap the wisest.

(III.ii.97-101)

Bassanio does not seek a secreted signified in the inscriptions or the metals themselves. He recognizes lead as signifying the redundancy of 'ornament' to symbolize a love which has already been realized: 'but thou, thou meagre lead / Which rather threaten'st than dost promise aught, / Thy paleness moves me more than eloquence, / And here choose I,—joy be the consequence!' (III.iii.104-7).

The process of choosing nevertheless presents dangers which are expressed as threats to the lovers' living bodies.

As Bassanio moves towards the caskets to make his choice Portia participates by announcing herself to be threatened at that moment by death. Invoking the story of Hercules' rescue of Hesione from the sea monster (Ovid, *Metamorphoses,* xi) she effects a metaphorical transformation on the scene. In this textual superimposition she becomes Hesione, and Bassanio Hercules; and just as Hesione was mortally threatened by the sea monster, so she is threatened with an emotional death if Bassanio fails to overcome the monstrous impositions of the will:

I stand for sacrifice,
The rest aloof are the Dardanian wives,
With bleared visages come forth to view
The issue of th' exploit: go Hercules!
Live thou, I live.

(III.ii.57-61)

If Hercules fails to slay the sea monster then Hesione will be its victim. The threat of death, albeit a figurative one, recalls Antonio's figurative death-in-silence at the start of the play.

Bassanio's response to discovering the picture of Portia focuses on his body; he speaks of the dissolution of the corporeal boundaries between himself as perceiving subject, and the picture as perceived object:

Fair Portia's counterfeit! What demi-god
Hath come so near creation? move these eyes?
Or whether (riding on the balls of mine)
Seem they in motion?

(III.ii.115-18)

Bassanio imagines the picture not simply as a static similitude but a source of power in its own right, with painted hair 't'entrap the hearts of men' (III.ii.122); and as it was being painted it threatened to disable the painter who was painting it, depriving him of his eyes:

but her eyes!
How could he see to do them? having made one,
Methinks it should have power to steal both his
And leave itself unfurnish'd.

(III.ii.123-6)

The picture, the image of a body, is imagined as entering into relationships with real bodies and capturing parts of them for itself. Bassanio's speech plays over the interrelationships of bodies and their representations. At this moment of most intense pleasure, Bassanio focuses on the tremulous relation of his body and the image of Portia's; and announces a moment of blissful physical merging with Portia. The bliss is the counterpart of erotic bliss, but it is doubly displaced: Bassanio's body moves only in his language, not his actions, and Portia appears as a picture not as herself. The fullness of erotic pleasure which his language implies falls away in the end as language's inability fully to represent experience reasserts itself. Bassanio ends by articulating a chain of representations—his praise, the picture of Portia, and Portia herself—which shows his desire pursuing its object along the chain and always failing to capture its fullness:

> yet look how far
> The substance of my praise doth wrong this shadow
> In underprizing it, so far this shadow
> Doth limp behind the substance.
>
> (III.ii.126-9)

Bassanio is completely in control of his discourse; indeed, his value as Portia's lover is demonstrated dramatically by this very discursive dominance and subtlety. This part of the scene, the expressive climax of Portia and Bassanio's love, achieves its dramatic persuasiveness through its intelligent self-consciousness about language. Bassanio's discourse advertises the inadequacy of language to capture the real; expressing love not as full of self-presence, but as something beyond and outside the play of language. It does not inscribe love directly, but speaks instead of the impossibility of love's full inscription in language, picture, or bodies.

Words fail Bassanio when Portia hands everything, including herself, over to him: 'Madam, you have bereft me of all words' (III.ii.175). The consequent 'confusion' in Bassanio's 'powers' (177) is a disruption of the normal workings of his body, and it is represented as the noise of a crowd in which the meanings of the separately spoken sentences of praise are lost in a blur of speech-noise:

> there doth appear
> Among the buzzing pleased multitude,
> Where every something being blent together,
> Turns to a wild of nothing, save of joy
> Express'd, and not expressed.
>
> (III.ii.179-83)

Bassanio's sense of joy has temporarily exceeded his body's ability to muster the power of language to capture and express it. The experience nevertheless exists as a confused energy inside his body which is stirred like the crowd, but unable to direct it to a coherent speech act. But Bassanio still communicates his feelings in the pre-linguistic state of the body's own workings, which form another kind of speech: 'Only my blood speaks to you in my veins' (III.ii.176). The body's blood-flow is the authenticating sign of his intense responsiveness which cannot at that moment find its way into language. These ambiguities are resolved by a simple return to the body, the note in the casket commanding the successful suitor to *'Turn you where your lady is, / And claim her with a loving kiss'* (III.ii.137-8). The body authenticates the moment. Gratiano's suggestion for a wager on the first boy the couples can produce anticipates the lovers' physical absorption into the social life of Venice.

At this moment when a double marriage is anticipated another body enters the scene which blocks that outcome. Bassanio receives a letter from Antonio giving news that he is subject to Shylock's forfeit. Bassanio describes the letter to Portia as a mutilated and dying body:

> Here is a letter lady,
> The paper as the body of my friend,
> And every word in it a gaping wound
> Issuing life-blood.
>
> (III.ii.262-5)

Bassanio represents the letter as Antonio's body, and that body in turn as a kind of writing. The paper marked with inked words is like a body cut with wounds from which flows its 'lifeblood'. Each wound is also 'gaping', a mouth shaped for speaking, or signalling pain. This is truly a speaking body. The letter's material signifiers—paper and inkmarks—produce meaning prior to its signifieds, and are more emotionally compelling. The wounds gaping like mouths are an emptiness that cries out for Bassanio's presence. Bassanio's strong writerly response, tracing a figurative dying body, shows his profound emotional responsiveness to Antonio's plight. However, the entry of this spectral body, represented in writing, disrupts the imminent marriage and signifies the emotional and practical obstacles that will have to be overcome before it can take place.[20] This letter has a similar power to the bond, for each calls in its debt, and each has as its real aim something in excess of what it seems to signify. In his letter Antonio's focus is on Bassanio, not on the money owed nor his own impending death: *'Sweet Bassanio, . . . my bond to the Jew is forfeit, and (since in paying it, it is impossible I should live), all debts are clear'd between you and I, if I might but see you at my death'* (III.ii.314-18). Antonio's letter points to the real nature of the favour he did Bassanio in borrowing money for his venture: it seeks the return in the form of love on Antonio's pledging of 'person'. Antonio's claim for Bassanio's presence represents the calling in of the excess of their agreement, that for Antonio is Bassanio's love. For Antonio the process is now in hand by which the writing of his body into the bond to maintain his place in Bassanio's affairs, now unexpectedly promises to realize the desires underlying it.

Antonio does not explicitly speak of his relation to Bassanio; but others do. Lorenzo had evidently been discussing the subject with Portia when he enters at the start of III.iv. His phrase 'god-like amity' (3), derives from Renaissance neo-platonic ideas of friendship, and shows 'the exalted tone of much Renaissance writing on male friendship'.[21] In such accounts of male friendship the sexual is banished, leaving only the spiritual.[22] However, the account which Portia proceeds to give of this kind of male friendship does recognize a particular sort of shared physicality in friendship:

> for in companions
> That do converse and waste the time together,
> Whose souls do bear an egall yoke of love,
> There must be needs a like proportion
> Of lineaments, of manners, and of spirit;
> Which makes me think that this Antonio
> Being the bosom lover of my lord,
> Must needs be like my lord. If it be so,
> How little is the cost I have bestowed

> In purchasing the semblance of my soul
> From out the state of hellish cruelty!
>
> (III.iv.11-21)

Her notion of friendship is that between friends who love equally there must also be a similarity of bodies, manners, and spirit. Two friends are supposed to be alike physically and temperamentally, and are also supposed to correspond in their souls. Portia can therefore call paying off Antonio's debt, 'purchasing the semblance of my soul', for she and Bassanio, now married, are one soul, and Antonio's soul exactly corresponds to Bassanio's. The conflict of friendship and marriage arises precisely out of two different kinds of merging that are represented by marriage and friendship. In Christian marriage two different bodies and souls are thought of as becoming one; in neo-platonic friendship two similar bodies and souls become as one in an identity of exact similarity. Bassanio is here poised between the conflicting demands of marriage and friendship. It is Portia's assuming the male sexual identity of Balthazar which enables her 'to displace Antonio's hold on Bassanio's affections and loyalties',[23] and to replace friendship with marriage.

The action in the courtroom is an interpretive contest over the bond. Shylock's refusal to tell the hostile court his reasons for pursuing the bond to its bloody conclusion in Antonio's body should be seen in the same light as Bassanio's warning to Gratiano, before they leave for Belmont, not to be 'too rude, and bold of voice' (II.ii.172) when he goes 'where [he is] not known' (175), and thus risk being 'misconst'red' (179). Shylock refuses to risk being 'misconst'red' by the court, and represses any historical account of himself. Instead he short-circuits the question by locating his motives in nature rather than culture, in corporeal humours not historical influence:

> You'll ask me why I rather choose to have
> A weight of carrion flesh, than to receive
> Three thousand ducats: I'll not answer that!
> But say it is my humour,—is it answer'd?
>
> (IV.i.40-3)

Shylock's refusal to answer has similar effects to Antonio's silence in the first scene in that both thereby become inscrutable to others. The incomprehensibility to the Christians of Shylock's seeking his bond is expressed as his having an irregular body which is both unnaturally hard and empty. The Duke calls him a 'stony adversary' (IV.i.4) and speaks of his being like those with 'brassy bosoms and rough hearts of flint' (IV.i.31). For Antonio Shylock's impenetrability is located at the vital organ of the heart: 'You may as well do any thing most hard / As seek to soften that—than which what's harder?—/ His Jewish heart!' (IV.i.78-80). And Gratiano demands, 'can no prayers pierce thee?' (IV.i.126). Along with hardness goes emptiness. The Duke wonders if Shylock can be 'void, and empty / From any dram of mercy' (IV.i.5-6). When Shylock's resistance is greatest to the persuasions of Portia/Balthazar and the insults of Gratiano and Antonio, he declares himself to be immune from the effect of their words. Secure in the absolute efficacy of the bond, he declares himself to be beyond the reach of language: 'by my soul I swear, / There is no power in the tongue of man / To alter me' (IV.i.236-7).

In the courtroom Antonio is willing to lose his life for Bassanio's sake: 'Grieve not that I am fall'n to this for you' (IV.i.262), he says. Facing death, Antonio makes his farewell to Bassanio; but his attention is actually focused beyond death, for the corporeal mutilation he is about to suffer is to have its real point of arrival in social discourse, as a narrative. He is not concerned with Shylock's malevolence, but rather at the way in which his death will be transformed into discourse.[24] Furthermore, his attention is directed not at Bassanio but at Portia who will hear the story of his death which Bassanio will tell. Antonio utters a string of imperatives which lay down the track and destination for the story which his death will produce, projecting a hypothetical process which runs from bodily mutilation through death to discourse:

> Commend me to your honourable wife,
> Tell her the process of Antonio's end,
> Say how I lov'd you, speak me fair in death:
> And when the tale is told, bid her be judge
> Whether Bassanio had not once a love.
>
> (IV.i.269-73)

Antonio projects a transformation of his death into a story and a question, in which the word 'love' is finally uttered. Were he to realize the scenario he projects, his love for Bassanio would be inscribed in his living body, and its truth proved by incisions which would be neither deletable nor reversible. The speech anticipates an exchange which would turn his physical death into social discourse aimed at recording and validating a certain meaning for it. On the brink of death, Antonio imagines a future scene in which his physical mutilation would be productive of a certain created value of 'love'. That authenticated love, passing through his physical body to a transcendent verbal body of Bassanio's discourse, would require Portia's response, interpretation, and judgement; and would thereby produce its own life-after-death effects. Antonio's rhetorical question would make Portia the judge in the case of the competing claims between her love and Antonio's for Bassanio; and in his scenario she would deliver and face a judgement already weighted against herself.

Of course, Portia-Balthazar releases Antonio from the bond. She takes the bond's signifiers and reduces them to their barest signifieds, at which point the bond breaks down in non-sense. When Portia prevents Shylock's forfeit by telling him that he may take 'a pound of flesh' and no more, she is setting limits to the meanings of words and to the interpenetration of bodies: words are defined with absolute literalness; the integrity of a body is defended. Exchange, one of the characteristic actions of the play, is halted: a pound of flesh is not taken in exchange for three thousand ducats.

It is then Shylock's turn to have his life endangered for the offence of seeking the life of a Venetian citizen: 'the offender's life lies in the mercy / Of the Duke only' (IV.i.351-2). Although the Duke's pardon frees him from the threat of judicial violence, it subjects him to the power of the court's words. Shylock is not beyond the reach of language as the court strips him of half his wealth, confirms the stealing of his daughter, and enforces his conversion to Christianity. The court does not destroy Shylock's physical body, but destroys instead the complex cultural body in which his identity inheres. By his forced conversion to Christianity (in which he will be silenced as the words of baptism are spoken over him) he loses the power to define himself as a Jew; at the same time as he loses the offspring of his body to Lorenzo, who 'lately stole his daughter' (IV.i.381). He protests at the destructiveness of the court's conditions:

> Nay, take my life and all, pardon not that,—
> You take my house, when you do take the prop
> That doth sustain my house: you take my life
> When you do take the means whereby I live.
>
> (IV.i.370-3)

The 'house', as a metaphor for life, has the double sense of building and clan; 'the image and the thing imaged fuse with great dramatic force'.[25] Shylock has earlier shown the same habit of fusing image and thing in the figure of his house as a body when he tells Jessica not to 'thrust [her] head into the public street / To gaze on Christian fools' (II.v.32-3):

> But stop my house's ears, I mean my casements,
> Let not the sound of shallow fopp'ry enter
> My sober house.
>
> (II.v.34-6)

His house is his body which he would defend from penetration by the sounds of Christian music. These links between house as body, clan, and life itself show the interconnectedness of the parts of Shylock's identity, and are precisely what the court destroys in its judgements on him.[26] The court's mercy in sparing his body must be set against its decisions which disintegrate his social identity: livelihood, religion, and succession will all be barred. Shylock's body is not destroyed but his self-identity is disintegrated and deleted, and this deletion is confirmed by Act V.

III

In the first four Acts the body is written into the interlocking struggles of personal desire and social practices; and its power is real but uncertain as long as those struggles continue. In Act V, out of the crises of entanglement posed by the interdependence of bodies, resolutions are offered which define the boundaries of body and spirit, and articulate what is socially legitimate and dominant. As Walter Cohen has shown, the dramatic effects of the last act are radical and extensive, as the 'construction of the pastoral world' of Belmont 'ideologically reconciles the socially irreconcilable. . . . The aristocratic fantasy of Act V, unusually sustained and unironic even for Shakespearean romantic comedy, may accordingly be seen as a formal effort to obliterate the memory of what has preceded.'[27] Shylock's person (and name) disappears from Act V along with traces of Jewishness. Lorenzo's reference to manna when he is told of the will of 'the rich Jew' (V.i.292) is the exception—'Fair ladies, you drop manna in the way / Of starved people' (V.i.294-5)—which shows the appropriation into Christian discourse of the Jewish element that with Shylock's undoing has been deleted from Belmont. Christian dominance is thereby confirmed.

Lorenzo's notion of music has effects which assume the interpenetration of corporeal and incorporeal: he calls for music to 'Creep in our ears' with 'touches of sweet harmony' (V.i.56-7), and directs Stephano, 'With sweetest touches pierce your mistress' ear' (V.i.67). But boundaries between bodies and the abstract harmonies of music are clearly established as he directs Jessica's (and the audience's) attention to the music of the spheres:

> Sit, Jessica,—look how the floor of heaven
> Is thick inlaid with patens of bright gold,
> There's not the smallest orb which thou behold'st
> But in his motion like an angel sings,
> Still quiring to the young-ey'd cherubins . . .
>
> (V.i.58-62)

The harmony of the spheres is a figure in Act V which effects ideological reconciliation. The spheres are a totalizing image which renders unimaginable anything which is not of it. It is thus a falsifying general analogy for the conflictual social scenes of Venice and Belmont grounded on differences of religion, citizenship, and race. Lorenzo goes on to define the relationship between the music of the orbs and its perception:

> Such harmony is in immortal souls,
> But whilst this muddy vesture of decay
> Doth grossly close it in, we cannot hear it.
>
> (V.i.63-5)

The play invokes the music of the spheres as an image of universal harmony, but it places the perception of that harmony in the soul, a human part which lies outside ordinary human consciousness; and simultaneously debases the body by calling it the 'muddy vesture of decay', an impediment to perceiving the 'highest' truth. In Lorenzo's rhetorical construction the idea of comprehensive harmony, located in 'cherubins' and human 'immortal souls', is concomitant with devaluing the human body. Heavenly bodies are supposed to produce music representing fullness and highest truth, while the corporeal is debased and the truth it can produce ignored.

In Act V words and bodies are redefined in the new circumstances of Belmont, a name which suggests 'the 'beautiful mountain' of a fairy-tale'[28], as well as the beautiful female pubic mound. The redefinition of the value of bodies is seen in the ring episode. Portia threatens to give her body to the lawyer since her husband has given the lawyer their ring:

> Since he hath got the jewel that I loved, . . .
> I will become as liberal as you,
> I'll not deny him any thing I have,
> No, not my body, nor my husband's bed.
>
> (V.i.224-8)

The threat expresses the impossibility of a wife's sharing her body with another man and still being a wife. Bassanio learns the lesson of bodily exclusivity that marriage signifies, and as part of this process friendship is subordinated to marriage. Portia's clear view of friendship sees that male friends exactly correspond—'a like proportion / Of lineaments, of manners, and of spirit' (III.iv.14-15)—and it is the impulses of friendship that prompted Antonio 'to lend [his] body for [Bassanio's] wealth' (V.i.249), and Bassanio to give the ring to Balthazar-Portia. Bassanio learns that in terms of marriage men are not identical and equivalent and therefore not freely exchangeable by their wives. Friendship, on the other hand, imagines men as equivalent to each other. In the microdrama of the return of the rings Bassanio is inducted into the ideology of marriage which represents each husband as separate and different, and accorded unique right of sexual access. Understanding this idea is said by Portia to be more than just a matter of words, but as being a fusion of words, ring, and body itself: she tells Bassanio that his 'wife's first gift' of the ring is 'A thing stuck on with oaths upon your finger, / And so riveted with faith unto your flesh' (IV.i.167-9). The ring riveted to flesh fixes the body's meaning within the ideology of marriage; it creates a self embodied in marriage. The separation of Antonio's body from the scene of his friendship with Bassanio is effected when he pledges his soul that Bassanio will be true to his wife:

> I once did lend my body for his wealth,
> Which but for him that had your husband's ring
> Had quite miscarried. I dare be bound again,
> My soul upon the forfeit, that your lord
> Will never more break faith advisedly.
>
> (V.i.249-53)

Antonio's body disappears from the scene and with it his material involvement in Bassanio's affairs. His penultimate words—'I am dumb' (279)—echo Shylock's defeated last words, 'I am content' (IV.i.389), and ominously return him to the silence in which he began.

The play ends with words and the body being put into parodic conflict. As the two married pairs prepare to leave the stage Gratiano sets up a question:

> —the first inter'gatory
> That my Nerissa shall be sworn on, is,
> Whether till the next night she had rather stay,
> Or go to bed now (being two hours to day) . . .
>
> (V.i.300-3)

The question is a real one inasmuch as the pleasure of the night will lie in talking about making love as well as in making love itself. No doubt consummation will take place, but for a moment consummation is teasingly delayed. In a play in which the body has passed fleetingly in and out of discourse it is appropriate that the telos of desire in the body should once more be deferred. Gratiano's last words bring back the body—'Well, while I live I'll fear no other thing / So sore as keeping safe Nerissa's ring' (V.i.306-7)—and recall the knowledge that bodies continue to produce problems of value and identity even after marriage.

Notes

1. All references are to the Arden edition of *The Merchant of Venice*, ed. J. R. Brown (London: Methuen, 1955). All other Shakespeare references are to *The Complete Works*, Compact Edition, gen. eds Stanley Wells and Gary Taylor (Oxford: Clarendon Press, 1988).

2. 'Fiction and friction', in *Shakespearean Negotiations: the Circulation of Social Energy in Renaissance England* (Oxford: Clarendon Press, 1988), p. 86.

3. ibid.

4. See Keir Elam, *Shakespeare's Universe of Discourse: Language-games in the Comedies* (Cambridge: Cambridge University Press, 1984), pp. 202-9, for an analysis of the discursive struggles of the courtroom scene.

5. Jonathan Goldberg, 'Shakespearean inscriptions: the voicing of power', in Patricia Parker and Geoffrey Hartman (eds), *Shakespeare and the Question of Theory* (New York and London: Methuen, 1985), p. 122.

6. Jacques Lacan, *Ecrits: a Selection,* trans. Alan Sheridan (London: Tavistock, 1977), p. 158: 'man defies his very destiny when he derides the signifier'.

7. For a full discussion of the play in terms of generation and production, see Marc Shell, *Money, Language and Thoughts: Literary and Philosophical Economies from the Medieval to the Modern Era* (Berkeley, Los Angeles and London: University of California Press, 1982), pp. 47-83.

8. ibid., p. 53.

9. Cf. King Lear's wish to discover if the body will show the source of guilt if it is anatomized: 'Then let them anatomize Regan; see what breeds about her heart. Is there any cause in nature that make these hard-hearts?', *King Lear,* III.vi.34-6.

10. *The Claim of Reason: Wittgenstein, Scepticism, Morality and Tragedy* (Oxford and New York: Clarendon Press and Oxford University Press, 1979), p. 479.

11. ibid., p. 480.

12. See note to I.i.79 of *The Merchant of Venice* ed J. R. Brown.

13. M. M. Mahood's note on these lines is 'lack of activity is only proper to a sexually impotent old man or a sexually unmarketable woman', *The Merchant of Venice* (Cambridge: Cambridge University Press, 1987), p. 62. She also notes that 'neat's tongue dried' is 'cured ox tongue (and so a withered penis incapable of excitement)', ibid.

14. Michel Foucault, *The Order of Things: an Archaeology of the Human Sciences* (London and New York: Tavistock, 1970), p. 41.

15. 'The theme of the three caskets', in *Collected Papers*, vol. 4 (London: Hogarth Press, 1925, pp. 245-56).

16. *Epithalamium,* 11.153-6, in *Poetical Works,* ed. J. C. Smith and E. de Selincourt (London: Oxford University Press, 1970).

17. Cf. John Donne's 'Aire and Angels', which uses the trope of the relation of angels to corporeal things to complicate and thereby diminish clear boundaries between flesh and spirit.

18. Shell, op. cit., p. 57.

19. ibid.

20. For a discussion of the love-versus-friendship *débat*-theme see Keith Geary, 'The nature of Portia's victory: turning to men in *The Merchant of Venice*', *Shakespeare Survey,* 37 (1984), pp. 55-68.

21. Note to III.iv.3. of *The Merchant of Venice,* ed. Mahood. For a full account of Renaissance ideas of friendship see 'The virtue of friendship and the plan of Book Four', in *The Works of Edmund Spenser: A Variorum Edition,* ed. Edwin Greenlaw et al., *The Faerie Queene,* Book Four, special editor Ray Heffner (Baltimore: Johns Hopkins Press, 1935), pp. 281-313, *passim.*

22. See, for instance, Sir Thomas Browne, *Religio Medici*: 'that part of our noble friends that we love is not that part that we embrace but that insensible part that our arms cannot embrace', in *The Works of Sir Thomas Browne,* ed. G. Keynes, vol. 1 (London: Faber & Gwyer, 1928), p. 92; quoted by Alan Bray, *Homosexuality in Renaissance England* (London: Gay Men's Press, 1982), p. 60.

23. Geary, op. cit., p. 64.

24. Cf. Hamlet's concern at the point of death that Horatio should 'Report me and my cause aright / To the unsatisfied' (V.ii.291-2); and Othello's providing an interpretation of his actions to be reported to the Venetian state after his death (V.ii.347-65).

25. Note to IV.i. 371 of *The Merchant of Venice,* ed. Mahood.

26. Other examples of Shylock's thinking of his identity as connected with his body occur when he calls the jewels Jessica stole 'two stones, two rich and precious stones' (II.viii.20), thus unconsciously associating them with his testicles and seed; and when he hears of his daughter's profligacy from Tubal: 'Thou stick'st a dagger in me' (III.i.100).

27. '*The Merchant of Venice* and the possibilities of historical criticism', *ELH,* 49 (1982), pp. 765-89; p. 777.

28. J. R. Brown, *Shakespeare and his Comedies,* 2nd edn (London: Methuen, 1962), p. 70.

Susan Oldrieve (essay date 1993)

SOURCE: Oldrieve, Susan. "Marginalized Voices in *The Merchant of Venice*." *Cardozo Studies in Law and Literature* 5, no. 1 (spring 1993): 87-105.

[*In the following essay, Oldrieve reads both Shylock and Portia as social outcasts alienated from the Christian and patriarchal world of Venice/Belmont in* The Merchant of Venice.]

I. INTRODUCTION

In *The Merchant of Venice,* Shylock and Portia both represent marginalized groups, the one an ethnic and religious minority, and the other women. As Marianne Novy points out,

> Women and Jews could be seen as symbolic of absolute otherness—alien, mysterious, uncivilized, unredeemed. Although women could be praised for being as virtuous or intelligent as men, or Jews for converting to Christianity or behaving as Christians ought, nevertheless femaleness and Jewishness as qualities in themselves had negative meanings in this tradition—both were associated with the flesh, not the spirit, and therefore with impulses toward sexuality, aggression, and acquisitiveness. . . .[1]

Novy argues that these were "all qualities becoming more evident in Renaissance society" and that in rejecting the Jew and finally repressing the power of women, the play reflects a desire to contain its own movement toward individualism.[2]

While I do not entirely agree with Novy's reading of Act V, her association of Jews and women as outsiders is significant. Their legal and economic conditions, as well as their emblematic connotations, support the analogy. Women were the property of their fathers, and Jews the property of their rulers. The mid-12th century "Laws of Edward the Confessor" (assuming that Shakespeare was adhering to English law, and placed his story in Venice as part of his poetic license) describe clearly the legal position of the Jew in England:

All Jews, wherever in the realm they are, must be under the King's liege protection and guardianship, nor can any of them put himself under the protection of any powerful person without the King's licence, because the Jews themselves and all their chattels are the King's. If therefore anyone detain them or their money, the King may claim them, if he so desire and if he is able, as his own.[3]

Similarly, in *The Merchant of Venice,* Portia is her father's property: even from the grave he has the legal and moral right to decide the most intimate concerns of her life. Furthermore, when married, she is expected to transfer control of her life and living from her father's hands to the hands of a man who might well be completely unknown to her.

Portia's first appearance onstage shows her struggling to balance her needs as an individual against the demands of the patriarchal society in which she lives. She knows she should conform to her father's will, but she desperately wants to control her choice of a husband. Harry Berger's excellent explication of the casket scene in Act III sensitively reveals Portia's conflict between independence and submission. He suggests that Portia is caught between her desire to give Bassanio clues about how to choose and her reluctance to betray her father's will. She is also torn between her desire for Bassanio and her anxiety about submitting herself to him. As Berger explains, "Portia plays the inquisitor, but this is a role which, if she were more crass, she could conceivably induce upon Bassanio, assigning him the function of torturing out of her the answers for deliverance (for her deliverance as well as his) which she would have too many scruples to offer voluntarily, not only the scruple about being forsworn but also the scruple about crowning Bassanio over her as her monarch."[4]

In spite of Portia's scruples and her determination to live by the rules, her discussion with Nerissa in Act I admits the possibility of rebellion against her father's authority. Whether the director chooses to emphasize the clues in the song or not, this scene and her tense conversation with Bassanio make us aware that Portia could choose to ignore her father's will and dispose of herself according to her own wishes. Shylock's situation seems much less flexible. He must convert or die.

While Novy believes that the play rejects the Jew,[5] it seems that in juxtaposing Shylock's dilemma with Portia's, Shakespeare suggests that it is possible for all "Others" to conform in public but at the same time to establish a private realm in which they can successfully satisfy their emotional needs. Berger concludes that Portia finally asserts her individuality and power by "mercifying" Antonio in the last scenes. She simply outgives both him and Bassanio, and in so doing puts them under her power.[6] My reading differs from Berger's in that I believe she exhibits this power not just for her own sake but also for Shylock's.

II. Shylock and the Christian Patriarchy

Shylock's counterpart in the Christian business world is Antonio, who represents the dominant élite. He is the successful businessman of Venice, totally immersed in the city's financial and social life. Antonio first appears surrounded by friends who are deeply concerned about his melancholia. In Act I, Bassanio's entrance with Lorenzo widens Antonio's socio-commercial circle. The men on stage are obviously part of a well-knit and familiar group who both do business and socialize with each other. Antonio is the most successful of them, and the most respected. A true "Old Boy Network" is portrayed during the friendly exchanges of I,i,57-73.[7] The stage is full of men of various ages who share common interests, values, and daily pursuits, and who give each other both the emotional and the financial support that enable them to retain their social and commercial security. Antonio is the center of their concern in every scene in which he or they appear, until Act V. Bassanio is the newest member of the group, favored by Antonio and encouraged by all the men to succeed in their world of commerce. When he says, "To you, Antonio, / I owe the *most* in money and in love" (emphasis added), his words imply that he has received help from others as well, but that Antonio is his primary mentor. Their conversation extends the tone of mutual bonding established at the rise of the curtain, culminating in Antonio's slightly reproachful, "You know me well . . . do but say to me what I should do / That in your knowledge may by me be done, / And I am prest unto it." (I,i,153-160) Antonio is willing to devote both his material and emotional resources to ensure Bassanio's success.

Whether Antonio is motivated by more than his mentorship and his enthusiasm for business cannot be told from the text alone.[8] However, the mentor-protégé relationship does not necessarily need overtones of homosexuality to radiate strong emotion. In such a relationship, the protégé's success is a reflection of the mentor's, and it can be difficult for the mentor to dissociate his professional self-image from the success or failure of the protegé. When Antonio is engulfed in his losses, he wishes to see Bassanio, because in so doing he can assure himself that he has not completely failed in his economic ventures: he can affirm that his loans to Bassanio have secured the young man's social and financial position. He rejects Bassanio's offers of sacrifice, telling him, "You cannot be better employed, Bassanio, / Than to live still and write mine epitaph." (IV,i,117-18) In writing Antonio's epitaph, Bassanio would preserve his friend's reputation, and through his success, carry on Antonio's role in the world.

In this sense, Bassanio is more Antonio's son, continuing the family name and tradition, than his lover.[9] Such a relation is borne out by one of Shakespeare's sources, *Il Pecorone,* where the relationship between the mentor and protégé is one in which a rejected younger son finds a surrogate father.[10] Bassanio and Antonio thus stand in comparison not to Portia and Bassanio, but to Portia and her father, and to Shylock and Jessica. The need to perpetuate one's estate—to control it after one's death by handing it on to an obedient child—is a motif that runs throughout the play. The will of Portia's father and Shylock's grief over the loss of both his daughter and, through her, his ducats, clearly reflect the play's concern with perpetuation. Antonio, too, can reflect this concern, particularly if a director follows Shakespeare's source and portrays him as an older man. Beneath Antonio's intense interest in Bassanio may be a homosexual attraction or a doting friendship, but he also may be motivated by a bachelor's desire for a surrogate child who will ensure his immortality.

III. Portia and Belmont's Patriarchy

Perpetuation is also an issue for Portia, as we move from a predominantly male world to a predominantly female world. Portia's father has tried to ensure that his daughter and his rich estate will continue to prosper after his death. While Antonio trusts Bassanio's judgment in spite of indications that his "son" wastes more money than he preserves, Portia's father takes the care of his estate totally out of his daughter's hands, completely disregarding her intelligence and common sense. Portia cannot even veto her father's choice of a husband, a right increasingly accepted in Elizabethan times.[11] Certainly with both her parents dead, and apparently competent of age and capable of managing the estate well, Portia could expect to have some influence over her marriage.

Portia chafes against this patriarchal control but eventually accepts it, partly out of trust and duty, and partly because she finds that it ultimately works to her advantage. When she discovers that her father's will has chased most of her distasteful suitors away, she resolves, "If I live to be as old as Sibylla, I will die as chaste as Diana, unless I be obtained by the manner of my father's will." (I,ii,104-6) David Sundelson argues that her submission to her father is a form of identification that enables her to cope with his death. She recreates him within herself by taking upon herself his characteristics and values.[12] Carol Leventen also argues that Portia internalizes her father's will, but attributes her motivation to cultural imperatives:

> Quite literally, Portia makes a virtue out of what once was perceived as necessity. In Freudian terms, Portia's words to Nerissa in I,ii and to Bassanio in III,ii, demonstrate the power of the superego: the internalisation of cultural imperatives. Guilt is so internalised that one can never "get away with it" because one punishes one's self; the sanctions are no longer "out there."[13]

With or without the influence of guilt, when Nerissa announces that at least some undesirable suitors have been driven away by Portia's father's demands, the will and the patriarchal and economic system it reflects seem to have worked for her. It is this success that makes her more willing to accept the demands of the patriarchal authority and to submit both her possessions and her person to her husband. The ring that she gives Bassanio is a symbol of her trust in him and in the institution of marriage in her patriarchal world. It is also, as Newman points out, "a representation of Portia's acceptance of Elizabethan marriage which was characterized by women's subjection, their loss of legal rights, and their status as goods or chattel."[14] A potential rebel at first, Portia conforms to the demands of her society and places her entire life and living into her husband's hands.

Her faith in the patriarchal view of marriage extends to Antonio and to the exclusively male socio-commercial relationships with which the play begins. She tells Lorenzo,

> . . . this Antonio,
> Being the bosom lover of my lord,
> Must needs be like my lord. If it be so,
> How little is the cost I have bestowed
> In purchasing the semblance of my soul
> From out the state of hellish cruelty!
>
> (III,iv,16-21)

Her trust in Bassanio makes her willing to trust Antonio, and her generous financial offers mimic the financial and emotional support the play's Christian merchants give each other. Portia becomes "one of the boys" even before she takes on her disguise as a male to defend her new group of friends from an outside threat.

What Portia does not realize at first is that Antonio is not exactly like her lord—or like what she has seen of Bassanio so far. Nor does she understand that the man who is threatening Bassanio's friend has been victimized by the Christian merchants just as she could have been victimized by her father's patriarchal control. Shylock is a businessman in Venice, too, but conducts his business very differently than do his Christian colleagues. Not only does he charge interest while Antonio does not, but he also for the most part works alone, without the social, financial, and emotional support of mainstream Venetians. Antonio is threatened by Shylock's business practices; he resorts first to vehement anti-semitism and then to the legal opportunities Portia affords him to eliminate that threat.

IV. The Contract and Its Enforcement

Both Shylock and Antonio are highly successful, and the fact that Antonio sends Bassanio to Shylock shows that even in Antonio's mind, Shylock is an important business force on the Rialto. Shylock says he hates Antonio because he "brings down the rate of usance," (I,iii,42) but also because he berates Shylock in public, "even there where merchants most do congregate." (I,iii,46) One result of Antonio's behavior would be to drive customers away from Shylock and into his own fold; therefore, his berating Shylock in public would reflect not just anti-semitism, but an anti-semitism used to give the Christian an economic advantage. If Antonio were not threatened professionally by Shylock's business abilities, he would have less motivation to denigrate him in front of customers.

Their rivalry emerges directly as they briefly vie for Bassanio early in scene three. Shylock has just told the Laban and Jacob story, parrying Antonio's pointed questions with a good joke underscoring his financial success. That Bassanio responds by laughing, as he does in the 1981 BBC television production of the play, is signaled by Shylock's line "But note me, signor."[15] Shylock has gotten Bassanio's attention and wishes to extend their moment of comraderie. Antonio immediately interrupts him with "Mark you this, Bassanio," drawing the young man's attention back to himself and reminding him to which camp he belongs.

For a short moment, then, Bassanio is caught between two potential mentors, and the rivalry between Shylock and Antonio becomes not just a matter of business practice and success, but of the gathering and losing of friendship and prestige. Shylock is not really interested in stealing Antonio's protegé from him; he seeks only professional respect for his way of doing business. His rival needs a loan and is willing to adhere to conditions he has vehemently denounced in public. Antonio, faced with his economic vulnerability and perhaps smarting from Shylock's ability to attract Bassanio's attention, berates Shylock's methods even as he is asking for help.

Shylock's bond proposal comes out of his emotional reaction to this insult. He has said that he wants to "catch him once upon the hip" (I,iii,43) for the way in which Antonio has damaged his business reputation; and here he finds himself subjected to worse scorn. He is justifiably angry, and he wants to find a way to stop Antonio's behavior once and for all. The unusual bond that he offers both satisfies his anger and will prevent future public outcry. He begins by accepting Antonio's way of doing things. The implication is that if he can compromise, Antonio should also, especially since he wishes to profit by Shylock's practice:

> To buy his favor I extend this friendship.
> If he will take it, so; if not, adieu.
> And for my love, I pray you, wrong me not.
>
> (I,iii,167-9)

If Antonio does not accept the loan without monetary interest, then he can no longer berate Shylock for demanding interest, for Shylock can counter Antonio's public criticism by claiming that he offered him a no-interest loan and was refused. And if Antonio is willing to "play" with Shylock by accepting the bond and the "merry sport" that it represents, then perhaps he will voluntarily come to treat Shylock with more respect. In either case, Shylock will get what he most desires: the silencing of Antonio's public criticism of his business practices.

On the other hand, Shylock is deeply and justifiably angered by Antonio's insults and some part of him would probably enjoy cutting into Antonio's "fair flesh." Because Shylock's social and legal position prevents him from taking a more direct action for revenge, his anger expresses itself in a dare that also allows Shylock the opportunity subtly to insult Antonio by stating that his "fair flesh" is worth less than an animal's.

Antonio accepts the dare, sure that he cannot lose and pleased that he may have pressured Shylock into conforming to the "proper" way of doing mercantile business. As long as Shylock operates according to his own rules, he threatens Antonio's business supremacy. When Antonio thinks Shylock may be persuaded to change his business practices, he no longer feels threatened; perhaps he believes that he can then compete with Shylock on his own terms and win.

In the trial scene, the Duke, speaking for "the world," (IV,i,17) also expects Shylock to play by Antonio's rules. Not only does he tell Shylock that everyone expects him to change his mind about exacting the forfeiture, but also to

> Forgive a moiety of the principal,
> Glancing an eye of pity on his losses
> That have of late so huddled on his back . . .
>
> (IV,i,26-28).

The Duke seems to have forgotten that Shylock is motivated by his own great losses. Not only has he lost ducats and jewels, but in losing Jessica, he has lost both a daughter and the means by which to control his estate after his death. Antonio can still hope to perpetuate his image in Bassanio, and Portia has behaved as an admirable image of her father and of Bellario her mentor, but Shylock has had all hope of the future torn from him. The Duke ignores Shylock's grief and tells him that loyalty to business associates—even if they have betrayed him—should come before personal concerns. Shylock refuses this argument, and in a forceful speech argues that his feelings are all that matter in this case. His private and personal emotions are going to take precedence over social and political amenities, and he is there to see that the system that allowed him to be humiliated is forced to recognize his personal experience.

Portia enters the scene in the service of that system, intent upon saving her husband's friend and punishing his enemy, upon showing that the feelings of the individual must give way to the larger cause of social harmony. Portia has her plan clearly worked out before she enters the courtroom. She hopes, like the Duke, that she can talk Shylock into relenting and conforming to the expectations of the establishment, but she is prepared to "throw the book at him" if he should not.

However, by defeating Shylock, Portia learns that the very system she upholds would make a victim of her as a woman and a mockery of the marriage to which she has trusted her life and living. The warnings begin with Bassanio's offer to sacrifice her for Antonio. Her aside, even if jocular in tone, expresses some concern over this offer, a concern echoed by Nerissa and by Shylock's comment about Christian husbands. Pausing only momentarily, Portia returns to her primary task and offers the Duke a chance to render the mercy he previously asked of Shylock. The Duke meets her expectations, but she does not allow him to speak for Antonio. "Ay for the state, not for Antonio" (IV,i,371) she says of the Duke's reducing Shylock's punishment to a fine. Antonio is to have his own opportunity to demonstrate the charity which he has so vehemently argued Shylock should show.

When Portia turns to Antonio, she asks for his demonstration of mercy, expecting it to exceed the Duke's. Instead, Antonio not only appropriates half Shylock's wealth, but proposes to settle it on his protegé Lorenzo, thus making Jessica, in effect, his rather than Shylock's daughter, and completely divesting Shylock of the right to control his estate. Portia, who has so painfully accepted the patriarchal right to dispose of a daughter, suddenly sees that when it suits them, powerful men care little about that right when it belongs to a member of a marginalized group. The father-daughter relationship for which she risked great unhappiness disappears in the game of power. This moment reminds Portia that she is the property of the dominant male. From the grave or in the courtroom, he has the legal right to pick her up or lay her down; she is completely subject to his whim. When Antonio demands Shylock's conversion, Portia suddenly recognizes the similarity between the Jew's plight and her own. That recognition gives her reason both to devise and to resolve the dilemma of the rings with which the play ends.

V. Forcing a Conversion

Shylock's conversion must be accounted for in any comprehensive reading of *The Merchant of Venice*. In the trial scene, when Antonio stipulates ". . . that for this favor / He presently become a Christian," (IV,i,384-5) the audience inevitably feels tremendous tension. From that point on, the dynamics of the scene depend heavily upon the characters' non-verbal reactions to Antonio's words. Interpretation of the subtext depends upon one's feelings about conversion in general and upon the relationship one sees between Shylock's forced conversion and the play's themes.

The Merchant of Venice reflects an era in which conversion resonated differently than it does today, and it is therefore useful to understand what a religious conversion might have meant to the Elizabethan audience of Shakespeare's play. Barbara Lewalski, Lawrence Danson, and others (including myself) have argued that Shylock's conversion reflects an allegorical representation of harmony; that because Shakespeare knew no Jewish people, he thought of the conversion of a Jew primarily in theological and abstract terms; and therefore, that Shylock's conversion was not meant to generate the degree of emotion it often elicits from the modern reader.[16] However, the issue of religious conversion in Elizabethan England was not merely a theological concern in which the Jew represented the Old Law and the Christian the New Law. It was a life experience for many in Shakespeare's own audience, and a political and social issue that affected their daily lives.

Henry VIII had required that his subjects repudiate the Pope, opening the door for the influence of zealous Continental Protestantism upon the English Church. The short reign of Edward VI continued the conversion from Catholicism to Protestantism, but Mary radically reversed that process. Under the influence of Mary and her Spanish husband, English men and women again found themselves worshipping as Catholics, or risking accusations of treason. When Elizabeth came to the throne, she came as a strong Protestant leader, soon to be excommunicated and marked for death by the Pope who encouraged all English Catholics to reject her as their sovereign. Nevertheless, most English people donned their Protestant cloaks in compliance with the orders of the state. Some Catholics retained their faith as secret recusants, caught between theological belief and national loyalty. Shakespeare's own father is believed to have been among these recusants,[17] indicating that the issues of religious conversion for political and social reasons may have been more experiential than theoretical for our playwright. If William Shakespeare were raised in a Catholic household that secretly held onto its faith in spite of Elizabeth's ascension to the throne, the playwright himself would have experienced having to disguise or change his faith, his heritage, and his manner of worship in order to comply with the law of the land or risk losing both his living and his life.

Religious conversion in Renaissance Europe was inextricable from political and social conformity and practical daily living, both for Christians and for Jews. If a person wanted to be socially accepted, politically safe, and economically stable, conformity to the politically correct religion of the day was imperative. Consequently, it is not surprising to find that Elizabethan anti-semitism, like that of its European cousins and medieval predecessors, was grounded upon the Jewish refusal to convert, that is, their refusal to conform to the political and religious unity of the state.[18]

However, just as there were English recusant Catholics who outwardly conformed to Protestantism, or earlier, Protestants accepting Catholic trimmings to please their monarch, so too, some Jews compromised by converting outwardly while practicing their preferred religion in secret. Such "converted" Jews were known as conversos, ostensible Christians whom everybody knew as Jews.

It is impossible to estimate how many such conversos were present in London while Shakespeare was there. One who was well-known was Dr. Roderigo Lopez, physician to the Queen, translator, and spy, best known for his grisly death as a (probably wrongfully) accused traitor in 1594. Richard Popkin argues that Shakespeare may have known of the Jewish hostage, Alonso Nuñez de Herrera (Abraham Cohen de Herrera) whose situation and learning were much discussed in certain Elizabethan court circles.[19] Also, both Cecil Roth and Maurice Freedman tell of small groups of Jews from Antwerp who settled in London and Bristol as conversos, officially either "Portuguese" or "Protestant" although even the authorities knew them to be Jewish. Evidently, these groups lived comfortably enough in England until 1609 when an internecine quarrel led one faction to report to the authorities that the other faction was practicing Judaism. The whole community was then expelled from England.[20] Once these groups were exposed, they became a threat to the political and social unity of the state and were expunged.

So to say that Shakespeare knew only of the theological treatment of Jews and their conversion is probably not entirely accurate. He may have known more than one Jewish converso. Certainly he knew conversion as a way to achieve political and social unity through at least an outward conformity. Thought of in this way, religious conversion becomes part of the larger theme of how individuals might cope with authoritarian political, social, and economic pressure. Shylock's dilemma is therefore not entirely different from Portia's. He struggles under the political and economic sanctions of Christian authority; she copes with a patriarchal system that similarly exerts economic and social control over individuals.

Christian mercy has been traditionally given as Antonio's motivation in his demand for Shylock's conversion. However, in the bond scene, Antonio was more concerned with Shylock's business practices—and weakening them—than with his religion, and there is no reason for him to have changed his motivation here. In forcing Shylock to become a Christian, he thinks he is demanding that Shylock give up his practice of charging interest. Since the court has already diminished Shylock's capital by as much as half, Antonio's demand for conversion would ideally force Shylock to stop charging interest. This would destroy Shylock's means of increasing that capital quickly, effectively eliminating Antonio's most threatening business rival. Rather than respond to Portia and the trial scene by rendering mercy, Antonio continues his business competition with the man and uses his rival's vulnerability to assert further dominance.

VI. Portia and Shylock Linked

I fully appreciated the reaction of Joanne Comerford, as Portia, during the trial scene of Peter Royston's staged reading of *Bonds—Made and Broken*.[21] She was shocked at both the Duke's and Antonio's offers of "mercy," and pained by the effect of her judgment upon Shylock. Portia suddenly sees how the law "being seasoned with a gracious voice, / Obscures the show of evil," (III,ii,76-77) and is horrified to have been a part of it. When she asks Shylock, "Art thou contented Jew? What dost thou say?" (IV,i,391) she is making a hopeless plea for a way out. Shylock, of course, cannot offer her one, but his concerned look draws attention to their common understanding of oppression. Shylock's "I am content" then becomes a fatherly response meant to indicate that sometimes conformity is the only choice that can be made. For a brief moment, Shylock regains a child—one who understands and will listen to him—and Portia a father.

After a moment of silence, the emotional connection between Portia and Shylock dissipates with Portia's somber "Clerk, draw up a deed of gift." (IV,i,392) Shylock, shaken by the swiftness of his defeat, asks leave to go and resignedly departs amid Gratiano's heartless taunts, a picture of personal emotion crushed beneath public displays of power. Portia's eyes follow him out the door as she realizes that her feelings as a woman have been just as easily dismissed by the dominant patriarchal system she has worked to support, and could as easily again be disregarded.

At this point, the winning party approaches to ask her to dinner. Impressed with this young "man," they want to make him part of their social and business circle. Suddenly aware of her femininity and of her distaste for the cliquishness of these men, Portia begs off, only to be accosted by Antonio and Bassiano, who try to pay her off for the work she has suddenly found so distasteful. She asks only that Bassanio recognize her when they meet again, a line that can be taken to express the hope that he will look past her feminine exterior to the personhood beneath, rather than to forget the humanity masked by her otherness as his friends forgot Shylock's. Novy argues that the pun on "know me,"

> which relates sexuality to recognition, anticipates her emphasis on sexual identity in the return to Belmont and her implicit victory over Antonio. In the trial, the threat of aggression has been removed by projection onto a scapegoat; at Belmont, it can be dissolved in play—mock hostility which unites the married couples more closely.[22]

The pun instead underscores the intimacy Portia requires and links to it the ability to see behind appearances to people's real feelings. Unless Bassanio can recognize her, he will never develop true intimacy with his wife. In Act V, Portia literalizes her point by making the sexual knowing contingent upon Bassanio's acceptance of her emotions, her intelligence, and her financial power.

Immediately after the trial scene, though, she only fears that Bassanio cannot be trusted to see beyond the materialistic comraderie of the business world. She therefore tests him by asking for his ring. Will he sacrifice his wife's trust to the demands of the "Old Boy Network?" He seems to pass the test at first, but immediately Antonio insists that their friendship take precedence over Bassanio's vows to his wife. When Gratiano brings her the ring, Portia finds that her fears were justified—business and power, coated with friendship, are more important to her husband than emotional, domestic bonds. Men count more than women. Berger points out that Bassanio's giving Antonio Portia's ring indicates "man's assumption that men are superior to women, that it is men who save each other and the world and who perform great deeds and sacrifices; the pledge to a woman can be superseded by the debt of gratitude owed a man."[23] When that exchange occurs in Act IV, Berger explains, "Once again we see how a culture dominated by the masculine imagination devalues women and asserts male solidarity against feminine efforts to breach the barrier. In her own way,

Portia is no less an outsider than Shylock and her "I stand for sacrifice" is finally not much different from Shylock's "I stand for judgment."[24] Too feisty and too angered by her experience in the courtroom to accept this subjugation, she resolves with Nerissa that "we'll outface them and outswear them too." (IV,i,17)

The ring plot thus becomes Portia's version of what Shylock wanted to accomplish in the trial scene, but, as Novy suggests, with the violence removed.[25] In the privacy of Belmont, Portia again takes control of her estate and her life, and ensures that her marriage to Bassanio will be conducted upon hers and not Antonio's terms or the terms of the patriarchal system under which she was wed. As Richard Weisberg explains, Portia is fed up with the mediation of others:

> The legal relationship adopted as a commercial matter by Antonio as the play began now threatens to mediate the most personal of human relationships. Portia, exhausted by her own courtroom tactics on behalf of the mediators, will have none of it. It is time for Bassanio to stand for himself; it is time for the couple, unhindered by third-person intervention, to consummate their marriage.[26]

Weisberg argues that Portia's annoyance comes from her disillusionment with social and legal mediation, and from her growing impatience with the way in which it has delayed the fulfillment (represented as sexual consummation) of Bassanio's commitment to her.[27]

I would argue, however, that her impatience arises from the way in which Antonio's world, including its legal system, ignores the humanity and emotional concerns of the outsider. Her husband was willing to sacrifice her for a business associate. Business competition easily displaced the father's right to dispose of his property—for which she had been willing to risk her life's happiness. Disguised as a man, she was accepted and admired for her perceptive logic and presence of mind; but she knows that as a woman she could never have exercised her intellectual gifts in the Venetian court any more than she had been permitted to exercise them in choosing a husband. The public world has denied her feelings, her intelligence, her right to life (Bassanio wishes she were dead for Antonio's sake). (IV,i,281-6) These experiences send her back to the privacy of Belmont determined to make her husband and his friends acknowledge—in both word and deed—the interests of those whom their public world has marginalized.

She does not again submit herself and her estate to male governance. Portia takes advantage of her private power over Bassanio's economic and patrilineal success to gain and maintain control over her life. Her husband must depend upon her chastity to maintain his reputation, his line of descent, and his control over his estate after his death. Only as long as her children are his children will Bassanio's public influence endure. Portia returns to Belmont as its mistress and retains her power as a woman and a wife to the close of the play. She also refuses to promise sexual fidelity until Antonio commits more to Bassanio's private and emotional well-being than he did to his public business ventures. She rebels not so much against her husband as against the Venetian values which Antonio has taught him. In order to purge those values from Belmont, she must ensure that Antonio as well as Bassanio is made to recognize the importance of people outside his commercial coterie. When Antonio offers his soul as surety for Bassanio's vows, Portia has won. The world of men has been forced to acknowledge the importance and power of woman.

VII. THE MOVE TO THE MARGINS

In Act V, Portia also sees to it that Antonio finds himself obliged to her for his life and living. Ronald Sharp suggests that the "return" of Antonio's ships is in fact a gift from Portia, one that she disguises as "good fortune."[28] It is difficult to imagine how Antonio's ships could have returned, since everyone on the Rialto—Solanio, Solario, and Tubal—seem certain that they have all sunk. However, even if the ships have survived, Portia's revelation that she was Balthasar and her control over the news about Antonio's good fortune force him to recognize that he is no longer center stage. There is more to the world than the Rialto, and his life depends upon the hidden power in the margins. He is duly humbled and perhaps even humiliated by the realization that the brilliant young clerk who saved his life was no more than a woman, and that this same woman wields more control over the life of his friend and over his business transactions than he can.

On another level, Newman explains that "Portia's unruliness of language and behavior exposes the male homosocial bond the exchange of women insures, but it also multiplies the terms of sexual trafficking so as to disrupt those structures of exchange that insure hierarchical gender relations and the figural hegemony of the microcosm/macrocosm analogy in Elizabethan marriage."[29] Portia's demand that her feelings and power be recognized disrupts not just Antonio's view of the world, but also that of patriarchy and authority in general. Her triumph in Act V is thus in some ways a recap of Shylock's powerful "gaping pig" speech of Act IV.

Ann Parten argues that the resolution of the ring plot and Gratiano's concluding pun on "Nerissa's ring" dissolve the fear that Portia will remain dominant.[30] Her point is convincingly stated, but for me that joke always falls flat, even amidst the most comic of performances. In contrast to the serious sexual and financial concerns that Portia's authority and dignified language have just laid to rest, it is simply too lewd to be funny. The time for such masculine flippancy is long past, left behind in Venice at the conclusion of the trial scene. Gratiano's tone seems uncomfortably out of place, as if an important point has just gone over his head. The joke's consequent failure seems to reinforce the powerlessness of the men in the face of Portia's strength. They may try to laugh off her threat to their exclusively male world, but their effort does not succeed. Sundelson's view of the joke as an uneasy effort to resist being engulfed by the feminine reflects more clearly my experience of the play.[31] Antonio doesn't lose Bassanio or his power to Shylock in public, but in private, he loses both to Portia.

Shylock's accepting his conversion stresses the necessity of submitting to authority, but the play's comic conclusion is comic because it holds out the hope that in spite of this necessity, ways can be found to retain control over personal and private concerns. It is for this that we all—male or female—enjoy Portia and Nerissa's putting down of Bassanio, Gratiano, and Antonio. The play would end upon a celebratory note except for the lingering regret over Shylock's fate. The public pain we have felt for him in Act IV still overshadows the private resolution in Act V too darkly for the play to feel wholly comic. Thinking of Shakespeare's own father, I am not sure that that pain should be resolved, but if a director wishes to convey a more fully comic closure, the text provides a way to make it possible.

When Lorenzo hears of Portia's return to Belmont, he asks who comes with her. Stephano replies, "None but a holy hermit and her maid." (V,i,33) Who is this holy hermit? Few productions bother with him at all, so why does Shakespeare mention him? Portia and Nerissa did say they were going to a convent during their husbands' absence, but in fact they went to visit Bellario, and then on to Venice. Where did they pick up a holy hermit?

The last person Portia and Nerissa saw before returning to Belmont was Shylock. Could Shylock be the holy hermit, disguised in a friar's robe like the "fantastical Duke of dark corners" in *Measure for Measure*? The idea is far-fetched if one conceives of the play as it has traditionally been staged, but given the Elizabethan experience of religious conversion, it is possible. In this context, Shylock, disguised in a way that identifies him as a converso, observes Portia exert in private the personal autonomy that he was forced to give up in public. She conveys his deed of gift to his daughter Jessica, humbles his enemy, and shows that conforming to authority need not entail total abdication of individual power. Although bound publicly to the role of wife, Portia maintains individual power in her home.

Disguised as a hermit, Shylock would also represent an outward conformity that does not necessitate abandonment of personal autonomy, either religious or economic. As long as Shylock maintains his Christian disguise, he will be free to go on believing and even practicing religion as he wishes. Roth reports that "During a lawsuit brought in 1596 against one of the Marrano merchants who had been trading with the Peninsula in partnership with an Englishman, the Jewish ceremonies observed at his home in Duke's Place, London, were alluded to in Court without any sense of incongruity and (what was more remarkable) without any untoward results."[32] Apparently, in some cases at least, the practice of Judaism was allowed in the private sphere, even when the authorities were aware that it was occurring.

Furthermore, in spite of the Christian injunctions against usury and Antonio's insistence that loans should be made freely and business conducted without the contamination of interest charges, it is likely that an Elizabethan Shylock could have continued to charge interest on his loans. In his chapter, "Property and the Grasp of Greed," Max James discusses 16th and 17th century treatises against usury. He explains that "even though both Stubs and Smith declare that the government placed a cap on interest rates at ten percent maximum to restrain greed, in actual fact, ten percent was usually the minimum, and many devices were used to circumvent the law and to charge a much higher percentage. . . ." He also points out that not all usurers were Jews: ". . . most usurers were merchants, and . . . merchants were often criticized and excoriated as severely as usurers."[33] According to Elizabethan legal practice, then, Shylock as a Christian merchant could have continued to charge at least ten percent interest. So, Antonio has not gained his presumed victory when he forced Shylock to convert. In Elizabethan society, even a judgment such as that rendered in the play would not have necessitated a change in Shylock's methods. Instead, Antonio's desire to live according to his period's economic ideals might have been seen by many in the Elizabethan audience as nice, but impractical. If so, then *The Merchant of Venice*, like *Richard II*, pits ideology against practicality. However one reads *Richard II*, the ideals that Antonio preaches in *The Merchant of Venice* are undercut by his satisfaction in victimizing Shylock. Seeing a disguised Shylock achieve his revenge both non-violently and practically might help to relieve an audience of any discomfort with which the last act might otherwise leave them.

As the lovers enter the house with Antonio trailing awkwardly behind, the hermit throws back his cowl. He walks slowly off stage, alone, isolated, and still in pain, but satisfied with the revenge he has observed, and resigned to his fate as actor of conformity, as converso, in an authoritarian world. Portia's private victory thus becomes Shylock's, and not just Shylock's, but also the victory of the public playwright/London actor torn between acknowledging the necessity for political and religious conformity and his personal drive to recognize and celebrate individual human experience.

Notes

1. Marianne L. Novy, "Giving, Taking, and the Role of Portia in *The Merchant of Venice*," 58 *Philological Quarterly* 137, 139 (1979).

2. *Id.*

3. Cecil Roth, *History of the Jews in England* (Oxford: Clarendon Press, 1964; reprinted 1978), p. 96. For Elizabethan women as their fathers' property, *see* Lawrence Stone, *The Family, Sex and Marriage in*

England 1500-1800 (London: Weidenfeld and Nicolson, 1977), pp. 180-191.

4. Harry Berger, "Marriage and Mercifixion in *The Merchant of Venice*," 32 *Shakespeare Quarterly* 155, 160 (1981).

5. Novy, *supra* note 1 at 151. Novy concludes her essay by stating that "Like the threat of Shylock, whose trial postpones the consummation of marriages, otherness may seem an obstacle to love and indeed Shylock's exorcism may be intended to remove it as an obstacle. But the acceptance of Portia's self-assertion that we find at the end of *The Merchant of Venice* is also a celebration of otherness and of the means it depends on—financial, sexual, verbal—to give and to receive."

6. *See* Berger, *supra* note 4 at 161-162.

7. William Shakespeare, *The Merchant of Venice,* David Bevington, ed. (New York: Bantam Books, 1988). Hereinafter, parenthetical line references will be in the text.

8. Karen Newman, "Portia's Ring: Unruly Women and Structures of Exchange in *The Merchant of Venice*," 38 *Shakespeare Quarterly* 19, 22 (1987). Karen Newman looks at *The Merchant of Venice* in the light of Lévi-Strauss' anthropological theory of cultural exchange (in which he defines the origin and sustenance of society to be the authorized exchange of women to ensure male bonding) and of Luce Irigaray's feminist critique of his theory. From this perspective, Newman concludes that "Instead of choosing one interpretation over the another, idealized male friendship or homosexuality, Irigaray's reading of Lévi-Strauss allows us to recognize in Antonio's relationship with Bassanio a homosocial bond, a continuum of male relations which the exchange of women entails."

9. *See* Stone, *supra* note 3 at p. 118. In concluding his chapter on "Family Characteristics," Stone explains that children were often sent out of the home to be raised by other families. As a result, nuclear family bonds were weakened so bonds based upon mutual political or economic interests could be strengthened. He writes that "This was a family group [which] was held together by shared economic status and political interests, and by the norms and values of authority and deference. This was a family type which was entirely appropriate to the social and economic world of the 16th century, in which property was the only security against total destitution, in which connections and patronage were the keys to success, in which power flowed to the oldest males under the system of primogeniture, and in which the only career opening for women was in marriage. In these circumstances the family structure was characterized by its hierarchical distribution of power, held together not by affective bonds but by mutual economic interests." To an Elizabethan audience, therefore, Antonio's paternal bond to Bassanio would seem much more logical and familiar than it does to us today.

10. *See* Bevington, ed., *supra* note 7 at 104 for a translation of this story.

11. *See* Max James, *"Our House is Hell": Shakespeare's Troubled Families* (New York: Greenwood Press, 1989), pp. 12-16. *See also* Stone, *supra* note 3 at p. 190.

12. David Sundelson, "The Dynamics of Marriage in *The Merchant of Venice*," 4 *Humanities in Society* 245-262 (1981).

13. Carol Leventen, "Patrimony and Patriarchy in *The Merchant of Venice*," *A Matter of Difference: Materialist Feminist Criticism of Shakespeare,* Valerie Wayne, ed., afterword by Catherine Belsey (Ithaca: Cornell University Press, 1991), p. 70.

14. Newman, *supra* note 8 at 25.

15. *The Merchant of Venice* (BBC television broadcast, 1981).

16. *See* Lawrence Danson, *The Harmonies of The Merchant of Venice* (New Haven: Yale University Press, 1978), pp. 165-169; Barbara K. Lewalski, "Biblical Allusion and Allegory in *The Merchant of Venice*," 13 *Shakespeare Quarterly* 327, 334 (1962); reprinted in *Twentieth Century Interpretations of The Merchant of Venice,* Sylvan Barnet, ed. (New Jersey: Prentice Hall, 1970), pp. 33-80. My reading exists in an unpublished essay, "Reconciliation and Closure in *The Merchant of Venice.*"

17. *See* F. W. Brownlow, "John Shakespeare's Recusancy: New Light on an Old Document," 40 *Shakespeare Quarterly* 186 (1989). The document naming John Shakespeare as a recusant is dated 1592, a date close to the earliest date of 1594 given for the composition of *The Merchant of Venice.* Brownlow also points out that the authorities tended to deal gently with most recusants, and that a common explanation for their absence from church was debt. In the law and social culture of Elizabethan England, there was evidently a connection between debt and religious nonconformity that may have laid the groundwork for Shakespeare's development of a similar connection in *Merchant.*

18. *See further* Daniel Lasker, *Jewish Philosophical Polemics Against Christianity in the Middle Ages* (New York: Ktav Publishing House, 1977); David Berger, *The Jewish-Christian Debate in the High Middle Ages: A Critical Edition of the Nizzabon Vetus* (Philadelphia: Jewish Publication Society of America, 5739-1979), pp. 30-32; Egal Feldman, *Dual Destinies: The Jewish Encounter with Protestant America* (Urbana: University of Illinois Press, 1990); and Rosemary Ruether, *Faith and Fratricide* (New York: The Seabury Press, Inc., 1974). Cecil Roth

19. Richard Popkin, "A Jewish Merchant of Venice," 40 *Shakespeare Quarterly* 329, 329-331 (1989).

20. *See* Roth, *supra* note 3 at 139-144 and Maurice Freedman, *A Minority in Britain: Social Studies of the Anglo-Jewish Community* (London: Mitchell Valentine, 1955), p. 9. Roth's chapter "The Middle Period" recounts the history of other Jewish groups in England, suggesting that they were not completely absent from England during Elizabeth's reign.

21. *Bonds—Made and Broken* (New York Bar Association reading, December 11, 1992). The reading was part of a symposium on "Legal Aspects of *The Merchant of Venice*." See "Editor's Preface" to this number.

22. Novy, *supra* note 1 at 147.

23. Berger, *supra* note 4 at 161.

24. *Id.*

25. *See* Novy, *supra* note 1 at 148-149.

26. Richard Weisberg, *Poethics, And Other Strategies of Law and Literature* (New York: Columbia University Press, 1992), p. 102.

27. *Id.* at 101.

28. Ronald A. Sharp, "Gift Exchange and the Economies of Spirit in *The Merchant of Venice*," 83 *Modern Philology* 250, 263 (1986).

29. Newman, *supra* note 8 at 32.

30. Anne Parten, "Re-establishing Sexual Order: The Ring Episode in *The Merchant of Venice*," 9 *Women's Studies* 145, 145-155 (1982).

31. *See* Sundelson, *supra* note 12 at 252-257.

32. Roth, *supra* note 3 at 141-142.

33. James, *supra* note 11 at 97-98.

Richard Abrams (essay date 1996)

SOURCE: Abrams, Richard. "The Gaping Pig—and Worse: Shylock's Christian Ducats." In *Afterimages: A Festschrift in Honor of Irving Massey,* edited by William Kumbier and Ann Colley, pp. 163-74. Buffalo, N.Y.: Shuffaloff, 1996.

[*In the following essay, Abrams explores the theme of sadness in* The Merchant of Venice, *noting that disappointment is Shylock's most telling characteristic.*]

My topic is sadness in *The Merchant of Venice,* my starting point—Jewish sadness, ultimately, though it is with Antonio's "inexplicable" sadness that the play begins.

> In sooth I know not why I am so sad.
> It wearies me, you say it wearies you;
> But how I caught it, found it, or came by it,
> What stuff 'tis made of, whereof it is born,
> I am to learn.
> And such a want-wit sadness makes of me
> That I have much ado to know myself.
>
> (1.1.1-7)[1]

Of course there have been attempts at explanation. Antonio anticipates losing Bassanio; he has presentiments of disaster, or "some sort of rich man's melancholy"; he is assailed by conscience for failing to live up to his Christian code.[2] All these explanations are suggestive and some work well in combination; collectively, they suggest Shakespeare's skill in moving the audience into the action. Still, to my mind, the received explanations all give Antonio too much credit. Whether they attribute his sadness to neurotic suffering or the operation of a higher instinct, they mark him as a man of sensibility, ratifying the character's own pretensions. By these accounts Antonio becomes not just *a* rich man, i.e., possibly self-made. Rather, as he tosses on his featherbed, they confirm him in his resemblance to the *born*-rich, especially his soon-to-be rival in love, whose princess-and-the-pea discriminatory refinement will appear in the next scene. While one might otherwise have taken Antonio merely for a successful businessman, his melancholy proclaims him the possessor of that most prized of status markers, *un cor gentil*. Like the pampered Portia whose "little body is aweary of this great world" (1.2.1-2), Antonio shows aristocratic veining in his propensity to distill sadness from the very air.

That Antonio's sadness may be partly an affectation is hinted early on, but by so boorish a spokesman as to have escaped a hearing. Advised that he has "too much respect upon the world," Antonio answers, "I hold the world but as the world, Gratiano—/ A stage where every man must play a part, / And mine a sad one" (1.1.77-79). Notwithstanding the egalitarian bow, Antonio patently views his sadness as tragically individualizing, as a cosmically assigned affliction, as not-of-this-world. That is to say, he already models the resemblance he will later play to the hilt, his resemblance to the "man of sorrows and acquainted with grief." Yet not everyone is stirred by the performance. Discounting Antonio's pretensions of otherworldly woe, Gratiano whistles as though he had just come through a train wreck, "Let me play the fool":

> Why should a man whose blood is warm within
> Sit like his grandsire cut in alabaster?
> . . . . .
> There are a sort of men whose visages
> Do cream and mantle like a standing pond,
> And do a willful stillness entertain
> With purpose to be dressed in an opinion
> Of wisdom, gravity, profound conceit—
> As who should say, 'I am Sir Oracle,
> And when I ope my lips, let no dog bark!'
>
> (1.1.83-94)

That Antonio postures for status becomes a distinct possibility, though even if Gratiano's instincts are right, we need not conclude that Antonio's sadness is entirely faked. At one level or another sadness is self-verifying; it is irreducible, like Descartes's doubt. Still, there's a gap between the sadness that worms its way in the heart and the sadness that's dug out for bait; Gratiano again: "fish not with this melancholy bait / For this fool gudgeon, this opinion" (101-02). Antonio's inclination to capitalize on grief will become evident when he uses his predicament with Shylock to bind Bassanio; and even in his entry, I would argue, he is already using sadness for effect. Despite its appearance of world-weary candor, Antonio's feckless apology constitutes a vigorous staking of social ground.

Addressing the "petty traffickers" of the Rialto, Salerio and Solanio, Antonio above all is courteous; he wears his sorrow lightly, prefers not to burden his companions. Yet Antonio will show identical courtesy when, joined by "worthier friends" (Bassanio, Lorenzo and Gratiano), he hurries Salerio and Solanio on their way ("Your worth is very dear in my regard. / I take it your own business calls on you" [1.1.62-63]).[3] The important point to bear in mind in negotiating scene 1's genteel hypocrisies is that this is Venice, where men are damned with the accusation, "You grow exceeding strange" (67). Thus, in fending off Salerio and Solanio's unwelcome inquiries, Antonio is chiefly concerned to avoid an appearance of difference lest the appearance result in an erosion of status. As sad as Antonio may be, and as different as that makes him, he insists that his sadness is not really his, that it's an *other*—indeed, an "it"—to which his own response respectably replicates his interlocutors': "It wearies me, you say it wearies you." Moreover, as Antonio dilates on his non-ownership of the thing of darkness he coincides with, his "it" takes on substance and a history:

> . . . how I caught it, found it, or came by it
> What stuff 'tis made of, whereof it is born,
> I am to learn.

An "it" you "find" or "come by," a sadness made of alien "stuff," no one can decently blame *you* for possessing. Hence, Antonio's unconscious rhetorical tactic of hypostatization allows him to hold his grief at arm's length, to keep "it" from infecting *him*. The figure of contagion is particularly apt in that the first and last terms of Antonio's sequence betray his conception of his sadness as having been "caught" or contracted from a foreign source, "born" elsewhere. In this respect, Antonio's opening lines already display the mechanism that drives his character: his penchant for scapegoating. If one believes oneself subject to foreign contagion, one may wish to expel the infected and infecting outsider; hence Antonio's antidote to sadness—to harass Shylock.[4] As has often been observed, Antonio's character suffers from a kind of albinism; for a title figure he is surprisingly bland and uninteresting. Yet if Antonio is customarily ineffectual, his wonted passivity throws in relief his occasional outbursts of vehemence. Only when Antonio loses himself in persecuting Shylock does he come to life; only by pursuing the remedy of viciousness can he escape the jaws of his own melancholy.

A play whose opening announces a sadness which soon mutates to its opposite implicitly invites its audience to seek the initially-evoked sadness elsewhere; thus, if Antonio's apology turns out to be turf-protection, his case invites comparison with other, possibly more authentic forms of sadness in the play. Consider, as a means to establish criteria for comparison, Edgar's famous remark in *King Lear,* "The worst is not / So long as we can say, 'This is the worst.'" Edgar's point, that by representing grief you belie it, is probably best borne out in Shakespeare's plays by Richard II when he abdicates his throne. Insisting that his grief is insupportable, Richard nonetheless possesses the presence of mind to send for a mirror to "show me what a face I have / Since it is bankrout of his majesty" (R2 [*Richard II*], 4.1.266-67). The impression is distasteful; we feel, with Bolingbroke, that we are watching shadow-play. And though Antonio's modest sadness is a far cry from Richard's grotesque exhibitionism, if I am right to argue that, in his own way, Antonio too is engaged in wan display, we may prefer to distrust all instances of *self*-exhibited sadness (at least, all onstage-instances), crediting only those cases in which, as Kafka writes, the subject weeps without knowing it ["weint er, ohne es su wissen"].[5] Thus, over against Edgar's systematic updates on his own reduction to nothingness, critics have frequently set up the touchstone of Edgar's father Gloucester's despondency. When Edgar rallies Gloucester's with the slogan, "Ripeness is all," Gloucester's pathetic response, "And that's true too," admits of no rebuttal (KL [*King Lear*], 5.2.8-11). The old man's obliging readiness to agree that his dejection may after all be needless reveals that he is *heaped.*

On this model *The Merchant of Venice* presents many instances of plain soreheartedness to set against Antonio's studied sorrow in the first scene. After Portia hears Bassanio in court affirm his willingness to sacrifice his new wife to save his friend, she returns home and remarks with weary understatement, "How far that little candle throws his beams! / So shines a good deed in a naughty world" (5.1.90-91). Indeed, even Antonio at play's end has grown sufficiently to offer a contrast with his more disingenuous act 1- self; observing the ills his manipulation has caused, he comments feebly, "I am th'unhappy subject of these quarrels" (238). And there is Jessica: more painful, even, than her and Lorenzo's guilt-ridden lovers' litany ("In such a night") is her isolation when Portia arrives home. As the gentiles gather at Belmont, Jessica simply recedes; she is "accepted" insofar as no one actively opposes her presence there, but neither does anyone speak to her, nor she to anyone, throughout the play's remainder. Finally, as an instance of abiding sadness—indeed, of passage to sadness's other side—we recall Old Gobbo asking the way to the house of his son and "Master Jew." (What a world of hopes, to judge by the name, must have been present at Launcelot's christening—all disappointed!) After Launcelot teases his poor blind father by giving him incomprehensible directions, the old man tries again:

> Be God's sonties, 'twill be a hard way to hit! Can you tell me whether one Launcelot that dwells with him [Shylock], dwell with him or no?
>
> (2.2.40-42)

Accustomed to hardship, Old Gobbo takes nothing for granted. Evidently he has seen so many disappointments that he builds an expectation of them into his inquiry. Even as he tags Launcelot—for reference's sake—as dwelling with Shylock, he questions whether Launcelot dwells with Shylock. The voice is a familiar one—or so it strikes us today. In its long exposure to an adversity which it domesticates, makes tolerable, the voice is one we've come to associate with Jewish humor.[6]

My association may not be as farfetched as it sounds. The basis of Launcelot's deception of his blind father in Jacob's deception of Isaac (down to the old man's feeling his son's head to identify him) is well-established, and to this may be added a second, less well-known allusion to the Jewish Bible. Though the Quarto and Folio stage-directions and speech-prefixes of *The Merchant of Venice* give the old man's name as "Gobbo," in the dialogue his name appears as "Iobbe," "an Italianized form of Job" according to the Arden editor (xxii). Hence, the poor, patient father becomes a type of long-suffering Jewry. (And the son—what a monicker! Lancelot Job: a macaronic oxymoron of a name!) The hint of Jewish suffering in Launcelot's "true-begotten father" is suggestive and points in an obvious direction. If scene 1 cues expectations of a sad Antonio only to surprise us with Antonio's ferocity two scenes later, then Shylock as Antonio's demonized counterpart may offer significant variation. Though the Venetians denigrate Shylock as Antonio's opposite, an "unfeeling man," nothing "harder" than "His Jewish heart" (4.1.63, 79-80), and though Antonio himself seems often bent on staging his own difference from the Jewish moneylender, many recent critics (drawing on such passages as Portia's "Which is the merchant here? and which the Jew?") have been duly skeptical, regarding the distinction on which Antonio's esteem depends as, largely, a self-serving fabrication.[7] Thus, though Antonio considers his own inexplicable sadness as his personal cross to bear (". . . every man must play a part, / And mine a sad one"), Shakespeare ironically brings out an aggravated version of the same emotion in the character the Venetians regard as Antonio's antithesis. When Shylock makes a play for sympathy on this ground, declaring "suffer'nce . . . the badge of all our tribe" (1.3.106), the exhibitionist factor, evident in "badge," cancels any pity we may feel. But at other times Shylock is less self-conscious, not only not knowing *why* he is sad (like Antonio), but not even knowing *that* he is sad. And at these times, I would argue, Shylock becomes truly affecting. He radiates a sadness that we are asked to recognize as his habitual mode.

Take the famous speeches. If I ask my students, books closed, why Shylock hates Antonio they will tell me that Antonio kicked and spat on him. But Shylock doesn't give that as his reason—at least not at first; he seems not always in full possession of the fact of his own persecution. Instead, in explanation he offers the reasons of the stereotyped Jew: "I hate him for he is a Christian; / But more, for that in low simplicity / He lends out money gratis" (1.3.38-40). In Antonio's phrase, Shylock, repressing, may be said to be made a want-wit by his sadness.

Or consider Shylock in court when he tauntingly explains his reasons for seeking revenge:

> Some men there are love not a gaping pig,
> Some that are mad if they behold a cat,
> And others, when the bagpipe sings i'th' nose,
> Cannot contain their urine
>
> (4.1.47-50)

Most hear this as a justification of anger but I hear it as a plaint. Timelessly, the bagpipe wails, and old men have trouble with their bladders. More historically, Shylock's images connect to Jewish suffering via the disturbing traditional figure of the *Judensau*, as Gustav Ungerer has shown, building on Irving Massey's understanding of the gaping pig not as a roast pig but the living barnyard animal, "stretching [its] jaws, almost as if . . . trying to loosen the joint . . . the same position [pigs] fall into when they squeal or scream" (11). When Shylock rages he "weeps without knowing it"; like Antonio incapable of deciphering his own sadness, he cannot say where he "caught" this grief, "What stuff 'tis made of, whereof it is born."

In my first example above, Shylock explains in soliloquy his reasons for hating Antonio; and in my second, though he addresses the court, he may as well still be in soliloquy for all the hearing he will receive. My point, as underscored by the quantity and variety of Shylock's actual and virtual soliloquies, is not only that Shylock is often alone in the play, but that he needs to be listened to, needs to be made sense of to himself. Again and again, in a character trait scanted by criticism, Shylock looks for love in the wrong places. In scene 3, just before clenching in hatred toward Antonio, he abandons his habitual sarcasm, becoming positively expansive on his favorite subject of the patriarchs. He seems to reach out for understanding, letting an insult pass (*Ant.*: "And what of him [Jacob]? Did he take interest?") as he continues his digression in a hopeful voice. For a moment we cannot be sure what Shylock is reaching for. Then, when a preaching Antonio interrupts him a second time ("Mark you this, Bassanio, / The devil can cite Scripture"), Shylock himself tells us: "I would be friends with you and have your love" (134). Only *now*, of course, Shylock is past wanting friendship; he is being manipulative, whereas moments before, in his relaxed storytelling mood, his explanation would almost have been true. (In this vein I might also cite Shylock's often-quoted justification of his revenge. Shylock is usually accused of "using" his humanity to justify evil. But from a standpoint of Jewish identity, i.e., Jewish pride, Shylock's assimilationist appeal for Christian sympathy to the dullards Salerio and Solanio, whom he far outclasses, is disappointingly complaisant, "a weak disabling of [him]self" [2.1.30]. Shylock gives away too much. Hath not a Jew . . . *brains*?)

And Shylock seeks understanding and love not just from Antonio but from Bassanio, all the while questioning why he should accept an invitation to Bassanio's feast (but he accepts anyway):

> I am bid forth to supper, Jessica.
> There are my keys. But wherefore should I go?
> I am not bid for love—they flatter me—
> But yet I'll go in hate
>
> (2.5.11-14)

Moments later, stung mildly by Launcelot's announced departure, Shylock even spends a good thought on the *Schnorrer*'s behalf: "The patch is kind enough, but a huge feeder" (44): well, *half*-a-thought, but that's still a half-thought more than Launcelot spends on Shylock. Finally, even from a source where Shylock might have expected kindness, he receives only pain. I am always astonished by Tubal's pleasure in twisting the knife. Though on the stage Tubal is generally played to a different effect, in reading the scene it's hard to escape the impression that Tubal finds something not altogether displeasing in his co-religionist's suffering.[8] (A Hasidic saying: "No man's beard ever grows grey worrying about another's troubles" [Jacobson, 19]).

The case of Shylock's intimate enemy Tubal brings us to the pivotal event in Shylock's life: his crushing betrayal by Jessica. Though Shakespeare so works the offstage scene of horrified discovery as to induce audiences to accept at face value Solanio's report of Shylock's confused passion, and thus to conclude that Shylock rates the loss of his money above (or on a par with) the loss of his flesh-and-blood—

> 'My daughter! O my ducats! O my daughter!
> Fled with a Christian! O my Christian ducats!
> Justice! the law! my ducats and my daughter!'
>
> (2.8.15-17)

—evidence elsewhere in the play points up the mean-spiritedness of this response. Critics have regularly noted the hate-filled Solanio's unreliability as a reporter of the crying old man he terms "the dog Jew" (14), and have noted, too, the evidence of Shylock's own curse on Jessica. Shylock wishes to bury his recovered jewels *with* his daughter, not to retrieve them (3.1.78-80): "A terrible curse—but it *is* a curse, and not an expression of greed. . . . In his self-punishing, self-pitying fury, Shylock calls down destruction on everything that he has lost" (Gross 74). To these, I would add two fresh pieces of evidence. Shakespeare's intent to entrap viciousness, to show complacency its face, appears in Salerio's adulatory description of Antonio not twenty lines later:

> A kinder gentleman treads not the earth.
> I saw Bassanio and Antonio part:
> Bassanio told him he would make some speed
> Of his return; he answered, 'Do not so.
> Slubber not business for my sake, Bassanio,
> But stay the very riping of the time . . .'
>
> (2.8.35-40)

Business! Although audiences stereotype Shylock as rating money above love, it is Antonio, rather, who does so; Antonio conceives Portia's wooing purely as a business proposition (a view in which Bassanio has encouraged him). Then, too, to recall our earlier discussion of Shylock's characterization, from what we have already seen of Shylock's reluctance to delve his hatred of Antonio, it is unsurprising that he cannot now locate the true source of his pain: namely, that Jessica seems no longer to love him, that she has left him naked to his enemies. Instead of gazing on that Medusa, Shylock self-protectively converts his grief to grievance. His sadness, again "want-wit," leaves him impotently raging, with "much ado to know [him]self."

I'd go further: a moment ago I quoted John Gross describing Shylock "call[ing] down destruction on everything that he has lost." Gross assimilates Jessica to the ducats. Petulant, Shylock wants to see the last of her and them, to have everything he once believed his own, now, finally and decisively, out of his life and heart. I think this gets it backwards. It's not Jessica as object that Shylock assimilates to the ducats. It's the ducats he assimilates to *her* in what he constitutes as *another* failed love-relationship. Shylock's lament for his lost ducats is usually read as containing a *lapsus linguae*: for "Christian ducats" *read* Christian daughter. But the idea that Shylock's money has betrayed him *along with* Jessica, that it *too* has converted to Christianity (cf. Portia: "Myself and what is mine to you and yours / Is now converted" [3.2.166-67]), is not without interest. If Shylock's money has sustained and protected him, if his "living" has long watched over his "life" (cf. 5.1.286), then his genial guardian now goes over to the enemy. *His* ducats, as they once seemed, betray him by becoming Christian; they can no longer be counted on to keep the wolf from the door.

In the Christianization of his ducats conceived as a kind of a tutelary deity (a reading strengthened, incidentally, by the association of the two sealed bags of ducats with testicles, hence, the protecting spirit of the *paterfamilias*) Shylock finds cause for despair. In the imagined betrayal of *things* there may be something nearly as wrenching as the betrayal of loved ones, especially if, as Freud and many before him have believed, those "things" are at bottom a stabler substitute *for* loved ones, undoing our narcissistic wounds with promises of their magical support.[9] To draw a Shakespearean analogy, among Richard II's griefs perhaps the unkindest cut is struck by Richard's horse "roan Barbary," who in a seeming betrayal permitted Bolingbroke to ride his back, and "Would . . . not stumble . . . fall down, / . . . and break the neck / Of that proud man" (*R2*, 5.5.78ff). Richard had already given up on people some while ago (cf. 4.1.168 ff). But for a dumb beast not to live up to its anthropomorphic potential—this is occasion for a woe that for once eludes even Richard's powers of articulate self-pity ("Forgiveness, horse! Why do I rail on thee" [5.5.90]).

I want to close on a speculative and sentimental note by musing—beyond the scope of what the play allows—on what could have made poor Shylock happy. Certainly not Jessica's continuing loyalty, which he took for granted till she left him; nor, after she betrays him, could he delight much in her return. At no time can his money-bags have provided great pleasure, but only security, especially if, as argued, his money draws its main significance from its surrogacy for love. (For Shylock to take solace in possessions, though, is not a total lost cause; Leah's ring is the obvious case, and beyond that, I for one would like to know what Shylock *collects*.) Of course, acceptance from Antonio and his kind is out of the question; and even if it were offered provisionally (say, as a result of his enforced conversion) Shylock would have to be "a soft and dull-eyed fool" (3.3.14), a dummy, to trust it. Yet lest my question by now seem frivolous, let me suggest that the play does at one point invite us to imagine Shylock brought closer to human community. Old Gobbo, who like no one else in *The Merchant of Venice* coins a term of respect for Shylock, is on his way to bringing "*Master* Jew," a gift when Launcelot intercepts him ("My master's very Jew. Give him a present? Give him a halter"). The unsolicited gift, "a dish of doves," falls within Kosher law and would appear to be offered entirely without ulterior motive.[10] If, in Shylock's view, even a Launcelot is "kind enough, but a huge feeder," then to Launcelot's father bringing food, the reservation would not apply. To be sure, Shylock would not know what to say to the poor blind rustic, and he might not think much of the cooking, but I suspect he would be touched by the kindness. It is pleasant to imagine a moment of fellow-feeling growing between the two old men, but that may be hoping for too much. At worst, though, not even "old Shylock" (as he fondly calls himself) could find cause for hurt in Old Gobbo's unexpected generosity. A pity the dish of doves never arrived! It was a kindness "lost / As offered mercy is" (*Cymb.* [*Cymbeline*], 1.3.3-4).

Notes

1. My text for *Merchant of Venice* and other Shakespearean citations is the individual play editions of *The Pelican Shakespeare*, general ed., A. Harbage; the text of *MV* is edited by Brents Stirling.

2. For Antonio's affliction by conscience, Danson (30-34 *et passim*); the citation is from Barber (180); the first three views are already evidenced by 1888 in the *Variorum* note on the passage, and have appeared with innumerable variations since then.

3. Ralph Berry has an interesting discussion of the tempo of social pressures in scene 1, though fails to discuss Antonio's motive of avoiding stigma.

4. Gillies comments that "Antonio as the ideal Venetian (*sic*) is . . . systematic in representing Shylock as other. More than just a 'Jew,' Shylock is a 'stranger,' an 'alien' and an 'infidel'. His Jewish otherness has [a] pandemic quality" (128). Further, "the confrontation between Antonio and Shylock amounts to a struggle over the political and economic heart of Venice. Thus the forum of Antonio's many assaults on Shylock is always the market-place. . . . Like Christ chasing the money-changers from the temple . . . Antonio seeks to recover the sacred core of the city from the twin abominations of 'interest' and intrusion" (129).

5. Franz Kafka, "Auf Der Galerie" (154-55); I thank Al Cook for rounding up the citation.

6. Old Gobbo's phrasing further tangs of Hebraism at 2.2.86-87, "Lord worshipped might he be, what a beard hast thou got!"

7. Typically, Novy writes, "But if in general Antonio denies or sublimates his own sexuality and instead supports Bassanio's pursuit of Portia, he also denies the acquisitiveness inherent in being a merchant and instead attacks Shylock, the double who shares and exaggerates his mercantile profession and marginal social status. Even in this respect, however, he generally presents himself as self-denying, patiently holding in check his hostility to Shylock everywhere but in the scene where he arranges the loan. In his verbal attack on Shylock there, his speech takes on unusual energy; this is the one scene in which Antonio does not speak about being sad. His temporary recovery resembles the relief from a sense of powerlessness and depression that modern psychologists have often found to be one function of anti-Semitic outbursts" (71).

8. In recent productions I've seen, Shylock is played (rightly, I feel) as a Jewish stereotype but then, compensatorily, Tubal is turned into nature's nobleman. The effect is reminiscent of the old television series, *All in the Family,* in which the producers presented a comically-bigoted Archie Bunker but then leaned over backwards to make the other characters impeccably liberal. Of Shylock's grudging fondness for Launcelot, Harley Granville-Barker writes, "he has a niggard liking for the fellow, is even hurt a little by his leaving, touched in pride, too, and shows it childishly: "Thou shalt not gormandize / As thou hast done with me," cited by Barber (191).

9. See Muensterberger for interesting and relevant Freudian discussion of the mania of collecting. For "hallowed" consumer items bringing "a benediction to the buyer," *WT* [*The Winter's Tale*], 4.4.594-95.

10. Hassel remarks that "As in no other Shakespearean play, characters so frequently refer to dining together that such dining becomes our sense of the natural Christian condition. Dinners are consistently focal points for celebration and companionship." He cites nine instances, concluding, "Like Communion these dinners celebrate and reward shared love" (193). My

own sense is that nothing so attractive is going on; most of Hassel's nine cases savor of "networking": sleazy characters "do lunch." Old Gobbo's reaching-out, on the other hand, which Hassel fails to mention, seems to me convivial in the radical sense, an attempt to extend community.

Works Cited

Barber, C. L. *Shakespeare's Festive Comedy.* Cleveland and New York: World Publishing Company, 1967; first. ed., 1959.

Berry, Ralph. "Discomfort in *The Merchant of Venice,*" in *Thalia: Studies in Literary Humor* (Ottawa) 1 (1978-79): 9-16.

Danson, Lawrence. *The Harmonies of "The Merchant of Venice."* New Haven and London: Yale University Press, 1978.

Gillies, John. *Shakespeare and the Geography of Difference.* Cambridge: Cambridge University Press, 1994.

Gross, John. *Shylock: A Legend and Its Legacy.* New York, London, etc: Simon and Schuster, 1992.

Hassel, R. Chris, Jr. *Faith and Folly in Shakespeare's Romantic Comedies.* Athens, Ga.: University of Georgia Press, 1980.

Jacobson, Howard. *Roots Schmoots: Journeys Among Jews.* Woodstock, New York: The Overlook Press, 1994.

Kafka, Franz. "Auf Der Galerie." In *Das Urteil und andere Erzahlungen* Frankfurt: Fischer, 1946.

Massey, Irving. *The Gaping Pig: Literature and Metamorphosis.* Berkeley, Los Angeles and London: University of Indiana Press, 1976.

Muensterberger, Werner. *Collecting: An Unruly Passion.* Princeton, N.J.: Princeton University Press, 1994.

Novy, Marianne L. *Love's Argument.* Chapel Hill, N.C.: University of North Carolina Press, 1984.

Shakespeare, William. *The Merchant of Venice.* Ed. John Russell Brown. Arden Edition of the Works of William Shakespeare. Cambridge, Mass.: Harvard University Press, 1959.

———. *The Variorum Merchant of Venice.* Ed. H. H. Furness. Philadelphia: Lippincott Company, 1888.

Ungerer, Gustav. "Shylock's Gaping Pig." In *Elizabethan and Modern Studies.* Presented to Professor Willem Schrickx. Ed. J. P. Vander Motten. Ghent: Seminarie voor Engelse en Amerikaanse Literatur, 1985, 267-76.

Samuel Ajzenstat (essay date 1997)

SOURCE: Ajzenstat, Samuel. "Contract in *The Merchant of Venice.*" *Philosophy and Literature* 21, no. 2 (October 1997): 262-78.

[*In the following essay, Ajzenstat evaluates* The Merchant of Venice *as a romantic comedy featuring a number of significant oppositions, the most fundamental being that between "the conditional and the unconditional."*]

The Merchant of Venice is widely interpreted as a Christian parable about the power of selfless love to raise us above the loveless inflexibilities of the legal and commercial orders.[1] The account I shall offer is the precise opposite of this interpretation: *The Merchant* makes more sense as a play about love's *inability* to allow us to dispense with a loveless realm of hard necessity and, even more, about love's dependence on a loveless realm for its own survival. But the rejection of the idealistic account does not make *The Merchant* a cynical play. It remains a romantic comedy because it shows that love does not require the myth of its invulnerability and all-conquering power to remain meaningful both in the here-and-now and as a pointer to something beyond it.

The Merchant intertwines two distinct stories, a very pleasant and a very unpleasant one. The pleasant story takes place in the beautiful estate of Belmont where the young Venetian nobleman Bassanio wins Portia's hand by passing the test specified in her father's will, picking from among a golden, a silver and a lead casket the one which contains her picture. The unpleasant story takes place in a dark, ugly Venice where the merchant Antonio, in order to finance his beloved friend Bassanio's trip to Belmont, puts himself under the power of Shylock, the Jewish moneylender whose hatred he has earned by reviling him as a Jew and a usurer. Antonio risks his life, pledging a pound of his flesh if the debt is unpaid. Shakespeare brings the two stories together by having Portia, disguised as a man, go to Venice to defend Antonio in the law courts. Shylock is defeated and forced to convert to Christianity and the victors return to Belmont. Shylock's daughter Jessica, having run away to marry the Christian, Lorenzo, is also allowed to make the passage from Venice to Belmont.

To idealistic critics, the two stories work against each other. However compassionate the Christians may think they are being by making Shylock convert, it is clear enough to us in the modern audience that they are destroying him. It takes something away from the beautiful triumph of pure love—which such critics think must be the point of the play—to see it purchased at the price of the destruction of someone for whom we have come to have considerable sympathy. Consequently, the play seems either to fall apart dramatically or to be a unity only if anti-semitic. Such critics adopt a number of expedients, trying to get us to see Shylock as a simple, generalized villain, or viewing the play as anti-semitic but falling back on the historicist, Shakespeare-couldn't-have-known-any-better line, or else arguing that the play's incoherence is praiseworthy because Shakespeare's human sympathy overcame his skill as a playwright. But once we recognize, as I shall argue, that the ubiquity of something less than love is as present in the love story taken by itself as it is in the Shylock story, the sense of incoherence disappears.

As for anti-semitism, it is surely an element in the play. But when we see it as a consequence of the Christian characters' attempt to separate themselves from what the play shows us to be an inseparable aspect of human life, we can understand that the play not only opposes anti-semitism but offers an astute philosophical analysis of it.

The play's fundamental opposition, often characterized as between love and commerce, is more revealingly seen as an opposition between a need for unconditional commitments and the equally pressing need to fence our commitments with conditions. The conditional is rooted in that aspect of ourselves—part of what we call justice—that tells us it is only fair for us to be self-interested enough to expect a return for what we give, reward for good, punishment for bad, measure for measure. Its basic metaphor is the contract. The unconditional is rooted in our sense of the grandeur of being able both to give and to get without demand of a return on either side, each entirely transcending need for the sake of the other. The Christian characters are not necessarily wrong to see the unconditional as spiritual perfection and the conditional as a taint on spiritual perfection. Their mistake—which the idealistic critics share—is to think that spiritual perfection is open to them. The mistake has two sides: the belief that they can distance themselves from what they find most dubious in commerce by identifying it with the Jew Shylock, and the belief that human love is sustainable without a conditional, tit-for-tat component. The play destroys both beliefs, the first in its way of telling the Shylock-Antonio story, the second in the Portia-Bassanio story. In both, we see the Christian characters being eased in the direction of a more rueful, less utopian conception of the spiritual possibilities open to them than they were reaching for at the beginning. At the same time our recognition that this reaching resulted in the casual and hypocritical demonization of others need not rob the Christian characters of our sympathy once we see that the harm they do comes from no worse a motive than the desire to be able to think well of themselves. The play shows us that the life of purely unconditional relationships, however exalted it may be, is unreachable and the attempt to reach it corrupting, but it resists a complacent reaction to the realization that this is how things must be. In a grand tradition, perhaps now on the wane, it is profoundly anti-utopian without quite letting us give up longing for a purer world. And though it is the Christian Portia who in many ways most fully represents the divided soul, Shakespeare will find a way of hinting that the spirit that blows through the play is an Old Testament spirit.

I

In *The Merchant,* as often in Shakespeare, issues emerge most clearly and subtly in incidental set pieces easily overlooked and sometimes cut in performance. Such episodes do not so much add to the plot as permit Shakespeare to comment unobtrusively on the main action. My account of the play hangs on four such episodes. The first of these, I wish to suggest, can best be seen as a "comment" on the demand in the trial scene that Shylock convert to Christianity. It occurs at the beginning of Act III, Scene v, when Shylock's daughter Jessica tells Launcelot Gobbo, the clown and ex-servant of Shylock, of her conversion to Christianity.

Audiences find Shylock's forced conversion extremely distressing. Yet this occurrence gives the true measure of Shakespearean irony—an irony more often saving than cynical. The saving irony here is that what is literally the cruelest persecution Shylock undergoes marks symbolically the collapse of the system which finds it useful to cast him as an object of persecution in the first place. Portia, we shall see, undergoes a similar turnabout. Both reversals reveal the instability of the Belmont-Venice dichotomy. This implication emerges not in the trial scene itself but in Launcelot's reaction to Jessica's talk of conversion. When she tells him that her husband, Lorenzo, "hath made me a Christian," the clown responds:

> Truly the more to blame he; we were Christians enow before, e'en as many as could well live one by another; this making of Christians will raise the price of hogs,—if we grow all to be pork eaters, we shall not shortly have a rasher on the coals for money.
>
> (III.v.19-23)

A bad joke, maybe. But a revealing one. Antonio may well think of Shylock's conversion in spiritual terms. Launcelot helps us see that it also has an economic consequence—a much more interesting one than the price of bacon.

What would be the economic consequence of a conversion of all Venetians to Christianity? Clearly, either that all money lending would cease, with the consequent collapse of the Venetian commercial empire—something that Antonio has already told us he is willing to give his life to avoid (III.iii.26-36)—or else that Christians would become moneylenders. Launcelot's joke points to the increasingly explicit entry of Christians into usury, henceforth to be dignified with the name of banking. Of course, for this to happen there is no literal need for the conversion of all or any Jews. What Shylock's conversion points to symbolically is not a spiritual change in Jews but a spiritual change in Christians.

It is not that Christians become moneylenders for the first time. In the twelfth century, St. Bernard had written: "We are pained to observe that where there are no Jews, Christian moneylenders 'Jew' worse than the Jews, if indeed these men may be called Christians and not rather baptized Jews." The historian who reports this statement comments that though "the Jews always formed a tiny minority of the people so engaged," squeamish Christians could console themselves with the fiction that Christian moneylenders must really be Jews.[2] The spiritual change that is taking place is that they will soon no longer need the fiction.

Some may wish to explain this ironically as nothing more than the replacement of traditional squeamishness with a modern complacency that does not worry itself over spiritual ambiguities. We cannot be sure that this is not the direction in which Shakespeare sees his characters heading; many of them have a strong streak of complacency. But we have yet to point to some hints in the play to suggest a different explanation of what is happening.

The explanation I wish to explore is well suggested in a remark of the American Protestant theologian Reinhold Niebuhr about St. Augustine's *The City of God*. Augustine speaks of two cities or ways of life, the city of God and the city of man, and has seemed to many of his readers to believe—just as the separation between the two "cities" of Belmont and Venice helps the Christian characters and idealistic critics of *The Merchant* to believe—that the human race can be fairly neatly divided into two categories: those who live in the community of unconditional love and those who live in the community of self-love and who, among other things, do the dirty work of law and order by which the ungodly control each other so that the godly can live in peace. Niebuhr offers a criticism which, whether or not fair to Augustine, seems to me to crystallize the movement of our play precisely:

> When Augustine distinguished between the "two loves" which characterize the "two cities," the love of God and the love of self, and when he pictured the world as a commingling of the two cities, he did not recognize that the commingling is due not to the fact that two types of people dwell together, but because the conflict between love and self-love is in every soul.[3]

For all that Belmont is a poor counterfeit of the city of God, Niebuhr's remark helps us see *The Merchant of Venice* as a parable in which the idea that pure Virtue and pure Vice are exemplified in "two types of people," Shylock and Portia, is replaced by the realization that vice and virtue are in conflict within each soul. This realization allows for a more concrete account of all human beings as unpurifiable mixtures of good and ill who, instead of pretending to banish contradiction from their hearts, will have to embark on the project of learning how to live torn by the struggle between the unconditional and the conditional.

To be able to see the play in these terms we must be able to keep alive our sense that there is something despicable about the conditional, contractual life. There must be something capable of moving us in Antonio's essential criticism of lending at interest:

> If thou wilt lend this money lend it not
> As to thy friends—for when did friendship take
> A breed for barren metal of his friend?
>
> (I.iii.127-129)

To say of the Renaissance Venetians that they wish to live golden spiritual lives full of beauty and mutual regard far above the life of crass, competitive money-grubbing but that they can see no way of doing so except through the proceeds of those crass activities is not to situate them historically or geographically but to understand them as exemplars of a more generally familiar dilemma. What hangs over Antonio's head surely is the injunction to "sell all you have and give to the poor." It makes him a better man and a worse one. He cannot live with it and he cannot live without it.

We may miss the advantages of the Belmont-Venice system, which are mainly two: first, that it keeps up the morale of at least some members of the society, by allowing them, however artificially, to think well of themselves without asking them to forgo the benefits of wealth. And secondly, along with this, that it is able to keep alive, even if only by lip-service and only among an elite, an exalted conception of human relationships. If they had been more honest with themselves both of these things might have been more difficult for them.

But Shakespeare does not endorse this self-deception. So, though he allows us to see, in spite of everything, the graces of Belmont, he also shows us the unworkability of the separation of Belmont from Venice. We have yet to see the fatal flaw that will bring the system crashing down. Before we can do so, we need a further understanding of how the basic principle at issue is brought into the play and an examination of Portia's role in bringing out the collapse of the social structure she is trying to save.

II

A second "incidental" episode points us towards a deeper view of what is at issue in *The Merchant*. Once more it involves Launcelot Gobbo, the play's wry philosopher-clown, and should also be read as a comic commentary on a serious scene, the only one in which Antonio and Shylock debate the issue of usury. In the comic episode, Launcelot meets his father coming to visit him (II.ii.31-94). The high-spirited son cannot resist confusing the blind old man. He first pretends not to be Launcelot, then, acknowledging that he is, kneels down and asks his blessing. The father, feeling the top of Launcelot's head expresses surprise that his son has grown such a long beard. Truly, as Launcelot remarks, "It is a wise father that knows his own child."

This episode is a comic acting out of the biblical scene (*Genesis* 27) in which Jacob wears goatskins so that his blind father Isaac will feel him, think he is his elder son, the hairy Esau, and be deceived into giving him Esau's blessing. The point of this scene begins to emerge when we recall the serious scene in which Shylock tells Antonio that by usury he is following Jacob's example and Antonio's reply that Jacob, unlike Shylock, did nothing unjust and was in any case guided by God (I.iii.66-90). The scene between Launcelot and his father functions as Shakespeare's invitation to us to consider Antonio's rosy, idealizing picture of Jacob as not quite what Scripture intended, indeed as a deep misunderstanding of the religious tradition.

It is not possible here to give a full account of the story of Jacob. Of all the Biblical patriarchs he most conspicuously lives out a double bind. In order to fulfill his spiritual calling of being one of the founders of a holy nation he must lie and cheat. At the same time, the God he serves with his lie is a god who demands truth so Jacob and his mother must be punished.

The biblical text lays out the structure of the punishment with wonderful clarity. In the story of Jacob's marriage, the same kind of trick he had used to supplant his elder brother (*Genesis* 29: 16-27) is used against him to supplant a younger of two sisters.

Reading Jacob's marriage to Leah as punishment suggests that his original act of lying was evil. But the story also suggests that the lie was necessary. This seems to be the reading that emerges from Launcelot's scene with his father, for just before their meeting Launcelot has been debating with himself whether he should obey his conscience and remain Shylock's servant or obey the devil and run off and enter Bassanio's service (II.ii.1-24). He decides that the devil's advice is altogether better just as his father enters. This suggests in a comic way that it may be necessary to disobey one's conscience.

This account can be usefully juxtaposed with the Shylock-Antonio debate.[4] Antonio thinks that Jacob did not cheat but could and did leave everything in God's hands, hence he cannot be used to justify usury. Shylock thinks that Jacob's practices were justified by their results. Neither of them seems to think of Jacob as morally ambiguous, doing what was both wrong and unavoidable. The idea of moral ambiguity is what Launcelot points towards. The scene between the Gobbos offers Shakespeare's account of Jacob in opposition to both Shylock's and Antonio's. The Jacob of this interpretation is, as it were, a combination of Shylock and Antonio within one person, practicing out of necessity what must also be seen as a falling away from perfection. That we are meant to take Jacob as a person who must suffer the consequences of a divided heart is suggested by his dream (*Genesis* 28: 11-15) of a ladder connecting a high place with a low place with beings moving up and down on it continually but never simply in an upward direction and never reaching God, who is not at the top of the ladder but above it.

The question, then, that the Shylock-Antonio part of the story poses for us is whether a full ethical life can be unified and consistent or must of necessity exhibit a tense and never quite consistent duality. Turning now from the Shylock story to the story of Portia's wedding, we shall see further reasons for reading *The Merchant* as a demonstration of inescapable human duality and the less than perfect but nevertheless genuine good available to us by living in terms of it.

III

The third of our set pieces is the ring episode at the very end of the play. The crisis past, the main characters (except, as often noted, Shylock) gather in Belmont. The atmosphere of relief is briefly disturbed when Portia and her maid Nerissa ask for the rings they had given their husbands and made them promise never to part with. Bassanio and Gratiano have reluctantly given the rings to the lawyer and his clerk who had saved Antonio. The women who, of course, were the lawyer and "his" clerk, and had demanded the rings to test their husbands, put the poor men through hell for a few moments. They can say truthfully that since the lawyer and his clerk now have the rings they will sleep only with them. But they soon take pity on Bassanio and Gratiano and tell all. The men promise, once more, never to part with the rings. As Nerissa and Gratiano run off to consummate their marriage, Gratiano ends the play with an obscene remark in which a ring on a finger represents the joining of sexual organs:

> Well, while I live I'll fear no other thing
> So sore, as keeping safe Nerissa's ring.

These jokey threats of tit-for-tat infidelity hold an important clue to the rest of the play. I do not doubt that Portia's marriage is a love match. But what does that imply in a play that is supposed to be pitting tit-for-tat contractualism against unconditional love? The inscription on the leaden casket, the one containing Portia's picture, makes reference to unconditional love by demanding of the chooser that he "give and hazard all he hath" (II.vii.16). Is Portia required to "give and hazard all [she] hath" or ought she to try, if possible, to state her conditions? Is a mating of souls spoiled if an element of tit-for-tat enters it? To think so would be remarkably similar to the idealistic attitude we have seen Antonio take towards money-lending (I.iii.128-129). But this is not Portia's answer. Among the different interpretations of her action, depending on whether we like or dislike her, it is open to us to believe that she states her conditions in the faith that she is not thereby relinquishing the unconditionality of her relationship with Bassanio. For all her bantering tone she delivers a deadly serious and, in the context of the rosy glow of dawn at Belmont, a very poignant threat: my sexual fidelity is conditional on yours. We need not think that she actually would retaliate in this way if the issue arose. She may well be incapable of it. All the more reason, we might say, to threaten.

It may be helpful to think about Bassanio and Portia in the light of some of our own recent confusions about marriage. The idealistic insistence that marriage should not state conditions on either side was one of the more permanent legacies of the counter-cultural revolution of the 1960s. A certain measure-for-measure backlash redeemed the legalities of marriage when many women found themselves facing such realities as the need for child support payments. In our times—and not only in ours—both unconditional love (as long as it lasts) *and* liberal contractualism have been applied to marriage with a vengeance and often with an uneasy sense that they were not quite compatible.

Realism about the need for guaranteed security would have been entirely unproblematic if the idealistic or utopian view were simply wrong. Unfortunately for any simple account, it seems to be as important for human beings to give and get unconditional love as it is for them to be able to hedge it around with conditions for the sake of security. Is it possible to satisfy both requirements?

The Merchant's last episode answers with a qualified yes. The yes is that the combination of self-surrender and self-preservation is a human necessity that we are able to cobble together. The qualification is that it is after all a kind of makeshift, an ambiguous joining of two very different spiritual attitudes, requiring considerable moral equilibrium—something Portia luckily possesses to a fault—so as not to be overwhelmed when utopian temptations make ordinary marriage seem like mere hypocrisy.

Right at the end, then, the play brings us gently back to the ubiquity of contract. The ring episode invites us to consider that pure unconditional love by itself cannot and never could provide the cement for normal, human relationships and yet can draw aid and support from the lower, or less idealistic, conditional part of ourselves. It suggests that even in our most personal and intimate relations we have to make room in our hearts for the external constraints of the contractual, even when it seems to us a less beautiful and more grasping way of life than the pure refusal to enforce conditions. But that the low can help the high to survive is part of what makes *The Merchant* a comedy—even if a bittersweet one.

In her marriage Portia gently calls a threat of retaliation to the aid of a love which an idealist or a romantic might think was incompatible with such threats. In retrospect she seems from the very beginning of the play to have been the sort of person who would be able to temper the demand for the unconditional with contractual realism. As such, rather than as a presumed agent of Christian mercy, she is an appropriate person to offer Shylock an acceptably contractual compromise when they confront each other in the courtroom. But the hostility of others has turned Shylock from a person who lives by conditionality into an agent of unconditional hatred in the service of which he has twisted the very idea of contract. After he refuses to accept twice his money back (IV.i.84-87), he is beyond the pale of the contractual and will have to be destroyed. The trial is a prefiguring of the collapse of the system under which Shylock was made a pariah. But that collapse will come too late to help him.

IV

The fatal flaw that will bring down the Belmont-Venice system is that it depends vitally on the participation of two people, Shylock and Portia, who can hardly be expected to be very pious towards it. They are both in a position to see through the roles they are expected to play as quite a bit less than God-given. Portia's golden existence in Belmont requires, at least as her father sees it, that she and her wealth be handed over to a man (or manager) whose main qualification is to be wised-up enough to the hypocrisies

Scenes from The Merchant of Venice.

of others so that he can survive his forays into Venice. Bassanio reflects in front of the caskets (III.ii.73-105) not on how good externally plain things may be inwardly but on how corrupt beautiful-looking things often are within, an odd reflection with which to win a woman he thinks both "fair, and (fairer than that word) / Of wondrous virtues" (I.i.162-163). The choice of the caskets is cunningly arranged to appear to reflect the values of Belmont—which are supposed to be Portia's—while actually attracting someone who not only has a fair amount of Venice in his soul but also knows how to hide it. For the protection of Belmont, Portia cannot be allowed to marry according to her own will. And Shylock is allowed to make a living in Venice only at the cost of ostracism and humiliation. Both have good cause to see the price they are paying in order to represent what the Christian males need them to represent, an allegory of pure Virtue versus "pure" Vice.

Because this allegory makes Shylock an outsider, it takes the chance that he may want to pull it down and will find the opportunity to do so in its own weakness, the inflexible legalism that underlies the commercial contract. But

Shakespeare adds a twist. As it turns out, the system can be saved only by someone who is as much an outsider as Shylock, someone as willing as he is, and as Antonio is not, to find a loophole in the letter of the law. That other outsider is, of course, Portia. What makes it impossible to see the confrontation between Shylock and Portia as a clash between law and mercy is simply that both of them use the law shamelessly for their own purposes. In a further irony it is Antonio, though a Christian, who is the play's committed legalist; he considers the commercial law of Venice untouchable:

> The duke cannot deny the course of law:
> For the commodity that strangers have
> With us in Venice, if it be denied,
> Will much impeach the justice of the state,
> Since that the trade and profit of the city
> Consisteth of all nations.
>
> (III.iii.26-31)

If Portia had had that much respect for the law she would have been unable to play with it enough to save it from the consequences of its own mechanical rigidity.[5] This suggestion seems outrageous to those critics who believe the Belmont-Venice allegory and therefore believe that Portia can only act on the highest standards of purity. These are the same critics—a surprisingly large number—who think it merely cynical to suggest that Portia gives Bassanio a hint as to which casket to choose by having a song containing rhymes for "lead" sung to him.[6] But once we are ready to take the play as teaching that we live in a world where we must be willing to marshal the impure on behalf of the pure if anything pure is to survive, it becomes extremely plausible to see the trial of the caskets as Portia's dry run for the trial of Antonio, a dry run in which she displays an understandable unscrupulousness, cheating her father as surely as Jacob cheated his—in her case in the interest of a true love.

Very gently Shakespeare here touches the theme of unscrupulousness in defense of a world where scruples are to have a chance to survive, a theme which becomes crucial in his histories. What is in question is Machiavelli's teaching that a legal order can be created and defended only by someone who does not feel bound by it, the unscrupulous founder who stands outside the law. The point is put delicately by King Henry V (a student of Falstaff in seeing through the law) to Katherine of France: "you and I cannot be confin'd within the weak list of a country's fashion; we are the makers of manners" (*Henry V*, V.ii.266).

Anyone who gets to know Portia must feel that she too, in her heart "cannot be confined within the weak list of a country's fashion." But in her dealings with Venice she thinks of herself as acting to save her country's fashion. It seems that though she has seen through the conventions of Venice she knows that the self-esteem of the man she loves depends on the maintenance of the world in which he has his noble status. The mixture of conditional and unconditional she is able to admit into her marriage—if indeed she knows she is doing it—she does not here force on the Christian males. It is against her will that she sows the seeds of destruction in the Belmont-Venice system's way of dealing with commerce.

The trial scene has an almost epic quality. Two great antagonists, Shylock and Portia clash, both empowered because they have seen through the laws of their community, he to pull down at least one of its pillars, she to save it. Victory is Portia's. But Shakespeare has one more saving twist of irony. Portia's victory like Shylock's conversion has a double meaning.

Portia the woman takes on in pretense the figure of a man just as Shylock the Jew takes on in pretense the figure of a Christian. She symbolically unfits herself to play the role mapped out for her in the society she is supposedly saving—even though she largely returns to playing it. Just as Shylock's conversion tells us that in the future Jews will not be able to be placed at the low end of the Belmont-Venice system, Portia's appearance in Venice in male dress tells us that she or her descendants will not willingly stay put on the pedestal in Belmont. Shakespeare is tangibly predicting the demise of the Belmont-Venice dichotomy.

But even if the dichotomy does die, we are not meant to think that love and contract simply join hands and become mutually supporting. It may be that to be able to love at all one must be able to state one's conditions. But it is not the case that in order to state one conditions one must be able to love. So, even when the conditional and the unconditional come to reside in the same heart, the conditional, especially in the form of commercial life, will retain an independence that the unconditional does not have. Love will need contract more than contract needs love. The melding of Venice and Belmont cannot eradicate the division between those we love and those we do not love. But it can stop us—sometimes—from believing that only those we do not love have contractualism in their souls. In this world at least, the conditional is a more inescapable power than the unconditional. The ubiquity of commerce may now open the way for Shylock to become a respectable businessman. The exclusiveness of love makes it extremely unlikely that he will ever be invited to even the new, more ambiguous Belmont.

V

Some hint of what Shakespeare may think of the social order whose death he anticipates lies in the references to Christian hypocrisy which the more cynical critics have noted in almost every scene of *The Merchant*.[7] To these critics they suggest simple condemnation of the Christians. More likely, I think, they are there to shore up the message that we live out our lives in a not quite harmonious double-mindedness.

But for many, double-mindedness is just a euphemism for hypocrisy and may well come to seem morally intolerable.

Is there anything that can ease the tension of living with the necessity of duplicity? Is dividedness the last word about us?

At one point Shakespeare suggests otherwise. This is the last of the episodes I shall consider. At the beginning of Act V, the scene that ends with the rings, Lorenzo, lying out under the stars at Belmont, speaks to Jessica of the music of the spheres:

> There's not the smallest orb which thou behold'st
> But in his motion like an angel sings,
> Still quiring to the young-ey'd cherubins;
> Such harmony is in immortal souls,
> But whilst this muddy vesture of decay
> Doth grossly close it in, we cannot hear it.
>
> (V.i.60-65)

Lorenzo elegantly calls up a world that transcends the double bind, that is harmonious rather than conflictual, but is unavailable to us while we wear "this muddy vesture of decay." For the idealists these words will be discredited by being spoken by a frivolous playboy consoling himself complacently for his own grossness with the drug of religion. But if the play is about double-mindedness it is appropriate that Lorenzo should speak these lines. When Lorenzo continues:

> The man that hath no music in himself,
> Nor is not moved with concord of sweet sounds,
> Is fit for treasons, stratagems and spoils . . .
> Let no such man be trusted
>
> (V.i.83-88)

he may think he is talking about someone like Shylock, who speaks of the "vile squealing of the wry-neck'd fife" (II.v.30) and the dire effect of the bagpipes (IV.i.49-50). But since he has just said that none of us can hear the real music, we are apparently all "fit for treasons, stratagems and spoils."

Here Lorenzo sums up the double-mindedness of the play and moves it for a moment to a cosmic plane. Lorenzo's dream is not unlike Jacob's. We only know what is low in our world because we have glimpsed something high. Our ability to see ourselves from above is an element of our worth even when what we see from that perspective is our worthlessness. Even if Lorenzo is not fit to speak these words or doesn't believe them in any but the most superficial sense, one would have to be an intensely serious deconstructionist not to be glad he says them or not to like him a little better for saying them.

VI

I have argued that *The Merchant of Venice* is best understood in the context of a tension between the conditional and the unconditional. A tension of this kind continues to reverberate through our philosophies and theodicies. We vacillate between thinking that goodness is rewarded and thinking that reward would demean it; of love we think both that it endures all but that we may demand good behavior from those who say they love us; in commerce, the profit motive can seem both reasonable and crass. One need not be a Christian to feel the tug of living like the lilies of the field. But one will also feel the tug of having a retirement savings plan at a respectable interest rate. Controlling the future, which requires laying down conditions, and letting the future look after itself, which is what makes unconditional commitment possible—both of them answer to something powerful in our natures that helps to define our self-understanding. Our hearts are torn by the tension between them.

The utopian cure for the torn human heart can hardly be better put than in Hamlet's "throw away the worser part of it / And live the purer with the other half" (*Hamlet*, III.iv.159-160), and many would identify that as *The Merchant*'s teaching. This is certainly how the Christian characters in the play see themselves. But much of Shakespeare's work can be seen as showing that we cannot "throw away the worser part" and that trying to do so is disastrous. But to let "the worser part" in the form of our less generous, more self-centered, more unscrupulous impulses run rampant would also be disastrous in the world of Shakespeare, who does not seem as optimistic as later thinkers that such impulses will act on each other as checks and balances. Instead, at least in *The Merchant*, a different sort of impulse—one of unconditioned love—is what offers a counterweight to the ungenerous, conditional impulses, though it also loses something by existing in tension with them. In *The Merchant* this counterweight operates, reasonably enough, only in what we would call the private world of marriage and personal friendship. The fate of the more public world of relations between strangers remains uncertain as it is seen moving in the direction of a more openly acknowledged contractualism. But the utopian cure is unambiguously set aside. If "the worser part" is the contractual life, then neither Portia nor Antonio can throw it away. Antonio projects it onto Shylock and in the process creates an implacable enemy who might well have destroyed him. And though the surface symbolism of Belmont suggests that the man who would win Portia must be a devotee of unconditional love who will "give and hazard all he hath." Portia has learned by the last scene that for her to give and hazard all she has would be hazardous indeed.

The world into which we are introduced at the beginning of *The Merchant* is both in Venice and in Belmont a make-believe world that depends on clear-cut social distinctions between Jews and Christians and between men and women based on clear-cut social roles. It is Shakespeare's anti-utopianism to show us that this world is a fool's paradise. But his anti-utopian attitude is not one of moralistic indignation. Post-Holocaust critics, anxious to acquit Shakespeare of the charge of anti-semitism, have tried to show him "taking sides" against the Christian characters. In fact, he does something more useful. Without moralizing, he offers an analysis, a brilliant piece of social science, identifying an important spiritual function that intolerance tries to serve and also showing—from our vantage point one might say predicting—exactly how the Venice-Belmont system comes to collapse. Nor does he flatten out the dilemma. Tit-for-tat contractualism is not seen as untainted. Nor does Shakespeare suggest, as some critics do, that money-lending itself is unambiguously moral as long as the rate of interest is not exorbitant and pounds of flesh are not brought into the bargain. Antonio despises Shylock long before there is any pound-of-flesh contract. Nor are the Christians condemned for wishing to think of themselves—however unrealistically—as untainted either by the profit motive or by a measure-for-measure conception of love relations. The project is simply shown collapsing under its own weight.

For some commentators the political teaching of *The Merchant of Venice* is that the society in which we live has been bought at the price of the driving out of love and friendship. But Lorenzo's and Jessica's rueful reflection in the final scene (V.i.1-22) on legendary lovers who came to a bad end—Troilus, Thisbe, Dido, Medea—is perhaps meant to remind us that there was never a time when love and friendship did not have a hard time maintaining themselves against the necessities of nature and commerce even while depending on those necessities for support. They do not list these lovers to give themselves an excuse for infidelity. Rather, having caught a hint of perfection in the night and the stars, they are pledging themselves not to betray the only life they can know just because it is mixed and imperfect. A few minutes later Portia, in the ring episode, will also pledge her loyalty to a life that is something less than the music of the spheres. That they can settle for less without forgetting the more is one of the things that after all makes *The Merchant of Venice* a comedy and not a tragedy.

Notes

1. Citations are to the Arden edition, *The Merchant of Venice*, edited by John Russell Brown (London: Methuen, 1971).

2. Lester K. Little, *Religious Poverty and the Profit Economy in Medieval Europe* (Ithaca: Cornell University Press, 1978), pp. 52, 56.

3. Robert McAfee Brown, ed., *The Essential Reinhold Niebuhr* (New Haven: Yale University Press, 1986), p. 135.

4. See Barbara K. Lewalski, "Biblical Allusion and Allegory in *The Merchant of Venice*" *Shakespeare Quarterly* 13 (1962): 327-43. Lewalski does not include Launcelot Gobbo's gloss on the Jacob story.

5. I adopt the general view that Portia uses a legal trick in her defense of Antonio since a contract that granted a pound of flesh would also grant the right to shed blood in taking the pound.

6. John Russell Brown, for example (note on III.ii.63, p. 80) says that such a hint "would belittle Bassanio and Portia and cheapen the theme of the play."

7. For a detailed, classic account of the "ironic" interpretation, see A. D. Moody, *Shakespeare: The Merchant of Venice* (London: Edward Arnold, 1964).

Alan Rosen (essay date 1997)

SOURCE: Rosen, Alan. "The Rhetoric of Exclusion: Jew, Moor, and the Boundaries of Discourse in *The Merchant of Venice*." In *Race, Ethnicity, and Power in the Renaissance,* edited by Joyce Green MacDonald, pp. 67-79. Cranbury, N.J.: Associated University Presses, 1997.

[*In the following essay, Rosen remarks on the rhetorical strategies of* The Merchant of Venice*'s racial outsiders, emphasizing Shylock's recursive and literal mode of speaking and the Prince of Morocco's eloquence as beyond "the borders of legitimate discourse" in the play.*]

In the 1590s, both Jew and Moor remained for English Christians exotic infidels, whose obstinate unbelief and cultural difference continued to challenge, boldly or surreptitiously, Christian hegemony in Europe.[1] In Shylock the Jew and the Prince of Morocco the Moor, *The Merchant of Venice* presents these two kinds of infidels and thus brings together within this problem comedy two groups for whom Renaissance England felt a special fascination and repulsion. That the play forges and exploits a link between the two groups is not self-evident, for Shakespeare assigns Shylock and Morocco to separate realms—Venice and Belmont respectively—and thereby seems to place in the background any meaningful association between Jew and Moor. I wish, however, to foreground this association and argue that the distinctive rhetoric of each character—for Shylock, plainness; for Morocco, eloquence—threatens in its own way to undermine the linguistic foundations of the play. Although this threat is contained, dramatic juxtaposition works to connect the two characters, blurring the boundaries between them. Once linked, shared aspects of their language challenge the play's discourse of insider/outsider while simultaneously reinforcing the threat that the infidels pose.

1

Despite varying assessments of Shylock's language, critics share two assumptions: first, Shylock is made by Shakespeare to speak differently from other characters in the play; second, he speaks more plainly than other characters.[2] This plain speaking is evidenced particularly in Shylock's propensity to repetition.

The play foregrounds Shylock's repetitions from his first appearance on stage in 1.3. For the scene quickly establishes a pattern in which Bassanio initiates and Shylock repeats the financial terms of the proposed agreement. Moreover, the constant pattern of Shylock's repetition makes the audience retroactively aware that, although Shylock speaks the first words of the scene—"Three thousand ducats"—even these words echo an implied off stage proposal by Bassanio.³ In the first eight lines of the scene, then, Shylock speaks words that are not his own.

This appropriation of another character's words at the moment of dramatic introduction blurs the distinctions that one expects to obtain between Bassanio and Shylock, noble Christian and miserly Jew,⁴ frustrating at least for a time the expectation that Jews speak differently, that they have in Sander Gilman's phrase "a hidden language" uniquely their own.⁵ By repeating Bassanio's words, Shylock also makes use of them. It is this aspect of use which, as Burckhardt and Shell have argued, is a defining characteristic of Shylock's approach to language as well as to money.⁶ From the very first utterance, then, Shylock's role is to keep things (and words) in circulation.

Shylock continues to echo Bassanio, yet he also introduces a note of self-repetition, a mode of iteration that becomes conspicuous in Shylock's next scene, in which he calls for Jessica several times. Although the repeated call serves at first as an anxious summons for his daughter, it is soon taken up by Lancelot, parodying Shylock's earnestness.⁷ In the next scenes, as Jessica flees, this pattern of repetition and parody intensifies.⁸ Solanio quotes Shylock repeating the features of his losses and Salerio notes that boys echo Shylock's repetitions (2.8.12-24). As Shylock repeats himself with increasing frequency, seemingly in search of a language to express his loss, other characters parody his iterations, resulting in what one critic refers to as the denial of "the right to coherent speech."⁹ Even as Shakespeare ritualizes Shylock's language, the choric procession of children simultaneously establishes a parody of that ritualization.

In act 3, the climax of Shylock's self-repetition, Shakespeare complicates the variations on this technique. To the Christians, Shylock responds to taunts with the "Hath not a Jew" speech, in which the repetitions are arranged in a complex rhetorical schema: "Hath not a Jew eyes? Hath not a Jew hands? . . ." (3.1.46-47). To Tubal the Jew, by contrast, Shylock merely repeats words, bereft of this larger rhetorical framework:

TUBAL.

Yes, other men have ill luck too. Antonio, as I heard in Genoa—

SHY.

What, what, what? ill luck, ill luck?

TUBAL.

—hath an argosy cast away coming from Tripolis.

SHY.

I thank God, I thank God! Is it true, is it true?

(3.1.77-81)

Shylock's repetitions embody language at a reduced and primitive level: "An even more primitive way than pun-ning," suggests Sigurd Burckhardt, "to strip words of their meanings is repetition. Say 'a rose is a rose is a rose' a few more times, and what you have is a meaningless sound, because you have torn the word out of its living linguistic matrix and so are left with nothing but a vile phonetic jelly."¹⁰ Repetition emphasizes material corporeality, "mak[ing] the word malleable, ready to take the imprint the poet wants to give it."¹¹

Burckhardt's emphasis on the corporeality of language enforces Shylock's association with the corporeal; a Jew, in other words, whose materiality symbolizes for Christians an unredeemed carnality, would fittingly speak a language itself carnal. Appropriately, Shylock reaches the climax of such "primitive" speech in the only scene in which he speaks at length with another Jew.

According to A. R. Braunmuller, however, the rhetorical strategies of Renaissance drama point in a different direction, not enforcing but subverting the conventional system of meaning.¹² Dramatists carried out this subversion by emphasizing "alliteration, repetition, echo, reversal,"—language that privileged sound over sense. "This similarity of sound," writes Braunmuller, "among words and phrases overrides the semantic, conventional, unthinkingly assumed difference between them."¹³ While these rhetorical strategies informed other modes of public discourse in Renaissance England, the plotted nature of drama exploited "patterned speech" in ways that significantly undermined conventional systems of linguistic meaning, keeping audiences in "a continuous rhetorical anxiety," a linguistic limbo "puzzling and possibly terrifying."¹⁴

Braunmuller's comments suggest that Shylock's discourse is not only to be viewed as signifying a perverse materiality but also as concretizing the vertiginous aspects of Renaissance dramatic rhetoric. Made to speak an ever more heavily patterned speech, Shylock embodies the unfamiliar system of meaning, the "continuous rhetorical anxiety," produced by this rhetoric. As he repeats more frequently, his idiom threatens to subsume the system of semantic difference which continues to inhere in the language of other characters. The repetitions of his repetitions—Solanio's account and the boys' cries—acknowledged the threat of Shylock's idiom but also keep it in check through parody. Seen in this light, the force of Shylock's meeting with Tubal is that here, as Shylock comes to repeat almost every line, there is no parody, no repetition of his repetition, no policing of his alternative system of meaning. At this point, not only does Shylock's passion for revenge endanger Antonio, but his iterative language, multiplying without check, threatens to overwhelm all other language.

But Shakespeare himself polices Shylock's phonic language. Just as the court scene defuses the danger that Shylock poses to Antonio's well-being, so it also constrains Shylock's language, compelling him to speak in proper rhetorical formulas.¹⁵ Even if Burckhardt and other ironic readers are correct in claiming that Shylock's courtroom rhetoric outshines that of Antonio and Portia, it is also the case that Shakespeare eliminates the subversive repetitions. Indeed, the elimination of what had become an increasingly frequent sign of Shylock's distinctiveness is startling and perplexing. The answer may lie in the way the institution of the courtroom shapes the language spoken.[16] For, as the play implies, the courtroom represents the Venetian law which allegedly applies equally to all. As the law applies to all equally, so, one may speculate, do all participants in the court proceedings share the same discourse. Hence, this legal discourse preempts Shylock's repetitions before they are set in motion.

If the courtroom eliminates the repetitions, there nevertheless remains an imagistic trace of the threat they posed. Telling the Duke why he cannot explain his passion for revenge, Shylock suggests that "Some men there are that love not a gaping pig; / Some that are mad if they behold a cat; / And others when the bagpipe sings in i'the nose / Cannot contain their urine: for affection / Masters oft passion, sways it to the mood / Of what it likes or loathes" (4.1.48-52). Shylock's list—pig, cat, and bagpipe—enumerates what are generally benign aspects of culinary, domestic, or musical culture. But what is benign to most makes dysfunctional an idiosyncratic few. In the case of the bagpipe, the special sound causes the victim to lose control of natural functions. This association of unnerving sound and a threat to control recalls the "rhetorical anxieties" which confronted the audience faced with "patterned speech," that is, repetition. Braunmuller indicated that, by replacing semantic difference with phonetic identity, repetition subverted the conventional system of linguistic meaning, a subversion which occasioned a "possibly terrifying" feeling in the audience. Similarly, the bagpipe foregrounds an unusual type of sound which assaults the listener, causing a breakdown of normal functioning. Both bagpipe and repetition figure in the play as sources of phonic subversion. Even though Shylock himself is no longer given to repetition, then, the analogy he chooses to represent his motivation continues to intimate the threat embodied by it. It is suggestive, furthermore, that the only other reference in the play to bagpipes comes in association with the creature most emblematic of repetition: "Now by two-headed Janus," says Solario, also trying to account for abnormal behavior, "Nature hath framed strange fellows in her time: / Some that will evermore peep through their eyes, / And laugh like *parrots* at a bagpiper" (1.1.50-53; emphasis added).[17]

2

The difference between Shylock's recursive speech and that of other characters has frequently been described in terms of plainness versus eloquence: where Shylock the Jew speaks unpoetically, realistically, plainly, the Christians in the play speak lyrically, beautifully, eloquently.[18] Most critics valorize eloquence, understanding Shylock's deviant plain-speaking as reinforcing his villainy. But the dichotomy drawn between plainness and eloquence has its proponents as well among those who see Shylock as the play's victim, a view culminating in Burckhardt's extended contrast between Antonio and Shylock. Suspicious of Antonio's flaccid grandiloquence, Burckhardt favors Shylock's plainness, supporting his reading by indicating that the play itself puts forth a hermeneutics of suspicion regarding eloquence. Additionally, Burckhardt argues that the plainness with which Shylock speaks registers Shakespeare's achievement as a dramatist: "But the qualities which make us rank Shylock's lines over Antonio's have long been accepted among the criteria by which we seek to establish the sequence of Shakespeare's plays, on the assumption that where we find them we have evidence of greater maturity and mastery."[19]

Though most critics have not shared Burckhardt's radical suspicion of eloquence in the play in general, they have shown a marked suspicion of the eloquence of one specific character: the Prince of Morocco. According to this view, Morocco's eloquence indicates his concern with appearances; just as his language is full of ornate rhetorical flourish, valuing surface over substance, so he chooses the gold casket, again valuing surface over substance.[20] Language reflects action, and vice versa. Besides testifying to Shakespeare's multilevel control of plot, this reading of Morocco's language often attempts to assign it a psychological or moral significance, confirming his unworthiness to win Portia.[21]

Initially, Shylock and Morocco seem as much separated by style as by setting, the rhetoric of the former shaped by the absence of ornament, that of the latter formed by the excess of it. But by associating Shylock with plainness and Morocco with eloquence, Shakespeare positions both outsiders at the opposite extremes of the rhetorical continuum, equally, if contrarily, pressing against the borders of legitimate discourse. On the one hand, this positioning allows the other characters in the play to speak comfortably within the limits that the Jew and Moor articulate. On the other hand, Shylock and Morocco are compelled linguistically as well as culturally to inhabit a place on the margins of discourse.

Having established this linguistic extravagance, glosses on Morocco amplify this suspicion of eloquence by indicating that his language recalls Marlowe's Tamburlaine, an intertextual resonance initially noted by M. C. Bradbrook and subsequently applied by numbers of readers.[22] Frank Whigham, for instance, sees Morocco

> handicapped by his race, his lack of sophistication and his outmoded style. The attribute of his style most relevant here is his lavish claims made for his own desert. In the early days of Elizabethan drama the non-European setting and character, presented with extensive rhetorical ornament, gave the exotic an incantatory power over Elizabethan audiences. In the courtly context, however, the imperialistic titanism of Tamburlaine is ill-adapted to purposes of wooing.[23]

This judgment implies that Shakespeare chose to outfit his suitor with a clumsy language, one more appropriate to conquest than romance. But the association with Marlowe also suggests that for Morocco's lines Shakespeare turned to an earlier, more primitive dramatic language. Morocco's eloquence, then, not only represents a psychological or moral flaw but also Shakespeare's parody of the bombastic vocabulary that Tamburlaine spoke and Marlowe wrote. Just as Bassanio displays his romantic merit by choosing the right casket, so does Shakespeare display his dramatic merit by surpassing his predecessors in the fit choice of language, not gaining the fortune of Belmont but rather containing the influence of his greatest competitor and asserting his authorial mastery.[24]

In his reading of the play, Freud also connects the casket scene with mastery, arguing that the choice of the caskets is actually the choice of a beautiful woman and that the scene dramatizes the attempt to master death—which here masquerades as its opposite, beauty.[25] The emphasis for Freud is on choice: "Choice stands in the place of necessity, of destiny. In this way man overcomes death, which he has recognized intellectually."[26] The casket scene registers the move from non-choice to choice, from a passive relation to what is determined to an active mastery over it. The scene becomes the site where psychological overcoming works in conjunction with stylistic mastery. In both instances, mastery is achieved by containing what is other: on the one hand, death represents the metaphysical other; on the other hand, Morocco (and Tamburlaine and Marlowe) represents the cultural other. Even these realms converge, however, in Morocco's second appearance, in which, after a speech replete with images of burial and death, Morocco chooses the casket containing "A carrion Death" (2.7.63). By having Morocco choose a death's head, Shakespeare links what is culturally other to what is metaphysically other, doubly enforcing repulsion while simultaneously mastering it.

While the play admittedly encourages the association of Morocco and Tamburlaine, it also questions the aptness of the parallel and consequently provokes doubt in Morocco's position as an absolute other. Significantly, Morocco styles himself as a kind of Hercules, the Renaissance ideal of a warrior (and a prototype of Tamburlaine as well),[27] a self-identification that would seem to reinforce his "titanic" status. But the association does not promote his warrior status but rather undermines it, for the Hercules that Morocco invokes renounces acting as a warrior, consenting instead to "play at dice" and be led by "blind Fortune" (2.1.36). Bassanio, moreover, is also identified with Hercules (3.2.53-62), and in this identification Shakespeare emphasizes the more familiar, martial side of the Greek hero. Tellingly, where Morocco's link to Hercules highlights an uncharacteristic submission, Bassanio's dramatizes a stereotypical aggression, provoking the audience to see not Morocco but Bassanio as the emblem of heroism, as the one who brings into the "courtly context . . . imperialistic titanism." This link to Bassanio via Hercules further destabilizes Morocco's status as Other, for it makes it difficult to clearly distinguish one suitor from another, effacing to a degree the difference between winner and loser and between familiar Venetian and exotic Moroccan.[28]

In the Prince of Morocco, Shakespeare represents a Moor who is liminal and transitional, coming between the demonization of Aaron in *Titus Andronicus* and the heroic, if problematic, characterization of Othello.[29] The critical dispute concerning two pivotal traits, color and religion, attests to this liminal status. Morocco is described as "tawny," a term which some critics argue indicates "light-skinned, as distinct from a 'blackamoor'";[30] others believe the linguistic and even dramatic evidence demonstrates that Morocco is black.[31] Morocco's religion is less subject to dispute; but the lack of an explicit religious designation has led at least one recent critic to assume that Morocco is Christian, a judgment which in essence nullifies his outsider status.[32] Morocco's position vis-à-vis stage and social history reinforces this transitional status. Significantly, Morocco is one of the first "non-villainous" Moors to appear on the English stage[33] a stage which had previously dramatized Moors as villains and in which blackness served as an emblem of evil. Morocco as a noble suitor contravenes this stereotype. Nevertheless, the representation of Morocco as an exotic "tawny" Moor continues to reinscribe the alien traits of previous stage Moors (including Shakespeare's own Aaron in *Titus Andronicus*) and thereby to provoke suspicion, particularly suspicion concerning sexual propriety that would be aroused in watching a black alien attempt to marry a white heroine.[34]

Although the play eschews the direct representation of the Moor as villain, it enforces suspicion of Morocco by linking him dramatically with Shylock the Jew, a strategy which blurs the boundaries between one outsider and the other. At the beginning of 1.3 Shylock enters the play, a Jew in a Christian world; at the beginning of act 2, Morocco enters, a black in a white world. As Shylock intrudes upon the homogeneity of Christian Venice, so Morocco intrudes upon the homogeneity of white Belmont. The discomfort caused by the intrusion of one enforces the discomfort caused by the intrusion of the other. In addition, reference to Morocco's "complexion" frames Shylock's first appearance. In 1.2, Portia shows her repulsion of Morocco by quipping, "If he have the condition of a saint, and the complexion of a devil, I had rather he should shrive me than wive me" (1.2.123); next Shylock has his scene (1.3); then act 2 begins by Morocco in effect answering Portia's quip: "Mislike me not for my complexion" (2.1.1).

Shylock's scene both postpones and substitutes for Morocco's. If we recall that prior to *MV* black men on the English stage were conventionally villains, the postponement of Morocco's arrival intensifies anxiety over what kind of black man will appear on stage. Where Portia's racial strictures initially seem to apply only to marriage in contrast to religion ("rather he should shrive me than wive me"), the substitution of Shylock for Morocco problematizes this formula, exposing the way the discourse of exclusion governs religion as well as matrimony. The substitution of one intruder for the other also means that Shylock arrives in a drama whose discourse is already in place to distinguish insider from outsider. Consequently, Shylock enters the play caught not only in the stage conventions associated with Jews but also in those associated with Moors.

The play further promotes this association of Jew and Moor by linking the way they themselves manipulate the discourse of insider/outsider. Morocco claims his right as a suitor by questioning the criterion chosen by Portia—"complexion of a devil"—and offering his own: "Let us make incision for your love / To prove whose blood is reddest" (2.1.6-7). As with the caskets, Morocco's new criterion also takes the form of a contest, a contest in which Portia would be compelled to distinguish one thing from another. The shift from "complexion" to "blood," from outer surface to inner substance, links Morocco's claim with the other gestures in the play (caskets, bonds, rings) which require one to go beneath a deceptive surface. More specifically, however, Morocco's contest prepares for Shylock's challenge to Salerio: "If you prick us, do we not bleed?" (3.1.58). Significantly, both Moor and Jew claim that what seems different on the surface can be better judged by what is beneath it; that the less favorable exterior which they present can be neutralized by reference to an interior dimension: the blood which flows in all people's veins.

By rejecting surface and privileging depth, Moor and Jew attempt to use the operative discourse of the play—outside/inside—to redefine their relation to other characters. This discourse works generally to make clear who is the resident and who the intruder. In the case of Morocco, his skin color excludes him from Portia's (and the Elizabethan audience's) favor. His ornamental language and choice of the golden casket allegedly betray a concern with surfaces that reinforces his rightful exclusion. In the case of Shylock, his literalism highlights concern with the letter rather than the spirit, with the outer form rather than the inner meaning. In this attempt to challenge their marginalization, then, Morocco and Shylock mobilize the very discourse that enforces the distinction between insider and outsider and which confers on them, Moor and Jew, the status of Other.

But this attempt to turn the discourse of exclusion back on itself fails, as both Morocco and Shylock use images of violence—"incision" and "pricking," acts committed with a sharp, invasive instrument—to exhibit their solidarity with the rest of human kind. The two intruders, moreover, are the ones who brandish weapons in the play, a detail which enforces the association of alien and violence. Even as Moor and Jew try to undermine and overcome the terms that set them apart from the Christian characters, these images of violence continue to dramatize the danger they pose, justifying their exclusion. The images of violence also enforce the fantasies of the audience, for the wounds which Morocco and Shylock envision are rhetorically inflicted upon themselves (Morocco will make an "incision" on himself; Shylock will be "pricked"), thereby substantiating the belief in an alien threat while simultaneously having the danger recoil upon those who are believed to threaten. Taken to its furthest point—as some critics have done—the recoil of the violence causes both Morocco and Shylock to undergo a symbolic castration (again scenically juxtaposed): the Moor, who has pledged not to marry, leaves Belmont uttering "farewell heat and welcome frost" (2.7.75); the Jew, whose fortune has been stolen, is reported to focus his grief on the loss of his "two stones, two rich and precious stones" (2.8.20).[35] The punishment, then, links the two intruders even as it renders them impotent.

This impotence no doubt underscores failure. Yet, through the eccentric discourse of its intruders, *MV* sets forth alternative systems of meaning that challenge more conventional ones: Shylock's repetitions begin to erode the order articulated by semantic difference,[36] while the juxtaposition of Moor and Jew indicates the attempt to rewrite the categories of exclusion. Neither challenge meets with success. But the play must work hard to neutralize the threat posed by these outsiders. Indeed, one may speculate that the threat to conventional meaning tested here in *MV* becomes more fully realized in the later tragedies, in which Shylock's repetitions modulate into Lear's maddened iterations and Morocco's eloquence informs Othello's captivating tales.

Notes

1. For a recent consideration of England and the Jews in the context of *The Merchant of Venice,* see James Shapiro, "Shakespeare and the Jews," The Parkes Lecture, University of Southhampton, 1992; and more generally, including the arrest and trial of Lopez, Cecil Roth, *History of the Jews in England* (Oxford: Oxford University Press, 1941). On England's relation to the Moors in the 1590s, see Jack D'Amico, *The Moor in English Renaissance Drama* (Tampa: University of South Florida Press, 1991).

2. See particularly B. I. Evans, *The Language of Shakespeare's Plays* (London: Chatto & Windus, 1964). Cf. C. L. Barber, *Shakespeare's Festive Comedy* (Princeton: Princeton University Press, 1959), 163-91; Thomas Fujimura, "Mode and Structure in *The Merchant of Venice,*" PMLA [*Publications of the Modern Language Association of America*] 81 (1966): 499-511; and Jane Donawerth, *Shakespeare and the Sixteenth-Century Study of Language* (Urbana: University of Illinois Press, 1984), 189-218. On the equivocal claims of "plainness" and "plain speaking," see Kenneth J. E. Graham, "'Without the form of justice': Plainness and the Performance of Love in *King Lear,*" *Shakespeare Quarterly* 42 (1991): 438-61.

3. This and all subsequent citations are from M. M. Mahood, ed., *The Merchant of Venice* (Cambridge: Cambridge University Press, 1987).

4. "Well, thou shalt see, thy eyes shall be thy judge, / The difference of old Shylock and Bassanio—" (2.5.1-2). The elaborate form of Shylock's salutation to Lancelot reinforces the fact that the difference between Shylock and Bassanio, while discernible, is not to be taken for granted.

5. Sander Gilman, *Jewish Self-Hatred: Anti-Semitism and the Hidden Language of the Jews* (Baltimore: Johns Hopkins University Press, 1986).

6. Sigurd Burckhardt, *Shakespearean Meanings* (Princeton: Princeton University Press, 1968). Marc Shell, "The Wether and the Ewe: Verbal Usury in *The Merchant of Venice*," *Kenyon Review*, n.s. 1 (1979): 65-92.

7. James Bulman notes in his volume on *The Merchant of Venice* in the Shakespeare in Performance series (Manchester: Manchester University Press, 1991), that in Komisarjevsky's iconoclastic production of *Merchant*, not only Lancelot but old Gobbo echoes Shylock here, creating a "double echo" (60).

8. For a discussion of parody as repetition, see Linda Hutcheon, *A Theory of Parody: The Teachings of Twentieth-Century Art Forms* (New York: Methuen, 1985).

9. Lawrence Normand, "Reading the Body in *The Merchant of Venice*," *Textual Practice* 5, no. 1 (1991): 57.

10. Burckhardt, *Shakespearean Meaning*, 29; Shell's attempt in "The Wether and the Ewe" to analyze Shylock's "verbal usury" sees puns (rather than repetition) as his emblematic verbal gesture, 66-67.

11. Burckhardt, *Shakespearean Meanings*, 30.

12. A. R. Braunmuller, "The Arts of the Dramatist," in *The Cambridge Companion to English Renaissance Drama*, ed. A. R. Braunmuller and Michael Hattaway (Cambridge: Cambridge University Press, 1990), 63-67.

13. Ibid., 63.

14. Ibid., 67.

15. Normand, "Reading the Body," 66.

16. From a different perspective than the one I am pursuing here, Lawrence Danson emphasizes the relation between courtroom and language in *The Harmonies of 'The Merchant of Venice'* (New Haven: Yale University Press, 1978).

17. Interestingly, the two-faced Janus also hints at repetition. Sarah Kofman has recently examined the Janus figure in relation to *The Merchant of Venice;* her analysis, however, does not consider repetition as such but emphasizes instead how doubleness is the real theme of the play. See "Conversions: *The Merchant of Venice* Under the Sign of Saturn," tran. Shaun Whiteside, in *Literary Theory Today*, ed. Peter Collier and Helga Geyer-Ryan (Cambridge: Cambridge University Press, 1990): 142-66.

18. See my remarks, note 4 above. On the issue of eloquence, see *Renaissance Eloquence: Studies in the Theory and Practice of Renaissance Rhetoric*, ed. James J. Murphy (Berkeley: University of California Press, 1983).

19. Burckhardt, *Shakespearean Meanings*, 209.

20. While critics generally say little about Morocco, the little they do say tends to comment on his eloquence. See, for example, Donawerth, *Shakespeare and the Sixteenth-Century Study of Language*, and Frank Whigham, "Ideology and Class Conduct in *The Merchant of Venice*," *Renaissance Drama*, n.s. 10 (1979): 93-115; also James Shapiro, "'Which the Merchant Here, and Which the Jew?': Shakespeare and the Economics of Influence," *Shakespeare Studies* 20 (1987): 269-79. While Emily Bartels, in "Making More of the Moor: Aaron, Othello, and Renaissance Refashionings of Race," *Shakespeare Quarterly* 41 (1990) does not discuss Morocco, she does note the role of eloquence in relation to Aaron of *Titus Andronicus*: "What threatens to undermine Aaron's function as an absolute sign of the Other is his cultural literacy and . . . his eloquence. . . . [But] Aaron's speech simultaneously declares his malign differentness." Aaron's "malign differentness," however, is betrayed not by exaggerated eloquence but by a "purposelessness that makes his villainy all the more insidious" (445). In contrast, such commentators as Donawerth or Shapiro suggest that Morocco's otherness is represented not by motivation (or its lack), but by style (or its excess).

21. A. D. Moody's small casebook on *The Merchant of Venice* (Woodbury, N.Y.: Barron's Educational Series, 1964) is the only commentary I have encountered which does not psychologically or morally justify Morocco's failure to choose the winning casket; on the contrary, Moody argues that Morocco deserves to win Portia.

22. See two discussions by M. C. Bradbrook, *Shakespeare and Elizabethan Poetry* (London: Chatto & Windus, 1951), 175-76; and "Shakespeare's Recollections of Marlowe," in *Shakespeare's Styles*, ed. Philip Edwards, Inga-Stina Ewbank, and G. K. Hunter (Cambridge: Cambridge University Press, 1980), 191.

23. Whigham, "Ideology and Class Conduct," 98-99.

24. James Shapiro focuses on the contention between Marlowe and Shakespeare in "'Which the Merchant Here, and Which the Jew'?"

25. Sigmund Freud, "The Theme of the Three Caskets," in *The Standard Edition of the Complete Psychological Works of Sigmund Freud*, ed. James Strachey (London: The Hogarth Press, 1955), 12:289-301.

26. Ibid., 299.

27. Renaissance views of Hercules, including the association with Tamburlaine, are documented in Eugene M. Waith, *The Herculean Hero in Marlowe, Chapman, Shakespeare and Dryden* (London: Chatto & Windus, 1962).

28. Raymond Waddington draws attention to the association of Hercules with Morocco and Bassanio, only to argue ingeniously that the shared attribution is meant not to link but to distinguish the two suitors and their contrasting views of fortune, in "Blind Gods: Fortune, Justice and Cupid in *The Merchant of Venice*," *ELH* 44 (1977): 458-77.

29. In her study of Shakespeare's Moors, Bartels argues that, in *Titus Andronicus*, the early Shakespeare unironically demonizes Aaron but, in *Othello*, the late Shakespeare exposes the process of demonization. Bartels notes, 435n, that she does not consider Morocco because he is a minor character.

30. Eldred Jones, *Othello's Countrymen: The African in English Renaissance Drama* (London: Oxford University Press, 1965); Mahood, *The Merchant of Venice*, 79.

31. G. K. Hunter, "Elizabethans and Foreigners," *Shakespeare Survey* 17 (1964): 37-52; Anthony Barthelemy, *Black Face, Maligned Race: The Representation of Blacks in English Drama from Shakespeare to Southerne* (Baton Rouge: Louisiana State University Press, 1987).

32. Michael Ferber, "The Ideology of *The Merchant of Venice*," *ELR* 20 (1990): 448.

33. Barthelemy, *Black Face*, 147.

34. Barthelemy emphasizes that even though Morocco is not a villain, he continues to present "an obvious and unwelcome sexual threat to Portia," a threat directly associated with his Moorishness (149-50).

35. Zvi Jagendorf links Morocco's departing words to castration in "Innocent Arrows and Sexy Sticks: The Rival Economies of Male Friendship and Sexual Love in *The Merchant of Venice*, *Hebrew University Studies in Literature and the Arts* 19, no. 2 (1991): 37. More graphically, Shell, "Wether and the Ewe," writes of Shylock's castration: "the two sealed bags and stones . . . are confused with his two testicles. . . . Shylock lost his *Geld* when Jessica 'gilded herself with ducats' (2.6.59-50) and has also been 'gelded'" (77).

36. I am currently at work on an article which will consider the application of other theories of repetition (e.g., Derrida, Freud, Deleuze, Miller) to Shylock's language. Additionally, James Shapiro argues that catastration plays a central role in the play and, more generally, in the image of the Jew in early modern England. See "Shakespeare and the Jews."

Marc Berley (essay date 1999)

SOURCE: Berley, Marc. "Jessica's Belmont Blues: Music and Merriment in *The Merchant of Venice*." In *Opening the Borders: Inclusivity in Early Modern Studies,* edited by Peter C. Herman, pp. 185-205. Cranbury, N.J.: Associated University Presses, 1999.

[*In the following essay, Berley examines Lorenzo's statements concerning music and harmony alongside Jessica's dark response to "sweet music," finding in this contradiction a thematic dissonance in* The Merchant of Venice.]

With Lorenzo's famous lines about harmony in *The Merchant of Venice,* Shakespeare offers, as he often does, his uncommon treatment of a Renaissance commonplace. Nevertheless, scholars have long agreed that Lorenzo's speech about harmony in the last scene of *Merchant* is a traditional praise of music that enacts dramatically the play's fully harmonious resolution. Long ago, C. L. Barber asserted that "No other comedy, until the late romances, ends with so full an expression of harmony as that which we get in the opening of the final scene of *Merchant*. And no other final scene is so completely without irony about the joys it celebrates."[1] This remains a standard reading of Lorenzo's speech and the final scene. In this essay, I mean to show that the play does not support such readings. A harmonious resolution "completely without irony" requires the harmonious assimilation of Jessica in Belmont; and Jessica is excluded from the celebration. What is most important, she excludes herself, with her response to Lorenzo's speech: "I am never merry when I hear sweet music" (5.1.69).[2] Critics have been hesitant to see the dark aspects of Jessica's last line. Shakespeare, however, builds a pattern of responses to music that culminates in Jessica's important response. Jessica is excluded from the musical celebration at Belmont, and the final scene makes *Merchant* an early comedy by Shakespeare that questions with ironic dissonance the joys some of its characters too forcibly celebrate.

James Hutton first identified Lorenzo's speech as merely a conventional mixture of speculative (chiefly Neoplatonic) musical theories in praise of music.[3] "Much has been written . . . about Lorenzo's almost too familiar lines," Hutton writes. "Everyone recognizes that the topics are traditional, but, if I am not mistaken, it is always assumed that Shakespeare himself has brought them together. . . . [I]t has not . . . been made clear that this speech not only contains traditional topics, but that the arrangement is traditional. . . . [I]n short," Hutton concludes, "we have here to do with a coherent literary theme that Shakespeare has taken bodily into his play . . . [s]o familiar a theme, indeed, that Shakespeare permits himself to treat it in a kind of shorthand." After quoting Ronsard on the subject of the "unmusical man," Hutton concludes that "It is as one more of these *laudes musicae* that an Elizabethan audience would hear Lorenzo's familiar words."[4]

Hutton's valuable study influenced the criticism of Lorenzo's speech and Shakespeare's allusions to speculative music in particular, as well as Renaissance discussions of music in general, in two important ways. First, scholars such as John Hollander, S. K. Heninger, and Lawrence Danson furthered Hutton's reductions: of Lorenzo's speech to Neoplatonic "shorthand"; of Lorenzo to Shakespeare; and of Shakespeare's view to Lorenzo's speech.[5] Second, they followed Hutton's assumption that Shakespeare's "shorthand treatment" is a version that typifies the thought of an age that extends from Ronsard to Milton.[6] Such readings of Lorenzo's speech fail to account for the considerable innovations, not only of *Merchant* but, more generally, of Shakespeare and Milton.[7]

Lorenzo's speech is filled with Neoplatonic elements, but it is not a disembodied summary of Neoplatonic treatises that "Shakespeare has taken bodily into his play." Lorenzo speaks for neither Shakespeare nor the play. Lorenzo speaks for himself, and the dramatic context of his speech is complex. The relationship between Jessica and Lorenzo and the pattern of allusions to music and merriment throughout the play provide the larger context in which not only Lorenzo's speech but also the general harmony of Belmont must be considered.

Jessica's response to both Lorenzo's speech and the music of Portia's musicians addresses crucial questions raised by what is anything but an unambiguous play that celebrates joys without irony. What precisely does Jessica mean when she says, "I am never merry when I hear sweet music" (5.1.69)? And what does her reply mean within the play? What, furthermore, is the relationship between music and merriment within the play? On this important question, Jessica, as much as Lorenzo, speaks for the play.

During the last forty years, various critics and diverse schools of criticism have either ignored Jessica or fit her into their readings. Even recent feminist studies do not give Jessica the attention she demands.[8] Some critics have suggested that the harmony of Belmont is suspect, but the matter—like Jessica—still has not been considered adequately. Jessica's last response, one of many reactions to music and talk about music within the play, is the most inharmonious, and important; for too long it has been attuned by scholars to the dazzling speech that surrounds it.

Shakespeare was, among other things, a brilliant and subtle orchestrator of dramatic form—and by the time of *Merchant,* he was getting mighty good. Indeed, he was beginning to write comedies in which problems—rendered with precise innovations of dramatic form—resist the dramatic resolution of the play. Shakespeare used this tension to involve his audience in its own moral and cultural dilemmas. Throughout *Merchant,* reactions to music form a coherent pattern, building tensions that climax in Lorenzo's speech and Jessica's reaction to it. Reactions to music—and talk about music—reveal the quality of merriment achieved by its characters. Finally, an audience's reaction to Lorenzo's speech reveals much about the quality of merriment an audience may achieve for itself.

. . . . .

We must begin any consideration of Lorenzo's speech by placing it within its immediate dramatic context, the echoic exchange of "In such a night . . ." that precedes it. The exchange centers on classical stories of love-turned-bitter; the subject speaks against the harmony of the echoic form. Lorenzo speaks of Troilus and Cressid, which turns Jessica to Thisbe. Lorenzo mentions Dido, which turns Jessica to Medea, and Jessica's insinuation that she has risked everything for him leads Lorenzo to their case:

> In Such a night
> Did Jessica steal from the wealthy jew,
> And with an unthrift love did run from Venice
> As far as Belmont.

Jessica speaks directly to the core of what seem to be real troubles:

> In such a night
> Did young Lorenzo swear he loved her well,
> Stealing her soul with many vows of faith,
> And ne'er a true one.
>
> (5.1.15-22)

If the others can be explained away as playful literary allusions, Jessica's last, direct charge cannot. Lorenzo responds with similar direction: "In such a night / Did pretty Jessica, like a little shrow / Slander her love, and he forgave it her." But Jessica appears unforgiving, concluding the exchange by remarking her unwillingness to conclude it: "I would out-night you, did nobody come: / But hark, I hear the footing of a man" (5.1.23-24). By 5.1, real trouble is afoot; playful banter has turned dark. Moreover, given the thematic analogies to the plot of Portia and Bassanio, this exchange between Jessica and Lorenzo has its further dark resonance.

The serious subject of the exchange pushes the limits of its playful banter, signaling a conflict between beautiful form and ugly content, between the charm of sound and the trouble of its meaning. The exchange ends with Jessica promising to "out-night" Lorenzo, interrupted by Portia's servant Stephano. Before Stephano is gone, Lorenzo begins a speculative speech about musical harmony. Rather than a disembodied piece of Neoplatonism, Lorenzo's speech is part of Shakespeare's intricately woven dramatic context. An attempt to make Jessica merry once again, the speech is spoken by the play's hottest lover at a time when his lady appears, with reason, to be getting cold. Lorenzo tries to effect a transition to a better, more harmonious aspect of "such a night." Using speech and music, Lorenzo tries to get Jessica to see that "such a night" *becomes* "the touches of sweet harmony" rather than the will to "out-night."

The "sweet power" of speech and music were deeply linked in Shakespeare's day. Both were considered modes of seduction, and Lorenzo now has need for grander, sweeter promises, bigger vows that might make Jessica forget about broken ones:

> Sweet soul, let's in, and there expect their coming.
> And yet no matter; why should we go in?

>   My friend Stephano, signify, I pray you,
>   Within this house, your mistress is at hand,
>   And bring your music forth into the air.
>   [*Exit Stephano.*]
>   Here will we sit and let the sounds of music
>   Creep in our ears; soft stillness and the night
>   Become the touches of sweet harmony.
>   Sit, Jessica. Look how the floor of heaven
>   Is thick inlaid with patens of bright gold.
>   There's not the smallest orb which thou behold'st
>   But in his motion like an angel sings,
>   Still quiring to the young-eyed cherubins;
>   Such harmony is in immortal souls,
>   But whilst this muddy vesture of decay
>   Doth grossly close it in, we cannot hear it.
>   [*Enter musicians.*]
>   Come ho, and wake Diana with a hymn!
>   With sweetest touches pierce your mistress' ear
>   And draw her home with music.
>   *Play music.*
>
>   (5.1.49-68)

Rather than mere Neoplatonic shorthand, the speech is dramatic recapitulation. Lorenzo first promises the "the touches of sweet harmony." The phrase seems at first to refer to actual music to be played by the musicians, but Lorenzo eventually links it to the heavenly harmony they cannot hear: "Such harmony" (which "is in immortal souls") refers back to the "sweet harmony" that ("whilst this muddy vesture of decay / Doth grossly close it in") they cannot hear. Six lines after offering Jessica heavenly harmony, Lorenzo begins to explain why he may offer only earthly discord. Lorenzo, in short, offers Jessica something he cannot provide, and the exchange of "In such a night . . ." suggests he has done this before. The speech is dazzling, but it confirms a pattern of promising more than he will deliver.

Lorenzo continues to elicit harmony where there appears to be discord, moving from musical speech to the power of music itself. After he tells Jessica that we cannot hear the music of the spheres, the musicians enter, and Lorenzo gives them specific directions. Speaking to Portia's musicians at Portia's house, Lorenzo is telling them to draw her home. But he is also speaking, in Neoplatonic terms, about the theory according to which the actual "sounds of music" can pierce the ear, touch the soul, and re-attune it, thereby drawing it home to the heavenly harmony. The Neoplatonic theory of the "sweet power of music"—namely, that music can penetrate one's soul and draw it to heaven—merely complicates the matter of wooing with false vows, for it is deeply related to seduction by false music, as well as, more generally, penetration of Jessica's body.

Lorenzo attempts to placate Jessica not by winning an old argument but by dazzling her with beautiful new promises and lascivious music—both of which had worked well before. As Robin Headlam Wells observes, "a man of eloquence is capable of persuading people to do whatever he wishes. However, the real mark of his power is not his ability to *force* people 'to yeeld in that which most standth against their will', but rather," as Thomas Wilson asserts in his influential *Arte of Rhetorique*, "his skill in inducing them 'to *will* that which he did.'"[9] Jessica, however, continues the tone she establishes during the echoic exchange by asserting that music does not make her merry. Given the common association of music and rhetoric, Shakespeare is juxtaposing—indeed, likening—the forced conversion of Shylock with Lorenzo's attempt to re-seduce Jessica in the final scene. Shylock never wills what Portia does, but Jessica early on appears to will what Lorenzo does. By the last scene, though, she has reasons not to, and Lorenzo has a need to steal her soul again. Stealing one's "soul with vows of faith" is akin to wooing one with music and musical language. Neoplatonic theory promises momentary ecstasy by penetration. But Jessica, as she says, won't be merry.

Lorenzo's speech has long been seen as traditional (Neoplatonic) praise of music, but it is only within this dramatic context that we can appreciate its significance. It cannot be seen as "the most purely religious utterance in the play."[10] Lorenzo offers a seductive speech. He knows to seize every opportunity to throw in the adjective *sweet*. But in Shakespeare's plays, such excess serves to mock precisely the subjects most relevant here. To be excessively sweet is not to be sweet at all; music becomes an illusion, and any love it induces becomes a foible. A good example is *Troilus and Cressida* 3.1. Similarly, in *Cymbeline*, Shakespeare has Cloten mock the hyperbole of both the Neoplatonic idea of penetration and the literary conventions derived from it. Cloten—like Lorenzo, but in direct, ribald, language—alludes to the musicians as surrogate seducers: "Come on, tune. If you can penetrate her with your fingering, so; we'll try with tongue too." Once they play, Cloten hedges: "So, get you gone. If this penetrate, I will consider your music the better; if it do not, it is a vice in her ears which horsehairs and calves' guts, nor the voice of unpaved eunuch to boot, can never amend" (2.3.11-31). Comically rendering the conflict between deceptively false and beautifully true music, Cloten razes the system of musical powers established by Neoplatonists such as Ronsard. The music shall prove itself good and powerful, says Cloten, only when it shall have penetrated his lady.

Shakespeare's interest in the prurient mocking of Neoplatonic theory is evident as early as *Love's Labor's Lost*. The King decrees that he and his lords will be "brave conquerors . . . / That war against your own affections," devoted to a contemplative life: "Our court shall be a little academe, / Still and contemplative in living art." Berowne, however, troubled by the prospect of there being no ladies, voices his doubt about the austerity: "But is there no quick recreation granted?" Offering a substitute, the King answers that in lieu of ladies the men shall recreate themselves by means of musical language:

>   Our court you know is haunted
>   With a refinèd traveller of Spain,
>   A man in all the world's new fashion planted,
>   That hath a mint of phrases in his brain;

One who the music of his own vain tongue
Doth ravish like enchanting harmony;
A man of complements, whom right and wrong
Have chose as umpire of their mutiny.

(1.1.159-66)

A man who "hath a mint of phrases in his brain" and a "vain tongue," a man who "ravish[es] like enchanting harmony" is a rhetorician. He may be an umpire of mutiny, but his skill points to another mutiny: between "quick recreation" (wine, women, and song) and slow moral "contemplation in living art" (recreation), between "purposing merriment" and enduring the much ado it takes to attain self-knowledge. This conflict is one of Shakespeare's major themes throughout his plays—another way of speaking about the mediation of appetite and reason, frenzy and self-rule, evasion of shame and painful self-reflection.

The music plays in Belmont, and Jessica responds, both to Lorenzo and to the music for which he has made his great Neoplatonic claims. Jessica tells Lorenzo—in language more subtle than the language of her father, but less than subtly—that all is not "sweet" for her in Belmont. Whereas Shylock sticks to his rough idiom, Jessica can adopt the harmonious utterance of the Italians; she can speak poetry, echo Lorenzo. But, finally, she answers in blunt prose to Lorenzo's dazzling blank verse; her response is poignantly unmusical in both its meaning and its form: "I am never merry when I hear sweet music." Jessica offers, in the manner of her father, rough idiom to Lorenzo's mellifluous "vows of faith."

Jessica's response puts Lorenzo in a predicament. Lorenzo resumes his speech, turning his focus to the Neoplatonic theory of the "unmusical man":

> The reason is, your spirits are attentive.
> For do but note a wild and wanton herd
> Or race of youthful and unhandled colts
> Fetching mad bounds, bellowing and neighing loud,
> Which is the hot condition of their blood:
> If they but hear perchance a trumpet sound,
> Or any air of music touch their ears,
> You shall perceive them make a mutual stand,
> Their savage eyes turned to a modest gaze
> By the sweet power of music. Therefore the poet
> Did feign that Orpheus drew trees, stones, and floods;
> Since naught so stockish, hard, and full of rage
> But music for the time doth change his nature.
> The man that hath no music in himself,
> Nor is not moved with concord of sweet sounds,
> Is fit for treasons, stratagems, and spoils;
> The motions of his spirit are dull as night,
> And his affections dark as Erebus.
> Let no such man be trusted. Mark the music.

(5.1.55-88)

With her last line, Jessica leaves Lorenzo to deliver a stock Neoplatonic answer that, rather than resolve the matter, shows that he is in deeper trouble than commonplace sweet-talk can get him out of.

In the two parts of his speech, Lorenzo speaks for himself, not for the play. Here we can begin to see Shakespeare's original, dramatic use of the commonplace praise of music. In the first part of his speech (while he is trying to charm Jessica), Lorenzo blames a universal human nature, the "muddy vesture of decay." After Jessica says she is not merry, in contrast, Lorenzo blames Jessica specifically, making the dark (Neoplatonic) suggestion that she has no music in herself—whether due to momentary attentiveness or the essential unmusicality of her Jewish soul. The two parts of Lorenzo's speech speak to an important question: is there something irreparably wrong with Jessica? Shakespeare never directly gives us an answer, but he has Lorenzo insinuate one early. Lorenzo alludes to the problem of Jessica's Jewish soul in 2.4; and by 5.1, Jessica has shown herself fit for treasons, stratagems, and spoils. According to Ronsard, the "unmusical man" is "not delighted and is not . . . sweetly ravished and transported," giving "proof thereby that he has a . . . depraved soul, and is to be guarded against as one not happily born."[11] *Merchant* raises important questions: is Jessica "unhappily born"? Can she be merry?

That Shylock cannot be happy is a basic fact required by the plot of the play. Jessica's happiness is a different matter—it is in no way certain, and its uncertainty is a central part of the play. One reason "Shylock's enforced baptism is disconcerting," as John Gross observes, "is that it is contrary to predominant Christian tradition. . . . The treatment meted out to Shylock belongs at the harsh end of the spectrum."[12] Jessica's failure to be merry, if the result of treatment that belongs to the kinder end of the spectrum, stands as a significant, ironic counterpoint to Shylock's defeat. And none of the darkness comes as a surprise by 5.1. The likely failure of Jessica's assimilation is, as we will see, registered with irony in every scene in which she appears before 5.1.

. . . . .

One can say with good reason, as has Frank Kermode, that *Merchant* is a play about justice, but *Merchant* is also chiefly a play about characters who seek, in their various ways, merriment. The theme befits a comedy, especially a play Kermode rightly links with *A Midsummer Night's Dream* and *Twelfth Night*.[13] Antonio begins the play by saying, "I know not why I am so sad," confessing that he has "much ado to know myself." His friend Solanio offers tautology as counsel, "Then let us say you are sad / Because you are not merry . . ." (1.1.47-48). In the second scene, Nerissa has to tell Portia, who has long been seeking merriment, to be careful not to let hastiness keep her from striking an Aristotelian "mean." It is in this context that one must see the attempts of all the characters to be merry—especially Jessica's.

The question whether "sweet music" should make Jessica "merry" contains within it the larger question on which the play is centered: what does it mean to be "merry"? *Merchant*, after all, is a play about conflicting attempts to be "merry"—and the antipodal world-views on which these attempts are based. The crux of the play, of course, is that Antonio and Shylock cannot both end the play "merry." The Christians are, as Bassanio himself exclaims to Gratiano, "friends / That purpose merriment" (2.2.189-90). For Shylock, who rejects such purposing, the possibility for merriment exists only in the "merry sport" of his "bond" (1.3.139-47). It is clear that the "merry sport" of the bond is not "merry." It is less clear, though clearly as true, that forcible conversion of a Jew is another form of "merry sport" that is not truly "merry" or "gentle"—and that such a lack of gentleness is as possible for gentiles as for Shylock "the Jew."

Merchant is a play about polarizing views that would make one the true and the other the false pursuit of merriment. But, as Maynard Mack observes in his essay, "Engagement and Detachment in Shakespeare's Plays," "the usual lesson of comedy [is] that overengagement to any obsessive single view of oneself or the world is to be avoided."[14] Shakespeare has written, I am arguing, a play that is neither a simple attack on Jews nor a subtle defense of them. *Merchant* depicts merciless Christians seeking merriment as well as a merciless Jew. The play considers not why one of the two pursuits is true, but why both potentially are destructive. And it is Jessica, I suggest, who most comes to feel, if not understand, the reasons why.

The pun on *gentle* and *gentile* made consistently in the play suggests that Shylock could improve his fortune by assimilating, by being *gentle*. The plot requires that we accept not only Shylock's forced conversion as a comic resolution, but also his forced response to Portia's question: "Art thou contented, Jew? What dost thou say?" Shylock says, "I am content" (4.1.391-92), and we all know he is not. Jessica, in stark contrast to her father, not only converts willingly but twice accepts this promise that a change of religion will bring a change of fortune: "O Lorenzo, / If thou keep promise, I shall end this strife, / Become a Christian and thy loving wife"; "I shall be saved by my husband. He hath made me a Christian" (2.3.20-22; 3.5.17-18). Jessica looks to conversion as an answer to her troubles, which appear to her to be rooted in her life with her repressive Jewish father. The first time we hear her, Jessica says, "Our house is hell" (2.3.1). Whereas Shylock's conversion is forced, Jessica's is willing—but her willingness is rooted in a flight from tedium. She gives away her father's turquoise ring, voiding with this gesture the union that made her a Jew, trading, symbolically, a world of rigidity for a world of lascivious joys. But when we see her in 5.1, the final scene of the play, sweet music—precisely the same music that first caused her to "thrust [her] head into the public street"—no longer makes Jessica merry. Forced to convert, and forced to speak, Shylock's penultimate utterance in the play—"I am content"—is clearly ironic. Jessica's last line—"I am never merry when I hear sweet music"—is also ironic. She cannot say *never*.

The dramatic counterpoint created by the last utterances of father and daughter is significant. Much depends on whether Jessica is truly unmerry at the end of the play—and whether her failure to be merry is a result of a failure in her (a natural failure of her impenetrable Jewish soul?) or a failure in Lorenzo. Shakespeare, moreover, provides us with a clear pattern that suggests that blame is to be placed on both Jessica and Lorenzo. On Jessica, not because her soul is Jewish, but because she avoids the truth that it is; on Lorenzo, because he seduces Jessica with promises he does not keep. Jessica's response to Lorenzo and his music suggests, moreover, the deeper falsehood of the promise of Christian harmony announced by Lorenzo in his speech. We must arbitrate these matters, and we do well to base any conclusions on careful consideration of larger patterns built within the play.

With Jessica, Shakespeare presents us with another Jew, one who willingly converts; yet, still, Lorenzo sees the need to account early for the possibility of her future misfortune:

> If e'er the Jew her father come to heaven,
> It will be for his gentle daughter's sake;
> And never dare misfortune cross her foot,
> Unless she do it under this excuse,
> That she is issue to a faithless Jew.
>
> (2.4.33-37)

Even before the two appear together in the play, Lorenzo warns that Jessica might not be "merry" even as his bride. The "excuse" will be Jessica's Jewish nature, which, despite her hope that marriage and conversion will change it, Lorenzo says plainly cannot be changed. Similarly, Launcelot helps Jessica leave her father, but not without telling her that "the sins of the father are to be laid upon the children" and "truly I think you are damned" (3.5.1-6).

Not only does it appear that something has changed for the worse between Jessica and Lorenzo in 5.1; to this point, the play has hinted consistently at the likelihood of such trouble. In the elopement scene, for example, the first scene in which Jessica and Lorenzo appear together, Gratiano and Salerio preface the elopement with foreboding truisms about love. As Salerio says, "O ten times faster Venus' pigeons fly / To seal love's bonds new-made than they are wont / To keep obligèd faith unforfeited" (2.6.5-7). Gratiano replies with his speech on the effects of "the strumpet wind," including his maxim "All things that are / Are with more spirit chasèd than enjoyed" (2.6.12-13). Indeed, as soon as Jessica reenters, Lorenzo quickly confirms what Gratiano had said, that "lovers ever run before the clock" (2.6.4): "What, art thou come? On, gentlemen, away! / Our masquing mates by this time for us stay" (2.6.58-59). It is time, says Lorenzo, to be in time for merriment, for merriment is fleeting.

The elopement scene shows a Jessica eager for merriment, but it also imparts misgivings about Jessica's self-knowledge, as well as deeper matters of shame and conscience that might come to her when she knows herself better. Jessica naively expects Lorenzo to change her Jewish identity and thus her fortune, as she says to Launcelot before leaving Shylock's house:

> Alack, what heinous sin is it in me
> To be ashamed to be my father's child
> But though I am a daughter to his blood,
> I am not to his manners. O Lorenzo,
> If thou keep promise, I shall end this strife,
> Become a Christian and thy loving wife!
>
> (2.3.16-21)

Jessica puts all her hope for future merriment in Lorenzo's vow and her associated conversion. In short, a new life hangs on the promise of a man. But Jessica confuses strife, which can end, with facts about her life that cannot be erased—facts which, if she refuses to acknowledge them, promise, rather, to increase her strife.

In saying farewell to her father, Jessica tries to change her identity, and hence her fortune: "Farewell; and if my fortune be not crost, / I have a father, you a daughter lost" (2.5.54-55). But in the elopement scene, ironically, Jessica shows herself to be very much "to his manners": while trying to rid herself of the shame of being her father's child, Jessica "gilds" herself with her father's ducats.

Whether a Jew can exchange her fortune by assimilating, by changing her manners, is a question central to the play. Jessica's "Here, catch this casket" (2.6.33) suggests her possession of an unburdened, merry spirit. She is rejecting a penurious, fruitless pursuit of merriment for a fruitful one. But the rest of what Jessica says in the elopement scene is laden with dark hints of repression: "I am glad 'tis night—you do not look on me—/ For I am much ashamed of my exchange" (2.6.34-35). Jessica then offers a truism that hints at the future troubles the blindness of love can bring: "But love is blind, and lovers cannot see / The pretty follies that themselves commit . . ." (2.6.36-37). Because Jessica sees the shame of cross-dressing ("my exchange"), the lines register a latent concern that what she does not see might in the future be of greater consequence. Jessica uses the word *shame* twice in this scene, and both times it resonates with her earlier mention of the "heinous sin. . . . To be ashamed to be my father's child":

> What, must I hold a candle to my shames?
> They in themselves, good sooth, are too too light.
> Why, 'tis an office of discovery, love—
> And I should be obscured."
>
> (2.6.43-44)

The lines have their obvious, as well as deeper, meaning. Clearly, Jessica wishes to hide her cross-dressing from her lover, and this seems natural. Jessica, however, appears overly concerned with her "shames," rather than naturally concerned with the single shame of cross-dressing. There is disparity, moreover, between Jessica's worry "I should be obscured" and Lorenzo's assurance, "So are you, sweet, / Even in the lovely garnish of a boy." Jessica, as Lorenzo says, is already obscured. Further, Lorenzo knows what he is getting—a pretty Jewish girl who is wearing pants and sporting the ducats of her "father Jew" (2.6.22). What Jessica seems anxious to obscure, rather, is a more general need to obscure herself. Lorenzo tells Jessica to "come at once," but Jessica—thinking her shames "too too light"—delays, risking, in effect, a greater light, the sun: "I will make fast the doores, and gild myself / With some moe ducats, and be with you straight" (2.6.49-50). Shakespeare highlights Jessica's worries about the exchange she makes with Lorenzo; the stakes are so high already that to gild herself with more ducats is worth the risk.

Gilded in her father's ducats, Jessica endeavors to close forever behind her the doors of her father's house. But the scene suggests that Jessica may not get away from her father's house with the mere consequence of the shame of cross-dressing. Like Launcelot, Jessica leaves her old master, Shylock, for a new one, Lorenzo. Indeed, Shakespeare has Launcelot offer his clownish wisdom on two subjects very important to Jessica: leaving one's Jewish master and the conscience that attends any attempted flight from one's identity. "Certainly my conscience will serve me to run from this Jew my master" (2.2.1), says Launcelot in his first line. He then encounters his father, Old Gobbo, and proceeds to ask him, "Do you know me, father?" The Launcelot-Gobbo subplot suggests, however glibly, that where identity, conscience, and shameful fathers are concerned, "Truth will come to light . . . in the end truth will out" (2.2.74).

Jessica seems, in short, to lack an understanding of the exchange she is making.[15] (Exchange, of course, is her father's hated skill.) Jessica seems, in fine, to cloak the "heinous sin" of being ashamed to be who she is under the shame of her cross-dressing. This becomes a common proto-Freudian theme in Shakespeare: to be ashamed to be ashamed of shame.

Jessica's identity—as a woman, as a lover, as a convert—appears to be in flux in 2.6. Jessica, like Lorenzo, knows only that she is her father's child. The central problem seems to be that Jessica does not know the true value of what she is giving Lorenzo in "exchange." Another problem is that she worries too little about what she is getting in Lorenzo.

The notion that love is an office of discovery suggests that, in time, through the foibles of blind love, there is truth to be known by Jessica—about Lorenzo and about herself. Just as there is irony in Jessica's last response to Lorenzo, so is irony in Jessica's first response to Lorenzo in the play, in the balcony scene: "Who are you? Tell me for more certainly, / Albeit I'll swear that I do know your tongue" (2.6.26-27). As the play goes on, it becomes clearer that Jessica knows the tongue, the dazzling vows, but not the man. By 5.1, there is the strong suggestion that something has happened since 3.5, that Lorenzo is the main reason Jessica is not merry when she hears sweet music. Self-knowledge and conscience appear to be other reasons.

. . . . .

Throughout *Merchant,* reactions to music are linked to one's merriment, for they display one's knowledge of oneself and the world. And, just as Shylock and Lorenzo offer competing theories about what will keep Jessica from being merry, they also offer competing views of music. Sensing "some ill a-brewing towards my rest," Shylock warns: "Jessica my girl, Look to my house" (2.5.15-17). Informed by Launcelot about "a masque," Shylock warns, more specifically, about the danger of music:

> What, are there masques? Hear you me, Jessica:
> Lock up my doors; and when you hear the drum
> And the vile squealing of the wry-necked fife,
> Clamber not you up to the casements then,
> Nor thrust your head into the public street
> To gaze on Christian fools with varnished faces;
> But stop my house's ears—I mean my casements;
> Let not the sound of shallow fopp'ry enter
> My sober house. By Jacob's staff I swear
> I have no mind of feasting forth to-night;
> But I will go. Go you before me, sirrah.
> Say I will come.
>
> (2.5.27-38)

Jessica is part of Shylock's house; her maidenhead is one of his doors. With words that anticipate, in both form and matter, Lorenzo's speech in 5.1, Shylock gives his daughter his last command: "Let not the sound of shallow fopp'ry enter / My sober house."

Jessica, we see, is called on to choose between these antithetical views. What is more important, Jessica is twice called upon to see through the discrepancy between form and content apparent in the articulation of each view. In the first instance, Jessica shuns her father's disharmonious "manners" and is led to a kind of merriment by the "vile squealing." Finally, however, at Belmont, music and musical speech lose their formerly seductive power: sweet music—and sweet vows—do not make Jessica merry. An untrue lover cannot speak persuasively about harmony, having already taught a harsh lesson about discord.

Shakespeare uses Lorenzo's speech to build dramatic tension; the end of the play puts Jessica back where she began. Just as Lorenzo's vows turn to lies, his seductive exhortations turn to commands. Lorenzo's commands replace Shylock's. They are more subtle, and tempered by the music of his speech, but they are commands: "Sit, Jessica. . . . Mark the music." Jessica's reaction to music is again her form of resisting the man who commands her, her rejection of a particular world-view that would govern her reaction to music, and thereby her reactions to all things. Moreover, Jessica's claim that she is never merry when she hears sweet music reveals that Shylock's view of music turns out to be more nearly true for her than Lorenzo's view.

Writing about Jessica and Lorenzo in 5.1. in his study *The Harmonies of The Merchant of Venice,* Lawrence Danson, following John Hollander in assuming that Lorenzo speaks for Jessica, writes that "[it is] this pair of lovers who speak about that music of the spheres which the play's other harmonies imitate."[16] Such a conclusion is based on the assumption that the talk about false vows is merely playful banter (Danson calls it "easy banter and serious intimacy"). The critical consensus represented by Barber and Danson is expressed by Kermode. *Merchant,* he writes, "begins with usury and corrupt love" and "ends with harmony and perfect love."[17]

As Danson knows, the question of Lorenzo's "moral fitness" is crucial to "our response to teasing banter at the opening of the fifth act." Danson sees that his fitness has "been established," but the only proof he can adduce is the encomium of a hot lover, Lorenzo's praise of Jessica in 2.6.52-57. Danson bases his assessment of Lorenzo's "moral fitness" on an assumption that his famous speech is an enactment of religious harmony: the "union of the Gentile husband and the daughter of the Jew suggests the penultimate stage of salvation history described by St. Paul."[18] But a Christian's theft of a soul "with many vows of faith / And ne'er a true one" speaks, ultimately, not for the "harmony in his immortal soul" but for the impenetrable grossness of his "muddy vesture of decay." Jessica's response that she is not merry is not a confirmation of her salvation—not even a playful one. We are reminded, after all, of the County Palatine, who "hears merry tales and smiles not" (1.2.44-45), whom Portia therefore deems unfit to marry.

. . . . .

An unambiguous resolution of the play requires harmony between Jessica and Lorenzo. And it is for this reason—a circular one—that scholars have for so long thrown Jessica over to the side of the Christians, despite what she says.[19] Gross is one critic who sees the darker aspects of Jessica's marriage to Lorenzo, and of the troubling edges in their dialogues; but even he suggests "[o]ne should not make too much of" it.[20] One should be reminded of Leo Spitzer's warning in *Classical and Christian Ideas of World Harmony* about the "harmonizing tendency" that frequently attends the study of ideas of Christian harmony.[21] Even if one persists in playing down Jessica's dissent, there is no justification for saying that Jessica speaks with Lorenzo—or that Lorenzo speaks for Jessica. Jessica says she is not merry; thereafter, she does not speak at all. She is present at the final celebration at Belmont, but she is not part of it.

As Norman Rabkin writes, "As the entire critical history of the play has made equally apparent, the play's ultimate resolution of [its] conflicts is anything but clear or simple." Even Rabkin, however, sees the critical challenge as a demand for allegiance on one of two sides; and he, too, reads Lorenzo's speech as the signal of harmonious resolution of Lorenzo's side: "On the one side, as we have seen, we find Shylock, trickery, anality, precise definition, possessiveness, contempt for prodigality" as well as "distrust of emotion and hatred of music, bad luck, and failure."

"On the other," writes Rabkin, "we find Portia, but also Antonio, Bassanio, Lorenzo, Jessica, and Gratiano; freedom, metaphorical richness of language, prodigality" as well as "love of emotion and music, supreme trickery, a fondness for bonds, good luck, success."[22] In this common reading, Jessica is thrown in—here, just before Gratiano—as Lorenzo's happily instructed wife.

Catherine Belsey, in "Love in Venice," appears ready to reverse the sway of this "harmonizing habit." But while she questions the assumptions of Barber and Danson, Belsey offers a sweeping description of love in Venice that leads her to reduce Lorenzo's talk about the "muddy vesture of decay" to putatively historical truths about the body and desire. Belsey writes that "the older understanding of love leaves traces in the text, with the effect that desire is only imperfectly domesticated" and the "consequence" that "Venice is super-imposed on Belmont." Belsey astutely identifies the consequence, but she ignores the particular exclusion of Jessica. She suggests that all the characters in the play look "back to a world, fast disappearing in the late sixteenth century, where love was seen as anarchic, destructive, dangerous."[23] Apparently, Belsey does not uphold Jessica's distinction between false and true vows. Belsey argues instead that the play speaks nostalgically (historically) about a desire that, in accordance with historical indicia, can no longer be fulfilled. According to Belsey, Jessica and Lorenzo, an otherwise harmonious couple, are deprived of an allegorical harmony, or granted only a trace of it—for, in the late sixteenth century, just as now, one may get no more than a trace of anything. *Merchant*, however, does not treat an essential crisis in the history of desire; it depicts the particular, contextualized problems the women in the play have with particular men.

There is something peculiarly wrong with all the male characters in *Merchant*. Portia shows herself to be superior to all the men in the play, and Jessica seems to be. Each, however, is hampered by her father's rules for choosing men, opposing sets of rules that specify different reactions to music, reactions that are central to the resolution of the play. Moreover, both Portia and Jessica are also morally flawed.

As we have seen, Jessica's response to Lorenzo's speech and the music of Portia's musicians raises questions that are crucial to any thorough reading of the play. Does Jessica's response to the music at the end of the beginning of act 5 confirm that a Jewish soul is "not happily born," unmusical? Or is Jessica's failure to be merry a good thing? Does she exhibit a noble melancholia that distinguishes her from those flighty wenches who, when they hear the strains of a lascivious lute, giggle, roll their eyes, and fall wholly for the man who brings the strains about—as Jessica once did? Do we listen now to a young woman whom love has discovered to herself, a woman made wiser by brief experience, a woman who is ready to register her dissenting view? And might she somehow speak for the play? These questions are necessary to any study of *Merchant*.

As Keith Geary writes, building on the insight of Rabkin, "We must, critics tell us, take sides either with Shylock or with Portia and the Christians, and stand by our choice." But such "black-and-white judgement seems peculiarly inappropriate to a play that argues the falsity of such neat and absolute distinctions," for *Merchant*, as Geary writes, "deals in shades of grey and continually raises the problem of appropriate response and judgement, most acutely, of course, in relation to Shylock."[24] Jessica, I am suggesting, is the character who most feels and portrays what becomes the obvious falsity of neat distinctions.

Merchant contrasts the Christians' gift for musical speech with the rough idiom of Shylock. Lorenzo is dazzling; Shylock is blunt. *Merchant*, however, demands that we distinguish the harmony of form ("In such a night . . .") from the force of real discord. At the same time, the play reveals to us our inability to distinguish them. Shylock's nasty "contempt for prodigality" and "hatred of music" is an extreme antithesis to the dangerous trust in music shown by the Christians. They demonstrate a Neoplatonic trust in music and musical language that becomes suspect. With Jessica's final rejection of Lorenzo's claims, the play suggests that the "sweet power" of "sweet music" is a potentially destructive illusion for Christians as well as Jews. The case of Portia is apposite.

Merchant is neither spoken for nor resolved by the seductive harmony Lorenzo so dazzlingly proclaims. As he does in other plays, Shakespeare involves the audience in the moral dilemma of the play. He compels us to take sides even as he warns of the dangers of doing so. In *Merchant* he gives us a character whose middle position is, even more dangerously, easy to ignore. By living between "Antipodes," by reacting nakedly to music, Jessica learns the most in the play, and yet she is the least pedantic character in the play. She is, moreover, the least likely to seduce us: as a Jew Jessica is eclipsed by her father; as a woman by Portia; as someone who might tell us something about being merry, she is eclipsed by Antonio; as someone who might tell us something about the "power of music," by Lorenzo. By the end of the play, Jessica can neither be disassociated from nor identified with her father—or Lorenzo.[25] Jessica's is the strange suffering of one who dares to live between the "Antipodes." A tug on the audience from two sides can make for great drama, but Shakespeare does even better in *Merchant*. If all the other characters demand our taking one side or another, Jessica does not, for she herself is tugged by both. As Launcelot says, her mother and father are Scylla and Charybdis: "Well, you are gone both ways" (3.5.15-16).

The wonder of the play, I am suggesting, is its ability to bring the audience around to Jessica's experience in the middle of undesirable extremes. In many ways, *Merchant* is a precursor of *Measure for Measure*—a comedy with a troubling comedic resolution; a comedy with a trenchant focus on the virtue of moving from Hebrew justice to Christian mercy; a comedy about the trouble Christians can have being merciful as they seek merriment. It would only be a few years, we must remember, before Shakespeare would write his "problem plays."

In *Merchant,* one character, a minor character, Jessica, tries unsuccessfully to arbitrate the merciless extremes of Jewish rigidity and Christian frivolity. Act 5 begins (and the play ends) by developing the problems the play presents, not by fully resolving them in a traditional praise of musical harmony. Lorenzo offers a dazzling speech by which we, like Jessica, are liable to be seduced. But Shakespeare allows us to see through Lorenzo, and forces us to consider large and important questions raised both by Jessica and the dramatic themes and tensions within the play. In the end, Lorenzo delivers a speech about heavenly harmony that succumbs to the earthly conflict it tries to resolve.

Merchant is a difficult play, and has long been a divisive one. Many critics have, along with Lorenzo, praised a pristine harmony; some critics have grudgingly acknowledged it; and a few critics have briefly remarked hints of discord.[26] But these various readings have persisted in seeing (or not seeing) Jessica in much the same way. When we examine Jessica and her role, moreover, we see that *Merchant* is a play about undesirable extremes over which even competing schools of criticism might come to some consensus.

We must remember, in the end, that Jessica's last line—like the second part of Lorenzo's speech—competes for our attention with the seductive sounds of the musicians. At the conclusion of a play that pushes its dramatic content to the limits of comic form, a play that juxtaposes the harmony of form with the reality of discord and coerced harmonies, we must listen with an ear to the seductive music of both Lorenzo's speech and Portia's musicians, and with our soul bent toward deeper, more speculative matters—in short, like Jessica, with attentive spirits.

Notes

1. Barber, *Shakespeare's Festive Comedy* (Princeton: Princeton University Press, 1959), 187.

2. I quote throughout from William Shakespeare, *The Complete Plays,* ed. Alfred Harbage (New York: Viking, 1969).

3. Hutton, "Some English Poems in Praise of Music," *English Miscellany* 2 (1950): 1-63.

4. Ibid., 1-5.

5. See Hollander, *The Untuning of the Sky* (Princeton: Princeton University Press, 1961); Heninger, *Touches of Sweet Harmony* (San Marino, California: The Huntington Library, 1974); Danson, *The Harmonies of The Merchant of Venice* (New Haven: Yale University Press, 1978).

6. See, for example, Nan Cooke Carpenter, *Music in the Medieval and Renaissance Universities* (New York: Da Capo Press, 1972) 147.

7. See Marc Berley, "Milton's Earthy Grossness: Music and the Condition of the Poet in 'L'Allegro' and 'Il Penseroso,' *Milton Studies,* ed. Albert C. Labriola, Vol. 30 (Pittsburgh: University Pittsburgh Press, 1993): 149-61.

8. Irene Dash, *Wooing, Wedding* and *Power* (New York: Columbia University Press, 1981), mentions neither Jessica nor *Merchant;* in *The Woman's Part: Feminist Criticism of Shakespeare,* ed. Carolyn Ruth Swift Lenz, Gayle Greene, and Carol Thomas Neely (Urbana: University Illinois Press, 1983), Jessica is mentioned in only one essay, and only once, in a typical sentence linking her choice of Lorenzo to her father's misfortune; Lisa Jardine, *Still Harping on Daughters* (1983; New York: Columbia University Press, 1989), mentions Jessica only once, to remark only the matter of her cross-dressing; *Women's Re-Visions of Shakespeare,* ed. Marianne Novy (Urbana: University Illinois Press, 1990) is a collection in which Jessica is not mentioned at all; in the few allusions to *Merchant* throughout the volume, it is Portia who is the subject.

9. Wells, *Elizabethan Mythologies* (Cambridge: Cambridge University Press, 1994), 5.

10. John Gross, *Shylock: A Legacy and Its Legend* (New York: Simon & Schuster, 1992), 99.

11. Hutton, "English Poems," 4.

12. Gross, *Shylock,* 91.

13. Kermode, *Shakespeare, Spenser, Donne* (London: Routledge, 1971), 210-15.

14. Mack, "Engagement and Detachment in Shakespeare's Plays," reprinted in *Everybody's Shakespeare* (Lincoln: University of Nebraska Press, 1993), 25.

15. Some criticism written from Marxist and cultural materialist perspectives sheds further light on Jessica's "exchange." Even these studies, however, do not give Jessica the attention she requires. See, for example, Karen Newman, "Portia's Ring: Unruly Women and Structure of Exchange in *The Merchant of Venice,*" *Shakespeare Quarterly* #38 (1987): 19-33. Newman offers intelligent analysis of the role of Portia's ring, as well as of "exchange" more generally. But Newman does not even mention Jessica's "exchange" as a point of comparison or contrast.

16. Hollander, *Untuning the Sky,* 151-52; Danson, *Harmonies,* 177.

17. Kermode, *Shakespeare, Spenser, Donne,* 215.

18. Danson, *Harmonies,* 178-84.

19. James Shapiro, *Shakespeare and the Jews* (New York: Columbia University Press, 1996), 158-59, remarks only briefly the possibility that Jessica "might revert to her Jewish nature." The possibility,

of course, is only hinted at; and it is part of Shakespeare's skill here to resist closure. To consider the matter fully, one has to pay more attention to the dramatic structure of the play than Shapiro does.

20. Gross, *Shylock,* 72.

21. Spitzer, *Classical and Christian Ideas of World Harmony,* ed. Anna Granville Hatcher (Baltimore: Johns Hopkins University Press, 1963), 4.

22. Rabkin, *Shakespeare and the Problem of Meaning* (Chicago: University Chicago Press, 1981), 28-29.

23. Belsey, "Love in Venice," *Shakespeare Survey* 44 (1991): 43.

24. Geary, "The Nature of Portia's Victory: Turning to Men in *The Merchant of Venice,*" *Shakespeare Survey* 37 (1984): 55.

25. One exception to the "harmonizing habit" is offered by John Picker, "Shylock and the Struggle for Closure," *Judaism* 43:2 (1994): 174-89, who considers with insight Jessica's response to Lorenzo's "musical illusion of happiness." Picker's consideration of music, however, is general and brief, for his subject is the more general one of closure. He concludes, moreover, by bringing Jessica too close to Shylock's world-view.

26. See, for example, Newman, "Portia's Ring," 32.

Richard H. Weisberg (essay date 1999)

SOURCE: Weisberg, Richard H. "Antonio's Legalistic Cruelty: Interdisciplinarity and *The Merchant of Venice.*" In *Un-Disciplining Literature: Literature, Law, and Culture,* edited by Kostas Myrsiades and Linda Myrsiades, pp. 180-89. New York: Peter Lang, 1999.

[*In the following essay, Weisberg appraises the legalistic elements of* The Merchant of Venice, *and finds "non-ironic" interpretations of the play's opposition between Christian mercy and rigid Judaic law to be reductive and misleading.*]

Introduction

The law and literature movement now involves hundreds of scholars across the disciplines.[1] Among the movement's contributions to scholarship and teaching in literature has been its attention to several well-worked "legalistic" stories. Particular success has been achieved in the debates about Melville's *Billy Budd, Sailor,* where an established critical perspective on Captain Vere has been challenged by recourse to legal materials and closer readings of the story's legalistic passages.[2]

In recent years, a similar methodology has been applied to *The Merchant of Venice.*[3] Abjuring the mainstream critical insistence on "non-ironic" readings of what is clearly one of Shakespeare's most complex and ironic plays, law and literature scholars have again simply noticed what the text affords in rich abundance: passages of legalistic complexity that—once engaged—reverse traditional patterns of understanding.

So, in *Poethics and Other Strategies of Law and Literature* (94-104), I endeavored to show that Act V's legalistic language—epitomized by Portia's rejection of Antonio's persistent intermeddling in her relationship with Bassanio—evokes Shylock and leaves the audience wondering at Belmont's new usages: "surety"; "deed of gift"; "inter'gatories." The Jew, with his insistence on oathkeeping, bonds, and the law, must be defeated at trial, for his verbal directness contradicts Christian linguistic maneuvering as much as his excessive legality offends their notion of "mercy"; yet he seems in the final act quite to have overpowered (on the level of language) the Christian characters and their earlier rejection of him. Portia will not tolerate yet another episode of Antonio's "suretyship" for his young friend, her new husband. She prefers, and will probably enforce on Belmont as best she can, the more directly committed system of the old Jewish moneylender, who has never been able to stomach "Christian intercessors" and their flouting of the law.

On this reading, however appropriate it is to the play's comic medium, which mandates the defeat of Shylock's bond, Portia is at trial always alert to the Jew's constancy and ethics in the domain of human relations. Although she briefly becomes a fellow traveler herself along the path of Christian distortions of law—where ostensible "mercy" quickly is debased to forms of legalized cruelty unimaginable in Jewish communities—she does so merely to solve the comedy's central problem and then to move ahead as ethically as she can toward her marriage to a typical Christian whom she happens to adore. But to do this, she must reject on the island of Belmont the nagging presence of Antonio, whose main aim is, precisely, to keep Bassanio from direct commitments to others.

Debate on many of these issues ensued in a spirited exercise of interdisciplinary wit, where the likes of Lawrence Danson and Jay Halio took on some lawyers at the Association of the Bar of the City of New York in late 1992 (*Proceedings*). And it has spilled over into a series of readings by professional actors in which a proper emphasis has been placed on the relationship of Act IV to Act V, with their legalistic origins of course in the "contract formation" scene, I,iii.[4]

Christian Legalism in the Trial Scene

What I like to call "the turn to legalism" among Christian characters in *The Merchant of Venice* begins midway through the trial scene itself. Looked at this way, the prevalent critical dichotomy between some rigid Jewish "law" and some more humane Christian "mercy" breaks down on the most obvious textual level.

Portia, perhaps fascinated by Shylock's excessive yet somehow solid insistence on his bond, is committed to undoing the moneylender's extreme application of what might otherwise be a righteous and ethical reliance on written law. But she is equally repulsed by the overly flexible oathbreaking of the Christian characters, which she sees in open court before her eyes when Bassanio and Gratiano assert their willingness to sacrifice their new wives to save the beleaguered Antonio. Like the old Jew, who remarks in a striking aside (as he is supposedly hell-bent at the time for vengeance), "These be the Christian husbands," Portia notes their willingness to compromise not only the marriage vows but tons of her own ducats, which Bassanio constantly offers the obdurate plaintiff. Later in this same Act, she will deduce that Antonio's baleful influence on Bassanio has moved the latter to give her the ring that symbolized those vows; the audience to the play will also compare that easy traducement to Shylock's ethical unwillingness to give his wife's ring away "for a wilderness of monkeys."[5] So Portia watches all these men in open court, and it cannot be that she wishes to adopt the easy oathbreaking of her spendthrift husband and his flighty circle of friends, nor that she comes to detest everything that Shylock represents in the domain of ethics and law.

Portia begins in court a process that carries her through to the Belmont of Act V: the emulation of Shylock's ethical system once—through her efforts—it has been drained of its excesses, which she perceives to be less legalistic than situational. She comes quickly to learn that Shylock's villainy consists in a Christian-imposed condition of ostracized resentment. Neither she nor any even-handed observer of the play as a whole needs find any *necessary* linkage of "legalism" to vengeance. On the contrary, she perceives the very opposite: the source of the deepest resentment and the most violent hatred derives from Christian applications to moral outsiders of a superficial and self-serving "mercy." Although personally unaware of Antonio's cruelty to Shylock on the Rialto, Portia will have sufficiently good reason to associate with the merchant this degradation of Christian love. Once the trial and its immediate aftermath reveal his threat to her values, she moves as graciously as possible to remove Antonio from her husband's circle. But this must await the "happy resolution" of Shylock's vengeful lawsuit.

It is clear to most analysts that Portia follows Shylock's legalistic method in open court, where she reads his bond so narrowly, so literally, that it cannot be enforced on its terms. Then, reveling perhaps in her mastery of a complex situation irresolvable by men, she hauls out a statute and continues, with an excess of zeal that parallels Shylock's in a way, to defeat his cause. This "Alien Statute" gives the state the right to take the Jew's life and half his property—but the Duke instantly forgives the former and virtually returns to Shylock all but a small "fine" for the latter. Touched perhaps by the state's graciousness, she turns to the merchant, who is entitled to the other half. Portia explicitly begs Antonio to make the theoretical Christian move beyond law for which she is better known to audiences than for her contractual legalisms. She asks him to undo the legalistic persecution of the Alien Statute by reducing its effect on his enemy: "What mercy can you render him, Antonio?" (IV. i. 394)

It is here that Antonio, ostensibly the model of Christian courtesy and otherwise the voice of what I have called Christian "mediation" (*Poethics*) throughout the play, might be fully expected to outdo the Duke's generosity.

Instead, Antonio proceeds to fail every test of moderation, mercy, and forgiveness that Portia has imposed upon him. (She was not, of course, privy to his earlier similar failure in rejecting Shylock's offer of friendship in I. iii.) She fathoms what happens when Christian intercessors are given sway over earthly law. She hears, feelingly, the following amazing cruelties, which—in the absence of legal understanding—critics have taken as signs of Christian generosity:

> So please my lord the Duke and all the court
> To quit the fine for one half of his goods,
> I am content, so he will let me have
> The other half in use, to render it
> Upon his death unto the gentleman
> That lately stole his daughter,
> Two things provided more: that for this favor
> He presently become a Christian;
> The other, that he do record a gift,
> Here in the court, of all he dies possessed
> Unto his son Lorenzo and his daughter.
>
> (IV. i. 396-406)

The chief hurdle to understanding this bizarre show of "mercy" is its opening two and one-half lines, which are "precatory"—they mean nothing at all to the law. Antonio merely reiterates the Duke's disposition of the half of Shylock's goods that are to go *to the state*! Antonio has no power over, nor any interest in, that half. Thus *he is in fact forgiving the "fine" that only the state has a right to get*. So Antonio begins his speech by winning the hearts of his listeners through a gracious disposition of that which he does not own.

The legally irrelevant opening rhetorical gambit might be understandable in one untrained in the law. But Antonio turns out to be no *ingenu*: his false generosity is but the preface to a highly legalistic maneuver that will totally destroy Shylock. Furthermore, the first two and one-half lines deliberately evoke earlier examples of Christian rhetoric masking self-interest, greed and theft. To take three such cases only: in Act I, Bassanio succeeds in getting Antonio's support for the loan of 3000 ducats not by using direct speech, such as "Lend me this; I'll pretty myself up, head over to Belmont, win the hand of the rich heiress and return to you not only this loan but the previous ones I have welched on." Instead, he uses the graceful image of the bow and arrow, a lovely figure that couches in ethereal language what is in fact a grimy purpose. In the same act, Shylock's usury is seen as evil, but the plundering of colonials engaged in by Antonio's ventures is masked by the romantic imagery of "ships at sea." As

Judith Koffler has masterfully shown in a leading law and literature piece on the play, the Christian contribution is one of elevated rhetoric, not improved human relations (116-34). And, finally, Lorenzo spirits away Jessica and much of Shylock's wealth, robing with some of the play's loveliest lines the breach of at least two Commandments.

So Antonio uses the opening moment of his response to Portia to do what he—and the Christians generally—are best at: rhetorical but not actual generosity. (Shylock's method, unfortunately for him, is that of the comedic villain but not always the earthly wrongdoer: he speaks what is on his mind, often in a more literal language than would please the Christians.) He merely mimics Bassanio, who throughout this same scene has managed to hide through rhetorical flourishes that the ducats he constantly offers Shylock are, of course, Portia's (and her avoiding the loss of this wealth goes a long way to explain why she instead brings Shylock down). How sweet of Antonio to forgive even the meager "fine" that the Duke fashioned for Venice ("Ay for the state," says Portia, "not for Antonio") as a way of reducing Shylock's penalty in the face of an already humiliating and procedurally questionable reversal of fortune. Generations of critics, if not necessarily the play's audiences, have been hoodwinked by the opening rhetorical move. The rest of the speech, replete with legalistic exactitude, usually goes unexamined.

Let us pay Shakespeare the compliment of understanding the substance of his merchant's "mercy" to Shylock. Antonio fleshes out the Alien Statute—and I've chosen my verb carefully—as follows:

1. Shylock must place half of his *present* wealth into a trust, with Lorenzo and Jessica receiving the principal at Shylock's death;

2. Shylock must convert to Christianity;

3. Shylock must pledge to will *all of his after-acquired* wealth to Lorenzo and Jessica.

To make this Draconian "mercy" more comprehensible—and putting aside for the moment Shylock's forced conversion—we'll assume that Shylock currently is worth 1,000,000 ducats. Recall that, under the Alien Statute, half of that was to go to the state, but that the Duke reduced the penalty to a fine of undetermined amount. We can assume further, then, that Shylock has been permitted by the state to keep 400,000 ducats and required by Venice to pay 100,000 as his fine.

Compared to that scenario, as we shall see, Antonio's disposition of Shylock's present wealth is by no means generous.

The "Shylock Trust"

The merchant, apparently knowledgeable in the intricacies of property law, seizes the half of the moneylender's present wealth under his dominion and places it in "use"—the Elizabethan and indeed the present synonym for a "trust." We will call this the "*Shylock Trust*." Shylock's wealth provides the *res,* or subject matter of the Trust (namely 500,000 ducats). Antonio will be the administrator of the trust (the "trustee"). Under his direction alone, subject only to a use of the wealth that will be deemed responsible by some eventual court of equity, the 500,000 ducats will be invested, and they will provide both income and preservation or growth of the principal itself. The Trust provides for two categories of "beneficiaries," the income beneficiary and the remaindermen, that is, those who will get the principal upon the death of Shylock.

Who gets the income from the Shylock Trust? Antonio's failure to name the income beneficiary is not fatal to the formation of the trust. In fact, he seems either to be giving Shylock the income benefit or else himself. This can be clarified later. What Antonio makes clear is that he is vesting the remainder interest, i.e., the right to take the principal upon Shylock's death, in Lorenzo and Jessica.

So—since this is the fairer reading of his words—if we assume that Antonio is keeping the income interest for himself, the Shylock Trust would be enforceable as follows:

1. 500,000 ducats, yielding approximately 5% a year, provides an annual income of some 25,000 ducats to Antonio for as long as Shylock lives. Antonio would thus be the income beneficiary *pur autre vie* (bad lawfrench for "for the life of another," i.e., for as long as Shylock lives).

2. Meanwhile, through careful investment, the 500,000 ducat principal is preserved. At Shylock's death, Jessica and Lorenzo get these monies. The Shylock Trust is terminated.

The "Shylock Will"

Antonio goes much further, however. Exceeding the terms of the Alien Statute, he insists that even Shylock's after-acquired wealth be subject to his command. Recall that Shylock, although elderly, is still active and successful on the Rialto. He may be stripped of 60% of his present wealth, but he may well go on to earn millions more. Furthermore, he may receive gifts from others or in some different manner acquire new property. The Alien Statute gives neither the state nor Antonio the right to control these future earnings or possessions. Antonio, drunk with legalistic power, grabs them anyway, imposing the following scheme: Shylock must pledge immediately that he will bequeath to Jessica and Lorenzo all of his after-acquired wealth. Of course, this permits him to continue to earn and to live from those earnings. (If he finally gets himself good legal counsel, which he now knows he should have done before going into court, Shylock may also be able to plan his estate so that there's nothing left when he dies. Or he may covertly amend his will, which lawfully may be done until the moment of his death, to leave his wealth to someone who has truly loved him.) On the other hand, if really forced to convert to Christianity, he may not be able to pursue his work as a moneylender. In any event, what is left in Shylock's estate at his death must presently be pledged to Lorenzo and Jessica.

Few late-twentieth-century audiences applaud Antonio's insistence upon Shylock's conversion to Christianity. Once heeded and understood, these property arrangements seem almost as odious. Shylock, whose acuity with language surpasses most of the Christian characters—but who errs, as we have seen, by refusing to adjust his own direct speech to their hypocritical patterns—knows that "You take my life / When you take the means whereby I live." Although the conversion must strike him as disgusting, its enforced effect plays equally upon his profession. Antonio, of course, also understands that Christians do not take money for interest; they leave this to the Jews, having monopolized other and more covert forms of plunder. Shylock is left only with what the Duke has provided him. And he must face the additional torment of being the enforced benefactor of a young couple he has every good reason to despise.

"These be the Christian mercies."

The Comedic Circle Squared: Mercy to Legalism to Law

Yet the play remains a comedy. As I have elsewhere argued, Shylock must be brought down; his comedic villainy consists in equal parts of vengeful excess, linguistic directness, and ethical precision. Oathkeepers and direct talkers, as everyone from Shakespeare and Molière to Stoppard and Ionesco know, do not fare well in a comic arena. Nor do monomaniacs, although that term is too strong for Shylock, whose obsession about the pound of flesh commences only as his daughter elopes and is mediated even at the trial by accurate reflections upon the Christians that are as keen as his sharpened knife. Shylock must fall because ethical behavior, which can often seem compulsive to an observer, sits poorly on a religious outsider trying to exert himself lawfully in a comedic environment.

The audience to a comedy wants and deserves the defeat of such a character. Having received that in the trial scene, in Act V it expects nothing but music, poetry, and conjugal bliss. Shakespeare provides, instead, discords, arguments, and still unconsummated marriages. These peculiar elements alone make the play "ironic" despite the flawed and even transparent attempts of mainstream critics to find harmonies, dances, and resolutions.[6]

As we have seen, the disharmonies of Act V conjoin with a strange move, led by Portia, to the language of law otherwise embodied in the play largely by the comedic villain himself. It is as though her dealings with the Christians during the trial have left her at least as exasperated with their cruelties as with the single excess she disguised herself to remedy. Now speaking in her own voice, she adopts for Belmont neither the "mercy" of her own most famous speech nor the legalisms of her (and Antonio's) victory over Shylock. Instead, she leads her world of Venice to *law*—to an insistence on the primacy of language used directly to promise and to commit one individual to another.

To do this, Portia must, of course, accomplish more than the mere imparting of legal language she has learned from Shylock. But even this is far from trivial. When the curtain virtually falls with Gratiano calling for an "inter'gatory"—formal legalized questioning under oath—as to whether he and Nerissa should finally bed down, the most extreme anti-Semitic Christian in the play has adopted Shylock's legalistic turn of phrase.

Portia must also, however, reject Antonio. There is little doubt, now that we have read carefully the trial scene and its aftermath in the giving away of the rings, that Portia sees Antonio as a direct threat to her still unconsummated relationship with Bassanio. When the merchant absurdly thrusts himself again between them, she is much too intelligent not to see the grotesque repetition of Antonio's earlier commercial mediation. She remains polite, but the following dialogue should be read as her ironic rejection of the mediated "surety" relationship that permits one party to stand in the place of another:

ANTONIO:

> I once did lend my body for his wealth,
> Which but for him that had your husband's ring
> Had quite miscarried. I dare be bound again,
> My soul upon the forfeit, that your lord
> Will never break faith advisedly.

PORTIA:

> Then you shall be his surety.

(V. i. 268-73)

A surety is, somewhat like a guarantor, a "middleman" who can be sued in the place of the actual debtor. The implications of Antonio's excessive, repetitive impulse to "stand in" for Bassanio are all too clear to Portia. She sees that the merchant's urge to mediate is as compulsive as the Jew's impulse to "stand on the law."

Which is better? For Portia, as for the thoughtful member of this play's audience, there is no easy answer. But she now feels empowered, in her own domain and voice, to try out the regime of law and to see if—stripped of an excess forced upon it by the mainstream culture—Jewish ethical modes might be less formalistic and less cruel than Christian "mercy" of the Antonio variety.

Conclusion

Law and literature crosses disciplinary borders to seek enlightenment where important sections of stories have remained mere inkblots to decades and even centuries of otherwise sentient readers. In the case of the text we have just been examining, law—as Shakespeare's precision in these matters makes clear—is meant to help identify character. We cannot emerge from Antonio's legalisms without wondering about his cruelty. If, instead, we stop reading the end of the trial scene before embracing the language of property law as it is given to us, we are likely to mistake Shylock's fidelity for intractability, Antonio's technical manipulation for graciousness, and Portia's increasing dislike of the merchant of Venice for a loving friendship or even a three-way "dance" of comedic alliance. The stakes are, at the least, the meaning and staging of Act V and, at the most, the comprehension of the play's values as attuned to those of the defeated litigant.

Notes

1. The author gratefully acknowledges the suggestions of Peter Alscher, Lawrence Danson, and Jay Halio, none of whom, however, is responsible for any of the opinions expressed in what follows.

2. See, for example, the *Symposium Issue* with articles on the story by Judith Koffler, Robin West, James Warren, Brook Thomas, Steven Mailloux, Richard Posner, Michael Hancher, and the present author, whose work on the story in the earlier *The Failure of the Word* has been discussed in Sealts 39-61 and Appendix 3: "With regard to Vere's conduct of Billy's trial and execution [our 1962 'generic text'] concluded—perhaps somewhat hastily—that Melville 'simply had not familiarized himself with [naval] statutes of the period'" (51). In a similar vein, see Milder 77-79.

3. See *Proceedings* with articles on the play by Peter Alscher, Jay Halio, Charles Spinosa, Susan Oldrieve, Clayton Koelb, Judge David B. Saxe, Marci Hamilton, and Daniel Kornstein. All these sources point to the origins of legal analysis of the play dating to the natural lawyer Von Ihering (who took Shylock's side in the late 19th century) and various English and American explanations of the *contract formation* scene (I. iii). My analysis below focuses on Antonio's disposition of Shylock's wealth in IV. i.

4. Productions influenced by lawyerly readings of the play include those of the Peter Royston Players (New York, 1992-93) and of the Hofstra Theater Department (1996).

5. The famous "ring plot" has been much discussed by critics and with recent excellence by Kahn 107-111. Kahn's view that Portia deems Antonio an unworthy rival for Bassanio's affections parallels mine here. But it is significant to me that Kahn barely touches on Shylock as a player in this plot, despite the text's obvious association of the Jew with values connecting ethical marital behavior to the ring, values everywhere betrayed by the Christians (led by Antonio) until Portia formally espouses them in Act V. Yet there, Kahn—allowing that "ironic similarities between Jew and Christian abound"—places these less in the realm of a positive morality in fact espoused by Portia than in the negative vengeance Portia displays toward her transgressing husband (110).

6. See Danson.

Works Cited

Danson, Lawrence. *The Harmonies of "The Merchant of Venice."* New Haven: Yale UP, 1978.

Kahn, Coppelia. "The Cuckoo's Note." In *Shakespeare's "Rough Magic."* Ed. Peter Erickson and Coppelia Kahn. Newark: Delaware UP, 1985.

Koffler, Judith. "Terror and Mutilation in the Golden Age." *Human Rights Quarterly* 5 (1983): 116-34.

Milder, Robert. "ARTICLE?" *American Literary Scholarship* (1982): 77-79.

"Proceedings of the Association of the Bar of the City of New York." *Cardozo Studies in Law and Literature* 5.1 (1993).

Sealts, Merton. *Beyond the Classroom: Essays on American Authors.* Columbia: U of Missouri P, 1996.

"Symposium Issue." *Cardozo Studies in Law and Literature* 1.1 (1989).

Weisberg, Richard H. *Poethics and Other Strategies of Law and Literature.* New York: Columbia UP, 1992.

———. *The Failure of the Word.* New Haven: Yale UP, 1984.

FURTHER READING

Criticism

Beiner, G. "The Merchant of Venice." In *Shakespeare's Agonistic Comedy: Poetics, Analysis, Criticism,* pp. 168-202. Cranbury, N.J.: Associated University Presses, 1993.
Evaluates *The Merchant of Venice* as an agonistic (or "punitive") comedy, with critical attention principally focused on the bond between Shylock and Antonio, Antonio's apparent defeat, the reversal of fortunes, and Shylock's punishment.

Berkowitz, Joel. "'A True Jewish Jew': Three Yiddish Shylocks." *Theatre Survey* 37, no. 1 (May 1996): 75-98.
Documents performances and interpretations of Shylock by Yiddish-speaking actors and directors in American theater during the first half of the twentieth century.

Boehrer, Bruce. "Shylock and the Rise of the Household Pet: Thinking Social Exclusion in *The Merchant of Venice.*" *Shakespeare Quarterly* 50, no. 2 (summer 1999): 152-70.

Traces parallels between Jessica's status in the society of *The Merchant of Venice* and that of pets (specifically dogs) in Elizabethan England.

Booth, Roy. "Shylock's Sober House." *Review of English Studies* 50, no. 197 (February 1999): 22-31.

Observes the symbolic function of Shylock's (i.e. a Jew's) house in *The Merchant of Venice* with a view to early modern English texts on the subject.

Chaudhuri, Sukanta. "Shakespeare and the Ethnic Question." In *Shakespeare and Cultural Traditions,* edited by Tetsuo Kishi, Roger Pringle, and Stanley Wells, pp. 174-87. Cranbury, N.J.: Associated University Presses, 1994.

Examines the anti-Semitic discourse of *The Merchant of Venice.*

Fischer-Lichte, Erika. "Theatre as Festive Play: Max Reinhardt's Production of *The Merchant of Venice.*" In *Venetian Views, Venetian Blinds: English Fantasies of Venice,* edited by Manfred Pfister and Barbara Schaff, pp. 169-80. Amsterdam: Rodopi, 1999.

Discusses Reinhardt's radical 1905 production of *The Merchant of Venice* at the Deutsches Theater in Berlin, in which he centered the setting of the play, rather than the characters, as the focus of the drama.

Gaudet, Paul. "'A Little Night Music': Intertextuality and Status in the Nocturnal Exchange of Jessica and Lorenzo." *Essays in Theatre* 13, no. 1 (November 1994): 3-14.

Probes allusions to classical romantic tragedies (stories such as those of Troilus and Cressida, Aeneas and Dido, and Jason and Medea) in the ostensibly comic interlude between Jessica and Lorenzo at the beginning of the final scene of *The Merchant of Venice.*

Geary, Keith. "The Nature of Portia's Victory: Turning to Men in *The Merchant of Venice.*" *Shakespeare Survey* 37 (1984): 55-68.

Investigates Portia's role in *The Merchant of Venice*—particularly while she is disguised as a man in the latter portions of the drama—in the context of the play's theme of love versus friendship.

Gross, John. *Shylock: A Legend and Its Legacy.* New York: Simon & Schuster, 1992, 386 p.

In-depth study of the origins of Shakespeare's Shylock and interpretations of the character on British and American stages from the early seventeenth century to the end of the twentieth.

Hassel, R. Chris, Jr. "'I Stand for Sacrifice': Frustrated Communion in *The Merchant of Venice.*" In *Faith and Folly in Shakespeare's Romantic Comedies,* pp. 176-207. Athens: University of Georgia Press, 1980.

Investigates elusive and ironic references to the religious holiday of Shrovetide and doctrinal controversies related to Christian Communion in *The Merchant of Venice.*

Holmer, Joan Ozark. *The Merchant of Venice: Choice, Hazard and Consequence.* London: Macmillan, 1995, 369 p.

Book-length examination of *The Merchant of Venice* that examines the play's aesthetic, religious, and economic contexts, and includes an extensive textual analysis.

Japtok, Martin and Winfried Schleiner. "Genetics and 'Race' in *The Merchant of Venice.*" *Literature and Medicine* 18, no. 2 (fall 1999): 155-72.

Appraises the ethnic categories of Jew and Moor in *The Merchant of Venice,* while acknowledging the anachronism of applying such terms as race and genetics to a Shakespearean text.

Jensen, Hal. Review of *The Merchant of Venice. Times Literary Supplement,* no. 5022 (2 July 1999): 20.

Reviews the 1999 Royal National Theatre production of *The Merchant of Venice,* observing that director Trevor Nunn's bleak interpretation illuminated the nuances of Shakespeare's characters, but obliterated the light-hearted qualities of the play.

Katz, David S. "Shylock's Gender: Jewish Male Menstruation in Early Modern England." *Review of English Studies* 50, no. 200 (November 1999): 440-62.

Concentrates on Shylock's character in light of the medieval and early modern myth that Jewish men menstruated.

Patterson, Steve. "The Bankruptcy of Homoerotic Amity in Shakespeare's *The Merchant of Venice.*" *Shakespeare Quarterly* 50, no. 1 (spring 1999): 9-32.

Reads Antonio as "a prototype of the lovesick homosexual."

Simon, John. Review of *The Merchant of Venice. New York* 33, no. 6 (14 February 2000): 141.

Comments on director Trevor Nunn's "problematic" updates to *The Merchant of Venice* for his National Theatre production.

Sokol, B. J. "Constitutive Signifiers or Fetishes in Shakespeare's *The Merchant of Venice*?" *International Journal of Psycho-Analysis* 76, no. 2 (1995): 373-87.

Psychoanalytic discussion of *The Merchant of Venice* that explains character anxieties in terms of post-Freudian object obsession.

Spinosa, Charles. "The Transformation of Intentionality: Debt and Contract in *The Merchant of Venice.*" *English Literary Renaissance* 24, no. 2 (spring 1994): 370-409.

Legalist-literary analysis of the trial scene in *The Merchant of Venice* that takes into account social developments related to English law courts at the beginning of the seventeenth-century.

Pericles

For further information on the critical and stage history of *Pericles,* see *SC,* Volumes 2, 15, 36, and 51.

INTRODUCTION

Pericles, likely composed in 1607 and considered Shakespeare's first romance, is a tale of loss and recovery based on "Apollonius of Tyre," an ancient legend with roots in Greek and Roman antiquity. Although *Pericles* was extremely popular during Shakespeare's time, and was often successfully re-staged and reprinted throughout the seventeenth century, it was neglected for two centuries thereafter. Long considered to be one of Shakespeare's least satisfying plays, critics have cited its flawed text, controversy over the play's authorship, lifeless characters, and shapeless plot as reasons for its marginalization. Recently, however, *Pericles* has enjoyed a revival in scholarly interest. Twentieth-century commentators continue to explore the play's questionable authorship, characterization, and major themes. *Pericles* also has experienced a revival on the stage, as productions of the play have had much success in the twentieth century.

Questions regarding the play's authorship continue to interest critics. Some scholars maintain that parts of *Pericles* are so flawed that they could not have been composed by Shakespeare. Proponents of this theory maintain that Shakespeare collaborated with another author, who wrote the somewhat inferior first two acts of the play. Other critics, such as James O. Wood (1977), contend that the play was written entirely by Shakespeare. Wood uses the theme of flattery as it appears in the second act of *Pericles* to support an argument for Shakespeare as the play's sole author, and as the basis for his assertion that the surviving text is an amalgam of an early draft by Shakespeare and his later revisions.

The character of Pericles as well as the other major characters in the play have also continued to attract the attention of modern scholars. John P. Cutts (1969) examines the character of Pericles, and suggests that the outer disharmony Pericles encounters reflects the inner disharmony of his own character. Annette C. Flower (1975) studies the disguises of the three main characters—Pericles, Marina, and Thaisa—and explores how the relationship between disguise and identity in *Pericles* reveals and defines character. Stephen J. Lynch (1993) focuses on Gower, who functions as the play's chorus, or narrator. Lynch argues that Gower serves as a "surrogate author" of the play, claiming that Shakespeare's use of Gower "involves a double strategy: a confession of authorial limitations matched with a claim to authorial elevation and mystification."

Just as scholarly interpretations of *Pericles* have proliferated, the twentieth century has seen a revival in productions of the play. J. Thomas Rimer (see Further Reading) studies Japanese productions of *Pericles,* showing how similar the traditional Japanese Noh and Kabuki forms are to the narrative and dramatic strategies represented in *Pericles.* Doreen Delvecchio and Antony Hammond (1998) trace the production history of the play from the seventeenth through the twentieth century. The critics remark on the opportunities the play offers for theatrical spectacle and musical embellishment, but find that a minimalist approach works equally well.

While some scholars still view *Pericles* as a dramatic failure, others, like T. S. Eliot, who called it a "very great play," have achieved a new, more positive understanding of the work. In his 1955 essay, Derek Traversi argues that *Pericles* is a complex transitional work, bridging the gap between the tragedies and the last bittersweet plays of loss, miracle, and restoration. Likewise, Harold Bloom (1988) maintains that the play represents Shakespeare's first attempt to fashion a play that was neither a comedy nor a tragedy, but could incorporate elements of both. Paul Dean (see Further Reading) argues that *Pericles* derives its unity from being a pilgrimage tale, echoing Biblical antecedents like *The Book of Jonah* and medieval models like Chaucer's *Canterbury Tales.* Critics argue, moreover, that *Pericles* is a play with universal themes. David Solway (1997) sees it as a "voyage through time to an atemporal destination," whose theme is the "universal dream of retrieval and atonement."

OVERVIEWS AND GENERAL STUDIES

Harold Bloom (essay date 1998)

SOURCE: Bloom, Harold. "*Pericles.*" In *Shakespeare: The Invention of the Human,* pp. 603-13. New York: Riverhead Books, 1998.

[*In the following essay, Bloom presents an overview of* Pericles, *concentrating on the last three acts.*]

Shakespeare was occupied with *Pericles* in the winter of 1607-8, though scholars are not able to define the precise nature of that occupation. The first two acts of the play are dreadfully expressed, and cannot have been Shakespeare's, no matter how garbled in transmission. We have only a very bad quarto, but the inadequacy of so much of the text is probably not the reason why *Pericles* was excluded from the First Folio. Ben Jonson had a hand in editing the First Folio, and he had denounced *Pericles* as "a mouldy tale." Presumably Jonson and Shakespeare's colleagues also knew that one George Wilkins was the primary author of the first two acts of the play. Wilkins was a lowlife hack, possibly a Shakespearean hanger-on, and Shakespeare may have outlined Acts I and II to Wilkins and told him to do the writing. Even by the standards of Shakespeare's London, Wilkins was an unsavory fellow—a whoremonger, in fact, a very relevant occupation for a coauthor of *Pericles,* though the superb brothel scenes are Shakespeare's work.

Pericles is not only uneven (and mutilated) but very peculiar in genre. It features choral recitations by a presenter, the medieval poet John Gower, who is atrocious in the first two acts but improves markedly thereafter. The play resorts to frequent dumb show, in the manner of *The Murder of Gonzago,* revised by Hamlet into *The Mousetrap.* Most oddly, it has only a sporadic continuity: we are given episodes from the lives of Pericles, his wife Thaisa, and their daughter Marina. The episodes do not necessarily generate one another, as they would in history, tragedy, and comedy, but Shakespeare had exhausted all of those modes. After *Antony and Cleopatra,* we have seen the retreat from inwardness in *Coriolanus* and in *Timon of Athens.*

It would be absurd to ask, What sort of personality does Shakespeare's Pericles possess? Libraries have been written on the personality of Hamlet, but Pericles has none whatsoever. Even Marina has every virtue but no personality: there cannot be that individual a pathos in the emblematic world of *Pericles, Prince of Tyre.* Shakespeare was not in flight from the human, but he had turned to representing something other than the shared reality of Falstaff and Rosalind, Hamlet and Cleopatra, Shylock and Iago. Pericles and Marina are a universal father and daughter; his only importance is that he is her father, who loses her and then receives her back again, and she matters only as a daughter, who suffers separation from her father, and then is restored to him. I am not suggesting that they are archetypes or symbols, but only that their relationship is all that interests Shakespeare. Lear is everything and nothing in himself, and Cordelia, in much briefer compass, also contains multitudes. Pericles is just real enough to suffer trauma, and Marina is strong enough to resist being debauched, but both scarcely exist as will, cognition, desire. They are not even passive beings. In that sense alone, the jealous Ben Jonson was right: Pericles and Marina are figures in a moldy tale, an old story always being retold.

Both performances of *Pericles* that I have attended, some thirty years apart, were student productions, and both confirmed what many critics long have maintained: even the first two acts are quite playable. Except for the astonishing recognition scene between Pericles and Marina in Act V, and the two grotesquely hilarious brothel scenes in Act IV, very little in the play can be judged dramatic, and yet performance somehow transfigures even the ineptitudes of George Wilkins. This puzzles me, because bad direction and bad acting have converted me to Charles Lamb's party: it is, alas, better, especially now, to read Shakespeare than to see him travestied and deformed. *Pericles* is the exception; it is the only play in Shakespeare I would rather attend again than reread, and not just because the text has been so marred by transmission. Perhaps because he declined to compose the first two acts, Shakespeare compensated by making the remaining three acts into his most radical theatrical experiment since the mature *Hamlet* of 1600-1601. *Pericles* consistently is strange, but it has nothing as startling as the gap in representation that Shakespeare cuts into *Hamlet* from Act II, Scene ii, through Act III, Scene ii. But then *what* is being represented in the last three acts of *Pericles*?

Gower, speaking the Epilogue, tells us that Pericles, Thaisa, and Marina are "Led on by heaven, and crown'd with joy at last," so that the play represents the triumph of virtue over fortune, thanks to the intercession of "the gods," which must mean Diana in particular. Shakespeare, in his final phase, frequently seems a rather belated acolyte of Diana. No dramatist, though, would have understood better than Shakespeare how impossible it is to bring off a staged representation of triumphant chastity, virginal or married. Shakespeare's poem *The Phoenix and the Turtle* is exactly relevant on this subject:

> Love hath reason, reason none,
> If what parts, can so remain.

Whether the heart's reasons can be staged was always Shakespeare's challenge, and kept his art a changing one. How to represent the mystery of married chastity—"If what parts, can so remain"—remained a perplexity to the end. Shakespeare's Gower and *Pericles* so remove us from our world (except for the whorehouse scenes!) that the play indeed answers the Bawd's rhetorical question: "What have we to do with Diana?" (IV.ii.148).

Essentially, there are only two deities in *Pericles,* Neptune and Diana, and Diana wins. What are we to make of that victory? Neptune has oppressed Pericles, almost in the pattern of Poseidon's operations against Odysseus. Northrop Frye, noting the processional form of *Pericles,* remarks that the play's manner of presenting its action makes it one of the world's earliest operas, and then compares it to Eliot's *The Waste Land,* and necessarily also to Eliot's "Marina." I suppose that Diana's triumph is operatic enough, as is Marina's victory over both the staff and the clientele of the brothel. Frye's reading of the play, rather like Wilson Knight's more baroque interpretation, seems to me a little remote from *Pericles*'s curious and deliberate emptiness, akin to much of *The Waste Land* and Eliot's "Marina."

Such an emptying-out of Shakespeare's characteristic richness is a *kenosis* of sorts; the most sophisticated of all poet-playwrights surrenders his greatest powers and originalities—God becoming man, as it were. Frye calls *Pericles* "psychologically primitive," but this is true only in the sense of Shakespeare's knowing abnegation of inwardness, not in asking the audience for a primitive response. Our participation is not uncritical; we give up the Shakespearean lifelike, but not the Shakespearean selfsame. Gower is there to keep telling us that this is a play, but so redundant a message takes us back from Pericles and Marina not to "mouldy tales" and the authority of the archetypal, but to Shakespeare himself. The audience does not attend without the foregrounding of knowledge as to who the playwright is, and how different *Pericles* is from the more than thirty plays preceding it. Nor can anyone now read *Pericles* without the awareness that the creator of Hamlet, Falstaff, and Cleopatra is giving us a protagonist who is merely a cipher, a name upon the page. Wonder is always where one starts and ends with Shakespeare, and Shakespeare himself, as poet-playwright, is the largest provocation to wonder in *Pericles*. One suspects that the scenario for the play originated with Shakespeare, but that he had some distaste for what was to go into the first two acts and casually assigned them to a crony, Wilkins.

Pericles begins at Antioch, where its founder and ruler, Antiochus the Great, gleefully piles up the heads of suitors for his unnamed daughter, executing them for not solving a riddle whose solution would reveal his ongoing incest with her. Getting the riddle right, Pericles of Tyre flees for his life. After making a voyage to Tharsus, to relieve starvation there, the colorless hero suffers his first shipwreck, and then finds himself ashore at Pentapolis, where he marries Thaisa, daughter of the local king. All this out of the way, Shakespeare himself takes over to start Act III. Pericles and Thaisa, who is about to deliver their infant daughter Marina, are voyaging back to Tyre; Neptune acts up, and we rejoice to hear Shakespeare's great voice as Pericles invokes the gods against the storm:

> The god of this great vast, rebuke these surges,
> Which wash both heaven and hell; and thou that hast
> Upon the winds command, bind them in brass,
> Having call'd them from the deep! O, still
> Thy deaf'ning, dreadful thunders; gently quench
> Thy nimble sulphurous flashes!
>
> [III.i.1-6]

That is Herman Melville's Shakespeare, though Ahab, if he spoke these lines, would convert them to defiance. Pericles is no Ahab, and endures the apparent death of Thaisa in giving birth to Marina. He then yields to the sailors' superstition that a corpse on board will sink the ship, meaning that his wife's coffin must go overboard. The farewell of Pericles to his bride also found its way to Melville's imagination.

> A terrible childbed hast thou had, my dear;
> No light, no fire: th'unfriendly elements
> Forgot thee utterly; nor have I time
> To give thee hallow'd to thy grave, but straight
> Must cast thee, scarcely coffin'd, in the ooze;
> Where, for a monument upon thy bones,
> And e'er-remaining lamps, the belching whale
> And humming water must o'erwhelm thy corpse,
> Lying with simple shells.
>
> [III.i.56-64]

Resolute to forfeit mimetic realism, Shakespeare never lets us know whether Thaisa is dead indeed. When, in the next scene, the lady is either revived or resurrected by Cerimon of Ephesus, where her coffin apparently has landed, she comes awake with the outcry "O dear Diana," thus invoking the particular goddess of the Ephesians. In the next scene, at Tharsus, commending the infant Marina's care and upbringing to the governor, Cleon, and his wife, Dionyza (whom Pericles had rescued from famine), the Prince of Tyre vows "by bright Diana" to remain unshorn until Marina be married. Subsequently, the restored Thaisa goes off to abide at the temple of Diana in Ephesus as the goddess's high priestess. The play's final reconciliations will conclude there, and I think it important to observe that Shakespeare avoids the patterns of Christian miracle plays in thus exalting Diana of the Ephesians. It is as though St. Paul never came to Ephesus: the divinity that haunts Shakespeare's late romances is located by him outside the Christian tradition. Shakespeare, in his dying, may have returned to his father's Catholicism, but like Wallace Steven's reputed deathbed conversion, this would have been another instance of the imaginative achievement going one way and the personal life quite another.

When I think of *Pericles,* I remember first not the final scene in Diana's temple, where Thaisa is reunited with Pericles and Marina, but the two superbly vivid episodes of Marina's defiance in the brothel, and then the sublime recognition scene between Marina and Pericles on board ship at the onset of Act V. If the remainder of *Pericles* were worthy of these great confrontations, then the play would stand with the strongest of Shakespeare's, which, alas, it does not. Act IV, at its best and worst, reads like a Jacobean *Perils of Pauline,* with Marina always on the verge of being either murdered or raped. For the crime of outshining their natural daughter, Marina's guardians arrange for Marina to be slaughtered by the seaside. In the nick, pirates arrive and rescue her, but only to sell Marina to a brothel in Mytilene. The great Flaubert, in his final days, is reported to have been considering for his next novel the ideal setting "a whorehouse in the provinces." Returning to the spirit of the wonderfully rancid *Measure for Measure,* Shakespeare surpasses all possible rivals in the gusto with which he portrays the oldest profession:

PAND.

> Boult!

BOULT.

> Sir?

PAND.

> Search the market narrowly; Mytilene is full of gallants. We lost too much money this mart by being too wenchless.

BAWD.

> We were never so much out of creatures. We have but poor three, and they can do no more than they can do; and they with continual action are even as good as rotten.

PAND.

> Therefore let's have fresh ones, whate'er we pay for them. If there be not a conscience to be us'd in every trade, we shall never prosper.

BAWD.

> Thou say'st true; 'tis not our bringing up of poor bastards, as I think I have brought up some eleven—

BOULT.

> Ay, to eleven; and brought them down again. But shall I search the market?

BAWD.

> What else, man? The stuff we have, a strong wind will blow it to pieces, they are so pitifully sodden.

PAND.

> Thou sayest true; there's two unwholesome, a' conscience. The poor Transylvanian is dead, that lay with the little baggage.

BOULT.

> Ay, she quickly pooped him; she made him roast-meat for worms. But I'll go search the market.
>
> [IV.ii.1-23]

Only in the brothel scenes does Shakespeare's mimetic art return, wonderfully refreshing in the stiff world of *Pericles*. Pandar, Bawd, and Boult have personalities; Pericles, Marina, and Thaisa do not. Before the formidable, indeed divine (being Diana-like) virtue of Marina, these splendid disreputables must yield, while inaugurating a mode of irony frequently imitated since. Pandar presages the stance of Peachum and Lockit in Gay's *The Beggar's Opera*: "If there be not a conscience to be us'd in every trade, we shall never prosper." The wind of mortality blows upon overworked whores and their Transylvanian client, and upon Shakespeare also (by some accounts). Anticipating a high market—a wealthy prospective client—for Marina, the Bawd makes the most poetic remark of the play: "I know he will come in our shadow, to scatter his crowns in the sun." But they do not know that Marina is in fact their nemesis. Men march out of the brothel asking one another, "Shall's go hear the vestals sing?," and soon enough the three worthies are in the position of the unhappy kidnappers in O. Henry's "The Ransom of Red Chief":

PAND.

> Well, I had rather than twice the worth of her she had ne'er come here.

BAWD.

> Fie, fie upon her! she's able to freeze the god Priapus, and undo a whole generation. We must either get her ravish'd or be rid of her. When she should do for clients her fitment and do me the kindness of our profession, she has me her quirks, her reasons, her master-reasons, her prayers, her knees; that she would make a puritan of the devil, if he would cheapen a kiss of her.

BOULT.

> Faith, I must ravish her, or she'll disfurnish us of all our cavalleria, and make our swearers priests.
>
> [IV.vi.1-12]

They are already defeated, and they know it; their comic despair exceeds their bravado, and neither they nor we believe that Boult will ever ravish her. The governor of Mytilene, Lysimachus, arrives, intending to be the designated taker of Marina's maidenhead, and departs in love with her, and in revulsion at his own purpose. Boult next falls before her, and goes forth to advertise to Mytilene that Marina will teach singing, weaving, sewing, and dancing, after she is lodged "amongst honest women," as soon she is. Clearly we have to regard Marina's chastity as being mystical or occult; it cannot be violated, because Diana protects her own. Marina, after her family's reunion, can be married to Lysimachus, both because he now knows that her social rank is at least as high as his own, and also because Diana (in *Pericles*) accepts married chastity as an alternative for her votaress. The comedy in the brothel scenes is among Shakespeare's most advanced; only the irony of Marina's invulnerable status maintains the dramatic structure's coherence, since we observe three sensible sexual pragmatists confronted by a magical maiden whom they cannot suborn, that being well beyond their power. They discover that indeed they have to do with Diana (to answer the Bawd's earlier question), who necessarily undoes them.

What remains is the summit of *Pericles,* the magnificent recognition scene between father and daughter, the one crucial event toward which the entire play has been plotted. Pericles, having been told by Cleon that Marina is dead, is in trauma. Unkempt and barely nourished, he lies on the deck of his ship, rather like Kafka's undead Hunter Gracchus on his death ship. But Gracchus is the Wandering Jew or Flying Dutchman, caught forever in cycle, and Pericles at last is on the verge of release from his passive yielding to a procession of catastrophes. Critics rather oddly compare Pericles and Marina to Antiochus the Great and his incestuous paramour, the nameless daughter, the supposed point being that Pericles and Marina evade incest. The danger is only in the critics, and not in the play, since it is Lysimachus who authorizes Marina to act as therapist for Pericles, and the reformed governor both is in love with the maiden and hardly desires to join himself to the profession of the gaudy trio of Pandar, Bawd, and Boult. It is in her mystical vocation as votaress of Diana that Marina approaches the comatose Prince of Tyre. Doubtless there is an implied contrast between incest and chaste father-daughter love, but it is too obvious for critical labor.

The 150 lines of the recognition scene (V.i.82-233) are one of the extraordinary sublimities of Shakespeare's art. From Marina's first address to her father—"Hail, sir! my lord, lend ear"—and his first traumatic response of pushing her back, through to Pericles's falling asleep to the music of the spheres, Shakespeare holds us rapt. I use that archaic phrase because of my experience as a teacher, observing the intense reaction of my students, which parallels my own. It is a lesson in delayed response that Shakespeare teaches, in this prolonged revelation of kinship. As the dialogue goes forward, it crests initially in Pericles's gathering awareness of the resemblance between his lost wife and the young woman standing before him:

> I am great with woe
> And shall deliver weeping. My dearest wife
> Was like this maid, and such a one
> My daughter might have been: my queen's square brows;
> Her stature to an inch; as wand-like straight;
> As silver-voic'd; her eyes as jewel-like
> And cas'd as richly; in pace another Juno;
> Who starves the ears she feeds, and makes them hungry
> The more she gives them speech.
>
> [V.i.105-13]

This begins by recapitulating the spirit of Marina's birth at sea, with the apparent death of Thaisa. But the accents of a man permanently in love with his wife's eyes, gait, voice break through in curiously Virgilian cadence (deliberate, I would think), and prepare us for a further tribute both to mother and to daughter:

> yet thou dost look
> Like Patience gazing on kings' graves, and smiling
> Extremity out of act.
>
> [V.i.137-39]

"Extremity" sums up all of Pericles's catastrophes; awe is a proper response to the tribute father makes to daughter, as her smile undoes the whole history of his calamities. Both here and ongoing, it is remarkable that Shakespeare never once allows Marina any affective reaction as the mutual recognition progresses. Pericles weeps as the names, first of Marina and then of Thaisa, are spoken by his daughter in her all-but-final lines in the play. But Marina remains grave, formal, and priestess-like, somberly saying, "Thaisa was my mother, who did end / The minute I began." By now we have accepted her occult status, and Pericles at least comes alive:

> O Helicanus, strike me, honour'd sir!
> Give me a gash, put me to present pain,
> Lest this great sea of joys rushing upon me
> O'erbear the shores of my mortality,
> And drown me with their sweetness. O, come hither,
> Thou that beget'st him that did thee beget;
> Thou that wast born at sea, buried at Tharsus,
> And found at sea again. O Helicanus,
> Down on thy knees! thank the holy gods as loud
> As thunder threatens us: this is Marina.
>
> [V.i.190-99]

It is as though, emerging from trauma, he requires a proof of his own fleshly mortality. His subsequent vision of Diana bids him on to Ephesus, and to a second scene of recognition, where he gratifies us by crying out to his wife, "O come, be buried / A second time within these arms." Here, at last, Marina expresses emotion, when she kneels to her mother: "My heart / Leaps to be gone into my mother's bosom." That formal kneeling somewhat qualifies her sentiment, since to kneel is not quite to leap into one's mother's arms. Still, Shakespeare has exhausted himself, and us, with the epiphany of Marina to Pericles, and wisely the play subsides with the announcement that Marina will marry Lysimachus, and the two will reign in Tyre. Pericles, after destroying Cleon and his wicked wife Dionyza, will take up royal rule in Pentapolis, where Thaisa's father has conveniently died. Gower comes on to wish us "New joy wait on you," and this inauguration of Shakespeare's late romances has reached conclusion. As M. C. Bradbrook observed, *Pericles* is "half spectacle and half vision." That is a very problematical formula, and Shakespeare took a high risk with this play. But what remained for him to accomplish? He had revived European tragedy, and vastly perfected comedy and dramatic chronicle. What remained was vision, tempered by the necessities of stage presentation. He went well beyond *Pericles* in the romances that followed it, but this play was the school where he learned his final art.

CHARACTER STUDIES

John P. Cutts (essay date 1969)

SOURCE: Cutts, John P. "Pericles' 'Downright Violence.'" *Shakespeare Studies* 4 (1969): 275-93.

[*In the following essay, Cutts argues that the outer disharmony Pericles encounters reflects the inner disharmony of his own character.*]

F. D. Hoeniger, in the introduction to his edition[1] of *Pericles*, asserts that G. Wilson Knight[2] is wrong in his argument that Pericles is somehow infected by the evil of Antiochus' daughter whom he tried to woo, and that Kenneth Muir's[3] suggestion that Thaisa upon suddenly marrying Pericles broke a vow to Diana is equally misleading, and that to seek for a moral cause of Pericles' troubles is to assume the role of Job's comforters. On the contrary I think that to take Hoeniger's own position that Pericles is the plaything of Fortune and the gods, that he is "an impeccably good man, man without defect," is to make of Pericles an unnecessary Job. From the totality of the play's structure one must be very uncomfortable with Pericles as a Job as I hope to be able to show by modifying, elaborating upon and adding to both Wilson Knight's and Muir's arguments.

The play's opening, couched in medieval terminology, would surely have us consider "man's infirmities" (I.ch.3) to teach "frail mortality to know itself" (I.i.43) as a restorative. Any estimate of the play's total impact will certainly have to allow for the striking effect of the reincarnation of the medieval poet, but he is surely there not simply as a makeshift device for holding the play's sprawling action together, nor is he explainable by the colorful garb he wears suggestive of the quaintness of an archaic world. Gower's presence makes certain that the audience be made aware of mortality and man's infirmities. One would be hard pressed to find an exemplum in medieval drama that treated of its main figure as an "impeccably good man, a man without defect."[4]

It is too easy to suggest that Pericles *accidentally* finds himself imbroiled in the discovery of Antiochus' incest, that he was innocent of any thought of wrongdoing when he approached Antiochus' court in the first place. It was hardly naïveté which led him to believe that he would be successful where many had failed before, that he would solve the riddle, Oedipus-like, win the daughter and become "son to great Antiochus" (I.i.27). He is in such a hurry[5] to interrupt Antiochus, who is about to unfold all the dangers and difficulties, that when Antiochus merely addresses him as "Prince Pericles" Pericles rushes in with "That would be son to great Antiochus." But even if we were to allow him genuine innocence *before* he reaches Antiochus' court there can surely be no doubt of his impetuousness, his rashness, and his infatuation with moral danger once he is there. All the visible signs around him cannot be mistaken for anything but what they are, powerful indications of death on an insidious scale. Thinking "death no hazard in this enterprise" (I.i.5) he is little removed from Hamlet's "I'll speak to it, though hell itself should gape / And bid me hold my peace" because his "fate cries out," or from Faustus' "Ile conjure though I die therefore" or from Hotspur's "Albeit I make a hazard of my head" in his drunk-with-choler mood. "Thus ready for the way of life or death" (I.i.55) Pericles awaits the "sharpest blow" (I.i.56). Antiochus, like Mephistopheles with Faustus, does not equivocate on the mortal dangers inherent in Pericles' presumption. He points out the skulls of "sometimes famous princes" (I.i.35) which advise Pericles to desist "for going on death's net, whom none resist" (I.i.41). Pericles is in a House of Death and cannot but be sensitive of this fact. It is instructive, I think, to see how at the end of the play, where there are so many cross-references to Antiochus' court, Lysimachus will try to excuse his presence in a brothel house by claiming that he had not brought "[t]hither a corrupted mind" (IV.vi.103), but he protests too much his innocence for us to be convinced; "For me, be you thoughten / That I came with no ill intent: for to me / The very doors and windows savour vilely" (IV.vi.108-110). The same criterion he used in judging Marina—"Why, the house you dwell in proclaims you to be a creature of sale" (IV.vi. 76-77)—must surely be exercised against himself. The house he has stepped into proclaims him to be a creature *buying,* and the Bawd, Pander and Boult evince no surprise at his seeking such a commodity.

Pericles' own terminology in the House of Death gives him away. To greet Antiochus' daughter, presented by the father as fit for "the embracements even of Jove himself" (I.i.8), as

> See, where she comes apparell'd like the spring
> Graces her subjects, and her thoughts the king
> Of every virtue gives renown to men!
>
> (I.i.13-15)

is to mistake the House of Death for the House of Life, and to invite consideration of Jove's immoral ventures rather than chaste behavior. Strangely enough Pericles himself sums up this confrontation with Antiochus' daughter by presuming "To taste the fruit of yon celestial tree" (I.i.22), thereby putting the whole situation in the context of Eden's tree of life or tree of death. Nor is this merely random rhetoric, for Antiochus' very next words place Pericles' quest in the context of Hercules' twelfth labor:

> Before thee stands this fair Hesperides,
> With golden fruit, but dangerous to be touch'd:
> For death-like dragons here affright thee hard.
> Her face, like heaven, enticeth thee to view.
>
> (I.i.28-31)

Jacobeans would hardly miss the Biblical implications of the fruit of that forbidden tree. *Comes' Mythologiae* (1567),[6] in which the meaning of the golden apples is explained as symbols of wealth which is given to men almost as a touchstone by which to test their souls,[7]

> quare praeclare dictum est a sapientibus diuitias tanquam lapidem indicem animi cuiusquam esse datas hominibus, quae viris bonis & prudentibus facultates essent

makes the message doubly clear. Pericles is entering into very great temptations. Like Guyon in Mammon's cave confronted with "a woman gorgeous gay, / And richly clad in robes of royaltye, / That neuer earthly Prince in such aray / His glory did enhaunce, and pompous pride display,"[8] and tempted to taste of the golden apples of this Proserpina's garden and to sit in her silver stool, Pericles is tempted by the magnificence, the wealth, and the power of Antiochus' daughter, but, unlike Guyon, he commits himself and asks for the passport, staking his whole "riches" (I.i.53) on the issue of the die. His easy couplet

> For death remember'd should be like a mirror
> Who tells us life's but breath, to trust it error
>
> (I.i.46-47)

could well be interpreted as a good man's recognition that he is dust and to dust shall return. But the mirror rhetoric is picked up again only a few lines later, after the anticlimax of the riddle, and heaven's countless eyes viewing man's acts are bidden not to peep through the blanket of the dark, but to hide their fires, to cloud their sights perpetually, not just because the *revelation* of the riddle causes Pericles to consider "There's nothing serious in mortality" as a consequence of Antiochus' action, but much more significantly if ironically because the "Fair glass of light" (I.i.77), Antiochus' daughter, in which he saw mirrored forth his conquest of magnificence, wealth and power, has now been shattered. Instead of that glorious image of himself he is now forced to acknowledge that like Pandora he has opened "this glorious casket stor'd with ill" (I.i.78), the gift of all the gods to his way of thinking, and let loose in the world that which will work no peace, no rest, no comfort, until his sea voyage of life returns him a belief again in that innocence which his action in the court of Antiochus lost—his Marina, a symbol of his own personality (not just a symbol of the fruition of his marriage with Thaisa),[9] and returns him a link again with human affairs, his purpose in life, his Thaisa—a symbol of his own personality, his link not just with his marriage partner but with his hold on life.

Surely when Pericles exclaims immediately after his mention of the casket that "[his] thoughts revolt; / For he's no man on whom perfections wait / That, knowing sin within, will touch the gate" (I.i.79-81), this can hardly refer only to his post-riddle revulsion against accepting Antiochus' daughter as a bride. It is true that Antiochus' anxious answer "touch not upon thy life" (I.i.88) interprets Pericles' response to the daughter in this light, but Antiochus must keep *drawing attention* to his own boldness, must have his deeds in the limelight. Like Aaron or much more subtly Iago, he must feel that he has been so clever in flouting all conventional morality. Getting away with it is not enough: he must have praise. This, I feel certain, is the deep significance of a riddle that is no riddle. As others have pointed out, there are far more potent examples throughout the play that deserve seriously to be considered as enigmatic conundrums. Pericles face to face with Marina at the end of the play describes her in terms that deliberately contrast with Antiochus' daughter:

> Who starves the ears she feeds, and makes them hungry
> The more she gives them speech.
>
> (V.i.112-113)

His "no man on whom perfections wait / That, knowing sin within, will touch the gate" is very powerfully suggestive of his own motives in succumbing to the temptation in the first place. That he should in any way either before or after temptation think of himself as a man on whom perfections wait is open to criticism. The remarkable imagery he uses for finally describing Antiochus' daughter:

> You are a fair viol, and your sense the strings
> Who, finger'd to make man his lawful music,
> Would draw heaven down and all the gods to hearken;
> But being play'd upon before your time,
> Hell only danceth at so harsh a chime
>
> (I.i.82-86)

operates on more than one level. Of course it functions as an encomium of chastity, as Prospero similarly suggests in his talk with Ferdinand over Miranda—"but / If thou dost break her virgin-knot before / All sanctimonious ceremonies may / With full and holy rite be administer'd, / No sweet aspersions shall the heavens let fall / To make this contract grow" (V.i.14-19). But much more significantly it represents, too, Pericles' own destruction of musical harmony. Everything from now on will be discord to varying degrees until the music of Marina makes it possible for him again to hear the music of the spheres, for him again to be tuned in to the normal thoroughfare of kingly responsibilities. The play abounds with musical references and terminology. Although I consider Hoeniger's claim "Though Shakespeare was fond of music, nowhere else did he use it as often and as widely except in the great play which *Pericles* so clearly anticipates, *The Tempest*" (p.lxxix) to be a little exaggerative especially when one considers *Twelfth Night*, yet his attempt to draw attention to the emphasis on music in *Pericles* is very sound. After mastering the riddle of Antiochus' court Pericles goes on to master the riddle of Simonides.

Pericles is described by Simonides as "music's master" (II.v.30) on the basis of his "sweet music this last night" (II.v.26), his "delightful pleasing harmony" (II.v.28). Hoeniger and others are led by Simonides' remarks to suggest that "Pericles should make a brief appearance on the stage with a musical instrument, no words spoken, somewhere between the end of this scene [i.e.,II.ii] and the opening of II.v." This is being too literal, and adds quite unnecessarily to the "textual corruption" theory which editors have for so long been at pains to "prove." Simonides immediately asks Pericles what he thinks of Thaisa and states that Pericles "must be her master" (II.v.38), and she his scholar. It seems clear to me that the musical entertainment of the previous evening which had so delighted Simonides' ears was the dance in which Pericles chose Thaisa as his partner at Simonides' request. Professor Long cleverly suggested as long ago as 1956[10] that this second dance in contradistinction to the dance of the Knights "Even in [their] armours, as [they] are address'd" (II.iii.94) is a duet involving Pericles and Thaisa only, and this is, I believe, right. Hoeniger's objection that Long in making much of the absence of "Ladies" in the scene's opening stage direction in the 1609 Quarto fails to take into account that "such omission means little in a play where so many stage directions are either missing or incomplete"[11] is well taken, but the argument does not stop there. It may well be as Long suggests that Pericles, having demonstrated his skills in tilting and in the artful sword-dance, is now examined for his fitness in the art of love, the last part of his "threefold chivalric test," despite Hoeniger's claim that there is little in the play to suggest such a test in stages. Structurally such a testing could well be paralleled with other testings Pericles undergoes. But I think that what is being appealed to is the distinction between antimasque and masque. The vanquished five knights dance in their armor; they are characterized by the "loud music" (II.iii.97) of the clashing of their armor, "too harsh for ladies' heads." That Pericles *may* be included in this armor dance is conceivable, of course, though I think it very unlikely. In the first place he has always drawn attention to himself by being on one side, not of the group, and secondly, Simonides specifically calls for the knights' dance in an effort to awake Pericles from his melancholy, as if it were an entertainment *for* Pericles. Immediately after the knights' dance Simonides approaches Pericles separately to offer Thaisa as his dancing partner. It is of course, possible, as Hoeniger suggests, that this corresponds to the revels[12] part of the masque in which the "courtier-masquers, after the 'Main,' danced with chosen members of their audience," though this would be awkward since it would be relegating Thaisa to the least elevated part of the masque. Much more likely is the probability that the vanquished knights are made by Simonides to dance as a foil to the main dance of Pericles and Thaisa, an antimasque to the main. By this procedure, antimasque to main masque. Pericles is afforded great dignity. It seems to me that Simonides is fixing this procedure himself, that it is part of his shoddy treatment of the knights. Since Pericles has been successful in the tourney, there is really no need to have to apologize to the disappointed knights by cooked up excuses "That for this twelvemonth she'll not undertake / A married life" (II.v.3-4), and that "One twelve moons more she'll wear Diana's livery: / This by the eye of Cynthia hath she vow'd, / And on her virgin honour will not break it" (II.v.10-12). Ironically Thaisa will wear Diana's livery for fourteen years! Simonides is inventing an excuse for ridding himself of the other knights, but making vows to the gods as his excuse is bound to bring such repercussions. Professor Muir has suggested that Thaisa's misfortunes are brought about by Diana, the play's presiding deity, who is incensed by Thaisa's breaking of her vow. This is not strictly true, as Hoeniger points out[13] by comparing Apollo's role in *The Winter's Tale,* which is a clear case of an incensed god actively interfering in human affairs. The problem with Thaisa is best tackled from Thaisa's own motivation and from her father's. The court of Simonides has its own riddle. "[P]rinces and Knights come / from all parts of the world to joust and tourney" (II.i.107-108) for the love of the King's daughter, only to be told that she will wear Diana's livery. Thaisa and Simonides seize on Pericles: Antiochus' daughter apparently approved of Pericles:

> Of all, 'say'd yet, may'st thou prove prosperous!
> f all, 'say'd yet, I wish thee happiness
>
> (I.i.60-61)

and though it is possible to conclude that she has said this to every suitor before, it does not diminish its effectiveness on a Pericles who imagines himself different from all the other applicants. If we concentrate on the dramatic structure of Antiochus' court and Simonides' court, likened as they are by Pericles joining in the lists and tourneying for the princess, then I think it becomes obvious that they represent two sides of one coin. At Antiochus' court Pericles is the brash, dashing, impetuous, ambitious, proud knight: at Simonides' the melancholy, retired, subdued, "mean knight." The "gentler gamester is the soonest / winner" (*Henry V,* III.vi.117-118).

Pericles can take no real credit for reading Antiochus' open book. His "blind mole—poor worm" (I.i.101,103) description of himself hardly fits the facts. He would like to hide behind his need to tell the world of Antiochus' incest, to warn others of oppressors, and to hide behind his fear for his own death at the hands of the tyrant, but the mole's activity is the result largely of ambition and pride, as is clearly evidenced by Shakespeare's use of the molehill in *3 Henry VI* where both Richard Plantagenet and Henry VI find themselves on molehills largely of their own making, Richard actively tunneling in the dark and casting "copp'd hills towards heaven" (*Per.*I.i.102), daring the force of the Lord's anointed, and Henry VI much more passively but no less inexcusably allowing Margaret and Suffolk to undermine England's power at home and abroad. Pericles' ambition to become "son to great Antiochus" and to solve the world's riddle has "cast / Copp'd hills towards heaven" and he will suffer for it by a kind of spiritual death. Antiochus, in toying with him, allowing him "[f]orty days" (I.i.117) longer, emphasizes his wilderness existence. Henceforth Pericles will "shun the danger" (I.i.143) of Antiochus, will flee from the symbol of his own destruction of peace of mind. Not an hour can "breed [him] quiet" (I.ii.6). His subjects for whom he professes kingly care sense his mental anxiety—"keep your mind, till you return to us, / Peaceful and comfortable" (I.ii.36-37), and, though they are sharply rebuked by Helicanus for "flattery" because "reproof, obedient and in order, / Fits kings, as they are men, for they may err" (I.ii.43-44), Helicanus himself "knows" ("but thou know'st this" [I.ii.78]), without being told, what Pericles has gone through at Antiochus' court as Pericles well realizes, because guilt is written all over his face.

Pericles tries to turn his anger against Helicanus' boldness in speaking disrespectfully about a king, but the anger Helicanus sees in Pericles' looks does not derive from Helicanus' breach of feudal etiquette. Pericles has "ground the axe [him]self" (I.ii.58) as much as Helicanus has, but the nearest he comes to recognizing this is to suggest that Antiochus will make pretence of wrong that Pericles has done him and all must feel war's blow "for mine *if* I may call offence" (I.ii.92; italics mine). His whole speech,

Raymond O'Neill as Antiochus Lord, Nicholas Pennell as Pericles, Joan Gaskell as Antiochus Woman, Nachum Buchman as Antiochus, Judith Cockman as Antiochus Woman, and Jack Wetherall as Antiochus Lord in Act I, scene i of the 1973 Stratford Festival production of Pericles.

I.ii.79-91, prior to this half-admission is full of fears and doubts acknowledging fears for his own safety but attributing doubts to Antiochus, when in point of fact it is he himself who is full of doubts too. When he delegates the responsibilities of government to Helicanus "whose wisdom's strength can bear it" (I.ii.119) and pleads that, although in exile himself and Helicanus at the head of the state, nevertheless "in our orbs we'll live so round and safe" (I.ii.122), it is not difficult to see in this a parallel with the musical imagery which opened the play on the appearance of Antiochus' daughter—"The senate-house of planets all did sit / To knit in her their best perfections." Both are stressing harmony and order and both represent anything but that. There is a neat parallel, too, in the way Pericles' and Thaisa's *dance* is stopped by Simonides with "Unclasp, unclasp" (II.iii.106) and in the very next scene Helicanus is described as knit in harmony with the rest of the peers of Pericles' kingdom—"we'll clasp hands: / When peers thus knit, a kingdom ever stands" (II.iv. 57-58)—after he has successfully argued that they should wait a twelvemonth longer for Pericles and not force him to take their present wish to make him king and thus cause him to "leap into the seas, / Where's hourly trouble for a minute's ease" (II.iv.43-44).

For the rest of the play Pericles will be a figure of varying degrees of disorder and discord. Delegating his responsibilities to Helicanus is *not* conducive to good government, as the play very well points out when the lords of Tyre understandably pester Helicanus with their overflowing griefs and desire to know whether Pericles "lives to govern [them]" (II.iv.31).

Before Pericles once again enters the lists to tourney for a princess he is put through an instructive performance at Tharsus, which is complaining about man's infirmities and asserting that to relate tales of others' griefs hoping to learn thereby how to forget its own is like blowing at fire in hope to quench it:

> For who digs hills because they do aspire
> Throws down one mountain to cast up higher.
>
> (I.iv.5-6)

This recalls the blind mole imagery of Pericles, and there are other correspondences. Tharsus, described as having towers which bore their "heads so high they kiss'd the clouds" (I.iv.24), "men and dames so jetted and adorn'd, / Like one another's glass to trim them by" (I.iv.26-27)—examples of pride similar to Pericles'—is a clear indication that a parallel with Tyre is intended. When Pericles enters Tharsus and plays savior to it by giving it "life whom hunger starv'd half dead" (I.iv.96), his cautionary remark that his gift horse should not be construed as another Trojan horse psychologically betrays him. He has opened up one casket of mischief at Antiochus' court and is trying to make amends now by opening up a casket of good. The citizens of Tharsus help to restore his former image for him by building "his statue to make him glorious" (II.ch.14), thinking that everything he utters is gospel truth. The whole process is not so much different from Bolingbroke's wish to keep his presence "like a robe pontificial" (III.ii.56) in his purpose to "lead out many to the Holy Land" to prevent people looking "[t]oo near unto [his] state" (*2 Hen.IV.*, IV.v.212) or his son's preoccupation with religious scruples whereby he can condemn the last of the Mortimer faction, the French, and the remnants of the Eastcheap world in a hardly understood effort to show penitence, though before Agincourt's immense odds Hal does verbalize his realization that:

> More will I do;
> Though all that I can do is nothing worth.
> Since that my penitence comes after all,
> Imploring pardon.
>
> (*Henry V*, IV.ii.308-311)

For Pericles the sojourn at Tharsus must necessarily be brief. The play's use of a Dumb Show to indicate Helicanus' warning to Pericles that "in Tharsus was not best / Longer for him to make his rest" aptly suggests that no matter how hard Pericles tries to give expression to his "savior" needs the real cause of his distress will not be dumb. Thoughts of what he did at Antiochus' court mount in virulence against him, tempests toss him, and symbolically strip him naked on the shores of life like Lear and Macbeth upon the blasted heath of their own making, but unlike them refusing to acknowledge *openly* any sinning but only being sinned against. His observation that "earthly man / Is but a substance that must yield" (II.i.2-3) to the elements and that he as "fits [his] nature" (II.i.4) does obey recalls Lear's similar submission to the elements and is another example of frail mortality being made to know itself. It looks like passiveness, putting up with bad fortune because that is all man can do, but the fishermen commenting on the situation draw attention to man's dual nature, half beast, half flesh, almost in terms of Lear's recognition:

> Down from the waist they are Centaurs,
> Though women all above:
> But to the girdle do the Gods inherit,
> Beneath is all the fiend's.
>
> *(IV.vi.126-129)*

The fishermen keep such a "jangling of the bells" (II.i.41) in the belly of the rich miser of a whale that the causer of the oppression cannot possibly forget how he has behaved. Pericles is moved to comment how "[t]hese fishers tell the infirmities of men" (II.i.49), thus affording us a link with the play's opening chorus, and yet he does not realize that in praising them for exposing men's wrongdoings, for they "recollect / All that may men approve or men detect" (II.i.50-51), he is ironically commenting upon himself. He the huge whale in his "wat'ry empire" has devoured all the "poor fry before him" in his determination to prove the only survivor of the Antiochus riddle, and at one mouthful too, one rapid stroke. One may indeed search the calendar in vain for an honest man as the fisherman suggests, and the sea was certainly a drunken knave casting Pericles in their way when they are discussing what honesty is. *Lear*'s "to-and-fro-conflicting wind and rain" (III.i.11)—"the tempest in [Lear's] mind" (III.iv.12)—becomes in *Pericles* a "vast tennis-court" (II.i.60), in which the waters and the wind have made Pericles "the ball / For them to play upon" (II.i.60-61). The tennis metaphor aptly fits Pericles, who must suffer many more setbacks before he realizes there is something wrong with his tennis-playing. The tennis metaphor tends to rob its user of the dignity he is striving for. Henry V is no more successful in trying to turn the Dauphin's tennis-balls to gun-stones because he claims he will "play a set / Shall strike his father's crown into the hazard" (I.ii.262-263), when in point of fact as the play shows and as Henry VI goes on to emphasize with his revealing

> I'll leave my son my virtuous deeds behind;
> And would my father had left me no more!
>
> *(3 Henry VI, II.ii.49-50)*

things "evil got had ever bad success" (*3 Henry VI*, II.ii.46). The end result of Henry V's tennis is to strike Bolingbroke's crown into the hazard.

Pericles reborn from the sea has not yet learned that he has "suffer'd like a girl" not like a man "[e]xtremity out of act" (V.i.137;139). His determination to enter the lists for good Simonides' daughter is basically to try to convince himself that his first entering of the lists in the play was equally as honest. The savior episode at Tharsus stilled his conscience for a while: the shipwreck episode makes him think of starting afresh all over again; but the episode with the fishermen ironically comments on the situation with "what a man cannot get, he may lawfully deal for with his wife's / soul" (II.i.113-114). The fishermen obviously refer first to a man's willingness to rent out his wife to another man in order to prosper in the world. When this is seen as a reflection on Pericles one is faced with the conclusion that Pericles is out to get something unlawfully at the expense of his "wife" to be. The last words of Pericles at this juncture, "This day I'll rise, or else add ill to ill" (II.i.165), surely emphasize the ironical overtones of what the fishermen have been saying. The rusty armor which they provide for him from the seas, this "garment" which they make for him "through the rough seams of / the water" (II.i.148-149), should remind him of his common humanity, his link with the ebb and flow of human suffering, but he turns it to his proud advantage in several ways. Identifying it as the armor of his father it becomes the symbol of his discovery of an identity, a father image, his evolution from a "wat'ry grave" (II.i.10) to a new life, which will soon find its expression in his attitude toward Simonides. Disastrously he treats it as an indication that his "shipwreck now's no ill, / Since [he has] here [his] father gave in his will" (II.i.132-133), and he clothes himself in steel despite "all the rapture of the sea" (II.i.154) and once more becomes in his own mind the knight-errant "looking for adventures in the world" (II.iii.83), mounting himself upon "a courser, whose delightful steps / Shall make the gazer joy to see him tread" (II.i.157-158), which powerfully recalls the concentration on outward magnificence contrasted with inward worth which the play emphasizes throughout. When Pericles has to admit that his equipment is yet "unprovided of a pair of / bases" (II.i.159-160) and has to accept a pair from one of the fishermen who brings him to the court himself this should be another reminder of his "human infirmity," instead of which "What [he has] been [he has] forgot to know" (II.i.71), and he behaves like the rich miser driving the poor fry of the fishermen before him and at last devouring their use at a mouthful.

When next we see Pericles he is playing the "mean Knight," the psychological opposite of his role in Antiochus' court. Now everything is humility. He counts on discerning people noticing how

> Opinion's but a fool, that makes us scan
> The outward habit by the inward man
>
> *(II.ii.55-56)*

and once again attempts to show up all the other "princes and Knights come / from all parts of the world to joust and tourney" (II.i.107-108) for a princess's love, but this time by excessive modesty, humility, and an appeal to inner worth. His reticence and non-participation make Simonides think that his "court / Ha[s] not a show might countervail [Pericles'] worth" (II.iii.55-56). He even goes so far as to tell Simonides that he "never aim'd so high to love [his] daughter" (II.v.47), which is almost in flat contradiction of his statement to the fishermen.

The tournament of Knights is a masterpiece of set organization. To consider this, however, as merely another piece of colorful pageantry as so often unfortunately is the prevailing approach,[14] as for instance is the case with the tournament in *Richard II,* is to miss the careful symbolism of the whole. The five Knights in the city of Pentapolis obviously call for careful scrutiny, and for us as well as Thaisa "to entertain / The labour of each Knight in his device" (II.ii.14-15). Thaisa is described at this point as "Beauty's child, whom Nature gat / For men to see, and seeing wonder at" (II.ii.6-7), which is a clear enough parallel with the description of Antiochus' daughter:

> Nature this dowry gave: to glad her presence,
> The senat-house of planets all did sit
> To knit in her their best perfections.
>
> (I.i.10-12)

The general description of the princely Knights as a "model which heaven makes like to itself; / As jewels lose their glory if neglected, / So princes their renowns if not respected" (II.ii.11-13) takes on particular significance in Pericles' case, for in the immediately preceding scene Pericles, girding himself with a *rusty* armor, refers to his new-found equipment as a "jewel hold[ing] his building on [his] arm" (II.i.155). Pericles has certainly lost his glory by neglecting matters that truly concern princes as models of heaven. His own actions have set him on a course not unlike that of an unruly meteor that cannot be brought back into obedient orb until its motion is linked again with the harmony of the spheres.

To compare the dramatist's description of the five Knights and their devices with the various descriptions and mottoes in Wilkins' *Painfull Adventures,* and then to suggest strongly that "Q provides an imperfect report with some lines missing and others replaced"[15] is surely to miss the point. Nor is the difference between the *full* description of the Knights in Wilkins and the less full description in the play to be explained away as "deliberate, in the interest of brevity."[16] The deliberate alteration of what passes for source material is usually attributable to *dramatic* necessity in a constructional sense. The alteration of Hotspur's age is effected not simply to telescope history and battles, but to afford a dramatic comparison and contrast between Hal and Hotspur of the same age and to make it possible for Bolingbroke to see in Hotspur an image of his own youthful ambition. I suggest that the play's alteration of the description of the Knights and their mottoes is deliberately calculated to take it out of *categorical* pointing, mere automatic listing, and to point the emphasis elsewhere. In one sense the description is obviously satirical. The elaborate outward show of the Knights contrasts immediately with the "rusty outside" of Pericles' outward show, but does it more accurately reflect the inward man of Pericles' inward show in five stages eventually summed up by the sixth? The technique is not all that different from the tedious brief show in *A Midsummer-Night's Dream* where the lovers are looking on at Pyramus and Thisbe without recognizing how much they are looking in a mirror.

The first, a Knight of Sparta with the black Ethiop reaching at the sun, and his motto of *Lux tua vita mihi* is interpreted by Simonides very simply as "He loves you well that holds his life of you" because Simonides considers it only from Thaisa's angle. More accurately surely this would mean Spartan courage of a stranger presuming to reach at the "Fair glass of light"—Pericles in Antiochus' court. If so, then "He loves you well that holds his life of you" ironically parallels Pericles' last summation of his love for Antiochus' daughter before the riddle is given to him: "But my unspotted fire of love to you, / Thus ready for the way of life or death, / I wait the sharpest blow" (I.i.54-56). The black Ethiop reaching for the sun figures the darkness and ignorance of the stranger seeking the light, and this again points rather to Pericles than to any other Knight, and to Pericles' own estimation of how he had no idea what he was getting himself into. Some of the Lords commenting later on Pericles make much of his being a stranger and of his appearance befitting one who has "practis'd more the whipstock than the lance" (II.ii.50).

The second contender, an armed Knight from Macedon "that's conquer'd by a lady," bearing his motto *Pue Per doleera kee per forsa,*[17] is not commented on by Simonides. That the motto is described by Thaisa as Spanish is perhaps best interpreted as Thaisa's mistake rather than the Quarto's. Macedon is surely meant to recall Alexander the Great; certainly Fluellen makes a great fuss over Macedon and Alexander "for / there is figures in all things" (*Henry V,* IV.vii.34-35), and it seems clear to me that the dramatist has deliberately cut down on the derivations of the five Knights so that Macedon and Sparta are the only two Greek ones remaining, Corinth and Athens having been dropped. Sparta and Macedon have immediate application in Spartan courage and Alexandrian cutting of the Gordian knot. "More by gentleness than by force" is surely more applicable to Pericles than to any of the five Knights, as he plays the gentler game. That he should be conquered by a lady might be interpreted also as an early indication that the overtures to love are made by Thaisa helped by her father, both of them intrigued by Pericles' obvious appeal to the inward rather than the outward man.

The third Knight, uncommented on by Simonides, and described as coming from Antioch, "his device, a wreath of chivalry" and his motto "*Me Pompey*[18] *provexit apex*" is surely a clear reflection of Pericles himself, who has come from his chivalric "adventure" at Antiochus' court where he hoped to reach the crown of triumph in solving the riddle.

Simonides' comments on the fourth Knight's device of a burning torch turned upside down and the motto *Qui me alit, me extinguit* that this shows "beauty hath his power and will, / Which can as well inflame as it can kill"

(II.ii.34-35) indicate how Simonides is interpreting it as he did the first Knight's, that is, from Thaisa's point of view. However, if we look at it as another description of Pericles it is not difficult to see how appropriate it is that Pericles should be extinguished by the self-same wax which was the cause of his light. In Antiochus' court he carried his torch aloft: in Simonides' he is turning it upside down—his elevated pride is turned to submissive humility.

The fifth and last of the Knights, uncommented on by Simonides, and described as a "hand environed with clouds, / Holding out gold that's by the touchstone tried" with a motto *Sic spectanda fides* is surely a neat summation of the need for Pericles to be tested not by words and aspirations only but by actual deeds also. Pericles has borne his head so high to kiss the clouds, hoping to seize the golden apples of Hesperides at Antiochus': now he must be put to the test of deeds not riddles at Simonides' court.

The derivations, where given, and the emblems and devices of all five Knights suggest ironical comments on Pericles' own condition. When he himself is introduced as a stranger with the device of a "wither'd branch, that's only green at top" and the motto *In hac spe vivo*, Simonides' interpretation of this pretty moral as "[f]rom the dejected state wherein he is, / He hopes by you his fortunes yet may flourish" (II.ii.45-46) makes the parallel with Antiochus' court—"That would be son to great Antiochus"—very effective. The black Ethiop reaching at the sun, the armed Knight that's conquered by a lady, the Knight drawn to this enterprise by the crown of the triumph, the burning torch upside down, the hand from the clouds holding gold to be tried—all reach their conclusion in the branch that's withered but yet maintaining a little life at top. Pericles on "set purpose" (II.ii.53) is trying to dissociate all the Antiochus experiences from himself and to revert to the significance of his father's rusty armor for confidence, and his emblem and motto represent the wish that he has not completely ruined his life but left a small vestige of hope.

I think it is entirely possible that the five Knights may represent the five senses. The first with his concentration on light (sun, *lux*) representing sight; the second with his emphasis on gentleness of a lady suggesting either touch or smell, but since the fifth clearly stands for touch, the second could presumably be smell. The third concentrates on drawing people from afar to this chivalric enterprise, and thus may be hearing. The fourth's concentration on feeding and extinguishing is obviously taste, and the fifth with its references to hand and touchstone clearly could stand for touch. If this allegorization is possible then it would certainly afford a very smooth yet subtle transition into the next scene—a banquet at which Thaisa is described as "queen o' th' feast" (II.iii.17).

Simonides and Thaisa have not made comments on each of the contenders, and I think the explanation of this lies in quite a different quarter than is represented by Hoeniger's asseverance that "It is a good guess that the King explained the motto in similar words [to those in Wilkins] in the uncorrupted text."[19] The dramatist is surely deliberately having Simonides and Thaisa *impatient* with all the Knights except Pericles, and Simonides' final statement of how foolish it is to "scan / The outward habit by the inward man" is a careful enough indication where he is prepared to exercise patience. Before long the play reveals how Simonides has had suspicions that the stranger "for aught [he] know[s], / May be (nor can [he] think the contrary) / As great in blood as [he] [him] self" (II.v. 77-79), and it is presumably on this intuition that he has been acting in promoting his daughter's advances to Pericles, and in commending her choice and decision to "wed the stranger knight." The whole business is not unlike Prospero's machinations whereby Ferdinand is secured for his daughter Miranda, though it is not so easy to see the initial stages of the process with Simonides. By the time he bids his daughter make advances to Pericles by taking the "standing-bowl of wine to him" (II.iii.65) even against her outward expression that this is unbecoming to a lady and even impudent:

> if befits not me
> Unto a stranger knight to be so bold;
> He may my proffer take for an offence,
> Since men take women's gifts for impudence
>
> (II.iii.66-69)

though, of course, her aside shows that she is secretly delighted at the opportunity to make advances to Pericles (II.iii.72), Simonides' interference is being clarified. Its real extent is not revealed, however, until Simonides palms off the other contenders for Thaisa's hand in marriage with spurious excuses. Thus he plainly shows his hand in securing this stranger, not a "wheeling and extravagant stranger" as in *Othello* where Brabantio hardly recognizes how he is "fixing" his daughter's marriage despite his "dream" of such a likely accident (I.i.142), but a Knight-errant who "only by misfortune of the seas / Bereft of ships and men, cast on this shore" (II.iii.89), according to Pericles' *own* report. The strength of the Quarto's use of "only" is obvious in this interpretation. One need not resort to suggestions that "*only* may well be corrupt,"[20] or to emend it to "newly" as Elze[21] conjectured.

Pericles hides behind his father figure, Simonides, and allows himself to be manipulated, deliberately keeping in the background and letting Simonides and Thaisa manage things the way they wish. He describes himself as a "glow-worm in the night, / The which hath fire in darkness, none in light" (II.iii.43-44). It is the *radiance* of Simonides' court which recalls his own father's splendor who "[h]ad princes sit like stars about his throne, / And he the sun" (II.iii.39-40) and contrasts with his own poor light. By this means he tries to eradicate from his mind his own self searching for a wife on *his* terms—the disastrous Antiochus affair—and tries to convince himself that the wife he is now gaining comes with his father's blessing and approval. Thaisa represents in this sense his tie and bind, his attempt to convince himself that he is part of normality, of normal human affairs. It is yet another attempt to combat his sense of guilt over his Antiochus experience.

When at the beginning of Act III the dumb show and chorus report "Antiochus and his daughter dead" and Pericles urgently summoned back to Tyre to prevent the men of Tyre from mutinying and placing the crown on Helicanus' head, it is highly significant that Pericles' attempts to comply immediately run him into a violent storm off Tharsus. The death of Antiochus and his daughter frees Pericles from the fear of death at Antiochus' hands, but does not free him from the conscience effects of that association. Try as hard as he can to get back to Tyre successfully with his bride, as if the whole Antiochus affair had never taken place, as if Thaisa were the bride he set out for in the first place and was bringing home to be his consort, the microcosmic storm belies his attempt to think all is as it had never been. How eloquently he calls upon the god of the great vast to rebuke the surges, to bind the winds in brass, to still the deafening, dreadful thunders, and to quench the storm's sulphurous flashes, but all this is "as a whisper in the ears of death / Unheard" (III.i.9-10). The storm that is within him will not subside. That which he gained so easily,[22] Thaisa, is just as rapidly snatched away, and his sea-sorrow is given visible embodiment in Marina. His grief has lingered long in the chambers of the sea, but now it is given birth, a local habitation and a name, and he must cast for ever from him the comforting thought that Thaisa made up for Antiochus' daughter, that his credit ledger with the gods cancels out his debit. All is suffering till ripeness be all. His "priestly farewell" (III.i.69) to Thaisa with Nestor (the cup) and Nicander (man's victory) as priestly assistants, attended by Lychorida (unbinding and loosing), is full of ceremonial implications that he must sacrifice (cup) his victory, his gaining of Thaisa, and give it to the gods. Temporarily his heart is in the coffin there with Thaisa, or already in the sea:

> Ay me whilst thee the sounding seas and shores
> Wash far away wherere thy bones are hurled. . . .
> Where thou perhaps under the whelming tide
> Visit'st the bottom of the monstrous world
>
> *(Lycidas)*

with the "belching whale." In some sense he has "ravin[ed] up / [His] own life's means" (*Macbeth*, II.iv.28-29), has devoured the poor fry before him, has engulfed others in his own tempestuous seas. His short-lived victory had been wrested out of his first sea-wrecking; the sea symbolically claims it back. And he finds himself willingly going back to Tharsus, ostensibly to leave his babe at "careful nursing" (III.ii.80) there, but subconsciously to take refuge in a place which still thinks of him as a savior, a place that had erected a statue to his glory. What irony it is that the next time he visits Tharsus, fourteen years later, he is presented with a monument with epitaphs in "glitt'ring golden characters" (IV.iii.44) expressing general praise of Marina. Since the audience knows Marina is alive Pericles' confrontation with a glorious statue monument is powerfully suggestive of mirror techniques. Pericles is made to see his life's statue, his savior role, turned into his death's monument, the destruction of his attempts to hide behind good deeds and to blame all his difficulties on the "wayward seas" (IV.iv.10). Deprived of Thaisa and Marina, he is back again in mind at Antiochus. He "bears / A tempest, which his mortal vessel tears" (IV.iv.29-30).

The concentration on Diana at this part of the play deliberately contrasts the unchaste atmosphere of the Antiochus affair, which will soon be set in very sharp relief by the brothel. Pericles is careful in his instructions to Cleon and Dioniza to look after Marina till she be married and to swear

> By bright Diana, whom we honour, all
> Unscissor'd shall this hair of mine remain,
> Though I show will[23] in't.
>
> *(III.iii.28-30)*

His wife Thaisa through the connivance of her father had put off his rivals by making a vow "on her virgin honour" to wear Diana's livery for twelve more months, and promptly married Pericles. There should be no wonder that when Thaisa is revived by Cerimon her first expression should be "O dear Diana" (III.ii.106), and her resolved intention to take a vestal livery in Diana's temple. Thaisa has offended against Diana and in her own mind will go on making reparation to Diana until Pericles come to Diana's temple and claim her in all proper religious propriety. Like Leontes in *The Winter's Tale* Pericles will "[n]ew woo [his] queen" (III.ii.156), but this time under the auspices of Diana.

The vision of Diana that comes to Pericles is surely prompted by his hope that by propitiating her deity for his part in the transgression—wedding a votaress of her order *before* the twelvemonth was up—he might somehow have Thaisa as miraculously restored to him as Marina was. Psychologically, too, it is obvious that he would make for Ephesus near whose coast Thaisa had been cast overboard. His mind is functioning not just along the lines of recovering a wife, however, but of a bridegroom meeting a bride as his very ready response to Lysimachus' hint that when they come ashore Lysimachus has a suit to prefer to Pericles indicates. Lysimachus "shall prevail, / Were it to woo [his] daughter" (V.i.259-260). That Pericles' explanation to Diana for his journeying in the past is little better than his explanation to Thaisa in her father's court should not disturb us. Pericles' awakening, recognition, restoration to harmony is worked out almost totally symbolically. He does not have glimpses of his real self, of his real wrongdoing as Lear does, but then he has the vision of Diana. The nearest he is made to come to an admission of disturbance is his expression that he was "frighted from [his] country" (V.iii.3) and then went on to wed Thaisa. At Simonides' court he had hidden behind the chivalric statement that he was trained in "arts and arms" (II.iii.82) and had been "looking for adventures in the world" when he was washed up on Simonides' shore. "Frighted" is *nearer* the truth, but a long way from it. His Antiochus affair in the House of Death, his Simonides' court affair in the House of "the gentler gamester is the soonest winner," his abandonment of Marina to the place where his image is made glorious—all these are nearer to the truth. He "puts on sackcloth" (IV.iv.29), swears never to wash his face, nor cut his hair—and these are "but the trappings and the suits of woe" (*Hamlet*, I.ii.86). They are indeed "actions that a man might play" (I.ii.84). Hamlet's indictment against the "inky cloak" as one of these actions could well be paralleled with the "banners sable" of Pericles' ship which is "trimm'd with rich expense" (V.Ch.19). He plays the man of grief in excessively rich *outer* show.

What his inner self should have been like is revealed by the play's concentration on Marina's "lasting storm," and how she endured it (IV.i.19). The fourth act is almost entirely devoted to her sea-changes, which she later claims "might equal" the stranger King's "if both were justly weigh'd" (V.i.88), and even Pericles is moved to believe that a comparison between her sufferings and his is possible, though, of course, his must be the greater or else she has suffered like a man and he like a girl.

When Marina, faced with her murderer-to-be, stresses her innocence in that she did never hurt Dioniza's daughter in all her life, never spoke a bad word, "nor did ill turn / To any living creature" (IV.i.75-76), never killed a mouse, hurt a fly or "trod upon a worm" (IV.i.78) against her will, she pleads from an innocence that is never in doubt, and contrasts sharply with her father's position in which he claims that like the poor worm he must die for telling the earth it is wronged with man's oppression. Marina's confrontation with Boult's court, the Mytilene brothel, is also in sharp distinction with her father's in Antiochus' court. The "sore terms" the brothel "stand[s] upon with the gods" (IV.ii.32) are known to the proprietors and customers of the establishment, whose one redeeming feature is that they acknowledge they would not do thus if they could "pick up some pretty / estate" (IV.ii.30-31), and thus keep their doors closed, because theirs is neither profession, trade, or calling. And indeed Boult is very willing to speak for himself and for the Pander and the Bawd in finding gold "tractable enough" (IV.vi.198).

What irony it is that the gold Marina thus buys herself out of the brothel with and with which the brothel people can begin to restore some kind of respect to themselves came from Lysimachus! Marina has indeed been brought to the brothel by "wayward fortune" that did "malign [her] state" (V.i.89), but has not lost faith in the gods whom she does not accuse but calls on their defence and commends her chastity into Diana's keeping (IV.iii.147). Her beauty is promulgated abroad through the market of the world as was Antiochus' daughter's, and prospective clients have been lured to "joust" for her, Monsieur Verolles, the pox, to try to "cut a caper at the proclamation" (IV.ii.105-106), a Spaniard to mouth-water "to bed to / her very description" (IV.ii.98-99), and "of every nation a traveller" (IV.ii.112) to scatter his crowns in the shadow of the brothel's sun. Each knows precisely why he is visiting a brothel and each is presented with some kind of riddle to try to excuse his presence there. The first two gentlemen clients visit what they took to be a bawd and hear "vestals sing" (IV.v.7), but could they not be said to be feeding on "mother's flesh which did [them] breed" (I.i.66), especially with regard to Monsieur Verolles who "brought his disease / [T]hither: here he does but repair it" (IV.ii.108-109). Lord Lysimachus (end of the battle for Marina and Pericles!) comes "disguis'd" to "do the deeds of darkness" (IV.vi.29) with some "wholesome iniquity" that a man "may deal withal, and / defy the surgeon" (IV.vi.24-25), as if "after a long voyage at sea" (IV.vi.42), and is faced with the riddle of how Marina could have been at the same trade "[e]'er since [she] can remember" (IV.vi.72), and tries to argue his way out of his embarrassing presence in a brothel by pleading an incorrupt mind, but the gold he gives her is another way of scattering his crowns. His very presence is his indictment.

The brothel episodes thus function as a foil for Pericles' behavior particularly in Antiochus' court. The riddle that man goes to solve is basically the riddle of his own going. It would be better not to let one's feet travel in that direction in the first place, but if one does fall then it is better to be able to buy oneself out by pleading

> best men are moulded out of faults,
> And, for the most, become much more the better
> For being a little bad.
>
> (*Measure for Measure*, V.i.437-439)

The clients visiting the brothel exhibit "man's infirmities" on a far smaller scale than Pericles visiting Antiochus' court. A little gold washes them clean, but Pericles' hands that opened Pandora's box "will rather / The multitudinous seas incarnadine / Making the green one red" (*Macbeth*, II.ii.60-62) wherever he travels. Coming back to reclaim his daughter after fourteen years of absence he does "[s]ail seas in cockles"[24] (IV.iv.2) trying to thwart the "wayward seas" (IV.iv.10) rather than admit his own waywardness, piloting his ship to Tharsus as modern emendators of the text will have us read whereas the original Quarto quite clearly suggests in its spelling and capitalization of "Pilat" ("this Pilat thought," IV.iv.18) a pun on the state of mind in which he is going to Tharsus, trying to wash his hands clean of any thought of not having done the right thing. And he symbolically finds his glorious image is dead, reads his own epitaph in Marina's monument—"wither'd in her spring of year" (IV.iv.25) recalling the withered branch again—and retreats into his scallop shell of unquiet while his lost innocence, Marina, will "never stint, / Mak[ing] raging battery upon shores of flint" (IV.iv.42-43), making "a batt'ry through his deafen'd ports, / Which now are midway stopp'd" (V.i.46-47).

It is fitting that it should be a Lysimachus who must persist in bringing the maid of Mytilene to the dumb statue of Pericles to try to breathe life into it once more. Like the fishermen earlier Lysimachus makes up this garment for Pericles through the rough seams of Mytilene's waters. The fishermen presented Pericles with the rusty armor of his father and equipped him with a pair of bases: Lysimachus presents him with a jewel of a maid who reminds him of his wife and daughter (V.i.106-108) and furnishes him with "her sweet harmony" (V.i.44). They both "tell the infirmities of men" (II.i.49) and the need for condolements, and both hope if Pericles thrives that he will "remember / from whence [he] had them" (II.150-151).

Marina's song certainly begins to soften the shores of Pericles' flint. The statue comes alive, and it is as if it has all been a dream. A sea of joys rushes in upon Pericles "[o]'erbear[ing] the shores of [his] mortality" (V.i.193). The recognition of another's griefs, his daughter's caused by his own misdeeds, makes him no longer boast that nothing could prove even the "thousandth part / Of [his] endurance" (V.i.135-136), but acknowledges of Marina, "[She] that beget'st him that did [her] beget" (V.i.195), the true answer to the riddle "[on] mother's flesh which did [him] breed," the recognition that man himself destroys the music of his life, and forgets the source from whence it came. When he hears the music of the spheres he is mentally back again in tune with the world and with the gods, and from there it is an easy transition to his vision of Diana.

The end of the play is full of echoes of its beginning. The Antiochus affair looms very large. That Pericles should be in conference with Marina shortly after the drama has shown her visited by the two Gentlemen and Lysimachus might vaguely suggest that Pericles is in their line, too. Indeed were he really tempted to do her violence as his initial pushing her back made her suspect, and her asking him "Whither will you have me" (V.i.176) echoing as it does the same question to Boult about to ravish her (IV.vi.153) shortly after she has related to him the story of the plot on her life and of the pirates bringing her to Mytilene, then the play's initial theme of incest would be rounded out in an extraordinary way. The kind of wife Pericles was looking for in Antiochus' court was a daughter image rather than a peer, a co-equal partner. As far as he himself was aware his pursuit of Antiochus' daughter was a means to Antiochus' wealth, a strong enough impediment to a marriage of true minds. When Marina's sea-sorrow fuses daughter and wife in one image for him it makes possible the beginning of the search for a real wife for herself alone. The return of his daughter could never be a sufficient substitute. In the temple of Diana all impurities of excessive material impediments in a plus sense as represented by the Antiochus' court affair, and of excessive material impediments in a minus sense as represented by the Simonides' court affair, are purged away, but man is still left with his infirmities that glorify the blessed gods. His mortal weakness is the gods' immortal strength.

Notes

1. See F. D. Hoeniger, ed., *Pericles* (New Arden Shakespeare, Cambridge, Mass. 1963; rev. ed. 1966), Introduction, p. lxxxi.

2. See G. Wilson Knight, *The Crown of Life* (London, 1958), pp. 32-75.

3. See Kenneth Muir, *Shakespeare as Collaborator* (New York, 1960), pp. 80-81.

4. Hoeniger, Introduction, pp. lxxx-lxxxi.

5. Thelma N. Greenfield, "A Re-Examination of the "Patient" Pericles," *Shakespeare Studies,* III (1967), 51-61, rightly takes exception to the prevalent view of Pericles as a type of the patient man, and less convincingly substitutes a view of Pericles as "the Renaissance descendant of the wily Greek traveler, a solver of riddles, a master of escape and incognito, skilled in the arts, and in his accomplishments and understanding a born ruler of men." Pericles is by no means a Ulysses, nor is he an Oedipus, but a prince of dark corners, avoiding, and retreating from princely responsibilities. I am grateful to Professor J. Leeds Barroll for allowing me to see Professor Greenfield's paper in galleys.

6. See Natalis Comitis, *Mythologiae* (Venetiis, 1568; foreword dated 1567—B.M. copy 704.d7), *Liber Septimus, Cap.* VII, 38-40, Sig. Iiiv. The version in the 1581 edition is the same.

7. See Douglas Bush, *Mythology & the Renaissance Tradition in English Poetry* (New York, 1963, new rev. ed.), p. 94 for the general importance of the *Mythologiae* for the Renaissance, and p. 98 for this allegorical interpretation of the golden apples.

8. See J. C. Smith and E. de Selincourt, eds., *The Poetical Works of Edmund Spenser* (London, rep. 1963), II, Canto VII, 44, p. 104.

9. See Hoeniger, Introduction, p. lxxxvi.

10. See S. H. Long, "Laying the Ghosts in *Pericles,*" SQ [*Shakespeare Quarterly*], VII (1956), 39-42.

11. See Hoeniger, p. 64 fn.

12. "Measures" line 103 but "revels" line 93. See Hoeniger, p. 65 fn. carry over.

13. Hoeniger, p. 70 fn.

14. Hoeniger lists Kyd's *Spanish Tragedy* and *Soliman and Perseda* together with Middleton's *Your Five Gallants*. His only Shakespearean analogy is *Troilus and Cressida,* I.ii, which is quite different in technique. Most critics tend to ignore this part of the play, or concentrate only on Pericles' own emblem, and that in a rather perfunctory manner. See Derek Traversi, *Shakespeare: The Last Phase* (Stanford, Cal., 1955), p. 24.

15. Hoeniger, pp. 51-52, footnote to beginning of II.ii.

16. Hoeniger, p. 182.

17. This has caused quite unnecessary confusion (See Hoeniger, p. 54). Critics have emended it to Spanish and to correct Italian. Hoeniger suggests that "the reporter or anyone else" may be responsible for these corruptions. In point of fact the Q spells the Italian

words as they sound, as for instance is the case later in this scene where Q has "Pompey" for "Pompae" and in IV.vi where the Q has "Caualereea" for "cavalleria." The only "corruption" is the first "e" of "doleera" which should be emeded to "c"; "e" for "c" is an Elizabethan common error.

18. I suggest "Pompey" may well indicate how the word was to be pronounced. See previous note.

19. Hoeniger, p. 55 fn.30.

20. Hoeniger, p. 63 fn. 88-89.

21. See *Englische Studien*, IX (1885), 282.

22. See Frank Kermode, ed., *The Tempest* (New Arden Shakespeare, Cambridge, Mass., 1958, 6th ed.), III.i.n.1-2 for the relevance of a passage in St. Augustine's *Confessions*: "Yea, the very pleasures of human life men acquire by difficulties. . . . It is . . . ordered, that the affianced bride should not at once be given, lest as a husband he should hold cheap whom, as betrothed, he sighed not after" (Book VIII.7-8).

23. Hoeniger accepts Theobald's and Malone's conjecture "show ill" and finds support in Wilkins, *The Painful Aduentures*: "himselfe in all vncomely," but I think this is quite unnecessary emendation. Pericles does show "will" in many ways, and showing "will" is showing "ill." If we emend do we not lose the possibility of the double meaning?

24. Not just the fairy tale atmosphere of the play as Hoeniger's note to line 2, p. 121, suggests.

Annette C. Flower (essay date 1975)

SOURCE: Flower, Annette C. "Disguise and Identity in *Pericles, Prince of Tyre*." *Shakespeare Quarterly* 26, no. 1 (winter 1975): 30-41.

[*In the following essay, Flower explores how the relationship between disguise and identity in* Pericles *reveals and defines character.*]

The paradox in *Pericles, Prince of Tyre* is the paradox of fantasy: that not "realism" but conscious illusion, artfully handled, can most satisfyingly interpret reality. A "mouldy tale" it may be, but such a label is not so much a charge of failure as a badge of success, for *Pericles* is meant to be a mouldy tale. Its mouldiness and its narrative basis are deliberately exploited. Even the structure of the play depends upon its kinship with narrative fiction, for Gower appears as presenter in order to *tell* the story, mediating between play and audience like a narrative persona; he interprets, manages, directs the play as we watch it.[1] The presence of Gower contributes to "that identification without sympathy, that detachment without irony"[2] which transforms Pericles' fantastic adventures into something we respond to as archetypal.

Pericles exploits narrative techniques, fairy-tale motifs, and dramatic conventions so as to call attention to these elements and thus present them in a new light. The fatal riddle, the bride's tournament, Snow White with her wicked stepmother and reluctant executioner, purity undefiled in a brothel, pirates and shipwrecks, and magician-doctors—mouldy tales indeed, but in being retold they "change / Into something rich and strange."

All romances might well be subtitled "The Triumph of Time," for always they operate on Feste's principle that "thus the whirligig of time brings in his revenges." In *Pericles*, not only does Gower, as romancer, transport the audience hither and thither in time as in space, but he insists upon the way time organizes his tale. The passage of time is to be fulfilled by imagination, "eched" by the fancy (III. Prol. ll. 11-13).[3] Furthermore, the action of the play is not only dependent upon the whirligig of time but is encompassed in the mimetic images of the dream and the tale. Pericles at first takes Marina's restoration for a dream (V.i.160-61). Upon finding that dream real, he falls asleep, lulled by the music of the spheres, to dream of Diana's instructions, dream instructions which lead, in waking life, to the recovery of Thaisa. The entire play is, of course, Gower's "song that old was sung," but within the plot, too, tale-telling is emphasized—Antiochus' fear that Pericles will "tell the world Antiochus doth sin" (I.i.146), Cleon's vain hope that "relating tales of others' griefs" may "teach us to forget our own" (I.iv.2-3), and his "discourse of our woes" (I.iv.18) to remind heaven of Tharsus' plight. The recognitions in Act V depend upon first Marina and then Pericles telling his story. Marina introduces her tale by saying, "If I should tell my history, it would seem / Like lies, disdain'd in the reporting" (V.i.117-18). According to Lysimachus, "She never would tell / Her parentage" (V.i.186-87) until now and, once recognized, she is enjoined to tell her story again to the dubious Helicanus (V.i.223-25). Pericles, commanded by Diana to tell his tale at Ephesus, does so, and the play ends with the promise of further tale-telling in Pericles' request that Cerimon explain the rescue of Thaisa (V.iii.84-85). The story is therefore not only framed as Gower's tale, but dependent upon being "told" by its own characters. Dream and tale-telling work together to provide distance, to give a remote and airless clarity within a shadowy landscape.

Even more central to this effect, however, are the disguises of the three major characters in *Pericles*. Like the other motifs in the play, these disguises are familiar devices adapted from prose romance and fairy-tale. Pericles, Thaisa, and Marina are all, at various times, deprived of their princehood by circumstance and must therefore function as private citizens. In doing so, each disguises himself: Marina by refusing to state her true identity, forcing others to deal with her simply as a captive virgin; Thaisa by adopting the role of priestess of Diana, the role best suited to the circumstances into which she has been thrust; and Pericles by assuming a whole series of roles, each suited to one aspect of the questing knight, but none, until the last, a full expression of his personality.

All of Pericles' experience in the play consists of playing parts, adopting the postures and points of view which allow him to adjust to circumstance, and to learn. His life, as we see it, is given to a quest for some form of wholeness which he himself cannot explain, and his quest takes the form of an exploration of the fragments which make up that whole, each fragment a life he lives, a role he plays.

Pericles appears first as the Prince of Tyre properly wooing the Princess of Antioch. The wooing is unsatisfactory, however, for the Princess of Antioch is not what she seems. Pericles' reaction to finding her a "glorious casket stor'd with ill" (I.i.77) is the first step in his "education," and the knowledge he gains from it is not merely the painful Renaissance truism that what seems fair may be far otherwise, but the more specific realization that royalty is particularly vulnerable to sins associated with disguise. "Kings are earth's gods; in vice their law's their will; / And if Jove stray, who dares say Jove doth ill?" (I.i.103-4). Since rulers are the lawmakers, they can use the law and their unique authority to justify their actions, to disguise their sin. Pericles recognizes the metaphoric relationship between hypocrisy and disguise when he remarks

> How courtesy would seem to cover sin,
> When what is done is like an hypocrite,
> The which is good in nothing but in sight!
>
> (I.i.121-23)

Rulers are, furthermore, peculiarly susceptible to the attempts of others to disguise the truth through flattery: "heaven forbid / That kings should let their ears hear their faults hid!" (I.ii.61-62).

Such knowledge arms Pericles for his further adventures, adventures which, as he suggests to the faithful deputy he leaves behind, will be both test and fulfillment:

> But in our orbs we'll live so round and safe
> That time of both this truth shall ne'er convince,
> Thou show'dst a subject's shine, I a true prince.
>
> (I.ii.122-24)

Ironically, for each to fulfill himself, to make his orb round, the two must reverse roles. Helicanus, the true subject, must deputize for Pericles, who must abandon rule in order to prove his princehood. The exchange tests both men, for just as Helicanus can prove himself a true subject only by refusing to abuse or usurp the authority lent him, so Pericles can prove himself a true prince only by avoiding the possibility of flattery (a possibility always present when the prince's rank is known) and by acting princely when he is not bolstered by the unquestionable authority of rule.

Therefore, after the rescue of Tharsus, which demonstrates magnanimity when it is easy for Pericles to be magnanimous, his testing begins. The shipwreck divests him of ships, followers, treasure, all the symbols of his princehood. Even, for the nonce, the armor which gives him an identity by linking him with his father is lost. Like Lear, though in a lower key, Pericles comes through the storm affirming only his essential mortality:

> Wind, rain, and thunder, remember earthly man
> Is but a substance that must yield to you;
> And I, as fits my nature, do obey you.
>
> (II.i.2-4)

He is stripped of all distinction, not only physically but spiritually:

> What I have been I have forgot to know;
> But what I am want teaches me to think on:
> A man throng'd up with cold. . . .
>
> (II.i.71-73)

From this recognition of an identity as "mere man," Pericles must earn his way back to princehood by being princely. From the fishermen Pericles receives not only food, shelter, and clothing, but, in their praise of Simonides, a reminder of the definition of the true prince, "our king the good Simonides" who "deserves so to be call'd for his peaceable reign and good government" (II.i.98, 100-101). Only after this reminder does Pericles recover his ancestral armor and with it, symbolically, his name, for in it he appears at court as "Pericles, / A gentleman of Tyre" (II.iii.87-88).

This is the role which Pericles sustains for the remainder of Act II, the role in which he must prove his worth through actions rather than title. In this act, the primary emphasis is upon the relationship between Pericles and Simonides; the courtship of Thaisa, with its counterpoint to Act I's courtship of Antiochus' daughter, is subordinate to the relationship between the two princes because Thaisa, like Antiochus' daughter, is a reflection of her father's reign. Simonides' identity as true prince is confirmed in his words to the courtiers who scorn Pericles' mean appearance in the tourney: "Opinion's but a fool, that makes us scan / The outward habit by the inward man" (II.ii.56-57). Simonides, as true prince, sees beyond "outward habit," appearances, and thus recognizes true worth in Pericles, the stranger

> . . . who, for aught I know,
> May be, nor can I think the contrary,
> As great in blood as I myself.
>
> (II.v.77-79)

Though he can distinguish between appearance and substance, Simonides is not beyond using illusions for his own ends. Like Prospero, though not at such length, he disguises his approval of the match between Pericles and Thaisa, seeming to oppose in order to test the resolution of the two. Thaisa, however, like her father, sees through seeming to the reality within—"To me he seems like diamond to glass" (II.iii.36)—and therefore she is steadfast, as is Pericles, who learned to see clearly in the first courtship.

Pericles comes to Pentapolis as a "new man," stripped of additions and distinctions of rank, wearing not the coronet of princehood but the armor which links him to his father. Thus his primary identity in Act II is that of a son, and in Simonides he finds a new father:

> Yon king's to me like to my father's picture,
> Which tells me in that glory once he was. . . .
> Where now his son's like a glowworm in the night,
> The which hath fire in darkness, none in light.
>
> (II.iii.37-38, 43-44)

At Antioch Pericles said he "would be son to great Antiochus" (I.i.26), but Antiochus was already "father, son, and husband mild" (I.i.68) to his daughter. Now, however, Pericles has learned to choose better in choosing a father; not only does he, after the experience with Antiochus, recognize the difference between the true and the false prince, but he also refers his judgment to the precedent of his own family identity, finding in Simonides not only a true king but a king who is "like to my father's picture." Pericles, Simonides, and Thaisa are all adept at seeing through surface appearance to the true worth that lies within.

The first two acts use disguise and the attendant illusion/reality devices primarily to make the distinction between worth and birth. Pericles proves his worth by being princely when his princehood is hidden. Simonides and Thaisa have the nobility of true princes, in contrast to Antiochus and his daughter, whose princehood itself is a disguise, a handsome outward show which conceals the corruption within. Both good and evil characters have used disguise and dissimulation to their own ends: Simonides' benevolent pretense of opposition has its counterpart in Antiochus' malevolent pretense of friendship. The theme of birth and worth is, however, only one facet of the motif of illusion and reality in the play, and the news which comes to Pentapolis that "Our heir-apparent is a king!" (III. Prol. l. 37) is not an end but merely a turning-point in Pericles' career. From this point onward, the concern is with seeming and reality not so much in people as in events. Pericles has learned to distinguish the true from the feigned in human behavior; for the rest of the play he undergoes a series of transformations based on a mistaken reading of circumstances—particularly the mistaken assumption that those who are said to be dead, who *seem* dead, really are dead.

In this latter part of the play, Pericles himself is subordinated first to Thaisa, then to Marina. His return to Tyre, and to the form, at least, of his princehood, is glossed over in two lines (IV. Prol. ll. 1-2). His only appearances in Acts III and IV are those in which he is victimized by the semblance of death: Thaisa's in Act III and Marina's in Act IV. As in the contrasted father-daughter pairs of Acts I and II and the contrasted monuments built by Cleon and Dionyza (a statue of Pericles as a reminder of his rescue of Tharsus and a tomb of Marina as a false proof of her death, the one a true imitation and the other a false show),

Pamela Brook as Marina, Pat Bentley-Fisher, Trudy Cameron, and Joan Gaskell as Whores, and Amelia Hall as Bawd in Act IV, scene ii of the 1973 Stratford Festival production of Pericles.

the two counterfeit deaths, though both deceive Pericles, are in contrast. Thaisa's seeming death is accidental, natural, and her restoration by Cerimon is benevolent. Marina's seeming death is the result of a deliberate, malevolent plot against her, and her rescue is equally malevolent in intention. Pericles himself, however, is as unaware of such distinctions as he is of the falsity of both deaths.

The death of Thaisa gives Pericles a new role to play, that of the sufferer. In the first storm we saw no suffering, only the aftermath in Pericles' acceptance of "mere" manhood. At that point, in fact, Pericles had nothing to lose but the external marks of rank, nothing that was of personal worth to him. The second storm, however, robs him, by the seeming death of Thaisa, of something that has become a part of himself, just as Marina is a "piece / Of your dead queen" (III.i.17-18). As he did after the first storm, Pericles accepts the inevitable:

> We cannot but obey
> The powers above us. Could I rage and roar
> As doth the sea she lies in, yet the end
> Must be as 'tis.
>
> (III.iii.9-12)

This acceptance, however, marks him as a sufferer, one to whom things happen that he cannot control. The death of

Thaisa is doubly a reversal: it seems to negate the justification of true worth and goodness in Acts I and II, and it forces Pericles into a kind of dependence both on "the powers above us" and on other people. That he accepts his suffering as a role is obvious in Pericles' immediately giving it a visible symbol in the vow to grow his hair.

> Till she be married, madam,
> By bright Diana, whom we honour all,
> Unscissor'd shall this hair of mine remain,
> Though I show ill in't. So I take my leave.
> Good madam, make me blessed in your care
> In bringing up my child.
>
> (III.iii.27-32)

In this speech, the acceptance of suffering imposed by "the powers above us" is explicitly linked with dependence upon others, specifically dependence upon Dionyza to nurture Marina.

Similarly, the false death of Marina evokes a response from Pericles in terms of appearance, for he,

> . . . in sorrow all devour'd,
> With sighs shot through and biggest tears o'ershower'd,
> Leaves Tharsus, and again embarks. He swears
> Never to wash his face nor cut his hairs;
> He puts on sackcloth, and to sea.
>
> (IV.iv.25-29)

Additional suffering, in the form of a second counterfeit death, calls for a further visible mark of the sufferer's role, in the unwashed face and the sackcloth of complete submission to exterior forces. It is in this guise, Job-like, that Pericles in Act V approaches restoration. From the depths of submission and self-abnegation symbolized in his sackcloth and unkempt appearance, he rises, at the discovery of Marina's identity, to a new affirmation of self: "I am Pericles of Tyre" (V.i.203) and immediately demands, "Give me fresh garments" (V.i.212).

The sequence of events in Pericles' restoration is significant. He recognizes Marina by circumstantial evidence in her story ("This is the rarest dream that e'er dull sleep / Did mock sad fools withal"—V.i.160-61) before her straight-forward claim, "I am the daughter to King Pericles, / If good King Pericles be" (V.i.177-78). There follows Pericles' famous recognition speech, with its assertion of the recreation of father by daughter and its ascription to the gods of benevolence and beneficence:

> O, come hither,
> Thou that beget'st him that did thee beget;
> Thou that wast born at sea, buried at Tharsus,
> And found at sea again! O Helicanus,
> Down on thy knees, thank the holy gods as loud
> As thunder threatens us. This is Marina.
>
> (V.i.193-98)

After this identification of Marina, Pericles at last proclaims his own identity: "I am Pericles of Tyre" (V.i.203). The two who are reunited were originally, if only for a moment, three, and the final test of Marina's reality is her identification of her mother as Thaisa, an identification which calls for a new identity for Pericles: "Now blessing on thee! Rise, thou art my child. / Give me fresh garments" (V.i.211-12). No longer sufferer but father, he must change his appearance to signify his change of role. The motif is reiterated when Lysimachus is presented to him; Pericles greets Lysimachus and again calls for a change of clothing: "I embrace you. / Give me my robes" (V.i.220-21). The transition from sufferer to father is swift and complete, for by the end of this scene Pericles reads, with an adroitness worthy of his "father" Simonides, the intentions of Lysimachus:

> You shall prevail,
> Were it to woo my daughter; for it seems
> You have been noble towards her.
>
> (V.i.259-61)

Having recovered Marina, having become a father (and having proved himself in this new role by his fatherly as well as princely recognition of Lysimachus' worth), Pericles must discover that he is still also a husband. Though the sequence differs and the scene is shorter, the recognition of Thaisa depends upon the same elements as that of Marina: both characters must assert their own identities, and the final confirmation rests upon remembering the name of a third person. This time, as instructed by Diana, Pericles first proclaims himself: "I here confess myself the King of Tyre" (V.iii.2) and tells his story, at which Thaisa makes the identification, "You are, you are—O royal Pericles!" (V.iii.14). Thaisa is identified first by Cerimon, then, recovering from her swoon, by her own claim, "That Thaisa am I, supposed dead / And drown'd" (V.iii.36-37). Despite his belief, however, Pericles demands, as he did of Marina, one further proof, the recollection of the name of the "ancient substitute" he left in Tyre, and Thaisa's identification of the regent as Helicanus is "Still confirmation" (V.iii.55), a confirmation reconfirmed in the presentation, "Embrace him, dear Thaisa; this is he" (V.iii.56). This completion, the final rounding of Pericles' orb which makes him not only prince but father and husband too, is marked by a final alteration of appearance: he will cut his hair and beard (V.iii.76-78).

The two recognition scenes, V.i and V.iii, are remarkable for the emphasis upon names. "My name is Marina" (V.i.141); "I am the daughter to King Pericles" (V.i.177); "This is Marina" (V.i.198); "I am Pericles of Tyre" (V.i.203); "My mother's name was Thaisa" (V.i.209); "Sir, 'tis the Governor of Mytilene" (V.i.216-17); "I here confess myself the King of Tyre" (V.iii.2); "You are, you are—O royal Pericles!" (V.iii.14); "This is your wife" (V.iii.18); "That Thaisa am I" (V.iii.36); "Look who kneels here . . . / Marina" (V.iii.47-48); "I have named him oft." "'Twas Helicanus then." / ". . . this is he" (V.iii.54, 56); "Lord Cerimon, my lord—this man" (V.iii.60). Appearances have been so deceptive, things have been so counter to what they seemed (thus Pericles first addresses Cerimon, at

V.iii.18, not conventionally as "reverend sir," but as "Reverend appearer"), that now no seeming identity is complete without the most basic affirmation, a name. Stripped of identity by the first storm, Pericles acknowledged himself a mere man, at the mercy of the elements of nature; after that admission he regained his father's armor, identity through ancestry, and thus his name, "Pericles, a gentleman of Tyre." He is stripped by the second storm of a more complex identity, not that family tie of ancestry which tells him who he is by who his father was, but the family ties of spousal and fatherhood which tell him what he is by what his posterity may be. He must again acknowledge subservience, not merely to natural elements, but to the gods who control nature and who may confuse in order to illuminate, disguise in order to reveal. Having established his first identity, his name, he now must use it, almost conjure with it, in order to regain his full identity. In the process of establishing that identity, Pericles' disguises have never been devices to conceal the truth; rather they have been roles which isolated and emphasized one aspect of that truth, until at last all his roles are integrated into a full identity.

Though both Thaisa and Marina also disguise themselves, adopting roles to suit their altered circumstances, Thaisa's disguise as a nun is subordinated to her disguise as a corpse. In Act II, of course, Thaisa's lack of disguise is emphasized in the stress on the congruity of personality and role. Thaisa is, in relation both to her father and to Pericles, the feminine counterpart to the true prince. In her, seeming and being are the same. Thus her disguise as a nun is appropriate:

> But since King Pericles,
> My wedded lord, I ne'er shall see again,
> A vestal livery will I take me to,
> And never more have joy.
>
> (III.iv.8-11)

Thaisa's identification with truth demands of her an alternate role expressive of her unworldliness, her devotion to something higher than human struggles. Her sense, too, of rebirth ("What world is this?"—III.ii.111) requires that she identify herself henceforth with the supernal. This identification with a transcendent chastity (the "vestal livery") motivates her recovery speech:

> O let me look!
> If he be none of mine, my sanctity
> Will to my sense bend no licentious ear,
> But curb it, spite of seeing. O, my lord,
> Are you not Pericles?
>
> (V.iii.29-33)

Chastity is frequently a central concern in regard to the princess or queen in Renaissance drama and is frequently, as here, associated with her identity as true prince, for in the Renaissance view, truth, troth, and chastity are, in the woman, inseparable attributes. It is, of course, this aspect of Thaisa which Marina assumes and vindicates in Act IV, just as in *The Winter's Tale* Perdita becomes the exponent of truth, troth, and chastity and thereby vindicates Hermione.

It is only to the audience and to Cerimon, however, that Thaisa reappears disguised as a votaress of Diana. To Pericles and Marina, Thaisa appears to be dead, for death, as Cerimon points out, "may usurp on nature many hours" (III.ii.87). This disguise, seeming so final, precipitates the last recognition of the play, but the disguise of death is primarily a passive role for Thaisa. It keeps her out of the center in the last three acts, much as her subordination to Simonides kept her from being central in Act II. In Acts IV and V, her function as touchstone of truth is transferred to Marina, whose disguise of death is anything but passive.

Marina's disguise is, in the structure of the play, the real counterpart to Pericles'. Like him she learns first the deceptions of those who appear princely; the duplicity of Dionyza, who claims to love both Pericles and Marina "with more than foreign heart" (IV.i.35), is, in Marina's experience, equivalent to the duplicity of Antiochus in Pericles' experience. Antiochus and his daughter, concealing their incestuous relationship under the semblance of correct, formal behavior, disguise evil as good, faithlessness as friendship, thus providing contrast to the genuine love and good will of Simonides and Thaisa. Cleon and Dionyza, though at first genuine in their gratitude, become dissemblers; Dionyza hides her jealousy and rancor under a semblance of love and, after Marina's presumed death (at the hands of Leonine—Falstaff's confidence that "the lion will not touch the true prince" seems to have gone awry), persuades Cleon to conceal the supposed murder under the bland report that Marina "died at night."

Confusing truth with seeming, Dionyza tells Cleon that Marina's murder will go undetected,

> Unless you play the pious innocent,
> And for an honest attribute cry out
> 'She died by foul play'.
>
> (IV.iii.17-19)

To her way of thinking, innocence on Cleon's part would be mere acting; he is already implicated in her crime. Unless he speaks out, the monument will speak for them:

> . . . her epitaphs
> In glittering golden characters express
> A general praise to her, and care in us
> At whose expense 'tis done.
>
> (IV.iii.43-46)

For Dionyza, appearance counts, not what lies within. In fact, she cannot any longer distinguish what lies within. Gower's comment on the dumb-show presentation of Marina's grave therefore works in two directions: "See how belief may suffer by foul show! / This borrowed passion stands for true old woe. . . ." (IV.iv.23-24). On one level a conventional apology for actors, these lines also furnish a commentary on Cleon and Dionyza, who "borrow" a passion they do not feel and so make a "foul show" of sympathy.

Like Antiochus, Dionyza professes friendship to hide hostility, besmirches the name of princehood, and forces the true prince to flee for her life. Furthermore Marina, like her father, is stripped of rank and thus thrown on the inner resources which prove her princehood through demonstrating her worth. Kidnapped and sold into a brothel, the ironic counterpart to Thaisa's vestal temple, Marina displays a chastity so complete "that she would make a puritan of the devil, if he should cheapen a kiss of her" (IV.vi.9-10). This militant chastity, in fact, ultimately wins her a respectable position as a teacher of needlework as well as the esteem of many of her would-be customers, including Lysimachus, who himself appears first in disguise (IV.vi.16), though his disguise is evidently such a familiar ruse to conceal his visits to the brothel that it fools no one.[4]

Throughout this portion of her career, Marina conceals her princehood, as Pericles concealed his in Act II, and insists upon the integrity of her identity as a virgin. For her, as for Thaisa, chastity is an essential element of feminine identity; thus she is unable to comprehend the Bawd who has purchased her from the pirates:

MAR.

    Are you a woman?

BAWD.

    What would you have me be, an I be not a woman?

MAR.

    An honest woman, or not a woman.

(IV.ii.82-84)

Marina's implication that a dishonest woman is, in fact, no longer a woman, has assumed a perverse disguise, is borne out in the Bawd's subsequent conversation. Having lost the honesty by which womanhood is identified, she has perverted all values, so that she sees good as evil. The fact that Marina "has here spoken holy words to the Lord Lysimachus" is to her "abominable" (IV.vi.132-33). Because she has no truth left, the report that Marina "makes our profession as it were to stink afore the face of the gods" (IV.vi.134-35) is to the Bawd a hanging matter, as though the truth of her profession's stench had no existence outside Marina's perception of it. And when Marina calls upon the gods for aid, the Bawd cries, "She conjures" (IV.vi.146).

The Bawd is, on the low-comic level, the logical extension of Antiochus and his daughter. Even the poxes and pestilences of which she speaks so gaily are the natural counterparts to the "fire from heaven" which strikes Antiochus and his daughter,

> . . . and shrivell'd up
> Their bodies, even to loathing; for they so stunk
> That all those eyes ador'd them ere their fall
> Scorn now their hand should give them burial.
>
> (II.iv.9-12)

Pericles, Marina, and Thaisa learn to "thank the holy gods as loud / As thunder threatens us"; Antiochus and his daughter, Cleon and Dionyza, and the Bawd have no regard for the truth that the gods represent, and therefore they become a stench in the nostrils of heaven. Ultimately, their disguises are a denial of truth, whereas the disguises of Pericles, Marina, and Thaisa are affirmations of truth. Therefore the Bawd's perverse insistence upon seeing the world upside-down is a constant mystification to Marina. When the Bawd attempts to teach her the duplicity proper to the trade—"Mark me: you must seem to do that fearfully which you commit willingly; to despise profit where you have most gain" (IV.ii.118-19)—Marina replies, "I understand you not" (IV.ii.123). For Marina, chastity and truth are inseparable, and it is her straightforward speaking of truth which preserves her chastity, as when she reminds Lysimachus of his own honor and her helplessness:

> If you were born to honour, show it now;
> If put upon you, make the judgment good
> That thought you worthy of it.
>
> (IV.vi.91-93)

In this respect, Marina belongs to a long line of Renaissance heroines, extending back to Dorothea and beyond, who function as touchstones of truth and honor in others because they are themselves embodiments of those virtues.

Because of this identification with an ideal of virtue, Marina's disguise shifts attention from *who* she is to *what* she is. Pericles, after the first shipwreck, acknowledged the helplessness of mere man in the face of the overwhelming forces that buffet him. Marina is, in ordinary terms, far more helpless than he, and she stresses this physical helplessness by her insistence upon being treated as exactly what she appears to be, a captive virgin. This vulnerability serves, however, as a foil to the internal strength with which she insists upon her truth and chastity, a moral strength which wins over not only the young bucks and the half-heartedly licentious Lysimachus but even the thoroughly corrupted Boult. This testing of Marina's integrity, like the testing of Pericles in Act II, is sealed by a mark of approval on the part of the local ruler. In Act II, Simonides, recognizing Pericles' worth, mused that he

> . . . for aught I know,
> May be, nor can I think the contrary,
> As great in blood as I myself.
>
> (II.v.77-79)

So now Lysimachus, recognizing Marina's worth, presents her to Pericles as

> . . . such a one that, were I well assur'd
> Came of gentle kind and noble stock,
> I'd wish no better choice, and think me rarely wed.
>
> (V.i.66-68)

Lysimachus is more cautious than Simonides in his praise, not willing to propose a marriage without some knowledge of blood-lines. But Lysimachus is an only-recently reformed frequenter of brothels, and has some justification for not trusting his intuitions too far.

It is, however, Lysimachus' recognition of her virtue, and of her extraordinary persuasiveness, which brings Marina face to face with Pericles. Characteristically straightforward, she introduces herself to Pericles the sufferer as one who, weaker as this world's power is measured, can claim equality of suffering:

> I am a maid,
> My lord, that ne'er before invited eyes,
> But have been gaz'd on like a comet. She speaks,
> My lord, that, may be, hath endur'd a grief
> Might equal yours, if both were justly weigh'd.
> Though wayward fortune did malign my state,
> My derivation was from ancestors
> Who stood equivalent with mighty kings;
> But time hath rooted out my parentage,
> And to the world and awkward casualties
> Bound me in servitude.
>
> (V.i.83-93)

It is this speech which rouses Pericles from his torpor; he seizes upon the two words, "fortune" and "parentage," which link him with Marina, and demands her story. Already he recognizes not only a kindred fortune but a literal kinship, for he begins "You are like something that—" (V.i.101) and, after Marina's claim that she is mortal and "No other than I appear" (V.i.104), he exclaims, "My dearest wife was like this maid, and such a one / My daughter might have been. . . ." (V.i.106-7). The final identification by names ("I am the daughter of King Pericles," "This is Marina," "I am Pericles of Tyre") is the culmination of a series of names which Pericles applies to Marina:

> Falseness cannot come from thee; for thou lookest
> Modest as Justice, and thou seem'st a palace
> For the crown'd Truth to dwell in.
>
> (V.i.119-21)

> . . . thou dost look
> Like Patience gazing on kings' graves, and smiling
> Extremity out of act.
>
> (V.i.136-38)

> O, I am mock'd,
> And thou by some incensed god sent hither
> To make the world to laugh at me.
>
> (V.i.141-43)

> But are you flesh and blood?
> Have you a working pulse, and are no fairy?
>
> (V.i.151-52)

The miraculous recovery of the seemingly dead Marina requires her identification with superhuman power: first with Justice, Truth, and Patience, virtues which she has come to represent; then, in a moment of doubt, with an illusion created by a malevolent god to trick Pericles into false hope; then with a changeling, another sort of false, illusionary child. Only in the climactic speech—

> O Helicanus,
> Down on thy knees, thank the holy gods as loud
> As thunder threatens us. This is Marina.
>
> (V.i.196-98)

—does Pericles accept Marina's human reality and articulate the right supernatural connection, enjoining Helicanus to "thank the holy gods" who not only threaten with thunder but bless with restoration.

Notes

1. As M. St. Clare Byrne reports it, Tony Richardson's 1958 production of *Pericles* used Gower as a conscious, visual link:

   > Downstage, almost in the proscenium arch, to right and left, there are stepped and bulwarked rostrums, suggesting the beak and stern of a rowing galley. Rowers, three a side, pull steadily. . . . In the background there is a patterning of cordage and sails and spars against open sky; and downstage, with the six rowers, is Edric Conner, the West Indian singer and actor, who sings and speaks Gower's linking narrative to this more intimate audience. . . . The continual reminder of the sea theme, which is the very thread upon which the plot is hung, is exactly right. It anchors the rambling yarn to an atmosphere, and enables us to see it all through the eyes of the seamen's crude and unsophisticated but vivid imaginations. As the story-teller weaves his spell, out of the background of ship and sky his magic summons the figures of his tale; and as they materialize he retires downstage, and when an episode ends he steps back into the scene, sometimes before the beings his fancy has evoked have all departed ("The Shakespeare Season at the Old Vic, 1957-58, and Stratford-upon-Avon, 1958," *SQ* [*Shakespeare Quarterly*], 9 [1958], 521).

   Though such a conception "modernizes" Gower, it preserves his function as intermediary.

2. John Arthos, *The Art of Shakespeare* (London and New York: Barnes & Noble, 1964), p. 156. Most of the section on *Pericles* in *The Art of Shakespeare* appeared first as "*Pericles, Prince of Tyre*: A Study in the Dramatic Use of Romantic Narrative," *SQ*, 4 (1953), 257-70.

3. All quotations are from Peter Alexander's edition of the *Complete Works* (London and Glasgow: Collins, 1951).

4. So much in *Pericles* is obvious reworking of material from Shakespeare's earlier plays that it is tempt-

ing here to look for a connection with *Measure for Measure*. Is Lysimachus a would-be Vincentio? Or is Vincentio a would-be Lysimachus?

Stephen J. Lynch (essay date 1993)

SOURCE: Lynch, Stephen J. "The Authority of Gower in Shakespeare's *Pericles*." *Mediaevalia: A Journal of Medieval Studies* 16 (1993): 361-78.

[*In the following essay, Lynch argues that Gower serves as the "surrogate author" of* Pericles, *claiming that Shakespeare's use of Gower "involves a double strategy: a confession of authorial limitations matched with a claim to authorial elevation and mystification."*]

The presence of so ancient a figure as Gower in so late a play as *Pericles* poses a series of immediate questions. Why, so late in Shakespeare's career, does he resort to a chorus? Why John Gower as chorus? Most importantly, what is the relationship between the choric Gower and the text of the play?

The first two questions can be addressed with a few brief, though tentative, remarks. A chorus seems requisite in part because of the very nature of the material as Shakespeare received it. The story of Apollonius of Tyre in Gower's *Confessio Amantis* (Book VIII) is structurally episodic, as well as temporally and geographically diverse—a sprawling and fragmented narrative requiring a framing devise in order to secure some measure of cohesion. Gower himself resorted to a type of choric framing throughout the *Confessio* by interjecting Latin headings between episodes of the stories.

John Gower serves as chorus primarily as an acknowledgement of literary debt. Indeed, Shakespeare follows the Confessio with notable fidelity, borrowing the plot sequence, several of the characters' names, and occasionally the very language of the poem. Moreover, Gower as chorus provides an archaic atmosphere to the play. If the woodcut illustration of Gower in George Wilkins' *Painfull Adventures of Pericles* (a prose romance apparently based on the play) is an accurate depiction of the choric Gower as he appeared on stage, he apparently wore an old-fashioned cap, wooden shoes, and held a staff and laurel.[1] "Ancient Gower" (1.Chor.2), in other words, looks ancient. Along with his medieval garb, Gower also makes frequent appeals to an archaic and antiquated poetic tradition which would license the loose structure, improbabilities and unsophisticated moralizing that inform and shape much of the play.[2]

Far more problematic, however, is the complex interplay between Gower and the text. As a conventional chorus, he is unconventionally distanced from the language of the play. In only one other play, *Henry V,* does Shakespeare make extensive use of a chorus, yet the chorus of the history play is far more integrated into the text, speaking the same idiom and verse form as the characters in the play proper. In *Pericles,* however, Gower the chorus stands "in the gaps" (4.4.8), disjointed from the play, speaking an archaic diction of end-stopped, rhymed, tetrameter couplets. Gower fulfills traditional choric obligations by providing background exposition along with much-needed temporal and geographical transitions. Yet, unlike the historical chorus, Gower appeals to distinctly outmoded aesthetic principles, and he comments on the play with an insistent and antiquated moral tone.

As author of the major source and choric presenter of the play, Gower seems strangely lacking in authority. He is often at pains to remind the audience of his literary indebtedness, that the story he presents is not his own: "To sing a song that old was sung, / From ashes ancient Gower is come," "I tell you what mine authors say" (1.Chor.1-2,20). He offers himself as subservient mediator for an authorial tradition that precedes and exceeds him. Allusions to sources and old books are no doubt traditional, yet Gower seems not merely indebted but apologetic, as he humbly confesses his poetic limitations before an audience whose "wit's more ripe" (1.Chor.12). He will manage, as he repeatedly tells us, only with our "patience" (5.3.102). While the chorus of *Henry V* emphasizes the limitations of the theater, Gower emphasizes the limitations of the chorus.

The choric Gower not only mimics the language and style of the source but often exceeds, even parodies, the source. His aphoristic couplets are distinctly more rigid and formulaic than what we find in the *Confessio*. Instead of animating the play, Gower's choric commentary tends to restrain the play. Wonder and mystery collapse for Gower into rigid and even trite moralization:

> Here have you seen a mighty king
> His child, I wis, to incest bring;
> A better prince and benign lord,
> That will prove aweful both in deed and word.
>
> (2.Chor.1-4)

Gower habitually reduces the dynamics of the play into simple proverbs:

> I'll show you those in trouble's reign,
> Losing a mite, a mountain gain.
>
> (2.Chor.7-8)

While the chorus of *Henry V* imaginatively expands the play, Gower's reductive commentary attempts to contain and restrain the play within neatly balanced and overly deterministic rhymes.

Yet if we feel unsatisfied with the quaint simplicities of Gower, so too does Gower. Indeed, he continually negates his own interpretive authority, as he deflects our attention to the play itself. Introducing the first dumb show, he aptly remarks, "What need I speak?" (2.Chor.16), and then, as he spies the entrance of Pericles, he apologizes for his intrusion, and defers to the authority of the text over himself:

> And here he comes. What shall be next,
> Pardon old Gower—this longs the text.
>
> (2.Chor.39-40)

Gower is surely a congenial guide and companion, an ever-helpful mediator between the play and the audience, but his cosmic vision leaves something to be desired. Rarely does he offer more than a track record of Fortune's ups and downs:

> Till fortune, tired of doing bad
> Threw him ashore, to give him glad.
>
> (2.Chor.37-38)

> But fortune, mov'd,
> Varies again; the grisled north
> Disgorges such a tempest forth . . .
>
> (3.Chor.46-48)

His poetic sensibility seems unvaryingly mechanical. When he does stumble upon "grace" and "wonder," he quickly scrambles to get back on solid ground, as when he introduces the mature Marina:

> . . . who hath gain'd
> Of education all the grace,
> Which makes her both the heart and place
> Of general wonder. But, alack,
> That monster Envy . . .
>
> (4.Chor.5-12)

The very instant "grace" and "wonder" enter his choric vocabulary, Gower turns upon the adversitive conjunction "But," and proceeds to launch into an antithetical account of 'monster Envy.'

Gower's gentle urging that we see in the play more than he sees, that we read beyond his reading, that we transcend his naive poetic sensibilities, seems eminently necessary when we are confronted by his exceedingly formulaic closing commentary on the play:

> In Antiochus and his daughter you have heard
> Of monstrous lust the due and just reward.
> In Pericles, his queen and daughter, seen,
> Although assail'd with fortune fierce and keen,
> Virtue preserv'd from fell destruction's blast,
> Led on by heaven, and crown'd with joy at last.
> In Helicanus may you well descry
> A figure of truth, of faith, of loyalty
> In reverend Cerimon there well appears
> The worth that learned charity aye wears.
> For wicked Cleon and his wife
>
> (5.3.86-96)

This attempt at final closure not only fails to close the play but seems strangely dissonant from the play. Gower's choric summation misrepresents more than represents what we have seen on stage. In what seems an overeager effort to achieve supreme balance and symmetry, Gower elevates quite minor characters (Helicanus and Cerimon) to major standing. The miracles in Act 5 are thwarted and restrained into strictures of end-stopped rhymed couplets. Gower becomes a chorus out of accord with the play, an author figure without authority or control over the text he presents. The sense of awe and wonder so prevalent in the play even before the final act—"What world is this?," "Is not this strange?," "Most rare" (3.2.108-10)—is noticeably absent in the commentary of Gower.

Shakespeare's presentation of Gower seems not only at odds with the play but at odds with Gower's presentation of Gower, or rather the narrator, in Book VIII of the *Confessio*. Genius, the narrator of the Apollonius story, also feels bound to an ancient and pre-existent story—"Of a cronike in daies gone . . . I rede thus," "To telle as olde bokes seyne," "as the cronikes seyne" (VIII.279-81, 1160, 1554)—but he exercises considerably more authority over the story he tells. When Genius intrudes upon the narrative, his commentary, though not absolute or definitive, is closely integrated into poem. He too may seem preoccupied with the rhythmic irregularity of Fortune:

> Fortune hath ever be muable
> And maie no while stonde stable.
> For nowe it heith, nowe it loweth,
> Nowe stant upright, nowe overthroweth,
> Nowe full of blisse, and nowe of bale . . .
>
> (VIII.593-97)

But unlike the mechanistic and myopic chorus of the play, the narrator of the poem is also capable of a language of wonder and marvel:

> But for to speake of the mervailes
> Which afterwarde to him befelle,
> It is a wonder for to telle.
>
> (VIII.984-86)

> At Ephesus the sea upcast
> The coffre, and all that was therin.
> Of great mervaile now begyn . . .
>
> (VIII.1164-66)

Gower's narrator apprehends a providential and mysterious order that lurks beyond the apparent waywardness of Fortune. Moreover, Gower's narrator, though moral, is considerably less moralistic. His closing summation of the narrative, though framed as a balanced contrast between noble Apollonius and wicked Antiochus, does not devolve into rigid formula:

> And in ensample his life was writte,
> That all lovers mighten witte
> Howe at laste it shal be sene
> Of love what thei wolden mene.
> For see nowe on that other side,
> Antiochus with all his pride,
> Whiche sette his love unkyndely,
> His ende had sodeynly,
> Set ageyn kynde upon vengeance,
> And for his lust hath his penance.
>
> (VIII.2007-16)

Moral Gower, no doubt—but the verse here, as throughout the poem, is not trite, reductive, or overly mechanistic.

Shakespeare's Gower, in contrast, seems considerably more medieval, more archaic, more quaint and naive than the medieval Gower. Instead of updating his source—Shakespeare's usual practice—Shakespeare backdates his play, making the play, or at least the choric Gower, more antiquated than the *Confessio* would suggest. It is not surprising that Dryden mistook the play as Shakespeare's earliest work, predating *Titus Andronicus*: "Shakespeare's own Muse her Pericles first bore; / The Prince of Tyre was elder than the Moor."[3] Downplaying the more wondrous apprehensions of Genius in the *Confessio*, Shakespeare develops in the figure of Gower a constricted and narrowed perspective.

Shakespeare's Gower does not merely stand in the gaps of the play, but occasionally enters into the very fabric and structure of the text. His dissonant choric commentary, ironically, is integrated into the play in that the play is periodically discordant with itself. Repeatedly, the flow of the action (and how rarely it flows) comes to a sudden halt as characters pause to provide choric and moral commentary, and, as with Gower, such choric remarks are usually off key, if not woefully insufficient. In other words, the play contains internal choruses that mimic the ineptitude of the external chorus. The three fishermen, for example, prove quite adept at extracting morality from fish. Fish live in the sea, the first fisherman expounds, "as men do a-land; the great ones eat up the little ones" (2.1.28-29). Pericles is quick to respond, "a pretty moral" (2.1.35). Yet the moral analogy of the fishermen seems partial at best—suited to the daughter-devouring Antiochus, but failing to account for the generosity of Pericles to Cleon, or the benign rule of Simonides, or even their own kindness towards Pericles.

Consistently in the play, interpretations prove misinterpretations, or at least under-interpretations. The white flags of Pericles' ships are mistaken by Cleon as signs of strategic deception. King Simonides' dissimulation with his daughter's letter seems to Pericles a scheme to undo him. Even the bawds prove hermeneutic incompetents, as they interpret Marina as a gift of fortune, only to find her more of a curse than a blessing—although finally she proves a profitable blessing but in a way they never anticipated. All of these misinterpretations, significantly, are the embellishments of Shakespeare upon the story in the *Confessio*.

Shakespeare also adds to the play an entire scene, without precedent in the poem, that is entirely preoccupied with interpretation. King Simonides systematically interprets and comments upon a series of emblematic shields presented by various knights. At the end of the line enters Pericles, holding a "withered branch, that's only green at top" (2.2.43). The King renders a prompt and self-confident interpretation:

> A pretty moral;
> From the dejected state wherein he is,
> He hopes by you his fortunes yet may flourish.
>
> (2.2.45-47)

Simonides seems to hit upon the meaning, perhaps even the precise meaning Pericles intended. Yet, the meaning of the "withered branch" is not permanently fixed by Simonides, but continues to exfoliate throughout the play, developing a semiotic richness that exceeds any single configuration. By Act 5, the branch, green at top, will come to suggest not merely Pericles' recuperation of his fortunes through marriage to Simonides' daughter, but his later recuperation of his apparently deceased daughter, as well as his still later recuperation of his wife in Diana's temple, along with his recovery of his sanity and spiritual health, the restoration and revival of his family and royal lineage, the political restitution and extension of his empire (to include not only Tyre but Pentapolis), and so forth. The branch far exceeds Simonides' reading of the branch. Like the choric Gower, Simonides fails to restrain or limit the textual free play of meaning.

The tendency in the play for characters to assume a Gower-like stance of not-so-authoritative choric authority is most evident in Pericles himself as he habitually pauses to interpret, and misinterpret, his experiences. After washing ashore in Pentapolis, he feels like a tennis ball randomly knocked about in the "vast tennis court" (2.1.60) of the sea, only to find his father's rusty armor has not-so-randomly been recovered in a fishing net. He then scrambles to reinterpret: "Thanks, fortune, yet, that, after all my crosses, / Thou givest me somewhat to repair myself" (2.1.123-24). Yet his reinterpretation proves but another in an ongoing series of interpretations of the nature of fortune and the sea.

Indeed, the sea is an almost constant presence in the play, and evolves as a recurrent metaphor that stubbornly eludes final interpretation. Fluid, tempestuous, protean—the sea suggests itself in a dizzying array of manifestations: tennis racket wielding Neptune as well as mother goddess and redeemer, tempestuous and tranquil, giver and taker of life, divider and reuniter of families, home to kings, maidens, and pirates. Especially in the early seventeenth century, the sea—in its geographical expansiveness and unfathomed depths—would suggest a realm of mystery and wonder, beyond final definition or containment. Even the more solid and substantive "ooze" (3.1.60) in which Thaisa is deposited, suggests an elusive fluidity. Appropriately, the god of the sea is described as "mask'd Neptune" (3.3.38)—hidden, inscrutable, beyond full comprehension.[4]

A sense of irreducible enigma is introduced in the very opening scene of the play, not just in the riddle, which seems surprisingly unenigmatic (especially compared to the more challenging riddle of the poem), but in the persistently enigmatic and slippery world that confronts Pericles. In the opening scene, Pericles, before interpreting the riddle, interprets the face of the princess of Antioch—and gets it all wrong:

See where she comes, appareled like the spring,
Graces her subjects, and her thoughts the king
Of every virtue gives renown to men!
Her face the book of praises, where is read
Nothing but curious pleasures.

(1.1.16-17)

Her pleasures, however, prove a bit too curious, and so Pericles is compelled to reread and reinterpret: "this glorious casket stor'd with ill" (1.1.78). As internal and inept chorus, Pericles persistently under-reads the texts of his world. He likewise mistakes the music of Antioch as heavenly and divine—mistakes it for the music of the spheres that will sound in Act 5.

Moreover, Pericles under-interprets the death's heads that hang as iconic and emblematic riddles on the wall in Antioch, taking them merely for a conventional *momento mori*: "For death remembered should be like a mirror, / Who tells us life's but breath, to trust it error" (1.1.46-47).[5] Pericles neglects to see any further association between the heads on the wall and the amorous impulses that drove him to Antioch. The heads of the failed suitors, however, might pose a riddle not just of human mortality but of the relations between love and death, signifying that illicit love leads to sterility and death. Pericles' "inflam'd desire . . . To taste the fruit of yon celestial tree" (1.1.21-22) clearly suggests an allegorical reenactment of spiritual death and the Fall of Man. Though Pericles makes a quick exit, never tasting the fruit, never actually falling into sin, he slips nevertheless by mistaking a lesser good for a greater good, attempting to find in the face of the princess—"beyond all wonder" (1.2.76)—a substitute for the wonders of heavenly paradise.

Pericles' initial hermeneutic failures cast doubt upon his supposedly definitive reading of Antiochus' riddle. His decoding of the riddle may function in the play not as an absolute confirmation of his role as reliable interpreter, but as a foil to his tendency to misread or under-read the more elusive riddles that confront him. Though Antiochus is impressed with Pericles' interpretive skill—"He hath found the meaning" (1.1.144)—Pericles untangles the riddle of Antiochus only to miss the riddles in his own life. He outwits the sphinx to stumble over his own feet.

The following scene strongly suggests that Pericles may not have fully resolved the riddle in Antioch. He enters the stage bemoaning for thirty-three lines his condition of "dull-ey'd melancholy" that "Makes both my body and soul to languish" (1.2.2,32), and he expresses bewilderment for the lack of any direct or immediate cause. He proceeds to consider and then dismiss a series of speculative causes for his melancholy, until he finally settles on what he takes to be the definitive root cause—fear of a military invasion by Antiochus. As a master of riddles, Pericles' interpretation of his aching melancholy seems remarkably unsubtle. It is worth noting that his melancholy is Shakespeare's addition to the story. In the *Confessio*, melancholy is felt not by the hero, Apollonius, but by the citizens of Tyre after they hear of his departure:

Whan that thei wist he was ago,
It is a pitee for to here.
They losten lust, they losten chere,
They toke upon hem suche penance,
There was no song, there was no daunce,
But every myrthe and melodie
To hem was then a maladie.

(VIII.484-88)

Shakespeare displaces the melancholy in his source from the citizens of Tyre to Pericles. The play thus renders the cause of Pericles' melancholy problematic, for while the citizens in the poem have a direct and definite cause for their melancholy, Pericles has not. Following immediately after his departure from Antioch, his melancholic depression seems linked, dramatically and psychologically, to his encounter with incest. His extreme revulsion—"my thoughts revolt" (1.1.72)—may emerge not only from the discovered putrification in his object of desire (the princess), but from an unconscious recognition of a potential putrification in his own desire. The "danger, which [he] fear'd, is at Antioch" (1.2.7) may not, after all, be confined to Antioch but may be lurking in himself, in a hidden and irrational obsession with incest—an enigmatic "sea" in his own nature. His melancholy, which he is quick to interpret and define, seems far more mysterious, far more of a riddle, than he comprehends.

Pericles' desire to find in the princess a "boundless happiness" (1.1.25) may indicate as well an unacknowledged longing for an illicit boundary-crossing happiness. An excessive passion, if not an incestuous passion, also characterizes the hero of the *Confessio* as he sets sail for Antioch:

Appolinus the prince of Tyre,
Whiche hath to love a great desire,
As he whiche in his high moode,
Was likinge of his hote blode,
A yonge, a freshe, a lustie knyght. . . .
To ship he goeth, the winde him driveth.

(VIII.383-93)

"Hote blode" and "winde" are conventional markers of unhinged and dangerous passions. A troubled sexuality also seems indicated in Apollonius when he leaves his daughter with Stangulio and Dionyse (Cleon and Dionyza), pledging never again to shave until his daughter is married:

And this avowe to god I make,
That I shall never for hir sake
My berde for no likynge shave,
Till it befalle, that I have
In covenable tyme of age
Besette hir unto mariage.

(VIII.1309-14)

He will not shave "for her sake." Such a course of action seems curious to say the least, and might suggest, whether Gower intended it or not, a fear in the hero of an incestuous fate—a fate that can best be avoided by assuming an uncouth and undesirable appearance until his daughter is wed and he is in the clear.

Shakespeare may have read, or misread, the *Confessio* as suggesting an incest anxiety in the hero.[6] Indeed, the play develops and expands upon such a possibility:

> Till she be married, madam,
> By bright Diana, whom we honor, all
> Unscissor'd shall this hair of mine remain,
> Though I show ill in 't.
>
> (3.3.29-32)

Pericles' vow to grow his hair takes the form of a vow to Diana—thus becoming, at least implicitly, a vow of chastity as well. Pericles will grow his hair, transform into a ragged outcast, and live chaste until his daughter marries. The goddess of chastity, barely mentioned in the source, emerges as a major figure in this play about the unchaste threat of incest. Diana is prayed to by Marina in the brothel and even appears to Pericles in a dream (an anonymous god appears in the poem). The chaste Diana protects Marina from the bawds and Pericles from himself.

In the final act, Shakespeare also expands upon the incestuous suggestions in his source. In the *Confessio,* father and daughter are reunited in an atmosphere that could lend itself to illicit temptations. The "yonge Thaise" enters alone into Apollonius' cabin, "so derke a place," to play music and "By all the weies, that she can, / To glad with this sory man" (VIII.1649-70). In his solipsistic despair, Apollonius rejects her, and even strikes her with his hand. She defends herself with an appeal to her noble lineage—an appeal that might evoke a sense of courtship:

> Avoy my lorde, I am a mayde,
> And if ye wyst, what I am,
> And out of what linage I cam,
> Ye wolde not be so salvage.
>
> (VIII.1704-07)

In the play, Pericles is revived from despair and reunited with his daughter in a scene that more explicitly develops an atmosphere of wooing and seduction. Like Leontes in the *Winter's Tale,* looking upon his grown daughter as a possible mate—"I'd beg your precious mistress, / Which he counts but a trifle" (5.1.223-24)—Pericles finds his daughter appealing for her resemblance to his beloved wife—"for thou lookest / Like one I loved indeed" (127-28). After being pushed away by Pericles, Marina appeals not only to her lineage but to her beauty, modesty, and power to elicit desire:

> I am a maid, my lord, that ne'er before
> Invited eyes, but have been gazed on
> Like a comet . . .
>
> My derivation was from ancestors
> Who stood equivalent with mighty kings.
>
> (5.1.87-94)

When Pericles finally recognizes Marina, he responds in a language of erotic rapture:

> O Helicanus, strike me, honor'd sir,
> Give me a gash, put me to present pain,
> Lest this great sea of joys rushing upon me
> O'erbear the shores of my mortality,
> And drown me with their sweetness. O, come hither,
> Thou that beget'st him that did thee beget.
>
> (5.1.195-200)

The cryptic final line, in which Pericles sees himself as both father and son to his daughter, recalls the perverse family relations in the riddle of Antiochus. Likewise, the evasive and riddling language of Marina earlier in the scene associates her with Antioch.[7] Amidst the background and looming threat of an erotics of incest, Pericles achieves an erotics of faith. Pericles and Marina re-enact the Christian mystery in which Christ proves, paradoxically, both father and son to Mary. Marina, a name repeatedly linked with the sea, can now be reinterpreted in association with the celestial virgin.

Sea imagery returns once again, with insistent repetition—"great sea of joys," "shores of my mortality," "drown me," "Thou that wast born at sea, buried at Tharsus, / And found at sea again!" (5.1.197-202). A thoroughly inexplicable and wondrous sea delivers Pericles from the threat of incest—a near miss—and redeems him from his desperate melancholy. This wonder of unbounded grace is then redoubled in the "great miracle" (5.3.59) of the final scene as Pericles is reunited with his wife in Diana's temple.

By tracing a series of incestuous suggestions in the text, I do not mean to argue that Pericles can be seen as a latent pervert who deserves all the suffering he gets until he is purged of wayward sexual desires. Indeed, how can we fault Pericles for not acknowledging in Act 1 an incestuous desire for a daughter he has yet to conceive? Such an analysis would reproduce the formulaic and reductive moralizing of the choric Gower. My point is not that incest is the firm ground that renders the text fully readable, but rather that incestuous desire lurks in the text as an elusive possibility—a possibility that belies the hasty and overly deterministic interpretations of Pericles. The riddle of incest that confronts him in Act 1 is not definitively unraveled and left behind in Antioch, but continues to surface in the semantic richness and free play of the text—despite the myopic limitations of the internal chorus, Pericles, and the external chorus, Gower. Beyond the riddle of Antiochus, lurks the riddle of Pericles, that neither Pericles, nor Gower, nor we can ever fully contain or resolve.

The play continually depicts Gower, along with the internal choruses, at odds with the dynamics of the text. Choric interpretations devolve into misinterpretations and under-interpretations. The text persistently eludes Gower's formulations of the text. His choric commentary always remains other than and less than the text itself. Gower functions in the play not as an ultimate frame, a fixed hermeneutic resting place of semantic equilibrium, but instead as a myopic foil to a text that proves too slippery and suggestive for choric authority or control.[8]

Yet the play does not merely parody Gower, for his role as authorial presenter inevitably suggests an association with the author of the play, Shakespeare—especially if Shakespeare played the role, which he probably did. As one of only two major choruses in Shakespeare's works, and the only chorus who is an author, Gower as chorus seems closely akin to Shakespeare as author. We know that at least one of Shakespeare's contemporaries blurred the identities of chorus and author: the title page to Wilkins' *Painfull Adventures* reads, "the true history of the play of Pericles, as it was lately presented by the worthy and ancient poet John Gower."

The romances in general seem concerned with the role and nature of the author, and often project author figures into the plays. Paulina appears in the final scene of the *Winter's Tale* as on stage playwright and director, orchestrating and commenting upon the action. Likewise, Prospero in the *Tempest* appears with book and staff (suggesting pen), writing and directing the internal plays within the play. If Gower appears as a surrogate for the author, what might Gower indicate about Shakespeare's sense, after some twenty years in the business, of his own authority over his texts?

Most obviously, Gower suggests Shakespeare's professional role as rewriter and dramatizer of ancient stories—stories composed by a succession of diverse authors. The text of *Pericles* provides a particularly good case in point: based on Gower's *Confessio,* the play was begun perhaps by another dramatist, and given to Shakespeare to revise and complete. Shakespeare's texts, even when his own, are not fully authorized by him, but are re-presentations of "olde bokes" and "cronikes" (VIII.1160,1554)—which are themselves re-presentations of still older texts. From a still wider cultural perspective, even Shakespeare's originality is not original but intertextual—enabled by and dependent upon multiple forms of cultural discourses. Language speaks, not the author. As Roland Barthes comments,

> We know now that a text is not a line of words releasing a single "theological" meaning (the "message" of the Author God) but a multi-dimensional space in which a variety of writings, none of them original, blend and clash. The text is a tissue of quotations drawn from the innumerable centres of culture.[9]

Like Gower the chorus, Shakespeare the author does not autonomously create but rather intervenes in a pre-existent field of discourse that always precedes and exceeds authorial formulation and containment.

Even more, as a man of the theatre, Shakespeare would exercise rather limited control over his works. Not only were the plays the property of the theater company, but, as live performances, his plays would be subject to the manifold uncertainties and contingencies that flesh is heir to—the variability of actors and acting conditions, as well as inevitable differences in audience response (both within any single audience and between different audiences). As a working playwright, Shakespeare must have repeatedly encountered an inevitable dissonance between authorial intention and dramatic execution, compounded by wide and often inexplicable differences in audience reception—a bewildering complex of variables, all shaping the performance and reception of a work, yet for the most part outside Shakespeare's range of authorial control. While a script on paper appears the same from day to day, performances on stage are always and inevitably different. Regardless of authorial intention—which itself would be diverse, inconsistent, and not fully conscious—the plays would generate their own free-floating textual and performative meaningfulness.

Off stage as well, Shakespeare's works, at least the printed poems and plays (in quarto editions), would achieve a high degree of textual autonomy. With the rise of printing in early modern Europe, mass-produced texts, severed from authorial presence and control, could be read and construed in an infinite variety of ways. The concurrent rise of Protestant individualism would only exacerbate the tendency, as texts (Scriptural or otherwise) would be subjected to private reading and an endless array of interpretive possibilities.

As presenter of a text that exceeds him; Gower may function as a confession of Shakespeare's authorial limitations. Yet at the same time, ironically, Gower may function as a claim to authorial control and mastery of another sort. For if the plays tended to mean other than what Shakespeare intended, they would also have meant more than he intended. Complementing the author's inability to control and restrain free-floating textuality is the author's ability to generate free-floating textuality. One of the great miracles in *Pericles* is that Gower, in spite of his limitations, manages to mediate a play that aspires to transcendent and timeless truth—even if the moments of transcendence remain outside his field of vision. Gower presents the text, and the text produces a bounty of surplus meaningfulness and semiotic excess beyond Gower's intentions. His narrow and naive perspective does not finally prevent the text from achieving a rarefied aesthetic status. The play does not pronounce the death of the author (or rather the stillbirth of the author as he emerged in early modern Europe), but rather makes a discreet claim to authorial transcendence.

Shakespeare's use of Gower thus involves a double strategy: a confession of authorial limitations matched with a claim to authorial elevation and mystification. Like Gower, Shakespeare serves as humble author function through which stories are told and retold again, yet like the choric Gower, Shakespeare, in spite of limitations, functions as an authorial medium through which eternal truth speaks.[10]

In the final act of the play, Pericles finds in Marina, even before he recognizes her, a truth transcending his desperate and confused melancholy:

Falseness cannot come from thee, for thou lookest
Modest as Justice, and thou seemest a palace
For the crown'd Truth to dwell in.

(5.1.123-25)

Yet thou dost look
Like Patience gazing on king's graves, and smiling
Extremity out of act.

(5.1.140-42)

Beyond Pericles' muddled world shimmers transcendent and Platonic truth—a beatific vision as Marina transfigures from fleshly self to radiant symbol of eternal virtues: Justice, Truth, Patience. It is one of several hieratic moments in the play when the shadowy world of existence figures forth a realm of pure essence.

It is a moment Pericles only barely understands, and Gower the chorus seems to miss altogether. Outside Gower's field of vision, the text intersects the divine. Gower succeeds not as controller or interpreter of the text but as mediator of truths beyond even his own apprehension. His lack of understanding may even serve as testimony to the supreme value of the text he presents—for the truth of the text proves too rarefied for ordinary or even choric comprehension. Through the use of Gower as surrogate author, Shakespeare reduces the role of the author to humble and unknowing mediator while mystifying the author as medium through which absolute truth speaks—if not loud and clear, then at least through a textual glass darkly. In a strategic move that finds its counterpart in Ben Jonson's publication of his collected works—a bold claim to literary standing—Shakespeare, a man who succeeded in elevating his civic status to that of gentleman, aspires beyond the craft of playwriting to a mystique of literary transcendence.

Notes

1. See F. David Hoeniger, "Gower and Shakespeare in Pericles," *Shakespeare Quarterly,* 33 (1982): 463.

2. For studies of Shakespeare's use of the choric Gower in *Pericles,* see Hoeniger, pp. 461-79; Kenneth J. Semon, "Pericles: An Order Beyond Reason," *Essays in Literature,* 1 (1974): 17-27; Walter F. Eggers, Jr., "Shakespeare's Gower and the Role of the Authorial Presenter," *Philological Quarterly,* 54 (1975): 434-43; and Richard Hillman, "Shakespeare's Gower and Gower's Shakespeare: The Larger Debt of *Pericles,*" *Shakespeare Quarterly,* 36 (1985): 427-37. For textual evidence of Shakespeare's use of the *Confessio Amantis,* see Geoffrey Bullough, *Narrative and Dramatic Sources of Shakespeare,* 6 (London, 1966), pp. 349-74. All references in this essay to the *Confessio Amantis* are from Bullough, pp. 375-423. References to Pericles are from *Complete Works of Shakespeare,* ed. David Bevington (London, 1980).

3. Quoted in Bullough, p. 349. The archaic style that apparently led Dryden to mistake *Pericles* for an early work could also be attributed to dual authorship. I do not intend to address the sticky issue of authorship in *Pericles,* except to say that if the first two acts were written by another dramatist, Shakespeare, in his revision and completion of the play, appropriated the style of the first two acts into the last three, thus achieving an overall unity and cohesion. The three dumb shows of the first half, for instance, are complemented by two more in the second half. Likewise the archaic Gower appears throughout (three times in Act 5), and though he speaks more lines of contemporary pentameter in the second half, his language is always distinctly old-fashioned. For studies of the play's deliberately archaic and medieval design, see Hoeniger, pp. 460-79, and Howard Felperin, *Shakespearean Romance* (Princeton, 1972), pp. 143-76.

4. For a discussion of "mask'd Neptune," see C. L. Barber and Richard Wheeler, *The Whole Journey: Shakespeare's Power of Development* (Berkeley, 1986), p. 311.

5. The iconic heads and other iconic stage images in the play are examined by Mary Judith Dunbar, "'To the Judgement of Your Eye': Iconography and the Theatrical Art of *Pericles*" in *Shakespeare, Man of the Theatre,* ed. Kenneth Muir, Jay L. Halio, and D. J. Palmer (Newark, 1983), pp. 86-97.

6. For a study of literary influence as a process of an author "misreading" his predecessor, see Harold Bloom, *The Anxiety of Influence* (London, 1973). Bloom argues that only poets after Milton felt such anxiety, but the tendency holds for Shakespeare as well.

7. As Coppelia Kahn remarks, Marina's "oblique, cryptic, enigmatic mode of speech links her to the riddling, incestuous princess of Antioch." See "The Providential Tempest and the Shakespearean Family" in *Representing Shakespeare,* ed. Murray M. Schwartz and Coppelia Kahn (Baltimore, 1980), p. 232.

8. The *Confessio* itself, with its structure of Latin headings interspersed throughout the text, might have suggested for Shakespeare the interplay between the choric frame and the text in *Pericles.* As Robert F. Yeager comments, "Gower's Latin hexameters attempt to enforce a single meaning on their context, while Chaucer's fictive narrators insist upon the opposite. . . . Yet each poet succeeds at his task: we are required to read the text itself as 'other,' as autonomous presence, actual and active—as sign, in short—rather than as transparent conduit or medium beyond, or through, which the fictive world potentially unfolds." See "English, Latin, and the Text as 'Other': the Page as Sign in the Work of John Gower" in *Text: Transactions of the Society for Textual Scholarship,* 3 (1987), p. 261.

9. Roland Barthes, "The Death of the Author" in *Image-Music-Text,* trans. Stephen Heath (New York, 1977), p. 146.

10. Steven Mullaney, examining Shakespeare's plays in light of the location of the Globe theater in the marginal and disreputable Liberties of London, also argues that Shakespeare aspires in *Pericles* to a transcendent status: "*Pericles* represents a radical effort to dissociate the popular stage from its cultural contexts and theatrical grounds of possibility—an effort to imagine, in fact, that popular drama could be a purely aesthetic phenomenon, free from history and from historical determination." See *The Place of the Stage* (Chicago, 1988), p. 147.

PRODUCTION REVIEWS

Doreen Delvecchio and Antony Hammond (essay date 1998)

SOURCE: Delvecchio, Doreen and Antony Hammond. Introduction to *Pericles, Prince of Tyre,* edited by Doreen Delvecchio and Antony Hammond, pp. 1-78. Cambridge: Cambridge University Press, 1998.

[*In the following excerpt, Delvecchio and Hammond trace the production history of* Pericles *from the seventeenth through the twentieth century.*]

PERFORMANCE AND RECEPTION

SEVENTEENTH CENTURY

From the beginning *Pericles* has been a play that has divided opinion. It is evident that it was a popular play on stage, and this success surely was at least in part owing to the opportunities it (like the other romances) offered for theatrical spectacle and musical embellishment. The implications for staging found in the quarto text are quite elaborate, though often ambiguous. Many of them are discussed in the Commentary, but this is a good place to remark on their scope.

The opening scene, with the grim display of severed heads, is one. Act 2 presents many challenges for staging, such as the location of King Simonides and Thaisa during the parade of the Knights and presentation of the impresas (2.2), and how exactly the stage was disposed for that scene. The royal party 'withdraws' at the end of the scene while the tilting takes place *offstage* and the main stage is set for the banquet in 2.3, an elaborate scene requiring torches and pages, and later music and dancing, all of which entail use of the maximum resources of the company. Unless 2.4 takes place on the upper stage (for which there is no evidence), there must also be a busy clearing of the banquet before the scene can take place.

Storms in the Elizabethan theatre were often accompanied by 'effects', of which the cannon-ball for thunder, fireworks for lightning, and some way of simulating wind sound were the commonest. In as tempestuous a play as *Pericles,* such effects were almost certainly used in 3.0-3.1, and probably also in 2.0-2.1. The staging of 3.1, however, demands the abandonment of all naturalistic criteria (which few editors seem capable of), so that the main stage becomes the deck of the ship, and the stage doors may be taken to lead below deck. Any attempt to use the stage otherwise would place the actors in a huddle upstage in what is plainly the 'biggest' scene in the play.

More elaborate staging occurs in 3.2, the sudden safe haven of Cerimon's house after the howling of the storm just ended, where in Thaisa's revival many properties are called for by Cerimon (and presumably supplied) and use is made of music. The disposition of the coffin on the stage is a bit of a puzzle, for its contents would be invisible to those in the yard unless it were raised and tilted, which seems unlikely.

There are more lively scenes in Act 4 such as the melodramatic frustration of Leonine's attempt to murder Marina by the Pirates' apparently instantaneous appearance and disappearance, and the sudden transition into the Miteline brothel; sandwiched between the two brothel scenes is the scene at Tarsus, and the visual display of Marina's tomb there, Pericles' mimed passion, and donning of sackcloth. The scenic requirements of Act 5 are complex, but probably best resolved by staging it like 3.1, with the main stage the deck of the ship, and the doors leading either to the ship's rail, or below decks, or both; this is the only scene in the play which seems to mandate use of a discovery space, though it would come in handy elsewhere (e.g. 4.4). The music of the spheres (played, no doubt, from the musicians' gallery) and the theophany of Diana comprise the single most spectacular scenic element in the play, though there is ample opportunity to make Diana's temple in the final scene a splendid tableau.

Companies in recent years who have staged the play in large, well-equipped theatres (RSC [Royal Shakespeare Company production] 1958, Stratford 1973 and 1986, National [The (Royal) National Theatre, London production] 1994) have seized upon all these opportunities, and invented many more (no director, apparently, can resist staging the Knights' joust between 2.2 and 2.3, even though the quarto is very careful to leave it out). We may confidently assume that the sharers at the Globe[1] seized with equal enthusiasm upon the play's scenographic potential, though as usual there are no useful eye-witness accounts.[2]

Early references to *Pericles* are mainly complimentary. The very rare pamphlet *Pimlyco. Or, Runne Red-Cap. Tis a mad world at Hogsdon* (1609, *STC* [*A Short-Title Catalogue of Books Printed in England, Scotland, & Ireland and of the English Books Printed Abroad*] 19936) is influenced by the play, since it involves a tribute to Skelton, and refers to 'learned *Gower*' on B2[r]; the reference to *Pericles* occurs on c1[r]:

Amazde I stood to see a Crowd
Of *Ciuill Throats* stretchd out so lowd:
(As at a *New-play*) all the *Roomes*
Did swarme with *Gentiles* mixt with *Groomes*.
So that I truly thought, all *These*
Came to see *Shore,* or *Pericles.*[3]

The Prologue to *The Hogge Hath Lost His Pearl* optimistically concludes:

And if it proue so happy as to please,
Weele say tis fortunat like Pericles.[4]

The views of the contrary party emerged presently. Ben Jonson, much disgruntled at the failure of his play *The New Inn,* attacked contemporary popular theatrical taste in the poem, 'The just indignation of the author . . .' (sometimes known as 'Ode to Himself', written in 1629 and appended to the printed text of his play). He singled *Pericles* out for particular condemnation:

No doubt some mouldy tale,
Like *Pericles*; and stale
As the Shrieves crusts, and nasty as his fishscraps, out
  of every dish,
Thrown forth, and rak't into the common tub

(lines 21-5)[5]

This poem was by no means Jonson's only diatribe against the kind of play he took *Pericles* to be, and the kind of play which was attracting audiences in droves, while they slighted what he regarded as his own more serious work. The best-known such attack is found in the Prologue to *Every Man in his Humour* (not printed in the first edition of 1601; included with the Folio of 1616):

He rather prays, you will be pleased to see
One such today as other plays should be;
Where neither *Chorus* wafts you ore the seas;
Nor creaking throne comes downe, the boyes to
  please;
Nor nimble squibbe is seene, to make afear'd
The gentlewomen; nor roul'd bullet heard
To say, it thunders; nor tempestuous drumme
Rumbles, to tell you when the storme doth come

(lines 13-20)

The tenor of this objection lies against abuses of the unities, and against the use of what we now call special effects. Jonson believed Shakespeare, by abusing principled dramaturgy in this way, to be belittling the dramatist's profession.[6] He returned to the fray in the Induction to *Bartholomew Fair,* where the 'author' declares 'Hee is loth to make Nature afraid in his *Playes,* like those that beget *Tales, Tempests,* and such like *Drolleries*' (lines 128-30). Jonson's attitude towards dramaturgy has served as a stick to beat *Pericles* with ever since.[7]

How long *Pericles* stayed in the King's Men's repertory is anyone's guess, but the continuing production of quarto editions suggests it remained popular. Two references suggest that its reputation as a successful play remained high even after the closure of the theatres. The first occurs in Samuel Sheppard's *The times Displayed* (1646); it is in the sixth sestiad which, unlike the others (which are religious debates), is a lament by Apollo on the degenerate state of poetry:

See him whose Tragick Sceans *EURIPIDES*
Doth equal, and with *SOPHOCLES* we may
Compare great *SHAKESPEAR ARISTOPHANES*
Never like him, his Fancy could display,
Witness [t]he Prince of *Tyre,* his Pericles,
His sweet and his to be admired lay
He wrote of lustful *Tarquins* rape shews he
Did understand the depth of Poesie.[8]

To be sure, this is a literary, not a theatrical, appreciation: though Sheppard began his literary life as Jonson's amanuensis in 1606, this is clearly an old man's literary retrospective (there is, for instance, no mention of the closing of the theatres).

A much more interesting, because often misrepresented, reference is found in John Tatham's prefatory poem to Brome's *A Joviall Crew* (1652):

There is a Faction (Friend) in Town, that cries,
Down with the *Dagon-Poet, Johnson* dies.
His works were too elaborate, not fit
To come within the Verge, or face of *Wit.*
Beaumont and *Fletcher* (they say) perhaps, might
Passe (well) for currant Coin, in a dark night:
But *Shakespeare* the *Plebean* Driller, was
Founder'd in's *Pericles,* and must not pass.
And so, at all men flie, that have but been
Thought worthy of Applause: therefore, their spleen.

(A4ᵛ)

The whole poem is quite clever, as such things go, attacking the malice of those that condemn 'the Beams that warm'd you, and the Stage'. If the two lines about Shakespeare are taken out of context, they appear condemnatory; in context, the implication is clear: *Pericles* was considered by Tatham a success.

But the climate was about to change. Downes says *Pericles* was acted at the Cock-pit in Drury Lane, by Rhodes's company, with Betterton in the title role, in the 1659-60 season.[9] Following this the play's long theatrical neglect began.[10] A modified version of Jonson's view prevailed: changing literary and theatrical fashion found romance plots and subjects outmoded;[11] and by the time Romanticism might have restored interest in *Pericles,* at least for its spectacular aspects, its virtue had been sullied by the doubts concerning its authorship.

NINETEENTH CENTURY

Samuel Phelps's production at Sadler's Wells in 1854, which ran for fifty-five performances, was a grand tribute to Victorian scenography. Phelps, normally a purist in his productions, cut Gower, all references to incest, and the brothel scenes; but according to the critic of the *Ath-*

enaeum, the scenery was 'several years in preparation, and the immediate expense of the production is scarcely less than 1,000 *l*'.[12] *The Times* treated the venture sardonically:

> Not a single opportunity is missed for hanging on a wondrous picture or group that shall hide the paucity of the dramatic interest. When Pericles is thrown upon the sands, it is with the very best of rolling seas . . . when the storm afterwards rocks his vessel, it rocks in real earnest, and spectators of delicate stomachs may have uneasy reminiscences . . . An admirably equipped Diana, with her car in the clouds, orders his course to her sacred city, to which he is conducted by a moving panorama of excellently-painted coast scenery. The interior of the temple, where the colossal figure of the many-breasted goddess stands in all its glory amid gloriously attired votaries, is the last 'bang' of the general magnificence.

However, 'the personages in general do little else than walk on and walk off the stage, without betraying or exciting an emotion'.[13] The last English production before the twentieth century was the bizarre John Coleman farrago at Stratford-upon-Avon. The veteran Coleman had produced his own revised script of *Pericles,* and the hard-pressed Frank R. Benson in a weak moment gave Coleman permission to produce it, and only ten days in which to do so. The results were catastrophic.[14]

TWENTIETH-CENTURY SPECTACLE

The twentieth century has seen the revival of the play's fortunes: a slow, hesitant revival which nonetheless has led to productions of *Pericles* having these days become a quite common theatrical event.[15] The Royal Shakespeare Company's 1947 production was a relic of an earlier age; director Nugent Monck omitted the first act, on the grounds that 'it is irrelevant and not the work of William Shakespeare', a curious portmanteau judgement. Barry Jackson's scenes were likewise old-fashioned. . . . In 1958 Tony Richardson directed a more complete version, in which Gower (Edric Connor) became a calypso singer; Richard Johnson played Pericles, Geraldine McEwan, Marina, and a young Edward de Souza, Lysimachus. The design was by Loudon Sainthill. . . .

Unfortunately, all productions since then by the major companies have treated *Pericles* as a lame-duck text, and both rearranged it and Wilkinsised it in varying degrees.[16] The last main-stage production at Stratford-upon-Avon was Terry Hands's in 1969, designed by John Bradley, which featured an unchanging bare stage dominated by a hanging dodecahedron which puzzled all reviewers, and very sixties-ish costuming, or lack thereof. . . . Emrys James played Gower as a Welsh bard, . . . , but the most unusual feature of the casting was the doubling of Thaisa and Marina by Susan Fleetwood. This peculiar idea necessitated the use of another actress for Marina in the final scene, and provoked an objection from Harold Hobson. By returning Fleetwood to Thaisa's part in the final scene, and by not attempting to age her, he wrote, the impression was given 'that Pericles is in danger of misbehaving with his own child. So the play appears to have come full circle, and to finish where it began, in incest. This is clean contrary to what I understand to be Mr Hands's intention.'[17]

Jean Gascon directed *Pericles* for the Shakespeare Festival (as it was then called) of Stratford, Ontario, in 1973, in a production that one reviewer not given to unnecessary enthusiasm called 'superlative theatre, and an illumination of the play that came as a revelation . . . not conflicting with one's own response to the written text, but making one aware that, by comparison, that response was meager and imaginatively undernourished'.[18] Nicholas Pennell was much admired as Pericles, as was Edward Atienza's voice-over Gower; whilst Leslie Hurry's storybook costumes also met with approval. In retrospect, however, it can be seen, even for its own time, to have been an old-fashioned production.

Arguably the best large-scale production of the play in recent years has been that at Stratford, Ontario in 1986. Director Richard Ouzounian clearly regarded the work with enthusiasm and, aided by an excellent cast, caught much of the play's appeal both as fairy-tale and as profound myth; all this despite the intrusion of some of the Oxford adaptation's fantasies. Like Tony Richardson, he emphasised Gower's otherness geographically and culturally: Renée Rogers belted out the choruses in pop—soul fashion, nearly becoming the star of the show in the process.[19] The resources of Guthrie's famous stage were often used to excellent advantage, as for instance when Pericles was cast upon the angry shore in Pentapolis, hurtling up from the vomitorium as if cast by a gigantic wave. Geraint Wyn Davies, as Pericles, contrived a more convincing progression from naïve youth to exhausted age than any other recent exponent, and the central scenes (2.2 and 2.3) were deftly handled, thanks to the excellent acting of Goldie Semple as Thaisa, and the wonderfully old-King-Cole-style Simonides of the inimitable William Needles.[20]

MINIMALISM

The tradition of spectacular production has thus been given every opportunity. The play works equally well, however, in more restrained or economical settings: it does not depend upon expensive sets and prodigies from the audiovisual departments to make its effect. Ron Daniels made his début with the Royal Shakespeare Company by directing it in 1979 at The Other Place, a carefully minimalist production, which was liked by reviewers in direct proportion to their dislike of *The Merry Wives of Windsor* on the main stage; Peter McEnery was much admired as Pericles. More recently, the Swan was in 1989 the venue for another directorial début, David Thacker's. This modest production, vaguely Georgian in costuming, reverted to 1958's idea of a West Indian Gower (Rudolph Walker), without the calypso music; he carried and referred to a big book, and remained on stage throughout.[21] Nigel Terry played a measured Pericles; many reviewers took objection to Cerimon's being played by a woman (Helen Blatch), a practice which seems now to have become inevitable. This is the only RSC production to have an archival videotape; it is a scandal that the tape is so poor that only a handful of brightly lit scenes can be made out at all: a twentieth-century equivalent of a 'bad quarto'.[22]

A remarkable student production (professionally directed: Mimi Mekler) by the joint Erindale-Sheridan Theatre and Drama Studies programme of the University of Toronto at Erindale showed how the minimalist approach can be carried to a surprisingly successful extreme (1993). The tiny, wingless theatre, and the small cast (eleven) were treated as opportunities for theatrical inventiveness, rather than as limitations. Cuts were relatively few: more of the text was retained, and in the original order, than in any of the professional productions described here. The small cast of course entailed elaborate doubling; the only actor who did not double was the Pericles. The set was a bare stage with one corner curtained off, with a raised platform, to become scenes 'within'. A cloth backdrop became a wall with the heads of the unsuccessful princes in 1.1 (leaning against it from behind, the actors seemed like bas-reliefs). The director's best ideas came in the Pentapolis scenes, the fairy-tale comic centre of the play, which Mekler treated admirably as a series of children's play-acting games. So, the rusty armour in 2.1 was a mesh gown with tin can tops sewn into it, which looked funny until all the Knights appeared so clad; their shields were dustbin lids, and their procession before Simonides and Thaisa joked up with swingy music; the combats were included, the funniest being when Pericles and a Knight shook hands, and then made their forefingers their swords. The brothel scenes were aided by the addition of two girls acting as tarts most suspicious of the unwanted newcomer; the appearance of the 'disguised' Lysimachus in a huge crow-beaked mask reduced the cast to hysterics. The sexual politics of the last Cleon-Dioniza scene were emphasised by having them in bed, with Dioniza using her sexuality to overcome Cleon's feeble moral resistance: a nice idea in juxtaposition with the brothel. All in all, this was a remarkable achievement, considering the limitations of the forces involved.[23] Perhaps *Pericles*' future fortunes lie in directions such as these.

NATIONAL *1994*

Curiously, the National (now Royal National) Theatre had not mounted *Pericles* until Phyllida Lloyd's production at the Olivier Theatre, May 1994. And certainly, this, the most recent staging of the play at the time of writing, gives cause for thinking that minimalism is the better choice. The production has become notorious for its cost (shades of Phelps) and for its problems with stage technology, which caused the cancellation of the first preview, and its opening without a dress rehearsal. A useful account of the production has been published[24] which, besides chronicling some of the difficulties, is helpfully illustrated.

The production epitomised the difficulties that the current approach to main-stage productions of the classics blunders into. It is assumed that today's visually oriented audiences, brought up on blockbuster movies and musicals, will tolerate classical theatre only if it is produced in a spectacular fashion. The technical facilities of modern theatres make directors feel obliged to use them (the tilting revolve in the Olivier was the cause of much of Lloyd's misery), and since for all sorts of practical reasons the cast has very little time to accustom themselves to their costumes, the lighting, and other technical aspects, the traditional ecology of the theatre—that it is a place for acting—is once more threatened, as it was in the worst days of nineteenth-century pictorialism. The play becomes the excuse for the display of technological gee-whizzery, rather than the technology's being placed at the service of the play. It is a sad tale, apologetically documented by Reynolds. . . .

The production earned mixed reviews and smallish audiences. Michael Billington rightly complained that Lloyd's emphasis on dance and music left the language undervalued, and that 'propulsive narrative is too often sacrificed to arresting detail' (*Guardian Weekly*, 26 June 1994). Others were referring to it as *Pericles—the Musical*; Benedict Nightingale in *The Times* (23 May 1994) gave a full, and devastating, description of all the visual effects in language recalling his predecessor's report on Phelps, 140 years before. However, despite the difficulties created by the staging, by some very strange costuming, and by the interpolation of some perfectly gratuitous 'production numbers', such as the roaring twenties musical interlude beginning the brothel scene, the performance had all sorts of genuine theatrical imagination. The use of simultaneous staging, especially of 3.3 and 3.4, was imaginative . . . , and at last there was a real theophany. . . . Though generally under-cast, there were some good performances, most especially Henry Goodman's audience-engaging, charming Gower. But overall, Lloyd's was as much an *adaptation* of the play as Lillo's, Phelps's, or Coleman's.

Clearly, the ecological balance between acting and *mise-en-scène* has swung to an extreme at present; it's time for another Jonson (or Guthrie, or Peter Brook) to give everyone what for, and begin the return swing.

Notes

1. There is a commonly held view that the scenographic characteristics of the last plays imply that they were originally written for the Blackfriars. But *Per.* [*Pericles*], which shares these characteristics, is too early for the Blackfriars; as the title page of the quarto makes clear, it was a Globe play. This casts doubt on the whole theory.

2. Hoeniger [*Pericles*, ed. F. D. Hoeniger, 1963 (Arden Shakespeare)], p. lxvi, quotes a letter from Sir Gerald Herbert, with its account of a court performance of *Per.* on 20 May 1619, but Herbert was much more interested in the fancy banquet than the play; the only useful information is that the long interval was taken after Act 2.

3. 'Shore' is perhaps the lost play by Chettle and Day performed by Worcester's Men in 1603, about Jane Shore, King Edward IV's celebrated mistress.

4. A3ᵛ (STC [*A Short-Title Catalogue of Books Printed in England, Scotland, & Ireland and of the English Books Printed Abroad 1475–1640*. First compiled by A. W. Pollard and G. R. Redgrave. Second edition, revised and enlarged, begun by W. A. Jackson and F. S. Ferguson, completed by Katherine F. Pantzer, 3 vols., 1986, 1976, 1991] 23658). The play was seen by Sir Henry Wotton on 21 February 1613.

5. The 'common tub' consisted of the unattractive leftovers from City feasts, collected for the poor.

6. The date of this Prologue is in dispute; Herford and Simpson [C. H. Herford and Percy Simpson, *Ben Jonson*, II vols., 1925-52] believe it to have been written during or shortly after the War of the Theatres, but there is no external evidence for this, and it might well express Jonson's mature dislike of the romances.

7. Most recently in Benedict Nightingale's review of the National 1994 production, which follows the grand tradition of theatre reviewing in berating *Pericles*' plot for its lack of realism (*The Times*, 23 May 1994).

8. Stanza 9, p. 22 (c3ᵛ).

9. *Roscius Anglicanus, or an Historical Review of the Stage,* 1708, p. 18.

10. Broken only by the three performances of Lillo's *Marina* in 1738.

11. Not that the other romances did better: *WT* [*The Winter's Tale*] was not performed; *Cym.* [*Cymbeline*], adapted by D'Urfey, was given twice. Only *Temp.* [*The Tempest*], first adapted by Davenant and Dryden, and subsequently further humiliated by Shadwell, and Webberised into a musical, was a roaring success.

12. October 1854. A thousand pounds in 1854 would have been the equivalent of perhaps £250,000 today.

13. 16 October 1854.

14. J. C. Trewin has a very entertaining account of it in his *Benson and the Bensonians* (1960), pp. 115-19.

15. No attempt is being made here to record all productions of the play. Productions in translation, and many professional, as well as semi-professional and amateur productions (with one exception), are necessarily and deliberately excluded. Details of many of these can be found in *Shakespeare Around the Globe: A Guide to Notable Postwar Revivals,* ed. Samuel L. Leiter, 1986, pp. 555-67; and in vol. XXI of Gale's *Shakespearean Criticism* series (1991).

16. In his chapter on *Pericles*, Roger Warren (*Staging Shakespeare's Late Plays,* 1990) provides an overview, often in fascinating detail, of the RSC [Royal Shakespeare Company production] 1969 and 1989 and Stratford 1986 productions, but his missionary view of the Oxford adaptation colours and distorts many of his statements and all of his opinions.

17. *Sunday Times,* 6 April 1969. No theatrical judgement, however sane, can 'scape whipping. Warren contrives to argue that incest 'is a possibility raised by the text itself, a danger narrowly averted' (p. 233). This seemingly incredible misprision arises from a doggedly post-modern misreading of 5.1.190 (see Commentary).

18. Berners W. Jackson, 'Shakespeare at Stratford, Ontario, 1973', *SQ* [*Shakespeare Quarterly*] 24 (1973), 408.

19. It is curious that no director has attempted to do the obvious, that is to show Gower as a familiar figure from the past, a celebrated storyteller whose speech and looks are of a previous age.

20. It is most regrettable that the absurd conditions imposed by Canadian Equity and endorsed by the Stratford Archive make it impossible to include photographs of this remarkable production.

21. A useful caution against over-reliance on reviews emerges here: Michael Coveney (*Financial Times,* 14 September 1989) condemned Walker as 'haltingly half-comprehensible'; Michael Billington (*Guardian,* same date) says he articulated beautifully. Billington was right: the videotape confirms it.

22. The tape of Stratford 1986 is equally frustrating, in a different way: for a vast chunk of the play the sound track is audible, but the video picture has disappeared in a jumble of mistracking. A plague on both their houses.

23. It seems to have shared many features with Ultz's production for the Theatre Royal, Stratford East (1983): see Leiter, *Shakespeare Around the Globe,* p. 557.

24. Peter Reynolds's *Pericles: Text Into Performance,* published by the Education Department of the National Theatre (undated, but obviously 1994).

THEMES

James O. Wood (essay date 1977)

SOURCE: Wood, James O. "Shakespeare, *Pericles,* and the Genevan Bible." *Pacific Coast Philology* 12 (October 1977): 82-9.

[*In the following essay, Wood uses the theme of flattery as it appears in the second act of* Pericles *to support an argument for Shakespeare as the play's sole author, and as the basis for the assertion that the surviving text is an amalgam of an early draft by Shakespeare and his later revisions.*]

The singular play *Pericles, Prince of Tyre,* published in quarto as Shakespeare's in 1609, somehow failed to appear in the Folio of 1623. Though it is universally agreed that much of the latter half could have been written only by Shakespeare, his total authorship has found only sporadic acceptance. Full attribution would significantly affect our view of the poet, for it would enable us to know him as the only begetter of his closing quaternion of magnificent romances, not a mere shaper of another man's creation, much less a pupil of Beaumont and Fletcher. While some may demur to T. S. Eliot's phrase, "that very great play *Pericles*,"[1] all will agree that the stone which the builders rejected, if the editors of the Folio did indeed exclude it, is the cornerstone of a new Shakespearean wing.

Opinion about the authorship has altered appreciably since mid-century. In 1930 E. K. Chambers asserted, regarding the two distinct parts of *Pericles,* "The most obvious thing about the play is that, as it stands, it cannot all be by one writer . . . [most of the earlier portion] does not read like Shakespeare at any stage of development."[2] A few years later George Lyman Kittredge observed, with heavier emphasis, "That *Pericles* is not all Shakespeare's is an obvious and undisputed fact . . . The first part cannot be his, except perhaps for an occasional touch."[3] However, a later trend toward an all-Shakespearean *Pericles* has been led by G. Wilson Knight, whose *The Crown of Life* was published in 1947; and the trend has continued despite the recent effort to revive the candidacy of George Wilkins as a collaborating playwright.[4] A good many now grant that the whole play may well be Shakespeare's but insist that the version we have is a memorial reconstruction and that the language is largely that of one or more reporters. A few, however, treat the language as Shakespeare's own throughout, a view that a recent computer analysis of the style tends to support.[5] As early as 1953 C. J. Sisson declared, "*Pericles* is all of a piece, and is Shakespeare's."[6] How? All of a piece?

It is necessary, and I believe ultimately possible, to rescue this Shakespearean text, piecemeal, from a heavy accumulation of imputations of corruption and alleged evidence of contemporary reporting and alien authorship. In the first scene, one significant passage, cited by some as the work of another poet or the garbling of a reporter, can be seen on careful inspection to be sound and distinctively Shakespearean.[7] In the fourth scene a substantial passage, of which the true text is alleged to be irrecoverable, can be vindicated by attention to a point in Shakespearean grammar.[8] As Sisson pointed out in 1953, "Never has a play of Shakespeare been dealt with so cavalierly by its editors."[9]

I wish now to review a scene which has been held up as the prime example of reportorial garbling. It is the second scene of the first act, in which the young Prince Pericles is lifted from a slough of despond by a wise old counsellor and is started on his epic travels. Its theme is brooding withdrawal and swift restoration to active life. It grew, in a mind like Shakespeare's, from a glimpse, in an admitted source of the play, of the prince "withdrawing himselfe into his studie."[10] One perceptive critic has said that if this scene "was not conceived by Shakespeare, he must have had a twin."[11]

As the scene opens, the tender, high-minded young prince has recently returned to Tyre from Antioch, whither he had gone in high hopes of winning the hand of the daughter of King Antiochus. He loved her at first sight; but, through a rather easy riddle given to him to solve, he has discovered that she and her father are living incestuously. The king has resolved to kill him, as he has killed previous suitors whose heads decorate his premises. Pericles has hastened home under cover of night.

Now, in the second scene, Pericles is shown in seclusion, asking certain lords to let none disturb him. Like a similar Shakespearean prince caught in a situation fraught with incest and murder, he lapses into paralyzing grief, "dull-eyde melancholie." His pensive self-description has distinct kinship with the well-known account of world-weariness that Hamlet gives to Rosencrantz and Guildenstern. Pericles is certain that Antiochus will overrun Tyre in order to destroy him and thus guard the heinous secret. As the prince is surrendering to utter despair, "Enter all the Lords to Pericles," and two sycophants, very probably the lords that he has asked to guard his solitude, speak to him unctuously:

1. Lord.

> Ioy and all comfort in your sacred brest.

2. Lord.

> And keepe your mind till you return to vs peacefull and comfortable.

> (I.ii.34-35)

The prince has thus far told nobody the cause of his condition; but the two lords are soothingly acquiescing in his withdrawal and his neglect of his royal function. At this point, however, one Helicanus, an old counsellor, soundly rebukes the toadies and takes the prince in hand. A contemporary playgoer and playwright, George Wilkins, in an often dilated and occasionally metrical account of the play in 1608, when it was a stage success but was as yet unpublished tells how Helicanus

> came hastily into the chamber to him, and finding him so distasting mirth, that he abandoned all familiar society, he boldly beganne to reproue him, and not sparingly tolde him, he did not wel so to abuse himselfe, to waste his body there with pyning sorrow, vpon whose safety depended the liues and prosperity of a whole kingdome, that it was ill in him to doe it, and no lesse in his counsell to suffer him . . . that while he

Martha Henry as Thaisa, Nicholas Pennell as Pericles, and Edward Atienza as Gower in Act II, scene iii of the 1974 Stratford Festival production of Pericles.

liued so shut vp, so vnseene, so carelesse of his gouernment, order might be disorder for all him.[12]

In the play, Helicanus' chiding speech begins with a word mocking the lord's blandishment:

H<small>EL</small>.

> Peace, peace, and giue experience tongue,
>   They doe abuse the King that flatter him. . . . . .
> When *signior* sooth here does proclaime peace,
> He flatters you, makes warre vpon your life.
>
> (I.ii.37-45)

Pericles, infuriated, dismisses all the others and turns on Helicanus, threatening him with "the dart in Princes frownes," shadowing the confrontation in which Lear says to Kent, "The bow is bent and drawne, make from the shaft" (*Lr.* I.i.145). Pericles is soon checked, however, by Helicanus, who counsels him to leave Tyre for a time and thus escape Antiochus and avert the ruthless invasion that is imminent. The strategy is as simple as the scene is clear.

It would seem obvious enough, without Wilkins' florid account, that Signior Soothe's fawning wish that Pericles' mind be kept "peacefull and comfortable" "till you return to vs" alludes to the prince's seclusion and virtual abdication of his kingly office. Most editors, however, "postulate major dislocations in this scene" (*Riverside Shakespeare*, 1974, p. 1486) and think that "the lines seem wildly disordered" (*Complete Pelican Shakespeare*, 1969, p. 1264), oddly supposing that the speaker is referring to Pericles' future travels, though these are thought of only later by Helicanus, and are then begun in secret. Further, we are told that there is no "apparent reason for the following remarks by Helicanus on flattery" (Riverside ed., p. 1486), that "there has been no flattery" (Pelican ed., p. 1288). This second misapprehension, transparent as the first, is dispelled by referring to any good English dictionary. A major aspect of flattery is *soothing* (OF. *flater*, to smooth, caress), a sense particularly frequent in Shakespeare. The comforting acquiescence of yes-men contributes to the ruin of a Richard II or a Richard Nixon. On this aspect of flattery a chapter of the Genevan Bible

(1560) which I believe was running in the poet's mind as he framed this scene is especially illuminating.

The sixth chapter of Jeremiah is a diatribe against false prophets who are soothing the fears of a people about to be invaded by a ruthless army. A reader versed in scripture, coming upon Helicanus' half-mocking "Peace, peace," thinks immediately of verse 14 (made proverbial in America by Patrick Henry): "Thei haue healed also the hurt of the daughter of my people with swete wordes, saying, Peace, peace, when there is no peace." In the margin beside this the Genevan editors make this comment: "The false Prophets comforted them by flatterings," confirming the use of "flatter" in *Pericles;* but what is startling is the fact that two of the words reiterated in the dialogue of the play, "comfort" and "flatter," seem to echo the marginal note. Apparently Shakespeare, like Milton, occasionally assimilated the marginal notes of the Genevan Bible.[13]

It has been observed by sharp-eyed Professor Jenijoy La-Belle that in the margin above Psalm 78 the Genevan editors placed the words "Mans ingratitude," a phrase that appears in Amiens' song in the banquet scene in *As You Like It* (II.vii) and nowhere else in Shakespeare. She also noticed that below the heading, in the text of the psalm, it is said that God "smote all the firstborne in Egypt" (verse 51); and recalling that Jaques, just before the banquet, said "I'le go sleepe if I can: if I cannot, I'le raile against all the first borne of Egypt" (1623 Folio, II.v.60-61), LaBelle evidently inferred some possible borrowing by Shakespeare.[14] We can strengthen the inference by looking a little further into the biblical text. Two other key phrases in Amiens' song, "benefits forgot" and "friend remembered not," echo verse 42 of the psalm, "Thei remembered not his hand" and its marginal comment, "The forgetfulnesse of Gods benefitts." This blending by Shakespeare of Genevan text and margin is similar to what we have noticed in *Pericles.*

Psalm 78 is a review of the account in Exodus of God's wonderful works in delivering the enslaved Israelites, followed by a jeremiad against their thanklessness. Prominent in the earlier half of the psalm is God's provision of food. After the people had walked dryshod across the bed of the Red Sea, they "spake against God." Could he "prepare a table in the wilderness?" they murmured (verse 19). I suggest that it was the preparation of a table in the Forest of Arden that drew the snatches of the psalm and its margin into the context of the play. To Jaques' remark about the firstborn of Egypt, Amiens replies that he is off to join the Duke, because "his banquet is prepared." Orlando then enters with Adam, who is keeping his vow to follow him "to the last gasp." Adam had given five hundred crowns, his life savings, to Orlando, saying

> Take that, and he that doth the Rauens feede,
> Yea prouidently caters for the Sparrow,
> Be comfort to my age.
>
> (II.iii.43-45)

(The raven is in Luke xii. 24; the sparrow is in Matt. x. 29.) The moment has now arrived for Adam to find the bread he has cast upon the waters.

Much has been said of late about Shakespeare and divine providence. Of course, in "Bible times" the laws of nature could be countermanded. For the Israelites a table was prepared in the wilderness when manna was sent down like rain (verse 24 of our psalm); and on a later well-known occasion loaves and fishes were multiplied. These we call miracles. In Shakespeare's romances, however, as in the modern world, God's bounty comes only through human agency or the operation of natural processes; yet it may be described as divine providence nonetheless. In the Judeo-Christian view nothing in life is purely accidental. Orlando and Adam arrive famished in the wilderness as a banquet is about to be served; Pericles' daughter Marina, like Hamlet, is saved by pirates from imminent death; Pericles arrives with a cargo of corn even as Cleon is praying for bread. These cases are simple; but the whole career of Pericles can be taken as a miracle play to show that, as he acknowledges at the opening of the second act, when washed ashore after shipwreck, the higher powers are good but inscrutable and must be accepted on faith.

The burden of Psalm 78, ingratitude, is notably recurrent in Shakespeare from first to last; and in *Pericles,* where manna is a conspicuous godsend, the treatment of the sin of sins is primitive and severe. Cleon, after receiving the cargo of corn, says to the prince that if any

> pay you with vnthankfulness in thought,
> Be it our Wiues, our Children, or our selues,
> The curse of heauen and men succeed their euils.
>
> (I.iv.102-104)

This is prophetic. Cleon's wife schemes (IV.i.) to murder Pericles' daughter and, in a scene (IV.iii.) distinctly suggesting *Macbeth,* persuades Cleon to condone the crime. The plot fails, but the conspirators are burned in their palace by their outraged subjects.

Our inspection of the second scene of *Pericles,* together with the new insights to which the study has led, asks greater editorial respect for the textual integrity of the play and for the accumulating evidence that *Pericles* is, as Sisson averred, all of a piece and is Shakespeare's. The statement of Chambers that a large part of the play "does not read like Shakespeare at any stage of development" declares its own subjectivity; it accords with the traditional view that Shakespeare began with the Henry VI plays and *The Comedy of Errors.* But such plays must have been preceded, I should think, by a good deal of practice. It is well known that Dryden said *Pericles* was Shakespeare's first play; Edmond Malone once thought that he wrote it about 1590-91, and I am not aware of any firm evidence that the original *Pericles* was written at a later date or by any other particular playwright. On the other hand, I have reason to believe that Shakespeare was acquainted with the main sources of the play when he wrote *The Comedy* of Errors. F. D. Hoeniger, the careful editor of the New Arden Edition, grants that there may have been a version of *Pericles* by Shakespeare extant in the 1590's.[15] I not only concur; I submit that we probably have the first two acts of it, virtually unchanged, in the 1609 quarto, as well as some pieces of the last three acts scattered among the superb revisions he made about the time of *King Lear*.

How the old manuscript of *Pericles* may have been preserved is an interesting speculation. There is reason to suspect that about 1604 it was in the company's archives or was at any rate accessible to John Day and George Wilkins.[16] Both C. J. Sisson[17] and Hardin Craig[18] have discovered evidence that the printer's copy for the 1609 quarto was at least in part in Shakespeare's handwriting. I think it all may have been; I am not an expert in Shakespearean spelling, and I know no one who is, but I have noticed a number of curious spellings common to the quarto of *Pericles* and other texts thought to be proximate to Shakespeare's autograph. At the point where the revising of the play begins, he seems to have taken a fresh sheet of paper for a thorough revision of the whole first scene of Act III where Pericles, on a ship's deck, rages Lear-like against the storm as his dying wife is giving birth to a daughter. From there on in the play, new work is mingled with old. Its printers may not have been very intelligent, but they seem to have been conscientious: only slight alterations were made when the quarto was reset for another printing by the same publisher in the same year. It would appear that the manuscript was not good printer's copy and not even a prompt copy of the play, but something a good deal more primitive.

E. K. Chambers' rejection of portions of *Pericles* as un-Shakespearean is in keeping with the consensus of his time; the recent transparent misapprehension of the second scene is harder to explain. True, there is a time-honored tradition among scholars that the text of the play is extremely corrupt (asserted by Malone, reaffirmed by Chambers),[19] which perhaps predisposes some to believe the worst about it; but this view is coming to be recognized as an exaggeration. Some of the appearance of corruption is due to old idiom and grammar, and some is due to the printer's copy with its difficult handwriting and intermittent revisions. But, if the language is direct Shakespeare, as I think it may well be, the theory of reportorial garbling is a chimera. Certainly I can think of no reason to believe the Riverside general editor's statement that "there is every reason to believe the quarto represents a memorially reconstructed version" (p. 1511). This theory, based partly on the attribution of wild disorder to the second scene, has prospered since the publication of an article by Philip Edwards in 1952.[20] Its curious survival serves to illustrate a tendency among editors (lately described as pathological)[21] to adopt plausible interpretations without critical examination.

While the verdict of a computer and a handful of scholar-believers may not find immediate wide acceptance among readers of *Pericles,* it may encourage greater editorial caution, and perhaps respect, in dealing with this hitherto undervalued text. In my own opinion, the text shows Shakespeare beginning to do to his own primitive play what he was doing, or perhaps had just done, to the chronicle history of *King Leir*. *Pericles* now stands, as it were, like a canvas of some great painter's apprenticeship, which the mature artist took from his attic and deftly perfected in a few prominent areas.

Notes

1. See G. Wilson Knight, *Neglected Powers* (London, Routledge, 1971), p. 490.

2. E. K. Chambers, *William Shakespeare* (Oxford, the Clarendon Press, 1930), I, 521.

3. G. L. Kittredge, ed., *The Complete Works of Shakespeare* (Boston, Ginn and Company, 1936), p. 1377.

4. See Roger Pryor, "The Life of George Wilkins," *Shakespeare Survey* 25 (1972), 137-52; and Willem Schrikx, "*Pericles* in a Book-List of 1619," *Shakespeare Survey* 29 (1976), 21-32.

5. See Louis Marder, "Stylometric Analysis and the *Pericles* Problem," *SNL* 26 (Dec. 1976), 46.

6. C. J. Sisson, *William Shakespeare, the Complete Works* (New York, Harper, 1954), p. 1206.

7. See my note, "Shakespeare's Hand in *Pericles*," *N& Q* [*Notes and Queries*] 219 (Apr. 1974), 132-33.

8. See my article, "The Shakespearean Language of *Pericles*," *ELN* [*English Language Notes*] 13 (Dec. 1975), 98-103.

9. Sisson, loc. cit.

10. Laurence Twine, *The Pattern of Painefull Aduentures*, Geoffrey Bullough, ed., *The Narrative and Dramatic Sources of Shakespeare's Plays*, VI (London, Routledge, 1966), 429.

11. D. A. Stauffer, *Shakespeare's World of Images* (New York, Norton, 1949), p. 347.

12. George Wilkins, *The Painefull Aduentures of Pericles Prince of Tyre*, ed. Kenneth Muir (University Press of Liverpool, 1967), p. 21.

13. A marginal note in the Genevan Bible seems also to underlie the reading "base Judean" in *Oth.*, V.i.347. See Richmond Noble, *Shakespeare's Biblical Knowledge* (London, Norton, 1935), pp. 90-93.

14. See Hallett Smith, *Shakespeare's Romances* (San Marino, The Huntington Library, 1972), p. 89.

15. F. D. Hoeniger, ed. *Pericles,* the new Arden Edition (London, Methuen, 1963), p. lxiv.

16. See my note cited above in footnote 7.

17. Sisson, loc. cit.

18. Hardin Craig, "*Pericles* and *The Painful Adventures*," *SP* [*Studies in Philology*] 45 (Oct. 1948), 605.

19. See Hoeniger, p. xxxii; and Chambers, I. 520.

20. Philip Edwards, "An Approach to the Problem of *Pericles*," ShS [*Shakespeare Survey: An Annual Survey of Shakespeare Study and Production*] 5 (1952), 25-54, esp. 26-27. The theory of radical corruption in this scene had appeared earlier. See Sina Spiker, "George Wilkins and the Authorship of *Pericles*," SP 30 (Oct. 1933), 560. My previous comments on the myth include "The Running Image in *Pericles*," ShakS [*Shakespeare Studies*] 5 (1969), 241, and "*Pericles*, I.ii." N&Q 212 (Apr. 1967), 141-42.

21. John C. Meagher, "The Pathology of Editorial Annotation," *Shakespeare 1971*, ed. Clifford Leech and J. M. R. Margeson (University of Toronto Press, 1972), pp. 244-59.

Constance Jordan (essay date 1992)

SOURCE: Jordan, Constance. "'Eating the Mother': Property and Propriety in *Pericles*." In *Creative Imitation: New Essays on Renaissance Literature in Honor of Thomas M. Green*, edited by David Quint, Margaret W. Ferguson, G. W. Pigman III, and Wayne Rebhorn, pp. 331-53. Binghamton, N.Y.: Medieval & Renaissance Texts & Studies, 1992.

[*In the following essay, Jordan argues that the incestuous relation of Antiochus and his daughter in* Pericles *constitutes a metaphoric representation of political tyranny, and that Antiochus represents Pericles's desire for absolute rule.*]

> Bot yit it is a wonder thing,
> Whan that a riche worthi king . . .
> Wol axe and cleyme proprete
> In thing to which he hath no riht,
> Bot onliche of his grete miht.
>
> (*Confessio amantis III*)

This essay begins with a question: Is there any basis for reading Shakespeare's last plays—focused as they are on monarchs caught up in familial strife, often expressed as inter-generational rivalry between males—in light of the contemporary debate on the proper form of government and specifically of the monarchy? In some measure we already have an answer. As the perceptive criticism of such scholars as David Bergeron and Leonard Tennenhouse has demonstrated, these plays refer allusively and sometimes directly to political or social conditions that obtained during the reign of James I. Topics at issue include the politics of royal marriages, the status of wards, the disposition of inherited property, and the circumstances in which particular families are ennobled.[1] My own investigation here is similarly focused. Read in the figured language of Jacobean political discourse, Shakespeare's *Pericles*, 1605—a dramatization of the relations between a royal father, daughter, and mother—acquires meaning as political theater. I am not suggesting that this meaning render sentimental our response to the representation of familial reconciliation and regeneration that for many audiences has given this play its chief appeal. But I will claim that to Shakespeare such actions were understood to affect political as well as personal life, and that he saw some point in representing them as thus doubly charged in this and his other romances. To Jacobean audiences particularly, mindful as they were of the analogy between the governments of the family and the state that was so frequently a feature of their political discourse, the bizarre conflict opening the action of *Pericles* would have presented a special interpretive challenge.

As P. Goolden has observed, the answer Pericles gives to Antiochus' riddle—incest—seems logically too easy; at the very least, it asks us to wonder why earlier suitors failed to discover it.[2] More pointedly, what it implies about Antiochus—that he is lawlessly lustful—also indicates a suitor's double jeopardy. He who answers the riddle correctly is just as doomed as he who does not. And finally, incest in and of itself appears to have little to do with the action that follows. If, therefore, this riddling incoherence is not to be attributed to an authorial blunder, it needs a subtle analysis, in fact the kind of analysis for which Jacobean audiences were well-prepared. When the image of incest is understood by reference to the language describing the nature of political rule, both domestic and civil—specifically one in which the monarch is to behave as a father to his children, the subjects, and as a husband to his wife, the commonwealth—it provides a basis for understanding the play's continuous appeal to ideas of legitimate government.

I

When James VI of Scotland acceded to the English throne in 1603, his new subjects would already have received sufficient indication that his conception of the monarchy was one they had not yet themselves experienced in practice. It had been succinctly set forth five years earlier in James's *True Law of Free Monarchies*, 1598, a short treatise addressed to his fellow Scots (although perhaps also with the neighboring English in mind) and it represented the reciprocal duties of the king and his subjects in hereditary (as opposed to elective) monarchies. Anyone acquainted with the elements of English law would instantly have recognized that James's *True Law*—resting as it did on the feudal presumption that all property was ultimately held of the king, a presumption which to James entailed the further claim that all property was finally the possession of the king—was grossly inconsistent with English legal practice and the kind of monarchy it had sustained during the previous decades of the sixteenth century. And the more astute might well have imagined that James's reign would be vexed by conflicts over property: the monarch's right to appropriate his subject's private property in the form of "impositions" or taxes, and also his right to administer, develop and control the property vested in the commonwealth without regard to the needs or desires of the people as a whole.

James I and his absolutist supporters regarded both kinds of monarchic rights as very largely unqualified. In 1603 Thomas Bilson, for example, insisted that "God hath allowed [monarchs] power over the goodes, lands, bodies and lives of their subjects: and what private men may not touch without Theft and Murder that Princes may lawfully dispose as Gods Ministers. . . ."[3] Constitutionalists, who had had the larger voice in the Tudor debate, took an opposing view. They spoke of the royal prerogative as controlled by the countervailing rights of the people: first, to determine when and how they, as individuals, should be taxed; and second, to be sustained and encouraged, as a whole, in their productive activities which included manufacture and trade—in short, the monarch was to increase the commonwealth for its sake not his own. For the monarch to exercise his power in the manner described by Bilson amounted to tyranny; John Ponet, writing his influential *Short Treatise of Politike Power* in 1556, had characterized tyranny as monarchic theft of the property of the people.[4] The constitutionalist case was supported in the first instance by the authority of the respected Sir John Fortescue, whose *Learned Commendation of the Politique Lawes of England,* in print in 1567, revealed that it was only outside England that "the princes pleasure standeth in force of a lawe. . . . [They] burden their subjectes withe chargeis: and also when they lust, do determine controversies of sueters as pleaseth them." In England, by contrast, "al kingely power muste been applyed to the wealthe of his kyngdome"; indeed, a king's own position is threatened if he does not respect his subjects' property:

> On the other syde that kynge is free and of myghte that is hable to defende his subjectes as well agaynste straungers as agaynste his owne people and also theire goods and possessions not onely from the violente and unlawefull invasions of their owne countrey menne and neighbours butte also from his own oppression and extortion thoughe such wilful lusts and necessities doe move him to the contrarie. For who can be more mighty or more free then he that is hable to conquere and subdue not onely others but also himselfe?[5]

The moralism in Fortescue receives a more specifically practical formulation in Ponet, who claims that "Princes are ordained to doo good, not to doo evil," and that an element in this "good" is the procurement of "wealthe and benefite [for] their subjectes" (26). This obligation is not discharged by monarchs who "will have all that their subjectes have common to themselves . . . no, not so muche as paie for those thinges, that in wordes they pretende to buie of their subjectes" (80). In a similar vein, the writer of the *Vindiciae contra tyrannos,* 1579, asserts that while the king is the "proprietor" of his "personal inheritance," he "is in no sense the proprietor of the royal patrimony or the public treasure, which is common known as the domain."[6] Only a tyrant asserts proprietorship of the commonwealth. And Nicholas Fuller, writing a year or two after *Pericles* was performed, simply declares that the "liberty of the [English] subject," established by the Magna Carta, guarantees that he cannot be deprived of his goods except by "some Act of Parliament." Like Sir Edward Coke, Fuller goes on to refer to the law that so protects the subject as his "inheritance": "the lawes of England are the high inheritance of the Realme by which both the King and the subjects are directed." This "inheritance" guarantees the actual inheritance of property: "the law admeasureth the kings prerogative so as it shall not extend to hurt the inheritance of the subjectes."[7]

These opposing positions on the monarch's relation to the property of the subject and the commonwealth were also inscribed in political debate in the figurative languages of the body politic and the monarch as patriarch. In his *Picture of a Perfit Common wealth,* 1600, Thomas Floyd states: the "commonwealth is a living body compact of sundry estates and degrees of men" and the king is its "soule." It is also the "mother of us all"; the king is a "Father over his children" who are his subjects; and by extension (as James himself had declared), the king is the husband of the commonwealth.[8] The king's position as both soul and patriarch allowed many commentators to play suggestively with the idea of monarchic "lust," "will," or "pleasure." As Fortescue had maintained, a monarch's "lust" drives him to act outside the law; hence lustfulness characterizes the behavior of the tyrant. In 1594 Robert Parsons could insist that a "Prince ruling by law is more than a man, or a man deifyed, and a Prince ruling by affections is lesse then a man or a man brutified."[9] Naturally, he ceases to be a king according to any way of conceptualizing the office. And Edward Forset, warning that the monarch, who is both head and heart of the body politic, is subject to "naturall fralities," associates these "sensuall and irrational mocions, rising out of the infectious mudd of flesh and bloud" with tyranny: such a monarch is prevented "from either attayning unto or retayning firmely the precise points of perfect Justice."[10] Parsons links royal "pleasure" specifically with the illicit appropriation of property: for a king to dispose of "mens goodes, bodies and lives" at his "pleasure" means that he is under "no law or accomptgiving whatsoever" (sig. D7). Here he follows Ponet who had declared that monarchs who are above the law have "absolute power," which is a "fulness of power, or prerogative to doo what they lust, and none may gaynesaye them." The exercise of this power is principally in relation to property: absolute monarchs "use their subjectes as they doo their beastes . . . getting their goodes from them by hoke or crooke . . . and spending it to the destruction of their subjects" (26). In sum, whether imagined in absolutist or constitutionalist terms, a monarch is obliged to rule rationally and without giving way to affections. For constitutionalists in particular, a monarch who abuses property rights is described in ways that define him as passionate ("lustful") rather than reasonable, self-indulgent ("sensuall") rather than disciplined, and governed by desire for "goodes" rather than a commitment to the good of his people.

The figurative languages of the body politic and patriarchy also allowed for a further degree of allusiveness. In the ordinary relations of economic and legal life, the concept of property and the manner in which it was held were complex; goods and land were obviously properties, but so in other senses were children and wives. Their status as kinds of possession referred not only to such institutions as the entail and the dowry by which property was transferred from one person to another, but also to hierarchical relations of power in which one party was subservient to another. Hence it was possible to see in allusions to the monarch as father and husband references to relations that went beyond those determined by kin and in fact extended to those characterizing government, perceived, as government so often was, in its relations to property. Hence, too, the relative density of these figurative languages: familial experience is here actually informing political meaning, as kinship relations are made to construct precise arguments on the nature of monarchic government. It is to familial experience that refinements in the terms of political discourse are indebted.

To the patriarch, both children and wife were possessions or properties. That they were not wholly at the disposal of their owner is suggested by a contemporary play of language now largely impossible. For Shakespeare and his audiences "property" meant both that which was owned and also that which was fitting or suitable. So Shakespeare writes in "The Phoenix and the Turtle," 1601, that "Property was thus appalled," meaning that propriety has not been observed, and in *Othello,* 1604, that to be "proper" is to be decorous.[11] This ambiguity is not simply gratuitous but actually inheres in the complex manner in which the concept of property was regarded at law during this period. I think it reflects actual differences in the ways in which property holders were considered to possess the property they claimed was theirs.

Objects were often considered to be owned outright; in such cases, an owner could claim a "full dominion" (*dominium plenum*) over them and do what he pleased with them. *Land* was more frequently owned by more than one party and in more than one sense; notably, it could be possessed as by a tenant, and be owned as by a landlord. In this case, the "dominion" of both tenant and landlord was qualified; the tenant's ownership was merely "of use" (*dominium utile*), and the landlord's right to dispose of the land at will was circumscribed by his tenant's right to its use. Both landlord and tenant had possessory rights, and each could claim a right of possession against the other. A comparable although not precisely similar reciprocity also characterized a father's possession of his child and a husband's of his wife. In the case of a child, paternal rights of ownership (effectively very extensive in the case of a noble daughter) extended to the right to dispose of the child at will but they were also legally circumscribed by the child's right to protection and nurturance. Originally a feature of Roman law, a child's right or *ius* against a parent was later incorporated into a broad notion of natural rights. The character of the father-child relationship, although in essence one between owner and property, did not entail classifying its weaker member as a mere object:

to put it another way, here property entailed propriety. Husbands also had proprietary rights over wives but these, too, were subject to qualification. A husband could "use" a wife sexually and he could make use of whatever of her dowry was real property to generate more property for the sake of their common good and that of their heirs. But in her person she was not subject to his governance as was a child; she could not be placed or disposed of as a child could. Her husband had to regard her as his spiritual equal; he was encouraged to regard her as a companion in life.[12]

To discriminate patriarchal rights of *dominium* is therefore to recognize in them an absence of *dominium plenum* altogether. A child is a possession that cannot be "used"; patriarchal governance in placing the child, or disposing of it in society, although virtually absolute, is not to be based on paternal interest. A wife, on the other hand, is controlled by a virtual *dominium utile:* she is property to be used, to be enjoyed, to be made generative and profitable, but by her claim to adult status, she cannot be placed or disposed of. Among the many striking features of incest is the way in which it conflates these distinctly different kinds of *dominium* and as a practical consequence transforms the right of the patriarch (both father and husband) to a *dominium plenum.* A woman who is both a child and a wife cannot claim unequivocally either a liberty from use or restrictions in governance. As a relation of property, incest signals the violation of fundamental proprieties. It follows that where incest is monarchic and monarchs are charged to observe property rights, incest becomes a figure of absolutist pretensions—or tyranny—as perceived from the point of view of a constitutionalist politics.

The significant elements of the image of monarchic incest are already apparent in both Ponet and the *Vindiciae.* Ponet, outlining the conditions of a *constitutional* monarchy, sees that its power is a "gift of God," analogous to that conferred on the husband in matrimony. The task of both monarch and husband is not only to "use" his wife but to be her "gracious Benefactor." That is, he is to use her to make her (and the couple) generative (42). And inasmuch as a monarch is a father to his subjects, his power is also limited. He is merely an "executor" of God's law. In any case, he cannot do what he "lusteth": for otherwise it might be said "that God allowed their [i.e., monarchs'] tyranie, robbery of their subjects, killing them without law, and so God [becomes] thautor of evil . . ." (43). Thus the offices of monarch and father allow for latitude in administering the law but not for license in using (and hence abusing) those subject to that law. The author of the *Vindiciae* extends the analogy between the wife and the commonwealth to a consideration of her "dowry" as the property of the commonwealth which is not to be compromised. In it, the *Vindiciae* claims, the people have a "proprietary right": "if the public patrimony or domain is truly called the 'dowry of the commonwealth,' and if the dissolution or waste of that dowry means that the commonwealth, the kingdom, and at last the king himself are lost, is there any legal principle imaginable that could make alienation of that dowry permissible?" (174-75).

The possibility that the riddle Pericles confronts as he discovers the spectacle of Antiochus married to his Daughter can be read as political metaphor is now I trust sufficiently attractive to be worth considering in some detail. (As a verbal statement, this riddle is further complicated by an apparent anomaly: the daughter is said to be a mother to her father. The meaning of this relationship is unclear until the end of the play.) The audience is asked to see the royal couple in three perspectives. In the relation of father and child is represented the relations of a monarch and his subject, or collectively his people. The question it asks is the nature of the rule of the father-king over his child-subject. In the relation of husband and wife, at issue is the extent of the husband-king's rights over his wife-commonwealth. And finally, the conflation of the roles of father and husband in incest asks the audience to recognize an image of violated rights of property and propriety—rights that, understood in the figured languages of the body politic and patriarchy, were established as a virtual guarantee of freedom from tyranny. In the view of constitutionalists such as Ponet, figurative and political incest is as illicit as its domestic counterpart. A monarch as father can administer to what he has proprietary rights over—his children and subjects—but they retain the right to the protection and the use of their property, including the property they have in their own person. Correspondingly, a monarch as husband can use his wife or the commonwealth—that is, the whole of the body politic of which he is the soul—in the interest of generation, to increase the wealth of the nation as a whole. Such use is comprehended in the monarch's prerogative, especially his right to regulate trade.[13] But it does not include absolute government. The commonwealth, the "mother" to whom the monarch is married, retains a degree of independence which is typically associated with the representatives of the people in Parliament and expressed as the right of that "body" to determine when the monarch can tax the people and by how much. In effect, this husbandry indicates a *dominium utile*; in the first instance, it is the people who own the property of the commonwealth. The actual language of the riddle used by the Daughter further clarifies the fate of the mother in incest. By "feeding on mother's flesh," the Daughter likens herself to the offspring of a viper, who was said to eat its way out of its mother, and so alludes to her appropriation of flesh that is properly her mother's, that is, her father's body (I.i.65-66). Read a second time, however, the image points to a second referent; now incest indicates the sterility of a kingdom in which the commonwealth, in this case the absent mother, is consumed by the illicit couple. The image refashions an earlier and more obviously political one in *1 Henry VI*: "Civil dissension is a viperous worm / That gnaws the bowels of the commonwealth" (III.i.71-72). The Daughter, an abused and abusing subject, is an agent in this consumption, an action that thwarts and so finally reverses the process of generation.

The most impressive and memorable authority upon which Shakespeare's Jacobean audience would have depended for these speculations was, of course, James I himself, and especially James I as a reader of Scripture. The biblical passage upon which both sides of the political debate frequently focused was that describing the advent of the monarch to the society of the Israelites in 1 Samuel. There, the prophet's picture of a monarch portrays him as a tyrant: like Antiochus, he treats his subjects as objects for his service and pleasure, and he regards their property as his. Constitutionalists, quite obviously, interpreted the biblical text as an argument against absolutism, as the prophet's warning to the people about the dangers of royal power. For James, however, 1 Samuel had to mean something else. In his *True Law*, tyrannical action on the part of the monarch, although recognized as "breaking" points of "equitie and justice," is justified because James interprets the prophet's words not as monitory but rather as hortatory.[14] The people are not to reject the monarchy on the grounds that it threatens tyranny but rather to steel themselves to bear the monarchy because it is divinely instituted.

To James royal power is both paternalistic and confers *dominium plenum* with no countervailing *iura*. As the *True Law* declares, a king is "naturall Father to all his Lieges. . . . As the Father, of his fatherly dutie, is bound to care for the nourishing, education, and vertuous government of his children, even so is the king bound to care for all his subjects" (55-56). Against the judgments and wishes of this father his children have no recourse: "can any pretence of wickenes or rigor on his part be a just excuse for his children to put hand to him?" (65). Reading 1 Samuel, James denies them all rights. Paraphrasing the prophet, he writes: "the best and noblest of your blood shall be compelled in slavish and servile offices to serve him [the king]: and not content of his owne patrimonie, [the king] will make up a rent to his owne use of your best lands, vineyards, orchards, and store of cattell: *So as inverting the Law of nature, and office of a King, your persons and persons of your posteritie, together with your lands, and all that ye possesse shall serve his private use, and inordinate appetite*" (58, my emphasis). James terms the monarch's right to steal an "allowable vertue"; in any case, his subjects or children are better off if their "mother," the "Commonwealth," is ruled by a tyrant than not ruled at all; better to be impoverished by the king's prerogative than to live lawlessly (66).[15] James rests his claim to absolute monarchy in Scotland on the "fact" of the legendary conquest of that country by the mythical King Fergus, from whose monarchic descendants all property in Scotland was subsequently held in a feudal manner. According to James, he and all later kings retained *dominium plenum* over the kingdom; their subjects depended for their use on his will: "the King is *Dominus omnium bonorum*, and *Dominus directus totius Dominii*, whose subjects being but his vassals, and from him holding all their lands as their over-lord who . . . chaungeth their holdings . . . without advice or authoritie of either Parliament or any other subalterin judiciall seate" (62). He means, of course, that the vassals of the king have effectively no proprietary rights at all, since there is no law, no "judiciall seate," by which they may be claimed.

In England such a sweeping view of the prerogative may well have been regarded as excessive even by absolutists, accustomed as the English people were to a different concept of property, and particularly in land. Most real property in England was held by a conveyance known as a "use." Functioning as a kind of trust, a use split the ownership of a property into two complementary types of possession: nominal and custodial, and actual and profitable. It signified a form of possession that entitled the possessor, who was called the *cestuy que use,* to enjoy or profit from his possession of a property; and it also signified the nature of the trust the possessor or *cestuy que use* placed in the nominal owner of that property, in whose name it was recorded and who was termed the *feoffee to a use.* The feoffee exercised a discretionary and executive governance over the property; the cestuy que use enjoyed its benefits. Uses were established for the purpose of evading the duties holders of property owed the crown; the feoffee was not liable because he was not in possession of the property, the cestuy que use (who was sometimes the original feoffor, but more often his heir to whose use the property had been entailed) was not liable because he did not own the property. Henry VIII declared uses invalid (for obvious reasons) but they gradually reappeared in the second half of the sixteenth century. The *idea* of a use seems to have acquired political meaning because it could be reconciled with general principles supporting a constitutionalist as opposed to an absolutist form of monarchy. What it suggested in the way of the distribution of rights between a feoffee and a cestuy que use was what constitutionalists claimed had existed from time immemorial between monarch and people, namely that the English commonwealth—the land and the property of its people—was originally the property of the people who had subsequently entrusted it to the monarch to hold for their benefit. They retained proprietary rights to its use; and the fruits of that use could be alienated from them only with their consent.[16] Their power in the form of rights was thus double. As subjects and children they could claim the monarch's paternal protection without allowing him to "use" their property; and as uxorial members of the body politic, they could claim a share in their own governance.

II

The incest of Antiochus can therefore be understood to represent what to Jacobean audiences versed in political argument was the typical form in which a tyranny was manifest—an abuse of proprietary rights. Gerard A. Barker suggests that Pericles confronts in Antiochus' incest his own ambition; Pericles, a prospective tyrant, desires to use his daughter and dispose of his wife, to organize political relations so that his pleasures end in the consumption rather than the generation of the commonwealth.[17] In the words of the Chorus, Gower, the play is a "restorative," a means to cure a disease. Since law was often referred to as the "physick" of the state, and magistrates were figured as "physicians," we may infer here that the state and the monarchy we are about to see on stage are ill (illegally governed) and in need of medication.[18] In other words, Gower has introduced a play in which the practices of proprietorship need reform; his language also implies that the reform will not be innovative but rather a return to, a restoration of, former practices. The illness in question—dramatized as incest and implied to be tyranny—is one affecting the generativity of a nation and its people; insofar as Pericles himself is a victim of disease, the play allows him a restorative. His education in the art of government is dramatized throughout the length of the play in continuous allusions to his responsibilities as husband and father—richly conceived figurations of aspects of royal government. Events at each stage of his journey represent a phase in his acquisition of royal discipline.

At Antioch, the Daughter of Antiochus, "clothed like a bride," appears to promise Pericles "nothing but curious pleasures" (I.i.6; 6). Pericles' description of his prospective union as a taste of the fruit of "yon celestial tree," a tree by definition reserved for immortals (I.i.21), suggests that this inference is presumptuous. To seek incestuous relations, and so to confound and ignore generation, is, of course, only the privilege of immortals. For mortals will, inevitably, "die in the adventure" (I.i.22). Helicanus' counsel to Pericles places him more directly in the position of guilty monarch. He hints at Pericles' complicity in Antiochus' sin when he claims he offers Pericles "reproof, obedient and in order": this "fits kings as they are men, for they may err" (I.ii.43, 44). The content of Helicanus' reproof is undeclared but in constitutionalist discourse, monarchic error was to be checked by the positive law to which they were as subject as their subjects were—always excepting legitimate uses of the prerogative.[19] And when Pericles later names Antiochus "tyrannous," Helicanus responds by suggesting that Antiochus may not be the only monarch guilty of this perversion: "Antiochus you fear / And justly too, I think, you fear the tyrant" (I.ii.84, 102, 103; my emphasis). Merely by paying suit to Antiochus, Pericles is, of course, inviting death: if he fails to answer the riddle, he is beheaded; if he succeeds, he will be similarly treated. The first result conveys the power of the tyrant, Antiochus; the second seems also to allude to the Platonic theory of knowledge as recognition. Pericles "knows" monarchic incest because he has already encountered it, presumably as an image of his own desire for absolute rule.

At Tharsus, Pericles contends with the economic consequences of Antioch; he learns there not of an incestuous child eating a mother, consuming a commonwealth, but conversely of mothers ready to eat children, a present generation consuming its future (I.iv.42-44). But if Tharsus, like Antioch, evokes a political problem, Pericles shows that he knows at least part of its solution. He feeds the people of Tharsus freely with grain he imports to them on his ship; in effect, he behaves as if the grain is theirs, not his. This action is politically significant (and unmotivated in other respects); I think it is meant to indicate a step in Pericles' reform of the tyrant latent within him. Apart from its magnificence, an aspect of monarchy that is represented later at Pentapolis by the government of his prospective father-in-law, King Simonides, Pericles' action recalls a feature of constitutional monarchies whose advocates argued that if the ship of state is piloted by the monarch, its owners are the people and its cargo is the commonwealth.[20] By dispensing food to a starving populace in this manner, Pericles demonstrates his respect for the concept of limited *dominium*; his proprietary rights are employed in the interest of subjects who need nourishment. Paradoxically, it is by such restraint that he achieves a degree of power that is typically reserved for an absolute monarch: at Tharsus, his word is taken as Scripture (and, by implication, divine law). As Gower says, "each man / Thinks all is writ he [Pericles] speken can" (II.Chorus, 11-12).

At Pentapolis, Pericles begins to work out what a proper relationship to a wife and child would be. He discovers in Thaisa a bride who, by "wishing him [and not her father] my meat," rectifies the incest at Antioch (II.iii.32). More important (since Thaisa is subject to the paternal *dominium* of Simonides), her wishes are respected in the matter of marriage. Despite a good deal of playful dissembling, Simonides receives her letter declaring her love for Pericles by rejoicing that her choice agrees with his, and adds, as if acknowledging her right to that choice: "Nay how *absolute* she's in't / Not minding whether I dislike or no!" (II.v.19-20; my emphasis). His restraint on this score is matched by his sense of the responsibilities of his office which extend to royal largess:

> Princes in this should live like gods above
> Who freely give to every one that come
> To honor them . . .
>
> (III.iii.59-61; cf. Pericles at Tharsus)

Winning Thaisa, Pericles benefits from her father's generosity and self-control; the wedding night ends with the beginning of a new generation: "by the loss of maidenhead, / A babe is moulded" (III.Chorus, 10, 11).

It is nevertheless also the case that at Pentapolis Pericles is not free of tendencies associated with tyranny. Returning to Tyre to deal with a threat to his life, he comes to Pentapolis shipwrecked, an image widely recognized as signifying political chaos and often implicating the monarch as a tyrant who will be destroyed as a consequence. A classic example is the reference of Shakespeare's Ulysses to waters lifting themselves above shores when degree is lost (*Troilus and Cressida,* I.iii.110-13). The fullest Shakespearean exposition is perhaps that of Suffolk and his co-conspirators, who accuse Gloucester of turning "peers" into "bondmen to [his] sovereignty," "*racking*" the commons, and "costing" the "public treasure"—actions which together explain why "The commonwealth hath daily run to *wrack*" (*2 Henry VI,* I.iii.124-31; my emphasis). Purely political indications include those of Coke to injustice as a "raging sea" that "drowns up" the "humble" lowlands in a "recureless wracke" while the "Hills and Mountains stand safe,"[21] and of Floyd, who pictures the tyrant, by definition unjust, as himself a victim of his own willful machinations:

> Like as a battered or crazed ship by letting in of water not only drowneth herselfe but all that are in her: so a king or a vitious tyrant, by using detestable enormities, destroyeth not himselfe alone but all others beside that are under his government.
>
> (sig. C12v)

Parsons notes merely that a "Prince" given to his own "will" is sure to "come to shipwreck" (sig. D). Pericles is able to approach Simonides and win Thaisa—that is, overcome the consequences of shipwreck—*only* by fortunate means: his wreck becomes "no ill" when fishermen plying their nets on the shore recover his father's armor with which he can compete for and win Thaisa: "Thanks, Fortune, yet, that, after all thy crosses, / Thou givest me somewhat to repair myself!" he exclaims (II.i.133; 121-22). And here a force yet more decisive is linked to Fortune: Time. While Fortune is variable, Time is inexorable in its laws, bringing forth generation after generation, denying mortals any other form of immortality. As Pericles observes of his own royal status before he marries Thaisa: "Time's the king of men; / He's both their parent, and he is their grave" (II.iii.45-46). Both references allude to powers beyond human control and effectively introduce to the play a second level of political discourse that will circumscribe its critique of absolutism as tyranny and reveal a basis upon which to construct an apology for absolutism as conducive to a stable political order. Such a revision proceeds by way of an emphasis on anarchy.

In sixteenth-century political thought, anarchic possibilities are almost always perceived to originate in the disaffection of the people, and democracy is often identified as mob rule. In a monarchy, a root cause of anarchy is the retirement of the monarch; hence anarchy is logically opposed to tyranny. In *Pericles,* the threat of anarchy is expressed initially in the exchange between the shipwrecked Pericles and the fishermen who provide his armor. They praise Simonides' "peaceable reign and good government," but they also complain of scarcity and injustice. Men on land, one claims, live as fish in the sea: "The great ones eat up the little ones. I can compare our rich misers to nothing so fitly as to a whale: a plays and tumbles, driving the poor fry before him, and at last devours them all at a mouthful" (II.i.29-32; 103). The comparison of societies on land and in the sea, perhaps proverbial, recalls Ponet's description of anarchy, a society without "politike power and autoritie," in which the "riche wold appresse the poore, and the poore seke the destruction of the riche . . . as . . . the great fishe eate up the small, and the weak seke revenge on the mightie; and so one seking the others destruction, all at leyngth should be undone and come to destruction" (10). The fishermen's conversation would seem intended to remind Pericles of the political chaos that lawlessness creates. If so, it either goes unheeded or is misunderstood; these fishermen ask Pericles not to forget them (and presumably also what they have said) but he does precisely this in Act III when he retires from public view. Apparently avoiding the excesses of tyranny, he forgets the rights of the subject to protection and the commonwealth to governance, and in effect invites anarchy. Attempting again to return to Tyre, Pericles encounters a second storm and shipwreck, gives up his wife, Thaisa, for dead, and abandons his daughter, Marina.

The scenes then taking place at Tharsus and Ephesus further reveal the dangers of anarchy as well as the redemptive effects of law now associated with an image new to the play, that of divinity working in and through time. In Ephesus, Thaisa is revived by the medicine of the physician, Cerimon, and secretly preserved in Diana's temple, actions that recall the critical role of the law and divine providence in securing the future of the commonwealth. In effect, Cerimon stands in for Pericles. As Forset remarks, law is the state's "physick," and the monarch is the "principall Phisicion for the redressing or remedying the maladies of the bodie politique" (sig. L; see also Floyd, sig. B, E7v). In Tharsus, Pericles naively counts on the "charity" of Cleon and Dionyza, its king and queen: Cleon has declared that the "common body" of his people will force him to do his duty, that is, to nourish Marina because Pericles has earlier nourished them (III.iii.21, 22). But the people prove to be both ignorant and powerless when confronted with Dionyza's "monster, Envy," and her henchman, Leonine, agrees to murder Marina (IV. Chorus, 12-14). Marina's abuse culminates in her being seized by pirates and sold to pimps in Mytilene: hence she is to be made the object of a common use. What is decisive in the fate of both wife and daughter is the nonfeasance of their respective husband and father. This is further realized as a kind of abdication. After Pericles hears of Marina's "death," he ceases to exercise any kind of *dominium*.

The prostitution with which Marina is threatened in the bawdy "house" at Mytilene parodically inverts the royal incest at Antioch and signifies its opposite politically. Here the royal daughter is up for sale; in other words, what she stands for—the subject's right to protection of his person and property—is left to be abused by persons who lack a proper sense of value, who evaluate everything including human beings in purely monetary terms. Pander complains that he and his associates "have lost too much money this mart by being too wenchless": and when Bawd observes that their "creatures" are "with continual action . . . even as good as rotten," he replies that what they need is a woman they can sell dearly: "Our credit comes not in like the commodity. . . . If in our youths we could pick up some pretty estate, 'twere not amiss to keep our door hatched" (IV.ii.4, 5; 8, 9; 30-33). Pander's intention is clearly to ruin estates, both in the sense of land and of rank. Marina's own resolve to "keep her virgin knot untied" [not undone, tied up] prevents her abuse. It is important that she does so not because she has the protection of the law—Pericles' officers do not arrive to rescue her—but because she speaks divine law (IV.ii.147; IV.v.4). It is at this point, also, that her identity as daughter acquires a broader and to some extent an ambiguous political meaning. She comes to stand not only for the subject in the sense of the governed as well as for his property but also, inasmuch as she is herself royalty, for the monarch who sustains the good order of society overall.

Her additional symbolic significance depends upon the recognition that at this point she embodies a political contradiction. Since women were categorically the political subordinates of men, a woman could be made generally to signify the politically subordinate. But royal women such as Marina who had, or might inherit, political authority, were in this respect anomalous—they represented both governor and governed. This anomaly explains Marina's role in Mytilene, where she confronts its governor, Lysimachus, who intends to use her sexually, and its pimps, Pander and Bawd, who intend to sell her. Each of her adversaries incarnates some aspect of anarchy: the governor abdicates his role as moral example (recalling by contrast Simonides, a "model which heaven makes like itself" [II.ii.11]), and the pimps clearly act as the greedy rabble. But Marina rejects them and their interests, her inferior and womanly status notwithstanding.

That Shakespeare shows a figure representing the politically subordinate resisting anarchy and even what might be termed class war by the only forms of resistance— prayer and "preaching"—admitted as lawful by absolutists, such as James I, in cases of tyranny indicates how complex a political scene he illustrates by the family relations of the play.[22] From Act III on, Shakespeare avoids entertaining notions that might seem further to challenge—or to pursue criticism of—the absolutist position that was so clearly under attack in the first two acts of the play. Not only is the political threat to be avoided in Acts III and IV that of mob rule rather than tyranny; it is overcome by a figure who is identified, whatever the qualifications, as a subordinate who appeals (and can appeal) only to heaven for justice. Recourse to divinity was the only form of resistance absolutists permitted.

The effects of Marina's "divine preaching" on the men who intend to use her distinguish differences in social rank. Her "gentlemen" suitors respond to her by espousing virtue. As one declares: "I'll do anything now that is virtuous, but I am out of the road of rutting for ever" (IV.v.8, 9). The governor of Mytilene, Lysimachus, is moved by Marina's appeal to his honor—"if you were born to honor, show it now"—and instantly becomes authoritative in a manner suitable to his office (IV.vi.92). No longer misled by his "corrupted mind," he damns Boult, the pimp's doorkeeper, and condemns his "house": "Your house, but for this virgin that doth prop it, / Would sink, and overwhelm you. Away" (IV.vi.119-20). And Boult is persuaded to reform because Marina introduces him to a new concept of authority and of wealth. Like any subordinate confronted with authority, Boult is wary of the power of his master. Asked to imagine who his worst (that is, his most feared) enemy might be, he answers "my master, or rather my mistress," and he implies that he cannot leave his profitable doorkeeping: "What would you have me do? go to the wars, would you? where a man may serve seven years for the loss of a leg, and have not money enough in the end to buy him a wooden one?" (IV.vi.159-60; 170-74). His question recasts the fishermen's complaint. Poor persons whose rights of property are not protected by a just monarch suffer from the anarchy they cannot help but create. Marina reminds Boult that he could "do anything" but what he does to earn a living, and, as if to indicate the propriety of her advice, she vows she will earn her living by teaching womanly arts and virtues, a promise later realized when we learn that, as Gower says: "pupils lacks she none . . . / . . . and her gain / She gives the cursed bawd" (V.Ch. 9-11). On persons of all ranks and offices, therefore, Marina's virtue, divinely inspired, has the effect of law. It brings about legally the reform of society. Thus she exercises what Ponet defines as a "politike power," for symbolically her "autoritie" is over "goodes, lands, possessiones, and all suche things as might bried controversies and discordes, and so hyndre and let, that he [God] might not be served" (8). Remarkably, she does not reform the *characters* of Pander and Bawd; she merely makes them stop using her illegally. Pericles later perceives her as "*Modest* as Justice . . . a palace / For the crowned truth to dwell in" (V.i.121-22; my emphasis).

To conform to the conventions of political theater, the play must conclude with the rehabilitation of its governing monarch. If we can say that Pericles successfully rejected tyranny by confronting Antiochus' riddle and winning Thaisa, so he must also reject the temptation to anarchy implicit in his retirement. Marina, summoned by the reformed and now her betrothed Lysimachus to cure this visiting king of his speechlessness with her speech (a "sacred physic" for which she will be paid), accuses him obliquely of forgetting his paternal duties:

> My derivation was from ancestors
> Who stood equivalent with mighty kings;
> But time hath rooted out my parentage,
> And to the world and awkward casualties
> Bound me in servitude. . . .
>
> (V.i.90-94)

Pericles comes to realize who Marina is, and so who he is, by understanding paradoxes that address the real ambiguity in the concept of monarchic property and propriety. In each case, he is asked to tolerate what appear to be irresolvable enigmas. He sees that Marina is like his wife and also like what his daughter would have been; that is, she doubles for the wife and yet is, with respect to their relationship, the inverse of the wife. Moreover, like the daughter that she is—to whom he must minister but whom he may not abuse—Marina "feeds" but also "starves" him with her riddling speech (V.i.112-13). He guesses that her story will make her like a man; his griefs are, by contrast, those suffered by a girl; because in his eyes hers is anticipated as the more heroic life, they symbolically exchange genders and generations (V.i.136-37). And finally they exchange roles of parent and child. Marina begets Pericles; to him, she is "Thou that beget'st him that did thee beget" (V.i.195).

There is a sense, however, in which Pericles' *dominium* over these women is still further qualified. After Marina and Thaisa reenter his life, he is not only actually, once again, a father and a husband; he also speaks of himself metaphorically as a son, a son of his daughter. This relationship has already been alluded to in Antiochus' riddle, in which the Daughter describes her incestuous state as a conflation of all three relationships—"He's father, son, and husband mild; / I mother, wife, and yet his child"—and it seems puzzling here to have it reappear (I.i.68-69). But in the political terms in which the incest riddle makes sense, Antiochus' being a son is, like his being a father and a husband, a corruption of relationship that independently is valid. According to constitutionalists, all monarchs must acknowledge the condition in which they, like their subjects, are *under* the laws of the commonwealth, nurtured and protected by them equally. The familial relationship describing this condition is that between brothers, the children of a single mother. It is, of course, this subservience of the monarch to a mother who is positive law and Parliament that absolutists decline to accept (cf. Ponet, 44); an aspect of the abuse that Antiochus inflicts upon the Daughter is comprehended in her capacity to figure his obligation to respect the terms of his sonship. For Pericles especially, Marina's "motherhood" reflects a more particular significance. In the last act, she is described as the image of Justice, as the image of Patience "smiling extremitie out of act," and as one who "sings like one immortal" (V.i.121, 138-39; V.Ch. 3). She is constantly identified with virtue; insofar as she is the agent of the restoration of her parents, she seems to be a heavenly virtue that both inspires mortals and is preserved in and by their goodness:

> In Pericles, his queen and daughter, seen,
> Although assail'd with fortune fierce and keen,
> Virtue [preserved] from fell destruction's blast,
> Led on by heaven, and crown'd with joy at last.
>
> (V.iii.87-90)

For Pericles to be her son is not, therefore, merely a matter of his acknowledging his place under the law, although such an acknowledgement is certainly implied. It is also, and preeminently, a matter of being under divine law, of being the child of a mother who is Justice and Patience personified.

To conclude: given the full scope and development of its political argument, *Pericles* represents a concept of the monarchy predictably within the limits of what would have been judged acceptable doctrine to absolutists such as James. To require that the monarch be beholden to divine law and behave virtuously—conditions of rule Pericles at last understands and accepts—presents no real threat to his prerogative. The repeated invocations to Patience in the last act, recalling Helicanus' advice to Pericles after he fled from Antioch, would have reminded the audience of absolutist prohibitions against active resistance. If the play opens by characterizing as abusive a monarch's appropriation of the property of his subjects and of the commonwealth in terms that suggest an endorsement of constitutionalism and a restricted use of the prerogative, it also signally fails to pursue these concerns in a manner critical of their specifically political importance. In the play's last acts, Shakespeare rather chooses to portray the monarch as restored to strength and to a proper relation to his people, to the commonwealth, and to law by a moral enlightenment, a position that forces the monarch to see in the very images of desire and power the signs of a necessary and concomitant frustration and weakness.

Shakespeare's representation of obedience is, moreover, conceptually bound up with an article of faith that had little representation in the resistance theories of constitutional monarchists—the notion that time is restorative, and, by implication, that history is providential—but that is implicit in theories of divine right and often a feature of absolutist apology. (The virtuous Marina is both the dramatic manifestation of the chaste Thaisa, who, for the period of Marina's divine preaching, is hidden in Diana's temple, and also the condition, in the sense of the manner as well as the means, of Thaisa's return to the secular world.) In 1605 this representation of what is in essence a political mystery would have appealed to many audiences. There was reason then to imagine that legitimacy had been restored to the English monarchy after a period of uncertainty during Elizabeth's last years. In its depiction of the dangers of anarchy and of time as restorative, therefore, the play also celebrates legitimacy. But however impressive its reliance on the concept of moral and providential forces in history, *Pericles* also ends with an image undoing monarchic incest. Given the language of kinship as political metaphor, this conclusion must be understood as a reminder to Jacobean audiences that the king who was both husband and father could claim, by these very identities, no more than a limited *dominium*.

Notes

1. See David Bergeron, *Shakespeare's Romances and the Royal Family* (Lawrence: Univ. of Kansas Press, 1985); Leonard Tennenhouse, *Power on Display* (New York: Methuen, 1986). This essay is part of my longer study of political thought in Shakespeare's last plays.

2. P. Goolden, "Antiochus' Riddle in Gower and Shakespeare," *Review of English Studies*, n.s. 6.23 (1955): 245-51. For a lucid study of incest and the English monarchy see Bruce Boehrer, *Incest and Monarchy*, forthcoming from the Univ. of Pennsylvania Press.

3. Thomas Bilson, *A Sermon preached at Westminster before the King and Queenes Majesties at their Coronations on Saint James his day* (London, 1603), sig. B4v. In quoting from sixteenth- and seventeenth-century editions I have normalized letters but not spelling or punctuation. For arguments on the question of monarchic rule, see i.a. J. C. Sommerville, *Politics and Ideology in England, 1603-1640* (London: Longmans, 1986). For a history of the notion of constitutionalism in England, see J. G. A. Pocock, *The Ancient Constitution and the Feudal Law*, 2nd edition (Cambridge: Cambridge Univ. Press, 1987). For a study of tyranny in Elizabethan and Stuart drama, see Rebecca Bushnell, *Tragedies of Tyrants* (Ithaca: Cornell Univ. Press, 1990). I am generally indebted to Gordon Schochet and the Folger Institute Center for the History of British Political Thought for introducing me to the study of sixteenth- and seventeenth-century political philosophy.

4. Ponet qualifies the authority of the monarch as father: he is merely an "executor" of God's power and not exempt from his laws. Were this not the case, it might be said that "God allowed their tyranie, robbery of their subjectes, killing them without lawe. . . ." *A Shorte Treatise of Politike Power* (London, 1556), ed. Winthrop S. Hudson (Chicago: Univ. of Chicago Press, 1942), 43. Subsequent references to this work will appear in my text.

5. Sir John Fortescue, *A Learned Commendation of the Politique Lawes of England* (London, 1567), sig. K6v, K7, L8v, M1.

6. *Vindiciae contra tyrannos,* trans. and ed. Julian H. Franklin, in *Constitutionalism and Resistance in the Sixteenth Century* (New York, 1969), 174-75.

7. Nicholas Fuller, *The Argument in the Case of Thomas Lad and Richard Maunsell* (London, 1607), sig. A3, A3v, B3v. See also *The Fift Part of the Reports of Sr. Edward Coke, Knight* (London, 1607), sig. A6. The work of Fuller and Forset (see below) appeared within a year or two of *Pericles*; I am assuming that they drew on a commonly shared, figurative language to describe political relations.

8. Thomas Floyd, *The Picture of a Perfit Common wealth* (London, 1600), sig. B, Bv, C6v. For James, see p. 15.

9. [Robert Parsons], *A Conference About the Next Succession to the Crowne of Ingland* (London, 1594), sig. C8v.

10. Edward Forset, *A Comparative Discourse of the Bodies Natural and Politique* (London, 1606), sig. C4v.

11. "Phoenix," line 37; *Othello*, V.ii.196. For Shakespeare's works I use *The Riverside Shakespeare* (Boston, 1974).

12. Concepts of property are very complicated during this period. For an overview of questions on real property, see G. E. Aylmer, "The Meaning and the Definition of 'Property' in Seventeenth-century England," *Past and Present* 86 (1980): 87-97, and the reply by Andrew Reeve, 139-43. For an analysis of *dominium* in relation to *ius*, see Richard Tuck, *Natural Rights Theories: Their Origin and Development* (Cambridge: Cambridge Univ. Press, 1989), 5-31. Christopher Hill points out that Renaissance

concepts of "freedom" in contrast to "servility"—i.e., the condition of being a "freeman" as opposed to a "servant"—refer to the self as "property" that the former condition guarantees and the latter abrogates. To have a "property in one's own person and labour" is to be free politically and economically: to have lost that property is to be a wage-earner, a servant, a pauper. See Hill, "Pottage for Freeborn Englishmen: Attitudes to Wage Labour in the Sixteenth and Seventeenth Centuries," in *Socialism, Capitalism and Economic Growth,* ed. C. H. Feinstein (London: Cambridge Univ. Press, 1967), 338-50. For the meaning of property in political thought, see J. G. A. Pocock, "Authority and Property: the Question of Liberal Origins," in *After the Reformation: Essays in honour of J. H. Hexter,* ed. William J. Bouwsma and Barbara C. Malament (Philadelphia: Univ. of Pennsylvania Press, 1980), 331-54. On woman and property in the Renaissance see my *Renaissance Feminism* (Ithaca, Cornell Univ. Press, 1990); and also Mary London Shanley, "Marriage Contract and Social Contract in Seventeenth-Century English Political Thought," *Western Political Quarterly* 32 (1979): 79-91.

13. On the monarch's duty to foster trade see Forset, sig. C3, and especially Willaim Fulbecke, *The Pandectes of the Law of Nations* (London, 1602), sig. S4-T4v on subsidies and royal "impositions" on imports and exports.

14. James I, *The True Law of Free Monarchies* in *The Political Works of James I,* ed. Charles Howard McIlwain (Cambridge: Harvard Univ. Press, 1918), 58.

15. James quite specifically links the monarch's right to his subject's property with the availability of nubile women. Property not bequeathed to heirs, he claims, is the property of the king: "If a person, inheritour of any lands or goods, dye without any sort of heires, all his landes and goods returne to the king. And if a bastard die unrehabled without heires of his bodie (which rehabling onely lyes in the kings hands) all that hee hath likewise returnes to the king. And as ye see it manifest, that the King is over-Lord of the whole land: so is he Master over every person that inhabiteth the same, having power over the life and death of every one of them" (63).

16. The law on "uses," in effect primitive trusts, is, like the laws on property in general, very complicated. For an overview, see Kenelm Edward Digby, *An Introduction to the History of the Law of Real Property,* 5th ed. (Oxford, 1897), 315-72. For seventeenth-century formulations, see John Cowell, *The Interpreter* (Cambridge, 1607), sig. Zzz3v.

17. Gerard A. Barker, "Themes and Variations in Shakespeare's *Pericles,*" *English Studies* 44 (1963): 401-7. My analysis of *Pericles* as political theater is not intended to represent the play as either political doctrine or religious dogma, or to suggest that Shakespeare was taking a particular side on the question of monarchic authority and power. I do claim that the contestatory nature of drama generally is in the case of this particular play manifest not only in what is obviously in conflict, that is kinship relations, but also in the political references such relations had in the larger context of the language of contemporary political thought. As this play demonstrates, the violence of tyrannical government can be forcefully conveyed by images of marital and paternal abuse. Shakespeare's portrait of Pericles as husband and father identifies in intimate settings those "moods" or states of mind that to Jacobeans were chiefly indicators of political attitudes as well as practices; cf. esp. Forset.

18. Floyd, sig. E7v; Forset, sig. L-L2.

19. This limitation is crucial; see i.a. Fortescue, *Learned Commendation,* sig. L5v; Fuller, *Argument,* sig. A2-A3v; Parsons, *A Conference,* sig. C3v-C8v.

20. *Vindiciae,* 124; cf. the action of the Duke of Gloucester, reported in *2 Henry VI,* III.i.115-18.

21. *The Lord Coke his Speech and Charge: with a Discoverie of the Abuses and Corruption of Officers* (London, 1607), sig. C8.

22. James claims that only God can punish an evil monarch: "Neither is it ever heard that any king forgets himselfe twoards God . . . but God with the greatnesse of the plague revengeth the greatnes of his ingratitude (70). See also Bilson on monarchs: "must wee not reject their yoke with violence but rather endure their swordes with patience that God may be Judge betweene Prince and People . . . (sig. B6v); and William Barlow: "it becomes not good subjectes to bee their owne *Revengers. Christianity* teacheth *Patience,* not *Rebellion.*" *A Brand, Titio Erepta* (London, 1607), sig. F. Even Ponet, although advocating the active resistance of magistrates to unlawful government, admonishes the people: "yet are not the poore people destitute all together of remedy: but God hathe lefte unto them two weapones, hable to conquere and destroie the greatest Tirane that ever was: that is, Penaunce and Praier" (124).

David Solway (essay date 1997)

SOURCE: Solway, David. "*Pericles* as Dream." *The Sewanee Review* 105, no. 1 (winter 1997): 91-5.

[*In the following essay, Solway examines the dreamlike qualities of* Pericles.]

> Some to the Lute, some to the Viol went,
> And others chose the Cornet eloquent.
> These practising the Wind, and those the Wire,
> To sing Mens Triumphs, or in Heavens quire.
>
> —Andrew Marvell, *Musicks Empire*

Pericles, despite its earlier composition and disputed status, best sums up, of all the late plays, the character of Shakespearean romance. Its schematic form, its "gaps" and archaisms, its unadorned outlines and loose texture enable the spectator to observe with minimal distraction the tragicomic Muse at work. Its subject then appears not as any peculiar or local set of circumstances—misunderstandings, departures, reconciliations—but as nothing less than the universal dream of retrieval and atonement. The romance may be regarded as a dream not only in its unrealistic or improbable character—the comedies would answer to this description too—but in its particular *themes* of the recovery of self and the domestication of time as well as in the curious structure which it exhibits.

If we consider *Pericles* sympathetically, resisting the temptation to dismiss it as partially spurious or inferior, we see that it resembles a kind of "thought experiment" or imaginary voyage through time to an atemporal destination. The voyage, pursued in two directions at once—forward to a redeemed and glorious future and backward to an ideal, lost condition—blends anticipation and memory, thought and dream, into a single mythic consummation. In the prologue to act 3 Gower poses the rhetorical question "Who dreamt, who thought of such a thing?"; and Lysimachus, in expressing his wonder and delight with Marina, uses similar language: "I did not think / Thou woulds't have spoke so well; ne'er dreamt thou coulds't." The play is intended "to take [delight] our imagination," but only if we empathize with the hero and consent to "think his pilot thought" as we navigate in the straits between experience and dream.

I

Marilyn French in *Shakespeare's Division of Experience* tells us that the romances "are shot through with dream devices like projection, surrogation, and transformation," but she is content to let the matter rest on this level of analytic abstraction. It may be more helpful in considering the dream structure of *Pericles* to recall in greater detail what Freud has to say about the architectonic of the dream. Here we find that the "dream work" (the shaping of the dream out of the "dream thoughts") is governed by the four functional principles of condensation, displacement, representability, and secondary elaboration.

By condensation is meant something like overdetermination—that is, each dream image is determined by several dream thoughts that contribute to the psychic density of that image. Such condensation is perhaps most evident in the charged latency of the pun, over which the romance enjoys no privileged monopoly but which nevertheless finds a most welcoming reception therein. For example, early in act 1 Pericles compares Antiochus' incestuous daughter to a viol played before her time and links the image with the concept of law in the locution *lawful music*. The suggestion is that a law has been *violated*, and an ear attuned to semantic concentricities may recall this earlier turbulence in Marina's "Never was waves nor wind more violent," uttered some acts later. A similar fusion of image and thought occurs when Pericles, comparing himself to a treetop that protects its subject and nourishing roots, confesses to a royal apprehensiveness that makes his body "pine." And Cerimon, the magus or dream-figure to whom we all appeal, clearly stands for the magical *ceremony* that controls, harmonizes, and redeems the elemental ferocity of Nature. Name, function, person, and idea dovetail into single presence.

Images can also be overloaded with contradictory meanings and associations. Fire is one of the "unfriendly elements" and is responsible with the other three for Marina's "chiding . . . nativity"; yet Thaisa is revived to music and fire, so that her "fire of life kindle[s] again." Similarly the "fair viol" that was played before its time is then played, so to speak, after its time in Cerimon's command—"The viol once more." From the standpoint of Nature the music to which Thaisa is revived is also not a lawful music. But where, earlier, social law had been violated, here it is natural law that is transcended by Asclepian sanction.

The image of the sea is equally susceptible of antithetic density: the destructive element, devouring ships and men with insatiable indifference, becomes "this great sea of joys" that is lethal only through its superabundance of sweetness.

Sometimes the paronomasia is not only to be found in the spry amalgamation of contraries, but in the incremental heightening of effect, as, for example, "He bears / A tempest which his mortal vessel *tears*" (italics mine). Here the related ideas of dismemberment and sorrow are brought close together—along with the complementary association of salt waters, uniting the violence of the sea with the bitter helplessness of its victims.

Displacement implies that the dream appears as "elsewhere centered," requiring the dreamer to discount the manifest content of his dream in favor of its latent content, its raison d'être or substratum of meaning. The manifest content of our play is the story of tribulation and suffering through which we trace Pericles' coming of age, his passing through life's manifold stages of adolescent fancy, tragic bereavement, and mature reconciliation—helped along, albeit, by several lotterylike windfalls.[1] The latent content is not any particular series of crises or adventures but the storm of life itself, whirring us from our friends, in which we detect the perennial search for a divine father, a Cerimon whose "blest infusions" redeem us from our disenfranchisement. The pressure of the reality principle is unremitting and is explicitly acknowledged by Pericles: "We cannot but obey / The powers above us," he admits with resignation. Yet the pleasure principle continues to operate, modestly triumphant in the numinous figure of Cerimon whom Pericles addresses: "Reverend sir, / The gods can have no mortal officer / More like a god than you."

We need not dwell unduly upon either of the two remaining structural rules since they are largely self-evident. The dream cannot tolerate abstraction but must be representable in visual and aural terms. Consequently *any* play resembles a dream in its sensuous manifestation, but the romance with its visions, hieratic choreography, and musical interludes would satisfy the dream criterion more vividly and appositely. As for secondary elaboration—the papering over of lacunae to give a semblance of logic or coherence—we have in *Pericles* the choric device of Gower to explain or explain away illogicalities, asking pardon for using "one language in each several clime" (for convenience) and declaring that he stands "i' th' gaps" in order to inform or "teach" his audience.

We note as well the preponderance of other recognizable dream features: time elasticities (see the beginning of act 4 in both *Pericles* and *The Winter's Tale*), sudden changes of place, unwarranted knowledge (Diana's revelation—or Jupiter's "book" in *Cymbeline*), magical retributions, and the like. But these are not, properly speaking, principles of organization. Here it suffices to say there can be little doubt that the four basic structural principles adumbrated by Freud—condensation, displacement, representability, and secondary elaboration—can be distinctly observed leavening the dream thought (or the play thought) into the finished product itself.

Admittedly these principles of organization may also apply to literature in general and to poetic drama in particular, but they are most robust and ubiquitous in the romance play with its patently thaumaturgic elements, its unabashed reliance on miracle and revelation, and its congenial atmosphere of transcendent intercessions.

II

Dreams, we are told, are circuitous and intricate ways of expressing fundamental conflicts in the human soul. Occasionally a solution is offered, waiting upon decipherment; more often, perhaps, the dream presents an impossible resolution that can be experienced only at one remove from reality, in the *locus amoenus* of a region without geotemporal coordinates (second star to the right and straight on till morning). The conflict in the dream that is *Pericles* is the eternal one going on between the destructive and capricious realm of Nature, the elemental world indifferent to human desires (signified by the tempest, the realm of the "masked Neptune"), and the world of spirit or imagination, of human longing for harmony and election (signified by music and vision).

The spectator responds to the play in precisely the same way as Pericles reacts to Marina's narrative: "This is the rarest dream that e'er dull sleep / Did mock sad fools withal." We recognize a world in which dreams, bearing their "goddess argentine," are visionary and evangelical and "wishes fall out as they're willed." But, if Pericles thinks he is dreaming Marina and the events she recounts, as in some sense he surely is, we may then ask: Who is dreaming the play? The author in his creative fit, we may reply; but we might also decide that the play is dreaming itself and that the characters are dreaming one another—or at least that both play and characters seem intended to give that impression. The play may be said to be dreaming itself in so far as it is a dream whose content is another dream—the dream of resolution, restoration, happiness, accompanied by celestial music. Further, if we are not *consciously* accountable for our dreams, there exists a very real sense in which our actual dreams may be conceived as dreaming themselves, that is, they proceed without the intervention of the controlling sensibility.

But the dreamer and the dream, the dancer and the dance, subsist in a web of complex intersections that cannot be so readily sundered, as Augustine had hoped when he thanked his God that he was not responsible for his dreams. So the play, as is more or less the case with every pastoral romance, represents the collective dream of desiring, impoverished humanity. *Ultimately it is the spectator who is dreaming the play*. Time becomes the medium of reunification: obstacles are overcome and discontinuities annealed. Illogicalities are explained away, suffering is redeemed, death conquered, envy and resentment transmuted by the dream alchemy into reconciliation and requited love.

The riddle with which the play opens, alluding to Antiochus' incestuous daughter as both a mother and a wife, finds its resolution toward the end in the (similar yet different) magnanimous contradiction of a daughter giving birth to a father: "Thou . . . beget'st him that did thee beget." Marina is restored to her father, restoring him in the act of restoration, and preparing for the climactic reunion with the mother and wife who is Thaisa. It is here that the *authentic riddle*—the riddle of time, loss, and separation—is solved in the dream of a sublime atonement. Thus the cherubim at the gate put down their flaming swords and receive the exile, "led on by heaven and crowned with joy," into his lost inheritance.

When the curtain falls, the dreamer awakens to find himself once again banished into the world of conflict and bereavement. But the memory persists of a magical compensatory realm in which Lord Cerimon, "this man / Through whom the gods have shown their power," may once again, as we dream the dream at two removes, "from first to last resolve" us.

Note

1. G. Wilson Knight (*The Crown of Life*) suggests that the play can be seen as providing "a panorama of life from adolescent fantasy and a consequent fall, through good works to a sensible and fruitful marriage, and thence into tragedy, with a reemergence beyond mortal appearances into some higher recognition and rehabilitation." Derek Traversi (*Shakespeare: The Last Phase*) thinks the play records "a symbolic pilgrimage in search of an ideal expressed in terms of devotion to chivalrous love." (Although as Traversi also thinks that Marina is betrothed to Cerimon rather than Lysimachus, one is a little disposed, perhaps, to question his authority.)

F. Elizabeth Hart (essay date 2000)

SOURCE: Hart, F. Elizabeth. "Cerimon's 'Rough' Music in *Pericles*, 3.2." *Shakespeare Quarterly* 51, no. 3 (fall 2000): 313-31.

[*In the following essay, Hart argues that analysis of the adjective "rough" in Cerimon's phrase "rough music" points to the mother goddess Diana as the controlling deity of the play.*]

Shakespeare's use of "rough" in *The Tempest* to describe the magic that Prospero must "abjure" (5.1.50, 51) has inspired debate over the adjective's meaning, some critics finding in it the key not only to Prospero's powers but to the play as a whole.[1] A less well-studied but similarly ambiguous use of "rough" occurs in the 1609 quarto of *Pericles* (Q1), where it modifies the "Musick" that precedes Cerimon's revival of Thaisa, Pericles's presumed-dead wife and queen (sig. E4ʳ).[2] Owing to the questionable status of Q1 *Pericles*, however, "rough" in this case has frequently been emended to "still" in important editions, including the Arden; the Cambridge; the Penguin; and, most recently, the Oxford, from which the word "still" has been adopted for mass pedagogical use by the *Norton Shakespeare*.[3] While rough music does present interpretive difficulties in the context of a dire medical emergency, I will argue here that its emendation is not necessary. Rough music may, in fact, be critical to an understanding of the healing powers of Cerimon, a minor character whom critics and directors often treat as an early modern practitioner of occult magic despite the classical setting and context in which he is presented.[4]

The Q1 passage in question appears as follows, featuring Cerimon as speaker:

> Well sayd, well sayd; the fire and clothes: the rough and
> Wofull Musick that we haue, cause it to sound beseech you:
> The Violl once more; how thou stirr'st thou blocke?
> The Musicke there: I pray you giue her ayre. . . .
>
> (sig. E4ʳ)

Bolstered by a parallel moment in *The Painfull Adventures of Pericles Prince of Tyre*, a 1608 novelized version of the play by the London innkeeper George Wilkins, some editors have substituted Wilkins's descriptor "still" on the assumption that "Wofull" music is more likely to be dulcet in tone than the "rough" of quarto description.[5] (The passage from Wilkins reads: "[T]hen calling softly to the Gentlemen who were witnesses about him, he bade them that they should commaund some *still* musicke to sound" [emphasis added].[6]) Of the various definitions the *Oxford English Dictionary* gives for *still*, the archaic meaning of "Subdued, soft, not loud" as applied to sounds does nicely complement the somberness implied in "wofull."[7] The phrase *still music* was even current in the seventeenth century, appearing, as it happens, in a stage direction in the final scene of *As You Like It* (5.4.106 s.d.). By contrast, the *OED*'s [*Oxford English Dictionary*] applicable meanings for *rough*—"discordant, harsh," "wanting grace or refinement, rude, unpolished, rugged"—all seem contradictory to the tone we might imagine for a scene of such solemnity. And according to the *OED*, the phrase *rough music* does not appear to have become current in the language until the early eighteenth century—except, it would seem, in the case of the skimmington or charivari, where rough music was an integral aspect of that specific ritual of social control.[8]

A preference for "still" would also seem to be supported by Cerimon's request that his assistants bring him a "Violl," apparently a reference to the stringed instrument familiar to us as a viola or violin. However, editors have differed in their glossing of this word, too, frequently emending "Violl" to "vial"—a container for medicine—and noting that in the parallel passage from John Gower's *Confessio Amantis*, one of two principal sources for *Pericles*, Cerimon is said to "put a licour in hir mouthe."[9] The confusion is heightened by the variable spellings of words for both senses. The *OED* notes that while *viol* was available as a spelling for the musical instrument, the spelling *violl* was more closely associated with a "vessel of a small or moderate size used for holding liquids" than it was with the instrument, whose spelling variations actually tended more toward our modern-day spelling of *vial*.[10] The spelling *violl* clearly means the musical instrument earlier in the play when Pericles conceives of Antiochus's daughter as a "faire Violl" whose "stringes . . . finger'd make [for] man his lawfull musicke" (sig. A3ᵛ). These orthographic variations aptly illustrate what Margreta de Grazia and Peter Stallybrass consider an added dimension of materiality in early modern texts, a materiality based on scribal and print slippage whose histories are "so specific that [they] cannot comply with modern notions of correctness and intelligibility."[11]

While the discussion that follows may seem like much ado over a minor passage in a play fraught with greater difficulties, the status of this passage as a genuine crux is supported by the fact that few editions agree on how to interpret it. Its possible relevance, as well, to the play's many other uses of music make the nature of the music represented in any given scene an issue of some thematic importance. Indeed, references to music are so numerous in *Pericles* that, as one critic puts it, "[T]here is scarcely any significant action in the play that is not directly related to music."[12] Critics stress music's restorative powers and its emblematic function—typical in all Shakespeare's romances—as symbols of divine harmony.[13] Music as a healing agent is mentioned, in fact, at the very beginning of the play, in the opening lines of Gower's first chorus:

> To sing a song that old was sung,
> From ashes ancient Gower is come,
> Assuming man's infirmities
> To glad your ear and please your eyes.
> It hath been sung at festivals,
> On ember eves and holy-ales;
> And lords and ladies in their lives

Have read it for restoratives.

(1.Cho.1-8)

These lines characterize the play as itself an old song that the medieval poet has returned from the dead specially to sing to this modern theater audience. Gower allies this song with "festivals," "ember eves and holy-ales," and points out its function within English folk tradition (both heard and "read") as a restorative. At the play's end, song as "sacred physic" (5.1.77) figures prominently in Marina's successful use of music to stir Pericles from his paralyzing melancholy. Its emblematic function emerges shortly afterwards as Pericles's ears are opened to the "music of the spheres" (l. 233), a "heavenly music" (l. 236) that signifies the play's newly harmonized analogies between human and cosmic orders.

My argument defending rough music will contradict none of these impressions of music's sacred and restorative qualities in the play. Rather, I extend this view by suggesting a classical context in which a rough music could indeed be understood as sacred—an aspect of an organized religious practice that Cerimon as a character may loosely represent. Although Cerimon speaks fewer than a hundred lines in the play, his key role as facilitator or master of ceremonies is apparent even in the sound of his name.[14] He presents himself early in 3.2 as a gentleman-physician who eschews the "tottering honor" of nobility for the "secret art" of nature's curatives—"the blest infusions / That dwells in vegetives, in metals, stones" (ll. 42, 34, 37-38). While it is understandable that some have interpreted these lines as an allusion to the occult, I would argue that the emphasis here lies not so much on magic as it does on "physic"—medicine—which Cerimon has used to "restore" the lives of his fellow Ephesians ("Your honor has through Ephesus poured forth / Your charity, and hundreds call themselves / Your creatures" [ll. 45-47], remarks the Second Gentleman). Cerimon confesses that his motive for studying physic has been to achieve "immortality"—to acquire proximity to, if not an actual identification with, the gods—far more than to enhance his nobility:

> I hold it ever
> Virtue and cunning were endowments greater
> Than nobleness and riches. Careless heirs
> May the two latter darken and expend,
> But immortality attends the former,
> Making a man a god.
>
> (ll. 28-33)

Although he is clearly not a deity, the play seems to hint at his near approach to the divine: upon Thaisa's awakening, the First Gentleman exclaims to Cerimon, "The heavens / Through you, increase our wonder and sets up / Your fame forever" (ll. 97-99). The final scene's reconciliations echo this wonder, underscoring Cerimon's success as an intercessor between human and divine. Pericles wonders "who to thank" for "this great miracle" of his wife's return (5.3.59, 60). Thaisa's response—"Lord Cerimon, . . . / Through whom the gods have shown their power"—provokes Pericles's declaration "The gods can have no mortal officer / More like a god than [Cerimon]" (ll. 61-62, 64-65).

In this essay I will suggest that "rough" as a descriptor for Cerimon's music hints at a link between the healing powers of his "secret art" and the mysteries of the archaic goddesses who were associated with the ancient city of Ephesus, the setting for all of Cerimon's appearances in the play. Cerimon calls on Apollo and Aesculapius to guide him (3.2.69, 114), but the god whom he most actively serves is Diana of Ephesus, to whose temple and wishes he obviously has access. According to recent scholarship on Roman religious culture, this Diana of Ephesus—as distinct from Ovid's Diana—is best understood with respect to the Mother-worship that flourished in the territory of Phrygia, the home province of Ephesus and also of ancient Troy. Included in the forms of Phrygian Mother-worship was a particularly jarring kind of music, often practiced by a conspicuous class of priest. The central deity defining this culture was Cybele, whose characteristics had been transferred over the centuries to Diana of Ephesus. The play's connection between Cerimon and rough music may thus indicate the nature of Cerimon's service to Diana, whose ties to the culture of Cybelian Mother-worship were available to the Renaissance through classical literature and commentary and through contemporary Italian mythography. Cerimon's proximity to Diana of Ephesus endows him with the healing powers that, historically speaking, were a principal function of the Asian mystery rites.

Before proceeding with an argument focused on a single disputed word in the text, I feel it necessary to address this play's troubled textual history; in particular, I hope to clarify my own position on the collaboration theories that have shaped most editors' approach to its analysis. Many readers, beginning in the first century after *Pericles* was written, have detected a difference in style between the play's first two and final three acts, a difference so marked that some of the play's earliest editors suspected a hand other than Shakespeare's at work in Acts 1 and 2. This suspicion is fed by the fact that *Pericles* was omitted from the First Folio of 1623, presumably (or so editors have speculated) because Heminge and Condell were aware that the play was not solely Shakespeare's. The lack of a Folio version makes all-important comparisons between contemporary editions impossible. This is unfortunate since the only period edition available to us, the 1609 quarto, suffers from erratic lineation, inconsistent spelling, scenes containing references to missing actions, and myriad other problems that recent editors have ascribed to poor memorial reporting or compositorial error (or both). To address these problems, editors have long resorted to importing words, phrases, and even stage directions from Wilkins's *Painfull Aduentures of Pericles Prince of Tyre,* assuming, since Wilkins's novel was obviously written to capitalize on the stage version's popularity, that it must claim some degree of authority. This logic has shifted in recent years to the conviction that Wilkins must have been Shake-

Powys Thomas as Cerimon, Scot Denton as Fisherman, Martha Henry as Thaisa, and Richard Monette and Daniel Buccos as Fishermen in Act III, scene ii of the 1973 Stratford Festival production of Pericles.

speare's mysterious collaborator, and much effort has gone into attempts to prove this hypothesis using computer-driven statistical analysis.[15]

But critics of the Wilkins collaboration theory—and indeed of the very idea of collaboration—are becoming increasingly vocal in their dissent, raising points that urge the debate back to its root assumptions. David Bergeron has commented, for instance, that "Part of the problem is the ancient one of Shakespearean criticism: when encountering poorly written passages or ones that offend morally, always postulate the possibility of another writer clandestinely at work."[16] New Cambridge editors Doreen DelVecchio and Antony Hammond reject not only the collaboration theory and the idea of Wilkins as collaborator but also a related theory that Q1 *Pericles* was a memorial text (and hence a "bad" quarto), assigning most of the problems that have led to these theories to compositorial error or "the usual errors of misreading a difficult script. . . ."[17] One of the original reasons for suspecting collaboration, the fact that *Pericles* does not appear in the First Folio, actually indicates little, say DelVecchio and Hammond, since the Folio does include other plays, such as *Henry VIII* and *Macbeth,* that we now know or suspect to be collaborative efforts. Furthermore, they argue, radical style changes occur throughout the canon and must always "be considered very carefully in . . . dramaturgical context, rather than in stylistic literary isolation," where "literary taste" becomes "an uncertain arbiter."[18] The New Cambridge editors may be the boldest among the dissenters, but their view finds support in the recent work of some new historicists, who have quietly disregarded the authorship issue altogether, demonstrating through their variety of readings that it is possible to find, if not stylistic unity, then at least a degree of ideological coherence that binds together the disputed portions of the play.[19]

The controversy has advanced to a level of complex and competing scenarios that are now met with equally complicated rejoinders. However, the arguments on both sides remain conjectural. For the purposes of my limited analysis, let me say that I find the dissenters' arguments more persuasive, especially considering that the origins of the debate are largely ideological. To compound this problem, it now seems that the idealism inherent in centuries of bardolatry is not the only ideology framing the discussion: DelVecchio and Hammond accuse the Oxford editors of operating "gleefully" in their use of statistical evidence to determine collaboration not just in *Pericles* but in a range of Shakespeare's plays, hinting that their desire to undercut Shakespeare's status is reactionary.[20] Where its "reconstruction" of the text of *Pericles* is concerned, the Oxford edition "carried the belief of the editors . . . that [Wilkins] is essentially *more reliable than Q* to extraordinary extremes, re-writing its text as the fancy took them, and for trivial reasons."[21] This charge is particularly true, I say, in the case of "rough music," which occurs in 3.2, the portion of the play which even the staunchest of collaboration theorists agree was probably written by Shakespeare.[22] Given the fact that no one seriously disputes Shakespeare's hand in 3.2, the ease with which editors have simply substituted "still" for "rough" in the passage in question strikes me as a symptom of a general unwillingness even to try to make sense of the problems we are faced with in Q1. While the argument I present below is equally speculative, it at least attempts to historicize rough music—to offer a classical context and meaning for the crux that goes beyond the limits of internal evidence.

In keeping, therefore, with this imperative to historicize, I contend that there is a context in which rough music may turn out to be peculiarly appropriate if we take into account 3.2's setting in Ephesus, the fact that in the ancient world Ephesus was the world-renowned center of worship for the goddess Diana, and the probability that the Ephesian Diana bore associations with a form of cult music well known to the Romans and notorious for its "savagery." Ephesus, though properly the domain of the Greek goddess Artemis, became more familiarly associated with Diana under Roman rule in the first century BC and continued to be associated with her in the Latin-leaning Renaissance. The prominence in *Pericles* of the Ephesian Diana, who appears to Pericles in a dream vision in 5.1, and of her famous temple, which serves as the backdrop for the play's final scene, should prompt our curiosity about the extent to which she was known to the early moderns. Ultimately, Diana figures in my argument by virtue of her overlay onto the much older Phrygian goddess Cybele whom Artemis supplanted in a synthesis of metaphors not unlike other syntheses that took place in the aftermath of Roman colonization.

There is evidence that Shakespeare and his audience would have recognized this Diana as distinct from Ovid's Diana, the chaste huntress and goddess of the moon to whom line glosses in modern editions typically refer. Post-Reformation, Bible-literate playgoers would have recognized Ephesus from the Acts of the Apostles, in which Paul's missionary activities in the city of Ephesus provoke a riot among the craftsmen of Diana's temple, who repeatedly cry out "Great *is* Diana of the Ephesians!"[23] The traditional reputation of Ephesus as an occult setting may derive initially from these passages in Scripture, where newly converted Christians who had used "curious artes" "broght their bokes, and burned them before all men."[24] Diana's perceived agency within early modern discourse on demonology is exemplified by Cambridge theologian James Mason's *The Anatomie of Sorcerie,* a book devoted to defining and cataloguing the "mischieuous deuice[s]" of those in Mason's acquaintance who were reputedly learned in the occult.[25] Mason's diatribe against the practices of "Charmers, Inchanters, and such like" begins with a reading from Acts 19:11-16 and dwells at length on the "superstitious" practices associated with Diana:

> And it is manifest by histories, that the Ephesians were giuen to such like superstition; for it is recorded in diuers authors: That in the Image *Diana,* which was worshipped at Ephesus, there were certaine obscure words, or sentences not agreeing together, nor depending one vpon another; much like vnto riddles written vpon the feete, girdle, and crowne of the said *Diana*: the which if a man did vse, hauing written them out, and carrying them about him, hee should haue good lucke in all his businesses: and hereof sprung the prouerbe, *Ephesiæ literæ*: where one vseth any thing which bringeth good successe.[26]

In citing the *Ephesiæ literæ* proverb, Mason shows the currency of folk wisdom in England that focused on the iconic details of Diana's temple statue—the "many-breasted Artemis" that scholars study to this day.

But there were other early modern discourses in which an Ephesian Diana would have been a distinct figure, including one that was far more ameliorative and which circulated among the literati—the discourse on ancient mythology. A familiar subject in the history of this period, the Renaissance "rediscovery" of paganism has been thoroughly documented by Jean Seznec and Don Cameron Allen.[27] Their studies, though fully comprehensive of classical culture, are noticeably marked by an emphasis on influences from Asia Minor, on what Seznec and Allen characterize as centuries of integration of "Oriental" mythology into medieval Europe's understanding of the classical narratives of Greece and Rome.[28] Their focus on the East has gained support in recent years from the classical history and literary scholarship of Walter Burkert, Robert Turcan, Margaret Doody, and M. L. West, each of whom explores different aspects of ancient, early Christian, and medieval cultures as they were influenced by eastern cultures.[29] Of these scholars, Burkert may prove the most relevant for early modern studies through his claim that the comparative loss of eastern elements from the modern inventory of classical mythology was a late development—an eighteenth-century phenomenon not to be assumed of earlier classicisms.[30] Early modern classicism, Burkert's and others' studies imply, may well have included elements of eastern cultures to a degree not obvious to us as we regard it through the prism of an eighteenth-century revisionism.

As Seznec and Allen have noted, the fifteenth and sixteenth centuries saw the composition and widespread translation of Italian-authored manuals detailing the iconographic features of classical mythological figures, encyclopedias of the pagan world modeled on Boccaccio's fourteenth-century *Genealogia deorum gentilium libri*.[31] These scrupulous compilations of ancient symbology became indispensable guides to pre-Christian belief which, as Allen declares, "no seventeenth-century scholar, man of letters, or artist could do without."[32] Some of these manuals actively focus attention on the gods and goddesses of Rome's eastern provinces, mingling them and occasionally confusing their functions with the gods and goddesses of official Roman origin. Three in particular—manuals by Vincenzo Cartari, Lilio Gregorio Giraldi, and Natale Conti—were popular among English artists, poets, playwrights, and masque composers. Of these, Cartari's *Imagines deorum* (translated in 1599 as *The Fovntaine of Ancient Fiction. Wherein is liuely depictured the Images and Statues of the gods and the Ancients*) was the most attuned to eastern religious culture, giving what Seznec calls "extraordinary prominence" to the "Oriental cults."[33] Cartari's influence on Jonson, Daniel, Marston, Chapman, and—speculatively, at least—on Shakespeare has been argued in the past by Seznec, D. J. Gordon, and John Peacock.[34]

Manuals such as Cartari's bespeak an early modern sensitivity that may account for the traditional popularity of the Apollonius tale—the Greco-Asian story on which *Pericles* is based—and, perhaps, the otherwise-puzzling popularity of Shakespeare's play in his day. Thought to be a folktale of Hellenistic Greece, the story of Apollonius survives in its earliest written form in a second- or third-century Latin manuscript entitled *Historia Apollonii regis tyri*. The Middle Ages produced hundreds of versions of this tale in numerous languages, including Russian, Hungarian, Icelandic, and Danish, as well as French, Italian, Spanish, and English. The fourteenth century saw its inclusion in the *Gesta Romanorum* and in Gower's *Confessio Amantis*, two prime sources of moralistic fables for generations of English writers. In writing *Pericles*, Shakespeare consulted not only Gower's poem but also a fictional account of Apollonius by Lawrence Twine, a sixteenth-century contemporary whose narrative *The Patterne of Painefull Adventures* was reprinted several times over the course of Shakespeare's career. Yet despite the tale's dissemination and longevity, it managed to preserve distinct marks of its ancient Greco-Asian origins, not least of which were a setting along the Aegean and the providential role of an eastern Mother goddess, Diana of Ephesus. This Diana remains a constant throughout the story's history, her function as a *dea ex machina* iterated in retellings from late antiquity to Gower and eventually to Twine, Wilkins, and Shakespeare.[35]

But the Apollonius tale was not the only available fictional account of the Ephesian Diana: the latter decades of the sixteenth century had seen the translation and publication of several other Greek and Roman novels composed in the Far-Eastern provinces of the Roman Empire between 100-600 AD.[36] That these works enjoyed a popular readership in the Renaissance is clear by their multiple translations and editions and by the sixteenth- and seventeenth-century commentaries they inspired.[37] While it is generally accepted that these fictions must have served as models for Shakespeare, what has been less obvious is their pattern of representations of divine providence—the extent, that is, to which they repeatedly represent eastern goddesses and Diana of Ephesus in particular as figures central to their spiritual economies. For example, both the *Historia Apollonii* and the *Confessio Amantis* end at the Ephesian temple of Diana; it is therefore no surprise that Shakespeare ends *Pericles* in the same place. But so, too, does Achilles Tatius's *Loves of Clitophon and Leucippe*, a narrative not identified as a source for Shakespeare but one that had only recently come to the attention of London readers when *Pericles* appeared on the stage.[38] In Tatius's story two lovers from the city of Tyre endure separation, enslavement, and tests of their chastity, only to be miraculously reunited in the temple of Diana at Ephesus. Similarly, in Heliodorus's *Aethiopian Historie*, a fiction translated in 1569 and a primary source for Sidney's *Arcadia*, the mysterious Ethiopian-born heroine is linked to both the Egyptian Isis and, by her own declaration of allegiance, Diana of Ephesus. William Adlington's 1566 translation of Apuleius's *The Golden Ass*, an acknowledged source for many of Shakespeare's plays, displays details of the culture of eastern goddess worship to an extent unmatched in classical literature. The eleventh book of Apuleius's novel represents the mysteries of Isis, who in a dream vision presents herself to the hero as a grand compendium of Mediterranean goddesses, including, she states, "the sister of the good Phœbus [Diana, who is] . . . now adored in the sacred places of Ephesus."[39] The direct intervention of Diana of Ephesus into the lives of Pericles and his fractured family, while a relatively unusual device in drama, is so typical in these novels as to constitute a literary motif.

As presented in these various sixteenth-century discourses, from the Bible and demonological tracts to mythographical manuals and popular fiction, Diana of Ephesus would have connoted an eastern persona for Shakespeare's audience, one distinct from the persona of her Ovidian counterpart. But how might Diana's Ephesian identity inform Cerimon's rough music in *Pericles*, 3.2? My sense is that the connection to rough music lies not so much in Diana herself but in the more archaic Cybele, some of whose traits, as I mentioned earlier, were passed to Diana by geographical coincidence. Cybele was one of the great Bronze Age Mother goddesses who for thousands of years had dominated in Greece, Syria, Canaan, and Egypt.[40] Like these other Mothers, Cybele of Phrygia was a dual personification of the earth and moon, representing nature and fertility, cosmic as well as earthly time, and the life-and-death cycles of both human and vegetative existence. During the classical era she was associated with a subordinated male companion, Attis, who served her as both lover and son, and whose mythical castration, death, and resurrection provided the basis for springtime agricultural festivals.

The history of Cybele under Roman rule is inseparable from the larger history of the eastern cults' slow incorporation into the mainstream of Roman culture.[41] Officially introduced to the city in 204 BC, Cybele was at first regarded as a foreigner, the favored deity of slaves, immigrants, and merchants from Asia who had congregated mostly in Italian port cities. But once a temple to her had been erected in Rome, the practices of her cult, along with others from the East, inspired devotion among a "mass of individuals" whom Robert Turcan describes as "receptive to . . . exotic forms of worship."[42] According to Turcan, "[E]astern religions . . . offered the attraction of strong feelings and emotions. Their liturgies excited and aroused the senses of those who were henceforth left cold by the strictly formalist worship of the Roman gods."[43] By the imperial period and particularly under Claudius, Cybele was "well and truly officialized," her image appearing on Roman coins and her status appropriated by Roman empresses, some of whom generated iconography of themselves either as or with symbolic images of the goddess.[44] For centuries, March was Cybele's festival month, marking the anniversary of her entry into Rome. When Claudius instituted an April festival in honor of Attis, there began a popular combined festival for both. The *hilaria* ("joy") that ended this festival took on "the air of an exuberant carnival," not unlike the later medieval Carnival with its emphasis on masquerade and its alternating phases of solemnity and release, the latter expressed in displays of mass abandon.[45]

Such details become relevant when we consider two aspects of Cybele's cult that earned it a reputation among Romans for "savagery," an opinion repeated in commentaries available to early modern students of Roman history. In such commentaries two traits become systematically linked and contribute to the construction of a general category of social other—the Phrygian—within Roman culture. The first such trait was the appearance and behavior of Cybele's priests, who, contrary to what we might expect, were mostly male. These priests, called *galli*, acknowledged the feminine roots of the cult by methodically effeminizing themselves, growing their hair long and wearing women's clothing in public appearances. But their most arresting display of self-emasculation—the spectacle in the frenzy of spring festivities that brought them universal renown—was self-castration in imitation of Attis. The Greeks had outlawed the castration of priests wherever Cybele's cult appeared on their mainland. But in Rome the practice, although strictly forbidden for Roman citizens, flourished among ethnic Phrygians and was often performed to the fascination of Roman crowds. Cybele's eunuchs thus gained lasting notoriety, casting a vivid image of gender transgression and sexual mutilation on the tableau of city life: "Once a year, during the April festivals, the galli were permitted to dance through the streets of Rome to the sounds of *auloi* and tambourines, in their exotic 'get-up,' with their feminine garments, long hair and amulets. At that time they were allowed to make door-to-door collections, for the upkeep of the temple and its emasculated staff."[46]

The second trait—the one most relevant to my argument defending rough music—was the riotous clangor of the Phrygian music, "the sounds of *auloi* and tambourines" noted just above. Harsh music had long been associated with Cybele's cult and mysteries. Iconography often placed her with certain musical instruments, the timbrel (tambourine) and cymbal predominantly but also the drum, horn, reed flute, twin flute, straight and curved pipes, and possibly a primitive form of organ.[47] These instruments were part of festival celebrations and so became popularly identified with the orgiastic elements in the cult—with the frenzy that in previous centuries had been likened by the Greeks to the mania of Dionysus.[48] Percussive music has been traced to Cybele's liturgy dating back to the seventh century BC, but given speculation that her Hittite name Kubaba meant "cymbal," it may go back even further.[49] Significantly for the purposes of my argument about Cerimon, such instruments played a key role in the performance of her mystery rites, whose text, according to early Christian observers, included the statement "'From the tambourine I have eaten; from the cymbal I have drunk'."[50]

The extent to which Cybele's priests were associated with their music is evident from Latin commentary, the abundance of which supports the probability that Cybele, her eunuchs, and their distinctive sound were similarly known and linked in the Renaissance. The authorities' attitudes range from hostility to the cult's popular following (Varro, Seneca, Tacitus, Cicero, Juvenal, and Augustine) to disdainful fascination with the spectacle of the *galli* (Lucretius, Ovid) to open admiration and a willingness to make use of Cybele's mythic ties to Rome—her guardianship over Phrygian Troy—in order to generate an ideology of empire and civilization (Virgil, Ovid). A description from Lucretius's *De rerum natura* offers an example of the quality of detail that would have been available to early modern Latin readers.[51] Here Lucretius narrates a clear association between Cybele's "Capon-priests" (so-called because capons, or gelded roosters, do not father offspring) and the "crashing and clashing" and "threats blared raw on the horn" that were, for the Romans, unmistakably Phrygian:

> Various peoples . . .
> Call upon "Mother Ida" and give her troops
> Of Phrygian followers, for, they say, from Phrygia
> The "phruited" fields first spread for all the world.
> Capon-priests they assign her—they wish to show
> That those who sully the Mother's Law, those found
> Ungrateful to their parents, are unworthy
> To bear their children live to the shores of light.
> Palm-thunder on drums drawn taut—the crashing and clashing
> Of cymbals about her—threats blared raw on the horn—
> With the pipe and the Phrygian tempo they whip to a frenzy
> And brandish the daggers, the signs of their fury and bloodshed,
> That the crowd of sinners in their thankless hearts
> Will quake with fear before her Majesty.[52]

Virgil, perhaps influenced by Lucretius, similarly describes the "Corybantes" (priests) of the "Mother goddess" as wielding their "Brazen ringing cups" in the sacred groves of Mount Ida.[53] And Ovid, in his *Fasti,* a source for Shakespeare's *Rape of Lucrece,* writes of feeling "daunted by the shrill cymbal's clash and the bent flute's thrilling drone" as the "unmanly" priests of "the Idean Mother" bear an effigy of the goddess through the streets of Rome.[54]

Negative descriptions of Cybele's cult outnumber and outweigh the sympathetic by far—Augustine even devotes entire sections of his *De civitate Dei* to criticizing it.[55] But evidently the hostility of Latin authorities did not always inspire the same response from Renaissance commentators. For example, among the Italian mythographical manuals discussed earlier, the *Imagines deorum* of Vincenzo Cartari displays deep respect for the eastern cults in its presentation of them. In the process of cataloguing the eastern deities and their symbolism, Cartari offers examples to show not only the details of Cybele's Phrygianism but also the status of Diana as inheritor of that Phrygianism. Cartari correlates Diana through her moon aspect first to Isis, then to Ceres, and finally to Cybele, noting that among Diana's featured icons is the "Timbrell of Cibele."[56] There are also literary precedents contemporary with Shakespeare's *Pericles* that represent the Mother cults of which Cybele/Diana was a part as ideologically useful to the construction of English national identity and sometimes even as a legitimate expression of quasi-Christian spirituality. Certain of the Elizabethan poets, including Spenser, imitated Virgil in exploiting the implications of Cybele's Trojan history and iconography.[57] And the popular translations of the Greek and Roman novels discussed earlier offered representations of pagan spirituality that may have been modeled specifically on the mystery rites of the East, including, as we have seen, those of Diana of Ephesus.[58] Of these narratives, the one most frequently cited as a source for Shakespeare, *The Golden Ass,* features elements in its Isis episode that resemble what I have been describing as Phrygian styles of ritual and celebration. The popularity of these novels suggests early modern interest in the mystery rites that they allude to or represent.

Archaeology has given scholars a sense of these mystery rites—who engaged in them, what occasion prompted them, and how they differed from or resembled the Christianity that superseded them. Walter Burkert writes that the eastern mysteries echoed the votive religions of primitive societies, in which individuals made vows to the gods in return for protections of a practical, worldly nature. The difficulties—seafaring and illness—that Burkert claims inspired the most votive offerings also happen to be prominently featured in the ancient Apollonius tale.[59] The mystery-like flavor of the original tale bears implications, I would say, for later renderings of it and for Shakespeare's rendering in *Pericles,* in which major characters periodically pledge oaths or offer prayers directly to Diana.

Returning now to my core argument, Cerimon's use of "secret art" to restore Thaisa in 3.2 implies the unfolding of not just a mystery rite but of a rite that is specifically Phrygian in character, an atmospherics that might have been sufficiently coded through Cerimon's call—in the midst of his performance of a miracle—for a "rough" kind of music. Acting as intercessor between the human and divine, Cerimon uses what in this context is a sacred music to heal human suffering, thereby fulfilling the role of priest. He is a human being who nevertheless becomes "like a god," a seer "Through whom the gods have shown their power" (5.3.65, 62). I am *not* suggesting that he is a eunuch, like the priests of Cybele—there are no such hints in the play. He is, however, a man exercising knowledge, access, and privilege within the domain of a known Phrygian Mother goddess.[60] His maleness, combined with the play's timely reference to rough music, provides just the right detail, even without a reference to castration, to enable an audience familiar with Diana to fill out this portrait of Cerimon as her priest. The adjective "rough" may open a window onto a quality of early modern classical eclecticism that scholars such as Burkert are now encouraging us to recognize.

The significance of rough music as an indicator of religious Phrygianism has an impact, no doubt, on other aspects of the play besides Cerimon. It is a curious thing that Pericles at times approximates the *appearance* of a priest of Cybele, more so than Cerimon, as a result of the oath Pericles makes to "bright Diana" (3.3.30) to grow his hair long.[61] Shakespeare places more emphasis on this oath than do either of his sources, having Pericles pledge it not once, as in Gower and Twine, but twice and on two separate occasions.[62] The result, after sixteen years of growth, is a striking stage focus on long and decidedly male hair. By representing Pericles's devotions to Diana in this appropriately gendered way, Shakespeare is able to gather all three family members—father as well as mother and daughter—into Cerimon's world of service to the Mother.

Such a matrix of devotions would complement current interpretations of the play's monarchical ideology in terms of the competing interests of the ruler and his commonwealth, figured as father and mother respectively. As Constance Jordan has articulated this configuration, the monarch-father must learn to bend his destructive impulses to the nurture of the commonwealth-mother if he is to avoid falling into tyranny. Such a bending requires the tempering effects of divine law, which Jordan locates in the empowered chastity of the daughter Marina.[63] To the extent that Marina's divinity stems from her own devotions to "her mistress Dian" (4.Cho.29)—"Diana aid my purpose!" (4.2.148)—then the ultimate source of power in the play is obviously Diana herself, this Mother of Phrygia whose "sacred physic" is repeatedly expressed in music. Consistent, however, with the play's classical context, the *forms* that Diana's music takes differ according to characters' gender and station, appearing variously and at appropriate moments in the "rough" percussions of the male priest Cerimon; in the "sweet" harmonics of the "vestal" Marina (5.1.46; 4.5.7); and ultimately in King Pericles's privileged experience of the "heavenly" "music of the spheres."

Notes

1. See Robert Egan, "'This Rough Magic': Perspectives of Art and Morality in *The Tempest*," *Shakespeare Quarterly* 23 (1972): 171-82; and Cosmo Corfield, "Why Does Prospero Abjure His 'Rough Magic'?" *SQ* 36 (1985): 31-48. Corfield casts the debate in these terms: "What is required is an account of *The Tempest* that will adequately explain why Prospero can 'prize' his magic at the beginning yet find it 'rough' at the end—an account that will adequately link his return to Milan with his magical disenchantment" (31). Unless otherwise indicated, quotations from Shakespeare follow *The Complete Works of Shakespeare,* ed. David Bevington, 4th ed. (New York: HarperCollins, 1992).

2. Quotations of Q1 follow the fascimile edition *Shakespeare's Plays in Quarto,* Michael J. B. Allen and Kenneth Muir, eds. (Berkeley: U of California P, 1981).

3. See the Arden Shakespeare *Pericles,* ed. F. D. Hoeniger (London: Methuen, 1963); the Cambridge Shakespeare *Pericles,* ed. J. C. Maxwell (Cambridge: Cambridge UP, 1956); *Pericles, Prince of Tyre,* ed. James G. McManaway (New York: Penguin, 1977); *William Shakespeare: The Complete Works,* ed. Stanley Wells and Gary Taylor (Oxford: Oxford UP, 1987); and *Pericles, Prince of Tyre* in *The Norton Shakespeare: Based on the Oxford Edition,* ed. Stephen Greenblatt, et al. (New York: W. W. Norton, 1997).

4. Walter Cohen, for instance, calls Thaisa's revival "quasi-magical" (*The Norton Shakespeare,* 2,712); and David Bevington groups Cerimon with "a number of mysterious artist-figures and magicians [of] the late romances" (1,400). Doreen DelVecchio and Antony Hammond complain that "all recent directors seem determined to ignore the text and make Cerimon some sort of witch-doctor" (*Pericles, Prince of Tyre,* ed. DelVecchio and Hammond [Cambridge: Cambridge UP, 1998], 72n).

5. The *Riverside* editors note this possibility but dismiss it as being "graphically very difficult" (1,514). Bevington does not mention "still" but provides a footnote explaining the apparent confusion generated by retaining Q1's "rough": "Cerimon may be apologizing for the only music he can provide at short notice" (1,418n). Similarly, the 1956 Cambridge edition posits no alternatives but attempts a conciliatory interpretation based on internal evidence: "Cerimon wants not soothing, sweet music, but stimulating music, music that will penetrate Thaisa's coma" (195). Hoeniger in his Arden edition flatly declares "rough" to be "manifestly wrong" but admits that "still" is also "quite uncertain" (91n). The Folger Library General Reader's edition uses "rough" without comment. To cite editions mentioned here that have not already been cited in full above: eds. G. Blakemore Evans and J. J. M. Tobin, *Pericles, Prince of Tyre* in *The Riverside Shakespeare,* 2d ed. (Boston and New York: Houghton Mifflin, 1997); and *Pericles, Prince of Tyre, The Folger Library General Reader's Shakespeare,* ed. Louis B. Wright and Virginia A. LaMar (New York: Washington Square Press, 1968).

6. George Wilkins, *The Painfull Adventures of Pericles Prince of Tyre* (London, 1608), quoted here from Geoffrey Bullough, *Narrative and Dramatic Sources of Shakespeare,* 8 vols. (London and Hanley: Routledge and Kegan Paul, 1957-75), 6:492-548, esp. 523.

7. *The Oxford English Dictionary,* 2d ed., prep. J. A. Simpson and E. S. C. Weiner (Oxford: Clarendon Press, 1989), *s.v. still.*

8. The *OED* traces the first use of *charivari* to the early eighteenth century, when presumably *rough music* also came into general usage. But as many are aware, the charivari ritual was performed well before the eighteenth century. If we assume that the word *charivari* accompanied the practice, then it seems unlikely that the rough music that attended it took hundreds of years to enter the language.

   Incidentally, there may be a genealogical connection between the cultural Phrygianism that this essay describes and the Roman festivities that are believed to have led to medieval Carnival. There may, in other words, be a genetic link between the classical rough music that this essay historicizes and the rough music associated with the European charivari, an acknowledged offshoot of Carnival culture. I will explore this link in a future study.

9. John Gower, *Confessio Amantis* (London, 1483), quoted here from Bullough, 6:400.

10. Examples from the *OED* include a ca. 1560-78 spelling of the musical instrument as both *viol* and *viall.* During the same time period the word for the glass container was spelled *vyol* (1550), *violl* (1609), and *viol* (1660).

11. Margreta de Grazia and Peter Stallybrass, "The Materiality of the Shakespearean Text," *SQ* 44 (1993): 255-83, esp. 257. About spelling variations in particular they write: "Until dictionaries fixed these boundaries, cognates blurred, phonetically and orthographically, without regard to the post-lexical determinations that subsequently divided them" (266).

12. William A. McIntosh, "Musical Design in *Pericles,*" *English Language Notes* 11 (1973): 100-106, esp. 101.

13. See McIntosh, passim; F. D. Hoeniger, "Musical Cures of Melancholy and Mania in Shakespeare," in *Mirror up to Shakespeare: Essays in Honour of G. R. Hibbard,* J. C. Gray, ed. (Toronto: U of Toronto P, 1984), 55-67; and DelVecchio and Hammond, eds., 71-73.

14. Hoeniger notes that the name appears in Shakespeare's sources and that the two scenes in which Cerimon's appearance is quantitatively significant, 3.2 and 5.3, are "ceremonious scenes" (3).

15. The first scholar to suggest Wilkins as Shakespeare's co-author was H. Dugdale Sykes in *Sidelights on Shakespeare* ([Stratford-upon-Avon: The Shakespeare Head Press, 1919], 143-204) and, again, briefly in *Sidelights on Elizabethan Drama* ([Oxford: Oxford UP, 1924], 12). Sykes's argument persuaded Hoeniger, who, in turn, convinced David J. Lake, MacDonald P. Jackson, M. W. A. Smith, and Gary Taylor of the probability of Wilkins's direct involvement. My remarks here cannot do justice to the complexity and sophistication of these scholars' arguments in favor of Wilkins. For an up-to-date review of the evidence, including the pertinent computer-based analyses, readers should consult Stanley Wells and Gary Taylor, *William Shakespeare: A Textual Companion* (New York: W. W. Norton, 1987), 556-60; and MacD. P. Jackson, "Rhyming in *Pericles*: More Evidence of Dual Authorship," *Studies in Bibliography* 46 (1993): 239-49, esp. 240n. For summaries of the difficulties (and not just the authorship issue) plaguing the text of *Pericles,* see Karen Csengeri, "William Shakespeare, Sole Author of *Pericles*," *English Studies* 71 (1990): 230-43, esp. 230-34; and Barbara Mowat, "The Theater and Literary Culture" in *A New History of Early English Drama,* John D. Cox and David Scott Kastan, eds. (New York: Columbia UP, 1997), 217-30, esp. 218-22.

16. David M. Bergeron, *Shakespeare's Romances and the Royal Family* (Lawrence: UP of Kansas, 1985), 117.

17. DelVecchio and Hammond, eds., 207. My brief summary of DelVecchio and Hammond's counterarguments cannot represent their full discussion.

18. DelVecchio and Hammond, eds., 11.

19. See, for instance, Constance Jordan, *Shakespeare's Monarchies: Ruler and Subject in the Romances* (Ithaca, NY, and London: Cornell UP, 1997), 35-67; and her essay "'Eating the Mother': Property and Propriety in *Pericles*" in *Creative Imitation: New Essays on Renaissance Literature in Honor of Thomas M. Greene,* David Quint, Margaret W. Ferguson, G. W. Pigman III, and Wayne A. Rebhorn, eds. (Binghamton: State University of New York, 1992), 331-53; Stuart M. Kurland. "'The care . . . of subjects' good': *Pericles,* James I, and the Neglect of Government," *Comparative Drama* 30 (1996): 220-44; and Dana Lloyd Spradley, "*Pericles* and the Jacobean Family Romance of Union" in *Assays: Critical Approaches to Medieval and Renaissance Texts,* Peggy A. Knapp and Gary F. Waller, eds., 7 vols. (Pittsburgh: Carnegie Mellon UP, 1992), 7:87-118. Jordan (*Shakespeare's Monarchies*) and Spradley both note the author issue in passing but decline to incorporate it into their analyses.

20. DelVecchio and Hammond, eds., 12.

21. DelVecchio and Hammond, eds., 209. I tend to agree and would add that Gary Taylor and MacDonald P. Jackson's editorial remarks in the *Companion* volume show signs of a distinctly circular logic, as when, for instance, our principal reason for suspecting Wilkins's involvement in the first place—Wilkins's novelized version of the play—becomes in their arguments a *result* of co-authorship, whose "significance" is heightened by the assumption of Wilkins's involvement (557). *The Painfull Aduentures* is declared to be a "substantive" text to the extent that the editors transfer entire vignettes of action into their version of the play, defending at least one of these transferences on the basis of imagined censorship and announcing that "*P. A.* gives us, in essence, the more dangerous and more dramatic original" (559). Its amalgamation with Q is said to return *Pericles* "closer to its state when it left the hands of its author(s)" (559), a statement that seems incautious at the least when removed from the context of Taylor and Jackson's *belief* in Wilkins's role.

22. See, for example, Jackson, "Rhyming in *Pericles*," 239, 246, and 248n.

23. Acts 19:23-27, 28, 34, 35; quotations follow *The Geneva Bible: A facsimile of the 1560 edition* (Madison: U of Wisconsin P, 1969). Acts and Paul's letter to the Ephesians are considered to be among Shakespeare's sources for *The Comedy of Errors,* a play also set in Ephesus and also related to *Pericles* by its use of Gower's *Confessio Amantis.*

24. Acts 19:19. For a similar point about the scriptural basis of the occult representation of Ephesus with respect to *The Comedy of Errors,* see Arthur F. Kinney, "Shakespeare's *Comedy of Errors* and the Nature of Kinds," *Studies in Philology* 85 (1988): 29-52; and Glyn Austen, "Ephesus Restored: Sacramentalism and Redemption in *The Comedy of Errors*," *Journal of Literature and Theology* 1-1 (1987): 54-69.

25. James Mason, *The Anatomie of Sorcerie. Wherein the Wicked Impietie of Charmers, Inchanters, and such like, is discouered and confuted* (London, 1612), sig. A2[r]. Mason explains in his preface "To the Reader" that "It was my chance to fall into communication with a notable supporter of those wicked vanities, which are spoken against in this booke: who not contented to practise the same himselfe, went about to perswade others thereunto. . . . Which when I heard, and vnderstood, considering that he was a man of place, and some learning, and therefore might preuaile the more in this mischieuous deuise: I determined to search out what authors had written concerning that matter" (sig. A2[r]).

26. Mason, sig. M3[v].

27. See Jean Seznec, *The Survival of the Pagan Gods,* trans. Barbara F. Sessions (Princeton, NJ: Princeton UP, 1953); and Don Cameron Allen, *Mysteriously*

Meant: The Rediscovery of Pagan Symbolism and Allegorical Interpretation in the Renaissance (Baltimore: Johns Hopkins UP, 1970).

28. In Seznec and Allen's usage the term *Oriental* refers to West Asia, the Near East, and Egypt, regions I will summarize henceforth as "eastern."

29. See Walter Burkert, *The Orientalizing Revolution: Near Eastern Influence on Greek Culture in the Early Archaic Age,* trans. Margaret E. Pinder and Walter Burkert (Cambridge, MA: Harvard UP, 1992); Robert Turcan, *The Cults of the Roman Empire,* trans. Antonia Nevill (Oxford: Blackwell, 1996); Margaret Anne Doody, *The True Story of the Novel* (New Brunswick, NJ: Rutgers UP, 1996); and M. L. West, *The East Face of Helicon: West Asiatic Elements in Greek Poetry and Myth* (Oxford: Clarendon Press, 1997).

30. See Burkert, 1-8, esp. 1-2.

31. The term *manuals* is Seznec's; see his chapters "The Science of Mythology in the Sixteenth Century" (219-56) and "The Influence of the Manuals" (279-323).

32. Allen, 233.

33. Seznec, 238; see also 239, 277, 285, and 289-95.

34. See Seznec, 313-15; D. J. Gordon, *The Renaissance Imagination,* Stephen Orgel, ed. (Berkeley: U of California P, 1975), 102-5, 134, 174-75, and 187-90; and John Peacock, "Ben Jonson's Masques and Italian Culture" in *Theatre of the English and Italian Renaissance,* J. R. Mulryne and Margaret Shewring, eds. (New York: St. Martin's Press, 1991), 73-94, esp. 76-77.

35. See Bullough, 6:418-19 and 471-74.

36. Margaret Doody makes an interesting case for calling these works "novels" as opposed to "romances" or "fictions," the generically vague designations that scholars generally use in trying to categorize them. Their status as precursors to medieval and early modern prose fiction—not to mention the eighteenth-century novel itself—is a central tenet of Doody's study.

37. See Doody, 213-50. Shakespeare's familiarity with these narratives has been the subject of at least three book-length studies: Carol Gesner, *Shakespeare & the Greek Romance: A Study of Origins* (Lexington: U of Kentucky P, 1970); Barbara A. Mowat, *The Dramaturgy of Shakespeare's Romances* (Athens: U of Georgia P, 1976); and J. J. M. Tobin, *Shakespeare's Favorite Novel: A Study of* The Golden Asse *As Prime Source* (Lanham, MD: UP of America, 1984). See also Martha L. Adams, "The Greek Romance and William Shakespeare," *Mississippi University Studies in English* 8 (1967): 43-52. Mowat's *Dramaturgy* posits their specific influence on Shakespeare's late plays, the romances and tragicomedies, which, according to Mowat, inherited from ancient fiction the narrative and dramaturgical elements that so markedly distinguish them from his earlier plays. Mowat demonstrates parallels between Shakespeare's late plays and many elements of plot, character, and theme in the ancient novels, which she describes as "complex—indeed contorted—in structure, dependent on surprise, suspense, numerous *dei ex machina*; filled with dream-visions and oracles and magic; much emphasis on chastity, a miraculous happy ending, and a realization on the part of the characters that they are pawns in the hands of fate" (129). Interestingly, because of its disputed authorship, Mowat declines to discuss *Pericles,* focusing instead on *Cymbeline, The Winter's Tale,* and *The Tempest.* A willingness, however, to consider the same indebtedness to ancient fiction in *Pericles* that she finds in the later three plays might further the case for single-authorship by demonstrating *Pericles*'s generic consistency. Peggy Muñoz Simonds takes this view as a critical commonplace, setting the ancient novel among the four "major literary ancestors" of tragicomedy and describing them as "esoteric romances of the Greeks and of the later Latin author Apuleius, all works that contain disguised information on the mystery cults of antiquity" (*Myth, Emblem, and Music in Shakespeare's* Cymbeline [Newark: U of Delaware P; London and Toronto: Associated University Presses, 1992], 32).

38. Achilles Tatius, *Loves of Clitophon and Leucippe* (London, 1597).

39. Apuleius, *The Golden Ass of Apuleius* (1566), trans. William Adlington (New York: Hogarth Press, 1966), 334.

40. The Mother goddesses in these four regions were Demeter, Ishtar/Innana, Astarte, and Isis, respectively. Studies of these and other of the Mothers have proliferated since the early twentieth century, beginning with Robert Briffault's *The Mothers: A Study of the Origins of Sentiment and Institutions* (3 vols. [New York: Macmillan, 1927]) and including Robert Graves, *The White Goddess: A Historical Grammar of Poetic Myth* (New York: Farrar, Straus and Giroux, 1948); Raphael Patai, *The Hebrew Goddess,* 3rd enl. ed. (Detroit: Wayne State UP, 1990); Marija Gimbutas, *The Gods and Goddesses of Old Europe 7000-3500* BC (Berkeley: U of California P, 1974); Gerda Lerner, *Women and History: Vol. 1, The Creation of Patriarchy* (Oxford: Oxford UP, 1986), 141-60; and Anne Baring and Jules Cashford, *The Myth of the Goddess: Evolution of an Image* (London: Penguin Books, 1991).

41. Turcan's recent *Cults of the Roman Empire* takes up the theme of the presence of "Oriental" cults in the West where earlier classicists, such as Franz Cumont, left off. The acknowledged expert on Cybele is Maarten J. Vermaseren, author of *Cybele and Attis: The Myth and the Cult* (London: Thames and Hudson, 1977).

42. Turcan, 16.

43. Turcan, 18.

44. Turcan, 47, 43, and 48.

45. Turcan, 46. Turcan writes: "Behind a triumphal procession . . . knights and senators, freedmen and dignitaries could be seen in procession, made up, masked, and clad in the most unexpected disguises. Flute-players, trumpeters, drummers and chanters of the Mother-cult brotherhood . . . helped to add sound to the masquerade which was followed by lavish feasting" (46).

46. Turcan, 37-38.

47. See Vermaseren, 29, 77, and 110.

48. "'To rave with the followers of Bacchus' was synonymous with 'to be carried away with the Corybants [the Greek name for Cybele's priests]'" (Turcan, 30).

49. See Vermasaren, 23. Scholars of the subject now tend to believe that the name actually refers to the black stone or "cube" that was Cybele's altar fetish, similar to the cubelike black "Ka'aba" stone of Mecca, which was worshiped in the name of a female deity until the advent of Islam. See Turcan, 29; and Baring and Cashford, 396.

50. Clement of Alexandria, quoted here from Vermaseren, 116.

51. Lucretius was rediscovered in the fifteenth century and became known, though not widely, in the sixteenth century. The first English translations of *De rerum natura* appeared in the second half of the seventeenth century, when interest arose in his atomistic materialism.

52. Lucretius, *On the Nature of Things (De rerum natura)*, ed. and trans. Anthony M. Esolen, (Baltimore and London: Johns Hopkins UP, 1995), 2:590.

53. Virgil, *The Aeneid*, trans. Robert Fitzgerald (New York: Vintage Books, 1983), 3.154-55. Cybele appears occasionally throughout *The Aeneid,* having provided Aeneas and his followers with lumber from the slopes of Mount Ida to build their ships bound for Italy; and serving, in Book 10, as the "Benignant / Lady of Ida" on whom Aeneas calls to be his "first patroness in combat" (ll. 348-52). Virgil's image of her "Wearing her crown of towers," riding "By chariot through the towns of Phrygia, / In joy at having given birth to gods" (6.1053-55) was later appropriated by Boccaccio in his *Genealogia deorum gentilium libri,* which popularized her in early modern Europe as an emblem of empire and civilization. Peter S. Hawkins writes in "From Mythography to Myth-making: Spenser and the *Magna Mater* Cybele" (*The Sixteenth Century Journal* 12.3 [1981]: 51-64) that the Virgilian Cybele "capture[d] the imagination of [sixteenth-century] poets," the "'Troynovants'" (55), including Spenser, to whom Hawkins's study is principally devoted.

54. Ovid, *Fasti,* trans. James George Frazer (New York: G. P. Putnam's Sons, 1936), 4.183-90.

55. In Augustine's *De civitate Dei,* see esp. Book 7, 25-26, but comments also appear sporadically throughout Books 1-10.

56. Vincenzo Cartari, *The Fovntaine of Ancient Fiction. Wherein is liuely depictured the Images and Statues of the gods and the Ancients, with their proper and perticular expositions,* trans. Richard Linche (London, 1599), sig. H4^v.

57. See Hawkins, passim.

58. The classics scholars Karl Kerenyi and Reinhold Merkelbach each published studies earlier this century (*Die Griechisch-Orientalische Romanliteratur in religionsgeschichtlicher Beleuchtung* [1927] and *Roman und Mysterium in der Antike* [1962], cited in Doody, 19) that asserted religious origins for the Greek narratives, tracing them to the mysteries of Isis, Dionysus, and Mithras in particular. Doody agrees that the novels "very openly and ostensibly present . . . the images and practices and rituals of the mystery cults" (161), but she takes issue with the "bias" of Merkelbach, especially toward the rites of the male divinities, pointing out the ubiquity of female deities in these fictions (164).

59. See Walter Burkert, *Ancient Mystery Cults* (Cambridge, MA: Harvard UP, 1987), 12-13 and 15.

60. Elsewhere in Shakespeare's works there are references to priests serving Diana; see, for instance, *Cymbeline,* where Iachimo complains that Imogen's sexual loyalty to Posthumus will leave Iachimo unsatisfied: "Should he make me / Live like Diana's priest betwixt cold sheets . . . ?" (1.6.133-37). In his note on this line, Bevington simply substitutes "priestess" for "priest," exemplifying a modern erasure of what Shakespeare apparently knew to be historical.

61. The full oath reads: "Till [Marina] be married, madam, / By bright Diana, whom we honor, all / Unscissored shall this hair of mine remain, / Though I show ill in 't" (3.3.29-32).

62. The second oath is offered secondhand in Gower's lines at 4.4.27-29.

63. See Jordan, "'Eating the Mother'," 349.

FURTHER READING

Criticism

Becker, Marvin B. "A Historian's View of Another Pericles." *Michigan Quarterly Review* 15, no. 2 (1976): 197-211.

Argues that for an understanding of *Pericles*, knowledge of the complex historical context of the play, especially with regard to the medieval idea of "spiritual education through misfortune," is essential.

Dean, Paul. "Pericles' Pilgrimage." *Essays in Criticism* 50, no. 2 (April 2000): 125-44.

Explores *Pericles* as a pilgrimage tale with Biblical and medieval antecedents.

Fawkner, H. W. "Miracle: The Muteness of Pericles." In *Shakespeare's Miracle Plays: Pericles, Cymbeline, and The Winter's Tale,* pp. 28-34. Rutherford, N.J.: Fairleigh Dickinson University Press, 1992.

Analyzes the role and significance of muteness in *Pericles.*

McJannet, Linda. "Genre and Geography: The Eastern Mediterranean in *Pericles* and *The Comedy of Errors.* In *Playing the Globe: Genre and Geography in English Renaissance Drama,* edited by John Gillies and Virginia Mason Vaughn, pp. 86-106. Madison: Fairleigh Dickinson University Press, 1998.

Traces the factual bases for Shakespeare's historical and geographical settings in *The Comedy of Errors* and *Pericles.*

McManaway, James G. Introduction to *Pericles, Prince of Tyre,* by William Shakespeare, edited by James G. McManaway, pp. 14-22. New York: Penguin Books, 1977.

Provides a solid introduction to *Pericles,* examining the play's strengths and weaknesses, as well as its sources and contexts.

Relihan, Constance C. "Liminal Geography: *Pericles* and the Politics of Place." *Philological Quarterly* 71, no. 3 (summer 1992): 281-99.

Explores the political significance of setting *Pericles* in Asia Minor, arguing that the play is a critique of James I as a ruler.

Rimer, J. Thomas. "The Longest Voyage of All: Shakespeare's *Pericles* in Japan." In *Pericles: Critical Essays,* edited by David Skeele, pp. 339-48. New York: Garland Publishing, Inc., 2000.

Surveys the development of Shakespearean theater in Japan, focusing on a 1976 production of *Pericles* in order to explore the affinity between Shakespearean theater and traditional Japanese theater forms.

Skeele, David, ed. *Pericles: Critical Essays.* New York: Garland Publishing, Inc., 2000, 348 p.

An essential volume containing a diversity of essays on *Pericles.*

Spradley, Dana Lloyd. "*Pericles* and the Jacobean Family Romance of Union." In *Assays: Critical Approaches to Medieval and Renaissance Texts,* edited by Peggy A. Knapp and Gary F. Walker, pp. 87-118. Pittsburgh: Carnegie Mellon University Press, 1992.

Interprets *Pericles* as a reenactment of a conflict regarding unity and power between King James and the English parliament.

Taylor, Gary. "The Transmission of *Pericles.*" *Papers of the Bibliographical Society of America* 80, no. 2 (1986): 193-217.

Proposes the text of *Pericles* was derived from a series of memorial reconstructions by actors who performed in the play at the Globe.

Traversi, Derek. "*Pericles, Prince of Tyre.*" In *Shakespeare: The Last Phase,* pp. 19-42. New York: Harcourt, Brace & Company, 1955.

Argues that in *Pericles* Shakespeare developed the dramatic forms and methods he would use successfully in the three following romances.

Welsh, Andrew. "Heritage in *Pericles.*" In *Shakespeare's Late Plays: Essays in Honor of Charles Crow,* edited by Richard C. Tobias and Paul G. Zolbrod, pp. 89-113. Athens: Ohio University Press, 1974.

Contends that Shakespeare used traditional elements such as riddling, tale-telling, and confronting the seven deadly sins in the construction of *Pericles.*

Religion and Theology

INTRODUCTION

Critics have adopted a variety of approaches to explore the religious and theological dimensions in Shakespeare's plays. They have identified specific religious themes, explicated biblical allusions, and shed light on numerous theological subtexts. Late twentieth-century commentators almost uniformly decline to speculate about whether Shakespeare held particular sectarian views and, if so, what these might be. Instead they focus on his treatment of religious disputes in early modern England and the controversies that split the Christian church and led to the Reformation. Throughout the period when Shakespeare was writing his plays, religious systems of thought continued to be unstable, and doctrinal issues were vigorously contested. Many critics find evidence of Shakespeare's familiarity with these conflicts—as well as with centuries of Christian discourse—in his histories, comedies, and tragedies.

In her assessment of the Christian aspects in Shakespearean tragedy, Helen Gardner (see Further Reading) emphasizes the dramatist's evident knowledge of the Bible and contemporary theological writings. Gardner maintains that some of the most characteristic features of Shakespearean tragedy—especially those found in *King Lear*—are closely associated with Christian attitudes toward the mysteries of human existence. René Fortin (1979) also examines *King Lear* and finds both Christian and secular interpretations of the play to be equally valid. Acknowledging that the play's final scene poses a unique challenge to Christian or redemptive readings of the tragedy, he suggests that the death of Cordelia, far from contradicting Christian doctrine, confirms the Catholic and Protestant notion of God's judgments as unknown and inexplicable. Similarly, Daryl Tippins (1997) proposes that *King Lear* may be viewed as either nihilistic or transcendent. Cautioning readers to be wary of basing a definitive interpretation of the play as a whole on a reading of its final scene, he claims that the seeming pessimism of this episode does not negate the effect of previous scenes that represent compassion, reconciliation, and Christian optimism.

Alan Sinfield (1980) maintains that optimistic humanism is a critical issue in *Hamlet,* and argues that the play depicts the disintegration of the notion that human reason by itself can form the basis of moral action. But, he further contends, it also shows that the Calvinist belief in providential justice is an equally inadequate response to the grim realities of this world. Ronald G. Shafer (1990) considers that Hamlet is only temporarily attracted to humanism and that ultimately the prince reaffirms his belief in Christian values and his reliance on the will of God. Both Robert N. Watson (see Further Reading) and Julia Reinhard Lupton (1997) discuss questions of religious differences and theological doctrine in *Othello*. Watson asserts that the play's rendering of Catholic theology is burlesque, intended to caricature the idea that salvation can be earned and to endorse instead the Protestant tenet that salvation is a gift from God, unrelated to individual merit. Lupton examines Shakespeare's depiction of the Moor as at once a Christian hero and a barbarian forever excluded from the covenant of universal brotherhood.

Some critics detect significant religious motifs in the comedies as well as the tragedies. For example, Paul A. Cantor (1987) asserts that in *The Merchant of Venice* these issues are more complex than is ordinarily recognized. The play does not merely represent Christianity's triumph over Judaism, he contends, for its near-tragic ending features the downfall of Antonio, the play's representative Christian, as well as Shylock, its representative Jew. Both G. M. Pinciss (1990) and Julia Brett (see Further Reading) assess the religious dimensions of another Shakespearean comedy, *Measure for Measure*. Pinciss reads the play in terms of the Protestant belief in the positive value of despair: that is, as an integral part of the struggle to progress from recognition of one's sins to a state of true penitence and the achievement of forgiveness and salvation. Brett is particularly concerned with the distinction between Christian allegorizations and Christian interpretations of *Measure for Measure*. She stresses the importance of appraising the play's religious features in the context of its corresponding concern with political or secular issues, especially with regard to the Duke's dual responsibility as spiritual guide and temporal ruler. Maurice Hunt (1993) and David N. Beauregard (1999) evaluate religious aspects of two other Shakespearean comedies: *Twelfth Night* and *All's Well that Ends Well*. Hunt calls attention to *Twelfth Night*'s many references to non-Christian forces shaping human destiny and to its satirical treatment of Puritanism, concluding that the play's support for the Anglican view of providence is ultimately indeterminate. Beauregard maintains that *All's Well* is steeped in the Roman Catholic theology of grace. He particularly remarks on the play's disparate treatment of Protestant and Catholic attitudes toward merit and free will.

Commentators have also found intimations of a number of different sectarian and doctrinal issues in Shakespeare's histories. For instance, Robert G. Hunter (1978) examines the various means Falstaff uses to keep up his hopes of preferment—both in this world and the next. Hunter also proposes that Hal's rejection of Falstaff may be read as the triumph of the Protestant ethic, for the new king turns his back on Sir John in order to carry out the responsibilities of the monarchy to which, he believes, God has called him. By contrast, Roy Battenhouse (1985) argues that Henry V demonstrates a remarkable talent for transferring onto other people's shoulders responsibilities that are rightly his. Moreover, Battenhouse contends, Henry surrounds himself with flatterers and assumes a spurious piety, thus demonstrating the shallowness of his commitment to Christian norms. In his discussion of anticlericalism in Shakespeare's histories, Jeffrey Knapp (see Further Reading) focuses on the pseudo piety of a series of English bishops—from *1 Henry VI* to *Henry V*—who are principally concerned not with saving souls but with inciting violence. James C. Bryant (1984) maintains that Shakespeare presents the religious quarrels in *King John* in a political context that diminishes their significance. In his judgment, the play is on the side of Protestantism to the extent that it upholds the notion that an English monarch rules only by the grace of God and therefore need not answer to any other temporal or spiritual authority. Finally, R. Chris Hassel, Jr. (1986) maintains that *Richard III* presents Richmond as God's chosen agent to liberate England from the heavy hand of Richard's rule. In his analysis of the parallels between this play and the Book of Revelation, Hassel emphasizes the dramatic motifs of prophecy, the Last Judgment, and the destruction of the Antichrist.

OVERVIEWS AND GENERAL STUDIES

Roy Battenhouse (essay date 1994)

SOURCE: Battenhouse, Roy. "Introduction: An Overview of Christian Interpretation." In *Shakespeare's Christian Dimension,* pp. 1-14. Bloomington: Indiana University Press, 1994.

[*In the following essay, Battenhouse surveys 150 years of commentary on the Christian aspects of Shakespeare's art.*]

Many ordinary readers have felt instinctively that Shakespeare and the Bible belong together. Yet inevitably there have been others who claim for the poet their own reductive beliefs, despite his burial in a church and a Last Will that names Christ his savior. At the turn of the present century, for instance, we find Shakespeare described by Churton Collins as a "theistical agnostic," and A. C. Bradley saying that he painted the world "without regard to anyone's beliefs." John Robertson (a celebrated Disintegrator) declared that Shakespeare was groping his way toward the "sanity" of Auguste Comte. And England's poet laureate John Masefield, when writing on *Shakespeare and the Spiritual Life* (1924), was confident that to the dramatist "orthodox religion" meant almost nothing, since he "held to no religion save that of humanity and his own great nature." A follow-up to this contention was voiced by D. G. James in his *Dream of Learning* (1951), where Christianity is equated with "a fierce censorship" and we are assured that Shakespeare "did not write as a Christian." Even more skeptical are some of today's deconstructionists who seem to say that any author's personal beliefs is irrelevant and also irrecoverable.

Nevertheless a growing body of scholarship tying Shakespeare's plays to Christian insights has been accumulating since the mid-nineteenth century, and so an overview of this history will be helpful as a background to some summary observations on the achievements the present anthology catalogs.

The religious contexts of action in Shakespearean drama are the focus of our anthology. They may help us recall that in Elizabethan England religion was considered the anchor of morals, and the God of Christian faith was generally believed to be the creator, sustainer, and judge of all mankind. The guidebook for understanding good and evil in all sorts and conditions of life was Holy Scripture, a capstone to testimonies provided universally in the Book of Nature. In such a context everyone's history could be one of journey toward self-knowledge and health, or else of opportunities squandered. Do not Shakespeare's stories imply this sense of history? Historical criticism in our time should be open to perceptions that a drama's horizons of understanding can be ultimately Christian in their outreach.

Of signal importance has been Hermann Ulrici's *Shakespeare's Dramatic Art,* which appeared in English translation in 1846 and grew to a third edition by 1880. Ulrici read Shakespeare as "a Christian in the truest sense" with a "Christian view of life." He saw the dramatist's achievement as a blending of the "idealistic art" of the Middle Ages with the realism of modern history; and with this perspective he had no difficulty in accepting the ending of *King Lear* as a salvation of soul for Lear and Gloucester in their coming to see the true nature of love after undergoing a purification. Similarly, Ulrici read *The Merchant of Venice* and *Measure for Measure* as showing that human virtue is possible only in and through an inner love that combines strictness with mercy. In all of Shakespeare's comedies he saw what he called a "dialectics of irony" employed to neutralize one-sided obsessions, and he defended Shakespeare's puns as intrinsic to this comic method. Thus a portrait of the poet as moral philosopher replaced the wild genius presumed by eighteenth-century critics.

In this altered context, English writers began to speak of Shakespeare as Christian, and studies soon appeared in tribute to the national poet's congruence with the Good Book. Of these the most substantial were Bishop Charles Wordsworth's *Shakespeare's Knowledge and Use of the Bible* (1864) written for the Anniversary ceremonies and expanded in a third edition of 1880; J. B. Selkirk's (*pseud.*

for James Brown) *Bible Truths with Shakespearian Parallels* (1872), which had a sixth edition by 1888; and, in America, William Burgess's *The Bible in Shakespeare* (Chicago, 1903; later reprints). Wordsworth devoted a long chapter to Shakespeare's biblical allusions and another to his "Religious Principles and Sentiments derived from the Bible." He disagreed with Mr. Bowdler's excising from *The Family Shakespeare* the clown's speech in *All's Well* about the narrow gate and the porter's speech in *Macbeth* about the primrose way. He noted that in the tragedies the catastrophe results from sinful passions such as revenge and jealousy. He concluded his book by saying that no other Elizabethan "has paid homage to Christianity as effectually as Shakespeare." Selkirk arranged parallel quotations from Shakespeare and the Bible on more than a hundred topics. He concluded that Shakespeare's genius had so assimilated and reproduced the Bible's great truths that his words seem to renew its authority. Burgess proclaimed Shakespeare a sincere believer of "the main doctrines of the Christian religion" and offered in evidence from the plays parallels filling 16 pages and 150 pages of quotations on topics such as Conscience, God's Attributes, Thankfulness, etc. He found eight references to Cain, a confused memory of the 23rd Psalm by Mistress Quickly, and "the very likeness of Ahab and Jezebel" in the Macbeths (here citing Thomas Eaton's *Shakespeare and the Bible,* 1857).

Are there shortcomings in these studies? By hindsight we can observe that some of the moral sentiments cited are less genuinely Christian than they sound. For instance, Iago's discourse on free will is listed by Selkirk among Shakespeare's Bible truths. Actually, however, Iago was here using a Pelagian language to lure Roderigo to enslave himself to his lustful passion. In other passages, even when the moral idea expressed is indeed Christian and may reflect Shakespeare's own faith, Selkirk fails to note that the speaker who voices it was actually using it hypocritically to mislead his listeners—as is the case, surely, in King Henry IV's reference to "Those blessed feet. . . . nailed / For our advantage to the bitter cross." Here the king puts piety on display when, for his political advantage, he is about to postpone the crusade he had promised his feet would make. This truth of the drama can be overlooked by readers who look to Shakespeare simply as a storehouse of moral sentiments.

Let me discern also a misapprehension by Burgess when noting Canterbury's reference in *Henry V* to the Book of Numbers. This indicates, says Burgess, Shakespeare's versatility in using Scripture. A wiser inference would be that the Archbishop is being characterized as an irresponsible exegete, who cites from Numbers a text which (a canny reader might know) is a half-truth since it omits the more pertinent passage in Numbers where Moses disallowed a daughter the right to inherit land from her father if she marries a foreigner. Shakespeare's ironic point, wholly missed by Burgess, is that Henry V has no valid claim to France. A bigger mistake regarding Henry V is made by Wordsworth. He misreads the whole character of this king's piety by failing to see the irony in Shakespeare's having him fulsomely ascribe his Agincourt victory to God's arm alone, right after we have seen the battle won by Henry's order to cut the throats of prisoners. The Victorian Bishop's uncritical feelings of patriotism along with his liking for moral sentiment have left a blindspot in his ability to see. When tabulating Bible allusions he can point us to Matthew 2 as the source for Henry's mention of "Herod's bloody-hunting slaughtermen" but without perceiving in Henry a kinship with Herod. This blindspot, I must add, was also in Ulrici's vision and caused his declaring that Henry's career stands for "the moral purification and amendment of man." Indeed, it can be said that the deceitfulness of this monarch's piety remained largely unexposed by literary critics until around 1950, when Professor Goddard focused his Quaker intelligence on the specifics of the action in Shakespeare's play. Only then did the possibility arise that our "country" poet might have viewed history with the irony of an Erasmus.

A disillusionment with romantic idealism emerged after World War I and was signalled by T. S. Eliot's *The Waste Land*. While this poem got its popularity from its truth-telling vignettes of hollow love quest, its anthropological diggings encompassed a scope of history from Agamemnon's times to the present day. And its author was eventually discovered to be, surprisingly, an apologist for Christian orthodoxy. His essays in appreciation of Lancelot Andrewes and Dante, while at the same time he questioned Arnold's humanism and Lambeth's churchmanship, made possible a revived scholarly attention to the history of religion and to medieval drama in particular, along with some modern experiments in churchyard drama, and some stageplays that hinted of Christian mysteries hidden in secular experience. Eliot himself proceeded not only to tell us that literary criticism needed to be "completed" by recourse to theological truths, but also to provide avenues to those truths in his *Four Quartets* begun in the 30s and concluded during World War II in the 40s.

Those two decades are usually described by historians of Shakespeare criticism as an era of "historical" approaches. That is true; but the wide range of history that was reinvigorating scholarship needs to be more fully appreciated. While some students were delving into the history of theatre in general, or of Elizabethan acting companies, or of medieval story conventions, others were looking into schoolbooks and Stratford schoolmasters (two of them of Catholic sympathies) during Shakespeare's boyhood, or assessing the extent of his familiarity with the Bible (42 of its books by R. Noble's count) and the Prayerbook, or reviewing the contents of the Elizabethan *Homilies* appointed for church use. The history of ideas became important with the publication of Lily B. Campbell's *Shakespeare's Tragic Heroes* (1930) and Howard Patch's *The Tradition of Boethius* (1935) and Willard Farnham's *The Medieval Heritage of Elizabethan Tragedy* (1936). And concurrently, scholars of Old English literature and the medieval poets began to re-estimate the Christian ingredients of *Beowulf* and the works of Cynewulf, Langland, and Chaucer. All this, when accompanied by the proddings from T. S. Eliot I have mentioned, provided challenging horizons for those of us who underwent our graduate training in the mid-30s.

Historic religion received an increasing attention during World War II when the B.B.C. put on the air some talks by C. S. Lewis, known for his witty *Screwtape Letters* but now offering the public a core of "mere Christianity." His *The Case for Christianity* appeared in 1946. Almost everybody in those years seemed interested in Christianity's relation to culture. A stream of books around that topic issued from both Protestant and Catholic scholars, but was fed especially by Maritain's *True Humanism* (1938), *Ransoming the Time* (1941), and *Christianity and Democracy* (1945), along with Gilson's various expoundings of the medieval philosophers. De Lubac launched his multi-volume *Exégèse Médiévale* in 1941; and after a while Protestant and Catholic presses alike were publishing each a series of translations from the Church Fathers. Also new journals cropped up with titles such as *The Christian Scholar* and *Christendom,* college courses on the metaphysical poets flourished, and literary critics were shown by Erich Auerbach's *Mimesis* (Eng. tr., 1953) the special qualities characteristic of Judaeo-Christian stylistics.

Shakespeare's relation to Catholic tradition was first probed in the mid-nineteenth century by Richard Simpson, whose papers were assembled and amplified in Henry S. Bowden's *The Religion of Shakespeare* (1899). The contention of this book was the probability of a personal sympathy for the Old Faith by Shakespeare. Bowden began with some distinctions between Catholic and Protestant doctrines, and then showed how biographical documents relating to Shakespeare can have a hidden religious explanation. His coverage of the plays was chiefly impressionistic, noting the Catholic tone of lines such as "Unhousel'd, disappointed, unanel'd" in *Hamlet*, or the reference by the Countess in *All's Well* to "her prayers, whom Heaven delights to hear," or Prospero's allusion to "her help, of whose soft grace" he has had aid. An overconcern for pious wording, however, misled Bowden to eulogize Henry V as an "ideal" king and to misattribute compassion to Pandulph in *King John*. His best insights are his likening the persecuted Catholics under Queen Elizabeth to the plight of Edgar in *King Lear,* and his reply to Harsnett by quoting Thomas More to the effect that occasional fraudulent miracles should not blind us to the reality of true miracles—the kind Bowden finds in the conversion of Lear, in the healing of the King of France by Helena, and in the cures by King Edward in *Macbeth*.

The argument that Shakespeare "retained a genuine esteem for certain aspects" of Catholicism was renewed by John Henry de Groot in his *The Shakespeares and "The Old Faith"* (1946). To Bowden's culling of Catholic phrases he added others; and as evidence of Shakespeare's familiarity with the Rheims *New Testament* he cited the words *cockle, narrow* gate, and not a hair *perished,* unique to that translation. But De Groot's important contribution was his convincing argument, based centrally on discoveries made by Herbert Thurston in 1923 and subsequently, that the Last Will and Testament of John Shakespeare, the poet's father, was indeed no forgery but reliable evidence of his probable contact with the Jesuit missioners, since the Will follows a formula for Testaments drawn up by St Charles Borromeo and imported into England by them. This historical evidence justified De Groot in postulating a home training of young William which could have included Catholic lore and its continuing witness in iconography, such as the wall tapestries referred to by Falstaff. Moreover, John Speed's reference in 1611 to the "papist" Robert Persons and "his poet" implies that the dramatist retained Catholic sympathies.

Mutschmann and Wentersdorf's *Shakespeare and Catholicism* (1952) explained why "religion mattered supremely to Shakespeare" and concluded, on the basis of a large array of evidence both historical and dramatic, that he was a secret Catholic all his life and may have died a papist. M. D. H. Parker in her *The Slave of Life* (1955) devoted an Appendix to capsulizing and reinforcing the biographical interpretations of Mutschmann and Wentersdorf, and in her earlier chapters she drew on doctrines in Augustine and Aquinas to account for the idea of justice that undergirds Shakespeare's dramaturgy. More recently, Peter Milward has summarized the biographical problem in his *Shakespeare's Religious Background* (1973), and in *Shakespeare Yearbook 1* (1990) has written of Shakespeare's affinities with Thomas More, and has termed the plays "a synthesis of tradition and reform" in which allusions to the contemporary religious scene "cry out from between the lines."

The horizons of history uncovered by the scholars I have just mentioned, it should be noted, are larger than those entertained by E. M. W. Tillyard in his *Elizabethan World Picture* (1943) and his *Shakespeare's History Plays* (1944). For although he attempted in the latter book a providential view of history, the sense of providence he relied on was that of Edward Hall's Protestant overview rather than that of Augustine's *City of God* (the textbook of More and Erasmus). Tillyard's unawareness of the difference can be seen to be, in retrospect, the cause of the difficulty he got into when interpreting Henry V. In following Hall's portrait of Henry as an ideal king, Tillyard complains, Shakespeare ends with a copybook hero whose platitudes depress us and whose coarseness suggests that the dramatist was "writing up something he had begun to hate." The play's "slack construction" suggests that its author "had written his epic of England and had no more to say on the matter." But are these remarks consistent with Tillyard's overall claim that the eight plays constitute a unified chain of moral interpretation? At odds with this is also his comment that in *3 Henry VI* Shakespeare failed to make his material significant because he got tired or bored. It seems to me Tillyard approximates a satisfactory reading only when he views Henry Richmond as a godly minister of England's deliverance from Richard's tyranny. Yet, even here, he does not see that Hall's tracing of the happy outcome to a "policy" suggested by Buckingham has been replaced by Shakespeare's scene of the Queen's rejecting of Richard's "policy" pleas. Is not Shakespeare revising Hall's sense of providence by relying on Thomas More's sense of it in the material Hall borrowed from More and tried to overlay with moralizing on the glory of national unity?

Richmond's prayer to the "gracious" eye of God is not recorded by Hall. And when Tillyard cites it, his surrounding commentary reveals a twentieth-century fear of identifying Shakespeare with any settled beliefs:

> If one were to say that in *Richard III* Shakespeare pictures England restored to order through God's grace, one gravely risks being lauded or execrated for attributing to Shakespeare personally the full doctrine of prevenient grace according to Calvin. When therefore I say that *Richard III* is a very religious play, I want to be understood as speaking of the play and not of Shakespeare. For the purposes of the tetralogy and most obviously for this play Shakespeare accepted the prevalent belief that God had guided England into her haven of Tudor prosperity. And he accepted it with his whole heart, as later he did not accept the supposed siding of God with the English against the French he so loudly proclaimed in *Henry V.*
>
> (p. 204)

This passage leaves unexplained what Shakespeare did "accept" (believe?) regarding Henry V's status within a providential order, and also it seems to say that Tillyard thinks Calvin the only available interpreter of divine providence, and that "Tudor prosperity" is its goal. If Tillyard had consulted Augustine or Boethius, however, he could have learned that political prosperity is not identical with divine blessing, and that providence punishes a sinner centrally with his own sin and the interior weariness it entails (as in the vanity of "idol ceremony" confessed by Henry). But instead Tillyard supposes a Shakespeare of shifting belief, one who put his heart into Hall's (implicitly Calvinist?) belief when writing *Richard III* but lost enthusiasm for it subsequently.

Understandably, many readers of Tillyard have been unsatisfied with his explanations. Yet what warrants our skepticism, I would say, is not the premise that Shakespeare's histories reflect a divine providence but rather Tillyard's version of providence. Moreover, to grasp Shakespeare's chain we need to read the eight plays in the order given them in the folio's text rather than in their order of composition. Beginning with Richard's disowning of the balm of grace and ending with Henry Richmond's turning to grace and sacrament, the cycle places Henry V at a midpoint in the downward spiraling, a place in England's history analogous to Julius Caesar's in Rome's history, whereas the later Henry Tudor is analogous to Rome's Constantine.

The historical approaches I have associated with post-Bradleyan criticism were accompanied by a concurrent attention to Shakespeare's language of symbolism. One may regard this development as an amplifying of Romanticism's focus on the poet as a questing Seer, and perhaps as a continuation of Keats's idea that "Shakespeare lived a life of allegory" on which his works comment. G. Wilson Knight became its spokesman in 1930 with his metaphorically titled *Wheel of Fire,* for which T.S. Eliot provided a Prefatory Note. Eliot here wrote of the need to grasp the "whole design" of a poetic drama and to read both character and plot with an understanding of the work's "subterrene or submarine music." He also emphasized that the greatest poetry speaks "on two planes at once," a sensory experience within which there moves a pattern of deeper meaning. Eliot was perhaps remembering Augustine's analysis of a logic we listen for under time-borne sounds.

Knight saw Shakespeare's plays as having a spatial-temporal patterning of Tempest and Music set forth in a language of parable. And the most striking essay in Knight's many volumes was his early "*Measure for Measure* and the Gospels." Here he uncovered the affinity of Shakespeare's drama to the parables of Jesus and defended the Duke of this play as embodying in his actions the ethical wisdom of Jesus. Knight was writing not from any knowledge of the history of theology but rather as a post-Romantic who valued human imagination as the key to insight into life; he found in Shakespeare a poet whose genius coincided here with that of Christ—each being, as Knight explained elsewhere, an independent pioneer who challenged "orthodox" morality. Knight's reliance simply on imaginative genius was later to betray him into uncritical admiration for the transrational poetry of Nietzsche, by the light of which his comments on the mystical humanism of Shakespeare became questionable. Nevertheless his emphasis on symbolism has done much to reinvigorate Shakespeare criticism. It has directed attention to dimensions of myth and miracle in Shakespeare's plays, besides encouraging the efforts of Northrop Frye to associate literary genres with seasonal phases in the cycle of human experience.

S. L. Bethell in *The Winter's Tale: A Study* (1947) probed more radically than either Knight or Frye. Noting this play's atmosphere of supernatural religion, he stated his conviction that Shakespeare wrote "from the standpoint of orthodox Christianity" while using archaic dramatic methods to put his audience into an experiencing of symbolic meanings. Bethell's earlier *Shakespeare and the Popular Dramatic Tradition* (1944) had called attention to a multiconsciousness in Shakespeare's language, tracing its source to medieval popular drama. Then in his *Literary Criticism and the English Tradition* (1948) he proceeded to emphasize that a poem's most significant level is the sequence of events it re-creates in the mind, a narrative that conveys by its author's attitude a criticism of life, for the grasping of which the real world must be co-present with the play world in the minds of the audience. Anticipating some of today's theorists, Bethell insisted that a work's quality of *insight* into human experience is what critics ultimately judge, and that in this matter there is no critical neutrality; there are only Christian critics and Marxist critics and Moslem critics—and critics who think themselves disinterested but who are really swayed unconsciously by the beliefs they have necessarily acquired by being members of a particular society in a particular place and time.... The 'pure critics' of today adhere in fact to the dogmatic position of nineteenth-century humanism, which has been for so long the atmosphere of English academic circles that it is taken for granted like the air itself.... The Christian, on the other hand, knows that ... assumptions, unexamined because scarcely realized as assumptions, are part of the lot of fallen man. Such dogma, untrue or unclear, reflects the curse of Adam, and against it we have only to set the revealed dogma which we experience as a partial clearing of vision.... The Christian critic has little reason for arrogance, and if he should fail to do justice in his calling the fault lies with him and not the Cause he has espoused.

(pp. 25-26)

A similarly Christian response to the special quality of Shakespeare's narrative language may be seen in Nevill Coghill's ground-breaking essay of 1950 on the medieval "Basis of Shakespearian Comedy." Citing Dante's explanation of the four levels of meaning possible in a story of human journey, Coghill defined Shakespearean comedy as a journey from misery to joy and illustrated the presence of an allegorical import in several of Shakespeare's comedies.

Meanwhile in 1946 there appeared in PMLA my essay arguing that Shakespeare's *Measure for Measure* was informed by Christianity's doctrine of Atonement. The Duke's role, I explained, is a secular analogue of St Luke's "He hath visited and redeemed his people" and is replete with imagery of a star-led shepherd and king of love who rescues the lost and ransoms the guilty by a conquest such as the Church Fathers describe when explicating the Atonement story. The play's whole action, as I read it, participates by analogy in the biblical cycle of sin, law, sentence, intervention, faith, suffering, and reconciliation. This reading was curtly dismissed by Tillyard, who preferred to view the play as an artistic failure. Yet other scholars—notably Barbara Lewalski, J. A. Bryant, and R. G. Hunter—turned to biblical typology as an under-structure of Shakespeare's art; and by 1969 I was able to argue that biblical "premises" (a baptised Aristotelianism) governed his depicting of tragedy. "Typological Criticism" was the label David Bevington aptly used when discussing Christian interpretations in the Introduction to his textbook *Shakespeare* (3rd edition, 1980). He credited it, however, only with serving the cause of "image" study and remarked that its dissenters had made it assume "a defensive posture." True, it has been elbowed to the sidelines during our post-Vietnam era. But in fact its leaven of insight has been quietly enlarging, as will be evident in the range of selections in my present anthology. Arthur C. Kirsch, for instance, has recently invoked the Atonement motif when explaining the structure of *Much Ado* and also of *Cymbeline*, while Frances Pearce has invoked it in her commentary on *All's Well*.

Crosscurrents among Christian interpreters do of course sometimes muddle its impact. Their variety needs to be taken into account. Roland M. Frye, for instance, brought a narrowly Protestant cast of mind to his book on *Shakespeare and Christian Doctrine* (1963), in which he assailed "The School of Knight," his label for followers of G. Wilson Knight, especially J.A. Bryant. In Frye's view they were translating Shakespeare "out of dramatic into theological terms" not allowed by Luther and Calvin for secular drama. He therefore spoke of "blatant abuses of criticism" in theological analyses of Shakespeare and insisted that the plays should be read as employing Christian doctrine only for local characterizations and not as "essential" to his art. This argument, while it gave a welcome handle to anti-Christian readers, ignored the use of typology by Elizabethan poets such as Spenser. It also raised the hackles of Professor Knight, who proceeded to charge Frye with grossly misrepresenting him as medieval whereas in fact he regarded Shakespeare as looking "ahead to Ibsen and Nietszche," and Knight's phrase "miniature Christs" was a "passing analogy" only. (See his *Shakespeare and Religion* [1967], pp. 293-303.) One can see in Knight's reply his own muddling of a Dionysian with a Christian ethic. Frye, on the other hand, was supposing that Christian typology is essentially irrelevant to everyday life. Barbara Lewalski, herself of Protestant sympathies, has commented on the error of Frye's stance (in a footnote to her essay on *Twelfth Night, infra*).

But did Bryant's treatment of Shakespeare's tragedies harbor sometimes an ambiguity akin to Knight's? One of Frye's objections was to Bryant's finding "redemptions" in the love-deaths of Antony and Cleopatra. Bryant describes the death of these lovers as a "selfless" expenditure which enabled them to achieve "the distinctively Christian ideal of humanity." May not some readers question whether the suicides are really "selfless" and resemble a Christian sacrifice? Bryant qualifies by saying they "never really see the parallel" between their human action and "that perfect action which might have saved them." Does he mean they grasped imperfectly the Christian ideal? I proposed rather, in 1969, that theirs is a parody version of true sacrifice. That is, they unwittingly enact a grotesque analogy to the Christian ideal. Swayed by Wilson Knight's view of Cleopatra, Bryant admired her "strong toil of grace" without noticing that hers is a "riggish" kind of grace beloved by worshipers of Isis. David Kastan, more recently, has commented on the tragic deceptiveness of Cleopatra's grace (see *infra*).

When interpreting Shakespeare's comedies Bryant made good use of biblical analogy, as have other subsequent critics alert to typology. Applying this approach to tragedy, however, can be more complex. For here an interpreter is tempted to go beyond seeing in the tragic hero a likeness to Saul or Jezebel or some other type of sinful Adamkind and imagine a change in the hero that results in a quasi-Christian serenity. A frequent divergence among practitioners of Christian criticism has been over whether Othello or Hamlet or Richard II can be supposed to have died a saved soul. While skeptics would simply rule out this question as irrelevant, the critics who tackle it do so sometimes unconvincingly.

Pertinent to this issue is some considering of a tragedy's traditional function of catharsis. Can a tragedy exercise our pity and fear if it ends with its hero triumphant? Critics such as O. B. Hardison and John Andrews discussed this. A purging of pity and fear, they argued, depends on our seeing some great failure or failures unintended by the tragic actor but fated by his mischoices. I myself agreed with this interpretation and proposed that ideally a spectator needs to be brought to say at the end of a tragedy, "There but for the grace of God go I." The auditor needs to arrive at a valid state of pity and fear through the story's cleansing us of muddied or crude modes of pity and fear. In a similar way, a comedy should exercise our emotion of laughter and bring us to a purged mode of joy. Both comedy and tragedy, if thus viewed, are intended to be educative in a therapeutic way—not chiefly in a moralistic or didactic way. Drama is properly an invitation to self-discovery. It is the telling of a story which engages our emotions and minds in their unpurged condition (what Bethell referred to as the crude assumptions of our fallen nature). Then it proceeds to refine these as we react to the story itself, unless we resist or obstruct that process. Do not our best theologians (both nowadays and in early church history) engage us with a story, a "narrative theology," and does not the dramatist Shakespeare make his appeal through some "old tale" of perennial relevance?

Francis Fergusson has been a critic helpful especially for understanding what Aristotle meant by the imitation of an action. Very simply, according to Fergusson, Aristotle was referring to a basic action of the human psyche, imitated by six means, plot being the foremost. Fergusson's essay on *Macbeth,* in 1951, defined the basic action of that play as a psychic impulse to "outrun the pauser, reason"—which we see the hero persist in to his own downward destruction. But also, in this unusual tragedy with dimensions more than Aristotelian, we see a counter-movement when Malcolm outruns the pauser reason in an upward and saving direction. Through an engraced faith he overcomes his rational hesitancy regarding the trustworthiness of Macduff, and then with him undertakes a rescue of Scotland under the aegis of "powers above." A restoring of civic health "by the grace of Grace" closes the action. Supplementing Fergusson, other critics have elaborated on how sin and grace condition the two contrasting directions of psychic action imitated in this drama. It is as if the dramatist were aware of St Paul's providential view of history in Rom 5:20, that where sin increases, grace abounds all the more, since we see an Adam-like tragic fall by Macbeth followed by a grace of intervention by Malcolm (whose mother on her knees "Died every day she lived") and by England's Edward, the Confessor-king.

For Christian critics there is significance in the fact that a typological reading of history was provided by St Paul's interpretation of the Red Sea crossing. Our forefathers, says Paul, were baptized in the cloud and in the sea (1 Cor 10:2) and drank of the Rock which is Christ. This means that they began to participate in Christian mystery when they escaped from Egyptian values and committed themselves to the faith of Moses. It means that the sea-experience of these pre-Christians was a washing analogous to Christian baptism. It means, by implication, that a washing or purgation can happen anywhere or anytime when a nation or a person undergoes some ordeal that dissolves an old orientation and gives birth to a new. In short, every tempest-moment in human experience can either drown or baptize, either wreck or educate. History is our schoolhouse, not a treadmill. Around that truth Shakespeare constructed his dramas.

King Lear is a foremost example. The spouting hurricanoes to which Lear bares his head serve to drown his pride. They dissolve it, as we see, into a madness like that of Nebuchadnezzar, who had to eat grass in order to discover grace. Critics who find in this play's hero an earnest of redemption—and there are today still many who do—see the saving process as under way but incomplete when the story closes tragic and open-ended. They see a purgation that involves his dying to a blind self and being raised out of that grave by a Cordelia who foreshadows Christ's role. And one recent critic, significantly, has outlined the logic of this story by invoking as its gloss the church's liturgy, for the eve on which candidates are prepared for Easter baptism. That liturgy, as reviewed by John Cunningham (in 1984 in *Christianity and Literature*) rehearses mankind's journey toward the Light in four stages: 1) into the wilderness; 2) into the baptistry; 3) out of the baptistry in new garments; and 4) at the gate of death, where the soul pants for a higher life. These are the stages Lear experiences analogously in his pagan Britain.

But if historical experience itself mediates baptisms, moments when an old order of life is replaced by a new, can we not apply this framework of understanding to our reading of England's history as dramatized in *Richard III?* By the end of *3 Henry VI* Shakespeare has depicted a national history reduced to a swirl; imagery of wind and tide predominate. At this point the Machiavel Richard turns those waters into a vortex of fraud that drowns almost the whole community in an ordeal of bloodshed. A nadir is reached when innocent babes are massacred, as if by a biblical Herod. But this very outrage causes the warring queens to unite in a sisterhood of weeping mothers, so to speak. Together they renounce their addiction to Fortune's favors and turn to a rescuer from overseas. A secret supporter of this conversion is Lord Stanley (ancestor of the Lord Derby who in Shakespeare's day was suspected of Catholic sympathies), and another supporter is the Bishop of Ely (from whom Thomas More acquired his sense of history). Ely's desertion worries Richard with an anxiety comparable, say, to that felt by ancient Pharaoh when Moses escaped. And in the final showdown at Bosworth, the famous cry of the defeated Richard, "A horse, my kingdom for a horse," echoes, I think, the Bible's tribute to God in Ex 15:21: "the horse and his rider he hath thrown into the sea." Shakespeare has a biblical sense of history. Critics such as Tom Driver, Edward Berry, and Emrys Jones have articulated this point with various kinds of evidence.

Even in Shakespeare's lighter comedies it can be seen that the Bible's Red Sea crossing has a secular analogy in the purgation that precedes a lover's achieving of an adult maturity. "True lovers have been ever crossed," says Hermia in *A Midsummer Night's Dream,* and in that comedy the cross is their night of misadventures in a moonlit woods. Idolatrous fancies enbondage them in follies until a corrective ointment frees their eyes and they escape from dotage into a daylight understanding. The barking dogs and hunters' horns which help them wake up have a function here like that in Shakespeare's *The Tempest,* where Ariel sings of watchdogs and chanticleer's cry when directing young Ferdinand's education. In both plays a cleansing of eyes and heart is a necessary preparation for marriage festival. This is the case also in the comedy of *Much Ado,* which depicts the victimization of lovers to ego-serving fashions until their folly is exposed and they repent it. Figuratively they must undergo a death and rebirth, as is emphasized in each of the plays I have mentioned. Until that crossing is made, the story in each play turns about the wayward antics of deluded questers—for instance, the trashing of marriage by Claudio in *Much Ado,* or the treacheries plotted by Antonio's party and Caliban's, or Titania's monstrous obsession and Bottom's dream.

Bottom's dream, by the way, has been discovered by Christian critics to be Shakespeare's travesty analogy of St Paul's experience. That is, Paul's report in 1 Cor 2:9 and 2 Cor 12:4 of experiencing a mystery that transcended his daily routine has its parody parallel in the experience Bottom reports in befuddled amazement over having experienced what "the ear of man hath not seen" and his tongue is "not able to conceive." Bottom's wondrous perception that "Man is but an ass" has its exemplification in the absurd Pyramus and Thisbe story, which ends with pathetic suicides. By contrast, the lovers in Shakespeare's main plot are able to substitute self-mockery for suicide, make a successful transition from self-love to self-knowledge, and then join in wedding festivities which conclude with a hallowing of the household. In metaphoric terms, they have had a crossover experience, a kind of sacramental transformation.

Imagery of death and rebirth, as a little reflection can tell us, is basic to the structure of Shakespeare's romances. In *All's Well* Helena pretends a death as part of her St Francis strategy for shaming Bertram to death while offering him a rebirth into true love. Hermione in *The Winter's Tale* simulates death in order to become in due time the disguised bearer of new life for Leontes; and at that play's very middle we hear an old shepherd say, "Now bless thyself: thou mett'st with things dying, I with things new-born." In *Cymbeline* Imogen must fall asleep in a grave and emerge as a disguised Fidele in order to re-win her husband while also converting Britain's king. In *The Tempest* Alonzo must be brought to a mudded state of guilty despair, and Caliban to a literal quagmire, before each of them can receive grace or become wise enough to seek it.

Pericles is the most spacious of Shakespeare's romances, traversing as it does a lifetime journey on the part of its hero, in voyages that involve two episodes of storm at sea and then a calm of melancholy before his being visited by a voice that touches on the music of the spheres and directs him to a temple of joy. The structure of this play—so Cynthia Marshall has recently argued (in 1991)—is a capsulized story of the human race through the Seven Ages of History discerned by St Augustine in the Bible and publicized in The *Golden Legend,* the people's manual of heroic adventure in medieval times. Thus, for instance, the first storm encountered by Pericles corresponds to that in the biblical Age of Noah; Pericles emerges from it with a recovered armor that symbolizes faith. A second storm accompanies his departure from Pentapolis and entails the seeming loss of a family member, as in the Age of Abraham. Many years later, however, a visiting of Pericles by Marina parallels the biblical Age of the Prophets that brings news of salvation. The poet Gower is the play's Chorus to guide us through what Marshall appropriately calls a Cosmic Overview.

We know that *Pericles,* along with *King Lear,* was on the repertoire of some touring actors who performed these plays in the country house of a Yorkshire Catholic family in 1610. Evidently, neither play in such circles was thought to be, as some moderns suppose, haphazardly episodic or destructive of Christian faith. Many evangelical Protestants, also, are likely to have welcomed these plays, since the biblical typology of *Pericles* is akin to that of those Protestants who chose to risk their lives in voyages to America, and we know (as pertinent to *King Lear*) that exorcism was practised in Puritan circles as well as Catholic ones (to the dismay of Samuel Harsnett, who had objected to exorcisings by the puritan John Darrell before turning his attack on the "papists"). These parties, alongside many Christians in general in the early seventeenth century, are not likely to have regarded *The Tempest,* as some of today's critics do, as a recording of European despotism, but rather to have perceived in it a meaning such as James Walter has expounded in an essay in PMLA (1983) which invokes Augustine's allegorical interpretation of Genesis as a key to the metaphors Shakespeare uses in telling the Tempest story of providence in history. As Kenneth Muir has remarked, contemporary voyage literature included William Strachey's account of a shipwreck in Bermuda which carried memories of Paul's shipwreck on an island in which not a hair perished (Acts 27:34).

There is abundant evidence, much more than I have here touched on, for taking seriously the Christian contexts of Shakespeare's dramatic art. But can it nowadays receive a fair hearing? Much of recent critical opinion is not encouraging. Near my desk is a series of books called

"The Critics Debate" published by Humanities Press International. T. F. Wharton on *Measure for Measure* (1989) begins debate by saying that this play's "imperfections are obvious." When he gets around to summarizing Christian interpretations he does this inaccurately and reductively, and then proceeds to cite with approval critics who help him argue that the Duke is a meddlesome manipulator with no holiness whatever. Bill Overton's review of *The Winter's Tale* (1989) avoids Wharton's dogmatic skepticism. Overton is painstaking in all his summaries of critics, and he praises Traversi, Bethell, and Knight for helping establish that the play is "worth the fullest attention." But he objects to their letting the play become a "symbolic vehicle for ultimate truths about life." He feels that Bethell has "imposed" a Christian perspective on the play. He believes more attention should be paid to "political questions" so as not to abstract the play from the processes of history. What he means by this is implied in his honest confession at the beginning of his study: "I practise no religion, and my politics are socialist." Plainly, his hermeneutical circle conditions his range of appreciation.

We can expect the Christian dimension of Shakespeare's work to be downplayed or misrepresented by readers whose habit patterns of sensibility resist the acknowledgment of Christian mystery. St Paul recognized that to rationalists the cross would seem scandalous, while to legalistic moralists it was a stumbling block. He had to appeal beyond these obstacles to a latent capacity in human beings to learn through crisis-experience the reality of a divinely reasonable love and its higher moral law. Shakespeare's plays still exercise occasionally a similar function for some of their spectators today. Insofar as this is the case, should we not be grateful that they serve both a timely need and a timeless value? There is after all within today's culture some "good soil" capable of bringing forth a thirtyfold harvest so to speak, and occasionally a hundredfold.

THEMES

Robert G. Hunter (essay date 1976)

Hunter, Robert G. "Shakespeare's Comic Sense as It Strikes Us Today: Falstaff and the Protestant Ethic." In *Shakespeare: Pattern of Excelling Nature*, edited by David Bevington and Jay L. Halio, pp. 125-32. Newark: University of Delaware Press, 1978.

[*In the following essay, originally presented in 1976, Hunter views Falstaff as the antithesis of the Protestant ethic.*]

If there are such things as antibodies (and I am told that there are), then let there be such things as antiembodiments and let Falstaff be one. Let him also be an embodiment (there is plenty of room), for Falstaff embodies a large part of my subject, Shakespeare's comic sense. Simultaneously he antiembodies the Protestant ethic. What he is, it is not. What it is, he is not. Did Shakespeare's comic sense serve the body politic by generating Falstaff in an attempt to immunize comparatively Merrie England against those foreign organisms, the Puritan Saints? If so, the attempt failed, and Shakespeare knew it would. The Henriad, I will maintain but not demonstrate, dramatizes, in the rejection of Falstaff, the victory of the Protestant ethic, presenting that social triumph as a psychological event, the decision of Henry the Fifth to labor in his vocation, to do his duty in that royal station to which it pleased God to call him.

Thus Falstaff came into being, almost four centuries ago, during the first insurgency of the Protestant ethic and, perhaps, in response to it. Today we are celebrating the bicentennial of one of that ethic's more elaborate offspring. And do we not sense today that we are living through the decadence and disappearance of the ethic, that we watch going down the great drain of history what Shakespeare saw coming up it? What will take the ethic's place? That seems to me one of today's more nagging questions, and I haven't the vaguest notion of its answer. But we might explore the question by consulting the comic sense of our particular oracle. Let us have a look first at the ethic and then at Falstaff as antiembodiment of it.

The phenomenon that I claim Falstaff antiembodies is authoritatively described and accounted for by Max Weber in *The Protestant Ethic and the Spirit of Capitalism*. Weber identifies the main characteristic of that ethic as "worldly asceticism . . . a fundamental antagonism to sensuous culture of all kinds." He sees the ethic as the result of two theological causes, one Lutheran and one Calvinist. The Lutheran cause is the "conception of the calling." In reacting against the monastic ideal Luther did not entirely repudiate the worthiness of ascetic self-denial. What he did was to replace the insistence upon withdrawal from the world with a "valuation of fulfilment of duty in worldly affairs as the highest form which the moral activity of the individual could assume." To this exaltation of the importance of laboring in one's vocation was added the Calvinist notion of absolute predestination. If you believe that humanity has been irretrievably divided into the elect and the reprobate, then it becomes a matter of some importance to convince yourself that you are a member of the right group. "In order to attain that confidence intense worldly activity is recommended as the most suitable means. It and it alone disperses religious doubts and gives certainty of grace." As a paradoxical result, Protestantism, which proclaims that works are useless as a means of gaining salvation, ends by finding them "indispensable as a means . . . of getting rid of the fear of damnation." "Getting rid of fear" is a key phrase for an understanding of the psychological power of the Protestant ethic and of Falstaff as a compendious alternative to that ethic. Hope of eternal life gets rid of the fear of death.

Faith in our election gets rid of the fear of eternal damnation, and contemplating the success of our worldly activity ratifies our faith in election. Success is evidence of salvation. The Protestant ethic is a superb strategy for getting rid of those fears which are inherent in the human condition, fears of time, of death, and of damnation. It is one of the greatest in what Freud calls "the great series of methods devised by the mind of man for evading the compulsion to suffer."

Falstaff is an anthology of such methods. I count and will try to define five, taking them in the order Shakespeare presents them to us. The first I label "living within appetite," the second "play," the third "success," the fourth "carnival," and the last, "hope." Of these the first, second, and fourth are in direct opposition to the ideals and practices of the Protestant ethic. The third and the last are distorted imitations of Protestant ethic methods and I will call them serious parodies, though it makes me uneasy to claim that anything about Falstaff is serious.

The first of Falstaff's methods is the most effective and also the most difficult to sustain. It is common to all of us, originates in infancy, and antedates the fear of time itself. Our first clock is appetite, and time first presents itself to us as that which intervenes between appetite and its satisfaction, and its rebirth. The time we thus perceive through appetite is circular in nature, a time of eternal return. A day is that which separates breakfast from breakfast. There is nothing to fear in time thus perceived as circular, as the element in which pleasure, the satisfaction of appetite, takes place. And much in the reality we begin to perceive outside our bodies appears to confirm the truth of time's circularity. The sun also ariseth, and the sun goeth down and hasteth to the place where he arose. Spring, summer, autumn, winter—spring. Not much of this appetitive, circular time has passed, however, before its passing forces upon us the knowledge that our understanding of time is incomplete. The bodies whose appetites we have satisfied change permanently. Today is not yesterday despite the similarity in breakfasts. Summer returns but last summer will never return. Time, we find, is rectilinear, the shortest possible distance between birth and death. With that discovery our fear of time is born, and our minds must devise methods for evading the suffering in that fear. The method of the Protestant ethic is to glorify time's rectilinearity, to proclaim time the element not of pleasure, but of duty, of the worldly achievement that ratifies faith in our election. This, however, is not Falstaff's way.

Henry IV, Part One opens with the King doing desperate battle against the implacability of rectilinear time. "Find we a time" is his plea. A time for peace, for the establishment of order, for the crusade, the achievement that will expiate Richard's murder and convince the King that his soul is saved after all. The second scene begins when Falstaff first waddles into our consciousness on the line, "Now, Hal, what time of day is it, lad?" a question whose total banality inspires Hal to a rather wonderful tirade on the question: "What a devil hast thou to do with the time of the day?", a question that Hal himself proceeds to answer: "Unless hours were cups of sack, and minutes capons, and clocks the tongues of bawds, and dials the signs of leaping-houses. . . ." Hal's conditional answers his interrogative. Falstaff's clock is Falstaff's paunch and the time it tells is circular, revolving from thirst to sack to thirst to sack. From hunger to capon to hunger to capon. From lust to wench to lust to fair, hot wench. Falstaff copes with the fact of time's linearity by stoutly denying it, by doing his best to live his life within the circular time of appetite. Such a life would be a life without fear of time, but of course no moderately conscious life can be so lived. It's not just that capons, sack, and wenches refuse to arrive on schedule—though that is annoying enough. The rectilinearity of time is constantly being forced upon our unwilling minds. Even our best friends are in the habit of saying things like "gallows," and when we try tactfully to change the subject to something pleasant like "a most sweet wench," they refuse to cooperate and we end up depressed, "as melancholy as a gib cat, or a lugged bear."

When this happens to Falstaff, he moves to his second strategy. He answers the reproaches of his superego with the exhilarating language of play—purely verbal play at first. Falstaff copes with melancholy by playing with Hal at finding similes for it: a gib cat, a lugged bear, an old lion, a lover's lute, the drone of a Lincolnshire bagpipe, a hare, the melancholy of Moor-ditch. Having thus put the forces of his conscience on the defensive, he proceeds to polish them off by employing his favorite play method, role-playing. Falstaff has the ability to make anything appear ridiculous by pretending to be it. Here he represses his own tendencies to contrition by pretending to be contrite: "But Hal, I prithee trouble me no more with vanity . . . thou hast done much harm upon me, Hal, God forgive thee for it: before I knew thee, Hal, I knew nothing, and now am I, if a man should speak truly, little better than one of the wicked." What Poins calls "Monsieur Remorse" is Falstaff's first and in some ways best role. Nowhere does Shakespeare make it clearer how the humorous man copes with the certainty of death and the possibility of damnation. By parodying his own fears, Falstaff answers the challenge Hamlet gives the skull of Yorick: he makes us laugh at that. But of course it is not just himself that Falstaff is mocking here. Monsieur Remorse is pretty clearly a Puritan gentleman. He is one of the Protestant Saints whom the Prince of Wales has so far misled as to make him doubt his own election and fear that his conduct indicts him as little better than one of the reprobate. Not only does Falstaff's role-playing purge him of his own melancholy, it accuses the Protestant ethic of being a role that the Puritan thinks (or pretends to think) he is playing in earnest. But it is not only the specific mockery, the parochial satire that the Protestant ethic would find offensive. Falstaff's roles release him from the depressing confines of reality and that, unless done religiously, will not do. Play in all its forms, from morris-dancing to the great Globe itself, is an inadmissible alternative to laboring soberly in one's vocation. But Falstaff, *homo ludens,* goes on playing. On Gadshill and in the tavern his roles increase and multiply: the young desperado ripping off the fat chuffs who batten on the commonwealth ("They hate us youth"); the battered survivor of a better time who sees a virile world of courage and honor among thieves degenerating, disintegrating around him: "Go thy ways, old Jack, die when thou wilt—if manhood, good manhood, be not forgot upon the face of the earth, then I am a shotten herring . . ."; and Sir John Fairbanks, Sr., driving before him two, four, seven, nine, eleven men in buckram; and finally, of course, the King, the Prince, himself. So Falstaff's Protean mind copes with itself, represses and escapes its fears by becoming not dying Jack Falstaff but anything and everything, turning all things to laughter.

But again this is not enough. On the morning after the night before the body whose appetites have been so assiduously satisfied informs the Protean mind that time is rectilinear and he is but Falstaff and a man: "Do I not bate? Do I not dwindle? Why, my skin hangs about me like an old lady's loose gown. I am withered like an old apple-john." And we get a reprise of Monsieur Remorse, rather more Romanist in his second version, I think. Clearly, sterner measures than play are called for. Living in appetite is the strategy of the infant. Play is the strategy of the child. Falstaff is never such a fool as to put away childish things. He knows he needs all the strategies he can get. While retaining the two I have already identified, he moves to those of the mature man and specifically to an antiversion of the Protestant ethic itself. Having parodied the remorse of the Puritan, he now more seriously parodies its results: the determination to labor in one's vocation.

When, in their first scene, Hal interrupts the finger flights of Monsieur Remorse to ask Jack Falstaff where they should take a purse tomorrow, he gets the reply, "'Zounds, where thou wilt, lad, I'll make one." Upon which the prince observes, "I see a good amendment of life in thee, from praying to purse-taking." Monsieur Remorse's rejoinder is a model of Christian forbearance: "Why, Hal, 'tis my vocation, Hal, 'tis no sin for a man to labor in his vocation." If one wished to be unfair to the Protestant ethic (and I do), one could say that Weber's description of the shift in Christian morality from the medieval exaltation of the monastic ideal to the seventeenth-century Puritan enshrinement of capitalist worldly asceticism is encapsulated in Hal's phrase "from praying to purse-taking." Falstaff's methods in purse-taking are not commercial and therefore his calling is not lawful. But he is not really a highwayman either. The night's exploits on Gadshill are closer to play than to vocation, an especially exciting game of cops-and-robbers. Ordinarily and whenever possible, Falstaff combines the crafts of the professional soldier and the confidenceman. He combines them very successfully. The £300 that he extorts from reluctant draftees compares favorably with the £250 Shakespeare is estimated to have made in a good year and very favorably indeed with the £20 annual salary of the Stratford schoolmaster. And Falstaff is a success on the battlefield as well. He does his duty by leading or somehow chivvying his soldiers into a position where they can be thoroughly peppered, and then he distinguishes himself by stabbing the corpse of Hotspur in the thigh. Does he expect anyone to believe that he and not Hal has killed Harry Percy? It doesn't matter, for there are distinct orders of success in lying. A liar may succeed because he is believed or because he cannot be contradicted. Falstaff is content with the more modest degree, and thus he achieves one of those reputations, common enough in fields other than the military, for having done something or other at some time or other.

The result of these successful labors is the Sir John Falstaff of *Henry the Fourth, Part Two:* Jack Falstaff with his familiars, John with his brothers and sisters, and Sir John with all Europe. Such are the secular rewards of laboring in one's vocation—self-fulfillment and a sense of one's identity confirmed by the respect of the community. And there is no strategy more successful than success for concealing from us our participation in the common human condition. For the Puritan, of course, the rewards of such laboring also include the conviction of one's election and a consequent faith in one's eternal salvation. Falstaff does not go that far, not by some distance. Indeed, his profession is an extension of his play. He has added a new dimension to his role-playing and has begun to pretend really to be what he is pretending to be. To what extent that makes him different from the rest of us, including the ethical Protestants, I must leave it to the subtler masters of the dramaturgical school of social psychology to decide. My point is that as a technique for dealing with our fears of time and death, becoming Sir John with all Europe works very well. Monsieur Remorse is no longer needed to repress the natterings of the superego. Being Sir John is enough.

Or almost enough, for again the body reminds us of our inevitable predicament. The owner of Sir John's urine may have more diseases than he knows for, but Sir John is aware of a good number of them: "A pox of this gout! or a gout of this pox! for the one or the other plays the rogue with my great toe." That great toe, long invisible to its owner's eye, is transmitting the body's tedious message: you cannot conquer time. Falstaff's fourth method for jamming that communication is related to all of the previous three. Carnival is an attempt to regain occasionally and temporarily the bliss of living within appetitive time. It is that period which society sets aside for sanctioned play, for humor, wit, and role-playing. It is the necessary holiday in which we may rest from doing our duties in that station to which it has pleased God to call us. Except, of course, that the Puritans recognized no such necessity. They were opposed to Carnival, but they were equally opposed to Lent—not because they found its lugubrious self-denials distasteful (though they knew there was no merit in them) but because they thought it should be Lent all the year round. Once more, Sir John embodies a different point of view. After a hard day's labor devoted to evading the Lord Chief Justice, placating Mistress Quickly, devising methods for bilking Master Dommelton the slops-maker, and avoiding the importunities of a dozen sweating captains—after such a day, the warrior deserves his repose. Wine, women, and song, sack and canary, Doll Tearsheet and Sneak's noise—all the components of an ideal saturnalia are present in the great festive scene of *Henry IV, Part Two*. But Shakespeare is here aiming to present us with the real as well as the ideal, and real saturnalia has indecorous results: vomit, urine, syphilis, and violence. Our women enter talking of wine and its effects and when asked how she is doing now, Doll replies, "Better than I was—hem!" That "hem," I suspect, is Shakespeare's suggestion to his boy-actor that he should indicate audibly but nonverbally why Doll is doing better than she was. Sir John enters with song: "When Arthur first in court," and urine: "Empty the jordan." A bout of wit follows between Doll and Falstaff on the subject of who is responsible for whose venereal disease. The episode with Pistol brings us to violence and Sir John's valor inspires Doll to ask her little, tidy, Bartholomew boar-pig when he will leave fighting a-days and foining a-nights and begin to patch up his old body for heaven. *Carpe diem* is a motto of carnival, but one of the things we ask of saturnalia is that it make us forget why it is that we want to seize the day. Doll's comment is malapropos and her most flattering busses cannot make Falstaff forget the consequences of linear time: "I am old. I am old." And finally, in spite of the fun and games with Hal and Poins, it looks as if Shakespeare were going to let Falstaff be frustrated by age and time and by the demands of his vocation, for "The man of action is called on" and must leave the sweetest morsel of the night unplucked. Farewells must be said: "Well, fare thee well. I have known thee these twenty-nine years, come peascod-time, but an honester and truer-hearted man. . . ." I thoroughly agree with the Arden editor's note on peascod-time: "The precision with which Mistress Quickly dates a 29-year-old meeting is entirely touching." Just how entirely that is, however, can be understood only if one apprehends the bawdy of "peascod," and to do that one must reverse the syllables. Doing so emphasizes that the time that finally triumphs here is appetitive and circular. Bardolph reenters with a command: "Bid Mistress Tearsheet come to my master." Poins was wrong: desire has not outlived performance. Codpiece time comes round again and Plump Jack lives!

This is a heartening conclusion to a brilliant scene and yet we suspect Shakespeare of suggesting that Falstaff is coming to the end of his strategies. This suspicion is strengthened by the King's magnificent speeches in the next scene on the book of fate, the revolution of the times, and the necessity of meeting one's necessities. The scene that follows informs us that old Double is dead and John of Gaunt, who loved him well, is dead and death is certain, very sure, all shall die, and that the one way left of coping with that perception seems to be to let one's shallow mind wander quickly to the price of a good yoke of bullocks at Stamford Fair. Yet Falstaff continues to labor cheerfully in his fraudulent vocation, and it is not until act 5, scene 3 that we discover that he has been doing battle with time and the prospect of death by employing one strategy more than the four we have already examined. Pistol interrupts senility's saturnalia in Gloucestershire with news of yet another death: the old king is dead as nail in door. Falstaff, whom Shallow and Silence have kept quietly amused to this point, now explodes with excitement: "I am Fortune's steward . . . I know the young King is sick for me . . . the laws of England are at my commandment . . . woe to my Lord Chief Justice!" This is the revelation of a life illusion. Since the first time we saw him in the second scene of the Henriad, Falstaff has never repeated to Hal or us his speculations on what will happen when the Prince becomes the King. We realize that he much overestimates Hal's devotion to sack and laughter, but we have small reason to know, until we find out, that Falstaff thinks Hal's accession will put the laws of England at Sir John's commandment. What here stands revealed is Falstaff's last strategy, his secular, temporal version of a religious faith in one's election to eternal salvation. Falstaff copes with his condition by living in hope, as which of us does not. We must cling to our faith in that intervening event (the doctorate, tenure, the professorship, retirement) which will with millennial effect transform the quality of our existence. Delusive hope was included in Pandora's box lest we should despair and destroy ourselves. What kills Sir John is the destruction of his delusive hope and the consequent knowledge that his future does not exist.

He would have died anyway. Falstaff, like everybody else, is killed by death. But that death is designed by Shakespeare to show us something. The King kills Falstaff's heart, but what impels the King to do so is the desire to do his royal duty by laboring in his vocation. I lack the time to demonstrate why I think Henry of Monmouth stands for the Protestant ethic but I believe that, consciously or not, Shakespeare has transposed into his early-fifteenth-century action the uncompleted spiritual and political struggles of the 1590s. Hal's psychomachia is a battle between Carnival and Lent, and Falstaff is on the losing side. Hal and the Protestant Ethic reject Falstaff, but Shakespeare does not reject Falstaff nor does he reject Hal for rejecting Falstaff.

Falstaff defines the Protestant Ethic by being what it isn't, but also by being a different variety of what it is: a means of coping with the fears engendered by the realities of the human condition. The ethic defeats Falstaff because of the superior strength that derives from the religious faith on which it is based—a faith that enables it to cope with our fears by denying that the realities that inspire them are ultimately real, by asserting that linear time will give way to eternity and that death is a transition to eternal life. Falstaff's being what he is, however, poses a great question to the ethic's answer: may not the ethic's faith be as illusory a strategy as any of Falstaff's, finally a form of delusive hope itself? Hal, in accepting his necessary form, must reject Falstaff because the Protestant ethical form cannot encompass the question Falstaff poses. But Shakespeare's art can and does. It encompasses, as always, question and answer and the questioning of the answer. And the questioning of the questioning, for what is the Falstaff action but a demonstration of the inevitable inadequacy of the strategies of which his character is composed? Shakespeare's sense, whether comical or tragical or tragical-comical-historical-pastoral, seems to me to be always interrogative. For me the great thing about Shakespeare's art is its ability simultaneously to reveal and accept our inadequacies, above all the inadequacy of our answers. The motto carved on the temple of our particular oracle is, "Your answers questioned here."

René E. Fortin (essay date 1979)

SOURCE: Fortin, René E. "Hermeneutical Circularity and Christian Interpretations of *King Lear.*" *Shakespeare Studies* 12 (1979): 113-25.

[*In the essay below, Fortin asserts that a Christian reading of* King Lear *is as compatible with the "facts" of the play as a secular one, but that neither one is authoritative. Noting that the death of Cordelia is the principal impediment for Christian interpreters, he suggests that the play's ending, far from contradicting Christian doctrine, confirms the Catholic and Protestant notion of God's judgments as unknown and inexplicable.*]

Attempts to redeem *King Lear* by appealing to intimations of Christian transcendence in the play have been summarily, if not vehemently, dismissed by secular critics. Christian critics, we are told by W. R. Elton and others, are simply wrong because they do not attend to the "facts" of the play; seeking to escape the dire significances of the tragic vision, they are in effect guilty of wishful thinking, of imposing their own a priori assumptions upon the play. "The record" of Lear interpretations, says Nicholas Brooke, "is of a long series of strenuous efforts to circumvent the pain; and it is accompanied by a will to release large and encouraging affirmations once the pain is evaded."[1] Brooke insists that the greatness of *King Lear* derives, rather, from the "perfect completion of its negation and in the superb energy with which it is enforced" (p. 77).

Recently, however, René Wellek has posed an intriguing question: whether it is possible to conclude that there is indeed a single correct interpretation of the tragedies.[2] Wellek's question is worthy of further consideration, for perhaps the root of the controversy between secular critics and "Christian" critics is the fact that our criticism lacks a solid hermeneutical base. It is quite evident that the typical interpretation of *King Lear* (and of the other tragedies as well) is offered as the "right" interpretation, setting forth the meaning of the tragedy all would derive if they would only see the plays aright. But perhaps we are now ready to awaken from our dogmatic slumber and reexamine the implicitly Lockean assumptions which have governed our critical practice. For time after time in the past several decades we have been cautioned that perception and cognition are highly complex activities and that the perceiving eye and mind are actively engaged in constituting or shaping the truth they are naively supposed merely to register.[3] The conceptual model of a purely objective critical encounter, such as that called for by Morris Weitz (a model which would have the critic as spectator attempting to "see the object exactly as it is"), seems highly questionable at this time.[4] It is now almost de rigueur in critical essays to offer ritual obeisance to E. H. Gombrich and his demonstration that our vision is largely a matter of projection, of seeing only what we are prepared to see.[5] Specifically in literature the now familiar paradigm of the "included spectator" indicates an awakening to the creative participation of the viewer of a play,[6] while Norman Rabkin's view of the complementarity of Shakespearean meanings has made remarkable inroads; Shakespearean structure, Rabkin tells us, sets up "the opposed elements as equally valid, equally desirable, and equally destructive, so that the choice the play forces the reader to make becomes almost impossible."[7] Specifically about *King Lear,* Rabkin states, "We find ourselves able at almost any point in the play to read it as godless or divine; these are the terms implicit in the action of *King Lear* and explicit in its language."[8] E. D. Hirsch, who has been a stalwart defender of "objective interpretation," nonetheless concedes the shaping role of the interpreter:

> The object of interpretation is precisely that which cannot be defined by the ontological status of a text, since the distinguishing characteristic of a text is that from it not just one but many disparate complexes of meaning can be construed. . . . the object of interpretation is no automatic given, but a task that the interpreter sets himself. He decides what he wants to actualize and what purpose his actualization should achieve.[9]

In this context Marvin Rosenberg's condescending observation about the "redemptionist" readers of *King Lear* impresses me as especially provocative: "All this [devastation] cannot prevent those who will from seeing exaltation in Lear's final vision of Cordelia's death, or from believing that what Lear has learned was worth the suffering. *We perceive what we are prepared to, need to, perceive*" [italics mine].[10] Rosenberg goes on, of course, to dismiss such a response as tawdry sentimentality and to offer the real, objective truth about *King Lear,* that it is a play which ends in totally unrelieved "general woe" (p. 326).

Rosenberg's observation, however, raises the intriguing question whether it is only the "redemptionist" readers who are to be numbered among "those who will"; for it is difficult to determine precisely how the secular critics can lay claim to an epistemological transcendence denied other critics. Perhaps we have here, as Maynard Mack has suggested, merely a sentimentality of a different kind.[11] I do not propose, I hasten to add, that secular readings of *King Lear* are wrong; indeed they are often quite persuasive and should be heeded. I wish rather to suggest that to consider the secular reading as exclusively valid is as much an act of dogmatic assertion as is the comforting vision offered by the Christian interpreters, since the assertion in either case is based upon a selection of evidence as well as a

Edwin Forrest as King Lear.

selective interpretation of that evidence. It is difficult, when one considers the Joseph's coat of *Lear* interpretations, to dismiss the specter of the hermeneutical circle so prominent in Bultmann's exegetical theory:

> All understanding, like all interpretation, is . . . continually oriented by the manner of posing the question and by what it aims at. . . . Consequently, it is never without presuppositions; that is to say, it is always directed by a prior understanding about which it interrogates the text. It is only on the basis of that prior understanding that it can, in general, interrogate and interpret.[12]

One need not follow Bultmann's speculation into the intellectual swamp of relativism to appreciate the usefulness of the caveat; if critical objectivity is at all possible, as E. D. Hirsch insists it is, one does not easily attain it.[13] Interpretations of Shakespeare's plays are, and will continue to be, colored by personal predispositions since an active, personal response is inherent in the critical effort. But that this is the case is not to be regretted, for the great diversity of interpretations is our most eloquent witness to the wealth of Shakespeare's world as well as our best defence against critical dogmatism.

The final scene of *King Lear* provides the best opportunity to pursue these questions, for in the death of Cordelia lies the most formidable challenge to any affirmative, religious view of the tragic experience. The Christian critic's attempt to wrest comfort from the dire outcome of the play is decisively repudiated by the secular critic because the events of the play—its "facts"—supposedly contradict the central tenets of Christianity. But what specifically are these tenets? If we examine closely the secular arguments, we find (1) that nothing short of poetic justice would validate a religious argument; (2) that a truly Christian play would have to dramatize the miraculous intervention of the gods or otherwise catch them red-handed as they intrude into the affairs of men; and (3) that the universe in which the tragic ordeal takes place would have to be transparently meaningful. Nicholas Brooke, for example, states: "I have never been clear what constitutes a 'Christian play.' I should have supposed that label would involve some effort to justify God's ways to men, to make the mysterious less inscrutable" (p. 74). He later adds, "Poetical justice has been dealt out to Oswald, but embarrassingly, the gods didn't do it themselves," just as it is Edgar—and not God—who provides the "miracle" that saves Gloucester (pp. 80, 78). Elton likewise attaches great importance to miracles as signs of God's benevolent Providence: "In an unprovidential universe, it is suggested, miracles are absent and prayers are generally [?] ineffective. Such mention of miracles dramatically recalls to the spectator their absence—a sharply contrasting beam of tenuous light in a grimly dark and God-forsaken world."[14] Finally, Rosenberg joins this chorus with his utter certitude about the vacancy of Lear's final vision: "On this ultimate stage of fools, no one—except possibly Lear dying in illusion—is so foolish as to see any evidence of divinity at work. . . . Death everywhere, of the good as well as the 'bad'" (pp. 325-26).

Such responses cannot be peremptorily dismissed even by the Christian interpreter, for the question of poetic justice and of the benign concern of the gods for man is at the very heart of the play. From the outset of *King Lear* the characters express faith in the concern and loving-kindness of the gods: the gods, Lear feels, will at once take his part against his daughters; Cornwall's servants pray that the blinding of Gloucester be speedily avenged; Albany sees the killing of Cornwall as evidence that the "justicers" are above; and Edgar constantly assures his father that the gods are sensitive to human anguish:

> . . . therefore, thou happy father,
> Think that the clearest gods, who make them honors
> Of men's impossibilities, have preserved thee.[15]
>
> (IV.vi.72-74)

What we notice, however, is a far less hospitable universe. As many commentators have pointed out, a conspicuous feature of the structure of *King Lear* is its irony, the rhythm of expectation and frustration to which the characters are subjected.[16] It has been too infrequently noted, however, that the viewer is himself victimized by the same ironies. Our familiarity with the play—we all know how it ends—has largely blunted these ironies for us; like trained hounds we have been over the course before and are not likely to be led astray by false scents, as Lear, Albany, and Edgar are. But the "naive spectator," the first-time viewer of the play, who lacks our synchronic, spatial sense of the play's form, would hardly be so fortunate—especially if he is familiar with the earlier *Leir*. The naive spectator, rather, is constantly being assured that all will be well; he is comforted by the discreet loyalty of Kent, by the early and persistent rumors of civil wars that will bring down the house divided of Goneril and Regan, by the tender care of Edgar (as Poor Tom) for his father, and especially by the perpetual promise of the return of Cordelia. What is especially noteworthy is how early the viewer is given these assurances: we hear of the "likely wars toward," for example, in the first lines of Act II, while Kent offers us the promise of the "almost miracle" of Cordelia's return in Act II, scene ii—significantly before Lear's ordeal begins in earnest. It is as if the play is taking great pains to buffer the viewer from anguish, assuring him that the darkness is only temporary.

The peculiar cruelty of *King Lear*, of course, is that this promise is violated, most glaringly in the manner in which Cordelia—"Great thing of us forgot" (V.iii.238)—dies. Though we do see some measure of what could be taken for "rough justice" in the deaths of Cornwall, Oswald, Edmund, Goneril, and Regan, there is in the death of Cordelia no poetic justice, no "dark and vicious place" (V.iii.174) to account for her murder, no discernible incense thrown upon her sacrifice. The viewer is tempted, after this unconscionable mischief of the wanton gods, to accept as his the "cheerless, dark and deadly" world described by Kent (V.iii.292).

But does the play insist that we do so? Do the "facts" of the play, particularly its excruciating final scene, make *King Lear* absolutely incompatible with a Christian worldview? Any critic intending to offer an unequivocal reading of its ending should recall that he is witnessing a play that has throughout insisted upon the problematics of seeing and that this theme dominates the final lines of Lear:

> Do you see this? Look on her. Look, her lips,
> Look there, look there.
>
> *(V.iii.312-13)*

Five times in his final fourteen words Lear refers to vision. As Rosenberg has aptly stated, *King Lear* dwells upon "the necessity and difficulty of seeing to know. . . . seeing and knowing are never certain in *Lear*, for the play's dialectic insists upon ambiguity" (p. 344). Thus Lear's final statement presents to the viewers the ultimate challenge to vision: everything depends upon what is actually seen—or not seen—in these final moments. But here is perhaps the most devastating irony of the play: we do not and cannot see what Lear sees. What we see is merely Lear seeing. Philip Hobsbaum is at least partially right in arguing that "we cannot, to put it crudely, know whether or not Lear dies smiling. At the end of the play we are in exactly the same position as the spectators on stage. . . . Most of the critics who have dealt with the play seem to me wrong in opting for one or the other of these possibilities [hope and despair]: the values are more complex than that."[17]

Hobsbaum's comment is particularly useful when we consider the scene in the light of Betrand Evans' concept of discrepant awarenesses, for the concept may be especially relevant, though in a different way than most would imagine.[18] For where comedy typically offers to the viewer a cognitive perspective superior to that of the central figure (*we* know, for example, that Cesario is really Viola), it is possible that in *King Lear* it is the central figure who has the privileged vision, with the viewer able to see only from afar. Such a conclusion would be supported by the logic of the play, which postulates suffering as a precondition to accurate vision:

> Let the superfluous and lust-dieted man,
> That slaves your ordinance, that will not see
> Because he does not feel, feel your pow'r quickly.
> . . .
>
> *(IV.i.67-69)*

Thus Lear, because he has suffered, may indeed see more than the survivors (Edgar, Kent, and Albany), who seem to see nothing more than "general woe" (V.iii.321), and more than the spectators, whose suffering is at best vicarious. In short, if we accept what Rosenberg has said, that the play dwells upon "the necessity and difficulty of seeing to know," then we must be careful about arrogating to ourselves a clarity of vision superior to that of Lear, for what he sees, or cannot see, must remain for us only a matter of inference.

In order to be convincing, a Christian reading of *King Lear* must bravely push on beyond the "redemption" scenes of Act IV and take in fully the devastatingly ironic death of Cordelia. It is true, as secular critics have argued, that the death of Cordelia suggests the failure of the gods to provide the "chance which does redeem all sorrows" (V.iii.268), the saving miracle that would attest to their beneficence. Their failure to do so is particularly agonizing because it has occurred in a universe that seemed to support a faith in poetic justice but which instead decisively reasserts its opaqueness; we are left blindly staring at that which passeth all understanding.

But for the Christian critic the opaqueness of the *Lear* world is no insurmountable obstacle, for the very structural ironies which purportedly impeach the Christian worldview provide, when seen from a different perspective, a strong support for a Christian reading. To begin with, if the absence of visible supernatural intervention is to be the cudgel to beat down Christian interpretations—or Christian interpreters—one had better take a second look at the traditional beliefs of Christianity, for it is not at all presumed in the mainstream of Christian orthodoxy that God will intervene on call for his faithful; nowhere is a God of sweetness and light promised to man on this earth. Saint Paul, for example, preaches constantly that God is beyond human knowing: "How incomprehensible are his judgments and how unsearchable his wayes" (Rom. 11:33).[19] St. Augustine similarly speaks of God's "hidden equity that cannot be searched out by any human standard of measurement, though its effects are to be observed in human affairs and earthly arrangements."[20] Moreover, in Shakespeare's own time Reformation theology, under the twin influences of St. Paul and St. Augustine, forcefully elaborated the concept of a "hidden God" whose power and purposes are not to be fathomed.[21] In the words of Luther, God is "He for whose will no cause or ground may be laid down as its rule or standard. . . . God is wholly incomprehensible and inaccessible to man's understanding."[22] It is true that commentators, especially in the Catholic tradition, insisted upon the rationality of God, but even these writers were careful to respect the *mysterium tremendum;* Richard Hooker, for example, was strongly influenced by St. Thomas Aquinas and was therefore eager to defend the "light of reason" against the fideistic and voluntaristic emphases of the Reformers, but he nevertheless writes:

> The book of this law [the eternal law of God] we are not either able nor worthy to open and look into. That little thereof which we darkly apprehend we admire, the rest with religious ignorance we humbly and meekly adore.[23]

The ordeal of Lear and the death of Cordelia are, to be sure, hard to cope with, but they do not contradict the image of God held in either Catholic or Protestant Christianity. In fact, an ear attuned to scripture would discern in Lear's ordeal resonances of the Book of Revelation:

> I knowe thy workes, that thou art nether colde nor hote;
>
> I wolde thou werest colde or hote. Therefore, because thou art lukewarm, and nether colde nor hote, it will come to passe, that I shall spewe thee out of my mouth.
>
> For thou saist I am riche and increased with goods, and have neede of nothing, and knowest not how thou art wretched and miserable, and poore, and blinde, and naked.
>
> (Rev. 3:15-17)

I think it is evident that the verses point to central themes of the play and suggest much about its imagery. The lesson that Lear learns in his suffering is that he has been morally callous; it is a lesson that he learns by becoming himself poor, naked, and—symbolically through his madness—blind. The suffering of Lear, seen against this background is at once punitive and propaedeutic, a necessary condition to his redemption:

> I counsel thee to bie of me golde tryed by fire, that thou maiest be made riche, and white raiment, that thou maiest be clothed and that thy filthie nakednes do not appeare: and anoint thine eyes with salve, that thou maist se.
>
> As manie as I love, I rebuke and chasten.
>
> (Rev. 3:18-19)

Lear's "wheel of fire," the garment in which he is clothed after his wanderings, and the regained sight which allows him to see the daughter he has rejected in his blindness assume a more specific significance in the light of this Scriptural passage. The suffering of Lear may be construed as the activity of a loving, albeit stern, God.

There still, of course, remains the death of Cordelia. It is true, as many critics have averred, that Christian interpretations generally ignore the final excruciating scene of the play: "This object poisons sight; / let it be hid" (*Oth.* V.ii.363-64). It is, however, equally true that secular interpreters tend to view the death of Cordelia as an isolated episode, apart from the rich context that the previous four acts of the play have provided.

Because this context has been effectively explored elsewhere, I shall limit myself to brief remarks about how it may support a Christian reading. First, what is especially remarkable about the final scene is its recapitulatory nature, its gathering up of themes which developed earlier in the play. It should be noted, for example, that the Lear whom we view in the final scene has come full circle, being in much the same position as he was in Act I: calling upon his one true daughter to utter the words needed to sustain value in his life and once again receiving as answer the silence which is the alpha and omega of the play:

> What is't thou sayst? Her voice was ever soft,
> Gentle and low, an excellent thing in woman.
>
> (V.iii.274-75)

But Cordelia's failure to speak now may be no more a denial of value than was her earlier silence, particularly when one construes that silence in the light of other themes and images. Above all, Lear's lament over the dead Cordelia, "And my poor fool is hanged" (V.iii.307), recalls the motif of folly which has been so prominent earlier in the play. We have seen folly constantly associated with virtue: in the Fool's poignant commitment to Lear despite his own worldly wisdom which counsels a different course; in the supererogatory loyalty of Kent, who serves Lear despite his unjust banishment; and particularly in the superfluity of Cordelia's loving forgiveness. Virtue, for all its foolishness, yet survives in an otherwise bleak world. The Christian reader will have little difficulty seeing in such instances of unlikely goodness reminiscences of the Pauline theme of Christian folly in the First Epistle to the Corinthians:

> For brethren, you se your calling, how that not manie wise men after the flesh, not manie mighty, not manie noble, are called. But God hathe chosen the foolish things of the worlde to confounde the wise, and God

> hathe chosen the weake things of the worlde, to confounde the mighty things.
>
> (1:26-27)[24]

It is part of the Pauline scheme of things that true virtue be seen as folly or otherwise unpublished; Cordelia directs us to this view when she calls upon "All blest secrets, / All you unpublished virtues of the earth" (IV.iv.15-16) to remedy her father's distress.[25] For a prominent feature of *King Lear* is that virtue, in a world overwhelmed by evil, chooses to or is compelled to conceal its presence, to operate covertly. The list of "unpublished virtues" in the play is impressive; it includes Kent and Edgar, who fulfill their obligations in disguise; Gloucester, who summons up unexpected moral strength to assist his king and to bear his own ordeal patiently; the servants of Cornwall, who unexpectedly lash out at the cruelty of their master; and finally, Cordelia, who can publish her love for her father neither at the beginning nor at the end of the play.

But does the list of unpublished virtues end there? No one, I think, will deny that the question Lear addresses to the dead Cordelia, "Why should a dog, a horse, a rat, have life, / And thou no breath at all?" (308-09), is really addressed to the gods who would allow such an abomination. The Christian interpreter, recognizing that Lear has been throughout his ordeal surrounded by goodness which he has had difficulty perceiving, may have warrant enough to see the dead Cordelia as but a further instance of a pattern which points beyond to the gods, the ultimate unpublished virtues of the world. The apparent absence of redeeming goodness has thus far proven to be no guarantee that it does not exist.

And thus a play which begins with a king announcing "darker purposes" which lead to the temporary loss of a daughter ends with a Higher Power (or powers) announcing infinitely darker purposes and apparently bringing the same victim to distress. The Christian viewer will accept the harsh fact that the world offers no cheap consolations but need not necessarily infer that God has forsaken that world.

Rather, the Christian reader who is responsive to the Biblical echoes of the play may view the play as an attempt to demythologize Christianity, to reassert the hiddenness of God against the presumptuous pieties and shallow rationalism of the Edgars and Albanys of the world. In the death of Cordelia the viewers are once more confronted with the Judaeo-Christian God who, from the Book of Job on, has chosen to remain hidden and refuses to render account of His "darker purposes" to man. As Ivor Morris has indicated, *King Lear* is preeminently a play of stripping—of clothing, of language, of social masks—in order to unveil what is most fundamentally real (p. 184); in Act V it is God himself who is stripped, divested of the conventional images man has created for him. The God who emerges in the final events of the play is not the majuscule God as prime mover and creator of all, nor God as supreme justicer, nor even the God of translucent love to whom Cordelia seems to point. He is rather an unaccommodated and unaccommodating God who refuses masks of any kind, who denies us either the explanations we seek or the miracles which would make such explanations unnecessary. He is the miniscule God of Pauline theology who denies both signs and wisdom:

> For seing the worlde by wisdome knewe not God in the wisdome of God, it pleased God by the foolishenes of preaching to save them that beleve:
>
> Seing also that the Jewes require a signe, and the Grecians seke after wisdome.
>
> But we preache Christ crucified: unto the Jewes a stumbling block, and unto the Grecians foolishnes.
>
> (1 Cor. 1:21-23)

For the Christian interpreter the death of Cordelia need not, cannot be explained away; as "stumbling block" it supports rather than contradicts Revelation, the true Biblical God, even and perhaps especially that of the New Testament, being a God of faith seen but through a glass darkly, whose promises are beheld from afar. The ending of *King Lear,* in short, presents a demythologized Christianity that offers mystery rather than justice and that is founded upon hope rather than fulfillment; once more the language of Paul offers the best commentary:

> For we are saved by hope: but hope that is sene, is not hope: for how can a man hope for that which he seeth?
>
> But if we hope for that we se not, we do with patience abide for it.
>
> (Rom. 8:24-25)

Such a Christian reading, again, is not intended as *the* authoritative reading of *King Lear;* it is offered, rather, in an attempt to show that a Christian response to the play may be in conformity with both the "facts" of the play and with the doctrines of Christianity. Such a response, however, does not invalidate the secular reading, since even the most adamantly Christian of interpreters must feel the force of Edgar's admonition to "speak what we feel, not what we ought to say" (V.iii.326). What *King Lear* strongly suggests is that the lion of tragedy need not be devoured by the lamb of theology, for as Paul Ricoeur has suggested, tragedy survives the most ardent hermeneutical efforts of Christian thinkers:

> Killed twice, by the philosophical Logos and by the Judaeo-Christian Kerygma, [tragedy] survived its double death. The theme of the wrath of God, the ultimate motive of tragic consciousness, is invincible to the arguments of the philosopher as well as of the theologian. . . . As soon as meaninglessness appears to swoop down intentionally on man, the schema of the wrath of God looms up and tragic consciousness is restored.
>
> (p. 326)

To assert that *King Lear* admits both secular and religious interpretations is not, however, to argue for critical relativism, to consider the play as a tabula rasa awaiting any critical impression whatever. We must, as Murray Krieger has stated, "accept the hermeneutical gap that separates every critique from the work," but we must do so without denying the intersubjective nature of poetic communication; "at some level," says Krieger, "in spite of persuasive epistemological skepticism, all of us share Dr. Johnson's hard-headed, rock-kicking impatience with the unbridgeable private worlds of solipsism."[26] It is evident that the play, despite its apparent multivalence, creates its unique frame of discourse, channeling inquiry into specific areas of speculation and compelling attention to clearly-defined overwhelming questions. Thus a Christian interpreter can agree with much that Brooke, Elton, Rosenberg, and Stampfer have observed about the play: *King Lear* indeed dramatizes man's quest for justice; the folly, callousness, and brutality of which humanity is capable; the apparent injustice which man may suffer. It also dramatizes the unlikely perdurance of virtue under the most trying of conditions, as well as the moral awakening of several under the pressure of adversity. Calculations about what all of this adds up to may differ, and differ markedly, but it is most probably true that any interpretation of the play which denies that these are central concerns is simply wrong.

The open form of tragedy, its respect for the limits of human experience, allows readers to draw different conclusions: enough is given to allow interpreters to "see feelingly," to infer an interpretation based upon their own personal experience of the play; but enough is withheld to compel respect for the tragic mystery, to remind us that our conclusions are, after all, nothing but inference. If we learn anything from *King Lear,* it is that we all must see in our way, that a personal response is mandated by the tragic structure, but that our own vision is necessarily limited. Perhaps this humbling truth, hermeneutical as well as theological in its implications, is the play's most valuable revelation.

Notes

1. Nicholas Brooke, "The Ending of King Lear," in *Shakespeare 1564-1964,* ed. Edward A. Bloom (Providence, R. I.: Brown Univ. Press, 1964), p. 77.

2. "A. C. Bradley, Shakespeare, and the Infinite," *Philological Quarterly,* 54 (1975), 98.

3. Perhaps the most useful survey of this problem is in E. D. Hirsch, Jr., *The Aims of Interpretation* (Chicago: Univ. of Chicago Press, 1976).

4. Cf. M. H. Abrams, "What is the Use of Theorizing About the Arts?" *In Search of Literary Theory,* ed. Morton W. Bloomfield (Ithaca, N. Y.: Cornell Univ. Press, 1972), pp. 31-35.

5. E. H. Gombrich, *Art and Illusion* (New York: Pantheon, 1960); see esp. ch. 9, "The Analysis of Vision in Art."

6. Robert Hapgood's "Shakespeare and the Included Spectator," *Reinterpretations of Elizabethan Drama,* ed. Norman Rabkin (New York: Columbia Univ. Press, 1969) is, of course, the seminal article.

7. Norman Rabkin, *Shakespeare and the Common Understanding* (New York: The Free Press, 1967), p. 12.

8. Ibid., pp. 10-11; for a similar view, see Helen Gardner, *Religion and Literature* (New York: Oxford Univ. Press, 1971), pp. 35-36, 86-87.

9. E. D. Hirsch, Jr., *Validity in Interpretation* (New Haven: Yale Univ. Press, 1967), pp. 24-25.

10. Marvin Rosenberg, *The Masks of King Lear* (Berkeley: Univ. of California Press, 1972), p. 326.

11. Maynard Mack, *King Lear in Our Time* (Berkeley: Univ. of California Press, 1965), p. 115.

12. Cited in Paul Ricoeur, *The Symbolism of Evil* (New York: Harper, 1967), p. 351.

13. See especially Hirsch's "Appendix I. Objective Interpretation," in *Validity in Interpretation,* pp. 209-44; the essay first appeared in *PMLA,* 75 (1960).

14. W. R. Elton, *King Lear and the Gods* (San Marino: Huntington Library, 1966), p. 236.

15. All references to the plays are to *The Complete Signet Classic Shakespeare,* ed. Sylvan Barnet (New York: Harcourt, 1972).

16. See, e. g., Elton's "Irony as Structure," pp. 329-34.

17. Philip Hobsbaum, *Theory of Criticism* (Bloomington: Indiana Univ. Press, 1970), p. 161.

18. See Bertrand Evans, *Shakespeare's Comedies* (London: Oxford Univ. Press, 1960), esp. p. viii.

19. All Biblical references are to the Geneva Bible (1560), facsimile ed. (Madison: Univ. of Wisconsin Press, 1969).

20. Cited in Morris, p. 147.

21. See Paul R. Sellin, "The Hidden God: Reformation Awe in Renaissance English Literature," in *The Darker Vision of the Renaissance,* ed. Robert Kinsman (Berkeley: Univ. of California Press, 1974), p. 175.

22. Cited in Morris, p. 147.

23. *Laws of Ecclesiastical Polity,* (New York: Everyman's Library, 1925), I, 153.

24. For a fuller treatment of the relevance of the Corinthian letters, see Roger Cox, *Between Heaven and Earth* (New York: Holt, 1969).

25. I have discussed the theme of "unpublished virtues" at greater length in "Shakespearean Tragedy and the Problem of Transcendence," *Shakespeare Studies,* 7 (1974), 307-25.

26. Murray Krieger, "The Critic as Person and Persona," in *The Personality of the Critic,* ed. Joseph P. Strelka (University Park: Pennsylvania State Univ. Press, 1973), pp. 87-88.

Alan Sinfield (essay date 1980)

SOURCE: Sinfield, Alan. "Hamlet's Special Province." *Shakespeare Survey* 33 (1980): 89-97.

[*In the following essay, Sinfield discusses the connection between Hamlet's reference to "a special providence in the fall of a sparrow" and the question of whether the play's conception of the world is pagan or Christian.*]

> We defy augury: there is a special providence in the fall of a sparrow. If it be now, 'tis not to come; if it be not to come, it will be now; if it be not now, yet it will come—the readiness is all. Since no man owes of aught he leaves, what is't to leave betimes? Let be.
>
> (*Hamlet,* v, ii, 210-16)[1]

> [God is] a Governor and Preserver, and that, not by producing a kind of general motion in the machine of the globe as well as in each of its parts, but by a special Providence sustaining, cherishing, superintending, all the things which he has made, to the very minutest, even to a sparrow.
>
> (Calvin, *Institutes of the Christian Religion*)[2]

> Fate guides us, and it was settled at the first hour of birth what length of time remains for each. Cause is linked with cause, and all public and private issues are directed by a long sequence of events. Therefore everything should be endured with fortitude, since things do not, as we suppose, simply happen—they all come.
>
> (Seneca, 'De Providentia')[3]

The first passage quoted, where Hamlet declares that 'there is a special providence in the fall of a sparrow', is of key importance in the longstanding critical debate about *Hamlet* and Christianity. The way we relate it to the attitudes represented in the quotations from Calvin and Seneca bears crucially upon our choice between three rival interpretations of the play. Bradley recognises Hamlet's phraseology here as Christian but regards its tone and the play generally as pagan in implication: Hamlet expresses 'that kind of religious resignation which, however beautiful in one aspect, really deserves the name of fatalism rather than that of faith in Providence, because it is not united to any determination to do what is believed to be the will of Providence.'[4] Roland Mushat Frye believes these lines show Hamlet 'relying upon an unmistakably Christian providence' and hence achieving true faith.[5] Roy W. Battenhouse agrees with Frye that the play has a Christian tendency but also with Bradley that Hamlet's own attitude is unChristian: 'A biblical echo, the sparrow reference, when found in this upside-down context, alerts us to the tragic parody in Hamlet's version of readiness.'[6] Hamlet is either a pagan in a pagan play, a good Christian in a Christian play, or a sinner in a Christian play.

A Senecan frame of reference seems appropriate in the first four acts of the play, for Hamlet's great need is Stoic tranquillity of mind. He values Horatio because he is 'A man that Fortune's buffets and rewards / Hast ta'en with equal thanks; . . . not a pipe for Fortune's finger / To sound what stop she please . . . not passion's slave' (III, ii, 65-70). By subduing his emotions Horatio frees himself from the effects of fortune and becomes the Stoics' wise and happy man.

It is not the principle of revenge which troubles Hamlet, but the achievement of a state of mind where he can do something coherent about it. Seneca declares,

> The good man will perform his duties undisturbed and unafraid; and he will in such a way do all that is worthy of a good man as to do nothing that is unworthy of a man. My father is being murdered—I will defend him; he is slain—I will avenge him, not because I grieve, but because it is my duty.
>
> (*Moral Essays,* 'De Ira', I, xii, 2)

Hamlet cannot act so calmly; he cannot focus sufficiently coolly upon any matter to determine a policy and carry it through. His most sustained venture is the mouse-trap play but it is all brilliant improvisation. He is nervous and excited before and wildly exuberant afterwards; he vaunts, 'Now could I drink hot blood' (III, ii, 380), but spares the praying King and strikes out recklessly, killing Polonius. Though he has the evidence he sought he leaves at Claudius's command for England. The issue which oppresses Hamlet is not how or whether to be revenged, but how to do anything purposeful at all. In the face of the manifold injunctions, distractions, plots and crimes which assail him he can hardly hold himself single-mindedly to any action.

Hamlet presents himself as an unsuccessful Stoic in his first exchange with Rosencrantz and Guildenstern. They perhaps engaged in light-hearted philosophical banter as students, but here the subtext is their manoeuvring to discover each other's purposes. Rosencrantz denies that Denmark is a prison; Hamlet replies, 'Why, then, 'tis none to you; for there is nothing either good or bad, but thinking makes it so' (II, ii, 248-50). This characteristically Stoic notion usually has a contrary import—that one can be happy and free if the mind chooses. Rosencrantz should be amused but is determined to turn the discussion to ambition. Hamlet replies, more earnestly, 'O God, I could be bounded in a nutshell and count myself a king of infinite space, were it not that I have bad dreams' (II, ii, 253-55). Compare the Chorus in Seneca's *Thyestes*: 'It is the mynde that onely makes a king . . . A kyng hee is that feareth nought at all. / Eche man him selfe this kyngdome geeves at hand.'[7]

It is of course Stoic to entertain suicide as a solution to intolerable emotional pressure. Horatio, at Hamlet's death, terms himself 'more an antique Roman than a Dane' (V, ii, 333). The secular manner in which Hamlet discusses it (III, i, 56-88) recalls the disputes between Oedipus and Antigone in Seneca's *Phoenissae* (1-319), and Deianira, the Nurse and Hyllas in *Hercules Oetaeus* (842-1030). For Seneca it is indeed a 'question' whether it is nobler to suffer or to kill oneself. Death is always the way out, yet it is base to flinch: 'The brave and wise man should not beat a hasty retreat from life.'[8] His main theme is that it is superstitious and irrational to fear death or what might follow it, but such anxieties preoccupy Hamlet, who again falls short of Stoic detachment.

For Seneca, the man who achieves Stoic self-mastery is godlike:

> the wise man is next-door neighbour to the gods and like a god in all save his mortality. As he struggles and presses on towards those things that are lofty, well-ordered, undaunted, that flow on with even and harmonious current, that are untroubled, kindly, adapted to the public good, beneficial both to himself and to others, the wise man will covet nothing low, will never repine.
>
> (*Moral Essays,* 'De Constantia', viii, 2)

Hamlet is perplexed and disillusioned at the failure of this ideal in others and in himself. Man is said to be 'in apprehension, how like a god! the beauty of the world! the paragon of animals! And yet, to me, what is this quintessence of dust?' (II, ii, 303-5). He ponders:

> Sure he that made us with such large discourse,
> Looking before and after, gave us not
> That capability and godlike reason
> To fust in us unus'd.
>
> (IV, iv, 36-9)

But Hamlet is far from such cool judgement and unimpressed by the divine qualities of himself or those around him.

The plausibility of the godlike Stoic hero is questioned in similar terms by Marston in the Antonio plays, which seem strongly to have influenced *Hamlet*. In *Antonio and Mellida* Andrugio affects indifference to the loss of his kingdom but falls at once into a rage when it is mentioned: 'Name not the Genoese; that very word / Unkings me quite, makes me vile passion's slave' (IV, i, 68-9). In *Antonio's Revenge* Pandulpho remains tranquil about the murder of his son for many scenes, but suddenly declares, 'Man will break out, despite philosophy. . . . I spake more than a god, / Yet am less than a man' (IV, iii, 69-75).[9] In fact the inadequacy of Stoicism is implicit in Seneca's writings, where alongside the godlike, rational man is an acute awareness of the difficulty of withstanding the adversities which afflict mankind. Miriam T. Griffin terms it 'the schizophrenia endemic in Stoic philosophy, with its vision of the *sapiens* and its code of behaviour for the *imperfectus*'.[10] In Seneca's plays there are almost no successful Stoics. The eschewal of passion is in theory a stance of strength and self-sufficiency, but it can easily seem a weak, fallback position—a retreat from the intolerable.

What is at issue in *Hamlet* is optimistic humanism—that strand in Renaissance thought which exalted man's capacity to achieve, through the exercise of rational powers, a moral stature which the incautious termed godlike. Even a man of Hamlet's intelligence and sensitivity cannot assert himself in this world and gain a workable degree of self-sufficiency, but is overwhelmed by emotional turmoil and the follies and crimes of his fellow men. When Ophelia laments his instability—'that noble and most sovereign reason, / Like sweet bells jangled, out of time and harsh' (III, i, 157-8)—she draws attention to the collapse of a whole world view.

It is usual and proper to contrast Hamlet with the other young men in the play. But we should notice also that Laertes is no more successful (he kills Hamlet but wishes he had not), and although Fortinbras is presumably elected king of Denmark, this is by chance not design—the throne he and his father fought and schemed for is gained not through their godlike qualities but by default. Only the stolid Horatio approaches the ideal, and when his test comes at the end of the play he is hardly dissuaded from suicide. It seems impossible to act meaningfully in a universe tragically ill-adapted to human kind. The only dignified option seems to be that offered in the plays of Seneca, Webster and Ford: a heroic death.

Thus far we have placed *Hamlet* in a secular context, but Protestant thinkers anticipated the failure of Stoicism. Calvin did not expect fallen men to achieve rationality and equanimity, let alone be godlike; he termed 'absurd' the Stoic hero 'who, divested of humanity, was affected in the same way by adversity and prosperity, grief and joy; or rather, like a stone, was not affected by anything' (*Institutes,* III, viii, 9). The error of 'philosophers generally' is that 'they maintain that the intellect is endued with reason, the best guide to a virtuous and happy life, provided it duly avails itself of its excellence, and exerts the power with which it is naturally endued' (*Institutes,* II, ii, 2). According to the Protestant analysis, we should not be surprised or disappointed at the collapse of the Stoic ideal in *Hamlet*.

Upon his return from England Hamlet seems to have accepted this view. He no longer expects to achieve mastery of himself or his circumstances. In the Graveyard he meditates upon a jester's skull, an emblem of the limits which confound mortal aspirations. The cause of his change seems to be the extraordinary turns events have taken—the appearance of the Ghost when Claudius seemed secure, the arrival of the players prompting the test of the king, Hamlet's felicitous discovery of the plot against his life and above all his amazing delivery through the pirates. The latter especially is so improbable, and so unnecessary to the plot, that we may suppose Shakespeare wishes the audience also to be impressed with the special interventions of providence. Hence when Hamlet describes how he discovered Claudius's letter and changed it he attributes the whole sequence to providence: 'There's a divinity that shapes our ends, / Rough-hew them how we will' (V, ii, 10-11). He was able to seal the altered instructions: 'Why, even in that was heaven ordinant' (V, ii, 48). Thus he reaches the assertion that 'there is a special providence in the fall of a sparrow' (V, ii, 212). In phraseology at least Stoic doctrine has been superseded by Christian.

The choice of Calvin to represent contemporary Protestant opinion should no longer need arguing. Amongst historians his influence upon the Elizabethan Church is scarcely disputed and several literary scholars have recently related it to plays of the period.[11] Calvin is particularly relevant here because he insisted upon the doctrine of providence in the strong form which it takes at this point in *Hamlet*. One axis of his theology is the impotence of fallen humanity; the other is God's total power to govern the world in accord with his divine (though incomprehensible) plan.

Moreover, it is against Stoic fate or fortune that Calvin is arguing when he speaks of special providence and the fall of a sparrow—both in the quotation with which we began and again during the supporting argument:

> The Christian . . . will have no doubt that a special providence is awake for his preservation, and will not suffer anything to happen that will not turn to his good and safety. . . . Hence, our Saviour, after declaring that even a sparrow falls not to the ground without the will of his Father, immediately makes the application, that being more valuable than many sparrows, we ought to consider that God provides more carefully for us.
>
> (*Institutes,* I, xvii, 6)

In Calvin's Latin the words are usually 'singularis providentia'; his French has alternately 'la providence singulière' and 'la providence spéciale'; the translation by Thomas Norton (1561) has both 'singular providence' and 'special providence' (see I, xvi, 1, 4, 7).

Whether the allusion and phraseology shared by Calvin and Hamlet necessarily imply predestination is not entirely clear. Christ's remark about the sparrow is problematic for Christians who assert free will—Erasmus in his argument against Luther is obliged to take it as 'hyperbole'.[12] Bertram Joseph notices the term 'special providence' in several divines (though not Calvin) and thinks it consistent with free will, but he misses the dominant thrust of the phrase and the Reformation when he explains, 'Calvinists, too, could agree . . . that God through His special providence creates the opportunity, and the individual, if he is the right man, will take it'.[13] But Calvin and Luther alike believed that God has predetermined all events, and of the theologians Joseph mentions—William Perkins, Hugh Latimer, Joseph Hall and Lancelot Andrewes—all but the last took the same view. This is the doctrine Elizabethans generally understood in the tenth, eleventh and seventeenth of the Thirty-Nine Articles. When it was challenged at Cambridge in 1595 Archbishop Whitgift (no puritan) sponsored the Lambeth Articles to affirm it; they had no official status but indicate the position of the Church establishment.

Hamlet's words sound like predestination: 'If it be now, 'tis not to come; if it be not to come, it will be now; if it be not now, yet it will come' (V, ii, 213-15); 'ordinant' (V, ii, 48) means 'directing, controlling'. Notice also that in the 'bad' First Quarto Hamlet is made to say, 'theres a predestiuate prouidence in the fall of a sparrow'. Even if this is no more than a faulty memorial construct it shows how one well-placed contemporary understood Shakespeare's meaning. However, my argument does not require that we take Hamlet's phrase as Calvinistic in the fullest sense, only that we see Hamlet proposing a high degree of divine intervention and suggesting predestination.

We seem to have arrived at a Protestant interpretation of *Hamlet:* the prince recognises the folly of humanistic aspiration and the controlling power of providence, and the shape of the action, with purposes eventually falling on the inventors' heads, confirms it. Some readers may wonder why, if the play is governed by providence, it is manifestly composed of 'carnal, bloody, and unnatural acts' (V, ii, 373) with very little of love, mercy and forgiveness. At this point our attention to Calvin is surely justified, for his account of earthly life is as grim as that of any tragedian:

> Various diseases ever and anon attack us: at one time pestilence rages; at another we are involved in all the calamities of war. Frost and hail, destroying the promise of the year, cause sterility, which reduces us to penury; wife, parents, children, relatives, are carried off by death; our house is destroyed by fire. These are the events which make men curse their life, detest the day of their birth, execrate the light of heaven, even censure God, and (as they are eloquent in blasphemy) charge him with cruelty and injustice.
>
> (*Institutes,* III, vii, 10)

Calvin does not repudiate this description of the human condition; nor does he throw any stress upon the consolation of an after-life. Instead he asserts through the concept of providence that all is due to the just will of God.

However dreadful and apparently unfair the affliction, 'the rule of piety is, that the hand of God is the ruler and arbiter of the fortunes of all, and, instead of rushing on with thoughtless violence, dispenses good and evil with perfect regularity' (*Institutes,* III, vii, 10). Calvin sustains this statement mainly by insisting that all men are fallen and sinful and so deserve the worst that can happen to them. Nevertheless, he distinguishes the sufferings of the wicked from those of believers. In the former case, 'God is to be understood as taking vengeance on his enemies, by displaying his anger against them, confounding, scattering, and annihilating them'; in the latter 'it is not properly punishment or vengeance, but correction and admonition' (*Institutes,* III, iv, 31). But all receive afflictions. Even theologians who denied predestination believed with Calvin that human suffering is caused by God intervening in the world to afflict and punish good and bad men. Lancelot Andrewes in his 'Sermon Preached at Chiswick in the Time of Pestilence' (1603) refers to providence and the sparrow to show that God must be the cause of the plague. He concludes, 'So our inventions beget sin, sin provokes the wrath of God, the wrath of God sends the Plague among us.'[14]

The violent and punitive providence of Calvin and even of Andrewes could certainly be the moving force behind the diseased action of Shakespeare's play. Thus it is that Hamlet can claim, with the deaths of his father, Polonius, Ophelia and Rosencrantz and Guildenstern in mind, 'there is a special providence in the fall of a sparrow'. That is how God was believed to manage affairs.

So *Hamlet* appears to be a Christian play in the Elizabethan sense of the term. We are slow to recognise this because we have been taught a more amiable conception of the Christian God. Indeed, dwelling upon the rigorous of Protestant doctrine produces an intriguing solution to the question of how Christian Elizabethans wrote and enjoyed such bleak tragedies. Perhaps it is not that they understood the plays differently from the modern reader: they too saw in *Hamlet* man's feeble attempts to act purposefully in a hostile world. But what they perceived as the working out in typical fashion of God's mysterious providential plan strikes us as bitterly tragic. We read the plays similarly but place them differently in relation to a shifting concept of Christianity.

A whole group of plays might fall within this insight. *The Jew of Malta, The Spanish Tragedy, Richard III, Antonio's Revenge, Macbeth* and *The Revenger's Tragedy* all suggest by the intricate, violent and inexorable way in which events work out that a deity of the Protestant stamp is in control, and the characters often invoke him. They call upon God to destroy the wicked and eventually he does; we need not take ironically their devout satisfaction. The sufferings of innocent by-standers are instances of the crosses we are required to bear.

Yet such an interpretation is not satisfactory for *Hamlet*, and the difficulties emanate from the very speech about providence and the sparrow. The issue is not the killing of the king, the moral status of which seems to be uncertain. Most Reformation Protestants would be pleased at the violent death of a manifest wrongdoer like Claudius, but they would question the action of the killer. Calvin was opposed to private vengeance though he believed that God works through it. However, like Aquinas, he was sympathetic to tyrannicide, at least when performed by lesser magistrates who 'by the ordinance of God' are the 'appointed guardians' of the people (*Institutes,* IV, xx, 31). Tudor propaganda, of course, saw rebellion as the worst of evils, but the Dutch and Huguenots developed from Calvin's hint a complete theory of controlled revolt. Already in the closet scene Hamlet regards himself as Heaven's 'scourge and minister' (III, iv, 175), and just before the appearance of Osric he recalls to Horatio Claudius's manifold crimes and asks,

>   is't not perfect conscience
> To quit him with this arm? And is't not to be damn'd
> To let this canker of our nature come
> In further evil?
>
> (V, ii, 67-70)

Politically, ethically, theologically it can be argued either way.

The more pressing problem is Bradley's sense that the tone and implication of Hamlet's speech, however Christian its terminology, are fatalistic. Some commentators feel that, having recognised God's controlling hand, Hamlet's proper course is to do nothing. This was not Protestant doctrine. Although predestination means that individual actions can make no difference Calvinists, always afraid of antinomianism, urged that the true Christian should show his delight in God's will by co-operating as far as he is able (*Institutes*, I, xvii, 3, 4). Hamlet believes that providence wants Claudius removed and that he should do it—'the interim is mine', he says (V, ii, 73). However, 'the readiness is all' refers not to action but to death. Hamlet plays with Osric (surely this scene is purposely desultory), competes with Laertes and makes no plans against the king. The final killing occurs in a burst of passionate inspiration and when Hamlet himself is, in effect, slain.

Consider also the context of the speech. Hamlet is not making a general statement about the rightness of God's control of the world, but sweeping aside Horatio's very reasonable suspicion about the duel. Thus he ignores Calvin's argument that 'the Lord has furnished men with the arts of deliberation and caution, that they may employ them in subservience to his providence, in the preservation of their life' (*Institutes*, I, xvii, 4). Hamlet's thought has a contrary tendency: he sees no point in troubling about what will happen. And this is implicit in the tone of the speech. Editors disagree about the last line; the Second Quarto has 'since no man of ought he leaves, knowes what ist to leave betimes, let be'. However we emend this, it sounds fatalistic.

Hamlet acknowledges divine determination of events, but without enthusiasm. Our theme turns back upon itself, for his resignation, like his earlier godlike aspiration, is Senecan, Stoic world weariness is felt despite the distinctively Protestant phraseology; the context, the tone of the speech and Hamlet's subsequent inactivity all recall the quotation from 'De Providentia' with which we began: 'it was settled at the first hour of birth what length of time remains for each. . . . Therefore everything should be endured with fortitude, since things do not, as we suppose, simply happen—they all come.' Playing upon the ambivalence in Seneca's work, Shakespeare is developing the sense of futility which often underlies the theory of rational self-sufficiency. And this is in the very teeth of Calvinist doctrine for, as I have observed, it is actually whilst repudiating Stoic fate that Calvin alludes to providence and the sparrow. The Stoics 'feign a universal providence, which does not condescend to take special care of every creature' (*Institutes,* I, xvii, 6; see also I, xvi, 8), and it is against such an impersonal force that Calvin and Hamlet maintain a 'special providence' which cares for every individual in every detail of his life.

The intricate working out of events obliges Hamlet to recognise the precise control of the Protestant God but he does not find in himself the joyful response theologians anticipated. Calvin distinguished Stoic patience, which accepts what happens because 'so it must be', and Christian, which cheerfully embraces God's will 'with calm and grateful minds' (*Institutes*, III, viii, 11). Hamlet contemplates God's intimate and pervasive direction of the universe with only Stoic patience. It makes him wonder; temporarily, when he is sending Rosencrantz and Guildenstern to their doom, it exhilarates him; but ultimately it depresses him. 'There is a special providence in the fall of a sparrow' and in the corruption and suffering of Denmark, and it inspires in Hamlet not joyful co-operation but weary acquiescence. His attitude provokes the thought that the world is unjustly governed by such a God.

Commentators have disagreed about Hamlet's attitude to providence because it is confused, but I believe purposefully. Shakespeare is exploiting the contradictions in Stoicism and the embarrassments in Calvinism. For those who assert a beneficent order in the universe there are two alternatives with the problem of evil. One is that God allows considerable freedom to his creation; the danger here is that things begin to get out of control, the sense of God's concern slips away and we might as well regard events as absurd or the work of blind fortune. The other alternative is that God is in complete control, but then he has to assume an awkwardly immediate responsibility for evil. Seneca tries to slide between these two positions, partly by saying different things at different times, partly by proposing controlling gods who do not concern themselves with details.

The dilemma should trouble all Christians but Calvin confronts it head on: his doctrine of providence asserts defiantly that God directs everything and that he is perfectly good. All unpleasantness in the world occurs immediately and justly by God's will, and mere men should not expect to understand. Yet Calvin tries to explain, and runs repeatedly into difficulties. For instance, is it fair that God refuses to allow a man like Claudius (or Dr Faustus) to repent?

> To some it seems harsh, and at variance with the divine mercy, utterly to deny forgiveness to any who betake themselves to it. This is easily disposed of. It is not said that pardon will be refused if they turn to the Lord, but it is altogether denied that they can turn to repentance, inasmuch as for their ingratitude they are struck by the just judgment of God with eternal blindness.
>
> (*Institutes*, III, iii, 24)

Calvin falls back continually upon assertion and divine inscrutability: 'The will of God is the supreme rule of righteousness, so that everything which he wills must be held to be righteous by the mere fact of his willing it' (*Institutes*, III, xxiii, 2).

Calvin argues rigorously from his first principles and with ample scriptural support, and creates a superbly self-contained system. But he cannot make it satisfy ordinary, common sense morality. It is not that one cannot easily assemble signs of the operations of such a deity in the world; what is unacceptable is the demand that we marvel at its goodness and mercy. My contention is that the paradoxes of Protestant theology provoked alarm and confusion and that it is apparent in *Hamlet* and other tragedies.

Evidence of humane objections to Protestant orthodoxy ranges from Andrewes's complaint that the Lambeth Articles make God appear unjust to the development by General Baptists from about 1600 of a doctrine of universal salvation. Robert Burton (who, it may be noted, condemns in Calvin's manner Seneca's concept of fate)[15] describes fully, among the 'Causes of Despair' in religion, how Calvin's favourite Biblical sentences

> terrify the souls of many; election, predestination, reprobation, preposterously conceived, offend divers, with a deal of foolish presumption, curiosity, needless speculation, contemplation, solicitude, wherein they trouble and puzzle themselves about those questions of grace, free will, perseverance, God's secrets.
>
> (*Anatomy of Melancholy*, III, 398-9)

Burton himself seems to hanker after a liberal theology: 'For how can he be merciful that shall condemn any creature to eternal unspeakable punishment . . . But these absurd paradoxes are exploded by our Church, we teach otherwise'—and he goes on to restate Calvinist orthodoxy (III, 423-4).

Surely we cannot overestimate the impact upon the Reformation mind of the Church's insistence upon attributing good and bad alike to a special providence whose justice cannot be demonstrated to the ordinary intellect. It has much to do, I believe, with the peculiar theological stance of many Elizabethan tragedies. We have observed that characters often call upon a violent deity whose controlling presence is eventually confirmed by the intricate working out of events. At the same time, the beneficence of this system is brought into question by our sympathy for the characters, by the provocative interweaving of Jove, revenge, fate and fortune with Christian divinities, by a pervasive fatalism and by the harshness of some attitudes attributed to the deity—in *Antonio's Revenge*, for instance, the ghost of Andrugio declares, 'Now looks down providence / T'attend the last act of my son's revenge' (V, i, 10-11). We may be able to demonstrate from the *Institutes* the broad compatibility of such plays with Protestantism but we cannot feel comforted by the world they present. Hence the appeal of Seneca to Elizabethan dramatists: Stoicism offers complex variations upon Christianity in respect of its estimate of man and its conception of divine power. All this manifests a deep unease with Christian doctrine as it was customarily preached. These writers have gone half-way with Calvin: they are convinced that men are fallen and in a fallen world but have only nominal confidence in God's redemptive goodness. They lurch back towards fatalism; it is a recipe for tragedy.

Hamlet presents this dissatisfaction with orthodox theology in an unusually coherent form. By undermining humanistic Stoicism and positing a controlling deity in words deriving from Calvin the play takes us to the brink of a Protestant affirmation, but Hamlet's fatalistic attitude encourages us to question divine justice. We understand and respect his reluctance to co-operate with a divinity whose doings are so arbitrary and overwhelming. Senecan resignation seems a reasonable response.

It will be felt that I have been teasing out strands in popular plays that only a theologian would recognise in the theatre. This is true: the disquiet of these writers with Protestant doctrine was probably scarcely formulated. Their plays do not present a coherent philosophy but a confused sense of alarm and wonderment at the mysterious ways of providence. However, Marlowe for one seems fully conscious of the distinction between pagan and Christian and how it may be used to suggest a critique of providence. *The Jew of Malta* concludes, 'So march away; and let due praise be given, / Neither to Fate nor Fortune, but to Heaven.'[16] Ferneze prefers Christian doctrine to pagan and attributes events to God's providence, but the action makes us wonder whether fate or fortune is not a more likely presiding deity. In *Hamlet* Christian statements supersede pagan ones in a theologically precise form, but the action remains ambiguous.

Notes

1. Plays by Shakespeare are quoted from the *Complete Works,* ed. Peter Alexander (London and Glasgow, 1951). Unattributed act, scene and line numbers are from *Hamlet.*

2. John Calvin, *Calvin's Institutes,* [trans. Henry Beveridge], (Florida, n.d.), I, xvi, 1.

3. Seneca, *Moral Essays,* trans. John W. Basore, 3 vols (Loeb edition, London and Cambridge, Mass., 1958), 'De Providentia', v. 7.

4. A. C. Bradley, *Shakespearean Tragedy* (1960), p. 116. See also H. B. Charlton, *Shakespearian Tragedy* (Cambridge, 1949), pp. 103-4.

5. *Shakespeare and Christian Doctrine* (Princeton, 1963), p. 231. See also Ivor Morris, *Shakespeare's God* (1972), pp. 422-30.

6. *Shakespearean Tragedy, its Art and its Christian Premises* (Bloomington, 1969), p. 250. See also Lily B. Campbell, *Shakespeare's Tragic Heroes* (New York, 1966), pp. 141-7.

7. *Seneca, his Tenne Tragedies,* ed. Thomas Newton (1581), 2 vols (New York, 1967), I, 67.

8. Seneca, *Ad Lucilium Epistulae Morales,* trans. Richard M. Gunmere, 3 vols (Loeb edition, Cambridge, Mass. and London, 1961), XXIV, 25.

9. Ed. G. K. Hunter (1965, 1966).

10. *Seneca, a Philosopher in Politics* (Oxford, 1976), p. 177.

11. See Frye, *Shakespeare and Christian Doctrine;* William R. Elton, *King Lear and the Gods* (San Marino, 1968); Dominic Baker-Smith, 'Religion and John Webster' in Brian Morris, ed., *John Webster* (1970); Paul R. Sellin, 'The Hidden God' in *The Darker Vision of the Renaissance,* ed. Robert S. Kinsman (Berkeley and London, 1974); Robert G. Hunter, *Shakespeare and the Mystery of the Gods* (Georgia, 1976).

12. *Luther and Erasmus: Free Will and Salvation,* ed. E. Gordon Rupp and Philip S. Watson (1969), pp. 83-4.

13. Bertram Joseph, *Conscience and the King* (1953), p. 139; also pp. 136-41.

14. Lancelot Andrewes, *Works,* 11 vols (Oxford, 1854), V, 224, 234.

15. *The Anatomy of Melancholy,* ed. Holbrook Jackson, 3 vols (1968), III, 385, 387.

16. *The Plays of Christopher Marlowe,* ed. Roma Gill (Oxford, 1971).

James C. Bryant (essay date 1984)

Bryant, James C. "Shakespeare's Use of Religious Controversy in *King John.*" In *Tudor Drama and Religious Controversy,* pp. 129-49. Macon, Ga.: Mercer University Press, 1984.

[*In the following essay, Bryant maintains that in* King John *Shakespeare was able to achieve a measure of objectivity in his treatment of late fifteenth-century religious disputes.*]

Shakespeare was too much an artist and too much a businessman to make himself vulnerable to either the antitheatre officials in London or the anti-Romanist agents at Court. He wrote for a popular audience and was completely dependent upon the pleasure of that general public during the last decade of the sixteenth century. It seems unlikely, therefore, that Shakespeare would have used the stage to support his private notions about religion. At first he seemed more interested in reflecting public taste, not in prescribing it.

Like other successful dramatists of his period, Shakespeare held the mirror up to not only nature but also contemporary attitudes, including the instinctive religious beliefs of his audience. That mirror reflected the attitudes and fears generated by the recent, infamous Spanish Armada and its resultant surge of anti-Roman Catholic hostility in the name of patriotism.

Hostility against Roman Catholic subversive activity reached an apex in 1591 when Elizabeth issued a proclamation against Jesuit missionary priests. Two years later the hostility against all Roman Catholics was so pronounced that Parliament passed the Act Against Recusants.

The Preamble of that document reflects the official view concerning Roman Catholics in England.

> For the better discovering and avoiding of all such traitorous and most dangerous conspiracies and attempts as are daily devised and practiced against our most gracious sovereign lady the queen's majesty and the happy estate of this commonweal, by sundry wicked and seditious persons, who, terming themselves Catholics, and being indeed spies and intelligencers, not only for her majesty's foreign enemies, but also for rebellious and traitorous subjects born within her highness's realms and dominions, and hiding their most detestable and devilish purposes under a false pretext of religion and conscience, do secretly wander and shift from place to place within this realm, to corrupt and seduce her majesty's subjects, and to stir them to sedition and rebellion. . . .[1]

The act, in short, provided that every English subject older than the age of sixteen, "being a popish recusant" and refusing to attend divine services of the Church of England, would be restricted to his place of residence, from which he was forbidden to travel more than a distance of five miles.

An anonymous play entitled *Troublesome Reign of King John* was printed in 1591, right in the midst of general anti-Roman Catholic hostility. It is as vitriolic as Bale's play. It was also in the midst of anti-Roman Catholic hostility that Shakespeare wrote his own *King John*, and for the same audience as the anonymous play. Since the days of Henry VIII's reformation of the Church of England, the historical King John had been regarded as a champion of English kings against the usurpation of Roman bishops. If Shakespeare did not have his fingers upon the pulse of the nation, it is impossible to explain why he chose such a subject as King John for a play at all.

It has been customary to say that Shakespeare's *King John* is a condensation of the anonymous *Troublesome Reign*, and that Shakespeare's play was written sometime during the years 1594-1597. But one editor, E. A. J. Honigmann, in the new Arden edition (1954), argues for an earlier date, 1590 or 1591. That would mean, of course, that Shakespeare's play would have had no necessary relationship to the *Troublesome Reign*, and that the *Troublesome Reign* could have been an expansion of Shakespeare's original. In view of the evidence we now have, there is as much to favor Honigmann's view as the traditional one. Should the earlier date theory prevail, all of the scholarship based upon Shakespeare's omission or toning down of the Roman Catholic derogation contained in the *Troublesome Reign* would have to be reevaluated.

Since placing a date on the writing of *King John* is an impossibility in view of present evidence, it seems far more beneficial to read Shakespeare's play without reference to the *Troublesome Reign*. And, of course, by reading *King John* as a self-contained whole, one is left with what is most desirable: Shakespeare's writing.

Shakespeare's *The Life and Death of King John*,[2] unlike most of the Tudor drama in which the religious controversy plays a significant part, successfully avoids many individual grievances of Protestants against Catholics by sustaining the essentially Anglican point of view in matters of church and state that had been brought down in history from the time of William the Conqueror. That is, in the controversy between England and Rome, neither the English Church nor the English nation was to be dominated by foreign powers.

Shakespeare, with remarkable restraint when one considers the anti-Roman Catholic temper during the period of the play's composition, presents the bitter conflict as a matter of politics rather than merely a religious quarrel. Consequently, he raises certain questions in the drama which lift the entire problem above the vitriolic charges and countercharges for which the sixteenth century is noted.

The questions Shakespeare raises in *King John* are these: Does a king rule his dominions by the grace of God or by the grace of the pope? Does a *de facto* king have the right to expect absolute loyalty and obedience from his subjects, even when his right to the succession is questionable? Is rebellion against the king ever justifiable, even when the king proves to be wicked and an enemy of the Church? Do foreign princes have the right to interfere with a Christian king's administration of his own dominions? Having been raised to hear questions such as these resolved by the enforced preaching of the *Book of Homilies*, Shakespeare's audience would have known the right answer to a man. Further, official censorship would have guaranteed the correct response by dramatists in their plays.

When Shakespeare stresses the political nature of the religious dispute with Rome, he is writing within the range of a wide historical background, thoroughly familiar to the audience during the last decade of the century. It is no accident, therefore, that *King John* begins with allusions to the question of usurpation. While the king may have succeeded by "borrowed Majesty," the problem of usurpation is dealt with on several levels as a recurring theme throughout the play.

From an Anglican point of view, however, the most detestable usurpation was perpetrated by the Roman papacy. One recalls that the queen had begun her reign upon the assumption that the popes had usurped ancient royal prerogatives by interfering with the internal affairs of England's citizens and her Church. Elizabeth's Act of Supremacy (1559) abolished all papal jurisdiction in England, so that "all usurped and foreign power and authority, spiritual and temporal" could be removed forever.[3] Her Royal Injunctions (1559) began by ordering all ecclesiastics to preach sermons against papal usurpation. It need not be surprising to learn that homilies and propaganda tracts of the period coupled the name of the pope with usurpation.

If English subjects were not convinced already, Pope Pius V's bull excommunicating and deposing Elizabeth (1570) reinforced the charge of usurpation. In that document Pius referred to himself as "chief over all nations and all kingdoms, to pluck up, destroy, scatter, dispose, plant and build . . ."[4] The presence of the papal legate, Cardinal Pandulph, onstage would have been a sufficient reminder to Shakespeare's audience that the question of Rome's usurpation was still a live issue.

In act 3 Shakespeare implicitly raises the question of whether a king rules in his own right by the grace of God, or whether he rules by permission of the pope. Pandulph, as legate from Rome, demands to know why King John defies the Holy Church by refusing to admit Stephen Langton, the pope's choice for England's archbishop of Canterbury. John answers as Henry VIII or Elizabeth would have answered: "What earthly name to interrogatories / Can task the free breath of a sacred king?" (3.1.147-148).

Ironically, Pandulph had made his entrance by addressing King John and King Philip of France as "you anointed deputies of Heaven!" Perhaps without realizing it, Pandulph gives lip service to the divine right of kings, while his message from the pope would seem to deny that right. It may be recalled that John Bale's *King John* had centered the stage action upon this very point: a king was God's anointed minister to rule over his people. As such, he was answerable to no other power under heaven. Henry's assumption of the title "Supreme Head" (1531) was an affirmation of the right to rule his own dominions in matters spiritual and temporal, answerable to God alone. Elizabeth recognized her function as "Supreme Governor as well in all spiritual or ecclesiastical things or causes, as temporal." Political tracts and certain official homilies had stressed the point that kings, whether good or evil, reigned by divine sanction. Consequently, when John answers the cardinal, his words carry the whole force of the English understanding of a king's divine right to rule his dominions without interference from any foreign power, temporal or spiritual.

John's antipapal remarks can be seen, within the context of the times, not as being derogatory to the Roman Catholic Church but as an expression of the Reformation position. That position sees the pope as merely the bishop of Rome and an Italian priest with no more legal rights in the king's dominions than any other ecclesiastic.

> Thou canst not, Cardinal, devise a name
> So slight, unworthy, and ridiculous
> To charge me to an answer, as the Pope.
> Tell him this tale; and from the mouth of England
> Add thus much more: that no Italian priest
> Shall tithe or toll in our dominions,
> But as we, under Heaven, are supreme head,
> So under Him that great supremacy,
> Where we do reign, we will alone uphold
> Without the assistance of a mortal hand.
> So tell the Pope, all reverence set apart
> To him and his usurped authority.
>
> (3.1.149-160)

The point is clear: John assumes the Anglican position that his authority to reign is independent of the pope's claims to the contrary. As Supreme Head of the Church in England, John does not require assistance from the pontiff. As Supreme Head he also retains Edward the Confessor's precedents of investing his own primate and administering ecclesiastical affairs in the national Church. Elizabeth had demonstrated her position when she wrote to Dr. Richard Cox, bishop of Ely, demanding his conformity: "You know what you were before I made you what you are now. If you do not immediately comply with my requests, I will unfrock you, by God."[5] Elizabeth did not unfrock Archbishop Grindal, but when he refused to comply with her wishes, she placed him under house arrest for five years and assumed his duties personally. Thus, John does not reply to Cardinal Pandulph as a spiritual subject of the Roman See, but as a "sacred king" who is subject only to God. Whenever the bishop of Rome attempts to interfere with this normal state of affairs, he does so by "usurped authority."

The whole issue became clear in the Restraint of Appeals Act (1533) in which the king of England is referred to as the embodiment of ancient power, under whom "spiritualty and temporalty, be bounden and ought to bear, next to God, a natural and humble obedience," for he rules by the sufferance of Almighty God and without restraint from any foreign powers. The act reiterates the statutes of the realm passed during the reigns of Edward I, Edward III, Richard II, Henry IV, and others, in an effort to preserve ancient royal prerogatives from the "annoyance" of the Roman See as well as "other foreign potentates."[6]

The important First Act of Succession (1534) began with the explanation that such legislation is necessary because "the Bishop of Rome, and see apostolic, contrary to the great and inviolable grants of jurisdictions given by God immediately to emperors, kings, and princes, in succession to their heirs, has presumed, in times past, to invest who should please them, to inherit in other men's kingdoms and dominions."[7] Significantly, the act acknowledged England as "an imperial realm," in which Henry VIII maintained the status of any other emperor: "*rex est imperator in regno suo.*" Clearly, Shakespeare's audience was prepared to share in King John's reply to Cardinal Pandulph and would have maintained that the king rules in his dominions without prerequisite permission from Rome.

King Philip probably represents a standard Roman Catholic response to John's bold defiance of papal jurisdiction: "Brother of England, you blaspheme in this" (3.1.161). After all, Pope Boniface VIII's famous *Unam Sanctam* bull (1302) was still in force as a reminder to loyal Roman Catholics that "it is altogether necessary to salvation for every human creature to be subject to the Roman pontiff."[8] Thus when King John derogates the papal office, he also defies the sacred decisions of Church Councils and popes over the course of several centuries.

But King John deviates from the general principle under discussion and alludes to certain objectionable features of Roman Catholic practices in a manner not characteristic of Shakespeare at his best. John answers Philip's charge:

> Though you and all the kings of Christendom
> Are led so grossly by this meddling priest,
> Dreading the curse that money may buy out,
> And by the merit of vile gold, dross, dust,
> Purchase corrupted pardon of a man
> Who in that sale sells pardon from himself,
> Though you and all the rest so grossly led
> This juggling witchcraft with revenue cherish,
> Yet I alone, alone do me oppose
> Against the Pope and count his friends my foes.
>
> (3.1.162-171)

Pardons and indulgences were among the chief objects of Luther's attack upon the Church, and they remained the objects of abuse and satire throughout the century. In John's derogation of the "meddling priest," the commonplace ridicule of the "curse that money may buy out" is not unlike similar attacks reflected in stage plays during the polemical period of the English Reformation. Elizabethans of the Settlement period would have understood John's implication of the Reformation position that while pardons may be purchased, it is for the profitable market of man and not sanctioned by Scripture, for only God has the power to pardon sin. Moreover, the allusion to indulgences as a part of "juggling witchcraft" is little different from official statutes of the realm which never seemed to tire of associating Roman Catholic practices with superstition.

The inclusion of such allusions at this point is further evidence of how closely Shakespeare reflects the attitudes of the Elizabethan Settlement of Religion. The audience may have seen John's solitary position among the temporal sovereigns of Europe as essentially the position of England during the period of the Counter-Reformation. For Shakespeare's audience, Elizabeth alone of the reigning princes was not "grossly led" by "witchcraft" to fill the coffers of Rome. Recent plots against the government not only placed English Roman Catholics under official surveillance as potential traitors, but almost of necessity "friends" of the pope became "foes" of the Protestant queen's government. Thus, John's anachronistic position had particular relevance for Shakespeare's audience because John's reply reflects precise English attitudes of the Reformation.

A second question Shakespeare's play raises demanded considerably more delicacy in handling on the stage: Does a *de facto* king have the right to expect absolute loyalty, even when his right to the succession is questionable? It required particular delicacy on Shakespeare's part because of the very tenuous claim to succession by the House of Tudor.

In the play, France accuses John of disregarding the natural order of succession by usurping the throne with utter disregard for Prince Arthur's more immediate right to the succession. John vindicates his role by implying that might makes right, "Our strong possession and our right for us" (1.1.39). Queen Mother Elinor responds to this significantly. "Your strong possession much more than your right, / Or else it must go wrong with you and me" (1.1.40-41).

When Elinor and Constance debate the relative merits of the right of succession, Elinor says, ". . . Thou unadvised scold, I can produce / A will that bars the title of thy son" (2.1.191-192).

Thus far the problem is one which no doubt had occurred to Shakespeare's audience. Not only had the right of the Scottish line been overlooked in the English succession, but Mary Stuart had bypassed her own son, by terms of her will, in favor of Philip II of Spain as heir apparent. Moreover, while Cardinal Pandulph's quarrel with John is not at first directly concerned with his "usurpation" or his right to succeed to the throne, Pope Pius V's *Regnans in excelis* (1570), excommunicating and deposing Elizabeth, had expressed the common Romanist position that Elizabeth was not the rightful successor to the throne. Pius's bull deprived the queen "of her pretended right to the aforesaid realm."

The first Tudor king had solved the problem about his right to succession, even when there remained the possibility of Yorkist heirs more immediate in the line of succession. Henry VII helped secure his position on the throne by a marriage with a descendant of Edward IV, and in 1495 he led Parliament to enact legislation making it no treason to obey a *de facto* king. John seems to share the Tudor point of view by asking a most significant question, "Doth not the crown of England prove the King?" (2.1.273).

The problem of a dubious access to the throne can not justify the attitude assumed by the citizens of Angiers. They will not recognize King John nor obey him until they are assured that he is the rightful king: ". . . but he that proves the King, / To him will we prove loyal" (2.1.270-271).

An Elizabethan audience would probably have felt that France's "usurpation" of England's right to obey a crowned king was, as it proved to be in the case of Lewis, a mere pretext for personal gain. By the same token, Roman Catholic charges that England's queen had no right to rule would probably have impressed the audience as being a variation on the same theme, except in this case for the personal advantage of the pope.

At any rate, the fact that a king ruled in England by sanction of the Parliament should have been sufficient to answer the question about dubious rights to succession, and this had been the most effective means of answering those who pressed Mary Stuart's claims.

A third question raised by Shakespeare's play provides more effective dramatic possibilities: Is rebellion against the king ever justifiable, even when the king proves to be wicked and an enemy of the Church? No matter how much Englishmen may have changed their point of view on this question before the year 1649 when King Charles I was beheaded by Parliamentary consent, Shakespeare's audience had been instructed over a long period of time in the doctrine that rebellion against the prince was among the gravest sins imaginable. It was a part of the doctrine of Tudor absolutism.

The most relevant part of the rebellion theme occurs in act 3 when Cardinal Pandulph excommunicates King John.

> Then, by the lawful power that I have,
> Thou shalt stand cursed and excommunicate.
> And blessèd shall he be that doth revolt
> From his allegiance to an heretic;
> And meritorious shall that hand be called,
> Canónizèd and worshipped as a saint,
> That takes away by any secret course
> Thy hateful life.
>
> (3.1.172-179)

Actually, such a charge against Roman Catholic policy had been at the heart of several plots to assassinate the queen, even extending to late in the century. For example, as late as 1594 one Hugh Cahill, an Irishman, is reported to have confessed voluntarily "that when at Brussels, Father Holt and others said it would be a most blessed thing to kill the Queen, as by it he would win Heaven, and become a saint if he should be killed; he that would do it would be chronicled for ever."[9]

Sir Edward Coke, solicitor general, described a number of Roman Catholic attempts to incite rebellion and kill the queen.

> To this end many needy and desperate young men are seduced by Jesuits and seminary priests with great rewards and promises to kill the Queen, being persuaded that it is glorious and meritorious, and that if they die in this action, they will inherit Heaven and be canonized as saints.[10]

Two pamphlets written probably by Cardinal Allen for distribution upon the occasion of the Spanish invasion (1588) are significant for the light they bring to this dark business. The first calls Elizabeth "an incestuous bastard, begotten and born in sin of an infamous courtesan," and it calls upon Roman Catholics in England to rise up in arms against the "infamous, depraved, accursed, excommunicate heretic."[11] The second, called *Declaration,* calls for the "deprivation and deposition" of the queen in the pope's name, and for those who help to capture "the said usurper or any of her accomplices," Plenary Indulgence is to be allowed.[12]

The point of view expressed in Allen's pamphlets is reinforced by Pope Gregory XIII's license for political assassination. Gregory had told a group of assassins that "whoever sends 'the Queen' out of the world with the pious intention of doing God service . . . gains merit."[13] Other allegations of ecclesiastical sanction of the assassination of Elizabeth are recorded by Holinshed in connection with various conspiracies centered around Mary Stuart's claims to the throne.[14]

The question of rebellion seems to fascinate Shakespeare. In the play, Pandulphus calls upon English citizens in the name of His Holiness to rebel against an heretical king. On the other hand, John Bale's thesis was that citizens never have a right to rebel, even when the king may be wicked, for rebellion against God's anointed minister is tantamount to rebellion against God Himself. Shakespeare seems to champion this doctrine in his plays, although it would have been practically impossible for him to have done otherwise in view of the vigilance of official censors.

The Northern Rebellion (1569) may have prompted the addition of the important homily "Against Disobedience and Wilful Rebellion" (1571) in the official *Book of Homilies.* It would have been difficult for any man in Shakespeare's audience to have escaped hearing this homily many times during his lifetime. Yet the homily is little more than a summation of absolutist doctrine extending from the first Tudor king and reiterated by statesmen and ecclesiastics of the New Faith for most of the century.[15] The homily repeats the point from Paul's epistle to the Romans that Bale's *King John* had expressed: "The powers that be are ordained of God. Whosoever therefore resisteth the power, resisteth the ordinance of God: and they that resist shall receive to themselves damnation" (Romans 13:1-2). The scriptural passage goes on to say that even wicked kings rule according to God's will and must be obeyed as though they were good. The homily further maintains that Satan is the author of rebellion.

The homily "Against Disobedience and Wilful Rebellion" discusses the possibility that the king may prove to be an enemy of the Church, and if he does, what should be the attitude of his subjects toward obeying his will? In the play, Cardinal Pandulph has stated the attitude of the papacy just as clearly as Pope Pius V had stated it in *Regnans in excelsis:* subjects are absolved from oaths of loyalty in such a case, and they are forbidden to obey an heretical sovereign. In 1580, however, Pope Gregory XIII qualified Pius's bull by allowing English Romanists to obey and accept Elizabeth as queen "*rebus sic stantibus.*" But, of course, the implication is that when the rebellion came, Roman Catholics in England were to be released from oaths of loyalty and participate in the rebellion against the queen's government.

But the homily states emphatically that subjects are no more qualified to judge the merits of their king than the foot is qualified to judge the head: the result could only be rebellion. And rebellion is the greatest of all mischiefs. Moreover, a rebel is worse than the worst prince, and rebellion is far worse than the worst government of the worst prince. Just as Bale had cited scriptural texts to indicate examples of good men who obeyed bad kings, the homily recites examples of those who obeyed wicked rulers, even when it meant great personal discomfort: for example, the Virgin, in advanced pregnancy, obeyed a decree of Caesar Augustus to submit to an official census. Indeed, says the homilist, rebellion represents a combination of all the sins against God and humanity.

Curiously, in the play John's subjects do not seem to rebel against him because of the cardinal's injunction. Shakespeare suggests rather that there are other motives more immediate than the pope's deposition. For example, Englishmen at large are in a state of unrest because they believe that King John is responsible for Prince Arthur's death. Hubert de Burgh relates to John the strange goings-on in the city and the widespread rumors circulating among the commoners: "Young Arthur's death is common in their mouths" (4.2.187). Even when the nobles are about to rebel against their king, it is not because of any religious dispute; it is because their king has abandoned what great princes must safeguard—magnanimity. Salisbury reflects the rumor concerning Arthur's death: "It is apparent foul play, and 'tis shame / That greatness should so grossly offer it" (4.2.93-94). It is after the nobles have discovered Arthur's dead body that Salisbury justifies his decision to rebel against his king upon the basis of John's wickedness.

> The King hath dispossessed himself of us.
> We will not line his thin bestainèd cloak
> With our pure honors, nor attend the foot
> That leaves the print of blood where'er it walks.
>
> (4.3.23-26)

By the time rebellion breaks out in earnest, King John has submitted to Rome and acknowledged England as a papal fief. But even before the king's submission, Pembroke implies that Pandulph's deposition did not alter John's status as England's king.

> This "once again," but that your Highness pleased,
> Was once superfluous. You were crowned before,
> That that high royalty was ne'er plucked off,
> The faiths of men ne'er stainèd with revolt.
> Fresh expectation troubled not the land
> With any longed-for change or better state.
>
> (4.2.3-8)

Indeed, it is not a question of rebellion caused by the pope's demands, but of rebellion that occurs against a king who apparently has proven himself an evil ruler by "murdering" Arthur.

While the commoners and nobles may seem to have just cause for rebellion against their king, Shakespeare continues to deal with the question by demonstrating the truth expressed in the homily "Against Disobedience and Wilful Rebellion." That is, rebellion is worse than the worst government of the worst prince. Salisbury, expressing the outrage of the "distempered lords," not only determines to cease obeying his king, but he also dedicates himself to vengeance.

> It is the shameful work of Hubert's hand,
> The practice and the purpose of the King;
> From whose obedience I forbid my soul,
> Kneeling before this ruin of sweet life,
> And breathing to his breathless excellence
> The incense of a vow, a holy vow,
> Never to taste the pleasures of the world,
> Never to be infected with delight

> Nor conversant with ease and idleness
> Till I have set a glory to this hand
> By giving it the worship of revenge.
>
> (4.3.62-72)

The practical consequence of rebellion in the realm is the invasion by the French. To Shakespeare's highly patriotic and freedom-loving audience, nothing could have been more detestable, except perhaps a similar invasion by the Spanish. One can imagine the effect upon the audience hearing the Bastard's account of French successes.

> All Kent hath yielded. Nothing there holds out
> But Dover Castle. London hath received,
> Like a kind host, the Dauphin and his powers.
> Your nobles will not hear you, but are gone
> To offer service to your enemy,
> And wild amazement hurries up and down
> The little number of your doubtful friends.
>
> (5.1.30-36)

John submits to Rome only because he seeks to avoid the bloodshed of his subjects. Yet as he submits, the Bastard reflects a thoroughly English spirit of Elizabethan patriotism in his response to the news of John's new peace with the papacy.

> Oh, inglorious league!
> Shall we, upon the footing of our land,
> Send fair-play orders and make compromise,
> Insinuation, parley, and base truce
> To arms invasive?
>
> (5.1.65-69)

It is almost too late when the rebels discover what a dear price England must pay for rebellion. With the Dauphin installed in London and refusing to cease hostilities, even after the pretext of invasion has been removed, the rebels realize, perhaps for the first time, that foreign domination by a greedy French prince will be the consequence of their own disloyalty and rebellion.

In such a case, rebellion proved to be worse than any alleged evil on the king's part. The rebels have committed an unnatural sin against God's laws in taking up arms against their anointed king and in betraying England to a foreign prince. Shakespeare underscores this point by assigning to the Bastard—here the voice of English nationalism—the most celebrated lines of the play.

> This England never did, nor never shall,
> Lie at the proud foot of a conqueror
> But when it first did help to wound itself.
> Now these her princes are come home again,
> Come the three corners of the world in arms,
> And we shall shock them. Naught shall make us rue
> If England to itself do rest but true.[16]
>
> (5.7.112-118)

Shakespeare's audience, if not convinced before, could hardly avoid a proper response to the question of justifiable rebellion, even in the case of a wicked king who may be an enemy of the Church. It is certainly possible that Shakespeare may have had English Roman Catholics in mind when he raised the question, since Cardinal Allen and the papacy assumed that Roman Catholics would rise up in armed rebellion when the anticipated foreign invasion of England began.

A fourth question raised by Shakespeare's play would have been timely while bringing into focus the case of John's submission to Rome and a clear example of Rome's policy with dissenting nations: Do foreign princes have the right to interfere with a king's administration of his own dominions?

The answer would have been easy for the highly nationalistic English of Shakespeare's day. But such an answer would have presupposed the whole controversy with the papacy reaching back to the days of William the Conqueror. William's case was well known: he was willing to accept the pope's spiritual jurisdiction, but he would not acknowledge Rome's temporal claims within his dominions. William insisted, successfully, upon the ancient right of English kings to appoint their own bishops (lay investiture). Yet when the German Henry insisted upon similar claims, Pope Hildebrand deposed him and forced his submission in the snow of Canossa. By acting as both governor of the Church in England and Defender of the Faith, William the Conqueror limited papal jurisdiction in England.

By the time Shakespeare's play was composed, the temporal claims of the papacy had increased to the point that loyal Roman Catholics could acknowledge as their sovereigns only those whom the papacy permitted. The right of a prince to rule in his dominions was dependent upon a prerequisite of obedience and loyalty to the Holy See. If a sovereign defected from such obedience, or if he succeeded to the throne without papal consent, the pope could depose him as a heretic and call upon loyal Catholic countries to effect the deposition.

On the other hand, throughout the Middle Ages England had maintained that while her kings owed spiritual fealty to Rome, the papacy had no right to interfere with the temporal administration of matters claimed by royal prerogatives from the time of Edward the Confessor. By the time of the English Reformation, the changed conception of papal jurisdiction could be regarded by England only as papal usurpation.

In the play, act 1 proposes a war between France and England on the pretext that John is a usurper. Consequently, France claims the right to invade England, if necessary, since John's usurpation "religiously provokes" such recourse. But Shakespeare makes it clear that France's real motive is more one of personal gain than religious provocation. As Philip confesses, France came to champion the widow Constance's claims for Arthur, but dropped the cause in favor of personal advantage and greed: ". . . In her right we came; / Which we, God knows, have turned another way / To our own vantage" (2.1.548-550).

The Bastard exemplifies the perceptive English subject as he comments upon France's apparent duplicity, "fickle France," and he rightly sees that commodity is the real motivating factor in France's enterprise. In act 3, Cardinal Pandulph almost parallels instances of papal policy by urging Prince Lewis to invade England.

> The bastard Faulconbridge
> Is now in England, ransacking the Church,
> Offending charity. If but a dozen French
> Were there in arms, there would be as a call
> To train ten thousand English to their side,
> Or as a little snow, tumbled about,
> Anon becomes a mountain. O noble Dauphin,
> Go with me to the King. 'Tis wonderful
> What may be wrought out of their discontent
> Now that their souls are topful of offense.
>
> (3.4.171-180)

But while Lewis agrees to invade England upon a religious pretext, Cardinal Pandulph appeals to Lewis's covetousness to enlist his aid in the papal enterprise. He tells the prince that when Arthur is dead, Lewis becomes heir to Arthur's claims because of his recent marriage to Lady Blanch: "You, in the right of Lady Blanch, your wife, / May then make all the claim that Arthur did" (3.4.142-143). Lewis, taken in by the cardinal's Machiavellian policy, agrees to invade England and says significantly, "Strong reasons make strong actions" (3.4.183).

Shakespeare makes it clear that Lewis's invasion of England, though under the pretext of restoring the realm to papal control, was actually motivated by personal gain. When Lewis sees the cardinal approaching his camp at St. Edmundsbury, he tells the English rebels of his holy enterprise.

> Look, where the holy legate comes apace
> To give us warrant from the hand of Heaven
> And on our actions set the name of right
> With holy breath.
>
> (5.2.65-68)

But even before the cardinal arrives, the Dauphin assures his English rebels that they will share with him in the spoils of victory.

> Come, come; for thou shalt thrust thy hand as deep
> Into the purse of rich prosperity
> As Lewis himself. So, nobles, shall you all
> That knit your sinews to the strength of mine.
>
> (5.2.60-63)

When Cardinal Pandulph comes onstage he tells the Dauphin that since King John has submitted to Rome there is no further need for war; consequently, Lewis should withdraw from England. Yet, and this is the crux, Lewis reveals that he has no intention of being ordered about by the cardinal.

Your Grace shall pardon me, I will not back.
I am too high-born to be propertied,
To be a secondary at control,
Or useful servingman and instrument
To any sovereign state throughout the world.

(5.2.78-82)

He also accuses Pandulph of being the instigator of the whole business.

Your breath first kindled the dead coal of wars
Between this chastised kingdom and myself
And brought in matter that should feed this fire;
And now 'tis far too huge to be blown out
With that same weak wind which enkindled it.
You taught me to know the face of right,
Acquainted me with interest to this land,
Yea, thrust this enterprise into my heart.

(5.2.83-90)

Then the Dauphin lowers the shield of hypocrisy upon which he had justified his invasion of England and reveals his true motivation.

And come ye now to tell me John hath made
His peace with Rome? What is that peace to me?
I, by the honor of my marriage bed,
After young Arthur, claim this land for mine;
And, now it is half-conquered, must I back
Because that John hath made his peace with Rome?
Am I Rome's slave?

(5.2.91-97)

Thus fired by his own covetousness, Lewis assumes a position not unlike that taken by John at the beginning of the play in his attitude toward Rome. Shakespeare demonstrates that Lewis's sense of holy mission is merely a pretext for invading England in his own right. When the papal legate tries to stop him, Lewis defies the legate and refuses to be ruled by Rome.

The parallel to Spanish Philip's pretext for the Armada is too apparent at this point to be ignored. While Philip claimed to be the champion of the papacy in restoring "heretical" nations to the Roman See, in the case of his invasion of England his motivation was that of pressing his claim to the English throne. He claimed the right of succession in England on three grounds: (1) his previous marriage to Mary Tudor, (2) his inheritance of the English throne from Mary Stuart's will, and (3) his descent from John of Gaunt. Shakespeare's play implies that foreign invasions of England in the name of the Holy Church are in reality no more than the personal ambitions of greedy princes. It is certainly true in the case of the Dauphin.

If Shakespeare's audience felt a sense of betrayal because of John's submission to Rome while foreign powers plundered the realm, it would have felt a pleasant relief when the Bastard announces that King John was not entirely serious about the whole business. The king has not submitted to Pandulph as thoroughly as it may have seemed.

For at hand,
Not trusting to this halting legate here,
Whom he hath used rather for sport than need,
Is warlike John; and in his forehead sits
A bare-ribbed Death, whose office is this day
To feast upon whole thousands of the French.

(5.2.173-178)

During the last battle, the rebellious English nobles return to John's camp, the Dauphin's armada is wrecked on Goodwin Sands, and King John himself is maliciously poisoned by a monk at Swinstead Abbey. Yet it is a victory for England, and the French forces are compelled to withdraw. Future hope for England becomes apparent in the magnanimous spirit of the king's son, Prince Henry.

Shakespeare's play supports the general Elizabethan consensus that all such efforts on the part of foreign powers to invade England were without legal and moral justification. They were, in fact, no more than instances of usurpation—whether they were initiated by the papacy or by covetous princes. King John's early response to King Philip's interference may very well reflect the attitude of Englishmen in this regard: "Alack, thou dost usurp authority" (2.1.118). It is, therefore, essential to understand the technical aspects of the political-religious point of view before one can appreciate how skillfully Shakespeare has managed the question he raises. His attitude in the play is thoroughly Protestant insofar as he denies the papacy any right to invade by force the dominions of a reigning Christian prince. Shakespeare also seems to vindicate the Protestant assumption that since kings rule as anointed ministers of God, they are not answerable to any foreign power, temporal or spiritual. No foreign princes have the right to interfere with a Christian king's administration of his own dominions.

In *King John* Shakespeare has used the highly charged materials of ecclesiastical controversy for their artistic value. By reducing the controversy to basic political questions and lifting them above the contemporary strife to an earlier, more remote period of English history, he is able to maintain a degree of objectivity missing in the writings of other dramatists who had used similar materials.

While Shakespeare does not seem to be a violent partisan of the Settlement position, one cannot avoid observing that he comes through as a wise and perceptive spokesman for his age. For example, while the traditional commentaries relegate to Shakespeare an uncommon tolerance for Roman Catholics and the Old Faith, it is difficult to ignore the fact that he has made of Cardinal Pandulph a character much darker than necessary—almost the Vice of the play. A careful study of the cardinal shows him to be the cause of discord and strife among nations. He is the instigator of rebellion, he demands that King Philip break his sacred vows of peace and friendship with England, he appeals to the Dauphin through dubious means to invade England, and he seems to serve all the while at the altar of Commodity. Lewis made these exact charges against the legate, and the cardinal himself confessed that he alone was responsible for the rebellion in England and the foreign invasion.

> It was my breath that blew this tempest up,
> Upon your stubborn usage of the Pope;
> But since you are a gentle convertite,
> My tongue shall hush again this storm of war
> And make fair weather in your blustering land.
>
> (5.1.17-21)

But, of course, not even the papal legate could restrain the forces of discord he had released. If one persists in the contention that Shakespeare was always fair in dramatizing the Old Faith, it is indeed difficult to explain his treatment of the cardinal.

What is nevertheless gratifying about Shakespeare's use of religious controversy in *King John* is that he universalizes the conflict on a purely human basis. Pandulph may function as a papal legate in the play, but at the same time he is a fallible human being, subject to invoking unworthy policy for what he considers a worthy end. By the same token, John may be a Christian prince, but he is also subject to the same disintegrating forces that enter into the experience of all mortals: he is covetous, often ignoble, and Machiavellian in policy, but he is no villain. When his land is torn apart by hostile armies, he submits to the pontiff to spare his subjects further bloodshed. King Philip leads his armies against England in the name of justice for Prince Arthur, but he is vulnerable to Commodity and soon forgets his worthy commission. The Dauphin invades England on behalf of Cardinal Pandulph, but he too serves Commodity.

The issues, therefore, are never a simple matter with Roman Catholics as Vices and Protestants as Virtues. Rather, each character pursues his own course through the drama as a fallible human being. Perhaps it is such an awareness of human character as this that separates Shakespeare from other Tudor dramatists.

Notes

1. See "Act Against Recusants," in Gee and Hardy, 498-508.

2. References to the play are to the text in G. B. Harrison, ed., *Shakespeare: The Complete Works* (New York: Harcourt, Brace, and World, 1952) 547-78.

3. See the "Supremacy Act of Elizabeth," in Bettenson, 332-33.

4. See "*Regnans in excelsis,*" in Bettenson, 340-41.

5. G. B. Harrison, ed., *The Letters of Queen Elizabeth* (London: Cassel and Company, 1935) 121.

6. See "Restraint of Appeals," in Gee and Hardy, 187-95.

7. See the "First Act of Succession," in Gee and Hardy, 232-43.

8. See the excerpt from *Unam Sanctam,* in Bettenson, 161-63.

9. G. B. Harrison, *Elizabethan Journals* (Ann Arbor: University of Michigan Press, 1955) 288.

10. Harrison, 289.

11. Philip Hughes, *The Reformation in England* (London: Hollis and Carter, 1950) 3:380.

12. Hughes, 3:381.

13. E. I. Watkin, *Roman Catholicism in England from the Reformation to 1950* (London: Oxford University Press, 1957) 37.

14. For example, the celebrated case of Dr. William Parry's treason produced as evidence the following letter from Cardinal di Como in Rome, dated 30 January 1584: "Monsignor, the Sanctity of our Lordship first has read the letters of your Lordship in full faith and cannot but praise the good disposition you profess towards the public welfare, for which his Sanctity exhorts you to persevere so that you might attain the ends that your Lordship promises. In order that you may be further assisted by that good spirit which moved you, he grants you his blessing and full forgiveness of all sins, as your Lordship has requested, assuring that besides the reward that your Lordship will have in heaven his Sanctity will also put himself in your debt recognizing the merits of your Lordship in the best manner, and so much more so because your Lordship shows great modesty in expecting nothing. So carry out your saintly and honored intentions and be well. Finally I offer you from my heart and wish you every good and happy success." Holinshed, 4:573. Translated from the Italian by Frida A. Norman, professor of Italina, Georgia State University, Atlanta GA.

15. Irving Ribner cites other Tudor documents in which this doctrine of absolutism appears: John Cheke's *The hurt of sedicion howe grevous it is to a communwelth* (1549, repeated in Holinshed in 1587), an Edwardian homily entitled *An Exhortation concerning good order and obedience to Rulers and Magistrates,* John Jewel's *Apologia Ecclesiae Anglicanae* (1562, 1564, 1581, 1591), John Whitgift's *Defence of the Answer to the Admonition Against the Reply of Thomas Cartwright,* Richard Hooker's *Of the Laws of Ecclesiastical Polity,* and Thomas Bilson's *True Difference Between Christian Subjection and Unchristian Rebellion* (1585). *The English History Play in the Age of Shakespeare* (Princeton: Princeton University Press, 1957) 311-12.

16. Compare the following passage from Holinshed's account of Campion's trial (1581): "This little Lland, God hauing so bountifullie bestowed his blessings vpon it, that except it prooue false within it selfe, no treason whatsoeuer can preuaile against it, and the pope being hereof verie well persuaded, by reason that all his attempts haue prooued of no effect: he

hath found out a meane, whereby he assureth himselfe to speed of his desire. Secret rebellion must be stirred here at home among our selues, the harts of the people must be obdurated against God and their prince: so that *when a foren power shall on a sudden inuade this realme, the subjects thus seduced most ioine with these in armes,* & so shall the pope atteine the sum of his wish." 4:449. (Italics mine.)

Roy Battenhouse (essay date 1985)

Battenhouse, Roy. "*Henry V* in the Light of Erasmus." *Shakespeare Studies* 17 (1985): 77 85.

[*In this essay, Battenhouse evaluates* Henry V *in terms of the principles set forth by the sixteenth-century Catholic humanist Erasmus in his* Praise of Folly *and* The Education of a Christian Prince, *contending that Shakespeare presents Henry as a monarch who repeatedly evades personal responsibility and only counterfeits the role of ideal Christian king.*]

In a Cambridge edition of *Henry V* in 1947, John Dover Wilson described Henry as a king inspired by religion. He even likened this hero's faith to "that of the martyrs." He judged Henry's bishops to be upright men, and he viewed the play's chorus as an "entreaty from the playwright's own lips." J. H. Walter, in his Arden edition seven years later, sought to bolster Wilson's interpretation. He provided, therefore, among other things, a tabulation of "parallels" between passages in the play and ideas of kingship he found in a treatise by Erasmus, the *Institutio Principis Christiani* (1516). But on examining closely Walter's so-called parallels, I find them misleading. Some of them fail to notice that a surface similarity to a precept by Erasmus may actually signal a counterfeiting of it. Others of the listed "parallels" simply bypass a big contrast between what Erasmus enjoins and what Henry does. Let me say, incidentally, that an excellent assignment for seminar students is to ask them to read the whole of Erasmus's *The Christian Prince* and assess King Henry in the light of it. When I do so, the students notice various disparities; and then I can direct class attention to *The Praise of Folly,* a work by Erasmus that Walter did not bother to consult. *Praise of Folly* (1511, expanded 1514) contains passages of satire on pseudo piety that fit remarkably with aspects of behavior the play exhibits in Henry and in his associates. Thus the true parallels are ironic ones. But this means that the view given of Henry by editors such as Wilson and Walter collapses if subjected to the light of Erasmus's comic sense and the Christian norms that underlie it. This essay illustrates this point.

Praise of Folly has a middle section aimed at what Erasmus calls the "theatrical pomp" of playacting bishops and princes who pretend to piety. Here he remarks that whereas charity should prompt bishops to "settle wars, resist wicked princes, and freely give not merely riches but even lifeblood for Christ's flock" (p. 111),[1] this responsibility is often retranslated. What we see instead, he says, are churchmen who fish for lands and defend these with fire and sword (pp. 110, 113). We see bishops for whom the function of "overseer" means keeping a sharp lookout for money. Instead of feeding the flock, they feed themselves. And whereas Chrysostom, Basil, and Jerome confuted pagans by leading good lives and performing miracles, there are nowadays bishops who consider miracles out of date and out of step with the times (pp. 94, 112). "They settle everything with the sword, just as if Christ has perished completely and would no longer protect his own in his own way" (p. 113).

In Shakespeare's play the bishops of Canterbury and Ely fit this portrait. They declare that miracles have ceased.[2] They are modern and secularized churchmen. Their concern is for temporal lands. Their aim is not to settle wars but to remove all "bars" that might hinder Henry's going to war. When Canterbury urges Henry to "unwind your bloody flag!" he is not thinking of Christ's blood or of giving his own for the flock. He is shrewdly sanctioning Henry's ambition in exchange for his own advantage. He can see clearly enough that if Henry takes one-quarter of England into France the bishops will be left with "thrice such powers" at home. Henry seems unaware that he will thus, in effect, hand over domestic rule to the bishops. Perhaps he has been lulled by Canterbury's smooth proposal: "While that the armed hand doth fight abroad, / Th' advised head defends itself at home." But these words imply, do they not, that if Henry chooses the role of "hand," Canterbury will accept the role of "head."

We are given also by the archbishop a lesson from the honeybees. A picture is elaborated of various classes of functionaries—masons, merchants, magistrates, and so forth, all contributing to "one purpose." But what is this purpose? Prominent in the picture are soldiers going merrily forth to take booty and bring home pillage. The hive has an emperor, but notice how he is depicted. He is described as "busied with his majesty." He "surveys" the building of "roofs of gold,"[3] and "poor mechanic porters," and the surly hum of a "sad-eyed Justice," whose one task is to give death sentences to idlers. Isn't this, indeed, a *sad* version of justice? In this community, if we examine the imagery, human beings have become "poor" mechanics toiling to the tune of gold and pillage. Such is Shakespeare's irony. He has Canterbury end the fable by boasting an ability to defend his nation's "name of hardiness and policy." Indeed so; hardiness and policy are this bishop's stock-in-trade, instead of a bishop's proper function of Christian overseer. And Henry, likewise, is only a surveyor, not a shepherd-watchman. When the fable depicts him as "busied with his majesty," do we recall perhaps Falstaff's early assessment (*1H4*, I.ii.15) that Prince Hal would have majesty but no grace? Not even enough, said Falstaff, to say grace before bread and butter. Divine grace has no representative in the archbishop's fable.

Harold C. Goddard, after noting that this fable mentions no churchmen and that it transforms bees communing with flowers into soldiers armed with stings, comments that the archbishop is as deficient in his science as in his symbolism. "What fun," he remarks, "Shakespeare must have had making such a fool of the Archbishop, knowing all the while that his audience would swallow his utterances as grave political wisdom."[4] I surmise, however, that Shakespeare hoped at least a few of his auditors would recognize the foolishness of such wisdom and hence would find amusement in the archbishop's distortion of traditional fable.

Might not learned auditors recall, for instance, that the fable as told by Vergil made no mention of roofs of gold, or of an emperor, or of merchants, or masons, or indeed of any "sad-eyed Justice"? Vergil's bees, it is true, league together "under the majesty of law" to serve the community in various ways—some watching over the gathering of food in the fields, others caring for the young, and others building honeycombs to fill with nectar before winter comes, while to still others "it has fallen by lot to be sentries at the gates," where they watch the rains of heaven, take the loads of incomers, and "in martial array" drive from the fold the lazy drones. But those details from the *Georgics,* Book IV, differ significantly from the amplifications provided by the archbishop. Vergil's "sentries" were neither mechanic porters nor soldiers marching abroad for booty.

T. W. Baldwin, when comparing Vergil with Shakespeare, has tried to account for the reshaping by bringing in some commentary by a sixteenth-century editor of Vergil, Willichius; but Baldwin has to admit that the Platonic classifications of office expounded by Willichius provide no more than perhaps a "suggestion" for Shakespeare's phraseology. "Apparently," says Baldwin, Canterbury's mention of "merchants who trade and soldiers who plunder for the good of their emperor are, like the emperor himself and the magistrates, Shakespeare's own modern application of Vergil's ancient generalization." Baldwin thinks this "modern application" accords with Shakespeare's "own fundamental concept of the English commonwealth."[5] I think we can say, rather, that it is shaped to accord ironically with Canterbury's modern concept, a concept that neither Vergil nor Willichius would have approved. And it is unlikely, I think, that Shakespeare approved of the kind of "empery" Henry resolves to display, namely, a bending of France "to our awe / Or break it all to pieces." This is a case of "commonwealth" gone askew.

Erasmus in his *Education of a Christian Prince* referred to the bees, but with an application far different from that of the archbishop. As Andrew Gurr has pointed out, Erasmus begins by saying that a young prince should be told that "the king [bee] never flies away" from the hive and that "it is the part of a good prince always to remain within the limits of his realm." Furthermore, Erasmus goes on to say, "Plato calls it sedition, not war, when Greeks war with Greeks; and if this should happen, he bids them fight with every restraint. What term should we apply, then, when Christians engage in battle with Christians, since they are united by so many bonds to each other? What shall we say when on account of a mere title . . . a war is waged?" Gurr, in citing these passages, has noted that Henry's practice reverses the views of Erasmus. Gurr observes also how the "one consent" preached by the archbishop incorporates a wide variety of motives that "work contrariously"; and if we spell out these motives they are a concern by the prelates to keep their lands, a concern by the nobles for personal glory, and Henry's concern to secure his insecure titles; thus the "one purpose" that unites is an obedience to commodity or self-interest as the mainspring of the action.[6] For Erasmus, however, commodity-serving was not the proper goal of a commonwealth.

At this point, let me add a mention of another commentary on the bees, that of John of Salisbury in *Policraticus,* VI.21-22. The twelfth-century John, after citing Vergil's saying that the ordering of a commonwealth should be borrowed from the bees, goes on to warn that the happiness of the whole cannot be lasting unless its head gives an undivided attention to the practice of justice. To illustrate a failure in this respect, John then describes the irresponsibility of Dido in too quickly bestowing favor on Aeneas, "an exile and a fugitive, of whose plight and motives she was ignorant." "With what curiosity," John exclaims, "did the ears of the chief men drink in the fabulous tales of a man who was striving to clear himself from blame, who was seeking his own glory and reaching out for something wherewith to captivate the minds of his hearers!" And so, with "smooth words" and "seductive flattery" the tales won for him hospitality, followed by the "frivolity of a hunt and other delights"—the eventual fruit of which was the city's destruction.[7] This story, I suggest, has aspects of analogy to the tactics of Henry in winning public acceptance and then instigating a foreign hunt that would ultimately prove ruinous to England's commonwealth.

But to return to Erasmus. In his *Praise of Folly* we find him jesting at courtiers who control a foolish crowd with silly tricks of fable. Was it a philosophical oration, he asks, or rather a childish cock-and-bull story, when a certain Roman flattered his audience with a story about the belly and its parts (p. 40)? Erasmus is referring here to a fable used by Menenius and reported by Livy. We may recall how Shakespeare, when dramatizing this fable in *Coriolanus,* highlighted the absurd primacy it gives to the belly, the "sink" of the body politic; Menenius depicted Belly as the giver of *all* public benefit.[8] Surely the honeybee fable, in the version given it by the archbishop, is similarly beguiling and likewise absurd.

Further, let us notice some commentary that may be pertinent to Canterbury's pronouncing on Henry's claim to France. In *Praise of Folly* Erasmus laughs at orators who indulge in quibbles, "put on display their syllogisms," ruffle their "theological feathers," and make "oracular pronouncements" that distort Holy Scripture "as if it were

Scenes from William Shakespeare's Henry V.

a lump of wax" (pp. 95, 104-05). These features can all be seen, I would say, in the argument Canterbury develops. As a follow-up to Henry's narrowing of the war question to a matter of Salic law, the archbishop evades large issues of justice by plunging instead into a morass of legal quibble and obscure logic. Then, when Henry interrupts to ask for some ground in conscience, the archbishop seizes on a biblical text, "Let the inheritance descend to the daughter," and from this he triumphantly concludes, "Stand for your own, unwind your bloody flag!" Henry's "own," however, as Goddard has pointed out, is nothing but a tombstone claim, now being revived eighty years after the fact. Moreover, let me comment on the archbishop's textual scholarship. Any reader who takes the precaution of looking into biblical law regarding female inheritance will make the interesting discovery that Canterbury has cited only half of what Moses said on this point. He has quoted the Book of Numbers 27:8 but has ignored Numbers 36:3, where in regard to the same case, Moses gave the ruling that a daughter who marries outside her tribe loses all right to her father's lands.[9] Do we wonder why the clarifying addition is not mentioned by the archbishop? Plainly, it would demolish his whole argument, since Henry's French great-grandmother married outside her tribe when she married the Englishman, King Edward. Half texts, of course, were notorious in sham scholarship. The Dr. Faustus of Marlowe's play exploits a half text, as does the wife of Bath in Chaucer's comedy. And Erasmus often lets his Stultitia use snippets of Scripture to concoct a foolish argument (for example, pp. 117-21). All this is part of the *sottie* tradition.

But let us turn next to folly as practiced by kings. What does Erasmus satirically say of kingly folly? Here is a sample:

> They will not listen to anyone except those who have learned the knack of saying such agreeable things as will not disturb their minds with any dutiful anxiety. They think they have fulfilled the whole duty of a prince if they constantly ride to the hunt, [and] if every day brings with it some newly contrived method of reducing their citizens' wealth and diverting it into their coffers—always, of course, finding suitable pretexts so that downright injustice may at least have some appearance of justice.
>
> *(p. 108)*

Can we not parallel this with Henry's foreign hunt and its pretexts? Shakespeare shows us a Henry who does not listen to anything in the archbishop's speech except what is agreeable to his own exploit already predetermined. Having traded behind the scenes for the archbishop's favor, Henry uses the public hearing only for some appearance of justice. Take care, he admonishes, "*how* you awake our sleeping sword." What he wishes to avoid is not the war but any personal responsibility for it. Indeed, throughout the play, Henry has a kind of genius for dodging responsibility by transferring it to others—for instance, when he says that the dauphin will be the cause of all the widows the war will make, or when he tells the citizens of Harfleur that *they* will be blamable for whatever massacre Henry's soldiers may perpetrate, or when at Agincourt he evades a question from Williams by twisting it so as to reduce a king's responsibility to that of a merchant. Such talk would not have satisfied Erasmus. His *Praise of Folly* warns that a king is "responsible for the integrity of all officials" and for watching carefully against deception, keeping in mind "the judgment of that king [that is, God] who before long will call him to account." If a king deviates from what a scepter properly signifies—namely, justice and an uncorrupted heart—should he not fear, asks Erasmus, lest "some clever wit" make a laughing stock of his deficiencies (pp. 107-08)? I find that remark interesting because it reminds me of how Falstaff made laughable the kingship of Henry IV by wittily depicting him with a dagger in place of a scepter. We can only surmise what Falstaff might have said of Henry V's order at Agincourt to kill all the prisoners. I can imagine Falstaff saying, "Tut, tut! Food for daggers!" That would have been a suitably Erasmian jest at such bloody business.

But since Falstaff has long ago been banished by the "new" Henry, Shakespeare provides as evaluators of the massacre of prisoners the king's now favored companions, a beef-witted Gower and a pseudo-learned Fluellen. Their praising of the king's heroism is comic, although unwittingly so on their part. It illustrates the kind of folly Erasmus attributes to the camp of falsely Christian war leaders who reduce all laws and religion to chaos. Such leaders, he says, never lack "learned flatterers who call this patent madness by the names of zeal, piety, and fortitude," having devised a way to allow someone to thrust cold steel into a brother's guts without any awareness of offense against Christ's precept of charity (p. 114). The irony of that observation, I think, helps us see Shakespeare's irony when he depicts Gower praising Henry as "gallant" and shows us Fluellen devising a way not merely to allow Henry's deed but also to flatter it with a "learned" comparison to the "magnanimity" of Alexander the Pig.[10] Fluellen's lisp of "Pig" for "Big" is unwittingly on target. So also is his notion that Henry's greatness is akin to that of the pagan Alexander. Fluellen is oblivious of any norm such as Christian charity, and in that respect his comic learning is analogous to that of the archbishop in Act I. The two bishops of Act I, and here in Act IV the two yokels English and Welsh, seem to me parallel dramatizations of social types, high and low, who supported Henry with their flattery. Erasmus would have appreciated the irony of Shakespeare's drama.

In *The Christian Prince* Erasmus devotes a chapter to warning against flattery, and elsewhere in this treatise he twice says that pagan princes such as Alexander are no proper model for Christian kingship. "What could be more senseless," he asks, "than for a man who has received the sacraments of the church to set up as an example for himself Alexander, Julius Caesar, or Xerxes?" (p. 203). And again, there is that admonition: "You have allied yourself with Christ—and yet will you slide back into the ways of Julius Caesar and Alexander the Great?" (p. 153). A prince with Christ in his heart, Erasmus goes on to say, will rather bear with losing something of his empire than avenge an injury at great loss to the state (p. 154). A Christian prince should put aside "feigned excuses" and should try wholeheartedly for means to avoid war (pp. 249, 256). Erasmus urges the prince to question first his own right; and then, even if this is established without a doubt, he should nevertheless ask himself, "Shall I be charged with such an outpouring of human blood; with causing so many widows; with filling so many homes with lamentation and mourning; with robbing so many old men of their sons? . . . Must I account for all these things before Christ?" (pp. 253-54).

Shakespeare's Henry, if we apply these norms of Erasmus', is clearly a backslider from Christian duty. At Harfleur he urges his men to behave "like so many Alexanders"; and instead of asking himself the questions Erasmus mentions, he licenses a "conscience wide as hell." To the town's women and children he threatens a massacre like that of "Herod's bloody-hunting slaughtermen." Shakespeare thus associates Henry with the archetypal tyrant of Bible story. And at Agincourt we see Henry neglecting to heed an Erasmus-like admonition by the plain soldier Williams. The king, says Williams, will have "a heavy reckoning to make when all those legs and arms and heads chopped off in battle shall join at the latter day." Disregarding this admonition, the disguised Henry ends his nighttime visit by giving jolly assurance as follows: "It is no English treason to cut French crowns, and tomorrow the king himself will be a clipper." Here "clipping"—in the triple sense of cutting off heads, purses, and coins—serves as a kind of counterfeit creed by which Henry cheers up his troops.

Ironically, Henry's afterthought is to envy the repose enjoyed by wretches of "vacant mind." But in whom have we seen a vacant mind? Not in Williams, surely, but rather in Henry's version of watchfulness, which has vacated all Christian sense of responsibility. His prayer before battle does likewise. After asking God to steel his soldiers' hearts and take from them a sense of reckoning, he asks pardon for his father's fault of crown-snatching but takes no look into his own similar purpose. In effect, Henry thus parodies the Bible's meaning of "watch and pray." He has substituted what he earlier referred to as "idol ceremony," whose only reward, he admitted, was "titles blown from adulation." Such a concept of kingship flies in the face of the norms of Erasmus.

Erasmus in *The Christian Prince* makes the point that what distinguishes "a real king from the actor" is a king's duty to be "like a father" to the state (p. 152) and like a physician who studies to heal it (p. 205). Moreover, he says, a king should be like a farmer who loves the land over which he rules, and therefore he should consider no work more magnificent than a beautifying of his country with good habits, just laws, and magistrates of integrity (pp. 205, 248). He should strive to preclude, says Erasmus, any need for the science of war, since in military service there is a "busy sort of time-wasting," destructive of values (p. 226). A prince's aim should be the welfare of his people. And this means, further, that he should marry someone from his own kingdom. Marriage to a foreigner for the sake of political alliance, Erasmus warns, can harbor future trouble. "It sometimes happens," he remarks, "that after long violent wars, after countless disasters, a marriage is finally arranged and the matter settled, but only after both parties are worn out from misfortunes" (p. 242).

In Shakespeare's play Henry's marriage to Katherine comes when the armies of France and England are both exhausted and does not ensure future peace. The epilogue tells us that what followed was misfortune for England. In the negotiations for the marriage we see the emphasis Henry puts on obtaining it, but we see also that he has failed to obtain the crown of France and must disguise this fact with a paper title. In such a situation the two kings are adroit "actors," but neither is the kind of "real king" Erasmus defined in terms of father, physician, and good farmer. Their warfare has dis-beautified the world's best garden, Burgundy tells us, by turning it into a tangle of weeds. And when he describes this disaster as a symbol of the unnatural savagery to which "ourselves and children" have been reduced, can we suppose that the pronoun "our" means the French only? In Henry's camp, more conspicuously than among the French, we have seen the "swearing and stern looks and meditating on nothing but blood" that Burgundy lists as evidence of moral decline. Erasmus would call this the result of a neglect of other sciences for the sake of frivolous war, a wasteful business. And Shakespeare has shown it to be the result of Henry's taking his father's advice to "waste the memory of former days" by busying *giddy* minds in foreign quarrels. But what a cost there is in such a policy! By setting English youth afire to "sell the pasture to buy the horse," Henry has proved himself a poor farmer and no lover of England. He has dazzled eyes by his playacting, but he has healed nothing. Erasmus perceived the folly of that kind of kingship, as does Shakespeare.

The chorus of Shakespeare's play, however, lacks a sense of irony. It represents simpleminded English opinion—or, may we say, it echoes the view preached by Stultitia in *Praise of Folly* when she declares war to be the fountainhead of all praiseworthy deeds (p. 35). Human opinion, Stultitia goes on to say, is the basis of happiness, since "the human mind is so constituted that it is far more taken with appearances than with reality" (p. 71). Therefore, we enjoy life, she explains, as a sort of play in which various people wear the costumes for their assigned parts; and this whole play would be spoiled if some petulant wiseman were to strip away the makeup to examine the wretched man underneath. Would we not rightly banish, she asks, anyone who interfered with the disguises and poetry of illusion that are necessary to performing the play of life? The only true prudence, she concludes, is to adapt to prevailing circumstances, "do as the Romans do," and run with the herd (pp. 43-44).

This Roman sense of values, which Erasmus has jestingly set forth, seems to me to be the operative faith of Shakespeare's chorus. Metaphors of history as a playhouse (and no accompanying sense of history as a time for pilgrimage) define the outlook of the chorus. Henry in the role of Mars, using his kingdom for a stage on which to create a "swelling scene," is the story the chorus invites us to aid with our imaginations. A London swarming to fetch in its Caesar, as in "antique Rome," sums up the narrator's vision of welfare achieved. He laments only that Shakespeare's stage is too limited to display the full story. To overcome this obstacle, he confesses at Agincourt his fear that the battle's name will be much disgraced by our seeing four or five ragged foils disposed in brawl ridiculous, unless we as audience bring to mind "true things by what their mockeries be." We must see beyond the visible scene!

But are we not here being nudged by Shakespeare to ask what the "true things" are? The chorus thinks they are the public legend of Agincourt, more glorious than Shakespeare's crude players can convey. Shakespeare, surely, views the matter differently. His underside meaning is that the ragged foils are a true imitation of the *moral* raggedness of Agincourt, whose participants were engaged indeed in a ridiculous brawl. Yet, as we sit and see the disgraceful business, can we not bring to mind "true things"—namely, the Christian norms that Agincourt disgraced and merely counterfeited? This double-sided art of statement is in the tradition of Chaucer and Erasmus. Shakespeare has simply allowed his play's naive narrator, the chorus, to say some things truer than the speaker knows. The truth about Henry's conquest is that it was more Roman than Christian, and more a popular imagination of benefit than a genuine achieving of benefit.

That Shakespeare's play invites an ironic view of Henry was perceived by William Butler Yeats in 1903 but has been elaborated chiefly since Goddard's seminal essay of 1951. Progressively this view has helped establish the critical objectivity of Shakespeare as an artist able to portray both the popular basis of Henry's fame and the tawdry virtues that made it possible in an age concerned more with Roman spectacle than with Christian responsibility. Ralph Berry discovered in the play's rhetoric thirty-eight instances where a speaker's *therefore* or its semantic equivalent is used to cover a "dubious or fallacious argument."[11] That kind of evidence, of course, coheres with the Erasmian sense of humor I have outlined. It coheres also with the English "giddy minds" to which Shakespeare's Henry IV referred, and with the kind of prince Shakespeare lets Falstaff preview comically as a "shallow" fellow, intent on "new silk and old sack" (*2H4*, II.iv.235 and I.ii.196). Shakespeare was apparently well aware that the Christianity of Henry was as hollow as the pseudo piety at which Erasmus aimed his praise of folly. To writers such as Erasmus, therefore, the dramatist probably turned for insights into the comedy of pagan values masquerading as Christian. The result was a play shaped to stimulate reappraisal of Henry through its canny combination of heroic myth and shady dealings.[12]

Notes

1. In citing from the *Praise of Folly*, my page references (given in parentheses) are to Clarence H. Miller's translation (New Haven: Yale Univ. Press, 1979); and my page references to *The Education of a Christian Prince* are to Lester K. Born's translation (New York: Columbia Univ. Press, 1936), the one used by J. H. Walter.

2. Such a view is characteristic of a *faithless* and shallow learning, as Shakespeare makes clear in *All's Well That Ends Well,* II.i.115 ff and II.iii.1-5. In Henry's case, however, there is the further irony that the archbishop is correct in ascribing Henry's change of manners to natural causes rather than miracle; for, in fact, Henry has experienced no inward conversion or new faith, no miracle of the Holy Spirit such as John's gospel (chap. 3) stipulates for a genuine Christian conversion. J. H. Walter, floundering on this point, is forced to argue (p. xxi) that miracle is not "doctrinally admissable," thus ignoring biblical

doctrine. When Walter then tries to associate the "consideration" that caused Henry's change with a meaning given this word in Saint Bernard's writings, the argument is empty, since Bernard had in mind a *spiritual* consideration, something quite different from Henry's politic planning to attract more eyes. Realistically, the Frenchmen in the play attribute to Henry a "discretion" like that of the Roman Brutus (II.iv.37), in other words, a worldly reasoning of pagan calculation.

3. Recall here Sidney's well-known phrase regarding the weak foundation of roofs of gold; see his *An Apology for Poetry,* in G. Gregory Smith, ed., *Elizabethan Critical Essays,* I (Oxford: Oxford Univ. Press), 177.

4. Goddard, *The Meaning of Shakespeare* (Chicago: Univ. of Chicago Press, 1951), p. 224.

5. Baldwin, *William Shakspere's Small Latine and Lesse Greeke,* II (Urbana: Univ. of Illinois Press, 1944), 472-78. Baldwin seems not to see the significance of the changes he reports. For instance, regarding the bees at the gate, he remarks that they become "Shakespeare's 'executors pale,' not acting on their own initiative as in Virgil, but in good English tradition carrying out the decree of a sad-eyed justice, who had thus to be inserted." How *good* is this alteration? Baldwin also ignores the fact that one of the classes Willichius lists as proper to a republic, the *sacerdotes,* is absent from the archbishop's fable. Might we surmise that perhaps, ironically, the "sad-eyed Justice" represents the reduced function the archbishop takes to be his?

6. Andrew Gurr, "*Henry V* and the Bees Commonwealth," *Shakespeare Survey,* 30 (1977), 61-72; the quotations are from Gurr, pp. 61 and 64.

7. *The Statesman's Book of John of Salisbury,* trans. John Dickinson (New York: Knopf, 1927), pp. 245-48.

8. Regarding Shakespeare's irony when dramatizing the Roman fable of Menenius, see my discussion in *Shakespearean Tragedy: Its Art and Its Christian Premises* (Bloomington: Indiana Univ. Press, 1969), pp. 341-50.

9. Goddard, p. 221. Holinshed had recorded in his chronicle that Edward III relinquished his claim to France in the treaty of Bretigny (1360). C. H. Hobday, in "Imagery and Irony in *Henry V,*" *Shakespeare Survey,* 21 (1968), 107-13, remarks, "To assume that Shakespeare regarded Henry's claim to the French throne as justified is to assume he was incapable of reasoning" (p. 111).

10. I comment on this comparison, along with other comic aspects of the play, in "*Henry V* as Heroic Comedy," in Richard Hosley, ed., *Essays on Shakespeare and Elizabethan Drama* (Columbia: Univ. of Missouri Press, 1962), pp. 163-82. See also Goddard, pp. 248-51, and Robert P. Merrix, "The Alexandrian Allusion in Shakespeare's *Henry V,*" *English Literary Renaissance,* 2 (1972), 321-33.

Like Erasmus, Shakespeare had inherited the Christian estimate of Alexander given by Saint Augustine in *The City of God,* IV.iv., which likens "kingdoms without justice" to piracies. After commenting that "in thefts the hands of underlings are directed by the commander," Augustine tells us of the excellent answer a pirate gave to the Macedonian Alexander who asked him how he dared molest the seas. The pirate replied, "How darest thou molest the whole world? But because I do it with a little ship only, I am called a thief: thou, doing it with a great navy, art called an emperor." On the other hand, Augustine's example of a good ruler is the Christian emperor Theodosius, who rescued the child Valentinian from a usurping tyrant and succored the church with wholesome laws (*City of God,* V.xxvi). Augustine's norms in chap. xxiv for ruling well include "reign justly"; "be slack to revenge, quick to forgive"; "use correction for the public good"; "do all things not for glory but for charity." These norms were probably those by which Shakespeare evaluated the morals of the kings he dramatized.

11. Berry, *The Shakespearean Metaphor* (London: Macmillan, 1978), pp. 48-60.

12. I think misleading the contention of Norman Rabkin in his *Shakespeare and the Problem of Meaning* (Chicago: Univ. of Chicago Press, 1981), pp. 33-62, that the play, like a gestaltist's trick drawing of a rabbit or a duck, "leaves us at a loss" by oscillating between two "alternative" and "irreconcilable" portraits of Henry. "The terrible fact about Henry," Rabkin thinks, "is that Shakespeare seems equally tempted by both its rival gestalts" because he is undergoing a "crisis of understanding and belief," a spiritual struggle that he would spend the rest of his career working through (pp. 61-62). This biographical hypothesis seems to me unwarranted, and I would say that artistically the copresence of popular illusion and disgraceful facts about Henry is evidence not of "irreconcilable" portraits but of correlative aspects of his delusory success. That is, unless Henry had had in his own day many auditors willing to revere a Mars-like hero of "famine, sword, and fire," his hunting expedition would have had no supporters and his massacre-acquired victory no public acclaim; and likewise, an Elizabethan appetite for such things, a readiness by many auditors to overlook or approve Henry's tactics, is correlative with this hero's "theatre" success. The symbiotic relationship between blind appetite in the public and pretenses by wretched heroes who thereby win veneration is one of the points Erasmus makes in his satire. Augustine, I may add, had made this same point in his *City of God* (II.xx), where his criticism of Roman culture was that a love of wealth and riot as constituting human happiness led people to honor as gods whoever

procured this kind of happiness, even though a reasonable creature would be offended if he surveyed the "impurities" and "waste" of the kings who achieved this happiness. It is likely that Shakespeare was familiar with *The City of God;* and if so, he must have been reminded of Rome's cultural flaw when he found in Holinshed and Hall a similar phenomenon—a lauding of Henry in the summary evaluations of these chroniclers, even though the episodes reported in their chronicle material contained unsavory details at which a reasonable reader might balk if not predisposed to approve Henry. Shakespeare thereupon decided, I suggest, to challenge a return to ethical reason through a strategy of both inflating the adulation of Henry and amplifying his evasive makeshifts, thus squeezing the reader's mind between the portrait's two layers of illusion and shoddy reality. This had been the technique of Erasmus for exposing worldly folly.

R. Chris Hassel, Jr. (essay date 1986)

SOURCE: Hassel, R. Chris, Jr. "Last Words and Last Things: St. John, Apocalypse, and Eschatology in *Richard III.*" *Shakespeare Studies* 18 (1986): 25-40.

[*In the following essay, Hassel calls attention to similarities in substance, style, and structure between* Richard III *and the Book of Revelation. Characterizing the play as a vivid depiction of earthly apocalypse, he remarks on its repeated allusions to the day of final judgment, the prophetic visions of Clarence, Richard, and Edmund, and the contrasting portraits of Richmond as an agent of divine retribution and Richard as a diabolic Antichrist.*]

Although attempts to understand Richard's Pauline allusions have become almost epidemic recently, they have also usually been interesting. John Dover Wilson holds the most traditional view: he sees them as part of Richard's gleeful hypocrisy, specifically his characteristic "mock-Puritan piety." Geoffrey Carnall thinks that Richard is "positively impersonating, with mischievous exhilaration, the unscrupulous Apostle of the Gentiles." Other connections are argued by John Harcourt, particularly a parallel to Acts 23:12, when certain Jews swore like Richard with Hastings that they would not eat "till they had killed Paul." Alistair Fox develops Harcourt's idea of "the theme of grace in its Pauline context." Paul, like Richard, was afflicted with thorns in the flesh, but with patience and humility he bore his infirmities, in fact gloried in them, and was therefore richly rewarded. "Unlike Paul, Richard cynically repudiates providence so that his outward deformity, instead of being an occasion for regeneration, becomes emblematic of inner distortion." As Harcourt suggests, "Man may accept grace or he may reject it; and therein, for Paul, lies his freedom or his misery. . . . Richard, freely avoiding grace, shapes his own destiny and others'."[1] Queen Elizabeth understands her vicious adversary in just such theological terms: "True: when avoyded grace makes Destiny" (l. 2998).[2]

Curious about other possible uses of these Pauline oaths, and about the one by St. John as well, I searched through Renaissance theological works for other Pauline commonplaces that might be applicable. One concerns Paul's confrontational temperament, his skills as a debater. John Calvin in his commentaries on Corinthians, Galatians, and Ephesians stresses the "earnestness and vehemence of Paul's confrontation of 'false doctrines' and 'false apostles,' the 'disputing'" that is so characteristic of these epistles. In similar terms, Martin Luther calls I Corinthians 15 "a whole long chapter in strong and solid proof of [one] article of faith and in refutation of their injurious prattle." The "Arguments" summarizing the contents of each of these Pauline epistles in the *Geneva Bible* make a similar point. In Galatians, Paul "earnestly reasoneth against . . . false Apostles"; in I Corinthians he skillfully sets "before their eyes the spiritual vertue, & heavenlie wisdome of the Gospel" and "correcteth divers abuses in their Church." A modern commentator also describes Paul as "a powerful dialectician . . . with the native temper of a debater."[3] We need only recall Richard's scenes with Lady Anne and Queen Elizabeth to acknowledge this possible if perverse connection to St. Paul. In the first encounter, Richard is as brilliant in debate as his predecessor, overwhelming both Anne's fury and her arguments with his own clever responses. Two of his oaths by St. Paul preface the debate. With Elizabeth, however, the result is reversed, spelling a diminishing wit and fortune that will culminate in despair and defeat at Bosworth Field. St. Paul's name is not invoked before this second encounter; neither are his dialectical skills.

A related irony may concern Richard's use of four of his five Pauline allusions to stifle debate or dissent. He threatens the Halberds: "Villaines set downe the Coarse, or by *S. Paul,* / Ile make a Coarse of him that disobeyes." Further: "Advance thy Halbert higher then my brest, / Or by *S. Paul* Ile strike thee to my Foote, / And spurne upon thee Begger for thy boldnesse" (ll. 211-12, 216-18). These first two oaths will brook no parley, and receive none. In the third case, Richard is again opposing himself to dissent in his Pauline oath: "By holy *Paul,* they love his Grace but lightly, / That fill his eares with such dissentious Rumors." Here, not a blow but an implied charge of treason is his threat against the queen and her allies. As she does in IV.iv, Elizabeth stands up to Richard here, defending herself against his "vile suspects" (ll. 511-12, 554) of slander and political intrigue. Finally, when Richard wants to cut off all dissent in the council chamber, he orders Hastings' head cut off with another Pauline oath: "Off with his Head; Now by Saint *Paul* I sweare, / I will not dine, untill I see the same" (ll. 2047-48). Herod-like, this ranting tyrant wants the head of the one man dumb or brave enough to question his evil. Of course, this Hastings is no John the Baptist. Still, Richard "will not dine" until he sees his head. Interestingly, when Richard first speaks to Hastings, before the Tower, he swears not by St. Paul but by St. John. Could he have meant the Baptist? At that same moment Richard has been protesting, prophet-like, against the king his brother's physical excesses: "O he hath kept an evill Diet long, / And over-much consum'd his Royall Person: / 'Tis very greevous to be thought upon" (ll. 147-49). Just before, he has been trying to get Brakenbury the Lieutenant to speak "naught" of Mistress Shore. Is this poor woman about to play her unwilling Salome to Hastings' unwitting Herod? Is Richard both Herod and John the Baptist in this strange interlude? The parts fit askew, but interestingly. I wouldn't put the scenario past Richard.

Though the Folio oath by St. John has often been emended to St. Paul, there are several good reasons to let it stand. The oath may refer to St. John the Baptist, but it may also refer to St. John the Evangelist, popularly thought in the Renaissance to have been the author of both the fourth Gospel and the Book of Revelation, or the Apocalypse of St. John.[4] Several close parallels between *Richard III* and the tone, structure, language, and vision of Revelation may make this the most pertinent of Richard's pious oaths.

Perhaps the most impressive connections to Revelation are the parallels between its "Argument" and that of the play. The *Geneva Bible* describes the contents of Revelation as

> a summe of . . . prophecies . . . adding also suche things as shulde be expedient, aswel to forewarne us of the dangers to come, as to admonish us to beware some, and encourage us against others. Herein therefore is lively set forthe . . . the providence of God for his elect, and of their glorie and consolation in the day of vengeance: how that the hypocrites which sting like scorpions the members of Christ, shalbe destroyed. . . . The livelie description of Antichrist is set forthe, whose time and power notwithstanding is limited, and albeit that he is permitted to rage against the elect, yet his power stretcheth no farther then to the hurt of their bodies: and at length he shal be destroyed by the wrath of God, when as the elect shal give praise to God for the victorie; neverthelees for a ceason God wil permit this Antichrist, and strompet under colour of faire speache and pleasant doctrine to deceive the worlde. . . . Satan that a long time was untied, is now cast with his ministers into the pit of fyre to be tormented for ever, where as contrariwise the faithful . . . shal enjoye perpetual glorie.[5]

Soften the theological edge a bit, and this could be the argument of *Richard III,* so often does it parallel the play in action, structure, tone, and meaning.

Margaret, of course, is our most extraordinary prophet of last things in the play, foretelling as she does most of the death, desolation, ruin, and decay that will occur before the promised end. When such diverse characters as Hastings, Rivers, Grey, Vaughan, and Buckingham all die, formally affirming the efficacy of her curses and the accuracy of her prophecies, the motifs of prophecy and eschatology are further strengthened. Their own prophecies and curses add still more potency to the common motifs of Revelation and *Richard III.* Of course, in Revelation, the prophetic visions pertain to the end of the world, eschatology, or last things. The seven seals unfold the plagues and portents that will accompany the second coming of Christ to reward and punish the quick and the dead. In *Richard III,* the scope is limited to the last days of the Wars of the Roses. Richard is only devilish, not the beast himself; Richmond is Christlike, not Christ. But these actors, like their actions and the tones of some of their apocalyptic speeches, are not unlike their counterparts in Revelation.

Buckingham, whose death comes second only to Richard's in the long, formal sequence of such prophesied judgments, directly links the dramatic motif of prophecy with apocalypse, eschatology, and doomsday:

Buc.

This is All-soules day (Fellow) is it not?

Sher.

It is.

Buc.

Why then Al-soules day, is my bodies doomsday
. . . . .
This, this All-soules day to my fearfull Soule,
Is the determin'd respit of my wrongs:
That high All-seer, which I dallied with,
Hath turn'd my fained Prayer on my head,
And given in earnest, what I begg'd in jest.
Thus doth he force the swords of wicked men
To turne their owne points in their Masters bosomes.
Thus *Margarets* curse falles heavy on my necke:
When he (quoth she) shall split thy heart with sorrow,
Remember *Margaret* was a Prophetesse:
Come leade me Officers to the blocke of shame,
Wrong hath but wrong, and blame the due of blame.

(*ll. 3382-84, 3390-3401*)

This All Souls' Day to which he twice alludes is November 2, "a liturgical day of the Roman rite, commemorating all the faithful departed." Its celebration is also rich in images of last things, last judgment, reward, and punishment at doomsday. One of the prescribed readings from the Catholic missal is the famous Pauline passage from I Corinthians 15; it occurs at "the last trumpet," and reads: "O death, where is thy sting?" The other is appropriately from John 5:25, 29, which reads: "The houre shal come, and now is, when the dead shal heare the voyce of the Sone of God. . . . And they shal come forthe, that have done good, unto the ressurection of life: but they that have done evil, unto the resurrection of condemnacion [judgment]."[6] Buckingham knows that his body is doomed to die this All Souls' day. With all of the crimes on his head, and in light of his own testimony to God's providence in the punishment of "wicked men," he is certainly worried about his immortal soul in the judgment to come. Unlike Richard, however, this liar and conspirator in murder does not die in despair, but in contrition. He humbly acknowledges, "Wrong hath but wrong, and blame the due of blame." There is hope yet for his spotted soul.

The "resurrection of condemnacion," judgment hereafter, is vividly described in Revelation 20:12, 13, 15:

> And I sawe the dead, bothe great & smal stand before God: and the bokes were opened, & another boke was opened, which is *the boke* of life, and the dead were judged of those things, which were written in the bokes, according to their workes. And the sea gave up her dead, which were in her, and death and hell delivered up the dead, which were in them: & they were judged everie man according to their workes. And whosoever was not founde written in the boke of life, was cast into the lake of fyre.

Hastings' works are none too good. Worse, they may have been "determined," just as this judgment has been prophesied. If so, Buckingham is a reprobate who will as surely as Richard be "cast into the lake of fyre" at the fearful "seconde death." Like All Souls' day, eschatology is much in Hastings' mind as he nears his first death.

Clarence and Richard both dream of last things, death, and judgment, as their own deaths approach. Clarence's dream of death actually comes across in a prophetic, visionary style reminiscent of Revelation:

> O Lord, me thought what paine it was to drowne,
> What dreadfull noise of water in mine eares,
> What sights of ugly death within mine eyes.
> Me thoughts, I saw a thousand fearfull wrackes:
> A thousand men that Fishes gnaw'd upon:
> Wedges of Gold, great Anchors, heapes of Pearle,
> Inestimable Stones, unvalewed Jewels,
> All scattred in the bottome of the Sea,
> Some lay in dead-mens Sculles, and in the holes
> Where eyes did once inhabit, there were crept
> (As 'twere in scorne of eyes) reflecting Gemmes,
> That woo'd the slimy bottome of the deepe,
> And mock'd the dead bones that lay scattred by.
>
> (ll. 857-69)

This is one of the most impressive pieces of visionary poetry in Shakespeare, or anywhere, for that matter. Clarence's dream of judgment is even more vivid, even more frightening:

> O then, began the Tempest to my Soule.
> I past (me thought) the Melancholly Flood,
> With that sowre Ferry-man which Poets write of,
> Unto the Kingdome of perpetuall Night.
> The first that there did greet my Stranger-soule,
> Was my great Father-in-Law, renowned *Warwicke,*
> Who spake alowd: What scourge for Perjurie,
> Can this darke Monarchy affoord false *Clarence?*
> And so he vanish'd. Then came wand'ring by,
> A Shadow like an Angell, with bright hayre
> Dabbel'd in blood, and he shriek'd out alowd
> *Clarence* is come, false, fleeting, perjur'd *Clarence,*
> That stabb'd me in the field by Tewkesbury:
> Seize on him Furies, take him unto Torment.
> With that (me thought) a Legion of foule Fiends
> Inviron'd me, and howled in mine eares
> Such hiddeous cries, that with the very Noise,
> I (trembling) wak'd, and for a season after,
> Could not beleeve, but that I was in Hell,
> Such terrible Impression made my Dreame.
>
> (ll. 880-99)

With Brakenbury, we are afraid to hear Clarence tell this terrible vision of last things. "Apocalyptic" is the best term for the eschatological style and content of his vision. Again and again, Renaissance theologians link apocalypse and eschatology. In a sermon on Revelation, George Gifford called it "First . . . a prophecie which openeth the state of things to come . . . even to the great day of the generall judgement." To Hugh Broughton, eschatology was the "Summe of the Argument" of Revelation: "Johns Apocalyps telleth, that Christ shewed the state to come, to the ende of the world." John Napier repeatedly discussed "the latter day" or last things, "the day of judgment and general resurrection" in his treatise on Revelation. Augustine Marlorat concluded of Revelation: "Finally it sheweth (and that most plenteously) what shall be the ende at length both of the chosen, and the reprobates."[7] Clarence's dreams of dead bones, reprobation, and judgment fit comfortably within this apocalyptic, eschatological context.

But the surest test here is aesthetic: the passage also shares the style and feeling of apocalyptic literature. Listen to similar passages from Revelation[8]:

> And I heard a great voyce out of the Temple, saying to the seven Angels, Go your wayes, and powre out the *seven* viales of the wrath of God upon the earth. And the first went, and powred out his vial upon the earth: and there fell a noysome, and a grievous sore upon the men, which had the marke of the beast, & upon them which worshipped his image. And the second Angel powred out his vial upon the sea, and it became as the blood of a dead man: and everie living thing dyed in the sea. And the thirde Angel powred out his vial upon the rivers & fountaines of waters, and they became blood. . . . And the fourth Angel powred out his vial on the sunne, and it was given unto him to torment men with heat of fyre. . . . And the fift Angel powred out his vial upon the throne of the beast, & his kingdome waxed darke, & they gnewe their tongues for sorowe. . . . And there were voyces, and thundrings, and lightnings, & there was a great earthquake, suche as was not since men were upon the earth.
>
> (Rev. 16:1-18)

In substance, however, the best visionary passages of Revelation usually describe the new Jerusalem, not hell. These have more of the abundant imagery of Clarence's first dream:

> And the buylding of the wall of it was of Jasper: and the citie was pure golde like unto cleare glasse. And the fundacions of the wall of the citie were garnished with all manner of precious stones: the first fundacion *was* Jasper: the second of Saphire: the third of a Chalcedonie: the fourth of an Emeraude: . . . the twelveth an Amethist. And the twelve gates *were* twelve pearles,

and everie gate *is* of one pearle, and the strete of the citie *is* pure gold, as shining glasse.

(Rev. 21:18-21)

In Clarence's vision, torment predominates over blessedness. Both speeches possess brilliant apocalyptic imagery.

Richard's tormenting dream is relentlessly judgmental, each witness concluding his little vision with "dispaire and dye." By force of will, Richard, unlike Clarence, resists these "afflictions" of a "coward Conscience," particularly as they concern judgment hereafter. His brief slip into contrition and confession, "Have mercy Jesu," is immediately countered by denial: "Soft, I did but dreame" (ll. 3640-41). There is no judgment hereafter. But even here, in Richard's mind and in his kingdom, the judgment is "Guilty, Guilty." There will be "to morrowes vengeance on the head of *Richard*" even if he can reject for a while the later tomorrows and tomorrows. Judgment hereafter sticks deep in Richard's mind. As he addresses his troops, the possibility of judgment slips out again: "March on, joyne bravely, let us too't pell mell, / If not to heaven, then hand in hand to Hell" (ll. 3668, 3782-83). Like the fallen in Revelation before the final harvest of God, Richard begins to "Feare God, . . . for the houre of his judgement is come"; he begins to hear the third Angel,

> saying with a loude voyce, If any man worship the beast and his image, and receive *his* marke in his forhead, or on his hand, The same shal drinke of the wine of the wrath of God, . . . and he shalbe tormented in fyre and brimstone before the holie Angels, & before the Lambe. And the smoke of their torment shal ascende evermore: & they shal have no rest day nor night, which worshippe the beast and his image, and whosoever receiveth the print of his name."
>
> (Rev. 14:9-11)

Richard, of all men, is marked his own forever. Richard's apocalyptic dream marks the beginning of his discovery of this eternity of torment.

In Revelation, Satan and his worldly allies are defeated in a final battle and cast into hell:

> And I sawe the beast, and the Kings of the earth, and their warriers gathered together to make battel against him, that sate on the horse & against his souldiers. But the beast was taken, . . . and them that worshiped his image. These bothe were alive cast into a lake of fyre, burning with brimstone. And the remnant were slayne with the sworde of him that sitteth upon the horse.
>
> (Rev. 19:19-21)

"A Horse, a Horse, my Kingdome for a Horse" (l. 3834). In *Richard III* we see the unhorsed Richard, God's enemy, slain by God's champion Richmond. His hellish hereafter has been widely predicted throughout the play. We have no reason to expect him to jump the life to come.

Like Revelation itself, Brother Edward has a double vision of last things. At the beginning of his end (II.i), his vision is all redemption: "I, every day expect an Embassage / From my Redeemer, to redeeme me hence. / And more to peace my soule shall part to heaven, / Since I have made my Friends at peace on earth." By the end, he is less sure: "O God! I feare thy justice will take hold / On me, and you; and mine, and yours for this" (ll. 1126-29, 1259-60). Revelation 21:8 warns that "the fearefull and unbeleving, and the abominable and murderers, & whoremongers, and sorcerers, & idolaters, & all liars shall have their parte in the lake, which burneth with fyre and brimstone, which is the seconde death." The *Geneva* gloss includes among these sinners "Thei which feare man more then God," and "Thei which mocke & jest at religion." How few of these sins have Richard and his brothers Clarence and Edward avoided. How accurate their mutual prophetic visions of last things. Like his brother Clarence, Edward may be weighted down with sins, but he is also contrite: Richard never is. Their family portrait makes an interesting apocalyptic tableau in the play.

To the many accurate prophecies and the vivid prophetic style in *Richard III* are added additional characteristics from the "Argument" of Revelation in the *Geneva Bible*: forewarnings of the dangers to come, and admonitions to avoid them. We need look no further than Hastings' fine valedictory for such an admonition:

> O momentarie grace of mortall men,
> Which we more hunt for, then the grace of God!
> Who builds his hope in ayre of your good Lookes,
> Lives like a drunken Sayler on a Mast,
> Readie with every Nod to tumble downe,
> Into the fatall Bowels of the Deepe.
>
> (ll. 2069-74)

The endless lamentations of the women, Clarence's and Buckingham's dying words, all of the ghosts speaking to Richard, and Richard's own despairing response to his dream are equally impressive admonitions "to beware" (*Geneva* "Argument"). The play is as full of them as it is of apocalyptic prophecy.

There is also presented in the apparently preordained victory of Richmond "the providence of God for his elect, and of their glorie and consolation in the day of vengeance" (*Geneva* "Argument"). Richmond certainly assumes his election, though with appropriate humility, throughout his portrayal in *Richard III*. His "couragious Friends" are urged to march "cheerely on" precisely because they march "in Gods name" (ll. 3419, 3427). Before the last battle, he prays with the faith and the humility of certain election:

> O thou, whose Captaine I account my selfe,
> Looke on my Forces with a gracious eye:
> Put in their hands thy bruising Irons of wrath,
> That they may crush downe with a heavy fall,
> Th' usurping Helmets of our Adversaries:
> Make us thy ministers of Chasticement,
> That we may praise thee in thy victory:
> To thee I do commend my watchfull soule,
> Ere I let fall the windowes of mine eyes:
> Sleeping, and waking, oh defend me still.
>
> (ll. 3551-60)

"That we may praise thee in thy victory" is a double promise of piety and humility that Richmond grandly keeps. The ghosts testify to his election, and to Richard's reprobation: "Be cheerefull *Richmond*"; "vertuous and holy be thou Conquerer"; "live and flourish"; "Sleepe, *Richmond,* / Sleep in Peace, and wake in Joy, / Good Angels guard thee from the Boares annoy"; finally: "God, and good Angels fight on *Richmonds* side" (ll. 3566ff.). The victorious Richmond proves full of grace in accepting the victory, gracious to his "Victorious Friends," and grateful to God: "God, and your Armes / Be prais'd, Victorious Friends; / The day is ours, the bloudy Dogge is dead" (ll. 3845-47). Later in the same speech we hear the conjunction of God's blessing of the elect and his vengeance on the reprobate that we associate with the Argument of Revelation:

> Smile Heaven upon this faire Conjunction,
> That long have frown'd upon their Enmity:
> . . . . .
> Now Civill wounds are stopp'd, Peace lives agen;
> That she may long live heere, God say, Amen.
>
> *(ll. 3866-67, 3886-87)*

What could be clearer, then, than Richmond's election "lively set forthe," and his "glorie and consolation in the day of vengeance" (*Geneva* "Argument"). Richmond is portrayed as chosen by God to deliver England from the devilish tyrant Richard. Like the Messiah in Revelation, he counts among his allies not only God but "good Angels," invoked by the ghosts of Buckingham, Clarence, and the two princes. "The Prayers of holy Saints and wronged soules" (l. 3707) are also among his impressive supernatural forces. In Revelation, first four angels, then seven participate in "the destruction of the wicked and comfort of the godlie." So do "the Saintes of God overcome them all, and sing divine songs unto God by whose power they get the victorie."[9]

Most impressive is Richmond's direct allusion to Revelation while he prays as God's minister of wrath, "Looke on my Forces with a gracious eye, / Put in their hands thy bruising Irons of wrath." Of God's Messiah, his champion "Faithful & True" in Revelation 19:11, it is said that "he shal rule them with a rodde of yron: for he it is that treadeth the wine presse of the fiercenes and wrath of almightie God." This allusion increases our sense of both the apocalyptic and the providential dimensions of Richmond's potency in *Richard III.* "And a crowne was given unto him, and he went forthe conquering that he might overcome" (Rev. 6:2). The conquering Messiah rides forth in Revelation on a "white horse, and he that sate upon him, was called, Faithful & true, & he judgeth and fighteth righteously" (Rev. 19:11). The conquering heroes of Revelation and *Richard III* bear interesting similarities, as do the forces they command.[10]

So do their antagonists. In Revelation as in *Richard III,* this is a day of vengeance as well as a day of victory. According to the *Geneva* "Argument," on this last day "the hypocrites which sting like scorpions the members of Christ, shalbe destroyed." Richard, in all his devilish splendor, is an impressive antichrist to Richmond's avenging Messiah. First, Richard, as a good antichrist, is given ironic connections to this Messiah. The murderers reply to Clarence's naive assumption of Richard's good offices: "Why so he doth, when he delivers you / From this earths thraldome to the joyes of heaven" (ll. 1080-81). God deliver us from such deliverers. Richard is also called "devil" more than once in the play. He proudly numbers among his allies the devil himself as well as his own "dissembling lookes" (l. 433). Further, Richard is associated through various animal symbols with his supernatural ally. Richard is overtly compared to what Lancelot Andrewes calls "the subtle serpent" with such epithets as "serpent," "viper," and "cockatrice." His mother's epithet, "Thou Toad, Thou Toade" (l. 2918), parallels Milton's Satan, "Squat like a Toad, close at the eare of Eve."[11] Richard himself invokes "the spleene of fiery Dragons" (l. 3822) as he concludes his battle oration. Marbeck stated this traditional connection to Satan: "we maie fitly understand by the Dragon, Satan himselfe the father of lies." Less precisely Satanic, but equally loathsome, malignant, or destructive, are the boar, the wolf, and the dog. As Andrewes said in another sermon, such animals are enemies to "our lives good," if not explicitly Satanic.[12] John Downame even called Satan a wild boar: "So also this wilde Boare would have broken downe the hedge which defended Job by tempting him to blaspheme God." Downame added this touch: "He is called a murderer and a man-slayer, as though this were his profession and occupation."[13] That is Downame's early seventeenth-century description of Satan, not Richard; the connection is stunning. If Richard is not the beast of Revelation, he is certainly one of his dragonish associates.

Unlike Richmond's dream of comfort and victory, Richard's "tormenting Dreame / Affrights [him] with a Hell of ougly Devills" (l. 696). In the deep of his prophetic dream, brother Clarence sees "dead bones," "Angells," "Furies," and a "Legion of foule Fiends." Such angelology and demonology is yet another characteristic of Revelation and of apocalyptic literature in general. Most Renaissance commentaries on Revelation discuss not only "the promised Messias" and the "most ugly monster, the divell," but the hosts of angels and devils at their command. Napier talked of "Gods Saints and holie servantes" combating "the Devill and all damned spirites" in the last days. Broughton described "Angel trumpeters [who] sound howe haile and fire is mixt with blood," and depicts "Michaels Angels" against the "wicked spirites" of the devil. John Donne preached an entire sermon on the angelology and demonology of Revelation. The sermon was preached on All Saints Day, with Revelation 7:2, 3 as its text.[14] Richard, Clarence, Richmond, the ghosts, and many of their companions in *Richard III* assume that they live in a similar universe of angels and devils.

In the last battle, Richard, like the antichrist described in the *Geneva* "Argument" of Revelation, "shalbe destroyed."

His power seems overwhelming. "Notwithstanding, [it] is limited . . . and at length he shal be destroyed by the wrath of God." Just as surely as Richmond's victory seems preordained, and is so interpreted by God's minister, so Richard in his brief reign is like the beast "permitted . . . to rage . . . [and] under colour of faire speache and pleasant doctrine to deceive the worlde" (Geneva "Argument"). Anne, Hastings, Buckingham, Clarence, Edward, the princes, Henry VI, his Edward, Margaret, Elizabeth, his own mother, and unnamed others all suffer his hypocrisy and his sting. "At length he shal be destroyed by the wrath of God."

As Richmond's election thunders through Act V, so does Richard's reprobation. The two are dancing very different steps on the same balance. Richard's foot is increasingly heavy: "I have not that Alacrity of Spirit / . . . that I was wont to have." Richmond's is light, "jocond" in fact, "In the remembrance of so faire a dreame." "True Hope is swift, and flyes with Swallowes wings." Richard's back is bent with "dispaire and dye." Richmond rises to "Successe, and Happy Victory." And then, of course, come victory and defeat. "God, and your Armes / Be prais'd, Victorious Friends; / The day is ours, the bloudy Dogge is dead." Richard is unhorsed and uncrowned. Richmond is made king, graced with the "long usurped Royalties" plucked "From the dead Temples of this bloudy Wretch."[15] In the Apocalypse, the antichrist that "a long time was untyed, is now cast with his ministers into the pit of fyre to be tormented for ever, where as contrariwise the faithful . . . shal enjoye perpetual glorie" (Geneva "Argument").

In the world of the play, the judgment is almost as definitive:

> Abate the edge of Traitors, Gracious Lord,
> That would reduce these bloudy dayes againe,
> And make poore England weepe in Streames of Blood;
> Let them not live to taste this Lands increase,
> That would with Treason, wound this faire Lands peace.
>
> (ll. 3881-85)

So much for Godless traitors. For the elect:

> O now, let *Richmond* and *Elizabeth*,
> The true Succeeders of each Royall House,
> By Gods faire ordinance, conjoyne together:
> And let thy Heires (God if thy will be so)
> Enrich the time to come, with Smooth-fac'd Peace,
> With smiling Plenty, and faire Prosperous dayes.
>
> (ll. 3875-80)

Revelation concludes its last days with similar separation of the elect and the reprobate, and similar distribution of rewards and punishments.

> He that is unjust, let him be unjust stil: & he which is filthie, let him be filthie stil: & he yt is righteous, let him be righteous stil: & he yt is holie, let him be holie still. And beholde, I come shortly, & my rewarde is with me, to give everie man according as his worke shalbe.
>
> (Rev. 22:11-12)

Holy forever, righteous forever; filthy forever, unjust forever. Such is the truth that lies behind Richard's despair and Richmond's joy, at least within the artifice of *Richard III.*

Such persistent parallels between the arguments of *Richard III* and Revelation are not meant to suggest influence so much as generic similarity. Richard and Richmond are neither antichrist nor Christ. Shakespeare's play is mostly about judgment here, Revelation about judgment hereafter. In the play the conflict is political and the characters human; in the Apocalypse the action and the actors are cosmological. But in Shakespeare's contrived but lively dramatization of fulfilled prophecies, moral admonitions, "the Providence of God for his elect," the threatening but limited time of Richard the dragon, and the final awesome torment and grace of punishment and reward, we have a striking portrayal in this world of the core events of the Apocalypse. Add to those similar "arguments" the apocalyptic visions of Clarence, Richard, and Edward, and Buckingham's direct connection of his death and judgment with All Souls' and doomsday, and the analogy becomes even more striking. In its characters' preoccupation with last words and last things, there is much of apocalypse and eschatology in this history play.

Richard spoke more profoundly than he knew when he upbraided the messengers in Act IV: "Out on ye Owles, nothing but Songs of Death?" (l. 3311). He is surrounded by intimations of apocalypse and eschatology. The characters around him are preoccupied with last words and last things. Elizabeth's overwhelming victory, Richmond's threatening attractiveness, a nagging system of lesser defeats, and the inscrutable hand of providence join these apocalyptic motifs in hymning Richard's ultimate doom. Richard's ironic oaths by St. Paul and St. John join their swelling chorus. His despair and death will provide the final descant.

Notes

1. John Dover Wilson, ed., *Richard III* (Cambridge: Cambridge Univ. Press, 1954), p. xx; Carnall, "Shakespeare's *Richard III* and St. Paul," *Shakespeare Quarterly,* 14 (1963), 188; I find Carnall's suggestion implausible, in my book *Faith and Folly in Shakespeare's Romantic Comedies* (Athens: Univ. of Georgia Press, 1980), pp. 9-13, I discuss the high esteem of St. Paul among most Renaissance Christians. Harcourt, "'Odde Old Ends, Stolne . . .': King Richard and St. Paul," *Shakespeare Studies,* 7 (1974), 88-89; Fox, "Richard III's Pauline Oaths: Shakespeare's Response to Thomas More," *Moreana,* 7 (1978), 20-21.

2. William Shakespeare, *The Tragedy of Richard the Third,* in *Mr. William Shakespeares Comedies, Histories, & Tragedies* (London: Isaac Jaggard & Ed. Blount, 1623). Throughout, quotations from *Richard III* will refer to this edition. The complex relationship of the quarto and the folio texts invites

such citation. Kristian Smidt's parallel text edition of *The Tragedy of King Richard the Third* (New York: Humanities Press, 1969) is an accurate and useful edition of both texts. I follow Smidt's Through Line numbering.

3. Calvin, *Commentary on the Epistles of Paul the Apostle to the Corinthians,* John Pringle, tr. (Grand Rapids: William B. Eerdmans, 1948), I, 38-39; *Commentaries on the Epistles of Paul to the Galatians and Ephesians,* William Pringle, tr. (Grand Rapids: William B. Eerdmans, 1957), pp. 15-19; Luther, *Works,* Hilton C. Oswald, ed. (St. Louis: Concordia Press, 1973), XXVI, 13; XXVIII, 60. *The Geneva Bible,* Lloyd E. Berry, ed. (Madison: Univ. of Wisconsin Press, 1969); subsequent Biblical quotations will refer to this edition and be cited in the text. See F. Schroeder, "Paul, Apostle, St.," *New Catholic Encyclopedia* (New York: McGraw-Hill, 1967), XI, 8.

4. See, for example, William Fulke, *A Defence . . . against . . . Gregory Martin,* C. H. Hartshorne, ed. (Cambridge: Parker Society, 1843), I, 34; Thomas Brightman, *The revelation of S. John . . . ,* 3rd ed. (Leyden: John Class, 1616), p. 4; and John Marbeck, *A Book of Notes and Commonplaces* (London: Thomas East, 1581), p. 555.

5. Subsequent references to this "Argument" to Revelation in the *Geneva Bible* will be cited in the text as *Geneva* "Argument."

6. "*In commemoratione omnium fidelium defunctorum.*" This quotation and the following citations are from *Missale Romanum, Jussu editum* (Venetiis, 1717), p. lviii; see also *The Cathedral Daily Missal,* Rudolph G. Bandas, ed. (St. Paul: E. M. Lohmann, 1961), p. 1878; and A. Cornides, "All Souls' Day," *New Catholic Encyclopedia,* I, 319. The biblical quotations come from the *Geneva Bible.*

7. George Gifford, *Sermons upon . . . Revelation* (London: Thomas Man & Toby Cooke, 1596), sig. A6r; Hugh Broughton, *A revelation of the holy Apocalyps* (Amsterdam [?], 1610), p. 13; John Napier, *A plaine discoverie of . . . Revelation* (Edinburgh: R. Walde-grave, 1594), p. 144; Augustin Marlorat, *A Catholike exposition upon . . . Revelation,* Arthur Golding, tr. (London: H. Binneman, 1574), p. 2. See also G. E. Ladd, "Apocalyptic as Eschatology," in *International Standard Bible Encyclopedia* (Grand Rapids: Wm. B. Eerdmans, 1979), I, 153-56; and M. Rist, "Apocolypticism," in *Interpreters' Dictionary of the Bible* (Nashville: Abingdon Press, 1962), I, 157-61.

8. See also Rev. 14:9-11.

9. *Geneva Bible,* marginal note, Rev. 15.

10. Christ as Messiah, deliverer of the faithful from the hands of the enemy, is a prominent feature of Revelation and its commentaries. Among many Renaissance comments: John Donne in a sermon on Rev. 7 called "this Angel [of Revelation] . . . our Saviour Christ himselfe." *The Sermons,* George R. Potter and Evelyn M. Simpson, eds. (Berkeley: Univ. of California Press, 1953-62), X, 47. See also Gifford, sig. A7v; Napier, pp. 162-64, 230; and Richard Bernard, *A key . . . for . . . revelation* (London: Felix Kyngston, 1617), pp. 188 ff.

11. Lancelot Andrewes, *Ninety-Six Sermons* (1843; rept. New York: AMS, 1967), V, 452; John Milton, *Paradise Lost,* in *The Works,* Frank Allen Patterson, ed. (New York: Columbia Univ. Press, 1931), vol. II, l. 800.

12. Marbeck, p. 315; Andrewes, II, 9; Gifford in a sermon analyzed swine and dogs as particularly degenerate animals. The swine neglect the truth; the dogs tear the truthful. Richard seems compatible. Milton compared Satan to a wolf in *Paradise Lost,* IV, 183. William Woods, *A History of the Devil* (New York: G. P. Putnam's Sons, 1974), pp. 121-22; and J. B. Russell, *The Devil* (Ithaca: Cornell Univ. Press, 1977), pp. 113, 116, mention these and other animals traditionally associated with evil in the Christian tradition.

13. John Downame, *The Christian Warfare Against the Devil, World, and Flesh,* 4th ed. (London: William Stansby, 1634), pp. 88-89. Several other details may be worth a note, though I have not been able to find Renaissance sources. Maximilian Rudwin, *The Devil in Legend and Literature* (Chicago: Open Court, 1931), p. 48, says: "The Devil is often represented with a hump. This deformity was caused, according to . . . Victor Hugo, . . . by the fact that, in escaping out of the sack in which the Devil carried them on his back to hell, the human souls left behind 'their foul sins and heinous crimes, a hideous heap, which, by the force of attraction natural to the Fiend, incrusted itself between his shoulders like a monstrous wen, and remained for ever fixed.'" In a similar vein, G. Wilson Knight, *The Sovereign Flower* (London: Methuen, 1958), p. 211, attributes to Richard and St. Paul a mutual lameness. Rudwin concurs (p. 49).

14. Gifford, sig. A7v; Napier, pp. 242-43; Broughton, pp. 13, 152-58; Donne, vol. 10, sermon 1; see also vol. 8, sermon 1; and Rist, I, 157-61.

15. Lines 3513-14, 3697-98, 3428, 3565-3623, *passim,* 3845-51.

Paul A. Cantor (essay date 1987)

SOURCE: Cantor, Paul A. "Religion and the Limits of Community in *The Merchant of Venice.*" *Soundings* 70, nos. 1-2 (spring-summer 1987): 239-58.

[*In the following essay, Cantor identifies devotion to religious principles as the quality that links Shylock and*

[*Antonio in* The Merchant of Venice, *asserting harmony is only achieved by the defeat of both the Jew and the merchant, whose commitment to the values of their respective religions threatens the traditional values of comedy.*]

I

The Merchant of Venice continues to be a controversial play, the most controversial of all Shakespeare's romantic comedies. Indeed for a comedy, the play deals with unusually weighty subject matter, raising fundamental issues about religion one would not expect to see brought up in a humorous context. Critics have come to view the play as portraying the conflict between Christianity and Judaism, but they disagree as to Shakespeare's evaluation of the conflict. Some see Shakespeare as siding exclusively with the Christians and treat Shylock as the pure villain of the piece. Others argue that Shakespeare is in fact sympathetic to Shylock and making a plea for religious toleration. The critics who take a purely negative view of Shylock tend to be the ones who discuss *The Merchant of Venice* as a comedy, viewing Shylock in the context of the tradition of comic villains. By contrast, critics who are sympathetic to Shylock often discuss the play as if it were a tragedy, concentrating on Shylock's role and dealing only with the serious themes. I want to argue that there are ways of treating *The Merchant of Venice* as a comedy and still viewing Shakespeare as sympathetic to Shylock. Indeed it is only by looking at Shylock in the context of the whole play—and that means in relation to the other characters and to its comic structure—that one can appreciate the complexity of Shakespeare's portrayal.

But *The Merchant of Venice* is not an ordinary comedy, and the tendency to discuss it as if it were a tragedy does have some basis in its peculiar nature. If Portia did not intervene in the Antonio-Shylock conflict, it would have some kind of tragic outcome. More than most comedies, *The Merchant of Venice* flirts with tragedy. Shakespeare appears to be trying a dramatic experiment: to see how far he can push a play toward tragedy and still bring about a comic ending. Many critics would say that he let the experiment go too far, allowing the character of Shylock to take over the play to the point where the comic ending becomes unsatisfactory. For the play to be a comedy, Shylock has to be the villain, in comic terms the blocking agent. In the conventional comic pattern, he is the old man who stands in the way of the young lovers and threatens to prevent their happiness. Because he interferes with the potential harmony of the community, he has to be eliminated by the end of the play. But if we come to sympathize with Shylock, it will interfere with our feeling of comic resolution. Above all, if we feel that Shylock stands for a genuine principle, we will have at least something of a tragic impression at the end of the play. We will sense that the community has re-established itself only at the cost of excluding a legitimate point of view and thus narrowing its horizons.

Shylock is not the only potentially tragic figure in the play. He is after all not even the title character. Shylock is the *Jew* of Venice; Antonio is the *merchant* of Venice. The popular confusion as to who the title character is reveals how over the years Shylock has come to steal the show, leaving Antonio in his shadow, neglected by audiences and critics alike. But only by taking into account Antonio's role can one fully understand Shylock's; for despite the surface conflict between the two characters, they have a hidden affinity. Antonio also does not fit comfortably into the comic world of the play. In the grip of his melancholy and world-weariness, Antonio, like Shylock, is basically a killjoy. In particular, he refuses to participate in the comedy of romance, and represents in his own way almost as much of a threat to the happiness of the young lovers as does Shylock. Antonio stands up for the value of male friendship, for the idea that friendship is a higher form of concord than romantic love. Thus for the comic ending to be possible and the lovers to be happily married, Antonio has to be defeated just as Shylock is. Act IV is devoted to the defeat of Shylock, Act V to the defeat of Antonio. Indeed, if Shylock were the only opposition to the comic resolution, the structure of *The Merchant of Venice* would be defective, since the main character would drop out with a whole act to go. Only if one sees the importance of Antonio in the play does the structure of *The Merchant of Venice* make sense. Before Portia can be happy in her marriage, she has to prove that Bassanio loves her more than he does Antonio. Thus Antonio ends up being excluded from the happy ending almost as much as Shylock is. But if that is the case, then the comic resolution of *The Merchant of Venice* cannot simply reflect, as many critics have claimed, the triumph of Christianity over Judaism, for Antonio is as much the representative Christian in the play as Shylock is the representative Jew.

Investigation of *The Merchant of Venice* ought to begin from this observation: the comic resolution is possible only at the expense of both Shylock and Antonio, the two characters who take life seriously in the play, which above all means the two characters who take religion seriously. It may at first seem odd to claim that Antonio is the representative Christian in the play. There are of course many characters in the play who espouse Christianity, but, as I will show, they act like pagans, concerned primarily with the gratification of their senses and using their Christian principles to attain that end. What makes Antonio and Shylock similar is that they are both men of religious principles, but that of course is also what causes them to come into conflict, since their principles differ. For the conflict to be resolved, characters like Portia must intervene, characters who are more flexible about their principles and are in fact willing to bend whatever principles they have for the sake of happiness. Hence, as important as the opposition between Antonio and Shylock may be, in some ways it is less basic to *The Merchant of Venice* than the opposition between both Antonio and Shylock, who get involved in a potentially tragic conflict, and characters like Portia and Bassanio, who find a way of resolving it comically. By analyzing both the differences and the similarities between Shylock and Antonio, I hope to shed new light on *The Merchant of Venice*. The best way of understanding the play may not be to seek to resolve the ambiguities which seem to pervade Shakespeare's characterization of Shylock, but rather to uncover the ambiguities which surround his portrayal of Antonio and indeed of all Venice. The complexity of Shakespeare's portrayal of Shylock is rooted in a deeper complexity in *The Merchant of Venice,* what one might call its ambiguity of genre, the way the play oscillates between tragedy and comedy.

II

The most thoroughgoing attempt I have seen to characterize Shylock and Antonio as products of their religious principles is Allan Bloom's essay, "Christian and Jew: *The Merchant of Venice.*" Bloom describes Shylock this way:

> Shylock holds that respect for obedience to the *law* is the condition for leading a decent life. . . . Righteousness is hence the criterion for goodness; if a man obeys the law to its letter throughout his life, he will prosper. . . . Justice is lawfulness; Shylock is a son of Moses. Along with this goes a certain positive temper; Shylock lives very much in this world. Money is a solid bastion of comfortable existence, not for the sake of pleasure or refinement, but for that of family and home. . . . Decent sobriety is the rule of life.

Bloom contrasts Antonio in these terms:

> Antonio . . . bases his whole life on generosity and love for his fellow man. For him, the law, in its intransigence and its indifference to persons, is an inadequate guide for life. . . . Equity and charity are more important than righteousness. . . . Calm calculation is beyond him. He makes promises he cannot keep, and his hopes are based on ships that are yet to come in. The restraint and coldness of the Jew are not his; his sympathies go out to all men, and he cares much for their affection.[1]

Bloom thus shows how Shakespeare's portrayal of Shylock and Antonio reflects the traditional opposition of Judaism and Christianity in terms of justice vs. mercy or obedience to the letter of the law vs. charity.

Out of these contrasting religious attitudes, the conflict between Shylock and Antonio over the issue of usury grows. Antonio's Christianity gives him an otherworldly perspective on life. For him material things have no real value; the only true value is spiritual. For Antonio a man's wealth is ultimately worthless to him. The only purpose it can serve is to allow him to do good deeds by lending a helping hand to his friends. For Antonio, charging interest on loans serves no purpose. By contrast, as Shakespeare characterizes Shylock's Judaism, it gives him a thisworldly orientation, in which whatever a man achieves, he must achieve on earth. Wealth becomes for Shylock one of life's few solid values, and amassing it becomes his way of demonstrating his virtue and talent. He finds a biblical precedent for his way of life in the Old Testament figure of Jacob and thus views his business as having a religious sanction: "thrift is blessing, if men steal it not" (I.iii.9).[2]

Shylock sees no reason to part with his money, unless he receives some consideration in return, namely an interest payment. Antonio and Shylock are never going to agree on the issue of usury, because it has become bound up with the fundamental differences in their ways of life. We are inclined to say that usury is a narrowly economic issue which should be left to economists to decide. What we find surprising and alien is that Antonio and Shylock regard usury as a religious issue. But for them religion is a comprehensive force, governing how they behave in all aspects of life. For them there are no narrowly economic issues: ultimately every issue is religious. In particular, the Bible has something to say about every ethical issue, and as strange as it seems to us today, their dispute over usury quickly turns into a dispute over how to read the Bible (I.iii.71-101).[3]

The clearest way of seeing the problem Antonio and Shylock face in living together in the same city is to realize that in effect they do not speak the same language. Shylock says of Antonio:

> He hates our sacred nation, and he rails
> Even there where merchants most do congregate
> On me, my bargains, and my well-won thrift,
> Which he calls interest.
>
> (I.iii.48-51)

What Shylock calls sound business practice, Antonio calls usury. Similarly, what Antonio calls generosity, Shylock calls wastefulness.

How then does Venice succeed in making men live together in peace within the city? Shakespeare presents Venice as a remarkable community: a great commercial republic, which brings together men from all over the world for the purposes of trade. The commercial interests of Venice dictate a cosmopolitan nature for the city, but that creates a problem. Men with different beliefs and values can easily come into conflict, as we have seen in the case of Antonio and Shylock. Venice brings men together for the sake of commerce and attempts to maintain the peace between them on the basis of commerce.[4] The city tries to get men to reduce their spiritual concerns, which are potentially divisive. Men differ—often bitterly and violently—as to what the Bible says. But they can agree as to what an account book says: the figures are there, totalled up in black and white for all to see. Thus Venice tries to get men more interested in their material concerns, because it is easier for them to agree as to what is to their mutual economic benefit. The harmony of Venice rests on what is today called the cash nexus.

In the traditional view, the harmony of a community rests on its members having a common nature. They have to share certain common concerns. Above all, they have to share the same beliefs about the fundamental things in life. The community is originally a community of believers, and hence community is based on friendship. Portia's comments in passing on the nature of friendship have interesting implications for our view of Venice:

>   in companions
> That do converse and waste the time together,
> Whose souls do bear an egall yoke of love,
> There must be needs a like proportion
> Of lineaments, of manners, and of spirit.
>
> (III.iv.11-15)

Antonio and Shylock do not have "a like proportion / Of lineaments, of manners, and of spirit" and hence their community cannot be based on friendship. Rather Venice uses economic ties to bind together its citizens. The key principle is this: you do not have to like a man in order to lend money to him; in fact when it comes to securing repayment, it may help if you do not like him. Antonio understands what it means to enter into a purely business relationship with Shylock:

> If thou wilt lend this money, lend it not
> As to thy friends, for when did friendship take
> A breed for barren metal of his friend?
> But lend it rather to thine enemy,
> Who if he break, thou mayest with better face
> Exact the penalty.
>
> (I.iii.132-137)

As bitter as this passage may be, it reveals what is attractive about economic ties to a city like Venice: they offer a way of binding together enemies as well as friends. As opposed to traditional communal ties, the cash nexus promises to be more stable and secure, and also to embrace a wider range of humanity.

Shylock gives the clearest statement of the principle of the Venetian community:

> I will buy with you, sell with you, talk with you, walk with you, and so following; but I will not eat with you, drink with you, nor pray with you.
>
> (I.iii.35-38)

Shylock reveals that there is no true communion in Venice: men may do business with each other, but they do not necessarily share the deepest side of their souls. That is why the law becomes so important in Venice. With no inner spiritual principle of allegiance, men in Venice have to be united by the external, objective principle of the law. Antonio understands the connection between the cosmopolitanism of Venice and its need for a strict rule of law:

> The Duke cannot deny the course of law;
> For the commodity that strangers have
> With us in Venice, if it be denied,
> Will much impeach the justice of the state,
> Since that the trade and profit of the city
> Consisteth of all nations.
>
> (III.iii.26-31)

The Venetians are not united in their beliefs about the highest things. Rather they are united on the lowest principle, the principle of the body, what all men share as human beings. Men disagree as to what conduces to their spiritual welfare, but it seems more likely that they will agree as to what conduces to their bodily welfare.[5] One can point to the body; one cannot point to the soul.

The result is that the tendency of Venice is to redirect its citizens from spiritual to material concerns in order to bring about social harmony. That is why most of the Christians in the play do not appear to take their Christianity very seriously. The typical Venetians we see, men like Bassanio or Gratiano, are chiefly concerned with marrying well. Since the Venetians are wrapped up in securing a good place in society, religion becomes a social amenity in their eyes. A well-bred man has to put on a religious front, but that is all. When Bassanio warns his companion to be on his best behavior, Gratiano reveals his attitude toward religion:

> If I do not put on a sober habit,
> Talk with respect, and swear but now and then,
> Wear prayer-books in my pocket, look demurely,
> Nay more, while grace is saying hood mine eyes
> Thus with my hat, and sigh and say amen,
> Use all the observance of civility,
> Like one well studied in a sad ostent
> To please his grandam, never trust me more.
>
> (II.ii.190-197)

This is a telling passage: for Gratiano, religion has become reduced to a matter of civility, something one pays lip service to in order to placate one's grandmother.

One must in fact look very carefully at the Venetians in *The Merchant of Venice* to see how deep their religious impulses run. To read many of the critics, one would think that Shylock is confronted with a community composed of Church Fathers, representing the Christian faith at its purest and most exalted level. But beneath the surface pieties commerce has taken over the lives of Shakespeare's Venetians. This is evident in their language: they constantly speak of things in commercial terms. Consider Bassanio's declaration of friendship:

> To you, Antonio,
> I owe the most in money and in love,
> And from your love I have a warranty
> To unburthen all my plots and purposes
> How to get clear of all the debts I owe.
>
> (I.i.130-134)

For Bassanio, money characteristically comes before love, and he mixes indiscriminately terms of business and terms of friendship. In the opening scene, when the various Venetian merchants see Antonio unhappy, they automatically assume that only business worries could upset a man this much. Salerio makes the most revealing comment about Antonio's distress:

> Should I go to church
> And see the holy edifice of stone,
> And not bethink me straight of dangerous rocks,
> Which touching but my gentle vessel's side

Would scatter all her spices on the stream,
Enrobe the roaring waters with my silks.

(I.i.29-34)

Even when he is in church, this Christian merchant is thinking about his merchandise, concerned more about the fate of his goods than the fate of his soul. One could not choose a better emblem for the mentality of Shakespeare's Venice.

This tendency of Venice is parodied in the behavior of the clown, Launcelot Gobbo. He finds himself torn between his interest as a Christian in having Jessica convert to the true faith and his interest as a consumer:

We were Christians enow before, e'en as many as could well live one by another. This making of Christians will raise the price of hogs. If we grow all to be pork-eaters, we shall not shortly have a rasher on the coals for money.

(III.v.21-26)

In worrying that "in converting Jews to Christians, you raise the price of pork" (III.v.35-36), Launcelot provides a comic equivalent of Venice's tendency to let economic considerations override the religious.

III

The typical Venetians may seem superficial by comparison with Antonio and Shylock. But the fact that they are concerned with material pleasures does not mean that they are to be condemned. The typical values of Venice are in fact the typical values of comedy. As critics such as Northrop Frye and C. L. Barber have shown, Shakespearean comedy celebrates vitality and natural energy.[6] The festive spirit and carnival atmosphere in the comedies reflect this fact. The comedies tend to dwell on the most natural and universal of human concerns: getting married, establishing a family, and living well. There is something life-enhancing about the prevailing spirit in Venice. One can see it in Bassanio's opening line: "Good signiors both, when shall we laugh?" (I.i.66). Both Shylock and Antonio stand in the way of Venice's enjoyment.[7] As shown by his opening lines, Antonio is just too somber:

In sooth, I know not why I am so sad;
It wearies me, you say it wearies you.

(I.i.1-2)

As the letter Antonio sends to Bassanio shows (III.ii), he has a way of interrupting other people's moments of happiness and ruining their enjoyment.

With his otherworldly temperament, Antonio is not himself interested in the pleasures of this world:

I hold the world but as the world, Gratiano,
A stage, where every man must play a part,
And mine a sad one.

(I.i.77-79)

Gratiano answers Antonio very much in the spirit of comedy—"Let me play the fool" (I.i.79)—giving an eloquent defense of the goal of enjoying life and dismissing Antonio's melancholy as mere posing. But Antonio's melancholy is not a mere pose. Claiming to be weary of the world, Antonio is willing to prove it by sacrificing himself for his friend Bassanio. He has in fact a kind of martyr complex:

I am a tainted wether of the flock,
Meetest for death; the weakest kind of fruit
Drops earliest to the ground, and so let me.
You cannot better be employ'd, Bassanio,
Than to live still and write mine epitaph.

(IV.i.114-118)

Here Antonio is most clearly modelling himself on Christ. His sentiments may be admirable in themselves, but they still threaten to disrupt the comic world. Portia knows that she has to save Antonio: if he were to die as a martyr to his friendship for Bassanio, it would poison her marriage forever.

Shylock equally contradicts the comic spirit of the play. At first sight he paradoxically seems to resemble the other Venetians more closely than Antonio does: like them he is concerned with obtaining wealth, not giving it away. But Shylock differs from the other Venetians in not wanting to use his wealth for the sake of pleasure. Making money has become part of Shylock's sober way of life. When he is threatened with the loss of his wealth, he refers to it as "the prop / That doth sustain my house" (IV.i.375-376). Wealth is what gives security and stability to Shylock's life: he sees it as the foundation of his family line. Hence Shylock is unwilling to squander his money on frivolous pursuits and is actively hostile to any form of merriment:

What, are there masques? Hear you me, Jessica:
Lock up my doors; and when you hear the drum
And the vile squeaking of the wry-neck'd fife,
Clamber not you up to the casements then,
Nor thrust your head into the public street
To gaze on Christian fools with varnish'd faces;
But stop my house's ears, I mean my casements;
Let not the sound of shallow fopp'ry enter
My sober house.

(II.v.28-36)

In short, Shylock rejects the whole world of music, dancing, and comic festivity. Both Shylock and Antonio understand dimensions of life that elude the average Venetian. But at the same time, they are both missing an integral element of life: the ability to enjoy it.

Indeed Shylock's concern with money threatens to turn into an obsession, as he tends to forget that money has only instrumental value. One can see this danger in what appears to be his most ridiculous moment: when he equates the loss of his daughter with the loss of his money:

"My daughter! O my ducats! O my daughter!
Fled with a Christian! O my Christian ducats!"

(II.viii.15-16)

This is the most satiric moment in the portrayal of Shylock, but critics often forget that we never actually see Shylock speak these words. This is in fact Solanio's *report* of what Shylock says and as such it is a caricature. For Shylock's own words on this theme, we must look later in the play:

> A diamond gone, cost me two thousand ducats in Frankford! The curse never fell upon our nation till now, I never felt it till now. Two thousand ducats in that, and other precious, precious jewels. I would my daughter were dead at my feet and the jewels in her ear! Would she were hears'd at my foot, and the ducats in her coffin! No news of them? Why, so—and I know not what's spent in the search.
>
> (III.i.83-92)

There is still something laughable in Shylock's miserly concern with the cost of the search, but the way he himself links his daughter with his ducats has a bitterness about it that silences laughter. We can see here how closely Shylock associates his financial fortunes with the fortunes of his family. His dream is to be able to continue his line by passing his wealth on to his Jewish daughter and hence his nightmare is to see her throw it away as a Christian. By the end of the scene, Shylock rises to a note of genuine pathos:

> Out upon her! Thou torturest me, Tubal. It was my turkis. I had it of Leah when I was a bachelor. I would not have given it for a wilderness of monkeys.
>
> (III.i.120-123)

Once we see that wealth has a deeper value for Shylock, he no longer appears as ridiculous as he did in Solanio's portrait.[8] In Solanio's version, Shylock seemed to reduce Jessica to the level of his ducats; in Shylock's own words we see that in fact the reason why his money is so important to him is that it is bound up with his feelings about his family.

This is a good example of the complexity of Shakespeare's portrait of Shylock. In the words of Solanio, Shakespeare first gives us a purely external, unsympathetic view of Shylock, in which he appears merely grotesque and ridiculous. But then Shakespeare in effect repeats the scene, allowing us to hear Shylock's own words and to see inside his soul. Once we get a feel for the intensity of Shylock's emotions, it is difficult to treat him as merely laughable. There is something warped and one-sided about Shylock. But he has managed to make a virtue of his limitations. He has in fact taken a limited form of virtue—thrift and industry—and pushed it to an extreme, pushed it to the point where it becomes problematic and brings him into conflict with society. Antonio displays a similar one-sidedness. He tries to make friendship into the whole of life, and his martyr's mentality prevents him from participating in the joys of Venetian society. Ultimately what makes Antonio and Shylock similar is their inability to take pleasure in the moment. They are both masters of what is today called delayed gratification. Both are always laying up treasure, Antonio in heaven, Shylock in his counting house. They thus both contradict the holiday spirit of Venice, perfectly expressed by Jessica when she describes Bassanio:

> He finds the joys of heaven here on earth,
> And if on earth he do not merit it,
> In reason he should never come to heaven!
>
> (III.v.76-78)

In their desire to have their heaven here on earth, the Venetians speak for the world of comedy, precisely the world which both Antonio and Shylock reject.

IV

Left to themselves, Antonio and Shylock could only destroy each other. Though they appear to have agreed to deal with each other for business purposes, their economic bond is only an illusion. In the end, neither allows his behavior to be governed by strictly economic motives. Shylock wants to use his economic relationship with Antonio to gain revenge, while Antonio uses the bond to express his love for Bassanio. If Shylock and Antonio behaved like pure economic men, they would be able to resolve their differences peacefully, especially once Shylock is offered his money back. But Shylock and Antonio turn out to be too much caught up in their principles to accept any monetary solution to their conflict. Hence the intervention of Portia becomes necessary to save the day. She does not feel bound by rules, as shown by the way she outwits her dead father's will, giving hints to Bassanio so that the one suitor she herself desires will win her hand.[9] In general, fathers do not fare well in the world of *The Merchant of Venice*.[10] Jessica flees her father, rejects his religion, and even robs him. Launcelot Gobbo makes fun of his father, leading him around by the nose. This is all part of the comic pattern of the play. Fathers represent the power of convention and have to be defeated for the spirit of comedy to prevail. Having outwitted her own father, Portia has to go on to defeat the main father in the play: Shylock.

In the powerful courtroom scene, Portia begins by appealing to Shylock's mercy. She gives a beautiful speech, and the sentiments she expresses are no doubt admirable. But in taking this speech at face value, critics have made far too much of it. Portia knows that the appeal to mercy is not going to affect Shylock. This speech is only her opening gambit, and as such it is a very rhetorical performance. It is precisely what it sounds like—a set speech. Indeed we have to check carefully to see how closely Portia abides by these sentiments later in the scene.[11] Earlier in the play she herself warned us to check her speeches against her deeds:

> If to do were as easy as to know what were good to do, chapels had been churches, and poor men's cottages princes' palaces. It is a good divine that follows his own instructions; I can easier teach twenty what were good to be done than to be one of the twenty to follow mine own teaching.
>
> (I.ii.12-17)

Here as elsewhere in the play, Shakespeare alerts us to the possibility that Portia may not always live up to the pieties she espouses. The fact is that Portia has a purpose to accomplish in the courtroom scene and she will do anything to bring about the result she desires. But she knows that she must not reveal her partiality. That is the lesson she learned from the test of the three caskets: she had to give the appearance of impartiality even while manipulating events to the outcome she wanted.[12]

In the courtroom scene, Bassanio wants to be open about the manipulation:

> Wrest once the law to your authority:
> To do a great right, do a little wrong,
> And curb the cruel devil of his will.
>
> (IV.i.215-217)

But Portia vehemently rejects this approach on legal grounds:

> It must not be, there is no power in Venice
> Can alter a decree established.
> 'Twill be recorded for a precedent,
> And many an error by the same example
> Will rush into the state. It cannot be.
>
> (IV.i.218-222)

But this appearance of impartiality is all part of Portia's strategy for getting Shylock on her side. Since she seems to be defending his cause, he begins to trust her. Portia thus lulls Shylock into a false sense of security. Only then does she spring her trap on him: he can take Antonio's flesh but not his blood. Portia has gotten Shylock to insist that whatever is not explicitly stated in the bond is not legally valid (IV.i.257-262) and hence his failure to include title to Antonio's blood in the agreement now bars him from spilling even one drop of it (IV.i.306-312). Portia traps Shylock in his own legalism: he is reduced to asking weakly: "Is that the law?" (IV.i.314).

Thus Portia is able to defeat Shylock by exploiting what was regarded in the Renaissance as the Jewish tendency to read the law literally, rather than figuratively as Christians were supposed to do. Having checked his attack on Antonio, Portia now moves swiftly against Shylock. Suddenly he is the one on trial, charged under a law prohibiting an alien from practicing against the life of a Venetian citizen. The court is prepared to sentence him to death and take away all his wealth. The Duke and Antonio combine to show Shylock mercy, sparing his life and not confiscating all his wealth. But Antonio takes it upon himself to determine who shall inherit Shylock's wealth and moreover he insists that Shylock convert to Christianity. Several critics have argued that in Elizabethan eyes forcing Shylock to convert would have been viewed as a true act of mercy, since it shows concern for the salvation of his soul. But Shakespeare does not have Antonio say a single word about the salvation of Shylock's soul, and certainly Shylock does not overflow with gratitude in recognition of the Christians' concern for his spiritual welfare.

Indeed Shakespeare is unusually restrained in showing Shylock's reaction to the way he has been treated. Shakespeare seems to have gone out of his way to leave it open how to interpret the outcome of this scene. Shylock's laconic response—"I am content" (IV.i.394)—is profoundly ambiguous. An actor or a director can interpret this line in a variety of ways, as anyone who has seen a number of productions of *The Merchant of Venice* can confirm. Said with resignation, the line can suggest that Shylock is genuinely capitulating to the Christians. But said with defiance—with clenched teeth as it were—the line can suggest that Shylock is unrepentant and unbowed. The fact is that Shakespeare never shows a converted Shylock at the end of *The Merchant of Venice*. It would have been possible for Shakespeare to stage such a conversion, or at least to have it reported as he does with Duke Frederick at the end of *As You Like It*. The notion of conversion or change of heart is basic to the movement of comedy and adds greatly to the feeling of comic resolution. But Shakespeare evidently drew the line at showing a converted Shylock. He presents Shylock as a principled man, and to renounce his Judaism would be to betray whatever integrity he has. In *A Midsummer Night's Dream*, Demetrius can give up Hermia and still be Demetrius. But Shylock cannot give up Judaism and still be Shylock. All along, the dispute between Shylock and Antonio has had greater depth than the romantic squabbles typical of Shakespearean comedy. They have been arguing not over who is the prettiest girl in Venice but over what are the fundamental values in life.

That is why Shylock makes a tragic impression in his final scene. We sense that Venice is forcibly imposing conformity, responding to a challenge to its beliefs by simply trying to eliminate the challenger. Venice ultimately finds it cannot include Shylock as Shylock in the community. The courtroom scene is powerfully dramatic precisely because Shakespeare's sympathies are evenly divided. The first half of the scene is weighted against Shylock; as long as he appears to be the cruel one, threatening Antonio's life, we want to see Shylock defeated. But once Portia turns the tables on Shylock, our sympathies are reversed. We feel that Shylock has been caught by a legal trick and now the supposedly merciful Christians can hardly wait to break his spirit. It is easy to imagine how Shakespeare could have written the scene to slant it completely against Shylock. The Christians could have been presented as more genuinely merciful to him and less eager to see him crushed.[13] But Shakespeare did not want a one-sided view of Shylock. As we have seen throughout the play, just when Shylock is beginning to look inhuman or ridiculous to us, Shakespeare throws in a touch to humanize or dignify him in our eyes. By the same token, just when we are warming up to Shylock, Shakespeare has him do or say something that chills our sympathy for him. Shylock's final moment in the play arouses mixed feelings in us no matter how we choose to interpret his last words. If he is really giving in, then he is doing so only as a broken man, as is suggested by his claim: "I am not well" (IV.i.396). If this is the case, then we have watched a once proud and forceful man humbled and crushed. If the actor playing Shylock manages to convey defiance with his final words, then we have to admire Shylock's integrity, the fact that he does not crack under pressure from Venice.

When all is said and done, Shylock is at his most impressive in his final scene, and it is impossible to dismiss him as the mere butt of a joke. Though he is obviously no King Lear, he has many elements of a tragic figure. Above all, he is ultimately destroyed by his own virtues. His highest claim on our admiration is his devotion to the law. More than any other character in the play, he takes justice seriously and it is important to bear in mind that in pursuing Antonio he genuinely believes that the law is on his side. Shylock is willing to stand or fall with the law.[14] Thus it is his law-abidingness which brings about the reversal in his fortunes. He accepts Portia as his judge, and hence accepts her judgment in the case. When the law appears to turn against him, he does not try to evade the consequences with oversubtle interpretations of the statutes. He tries to maintain his dignity in the scene. In particular we never see Shylock begging for mercy or grovelling before the court.

Moreover, the Venetians cannot claim to have clean hands in the scene. Shylock is able to turn most of their arguments against them. For all their talk of mercy, they are, as Shylock points out, slaveholders (IV.i.90-93). And whatever Shylock is, they have made him that way. If he acts inhumanely, the reason is that the Venetians have not treated him as a human being, or as Shylock succinctly puts it: "since I am a dog, beware my fangs." (III.iii.7.). Though it would be going too far to call Shylock a tragic hero, our response to him involves the kind of complexity we feel in responding to the great tragic figures in Shakespeare (which explains why he has provoked almost as much critical debate as they have). We can admire certain qualities in Shylock without thinking that he would be a particularly pleasant person to have around. Shylock does not fit into the Venetian community, but perhaps that shows that something is lacking in Venice. As always, Shakespeare's viewpoint cannot simply be identified with that of any of his characters. Too often critics have been concerned with the question of whether Shakespeare was for or against Shylock. That is not the point: a dramatist does not have to give a verdict the way a judge does. *The Merchant of Venice* is a great drama, and not a cheap melodrama, precisely because Shakespeare can see what is good and bad in both Shylock and his antagonists.

V

By the same token, to defend Shylock does not require us to attack Portia. Because Shakespeare is a good dramatist, we can appreciate why they both act the way they do. Portia does what she has to do in the courtroom scene to save the situation. But we should recognize that she goes about her task very cleverly, indeed shrewdly. There is no use getting sentimental about her as so many critics have done. Throughout the play we see that she is not averse to manipulating people to get what she wants. In Act V, Portia completes her triumph by defeating Antonio, who in light of his relationship with Bassanio may be regarded as the final father-figure in the play. The comedy of the rings shows Antonio that he has gotten everyone in trouble by insisting that a man should be more loyal to his best friend than to his wife. In effect, Antonio has to remarry Bassanio and Portia, giving his consent to a union that will take his friend away from him.[15] Hence Antonio ends up almost as isolated as Shylock, literally the odd man out in the final scene. As the three couples march off, presumably to bed, Antonio is left standing on stage alone.[16]

It is possible to assimilate *The Merchant of Venice* to the standard pattern of comedy. The play deals with the elimination of whatever stands in the way of the satisfaction of the desires of the young lovers. By the end of the play, the characters are free to love and procreate. This was not so at the beginning, when Venetian society seemed threatened with sterility. As we have seen, there are two blocking agents in the play: Antonio and Shylock. Antonio's melancholy threatens to spoil the festive spirit of comedy. Moreover, he represents an extreme ideal of male friendship, which would keep the society of men together in necessarily sterile relationships. Shylock is equally opposed to the festive spirit, repelled by the thought of anybody enjoying himself. And he wants to breed money, not human beings. The chilling and killing hand of the law is perhaps best represented by the will of Portia's dead father. At the beginning of the play, it seems as if she will never get married. All the various forms of law and custom which inhibit the lovers have to be thrust aside in the course of the play in order to liberate the natural energies of the community.

But *The Merchant of Venice* does not make the same impression as most straightforward comedies. The reason is that in Shylock and Antonio Shakespeare experimented with using characters who have more depth than we normally expect in a comedy. Usually the blocking agents in a comedy are made to look purely ridiculous. They have no real principle to champion against the young lovers, but seem to oppose them merely for the sake of opposition. Moreover, the blocking agents are usually allowed to participate in the fun at the end of the play. Frequently they are brought to repent and reform in order to join the crowd. The conversion of Scrooge at the end of Dickens' *A Christmas Carol* is typical of this sort of movement. The stony old man suddenly turns out to have a melting heart. But this is not what happens with Antonio and Shylock. They give in but never clearly admit that they were wrong. Neither has a moment of recognition and neither, in Northrop Frye's terms, discovers a new social identity for himself.[17] In particular, Antonio remains a bachelor. Above all, neither Shylock nor Antonio undergoes a change of heart at the end of the play. Hence they do not fit into the happy ending, Shylock not at all and Antonio only barely. They both remain isolated from the final harmony, thereby indicating that it is somehow limited. Their opposition to the youthful passionate characters is not simply based in crotchetiness or cantankerousness. They are not just mean-spirited old men who do not want anyone else to have fun. Their opposition to the comic world is a principled opposition, rooted as we have seen in religious principles, and that makes us take them seriously.

In the tragic world to which they seem at first confined, Antonio and Shylock are bitterly opposed to each other. But from a higher perspective they are united against the whole comic world of the play. Antonio and Shylock have different principles, but at least they are both principled men. Only in the context of a comedy does their integrity look like inflexibility or stubbornness. They are opposed by characters like Portia, Bassanio, and Gratiano, who are not obsessed with principles, and will in fact adapt their principles whenever they stand in the way of success in life. What would come across as pliancy and lack of integrity in a tragedy appears as healthy flexibility and adaptability in a comedy.

Critics have understandably been concerned with the opposition between Christianity and Judaism in *The Merchant of Venice* and hence with the conflict between Antonio and Shylock. But as we have seen, a more fundamental opposition is at work in the play, which can be formulated in a variety of ways: Antonio and Shylock vs. the rest of the characters, the spirit of tragedy vs. the spirit of comedy, the world of religious principles vs. the world of nature and vitality. The attempt to read *The Merchant of Venice* as if it were some kind of sectarian debate, pitting one religion against another, has led to seemingly endless controversy. As I have tried to show, a more fruitful approach may be to raise the discussion to a higher level and view the play as a more comprehensive reflection on the problematic place of religion in general in social life, an enquiry in which aspects of both Christianity and Judaism are called into question.

Notes

1. Allan Bloom, *Shakespeare's Politics* (New York: Basic Books, 1964) 18-19. Throughout this essay, I am heavily indebted to Bloom's discussion of *The Merchant of Venice*.

2. The edition of Shakespeare I have used is G. Blakemore Evans, ed., *The Riverside Shakespeare* (Boston: Houghton Mifflin, 1974).

3. For a discussion of theological views on the subject of usury in relation to *The Merchant of Venice*, see W. H. Auden, "Brothers & Others," *The Dyer's Hand and Other Essays* (New York: Vintage Books, 1968) 233-237.

4. See Bloom 15-16.

5. Bloom (23) demonstrates the focus on the body in Venice by analyzing Shylock's "Hath not a Jew eyes?" speech (III.i.59-71): "if one looks at the list of similar characteristics on which Shylock bases his claim to equality with his Christian tormentors, one sees that it includes only things which belong to the body." See also 33, note 17: "Shylock characteristically mentions laughter as a result of tickling. He and Antonio would not laugh at the same jokes."

6. See Northrop Frye, *A Natural Perspective* (New York: Columbia University Press, 1965) and C. L. Barber, *Shakespeare's Festive Comedy* (Princeton: Princeton University Press, 1959).

7. See Auden 233.

8. See Bloom 22.

9. See Bloom 26: Portia "lets Bassanio know how to choose by the song. . . . It depreciates the senses, and its meaning is clear. Moreover, the first rhyme is 'bred' with 'head,' which also rhyme with 'lead.'" For confirmation of this point, see Leslie A. Fiedler, *The Stranger in Shakespeare* (New York: Stein and Day, 1972) 113-115, and Barbara Tovey, "The Golden Casket: An Interpretation of *The Merchant of Venice*," in John Alvis and Thomas G. West, eds., *Shakespeare as Political Thinker* (Durham, North Carolina: Carolina Academic Press, 1981) 215-216.

10. See Fiedler 86.

11. See Fiedler 131.

12. See Bloom 26-27.

13. See René Girard, "'To Entrap the Wisest': A Reading of *The Merchant of Venice*," in Edward Said, ed., *Literature and Society* (Baltimore: Johns Hopkins University Press, 1979) 107-108, 111-112. Approaching *The Merchant of Venice* from a very different perspective from mine, namely his theory of mimetic desire and the monstrous double, Girard arrives at similar conclusions about the apparent differences and hidden similarities between Shylock and the other Venetians.

14. See Bloom 13, 24, and Girard 112.

15. See Bloom 29, Fiedler 135, and Tovey 230.

16. See Fiedler 87-88 and Auden 233-234.

17. See Frye 78.

G. M. Pinciss (essay date 1990)

Pinciss, G. M. "The 'Heavenly Comforts of Despair' and *Measure for Measure*." *Studies in English Literature, 1500-1900* 30, no. 2 (spring 1990): 303-13.

[*In the following essay, Pinciss contends that in his role as friar, Duke Vincentio assays the spiritual well-being of each of the central characters in* Measure for Measure, *successfully guiding Claudio, Angelo, and Isabella from a state of religious despair to a renewed faith in God's forgiveness and their own salvation.*]

I

To a modern audience the notion expressed in *Measure for Measure* that being reduced to a state of despair can result in "heavenly comforts" (IV.iii.109) sounds paradoxical if not down-right contradictory; like the imprisoned Claudio sentenced to die, we might well ask "What's the comfort?" (III.i.53).[1] Yet the words come from the ruler of Vienna, who combines political power and religious authority. To his mind this painful spiritual condition is highly desirable. And his view is scarcely idiosyncratic: the benefits that can come out of despair are hard to overestimate, for the belief that losing hope in one's salvation can be a necessary first step to gaining it is confirmed in the Articles of the Church of England and in the sermons of influential English clergymen in the late sixteenth century.

In Renaissance thinking, despair can produce two opposing spiritual states. On the one hand, unqualified despair, doubting God's power to grant remission for one's sins and demonstrating a lack of faith, results in eternal damnation. But on the other hand, qualified despair can be positive, marking the very start of one's spiritual recovery.[2] According to Susan Snyder, both Luther and Calvin found "a kind of self-despair as prerequisite to salvation," and, no doubt with their encouragement, Protestant sermons stressed the need for fallen humanity, aware of its unworthiness, to be reborn through the experience of positive despair to a complete dependence on God: in the words of William Tyndale, "For except thou have borne the cross of adversity and temptation, and hast felt thyself brought unto the very brim of desperation, yea, and unto hell-gates . . . , it shall not be possible for thee to think that God is righteous and just."[3] Despair, as Robert Burton explained in *The Anatomy of Melancholy,* could affect even "God's best children."[4] As a result, the spiritual struggle of working through a deeply troubled conscience to arrive at a renewed faith in God is a process much discussed in the devotional literature of Shakespeare's time.[5] According to such ministers as Robert Cleaver, rector of Drayton, Oxfordshire, in 1598, "hearts must bee crushed and broken," for "till the heart bee broken for sinne, there can be no plaine confession of sinne, and therefore no repentance."[6] With similar imagery the anonymous author of *The Sicke-mans Comfort* (1590) describes how the truly penitent can acquire faith in the power of God's merciful forgiveness of sin:

> once made conscience-stricken by the enormity of his sins, "pearced to the heart with sorowe, we must then laye to his wounde some asswaging medicine, & do as the Masons do when they hewe their stone: first they give great blowes with their hammer . . . & then they poolish it over so . . . that the strokes are no more seen: so must we do, after we have handled the sick patient roughly & thrust him downe to hel by the rigorous threats of the lawes: we must comfort him, and fetch him againe by the sweete amiable promises of the Gospel, to the end that the sowplenes of this oyle may asswage the nipping sharpnes of the law."
>
> (p. 61)[7]

The same spiritual condition is also discussed by the influential William Perkins, fellow of Christ's College and popularizer of Calvin's doctrines, when he encourages his congregation to experience the state of "holy desperation" felt by the truly penitent before they throw themselves on the mercy of God. Perkins warns his audience, moreover, that even among the Elect lapses of faith or "spiritual desertions" are common: "This sorte of desertions, though it bee but for a time, yet no part of a Christian man's life is free from them; and very often taking deepe place in the heart of man, they are of long continuance."[8] Naturally, there is great danger that the despairing soul might so doubt God's mercy that he believes his sins cannot be forgiven. Failure to believe in God's forgiveness and in the sacrifice of Christ constitutes a loss of Christian faith, and, as a consequence, such a despairing soul is bound for hell eternally.

Since despair was an important concern for Renaissance Englishmen, the manifestations of this spiritual state were frequently demonstrated in contemporary literature. For instance, Spenser's Redcrosse Knight is saved from Despair's persuasive argument in favor of self-destruction only by Una's reminder of the forgiveness and salvation promised in the New Testament (*Faerie Queene* I.ix.53).[9] In the theater the negative power of despair is dramatized in Marlowe's *Doctor Faustus*. In the words of its hero: "My heart is hardened, I cannot repent," and, in consequence, he realizes: "damned art thou, Faustus, damned; despair and die!" For other characters, however, despair can revive hope by taking away everything but what is ultimately the only essential—trust in God alone. Unlike Faustus, those predestined to be saved will progress out of despair to arrive at true repentance, forgiveness, and the remission of sins. This process is shown by Edgar's treatment of his father in *King Lear*. Gloucester must be brought to understand the need to trust in divine providence—"thy life's a miracle"—and to believe that heaven alone determines the timing and conditions of our arrival and departure, our "coming hither" as well as our "going hence."[10]

Recognizing the widely held Renaissance belief in the benefits of despair we can better understand the behavior and intentions of the curious ruler of Vienna in *Measure for Measure,* one who "would have dark deeds darkly answered."[11] We should keep in mind that this discussion of Protestant theological notions is especially appropriate here, for, as Louise Schleiner points out, in no other play of Shakespeare's do we find that the "central characters evoke specific biblical passages and theological concepts to explain their crucial deeds; in no other are the allusions so prominent; in no other do they define so distinct and consistent a pattern. . . . This is Shakespeare's most theological play."[12]

II

If not the central figure, Duke Vincentio is surely the moving force of the action in *Measure for Measure.* Although the deceptions and deceits by which he operates have aroused considerable criticism and complaint, most of his motives are generally regarded as straightforward.[13] On some occasions at least, his behavior is unambiguous and laudable. By feigning absence from his city, he can test the character of his deputy, Angelo; by using the bed-trick and replacing Isabella with Mariana, Angelo's former fiancée, the Duke can order Angelo to marry her; and by substituting Ragozine, a notorious pirate who died of a "cruel fever," for Claudio, Isabella's brother, the Duke can save the young man's life.

But Duke Vincentio's actions and intervention are not so easily understood in every instance. In fact, a number of times his words and actions strike one as irrational or perverse. In particular, he seems nearly obsessed with teaching men to confront their death.[14] It is a lesson he repeats almost compulsively. He lectures Claudio on the need to "be absolute for death"—even eavesdropping to learn if his sermon has been effective—and he does not leave until Claudio is, in the Duke's words, "resolved to die" (III.ii.242). The Duke also intends to deal with the drunken prisoner Barnardine to "persuade this rude wretch willingly to die" (IV.iii.80). And, before the Duke is through with him, Angelo, too, says he is very ready to end his life: "I crave death more willingly than mercy; / 'Tis my deserving, and I do entreat it" (V.i.474-75).

The Duke's eccentricities are evident not only in these examples of his meddling but also in his treatment of Isabella. His explanation for his treatment of her appears cruel, if not almost incomprehensible. Although one may not approve, one can understand that he keeps from her the truth of her brother's fate in order to test her capacity to forgive Angelo: will she join Mariana and plead for the deputy's life even when Isabella believes him responsible for her brother's death? But Duke Vincentio's expressed motive for deceiving her, verbalized in soliloquy, is, in the judgment of Philip Edwards, an "appalling justification."[15] According to what the Duke tells us, he "will keep her ignorant of her good, / To make her heavenly comforts of despair, / When it is least expected" (IV.iii.108-10). For Edwards, "God works in mysterious ways, but this beats all—willingly to cause despair in order to show the beauty of divine consolation." Other students of this play also express irritation with the Duke's behavior. Harriett Hawkins finds his action "so patronizing as to be more infuriating, in intent, than satisfying when dramatically realized."[16] And Richard A. Levin thinks that when the Duke claims he will make "heavenly comforts of despair," his "rationale seems strained, his cruelty sadistic."[17] The reaction of these critics to the Duke's words is quite understandable, for if his language is divorced from its theological meaning, then the comic intrigues that will result in a happy ending—"the beauty of divine consolation"—cannot be reconciled with the notion of providential intervention into human affairs that is also being implied here—"willingly to cause despair." To quote Edwards once more, "The distance between the contrivances necessary for the fulfilment of the comedy and the workings of God which they are meant to suggest is impossibly great."[18] In effect, the concept of the fortunate fall does not usually include the notion that a masochistic Providence takes as much delight to chastise humanity as to save it.

Yet by appreciating that out of a qualified despair can come positive spiritual growth, we may be better able to explain the Duke's course of action. And we should recall that at this point in the play the Duke, now dressed as a friar, may well be providing some religious instruction by what he does. His insistence on the "comforts of despair" expresses what he has in mind since, as we have seen, Christian theology teaches that through despair we can acquire the faith to believe that we will be saved not through our goodness but God's.

III

Regarded in this context, the Duke-as-friar tests the spiritual health of each of the principal characters in the play, acting the part of religious teacher. First in his interview with Juliet, Claudio's pregnant fiancée, he evaluates her spiritual state and approves of her resolution, combining repentance and acceptance. The state of her conscience and her penance reflect her concern for her spiritual condition rather than for her self-image or her reputation in the world: "I do repent me as it is an evil, / And take the shame with joy" (II.iii.35-36).

Next he turns to Claudio in an effort to make him understand that peace can be achieved only through the same combination of repentance and acceptance. Claudio thinks he has learned the friar's lesson: "To sue to live, I find I seek to die, / And seeking death, find life. Let it come on" (III.i:42-43). But his willingness to "let it come on" is difficult to sustain. When Isabella tells him that Angelo has offered to exchange Claudio's life for her chastity, Claudio remembers that "death is a fearful thing," and he pleads with his sister to save him by yielding to the deputy.[19] Once more the Duke must urge Claudio to become reconciled to his plight: "Do not satisfy your resolution with hopes that are fallible." And once more Claudio will seek for pardon and resignation: "I am so out of love with life, that I will sue to be rid of it." Through the Duke's efforts, Isabella's brother "most willingly humbles himself to the determination of justice" and has "discredited" the "many deceiving promises of life" (III.ii.237-40). Having been brought to this positive state of despair, Claudio is ready for the rebirth that will be enacted in the final scene of the play.

With the prisoner Barnardine, "a man that apprehends death no more dreadfully but as a drunken sleep," who is both "insensible of mortality, and desperately mortal" (IV.ii.140-43), the ruler of Vienna has a more difficult time. His offers of comfort and prayer are rejected out of hand, and with comic determination Barnardine swears he "will not die today for any man's persuasion." To spare him from damnation, Barnardine's jailors grant the Duke-as-friar more time so that he can "persuade this rude wretch willingly to die" (IV.iii.80). Although we watch Duke Vincentio effectively lead some souls onto the path of salvation, we are never witnesses of his success in this instance. After all, not everyone will despair, not everyone will find comfort, and not everyone, ultimately, will be saved; in truth, Barnardine seems rather one of those "unfit to live or die." The final resolution for the Duke in the closing moments of the play is to offer Barnardine pardon for his crimes on earth, extending to him the utmost mercy and leaving him to make his own peace with heaven.

Unlike his failure with Barnadine, the Duke causes Angelo to experience a series of emotional states that ultimately affect his spiritual well-being. Although a man of conscience and moral awareness, Angelo has yielded to the temptations of lust and power. Forced to confront the painful truths of his actions, he suffers from both shame and guilt. These emotions lead him to a new sense of self and enable him to have his turn at the positive aspects of despair. His feelings of sorrow, regret, self-hatred, and repentance leave him in his own self-estimation deserving of death:

> I am sorry that such sorrow I procure,
> And so deep sticks it in my penitent heart
> That I crave death more willingly than mercy:
> 'Tis my deserving, and I do entreat it.
>
> (V.i.472-75)

This acknowledgement of his guilt and worthlessness is preparatory to his reformation, a necessary preliminary to understanding that salvation can be attained only through acceptance and faith.

Publicly admitting his guilt and still believing himself responsible for Claudio's death, Angelo has now arrived at the point where his character can be reformed:

> No longer session hold upon my shame,
> But let my trial be mine own confession.
> Immediate sentence, then, and sequent death
> Is all the grace I beg.
>
> (V.i.369-72)

In this spiritual state he can only turn to God with absolute dependence on His mercy; like Claudio, he must learn that salvation arrives through despair. As the Duke says, "your evil quits you well."

In the same final scene, the Duke determines that Lucio, the slanderer and wastrel, is to be put to death after he has been married to "one whom he begot with child," a judgment that recalls Claudio's original plight as well as the Duke's sentence on Angelo before the intercession of Mariana and Isabella. Ultimately, Lucio's life, like Angelo's, will be spared by the pleas of a woman who loves him, Kate Keepdown; and by confronting his own death, Lucio, too, will be granted the opportunity to be reborn to a new and reformed life.

IV

The positive aspects of despair are fostered by Duke Vincentio not only in the men but also in Isabella, whose development is carefully monitored by him. The men in the play must be brought to confront their own end, but in her case Isabella must confront the deaths of others. Believing her brother executed at Angelo's order, she must respond to the Duke's sentence of "An Angelo for Claudio, death for death" (V.i.407). The severity of this command perfectly reflects the severity of her attitudes in the early scenes—her desire for even greater strictness among the nuns of her convent, her prudishness about sexuality, her intolerance for human frailty. The Isabella of the first half of the play might well be expected to approve of the justice of "death for death"; in Mary Lascelles's words, "There is a singular rigidity in her bearing."[20]

Yet by the end of the play Isabella supports Mariana's plea for mercy and argues that Angelo should be forgiven. Like her brother and the deputy, Isabella has reached a new understanding of life, and like them she has grown under the tutelage of the Duke. For one "in probation of a sisterhood," she has had to deal directly with some of the more seamy aspects of human relations, exactly those furthest removed from her fastidious and priggish nature. . . .

Then, for reasons that the Duke never makes clear and even against her own instincts—"To speak so indirectly I am loth" (IV.vi.i)—Isabella must publicly admit to committing "what I abhor to name," "a vice that most I do abhor":

> the vile conclusion
> I now begin with grief and shame to utter.
> He would not, but by gift of my chaste body
> To his concupiscible intemperate lust,
> Release my brother; and after much debatement
> My sisterly remorse confutes mine honour,
> And I did yield to him.
>
> (V.i.98-104)

The shame and embarrassment of her situation are compounded, for the Duke, sitting in judgment, rejects her accusation and orders her to prison.

As in his treatment of Claudio and Angelo, Duke Vincentio's intention in all of this is constant: he has told Isabella that her experience is "a physic / That's bitter to sweet end." He has repeatedly encouraged her: "Show your wisdom, daughter, / In your close patience" and, rather than give way to anger, "give your cause to heaven." His instruction and her experience have clearly taken root, for Isabella, as she is arrested, expresses the kind of trust in Providence that the Duke nurses out of the far side of despair:

> O you blessed ministers above,
> Keep me in patience, and with ripen'd time
> Unfold the evil which is here wrapped up
> In countenance!
>
> (V.i.118-21)

As Darryl Gless explains, "the Duke's manipulations of Isabella result in a loss of all hope in worldly aid and a consequent real and utter dependence on divine ordinance."[21]

This complete trust in heaven to resolve matters that are beyond the power of men to understand or control is the positive outcome of despair: to use Duke Vincentio's own words, "Do not satisfy your resolution with hopes that are fallible" (III.i.167-68). Instead, one must rely on faith alone, a faith that is both tested and strengthened through despair. In the words of Richard Hooker: "Too much honey doth turn to gall; and too much joy even spiritually would make us wantons. Happier a great deal is that man's case, whose soul by inward desolation is humbled, than he whose heart is through abundance of spiritual delight lifted up and exalted above measure."[22]

Shakespeare dramatizes how the chief characters in this play, following different paths, all arrive at a point where they despair of their own powers. Stripped of all earthly assurance, they must learn to trust in heaven to achieve positive spiritual growth, to become in Hooker's words "happier a great deal." Only out of despair can they receive those "heavenly comforts" that come when "least expected." Through the good offices of the Duke, the action of *Measure for Measure* traces this spiritual progress.

Notes

1. All references to *Measure for Measure* are to the Arden edition, ed. J. W. Lever (London: Methuen, 1965).

2. In the section on Faith (#31) in the *Institutes of the Christian Religion,* Calvin wrote that only after the penitent "have divested themselves of all arrogance through recognition of their own poverty, have wholly cast themselves down, and have plainly become worthless to themselves, then at last they may begin to taste the sweetness of mercy which the Lord holds out to them" (trans. and annotated by Ford Lewis Battles, Grand Rapids: William B. Eerdmans, 1986), pp. 63-64. For a discussion of the progression from despair to a state of "assurance of salvation," see M. M. Knappen, *Tudor Puritanism* (Chicago: Univ. of Chicago Press, 1970), pp. 393ff. As Rowland Wymer explains, "The sorrow for sin which could bring a person to despair was also a necessary first step to achieving a state of grace." *Suicide and Despair in the Jacobean Drama* (New York: Harvester Press, 1986), p. 6. For an allied discussion see Martha Tuck Rozett, *The Doctrine of Election and the Emergence of Elizabethan Tragedy* (Princeton: Princeton Univ. Press, 1984). Susan Snyder has pointed out: "The whole Protestant emphasis on man's complete unworthiness and helplessness tended to reinforce the paradox of despair, to make it at once more necessary and more terrible. Luther in particular, proceeding from his own past agonizings over the inadequacies of confession and penance and the awful justice of God, his sudden seizures and black despondencies, placed despair of self at the very core of Christian experience." "The Left Hand of God: Despair in Medieval and Renaissance Tradition," *Studies in the Renaissance* 12 (1965):18-59, 23-24.

3. Snyder, p. 28. William Tyndale, "Prologue Upon the Epistle of St. Paul to the Romans," *Doctrinal Treatises* as quoted in Wymer, p. 6.

4. According to Article 16 of the Thirty-nine Articles, which defined the doctrines of faith of the Church of England: "After we have received the Holy Ghost, we may depart from grace given, and fall into sin, and by the grace of God we may arise again and amend our lives. And therefore they are to be condemned which say, they can no more sin as long as they live here, or deny place of forgiveness to such as truly repent." *The Book of Common Prayer* (Oxford: Oxford Univ. Press, 1928).

5. For a discussion of these works and their popularity, see Louis B. Wright, *Middle-Class Culture in Elizabethan England* (Chapel Hill: Univ. of North Carolina Press, 1935), ch. 8, and Beach Langston's account of books of devotion for the comfort of the dying (pp. 112-18) in "Essex and the Art of Dying," *HLQ* 13 (1950):109-29.

6. Robert Cleaver, *Four Godlie and Fruitful Sermons: two preached at Draiton in Oxfordshire* (1611).

7. As quoted by Langston, pp. 115-16.

8. William Perkins, *Works* 1:455-69 (1616-1618); *A treatise tending unto a declaration whether a man bee in the estate of damnation, or in the estate of grace* (London, 1591), pp. 6-7.

9. For further discussion, see James Nohrnberg, *The Analogy of The Faerie Queene* (Princeton: Princeton Univ. Press, 1976), pp. 152-55, and Kathleen Williams, *Spenser's World of Glass* (Berkeley: Univ. of California Press, 1966), p. 27.

10. One can suggest a number of reasons why Shakespeare frequently presents characters who struggle with their despair: it was a concern of widespread interest for his audience; it often affected men in an extremely emotional and therefore highly dramatic manner; and since it is a subject of *Corinthians,* one of his favorite New Testament books, it may have attracted him personally.

11. A problematic work whose central character is a ruling duke disguised as a friar naturally raises questions about the nature of political power as well as religion. As a consequence this play is especially appealing to new historicists, for example Stephen Greenblatt, *Shakespearean Negotiations* (Berkeley: Univ. of California Press, 1988), and Leonard Tennenhouse, *Power on Display: The Politics of Shakespeare's Genres* (New York: Methuen, 1986). Greenblatt's discussion, for example, analyzes how both the church and the state benefitted from keeping the public "in a condition of what we may call salutary anxiety. . . . For the ruling elite believed that a measure of insecurity and fear was a necessary, healthy element in the shaping of proper loyalties, and Elizabethan and Jacobean institutions deliberately

evoked this insecurity. Hence the church's constant insistence upon the fear and trembling . . . that every Christian should experience; hence too the public and increasingly spectacular character of the punishments inflicted by the state" (pp. 135-36). Ultimately, in Greenblatt's view, "the duke's strategy has not changed the structure of feeling or behavior in Vienna in the slightest degree," and the play dramatizes Shakespeare's "ironic reflections on salutary anxiety" (pp. 141-42). Other critical approaches continue to find this play especially congenial: the psychoanalytic in Meredith Skura's *The Literary Use of Psychoanalysis* (New Haven: Yale Univ. Press, 1981) and the literary and symbolic in Paul Hammond's "The Argument of *Measure for Measure*," *ELR* 16 (1986):496-519, and in Alexander Leggatt's "Substitution in *Measure for Measure*," *SQ* 39 (1988):342-59.

12. Louise Schleiner, "Providential Improvisation in *Measure for Measure*," *PMLA* 97, 2 (March 1982):227.

13. For a discussion of the Duke's character and a summary of critical judgments about him, see Cynthia Lewis, "'Dark Deeds Darkly Answered': Duke Vincentio and Judgment in *Measure for Measure*," *SQ* 34 (1983):271-89.

14. For a discussion of the various attitudes toward death expressed in the play, see Phoebe S. Spinrad, "*Measure for Measure* and the Art of Not Dying," *TSLL* 26 (1984):74-93.

15. Philip Edwards, *Shakespeare and the Confines of Art* (London: Methuen, 1968), p. 118.

16. Harriett Hawkins, *Measure for Measure, Twayne's New Critical Introductions* (Boston: Twayne, 1987), pp. 104-105.

17. Richard A. Levin, "Duke Vincentio and Angelo: Would 'A Feather Turn the Scale'?" *SEL* 22 (Spring 1982):257-70, 268.

18. Philip Edwards, pp. 118-19.

19. In his article "More Light on *Measure for Measure*," *MLQ* 23 (1962):309-22, Warren D. Smith finds, interestingly enough, that fourteen critics approve and thirteen disapprove of Isabella's conduct with her brother in this scene.

20. Mary Lascelles, *Shakespeare's "Measure for Measure"* (London: Athlone Press, 1953), p. 88.

21. Darryl J. Gless, *Measure for Measure, the Law, and the Convent* (Princeton: Princeton Univ. Press, 1979), p. 190.

22. Richard Hooker, *Sermon on the Certainty and Perpetuity of Faith in the Elect,* included with *Of the Laws of Ecclesiastical Polity* (New York: Dutton, 1907), 1:6.

Ronald G. Shafer (essay date 1990)

SOURCE: Shafer, Ronald G. "Hamlet: Christian or Humanist?" *Studies in the Humanities* 17, no. 1 (June 1990): 21-35.

[*In the essay below, Shafer charts what he sees as Hamlet's temporary abandonment of Christian principles for the precepts of humanism—and his ultimate reversion to orthodox religious values. In his humanistic phase, the critic proposes, Hamlet is arrogant and egotistical, elevating his own volition above God's sovereignty, but after he acknowledges the righteousness of Christian morality, he humbly submits himself to God's will and becomes an agent of divine retribution.*]

A good starting point for understanding the moral dimension of Shakespeare's *Hamlet* is with Irving Ribner's *Patterns in Shakespearean Tragedy* (1960). Ribner maintains that Shakespeare fashioned all of the elements of the play in such a way as to produce "the emotional equivalent of a Christian view of human life"; it is, thus, "an affirmation of a purposive cosmic order" (65). Hamlet's problem involves his denial of a "purposive and benevolent God" (66) and his failure to realize that "the punishment of the wicked" is God's "own prerogative" (67). To Ribner, the chief issue in the play is whether Hamlet will let "his Christian religion . . . guide him" (68) and become "a passive instrument in the hands of God" (69). To be victorious, Hamlet must do nothing but recognize that faith alone "frustrates" evil along with man's "cultivation of his own goodness" (72). Because Hamlet has not learned to believe in divine Providence, he is frustrated in his attempt to kill Claudius; he must recognize "the inability of man to execute the judgment of God" (77). Hamlet, at last attaining this moral insight, realizes "that heaven has preserved him," faces death heroically, and submits to the will of God (80). Because he has completely yielded to his Sovereign Lord, he is finally able to destroy Claudius, "as a lawful act of public duty, that of a minister of God" (81). Hamlet at the end of the play is a "passive instrument in the hands of divine providence" (81). Thus, the play does not record man's defeat, but his "victory and salvation" (82) over the "mole of nature" which for Ribner is "original sin which beclouds man's reason" (83); "Without this struggle there can be no knowledge and no salvation" (88). For Ribner, however, the conflict is between original sin and submission to God's will and agency; I would characterize the conflict as being between two competing philosophies, Christianity and humanism.

To Shakespeare's contemporaries, the philosophy of humanism extolled human values and individual perception as truth. Man was deified because the philosophy enthroned his thinking over the law of God; in effect, it dethroned God as Sovereign of the universe. Such a philosophy seems to be the prevailing vision of *Hamlet,* and while humanistic thinking in the play is not confined to Hamlet himself, he does seem to embody its tenets. For instance, he believes that *he* is born to set right the Danish court—no talk here of "the Most High who ruleth in the kingdom of men and giveth it to whomsoever He will" (Daniel 4: 25); he rejects the notion that death is the vanquished foe which ushers in the new eternal state; he rejects God's moral law against suicide; he wishes to erase all commandments from his brain except the ghost's command to seek revenge. Hamlet would appear, in short, to be a first-order humanist, since for him personal thinking is the touchstone of truth and morality. A providentially-ordered world, in which God's will ought to prevail over man's temporal and capricious will, is a dimly recollected illusion.

Yet this view of Hamlet's humanism, which seems to yield in many ways a convincing and, to the modern mind, a satisfactory reading of the play is simplistic at best. An examination of biblical analogues in the play leads to an opposite view. Hamlet is at one point the humanist incarnate in the play, but is that philosophy characteristic of him? I will argue that Hamlet's humanism is a temporary flirtation which he resorts to during the trauma at the Danish court, that it disguises his strong affinity for orthodox and Christian values, that his dark night of the soul is caused by the influence of humanism and the rejection of his Christianity, and that he finally rejects this humanistic stance at the end of his life when he again reverts to traditional, Christian values.

This progression is worked out against a biblical backdrop which, always present though generally muted, offers a profound commentary upon the action of the play. Before charting this progression, however, we would do well to sample the play's rich biblical texture. Ophelia, for example, tells Polonius that Hamlet had buttressed his claims of love for her "With almost all the holy vows of heaven" (I. iii. 115), indicating a Hamlet steeped in traditional religious dogma: that is some young prince whose protestations of love are set in a religious framework! She tells Laertes not to show her "the steep and thorny way to heaven" (I. iii. 48)—certainly a biblical paraphrase of Christ's reference to the narrow way (Matthew 7: 14)—if he will not follow it himself. After the "To be" speech she invokes heaven twice to help Hamlet (III. ii. 135, 142), and during her madness her religious references intensify. As with most of Shakespeare's characters during fits of madness, the true terrain of her mind is then disclosed. Ophelia is no exception. In one song she laments that a maid fell from innocence, and in a later song ("And will 'a not come again") she sings, "God 'a' mercy on his soul," adding at the end of the song, "And of all Christians' souls, I pray God" (IV. v. 200-01). Ophelia's speech, in short, is laced with traditional, recognizable religious references.

Hamlet's use of biblical cognates is just as insistent. Upon seeing the ghost, he cries, "Angels and ministers of grace defend us!" (I. iv. 39). Past theological training serves him well and reminds him that the ghost may not be a ghost at all but a corporealized spirit being, possibly demonic. When he hears Rosencrantz say that the world has grown honest, he retorts, "then is doomsday near" (II. ii. 238). It takes no biblical scholar to refer to a religious event as commonplace as doomsday, but that he employs this eschatological term does offer a glimpse into his soul and an insight into his penchant for couching experience in religious terminology. It does, on the other hand, take a person with some in-depth familiarity with the Bible to call Polonius a Jephthah (II. ii. 411), an obscure biblical allusion found in the Book of Judges (Chapters 11 and 12). He counsels the players not to "out-herod Herod" (III. ii. 14), and he tells Ophelia that "virtue cannot so inoculate our old stock" (III. i. 118-19), a fairly obvious biblical throwback to the Pauline dialectic of the old and new man, which appears throughout the Pauline epistles. After the "To be" speech he entreats Ophelia to remember his sins in her prayers: ". . . in thy orisons / Be all my sins rememb'red" (III. i. 90-91). Would a person who really believed that man was the quintessence of dust in a godless world, where nothing was right or wrong except one's perception of it, have bothered?

Such biblical echoes are numerous in Hamlet's speeches, but they increase after the staging of *Gonzago*. During the speech Hamlet utters when Claudius is at prayer, he makes no fewer than four references to heaven. As he struggles to kill Claudius, his affinity for the moral law keeps appearing in the form of biblical phraseology. An interesting psychological truth is present here: Hamlet, drawing nearer to the destruction of Claudius, deliberately forsakes years of religious training and the moral law that had been the very basis of his life. As his conscious mind denounces that standard, his unconscious mind resorts to it all the more vehemently and feeds the conscious mind with biblical language. The two standards war in his mind. Such a classic irony: as he nears the fulfillment of his death plan, his spiritual nature asserts itself. Hamlet, oblivious to this war, registers only a profound depression because he has grieved the higher law of love.

Moments later in Gertrude's bedroom, he refers in quick succession to the cross (III. iv. 15), religion (l. 48), heaven (ll. 49, 60), judgment (l. 71), the devil (ll. 77, 169), virtue (l. 167), angel (l. 169), and grace (l. 151)—all stock in trade words from orthodox Christianity. He reminds us of a clergyman, armed with text, when he says to Gertrude, "Confess yourself to heaven, / Repent what's past, avoid what is to come" (III. iv. 156-57)—not a great deal different from John the Baptist or St. Paul preaching to wicked mankind. The anomaly is that this God-denying, Bible-rejecting, Claudius-destroying prince would admonish Gertrude with exclusively biblical precepts. Why is he so insistent that she align her life with such precepts when he is so far astray from them himself and when he denies their existence? Is he that hypocritical, or is the cry for her to repent actually a cry directed, albeit unknowingly, at his own soul? Is he holding up the mirror to Gertrude, or is the spirit part of Hamlet, his new man nature, holding up the mirror to the carnal part, his old man nature? I contend the latter as much as the former, which causes a radical change in Hamlet's behavior at the end of the play.

The biblical language continues into Act IV. When Hamlet talks with Claudius, he tells the king that Polonius is in heaven and that "man and wife is one flesh" (IV. iii. 56), an overt use of precise biblical wording. He refers to man's thinking as a "capability and god-like reason" (IV. iv. 38) which is not to go unused. Although his thinking is not "god-like" during his bout with humanism, he nevertheless realizes that man's reasoning is supposed to be sovereign, and he is enough of a renaissance biblical scholar to know that Satan kindles the carnal, unregenerated nature in man, just as God kindles the spiritually regenerated nature. In several different instances he inveighs against man's longing for greed and fame, the things of this temporal world, as when he says that Fortinbras' men will fight in Poland for an "eggshell" which is merely "tomb enough and continent / To hide the slain" (IV. iv. 64-65). The spirit part of him realizes that Alexander and Caesar are ashes used to stop a beer barrel (V. i. 207-14). These sound like the reflections of one preaching against the allurements of the carnal life which oppose the walk in the spirit. Though his conscious mind is tempted by the ghost to destroy, Hamlet cannot totally walk away from years of such spiritual indoctrination: in his mind he knows that the spiritual walk cannot be achieved in the energy of the flesh, but his actions are, for a time, inconsistent with that realization.

Of all Hamlet's speeches that resonate with a biblical tone, his instruction to Polonius on caring for the players is most remarkable:

> God's bodkin, man, much better! Use every man after his desert, and who shall scape whipping? Use them after your own honor and dignity. The less they deserve, the more merit is in your bounty.
>
> (II. ii. 529-32).

Here he instructs Polonius not to requite men in accord with what is due them, but in accord with his own personal sense of honor—that is, give more than they deserve, do unto them as you would have them do unto you, the Golden Rule again. Man is to be rewarded not for what he deserves or for what his performance merits but in a way that patterns God's love and grace.

The play is thus steeped in this religious thought and language, and that language extends to all characters, not just Ophelia and Hamlet. Polonius says anyone can "sugar o'er / The devil" (III. i. 48-9); the player queen speaks at length of fidelity in marriage (III. ii. 176-83); Claudius knows his offence is rank and smells to heaven (III. iii. 36); Gertrude knows she has violated Holy Writ by marrying her husband's brother: "Thou turn'st mine eyes into my very soul, / And there I see such black and grained spots / As will not leave their tinct" (III. iv. 90-93); when the grave diggers refer to Christian burial, the one in disbelief says to the other: "What, art a heathen? How dost thou understand the Scripture?" (V. i. 35-36).

Because Hamlet's soul, like the world of Denmark, is steeped in scriptural theology, the pertinent issue is what happens to Hamlet when he forsakes this teaching, when he abandons what Ophelia calls his "*sovereign* reason" (III. i. 160; my emphasis). The essence of Hamlet's thinking is its sovereign nature, a mind predicated on divine truth which provides him with an anchored base to withstand the raging vicissitudes of life, including the Danish court. When he disavows that theological standard, he is unmoored, indecisive, and disenchanted with life. Despite its attractiveness on the surface, a life grounded in his own standards overwhelms him, for it causes all action and thought to become arbitrary. A multiplicity of choices crushes him. Why act with determination when the next minute might reverse this decision? Harmony and equilibrium give way to a paralysis of the will. It is easier to drift than to decide, easier to revert to the carnal nature's ancestral voice of revenge than to assert the spirit nature's voice of love. The tides of mankind are toward the former, not the latter.

Having sampled the biblical analogues in the play, we are now able to note how the play carefully maps out Hamlet's transformation from a providentially governed standard to a humanistic one. Early in Act I, Marcellus comments that "Something is rotten in the state of Denmark" (I. iv. 89). Horatio immediately responds by standing on the belief he—and Hamlet too—has always known, "Heaven will direct it" (I. iv. 90), thereby invoking the old sovereign standard: anything amiss in the kingdom of men will be rectified by an ever-present God. Not so with Hamlet: seeing the ghost, he responds, "whiles memory still holds a seat / In this distracted globe," he will "wipe away all trivial fond records, / All saws of books, all forms, all pressures past / That youth and observation copied there" (I. v. 97-102). Hamlet will eradicate all previous learning which, in a moment, he reduces to trivial and foolish records, even though they have steadied him through all the perilous shoals of his life to this point. In a telling line he says that "thy commandment all alone shall live / Within the book and volume of my brain, / Unmix'd with baser matter" (I. v. 103-05). He will permit the ghost's new commandment to hate and kill supersede God's commandment to love and forgive. And, hypocritically, he enjoins heaven's blessings upon this abandonment of heaven's plan: "Yes, by heaven" (I. v. 105). This manifestation of his self-idolatry again reveals the struggle in Hamlet's heart: as he disavows the old morality he continues to use its lexicon, as evidenced in the word "commandment." Ages of spiritual osmosis cannot be shed in a moment of even herculean self-resolve. In this same speech he says he wishes to erase all recollections from "the table of my memory," an interesting use of the table metaphor that recalls the Pauline letter to the Corinthians, when St. Paul says that the Spirit of the living God is written "not in tables of stone, but in fleshy tables of the heart" (II Cor. 3: 3). This is another illustration of the paradoxical Hamlet: he denounces the biblical ethic with biblical language. But equally important to our purpose here is to note the dramatic polarization of Horatio and Hamlet's responses: for Horatio, Heaven will direct anything amiss in the affairs of men, whereas Hamlet, by changing the commandment of the heart, will set it right himself without the assistance of Jehovah God.

The foregoing constitutes the first stage in his shift away from a sovereignly governed world. He fails to realize that God is in control, fashions his own vision of rectifying the state, and forsakes the command to love. His excessive lamentation over his father's death, which indicates an obdurate heart and failure to accept Heaven's will, reveals a deepening of the humanistic hold on his thinking. As is typical in Shakespeare's mature dramas, the person in the play one would least suspect, Claudius, articulates a profound truth when he speaks of Hamlet's "unmanly grief" and "a will most incorrect to Heaven" (I. ii. 94-95). Again, Hamlet is too enamored of his own heartbeat. His will that his father live predominates over God's will that he not live. That appears to be a subtle shift, but in point of fact it bespeaks a psychic change of the first magnitude: he has just crossed the great spiritual divide. Proof of that is his own admission, once he perceives reality solely from the viewpoint of a humanist standard, that the world is weary, stale, flat, and unprofitable. The longer this illusion exists, the greater the psychic damage it creates in Hamlet and those he poisons with it. Once he forsakes the notion of a world in which man has an ordered place, in which all works together for good, in which no problem is given man above what he is able to bear, in which no dilemma comes to man except that which God allows to filter through His own permissive will with the expressed intent of strengthening spirituality—once Hamlet forsakes that comforting ideology, he has no alternative but despair, and thus he contemplates his own death. Prior to his decision that self instead of God sat on the throne of his life, harmony existed. He was, as Ophelia tells us, "th' expectancy and rose of the fair state, / The glass of fashion and the mold of form, / Th' observ'd of all observers" (III. i. 155-57), living in a world where man, noble in reason, lived in a "goodly frame" (II. ii. 299, 305). Now his typically resilient optimism has been so effaced by humanism that he predicts future as well as present gloom: "it is not nor it cannot come to good" (I. ii. 158).

If the underpinnings of the play center on the dissolution of a religious morality in the heart of Hamlet, it comes as no surprise that Shakespeare spends some bit of time developing its opposite, the new creed of humanism. One of its obvious ideologues is Polonius who, in his parting words to Laertes (I. iii. 58-81), offers precepts that on the surface appear to be wholesome, even theological, but when perceived in the context of this thesis are age-old standbys of humanistic thought. Polonius instructs Laertes to be aware of his dress since appearance indicates the nature of the man inside. Is there any play when Shakespeare did not systematically attack that premise? He tells Laertes to avoid quarrels but when ensnared in one to manage it so as to win, another insight into his inverse of the Golden Rule. The quintessential humanist text of the play occurs at the end of this speech, "This above all: to thine own self be true." In this speech, supposedly the clarion call to truth, lay the tragic root of Hamlet's demise, for his being true to self has actually caused him to be false to many; and once he begins the process of internalizing all reality and measuring it against the yardstick of self, he unwittingly loses himself in the labyrinthine jungle of self, an exemplar of the nation of Israel during the reign of the judges: "Every man did that which was right in his own eyes" (Judges 17: 6). Free from carrying the yoke of religious precept and bearing the bondage of servile responsibility to it, he learns in retrospect a profound paradox: that yoke had been real freedom, not enslavement, and the seeming freedom of living life by personal morality is incarceration.

Besides leading to perverse judgment, Polonius' advice occasions the play's supreme irony: the shallow thinking which Hamlet most acidly mocks is that of Polonius, yet it is Polonius' dictum, be true to self, that Hamlet, of all the characters in the play, follows most religiously. This irony has its equal: the self-centered action Hamlet rejects the most is Claudius' killing of Hamlet's father, yet in severing himself from the old Christian standard, which exists only in those who patiently wait on a sovereign God, Hamlet condemns himself to follow this same pattern of murder. Hating Polonius' babble, he nevertheless adheres to its command and becomes a babbler himself; hating Claudius' action of being a murderer, he nevertheless attempts to follow suit and becomes a murderer too. Polonius is the spokesman for the new creed of humanism, Claudius is a convert to it, and Hamlet, ironically, is the disciple who follows the lead of his mentors. Is this the utopia of freedom which he felt his severance from a Christian standard would create?

Certainly we would appear to be at the heart of one of the play's many philosophic messages. To live one's life at the center of God's will is to know certainty amid oceans of doubt—as Hamlet always did—while to step out of that will in a brazen assertion of self-will is to be pummeled by the billowing waves. Prior to his rejection of God's will, which occurs when he seeks his personal revenge (I. v. 32), Hamlet was the jewel of the nation, the paragon of sovereign reason. After his fall he becomes the curse of the nation with a reason "like sweet bells jangled" (III. i. 161). If the self is to be the new arbiter of morality and the old moral code is no longer operative, then man is left to rely on his reason alone, to devise his own system of right and wrong. If it is not God's standard, it has to be man's; there are only two options. When Hamlet says this, "for there is nothing either good or bad but thinking makes it so" (II. ii. 249-50), he is not speaking in iambic pentameter—the line, that is, is not blocked off in poetry. In fact, all of Hamlet's speeches after his "O cursed spite, That ever I was born to set it right" (I. v. 189-90) appear in prose and not poetry, even though *all* other characters in these intervening scenes speak in poetry. How telling that Hamlet the poet speaks in prose, and how ironic that the linguistic alteration is the aftermath of his arrogant humanistic declaration. Is this accidental or the product of conscious artistry? I maintain that the loss of poetic

David Garrick as Hamlet.

eloquence mirrors Hamlet's psychic disarray. The life has gone out of the line, just as the soul has gone out of the man.

This change in language may be irrelevant to us, but we must note the Elizabethan attitude toward language. David Bevington is helpful on this point:

> A key to understanding Shakespeare's language is to appreciate the attitude toward speech accepted by him and his contemporaries. Speech was traditionally and piously regarded as God's final and consummate gift to man. Speech was thus to Elizabethans a source of enormous power for good or ill. Truth, if truly uttered, was bound to prevail. To have heard truth and to have rejected it was an unnatural thing, a sign that Satan had entered the obdurate heart and had caused it to reject God's truth. Christians were bound to preach the Word, and to destroy that heretic who persisted in rejecting it. Hence the struggle to excel in eloquent utterance.
>
> (Eastman 79)

Hamlet's continuing humanism causes him to regard events as the product of chance, "outrageous fortune" in his phrase; divine orchestration is not even considered. Death, the arch enemy, is from his point of view just as purposeless, "the undiscover'd country from whose bourn / No traveler returns (III. i. 80-81). This is Hamlet the humanist: wanting to die, rejecting God's will, quarreling with friends, seeing the world as cursed and chance-controlled, losing his poetic brilliance, perceiving himself as the harmony-restoring prince, delaying and mad.

He does not condemn himself to languish forever in this unhappy key. When his Christian values gain the ascendancy, he is able once again to gain control of his life. But the process is slow; it commences in the bedroom scene with Gertrude. He tells his mother that Heaven is, regarding her marriage to Claudius, "thought-sick at the act" (III. iv. 52) and that her sexual honeying is inappropriate. He is the moralist here who, as a result of being brought face to face with Gertrude's frailty, returns to his ante-humanist self. He is as Christian and moral in her presence as he had earlier been humanistic. The moral touchstone he uses to measure her spiritual ineptitudes condemns his own. Castigating her for the splinter in her eye forces him to an awareness of the log in his own. Gertrude knows Hamlet is turning her eyes into her soul, but she could never guess the extent to which he is turning his own eyes inward as well. The double standard finally reveals itself during this exchange. Granted, Gertrude's physical appetite may have clouded her judgment, but hers was no greater sin than Hamlet's contemplated murder of Claudius and his actual murders of Rosencrantz and Guildenstern. Perhaps there was room for Gertrude to assume a greater virtue, but her behavior was no worse than Hamlet's treatment of Ophelia during the staging of the play or, for that matter, than his treatment of his own mother.

The confrontation with Gertrude only partly explains his reversion to Christianity. The second appearance of the ghost is so shocking to Hamlet that it instinctively forces him back to his true self. Upon seeing the ghost, he blurts out a characteristic line: "Save me, and hover o'er me with your wings, / You heavenly guards!" (III. iv. 107-08). The line offers an insight into the true nature of Hamlet's soul: when confronted with real horror, he cries out to the angels to protect him, a ludicrous act, he indicated earlier, since angels are not a reality in a chance-controlled life. The appearance of the ghost strips Hamlet of his proud posturing of might and valor, rids him of his pompous talk of setting aright the realm, and discovers a scared young man whose reflexive response reveals an affinity for the God-ordered world, complete with ministering angels, which he, in an earlier egotistical moment, had forsworn.

Thus the dormant moral virtues in Hamlet's soul are awakened. The humanistic bent quickly demythologized, he fires at Gertrude a few volleys of biblical precepts. He says she ought "for love of grace" (III. iv. 151) to confess herself to heaven, to assume a virtue if she does not really possess it, and to refrain from illicit sexual union, when not much earlier he had spoken of fortune and absence of right or wrong, except as these exist in the mind. Hamlet, who previously indicated that morality exists internally in the human mind, not externally in the revealed and inspired Word of God, suddenly declares himself a spokesman for orthodox Christian values.

Hamlet's confrontation in the bedroom with his mother and the ghost enables him to see through the illusions that self-based wisdom has spawned. They are the watershed events that help him pulverize his own "puffed and libertine" humanistic illusions. Once their power is mitigated, he becomes a vessel capable of use by God, once again able to reactivate Christian values. In that humbled state, during which he is emptied of self, he is led to a revelation concerning the death of Polonius: "I do repent; but heaven hath pleas'd it so / To punish me with this, and this with me, / That I must be their scourge and minister" (III. iv. 180-82). Hamlet concludes that Heaven, not Hamlet, has orchestrated these events both to chastize the heady prince for his willful disobedience and to make him, in Bevington's gloss, the "agent of heavenly retribution." It was, in short, Hamlet's intent to rid the kingdom of evil and set it straight in his way and in his time frame. That exalted humanistic intent has enabled him to accomplish little: instead of getting rid of Claudius, he merely delays and delays some more, experiences fractured relationships with Ophelia, Laertes, Rosencrantz, and Guildenstern, and directly or indirectly causes the deaths of Ophelia, Gertrude, Rosencrantz, and Guildenstern. But later, it "pleases" Heaven to use him as the "scourge" to purge the realm.

At the very moment Hamlet is disavowing belief in and boasting of his severance from God, God was holding Hamlet in His hand and tooling him to become the instrument to accomplish His will. Evil must be eradicated from the realm, and Hamlet will indeed be the agent to accomplish it, but only when he does it according to God's will and time frame, not his own. In perhaps the play's key line for supporting this thesis, Hamlet says, "There's a divinity that shapes our ends, / Rough-hew them how we will" (V. ii. 10-11). What a chasm between that statement and his earlier statement that HE would shape events in the Danish kingdom toward order. This reference to a divinity-controlling universe is not the only evidence of Hamlet's radical return to Christianity. In regard to the presence of his dead father's seal on his person, which enabled him to prepare a new commission, Hamlet says, "even in that was heaven ordinant" (V. ii. 48). That is, God took care of even this minuscule detail, a point of view that totally contradicts his assessment of God during his humanistic phase, when he averred that one could only hope to dodge the slings and arrows of outrageous fortune.

This reassertion of a governing divinity also causes Hamlet to think anew regarding the death of Claudius. Earlier it was "my revenge," Hamlet's personal desire to destroy taking precedence over and acting independently of God's will. Now he says it is "perfect conscience" (V. ii. 67) to repay him, thereby signalling a radical shift in motive. Retaliation will not be the typical act of selfish revenge flowing out of a mind drunk with hate. If he is to destroy Claudius now, it will be the inevitable, God-sanctioned justice that flows out of a conscience made perfect by Hamlet's denial of his egotistical humanism and by his waiting on God.

Other actions at the end of the play further document this change in Hamlet. Whereas in his earlier self-assertive stage he jumped into the grave to fight Laertes—"But I am very sorry, good Horatio, / That to Laertes I forgot myself" (V. ii. 75-76)—now he is governed not by personal passion but by a Christ-like meekness. The desire for revenge is replaced here by the desire to forgive. He admits events had whipped him earlier into a "tow'ring passion" (V. ii. 80), but now before the duel he nobly confesses to Laertes, "Give me your pardon, sir. I have done you wrong" (V. ii. 224). This spirit of love for others makes him decidedly Christ-like, as does his reference to his heavy heart—"But thou wouldst not think how ill all's here about my heart" (V. ii. 210-11). A difficult line, it cannot be explicated with any certainty, but it is interesting to note the similarity to the statement made by Christ who, right before facing His cross and self-destruction, also referred to His heavy heart: "My soul is exceeding sorrowful, even unto death" (Matt. 26: 38). Both Christ and Hamlet die sacrificially, both purge evil from the social order by that death, both do not deserve death, both allude to a heavy heart, both are profoundly misunderstood, both seek personal will first—Christ had first requested His cup pass from Him before surrendering to God's will, just as Hamlet seeks his way first as well—and both attain a higher spirituality because of the adversity: certainly, Hamlet attains a higher spirituality because of his suffering, just as Christ was made perfect through suffering, as the writer of Hebrews explains: "For it became him [God] . . . to make the captain of their salvation [Jesus Christ] perfect through sufferings" (2: 10).

This array of religious references surrounding Hamlet clearly delineates his transformation. Immediately after he refers to his heavy heart, he says, "we defy augury" (V. ii. 217). Only belief in a shaping divinity will do for the regenerated Hamlet. Immediately thereafter, he says, "There is special providence in the fall of a sparrow" (V. ii. 217-18). Hamlet, even in his humanistic heyday, betrayed his soul's real first-love through language steeped in biblical antecedents, but by Act V it is not just vague biblical resonances but direct echoes of the language of Christ. The thought of God noting the fall of the sparrow hearkens back to Christ's statement in Matthew 10: 29, but the line is interesting for a second reason: it comes in the context of Hamlet and Horatio's discussion of Hamlet's duel with Laertes which Horatio says Hamlet will lose. Hamlet disagrees but concedes that even if he does, there is a "special providence in the fall of a sparrow," thereby equating himself with a sparrow. That he calls himself a sparrow, a bird not held in high esteem by Elizabethans, suggests his emergent humility at the end of the play; he has come a long way from the proud prince who would singlehandedly set right the court and defy God in the process.

Building on the thought that a loving sovereign God cares for the destiny of a sparrow, Hamlet utters a line that more fully than any other in the play documents his about-face from his earlier humanism. In the "To be" speech he laments that death is the powerful foe that overshadows all human life and ultimately makes cowards of us all in our earthly enterprises. Now he says,

> If it be now, 'tis not to come;
> If it be not to come; it will be now;
> If it be not now; yet it will come.
>
> (V. ii. 218-20)

This is God's Hamlet. No childish whimpering about the injustice of God's having fixed His canon against self-slaughter, no perverse fear about the undiscovered country. Rather, we see a stoic acceptance that flows out of a heart prepared to face death. Rejecting death indicates an obdurate heart stubbornly pitched against God's will; accepting death reveals a heart mature in its spiritual walk, a heart that knows that the deceptive baubles of this world are gilded illusions that distract one from his quest for spiritual enlightenment: "The readiness is all" (V. ii. 22). The message of the play is that only the spiritually mature can see this while the rest of us have trouble acquiescing to the arch enemy at any time. For Hamlet the days of mental anguish are past; he is the compliant servant about to do the bidding of his Lord.

Characteristically, Shakespeare offers a figurative encapsulation of Hamlet's winning over humanistic darkness and progressing into the kingdom of light. Claudius promises Hamlet a pearl if he makes the first hit. That seems a fairly innocuous detail in the larger flow and sweep of *Hamlet,* but sensitized to the biblical backdrop we look again at the metamorphosis in Hamlet: he knows God sees sparrows fall and governs nations; he begs his mother to repent; he forgives Laertes and begs Laertes to forgive him; he confesses genuine love for Ophelia (V. i. 268); he inquires about Gertrude's well-being during the duel (V. ii. 311); he calls Laertes his "brother" (V. ii. 241), just as Christ had said those who do the will of the Father are his brothers (Mark 3: 35). At the end of the play, in short, he is living in the kingdom of God. Now we consider the pearl again. Hamlet will give all for that pearl, because attaining the pearl, which cannot be won if he does not duel, means certain death, owing to Claudius' chicanery. This closely parallels Christ's story of the pearl of great price: "Again, the kingdom of heaven is like unto a merchant man, seeking goodly pearls: who, when he found one pearl of great price, went and sold all that he had, and bought it" (Matt. 13: 45-46). The merchant gave all he had to obtain the pearl, just as Hamlet must give all, including his life. Hamlet wins the pearl because only he dies to self, dies to humanism, and sacrifices all. Hamlet's right view of God gives him a right view of fellow man: he loves man so much he will lay down his life for him. Only the unblemished sheep, the most perfect specimen, is used for sacrifice; only that man who makes it to the lofty summit of self-annihilation is consecrated enough to be used of God for this high calling. Hamlet has moved the whole way from total self-indulgence to total self-obliteration.

Proud Hamlet with all that intelligence and creative power at his beck, is powerless in his God-denying days to eradicate the vicious evil that rots the kingdom. Broken Hamlet, who has been sifted by untold adversity, much of which he causes himself, is the pliable clay that can be molded as the master potter wills. The same sun that hardens the clay melts the wax. In this reading of the play one of the central messages centers on the uselessness of the impetuous, those who rush precipitously into blind action, in contrast to those who wait on the great I Am, for this waiting activates Him in the affairs of men; and once activated it matters little how many backup plans Claudius devises—poisoned cup, poisoned dagger—God will see that good wins over evil. Claudius was a formidable opponent for Hamlet, but against a Hamlet backed by God he is a whirling speck of nothingness: "if thou shalt indeed . . . do all that I speak, then I [God] will be an enemy unto thine enemies, and an adversary unto thine adversaries" (Exodus 23: 22).

Just as the pearl in the cup has a rich metaphorical application, so does the cup itself. Gertrude drinks from the cup, and immediately after Hamlet says, "I dare not drink yet, madam; by and by" (V. ii. 296). A seemingly vacuous line, it too assumes monumental significance when given a biblical exegesis. Christ also made reference to drinking from the cup on two separate occasions—when He asked James and John, who wanted to sit on either side of Christ in Heaven, if they were "able to drink of the cup that I shall drink of" (Matthew 20: 22), and when He prayed to God in Gethsemane to "let this cup pass from me" (Matthew 26: 39). He wished not to drink from the cup but later did, a reference to His crucifixion. Hamlet also says he will drink from the cup but only when he too is ready, that is, after he has been killed sacrificially to cleanse the realm of evil. In his dying speech he says to Horatio, "Give me the cup" (V. ii. 345), another parallel to Christ.

Does Fortinbras' command that Hamlet be given a soldier's burial square with this reading? In a humanistic reading of the play, Hamlet's military burial proved he had become his war-like father; the warrior/soldier in him had triumphed over the artist/creator. But in the context of this interpretation we are obligated to ask which soldier it is— the Danish soldier of war or the Pauline soldier of the cross with the breastplate of righteousness and his loins girt about with truth? The heavy use of biblical analogues lends credence to the latter. Fortinbras says, "Bear Hamlet, like a soldier, to the stage" (V. ii. 398), much like St. Paul had told Timothy to "endure hardness, like a good soldier of the cross" (II Timothy 2: 3).

Earlier, mad Ophelia had said, "Lord, we know what we are, but know not what we may be" (IV. v. 43-44). This provides a statement of the theme of the play: Hamlet suffers self-delusion, thinking he knows himself well. By the end, his odyssey from self-indulgence to enlightenment teaches him to define himself and his life, not in terms of immediate circumstances that surround him, however overwhelming those might be, not in terms of where he has been or is currently, but in terms of what the special Providence Who shapes our ends can work out in his life and lead him toward in the future. His journey from Christianity to humanism and return is complete by the end of the play. No wonder his last words are, "The rest is silence" (V. ii. 360). He makes it back to Christianity; once one attains that degree of Christlikeness there is nothing to be said, not even in the face of death.

Works Cited

Eastman, Arthur M. *A Short History of Shakespearean Criticism.* Lanham, NY: University Press, 1985.

Ribner, Irving. *Patterns in Shakespearean Tragedy.* London: Methuen, 1960.

Shakespeare, William. *The Complete Works of Shakespeare.* Ed. David Bevington. Glenview, IL: Scott Foresman, 1980.

Maurice Hunt (essay date 1993)

SOURCE: Hunt, Maurice. "The Religion of *Twelfth Night*." *CLA Journal* 37, no. 2 (1993): 189-203.

[*In the following essay, Hunt discusses the attitudes toward providence expressed by various characters in* Twelfth Night, *as well as the play's satirical treatment of Puritanism.*]

Much has been written about the Christian allusions in *Twelfth Night*, especially those to the Feasts of Epiphany and Candelmas. Foremost among critics adopting a Christian perspective is R. Chris Hassel, who has illustrated the relevance for the play of certain liturgical events in the Church year.[1] Recently Shakespeare's comic staging of the Annunciation has been demonstrated in *Twelfth Night*.[2] Yet despite these Christian allusions (and other, more generalized ones to the idea of being a good steward of one's talents), the religion of *Twelfth Night* is not as consistently Christian as might be supposed. Characters' references to Jove, Fate, Fortune, and Time as the providence of the play's world cause playgoers to question whether Shakespeare intended to represent a single deity consistently ruling the play's events. Not all of the allusions to non-Christian ruling forces can be interpreted as foils calculated to make the staging of the true doctrine of the Epiphany appear brighter. Several of the allusions, especially those spoken by Viola, make the Christian religion represented in *Twelfth Night* less doctrinaire than critics have claimed. In particular, Shakespeare satirizes certain self-serving Puritan notions of Providence in order to highlight a more authoritative Providence that works generally rather than specifically through the natural causation of Time and Fortune. While this idea of Providence appears in the prose romances underlying the plots of Shakespeare's comedies, it also conforms to Hooker's description of a somewhat vague, generalized Christian Providence that operates remotely through this world's natural agents, such as time and tempest. After satirizing traits of Puritanism, Brownism, and Catholicism in *Twelfth Night,* Shakespeare approximates an Anglican perspective on Providence, but only in an ambiguous manner.

While amounting to a kind of fantasy land, the Illyria of *Twelfth Night* appears to be under God's jurisdiction, as the theological overtones of the play's title implies. Characters as different as Viola and Sir Andrew swear by or mention the Christian God. When Olivia vainly lifts her veil to show Cesario her face, Viola exclaims that it is "Excellently done, if God did all" (I.v.239).[3] When, at Sir Toby's urging, Sir Andrew pens a challenge to Cesario, he concludes by writing "*Fare thee well, and God have mercy upon one of our souls*" (III.iv.167-68). Confronted by the duellist whom Sir Toby has built up into a formidable adversary, Viola murmurs an aside, "Pray God defend me" (III.iv.307). Characters' references to the devil, heaven, and hell complement their allusions to God. For example, in his "catechism" of Olivia, Feste says of her dead brother, "I think his soul is in hell, madonna" (I.v.66); she replies, "I know his soul is in heaven, fool" (I.v.67). Perhaps surprisingly, the character who most often mentions God is not Viola but Feste. Concerning Maria's punning contest with him, Feste concludes, "Well, God give them wisdom that have it; and those that are fools, let them use their talents" (I.v.14-15). And when Malvolio judges that "Infirmity, that decays the wise, doth ever make the better fool," Feste quips, "God send you, sir, a speedy infirmity, for the better increasing your folly" (I.v.76-77). Feste's catechism of Olivia and his repeated reference to her as "Madonna" deepen the Christian overtones of his character. And yet as the mockery of this catechism and his role as the false curate Sir Topas suggest, the association of Feste and Christianity does not appear a serious one.[4] Characters such as Viola frequently depict Feste's wit as barren and dry. This barrenness qualifies the spiritual advice that, disguised as the bogus prelate, he gives Malvolio, who is confined to a dark room.

After Maria hurriedly tells him to put on a gown and beard and make believe he is Sir Topas, Feste jokes, "Well, I'll put it on, and I will dissemble myself in't, and I would I were the first that ever dissembled in such a gown" (IV.ii.4-6). By means of these remarks, Shakespeare calls attention to the falsity of Feste's Christian persona. The errors in his Christian doctrine compound this falsity. Supposedly testing Malvolio's sanity by asking him what he thinks of Pythagoras's opinion concerning wild fowl, Feste receives the correct reply—"That the soul of our grandam might haply inhabit a bird" (IV.ii.53-54). When he asks his dupe what he thinks of Pythagoras's opinion, Malvolio implicitly endorses Christian doctrine, which does not include that of reincarnation: "I think nobly of the soul, and no way approve his opinion" (IV.ii.56-57). Feste, however, affirms the non-Christian principle of reincarnation when he replies, "Fare thee well: Remain thou still in darkness. Thou shalt hold th' opinion of Pythagoras ere I will allow of thy wits, and fear to kill a woodcock lest thou dispossesss the soul of thy grandam. Fare thee well" (IV.ii.58-62). By speaking of the wild fowl as a woodcock, the Elizabethan aviary type of silliness, Feste indirectly calls Malvolio fool by heredity. Nevertheless, Feste's doctrine separates him from the Christian role he plays. In fact, his allusion to the transmigration of souls acts as a foil to the preferred epiphanies of the play. Rather than the sudden manifestations of a redemptive, hidden identity, such as those seen in Sebastian, Olivia, and Viola in the last scenes of the play, Feste's notion of reincarnation leads auditors away from the play's focus upon the epiphany of spiritual incarnation.

Regarded from the perspective of the topsy-turvy customs of *Twelfth Night*—a time when asses ceremoniously progressed down cathedral aisles and when "naturals," or village idiots, impersonated the parish priest[5]—Feste's assumed and mistaken Christianity plays its part in a dramatic design with a relatively solemn religious conclusion: the celebration of the epiphanic occasion when divinity within mankind first became apparent.[6] Nevertheless, specific challenges to Christianity as a whole within *Twelfth Night* question the conclusion that Feste's playing *Sir Topas* finds its place neatly within an orthodox Christian ritual. For example, at one point Sir Andrew asserts that he has "no more wit than a Christian or an ordinary man has" (I.iii.82-83). Equally qualifying of standard Christian orthodoxy read into the play are the characters' many allusions to different ruling deities and non-Christian schemes. Even characters who mention God speak of other providences, a fact which clouds readings that claim that the play categorically celebrated the Epiphany in secular forms.

"Thou has spoke for us, madonna," Feste at one point tells Olivia, "as if thy eldest son should be a fool: whose skull Jove cram with brains" (I.v.113-15). Feste refers to the classical deity again in his response to Viola's gift of a coin: "Now Jove, in his next commodity of hair, send thee a beard" (III.i.45-46). Moreover, Viola, upon landing on the Illyrian seacoast, tells the Captain that she believes her brother "is in Elysium" (I.ii.4). Granted that the word "heaven" would not have juxtaposed itself as melodiously with the mention of Illyria in the preceding verse, Shakespeare makes his heroine's classical term for the afterlife more understandable by giving her initially a belief in Chance rather than Providence. "Perchance he is not drown'd," she states; "What think you, sailors?" (I.ii.5). The subsequent dialogue stresses the absence of faith in Providence. "It is perchance that you yourself were sav'd," the Captain remarks. "O my poor brother! and so perchance may he be." Viola replies. "True, madam," the Captain continues, "and to comfort you with chance,"

> Assure yourself, after our ship did split,
> And you and those poor number sav'd with you
> Hung on our driving boat, I saw your brother,
> Most provident in peril, bind himself
> (Courage and hope both teaching him the practice)
> To a strong mast that liv'd upon the sea;
> Where, like Arion on the dolphin's back,
> I saw him hold acquaintance with the waves
> So long as I could see.
>
> (I.ii.6-17)

Interestingly, Chance rules earthly affairs in the Captain's account; in his opinion, it is mankind, not God, who acts providentially in times of peril. "Provident in peril," self-reliant Sebastian bound himself to a mast. If anything, the metaphysics implicit in the Captain's speech is existential. Rather than comforting Viola with Chance, the Captain has comforted her with a portrait of a hopeful, brave brother who enacts his own providence in a world of accident.

The Captain's portrait of shipwreck vaguely resembles Sir Philip Sidney's speaking picture in the *Arcadia* of Pyrocles and Musidorus afloat amid the wreckage of their ship. The nonspecific resemblance reminds the playgoer that the conventions of Elizabethan romance undergird *Twelfth Night*. John F. Danby has described Sidneyan romance (and the English Renaissance literature derived from it) as composed of a series of concentric rings, the innermost dominated by characters' mistaken belief in Chance and Fate and the outermost ruled by Nature and Christian Providence, which directs heroes to a prosperous end despite their erroneous trust in Fortune or Fate. In the literal unfolding of Sidneyan romance and its derivatives, the hero and heroine usually pass from the belief in Chance or Fate to the conviction of Providence, a guiding design which is Christian in its overtones if not always in its name.[7] Granted Shakespeare's portrayal of Viola's endorsement of Chance, the playgoer might expect the later staging of her recognition of Providence as the Art of God that directs apparently lethal events such as shipwrecks to unexpectedly joyous conclusions.

That acknowledgement, however, does not occur in *Twelfth Night*. Or if it does, its staging is so ambiguous as to be unrecognizable. When she is not trusting her own quick wits, Viola relies upon Time and Fortune for her salvation. Once resolved to serve Orsino as Cesario, a musical eunuch, Viola exclaims, "What else may hap, to time I will commit" (I.ii.60). Her trusting Time in this case elaborates her previous wish that she "might not be deliver'd to the world" until she has made her "own occasion mellow" (I.ii.42-43)—where "mellow" connotes a benign ripeness created by Time. In Ilyria, Viola turns not to God or Providence but to Time as the agent of a ripening process, a process which will present her with opportune moments that might be seized and wrought into her happiness. In this respect, she is the female counterpart of the young man of the sonnets who read Shakespeare's *carpe diem* advice. When opportune moments do not materialize as quickly as Viola may have supposed, she never loses her faith in Time: "O time, thou must untangle this, not I" (II.ii.38), she laments concerning the barren love triangle formed by Orsino's, Olivia's, and her own unrequited affections. And when she first realizes that Olivia may have fallen in love with Cesario, she remarks, "Fortune forbid my outside have not charm'd her" (II.ii.17). These references in Viola's speech may convince playgoers that Shakespeare was either careless or unconcerned with dramatizing a single ruling deity in *Twelfth Night,* a deity comparable to the Jupiter of *Cymbeline* or the Apollo of *The Winter's Tale.*

Nevertheless, Shakespeare's sustained satire of a Puritan notion of Providence suggests that *Twelfth Night,* in its broader strokes, apparently conforms to a single metaphysical design, that of Elizabethan Anglicanism. An anti-Puritan bias surfaces in one of Sir Andrew's casual comments. Hearing Sir Toby maintain that only "some laudable attempt, either of valour or policy" on Sir Andrew's part can regain Olivia's supposed affection for the knight, Sir Andrew replies, "An 't be any way, it must be with valour, for policy I hate: I had as lief be a Brownist as a politician" (III.ii.29-31). In the words of G. L. Kittredge, a Brownist was a "follower of Robert Browne, an extreme Puritan, founder of the Congregational form of church government (59).[8] Through Sir Toby's remark, Shakespeare associates Puritanism with the practice of an Italianate vice, policy.[9] In *The Picture of a Puritane (1605),* a dialogue between a Protestant and a Puritan (to the extreme disadvantage of the latter character), Oliver Ormerod has the Protestant tell the Puritan, "For it is not unknown to any that hath had any dealing with you in wordly affairs, how crafty and subtle you are in all your dealing."[10] Malvolio, the puritanical character in the play, prides himself upon both his knowledge and practice of policy. "Marry sir, sometimes he is a kind of Puritan" (II.iii.140), Maria asserts. "The devil a Puritan that he is, or anything constantly, but a time-pleaser, an affection'd ass that cons state without book, and utters it by great swarths" (II.iii.146-49). Like Viola, Malvolio, in Maria's remark, trusts in time; pleasing time, however, is not the same thing as mellowing time or seizing the opportune moment. Shakespeare reverses the Elizabethan stock identification of policy as a "bad" Catholic (Italian/Spanish) practice by having Maria, whose name has Catholic overtones (especially strong in the context of the play's allusions to the Annunciation and Madonna), justly practice upon the Puritan Malvolio, "out-policying" and punishing the politician who delights in secret codes and love-games. Part of Maria's gulling of Malvolio invloves satirizing the narrow, self-serving idea of Providence as the economic reward of the religious elect.

In the case of Malvolio, this narrow idea is associated with the god Jove. Analysis of *Twelfth Night* discovers that passive or deluded characters regularly swear by Jove or Fate. For example, in act I, passive, withdrawn Olivia calls upon Fate to bestow Cesario upon her: "Fate, show thy force; ourselves we do not owe. / What is decreed must be: and be this so" (I.v.314-15). Sharply contrasting with Viola, who seizes the moment to disguise herself so that she may be protected by Orsino, inactive Olivia imagines Fate seizing Cesario and herself to forge a love bond. Likewise, Sebastian's depression over the loss of his sister and his worldly goods expresses itself in a belief in Fate. "My stars shine darkly over me," he tells Antonio; "the malignancy of my fate might perhaps distemper yours" (II.i.3-5). Rather than Fate, Malvolio credits Jove with ruling his life, giving him Olivia as a wife. Herschel Baker has noted that English Puritans "insisted that providence be acknowledged as the surest sign of God's sovereignty."[11] The delusion springing from Malvolio's self-love includes a non-Christian deity intent on materially rewarding the egotistical "Puritan." Significantly, it is Maria who plants this idea of providence in his imagination. The first verses of the forged "coded" letter that Malvolio reads aloud name the father of the gods:[12]

> *Jove knows I love;*
> *But who?*
> *Lips, do not move,*
> *No man must know.*
>
> (II.v.98-101)

In the letter itself, Malvolio reads, "*Thy fates open their hands, let thy blood and spirit embrace them*" (II.v.146-47). And at the end, he reads, "*Go to, thou art made, if thou desir'st to be so. If not, let me see thee a steward still, the fellow of servants, and not worth to touch Fortune's fingers*" (II.v.154-57). Maria signs the letter *"The Fortunate Unhappy"* (II.v.159). By implying that Fortune has given Malvolio the opportunity to woo Olivia, Maria has appealed to Malvolio's irreligious belief that Chance rules mortal affairs. Even before he sees the dropped letter, musing upon Olivia, he murmurs to himself, "'Tis but fortune, all is fortune" (II.v.23). And yet the letter's reference to Jove changes metaphysically irresolute Malvolio's idea of the deity ruling all human things. Deluded into believing that Olivia loves him, Malvolio thanks his stars, his horoscope, for his happiness, quickly qualifying his belief in astrological determinism by adding the name of the god appearing in the letter: "Jove and my stars be praised" (II.v.173-74). And when he continues to read and discovers that presumably Olivia would have him continually smile in her presence, he concludes, "Jove, I thank thee. I will smile" (II.v.178).

That Shakespeare intends these non-Christian references to manifest a certain irresoluteness, even error in religious belief, is indicated by a remark of Maria's in act III. Referring to Malvolio's yellow stockings, cross-gartering, and silly smiling, she tells her fellow plotters, "If you desire the spleen, and will laugh yourself into stitches, follow me. Yond gull Malvolio is turned heathen, a very renegado; for there is no Christian that means to be saved by believing rightly can ever believe such impossible passages of grossness. He's in yellow stockings" (III.ii.65-70). Kittredge notes that by the turn of the seventeenth century cross-gartering was a fashion associated only with old men and Puritans, while Queen Elizabeth disliked the color yellow because it appeared in the flag of Spain (48).

Maria implies that her forged letter, which has been called an epistle, amounts to a religious tract testing the Christian faith of its reader. Crediting Jove and his stars rather than God or Providence for the gift of Olivia, Malvolio fails the test. Regarded from an Anglican viewpoint, Malvolio is a heathen, a renegade to the true English church. His stockings suggest allegiances to both the Puritan and Catholic faiths, a doctrinal impossibility in keeping with the mad atmosphere of Illyria.

Shakespeare focuses the crassness latent in some Puritans' notion of Providence by having Malvolio thank Jove for making him materially rich. Regarding Olivia's sending of Sir Toby to him as a veiled fulfillment of part of the letter, Malvolio assumes that he and Olivia have engaged in a secret duet of policy: "O ho! do you come near me now? No worse man than Sir Toby to look to me! This concurs directly with the letter" (III.iv.64-66). Malvolio's deity delights in the practice of policy and rewards subjects who do likewise for their own materialistic ends. "I have limed her," Malvolio gloats, "but it is Jove's doing, and Jove make me thankful" (III.iv.74-75). "Well, Jove, not I, is the doer of this, and he is to be thanked" (III.iv.83-84). It will be recalled that Malvolio's selfish attraction to Olivia is not so much to her person as to her riches. His fantasies of married life with her revolve not around her beauteous person but around "Count Malvolio" (II.v.35), sitting in a "branched velvet gown," "having come from a day-bed, where [he has] left Olivia sleeping," later playing with "some rich jewel" while he lords it over Sir Toby and the lighter folk (II.v.47-81). Malvolio's thanking Jove for the expected fulfillment of a materially enriching destiny highlights the unchristian idea of a self-centered providence, one associated in *Twelfth Night* with Elizabethan Puritans rising through commerce and time-pleasing and thanking the supreme deity for their riches.

In *The Redemption of Time* (1606), the Banbury Puritan William Whatley argues that men should "buy out the Time, to traffique with it, as men do with wares . . . Good hours and opportunities and merchandize of the highest rate and price: and whosoever will have his soul thrive, must not suffer any of these bargains of Time to pass him, but must buy up, and buy out all the minutes thereof."[13] Concerning this passage, G. F. Waller has concluded that "the accommodation of Puritanism to the merchant's appreciation of the commercial value of time is plain" (24). For a Puritan like Whatley, God's Providence presents moments that the elect recognize and personally seize for their material gain. Foolishly Malvolio has made the discovered "epistle" signify what he selfishly wills it to mean; Shakespeare implicity satirizes the Puritan practice of interpreting scripture by no other light than that afforded by the solitary reader's crass needs and desires.

Olivia's belief that Satan possesses Malvolio after he has conformed his behavior to his willful reading of the epistle further defines Shakespeare's attitude toward the notion of Providence represented by the gull. When Sir Toby, Fabian, and Maria torment Malvolio by assuming that he is mad, they urge him to defy the devil through the power of prayer. "My prayers, minx?" (III.iv.122), Malvolio surlily responds to Maria. "No, I warrant you, he will not hear of godliness" (III.iv.123), she concludes, focusing the general irreligion apparent in Malvolio throughout the episode of his gulling. Olivia's single reference to Christian deity—"God comfort thee!" (III.iv.32)—addresses Malvolio's supposed madness; by altering Olivia's faith in this one instance, Shakespeare throws into relief the ungodly opinions that have prompted Malvolio to act as though he were possessed by the Devil. The playwright continues to stress the sacrilegious attitudes fueling Malvolio's "madness" when Feste in act V, referring to Malvolio's letter to Olivia, asserts, "[B]ut as a madman's epistles are no gospels, so it skills not much when they are delivered" (V.i.285-87). By couching his explanation of the tardiness of delivery in this religious language, Feste (and Shakespeare through him) reminds playgoers of the sacrilegious epistle catalyzing Malvolio's ungodly beliefs and behavior, which are based in an unpleasant egotism at odds with the charitable messages of the true gospel.

Nevertheless, Malvolio's only explicit reference to Christian deity appears in his "mad" epistle. His letter to Olivia begins "*By the Lord, madam*" (V.i.301). By this salutation, Shakespeare may be suggesting that Malvolio's suffering has amounted to a kind of purgatory, refining his faith into a less self-serving and more orthodox form of worship. Such a refinement of faith would complement that which occurs within Olivia in the later scenes of *Twelfth Night*. In keeping with the play's celebration of the Epiphany (the Festival of Light), Olivia characterizes her imminent marriage to Sebastian in the following terms: "Then lead the way, good father," she tells the priest who will unite them; "and heavens so shine / That they may fairly note this act of mine!" (IV.iii.34-35). Not Fate, not the stars (those divine forces invoked by Olivia earlier)—but a true priest gives her Sebastian in wedlock, a marriage celebrated under a "consecrated roof" (IV.iii.25) in an orthodox religious fashion (V.i.148-61).

And what of Viola? Do the events of the play refine her faith into a conviction more recognizably Christian than her early references to Elysium, Fortune, and Time suggest? When Antonio first mistakes her for Sebastian, calling her by her brother's name, Viola, once she is alone on the stage, ecstatically exclaims,

> He nam'd Sebastian. I my brother know
> Yet living in my glass; even such and so
> In favour was my brother, and he went
> Still in this fashion, colour, ornament,
> For him I imitate. O if it prove,
> Tempests are kind, and salt-waves fresh in love!
>
> (III.iv.389-94)

Tempests and the sea remain the most specifically defined agents of Providence in Viola's world view. She never moves beyond the outer ring of Nature of God, who, in the scheme of Sidneyan romance, orders Nature by his divine Art.

In this respect, Shakespeare's characterization has an Anglican, specifically a Hookerian cast. "Nature therefore is nothing else but God's instrument" Hooker argued in *Of the Laws of Ecclesiastical Polity*.[14] What is Providence to God, working His will through natural agents and processes, goes by different names among men:

> Only thus much is discerned, that the natural generation and process of all things receiveth order of proceeding from the settled stability of divine understanding. This appointeth unto them their kinds of working; the disposition whereof in the purity of God's own knowledge and will is rightly termed by the name of Providence. The same being referred unto the things themselves here disposed by it, was wont by the ancient to be called natural Destiny.[15]

Like Shakespeare in *Twelfth Night,* Hooker sees no contradiction between Providence and Destiny, simply because God works generally (that is, remotely) through natural agents such as sea tempests rather than by miracle or direct relevation to form designs that people at different times in different cultures name variously. "The manner of this divine efficiency, being far above us," Hooker states, "we are no more able to conceive by our own reason, than creatures unreasonable by their sense are able to apprehend after what manner we dispose and order the course of our affairs" (159). Thus Viola, unable to grasp directly the pattern of Providence, reasons that its agents, tempests and salt waves, are fresh in love. Still, the joyous design is God's: "Those things which nature is said to do, are by divine art perform'd, using nature as an instrument; nor is there any such art or knowledge divine in nature herself working, but in the Guide of nature's work" (159). Performed most likely on Twelfth Night (January 6th) and definitely on Candlemas (February 2, 1602),[16] *Twelfth Night,* after all, celebrates in delightful secular form key events in God's design such as the Epiphany and the Purification of the Virgin Mary.

Along with salt waves and tempests, the Anglican God as defined by Hooker realizes His Providence through the agency of time, which Viola chiefly trusts to work her happiness. Unlike Malvolio's conception of Jove's providence, Viola's idea of providence has no place for the reward of narrow, self-serving motives. Tempests and sea storms reward the needs and wishes of suffering mortals when characters are self-sacrificing in the pursuit of others' happiness. Such an assumption may or may not have matched Shakespeare's idea of Anglican Providence. Viola's idea of providence is less knowable, more truly mysterious than Hooker's admittedly removed God. It looks ahead to the enigmatic agents guiding the characters on Prospero's island—and perhaps Prospero himself.

Notes

1. See both *Renaissance Drama and the English Church Year* (Lincoln: U of Nebraska P, 1979) 77-89, 94-101; and *Faith and Folly in Shakespeare's Romantic Comedies* (Athens: U of Georgia P, 1980) 149-75, esp. 149-53, 162, 166-67.

2. Maurice Hunt, "*Twelfth Night* and the Annunciation," *Papers on Language and Literature* 25 (1989): 264-71.

3. All quotations of *Twelfth Night* are taken from the Arden edition, ed. J. M. Lothian and T. W. Craik (London: Methuen, 1975).

4. For the contrary view—that Feste's foolishness as curate exemplifies an Erasmian or Pauline wisdom—see R. Chris Hassel, Jr., *Faith and Folly* 149, 150, 153, 164-165, 169-75.

5. The topsy-turvy customs are described by C. L. Barber, *Shakespeare's Festive Comedy* (1959; Cleveland: World, 1963) 25; and by Marion B. Smith, *Dualities in Shakespeare* (Toronto: U of Toronto P, 1966) 114.

6. The epiphanic motif in *Twelfth Night* has been elucidated by, among others, John Hollander, "*Twelfth Night* and the Morality of Indulgence," *Sewanee Review* 67 (1959): 234; Barbara K. Lewalski, "Thematic Patterns in *Twelfth Night,*" *Shakespeare Studies* 1 (1965): 177-78; Smith 110-22; Richard Henze, "*Twelfth Night:* Free Disposition on the Sea of Love," *Sewanee Rivew* 83 (1965): 267-68; Hassel, *Renaissance Drama* 77-86; and Cynthia Lewis, "Viola, Antonio, and Epiphany in *Twelfth Night,*" *Essays in Literature* 13 (1986): 187-99.

7. See *Poets on Fortune's Hill: Studies in Sidney, Shakespeare, Beaumont, and Fletcher* (1952: Port Washington, NY: Kennikat Press, 1966) 74-107.

8. *Twelfth Night,* ed. George Lyman Kittredge and rev. by Irving Ribner, The Kittredge Shakespeares (Waltham, MA; Ginn, 1966) 59. For negative contemporary portrayals of Brownism, including the belief that two notorious 1607 murderers (Wilson and Petterton) were Brownists, consult G. B. Harrison, *A Second Jacobean Journal, Being a Record of Those Things Most Talked of During the Years 1607 to 1610* (Ann Arbor: U of Michigan P, 1958) 23, 112.

9. For the Puritanical case of Brownism, see G. B. Harrison, *A Jacobean Journal, Being a Record of Those Things Most Talked of During the Years 1603-1606* (London: George Routledge & Sons, 1946) 176. In *Basilikon Doron* (1603), King James equates Brownists with Puritans: "Of this special sect I principally mean, when I speak of Puritans; divers of them, as Browne, Penrie, and others, having at sundry times come in Scotland, to sow their people amongst us . . . ." (Lawrence Sasek, ed., *Images of English Puritans: A Collection of Contemporary Sources* [Baton Rouge: Louisiana UP, 1989] 219).

10. Quoted in Sasek 248.

11. *The Wars of Truth* (Cambridge: Harvard UP, 1952) 15.

12. Harold Bayley, in *A New Light on the Renaissance* (1909; New York: Benjamin Blom, 1967), has

demonstrated that secret paper codes were a practice of certain Medieval and Renaissance dissenting sects.

13. Quoted by G. F. Waller, *The Strong Necessity of Time: The Philosophy of Time in Shakespeare and Elizabethan Literature* (The Hague: Mouton, 1976) 24.

14. *Of the Laws of Ecclesiastical Polity* (London: Dent, 1907) 160.

15. Hooker 159-60. For a description of sixteenth- and seventeenth-century Protestant ideas of Providence, see Wilbur Sanders, *The Dramatist and the Received Idea: Studies in the Plays of Marlowe and Shakespeare* (Cambridge: Cambridge UP, 1968) 110-20.

16. A performance of *Twelfth Night* on Candlemas, February 2, 1602, is noted in the diary of the lawyer and playgoer John Manningham.

Julia Reinhard Lupton (essay date 1997)

SOURCE: Lupton, Julia Reinhard. "*Othello* Circumcised: Shakespeare and the Pauline Discourse of Nations." *Representations* 57 (winter 1997): 73-89.

[*In this essay, Lupton maintains that in* Othello *religious difference is more significant than racial difference, for—according to Renaissance doctrine—if the Moor was a Muslim rather than a pagan before his conversion to Christianity, he is forever barred from the congregation of universal brotherhood.*]

In his essay "Is There a Neo-Racism?" Etienne Balibar proposes that we now live under a new ideology of the nations, a "racism-without-races" that promotes various forms of ethnic cleansing under the alibi of "cultural" identity, purity, or autonomy, a discourse that co-opts and neutralizes the postwar vocabulary of liberal humanism and pluralism. Balibar links this *neoracism* of the late modern to the *protoracism* of the early modern period:

> A racism which does not have the pseudo-biological concept of race as its main driving force has always existed, and it has existed at exactly this level of secondary theoretical elaborations. Its prototype is anti-Semitism. Modern anti-Semitism—the form which begins to crystallize in the Europe of the Enlightenment, if not indeed from the period in which the Spain of the *Reconquista* and the Inquisition gave a statist, nationalistic inflexion to theological anti-Judaism—is *already* a "culturalist" racism. . . . in many respects the whole of current differentialist racism may be considered, from the formal point of view, *as a generalized anti-Semitism*. This consideration is particularly important for the interpretation of contemporary Arabaphobia, especially in France, since it carries with it an image of Islam as a "conception of the world" which is incompatible with Europeanness.[1]

Mapping contemporary neo-racism onto the deep structures of anti-Semitism, Balibar derives the anti-Islamic strain in contemporary politics from the long tradition of anti-Jewish thought in Western historiography. Following Balibar's diagnosis, I argue here that Shakespeare's *Othello* provides a canonical articulation of this protoracism insofar as the play fashions the Muslim in the image of the Jew according to the protocols of Pauline exegesis; in Balibar's terms, *Othello* stages a "culturalist" rather than biologistic ordering of intergroup relations, a religiously grounded discourse barely visible from the vantage point of the modern racial theories that have since displaced it, yet intermittently readable in the strange light of the neoracism that has emerged in recent years.

A fundamental religious ambiguity vexes the racialization of Othello throughout the play; although his professed Christianity authorizes Othello's place in Venice, the play never decisively determines whether he has converted from a pagan religion or from Islam. I argue that the black Centile of a universal church undergirds *Othello*'s opening narrative of international romance, but that this divine comedy of pagan conversion is continually shadowed by the more troubling possibility of Othello's entrance into Christianity via its disturbing neighbor, Islam. This secondary scenario, which subsumes Islam within what Balibar calls "*a generalized anti-Semitism*," situates the Moor in both greater proximity with and greater resistance to Christian Revelation than the pagan, who is conceived as a blank slate more open to a transformative Christian reinscription. These categories and their peculiar constellation in the play are inherited from Saint Paul's division of humanity into Greek, Jew, and barbarian, national differences that are sublated in the ideal of the universal church. Yet this is an always-future universality, which is projected by the continued dialectic between the open embrace of the Christian message on the one hand and the residual ethnic exclusivism represented by the Jews on the other, a tension that provides a foundational mapping of the Western ethno-political field. In the typological schemes of the Renaissance, Islam represents a double scandal, the catastrophic bastardization of both Christian universalism—through the seductive danger of the Islamic world mission—and Jewish particularism, represented by Muslim allegiance to ritual laws and to an Abrahamic monotheism without Christ.

Disclosing the play's reliance on the Pauline division of the nations necessarily reorients the current color-based approach to the play, in which the scandal of "monstrous" miscegenation inherited from the nineteenth-century racial Imaginary has come to govern *Othello*'s economy of differences.[2] Indeed, if we insist on grafting the typically modern question of Othello's color onto the problem of Othello's religion, the results might not fall where we expect them. Looking from Venice west and far to the south, toward pagan Africa and the New World, Othello would appear darker skinned, barbarian, and perhaps more capable of a full conversion because of his religious innocence. Looking east, toward Arabia and Turkey, and to the northern parts of Africa, Othello would become a Muslim-turned-Christian, probably lighter skinned than his

Gentile version, inheritor of a monotheistic civilization already marked by frequent contacts with Christian Europe and hence more likely to go renegade. Whereas for the modern reader or viewer a black Othello is more subversive, "other," or dangerous, in the Renaissance scene a paler Othello more closely resembling the Turks whom he fights might actually challenge more deeply the integrity of the Christian paradigms set up in the play as the measure of humanity. Critics have rightly decried the nineteenth-century movement to "whiten" or "orientalize" Othello.[3] It is certainly not my intention to return to such a project but rather to insist that this move in the nineteenth century took place within an already racialized discourse, whereas in *Othello* religious difference is more powerfully felt than racial difference, which was only then beginning to surface in its virulent modern form. Rather than deciding what color Othello "really" is, I argue that the play initially draws moral and physiological "blackness" away from the diabolical and bestial imagery manipulated by Iago into the more positive circuit of the Gentile barbarian, a recuperation that in turn is undercut by the potential attraction between the "Moor" and the "Mohammedan." Shakespeare does not use Christianity to rise above color-based racism so much as his play renders visible the blindspot of *ethnos* that mortgages the inclusive vision of Christian humanism, a blindspot marked above all by the unerasable yet nongenetic scar of circumcision in Shakespeare's Venetian plays.

Entries into Covenant

Othello, one of Shakespeare's middle tragedies, has often been read as a rewriting of *The Merchant of Venice:* both are set in the mercantile city-state of Venice, both employ clearly marked "others," and both use the theme of conspicuous exogamy to heighten the conventional comedic situation of young lovers blocked by an old father. *Merchant* exhibits a comedic structure sharply typological in its countering of Jewish justice and Christian mercy, a set of scriptural coordinates more carefully submerged yet all the more powerfully at work in *Othello* as well. Iago's cry to Brabantio, "Look to your house, your daughter, and your bags," clearly recalls Shylock's wail, "'My daughter! O my ducats! O my daughter,'" and Brabantio, like Shylock, is promised "the bloody book of the law" in recompense for the loss of his daughter.[4] Yet Brabantio of course is no Jew, but one of the "brothers of the state," a citizen and senator in this Christian maritime republic (*Othello* 1.2.98). The figure of Brabantio instantiates the type not so much of the Jew per se as of the *Jewish Christian* addressed by Saint Paul in his epistles to the Romans and the Galatians.

Paul opens the Epistle to the Romans by insisting on the inclusiveness of his message:

> I am under obligation *both to Greeks and to barbarians,* both to the wise and to the foolish; so I am eager to preach the gospel *to you also who are in Rome.* For I am not ashamed of the gospel; it is the power of God for salvation to every one who has faith, *to the Jew first and also to the Greek.*[5]

In the first line, Paul expresses his obligation "to Greeks and to barbarians," taking up the Hellenistic division of the world between civilized Greek-speakers and inarticulate non-Greeks. Paul then extends his message to the Christian community in Rome, implicitly linked here to the Greeks as the modern inheritors of classical culture.[6] The next verse moves from the Hellenistic opposition between Greeks and barbarians to the Hebraic division of peoples between Jews and Gentiles; Paul's judicious phrasing, "to the Jew first and also to the Greek," recognizes the historical priority of the Jews in the reception of Revelation, yet insists as well on the necessary dissemination of that message to the second, larger group of Greeks. The Hellenistic and Hebraic theories of the nations condensed in Paul's address to the Romans likely responds to the unhappy split of his audience between Gentile and Jewish converts to Christianity, the first group having no natural relation to the Hebrew Scriptures so central to Pauline hermeneutics, and the second circle still deeply invested in the laws of the Torah.[7] Finally, these lines, like the epistle in general, acknowledge and reconcile the claims of both groups in the new church by presenting faith as the common sign of righteousness for all Christians.

The legacy of Romans to the Western discourse of the nations is caught between Paul's urge to discount the legal observances of contemporary Jews on the one hand and to grant historical significance to the Jews as a people on the other, impulses that equally stem from Paul's sense of the Jews as an *ethnos,* a tribe or nation bound by a common language, law, and genealogy. Unlike Galatians, Romans does not forbid the observance of Jewish laws such as circumcision, but makes them *adiaphora,* matters of doctrinal indifference; put otherwise, such practices are (merely) *cultural*—belonging to the domain of communal custom, which, though not harmful and sometimes even positively good, nonetheless have no significance in the drama of salvation. In Daniel Boyarin's judgment, although Paul's project "is not anti-Semitic (or even anti-Judaic) in intent, it nevertheless has the effect of depriving continued Jewish existence of any reality or significance in the Christian economies of history."[8] The triumph of the Gentile mission, by no means a given in Paul's historical moment, would eventually lead to the forthrightly anti-Jewish interpretation of Paul in the Church Fathers and Reformation theologians.[9] Yet European modernity also owes to Paul the knitting of the Hebrew Bible, reconceived as the Old Testament, into the scriptural canon and exegetical consciousness of Gentile Christianity. As Hans Hübner has argued, Paul remained invested in "the theological relevance [of] the history of Israel";[10] Paul's typological revaluation of the Torah, like his relativization of Jewish law, also springs from his cultural reading of Judaism, which, as the archetypal *ethnos,* coheres as a historical entity capable of modeling forth a comparable integrity for other nations and for the church in Christian historiography.[11]

The Epistles divide the Jew between three basic types: those Jews who, like Paul, converted to Christianity; those

Jews who remained Jewish, not accepting Jesus as the Messiah; and the ancient Israelites of the Hebrew Bible whose lives and words typologically predict the events of the new era. Whereas the Shylock of Shakespeare's earlier Venice is a figure of obdurate intransigence to Christian conversion in the typological tradition of Esau and Laban, Brabantio takes the rather different part of the Jewish Christians in Paul's epistle. Brabantio excludes Othello from the "nation of our wealthy, curlèd darlings" (*Othello* 1.2.69), implicitly equating "nation" with *natio* or birth; similarly, when Brabantio refers so confidently to his "brothers of the state," we are left with the religious question, "Who is my brother?"[12] Brabantio, like the Jewish Christians of Paul's Epistle to the Romans, would presumably restrict the circle of brothers to native Venetians, to those tied to him by blood and custom. Yet Brabantio, as a type of the Judaized Christian rather than a Jew proper, is not a villain; unlike Shylock or Barabas, Brabantio appears clannish but not evil, myopically wed to external appearances, "to all things of sense" (1.2.65), but not without the Abrahamic virtue of hospitality that helped lead to the present crisis.

Othello, by extension, takes the roles of Gentile and barbarian in Paul's divisions of the human kingdom. Othello's entry into the play as a convert to Christianity initially stations him in the tradition of the three kings at the Epiphany, often represented as the European, African, and Asian recipients of Christianity's world message in Renaissance iconography. Bearing exotic offerings of frankincense and myrrh to the manger of the Christ child, the African king Balthazar brings the gifts of his culture in the sense of *giving them up,* ceding a measure of cultural identity in the act of conversion.[13] The three kings were typologically keyed to the three sons of Noah, taken as the forefathers of the world's white, black, and yellow peoples; in such a scheme, Othello-as-Balthazar becomes the epochal negation of Ham, father of the black nations. In patristic and rabbinic traditions, Ham brought the curse of blackness onto his descendants by sleeping with his wife on the ark; Shakespeare, however, is careful to show Othello and Desdemona arriving from the "high-wrought flood" (*Othello* 2.1.2) and "enchafèd flood" (2.1.17) on *separate ships,* redeeming rather than repeating Ham's transgression.[14] In these early scenes, the black Othello functions as the living symbol of Christian universalism, a social and spiritual vision that stands as the test of Brabantio's "Judaizing" constructions of national brotherhood. Whereas in *Merchant,* Jessica's elopement with Lorenzo from the house of Shylock stages the historic shift from Judaism to Christianity, in *Othello* the marriage of a barbarian groom to a Christian bride figures forth the extension of the Christian message from European Gentiles to all the nations of the world. From this typological perspective, the marriage of white and black, of Greek and barbarian, far from representing a monstrosity or scandal, assumes almost cosmic significance, its harmonies resonating with the exultant coloratura of the Song of Songs.

This epochal scene of Gentile conversion, I argue, initially controls the play of black-white imagery in the drama. Iago uses bestial and demonic images of blackness in order to deform and prejudice Brabantio's—and by extension the audience's—reception of the elopement. Iago in turn has his own strange links to the world of *Merchant:* his famous negation of the Jewish God's unspeakable name, "I am not what I am" (*Othello* 1.1.67), flags him as the Devil of the play and roots him in a parodically Old Testament *ethos* of historical *ressentiment,* seasoned by the damaged pride and nurtured spite of all the Cains, Ishmaels, and Esaus passed over in the Bible for younger favored sons. It is Iago, for example, who warns Brabantio about "your house, your daughter, and your bags," as if the character of Iago were responsible for raising the spirit of *The Merchant of Venice* into *Othello*. Even Iago's infamous image of bestial cross-coupling, "an old black ram / Is tupping your white ewe" (1.1.90-91), echoes *Merchant*'s most egregious pun, that between "ewes" and "Iewes,"[15] irradiating the play's most cited example of color-based racism with an animus of a different color. Iago's presentation of blackness as the sign of a savage, unredeemable nature is soon marked by the play as historically bankrupted through the epochal weight granted to Othello as a latter-day Balthazar (the name chosen by Portia in *Merchant*'s trial scene), a Christian soldier who traces "his life and being / From men of royal siege" (*Othello* 1.2.21-22), an exegetical genealogy that derives his noble personage from the three kings of a global Epiphany.[16]

It would be easy enough, however, to love this vision of Christian humanism not wisely but too well. In Shakespeare's Venetian plays, Christian-humanist discourse always operates as a *universalism minus the circumcised,* a set that excludes not the unconverted pagans of the New World but rather the Jews and the Muslims, strict monotheisms existing not far away but close at hand. Judaism and Islam stem from the same Abrahamic lineage as Christianity; the three groups are, in the Muslim phrase, "people of the book," religions organized around revealed Scriptures that share many of the same prophets and patriarchs. Othello's role as defender of the faith against the Mohammedan Turks is faulted by the possibility that he has converted to Christianity from Islam, an entry into a covenant that would trace a different arc from that of the Gentile barbarian, locating the pre-Christian Othello not *ante legem*—before or outside the revealed law that singled out the Jews from the nations of the world—but *sub lege,* under a stringent monotheism untempered by Christ's love.[17] John Pory's appendix to his 1600 translation of Leo Africanus's *History and Description of Africa* lists four religions on the dark continent, "Gentiles, Iewes, Mahumetans, and Christians,"[18] a catalog that clearly distinguishes "Mahumetans" from "Gentiles." *The Policy of the Turkish Empire,* an anonymous tract from 1597, differentiates between Muslim monotheism and Gentile polytheism: "Touching the Godhead, [Muslims] acknowledge both with the Iews and Christians that there is one onely God: Wherein they differ from the Gentiles, who had their multiplicitie of Gods."[19] Such passages separate Islam out from paganism and correlate it with Judaism based on the two religions' scriptural, legal, and monotheistic bases.

In Christian typology, the Muslim was bound to the Jew through the figure of Ishmael. For Saint Paul, Ishmael is the type of the carnal Israel or modern Jew:

> For it is written that Abraham had two sons, one by a slave and one by a free woman. But the son of the slave was born according to the flesh, the son of the free woman through promise. Now this is an allegory: these women are two covenants. One is from Mount Sinai, bearing children for slavery; she is Hagar. Now Hagar is Mount Sinai in Arabia; she corresponds to the present Jerusalem, for she is in slavery with her children.
>
> (Gal. 4.22-25)

With the rise of Islam, the figure of Ishmael as a negative type of the Jew was transferred onto Mohammed, a translation already authorized by the Islamic appropriation of Ishmael for its own prophetic genealogy. Christian typologists also used Esau, Pharaoh, and Herod to couple the Jew and the Muslim as carnal children of Abraham facing each other across the world-historic break effected by the Incarnation.[20] Islam, the youngest of the three Abrahamic religions, represented to Renaissance Christianity a kind of Judaism after the fact, a redoubling of Jewish intransigence in the face of Christian revelation. As such, Islam executed a second, even crueler affront to Christianity's historical vision of epochal succession, since modern Judaism (from the Christian perspective) is merely a residual carryover from an earlier moment, but Islam from its very inception carried out its proselytizing mission in full knowledge of Christian teachings. The rapid expansion of Islam, however, presented the inverse of Judaism's dispersed, sequestered, and inward-looking communities. The third Revelation announced by Islam rejected the particularism associated with Judaism in favor of the universalism pioneered by Christianity; like the rulers of European Christendom, the Arab and then Turkish empires used the theme of spiritual equality among the nations to support their religious and political projects.[21]

Brabantio's warning against "bondslaves and pagans" (*Othello* 1.2.101) acknowledges the two possible avenues of Othello's entry into Christianity. More than simply synonyms, the pointedly paired words represent distinct locations in the play's conceptual geography of the nations: the bondslave names the condition of Hagar, her offspring, and his Ishmaelite progeny, while the pagan identifies the state of the Gentile barbarian, potential recipient of the expanded Pauline mission. Whereas the first acts of the play establish Othello as Christian soldier and devoted husband, the middle movement of the tragedy instigates a crisis in both the marital and the religious covenants that bind Othello to Venice. If the remainder of the play charts Othello's increasing distance from the role of the African king established in act one, we must pay attention to the effects that these competing scripts for the entry into covenant have on Othello's tragic exit from it.

As the play progresses, is Othello, as critics have frequently suggested, *paganized*—made exotic, savage, and barbaric—or is he also *Islamicized and Judaized*, brought back into contact with a law that should have been dissolved by the rite of baptism? In the play, paganization describes Othello's decline into gullibility, madness, and cruelty, a process emblematized by the infamous handkerchief, its subtle fabric woven out of the iconography of the Gentile gods. Even as Othello descends into pagan fury, however, he also begins to "turn Turk" (2.3.164), a phrase that names Islamicization as a tragic trajectory that runs alongside the path of barbarization, paralleling, elaborating, and deviating from it. This second path reverts not to anarchy *ante legem* but to a tyranny *sub lege*, a transformation embodied by Othello's increasing identification with a jealous justice that must be executed at any cost, a law driven by the fierce monogamy of an immoderate monotheism.

This process climaxes in Othello's anguished retort to Desdemona's denials:

> Thou dost stone my heart,
> And makes me call what I intend to do
> A murder, which I thought a sacrifice.
>
> (5.2.67-69)

Othello's "sacrifice" simultaneously identifies him with the old law, ruled by the Lord "whose name is Jealous" (Exod. 34.14), and indicates the law's epochal supercession by Desdemona's obedient love, insofar as her death resonates with (though by no means simply instantiates) that of Christ. Whereas studies of race in the play tend to emphasize the movement of paganization, feminist critics have noted Othello's increasing association with justice, usually understood as the masculinist tenets of Judeo-Christian patriarchy.[22] My point is somewhat different: Othello's justice, like that of Shylock, serves to separate the Semitic strands out of the Judeo-Christian synthesis even while grotesquely reinforcing the authority of the husband; although Othello's increasing alliance with the law is indeed patriarchal, I would insist on the Abrahamic (Judeo-Islamic) connotations of the word *patriarch*.[23]

OTHELLO CIRCUMCISED

Othello's final autobiography stages his double placement in the narratives of paganization and Islamicization:

> Then must you speak
> Of one that loved not wisely but too well;
> Of one not easily jealous but, being wrought,
> Perplexed in the extreme; of one whose hand,
> Like the base Indian [Iudean],[24] threw a pearl away
> Richer than all his tribe; of one whose subdued eyes,
> Albeit unusèd to the melting mood,
> Drops tears as fast as the Arabian trees
> Their medicinable gum. Set you down this:
> And say besides that in Aleppo once,
> Where a malignant and a turbaned Turk
> Beat a Venetian and traduced the state,

I took by th'throat the circumcisèd dog
And smote him, thus.

(5.2.353-66)

In the exotic parable of the base Indian, the rejected pearl condenses the murder of Desdemona with Othello's departure from Christianity. The first simile is swiftly followed by the reference to tears that drop "as fast as the Arabian trees / Their medicinable gum," an elaborate circumlocution for myrrh. As nativity gift (Matt. 2.11), myrrh manifests the economy of conversion, in which the Gentile kings bring the precious distillations of their countries in exchange for a place in the Christian order. In the wake of Desdemona's murder, the myrrh also functions as a figure of Othello's regret and repentance for having reneged on that contract, becoming the medium of a "melting mood" that dissolves the universalist iconography of Epiphany into the scene of conversion's *re*version back into the strange substances that distinguish the nations. As the symbol of the Epiphany and its dissolution, the myrrh tree situates Othello in a pagan scene, darkening his skin in its allusive shade.

Yet, as critics have pointed out, the Folio text's substitution of "Iudean" for "Indian" installs Othello's tragedy within another set of mytho-historical coordinates. Since Lewis Theobald's eighteenth-century edition, editors and critics have occasionally favored the Folio reading, referring it to Judas's betrayal of Christ and to the Herod-Mariam story of jealous murder, taken from Josephus's *Jewish War* and *Antiquities of the Jews* as the material for several neo-Senecan dramas.[25] Like Brabantio's restricted use of "nation," the "tribe" of the "base Iudean" implies a circumscribed and *circumcised* worldview in which the Christian pearl finds no proper place, a rejection that stems not from the ignorance of the Indian but from the knowledge of good and evil brought about by the law.[26] Moreover, if we read "base Iudean" in terms of the Herod and Mariam story, a now familiar typological scenario takes shape within the confines of the simile. Herod, an Idumean descended from Esau, is a type of the latter-day Muslim as well as the inveterate Jew, and his maligned but faithful wife Mariam, a sacrificial victim in the Christological pattern shared with Desdemona, represents the righteous remnant who makes possible the historic transition into the new era.[27]

Rather than selecting "Iudean" over "Indian," I follow Edward Snow in insisting instead that "each variant suggests a different side of Othello."[28] "Indian" describes the more broadly drawn, more theatrically powerful movement of the drama as the tragic breakdown of Gentile conversion, yet the almost effortless substitution of "Indian" by "Iudean" follows the path of Islamicization that falls out of the play's dominant turn toward barbarism, articulating both paganism and Islam as the starting points of two separate itineraries into and out of Christianity. Othello's recollection of the Turk in Aleppo flows out of this auxiliary reading. As critics have often argued, Othello's reenactment of his earlier heroics both identifies him with the Turk and kills off that identification in the act of suicide, reasserting Othello's allegiance to the Christian ethics whose standard he has borne. Yet these readings too often identify the Turk simply as a "barbaric enemy," "the Infidel," or one of a "proliferating series of exoticized others."[29] To the contrary, it is my project to distinguish the Judean from the Indian, the Jew and the Muslim from the Gentile pagan.

As Lynda Boose, one of the few critics to move beyond the pagan reading, has pointed out, circumcision rather than skin color is the trait that Othello "invokes as the final, inclusive sign of his radical Otherness."[30] Iago had already evoked an epochal reading of circumcision when he advised Cassio to elect Desdemona as his petitioner:

And then for her
To win the Moor—were't to renounce his baptism,
All seals and symbols of redeemèd sin—
His soul is so enfettered to her love
That she may make, unmake, do what she list.

(*Othello* 2.3.336-40)

The phrase "*seals and symbols* of redeemèd sin" links baptism to Saint Paul's reading of circumcision as "a *sign or seal*" of faith (Rom. 4.11).[31] In Judaism, circumcision has a performative or constitutive function; it is a "seal" in the sense of an official imprimatur that validates and authenticates the contract between man and God.[32] *Brit milah,* "the covenant of circumcision," operates as a kind of signature, since it ratifies a contract and confers a Hebrew name; written on the body of the infant, this name at once identifies the child's absolute uniqueness and situates him in a network of genealogical relations.

For Paul, however, circumcision becomes an outward mark designed to reflect an internal condition of faith, a "sign" in the sense of an external indication. In Paul's words, "he is not a real Jew who is one outwardly, nor is true circumcision something external and physical. He is a Jew who is one inwardly, and real circumcision is a matter of the heart, spiritual and not literal" (Rom. 2.28-29). In the new era, circumcision is relegated to the status of a fallen sign (a mark that may or may not manifest a corresponding inner condition) and a merely legal seal (a bodily signature that establishes a purely formal covenant unmediated by spirit). In the dialectic of Christian history, circumcision gives way to baptism, a sacrament that leaves no bodily trace of its operation, its transparent and reflective waters dissolving the blood and erasing the scar of circumcision's violently inscriptive cut.

In the judgment of James Shapiro, "More than anything else in the sixteenth century . . . Paul's ideas about circumcision saturated what Shakespeare's contemporaries thought, wrote, and heard about circumcision."[33] I would add that it was above all the rite of circumcision in its Pauline articulation that emblematized the affiliation between the Jew and the Muslim in Christian typological thought. The author of the *Policy of the Turkish Empire* lays out the status of the law in the three religions:

For as the Iews had a particular lawe given unto them and published by God himselfe in mount Sinai . . . So have the Turkes (in imitation of the same) certaine lawes and precepts or Commandements laide downe in their Alcoran . . . Which argueth that their confidence and hope of salvation consisteth chiefely in the pietie and merite of their vertuous life, and good deedes: And that they doe not much differ in that point from the opinion of some Christians, who do attribute their salvation unto their merites.[34]

The passage sets up Islamic law as a belated version of the Torah and an alienating mirror of the Catholic Church. The author goes on to single out circumcision as a law that had once been "a most holy and sacred sacrament," but "is nowe converted . . . to a most idle and vaine ceremony" among Jews and Muslims.[35] The tract, though strongly polemical, actually makes some progress in depicting basic Islamic tenets and practices, differing on many points from the fantastic accounts disseminated from medieval sources. If the typological perspective threatens to make Islam disappear into Judaism, reductively appropriating the one religion to the more familiar paradigms of the other, I would also insist that the special historical consciousness born of typology—the interest in coherent epochs or "cultures" fundamental to Western philosophies of history—also helps account for the tract's relative success in depicting a foreign worldview. In the *Policy of the Turkish Empire,* the assimilative-reductionist and descriptive-historiographical poles of typological consciousness exist in something of a balance; the same might be said for the mimetic successes of *The Merchant of Venice* and their further elaboration in *Othello.*

Ron Canada as Iago and Patrick Stewart as Othello in the 1997 Shakespeare Theatre production of Othello.

Christopher Marlowe's *Jew of Malta,* on the other hand, with its more naked debts to medieval drama, lies toward the allegorical side of the typological continuum; in Marlowe's play, the cut of circumcision equates Jew and Muslim with an exemplary if reductive clarity that Shakespeare transmits in more sublimated forms. The Jew Barabas chooses as his slave, partner-in-crime, and successor the Muslim Ithamore by acknowledging their affiliation: "Make account of me / As of thy fellow; we are villains both: / Both *circumcisèd,* we hate Christians both."[37] The fellowship between the Jew and the Muslim has been signed and sealed in advance by the shared mark of circumcision, a permanent bodily sign that establishes membership in a group but, unlike racial traits such as skin color, is produced through the deliberate execution of ritual law. The name Ithamore is itself borrowed from the Old Testament, where "Ithamar" appears as the youngest son of Aaron (Exod. 6.23); by intensifying "-mar" into "-more," Marlowe has effectively Islamicized this type of the Jewish priest, semantically flagging the link between Judaic and Muslim law according to the habits of Christian typology.[38]

In appointing himself both confessor and executioner of Desdemona, Othello struggles to assume a priestly as well as a judicial function, becoming an "Ithamore," a Moorish son of Aaron, but in a higher, more interiorized, mimetic register than that elaborated in Marlowe's farcical morality play. In his suicide speech, Othello's drawn sword at once points outward to circumcision as the trait identifying the object of his scorn, and reflexively *re*turns it onto Othello's own body as the very means of death, a final stroke that cuts off his life by turning the Turk into and onto himself. In one arc of its meaning, this cut redeems the Moor in death, restoring him to the history of Venice as one who has "done the state some service" and who, like Mary Magdalene, has "loved not wisely but too well." From this perspective, circumcision functions as the emblem of Christian typology par excellence, the vehicle of world-historical cancellation that allows for the reconversion of the Moor to Christianity. Othello's suicide, that is, functions as a martyrological baptism in blood, an act that completes and terminates the era of the law; through his suicide, Othello has become literally "circumcised in the heart," not unlike Antonio in Shakespeare's earlier Venetian play. At the same time, the cut that (re)circumcises Othello does not disappear into its typological sublations. Instead it reinstates the Hebraic function of the signature, the written letters of a legally ratifying and subjectively identifying mark that dislodges Othello from the Christian historical order by locating him in a different covenant. In this sense, the suicide effects a circumcision according to the Judeo-Islamic rather than the Pauline-internal paradigm, constituting a self-validating signature that separates out Islam as a historico-theological position distinct from paganism, a regime defined by the singular imprint of circumcision as the persistent "seal and symbol" of the law. With this ritual gesture, Othello signs his final autobiography, exacerbating and inflaming as much as redeeming that ancient scar in the Pauline discourse of nations. This momentary positing of Islam as its own dispensation both exceeds the typological vision (which would reduce Islam to its own categories of faith and nationhood) and is itself anticipated by the historiographical impulse of Christianity as a narrative of epochal relations.

Paul's ethno-political theology can accommodate the vast differences between the Greek and the barbarian, but not the very little difference between the circumcised and the uncircumcised. In *Othello*—Shakespeare's second letter to the Venetians—Christian universalism, circling around the black body of the Gentile convert, has the capacity to envision if not realize a world of *racial* equality. It is worth asserting here that Christianity, like Islam, is a world religion, not a race, and does not belong to any civilization as either its special heritage or its colonial weapon, to whatever degree it has been used as such. What Shakespeare's Pauline Christianity—and this is a paradox besetting all revealed religions—has more difficulty imagining is a world of *religious* equality among the people of the book, an equality in which circumcision, maintained as an external mark of covenant not erased through spiritualization, could be accounted for rather than discounted by Christianity's historical scheme. In *Othello,* the romance of Gentile conversion supports the dream of a universal brotherhood that allows Shakespeare to set up and see through the black-white opposition. Yet this Christian-humanist discourse always operates as a universalism minus the circumcised; the Jew and the Muslim are subtracted from the nations of the world ingathered by Christianity, singled out and cut off by the ritual stroke through which they continue to distinguish themselves. Odd as it may seem to contemporary readers caught up in the horizon of modern racism, it is Othello's religious rather than racial traits that prove more intractable in the Christian vision staged by Shakespeare's play, an obduracy that points in turn to the vicissitudes of Renaissance *protoracism* in the shapes of *neoracism* that have emerged at the end of our bloody century.

Notes

1. Etienne Balibar, "Is There a Neo-Racism?" in Etienne Balibar and Emmanuel Wallerstein, *Race, Nation, Class: Ambiguous Identities,* trans. Chris Turner (London, 1991), 23-24.

2. The groundwork for this orientation was laid by the historical criticism of Eldred Jones, *Othello's Countrymen: The African in English Renaissance Drama* (London, 1965), and G. K. Hunter, "Othello and Colour Prejudice," in *Dramatic Identities and Cultural Tradition: Studies in Shakespeare and His Contemporaries* (Liverpool, Eng., 1978), as well as the political and psychoanalytic myth criticism of Leslie A. Fiedler, *The Stranger in Shakespeare* (New York, 1972). In the recent wave of essays, the black-white opposition has been most fruitfully explored by Arthur Little, "'An essence that's not seen': The Primal Scene of Racism in *Othello*," *Shakespeare Quarterly* 44, no. 3 (Fall 1993): 304-24, and Jonathan Crewe, "Out of the Matrix: Shakespeare's Race-Writing," *Yale Journal of Criticism* 8, no. 2 (1995): 13-29. Karen Newman, "'And wash the Ethiop white': Femininity and the Monstrous in *Othello*," in *Shakespeare Reproduced: The Text in History and Ideology,* ed. Jean E. Howard and Marion F. O'Connor (New York, 1987); Patricia Parker, "Fantasies of 'Race' and 'Gender': Africa, *Othello,* and Bringing to Light," in Margo Hendricks and Patricia Parker, *Women, "Race," and Writing in the Early Modern Period* (London, 1994); and Michael Neill, "Unproper Beds: Race, Adultery, and the Hideous in *Othello*," *Shakespeare Quarterly* 40, no. 4 (Winter 1989), have focused on monstrosity and miscegenation. Stephen Greenblatt, *Renaissance Self-Fashioning from More to Shakespeare* (Chicago, 1980); Parker; Newman; and Emily Bartels, "Making More of the Moor: Aaron, Othello, and Renaissance Refashionings of Race," *Shakespeare Quarterly* 41, no. 4 (Winter 1990), have excavated travel narratives as sources and models of *Othello*'s protocolonial practice, a dimension emphasized from a postcolonial angle in Ania Loomba, "The Color of Patriarchy: Critical Difference, Cultural Difference, and Renaissance Drama," in Hendricks and Parker, *Women, "Race," and Writing;* and Ania Loomba, *Gender, Race, Renaissance Drama* (Manchester, Eng., 1989). Bartels assumes that Othello was a Muslim, but does not develop the tensions between race and religion, a dynamic on which Lynda Boose, "'The Getting of a Lawful Race': Racial Discourse in Early Modern England and the Unrepresentable Black Woman," in Hendricks and Parker, *Women, "Race," and Writing,* has reflected suggestively.

3. See Neill, "Unproper Beds," 385.

4. *Othello,* ed. David Bevington (New York, 1980), 1.1.82; *The Merchant of Venice,* ed. John Russell Brown (London, 1955), 2.7.15; *Othello* 1.3.69-71. (All subsequent citations of these plays are from these editions.)

5. Rom. 1.14-16, in Wayne Meeks, ed., *The Writings of St. Paul* (New York, 1972). (All subsequent citations of Paul are from this edition; emphasis added.)

6. As Wayne Meeks comments, Paul "looks to Rome . . . as the center of the known world, and his visit there becomes a symbol for the universality of his mission 'among all the Gentiles' (Rom. 1.5)"; Meeks, *Writings of St. Paul,* 66.

7. According to modern scholars of Paul, the Jewish community in Rome, including those who had

converted to Christianity, had been exiled by Claudius around 49 C.E. and returned to the city with the accession of Nero in 54, a return that may have led to tensions between Gentile and Jewish Christians in the Roman church at the time of Paul's letter; Meeks, *Writings of St. Paul,* 67. Hans Hübner summarizes and rejects this argument, taking what seems to be a minority position, namely that Paul's more tolerant attitude toward Jewish law in Romans (as compared to Galatians) reflects a change of heart rather than of rhetorical situation; Hans Hübner, *Law in Paul's Thought,* ed. John Riches, trans. James C. G. Greig (1978, reprint: Edinburgh, 1984), 5.

8. Daniel Boyarin, *A Radical Jew: Paul and the Politics of Identity* (Berkeley, 1994), 32.

9. The twentieth century has seen a more balanced look at Paul's Jewish sources as well as a salutary extrication of Paul from the anti-Jewish exegetical traditions founded on his epistles by figures such as Martin Luther. On Paul and Judaism, see W. D. Davies, *Paul and Rabbinic Judaism: Some Rabbinic Elements in Pauline Theology* (1955, reprint: New York, 1967), and E. P. Sanders, *Paul, the Law, and the Jewish People* (Philadelphia, 1983); for examples of revisionist Christian readings of Paul in the wake of the Holocaust, see Alan Davies, ed., *Antisemitism and the Foundations of Christianity* (New York, 1979). For a brief history of Pauline scholarship in light of the Jewish question, see Boyarin, *Radical Jew,* 39-56.

10. Hübner, *Law,* 56.

11. Erich Auerbach, in his still definitive essay on typological interpretation, writes that this exegetical principle insured that the Old Testament became part of European civilization; Erich Auerbach, "Figura," in *Scenes from the Drama of European Literature* (1959, reprint: Minneapolis, Minn., 1984), 52. See also Karl Löwith on the importance of the Biblical idea of the nation for Western historiography; Karl Löwith, *Meaning in History* (Chicago, 1949), 195-96.

12. The distinction between "brother" and "stranger" established in Deuteronomy is of course crucial to the intergroup economy of *The Merchant of Venice;* whereas the Jew distinguishes "brother" and "stranger," not lending money to the one but permitting it to the other, the Christian is supposed to take all men as his brother; Marc Shell, *Money, Language, and Thought* (Baltimore, 1982), 51. Brabantio presumably concurs with Roderigo's assessment that the Moor is "an extravagant and wheeling stranger" (*Othello* 1.1.139)—not included in the Venetian brotherhood.

13. Peter Erikson, "Representations of Blacks and Blackness in the Renaissance," *Criticism* 34, no. 4 (Fall 1993): 499-527. Shakespeare uses epiphany imagery in his description of Morocco's love of Portia: "'Who chooseth me shall gain what many men desire.' / Why, that's the lady, all the world desires her. / From the four corners of the earth they come / To kiss this shrine, this mortal breathing saint" (*Merchant* 2.7.37-40). With the exception of Erikson, recent critics of *Othello* ignore this strand of racial iconography. Loomba, *Gender,* 42; Anthony Barthelemy, *Black Face, Maligned Race: The Representation of Blacks in English Drama from Shakespeare to Southerne* (Baton Rouge, La., 1987), 3-4; and Little, "Primal Scene," 308, emphasize the equation of blackness with evil and devilishness in the Christian tradition but do not note the countertheme of Gentile conversion.

14. Hunter cites Bede's commentary on St. Matthew: "Mystice autem tres Magi tres partes mundi significant, Asiam, Africam, Europam, sive humanum genus, quod a tribus filiis Noe seminarium sumpsit"; Hunter, "Othello and Colour Prejudice," 50. For the patristic tradition on Ham, see Augustine *City of God,* ed. David Knowles, trans. Henry Bettenson (Harmondsworth, Eng., 1972), 16.11; for the rabbinic tradition, see *Genesis Rabbah,* in *Midrash Rabbah,* trans. H. Freedman (London, 1983), 1:36-37. For another Renaissance figure of the African king as a symbol of the universality of the Christian message, see Thomas Middleton's 1613 masque, *The Triumph of Truth,* in which the conversion to Christianity of a "king of the Moors" epitomizes the "triumph of truth" announced in the masque's title. His visit to England is a modern epiphany narrative: "Nor could our desires rest till we were led / Unto this place, where those good spirits were bred"; Thomas Middleton, *The Triumph of Truth,* in *The Works of Thomas Middleton,* ed. A. H. Bullen (New York, 1964), 7:248. Samuel Chew comments on the masque in *The Crescent and the Rose: Islam and England During the Renaissance* (1937, reprint: New York, 1965), 463-65. The Ham story has received much play in recent criticism of *Othello* as a primal scene of Renaissance racism in Newman, "Femininity and the Monstrous," 146-47; Barthelemy, *Black Face,* 3; and Little, "Primal Scene," 308. I have not seen mention, however, of the way that Shakespeare stages the "flood" near Cyprus as the typological antidote to the Old Testament story, effectively replacing Ham with Balthazar.

15. Shell, *Money,* 49.

16. The foundations of this humanist reading of race in *Othello* were laid by Eldred Jones, who argued that the first scenes of the play introduce us to Othello through the jaundiced eyes of Iago in order to correct his contaminating language with the figure cut by Othello himself, and by G. K. Hunter, who demonstrated that the universalist dream of a world Christianity is what makes possible act one's judicious weighing of Iago's conventional stereotypes against Othello's natural dignity: Jones, *Othello's*

Countrymen, 87-93; Hunter, "Othello and Colour Prejudice," 49.

17. The period *ante legem* dates from Adam to Moses, *sub lege* from Moses to Christ, and *sub gratia* from Christ onward; Howard Hibbard, *Michelangelo*, 2d ed. (New York, 1974), 99-125.

18. John Pory, "A summarie discourse of the manifold Religions professed in Africa," appended to Leo Africanus, *The History & Description of Africa* (1600), trans. John Pory, ed. Robert Brown (London, 1896), 3:1001-50.

19. *The Policy of the Turkish Empire* (London, 1597), 15.

20. On Arab genealogy in Christian exegesis, see Norman Daniels, *Islam and the West: The Making of an Image* (Edinburgh, 1960), 128. On the reading of Pharaoh and Herod as Muslims, see Chew, *Crescent*, 390, 395.

21. Bernard Lewis, *Race and Color in Islam* (New York, 1970), 1-28.

22. See Lynda Boose, "Othello's Handkerchief: 'The Recognizance and Pledge of Love,'" *English Literary Renaissance* 5, no. 3 (Autumn 1975): 372-73.

23. For Othello's identification with an angry or untempered justice, see also *Othello* 2.3.69-72 and 5.1.1-3. In an unpublished lecture, Joseph Chaney has productively linked Othello's jealousy to that of the "Judeo-Christian God"; Joseph Chaney, "Othello's Jealousy and the Triangle of Desire" (lecture delivered at Indiana University, South Bend, Ind., March 1994). Monogamy and monotheism are firmly linked in the Jewish tradition, for example in the keying of the commandment against idolatry to the parallel commandment against adultery in the adjoining tablet; Avroham Chaim Feuer, *Aseres Hadibros/ The Ten Commandments: A New Translation with Commentary Anthologized from Talmudic, Midrashic, and Rabbinic Sources* (New York, 1981), 33. Boose notes the Deuteronomic sources for the "sacrifice" of an adulterous woman, but does not single out the specifically Old Testament provenance of the law (Deuteronomy being an especially charged text in the typological economy of *Merchant*); Boose, "Othello's Handkerchief," 372.

24. As editor David Bevington notes, the Quarto gives "Indian" (selected in most modern editions), but the Folio gives "Iudean," chosen by some editors and critics; *Othello*, 126 n.

25. Critics who prefer "base Iudean" include Richard S. Veit, "'Like the Base Judean': A Defense of an Oft-Rejected Reading in *Othello*," *English Literary Renaissance* 10, no. 3 (Autumn 1980), and Gordon Braden, who reads *Othello* in the context of Herod-Mariam dramas; Gordon Braden, *Renaissance Tragedy and the Senecan Tradition: Anger's Privilege* (New Haven, Conn., 1985), 153-71. Edward Snow provides a powerful defense of retaining both readings; Edward Snow, "Sexual Anxiety and the Male Order of Things in *Othello*," *Shakespeare Quarterly* 26 (1975): 412; citing Veit, he points out that "the word 'tribe' is never used in connection with Indians in Shakespeare. It primarily connotes 'clan' for him, often in connection with the 'tribes of the world'" (412). Fiedler, *Stranger*, 195-56, makes a strong case for "Iudean," but then chooses "Indian" instead. Josephus's accounts of the Herod-Mariam romance are excerpted in Elizabeth Cary's *The Tragedy of Mariam: The Fair Queen of Jewry*, ed. Barry Weller and Margaret W. Ferguson (Berkeley, 1994).

26. See St. Paul: "If it had not been for the law, I should not have known sin"; Rom. 7.7.

27. Dympna Callaghan provides a related reading of the Herod-Mariam story in her inter-pretation of Cary's *Tragedie of Mariam*; Callaghan, however, emphasizes not the typological split between the intransigent modern Jew and the successful Jewish convert (the Esau-Jacob pair), but rather the "racialization" or blackening of Herod and the concomitant whitening of Mariam. Crudely put, in Callaghan's reading, racial difference precedes and governs religious difference; Dympna Callaghan, "Re-reading Elizabeth Cary's *The Tragedie of Mariam, Faire Queene of Jewry*," in Hendricks and Parker, *Women, "Race," and Writing*. In my reading, religious difference precedes and governs racial difference.

28. Snow, "Sexual Anxiety," 412.

29. Braden, *Renaissance Tragedy*, 169; Loomba, *Gender, Race, Renaissance Drama*, 48; Parker, "Fantasies of 'Race' and 'Gender,'" 98.

30. Boose, "Racial Discourse," 40.

31. In Rom. 4, Paul notes that the declaration of Abraham's faith in Genesis 15.6 ("And he believed the Lord; and he reckoned it to him as righteousness") precedes by several chapters God's institution of the rite of circumcision (Gen. 17.11). From this, Paul argues that Abraham "received circumcision as a sign or seal of the righteousness which he had by faith while he was still uncircumcised" (Rom. 4.11).

32. In a related argument, Boyarin, *Radical Jew*, 37, cites midrashim that depict circumcision as a writing of God's name on the body.

33. James Shapiro, *Shakespeare and the Jews* (New York, 1996), 117.

34. *Policy of the Turkish Empire*, 15.

35. Ibid., 23. In Islam, circumcision is a custom rather than a law, though I have not seen this point acknowledged in the Elizabethan literature on Islam, which generally assimilates the Moslem practice to the more familiar Jewish one.

36. Chew, *Crescent*, 443-44.

37. Christopher Marlowe, *The Jew of Malta*, in Russell A. Fraser and Norman C. Rabkin, eds., *Drama of the English Renaissance*, vol. 1, *The Tudor Period* (New York, 1976), 225-27 (emphasis added).

38. Editors Fraser and Rabkin note the borrowing; ibid., 276 n. In *Titus Andronicus*, Shakespeare would clarify Marlowe's allusive conflation of the two identities by simply naming his Moor "Aaron," substituting the familiar father for the obscure son.

Darryl Tippins (essay date 1997)

SOURCE: Tippins, Darryl. "'Can you make no use of nothing?': Nihilism and Meaning in *King Lear* and *The Madness of King George*." In *Performance for a Lifetime*, edited by Barbara C. Ewell and Mary A. McCay, pp. 159-80. New Orleans: Loyola University New Orleans, 1997.

[*In the following essay, Tippins offers a reading of* King Lear *that attempts to mediate between absurdist or pessimistic interpretations of the play and religious or redemptive ones.*]

> At the heart of any dialogue is the conviction that what is exchanged has meaning.
> —Michael Holquist

> And yet this nothing / is the seed of all—heaven's clear / eye, where all the world's wonders appear.
> —Wendell Berry

Fierce debates rage over the ultimate meaning and purpose of Shakespeare's greatest tragedy, *King Lear*. On the one hand, the so-called "Idealists" (that is, the humanists and Christian readers) value the play as a story of redemptive suffering. A. C. Bradley spoke for this group when he maintained that Lear died, not in despair, but in ecstasy, believing that Cordelia was alive (252-53). Joseph Summers argued a different kind of hopeful ending: though Lear dies knowing that Cordelia was indeed dead, he dies knowing that what she taught him about love is "truly more alive than anything else in his world" (Summers 92). Many others agree that the play is ultimately meaningful and supportive of great Christian, or at least traditional, ethical themes—love, mercy, forgiveness, renunciation, and so forth. Stanley Wells summarizes:

> Uncompromisingly the play acknowledges the power of evil, the inevitability of death, the fragility of the human body, while also asserting the spiritual values that can give meaning to life.

On the other hand stand the skeptical Shakespeareans who are now ascendant. William R. Elton argues forcefully that this tragedy is certainly not an optimistic Christian drama, but a pagan story of "all-dissolving chaos" (338). Nicholas Brooke concurs: Lear's "final retreat to madness" makes it "impossible to retain any concept of an ordered universe" ("The Ending" 85). In fact, he argues, the last act "shatters the foundations of faith itself" (qtd. in Wells 248). Recent materialist critics like Jonathan Dollimore argue forcefully that the play undermines all notions of transcendent value, including the very construct called "humanity"; those who find a meaningful end in Lear are guilty of "essentialist mystification" (202). "All moral structures," claims Nicholas Brooke, "whether of natural order or Christian redemption, are invalidated by the naked fact of experience" (*Shakespeare* 59-60). Harold Bloom concurs: "Shakespeare's darkest tragedies, Lear and Macbeth, do not yield to Christianization" (51). A. L. French finds the Bradleyan salvationist interpretation "distasteful in itself as well as absurdly inappropriate to the spirit of Shakespeare's play" (144). Absurdist, nihilist, and materialist readings constitute the Lear orthodoxy of the late twentieth century, it seems.

One wonders: is it possible to negotiate between these agonistic positions? The answer is, yes, one can. Each camp seems to have gotten in touch with one powerful dimension of the play, championing it to the exclusion of other dimensions. The nihilists gravitate towards Kent's profoundly negative point of view, "All is cheerless, dark, and deadly," while the idealists defer to Edgar's "The gods are just," and while the so-called Redemptivists soften or disallow the play's dark tones. Pechter maintains: "What Tate and the Redemptivists . . . attempt to do is to protect us from the play, render us invulnerable—whether through plot changes or through the imposition of systems of meaning—to the extraordinary power of *King Lear* to make us suffer" (182).

Pechter criticizes those who, like Bradley, argue that the play contains something affirmative about life. These Redemptivists often make Edgar the authorial mouthpiece; and, like Edgar, they attempt "to control experience by reorganizing it into 'patterns' of significance" (182). Both readings slip into precisely the kind of absolutism that the play itself resists, but a more sophisticated alternative would be one neither naively optimistic nor absolutely pessimistic, and would instead welcome the play's abundance of positive and negative elements.

For what if *Lear* is neither naively optimistic nor lacking a system of meaning? What if this play has a "pattern" of significance, but this significance proves to be darkly meaningful? What if the work operates in a mysterious, paradoxical realm where *conflicting realities* co-exist? I maintain that the play is dialectical, with ever-shifting points of view. Jay L. Halio marks out this more inclusive position:

> *King Lear* thus offers powerful, imaginative rendering of conflicting and sometimes complementary attitudes and beliefs. If none dominates the action, our final impression of the play must remain what A. C. Bradley called a "mystery we cannot fathom."

(15)

In contrast some Redemptivists and some nihilists generally suppress those elements in the play that do not fit their monological thesis of salvation or chaos. A. C. Bradley long ago acknowledged this slipping into reductionism when he accused Swinburne of emphasizing "only certain aspects of the play and certain elements in the total impression" (278). Norman Rabkin has eloquently warned against the same problem in approaching *The Merchant of Venice*. Surely Bradley is right in arguing that the total impression is bigger than either the elements of darkness or of light. We must reach for a reading that, paradoxically, can allow for salvation *and* for chaos.

One way to preserve the paradoxical mystery of *King Lear* while making some sense of the debate about the play's alleged paganism, or nihilism, or absurdity on the one hand—or its Christian-humanist-idealist vision on the other—is to acknowledge a major mythic pattern that lies within the play, a trope that is at once pagan, Hebraic, Christian, and even, in a particular sense, "nihilistic." I refer to "kenosis," a concept which allows one to see how the play can at once be religious, yet also pessimistic, and even nihilistic. A "kenotic" reading of the play uniquely avoids the implicit optimism of orthodox idealist readings while refusing an absurdist interpretation as well. In other words, kenosis makes possible a complex, dialectical view of the play which resists reduction. If a kenotic vision lies back of this grand work, then the contending critics are partly right, partly wrong.

Despite significant differences among the ancient Hebrews and Greeks (and later the Hellenized Christians who composed the Greek New Testament), they shared a vision of human experience as profoundly kenotic. *Kenosis* is based on the Greek verb *kevow*, which means "to make empty; to deprive of content or possession; to be desolate; to nullify, destroy; to come to nothing" (Kittel and Friedrich 3: 661).

Of course, the breaking or the "emptying" of an earthly king or a godlike hero has long been a familiar literary pattern. Classical male heroes and protagonists (like Oedipus, Kreon, and Jesus Christ) undergo a trial in which they lose their royal status, are emptied and humiliated, reduced to "nothing," and as a result gain something (wisdom, honor, glory, understanding, and so forth). After being broken, maddened, blinded, stripped, thwarted, and emptied, the hero often finds his true voice, his vision, his vocation, his redemption, even though it may require his death.

The kenosis myth is very rich, complicated, and ancient. One authority on the subject, Ralph P. Martin, traces the idea of the kenotic descent of the divine hero to ancient Hellenistic legends (76-80). It appears in several Athenian dramas like *Antigone, Ajax,* and the *Suppliant Maidens;* yet the kenotic trope, while centuries old, has in recent years been largely forgotten in literary circles. It is crucial to much literature steeped in the Christian tradition, and as we shall see with Alan Bennett's recent play and screenplay *The Madness of King George,* the theme enjoys continuing significance in contemporary drama.

In this essay I wish to show how a recent kenotic drama can assist us in reading *King Lear* with fresh eyes. By comparing Shakespeare's and Bennett's uses of kenotic ideas, not only do we discern the continuing vitality of kenosis as a literary theme, but we also discover how the kenotic trope gives these works special shape and value. The Bennett play serves as a kind of commentary on Shakespeare's work, exposing latent kenotic motifs in the Renaissance play that have been masked by time and forgetting.

Additionally, through Bennett's remarkable appropriation of Shakespeare's plot, we discover a potent reply to critics who insist on *Lear*'s absurdism or nihilism. Bennett's fictional players function as an audience for *King Lear*. King George, in particular, "listens in" on the Shakespearean plot and then appropriates it in illuminating ways—just as Hamlet hears and appropriates the First Player's tragic speech in interesting and significant ways (*Hamlet* II.ii). Ultimately, *The Madness of King George* is a creative (re)interpretation of *King Lear*. Through the intertextual "dialogue" of these two plays we are not only presented a picture of the dynamics of theatrical experience, but we are provided telling cues for reading *King Lear* for ourselves. A play, we recall, not only *contains* dialogue; it is a dialogue—with a living audience—and all dialogue presupposes meaning. "At the heart of any dialogue is the conviction that what is exchanged has meaning" (Holquist 38). Alan Bennett, through his mad protagonist, teaches us once again how to dialogue with Shakespeare's great tragedy *in a meaningful way.*

When the ancient world was Christianized, kenosis entered with full force into Western thought and literature; indeed, Jesus Christ came to be seen as the supreme kenotic hero. St. Paul in his Philippian epistle described Jesus Christ as having experienced the truest form of kenosis (Philippians 2:5-11). Kenotic descent was a theme that apparently enamored St. Augustine; it appears as a recurring metaphor in the *Confessions*. Stories of saints and heroes who are stripped and humiliated, in imitation of Christ, became standard in the Middle Ages. As a number of authorities have shown, interest in kenotic themes flourished in the Reformation, generating extensive discussion of the theme. Kenotic literature abounds in the Renaissance, most notably in John Milton's drama *Samson Agonistes,* but also in the work of George Herbert and John Donne. The endurance of the kenotic trope in Western literature is truly remarkable, stretching from the ancient Greeks to Harold Bloom.

Either intuitively or through his exposure to Scripture, liturgy, and sacred art, Shakespeare knew the paradigm well. Kenotic language circulates through his plays, allowing the exploration of a number of motifs central to the hero's tragic descent. As the Shakespearean hero encounters his dark experience, he is forced into a radical mortification, self-forgetfulness, and—above all—self-annihilation or "nothingness" (which James L. Calderwood calls "creative uncreation"). For example, Richard II, shortly before his execution, describes himself as one who must undergo the curriculum of suffering and become "nothing"—a central kenotic motif:

> But what e'er I be,
> Nor I, nor any man but man is,
> With nothing shall be pleas'd, till he be eas'd
> With being nothing.
>
> (Richard II 5. 5. 38-41)

"Kenotic impulses" such as the one that appears in Richard can be found in most of Shakespeare's tragic heroes, as Fortin argues (80-94). However, an examination of *King Lear* reveals that it is the most kenotic Shakespearean play of all.

Metaphor is often an efficient and effective mode of entry into a text, argues Madelon Golhke Sprengnether: "It is metaphor that allows us to subread, to read on the margins of discourse, to analyze what is latent or implicit in the structures of consciousness or of a text" (46). Hence, the kenotic trope helps us to "subread," to read on the margins and discover latent and implicit structures in Shakespeare's text. Kenosis is not a single figure of speech; it actually entails a series of related figures, including concepts of emptying (indeed, pouring out to the point that one is hollow or "nothing"); *impoverishment; divestiture; occultation* (or concealment, hiddenness); *depotentiation* (loss of power); *torture; descent;* and *journeys into exile.* Of course, many of these figures are prominent in *King Lear.*

Motifs of *emptiness* and *nothingness* abound in the play. Defining "the quality of nothing" is the play's unspoken query (Gloucester, 1. 2. 33). "The word [nothing] reverberates throughout the first half of the play," observes Halio (114). "Nothing almost sees miracles" (2. 2. 148). The Fool notes and names Lear's kenotic fall: "now thou art an O without a figure. I am better than thou art now; I am a fool, thou art nothing" (1.4. 152). Like an ancient Greek figure, like Christian protagonists before him, Lear is moving towards the very death of the self. "O ruin'd piece of nature! This great world / Shall so wear out to naught" (4. 5. 135).

Postmodernists may detect in such passages a Nietzschean nihilism, but emptiness is not necessarily negative, as the contemplative tradition associated with the *via negativa* shows. "Nothingness" may become space for the spirit; it may mark the nadir of self, signaling the possibility of new growth. Hence, Kierkegaard writes: "God creates everything out of nothing—and everything which God is to use he first reduces to nothing" (45). Calderwood observes perceptively: "Something frequently comes of nothing in *King Lear*" (6).

Early in the play, the imperceptive and childish monarch speaks an apparently logical maxim: "Nothing will come of nothing" (1. 1. 85). But of course Lear is wrong on this point, as he is wrong about almost everything. It is the Fool who corrects him through his brilliant question—indeed the most haunting of the play: "*Can you make no use of nothing, nuncle?*" (1. 4. 115, my emphasis). Derek Peat argues that the play "forces every spectator to choose between the contrary possibilities it holds in unresolved suspension" (qtd. in Wells 248). I would amend Peat's insight to say that the play invites every spectator to consider the mysterious connections between contrarieties—specifically, to find the paradoxical relation of "nothing" to "something." If Maynard Mack is correct in saying that the Fool is offering "dramatic short-hand . . . for goings-on in the King's brain" (Mack 245-46), then Lear's dialogue with the Fool reflects the monarch's psychic wrestling over his own baffling kenotic experience. "What does it mean to be emptied, to become nothing, in this horrific fashion?" Lear is more or less asking himself. Lear's encounter with darkness teaches him (and spectators as well) to make use of "nothing." He is learning the same lesson that Yeats's Crazy Jane attempts to teach the Bishop:

> But love has pitched his mansion in
> The place of excrement;
> For nothing can be sole or whole
> That has not been rent.

After he is reduced to the status of a "poor, bare fork'd animal" (and after the Fool disappears), Lear is paradoxically invested with new faculties and powers. After his kenotic humiliations, he thinks more of others, and he consistently demonstrates compassion towards Gloucester, Kent, Tom o'Bedlam, and Cordelia. The holocaust of bodies in the final scene in no way undercuts the fact of Lear's changed behavior or heightened insights.

Throughout the play, O's, circles, and spheres abound (bleeding rings, the wheel of fire, bonds, the globe's "thick rotundity," Wheel of Fortune, precious stones [i.e. eyeballs], crowns, and so forth). These figures are freighted with double meanings; they may be empty or full. In Medieval and Early Modern terms the circle is perfectly ambiguous, signifying either *lack* or *fullness—absence* or *presence*. As the Fool makes plain, the egg (one of the play's most "fertile" O's) and the crown are polysemous: either one may be full or empty (1.4.120 ff.). The Fool tells us that the monarch's "crown" (meaning, variously, Lear's bald head, the royal coronet, and, by extension, the kingdom or the crown's domain) is not worth the two halves of an eggshell: "Nuncle, give me an egg, and I'll give thee two crowns" (1. 4. 120). The Fool suggests that the crown (i.e., head, coronet, imperial domain) is worthless because the king himself has profligately emptied his head, his office, and his lands. That is to say, Lear is not merely the victim of kenotic emptying; he is the very agent of it. The Fool is emphatic: "thou clovest thy crown i'th'middle and gav'st way both parts" (1. 4. 123-24).

Circles and O's suggest the hollow, the empty, the void; but also the seed of transcendent hope. According to John

Donne, man's life, properly considered, is a circle, "an endlesse, and perfect Circle . . . for immortality, and eternity are a Circle too" (2: 199-200); and the circle is a symbol of perfection, "one of the most convenient Hieroglyphicks of God." In such an economy, O's and "emptiness" may well be signs of ultimate meaning and purpose. Thus, the very passages that skeptical critics use to "prove" the play's nihilism equally suggest the play's transcendent kenoticism. "Can you make no use of nothing?," then, is sharply double-edged. Lear first answers the question "no," but by Act 4 Scene 6 in the arms of his beloved Cordelia, he discovers a "yes." And if this "yes" becomes "no" once again, with the gratuitous slaughter of Cordelia ("Never, never, never, never, never" [5. 3. 282]), why should this seemingly final "no" have the last word? The oscillating movements of the play invite the spectator to consider the possibility of "no," and "yes." In "The Slip" Wendell Berry suggests how kenosis preserves the mysterious, life-affirming paradox of the yes *and* no: "And yet this nothing is the seed of all." Something accrues to the audience through the process of watching the tragic, kenotic ordeal. The play, in one sense, does not end on the stage. It lives on and is completed *in us*.

"Nothing will come of nothing" ("Ex nihilo nihil fit") Lear tells Cordelia early in the play (1. 1. 85). But this is the claim of a sadly blind and deaf old man. Had Lear been more alert, he might have heard the heartfelt *fullness* in Cordelia's apparent verbal emptiness. He might have discerned the creative love in the apparent absence of love. Paradox reigns supreme here, for Cordelia is full while her sisters are merely fulsome. In fact, as the play's next four acts reveal, a world of action is born of Cordelia's pregnant silence, just as Lear's own spiritual hollowness is the "mother" of disaster (2. 4. 52). Note even here the implied hollowness: According to Harsnett the disorder called "mother" or "hysterica passio" is caused by "the wind in the bottome of the belly."

Impoverishment, loss of wealth, and the symbolic loss of spiritual and psychic qualities is another prominent kenotic figure, and it is most often associated with Cordelia. Just as Cordelia loses all but gains the French monarch, so Lear must lose his jewel in order to grow and learn. Fittingly, biblical kenotic language circulates through Cordelia's speeches and in speeches about her. France paraphrases St. Paul's language of kenosis from 2 Corinthians 6:10 and 8:9 in a speech which John Reibetanz calls "rhymed paradox" (qtd. in Halio 109):

> Fairest Cordelia, that art most rich being poor,
> Most forsaken, and most loved despised,
> Thee and thy virtues here I seize upon.
> Be it lawful I take up what's cast away.
> Bid them farewell, Cordelia, though unkind;
> Thou losest here a better where to find.
>
> (1. 1. 245-48, 255-56)

Kenosis is also illustrated figuratively through the putting on and the taking off of garments—*investiture and divestiture*. In *Lear* as in so much of Shakespeare, the changing (or loss) of one's apparel oft proclaims the man. "Through tattered clothes great vices do appear: Robes and furr'd gowns hide all" (4. 6. 156-57) says Lear. They hide not only the corruption and hollowness of the self, but also humanity's tragic vulnerability. Nakedness marks the beginning of a new identity.

Kenosis is also suggested by *depotentiation,* the loss of power. Sometimes the depletion of power is suggested by the loss of sexual potency; at other times spiritual depotentiation is dramatized by the loss of authority or physical strength. Lear's loss of power is systematic, inexorable, and extreme—he loses his kingdom, his family, his retainers, his property, his Fool, his wits, his very self. He becomes a "poor, bare, fork'd animal." Loss of control over one's own body through imprisonment and torture (such as crucifixion) is the ultimate manifestation of depotentiation—what Simone Weil calls *malheur.* Edgar, upon seeing Lear on the heath, remarks tellingly, "O thou side-piercing sight!" (4. 5. 84). Lear's torture is the equivalent of crucifixion:

> He hates him
> That would upon the rack of this tough world
> Stretch him out longer.
>
> (5. 3. 288-90)

A final prominent kenotic metaphor has been called the "*dramatic parabola*" (Brunner 561-63). According to this trope, the hero descends, or journeys into exile. In Pauline theology, the Son of God leaves the precincts of heaven to descend to earth. He undergoes stages of descent—first to the level of humanity, then to the level of a slave, and finally to the level of a criminal shamefully executed (Philippians 2:5-11). Since the 5th century of the Common Era, the kenotic journey has often been viewed as an exile from home with a final return. St. Augustine melded the journey of the Prodigal Son (Luke 15) with the Neoplatonic myth of the soul's exile from the realm of the Ideal in telling his own story of fall and redemption (Chadwick xxiv). The Medieval idea of the Wheel of Fortune (another circle, of course) also allowed poets to suggest the same theme, which implicitly offers hope, for if one is going down, one can always wait stoically for the upward turn. Edgar is the voice of this ancient version of kenotic promise:

> To be worst,
> The low'st and most dejected thing of fortune,
> Still stands in esperance, lives not in fear.
>
> (4. 1. 2-4).

Edgar also implies an affirmative answer to the Fool's query. One can make use of "nothing" by facing the blasts of airy nothing (storms of life) and finding cause for laughter:

> The worst returns to laughter. Welcome, then,
> Thou unsubstantial air that I embrace:

> The wretch that thou hast blown unto the worst
> Owes nothing to thy blasts.
>
> (4. 1.6-9)

If one accepts kenotic structure in *Lear,* "insubstantial air" and "nothing" can be read at once negatively and positively.

While the kenotic trope typically implies both descent and ascent, the *Lear* plot appears to move only downward. Dreams of ascent and return are never fulfilled, though the play's principal characters often imagine happy endings. A special problem of this play is that one can *never* say when one has actually hit bottom. The abyss of terror is deeper than Lear ever imagined. Part of the particular horror of *Lear* is the constant arousal of expectations that, at last, Lear has reached bottom or the outer boundaries of spiritual banishment, when he has not. Shakespeare, we know, revised the preexisting Lear plot precisely in order to defeat Lear's—and the audience's—expectations of an early, if not a pleasing, resolution.

Lear's reunion with Cordelia is the finest case in point. It is singularly important, as Susan Snyder and others have pointed out, that this delicate scene of reunion recalls the classic story of the Prodigal Son's reunion with his father (Snyder 361-69; Tippens, "Prodigal Son" 57-77). Shakespeare casts Lear as a kind of returning prodigal, the "child-changed" father/son who has lived among "rogues forlorn." Cordelia, as gracious, forgiving parent, asks her prodigal father:

> And wast thou fain, poor father,
> To hovel thee with swine and rogues forlorn
> In short and musty straw?
>
> (4. 6. 35-37)

Of course, in kenotic plots, the hero is supposed to enjoy a homecoming, a vindication, even a glorification. In the Philippian hymn text, after humiliation, crucifixion, and death, the writer can say, "Therefore, hath God highly exalted him. . . ." No doubt any audience attuned to the kenotic pattern hopes for just such a restoration. Indeed, Lear himself expects it:

> Thou shalt find
> That I'll resume the shape which thou dost think
> I have cast off forever.
>
> (1. 4. 263-65).

Lear supposes that such a life as his will yield a glorious return, for upon such sacrifices "[t]he gods themselves throw incense" (5. 3. 21). The pattern is clear, the expectation logical—but utterly mistaken. The wheel has not yet turned full circle. Edgar's question haunts this scene of surreptitious bliss, "Who is 't can say, 'I am the worst?'" (4. 1. 25). Lear's kenotic story prepares us for the upward movement that never arrives—or at least that does not arrive with any clarity. Yet this does not mean that such a movement is not possible; it just means "not yet." In this respect, the play is anything but optimistic Christian drama. The exile is longer, the fall more profound, the stripping more thorough than anyone imagined. And that is what makes the story tragic.

So, how shall we judge *King Lear*? Is it Christian, humanist, existentialist, or absurdist? Perhaps we need to trouble the categories a bit. Louis A. Ruprecht, Jr., in his work *Tragic Posture and Tragic Vision,* argues that ancient Christians and Hellenistic dramatists shared a surprisingly similar view of the world. For example, as interpreters of the Gospel of Mark have recently shown, St. Mark's story is far darker than many have supposed (see, for example, Stephen Moore's, *Literary Criticism and the Gospels* and *Mark and Luke in Poststructuralist Perspectives*). Belief in resurrection does not automatically cancel the tragic sense, nor does the absence of death in the final act necessarily signify the comic. Indeed, many Greek tragedies do not end in a series of deaths, yet they are universally seen as tragic, argues Ruprecht. "Teleology," the concern for endings, has been over-emphasized. If one considers the tone of the Gospel of Mark, for example, (which ends, not incidentally, with the stark sentence, "for they were afraid") and the Oedipus cycle, we see that both types of literature (gospel and tragedy) share a common view:

> "Tragedy shows us pain and brings us pleasure in the process." Which is to say that suffering teaches, and *that* really is the tragic in tragedy. *You never gain something but that you lose something.*
>
> (Ruprecht 97)

Many have tried to determine the meaningfulness of *King Lear* according to the final mental or spiritual disposition of the protagonist. Does Lear die in hope, in despair, or in delirium? The truth is, the final scene is susceptible to radically different interpretations. Actor, director, and spectator have considerable freedom to construe Lear's end.

But of course we do not have to know what was in the dying Lear's mind to come to grips with the play's meaning. Peter Brooks warns against making too much of any narrative's conclusion. The ending "does not abolish the movement, the slidings, the errors and partial recognitions of the middle. . . . The end] is not the exclusive truth of the text, which must include the processes along the way . . ." (711, 713). The final scene of recognition "cannot abolish textuality, does not annul the middle which, in its oscillation between blindness and recognition, between origin and endings, is the truth of the narrative text" (719). Ruprecht states boldly: "Tragedy has no interest in the end" (97). Brooks and Ruprecht make us wary of founding the "final" meaning of *King Lear* on a single reading of the conclusion, whatever that reading may be. Indeed, the play's final moment, overwhelming as it is, cannot entirely cancel previous scenes of charity, reconciliation, and even hope. The best interpretation of Lear maintains the "counterpoint of ever-shifting response" (Rabkin 30).

Quite apart from the death scene, what we *can* know is the quality of Lear's suffering. We *can* see the oscillations between blindness and insight. We *can* see how the kenotic ordeal alters him. We *can* watch Lear significantly alter his treatment of Cordelia and friends. We *can* see that *you never gain something but that you lose something*. We *can* see that destruction is necessary for recreation, that "nothing can be sole or whole / That has not been rent" (Yeats). "Life peers through the hollow eyes of death. The dry bones are made fruitful. . . . rebirth is founded on destruction. *Mors vitae initium*. The beginning of life is death" (Fraser 131). What is this truth? Is this orthodox faith? Yes, perhaps, but this is no naively optimistic faith. The fact of suffering overwhelms any cheer we might muster. Is it nihilism? Yes, perhaps, but this is not an "empty" nihilism, but a pregnant darkness such as one finds in *The Cloud of Unknowing* or John of the Cross, who declares that *something can come from nothing*.

Of course, such a darkly positive reading of the play is not inevitable. The something that comes from nothing is never writ large. It is a seed growing secretly. In Gospel language: "Very truly, I tell you, unless a grain of wheat falls to the earth and dies, it remains just a single grain; but if it dies, it bears much fruit" (John 12:24). It is voiced in the enigmatic sayings of fools, madmen, and prophets. Reality is too thick to be plain; as mad King George explains, there is a mist over the eyes. Hence, a materialist or nihilist reading is always conceivable, for the reading, finally, derives from the fullness or the emptiness of the spectator who bears significant responsibility for completing the play's meaning, much as Shakespeare asserted in earlier plays like *Henry V* and *Midsummer Night's Dream*: "Work, work your thoughts, and therein see. . . ." says the Chorus in *Henry V*. Without imagination, which in Shakespeare is very close to faith, the spectator misses the possibilities. Despairing readers may hold to their interpretations, but they should acknowledge that their dark readings derive from their milieu as much as from the text. And they might refrain from scorning readings which manage to find a constellation of meaning through connecting the few points of light in Lear's dark firmament. Skeptical interpreters may still counter that "meaningful" readings belong to a defunct Christian past. In a postmodern setting how is a coherent reading possible? Alan Bennett's masterful screenplay suggests one answer.

The Madness of King George illustrates how a later work can cast a backward light on a literary predecessor, casting both in fresh perspectives. *King George* not only echoes and parallels *King Lear* in important ways; Bennett's drama also teaches us to see rich possibilities in the precursor text. Both plays center on parent-child conflicts in British monarchical households. Both center on a protagonist who undergoes a trial of fire that changes the protagonist forever. Like Lear, George is an English monarch who "hath ever but slenderly known himself"; and though his children are no matches for Goneril, Regan, or Edmond, the Prince of Wales actively plots to seize the crown. Like Lear, George is dethroned, humiliated, and exiled.

Yet the connections between *King Lear* and *King George* extend far beyond details of plot. The deepest affinities appear when one observes the kenotic tropes of blindness, madness, and stripping. That Alan Bennett casts George as Lear redivivus becomes apparent after George is declared mad and is removed from power. Like Lear, in his madness George speaks a kind of inspired wisdom. He tells his frightened daughter: "Papa's not mad, my darling. No, no. He has just lost himself, that's all" (37). After being deposed, he sounds strikingly like Lear in his imperious declarations. Tortured with savage medical treatments, he shouts: "No! I am the Lord's anointed!" (42).

Like Gloucester and Lear, George's vision (both literal and spiritual) fails him. In a rich elegiac moment echoing Gloucester's "I stumbled when I saw," George says mournfully:

> I am not mad. I can't see. There is a mist. Oh, the Queen, missed, oh, oh, missed her, gone gone gone gone. . . .
>
> (43)

In George's confusion of homophones ("mist—missed") we are reminded of Lear's deep grief over losing Cordelia and Gloucester's sorrow at mistreating Edgar; and in George's elegiac repetitions of "gone, gone, gone, gone" and "no, no, no, no" (19), we hear echoes of Lear's "kill, kill, kill, kill, kill!" (4. 5. 179), "Howl, howl, howl, howl!" (5. 1. 231), and "Never, never, never, never, never" (5. 2. 282). As the medical tortures proceed apace at Kew, George becomes increasingly an image of Shakespeare's kenotic protagonist. The stage directions make the parallel explicit: "The King, cloaked and bearded now, looks like Lear" (57). Lear haunts the screenplay, serving as echo and commentary, an echoing and commentary that work in two directions.

King George's kenotic emptying is almost as extreme as Lear's. George is described as a "wretched moaning figure" who suffers intolerably at the hands of what he calls his "doctormentors" (44). As in *Lear*, the kenotic humiliations are revealed through a series of tropes, including the divestiture and investiture of clothing. In a scene recalling Lear on the heath, George runs half naked from the castle; and later he is quite literally stripped by his caretakers. When his sanity appears to return, he is given appropriate garments once again. He also makes the journey of the dramatic parabola—away from Westminster and Windsor—towards austere, cold, and remote locations. He rages through a heath-like expanse, and he descends to a kind of death, an image which is further developed when the Queen warns that her husband's deposition is his "death warrant" (65).

The kenotic trope of pouring out, emptying, and evacuation is suggested symbolically in numerous ways. George attempts to evacuate his tormented mind: "I have to empty my head of words," he says (38); and the evacuation of George's body (fourteen bowel movements [20]) is a painfully gruesome physical kenosis. One of the most unbearable moments occurs when the King can literally no longer contain himself and is reduced to utter humiliation as his servants look on helplessly. The King wastes away so completely in fact that, in his own thinking, he has become nothing: "Nobody sees me. I am not here" (55). However, as in *Lear,* nothingness is not the end of the matter, but the beginning, the sign of potential renewal, the reconstruction of the self.

Just as emptiness can be a sign of fullness, so madness proves its opposite. The categories of madness and sanity are slippery and ad hoc in George's universe as in Lear's. In both plays there is a subversive interrogation of assumptions. Power and authority are not *contradictory* to madness, but rather *forms* of it. Hence, Dr. Willis's remark: "Do you know, Mr. Greville, the state of monarchy and the state of lunacy share a frontier" (48). In the Regency Crisis of the 1780s, Bennett finds a narrative that portrays the postmodern crisis of identity. Is George mad? How can one tell? In a move reminiscent of Foucault, Bennett suggests that madness, like the self, is a construct. The only relevant questions about George are: Can he *perform*? Can he *seem*? Can he *act* like a monarch? "Monarchy is a performance," Bennett explains in his introduction to the play, "and part of the King's illness consists in his growing inability to sustain that performance" (Bennett xxix).

At the critical moment when George apparently begins to regain his senses, Chancellor Thurlow discovers the King reading and performing the reunion of Cordelia and Lear from Act 4, Scene 6. George insists that Thurlow join him in the performance; and Thurlow, at George's insistence, takes Cordelia's part. Greville plays the doctor, and the King, of course, plays Lear:

THURLOW: (As CORDELIA)

> "O you kind gods
> Cure this great breach in his abused nature.
> Th'untuned and jarring senses, O wind up,
> Of this child-changed father."

KING:

> That's very good. "Child-changed father" is very
>   good.

The scene continues with the King's elaborate pantomime of Lear waking:

KING: (As LEAR)

> "You do me wrong to take me out o' th' grave.
> Thou are a soul in bliss, but I am bound
> Upon a wheel of fire, that mine own tears
> Do scald like molten lead."
> Oh, it's so true!
> "Pray you do not mock me.
> I am a very foolish, fond old man.
> And, to deal plainly,
> I fear I am not in my perfect mind."

(69-71)

In his outburst "Oh, it's so true!" George's recognition is evident. Immediately, the others notice George's new (or renewed) rationality. Thurlow remarks, "Your Majesty seems more yourself," to which the King replies:

> Do I? Yes, I do. I have always been myself even when
> I was ill. Only now I seem myself. That's the important
> thing. I have remembered how to seem. What, what?

(71)

In the "What, what?" tag Thurlow, Greville, and the audience find the signal that the King's madness has lifted. He is himself, whatever that "self" may be, yet he is more than his former self. In numerous ways, George has changed. He is less dictatorial, less self-centered, and more understanding of his role and the role of the royal family. Like Lear and Gloucester before him, he comes to see things "feelingly," remarking "Love, that is the keynote" (75).

Bennett's play appears to end more optimistically than *King Lear;* yet even here Bennett's play shares an important common element with Shakespeare's tragedy. Like *Lear, King George* ends in ambiguity. If Bennett's play teaches us anything, it is that one must be wary of appearances. A close scrutiny of the final scene reveals that George's recovery of the throne and health is ambiguous. Like the rest of George's royal life, the glorious reception before St. Paul's is brilliant theatrics, "seeming." Even as George smiles and waves to the people, we cannot even be sure that he is cured of his malady. A stage direction indicates that George's mental health is at best precarious: "The KING makes the faintest shudder; fear shows in his eyes. He cannot tell if he is still ill or not" (80). "Presume not I am the thing I was," he tells Dr. Willis (80); but of course we are not at all clear what thing George was, or now is. The reality of George is either unimportant or unavailable to us as spectators, just as it is unavailable to George himself. The construct of the self, the seeming, the performance of the King is the only "reality" we have.

Consequently, the play's conclusion is disturbingly unclear and charged with irony. On the steps of St. Paul's Cathedral, the royal family present themselves as exemplars of and to the kingdom. As Handel's music swells, the family puts on the play that everyone expects. And George exhorts his family in terms etched in irony:

> We must try to be more a family. There are model farms
> now, model villages, even model factories. Well, we
> must be a model family for the nation to look to.

(81)

"Who could think they are not happy?" the stage directions darkly inquire. To underscore the irony of the final scene, this caption concludes the play:

> The colour of the King's urine suggests he was suffer-
> ing from porphyria, a physical illness that affects the

nervous system. The disease is periodic, unpredictable—and hereditary.

(81)

The film suggests that madness and confusion are expected features of the British royal family—and, by extension, madness and confusion are genetic traits of the human family. In fact *The Madness of King George* questions our ability to rise above our "unpredictable" and "hereditary" condition.

In stressing the many parallels between Bennett's play and Shakespeare's, I have obviously ignored important differences. Each artistic work is a unique creation, arises uniquely from its own milieu; yet I do wish to argue that, in current debates about *King Lear*'s meaning, Bennett's play can be pressed into useful service. In two respects, at least, *King George* helps us become better readers of *King Lear*. First, Bennett's play recalls us to the classic trope of kenosis. In this contemporary play of a child-changed father we are called back to the story of a hero who undergoes a radical descent that ultimately proves meaningful. According to Sprengnether's terms, the kenotic metaphor helps us "to read on the margins" and uncover "latent or implicit" motives in Shakespeare's tragedy (46).

In a second way *King George* assists our reading of *Lear* by illustrating why Shakespeare's tragedy cannot, finally, be read as an absurdist or nihilistic text. As we watch old George respond to the drama of *Lear,* we see how theatrical experience belies current nihilistic interpretations. In fact, George responds empathically to Lear in much the way actors and spectators have for over three centuries. Both plays reveal that empathy with another's suffering is "natural" and "normative," and certainly better than selfish indifference or cruelty. Indeed, Kent is the embodiment of this value. He feels with and for the good characters—Lear and Cordelia, above all. If Kent goes off to die or commit suicide, as some maintain ("I have a journey, sir, shortly to go: / My master calls me, I must not say no," 5.3. 295-96), it is not because he is indifferent to humanistic values like love, compassion, and loyalty. Rather, he departs precisely because these are inalienable qualities of his character. In the same way, we follow Lear with interest precisely because he transcends himself, abandoning his narcissism and learning to value others. Lear's discovery of others' needs is "meaningful." The fact that the objects of his love, the Fool and Cordelia, are torn from him does not diminish our certainty that it is better to love than not to love.

In other ways both plays imply that compassion for suffering is superior to cruelty. In fact, as we see cruelty enacted, we do not move to a position where human actions do not matter (an absurdist position); indeed, these texts ask us to re-double our conviction that benevolence and cruelty are quite different realities. *Pity presupposes that humans matter.* Suffering in *King Lear* may appear wanton or inexplicable, but no spectator views it as irrelevant. If readers arrived at a position in which cruelty or evil were just names for things they found personally distasteful, then the play could certainly be called absurdist. But who can read the play in this way?

Lear questions, "Why should a dog, a horse, a rat, have life / And thou no breath at all?" (5.3. 307-8). Such a question only makes sense in a meaningful universe. In a truly absurdist world, where all values have been rendered subjective or beyond definition, such questions fade into nonsense; but Lear dies believing that a human life ought to count more than a rat's life. He is still in the grip of a fundamental polarity (human/not human). Valuing the human, he knows that it is wrong for the good Cordelia to die; so does King George, and so do the viewers. That is why Thurlow pronounces *King Lear* "so damned tragic" (73). That is why *King Lear* ends with so much "meaning." As long as we care, we defy absurdity.

Thus, Alan Bennett's strange serio-comic play *The Madness of King George* is a commentary which explains why Shakespeare's tragedy cannot, finally, be read as an absurdist or nihilistic text. As we watch old George respond to the play, we see that he stands for all audiences who find meaning in Shakespeare's tragedy. In that uncanny intertextual moment when George reenacts Lear's encounter with Cordelia, the audience observes one suffering kenotic victim peering into the life of another; and so George III finds himself in Lear and is mysteriously changed in the process. In this creative, hermeneutic moment, Bennett has provided a path—and an answer—for critic and play-goer alike. What *Lear* does for George III, *Lear* has done for audiences for centuries. Shakespeare's tragedy shows us the continuing power of the kenotic trope, and it shows us how, in the mad protagonist's hollowing out, we are mysteriously made full.

Works Cited

Airay. *Lectures upon the Whole Epistle of St. Paul to the Philippians.* Ed. Christopher Potter. London, 1618.

Battenhouse, Roy. *Shakespearean Tragedy: Its Art and Christian Premises.* Bloomington: Indiana UP, 1969.

Bennett, Alan. *The Madness of King George.* New York: Random House, 1995.

Berry, Wendell. "The Slip." *The New Oxford Book of Christian Verse.* Ed. Donald Davie. Oxford: Oxford UP, 1981. 300-301.

Bethel, S. L. *Shakespeare and the Popular Dramatic Tradition.* 1944. Durham: Duke UP, 1977.

Bloom, Harold. *Western Canon: The Books and School of the Ages.* New York: Harcourt Brace, 1994.

———. *The Anxiety of Influence.* New York: Oxford UP, 1973.

Bradley, A. C. *Shakespearean Tragedy.* 2nd ed. 1904. London: Macmillan, 1956.

Brooke, Nicholas. "The Ending in King Lear," in *Shakespeare: 1564-1964* Ed. Edward A. Bloom (Hanover: U. Press of New England, 1964): 85.

———. *Shakespeare: King Lear*. London: Edward Arnold, 1963.

Brooks, Peter. "Freud's Masterplot." *The Critical Tradition*. Ed. David H. Richter. New York: Bedford/St. Martin's, 1989.

Brunner, Emil. *The Mediator: A Study of the Central Doctrine of the Christian Faith*. New York: Macmillan, 1934.

Bryant, J. A. *Hippolyta's View*. Lexington: U. of Kentucky Press, 1961.

Calderwood, James L. "Creative Uncreation in *King Lear*." *Shakespeare Quarterly* 37 (1986): 5-19.

Campbell, Oscar J. "The Salvation of Lear." *ELH* 15 (1948): 93-109.

Chadwick, Henry, ed. and trans. *Confessions*. By Augustine. Oxford: Oxford UP, 1991.

Cunningham, John. "King Lear, the Storm, and Liturgy," *Christianity and Literature* Fall 1984: 9-30.

Dawe, Donald G. *The Form of a Servant: A Historical Analysis of the Kenotic Motif*. Philadelphia: Westminster, 1963.

Dollimore, Jonathan. *Radical Tragedy: Religion, Ideology and Power in the Drama of Shakespeare and His Contemporaries*. New York: Harvester Wheatsheaf, 1984.

Donne, John. *The Sermons of John Donne*. Eds. George R. Potter and Evelyn Simpson. Berkeley: U. of Cal. Press, 1953-62.

Elton, William R. *"King Lear" and the Gods*. 1966. Lexington: U Press of Kentucky, 1988.

Fortin, René. "The Two Voices of Shakespearean Tragedy." *Shakespeare Quarterly* 32 (1981): 80-94.

Fowler, Robert M. *Let the Reader Understand: Reader-Response Criticism and the Gospel of Mark*. Minneapolis: Augsburg Fortress, 1991.

Fraser, Russell. *Shakespeare's Poetics in Relation to King Lear*. London: Routledge & Kegan Paul, 1962.

French, A. L. *Shakespeare and the Critics*. London: Cambridge UP, 1972.

Geneva Bible. 1560. Madison: U. of Wisconsin Press, 1969.

Guilfoyle, Cherrell. "The Redemption of King Lear." *Comparative Drama* 23 (Spring 1989): 50-69.

Halio, Jay L., ed. *The Tragedy of King Lear*. By William Shakespeare. Cambridge: Cambridge UP, 1992.

Harmon, William and C. Hugh Holman. *A Handbook to Literature*. 7th ed. Upper Saddle, N. J.: Prentice Hall, 1996.

Hassel, R. Chris. *Renaissance Drama and the English Church*. Lincoln: U. of Nebraska Press, 1979.

Holquist, Michael. *Dialogism: Bakhtin and His World*. London: Routledge, 1990.

Holloway, John. *The Story of the Night*. London: Routledge and Kegan Paul, 1961.

Kierkegaard, Søren. *The Journals of Kierkegaard*. Ed. Alexander Dru. New York: Harper, 1959.

Kirby, Ian J. "The Passing of King Lear." *Shakespeare Survey* 41 (1988): 145-58.

Kittel, Gerhard and Gerhard Friedrich, eds. *Theological Dictionary of the New Testament*. Grand Rapids: Eerdmans, 1985.

Klause, John L. "George Herbert, *Kenosis*, and the Whole Truth" in *Allegory, Myth, and Symbol*. Ed. Morton W. Bloomfield. Harvard English Studies 9. Cambridge: Harvard UP, 1981. 209-225.

Kott, Jan. *Shakespeare Our Contemporary*. Trans. Boleslaw Taborski. Garden City: Doubleday, 1966.

Mack, Maynard. *Everybody's Shakespeare: Reflections Chiefly on the Tragedies*. Lincoln: U. of Nebraska Press, 1993.

Martin, Ralph P. *Carmen Christi: Philippians ii. 5-11 in Recent Interpretation and in the Setting of Early Christian Worship*. Cambridge: Cambridge UP, 1967.

Moore, Stephen D. *Literary Criticism and the Gospels*. New Haven: Yale UP, 1989.

———. *Mark and Luke in Poststructuralist Perspectives: Jesus Begins to Write*. New Haven: Yale UP, 1992.

Muir, Kenneth, ed. *King Lear*. By William Shakespeare. London: Methuen, 1972.

Nicolson, Marjorie H. *The Breaking of the Circle*. Rev. ed. New York: Columbia UP, 1960.

Pechter, Edward. "On the Blinding of Gloucester." *ELH* 45 (1978): 181-200.

Rabkin, Norman. *Shakespeare and the Problem of Meaning*. Chicago: U. of Chicago Press, 1981.

Ribner, Irving. *Patterns in Shakespearean Tragedy*. London: Methuen, 1960.

Roche, Thomas P. "'Nothing almost sees miracles': Tragic Knowledge in King Lear" in *On King Lear*. Ed. Lawrence Danson, Princeton: Princeton UP, 1981.

Ruprecht, Louis A., Jr. *Tragic Posture and Tragic Vision*. New York: Continuum, 1994.

Shakespeare, William. *The Riverside Shakespeare*. Ed. by G. Blakemore Evans. Boston: Houghton Mifflin, 1974.

Snyder, Susan. "*King Lear* and the Prodigal Son," *SQ* 17 (1966): 361-69.

Sprengnether, Madelon Gohlke. "'I Wooed Thee with My Sword': Shakespeare's Tragic Paradigms" *Shakespeare's Late Tragedies.* Ed. Susanne L. Wofford. Upper Saddle: Prentice Hall, 1996. 46-60.

Summers, Joseph. "'Look there, look there!' The Ending of *King Lear*," in *English Renaissance Studies Presented in Honour of Dame Helen Gardner.* . . . Oxford: Clarendon, 1980.

Tippens, Darryl. "The Kenotic Experience of *Samson Agonistes.*" Milton Studies 22 (1987): 173-194.

———. "Shakespeare and the Prodigal Son Tradition." *Explorations in Renaissance Culture* 14 (1988): 57-77.

Wells, Stanley. *Shakespeare: A Bibliographical Guide.* New Edition. Oxford: Clarendon Press, 1990.

Wittreich, Joseph. *"Image of that Horror": History, Prophecy, and Apocalypse in King Lear.* San Marino, Cal.: Huntington Library, 1984.

David N. Beauregard (essay date 1999)

SOURCE: Beauregard, David N. "'Inspirèd Merit': Shakespeare's Theology of Grace in *All's Well that Ends Well.*" *Renascence* 51, no. 4 (summer 1999): 219-39.

[*In the essay below, Beauregard asserts that Roman Catholic teachings regarding sin, repentance, and salvation are central to the plot and characterization of* All's Well that Ends Well. *The first half of the play is concerned with the concepts of miracle and merit and the second with pilgrimage and prayer, the critic contends, and together the two parts delineate the Catholic doctrines of grace, merit, and free will.*]

Ever since the publication of Roland M. Frye's *Shakespeare and Christian Doctrine* (1963), interest in the role of theology in Shakespearean drama has suffered an unfortunate decline. Frye made the influential claim that Shakespeare held the mirror "up to nature, and not to saving grace" (267), arguing that Shakespearean drama was autonomous and confined to the temporal sphere "independent of theological systems" (268). The inadequacies of Frye's thesis are manifold,[1] but they become particularly evident when one considers the theological anthropology implicit in Shakespeare's dramatic practice, especially the operations of sin, penitence, and grace, not to mention various religious roles (abbess, pilgrim, novice, friar), confessional scenes, and theological shading of sources.[2] While one can agree with Frye's emphasis on nature, or "virtue's own feature" (*Hamlet* 3.2.22-23), as the main object of Shakespearean mimesis, it seems equally clear that Shakespeare never intended to exclude "saving grace" from his dramatic representations. Theology is reflected in the mirror, not excluded from it.

To be sure, Elizabethan censorship had effectively forced religious and political controversy from the stage. As the role of theology in popular drama was marginalized, the theater took a more ethical turn. In 1572 the Queen's Privy Council instructed London officials to allow "such plays, interludes, comedies, and tragedies as may tend to repress vice and extol virtue" (Yachnin 18-24). A decade later, with more philosophical sophistication, both Edmund Spenser and Philip Sidney laid out a similar program for poetry—the "figuring foorth" or representation of "notable images of vertues, vices, or what els [that is, passions]" so that the audience may see and love "the forme of goodnes" (Smith 1: 160, 166, 173). This is in full accord with Shakespeare's dramatic poetic of "hold[ing] the mirror up to nature, to show virtue her own feature, scorn [pride] her own image" (Beauregard, *Virtue's Own Feature* 21-35). Nevertheless, such an ethically focused program, whether for poetry or drama, necessarily carried with it concomitant theological notions of sin, repentance and grace. It would have been virtually impossible for Shakespeare to have remained free of the theological orientation of Elizabethan culture. It is important to realize, moreover, that, as an external regulating force, the official censors were permissive, inconsistent, and often ineffectual, although no doubt their activity had the interior effect of causing writers to exercise some measure of self-censorship (Clare 211-15). Thus, in order to escape censorship and personal penalty, Shakespeare had to avoid explicit theological expression, in the form of doctrinal controversy or declamation, but he could expect some latitude and tolerance in the representation of Catholic matters on the stage. The example of *Sir Thomas More* (ca. 1592-3), a play in which Shakespeare had a hand, confirms this. Sir Edmund Tilney, Master of the Revels and censor from 1579 to 1610, wrote in the margin of the manuscript "Leave out the insurrection wholy and the Cause ther off and begin with Sir Thomas Moore att the mayors session [a succeeding scene]" (Clare 32). Tilney objects to potentially seditious matter, but not to the sympathetically portrayed figure of Thomas More (Dutton 81).[3] In other respects as well, we can discern a certain latitude given to theological expression. The final scene of Marlowe's *Doctor Faustus,* for example, is suffused with theological implications regarding prayer, grace, and salvation. And Prospero's project in *The Tempest* (4.1.68-82; 5.1.28-32) is to bring men from sin to "heart's sorrow" and "penitence," the first step in the sacrament of penance. If theological controversy was steadily marginalized on the Elizabethan stage, the formal purpose and the moral images of drama still carried considerable theological force.

All's Well That Ends Well (ca. 1601-5) is a case in point. I shall argue in this essay that Shakespeare was well versed in theology and that a Roman Catholic—and not a Reformed—theology of grace informs the dialogue and action of *All's Well That Ends Well.*[4] This is not to claim that the play is primarily concerned with the explicit representation of Christian doctrine. Rather it is to claim that several references to theological doctrines appear in the speech of both primary and secondary characters, and that, taken in conjunction with Helena's two roles as miracle-worker and pilgrim, they present us with a play infused with a Catholic theology of grace.

To be more specific, Shakespeare presents us with a theologically charged drama that holds the mirror up to nature, but also to the operations of grace. His central concern is to represent "ambitious love" ingeniously achieving its deserved reward, but implicit in that representation is a Roman Catholic theology of grace. Thus, Helena, in her two roles as miracle-worker and pilgrim, speaks in the theological language of Roman Catholic doctrine and devotional practice. Basic to both halves of the play is the Catholic notion of merit, of reward given for virtuous behavior, which is dramatically rendered by the heroine's being twice rewarded for accomplishing two impossible tasks, first through divine grace and then through human effort. In part one, the low-born Helena, who ambitiously aspires to the love of Bertram, cures the hopelessly ill King through "inspirèd merit" and so is raised in title and rewarded with the hand of Bertram in marriage. In part two, despised by Bertram who flees to Florence and sets impossible conditions for their marriage (to get his ring and produce a child by him), Helena conspires by an ingenious bed-trick to again achieve her reward, the consummation of her marriage to Bertram, who is, as she says in the final scene, "doubly won" (5.3.315). The double victory of the virtuous Helena, then, shows us that, as the King makes clear in his central discourse (2.3.117-44), true nobility lies in virtue, not inherited rank, and that the exercise of virtue merits its reward.

What evidence of Shakespeare's theology is there in *All's Well?* To begin with, it is strikingly evident that the play contains numerous references to Roman Catholic theological doctrines and devotional practices. Since Shakespeare was brought up by Roman Catholic parents and was probably taught by Roman Catholic schoolmasters (Schoenbaum 65-66), the most likely explanation for these various references is that they are either the residue of his background and education or, because *All's Well* is a rather late play, the natural expression of a continuing belief. Revisionist historians of the English Reformation have convincingly argued that considerable popular resistance prevented the old religion from being uprooted until the 1580s, precisely the formative period of Shakespeare's youth (Todd 26-28; Duffy 1-8, 565-93). In any case, for whatever reason, there are undeniably a series of Roman Catholic references in *All's Well*. When Parolles remarks that "virginity murders itself, and should be buried in highways out of all sanctified limit" (1.1.140-42), he refers to the Roman Catholic refusal to allow suicides burial in consecrated ground, a refusal which was still customary but not yet specified in canon law within the Church of England (Noble 84). Later in the play, there are references to pilgrimage (3.4.4-17; 3.5.94-97; 4.3.47-49), to penitential vows (3.4.7; 3.5.95), to penance done in satisfaction for sin (3.4.6-7), to the requirements of auricular confession (4.3.108-11), and arguably to the Blessed Virgin Mary as intercessor (3.4.25-29). These matters were all particularly offensive to the ears of Reformed theologians. Furthermore, in the last act (5.3.57-58), the King remarks that Bertram's love for Helena will strike out numerous of his sins in "the great compt" (i.e., at the Last Judgment, as the great accounting for sin, implying the tallying up of sins over against merits). There is also his description of Helena as swearing by the saints (5.3.109), and there is Parolles' reference to Limbo (5.3. 263). Finally, there is the fact that, in four if not five of her last scenes, Helena appears dressed as a Catholic pilgrim (3.5; 3.7; 4.4; 5.1). On the other side of the question, one might argue that Lavatch's simile "as the nun's lip to the friar's mouth" (2.2.25-26) is an anti-Catholic expression, but this satirical jibe cannot be unequivocally construed as evidence of a Reformed sensibility at work, since it is critical of an abuse of the vow of chastity but not of Roman Catholic religious life in itself.

Apart from these minor references in *All's Well*, Shakespeare's theology of grace comes into even sharper focus when we direct our attention to four interrelated topics: miracle and merit, pilgrimage and prayer. These four theological topics shape the very substance of the action and characterization. To be sure, Shakespeare took over his story from Boccaccio, but he enhances his source, first making Helena a miracle-worker and then elaborating on her pilgrimage. When the minor references mentioned above are taken in conjunction with the development of Helena's two roles, they point to a Roman Catholic theology of grace informing the speech and action of the play. Moreover, they represent a doctrinal-devotional complex attacked by the Reformers. Fortunately for our purposes, the two-part structure into which the play falls conveniently lends itself to laying out the evidence for these claims. As Helena undertakes the curing of the King, the first part of the play focuses on the topics of miracle and merit, and the second part brings into play the topics of pilgrimage and prayer as she attempts to win back Bertram.

First, then, Shakespeare's treatment of the miraculous. A comparison of the first part of the play with its source points up a significant development that warrants some consideration. In Boccaccio's *Decameron* (3.9) and in William Painter's translation, *The Palace of Pleasure* (1566; rpt. Hunter, *All's Well*), the curing of the king is described some ten times as a "healing," to be accomplished in eight days with the aid of God. But when in *All's Well* Helena proposes to cure the King, she promises to do so in much more rapid fashion. Shakespeare shortens the time of the cure from eight days to less than two days (2.1.162-70). In so doing, he clearly emphasizes its miraculous nature

> There's something in't [Helena's healing "remedy"]
> More than my father's skill, which was the great'st
> Of his profession, that his good receipt
> Shall for my legacy be sanctified
> By th' luckiest stars in heaven . . .
>
> (1.3.240-44)

Helena's power to cure is something beyond mere professional skill, something beyond nature and attributable to the order of grace. Thus, when Helena proposes her cure to the King, Shakespeare has her appeal to the miraculous precedent of Moses' parting of the Red Sea (2.1.140-43), and after the king is cured she directly tells LaFew and Parolles that "Heaven hath through me restored the King to health" (2.3.63-64). Shakespeare develops Boccaccio's cursory references to God's "healing" grace into something considerably more miraculous.

Indeed, in order to increase the sense of the marvelous and the miraculous, Shakespeare subsequently adds the choral-like musing of LaFew as a reaction to Helena's curing of the King. Appropriately, LaFew's reflections are invested with an appreciative sense of philosophical causality and the limits of human knowledge or "*scienza*":

> They say miracles are past, and we have our philosophical persons, to make modern and familiar, things supernatural and causeless. Hence is it that we make trifles of terrors, ensconcing ourselves into seeming knowledge when we should submit ourselves to an unknown fear.
>
> (2.3.1-6; see also 2.1.179-80)

Here the relevant question is of course: who are "they"? and who are "our philosophical persons"? LaFew's exchange with Parolles has been taken in part as a reference to the Paracelsian attack on the more academic Galenists, whose herbal treatments are clearly not in line with Helena's more chemically-specific method of curing the king (Stensgaard 173-83). But while this closely argued line of interpretation convincingly makes of Helena a Paracelsian medical practitioner, it also improbably reduces Shakespeare to a mere Paracelsian theologian (183-88). Clearly, the LaFew passage extends to the skeptical minds of the day, whether to the natural philosophers or the followers of Montaigne. The "modern philosophical person," i. e., the natural philosopher or the skeptic, reduces reality, which has its supernatural dimension beyond the senses, to what is "familiar" and "trifling" and "seeming," that is, to secondary causes apparent to the senses. The naturalistic-skeptical mentality is here under attack for its refusal to transcend the senses and for its unwillingness to face the supernatural dimension of reality, which ought to inspire an "unknown fear" because of its terrifying proportions, proportions particularly evident from miracles. The fullest dramatic rendering of this philosophical deficiency is of course the opening scene of Hamlet where the initially skeptical Horatio confronts the ghost of Hamlet's father:

BERNARDO:
> How now, Horatio? You tremble and look pale.
> Is not this [the Ghost] something more than fantasy? What think you on't?

HORATIO:
> Before my God, I might not this believe
> Without the sensible and true avouch
> Of mine own eyes.
>
> (1.157-62)

Hamlet's later observation underlines the point: "There are more things in heaven and earth, Horatio, Than are dreamt of in your philosophy" (1.5.175-76). Reality for Shakespeare extends well beyond the confines of human sensibility.

We should note here that Reformed theologians generally rejected post-Scriptural miracles, especially as part of the devotional complex generating and sustaining pilgrimages and shrines (Hillerbrand, "Miracles"). They would have particularly objected to the notion of a miracle worked through human agency or the intercession of the saints. Whereas faith in miracles coming directly through God's grace was acceptable to the Reformers, belief in miracles coming through the mediated intercession of saints was not. Thus, Shakespeare's representation of a miracle worked through the mediation of Helena, quite consonant with her later undertaking of a pilgrimage in search of mediatory intercession at the shrine of St. James, suggests a theology that is more than merely Paracelsian and not at all Reformed.

Shakespeare's second development of his source has to do with the doctrine of merit. Given the proper historical context, the doctrinal perspective operative in the play can be easily determined. Broadly speaking, there were current in the sixteenth century two theologies of grace. One was Roman Catholic and can be found in such sources as Aquinas' *Summa,* the decrees of the Council of Trent, the works of Robert Bellarmine, and so on. The other was the expression of Reformed theology, emanating from the works of Luther and Calvin, in which the Elizabethan settlement was grounded (Wallace 29-78). As the Council of Trent made clear, there were several Roman Catholic doctrines regarding grace and works, but three in particular warrant our attention: one, that in justification God's grace is always primary, since justification is initiated by God and merited by Christ; two, that justification involves a real interior (rather than an imputed and extrinsic) change in the sinner in which he is truly made just and given "new life"; and three, that following justification an increase of grace can be merited by "works" (Molinski 956). Aquinas clearly delineates the nature of merit in relation to justice, taken in the Aristotelian sense as a kind of equality. Where there are equals, merit holds simply and absolutely (*de condigno*), as reward due in justice for work done. Where there are unequals, merit obtains proportionately (*de congruo*), as a kind of reward for which God has allotted one a power of operation:

> Merit and reward refer to the same, for a reward means something given anyone in return for work or toil, as a price for it. . . . Now justice is a kind of equality . . . and hence justice is simply between those that are simply equal; but where there is no absolute equality between them, neither is there absolute justice, but there may be a certain manner of justice
>
> . . . Now it is clear that between God and man there is the greatest inequality. . . . Hence there can be no justice of absolute equality between man and God, but only of a certain proportion. . . . Hence man's merit

with God only exists on the presupposition of the Divine ordination, so that man obtains from God, as a reward of his operation, what God gave him the power of operation for, even as natural things by their proper movements and operations obtain that to which they were ordained by God.

(ST 1a2ae, 114.1)

It is important to note that several of the key words in the play—inequality, "fate" and freedom, merit and reward—resonate with this passage.

Hence, in relation to the first principle, the primacy of God's grace in initiating justification, Luther was in fact recovering an older doctrine over against the semi-Pelagianism of theologians like Gabriel Biel, who maintained that human beings through their own efforts could "earn" the initial grace of justification. In relation to the second and third principles, however, Luther departed from the traditional doctrine in making out justification to be purely extrinsic and imputed. The sinner remained a sinner, and there was no interior change. Furthermore, he allowed no place for human merit since all was due to God's grace (Wallace 63; Allison 178-89). With consummate clarity, Richard Hooker, in his "A Learned Discourse of Justification" (1612), summed up the essential distinction and difference between the two positions, employing a distinction between the grace of justification and that of sanctification:

> The righteousnes wherewith we shalbe clothed in the world to comme, is both perfecte and inherente: that whereby here we are justefied is perfecte but not inherente, that whereby we are sanctified, inherent but not perfecte. . . . This grace they [Roman Catholics] will have to be applied by infusion . . . so the soule mighte be rightuous by inherente grace, which grace they make capable of increase . . . the augmentacion whereof is merited by good workes, as good workes are made meritorious by it. . . . But the rightuousnes wherein we muste be found if we wilbe justefied, is not our owne, therefore we cannott be justefied by any inherente qualitie. . . . Then although in ourselves we be altogether synfull and unrighteous, yett even the man which in him selfe is ympious, full of inequity, full of synne, hym god beholdeth with a gratious eye, putteth awaie his syn by not ymputing it, taketh quite awaie the ponishemente due therunto by pardoninge it, and accepteth him in Jesus Christe as perfectly rightuous as if he had fulfilled all that was comaunded hym in the law.

(5:109-13)

In other words, there is a future righteousness which will be perfect and inherent, a present righteousness in this world which is perfect but not inherent (i. e., Christ's perfect righteousness is imputed to sinners), and a present sanctification in this world which is imperfect and inherent (i. e., presently man is a sinner imperfectly sanctified; see Gibbs, "Justification" 216). Thus both sides agreed that justification comes through faith in Christ, but they disagreed on the nature of justification (extrinsic vs. intrinsic) and sanctification (imperfect vs. perfect). Moreover, they disagreed on the subject of "good works": on the Catholic side, merit and satisfaction were possible after justification; on the Protestant side, they were not because they appeared to undermine the merits and satisfaction of Christ in effecting salvation.

With these doctrinal differences in mind, we can return to Shakespeare's second development of his source, his greater emphasis on the theological notion of merit. What in Boccaccio and Painter is simply the heroine's clever exercise of human "policy" becomes in Shakespeare a virtuous action meriting reward. (However, Boccaccio's heroine refers to "recompense" [*merito*] twice, and in the original Italian the King possibly plays on the word [*mariteremo*, "we will give in marriage"; *marito*, "husband"] and refers to the husband Giletta has "deserved" [*guadagnato*] as a "reward" [*guiderdon*].) Shakespeare's fuller emphasis required some significant alteration of the action. We have mentioned above the distinction between condign and congruous merit, notions which Shakespeare consciously plays on in *Love's Labor's Lost* (1.2.13, 25) and which depend on equality and inequality between giver and receiver. This distinction, which conditions some courtly literature (Langer 233), enables us to make sense of Shakespeare's more pronounced emphasis on Helena's social inferiority to Bertram. Boccaccio makes little of his heroine's difference in social rank, other than to make it the basis for Beltramo's initially scornful rejection of Giletta as his wife. By contrast, Shakespeare first makes it the basis of Helena's despair over her "ambitious love" before she even sets out to pursue Bertram (1.1.86-94). Then, in view of this disparity of social station, he gives more prominence to the theme of reward and "desert," both with the King's discourse on virtue as the true nobility, justifying his raising Helena to be Bertram's equal in rank (2.3.117-44), and with Helena's final remark on Bertram's being "doubly won" (5.3.315).

The theme of merit extends to other aspects of the play as well. Along these lines, the recent claim that there are certain tensions and oppositions in the play—between divine power and human weakness, election and free will, and grace and earned reward (Lewis 151)—deserves extended consideration. All three of these alleged oppositions touch on the doctrine of merit, and in the light of that doctrine we can perceive a unified theology of grace in the play's dialogue and action. With respect to the first of these supposed oppositions, it seems evident at specific points in *All's Well* that divine power and human weakness are not in oppositional tension—in either Roman Catholic or even Reformed doctrine—but that in a complementary way God's power is mediated through Helena's action. This notion, repeated more than once in the play, would have been acceptable to the Catholic and even perhaps to the Reformed sensibilities in Shakespeare's audience. The complementarity of divine power and human weakness finds its first expression when Helena approaches the King and he refuses her aid:

> He that of greatest works is finisher
> Oft does them by the weakest minister.
> So holy writ in babes hath judgment shown
> When judges have been babes; great floods have flown
> From simple sources, and great seas have dried
> When miracles have by the great'st been denied.
>
> (2.1.138-43)

Having made her offer to cure the king, Helena uses another telling phrase—"The great'st grace lending grace" (2.1.162)—in claiming to the King that she can cure him in two days. What this phrase indicates is that her gift for healing is simply the power of God enabling her to act. And the notion of such complementarity is repeated in the King's response that "Methinks in thee some blessed spirit doth speak / His powerful sound within an organ weak" (177-78). It reappears two scenes later when LaFew and Parolles remark on the appearance of the "Very hand of heaven. . . . In a most weak—And debile minister" (2.3.31-34). What all these phrases suggest is a complementary relation between divine power and human action rather than an oppositional one, since divine power works through weak human beings, "lending" them grace, and not in spite of them.

If it is difficult to find any real opposition between divine power and human weakness in *All's Well,* so also it is hard to see where election and free will are necessarily at odds. It may seem that Helena at first sounds what from the perspective of Reformed theology appears to be an initially "Pelagian" note of confidence in the power of human action, at odds with the notion of God's grace as accomplishing all without regard to human merit:

> Our remedies oft in ourselves do lie
> Which we ascribe to heaven. The fated sky
> Gives us free scope, only doth backward pull
> Our slow designs when we ourselves are dull.
>
> (1.1.216-19)

As Richard Stensgaard has suggested (186), this seems to be inconsistent with Helena's later statement that only with the "help of heaven" has the King's cure been effected (2.1.154). But it is inconsistent only if we assume the perspective of Reformed theology and its doctrine of "*sola gratia*." Here Helena clearly speaks in a manner quite consistent with Roman Catholic theology, in which the mystery of predestination ("The fated sky") does not obliterate free will. Heaven after all "gives us free scope," a phrase clearly expressing divine provision for the exercise of human freedom. The Council of Trent in its sixth session (January 1547) condemned the notion that grace alone is conducive to salvation and that free will is a mere fiction:

> Can. 4. If anyone says that man's free will moved and aroused by God, by assenting to God's call and action, in no way cooperates toward disposing and preparing itself to obtain the grace of justification, that it cannot refuse its assent if it wishes, but that, as something inanimate, it does nothing whatever and is merely passive, let him be anathema.
>
> (Schroeder 42-43)

Free will here is something both passive and active—it is "moved" and "aroused," so that it can "assent," "cooperate," "dispose" and "prepare" itself—but it is not something "merely passive." Of further interest are the similar comments of Aquinas that free will is insufficient unless it is moved and helped by God (ST 1a.83.1) and that "we can admit the existence of fate (*fatum*)" inasmuch as "all that happens here below is subject to Divine Providence, as being pre-ordained" (ST 1a.116.1).

A comparable passage from "The Thirty-Nine Articles" will illustrate the difference between the Roman Catholic and Reformed views on free will:

> The condition of Man after the fall of Adam is such, that he cannot turn and prepare himself, by his own natural strength and good works, to faith, and calling upon God. Wherefore we have no power to do good works pleasant and acceptable to God, without the grace of God by Christ preventing [i.e., going before] us, that we may have a good will, and working with us, when we have that good will.
>
> (Leith, "Of Free Will" 270)

Here the emphasis is on what man cannot do—"turn and prepare himself," "do good works"—so that he is powerless to perform works pleasing to God. It will not do to see an absolute opposition here, but there is clearly a difference of emphasis. Trent is vindicating free will, the Articles are vindicating grace. Trent has a more active conception of human cooperation, the Articles a more passive one. Helena's phrase "gives us free scope," suggesting as it does some autonomy in human freedom, seems closer to Trent than to the Articles.

In accord with this conception of the complementary relation between divine power and human weakness, enabling human beings to act freely, is the doctrine of Trent regarding divine grace and human merit. The Council, again in its sixth session (January 1547), dealt with the subject of merit in terms suggestive of the very title of Shakespeare's play:

> . . . *Do not lose your confidence, which hath a great reward* [Heb. 10.35]. Hence, to those who work well *unto the end* [Matt. 10.22] [*Atque ideo bene operantibus "usque in finem"*] and trust in God, eternal life is to be offered, both as a grace mercifully promised to the Sons of God through Christ Jesus, and as a reward promised by God Himself, to be faithfully given to their good works and merits. . . . For since Christ Jesus Himself, as the head into the members and the vine into the branches, continually infuses strength into those justified, which strength always precedes, accompanies and follows their good works, and without which they could not in any manner be pleasing and meritorious before God, we must believe that nothing further is wanting to those justified to prevent them from being considered to have, by those very works which have been done in God, fully satisfied divine law . . . and to have truly merited eternal life. . . .
>
> (Schroeder 40-41)

Not surprisingly, Shakespeare seems clearly conscious of the play's title and its connection with salvation, since he plays on the word "well" in relation to "heaven" for a dozen lines in Act 2.4.

As for the doctrine of merit itself, early on in the very first scene there is some suggestion of it in the Countess' description of Helena: "She derives her honesty and achieves her goodness" (1.1.44-45). That is, the inheritance of a good disposition complements virtuous achievement and merit. And later when the King waves Helena's offer of help aside, she herself goes on to use terms that clearly and explicitly unite divine grace and human merit:

> Inspirèd merit so by breath is barred.
> It is not so with Him that all things knows
> As 'tis with us that square our guess by shows;
> But most it is presumption in us when
> The help of heaven we count the act of men.
>
> (2.1.150-54)

The meritorious nature of Helena's miraculous cure is here especially apparent in the phrase she uses to describe her action—"inspirèd merit"—an action inspired by God and meritorious for herself. Far from accomplishing all without reference to free will, grace—"the help of heaven"—enables Helena to meritoriously cure the King and thus receive her reward, much in the manner described by Trent.

To sum up—certain speeches and phraseology in the first part of *All's Well* create a sense of divine grace that goes well beyond Boccaccio and Painter. The Countess' description of Helena—"she derives her honesty and achieves her goodness"—affirms the value of human effort. More prominently, Helena's remark about "inspirèd merit" is clearly Roman Catholic in its sense of divine grace empowering human meritorious action, and her conception of "the greatest Grace lending grace" suggests a certain autonomy—and therefore human freedom and merit—in human action. All three phrases go beyond the theological commonplace of divine grace working through human agents, implicit in the allusions to the Scriptural figures of Daniel and Moses (2.1.140-43) and such remarks as the King's "Methinks in thee some blessèd spirit doth speak / His powerful sound within an organ weak" (2.1.177-78). Equally important, the play's action precisely and coherently reflects a Roman Catholic theology of grace, with Helena "working" a miracle with the aid of grace and meritoriously being "rewarded" by the King with the hand of Bertram. As a point of comparison, one might cite Spenser's commentary on the Red Cross Knight's victory over the Dragon, described in terms acceptable to Reformed theology:

> Ne let the man ascribe it to his skill,
> That thorough grace hath gainéd victory.
> If any strength we have it is to ill,
> But all the good is Gods, both power and eke will.
>
> (1.10.6-9)

By contrast with Spenser, Shakespeare seems inclined to acknowledge human weakness in the Reformed manner but in conformity with the Council of Trent to affirm the power of free will and human merit.

In the second half of the play, the Catholic notions of grace and merit carry over, albeit in a minor key, into the themes of pilgrimage and prayer. The action is clearly fashioned in parallel form. Just as Bertram uses deception in going off to war, informing his mother and Helena by letter, so Helena, also informing the Countess by letter, undertakes her pilgrimage as a deceptive ruse that allows her to draw near Florence and Bertram. Both the cowardly braggart Parolles and the fearless but lustful Bertram are duped, the former by the drum incident, the latter by the bed-trick. Again, it seems Shakespeare is primarily interested in Helena's "ambitious love" and the ingenuity with which she achieves her desire. But her costume as a pilgrim and her description of her pilgrimage carry with them the undeniable features of the Roman Catholic theology of grace.

With respect to pilgrimages, it is important to realize the confluence of Catholic doctrine and devotional practice. Through the late Middle Ages and into the Renaissance, when they were reformulated by the Council of Trent, the doctrines of grace were inseparably linked with miracles, saints, shrines, pilgrimages, and vows—and, we might add, with works of satisfaction for sin:

> Two dominant perceptions governed the notion concerning [miracles]: first, that miracles were performed by God through the intercession of the saints; second, that the saints' aid was attained through an exchange. Seeking help in hopeless circumstances, the faithful approached the saints at local shrines with prayers and vows of pilgrimages and votive gifts. In return, they received intercession for their devotion.
>
> (Hillerbrand, "Miracles")

All of these elements are captured in part two of *All's Well* when Helena supposedly undertakes "with sainted vow" her pilgrimage to the shrine of St. Jacques (compare Calvin on "votive pilgrimages" [Inst. 4.13.7] as "not only empty and fleeting but full of manifest impiety"). Consistent with her previous phraseology of "inspirèd merit," she is conscious of the meritorious nature of penitential action in the amendment of faults:

> I am Saint Jaques' pilgrim, thither gone.
>   Ambitious love hath so in me offended
> That barefoot plod I the cold ground upon,
>   With sainted vow my faults to have amended.
>
> (3.4.4-7)

And clearly her letter expresses the hope that a pilgrimage will obtain intercession from the saint in order to rescue Bertram from "the bloody course of war."

A pilgrimage to Spain, the invocation of Saint James, the penitential practice of walking barefoot on the cold ground, a "sainted vow," the amendment of faults. These notions and practices are not the staples of Reformed doctrine. The Reformers, in fact, considered the intercessory miracles reported at shrines as illusions and frauds, and they attacked the doctrine of intercession as well as the whole complex of doctrines surrounding pilgrimages to the shrines of saints (Hillerbrand, "Miracles"). Moreover, such things were important enough to call forth condemnation in *The Thirty-Nine Articles* appended to *The Book of Common Prayer*:

> The Romish Doctrine concerning Purgatory, Pardons, Worshipping and Adoration, as well of Images as of Relics, and also Invocation of Saints, is a fond thing, vainly invented, and grounded upon no warranty of Scripture, but rather repugnant to the Word of God.
>
> (No. XXII; Leith 274)

With this article in mind, it is extremely difficult to see Shakespeare's theology as consonant with Reformed doctrine in general and Church of England doctrine in particular.

Furthermore, consistent with this notion of pilgrimage, the conception of prayer in the play is also distinctively Roman Catholic, including as it does some notion of active "works" and satisfaction for sin. Helena undertakes her pilgrimage in order to pray at the shrine of St. Jacques and to do penance. Prayer is conceived of as "working" an effect, as an act of intercession, and as a means to amending faults. Thus, in blessing Bertram, the Countess speaks of what her prayers will "pluck down" (1.1.69), and she later proclaims that she will "pray God's blessing into thy [Helena's] attempt" to cure the King (1.3.253). Such a conception of prayer assigns it an active function of "working" an effect, contrary to the Reformed conception of prayer as a passive and powerless appeal to God for mercy.

This active conception is again in evidence later in the play when, after having received the letter from Helena informing her that she has gone on pilgrimage, the Countess exclaims against Bertram "What angel shall bless this unworthy husband?" She then proceeds to remark that only "her prayers, whom heaven delights to hear / And loves to grant" (either Helena's prayers or more probably the Blessed Virgin Mary's) can "reprieve him [Bertram] from the wrath of greatest justice" (3.4.25-29). The conception of prayer effecting by intercession the "reprieve" of a sinner is distinctly Roman Catholic. Again, the context seems to prevent us reading Helena as the mentioned "angel," since the Countess' steward has just spoken of the impossibility of pursuing and overtaking Helena, who seems to be intent on her own death (17). In the absence of a human means of preventing her, the Countess turns to a supernatural means for solution. Helena's mediation is no longer possible. Therefore the Countess desperately imagines another source of mediation. The lines seem clearly to refer to a woman greater than Helena, a woman of angelic stature, general intercessory power, and unique favor in the eyes of heaven—that is, Mary, the mediatrix of all graces (Hunter, *Comedy of Forgiveness* 129-30). Even if we take the Countess' phrase "what angel" as referring to Helena, her words are not in keeping with the Elizabethan "Homily concerning Prayer," which informs us that

> . . . we must call neither vpon Angel, nor yet vpon Saint, but onely and solely vpon GOD. . . . For to say that we should beleeue either in Angel or Saint or in any other liuing creature, were mere horrible blasphemie against GOD and his holy Word. . . .
>
> (*Certaine Sermons* 1:114)

The tradition of Mary as mediatrix, again a notion repulsive to Reformed theologians, was well known in Shakespeare's time. At about the same time (1608) that *All's Well* was written, John Donne, for example, was writing in very similar terms about Mary as mediatrix:

> As her deeds were
> Our helpes, so are her prayers; nor can she sue
> In vaine, who hath such titles unto you.
>
> ("A Litanie" ll.43-45; see Dubinski 18-24; Klawitter 131-33)

Donne was aware, as his letter to Henry Goodyere indicates, that in these lines he was striking a "*via media*" between Rome and Geneva, conceding to the former praise of the saints and to the latter a "rectified devotion" by avoiding invocation with the "*ora pro nobis*" refrain (Lewalski 260-61). But Shakespeare's lines contain a more forceful conception of intercession than Donne's: Mary's prayer is envisioned not merely as a suing for grace, but as actually effecting a "reprieve" for Bertram.

Finally, in addition to the notion of prayer as working an effect, the conception of satisfaction for sin is operative in Helena's intention to do penance for the sin of her "ambitious love." She writes that she intends "to barefoot plod . . . the cold ground upon, / With sainted vow my faults to have amended" (3.4.4-7), and when she reaches Florence, she is brought to the other "enjoined penitents," i. e., pilgrims who have vowed to do penance. Such physical penance is of course another form of "works" repudiated by Reformed theologians. The notion is not confined to *All's Well;* we find it also in *The Winter's Tale* when Cleomenes exclaims to Leontes:

> Sir, you have done enough, and have performed
> A saint-like sorrow. No fault could you make
> Which you have not redeemed—indeed, paid down
> More penitence than done trespass.
>
> (5.1.1-4)

In Cleomenes' eyes, "faults" and "trespasses" can be paid for and "redeemed" by the performance of penitential deeds with "saint-like sorrow." Two of the three parts of the Roman Catholic sacrament of penance—contrition, confession, and satisfaction—are here in evidence: namely, sorrow for sin, and the redemptive power of penitential acts, of satisfaction "paid down" for sin. This is not compatible with what we consistently find in Luther's *Babylonian Captivity of the Church,* Calvin's *Institutes* (see 3.4.25), Hooker's *Laws of Ecclesiastical Polity* (5.5.6), and *The Thirty-Nine Articles:*

> The Offering of Christ once made is that perfect redemption, propitiation, and satisfaction, for all the sins of the whole world, both original and actual; and there is none other satisfaction for sin, but that alone.
>
> (No. XXXI; Leith 277)

Since Christ has made satisfaction once for all, there is no need to "pay down" additional human satisfaction for sin. When Reformed theology speaks of "satisfaction," it means not the performance of penitential actions, like Helena's walking barefoot on the cold ground, but rather something quite different: "that we cease from euill, and doe good, and if wee haue done any man wrong, to endeauour our selues to make him true amends" ("The second part of the Homily of Repentance" *Certaine Sermons* 2:269). It should be mentioned that in the interests of a "*via media*," Hooker makes some allowance for works of satisfaction being contrary to and effectually curing the deeds of sin. But he talks in largely the same manner as the homily, distinguishing between satisfaction made to God, man, and Church, the first having been made by Christ, and the latter two consisting of restitution and amendment of life (6.5.2-9, esp. 6-8; see also Gibbs, "Repentance" 68). In neither source is there any mention of penitential satisfaction being undertaken with a "sainted vow."

Both parts of *All's Well,* then, reflect a Roman Catholic theology of grace. In part one, we have the presentation of the King's cure as miraculous, Helena's role as miracle-worker, and her words ascribing her miraculous cure to "inspirèd merit." In part two, we have her role as pilgrim, along with her sonnet-letter describing her pilgrimage as undertaken by "sainted vow" for the amendment of faults, the Countess' allusion to the intercessory power of the Virgin Mary, the conception of prayer as working an effect, and the notion of penance as satisfaction for sin. All these elements in the play, together with the several other references to Roman Catholic doctrine, provide compelling evidence of the sensibility of a "church papist" at work. Moreover, it seems that Shakespeare shaped the action to represent by analogy the operations of merit *de congruo* in part one, with the "unequal" Helena being "proportionately" rewarded with a raise in station by the King, and merit *de condigno* in part two, when having achieved equality of station she fulfills Bertram's terms and so gains a reward due in justice for labor done. In short, a Roman Catholic theology of grace pervades the play at every level.

In any event, the theological dimension of *All's Well* seriously challenges some conventional views of Shakespeare: that his plays sharply separate the secular order of nature from the order of grace, that he embraced the skepticism of Montaigne and the "new philosophers," and that he was most probably a conforming member of the Church of England. All these views run contrary to what we find in *All's Well*—the notions of miracle, pilgrimage, penitential vows, intercessory prayer, and "inspirèd merit," all emanating from the mindset of a Roman Catholic. Shakespeare again appears here to fit the profile of a discreet "church papist," more than that of a devout member of the Church of England or a secularized skeptic (Taylor 297-98; Beauregard, "New Light" *passim*).

Notes

1. There is something intrinsically problematic in Frye's claim that Shakespeare was "capable of treating the temporal and secular order independent of theological systems" (268). As two of Frye's critics have pointed out, this would have been virtually impossible in Elizabethan England, saturated as it was with liturgical ceremony and theological discourse (Hassel ix-xv; Shuger 46). This deep and central flaw stems from Frye's adoption of certain oppositions in Reformed theology between nature and grace, the temporal and spiritual orders. Thus he argued that Shakespeare's universality stood in opposition to Christianity (conceived of as sectarian by Frye), that classical ethics was more universal than an "exclusively" Christian ethics, that the temporal order is sharply separate from the order of grace, and that, consequently, literature was independent of theology. The complementary relation of these oppositions in Roman Catholic theology was never considered—Aquinas, whose ethics "inclusively" unites classical and Christian sources, was excluded because "his works were not in print in sixteenth century England" (11). But Aquinas' works, often cited by English theologians such as Hooker and Perkins, were printed on the continent and were available in such places as St. Paul's churchyard and St. John's College library, as has been demonstrated by recent scholarship (see Beauregard, *Virtue's Own Feature* 37-40).

Another major flaw in Frye's study is his reductive conception of a "universal" Shakespeare, universal not in the classical sense of representing the essential forms of "nature," but universal in the expurgatory sense of being an uncontroversial poet, undetermined by any theological system, and "equally accessible" to Christians and virtuous heathen (272). Shakespeare's inoffensively "secular" art thus transcends the history and religious divisions of his time, but we are assured that he was a conforming member of the Church of England, whose "broad and inclusive" character, however, prevents us from determining his personal faith (3-4). This conception jars with Frye's eccentric catalogue of theological topics, which shows that Shakespeare had an extensive knowledge of Christian doctrine. But the catalogue excludes theologically specific references to Limbo, pilgrimage, penitential vows, merit, satisfaction for sin, and auricular confession—to name those that occur in *All's Well*—and such crucial theological topics as justification, grace, purgatory, Franciscan religious life, nuns, saints, etc., all of which had been carefully catalogued by Mutschmann and Wentersdorf (213-365). The overall result is to expurgate the scandalously Catholic references from Shakespeare's theology.

2. See, for example, Shakespeare's toning down of his anti-Catholic sources in *King John,* and his transformation of his sources in *Measure for Measure.* Cinthio and Whetstone present us with a virginal heroine who is seduced by a magistrate and then is married to him. Shakespeare decks Isabella out as a novice in the Poor Clares, preserves her virginity, and has her remain silent when she is offered marriage (Beauregard, *Virtue's Own Feature* 153-55).

3. Tilney seems to have been mainly concerned with inflammatory language and possible insurrections, not with ideas and the promotion of ideological orthodoxy (Dutton 80). It has even been argued that between 1590 and 1625 the theater had come to be seen as politically powerless and disinterested, so that the authorities "do not seem to have thought it possible for the players seriously to disrupt the political order" (Yachnin 2-3, 23). Here we see part of the solution to the problem of how it was that Roman Catholic roles, whether of Helena as miracle-worker and pilgrim or Isabella as novice, were played before an Elizabethan or Jacobean audience. The problem recurs with Shakespeare's favorable portrayal of Franciscan friars—Friar Laurence in *Romeo and Juliet,* Friar Francis in *Much Ado About Nothing,* and Friar Peter in *Measure for Measure.* Except for Shakespeare and John Ford, English Renaissance dramatists depict Franciscan friars as "duplicitous, immoral, and satanic" (Voss 5). Thus, as far as official censorship is concerned, Tilney did not object to certain theologically sensitive roles being played on the stage, but rather to seditious matter.

If we consider the makeup of the audience, several other considerations bear on the problem. First of all, Shakespeare's plays were sometimes put on before Catholic audiences. In 1604 *Love's Labors Lost* was put on at Southampton House, a notorious Catholic center where in 1605 "above two hundredeth pounds worth of popish bookes [were] taken about Southampton house and burned in Poules Churchyard" (Akrigg 255, 181). In 1609-10, *King Lear* and *Pericles* were put on by Catholic players, Cholmeley's Men, at recusant houses in Yorkshire (Milward 78). A more important consideration is that in many respects English audiences were still Catholic or well disposed toward Catholicism. In July of 1603, a Spanish diplomatic report on King James' "Councillors of State . . . and other notables" identified a quarter of them as favorably disposed to Catholicism and in November of 1604, a second report by the Constable of Castile found "grounds for optimism in the favorable reports about King James and Queen Anne, the known Catholic sympathies among many aristocrats and the increasing number of Catholics" (Loomie 1: 1-10; 26-44, esp. 36). This latter report estimates that the religious makeup of England was one-third Catholic and that, of the other two sects, the Protestants were losing numbers and the Puritans increasing. Since those attending plays cannot have shared the Puritan hostility to the stage, it seems reasonable to suppose that Catholic figures on the stage were simply tolerated (as with Tilney), especially if they were marginal characters or presented in a dramatically ambiguous way. The Protestant revolution was far from complete, and, as Patrick Collinson and others have shown, a truly Protestant literary culture, based on the "plain truth" of the Bible, was still in the process of formation (34-37). Dramatic performance was affected, then, by a variety of complex circumstances that preclude our thinking of Shakespeare's plays as always and everywhere under the eye of rigorous Protestant censorship and a predominantly Protestant audience.

4. From time to time Shakespearean critics have suggested the relevance of the theology of grace to *All's Well,* but for various reasons have never undertaken a full exploration. In 1950 E. M. W. Tillyard viewed Helena and Bertram broadly as the representatives of "heavenly grace and natural, unredeemed, man respectively" (108), but did not pursue the matter further. Some ten years later, Roland M. Frye made the general claim that "sin is, after all, a universal element of human experience where saving grace is not," and so he concluded dismissively that "the theology of sin thus appears to have been quite serviceable to Shakespeare, whereas the theology of grace was less so," declining to include grace in his list of theological topics (115). Shortly thereafter, Robert G. Hunter also saw Helena as "the instrument of God's grace" (114, 128), but made the questionable claim that the orthodoxy of the English Reformation "was very close to the *Summa* when it came to the forgiveness of sins" (20, 244). More recently, David Palmer has claimed that the play alludes to the Reformed doctrines of man's depravity, "the natural inferiority and weakness of women," and free will "as conformable with God's will" (97-103). Other critics have examined *All's Well* from the standpoint of Scriptural sources, and have discerned in it New Testament images, allusions to Old Testament types of baptism, and types of the Old Testament prophets and the Prodigal Son (Sexton 262-3; Haley 104-5; Milward 172-79). Finally, using a New Critical model of drama taken to its now commonplace skeptical extreme, one critic has conceived the play as presenting the Reformed and "Christian humanist" (i. e., Roman Catholic) conceptions of grace "in consistent tension," claiming that it "first promotes one seeming truth and then substitutes its antithesis" (Lewis 151-56). In short, when it comes to the theology of grace in Shakespeare, some confusion reigns among critics,

and the confusion obscures a clearly Catholic feature of Shakespeare's work.

Works Cited

Akrigg, G. P. V. *Shakespeare and the Earl of Southampton*. Cambridge: Harvard UP, 1968.

Allison, C. F. *The Rise of Moralism: The Proclamation of the Gospel from Hooker to Baxter*. New York: Seabury, 1966.

Aquinas, Thomas. *Summa Theologica*. Trans. Fathers of the English Dominican Province. 3 vols. New York: Benziger Brothers, 1948.

Beauregard, David N. "New Light on Shakespeare's Catholicism: Prospero's Epilogue in The Tempest." *Renascence* 49.3 (1997): 159-74.

———. *Virtue's Own Feature: Shakespeare and the Virtue Ethics Tradition*. Newark: U Delaware P, 1995.

Calvin, John. *Institutes of the Christian Religion*. Trans. Ford Battles. 2 vols. Philadelphia: Westminster Press, 1960.

Certaine Sermons or Homilies: Appointed to be Read in Churches in the Time of Queen Elizabeth I (1547-1571). Ed. Mary Ellen Rickey and Thomas B. Stroup. 2 vols. Gainesville: Scholar's Facsimiles & Reprints, 1968.

Clare, Janet. *'Art made tongue-tied by authority': Elizabethan and Jacobean Dramatic Censorship*. Manchester: Manchester UP, 1990.

Collinson, Patrick. "Protestant Culture and the Cultural Revolution." *Reformation to Revolution: Politics and Religion in Early Modern England*. Ed. Margo Todd. London: Routledge, 1995. 33-52.

Dubinski, Roman. "Donne's 'A Litanie' and the Saints." *Christianity and Literature* 41 (1991): 5-26.

Duffy, Eamon. *The Stripping of the Altars: Traditional Religion in England 1400-1580*. New Haven: Yale UP, 1992.

Dutton, Richard, *Mastering the Revels: The Regulation and Censorship of English Renaissance Drama*. Iowa City: U Iowa P, 1991.

Frye, Roland M. *Shakespeare and Christian Doctrine*. Princeton: Princeton UP, 1963.

Gibbs, Lee W. "Richard Hooker's *Via Media* Doctrine of Justification." *Harvard Theological Review* 74 (1981): 211-20.

———. "Richard Hooker's *Via Media* Doctrine of Repentance." *Harvard Theologue Review* 84 (1991): 59-74.

Haley, David. *Shakespeare's Courtly Mirror: Reflexivity and Prudence in All's Well That Ends Well*. Newark: U Delaware P, 1993.

Hassel, R. Chris. *Faith and Folly in Shakespeare's Romantic Comedies*. Athens, GA: U Georgia P, 1980.

Hillerbrand, Hans, ed. *Oxford Encyclopedia of the Reformation*. 4 vols. New York: Oxford UP, 1996.

Hooker, Richard. *The Works of Richard Hooker*. Gen. ed. W. Speed Hill. 5 vols. Cambridge: Harvard UP, 1981-90.

Hunter, G. K., ed. *All's Well That Ends Well*. London: Methuen, 1959.

Hunter, Robert G. *Shakespeare and the Comedy of Forgiveness*. New York: Columbia UP, 1965.

Klawitter, George. "John Donne's Attitude toward the Virgin Mary: The Public versus the Private Voice" in *John Donne's Religious Imagination: Essays in Honor of John Shawcross*. Ed. Frances Malpezzi and Raymond Frontain. Conway, AR: U Central Arkansas P, 1995.

Langer, Ullrich. "Merit in Courtly Literature: Castiglione, Rabelais, Marguerite de Navarre, and Le Caron." *Renaissance Quarterly* 41 (1988): 218-41.

Leith, John H., ed. *Creeds of the Churches: A Reader in Christian Doctrine from the Bible to the Present*. 3rd ed. Atlanta: John Knox, 1982.

Lewalski, Barbara. *Protestant Poetics and the Seventeenth Century Religious Lyric*. Princeton: Princeton UP, 1979.

Lewis, Cynthia. "'Derived Honesty and Achieved Goodness': Doctrines of Grace in *All's Well That Ends Well*." *Renaissance and Reformation* 26 (1990): 147-70.

Loomie, Albert J. *Spain and the Jacobean Catholics*. 2 vols. London: Catholic Record Society, 1973.

Milward, Peter. *The Catholicism of Shakespeare's Plays*. Tokyo: Renaissance Institute, 1997.

Molinski, Waldemar. "Merit." *Encyclopedia of Theology: The Concise Sacramentum Mundi*. Ed. Karl Rahner. New York: Seabury, 1975. 955-58.

Mutschmann, H., and K. Wentersdorf. *Shakespeare and Catholicism*. New York: Sheed and Ward, 1952.

Noble, Richmond. *Shakespeare's Biblical Knowledge and Use of the Book of Common Prayer*. New York: Octagon, 1970.

Palmer, David. "Comedy and the Protestant Spirit in Shakespeare's *All's Well That Ends Well*." *Bulletin of the John Rylands Library* 71 (1989): 95-107.

Schoenbaum, Samuel. *William Shakespeare: A Compact Documentary Life*. Rev. ed. New York: Oxford, 1987.

Schroeder, H. J., ed. *The Canons and Decrees of the Council of Trent*. New York: Herder, 1941. Latin text from Denzinger, Henricus, and Schonmetzer, Adolphus, eds. *Enchiridion Symbolorum Definitionum et Declarationum de rebus fidei et morum*. 36th ed. Rome: Herder, 1976.

Sexton, Joyce. "'Rooted Love': Metaphors for Baptism in *All's Well That Ends Well*." *Christianity and Literature* 43 (1994): 261-87.

Shakespeare, William. *The Complete Works of Shakespeare.* Ed. David Bevington. 4th ed. updated. New York: Longman, 1996.

Shuger, Debora K. "Subversive Fathers and Suffering Subjects: Shakespeare and Christianity." *Religion, Literature, and Politics in Post-Reformation England, 1540-1688.* Ed. Donna Hamilton and Richard Strier. Cambridge: Cambridge UP, 1996. 46-69.

Smith, G. Gregory. *Elizabethan Critical Essays.* 2 vols. London: Oxford UP, 1904; rpt. 1964.

Stensgaard, Richard K. "*All's Well That Ends Well* and the Galenico-Paracelsian Controversy." *Renaissance Quarterly* 25 (1972): 173-88.

Taylor, Gary. "Forms of Opposition: Shakespeare and Middleton." *English Literary Renaissance* 24 (1994): 283-314.

Tillyard, E. M. W. *Shakespeare's Problem Plays.* Toronto: U Toronto P, 1950.

Todd, Margo, ed. *Reformation to Revolution: Politics and Religion in Early Modern England.* London: Routledge, 1995.

Voss, Paul. "The Antifraternal Tradition in English Renaissance Drama." *Cithara* 33 (1993): 3-15.

Wallace, Dewey D. Jr. *Puritans and Predestination: Grace in English Protestant Theology, 1525-1695.* Chapel Hill: U North Carolina P, 1982.

Yachnin, Paul. *Stage-Wrights: Shakespeare, Jonson, Middleton, and the Making of Theatrical Value.* Philadelphia: U Pennsylvania P, 1997.

FURTHER READING

Criticism

Brett, Julia. "'Grace is grace, despite of all the controversy': *Measure for Measure,* Christian Allegory, and the Sacerdotal Duke." *Ben Jonson Journal* 6 (1999): 189-207.

Provides an extensive review of religious and political readings of *Measure for Measure.*

Diehl, Huston. "'Infinite Space': Representation and Reformation in *Measure for Measure.*" *Shakespeare Quarterly* 49, no. 4 (winter 1998): 393-410.

Maintains that in *Measure for Measure* Shakespeare appropriated Calvinist theories of representation, epistemology, judgment, and reformation to explore the nature of his dramatic art and legitimate the stage.

Gardner, Helen. "Shakespearian Tragedy." In *Religion and Literature,* pp. 61-89. New York: Oxford University Press, 1971.

Asserts that Shakespeare's tragedies comprise unique expressions of his imaginative response to centuries of Christian thought and tradition.

Geller, Lila. "*Cymbeline* and the Imagery of Covenant Theology." *Studies in English Literature, 1500-1800* 20, no. 2 (spring 1980): 241-55.

Argues that the covenant motif is the central unifying principle of *Cymbeline,* suggesting that the play's themes and dramatic action replicate the contract between God and man that leads to salvation.

Greenblatt, Stephen. "Shakespeare and the Exorcists." In *After Strange Texts: The Role of Theology in the Study of Literature,* edited by Gregory S. Jay and David L. Miller, pp. 101-23. University: University of Alabama Press, 1985.

Examines the relation between *King Lear* and *A Declaration of Egregious Popish Impostures* (1603), Samuel Harsnett's attack on the Catholic practice of exorcism. Greenblatt contends that, particularly through the agency of Edgar as Poor Tom, the play endorses Harsnett's central argument that the notion of demonic possession is fraudulent and that exorcism is a form of theatrical illusion.

Hunter, G. K. "Shakespeare and the Church." In *Shakespeare's Universe: Renaissance Ideas and Conventions,* edited by John M. Mucciolo, pp. 21-8. Aldershot, England: Scolar Press, 1996.

Asserts that although it is evident that Shakespeare was thoroughly conversant with Catholic vocabulary and sensitive to its historical reverberations, it cannot be determined, on the basis of the attitudes represented in his plays, whether he was a Catholic or a Protestant—or even whether he cared deeply about the doctrinal differences between the two churches.

Kaula, David. "'Let Us Be Sacrificers': Religious Motifs in *Julius Caesar.*" *Shakespeare Studies* 14 (1981): 197-214.

Suggests that Christian allusions in *Julius Caesar* obliquely reflect sixteenth-century religious controversies and imply Shakespeare's skeptical view of religious extremism—whether Protestant or Catholic. Kaula calls particular attention to Cassius's characterization of Caesar as a virtual demon or Antichrist, Antony's similarly propagandistic portrait of him as the savior of Rome, and Brutus's vision of the assassination as a sacramental action.

———. "*Hamlet* and the Image of Both Churches." *Studies in English Literature 1500-1900* 24, no. 2 (spring 1984): 241-55.

Links the juxtaposition of polar opposites—especially Christ and Antichrist—found in Revelation and in sixteenth-century Protestant polemical literature to the oppositions featured in several apocalyptic passages in *Hamlet.*

Keefer, Michael H. "Accommodation and Synecdoche: Calvin's God in *King Lear.*" *Shakespeare Studies* 20 (1988): 147-68.

Perceives a darkly ironic association between Calvin's conception of God and the dramatic world of *King Lear*. Emphasizing Calvin's apprehension of God's will as absolute and utterly incomprehensible, Keefer reads Shakespeare's tragedy as a bleak representation of the chasm separating natural law and divine providence.

Knapp, Jeffrey. "Preachers and Players in Shakespeare's England." In *Preachers and Players in Shakespeare's England,* edited by Christopher Ocker, pp. 1-27. Berkeley: Center for Hermeneutical Studies, 1995.

Evaluates the anticlericalism of Shakespeare's history plays, tracing the progression of Shakespeare's increasingly dark representation of English bishops from *1 Henry VI* to *Henry V*.

Lewis, R. W. B. "Shakespeare's *Pericles*." In *Literary Reflections,* pp. 28-43. Boston: Northeastern University Press, 1993.

Observes that although the religious dimension of *Pericles* is chiefly expressed in pagan terms, the play's miraculous conclusion alludes to the Christian humanist conception of grace.

Lynch, Stephen J. "Sin, Suffering, and Redemption in *Leir* and *Lear*." *Shakespeare Studies* 18 (1986): 161-74.

Argues that despite its pagan setting, Shakespeare's *Lear* is more deeply concerned with spiritual issues than is its source: the ostensibly Christian *True Chronicle Historie of King Leir*. Lynch maintains that Lear's sins are more heinous than his predecessor's, his suffering more extreme, and his redemption more thorough and profound.

Maguin, Jean-Marie. "The Anagogy of *Measure for Measure*." *Cahiers Élisabéthains* 16 (October 1979): 19-26.

Finds that the key to the spiritual or mystical significance of *Measure for Measure* is the representation of Isabella and Angelo as religious archetypes. Maguin suggests that it is Isabella's betrothal to Christ that rouses the devil in Angelo and compels him to desecrate that which is pure.

Marx, Steven. "Holy War in *Henry V*." *Shakespeare Survey* 48 (1995): 85-97.

Calls attention to some similarities between biblical descriptions of holy war and the complex representation of war, politics, and religion in *Henry V*.

Matheson, Mark. "*Hamlet* and 'A Matter Tender and Dangerous.'" *Shakespeare Quarterly* 46, no. 4 (1995): 383-97.

Argues that Hamlet subscribes to the Renaissance concept of Christian humanism, which, with its emphasis on reason, represents a rejection of the medieval Catholic precepts espoused by the Ghost. However, the critic maintains that in the final scene the prince expresses a new-found belief in both the reliability of individual conscience as a basis for action and in the range and power of providence—an attitude that links him with radical Protestantism.

Muir, Kenneth. "The Advantages and Disadvantages of Secularity." In *Parallel Lives: Spanish and English National Drama 1580-1680,* pp. 211-23. Lewisburg, Pa.: Bucknell University Press, 1991.

Maintains that the principal difference between the golden age of drama in Spain and England is that Spanish playwrights were invariably Catholics writing for a Catholic audience, while English playwrights wrote for a secular theater and a religiously diverse audience. Muir outlines the impact of religious orthodoxy on the work of the Spanish dramatist Calderón and compares this with the way Shakespeare's freedom from doctrinal constraints allowed him to express his characters' convictions on the basis of dramatic logic—without revealing his own beliefs.

Nelson, Timothy G. A. "The Fool as Clergyman (and Vice-versa): An Essay on Shakespearian Comedy." In *Jonson and Shakespeare,* edited by Ian Donaldson, pp. 1-17. London: Macmillan, 1983.

Calls attention to the complementary and contradictory roles of pious fools and farcical priests in Shakespeare's comedies. Nelson's discussion focuses on Sir Hugh Evans in *The Merry Wives of Windsor,* Touchstone, Feste, and Olivia's priest in *Twelfth Night,* Lavache in *All's Well that Ends Well,* and the Friar in *Much Ado about Nothing*.

Poole, Kristen. "Saints Alive! Falstaff, Martin Marprelate, and the Staging of Puritanism." *Shakespeare Quarterly* 46, no. 1 (spring 1995): 47-75.

Documents Falstaff's links to Sir John Oldcastle, a fourteenth-century antagonist of religious orthodoxy, and to "Martin Marprelate," the imaginary author of late sixteenth-century tracts that ridiculed the established church.

Rees, Joan. "Falstaff, St. Paul, and the Hangman." *Review of English Studies* n.s. 38, no. 149 (February 1987): 14-22.

Regards St. Paul's epistle to the Ephesians, with its warnings of dire consequences for those who do not observe restraint and sobriety in every aspect of their lives, as a discreet subtext of *1* and *2 Henry IV*.

Richmond, Hugh M. "*Richard III* and the Reformation." *Journal of English and Germanic Philology* 83, no. 4 (October 1984): 509-21.

Asserts that Shakespeare's references to traditional religious topics and vocabulary in *Richard III* do not discredit religion but heighten the audience's awareness of it. Richmond also compares Richard's unflinching insight into his own depravity to the Puritan propensity for pitiless self-examination.

Schwindt, John. "Luther's Paradoxes and Shakespeare's God: The Emergence of the Absurd in Sixteenth-Century Literature." *Modern Language Studies* 15, no. 4 (fall 1985): 4-12.

Places Shakespeare's tragic perspective in the context of the view of the human condition developed by Martin Luther and his contemporaries. Schwindt does not claim that Luther's theology directly influenced Shakespeare, but he does suggest that it foreshadows the dramatist's tragic vision of a world where the only way to endure is to abandon reason and turn to faith.

Slights, Camille Wells. "The Politics of Conscience in *All Is True* (or *Henry VIII*)." *Shakespeare Survey* 43 (1991): 59-68.

Reads *Henry VIII* as a complex interrogation of Protestant reliance on individual conscience rather than external authority to resolve moral questions.

Vitkus, Daniel J. "Turning Turk in *Othello*: The Conversion and Damnation of the Moor." *Shakespeare Quarterly* 48, no. 2 (summer 1997): 145-76.

Maintains that *Othello* draws on early modern anxiety about Turkish imperialism as well as on stereotypes linking Islam with violence, tyranny, and religious conversion, and suggests that the Moor's suicide firmly establishes his identity as an infidel.

Waddington, Raymond B. "Lutheran Hamlet." *English Language Notes* 27, no. 2 (1989): 27-42.

An explication of Hamlet's "diet of worms" speech (IV.iii.19-25) as an allusion to the 1521 Edict of Worms, which condemned Martin Luther as a heretic. Remarking on the parallels between the Danish prince and the leader of the Protestant Reformation—particularly their shared traits of profound melancholy and obsessive concern with the depravity of human nature—Waddington considers the possibility that Shakespeare modeled Hamlet after Luther.

Watson, Robert N. "*Othello* as Protestant Propaganda." In *Religion and Culture in Renaissance England*, edited by Claire McEachern and Deborah Shuger, pp. 234-57. Cambridge: Cambridge University Press, 1997.

Describes a subliminal Christian allegory in *Othello* whose purpose is to parody the Catholic theology of salvation through good works and thereby strengthen the Protestant loyalties of his original audience.

Willis, Paul J. "'Tongues in Trees': The Book of Nature in *As You Like It*." *Modern Language Studies* 18, no. 2 (summer 1988): 65-74.

Examines the religious function of the Forest of Arden in *As You Like It* as a version of the book of nature: that is, as a text analogous to the scriptures in revealing the glory of God.

Wittreich, Joseph. "Image of That Horror': The Apocalypse in *King Lear*." In *The Apocalypse in English Renaissance Thought and Literature*, edited by C. A. Patrides and Joseph Wittreich, pp. 175-206. Manchester: Manchester University Press, 1984.

Explores the implications of apocalyptic motifs, images, and ideas in *King Lear*. The play's apocalyptic framework does not support or discredit either Christian or non-Christian readings, Wittreich asserts, but it does enhance *Lear*'s representation of sacred and secular history.

———. "Angling in the Lake of Darkness." In *Image of that Horror: History, Prophecy, and Apocalypse in King Lear*, pp. 3-13. San Marino, Calif.: Huntington Library, 1984.

The opening chapter of a book-length treatment of *King Lear* that approaches the play from the perspective of the Book of Revelation in particular and the prophetic tradition in general. Wittreich contends that in its terrifying evocation of the Last Judgment, *Lear* represents the climactic expression of Shakespeare's view of history as a recital of all the circumstances of human tragedy.

Womersley, David. "Why Is Falstaff Fat?" *Review of English Studies* n.s. 47, no. 185 (1996): 1-22.

Argues that on the eve of the battle of Agincourt in *Henry V*, the king becomes aware of his spiritual unworthiness, rejects Catholic theology and practices, and submits to the will of God.

Shakespearean Criticism
Cumulative Character Index

The Cumulative Character Index identifies the principal characters of discussion in the criticism of each play and non-dramatic poem. The characters are arranged alphabetically. Page references indicate the beginning page number of each essay containing substantial commentary on that character.

Aaron
Titus Andronicus **4**: 632, 637, 650, 651, 653, 668, 672, 675; **27**: 255; **28**: 249, 330; **43**: 176; **53**: 86, 92

Achilles and Patroclus
Troilus and Cressida **60**: 105

Adonis
Venus and Adonis **10**: 411, 420, 424, 427, 429, 434, 439, 442, 451, 454, 459, 466, 473, 489; **25**: 305, 328; **28**: 355; **33**: 309, 321, 330, 347, 352, 357, 363, 370, 377; **51**: 345, 377

Adriana
The Comedy of Errors **16**: 3; **34**: 211, 220, 238; **54**: 189

Aemelia
The Comedy of Errors **66**: 1

Albany
King Lear **32**: 308

Alcibiades
Timon of Athens **25**: 198; **27**: 191

Angelo
Measure for Measure
anxiety **16**: 114
authoritarian portrayal of **23**: 307; **49**: 274
characterization **2**: 388, 390, 397, 402, 418, 427, 432, 434, 463, 484, 495, 503, 511; **13**: 84; **23**: 297; **32**: 81; **33**: 77; **49**: 274, 293, 379;**65**: 100
hypocrisy **2**: 396, 399, 402, 406, 414, 421; **23**: 345, 358, 362
repentance or pardon **2**: 388, 390, 397, 402, 434, 463, 511, 524; **60**: 12

Anne (Anne Boleyn)
Henry VIII See **Boleyn**

Anne (Anne Page)
The Merry Wives of Windsor See **Page**

Anne (Lady Anne)
Richard III **52**: 223, 227, 239, 249, 280

Antigonus
The Winter's Tale
characterization **7**: 394, 451, 464
death (Act III, scene iii) **7**: 377, 414, 464, 483; **15**: 518, 532; **19**: 366

Antipholus of Ephesus
The Comedy of Errors
crisis of identity **66**: 51
as ideal ego of Antipholus of Syracuse **66**: 17
as Shakespeare's ego **66**: 1

Antipholus of Syracuse
The Comedy of Errors
characterization **66**: 1, 17, 51
madness **66**: 22
search for self **66**: 1, 17
as Shakespeare's alter ego **66**: 1

Antonio
The Merchant of Venice
excessive or destructive love **4**: 279, 284, 336, 344; **12**: 54; **37**: 86
love for Bassanio **40**: 156; **66**: 63, 78, 127, 135
melancholy **4**: 221, 238, 279, 284, 300, 321, 328; **22**: 69; **25**: 22; **66**: 78, 127, 153
pitiless **4**: 254
as pivotal figure **12**: 25, 129; **66**: 91
as representative Christian **66**: 292
versus Shylock **53**: 187; **66**: 153, 180
Twelfth Night **22**: 69; **60**: 115

Antonio and Sebastian
The Tempest **8**: 295, 299, 304, 328, 370, 396, 429, 454; **13**: 440; **29**: 278, 297, 343, 362, 368, 377; **45**: 200; **60**: 129; **61**: 338

Antony
Antony and Cleopatra
characterization **6**: 22, 23, 24, 31, 38, 41, 172, 181, 211; **16**: 342; **19**: 270; **22**: 217; **27**: 117; **47**: 77, 124, 142; **58**: 2, 41, 118, 134
Caesar, relationship with **48**: 206
Cleopatra, relationship with **6**: 25, 27, 37, 39, 48, 52, 53, 62, 67, 71, 76, 85, 100, 125, 131, 133, 136, 142, 151, 161, 163, 165, 180, 192; **27**: 82; **47**: 107, 124, 165, 174
death scene **25**: 245; **47**: 142; **58**: 41; **60**: 46
dotage **6**: 22, 23, 38, 41, 48, 52, 62, 107, 136, 146, 175; **17**: 28
nobility **6**: 22, 24, 33, 48, 94, 103, 136, 142, 159, 172, 202; **25**: 245
political conduct **6**: 33, 38, 53, 107, 111, 146, 181
public vs. private personae **6**: 165; **47**: 107; **58**: 41; **65**: 270
self-knowledge **6**: 120, 131, 175, 181, 192; **47**: 77
as superhuman figure **6**: 37, 51, 71, 92, 94, 178, 192; **27**: 110; **47**: 71
as tragic hero **6**: 38, 39, 52, 53, 60, 104, 120, 151, 155, 165, 178, 192, 202, 211; **22**: 217; **27**: 90
Julius Caesar
characterization **7**: 160, 179, 189, 221, 233, 284, 320, 333; **17**: 269, 271, 272, 284, 298, 306, 313, 315, 358, 398; **25**: 272; **30**: 316
funeral oration **7**: 148, 154, 159, 204, 210, 221, 238, 259, 350; **25**: 280; **30**: 316, 333, 362

Apemantus
Timon of Athens **1**: 453, 467, 483; **20**: 476, 493; **25**: 198; **27**: 166, 223, 235

Arcite
The Two Noble Kinsmen See **Palamon and Arcite**

Ariel
The Tempest **8**: 289, 293, 294, 295, 297, 304, 307, 315, 320, 326, 328, 336, 340, 345, 356, 364, 420, 458; **22**: 302; **29**: 278, 297, 362, 368, 377

Armado
Love's Labour's Lost **23:** 207

Arthur
King John **9:** 215, 216, 218, 219, 229, 240, 267, 275; **22:** 120; **25:** 98; **41:** 251, 277; **56:** 345, 357

Arviragus
Cymbeline See **Guiderius and Arviragus**

Audrey
As You Like It **46:** 122

Aufidius
Coriolanus **9:** 9, 12, 17, 19, 53, 121, 148, 153, 157, 169, 180, 193; **19:** 287; **25:** 263, 296; **30:** 58, 67, 89, 96, 133; **50:** 99

Autolycus
The Winter's Tale **7:** 375, 380, 382, 387, 389, 395, 396, 414; **15:** 524; **22:** 302; **37:** 31; **45:** 333; **46:** 14, 33; **50:** 45

Banquo
Macbeth **3:** 183, 199, 208, 213, 278, 289; **20:** 279, 283, 406, 413; **25:** 235; **28:** 339

Baptista
The Taming of the Shrew **9:** 325, 344, 345, 375, 386, 393, 413; **55:** 334

Barnardine
Measure for Measure **13:** 112; **65:** 30

Bassanio
The Merchant of Venice **25:** 257; **37:** 86; **40:** 156; **66:** 63, 135

the Bastard
King John See **Faulconbridge (Philip) the Bastard**

Beatrice and Benedick
Much Ado about Nothing
 Beatrice's femininity **8:** 14, 16, 17, 24, 29, 38, 41, 91; **31:** 222, 245; **55:** 221
 Beatrice's request to "kill Claudio" (Act IV, scene i) **8:** 14, 17, 33, 41, 55, 63, 75, 79, 91, 108, 115; **18:** 119, 120, 136, 161, 245, 257; **55:** 268
 Benedick's challenge of Claudio (Act V, scene i) **8:** 48, 63, 79, 91; **31:** 231
 Claudio and Hero, compared with **8:** 19, 28, 29, 75, 82, 115; **31:** 171, 216; **55:** 189
 marriage and the opposite sex, attitudes toward **8:** 9, 13, 14, 16, 19, 29, 36, 48, 63, 77, 91, 95, 115, 121; **16:** 45; **31:** 216; **48:** 14
 mutual attraction **8:** 13, 14, 19, 24, 29, 33, 41, 75; **48:** 14
 nobility **8:** 13, 19, 24, 29, 36, 39, 41, 47, 82, 91, 108
 popularity **8:** 13, 38, 41, 53, 79
 transformed by love **8:** 19, 29, 36, 48, 75, 91, 95, 115; **31:** 209, 216; **55:** 236
 unconventionality **8:** 48, 91, 95, 108, 115, 121; **55:** 221, 249, 268
 vulgarity **8:** 11, 12, 33, 38, 41, 47

 wit and charm **8:** 9, 12, 13, 14, 19, 24, 27, 28, 29, 33, 36, 38, 41, 47, 55, 69, 95, 108, 115; **31:** 241; **55:** 199

Belarius
Cymbeline **4:** 48, 89, 141

Benedick
Much Ado about Nothing See **Beatrice and Benedick**

Berowne
Love's Labour's Lost **2:** 308, 324, 327; **22:** 12; **23:** 184, 187; **38:** 194; **47:** 35

Bertram
All's Well That Ends Well
 characterization **7:** 15, 27, 29, 32, 39, 41, 43, 98, 113; **26:** 48; **26:** 117; **48:** 65; **55:** 90
 conduct **7:** 9, 10, 12, 16, 19, 21, 51, 62, 104; **50:** 59; **55:** 143, 154
 physical desire **22:** 78
 transformation or redemption **7:** 10, 19, 21, 26, 29, 32, 54, 62, 81, 90, 93, 98, 109, 113, 116, 126; **13:** 84

Bianca
The Taming of the Shrew **9:** 325, 342, 344, 345, 360, 362, 370, 375
 Bianca-Lucentio subplot **9:** 365, 370, 375, 390, 393, 401, 407, 413, 430; **16:** 13; **31:** 339; **64:** 255

the boar
Venus and Adonis **10:** 416, 451, 454, 466, 473; **33:** 339, 347, 370

Boleyn (Anne Boleyn)
Henry VIII **2:** 21, 24, 31; **41:** 180; **61:** 119, 129

Bolingbroke
Richard II See **Henry (King Henry IV, previously known as Bolingbroke)**

Borachio and Conrade
Much Ado about Nothing **8:** 24, 69, 82, 88, 111, 115

Bottom
A Midsummer Night's Dream
 awakening speech (Act IV, scene i) **3:** 406, 412, 450, 457, 486, 516; **16:** 34; **58:** 181
 folly of **46:** 1, 14, 29, 60
 his dream **60:** 142
 imagination **3:** 376, 393, 406, 432, 486; **29:** 175, 190; **45:** 147
 self-possession **3:** 365, 376, 395, 402, 406, 480; **45:** 158
 Titania, relationship with **3:** 377, 406, 441, 445, 450, 457, 491, 497; **16:** 34; **19:** 21; **22:** 93; **29:** 216; **45:** 160; **58:** 203, 215
 transformation **3:** 365, 377, 432; **13:** 27; **22:** 93; **29:** 216; **45:** 147, 160

Brabantio
Othello **25:** 189

Brutus
Coriolanus See **the tribunes**
Julius Caesar **50:** 194, 258

 arrogance **7:** 160, 169, 204, 207, 264, 277, 292, 350; **25:** 280; **30:** 351
 as chief protagonist or tragic hero **7:** 152, 159, 189, 191, 200, 204, 242, 250, 253, 264, 268, 279, 284, 298, 333; **17:** 272, 372, 387
 citizenship **25:** 272
 funeral oration **7:** 154, 155, 204, 210, 350
 motives **7:** 150, 156, 161, 179, 191, 200, 221, 227, 233, 245, 292, 303, 310, 320, 333, 350; **25:** 272; **30:** 321, 358
 nobility or idealism **7:** 150, 152, 156, 159, 161, 179, 189, 191, 200, 221, 242, 250, 253, 259, 264, 277, 303, 320; **17:** 269, 271, 273, 279, 280, 284, 306, 308, 321, 323, 324, 345, 358; **25:** 272, 280; **30:** 351, 362
 political ineptitude or lack of judgment **7:** 169, 188, 200, 205, 221, 245, 252, 264, 277, 282, 310, 316, 331, 333, 343; **17:** 323, 358, 375, 380; **50:** 13
 self-knowledge or self-deception **7:** 191, 200, 221, 242, 259, 264, 268, 279, 310, 333, 336, 350; **25:** 272; **30:** 316; **60:** 46
 soliloquy (Act II, scene i) **7:** 156, 160, 161, 191, 221, 245, 250, 253, 264, 268, 279, 282, 292, 303, 343, 350; **25:** 280; **30:** 333
The Rape of Lucrece **10:** 96, 106, 109, 116, 121, 125, 128, 135

Buckingham
Henry VIII **22:** 182; **24:** 129, 140; **37:** 109

Bushy, Bagot, and Greene
Richard II **58:** 259

Cade (Jack [John] Cade)
Henry VI, Parts 1, 2, and 3 **3:** 35, 67, 92, 97, 109; **16:** 183; **22:** 156; **25:** 102; **28:** 112; **37:** 97; **39:** 160, 196, 205

Caesar
Antony and Cleopatra **65:** 270
 Antony, relationship with as leader **48:** 206
Julius Caesar **50:** 189, 230, 234
 ambiguous nature **7:** 191, 233, 242, 250, 272, 298, 316, 320
 ambitious nature **50:** 234
 arrogance **7:** 160, 207, 218, 253, 272, 279, 298; **25:** 280
 idolatry **22:** 137
 leadership qualities **7:** 161, 179, 189, 191, 200, 207, 233, 245, 253, 257, 264, 272, 279, 284, 298, 310, 333; **17:** 317, 358; **22:** 280; **30:** 316, 326; **50:** 234
 as tragic hero **7:** 152, 200, 221, 279; **17:** 321, 377, 384
 weakness **7:** 161, 167, 169, 179, 187, 188, 191, 207, 218, 221, 233, 250, 253, 298; **17:** 358; **25:** 280

Caius, Doctor
The Merry Wives of Windsor **47:** 354

Caliban
The Tempest **8:** 286, 287, 289, 292, 294, 295, 297, 302, 304, 307, 309, 315, 326, 328, 336, 353, 364, 370, 380, 390, 396, 401, 414, 420, 423, 429, 435, 454; **13:** 424, 440; **15:** 189, 312, 322, 374, 379; **22:** 302; **25:** 382; **28:** 249; **29:** 278, 292, 297, 343, 368, 377, 396; **32:** 367; **45:** 211, 219, 226, 259; **53:** 45, 64; **61:** 307, 356, 362

Calphurnia
  Julius Caesar
  Calphurnia's dream **45:** 10

Cambridge
  Henry V See **traitors**

Canterbury and the churchmen
  Henry V **5:** 193, 203, 205, 213, 219, 225, 252, 260; **22:** 137; **30:** 215, 262; **66:** 280

Capulet
  Romeo and Juliet **65:** 201

Cardinal Wolsey
  Henry VIII See **Wolsey**

Casca
  Julius Caesar
  as Cynic **50:** 249
  as proto-Christian **50:** 249

Cassio
  Othello **25:** 189

Cassius
  Julius Caesar **7:** 156, 159, 160, 161, 169, 179, 189, 221, 233, 303, 310, 320, 333, 343; **17:** 272, 282, 284, 344, 345, 358; **25:** 272, 280; **30:** 351; **37:** 203; **60:** 46

Celia
  As You Like It **46:** 94

the changeling
  A Midsummer's Night Dream **58:** 162, 167

Cerimon
  Pericles **66:** 236

Chorus
  Henry V
  role of **5:** 186, 192, 226, 228, 230, 252, 264, 269, 281, 293; **14:** 301, 319, 336; **19:** 133; **25:** 116, 131; **30:** 163, 202, 220

the churchmen
  Henry V See **Canterbury and the churchmen**

Cinna
  Julius Caesar
  as poet **48:** 240

Claudio
  Much Ado about Nothing
  boorish behavior **8:** 9, 24, 33, 36, 39, 44, 48, 63, 79, 82, 95, 100, 111, 115; **31:** 209
  credulity **8:** 9, 17, 19, 24, 29, 36, 41, 47, 58, 63, 75, 77, 82, 95, 100, 104, 111, 115, 121; **31:** 241; **47:** 25
  mercenary traits **8:** 24, 44, 58, 82, 91, 95
  noble qualities **8:** 17, 19, 29, 41, 44, 58, 75; **55:** 232
  reconciliation with Hero **8:** 33, 36, 39, 44, 47, 82, 95, 100, 111, 115, 121; **55:** 236
  repentance **8:** 33, 63, 82, 95, 100, 111, 115, 121; **31:** 245
  sexual insecurities **8:** 75, 100, 111, 115, 121
  Measure for Measure **60:** 12

Claudius
  Hamlet **13:** 502; **16:** 246; **21:** 259, 347, 361, 371; **28:** 232, 290; **35:** 104, 182; **44:** 119, 241; **59:** 62

Cleopatra
  Antony and Cleopatra
  Antony, relationship with **6:** 25, 27, 37, 39, 48, 52, 53, 62, 67, 71, 76, 85, 100, 125, 131, 133, 136, 142, 151, 161, 163, 165, 180, 192; **25:** 257; **27:** 82; **47:** 107, 124, 165, 174
  characterization **47:** 77, 96, 113, 124; **58:** 24, 33, 59, 118, 134
  contradictory or inconsistent nature **6:** 23, 24, 27, 67, 76, 100, 104, 115, 136, 151, 159, 202; **17:** 94, 113; **27:** 135
  costume **17:** 94
  creativity **6:** 197; **47:** 96, 113
  death **6:** 23, 25, 27, 41, 43, 52, 60, 64, 76, 94, 100, 103, 120, 131, 133, 136, 140, 146, 161, 165, 180, 181, 192, 197, 208; **13:** 383; **17:** 48, 94; **25:** 245; **27:** 135; **47:** 71; **60:** 46
  histrionic nature **65:** 270
  personal attraction of **6:** 24, 38, 40, 43, 48, 53, 76, 104, 115, 155; **17:** 113
  self-knowledge **47:** 77, 96
  staging issues **17:** 94, 113
  as subverter of social order **6:** 146, 165; **47:** 113
  suicide **58:** 33
  as superhuman figure **6:** 37, 51, 71, 92, 94, 178, 192; **27:** 110; **47:** 71, 174, 192; **58:** 24
  as tragic heroine **6:** 53, 120, 151, 192, 208; **27:** 144
  as voluptuary or courtesan **6:** 21, 22, 25, 41, 43, 52, 53, 62, 64, 67, 76, 146, 161; **47:** 107, 174; **58:** 24

Cloten
  Cymbeline **4:** 20, 116, 127, 155; **22:** 302, 365; **25:** 245; **36:** 99, 125, 142, 155; **47:** 228

Collatine
  The Rape of Lucrece **10:** 98, 131; **43:** 102; **48:** 291; **59:** 180

Cominius
  Coriolanus **25:** 245

Conrade
  Much Ado about Nothing See **Borachio and Conrade**

Constance
  King John **9:** 208, 210, 211, 215, 219, 220, 224, 229, 240, 251, 254; **16:** 161; **24:** 177, 184, 196

Cordelia
  King Lear
  attack on Britain **25:** 202
  characterization **2:** 110, 116, 125, 170; **16:** 311; **25:** 218; **28:** 223, 325; **31:** 117, 149, 155, 162; **46:** 218, 225, 231, 242; **61:** 220, 230
  as Christ figure **2:** 116, 170, 179, 188, 222, 286
  death of **60:** 2; **66:** 260
  gender identity **48:** 222
  rebelliousness **13:** 352; **25:** 202; **61:** 194
  on stage **11:** 158
  transcendent power **2:** 137, 207, 218, 265, 269, 273
  women, the Christian ideal of **48:** 222

Corin
  As You Like It See **pastoral characters**

Coriolanus
  Coriolanus
  ambition **64:** 40
  anger or passion **9:** 19, 26, 45, 80, 92, 157, 164, 177, 189; **30:** 79, 96
  as complementary figure to Aufidius **19:** 287
  death scene (Act V, scene vi) **9:** 12, 80, 100, 117, 125, 144, 164, 198; **25:** 245, 263; **50:** 110; **60:** 46
  as epic hero **9:** 130, 164, 177; **25:** 245; **50:** 119; **64:** 2
  immaturity **9:** 62, 80, 84, 110, 117, 142; **30:** 140
  inhuman attributes **9:** 65, 73, 139, 157, 164, 169, 189, 198; **25:** 263
  internal struggle **9:** 31, 43, 45, 53, 72, 117, 121, 130; **44:** 93; **64:** 62, 103
  introspection or self-knowledge, lack of **9:** 53, 80, 84, 112, 117, 130; **25:** 296; **30:** 133
  isolation or autonomy **9:** 53, 65, 142, 144, 153, 157, 164, 180, 183, 189, 198; **30:** 58, 89, 111; **50:** 128; **64:** 62
  manipulation by others **9:** 33, 45, 62, 80; **25:** 296
  as military leader **48:** 230
  modesty **9:** 8, 12, 19, 26, 53, 78, 92, 117, 121, 144, 183; **25:** 296; **30:** 79, 96, 129, 133, 149
  narcissism **30:** 111
  noble or aristocratic attributes **9:** 15, 18, 19, 26, 31, 33, 52, 53, 62, 65, 84, 92, 100, 121, 148, 157, 169; **25:** 263; **30:** 67, 74, 96; **50:** 13; **64:** 25
  pride or arrogance **9:** 8, 11, 12, 19, 26, 31, 33, 43, 45, 65, 78, 92, 121, 148, 153, 177; **30:** 58, 67, 74, 89, 96, 129
  punishment of **48:** 230
  reconciliation with society **9:** 33, 43, 45, 65, 139, 169; **25:** 296
  as socially destructive force **9:** 62, 65, 73, 78, 110, 142, 144, 153; **25:** 296
  soliloquy (Act IV, scene iv) **9:** 84, 112, 117, 130
  as tragic figure **9:** 8, 12, 13, 18, 25, 45, 52, 53, 72, 80, 92, 106, 112, 117, 130, 148, 164, 169, 177; **25:** 296; **30:** 67, 74, 79, 96, 111, 129; **37:** 283; **50:** 99; **64:** 25, 40, 79
  traitorous actions **9:** 9, 12, 19, 45, 84, 92, 148; **25:** 296; **30:** 133
  as unsympathetic character **9:** 12, 13, 62, 78, 80, 84, 112, 130, 157; **64:** 79

the courser and the jennet
  Venus and Adonis **10:** 418, 439, 466; **33:** 309, 339, 347, 352

Cranmer
  Henry VIII
  prophesy of **2:** 25, 31, 46, 56, 64, 68, 72; **24:** 146; **32:** 148; **41:** 120, 190; **56:** 196, 230, 248, 273

Cressida
  Troilus and Cressida
  as ambiguous figure **43:** 305

inconsistency **3:** 538; **13:** 53; **16:** 70; **22:** 339; **27:** 362
individual will vs. social values **3:** 549, 561, 571, 590, 604, 617, 626; **13:** 53; **27:** 396; **59:** 234, 272
infidelity **3:** 536, 537, 544, 554, 555; **18:** 277, 284, 286; **22:** 58, 339; **27:** 400; **43:** 298
lack of punishment **3:** 536, 537
as mother figure **22:** 339
objectification of **43:** 329; **59:** 323; **65:** 290
as sympathetic figure **3:** 557, 560, 604, 609; **18:** 284, 423; **22:** 58; **27:** 396, 400; **43:** 305; **59:** 234, 245
as a Trojan **59:** 257

Cymbeline
Cymbeline
    characterization **61:** 54

Dark Lady
Sonnets **10:** 161, 167, 176, 216, 217, 218, 226, 240, 302, 342, 377, 394; **25:** 374; **37:** 374; **40:** 273; **48:** 346; **51:** 284, 288, 292, 321; **62:** 121

the Dauphin
Henry V See **French aristocrats and the Dauphin**

Desdemona
Othello
    as Christ figure **4:** 506, 525, 573; **35:** 360
    culpability **4:** 408, 415, 422, 427; **13:** 313; **19:** 253, 276; **35:** 265, 352, 380
    innocence **35:** 360; **43:** 32; **47:** 25; **53:** 310, 333
    as mother figure **22:** 339; **35:** 282; **53:** 324
    passivity **4:** 402, 406, 421, 440, 457, 470, 582, 587; **25:** 189; **35:** 380
    spiritual nature of her love **4:** 462, 530, 559
    staging issues **11:** 350, 354, 359; **13:** 327; **32:** 201

Diana
Pericles
    as symbol of nature **22:** 315; **36:** 233; **51:** 71; **66:** 236

Dogberry and the Watch
Much Ado about Nothing **8:** 9, 12, 13, 17, 24, 28, 29, 33, 39, 48, 55, 69, 79, 82, 88, 95, 104, 108, 115; **18:** 138, 152, 205, 208, 210, 213, 231; **22:** 85; **31:** 171, 229; **46:** 60; **55:** 189, 241

Don John
Much Ado about Nothing See **John (Don John)**

Don Pedro
Much Ado about Nothing See **Pedro (Don Pedro)**

Dromio Brothers
Comedy of Errors **42:** 80; **54:** 136, 152; **66:** 1

Duke
Measure for Measure
    as authoritarian figure **23:** 314, 317, 347; **33:** 85; **49:** 274, 300, 358; **65:** 19, 30, 45, 80, 100
    characterization **2:** 388, 395, 402, 406, 411, 421, 429, 456, 466, 470, 498, 511; **13:** 84, 94, 104; **23:** 363, 416; **32:** 81; **42:** 1; **44:** 89; **49:** 274, 293, 300, 358; **60:** 12; **65:** 30
    as dramatic failure **2:** 420, 429, 441, 479, 495, 505, 514, 522
    godlike portrayal of **23:** 320; **65:** 14, 91
    noble portrayal of **23:** 301; **65:** 53
    speech on death (Act III, scene i) **2:** 390, 391, 395
    as spiritual guide **66:** 300
Othello **25:** 189

Duncan
Macbeth **57:** 194, 236

Edgar
King Lear **28:** 223; **32:** 212; **32:** 308; **37:** 295; **47:** 9; **50:** 24, 45
Edgar-Edmund duel **22:** 365

Edmund
King Lear **25:** 218; **28:** 223
Edmund's forged letter **16:** 372

Edmund of Langley, Duke of York
Richard II See **York**

Elbow
Measure for Measure **22:** 85; **25:** 12

Elbow (Mistress Elbow)
Measure for Measure **33:** 90

elder characters
All's Well That Ends Well **7:** 9, 37, 39, 43, 45, 54, 62, 104

Elizabeth I
Love's Labour's Lost **38:** 239; **64:** 166, 179

Emilia
Othello **4:** 386, 391, 392, 415, 587; **35:** 352, 380; **43:** 32
The Two Noble Kinsmen **9:** 460, 470, 471, 479, 481; **19:** 394; **41:** 372, 385; **42:** 361; **58:** 322, 338, 345, 356, 361

Enobarbus
Antony and Cleopatra **6:** 22, 23, 27, 43, 94, 120, 142; **16:** 342; **17:** 36; **22:** 217; **27:** 135

Evans, Sir Hugh
The Merry Wives of Windsor **47:** 354

fairies
A Midsummer Night's Dream **3:** 361, 362, 372, 377, 395, 400, 423, 450, 459, 486; **12:** 287, 291, 294, 295; **19:** 21; **29:** 183, 190; **45:** 147

Falstaff
Henry IV, Parts 1 and 2
    characterization **1:** 287, 298, 312, 333; **25:** 245; **28:** 203; **39:** 72, 134, 137, 143; **48:** 117, 151; **57:** 120, 156
    as comic figure **1:** 287, 311, 327, 344, 351, 354, 357, 410, 434; **39:** 89; **46:** 1, 48, 52; **57:** 120
    as comic versus tragic figure **49:** 178
    as coward or rogue **1:** 285, 290, 296, 298, 306, 307, 313, 317, 323, 336, 337, 338, 342, 354, 366, 374, 391, 396, 401, 433; **14:** 7, 111, 125, 130, 133; **32:** 166
    as deceiver deceived **47:** 308
    diminishing powers of **47:** 363
    dual personality **1:** 397, 401, 406, 434; **49:** 162
    female attributes **13:** 183; **44:** 44; **47:** 325; **60:** 154
    Iago, compared with **1:** 341, 351
    as Jack-a-Lent **47:** 363
    Marxist interpretation **1:** 358, 361
    moral reformation **60:** 26
    as outlaw **49:** 133
    as parody of the historical plot **1:** 314, 354, 359; **39:** 143
    as positive character **1:** 286, 287, 290, 296, 298, 311, 312, 321, 325, 333, 344, 355, 357, 389, 401, 408, 434
    rejection by Hal **1:** 286, 287, 290, 312, 314, 317, 324, 333, 338, 344, 357, 366, 372, 374, 379, 380, 389, 414; **13:** 183; **25:** 109; **39:** 72, 89; **48:** 95; **57:** 147; **66:** 256
    as satire of feudal society **1:** 314, 328, 361; **32:** 103
    as scapegoat **1:** 389, 414; **47:** 358, 363, 375; **57:** 156
    stage interpretations **14:** 4, 6, 7, 9, 15, 116, 130, 146; **47:** 1
    as subversive figure **16:** 183; **25:** 109
Henry V **5:** 185, 186, 187, 189, 192, 195, 198, 210, 226, 257, 269, 271, 276, 293, 299; **28:** 146; **46:** 48; **60:** 26
The Merry Wives of Windsor
    characterization in 1 and 2 Henry IV, compared with **5:** 333, 335, 336, 337, 339, 346, 347, 348, 350, 373, 400; **18:** 5, 7, 75, 86; **22:** 93
    diminishing powers **5:** 337, 339, 343, 347, 350, 351, 392
    as Herne the Hunter **38:** 256, 286; **47:** 358
    incapability of love **5:** 335, 336, 339, 346, 348; **22:** 93
    personification of comic principle or as Vice figure **1:** 342, 361, 366, 374; **5:** 332, 338, 369, 400; **38:** 273
    recognition and repentance of follies **5:** 338, 341, 343, 348, 369, 374, 376, 397
    sensuality **5:** 339, 343, 353, 369, 392
    shrewdness **5:** 332, 336, 346, 355
    threat to community **5:** 343, 369, 379, 392, 395, 400; **38:** 297
    as unifying force **47:** 358
    vanity **5:** 332, 339
    victimization **5:** 336, 338, 341, 347, 348, 353, 355, 360, 369, 373, 374, 376, 392, 397, 400; **59:** 144
    as villain **47:** 358

Faulconbridge, (Philip) the Bastard
King John **41:** 205, 228, 251, 260, 277; **48:** 132; **56:** 306
    as chorus or commentator **9:** 212, 218, 229, 248, 251, 260, 271, 284, 297, 300; **22:** 120
    as comic figure **9:** 219, 271, 297; **56:** 365
    development **9:** 216, 224, 229, 248, 263, 271, 275, 280, 297; **13:** 158, 163; **56:** 335
    as embodiment of England **9:** 222, 224, 240, 244, 248, 271
    heroic qualities **9:** 208, 245, 248, 254, 263, 271, 275; **25:** 98; **56:** 348
    political conduct **9:** 224, 240, 250, 260, 280, 297; **13:** 147, 158; **22:** 120; **56:** 314

Fenton
The Merry Wives of Windsor
    Anne Page-Fenton plot **5**: 334, 336, 343, 353, 376, 390, 395, 402; **22**: 93

Ferdinand
The Tempest **8**: 328, 336, 359, 454; **19**: 357; **22**: 302; **29**: 362, 339, 377

Feste
Twelfth Night
    characterization **1**: 558, 655, 658; **26**: 233, 364; **46**: 1, 14, 18, 33, 52, 60, 303, 310
    role in play **1**: 546, 551, 553, 566, 570, 571, 579, 635, 658; **46**: 297, 303, 310
    song **1**: 543, 548, 561, 563, 566, 570, 572, 603, 620, 642; **46**: 297
    gender issues **19**: 78; **34**: 344; **37**: 59

Flavius and Murellus
Julius Caesar **50**: 64

Fluellen
Henry V **30**: 278; **37**: 105

Fool
King Lear **2**: 108, 112, 125, 156, 162, 245, 278, 284; **11**: 17, 158, 169; **22**: 227; **25**: 202; **28**: 223; **46**: 1, 14, 18, 24, 33, 52, 191, 205, 210, 218, 225; **61**: 176

Ford, Francis
The Merry Wives of Windsor **5**: 332, 334, 343, 355, 363, 374, 379, 390; **38**: 273; **47**: 321

Ford, Mistress Alice
The Merry Wives of Windsor **47**: 321

Fortinbras
Hamlet **21**: 136, 347; **28**: 290

French aristocrats and the Dauphin
Henry V **5**: 188, 191, 199, 205, 213, 281; **22**: 137; **28**: 121

Friar
Much Ado about Nothing **8**: 24, 29, 41, 55, 63, 79, 111; **55**: 249

Friar John
Romeo and Juliet See **John (Friar John)**

Friar Lawrence
Romeo and Juliet See **Lawrence (Friar Lawrence)**

the Friend
Sonnets **10**: 279, 302, 309, 379, 385, 391, 394; **51**: 284, 292, 300, 304, 316, 321; **62**: 121; **65**: 259, 345

Ganymede
The Winter's Tale **48**: 309

Gardiner (Stephen Gardiner)
Henry VIII **24**: 129

Gaunt
Richard II **6**: 255, 287, 374, 388, 402, 414; **24**: 274, 322, 325, 414, 423; **37**: 222; **52**: 174, 183

Gertrude
Hamlet **21**: 259, 347, 392; **28**: 311; **32**: 238; **35**: 182, 204, 229; **43**: 12; **44**: 119, 160, 189, 195, 237, 247; **59**: 39, 62, 74
    death monologue **48**: 255

Ghost
Hamlet **1**: 75, 76, 84, 85, 128, 134, 138, 154, 171, 218, 231, 254; **16**: 246; **21**: 17, 44, 112, 151, 334, 371, 377, 392; **25**: 288; **35**: 152, 157, 174, 237; **44**: 119; **59**: 2, 10

Gloucester
King Lear **46**: 254

Gobbo, Launcelot
The Merchant of Venice **46**: 24, 60; **53**: 187, 214; **66**: 158

Goneril
King Lear **31**: 151; **46**: 231, 242; **61**: 160

Gonzalo
The Tempest **22**: 302; **29**: 278, 343, 362, 368; **45**: 280

Gower chorus
Pericles **2**: 548, 575; **15**: 134, 141, 143, 145, 149, 152, 177; **36**: 279; **42**: 352; **66**: 208

Grey
Henry V See **traitors**

Guiderius and Arviragus
Cymbeline **4**: 21, 22, 89, 129, 141, 148; **25**: 319; **36**: 125, 158

Hal
Henry IV, Parts 1 and 2; Henry V See **Henry (King Henry V, formerly known as Prince Henry [Hal] of Wales)**

Hamlet
Hamlet
    as a fool **46**: 1, 29, 52, 74
    compared to Vindice **59**: 10
    death of **60**: 96
    delay **1**: 76, 83, 88, 90, 94, 98, 102, 103, 106, 114, 115, 116, 119, 120, 148, 151, 166, 171, 179, 188, 191, 194, 198, 221, 268; **13**: 296, 502; **21**: 81; **25**: 209, 288; **28**: 223; **35**: 82, 174, 212, 215, 237; **44**: 180, 209, 219, 229; **59**: 10
    divided nature **16**: 246; **28**: 223; **32**: 288; **35**: 182, 215; **37**: 241; **59**: 2
    elocution of the character's speeches **21**: 96, 104, 112, 127, 132, 172, 177, 179, 194, 245, 254, 257
    and identity (nature of) **59**: 18
    madness **1**: 76, 81, 83, 95, 102, 106, 128, 144, 154, 160, 234; **21**: 35, 50, 72, 81, 99, 112, 311, 339, 355, 361, 371, 377, 384; **35**: 117, 132, 134, 140, 144, 212; **44**: 107, 119, 152, 209, 219, 229
    meeting with the pirates (Act IV, scene vi) **59**: 56
    melancholy **21**: 99, 112, 177, 194; **35**: 82, 95, 117; **44**: 209, 219
    as negative character **1**: 86, 92, 111, 171, 218; **21**: 386; **25**: 209; **35**: 167; **59**: 10
    reaction to his father's death **22**: 339; **35**: 104, 174; **44**: 133, 160, 180, 189
    reaction to Gertrude's marriage **1**: 74, 120, 154, 179; **16**: 259; **21**: 371; **22**: 339; **35**: 104, 117; **44**: 133, 160, 189, 195
    religion **48**: 195
    romantic aspects of the character **21**: 96; **44**: 198; **59**: 47
    as scourge or purifying figure **1**: 144, 209, 242; **25**: 288; **35**: 157; **59**: 26, 62, 79; **66**: 305
    sentimentality vs. intellectuality **1**: 75, 83, 88, 91, 93, 94, 96, 102, 103, 115, 116, 120, 166, 191; **13**: 296; **21**: 35, 41, 44, 72, 81, 89, 99, 129, 132, 136, 172, 213, 225, 339, 355, 361, 371, 377, 379, 381, 386; **25**: 209; **44**: 198
    soliloquies **1**: 76, 82, 83, 148, 166, 169, 176, 191; **21**: 17, 31, 44, 53, 89, 112, 268, 311, 334, 347, 361, 384, 392; **25**: 209; **28**: 223; **44**: 107, 119, 229
    as a stoic at the end **54**: 96; **66**: 266
    theatrical interpretations **21**: 11, 31, 78, 101, 104, 107, 160, 177, 179, 182, 183, 192, 194, 197, 202, 203, 208, 213, 225, 232, 237, 249, 253, 254, 257, 259, 274, 311, 339, 347, 355, 361, 371, 377, 380; **44**: 198
    virility **21**: 213, 301, 355

Hector
Troilus and Cressida
    combat with Ajax **59**: 251
    as a Trojan **59**: 257

Helena
All's Well That Ends Well
    as agent of reconciliation, renewal, or grace **7**: 67, 76, 81, 90, 93, 98, 109, 116; **55**: 176; **66**: 335
    as dualistic or enigmatic character **7**: 15, 27, 29, 39, 54, 58, 62, 67, 76, 81, 98, 113, 126; **13**: 66; **22**: 78; **26**: 117; **48**: 65; **54**: 30; **55**: 90, 170, 176
    desire **38**: 96; **44**: 35; **55**: 109, 170
    as "female achiever" **19**: 113; **38**: 89; **55**: 90, 101, 109, 122, 164
    pursuit of Bertram **7**: 9, 12, 15, 16, 19, 21, 26, 27, 29, 32, 43, 54, 76, 116; **13**: 77; **22**: 78; **49**: 46; **55**: 90
    virginity **38**: 65; **55**: 131, 176
    virtue and nobility **7**: 9, 10, 12, 16, 19, 21, 27, 32, 41, 51, 58, 67, 76, 86, 126; **13**: 77; **50**: 59; **55**: 122
A Midsummer Night's Dream **29**: 269; **58**: 194;
    relationship with Hermia **60**: 142

Henry (King Henry IV, previously known as Bolingbroke)
Henry IV, Parts 1 and 2 **39**: 123, 137
    effectiveness as ruler **49**: 116
    guilt **49**: 112
    historical context **49**: 139
    illegitimacy of rule **49**: 112, 133, 137
    power **49**: 139
    as tragic figure **49**: 186
    as usurper **49**: 116, 137
Richard II
    Bolingbroke and Richard as opposites **24**: 423
    Bolingbroke-Mowbray dispute **22**: 137
    comic elements **28**: 134
    guilt **24**: 423; **39**: 279

language and imagery **6:** 310, 315, 331, 347, 374, 381, 397; **32:** 189; **58:** 301
as Machiavellian figure **6:** 305, 307, 315, 331, 347, 388, 393, 397; **24:** 428
as politician **6:** 255, 263, 264, 272, 277, 294, 364, 368, 391; **24:** 330, 333, 405, 414, 423, 428; **39:** 256; **52:** 124
Richard, compared with **6:** 307, 315, 347, 374, 391, 393, 409; **24:** 346, 349, 351, 352, 356, 395, 419, 423, 428; **52:** 108, 124; **58:** 241
seizure of Gaunt's estate **49:** 60
his silence **24:** 423
structure, compared with **39:** 235
usurpation of crown, nature of **6:** 255, 272, 289, 307, 310, 347, 354, 359, 381, 385, 393; **13:** 172; **24:** 322, 356, 383, 419; **28:** 178; **52:** 108, 124

Henry (King Henry V, formerly known as Prince Henry [Hal] of Wales)
Henry IV, Parts 1 and 2
and betrayal **49:** 123
as the central character **1:** 286, 290, 314, 317, 326, 338, 354, 366, 374, 396; **39:** 72, 100
compared with the fair friend of the sonnets **60:** 154
dual personality **1:** 397, 406; **25:** 109, 151; **48:** 95; **49:** 112, 139, 153, 162; **57:** 130
as Everyman **1:** 342, 366, 374
from audience's perspective **49:** 153; **57:** 116
from Henry's perspective **49:** 153
fall from humanity **1:** 379, 380, 383
general assessment **1:** 286, 287, 289, 290, 314, 317, 326, 327, 332, 357, 397; **25:** 245; **32:** 212; **39:** 134; **48:** 151; **57:** 116, 130; **65:** 306
as ideal ruler **1:** 289, 309, 317, 321, 326, 337, 342, 344, 374, 389, 391, 434; **25:** 109; **39:** 123; **47:** 60; **60:** 154
as Machiavellian ruler **47:** 60
as negative character **1:** 312, 332, 333, 357; **32:** 212
as outlaw **49:** 112
piety **66:** 280
preparation for rule **49:** 112; **57:** 116, 130
reformation **57:** 160
as restorer of law **49:** 133
Richard II, compared with **1:** 332, 337; **39:** 72
Henry V
brutality and cunning **5:** 193, 203, 209, 210, 213, 219, 233, 239, 252, 260, 271, 287, 293, 302, 304; **30:** 159; **43:** 24
characterization in 1 and 2 Henry IV contrasted **5:** 189, 190, 241, 304, 310; **19:** 133; **25:** 131; **32:** 157
chivalry **37:** 187
courage **5:** 191, 195, 210, 213, 228, 246, 257, 267
disguise **30:** 169, 259
education **5:** 246, 267, 271, 289; **14:** 297, 328, 342; **30:** 259
emotion, lack of **5:** 209, 212, 233, 244, 264, 267, 287, 293, 310
as heroic figure **5:** 192, 205, 209, 223, 244, 252, 257, 260, 269, 271, 299, 304; **28:** 121, 146; **30:** 237, 244, 252; **37:** 187; **49:** 194, 200, 236, 247
humor **5:** 189, 191, 212, 217, 239, 240, 276
intellectual and social limitations **5:** 189, 191, 203, 209, 210, 225, 226, 230, 293; **30:** 220
interpersonal relations **5:** 209, 233, 267, 269, 276, 287, 293, 302, 318; **19:** 133; **28:** 146

mercy **5:** 213, 267, 289, 293
mixture of good and bad qualities **5:** 199, 205, 209, 210, 213, 244, 260, 304, 314; **30:** 262, 273; **49:** 211
piety **5:** 191, 199, 209, 217, 223, 239, 257, 260, 271, 289, 310, 318; **30:** 244; **32:** 126
public vs. private selves **22:** 137; **30:** 169, 207
self-doubt **5:** 281, 310
slaughter of prisoners **5:** 189, 205, 246, 293, 318; **28:** 146
speech **5:** 212, 230, 233, 246, 264, 276, 287, 302; **28:** 146; **30:** 163, 227

Henry (King Henry VI)
Henry VI, Parts 1, 2, and 3
characterization **3:** 64, 77, 151; **39:** 160, 177; **47:** 32
source of social disorder **3:** 25, 31, 41, 115; **39:** 154, 187
as sympathetic figure **3:** 73, 143, 154; **24:** 32

Henry (King Henry VIII)
Henry VIII
as agent of divine retribution **2:** 49
characterization **2:** 23, 39, 51, 58, 60, 65, 66, 75; **28:** 184; **37:** 109; **56:** 242; **61:** 119, 136
incomplete portrait **2:** 15, 16, 19, 35; **41:** 120; **56:** 209
as realistic figure **2:** 21, 22, 23, 25, 32

Henry (Prince Henry)
King John **41:** 277; **56:** 348

Hermia
A Midsummer Night's Dream **29:** 225, 269; **45:** 117; **58:** 194
relationship with Helena **60:** 142

Hermione
The Winter's Tale
characterization **7:** 385, 395, 402, 412, 414, 506; **15:** 495, 532; **22:** 302, 324; **25:** 347; **32:** 388; **36:** 311; **47:** 25; **49:** 18; **57:** 319
restoration (Act V, scene iii) **7:** 377, 379, 384, 385, 387, 389, 394, 396, 412, 425, 436, 451, 452, 456, 464, 483, 501; **15:** 411, 412, 413, 518, 528, 532; **49:** 18; **57:** 294, 367; **60:** 2, 40
sex as identity **48:** 309
supposed death **25:** 339; **47:** 25
trial of **49:** 18

Hero
Much Ado about Nothing **8:** 13, 14, 16, 19, 28, 29, 44, 48, 53, 55, 82, 95, 104, 111, 115, 121; **31:** 231, 245; **47:** 25; **55:** 209

Hippolyta
A Midsummer Night's Dream **48:** 23

Holofernes
Love's Labour's Lost **23:** 207

Horatio
Hamlet **44:** 189
stoic perfection, example of **48:** 195

Hostess
Henry IV, Parts 1 and 2 **60:** 26

Hotspur
Henry IV, Parts 1 and 2 **25:** 151; **28:** 101; **39:** 72, 134, 137; **42:** 99; **60:** 154
and prisoners of war **49:** 137
versus Henry **49:** 137
Henry V **5:** 189, 199, 228, 271, 302

Humphrey
Henry VI, Parts 1, 2, and 3 **13:** 131; **56:** 187

Iachimo
Cymbeline **25:** 245, 319; **36:** 166; **47:** 274

Iago
Othello
affinity with Othello **4:** 400, 427, 468, 470, 477, 500, 506; **25:** 189; **44:** 57
as conventional dramatic villain **4:** 440, 527, 545, 582; **53:** 238
as homosexual **4:** 503; **53:** 275
Machiavellian elements **4:** 440, 455, 457, 517, 545; **35:** 336, 347; **65:** 327
motives **4:** 389, 390, 397, 399, 402, 409, 423, 424, 427, 434, 451, 462, 545, 564; **13:** 304; **25:** 189; **28:** 344; **32:** 201; **35:** 265, 276, 310, 336, 347; **42:** 273; **53:** 246, 275, 324
revenge scheme **4:** 392, 409, 424, 451; **65:** 327
as scapegoat **4:** 506
as victim **4:** 402, 409, 434, 451, 457, 470

Imogen
Cymbeline **4:** 21, 22, 24, 29, 37, 45, 46, 52, 56, 78, 89, 108; **15:** 23, 32, 105, 121; **19:** 411; **25:** 245, 319; **28:** 398; **32:** 373; **36:** 129, 142, 148; **47:** 25, 205, 228, 245, 274, 277; **61:** 34, 45, 76
reawakening of (Act IV, scene ii) **4:** 37, 56, 89, 103, 108, 116, 150; **15:** 23; **25:** 245; **47:** 252

Isabella
Measure for Measure **2:** 388, 390, 395, 396, 397, 401, 402, 406, 409, 410, 411, 418, 420, 421, 432, 437, 441, 466, 475, 491, 495, 524; **16:** 114; **23:** 278, 279, 280, 281, 282, 296, 344, 357, 363, 405; **28:** 102; **33:** 77, 85; **60:** 12; **65:** 28, 53, 72, 100

Jack [John] Cade
Henry VI, Parts 1, 2, and 3 See **Cade**

the jailer's daughter
The Two Noble Kinsmen **9:** 457, 460, 479, 481, 486, 502; **41:** 340; **50:** 295, 305, 310, 348, 361; **58:** 338, 371

Jaques
As You Like It
love-theme, relation to **5:** 103; **23:** 7, 37, 118, 128
as malcontent **5:** 59, 70, 84
melancholy **5:** 20, 28, 32, 36, 39, 43, 50, 59, 63, 68, 77, 82, 86, 135; **23:** 20, 26, 103, 104, 107, 109; **34:** 85; **46:** 88, 94; **57:** 31
pastoral convention, relation to **5:** 61, 63, 65, 79, 93, 98, 114, 118
Seven Ages of Man speech (Act II, scene vii) **5:** 28, 52, 156; **23:** 48, 103, 105, 126, 138, 152; **46:** 88, 156, 164, 169
Shakespeare, relation to **5:** 35, 50, 154; **48:** 42

as superficial critic **5:** 28, 30, 43, 54, 55, 63, 65, 68, 75, 77, 82, 86, 88, 98, 138; **34:** 85

the jennet
Venus and Adonis See **the courser and the jennet**

Jessica
The Merchant of Venice **4:** 196, 200, 228, 293, 342; **48:** 54, 77; **53:** 159, 211; **66:** 171

Joan of Arc
Henry VI, Parts 1, 2, and 3 **16:** 131; **32:** 212; **60:** 33

John (Don John)
Much Ado about Nothing **8:** 9, 12, 16, 17, 19, 28, 29, 36, 39, 41, 47, 48, 55, 58, 63, 82, 104, 108, 111, 121

John (Friar John)
Romeo and Juliet
  detention of **5:** 448, 467, 470

John (King John)
King John **41:** 205, 260
  death **9:** 212, 215, 216, 240; **56:** 345
  decline **9:** 224, 235, 240, 263, 275
  Hubert, scene with (Act III, scene iii) **9:** 210, 212, 216, 218, 219, 280
  moral insensibility **13:** 147, 163
  negative qualities **9:** 209, 212, 218, 219, 229, 234, 235, 244, 245, 246, 250, 254, 275, 280, 297; **56:** 325
  positive qualities **9:** 209, 224, 235, 240, 244, 245, 263

John of Lancaster, Prince
Henry IV **49:** 123
  and betrayal **49:** 123

Julia
The Two Gentlemen of Verona **6:** 450, 453, 458, 476, 494, 499, 516, 519, 549, 564; **40:** 312, 327, 374; **54:** 325, 332

Juliet
Romeo and Juliet See **Romeo and Juliet**

Launcelot Gobbo
The Merchant of Venice See **Gobbo**

Kate
The Taming of the Shrew
  characterization **32:** 1; **43:** 61; **64:** 244, 296, 343, 352
  final speech (Act V, scene ii) **9:** 318, 319, 329, 330, 338, 340, 341, 345, 347, 353, 355, 360, 365, 381, 386, 401, 404, 413, 426, 430; **19:** 3; **22:** 48; **54:** 65; **55:** 299, 331; **64:** 296
  love for Petruchio **9:** 338, 340, 353, 430; **12:** 435; **55:** 294
  portrayals of **31:** 282
  shrewishness **9:** 322, 323, 325, 332, 344, 345, 360, 365, 370, 375, 386, 393, 398, 404, 413; **64:** 283
  transformation **9:** 323, 341, 355, 370, 386, 393, 401, 404, 407, 419, 424, 426, 430; **16:** 13; **19:** 34; **22:** 48; **31:** 288, 295, 339, 351; **55:** 294, 315; **64:** 233, 244, 273, 283, 320

Katherine
Henry V **5:** 186, 188, 189, 190, 192, 260, 269, 299, 302; **13:** 183; **19:** 217; **30:** 278; **44:** 44
Henry VIII
  characterization **2:** 18, 19, 23, 24, 38; **24:** 129; **37:** 109; **41:** 180; **61:** 119, 136
  Hermione, compared with **2:** 24, 51, 58, 76
  politeness strategies **22:** 182; **56:** 262
  religious discourse **22:** 182
  as tragic figure **2:** 16, 18

Kent
King Lear **25:** 202; **28:** 223; **32:** 212; **47:** 9

King
All's Well That Ends Well **38:** 150; **55:** 148

King Richard II
Richard II See **Richard**

King Richard III, formerly Richard, Duke of Gloucester
Richard III See **Richard**

Lady Macbeth
Macbeth See **Macbeth (Lady Macbeth)**

Laertes
Hamlet **21:** 347, 386; **28:** 290; **35:** 182; **59:** 26

Launce and Speed
The Two Gentlemen of Verona
  comic function of **6:** 438, 439, 442, 456, 458, 460, 462, 472, 476, 478, 484, 502, 504, 507, 509, 516, 519, 549; **40:** 312, 320

Lavatch
All's Well That Ends Well **26:** 64; **46:** 33, 52, 68; **55:** 143

Lavinia
Titus Andronicus **27:** 266; **28:** 249; **32:** 212; **43:** 1, 170, 239, 247, 255, 262; **62:** 225, 233, 242

Lawrence (Friar Lawrence)
Romeo and Juliet
  contribution to catastrophe **5:** 437, 444, 470; **33:** 300; **51:** 253; **60:** 96
  philosophy of moderation **5:** 427, 431, 437, 438, 443, 444, 445, 458, 467, 479, 505, 538
  as Shakespeare's spokesman **5:** 427, 431, 437, 458, 467

Lear
King Lear **61:** 176
  curse on Goneril **11:** 5, 7, 12, 114, 116
  death of **60:** 2; **66:** 260
  love-test and division of kingdom **2:** 100, 106, 111, 124, 131, 137, 147, 149, 151, 168, 186, 208, 216, 281; **16:** 351; **25:** 202; **31:** 84, 92, 107, 117, 149, 155; **46:** 231, 242; **61:** 194
  madness **2:** 94, 95, 98, 99, 100, 101, 102, 103, 111, 116, 120, 124, 125, 149, 156, 191, 208, 216, 281; **46:** 264
  as scapegoat **2:** 241, 253
  self-knowledge **2:** 103, 151, 188, 191, 213, 218, 222, 241, 249, 262; **25:** 218; **37:** 213; **46:** 191, 205, 225, 254, 264; **54:** 103; **60:** 65, 75; **61:** 215, 220, 250
  spiritual regeneration **54:** 103; **60:** 65, 75

Leontes
The Winter's Tale
  characterization **19:** 431; **43:** 39; **45:** 366
  jealousy **7:** 377, 379, 382, 383, 384, 387, 389, 394, 395, 402, 407, 412, 414, 425, 429, 432, 436, 464, 480, 483, 497; **15:** 514, 518, 532; **22:** 324; **25:** 339; **36:** 334, 344, 349; **44:** 66; **45:** 295, 297, 344, 358; **47:** 25; **57:** 294
  Othello, compared with **7:** 383, 390, 412; **15:** 514; **36:** 334; **44:** 66; **47:** 25
  repentance **7:** 381, 389, 394, 396, 402, 414, 497; **36:** 318, 362; **44:** 66; **57:** 294

Lord Chief Justice
Henry IV
  as keeper of law and justice **49:** 133

Lorenzo
The Merchant of Venice **66:** 171

the lovers
A Midsummer's Night Dream **58:** 151, 169

Lucentio
The Taming of the Shrew **9:** 325, 342, 362, 375, 393

Lucio
Measure for Measure **13:** 104; **49:** 379; **65:** 19

Lucrece
The Rape of Lucrece
  chastity **33:** 131, 138; **43:** 92
  as example of Renaissance virtù **22:** 289; **43:** 148
  heroic **10:** 84, 93, 109, 121, 128; **59:** 175, 193
  patriarchal woman, model of **10:** 109, 131; **33:** 169, 200
  Philomela **59:** 193
  self-perception **48:** 291
  self-responsibility **10:** 89, 96, 98, 106, 125; **33:** 195; **43:** 85, 92, 158; **59:** 206
  unrealistic **10:** 64, 65, 66, 121
  verbose **10:** 64, 81, 116; **25:** 305; **33:** 169
  as victim **22:** 294; **25:** 305; **32:** 321; **33:** 131, 195; **43:** 102, 158; **59:** 175, 180, 189, 193, 206

Macbeth
Macbeth
  ambition **44:** 284, 324; **57:** 256; **65:** 317
  characterization **20:** 20, 42, 73, 107, 113, 130, 146, 151, 279, 283, 312, 338, 343, 379, 406, 413; **29:** 139, 152, 155, 165; **44:** 289; **57:** 189, 194, 236, 263, 267
  courage **3:** 172, 177, 181, 182, 183, 186, 234, 312, 333; **20:** 107; **44:** 315
  despair **65:** 297
  disposition **3:** 173, 175, 177, 182, 186; **20:** 245, 376
  imagination **3:** 196, 208, 213, 250, 312, 345; **20:** 245, 376; **44:** 351; **65:** 226
  as "inauthentic" king **3:** 245, 302, 321, 345
  inconsistencies **3:** 202
  as Machiavellian villain **3:** 280; **57:** 236
  manliness **20:** 113; **29:** 127, 133; **44:** 315; **57:** 256

psychoanalytic interpretations **20**: 42, 73, 238, 376; **44**: 284, 289, 297, 324; **45**: 48, 58; **57**: 267
Richard III, compared with **3**: 177, 182, 186, 345; **20**: 86, 92; **22**: 365; **44**: 269
as Satan figure **3**: 229, 269, 275, 289, 318
self-awareness **3**: 312, 329, 338; **16**: 317; **44**: 361; **57**: 256; **60**: 46
as sympathetic figure **3**: 229, 306, 314, 338; **29**: 139, 152; **44**: 269, 306, 337
as tragic hero **44**: 269, 306, 315, 324, 337; **57**: 267

Macbeth (Lady Macbeth)
Macbeth
ambition **3**: 185, 219; **20**: 279, 345
characterization **20**: 56, 60, 65, 73, 140, 148, 151, 241, 279, 283, 338, 350, 406, 413; **29**: 109, 146; **57**: 256, 263
childlessness **3**: 219, 223; **48**: 214
good and evil, combined traits of **3**: 173, 191, 213; **20**: 60, 107
inconsistencies **3**: 202; **20**: 54, 137
influence on Macbeth **3**: 171, 185, 191, 193, 199, 262, 289, 312, 318; **13**: 502; **20**: 345; **25**: 235; **29**: 133; **57**: 263
psychoanalytic interpretations **20**: 345; **44**: 289, 297; **45**: 58
sleepwalking scene **44**: 261
as sympathetic figure **3**: 191, 193, 203

Macduff
Macbeth **3**: 226, 231, 253, 262; **25**: 235; **29**: 127, 133, 155; **57**: 194

MacMorris
Henry V **22**: 103; **28**: 159; **30**: 278

Malcolm
Macbeth **25**: 235
fatherhood **48**: 214

Malvolio
Twelfth Night
characterization **1**: 540, 544, 545, 548, 550, 554, 558, 567, 575, 577, 615; **26**: 207, 233, 273; **46**: 286; **62**: 339, 348
forged letter **16**: 372; **28**: 1
punishment **1**: 539, 544, 548, 549, 554, 555, 558, 563, 575, 577, 590, 632, 645; **46**: 291, 297, 338
as Puritan **1**: 549, 551, 555, 558, 561, 563; **25**: 47; **66**: 312
role in play **1**: 545, 548, 549, 553, 555, 563, 567, 575, 577, 588, 610, 615, 632, 645; **26**: 337, 374; **46**: 347; **62**: 339

Mamillius
The Winter's Tale **7**: 394, 396, 451; **22**: 324

Margaret
Henry VI, Parts 1, 2, and 3
characterization **3**: 18, 26, 35, 51, 103, 109, 140, 157; **24**: 48
Suffolk, relationship with **3**: 18, 24, 26, 157; **39**: 213
Richard III **8**: 153, 154, 159, 162, 163, 170, 193, 201, 206, 210, 218, 223, 228, 243, 248, 262; **39**: 345; **62**: 2, 14, 18, 31, 52, 78

Mariana
Measure for Measure **65**: 53

Marina
Pericles **37**: 361; **51**: 118; **66**: 201

Menenius
Coriolanus **9**: 8, 9, 11, 14, 19, 26, 78, 80, 106, 148, 157; **25**: 263, 296; **30**: 67, 79, 89, 96, 111, 133

Mercutio
Romeo and Juliet
bawdy **5**: 463, 525, 550, 575
death **5**: 415, 418, 419, 547; **33**: 290
relationship with Romeo **65**: 142, 151
as worldly counterpart to Romeo **5**: 425, 464, 542; **33**: 290; **51**: 195

minor characters
Richard III **8**: 154, 159, 162, 163, 168, 170, 177, 184, 186, 201, 206, 210, 218, 223, 228, 232, 239, 248, 262, 267

Miranda
The Tempest **8**: 289, 301, 304, 328, 336, 370, 454; **19**: 357; **22**: 302; **28**: 249; **29**: 278, 297, 362, 368, 377, 396; **53**: 64

Mistress Elbow
Measure for Measure See **Elbow (Mistress Elbow)**

Mistress Quickly
Henry V See **Quickly**

Mortimer
Henry IV, Parts 1 and 2 **25**: 151

Norfolk
Henry VIII **22**: 182

Northumberland
Richard II **24**: 423

Nurse
Romeo and Juliet **5**: 419, 425, 463, 464, 575; **33**: 294

Oberon
A Midsummer Night's Dream **58**: 151, 162, 167, 203
as controlling force **3**: 434, 459, 477, 502; **29**: 175; **60**: 142

Octavius
Antony and Cleopatra **6**: 22, 24, 31, 38, 43, 53, 62, 107, 125, 146, 178, 181, 219; **25**: 257; **58**: 33
Julius Caesar **30**: 316

Olivia
Twelfth Night **1**: 540, 543, 545; **46**: 286, 324, 369; **47**: 45; **62**: 325, 343

Ophelia
Hamlet **1**: 73, 76, 81, 82, 91, 96, 97, 154, 166, 169, 171, 218, 270; **13**: 268; **16**: 246; **19**: 330; **21**: 17, 41, 44, 72, 81, 101, 104, 107, 112, 136, 203, 259, 347, 381, 386, 392, 416; **28**: 232, 325; **35**: 104, 126, 140, 144, 182, 238; **44**: 189, 195, 248; **59**: 31, 39
in art **48**: 255
death **48**: 255
as icon **48**: 255

influence on popular culture **48**: 255
as Mary Magdalen **59**: 68

Orlando
As You Like It
as ideal man **5**: 32, 36, 39, 162; **34**: 161; **46**: 94
relationship with Rosalind/Ganymede **60**: 115
as younger brother **5**: 66, 158; **46**: 94

Orsino
Twelfth Night **46**: 286, 333; **47**: 45; **62**: 343

Othello
Othello
affinity with Iago **4**: 400, 427, 468, 470, 477, 500, 506; **25**: 189; **35**: 276, 320, 327
as conventional "blameless hero" **4**: 445, 486, 500; **53**: 233, 238, 298, 304
conversion to Christianity **66**: 317
credulity **4**: 384, 385, 388, 390, 396, 402, 434, 440, 455; **13**: 327; **32**: 302; **47**: 25, 51; **65**: 327
Desdemona, relationship with **22**: 339; **35**: 301, 317; **37**: 269; **43**: 32; **53**: 315
divided nature **4**: 400, 412, 462, 470, 477, 493, 500, 582, 592; **16**: 293; **19**: 276; **25**: 189; **35**: 320; **53**: 268, 289, 343
egotism **4**: 427, 470, 477, 493, 522, 536, 541, 573, 597; **13**: 304; **35**: 247, 253
self-destructive anger **16**: 283; **53**: 324
self-dramatizing or self-deluding **4**: 454, 457, 477, 592; **13**: 313; **16**: 293; **35**: 317; **60**: 46
self-knowledge **4**: 462, 470, 477, 483, 508, 522, 530, 564, 580, 591, 596; **13**: 304, 313; **16**: 283; **28**: 243; **35**: 253, 317; **53**: 233, 343
spiritual state **4**: 483, 488, 517, 525, 527, 544, 559, 564, 573; **28**: 243; **35**: 253; **54**: 119; **60**: 46

Page, Anne
The Merry Wives of Windsor **47**: 321
Anne Page-Fenton plot **5**: 334, 336, 343, 353, 376, 390, 395, 402; **22**: 93; **47**: 308

Page, Mistess Margaret
The Merry Wives of Windsor **47**: 321

Painter
Timon of Athens See **Poet and Painter**

Palamon and Arcite
The Two Noble Kinsmen **9**: 474, 481, 490, 492, 502; **50**: 295, 305, 348, 361; **58**: 322, 338, 345, 356, 361

Pandarus
Troilus and Cressida **59**: 245

Parolles
All's Well That Ends Well
characterization **7**: 8, 9, 43, 76, 81, 98, 109, 113, 116, 126; **22**: 78; **26**: 48, 73, 97; **26**: 117; **46**: 68; **55**: 90, 154
exposure **7**: 9, 27, 81, 98, 109, 113, 116, 121, 126
Falstaff, compared with **7**: 8, 9, 16

pastoral characters (Silvius, Phebe, and Corin)
As You Like It **23:** 37, 97, 98, 99, 108, 110, 118, 122, 138; **34:** 147; **60:** 115

Paulina
The Winter's Tale **7:** 385, 412, 506; **15:** 528; **22:** 324; **25:** 339; **36:** 311; **57:** 319

Pedro (Don Pedro)
Much Ado about Nothing **8:** 17, 19, 48, 58, 63, 82, 111, 121

Perdita
The Winter's Tale
characterization **7:** 395, 412, 414, 419, 429, 432, 452, 506; **22:** 324; **25:** 339; **36:** 328; **43:** 39
reunion with Leontes (Act V, scene ii) **7:** 377, 379, 381, 390, 432, 464, 480

Pericles
Pericles **66:** 201
characterization **36:** 251; **37:** 361
patience **2:** 572, 573, 578, 579
suit of Antiochus's daughter **2:** 547, 565, 578, 579; **51:** 126; **66:** 190
Ulysses, compared with **2:** 551

Petruchio
The Taming of the Shrew
admirable qualities **9:** 320, 332, 341, 344, 345, 370, 375, 386; **55:** 294
audacity or vigor **9:** 325, 337, 355, 375, 386, 404; **64:** 266
characterization **32:** 1
coarseness or brutality **9:** 325, 329, 365, 390, 393, 398, 407; **19:** 122; **43:** 61; **64:** 283
as lord of misrule **9:** 393; **50:** 64; **55:** 322
love for Kate **9:** 338, 340, 343, 344, 386; **12:** 435
portrayals of **31:** 282
pragmatism **9:** 329, 334, 375, 398, 424; **13:** 3; **31:** 345, 351
as rhetorician **64:** 273, 296
taming method **9:** 320, 323, 329, 340, 341, 343, 345, 355, 369, 370, 375, 390, 398, 407, 413, 419, 424; **19:** 3, 12, 21; **31:** 269, 295, 326, 335, 339; **55:** 334; **64:** 233, 239, 266, 273, 283, 333, 352

Phebe
As You Like It See **pastoral characters**

Pistol
Henry V **28:** 146

plebeians
Coriolanus **9:** 8, 9, 11, 12, 15, 18, 19, 26, 33, 39, 53, 92, 125, 153, 183, 189; **25:** 296; **30:** 58, 79, 96, 111

Poet and Painter
Timon of Athens **25:** 198

the poets
Julius Caesar **7:** 179, 320, 350

Polixenes
The Winter's Tale
Leontes, relationship with **48:** 309

Polonius
Hamlet **21:** 259, 334, 347, 386, 416; **35:** 182

Porter
Henry VIII **24:** 155
Macbeth **3:** 173, 175, 184, 190, 196, 203, 205, 225, 260, 271, 297, 300; **20:** 283; **60:** 89

Portia
The Merchant of Venice **4:** 194, 195, 196, 215, 254, 263, 336, 356; **12:** 104, 107, 114; **13:** 37; **22:** 3, 69; **25:** 22; **32:** 294; **37:** 86; **40:** 142, 156, 197, 208; **49:** 27; **66:** 63, 91, 124, 144

Posthumus
Cymbeline **4:** 24, 30, 53, 78, 116, 127, 141, 155, 159, 167; **15:** 89; **19:** 411; **25:** 245, 319; **36:** 142; **44:** 28; **45:** 67, 75; **47:** 25, 205, 228; **61:** 34, 45, 76

Prince Henry
King John See **Henry (Prince Henry)**

Prospero
The Tempest
characterization **8:** 312, 348, 370, 458; **16:** 442; **22:** 302; **45:** 188, 272; **61:** 307
as God or Providence **8:** 311, 328, 364, 380, 429, 435
magic, nature of **8:** 301, 340, 356, 396, 414, 423, 458; **25:** 382; **28:** 391; **29:** 278, 292, 368, 377, 396; **32:** 338, 343; **61:** 272
psychoanalytic interpretation **45:** 259
redemptive powers **8:** 302, 320, 353, 370, 390, 429, 439, 447; **29:** 297; **61:** 326, 338
as ruler **8:** 304, 308, 309, 420, 423; **13:** 424; **22:** 302; **29:** 278, 362, 377, 396; **61:** 315
self-control **8:** 312, 414, 420; **22:** 302; **44:** 11
self-knowledge **16:** 442; **22:** 302; **29:** 278, 292, 362, 377, 396
as Shakespeare or creative artist **8:** 299, 302, 308, 312, 320, 324, 353, 364, 435, 447; **61:** 280, 288
as tragic hero **8:** 359, 370, 464; **29:** 292

Proteus
The Two Gentlemen of Verona **6:** 439, 450, 458, 480, 490, 511; **40:** 312, 327, 330, 335, 359; **42:** 18; **54:** 325, 332

Puck
A Midsummer Night's Dream **45:** 96, 158

Quickly (Mistress Quickly)
Henry V **5:** 186, 187, 210, 276, 293; **30:** 278

Regan
King Lear **31:** 151; **46:** 231, 242; **61:** 160

Richard (King Richard II)
Richard II
artistic temperament **6:** 264, 267, 270, 272, 277, 292, 294, 298, 315, 331, 334, 347, 368, 374, 393, 409; **24:** 298, 301, 304, 315, 322, 390, 405, 408, 411, 414, 419; **39:** 289
Bolingbroke, compared with **24:** 346, 349, 351, 352, 356, 419; **39:** 256; **52:** 108, 124; **58:** 275
characterization **6:** 250, 252, 253, 254, 255, 258, 262, 263, 267, 270, 272, 282, 283, 304, 343, 347, 364, 368; **24:** 262, 263, 267, 269, 270, 271, 272, 273, 274, 278, 280, 315, 322, 325, 330, 333, 390, 395, 402, 405, 423; **28:** 134; **39:** 279, 289; **52:** 169; **58:** 229, 241, 253, 259, 267, 307
dangerous aspects **24:** 405; **58:** 253
death of **60:** 21
delusion **6:** 267, 298, 334, 368, 409; **24:** 329, 336, 405
homosexuality **24:** 405
kingship **6:** 253, 254, 263, 272, 327, 331, 334, 338, 364, 402, 414; **24:** 278, 295, 336, 337, 339, 356, 419; **28:** 134, 178; **39:** 256, 263; **52:** 169; **58:** 241, 275
language and imagery **58:** 301
loss of identity **6:** 267, 338, 368, 374, 381, 388, 391, 409; **24:** 298, 414, 428
as martyr-king **6:** 289, 307, 321; **19:** 209; **24:** 289, 291; **28:** 134
nobility **6:** 255, 258, 259, 262, 263, 391; **24:** 260, 263, 274, 280, 289, 291, 402, 408, 411
political acumen **6:** 263, 264, 272, 292, 310, 327, 334, 364, 368, 374, 388, 391, 397, 402, 409; **24:** 405; **39:** 256
private vs. public persona **6:** 317, 327, 364, 368, 391, 409; **24:** 428
role in Gloucester's death **52:** 108, 124
role-playing **24:** 419, 423; **28:** 178
seizure of Gaunt's estate **6:** 250, 338, 388
self-dramatization **6:** 264, 267, 307, 310, 315, 317, 331, 334, 368, 393, 409; **24:** 339; **28:** 178; **60:** 21
self-hatred **13:** 172; **24:** 383; **39:** 289
self-knowledge **6:** 255, 267, 331, 334, 338, 352, 354, 368, 388, 391; **24:** 273, 289, 411, 414; **39:** 263, 289; **60:** 21, 46
spiritual redemption **6:** 255, 267, 331, 334, 338, 352, 354, 368, 388, 391; **24:** 273, 289, 411, 414; **52:** 124; **60:** 21, 46

Richard (King Richard III, formerly Richard, Duke of Gloucester)
Henry VI, Parts 1, 2, and 3
characterization **3:** 35, 48, 57, 64, 77, 143, 151; **22:** 193; **39:** 160, 177
as revenger **22:** 193
soliloquy (3 Henry VI, Act III, scene ii) **3:** 17, 48
Richard III
ambition **8:** 148, 154, 165, 168, 170, 177, 182, 213, 218, 228, 232, 239, 252, 258, 267; **39:** 308, 341, 360, 370, 383; **52:** 201, 223
attractive qualities **8:** 145, 148, 152, 154, 159, 161, 162, 165, 168, 170, 181, 182, 184, 185, 197, 201, 206, 213, 228, 243, 252, 258; **16:** 150; **39:** 370, 383; **52:** 272, 280; **62:** 104
credibility, question of **8:** 145, 147, 154, 159, 165, 193; **13:** 142
death **8:** 145, 148, 154, 159, 165, 168, 170, 177, 182, 197, 210, 223, 228, 232, 243, 248, 252, 258, 267
deformity as symbol **8:** 146, 147, 148, 152, 154, 159, 161, 165, 170, 177, 184, 185, 193, 218, 248, 252, 267; **19:** 164; **62:** 110
inversion of moral order **8:** 159, 168, 177, 182, 184, 185, 197, 201, 213, 218, 223, 232, 239, 243, 248, 252, 258, 262, 267; **39:** 360; **52:** 205, 214
as Machiavellian villain **8:** 165, 182, 190, 201, 218, 232, 239, 243, 248; **39:** 308, 326, 360, 387; **52:** 201, 205, 257, 280, 285; **62:** 2, 60, 78, 110

as monster or symbol of diabolic **8:** 145, 147, 159, 162, 168, 170, 177, 182, 193, 197, 201, 228, 239, 248, 258; **13:** 142; **37:** 144; **39:** 326, 349; **52:** 227, 272; **66:** 286
other literary villains, compared with **8:** 148, 161, 162, 165, 181, 182, 206, 213, 239, 267
role-playing, hypocrisy, and dissimulation **8:** 145, 148, 154, 159, 162, 165, 168, 170, 182, 190, 206, 213, 218, 228, 239, 243, 252, 258, 267; **25:** 141, 164, 245; **39:** 335, 341, 387; **52:** 257, 267; **62:** 78
as scourge or instrument of God **8:** 163, 177, 193, 201, 218, 228, 248, 267; **39:** 308; **62:** 60
as seducer **52:** 223, 227; **62:** 91, 104
self-esteem **52:** 196; **62:** 78
as Vice figure **8:** 190, 201, 213, 228, 243, 248, 252; **16:** 150; **39:** 383, 387; **52:** 223, 267; **62:** 78

Richard Plantagenet, Duke of York
Henry VI, Parts 1, 2, and 3 See **York**

Richmond
Richard III **8:** 154, 158, 163, 168, 177, 182, 193, 210, 218, 223, 228, 243, 248, 252; **13:** 142; **25:** 141; **39:** 349; **52:** 214, 257, 285; **66:** 286

the Rival Poet
Sonnets **10:** 169, 233, 334, 337, 385; **48:** 352

Roman citizenry
Julius Caesar
portrayal of **7:** 169, 179, 210, 221, 245, 279, 282, 310, 320, 333; **17:** 271, 279, 288, 291, 292, 298, 323, 334, 351, 367, 374, 375, 378; **22:** 280; **30:** 285, 297, 316, 321, 374, 379; **37:** 229

Romeo and Juliet
Romeo and Juliet
characterization **65:** 159
death-wish **5:** 431, 489, 505, 528, 530, 538, 542, 550, 566, 571, 575; **32:** 212
first meeting (Act I scene v) **51:** 212
immortality **5:** 536
Juliet's epithalamium speech (Act III, scene ii) **5:** 431, 477, 492
Juliet's innocence **5:** 421, 423, 450, 454; **33:** 257; **65:** 201
maturation **5:** 437, 454, 467, 493, 498, 509, 520, 565; **33:** 249, 257; **65:** 159
rebellion **25:** 257
reckless passion **5:** 419, 427, 431, 438, 443, 444, 448, 467, 479, 485, 505, 533, 538, 542; **33:** 241
Romeo's dream (Act V, scene i) **5:** 513, 536, 556; **45:** 40; **51:** 203
Rosaline, Romeo's relationship with **5:** 419, 423, 425, 427, 438, 498, 542, 575

Rosalind
As You Like It **46:** 94, 122
Beatrice, compared with **5:** 26, 36, 50, 75
charm **5:** 55, 75; **23:** 17, 18, 20, 41, 89, 111
disguise, role of **5:** 75, 107, 118, 122, 128, 130, 133, 138, 141, 146, 148, 164, 168; **13:** 502; **23:** 35, 42, 106, 119, 123, 146; **34:** 130; **46:** 127, 134, 142; **57:** 23, 40
femininity **5:** 26, 36, 52, 75; **23:** 24, 29, 46, 54, 103, 108, 121, 146

as Ganymede **60:** 115
love-theme, relation to **5:** 79, 88, 103, 116, 122, 138, 141; **23:** 114, 115; **34:** 85, 177

rustic characters
As You Like It **5:** 24, 60, 72, 84; **23:** 127; **34:** 78, 161
A Midsummer Night's Dream **3:** 376, 397, 432; **12:** 291, 293; **45:** 147, 160

Scroop
Henry V See **traitors**

Sebastian
The Tempest See **Antonio and Sebastian**

Shylock
The Merchant of Venice
alienation **4:** 279, 312; **40:** 175; **48:** 77; **49:** 23, 37; **66:** 91
ambiguity **4:** 247, 254, 315, 319, 331; **12:** 31, 35, 36, 50, 51, 52, 56, 81, 124; **40:** 175; **53:** 111; **66:** 87, 110, 117
ghettoization of **53:** 127; **66:** 78
forced conversion **4:** 209, 252, 268, 282, 289, 321; **66:** 110, 144, 180, 292
Jewishness **4:** 193, 194, 195, 200, 201, 213, 214, 279; **22:** 69; **25:** 257; **40:** 142, 175, 181; **48:** 65, 77; **66:** 87, 110, 117, 126, 292
master-slave relationship **53:** 136
motives in making the bond **4:** 252, 263, 266, 268; **22:** 69; **25:** 22; **66:** 59, 110
as outsider **53:** 127, 224; **66:** 87, 144, 158, 165
as Puritan **40:** 127, 166
as scapegoat figure **4:** 254, 300; **40:** 166; **49:** 27
as traditional comic villain **4:** 230, 243, 261, 263, 315; **12:** 40, 62, 124; **40:** 175; **66:** 87, 117
as tragic figure **12:** 6, 9, 10, 16, 21, 23, 25, 40, 44, 66, 67, 81, 97; **40:** 175; **66:** 87, 117, 124, 126, 153, 180, 292

Sicinius
Coriolanus See **the tribunes**

Silvia
The Two Gentlemen of Verona **6:** 450, 453, 458, 476, 494, 499, 516, 519, 549, 564; **40:** 312, 327, 374; **54:** 325, 332

Silvius
As You Like It See **pastoral characters**

Sly
The Taming of the Shrew **9:** 320, 322, 350, 370, 381, 390, 398, 430; **12:** 316, 335, 416, 427, 441; **16:** 13; **19:** 34, 122; **22:** 48; **37:** 31; **50:** 74; **64:** 244, 343, 352

soldiers
Henry V **5:** 203, 239, 267, 276, 281, 287, 293, 318; **28:** 146; **30:** 169

Speed
The Two Gentlemen of Verona See **Launce and Speed**

Stephano and Trinculo
The Tempest

comic subplot of **8:** 292, 297, 299, 304, 309, 324, 328, 353, 370; **25:** 382; **29:** 377; **46:** 14, 33

Stephen Gardiner
Henry VIII See **Gardiner**

Talbot
Henry VI, Parts 1, 2, and 3 **39:** 160, 213, 222; **56:** 85, 145; **60:** 33

Tamora
Titus Andronicus **4:** 632, 662, 672, 675; **27:** 266; **43:** 170; **62:** 233

Tarquin
The Rape of Lucrece **10:** 80, 93, 98, 116, 125; **22:** 294; **25:** 305; **32:** 321; **33:** 190; **43:** 102; **59:** 180
Petrarchan lover **48:** 291
platonic tyrant **48:** 291
Satan role **48:** 291

Thaisa
Pericles **66:** 201

Thersites
Troilus and Cressida **13:** 53; **25:** 56; **27:** 381; **59:** 265

Theseus
A Midsummer Night's Dream
characterization **3:** 363; **58:** 151, 220
Hippolyta, relationship with **3:** 381, 412, 421, 423, 450, 468, 520; **29:** 175, 216, 243, 256; **45:** 84
as ideal **3:** 379, 391
"lovers, lunatics, and poets" speech (Act V, scene i) **3:** 365, 371, 379, 381, 391, 402, 411, 412, 421, 423, 441, 498, 506; **29:** 175
as representative of institutional life **3:** 381, 403; **51:** 1

Time-Chorus
The Winter's Tale **7:** 377, 380, 412, 464, 476, 501; **15:** 518

Timon
Timon of Athens
comic traits **25:** 198
as flawed hero **1:** 456, 459, 462, 472, 495, 503, 507, 515; **16:** 351; **20:** 429, 433, 476; **25:** 198; **27:** 157, 161
death of **60:** 46
misanthropy **13:** 392; **20:** 431, 464, 476, 481, 491, 492, 493; **27:** 161, 175, 184, 196; **37:** 222; **52:** 296, 301
as noble figure **1:** 467, 473, 483, 499; **20:** 493; **27:** 212

Titania
A Midsummer Night's Dream **29:** 243; **58:** 151, 162, 167, 203

Titus
Titus Andronicus **4:** 632, 637, 640, 644, 647, 653, 656, 662; **25:** 245; **27:** 255; **62:** 258

Touchstone
As You Like It
callousness **5:** 88
comic and farcical elements **46:** 117

as philosopher-fool **5:** 24, 28, 30, 32, 36, 63, 75, 98; **23:** 152; **34:** 85; **46:** 1, 14, 18, 24, 33, 52, 60, 88, 105
relation to pastoral convention **5:** 54, 61, 63, 72, 75, 77, 79, 84, 86, 93, 98, 114, 118, 135, 138, 166; **34:** 72, 147, 161
satire or parody of pastoral conventions **46:** 122
selflessness **5:** 30, 36, 39, 76

traitors (Scroop, Grey, and Cambridge)
Henry V **16:** 202; **30:** 220, 278

the tribunes (Brutus and Sicinius)
Coriolanus **9:** 9, 11, 14, 19, 33, 169, 180

Trinculo
The Tempest See **Stephano and Trinculo**

Troilus
Troilus and Cressida
contradictory behavior **3:** 596, 602, 635; **27:** 362
Cressida, relationship with **3:** 594, 596, 606; **22:** 58; **59:** 245, 261
integrity **3:** 617
opposition to Ulysses **3:** 561, 584, 590
as a Trojan **59:** 257
as unsympathetic figure **18:** 423; **22:** 58, 339; **43:** 317; **59:** 261
as warrior **3:** 596; **22:** 339

Ulysses
Troilus and Cressida **59:** 245
speech on degree (Act I, scene iii) **3:** 549, 599, 609, 642; **27:** 396

Valentine
The Two Gentlemen of Verona **54:** 325, 332

Venetians
The Merchant of Venice **4:** 195, 200, 228, 254, 273, 300, 321, 331

Venus
Venus and Adonis **10:** 427, 429, 434, 439, 442, 448, 449, 451, 454, 466, 473, 480, 486, 489; **16:** 452; **25:** 305, 328; **28:** 355; **33:** 309, 321, 330, 347, 352, 357, 363, 370, 377; **51:** 335, 352, 377, 388

Viola
Twelfth Night **26:** 308; **46:** 286, 324, 347, 369; **60:** 115, 129; **62:** 308, 319, 325; **66:** 312

Virgilia
Coriolanus **9:** 11, 19, 26, 33, 58, 100, 121, 125; **25:** 263; **30:** 79, 96, 133; **50:** 99

Volumnia
Coriolanus
Coriolanus's subservience to **9:** 16, 26, 33, 53, 62, 80, 92, 100, 117, 125, 142, 177, 183; **30:** 140, 149; **44:** 79
influence on Coriolanus **9:** 45, 62, 65, 78, 92, 100, 110, 117, 121, 125, 130, 148, 157, 183, 189, 193; **25:** 263, 296; **30:** 79, 96, 125, 133, 140, 142, 149; **44:** 93; **64:** 72
as noble Roman matron **9:** 16, 19, 26, 31, 33; **64:** 72

personification of Rome **9:** 125, 183; **50:** 119

Wat the hare
Venus and Adonis **10:** 424, 451

the Watch
Much Ado about Nothing See **Dogberry and the Watch**

Williams
Henry V **13:** 502; **16:** 183; **28:** 146; **30:** 169, 259, 278

witches
Macbeth
and supernaturalism **3:** 171, 172, 173, 175, 177, 182, 183, 184, 185, 194, 196, 198, 202, 207, 208, 213, 219, 229, 239; **16:** 317; **19:** 245; **20:** 92, 175, 213, 279, 283, 374, 387, 406, 413; **25:** 235; **28:** 339; **29:** 91, 101, 109, 120

Wolsey (Cardinal Wolsey)
Henry VIII **2:** 15, 18, 19, 23, 24, 38; **22:** 182; **24:** 80, 91, 112, 113, 129, 140; **37:** 109; **41:** 129; **56:** 248, 262; **61:** 44

York (Edmund of Langley, Duke of York)
Richard II **6:** 287, 364, 368, 388, 402, 414; **24:** 263, 320, 322, 364, 395, 414; **39:** 243, 279; **58:** 241

York (Richard Plantagenet, Duke of York)
Henry VI, Parts 1, 2, and 3
death of **13:** 131; **60:** 33

Shakespearean Criticism
Cumulative Topic Index

The Cumulative Topic Index indentifies the principal topics of discussion in the criticism of each play and non-dramatic poem. The topics are arranged alphabetically. Page references indicate the beginning page number of each essay containing substantial commentary on that topic. A parenthetical reference after a topic indicates that the topic is extensively discussed in that volume.

absurdities, inconsistencies, and shortcomings
  The Two Gentlemen of Verona **6:** 435, 436, 437, 439, 464, 507, 541, 560; **54:** 295, 311

accident or chance
  Romeo and Juliet **5:** 418, 444, 448, 467, 470, 487, 573

acting and dissimulation
  Richard II **6:** 264, 267, 307, 310, 315, 368, 393, 409; **24:** 339, 345, 346, 349, 352, 356

adaptations
  Othello **65:** 327

adolescence
  Romeo and Juliet **33:** 249, 255, 257

adultery
  The Comedy of Errors **34:** 215

aggression
  Coriolanus **9:** 112, 142, 174, 183, 189, 198; **30:** 79, 111, 125, 142; **44:** 11, 79

alchemy
  The Phoenix and Turtle **64:** 211

alienation
  Timon of Athens **1:** 523; **27:** 161

allegorical elements
  Antony and Cleopatra **52:** 5
  King Lear **16:** 311; **61:** 215
  Measure for Measure **52:** 69; **65:** 14
  The Merchant of Venice **4:** 224, 250, 261, 268, 270, 273, 282, 289, 324, 336, 344, 350

  The Phoenix and Turtle **10:** 7, 8, 9, 16, 17, 48; **38:** 334, 378; **51:** 138, 188; **64:** 198, 209, 211
  The Rape of Lucrece **10:** 89, 93
  Richard II **6:** 264, 283, 323, 385
  Richard III **52:** 5; **62:** 60
  The Tempest **8:** 294, 295, 302, 307, 308, 312, 326, 328, 336, 345, 364; **42:** 320; **61:** 326
  Troilus and Cressida **52:** 5
  Venus and Adonis **10:** 427, 434, 439, 449, 454, 462, 480; **28:** 355; **33:** 309, 330

ambiguity
  Antony and Cleopatra **6:** 53, 111, 161, 163, 180, 189, 208, 211, 228; **13:** 368
  Hamlet **1:** 92, 160, 198, 227, 230, 234, 247, 249; **21:** 72; **35:** 241; **66:** 266
  King John **13:** 152; **41:** 243
  Measure for Measure **2:** 417, 420, 432, 446, 449, 452, 474, 479, 482, 486, 495, 505; **65:** 14, 19
  The Merchant of Venice **66:** 91, 124
  A Midsummer Night's Dream **3:** 401, 459, 486; **45:** 169
  Richard III **44:** 11; **47:** 15
  Sonnets **10:** 251, 256; **28:** 385; **40:** 221, 228, 268
  Troilus and Cressida **3:** 544, 568, 583, 587, 589, 599, 611, 621; **27:** 400; **43:** 305
  Twelfth Night **1:** 554, 639; **34:** 287, 316
  Venus and Adonis **10:** 434, 454, 459, 462, 466, 473, 480, 486, 489; **33:** 352; **51:** 368, 377, 388

ambition or pride
  Coriolanus **64:** 40
  Henry IV, Parts 1 and 2 **57:** 94
  Henry VIII **2:** 15, 38, 67
  Macbeth **44:** 284, 324
  Richard III **52:** 201, 223

ambivalent or ironic elements
  Henry VI, Parts 1, 2, and 3 **3:** 69, 151, 154; **39:** 160; **56:** 131

  Richard III **44:** 11
  Troilus and Cressida **43:** 340; **59:** 287

amorality, question of
  The Two Noble Kinsmen **9:** 447, 460, 492

amour-passion or Liebestod myth
  Romeo and Juliet **5:** 484, 489, 528, 530, 542, 550, 575; **32:** 256; **51:** 195, 219, 236; **65:** 214

amputations, significance of
  Titus Andronicus **48:** 264

anachronisms
  Cymbeline **65:** 251
  Julius Caesar **7:** 331; **65:** 251

androgyny
  Antony and Cleopatra **13:** 530
  As You Like It **23:** 98, 100, 122, 138, 143, 144; **34:** 172, 177; **46:** 134; **57:** 13
  Romeo and Juliet **13:** 530
  Twelfth Night **60:** 129

anti-Catholic rhetoric
  King John **22:** 120; **25:** 98; **66:** 271

anti-romantic elements
  As You Like It **34:** 72

antithetical or contradictory elements
  Macbeth **3:** 185, 213, 271, 302; **25:** 235; **29:** 76, 127; **47:** 41

anxiety
  Romeo and Juliet **13:** 235; **60:** 96

appearance, perception, and illusion
  A Midsummer Night's Dream **3:** 368, 411, 425, 427, 434, 447, 459, 466, 474, 477, 486, 497, 516; **19:** 21; **22:** 39; **28:** 15; **29:** 175,190; **45:** 136

Appearance versus Reality (Volume 34: 1, 5, 12, 23, 45, 54)
  All's Well That Ends Well **7:** 37, 76, 93; **26:** 117
  As You Like It **34:** 130, 131; **46:** 105; **57:** 35, 40
  The Comedy of Errors **34:** 194, 201
  Coriolanus **30:** 142
  Cymbeline **4:** 87, 93, 103, 162; **36:** 99; **47:** 228, 286
  Hamlet **1:** 95, 116, 166, 169, 198; **35:** 82, 126, 132, 144, 238; **44:** 248; **45:** 28
  Macbeth **3:** 241, 248; **25:** 235
  The Merchant of Venice **4:** 209, 261, 344; **12:** 65; **22:** 69; **66:** 59, 91
  Much Ado about Nothing **8:** 17, 18, 48, 63, 69, 73, 75, 79, 88, 95, 115; **31:** 198, 209; **55:** 259, 268
  The Taming of the Shrew **9:** 343, 350, 353, 365, 369, 370, 381, 390, 430; **12:** 416; **31:** 326; **55:** 278, 299, 334
  Timon of Athens **1:** 495, 500, 515, 523; **52:** 311, 329
  The Two Gentlemen of Verona **6:** 494, 502, 511, 519, 529, 532, 549, 560
  Twelfth Night **34:** 293, 301, 311, 316
  The Winter's Tale **7:** 429, 446, 479; **57:** 336

appetite
  Twelfth Night **1:** 563, 596, 609, 615; **52:** 57

archetypal or mythic elements
  Macbeth **16:** 317

archetypal structure
  Pericles **2:** 570, 580, 582, 584, 588; **25:** 365; **51:** 71, 79

aristocracy and aristocratic values
  As You Like It **34:** 120
  Hamlet **42:** 212
  Julius Caesar **16:** 231; **22:** 280; **30:** 379; **50:** 194, 196, 211

art and nature
  See also **nature**
  Pericles **22:** 315; **36:** 233
  The Phoenix and Turtle **10:** 7, 42; **64:** 209

art versus nature
  See also **nature**
  As You Like It **5:** 128, 130, 148; **34:** 147; **57:** 35, 75
  The Tempest **8:** 396, 404; **29:** 278, 297, 362; **61:** 356
  The Winter's Tale **7:** 377, 381, 397, 419, 452; **36:** 289, 318; **45:** 329; **57:** 278

artificial nature
  Love's Labour's Lost **2:** 315, 317, 324, 330; **23:** 207, 233; **54:** 234, 248, 257, 263

Athens
  Timon of Athens **27:** 223, 230

Athens and the forest, contrast between
  A Midsummer Night's Dream **3:** 381, 427, 459, 466, 497, 502; **29:** 175

assassination
  Julius Caesar **7:** 156, 161, 179, 191, 200, 221, 264, 272, 279, 284, 350; **25:** 272; **30:** 326

audience interpretation
  Julius Caesar **48:** 240

audience perception
  The Comedy of Errors **1:** 37, 50, 56; **19:** 54; **34:** 258; **54:** 136, 144
  King Lear **19:** 295; **28:** 325; **61:** 176
  Richard II **24:** 414, 423; **39:** 295
  Pericles **42:** 352; **48:** 364

audience perception, Shakespeare's manipulation of
  The Winter's Tale **7:** 394, 429, 456, 483, 501; **13:** 417; **19:** 401, 431, 441; **25:** 339; **45:** 374

audience perspective
  All's Well That Ends Well **7:** 81, 104, 109, 116, 121

audience response
  Antony and Cleopatra **48:** 206; **58:** 88
  Hamlet **28:** 325; **32:** 238; **35:** 167; **44:** 107
  Julius Caesar **7:** 179, 238, 253, 255, 272, 316, 320, 336, 350; **19:** 321; **48:** 240
  Macbeth **20:** 17, 400, 406; **29:** 139, 146, 155, 165; **44:** 306
  Measure for Measure **48:** 1
  Richard II **58:** 293
  The Two Noble Kinsmen **58:** 330

audience versus character perceptions
  The Two Gentlemen of Verona **6:** 499, 519, 524

authenticity
  The Phoenix and Turtle **10:** 7, 8, 16; **64:** 217
  Sonnets **10:** 153, 154, 230, 243; **48:** 325; **62:** 128

Authorship Controversy (Volume 41: 2, 5, 18, 32, 42, 48, 57, 61, 63, 66, 76, 81, 85, 98, 110)
  Cymbeline **4:** 17, 21, 35, 48, 56, 78
  Henry VI, Parts 1, 2, and 3 **3:** 16, 18, 19, 20, 21, 26, 27, 29, 31, 35, 39, 41, 55, 66; **24:** 51; **56:** 77
  Henry VIII **2:** 16, 18, 19, 22, 23, 27, 28, 31, 35, 36, 42, 43, 44, 46, 48, 51, 58, 64, 68; **41:** 129, 146, 158, 171
  Love's Labour's Lost **2:** 299, 300; **32:** 308
  Pericles **2:** 538, 540, 543, 544, 545, 546, 548, 550, 551, 553, 556, 558, 564, 565, 568, 576, 586; **15:** 132, 141, 148, 152; **16:** 391, 399; **25:** 365; **36:** 198, 244; **66:** 219, 236
  Timon of Athens **1:** 464, 466, 467, 469, 474, 477, 478, 480, 490, 499, 507, 518; **16:** 351; **20:** 433
  Titus Andronicus **4:** 613, 614, 615, 616, 617, 619, 623, 624, 625, 626, 628, 631, 632, 635, 642; **62:** 208, 254
  The Two Gentlemen of Verona **6:** 435, 436, 437, 438, 439, 449, 466, 476
  The Two Noble Kinsmen **58:** 330

  Shakespeare not a co-author **9:** 445, 447, 455, 461
  Shakespearean portions of the text **9:** 446, 447, 448, 455, 456, 457, 460, 462, 463, 471, 479, 486; **41:** 308, 317, 355; **58:** 330
  Shakespeare's part in the overall conception or design **9:** 444, 446, 448, 456, 457, 460, 480, 481, 486, 490; **37:** 313; **41:** 326; **50:** 326

autobiographical elements
  As You Like It **5:** 25, 35, 43, 50, 55, 61
  The Comedy of Errors **1:** 16, 18
  Cymbeline **4:** 43, 46; **36:** 134
  Hamlet **1:** 98, 115, 119; **13:** 487
  Henry VI, Parts 1, 2, and 3 **3:** 41, 55
  King John **9:** 209, 218, 245, 248, 260, 292
  King Lear **2:** 131, 136, 149, 165
  Measure for Measure **2:** 406, 410, 414, 431, 434, 437
  A Midsummer Night's Dream **3:** 365, 371, 379, 381, 389, 391, 396, 402, 432
  Othello **4:** 440, 444
  Pericles **2:** 551, 554, 555, 563, 581; **66:** 208
  The Phoenix and Turtle **10:** 14, 18, 42, 48; **51:** 155; **64:** 217, 225
  Sonnets **10:** 159, 160, 166, 167, 175, 176, 182, 196, 205, 213, 215, 226, 233, 238, 240, 251, 279, 283, 302, 309, 325, 337, 377; **13:** 487; **16:** 461; **28:** 363, 385; **42:** 296; **48:** 325
  The Tempest **8:** 302, 308, 312, 324, 326, 345, 348, 353, 364, 380; **61:** 272
  Timon of Athens **1:** 462, 467, 470, 473, 474, 478, 480; **27:** 166, 175
  Titus Andronicus **4:** 619, 624, 625, 664
  Troilus and Cressida **3:** 548, 554, 557, 558, 574, 606, 630; **59:** 225
  Twelfth Night **1:** 557, 561, 599; **34:** 338
  The Winter's Tale **7:** 395, 397, 410, 419

avarice
  The Merry Wives of Windsor **5:** 335, 353, 369, 376, 390, 395, 402

battle of Agincourt
  Henry V **5:** 197, 199, 213, 246, 257, 281, 287, 289, 293, 310, 318; **19:** 217; **30:** 181

battle of the sexes
  Much Ado about Nothing **8:** 14, 16, 19, 48, 91, 95, 111, 121, 125; **31:** 231, 245; **55:** 199

bawdy elements
  As You Like It **46:** 122
  Cymbeline **36:** 155

bear-baiting
  Twelfth Night **19:** 42

beauty
  Sonnets **10:** 247; **51:** 288
  Venus and Adonis **10:** 420, 423, 427, 434, 454, 480; **33:** 330, 352

bed-trick
  All's Well That Ends Well **7**: 8, 26, 27, 29, 32, 41, 86, 93, 98, 113, 116, 126; **13**: 84; **26**: 117; **28**: 38; **38**: 65, 118; **49**: 46; **54**: 52; **55**: 109, 131, 176
  Measure for Measure **13**: 84; **49**: 313; **54**: 52

Beginnings and Endings in Shakespeare's Works (Volume 54: 2, 6, 19, 24, 30, 35, 39, 43, 52, 58, 65, 75, 84, 96, 103, 110, 114, 119, 125**)**
  All's Well That Ends Well **54**: 30, 52
  Antony and Cleopatra **54**: 6
  Coriolanus **54**: 6
  Hamlet **54**: 2, 6, 19, 96; **59**: 18, 74
  Henry VIII **54**: 35
  Julius Caesar **54**: 6
  King Lear **54**: 2, 6, 103, 110, 114; **60**: 46, 65, 75; **61**: 262; **66**: 260, 326
  Love's Labour's Lost **54**: 58; **64**: 122, 145
  Macbeth **54**: 2, 6, 84
  Measure for Measure **54**: 52, 65
  The Merchant of Venice **54**: 52, 65
  Othello **54**: 2, 6, 119; **60**: 2, 91
  Pericles **54**: 35
  Romeo and Juliet **54**: 6, 125
  Richard III **54**: 84
  The Taming of the Shrew **54**: 58, 65; **64**: 244, 327
  The Tempest **54**: 19
  Troilus and Cressida **54**: 84
  Twelfth Night **54**: 19
  The Two Gentlemen of Verona **54**:
  The Two Noble Kinsmen **54**: 35

Biblical references
  Henry IV, Parts 1 and 2 **57**: 147

bird imagery
  The Phoenix and Turtle **10**: 21, 27; **38**: 329, 350, 367; **51**: 145, 181, 184; **64**: 198, 205, 217

body, role of
  Troilus and Cressida **42**: 66; **59**: 287, 306

body politic, metaphor of
  Coriolanus **22**: 248; **30**: 67, 96, 105, 125; **50**: 105, 110, 119, 140, 145, 152; **64**: 8

bonding
  The Merchant of Venice **4**: 293, 317, 336; **13**: 37

British nationalism
  See also **nationalism and patriotism**
  Cymbeline **4**: 19, 78, 89, 93, 129, 141, 159, 167; **32**: 373; **36**: 129; **45**: 6; **47**: 219, 265; **61**: 54
  Henry VIII **61**: 92, 111

brutal elements
  A Midsummer Night's Dream **3**: 445, 491, 497, 511; **12**: 259, 262, 298; **16**: 34; **19**: 21; **29**: 183, 225, 263, 269; **45**: 169

Cade scenes
  Henry VI, Parts 1, 2, and 3 **50**: 45, 51; **56**: 117, 122, 131, 180

Caesarism
  Julius Caesar **7**: 159, 160, 161, 167, 169, 174, 191, 205, 218, 253, 310; **30**: 316, 321; **50**: 196, 234

Calvinist implications
  Hamlet **48**: 195; **66**: 266

capriciousness of the young lovers
  A Midsummer Night's Dream **3**: 372, 395, 402, 411, 423, 437, 441, 450, 497, 498; **29**: 175, 269; **45**: 107

caricature
  The Merry Wives of Windsor **5**: 343, 347, 348, 350, 385, 397

carnival elements
  Henry IV, Parts 1 and 2 **28**: 203; **32**: 103
  Henry VI, Parts 1, 2, and 3 **22**: 156
  Richard II **19**: 151; **39**: 273

casket scenes
  The Merchant of Venice **49**: 27; **66**: 59, 63, 78, 135

Catholic components
  Henry IV, Parts 1 and 2 **57**: 167

censorship
  Richard II **24**: 260, 261, 262, 263, 386; **42**: 118; **52**: 141, 144

ceremonies, rites, and rituals, importance of
  See also **pageantry**
  Coriolanus **9**: 139, 148, 169
  Hamlet **13**: 268; **28**: 232
  Julius Caesar **7**: 150, 210, 255, 259, 268, 284, 316, 331, 339, 356; **13**: 260; **22**: 137; **30**: 374; **50**: 258, 269
  A Midsummer Night's Dream **58**: 189
  Richard II **6**: 270, 294, 315, 368, 381, 397, 409, 414; **24**: 274, 356, 411, 414, 419
  Titus Andronicus **27**: 261; **32**: 265; **48**: 264; **62**: 254
  The Two Noble Kinsmen **9**: 492, 498

change
  Henry VIII **2**: 27, 65, 72, 81

characterization
  As You Like It **5**: 19, 24, 25, 36, 39, 54, 82, 86, 116, 148; **34**: 72; **48**: 42; **65**: 336
  The Comedy of Errors **1**: 13, 21, 31, 34, 46, 49, 50, 55, 56; **19**: 54; **25**: 63; **34**: 194, 201, 208, 245; **54**: 144, 176
  Henry IV, Parts 1 and 2 **1**: 321, 328, 332, 333, 336, 344, 365, 383, 385, 389, 391, 397, 401; **19**: 195; **39**: 123, 137; **42**: 99, 162; **49**: 93; **57**: 88, 120, 156, 167, 181
  Henry V **5**: 186, 189, 192, 193, 199, 219, 230, 233, 252, 276, 293; **30**: 227, 278; **42**: 162
  Henry VI, Parts 1, 2, and 3 **3**: 18, 20, 24, 25, 31, 57, 64, 73, 77, 109, 119, 151; **24**: 22, 28, 38, 42, 45, 47; **39**: 160; **47**: 32
  Henry VIII **2**: 17, 23, 25, 32, 35, 39; **24**: 106
  King John **9**: 222, 224, 229, 240, 250, 292; **41**: 205, 215; **56**: 365
  King Lear **2**: 108, 125, 145, 162, 191; **16**: 311; **28**: 223; **46**: 177, 210
  Love's Labour's Lost **2**: 303, 310, 317, 322, 328, 342; **23**: 237, 250, 252; **38**: 232; **47**: 35; **64**: 140, 166
  Macbeth **20**: 12, 318, 324, 329, 353, 363, 367, 374, 387; **28**: 339; **29**: 101, 109, 146, 155, 165; **45**: 67; **47**: 41; **57**: 189, 194, 236, 256, 263, 267
  Measure for Measure **2**: 388, 390, 391, 396, 406, 420, 421, 446, 466, 475, 484, 505, 516, 524; **23**: 299, 405; **33**: 77; **65**: 2, 14, 38
  The Merry Wives of Windsor **5**: 332, 334, 335, 337, 338, 351, 360, 363, 366, 374, 379, 392; **18**: 74, 75; **38**: 264, 273, 313, 319
  The Tempest **8**: 287, 289, 292, 294, 295, 308, 326, 334, 336; **28**: 415; **42**: 332; **45**: 219; **65**: 311
  Titus Andronicus **4**: 613, 628, 632, 635, 640, 644, 647, 650, 675; **27**: 293; **43**: 170, 176,;
  Troilus and Cressida **3**: 538, 539, 540, 541, 548, 566, 571, 604, 611, 621; **27**: 381, 391; **59**: 234, 245, 251, 257, 261, 265, 272; **65**: 290
  Twelfth Night **1**: 539, 540, 543, 545, 550, 554, 581, 594; **26**: 257, 337, 342, 346, 364, 366, 371, 374; **34**: 281, 293, 311, 338; **46**: 286, 324; **65**: 336
  The Two Gentlemen of Verona **6**: 438, 442, 445, 447, 449, 458, 462, 560; **12**: 458; **40**: 312, 327, 330, 365; **54**: 338
  The Two Noble Kinsmen **9**: 457, 461, 471, 474; **41**: 340, 385; **50**: 305, 326
  The Winter's Tale **47**: 25

chastity
  A Midsummer Night's Dream **45**: 143

Chaucer's Criseyde, compared with
  Troilus and Cressida **43**: 305

chivalry
  Troilus and Cressida **16**: 84; **27**: 370, 374
  The Two Noble Kinsmen **50**: 305, 348

Christian elements
  See also **religious, mythic, or spiritual content**
  As You Like It **5**: 39, 98, 162; **57**: 31
  Coriolanus **30**: 111
  King Lear **2**: 137, 170, 179, 188, 191, 197, 207, 218, 222, 226, 229, 238, 249, 265, 286; **22**: 233, 271; **25**: 218; **46**: 77; **52**: 95; **60**: 75; **61**: 194, 262; **66**: 326
  Macbeth **3**: 194, 239, 260, 269, 275, 286, 293, 297, 318; **20**: 203, 206, 210, 256, 262, 289, 291, 294; **44**: 341, 366; **47**: 41; **57**: 236
  Measure for Measure **2**: 391, 394, 399, 421, 437, 449, 466, 479, 491, 511, 522; **48**: 1; **49**: 325; **60**: 12; **65**: 53; **66**: 300
  The Merchant of Venice **52**: 89
  Much Ado about Nothing **8**: 17, 19, 29, 55, 95, 104, 111, 115; **31**: 209; **55**: 228
  The Phoenix and Turtle **10**: 21, 24, 31; **38**: 326; **51**: 162, 171, 181; **64**: 211, 217, 225
  The Rape of Lucrece **10**: 77, 80, 89, 96, 98, 109; **59**: 165

Sonnets **10:** 191, 256
Titus Andronicus **4:** 656, 680
Twelfth Night **46:** 338; **66:** 312
The Two Gentlemen of Verona **6:** 438, 494, 514, 532, 555, 564
The Winter's Tale **7:** 381, 387, 402, 410, 417, 419, 425, 429, 436, 452, 460, 501; **36:** 318; **60:** 40

as Christian play
King Lear **48:** 222; **66:** 260

Chorus, role of
Henry V **49:** 194, 200, 211, 219, 260

church versus state
King John **9:** 209, 212, 222, 235, 240; **22:** 120; **66:** 271

civilization versus barbarism
Titus Andronicus **4:** 653; **27:** 293; **28:** 249; **32:** 265; **62:** 265, 270

Clarissa, (Samuel Richardson), compared with
King Lear **48:** 277
Measure for Measure **48:** 277
Othello **48:** 277
Titus Andronicus **48:** 277

class distinctions, conflict, and relations
General Commentary **50:** 1, 34
Coriolanus **64:** 94
Henry V **28:** 146
Henry VI, Parts 1, 2, and 3 **37:** 97; **39:** 187; **50:** 45, 51; **56:** 117, 131
The Merry Wives of Windsor **5:** 338, 343, 346, 347, 366, 390, 395, 400, 402; **22:** 93; **28:** 69
A Midsummer Night's Dream **22:** 23; **25:** 36; **45:** 160; **50:** 74, 86
The Taming of the Shrew **31:** 300, 351; **50:** 64, 74; **55:** 342
The Two Noble Kinsmen **50:** 295, 305, 310

classical influence and sources
The Comedy of Errors **1:** 13, 14, 16, 31, 32, 43, 61; **54:** 169
The Tempest **29:** 278, 343, 362, 368; **61:** 362

Clowns and Fools in Shakespeare's Works (**Volume 46:** 1, 14, 18, 24, 29, 33, 48, 52, 60)
As You Like It **5:** 24, 28, 30, 32, 36, 39, 54, 61, 63, 72, 75, 76, 77, 79, 84, 86, 93, 98, 114, 118, 135, 138, 166; **23:** 152; **34:** 72, 85, 147, 161; **46:** 88, 105, 117, 122
King Lear **2:** 108, 112, 125, 156, 162, 245, 278, 284; **11:** 17, 158, 169; **22:** 227; **25:** 202; **28:** 223; **46:** 191, 205, 210, 218, 225
Twelfth Night **1:** 543, 548, 558, 561, 563, 566, 570, 572, 603, 620, 642, 655, 658; **26:** 233, 364; **46:** 297, 303, 310

colonialism
Henry V **22:** 103
A Midsummer Night's Dream **53:** 32

The Tempest **13:** 424, 440; **15:** 228, 268, 269, 270, 271, 272, 273; **19:** 421; **25:** 357, 382; **28:** 249; **29:** 343, 368; **32:** 338, 367, 400; **42:** 320; **45:** 200, 280; **53:** 11, 21, 45, 67; **61:** 297, 307
Titus Andronicus **62:** 270

combat
King Lear **22:** 365
Macbeth **22:** 365

comedy of affectation
Love's Labour's Lost **2:** 302, 303, 304; **23:** 191, 224, 226, 228, 233

comic and tragic elements, combination of
King Lear **2:** 108, 110, 112, 125, 156, 162, 245, 278, 284; **46:** 191
Measure for Measure **16:** 102; **65:** 2, 111
Romeo and Juliet **5:** 496, 524, 528, 547, 559; **46:** 78
Troilus and Cressida **43:** 351

comic and farcical elements
All's Well That Ends Well **26:** 97, 114; **48:** 65; **55:** 148, 154, 164
Antony and Cleopatra **6:** 52, 85, 104, 125, 131, 151, 192, 202, 219; **47:** 77, 124, 149, 165; **58:** 41
The Comedy of Errors **1:** 14, 16, 19, 23, 30, 34, 35, 43, 46, 50, 55, 56, 59, 61; **19:** 54; **26:** 183, 186, 188, 190; **34:** 190, 245; **54:** 136, 144, 189; **66:** 17, 31, 38
Coriolanus **9:** 8, 9, 14, 53, 80, 106
Cymbeline **4:** 35, 56, 113, 141; **15:** 111, 122; **47:** 296
Henry IV, Parts 1 and 2 **1:** 286, 290, 314, 327, 328, 336, 353; **19:** 195; **25:** 109; **39:** 72; **57:** 120
Henry V **5:** 185, 188, 191, 192, 217, 230, 233, 241, 252, 260, 276; **19:** 217; **28:** 121; **30:** 193, 202
The Merry Wives of Windsor **5:** 336, 338, 346, 350, 360, 369, 373; **18:** 74, 75, 84; **59:** 105
A Midsummer Night's Dream **58:** 169
Richard II **24:** 262, 263, 395; **39:** 243
Twelfth Night **26:** 233, 257, 337, 342, 371; **51:** 1; **52:** 57
Venus and Adonis **10:** 429, 434, 439, 442, 459, 462, 489; **33:** 352; **51:** 377

comic form
As You Like It **46:** 105; **51:** 1; **57:** 2
Love's Labour' Lost **54:** 257, 263
Measure for Measure **2:** 456, 460, 479, 482, 491, 514, 516; **13:** 94, 104; **23:** 309, 326, 327; **49:** 349; **65:** 2

comic resolution
As You Like It **52:** 63
Love's Labour's Lost **2:** 335, 340; **16:** 17; **19:** 92; **38:** 209; **51:** 1; **54:** 240, 248, 274; **64:** 122, 145, 154

comic, tragic, and romantic elements, fusion of
The Winter's Tale **7:** 390, 394, 396, 399, 410, 412, 414, 429, 436, 479, 483, 490, 501; **13:** 417; **15:** 514, 524, 532; **25:** 339; **36:** 295, 380; **57:** 347

commodity
King John **9:** 224, 229, 245, 260, 275, 280, 297; **19:** 182; **25:** 98; **41:** 228, 269; **56:** 335

communication, failure of
Troilus and Cressida **43:** 277

compassion, theme of
The Tempest **42:** 339

complex or enigmatic nature
The Phoenix and Turtle **10:** 7, 14, 35, 42; **38:** 326, 357; **51:** 145, 162; **64:** 205, 209, 255

composition date
The Comedy of Errors **1:** 18, 23, 34, 55
Henry VIII **2:** 19, 22, 35; **24:** 129
Pericles **2:** 537, 544
Sonnets **10:** 153, 154, 161, 166, 196, 217, 226, 270, 277; **28:** 363, 385
Twelfth Night **37:** 78

conclusion
All's Well That Ends Well **38:** 123, 132, 142; **55:** 148, 154, 170
Love's Labour's Lost **38:** 172; **54:** 240, 248, 274
Troilus and Cressida **3:** 538, 549, 558, 566, 574, 583, 594
  comedy vs. tragedy **43:** 351; **59:** 278

conflict between Christianity and Judaism
The Merchant of Venice **4:** 224, 250, 268, 289, 324, 344; **12:** 67, 70, 72, 76; **22:** 69; **25:** 257; **40:** 117, 127, 166, 181; **48:** 54, 77; **53:** 105, 159, 214; **66:** 87, 110, 126, 127, 153, 158, 180

conflict between idealism and pragmatism
Hamlet **60:** 71

conscience
Cymbeline **61:** 136
Macbeth **52:** 15
Richard III **8:** 148, 152, 162, 165, 190, 197, 201, 206, 210, 228, 232, 239, 243, 252, 258; **39:** 341; **52:** 5, 196, 205

as consciously philosophical
The Phoenix and Turtle **10:** 7, 21, 24, 31, 48; **38:** 342, 378

conspiracy or treason
The Tempest **16:** 426; **19:** 357; **25:** 382; **29:** 377
Henry V **49:** 223

constancy and faithfulness
The Phoenix and Turtle **10:** 18, 20, 21, 48; **38:** 329; **64:** 209

construing the truth
Julius Caesar **7:** 320, 336, 343, 350; **37:** 229

consummation of marriage
Othello **22:** 207

contemptus mundi
Antony and Cleopatra **6:** 85, 133

contractual and economic relations
Henry IV, Parts 1 and 2 **13:** 213
Richard II **13:** 213; **49:** 602

contradiction, paradox, and opposition
As You Like It **46:** 105
Romeo and Juliet **5:** 421, 427, 431, 496, 509, 513, 516, 520, 525, 528, 538; **33:** 287; **44:** 11; **65:** 208
Troilus and Cressida **43:** 377; **59:** 318

contrasting dramatic worlds
Henry IV, Parts 1 and 2 **14:** 56, 60, 61, 84, 105; **48:** 95; **49:** 162; **57:** 183
The Merchant of Venice **44:** 11; **66:** 78, 158

contrasts and oppositions
Othello **4:** 421, 455, 457, 462, 508; **25:** 189

corruption in society
As You Like It **46:** 94; **57:** 35
King John **9:** 222, 234, 280, 297

costume
As You Like It **46:** 117
Hamlet **21:** 81
Henry VIII **24:** 82, 87; **28:** 184
Richard II **24:** 274, 278, 291, 304, 325, 356, 364, 423
Romeo and Juliet **11:** 505, 509
Troilus and Cressida **18:** 289, 371, 406, 419; **59:** 323

counsel
The Winter's Tale **19:** 401

Court of Love
The Phoenix and Turtle **10:** 9, 24, 50

court society
The Winter's Tale **16:** 410; **57:** 305, 336

courtly love
Troilus and Cressida **22:** 58; **59:** 349

courtly love tradition, influence of
Romeo and Juliet **5:** 505, 542, 575; **33:** 233

courtship and marriage
See also **marriage**
As You Like It **34:** 109, 177; **48:** 32; **51:** 44
Much Ado about Nothing **8:** 29, 44, 48, 95, 115, 121, 125; **31:** 191, 231; **51:** 33, 44; **55:** 209

credibility
Twelfth Night **1:** 540, 542, 543, 554, 562, 581, 587

critical history
Henry IV, Parts 1 and 2 **42:** 185; **48:** 167

cross-dressing
Twelfth Night **62:** 297, 319

cynicism
Troilus and Cressida **43:** 298

dance
Henry VI, Parts 1, 2, and 3 **22:** 156

dance and patterned action
Love's Labour's Lost **2:** 308, 342; **23:** 191, 237

dark elements
All's Well That Ends Well **7:** 27, 37, 39, 43, 54, 109, 113, 116; **26:** 85; **48:** 65; **50:** 59; **54:** 30; **55:** 164, 170
Twelfth Night **46:** 310

Death (Volume **60:** 2, 12, 21, 26, 33, 46, 71, 91)
Antony and Cleopatra **60:** 46
Coriolanus **60:** 46
Hamlet **60:** 46
Henry IV, Parts 1 and 2 **60:** 26
Henry V **60:** 26
Henry VI, Parts 1, 2, and 3 **60:** 33
Julius Caesar **60:** 46
King Lear **60:** 2, 46, 65, 75
Macbeth **60:** 46, 84
Measure for Measure **60:** 12
Othello **60:** 2, 46, 91
Richard II **60:** 21, 46
Romeo and Juliet **60:** 96
Timon of Athens **60:** 46
The Winter's Tale **60:** 2, 40

death, decay, nature's destructiveness
Antony and Cleopatra **47:** 71
As You Like It **46:** 169
Hamlet **1:** 144, 153, 188, 198, 221, 242; **13:** 502; **28:** 280, 311; **35:** 241; **42:** 279; **60:** 71, 91, 194
King Lear **2:** 93, 94, 101, 104, 106, 109, 112, 116, 129, 131, 137, 143, 147, 149, 156, 160, 170, 179, 188, 197, 207, 218, 222, 226, 231, 238, 241, 245, 249, 253, 265, 269, 273; **16:** 301; **25:** 202, 218; **31:** 77, 117, 137, 142; **46:** 264
Love's Labour's Lost **2:** 305, 331, 344, 348; **64:** 145
Measure for Measure **2:** 394, 452, 516; **25:** 12; **49:** 370
Venus and Adonis **10:** 419, 427, 434, 451, 454, 462, 466, 473, 480, 489; **25:** 305; **33:** 309, 321, 347, 352, 363, 370

decay of heroic ideals
Henry VI, Parts 1, 2, and 3 **3:** 119, 126; **56:** 95

deception, disguise, and duplicity
As You Like It **46:** 134; **57:** 40, 45
Henry IV, Parts 1 and 2 **1:** 397, 406, 425; **42:** 99; **47:** 1, 60; **48:** 95
The Merry Wives of Windsor **5:** 332, 334, 336, 354, 355, 379; **22:** 93; **47:** 308, 314, 321, 325, 344
Much Ado about Nothing **8:** 29, 55, 63, 69, 79, 82, 88, 108, 115; **31:** 191, 198; **55:** 236
Pericles **66:** 201
Sonnets **25:** 374; **40:** 221
The Taming of the Shrew **12:** 416

Deconstructionist interpretation of
Pericles **48:** 364

despair
Macbeth **65:** 297

deposition scene
Richard II **42:** 118

Desire (Volume **38:** 1, 19, 31, 40, 48, 56)
All's Well That Ends Well **38:** 96, 99, 109, 118; **55:** 122
As You Like It **37:** 43; **52:** 63; **60:** 115
Henry IV, Parts 1 and 2 **60:** 129
Love's Labour's Lost **38:** 185, 194, 200, 209
The Merchant of Venice **22:** 3; **40:** 142; **45:** 17; **66:** 135
The Merry Wives of Windsor **38:** 286, 297, 300
Romeo and Juliet **51:** 227, 236
Troilus and Cressida **43:** 317, 329, 340; **59:** 337
Twelfth Night **60:** 115

disappointment, theme of
The Merchant of Venice **53:** 211; **66:** 153

discrepancy between prophetic ending and preceding action
Henry VIII **2:** 22, 25, 31, 46, 49, 56, 60, 65, 68, 75, 81; **32:** 148; **41:** 190; **56:** 273

disillusioned or cynical tone
Troilus and Cressida **3:** 544, 548, 554, 557, 558, 571, 574, 630, 642; **18:** 284, 332, 403, 406, 423; **27:** 376; **59:** 234

disorder
Troilus and Cressida **3:** 578, 589, 599, 604, 609; **18:** 332, 406, 412, 423; **27:** 366; **54:** 84; **55:** 48; **59:** 251; **65:** 226

disorder and civil dissension
Henry VI, Parts 1, 2, and 3 **3:** 59, 67, 76, 92, 103, 126; **13:** 131; **16:** 183; **24:** 11, 17, 28, 31, 47; **25:** 102; **28:** 112; **39:** 154, 177, 187, 196, 205; **56:** 80, 110

displacement
All's Well That Ends Well **22:** 78
Measure for Measure **22:** 78

divine providence
Cymbeline **61:** 144

divine right versus justice
Henry IV **49:** 116; **57:** 88, 130

divine vs. worldly
King Lear **49:** 1

divine will, role of
Romeo and Juliet **5:** 485, 493, 505, 533, 573

domestic elements
As You Like It **46:** 142
Coriolanus **42:** 218; **50:** 145
Venus and Adonis **51:** 359

double-plot
 King Lear **2:** 94, 95, 100, 101, 104, 112, 116, 124, 131, 133, 156, 253, 257; **46:** 254
 Troilus and Cressida **3:** 569, 613

doubling of roles
 Pericles **15:** 150, 152, 167, 173, 180

dramatic elements
 Sonnets **10:** 155, 182, 240, 251, 283, 367
 Venus and Adonis **10:** 459, 462, 486

dramatic shortcomings or failure
 As You Like It **5:** 19, 42, 52, 61, 65
 Love's Labour's Lost **2:** 299, 301, 303, 322; **54:** 240, 248
 Romeo and Juliet **5:** 416, 418, 420, 426, 436, 437, 448, 464, 467, 469, 480, 487, 524, 562

dramatic structure
 The Comedy of Errors **1:** 19, 27, 40, 43, 46, 50; **26:** 186, 190; **34:** 190, 229, 233; **37:** 12; **54:** 136, 155, 189
 Cymbeline **4:** 17, 18, 19, 20, 21, 22, 24, 38, 43, 48, 53, 64, 68, 89, 116, 129, 141; **22:** 302, 365; **25:** 319; **36:** 115, 125; **60:** 240; **61:** 2
 Othello **4:** 370, 390, 399, 427, 488, 506, 517, 569; **22:** 207; **28:** 243; **53:** 261
 The Winter's Tale **7:** 382, 390, 396, 399, 402, 407, 414, 429, 432, 473, 479, 493, 497, 501; **15:** 528; **25:** 339; **36:** 289, 295, 362, 380; **45:** 297, 344, 358, 366; **57:** 278, 285, 347

 as dream-play
  A Midsummer Night's Dream **3:** 365, 370, 372, 377, 389, 391; **29:** 190; **45:** 117; **58:** 181
  Pericles **66:** 233

Dreams in Shakespeare (Volume 45: 1, 10, 17, 28, 40, 48, 58, 67, 75)
 Antony and Cleopatra **45:** 28
 Cymbeline **4:** 162, 167; **44:** 28; **45:** 67, 75
 Hamlet **45:** 28
 Julius Caesar **45:** 10
 A Midsummer Night's Dream **45:** 96, 107, 117
 Richard III **62:** 14, 18
 Romeo and Juliet **45:** 40
 The Tempest **45:** 236, 247, 259

dualisms
 Antony and Cleopatra **19:** 304; **27:** 82; **58:** 2, 71, 79, 105
 Cymbeline **4:** 29, 64, 73

duration of time
 As You Like It **5:** 44, 45
 A Midsummer Night's Dream **3:** 362, 370, 380, 386, 494; **45:** 175

economic relations
 Henry V **13:** 213

economics and exchange
 Coriolanus **50:** 152

 The Merchant of Venice **40:** 197, 208; **53:** 116; **66:** 59, 78

editorial and textual issues
 Sonnets **28:** 363; **40:** 273; **42:** 296

education
 All's Well That Ends Well **7:** 62, 86, 90, 93, 98, 104, 116, 126
 The Two Gentlemen of Verona **6:** 490, 494, 504, 526, 532, 555, 568

education or nurturing
 The Tempest **8:** 353, 370, 384, 396; **29:** 292, 368, 377

egotism or narcissism
 Much Ado about Nothing **8:** 19, 24, 28, 29, 55, 69, 95, 115; **55:** 209
 Twelfth Night **60:** 265, 270, 287

Elizabeth, audience of
 Sonnets **48:** 325

Elizabeth's influence
 The Merry Wives of Windsor **5:** 333, 334, 335, 336, 339, 346, 355, 366, 402; **18:** 5, 86; **38:** 278; **47:** 344

Elizabethan and Jacobean politics, relation to
 Cymbeline **61:** 54, 76
 Hamlet **28:** 232; **28:** 290, 311; **35:** 140; **58:** 79, 134

Elizabethan attitudes, influence of
 Richard II **6:** 287, 292, 294, 305, 321, 327, 364, 402, 414; **13:** 494; **24:** 325; **28:** 188; **39:** 273; **42:** 118; **52:** 141, 144; **58:** 283, 293

Elizabethan betrothal and marriage customs
 Measure for Measure **2:** 429, 437, 443, 503; **49:** 286; **65:** 80

Elizabethan commerce
 Cymbeline **61:** 76

Elizabethan culture, relation to
 General Commentary **50:** 34; **53:** 169; **56:** 2, 3, 15, 47
 Antony and Cleopatra **47:** 103; **58:** 118
 As You Like It **5:** 21, 59, 66, 68, 70, 158; **16:** 53; **28:** 46; **34:** 120; **37:** 1; **46:** 142; **57:** 23, 31, 64, 75
 The Comedy of Errors **26:** 138, 142; **34:** 201, 215, 233, 238, 258; **42:** 80; **54:** 169, 200; **66:** 22, 51
 Hamlet **1:** 76, 148, 151, 154, 160, 166, 169, 171, 176, 184, 202, 209, 254; **13:** 282, 494; **19:** 330; **21:** 407, 416; **22:** 258; **59:** 74
 Henry IV, Parts 1 and 2 **19:** 195; **48:** 117, 143, 151, 175
 Henry V **5:** 210, 213, 217, 223, 257, 299, 310; **16:** 202; **19:** 133, 233; **28:** 121, 159; **30:** 215, 262; **37:** 187; **49:** 260
 Julius Caesar **16:** 231; **30:** 342, 379; **50:** 13, 211, 269, 280

 King Lear **2:** 168, 174, 177, 183, 226, 241; **19:** 330; **22:** 227, 233, 365; **25:** 218; **46:** 276; **47:** 9; **49:** 67; **61:** 172, 176, 187, 194
 Love's Labour's Lost **64:** 122
 Measure for Measure **2:** 394, 418, 429, 432, 437, 460, 470, 482, 503
 The Merchant of Venice **32:** 66; **40:** 117, 127, 142, 166, 181, 197, 208; **48:** 54, 77; **49:** 37; **53:** 105, 111, 116, 127, 159; **66:** 117, 144
 A Midsummer Night's Dream **50:** 86; **58:** 220
 Much Ado about Nothing **8:** 23, 33, 44, 55, 58, 79, 88, 104, 111, 115; **51:** 15; **55:** 209, 241, 259
 The Rape of Lucrece **33:** 195; **43:** 77
 Richard II **58:** 267, 275
 Richard III **62:** 66
 The Taming of the Shrew **31:** 288, 295, 300, 315, 326, 345, 351; **55:** 315, 322, 334; **64:** 296, 327, 333, 343
 Timon of Athens **1:** 487, 489, 495, 500; **20:** 433; **27:** 203, 212, 230; **50:** 13; **52:** 320, 354
 Titus Andronicus **27:** 282; **62:** 233, 270
 Troilus and Cressida **3:** 560, 574, 606; **25:** 56; **59:** 225, 295, 306
 Twelfth Night **1:** 549, 553, 555, 563, 581, 587, 620; **16:** 53; **19:** 42, 78; **26:** 357; **28:** 1; **34:** 323, 330; **46:** 291; **51:** 15; **62:** 319, 348

Elizabethan dramatic conventions
 Cymbeline **4:** 53, 124
 Henry VIII **24:** 155; **56:** 196, 248

Elizabethan literary influences
 Henry VI, Parts 1, 2, and 3 **3:** 75, 97, 100, 119, 143; **22:** 156; **28:** 112; **37:** 97; **56:** 162, 180

Elizabethan love poetry
 Love's Labour's Lost **38:** 232

Elizabethan poetics, influence of
 Romeo and Juliet **5:** 416, 520, 522, 528, 550, 559, 575; **65:** 185

Elizabethan politics, relation to
 Hamlet **60:** 346
 Henry IV, Parts 1 and 2 **22:** 395; **28:** 203; **47:** 60; **48:** 117, 143, 167, 175; **57:** 88, 94
 Henry VIII **22:** 395; **24:** 115, 129, 140; **32:** 148; **56:** 201, 248
 King John **48:** 132; **56:** 306, 314, 325; **60:** 295, 329; **66:** 271
 Macbeth **60:** 357
 Richard III **22:** 395; **25:** 141; **37:** 144; **39:** 345, 349; **42:** 130; **52:** 201, 214, 257; **62:** 2

Elizabethan setting
 The Two Gentlemen of Verona **12:** 463, 485

Elizabethan society
 The Merry Wives of Windsor **47:** 331

Epicureanism
 Julius Caesar **50:** 249

emulation or rivalry
Julius Caesar **16:** 231; **50:** 211

England and Rome, parallels between
Coriolanus **9:** 39, 43, 106, 148, 180, 193; **25:** 296; **30:** 67, 105

English language and colonialism
Henry V **22:** 103; **28:** 159

English Reformation, influence of
Henry VIII **2:** 25, 35, 39, 51, 67; **24:** 89; **56:** 201; **61:** 92

epic elements
Henry V **5:** 192, 197, 246, 257, 314; **30:** 181, 220, 237, 252

erotic elements
A Midsummer Night's Dream **3:** 445, 491, 497, 511; **12:** 259, 262, 298; **16:** 34; **19:** 21; **29:** 183, 225, 269; **58:** 194
Venus and Adonis **10:** 410, 411, 418, 419, 427, 428, 429, 442, 448, 454, 459, 466, 473; **25:** 305, 328; **28:** 355; **33:** 321, 339, 347, 352, 363, 370; **51:** 345, 352, 359, 368

as experimental play
Romeo and Juliet **5:** 464, 509, 528

Essex Rebellion, relation to
Richard II **6:** 249, 250; **24:** 356; **58:** 293

ethical or moral issues
King John **9:** 212, 222, 224, 229, 235, 240, 263, 275, 280; **56:** 335
King Lear **52:** 1, 95
Measure for Measure **52:** 69; **65:** 72
Twelfth Night **52:** 57

ethnicity
The Winter's Tale **37:** 306

Euripides, influence of
Titus Andronicus **27:** 285

evil
See also **good versus evil**
Macbeth **3:** 194, 208, 231, 234, 239, 241, 267, 289; **20:** 203, 206, 210, 374; **52:** 23; **57:** 267
Othello **52:** 78
Richard III **52:** 78
Romeo and Juliet **5:** 485, 493, 505
Titus Andronicus **53:** 86, 92

excess
King John **9:** 251

fable of the belly
Coriolanus **50:** 13, 110, 140

fame
Coriolanus **30:** 58

family honor, structure, and inheritance
Richard II **6:** 338, 368, 388, 397, 414; **39:** 263, 279
Richard III **8:** 177, 248, 252, 263, 267; **25:** 141; **39:** 335, 341, 349, 370

family, theme of
Cymbeline **44:** 28

fancy
Twelfth Night **1:** 543, 546

as farce
The Taming of the Shrew **9:** 330, 337, 338, 341, 342, 365, 381, 386, 413, 426; **55:** 357; **64:** 233

farcical elements
See **comic and farcical elements**

fate
Richard II **6:** 289, 294, 304, 352, 354, 385
Romeo and Juliet **5:** 431, 444, 464, 469, 470, 479, 480, 485, 487, 493, 509, 530, 533, 562, 565, 571, 573; **33:** 249; **54:** 125

Fathers and Daughters (Volume 36: 1, 12, 25, 32, 37, 45, 70, 78)
As You Like It **46:** 94
Cymbeline **34:** 134
King Lear **34:** 51, 54, 60
    cruelty of daughters **2:** 101, 102, 106; **31:** 84, 123, 137, 142
Pericles **34:** 226, 233
The Winter's Tale **34:** 311, 318, 328

Feast of the Lupercal
Julius Caesar **50:** 269

female identity
See also **Gender Identity and Issues**
Macbeth **57:** 256

feminine power, role of
Macbeth **57:** 242

Feminist Criticism (Volume 55: 1, 16, 27, 37, 48, 56, 68, 78)
General Commentary **55:** 1, 16, 27, 56, 68, 78
As You Like It **23:** 107, 108
Comedy of Errors **42:** 93
Hamlet **55:** 56; **59:** 31, 39
King Lear **55:** 68
Love's Labour's Lost **42:** 93
Measure for Measure **23:** 320; **55:** 16, 68; **65:** 61
Merchant of Venice **55:** 27
A Midsummer Night's Dream **48:** 23
The Rape of Lucrece **59:** 165, 189, 193
Troilus and Cressida **55:** 37, 48; **59:** 337

feminism
As You Like It **57:** 2, 13

festive or folklore elements
Twelfth Night **46:** 338; **51:** 15

feud
Romeo and Juliet **5:** 415, 419, 425, 447, 458, 464, 469, 479, 480, 493, 509, 522, 556, 565, 566, 571, 575; **25:** 181; **51:** 245; **65:** 201

fire and water
Coriolanus **25:** 263

flattery
Coriolanus **9:** 26, 45, 92, 100, 110, 121, 130, 144, 157, 183, 193; **25:** 296
Henry IV, Parts 1 and 2 **22:** 395
Henry VIII **22:** 395
Richard III **22:** 395

folk drama, relation to
The Winter's Tale **7:** 420, 451; **57:** 356

folk elements
The Taming of the Shrew **9:** 381, 393, 404, 426

folk rituals, elements and influence of
Henry VI, Parts 1, 2, and 3 **39:** 205
The Merry Wives of Windsor **5:** 353, 369, 376, 392, 397, 400; **38:** 256, 300

food, meaning of
The Comedy of Errors **34:** 220
Troilus and Cressida **43:** 298; **59:** 306

forest
The Two Gentlemen of Verona **6:** 450, 456, 492, 514, 547, 555, 564, 568

Forest of Arden
As You Like It
    as "bitter" Arcadia **5:** 98, 118, 162; **23:** 97, 98, 99, 100, 122, 139
    Duke Frederick's court, contrast with **5:** 46, 102, 103, 112, 130, 156; **16:** 53; **23:** 126, 128, 129, 131, 134; **34:** 78, 102, 131; **46:** 164; **57:** 64; **65:** 255, 285
    pastoral elements **5:** 18, 20, 24, 32, 35, 47, 50, 54, 55, 57, 60, 77, 128, 135, 156; **23:** 17, 20, 27, 46, 137; **34:** 78, 147; **46:** 88
    as patriarchal society **5:** 168; **23:** 150; **34:** 177; **57:** 2
    as source of self-knowledge **5:** 98, 102, 103, 128, 130, 135, 148, 158, 162; **23:** 17; **34:** 102; **57:** 35
    as timeless, mythical world **5:** 112, 130, 141; **23:** 132; **34:** 78; **37:** 43; **46:** 88; **65:** 255
    theme of play **46:** 88

forgiveness or redemption
Henry IV, Parts 1 and 2 **57:** 116
Venus and Adonis **51:** 377
The Winter's Tale **7:** 381, 389, 395, 402, 407, 436, 456, 460, 483; **36:** 318

free will versus fate
Macbeth **3:** 177, 183, 184, 190, 196, 198, 202, 207, 208, 213; **13:** 361; **44:** 351, 361, 366, 373; **54:** 6; **65:** 317
The Two Noble Kinsmen **9:** 474, 481, 486, 492, 498

freedom and servitude
The Tempest **8:** 304, 307, 312, 429; **22:** 302; **29:** 278, 368, 377; **37:** 336

French language, Shakespeare's use of
Henry V **5:** 186, 188, 190; **25:** 131

Freudian analysis
A Midsummer Night's Dream **44:** 1

friendship
See also **love and friendship** and **love versus friendship**
Coriolanus **30:** 125, 142
Sonnets **10:** 185, 279; **28:** 380; **51:** 284, 288
The Two Noble Kinsmen **9:** 448, 463, 470, 474, 479, 481, 486, 490; **19:** 394; **41:** 363, 372; **42:** 361; **58:** 345, 356, 371

Gender Identity and Issues (Volume 40: 1, 9, 15, 27, 33, 51, 61, 65, 75, 90, 99)
All's Well That Ends Well **7:** 9, 10, 67, 126; **13:** 77, 84; **19:** 113; **26:** 128; **38:** 89, 99, 118; **44:** 35; **55:** 101, 109, 122, 164
Antony and Cleopatra **13:** 368; **25:** 257; **27:** 144; **47:** 174, 192; **53:** 67, 77; **58:** 59
As You Like It **46:** 127, 134; **57:** 13, 23, 45
The Comedy of Errors **34:** 215, 220
Coriolanus **30:** 79, 125, 142; **44:** 93; **50:** 128
Hamlet **35:** 144; **44:** 189, 195, 198; **59:** 31, 39
Henry IV, Parts 1 and 2 **13:** 183; **25:** 151; **44:** 44; **48:** 175; **60:** 154
Henry V **13:** 183; **28:** 121, 146, 159; **44:** 44
Julius Caesar **13:** 260
Macbeth **57:** 256
The Merchant of Venice **40:** 142, 151, 156
Othello **32:** 294; **35:** 327; **53:** 255, 268, 310
A Midsummer Night's Dream **53:** 1; **58:** 215
The Rape of Lucrece **53:** 1; **59:** 189, 193, 206
Richard II **25:** 89; **39:** 295
Richard III **25:** 141; **37:** 144; **39:** 345; **52:** 223, 239; **62:** 41
Romeo and Juliet **32:** 256; **51:** 253; **65:** 119, 142, 190
Sonnets **37:** 374; **40:** 238, 247, 254, 264, 268, 273; **53:** 1
The Taming of the Shrew **28:** 24; **31:** 261, 268, 276, 282, 288, 295, 300, 335, 351; **55:** 278, 299, 305, 315, 322, 357; **64:** 320, 327, 333, 343, 352
Titus Andronicus **62:** 242
The Tempest **53:** 64, 67
Twelfth Night **19:** 78; **34:** 344; **37:** 59; **42:** 32; **46:** 347, 362, 369; **60:** 129; **62:** 297, 319, 325
The Two Gentlemen of Verona **40:** 374
The Two Noble Kinsmen **42:** 361

genre
All's Well That Ends Well **48:** 65
As You Like It **5:** 46, 55, 79
The Comedy of Errors **34:** 251, 258; **66:** 38
Coriolanus **9:** 42, 43, 53, 80, 106, 112, 117, 130, 164, 177; **30:** 67, 74, 79, 89, 111, 125; **50:** 99; **64:** 2, 8, 18
Cymbeline **61:** 2
Hamlet **1:** 176, 212, 237
Love's Labour's Lost **38:** 163

The Merchant of Venice **4:** 191, 200, 201, 209, 215, 221, 232, 238, 247; **12:** 48, 54, 62; **54:** 65; **66:** 292
Merry Wives of Windsor **59:** 111
Much Ado about Nothing **8:** 9, 18, 19, 28, 29, 39, 41, 44, 53, 63, 69, 73, 79, 82, 95, 100, 104; **48:** 14; **55:** 232, 268
Richard III **8:** 181, 182, 197, 206, 218, 228, 239, 243, 252, 258; **13:** 142; **39:** 383; **52:** 239; **62:** 2, 41
The Taming of the Shrew **9:** 329, 334, 362, 375; **22:** 48; **31:** 261, 269, 276; **55:** 278; **64:** 239
Timon of Athens **1:** 454, 456, 459, 460, 462, 483, 492, 499, 503, 509, 511, 512, 515, 518, 525, 531; **27:** 203
Troilus and Cressida **3:** 541, 542, 549, 558, 566, 571, 574, 587, 594, 604, 630, 642; **27:** 366; **59:** 278
The Two Gentlemen of Verona **6:** 460, 468, 472, 516; **40:** 320

genres, mixture of
Timon of Athens **16:** 351; **25:** 198

gift exchange
Love's Labour's Lost **25:** 1; **64:** 122

good versus evil
See also **evil**
Measure for Measure **2:** 432, 452, 524; **33:** 52, 61; **52:** 69
The Tempest **8:** 302, 311, 315, 370, 423, 439; **29:** 278 297; **61:** 338, 362

grace
The Winter's Tale **7:** 420, 425, 460, 493; **36:** 328

grace and civility
Love's Labour's Lost **2:** 351; **64:** 114

Greece
Troilus and Cressida **43:** 287

grotesque or absurd elements
Hamlet **42:** 279
King Lear **2:** 136, 156, 245; **13:** 343; **52:** 1

handkerchief, significance of
Othello **4:** 370, 384, 385, 396, 503, 530, 562; **35:** 265, 282, 380

Hercules Furens (Seneca) as source
Othello **16:** 283

heroism
Henry V **49:** 194, 200, 211, 236

Hippolytus, myth of
A Midsummer Night's Dream **29:** 216; **45:** 84

historical accuracy
Henry VI, Parts 1, 2, and 3 **3:** 18, 21, 35, 46, 51; **16:** 217; **24:** 16, 18, 25, 31, 45, 48
Richard III **8:** 144, 145, 153, 159, 163, 165, 168, 213, 223, 228, 232; **39:** 305, 308, 326, 383

historical allegory
The Winter's Tale **7:** 381; **15:** 528
The Merchant of Venice **53:** 179, 187

historical and dramatic elements
Henry IV **49:** 93

historical and romantic elements, combination of
Henry VIII **2:** 46, 49, 51, 75, 76, 78; **24:** 71, 80, 146; **41:** 129, 146, 180; **56:** 196, 201

historical content
Henry IV, Parts 1 and 2 **1:** 310, 328, 365, 366, 370, 374, 380, 387, 421, 424, 427, 431; **16:** 172; **19:** 157; **25:** 151; **32:** 136; **39:** 143; **48:** 143, 167; **57:** 137
Henry V **5:** 185, 188, 190, 192, 193, 198, 246, 314; **13:** 201; **19:** 133; **25:** 131; **30:** 193, 202, 207, 215, 252
King John **9:** 216, 219, 220, 222, 235, 240, 254, 284, 290, 292, 297, 300, 303; **13:** 163; **32:** 93, 114; **41:** 234, 243; **56:** 286, 296, 306, 357; **60:** 329
The Tempest **8:** 364, 408, 420; **16:** 426; **25:** 382; **29:** 278, 339, 343, 368; **45:** 226; **53:** 21, 53; **61:** 297

historical determinism versus free will
Julius Caesar **7:** 160, 298, 316, 333, 346, 356; **13:** 252

historical elements
Cymbeline **47:** 260

historical epic, as epilogue to Shakespeare's
Henry VIII **2:** 22, 25, 27, 39, 51, 60, 65

historical epic, place in or relation to Shakespeare's
Henry IV, Parts 1 and 2 **1:** 309, 314, 328, 374, 379, 424, 427
Henry V **5:** 195, 198, 205, 212, 225, 241, 244, 287, 304, 310; **14:** 337, 342; **30:** 215
Henry VI, Parts 1, 2, and 3 **3:** 24, 59; **24:** 51; **48:** 167; **56:** 95

historical principles
Richard III **39:** 308, 326, 387

historical relativity, theme of
Henry VIII **41:** 146; **56:** 220; **61:** 111

historical revisionism
Henry VI, Parts 1, 2, and 3 (**56:** 85, 110, 122, 131, 145

historical sources, compared with
Richard II **6:** 252, 279, 343; **28:** 134; **39:** 235; **49:** 60; **58:** 259, 275, 283

historiography
General Commentary **56:** 3, 15, 25, 47, 53, 60
Henry IV, Parts 1 and 2 **56:** 2, 15, 25
Henry V **56:** 2, 15
Henry VI, Parts 1, 2, and 3 **56:** 2, 25

Henry VIII **37**: 109, 201, 209, 230; **61**: 92, 101, 111
Richard II **56**: 2, 15
Richard III **56**: 2

homoerotic elements
As You Like It **46**: 127, 142; **57**: 23; **60**: 115
Henry V **16**: 202
Sonnets **10**: 155, 156, 159, 161, 175, 213, 391; **16**: 461; **28**: 363, 380; **37**: 347; **40**: 254, 264, 273; **51**: 270, 284; **62**: 128

Homosexuality (Volume 60: 105, 115, 129, 142, 154)
As You Like It **46**: 127, 142; **57**: 13; **60**: 115
Henry IV, Parts 1 and 2 **60**: 154
Measure for Measure **42**: 1
The Merchant of Venice **22**: 3, 69; **37**: 86; **40**: 142, 156, 197; **66**: 127
A Midsummer Night's Dream **60**: 142
Sonnets **60**: 105
Troilus and Cressida **60**: 105
Twelfth Night **22**: 69; **42**: 32; **46**: 362; **60**: 115, 129
The Winter's Tale **48**: 309

honor or integrity
Coriolanus **9**: 43, 65, 73, 92, 106, 110, 121, 144, 153, 157, 164, 177, 183, 189; **30**: 89, 96, 133; **64**: 2
Henry VIII **61**: 101

hospitality
The Winter's Tale **19**: 366

as humanistic play
Henry VI, Parts 1, 2, and 3 **3**: 83, 92, 109, 115, 119, 131, 136, 143

hunt motif
Venus and Adonis **10**: 434, 451, 466, 473; **33**: 357, 370

hypocrisy
Henry V **5**: 203, 213, 219, 223, 233, 260, 271, 302

ideal love
See also **love**
Cymbeline **61**: 34, 45
Romeo and Juliet **5**: 421, 427, 431, 436, 437, 450, 463, 469, 498, 505, 575; **25**: 257; **33**: 210, 225, 272; **51**: 25; **51**: 44, 195, 203, 219

idealism versus pragmatism
Hamlet **16**: 246; **28**: 325

idealism versus realism
See also **realism**
Love's Labour's Lost **38**: 163
Othello **4**: 457, 508, 517; **13**: 313; **25**: 189; **53**: 350

identities of persons
Sonnets **10**: 154, 155, 156, 161, 166, 167, 169, 173, 174, 175, 185, 190, 191, 196, 218, 226, 230, 233, 240; **40**: 238; **62**: 128

identity
The Comedy of Errors **34**: 201, 208, 211; **54**: 155, 169, 200
Coriolanus **42**: 243; **50**: 128
A Midsummer Night's Dream **29**: 269; **58**: 215
The Two Gentlemen of Verona **6**: 494, 511, 529, 532, 547, 560, 564, 568; **19**: 34

illusion
The Comedy of Errors **1**: 13, 14, 27, 37, 40, 45, 59, 63; **26**: 188; **34**: 194, 211; **54**: 169, 200

illusion versus reality
Love's Labour's Lost **2**: 303, 308, 331, 340, 344, 348, 356, 359, 367, 371, 375; **23**: 230, 231

imagery
Venus and Adonis **10**: 414, 415, 416, 420, 429, 434, 449, 459, 466, 473, 480; **25**: 328; **28**: 355; **33**: 321, 339, 352, 363, 370, 377; **42**: 347; **51**: 335, 388

imagination and art
A Midsummer Night's Dream **3**: 365, 371, 381, 402, 412, 417, 421, 423, 441, 459, 468, 506, 516, 520; **22**: 39; **45**: 96, 126, 136, 147

immortality
Measure for Measure **16**: 102

imperialism
Antony and Cleopatra **53**: 67, 77
Henry V **22**: 103; **28**: 159
The Merchant of Venice **53**: 116

implausibility of plot, characters, or events
All's Well That Ends Well **7**: 8, 45
King Lear **2**: 100, 136, 145, 278; **13**: 343
The Merchant of Venice **4**: 191, 192, 193; **12**: 52, 56, 76, 119
Much Ado about Nothing **8**: 9, 12, 16, 19, 33, 36, 39, 44, 53, 100, 104
Othello **4**: 370, 380, 391, 442, 444; **47**: 51

inaction
Troilus and Cressida **3**: 587, 621; **27**: 347

incest, motif of
Pericles **2**: 582, 588; **22**: 315; **36**: 257, 264; **51**: 97, 110; **66**: 190, 224

inconsistencies
Henry VIII **2**: 16, 27, 28, 31, 60

inconsistency between first and second halves
Measure for Measure **2**: 474, 475, 505, 514, 524; **49**: 349, 358

induction
The Taming of the Shrew **9**: 320, 322, 332, 337, 345, 350, 362, 365, 369, 370, 381, 390, 393, 407, 419, 424, 430; **12**: 416, 427, 430, 431, 441; **19**: 34, 122; **22**: 48; **31**: 269, 315, 351; **55**: 331, 357; **64**: 244, 255, 343

as inferior or flawed play
Henry VI, Parts 1, 2, and 3 **3**: 20, 21, 25, 26, 35
Pericles **2**: 537, 546, 553, 563, 564; **15**: 139, 143, 156, 167, 176; **36**: 198; **51**: 79; **66**: 186
Timon of Athens **1**: 476, 481, 489, 499, 520; **20**: 433, 439, 491; **25**: 198; **27**: 157, 175; **52**: 338, 349

infidelity
Troilus and Cressida **43**: 298; **55**: 37, 48; **59**: 251

innocence
Macbeth **3**: 234, 241, 327; **57**: 267
Othello **47**: 25
Pericles **36**: 226, 274

innocence to experience
The Two Noble Kinsmen **9**: 481, 502; **19**: 394

Ireland, William Henry, forgeries of
Sonnets **48**: 325

Irish affairs
Henry V **22**: 103; **28**: 159

ironic or parodic elements
The Two Gentlemen of Verona **6**: 447, 472, 478, 484, 502, 504, 509, 516, 529, 549; **13**: 12; **54**: 295, 307
Henry VIII **41**: 129; **56**: 220

irony
All's Well That Ends Well **7**: 27, 32, 58, 62, 67, 81, 86, 109, 116
Antony and Cleopatra **6**: 53, 136, 146, 151, 159, 161, 189, 192, 211, 224
As You Like It **5**: 30, 32, 154
Coriolanus **9**: 65, 73, 80, 92, 106, 153, 157, 164, 193; **30**: 67, 89, 133
Cymbeline **4**: 64, 77, 103
Henry V **5**: 192, 210, 213, 219, 223, 226, 233, 252, 260, 269, 281, 299, 304; **14**: 336; **30**: 159, 193; **66**: 280
Julius Caesar **7**: 167, 257, 259, 262, 268, 282, 316, 320, 333, 336, 346, 350
The Merchant of Venice **4**: 254, 300, 321, 331, 350; **28**: 63; **66**: 91, 158, 171
Much Ado about Nothing **8**: 14, 63, 79, 82; **28**: 63
The Rape of Lucrece **10**: 93, 98, 128
Richard II **6**: 270, 307, 364, 368, 391; **24**: 383; **28**: 188
Sonnets **10**: 256, 293, 334, 337, 346; **51**: 300
The Taming of the Shrew **9**: 340, 375, 398, 407, 413; **13**: 3; **19**: 122; **55**: 278, 299, 322
The Two Noble Kinsmen **9**: 463, 481, 486; **41**: 301; **50**: 348
The Winter's Tale **7**: 419, 420

the island
The Tempest **8**: 308, 315, 447; **25**: 357, 382; **29**: 278, 343

Italian influences
Sonnets **28**: 407; **62**: 121, 146

Jacobean culture, relation to
  Antony and Cleopatra **58:** 79, 134
  Coriolanus **22:** 248; **64:** 25
  Macbeth **19:** 330; **22:** 365; **57:** 218, 256; **60:** 340, 357
  Pericles **37:** 361; **51:** 86, 110; **66:** 224
  The Winter's Tale **19:** 366, 401, 431; **25:** 347; **32:** 388; **37:** 306; **57:** 305, 336, 356

Jacobean court and politics
  Henry VIII **61:** 92

jealousy
  The Merry Wives of Windsor **5:** 334, 339, 343, 353, 355, 363; **22:** 93; **38:** 273, 307
  Othello **4:** 384, 488, 527; **35:** 253, 265, 282, 301, 310; **44:** 57, 66; **51:** 30
  The Winter's Tale **44:** 66; **47:** 25

Jonsonian humors comedy, influence of
  The Merry Wives of Windsor **38:** 319; **59:** 105

judicial versus natural law
  Measure for Measure **2:** 446, 507, 516, 519; **22:** 85; **33:** 58, 117; **49:** 1, 293

justice
  As You Like It **46:** 94
  Henry IV **49:** 112, 123; **57:** 137
  King Lear **49:** 1
  Othello **35:** 247

justice and mercy
  Measure for Measure **2:** 391, 395, 399, 402, 406, 409, 411, 416, 421, 437, 443, 463, 466, 470, 491, 495, 522, 524; **22:** 85; **33:** 52, 61, 101; **49:** 1, 274, 293, 300; **65:** 14, 30, 91
  The Merchant of Venice **4:** 213, 214, 224, 250, 261, 273, 282, 289, 336; **12:** 80, 129; **40:** 127; **49:** 1, 23, 27, 37; **66:** 180
  Much Ado about Nothing **22:** 85

justice, divine vs. worldly
  King Lear **49:** 67, 73; **60:** 185

juxtaposition of opposing perspectives
  As You Like It **5:** 86, 93, 98, 141; **16:** 53; **23:** 119; **34:** 72, 78, 131

Kingship (Volume 39: 1, 16, 20, 34, 45, 62)
  Henry IV, Parts 1 and 2 **1:** 314, 318, 337, 366, 370, 374, 379, 380, 383, 424; **16:** 172; **19:** 195; **28:** 101; **39:** 100, 116, 123, 130; **42:** 141; **48:** 143; **57:** 88, 94, 108, 137, 160; **65:** 306
  Henry V **5:** 205, 223, 225, 233, 239, 244, 257, 264, 267, 271, 287, 289, 299, 302, 304, 314, 318; **16:** 202; **22:** 137; **30:** 169, 202, 259, 273; **42:** 141; **49:** 200; **66:** 280
  Henry VI, Parts 1, 2, and 3 **3:** 69, 73, 77, 109, 115, 136, 143; **24:** 32; **39:** 154, 177, 187; **47:** 32
  Henry VIII **2:** 49, 58, 60, 65, 75, 78; **24:** 113; **41:** 129, 171; **56:** 242; **61:** 92, 119
  King John **9:** 235, 254, 263, 275, 297; **13:** 158; **19:** 182; **22:** 120; **56:** 314
  Richard II **6:** 263, 264, 272, 277, 289, 294, 327, 354, 364, 381, 388, 391, 402, 409, 414; **19:** 151, 209; **24:** 260, 289, 291, 322, 325, 333, 339, 345, 346, 349, 351, 352, 356, 395, 408, 419, 428; **28:** 134; **39:** 235, 243, 256, 263, 273, 279, 289; **42:** 173; **58:** 275, 301
  Richard III **39:** 335, 341, 345, 349

knighthood
  The Merry Wives of Windsor **5:** 338, 343, 390, 397, 402; **47:** 354

knowledge
  Love's Labour's Lost **22:** 12; **47:** 35

language and imagery
  All's Well That Ends Well **7:** 12, 29, 45, 104, 109, 121; **38:** 132, 65
  Antony and Cleopatra **6:** 21, 25, 39, 64, 80, 85, 92, 94, 100, 104, 142, 146, 155, 159, 161, 165, 189, 192, 202, 211; **13:** 374, 383; **25:** 245, 257; **27:** 96, 105, 135; **58:** 79, 88, 118
  As You Like It **5:** 19, 21, 35, 52, 75, 82, 92, 138; **23:** 15, 21, 26; **28:** 9; **34:** 131; **37:** 43; **48:** 42; **57:** 35, 56
  The Comedy of Errors **1:** 16, 25, 39, 40, 43, 57, 59; **34:** 233; **54:** 152, 162; **66:** 17, 31, 38
  Coriolanus **9:** 8, 9, 13, 53, 64, 65, 73, 78, 84, 100, 112, 121, 136, 139, 142, 144, 153, 157, 174, 183, 193, 198; **22:** 248; **25:** 245, 263; **30:** 111, 125, 142; **37:** 283; **44:** 79; **64:** 2, 89, 94, 103
  Cymbeline **4:** 43, 48, 61, 64, 70, 73, 93, 108; **13:** 401; **25:** 245; **28:** 373, 398; **36:** 115, 158, 166, 186; **47:** 205, 286, 296; **60:** 240
  Hamlet **1:** 95, 144, 153, 154, 160, 188, 198, 221, 227, 249, 259, 270; **22:** 258, 378; **28:** 311; **35:** 144, 152, 238, 241; **42:** 212; **44:** 248; **52:** 35; **59:** 42, 47, 56, 62, 74
  Henry IV, Parts 1 and 2 **13:** 213; **16:** 172; **25:** 245; **28:** 101; **39:** 116, 130; **42:** 153; **47:** 1; **57:** 137
  Henry V **5:** 188, 230, 233, 241, 264, 276; **9:** 203; **19:** 203; **25:** 131; **30:** 159, 181, 207, 234; **30:** 159, 181, 207, 234
  Henry VI, Parts 1, 2, and 3 **3:** 21, 50, 52, 55, 57, 66, 67, 71, 75, 76, 97, 105, 109, 119, 126, 131; **24:** 28; **37:** 157; **39:** 213, 222; **56:** 154, 162, 172, 180
  Henry VIII **41:** 180, 190; **56:** 262, 273
  Julius Caesar **7:** 148, 155, 159, 188, 204, 207, 227, 242, 250, 277, 296, 303, 324, 346, 350; **13:** 260; **17:** 347, 348, 350, 356, 358; **19:** 321; **22:** 280; **25:** 280; **30:** 333, 342; **50:** 196, 258
  King John **9:** 212, 215, 220, 246, 251, 254, 267, 280, 284, 292, 297, 300; **13:** 147, 158; **22:** 120; **37:** 132; **48:** 132; **56:** 286
  King Lear **2:** 129, 137, 161, 191, 199, 237, 257, 271; **16:** 301; **19:** 344; **22:** 233; **46:** 177; **61:** 215, 230
  Love's Labour's Lost **2:** 301, 302, 303, 306, 307, 308, 315, 319, 320, 330, 335, 344, 345, 348, 356, 359, 362, 365, 371, 374, 375; **19:** 92; **22:** 12, 378; **23:** 184, 187, 196, 197, 202, 207, 211, 221, 231, 233, 237, 252; **28:** 9, 63; **38:** 219, 226; **54:** 225, 274; **64:** 114, 145, 192
  Macbeth **3:** 170, 193, 213, 231, 234, 241, 245, 250, 253, 256, 263, 271, 283, 300, 302, 306, 323, 327, 338, 340, 349; **13:** 476; **16:** 317; **20:** 241, 279, 283, 367, 379, 400; **25:** 235; **28:** 339; **29:** 76, 91; **42:** 258; **44:** 366; **45:** 58; **65:** 317
  Measure for Measure **2:** 394, 421, 431, 466, 486, 505; **13:** 112; **28:** 9; **33:** 69; **49:** 370
  The Merchant of Venice **4:** 241, 267, 293; **22:** 3; **25:** 257; **28:** 9, 63; **32:** 41; **40:** 106; **53:** 169; **66:** 165
  The Merry Wives of Windsor **5:** 335, 337, 343, 347, 351, 363, 374, 379; **19:** 101; **22:** 93, 378; **28:** 9, 69; **38:** 313, 319; **59:** 89
  A Midsummer Night's Dream **3:** 397, 401, 410, 412, 415, 432, 453, 459, 468, 494; **22:** 23, 39, 93, 378; **28:** 9; **29:** 263; **45:** 143, 169, 175; **48:** 23, 32; **58:** 181, 186, 194
  Much Ado about Nothing **8:** 9, 38, 43, 46, 55, 69, 73, 88, 95, 100, 115, 125; **19:** 68; **25:** 77; **28:** 63; **31:** 178, 184, 222, 241, 245; **48:** 14; **55:** 199, 259
  Othello **4:** 433, 442, 445, 462, 493, 508, 517, 552, 587, 596; **13:** 304; **16:** 272; **22:** 378; **25:** 189, 257; **28:** 243, 344; **42:** 273; **47:** 51; **53:** 261
  Pericles **2:** 559, 560, 565, 583; **16:** 391; **19:** 387; **22:** 315; **36:** 198, 214, 233, 244, 251, 264; **51:** 86, 99; **66:** 233
  The Rape of Lucrece **10:** 64, 65, 66, 71, 78, 80, 89, 93, 116, 109, 125, 131; **22:** 289, 294; **25:** 305; **32:** 321; **33:** 144, 155, 179, 200; **43:** 102, 113, 141; **59:** 159, 175, 212
  Richard II **6:** 252, 282, 283, 294, 298, 315, 323, 331, 347, 368, 374, 381, 385, 397, 409; **13:** 213, 494; **24:** 269, 270, 298, 301, 304, 315, 325, 329, 333, 339, 356, 364, 395, 405, 408, 411, 414, 419; **28:** 134, 188; **39:** 243, 273, 289, 295; **42:** 173; **52:** 154, 157, 169, 174, 183; **58:** 253, 267, 293, 301, 307; **60:** 21
  Richard III **8:** 159, 161, 165, 167, 168, 170, 177, 182, 184, 186, 193, 197, 201, 206, 218, 223, 243, 248, 252, 258, 262, 267; **16:** 150; **25:** 141, 245; **39:** 360, 370, 383; **47:** 15; **52:** 285, 290; **62:** 14, 66, 71, 91, 104
  Romeo and Juliet **5:** 420, 426, 431, 436, 437, 456, 477, 479, 489, 492, 496, 509, 520, 522, 528, 538, 542, 550, 559; **25:** 181, 245, 257; **32:** 276; **33:** 210, 272, 274, 287; **42:** 266; **51:** 203, 212, 227; **65:** 119, 159, 185, 208, 214
  Sonnets **10:** 247, 251, 255, 256, 290, 353, 372, 385; **13:** 445; **28:** 380, 385; **32:** 327, 352; **40:** 228, 247, 284, 292, 303; **51:** 270, 304; **62:** 153, 159, 170, 180, 196; **65:** 259, 277
  The Taming of the Shrew **9:** 336, 338, 393, 401, 404, 407, 413; **22:** 378; **28:** 9; **31:** 261, 288, 300, 326, 335, 339; **32:** 56; **64:** 273, 296, 352
  The Tempest **8:** 324, 348, 384, 390, 404, 454; **19:** 421; **29:** 278; **29:** 297, 343, 368, 377; **61:** 280, 288
  Timon of Athens **1:** 488; **13:** 392; **25:** 198; **27:** 166, 184, 235; **52:** 329, 345, 354

Titus Andronicus **4:** 617, 624, 635, 642, 644, 646, 659, 664, 668, 672, 675; **13:** 225; **16:** 225; **25:** 245; **27:** 246, 293, 313, 318, 325; **43:** 186, 222, 227, 239, 247, 262; **62:** 225, 254
Troilus and Cressida **3:** 561, 569, 596, 599, 606, 624, 630, 635; **22:** 58, 339; **27:** 332 366; **42:** 66; **59:** 287, 295, 306, 318
Twelfth Night **1:** 570, 650, 664; **22:** 12; **28:** 9; **34:** 293; **37:** 59; **62:** 343
The Two Gentlemen of Verona **6:** 437, 438, 439, 445, 449, 490, 504, 519, 529, 541; **28:** 9; **40:** 343
The Two Noble Kinsmen **9:** 445, 446, 447, 448, 456, 461, 462, 463, 469, 471, 498, 502; **41:** 289, 301, 308, 317, 326; **50:** 310; **58:** 322, 330
The Winter's Tale **7:** 382, 384, 417, 418, 420, 425, 460, 506; **13:** 409; **19:** 431; **22:** 324; **25:** 347; **36:** 295; **42:** 301; **45:** 297, 344, 333; **50:** 45; **57:** 278, 285, 319, 347

language versus action
Titus Andronicus **4:** 642, 644, 647, 664, 668; **13:** 225; **27:** 293, 313, 325; **43:** 186; **62:** 225

Law and Justice (Volume **49:** 1, 18, 23, 27, 37, 46, 60, 67, 73)
Henry IV **49:** 112,116,123,133,137
Henry V **49:** 223, 236, 260
Henry VIII **61:** 92
Measure for Measure **49:** 274, 286, 293
The Merchant of Venice **53:** 169; **66:** 180
Othello **53:** 288, 350

law versus passion for freedom
Much Ado about Nothing **22:** 85

laws of nature, violation of
Macbeth **3:** 234, 241, 280, 323; **29:** 120; **57:** 242, 263; **65:** 226

legal issues
King Lear **46:** 276

legitimacy
Henry VI, Parts 1, 2, and 3 **3:** 89, 157; **39:** 154
Henry VIII **37:** 109; **56:** 209, 220, 230
Macbeth **60:** 340

legitimacy or inheritance
King John **9:** 224, 235, 254, 303; **13:** 147; **19:** 182; **37:** 132; **41:** 215; **56:** 325, 335; **60:** 295, 329

liberty versus tyranny
Julius Caesar **7:** 158, 179, 189, 205, 221, 253; **25:** 272

love
See also **ideal love**
All's Well That Ends Well **7:** 12, 15, 16, 51, 58, 67, 90, 93, 116; **38:** 80; **51:** 33, 44
As You Like It **5:** 24, 44, 46, 57, 79, 88, 103, 116, 122, 138, 141, 162; **28:** 46, 82; **34:** 85

King Lear **2:** 109, 112, 131, 160, 162, 170, 179, 188, 197, 218, 222, 238, 265; **25:** 202; **31:** 77, 149, 151, 155, 162; **61:** 220, 237
Love's Labour's Lost **2:** 312, 315, 340, 344; **22:** 12; **23:** 252; **38:** 194; **51:** 44
The Merchant of Venice **4:** 221, 226, 270, 284, 312, 344; **22:** 3, 69; **25:** 257; **40:** 156; **51:** 1, 44; **66:** 63, 127
  sacrificial love **13:** 43; **22:** 69; **40:** 142
A Midsummer Night's Dream
  passionate or romantic love **3:** 372, 389, 395, 396, 402, 408, 411, 423, 441, 450, 480, 497, 498, 511; **29:** 175, 225, 263, 269; **45:** 126, 136; **51:** 44; **58:** 175
Much Ado about Nothing **8:** 24, 55, 75, 95, 111, 115; **28:** 56; **51:** 30
Othello **4:** 412, 493, 506, 512, 530, 545, 552, 569, 570, 575, 580, 591; **19:** 253; **22:** 207; **25:** 257; **28:** 243, 344; **32:** 201; **35:** 261, 317; **51:** 25, 30; **53:** 315; **54:** 119
The Phoenix and Turtle **10:** 31, 37, 40, 50; **38:** 342, 345, 367; **51:** 145, 151, 155; **64:** 209, 211, 217
Sonnets **10:** 173, 247, 287, 290, 293, 302, 309, 322, 325, 329, 394; **28:** 380; **37:** 347; **51:** 270, 284, 288, 292; **62:** 153, 170
The Tempest **8:** 435, 439; **29:** 297, 339, 377, 396
Twelfth Night **1:** 543, 546, 573, 580, 587, 595, 600, 603, 610, 660; **19:** 78; **26:** 257, 364; **34:** 270, 293, 323; **46:** 291, 333, 347, 362; **51:** 30; **52:** 57; **62:** 297
The Two Gentlemen of Verona **6:** 442, 445, 456, 479, 488, 492, 494, 502, 509, 516, 519, 549; **13:** 12; **40:** 327, 335, 343, 354, 365; **51:** 30, 44
The Two Noble Kinsmen **9:** 479, 481, 490, 498; **41:** 289, 301, 355, 363, 372, 385; **50:** 295, 361; **58:** 345, 356, 371
The Winter's Tale **7:** 417, 425, 469, 490; **51:** 30, 33, 44

love and friendship
See also **friendship**
Julius Caesar **7:** 233, 262, 268; **25:** 272

love and honor
Troilus and Cressida **3:** 555, 604; **27:** 370, 374; **59:** 251, 257, 337

love and passion
Antony and Cleopatra **6:** 51, 64, 71, 80, 85, 100, 115, 159, 165, 180; **25:** 257; **27:** 126; **47:** 71, 124,, 174, 192; **51:** 25, 33, 44; **58:** 2, 41, 105; **60:** 179, 222

love and reason
See also **reason**
Othello **4:** 512, 530, 580; **19:** 253

Love and Romance (Volume **51:** 1, 15, 25, 30, 33, 44)
Pericles **51:** 71
The Phoenix and Turtle **51:** 145, 151, 155
Romeo and Juliet **51:** 195, 203, 212
Sonnets **51:** 284, 288, 292; **65:** 277
Venus and Adonis

  The Rhetoric of Desire **51:** 345, 352, 359, 368

love and time
Antony and Cleopatra **65:** 235
Romeo and Juliet **65:** 235

love, lechery, or rape
Troilus and Cressida **43:** 357

love versus fate
Romeo and Juliet **5:** 421, 437, 438, 443, 445, 458; **33:** 249

love versus friendship
See also **friendship**
Romeo and Juliet **65:** 142
The Two Gentlemen of Verona **6:** 439, 449, 450, 458, 460, 465, 468, 471, 476, 480; **40:** 354, 365; **54:** 295, 307, 325, 344

love versus lust
Sonnets **65:** 277
Venus and Adonis **10:** 418, 420, 427, 434, 439, 448, 449, 454, 462, 466, 473, 480, 489; **25:** 305; **28:** 355; **33:** 309, 330, 339, 347, 357, 363, 370; **51:** 359

love versus reason
See also **reason**
Love's Labour's Lost **54:** 225, 234
Sonnets **10:** 329

love versus war
Troilus and Cressida **18:** 332, 371, 406, 423; **22:** 339; **27:** 376; **59:** 234, 251, 257

Machiavellianism
Henry V **5:** 203, 225, 233, 252, 287, 304; **25:** 131; **30:** 273; **60:** 304
Henry VI, Parts 1, 2, and 3 **22:** 193; **60:** 304
King John **60:** 304
Macbeth **52:** 29; **57:** 236

Madness (Volume **35:** 1, 7, 8, 24, 34, 49, 54, 62, 68)
Hamlet **19:** 330; **35:** 104, 117, 126, 132, 134, 140, 144; **59:** 31
King Lear **19:** 330
Macbeth **19:** 330
Othello **35:** 265, 276, 282
Twelfth Night **1:** 554, 639, 656; **26:** 371

Magic and the Supernatural (Volume **29:** 1, 12, 28, 46, 53, 65)
The Comedy of Errors **1:** 27, 30; **54:** 215; **66:** 22
Macbeth
  supernatural grace versus evil or chaos **3:** 241, 286, 323
  witchcraft and supernaturalism **3:** 171, 172, 173, 175, 177, 182, 183, 184, 185, 194, 196, 198, 202, 207, 208, 213, 219, 229, 239; **16:** 317; **19:** 245; **20:** 92, 175, 213, 279, 283, 374, 387, 406, 413; **25:** 235; **28:** 339; **29:** 91, 101, 109, 120; **44:** 351, 373; **57:** 194, 242
A Midsummer Night's Dream **29:** 190, 201, 210, 216

The Tempest **8**: 287, 293, 304, 315, 340, 356, 396, 401, 404, 408, 435, 458; **28**: 391, 415; **29**: 297, 343, 377; **45**: 272; **61**: 326, 356
Sonnets
   occult **48**: 346
The Winter's Tale
   witchcraft **22**: 324

male discontent
The Merry Wives of Windsor **5**: 392, 402

male domination
Love's Labour's Lost **22**: 12
A Midsummer Night's Dream **3**: 483, 520; **13**: 19; **25**: 36; **29**: 216, 225, 243, 256, 269; **42**: 46; **45**: 84; **58**: 203, 220; **60**: 142

male/female relationships
As You Like It **46**: 134
The Comedy of Errors **16**: 3
Love's Labour's Lost **54**: 284; **64**: 154
The Rape of Lucrece **10**: 109, 121, 131; **22**: 289; **25**: 305; **43**: 113, 141; **59**: 180, 193
Troilus and Cressida **16**: 70; **22**: 339; **27**: 362; **59**: 349

male sexual anxiety
Love's Labour's Lost **16**: 17

manhood
Macbeth **3**: 262, 309, 333; **29**: 127, 133; **57**: 242, 256, 263

Marlowe's works, compared with
Richard II **42**: 173

marriage
See also **courtship and marriage**
The Comedy of Errors **34**: 251
Cymbeline **61**: 34, 45
Hamlet **22**: 339; **51**: 44; **54**: 215
Love's Labour's Lost **2**: 335, 340; **19**: 92; **38**: 209, 232; **51**: 1, 44
Measure for Measure **2**: 443, 507, 516, 519, 524, 528; **25**: 12; **33**: 61, 90; **49**: 286; **51**: 44; **65**: 80
The Merry Wives of Windsor **5**: 343, 369, 376, 390, 392, 400; **22**: 93; **38**: 297; **51**: 44; **59**: 95
A Midsummer Night's Dream **3**: 402, 423, 450, 483, 520; **29**: 243, 256; **45**: 136, 143; **48**: 32; **51**: 1, 30, 44; **58**: 175
Othello **35**: 369; **51**: 44;
The Taming of the Shrew **9**: 322, 325, 329, 332, 329, 332, 334, 341, 342, 343, 344, 345, 347, 353, 360, 362, 375, 381, 390, 398, 401, 404, 413, 426, 430; **13**: 3; **19**: 3; **28**: 24; **31**: 288; **51**: 44; **55**: 315, 331; **64**: 239, 320
Titus Andronicus
   marriage as political tyranny **48**: 264
Troilus and Cressida **22**: 339; **51**: 44
The Two Gentlemen of Verona **48**: 32
The Two Noble Kinsmen **58**: 338, 345, 356

martial vs. civil law
Coriolanus **48**: 230

Marxist criticism
Hamlet **42**: 229
King Lear **42**: 229; **55**: 16
Macbeth **42**: 229; **55**: 16
Othello **42**: 229

masculine identity
Henry VIII **61**: 129

masque elements
The Two Noble Kinsmen **9**: 490
The Tempest **42**: 332

master-slave relationship
Troilus and Cressida **22**: 58; **59**: 265

mediation
The Merry Wives of Windsor **5**: 343, 392

as medieval allegory, drama, or morality play
Hamlet **59**: 68
Henry IV, Parts 1 and 2 **1**: 323, 324, 342, 361, 366, 373, 374; **32**: 166; **39**: 89; **47**: 60
Measure for Measure **2**: 409, 421, 443, 466, 475, 491, 505, 511, 522; **13**: 94; **60**: 12
Timon of Athens **1**: 492, 511, 518; **27**: 155

medieval chivalry
Richard II **6**: 258, 277, 294, 327, 338, 388, 397, 414; **24**: 274, 278, 279, 280, 283; **39**: 256
Troilus and Cressida **3**: 539, 543, 544, 555, 606; **27**: 376; **59**: 349

medieval dramatic influence
All's Well That Ends Well **7**: 29, 41, 51, 98, 113; **13**: 66
King Lear **2**: 177, 188, 201; **25**: 218
Othello **4**: 440, 527, 545, 559, 582

medieval homilies, influence of
The Merchant of Venice **4**: 224, 250, 289

medieval influence
Romeo and Juliet **5**: 480, 505, 509, 573

medieval literary influence
Henry VI, Parts 1, 2, and 3 **3**: 59, 67, 75, 100, 109, 136, 151; **13**: 131
Titus Andronicus **4**: 646, 650; **27**: 299

medieval mystery plays, relation to
Macbeth **44**: 341; **57**: 194

medieval physiology
Julius Caesar **13**: 260

mercantilism and feudalism
Richard II **13**: 213

merit versus rank
All's Well That Ends Well **7**: 9, 10, 19, 37, 51, 76; **38**: 155; **50**: 59

Messina
Much Ado about Nothing **8**: 19, 29, 48, 69, 82, 91, 95, 108, 111, 121, 125; **31**: 191, 209, 229, 241, 245

metadramatic elements
As You Like It **5**: 128, 130, 146; **34**: 130
Henry V **13**: 194; **30**: 181; **49**: 200, 211
Love's Labour's Lost **2**: 356, 359, 362
Measure for Measure **13**: 104
A Midsummer Night's Dream **3**: 427, 468, 477, 516, 520; **29**: 190, 225, 243; **50**: 86
The Taming of the Shrew **9**: 350, 419, 424; **31**: 300, 315
The Winter's Tale **16**: 410

metamorphosis or transformation
The Merry Wives of Windsor **47**: 314
Much Ado about Nothing **8**: 88, 104, 111, 115; **55**: 209, 228
The Taming of the Shrew **9**: 370, 430

metaphysical poem
The Phoenix and Turtle **10**: 7, 8, 9, 20, 31, 35, 37, 40, 45, 50; **51**: 143, 171, 184; **64**: 211, 225

Midlands Revolt, influence of
Coriolanus **22**: 248; **30**: 79; **50**: 140, 172; **64**: 8

military and sexual hierarchies
Othello **16**: 272

mimetic desire
A Midsummer Night's Dream **60**: 172, 245

mimetic rivalry
The Two Gentlemen of Verona **13**: 12; **40**: 335; **54**: 332
Troilus and Cressida **60**: 172

as "mingled yarn"
All's Well That Ends Well **7**: 62, 93, 109, 126; **38**: 65

Minotaur, myth of
A Midsummer Night's Dream **3**: 497, 498; **29**: 216

as miracle play
Pericles **2**: 569, 581; **36**: 205; **51**: 97

misgovernment
Measure for Measure **2**: 401, 432, 511; **22**: 85
Much Ado about Nothing **22**: 85; **55**: 241

misogyny
King Lear **31**: 123
Measure for Measure **23**: 358

misperception
Cymbeline **19**: 411; **36**: 99, 115; **47**: 228, 237, 252, 277, 286, 296

mistaken identity
  The Comedy of Errors **1**: 13, 14, 27, 37, 40, 45, 49, 55, 57, 61, 63; **19**: 34, 54; **25**: 63; **34**: 194; **54**: 162, 176, 189, 215

modernization
  Richard III **14**: 523

Montaigne's Essais, relation to
  Sonnets **42**: 375
  The Tempest **42**: 339

moral choice
  Hamlet **52**: 35
  Julius Caesar **7**: 179, 264, 279, 343

moral corruption
  Macbeth **52**: 15, 23, 78
  Othello **52**: 78
  Troilus and Cressida **3**: 578, 589, 599, 604, 609; **18**: 332, 406, 412, 423; **27**: 366; **54**: 84; **59**: 261, 265

moral corruption of English society
  Richard III **8**: 154, 163, 165, 177, 193, 201, 218, 228, 232, 243, 248, 252, 267; **39**: 308; **52**: 201

moral inheritance
  Henry VI, Parts 1, 2, and 3 **3**: 89, 126

moral intent
  Henry VIII **2**: 15, 19, 25; **24**: 140; **54**: 35; **61**: 92, 101, 144

moral lesson
  Macbeth **20**: 23

moral relativism
  Antony and Cleopatra **22**: 217; **27**: 121

moral seriousness, question of
  Measure for Measure **2**: 387, 388, 396, 409, 417, 421, 452, 460, 495; **23**: 316, 321

Morality in Shakespeare's Works (Volume 52: 1, 5, 15, 23, 29, 35, 43, 57, 63, 69, 78, 89, 95)
  Antony and Cleopatra **52**: 5
  As You Like It **52**: 63; **57**: 13
  Henry V **5**: 195, 203, 213, 223, 225, 239, 246, 260, 271, 293
  Macbeth **52**: 29
  The Merchant of Venice **52**: 89
  The Merry Wives of Windsor **5**: 335, 339, 347, 349, 353, 397; **59**: 132
  Richard III **52**: 5
  The Tempest **52**: 43; **61**: 338
  Troilus and Cressida **52**: 5; **59**: 251, 257
  The Two Gentlemen of Verona **6**: 438, 492, 494, 514, 532, 555, 564
  Venus and Adonis **10**: 411, 412, 414, 416, 418, 419, 420, 423, 427, 428, 439, 442, 448, 449, 454, 459, 466; **33**: 330

multiple endings
  Henry IV **49**: 102

multiple perspectives of characters
  Henry VI, Parts 1, 2, and 3 **3**: 69, 154; **56**: 131

music
  The Merchant of Venice **66**: 171
  The Tempest **8**: 390, 404; **29**: 292; **37**: 321; **42**: 332; **61**: 315
  Twelfth Night **1**: 543, 566, 596

music and dance
  A Midsummer Night's Dream **3**: 397, 400, 418, 513; **12**: 287, 289; **25**: 36
  Much Ado about Nothing **19**: 68; **31**: 222
  Pericles **66**: 236

mutability, theme of
  Sonnets **42**: 375

Myth in Shakespeare's Works (Volume 60: 169, 172, 179, 185, 194, 205, 214, 222, 231, 240, 245, 254, 259, 265, 270, 276, 281, 287)
  All's Well That Ends Well **60**: 169
  Antony and Cleopatra **60**: 222
  Coriolanus **60**: 205
  Cymbeline **60**: 240
  King Lear **60**: 185
  Macbeth **60**: 169, 214
  Measure for Measure **60**: 281
  The Merchant of Venice **60**: 276
  A Midsummer Night's Dream **60**: 172, 245, 259
  Romeo and Juliet **60**: 96
  The Taming of the Shrew **60**: 281
  Titus Andronicus **60**: 276
  Troilus and Cressida **60**: 172
  Twelfth Night **60**: 265, 270, 287
  The Winter's Tale **60**: 254, 281

mythic or mythological elements
  See also **religious, mythic, or spiritual content**
  All's Well That Ends Well **60**: 169
  Antony and Cleopatra **60**: 222
  Coriolanus **60**: 205
  Cymbeline **60**: 240
  King Lear **60**: 185
  Macbeth **60**: 169, 214
  Measure for Measure **60**: 281
  The Merchant of Venice **60**: 276; **66**: 63
  A Midsummer Night's Dream **58**: 194; **60**: 172, 245, 259
  Richard II **52**: 154, 157, 169
  Romeo and Juliet **60**: 96
  The Taming of the Shrew **60**: 281
  Titus Andronicus **60**: 276
  Troilus and Cressida **60**: 172
  Twelfth Night **60**: 265, 270, 287
  The Winter's Tale **60**: 254, 281

mythological allusions
  As You Like It **46**: 142; **60**: 231
  Antony and Cleopatra **16**: 342; **19**: 304; **27**: 110, 117; **47**: 71, 192; **60**: 179, 222

naming, significance of
  Coriolanus **30**: 58, 96, 111, 125

narrative strategies
  The Rape of Lucrece **22**: 294

nationalism and patriotism
  See also **British nationalism**
  Henry V **5**: 198, 205, 209, 210, 213, 219, 223, 233, 246, 252, 257, 269, 299; **19**: 133, 217; **30**: 227, 262; **49**: 219, 247
  Henry VI, Parts 1, 2, and 3 **24**: 25, 45, 47; **56**: 80
  King John **9**: 209, 218, 222, 224, 235, 240, 244, 275; **25**: 98; **37**: 132
  The Merry Wives of Windsor **47**: 344
  The Winter's Tale **32**: 388

naturalism
  All's Well That Ends Well **60**: 169
  Macbeth **60**: 169

nature
  See also **art and nature** and **art versus nature**
  As You Like It **46**: 94
  The Tempest **8**: 315, 370, 390, 408, 414; **29**: 343, 362, 368, 377; **61**: 362
  The Winter's Tale **7**: 397, 418, 419, 420, 425, 432, 436, 451, 452, 473, 479; **19**: 366; **45**: 329

nature as book
  Pericles **22**: 315; **36**: 233

nature, philosophy of
  Coriolanus **30**: 74

negative appraisals
  Cymbeline **4**: 20, 35, 43, 45, 48, 53, 56, 68; **15**: 32, 105, 121
  Richard II **6**: 250, 252, 253, 255, 282, 307, 317, 343, 359
  Venus and Adonis **10**: 410, 411, 415, 418, 419, 424, 429

Neoclassical rules
  As You Like It **5**: 19, 20
  Henry IV, Parts 1 and 2 **1**: 286, 287, 290, 293
  Henry VI, Parts 1, 2, and 3 **3**: 17, 18
  King John **9**: 208, 209, 210, 212; **56**: 365
  Love's Labour's Lost **2**: 299, 300
  Macbeth **3**: 170, 171, 173, 175; **20**: 17
  Measure for Measure **2**: 387, 388, 390, 394; **23**: 269
  The Merry Wives of Windsor **5**: 332, 334
  Romeo and Juliet **5**: 416, 418, 426
  The Tempest **8**: 287, 292, 293, 334; **25**: 357; **29**: 292; **45**: 200
  Troilus and Cressida **3**: 537, 538; **18**: 276, 278, 281
  The Winter's Tale **7**: 376, 377, 379, 380, 383, 410; **15**: 397

Neoplatonism
  The Phoenix and Turtle **10**: 7, 9, 21, 24, 40, 45, 50; **38**: 345, 350, 367; **51**: 184
  Sonnets **10**: 191, 205

nightmarish quality
  Macbeth **3**: 231, 309; **20**: 210, 242; **44**: 261

nihilistic elements
  King Lear **2:** 130, 143, 149, 156, 165, 231, 238, 245, 253; **22:** 271; **25:** 218; **28:** 325
  Macbeth **65:** 297, 317
  Timon of Athens **1:** 481, 513, 529; **13:** 392; **20:** 481
  Troilus and Cressida **27:** 354

nihilistic or pessimistic vision
  King Lear **49:** 67; **66:** 326

"nothing," significance of
  Much Ado about Nothing **8:** 17, 18, 23, 55, 73, 95; **19:** 68; **55:** 259

nurturing or feeding
  Coriolanus **9:** 65, 73, 136, 183, 189; **30:** 111; **44:** 79; **50:** 110

oaths, importance of
  Love's Labour's Lost **54:** 257, 284
  Pericles **19:** 387

obscenity
  Henry V **5:** 188, 190, 260

Oldcastle, references to
  Henry IV, Parts 1 and 2 **48:** 117

omens
  Julius Caesar **22:** 137; **45:** 10; **50:** 265, 280
  Richard III **62:** 14, 18

oppositions or dualisms
  King John **9:** 224, 240, 263, 275, 284, 290, 300

order
  Henry V **5:** 205, 257, 264, 310, 314; **30:** 193
  Twelfth Night **1:** 563, 596; **34:** 330; **46:** 291, 347

order versus disintegration
  Titus Andronicus **4:** 618, 647; **43:** 186, 195

other sonnet writers, Shakespeare compared with
  Sonnets **42:** 296

Ovid, compared with
  Venus and Adonis **51:** 335, 352

Ovid, influence of
  A Midsummer Night's Dream **3:** 362, 427, 497, 498; **22:** 23; **29:** 175, 190, 216
  Titus Andronicus **4:** 647, 659, 664, 668; **13:** 225; **27:** 246, 275, 285, 293, 299, 306; **28:** 249; **43:** 195, 203, 206

Ovid's Metamorphoses, relation to
  Measure for Measure **60:** 281
  The Merchant of Venice **60:** 276
  A Midsummer Night's Dream **60:** 172
  The Taming of the Shrew **60:** 281
  Titus Andronicus **60:** 276
  Twelfth Night **60:** 265, 270, 287

  The Winter's Tale **42:** 301; **57:** 319, 367; **60:** 281
  Venus and Adonis **42:** 347

pagan elements
  King Lear **25:** 218

pageantry
  See also **ceremonies, rites, and rituals, importance of**
  Henry VIII **2:** 14, 15, 18, 51, 58; **24:** 77, 83, 84, 85, 89, 91, 106, 113, 118, 120, 126, 127, 140, 146, 150; **41:** 120, 129, 190

paradoxical elements
  Coriolanus **9:** 73, 92, 106, 121, 153, 157, 164, 169, 193
  Hamlet **59:** 47

parent-child relations
  Coriolanus **60:** 205
  A Midsummer Night's Dream **13:** 19; **29:** 216, 225, 243

pastoral convention, parodies of
  As You Like It **5:** 54, 57, 72

pastoral convention, relation to
  As You Like It **5:** 72, 77, 122; **34:** 161; **37:** 1

pastoralism
  Cymbeline **61:** 18

pastoral tradition, compared with
  A Lover's Complaint **48:** 336

patience
  Henry VIII **2:** 58, 76, 78
  Pericles **2:** 572, 573, 578, 579; **36:** 251

patriarchal claims
  Henry VI, Parts 1, 2, and 3 **16:** 131; **25:** 102

patriarchal or monarchical order
  King Lear **13:** 353, 457; **16:** 351; **22:** 227, 233; **25:** 218; **31:** 84, 92, 107, 117, 123, 137, 142; **46:** 269; **61:** 172, 237
  Love's Labour's Lost **64:** 192

patriarchy
  General Commentary **55:** 78
  Cymbeline **32:** 373; **36:** 134; **47:** 237; **51:** 25
  Henry V **37:** 105; **44:** 44
  Henry VIII **61:** 129
  A Midsummer Night's Dream **60:** 259
  The Rape of Lucrece **59:** 189, 206
  Romeo and Juliet **65:** 119, 190
  The Taming of the Shrew **64:** 327
  Titus Andronicus **50:** 13
  Troilus and Cressida **22:** 58; **59:** 272, 337, 349

patriotism
  See **nationalism and patriotism**

Pattern of Painful Adventures **(Lawrence Twine), compared with**
  Pericles **48:** 364

Pauline doctrine
  A Midsummer Night's Dream **3:** 457, 486, 506

pedagogy
  Sonnets **37:** 374
  The Taming of the Shrew **19:** 122

perception
  Othello **19:** 276; **25:** 189, 257; **53:** 246, 289

performance history
  The Taming of the Shrew **31:** 282; **55:** 357

performance issues
  See also **staging issues**
  Julius Caesar **50:** 186
  King Lear **2:** 106, 137, 154, 160; **11:** 10, 20, 27, 56, 57, 132, 136, 137, 145, 150, 154; **19:** 295, 344; **25:** 218; **61:** 187
  The Merchant of Venice **66:** 123, 124
  Much Ado about Nothing **18:** 173, 174, 183, 184, 185, 186, 187, 188, 189, 190, 191, 192, 193, 195, 197, 199, 201, 204, 206, 207, 208, 209, 210, 254; **55:** 221
  Sonnets **48:** 352
  The Taming of the Shrew **12:** 313, 314, 316, 317, 337, 338; **31:** 315; **55:** 357
  Sonnets **62:** 159

pessimistic elements
  Timon of Athens **1:** 462, 467, 470, 473, 478, 480; **20:** 433, 481; **27:** 155, 191

Petrarchan poetics, influence of
  Hamlet **59:** 47
  Love's Labour's Lost **64:** 154
  Romeo and Juliet **5:** 416, 520, 522, 528, 550, 559, 575; **32:** 276; **51:** 212, 236

philosophical elements
  Julius Caesar **7:** 310, 324; **37:** 203
  Twelfth Night **1:** 560, 563, 596; **34:** 301, 316; **46:** 297

physical versus intellectual world
  Love's Labour's Lost **2:** 331, 348, 367

pictorial elements
  Venus and Adonis **10:** 414, 415, 419, 420, 423, 480; **33:** 339

Platonic elements
  A Midsummer Night's Dream **3:** 368, 437, 450, 497; **45:** 126

play-within-the-play, convention of
  Henry VI, Parts 1, 2, and 3 **3:** 75, 149
  The Merry Wives of Windsor **5:** 354, 355, 369, 402
  The Taming of the Shrew **12:** 416; **22:** 48

plebians
  Coriolanus **50:** 13, 105, 189, 196, 230; **64:** 94

plot
  Love's Labur's Lost **54:** 225
  Twelfth Night **62:** 297, 339, 343, 348

The Winter's Tale **7**: 376, 377, 379, 382, 387, 390, 396, 452; **13**: 417; **15**: 518; **45**: 374; **57**: 285

plot and incident
Richard III **8**: 146, 152, 159; **25**: 164

Plutarch and historical sources
Coriolanus **9**: 8, 9, 13, 14, 16, 26, 39, 92, 106, 130, 142, 164; **30**: 74, 79, 105; **50**: 99

poet-patron relationship
Sonnets **48**: 352; **62**: 128

poetic justice, question of
King Lear **2**: 92, 93, 94, 101, 129, 137, 231, 245; **49**: 73
Othello **4**: 370, 412, 415, 427

poetic style
Sonnets **10**: 153, 155, 156, 158, 159, 160, 161, 173, 175, 182, 214, 247, 251, 255, 260, 265, 283, 287, 296, 302, 315, 322, 325, 337, 346, 349, 360, 367, 385; **16**: 472; **40**: 221, 228; **51**: 270

political and social disintegration
Antony and Cleopatra **6**: 31, 43, 53, 60, 71, 80, 100, 107, 111, 146 180, 197, 219; **22**: 217; **25**: 257; **27**: 121

political content
Titus Andronicus **43**: 262

Politics (Volume 30: 1, 4, 11, 22, 29, 39, 42, 46, 49)
General Commentary **56**: 3
Coriolanus **9**: 15, 17, 18, 19, 26, 33, 43, 53, 62, 65, 73, 80, 92, 106, 110, 112, 121, 144, 153, 157, 164, 180; **22**: 248; **25**: 296; **30**: 58, 67, 79, 89, 96, 105, 111, 125; **37**: 283; **42**: 218; **48**: 230; **50**: 13, 140, 172; **64**: 8, 18, 25, 79, 94
Cymbeline **61**: 54
Hamlet **44**: 241
Henry IV, Parts 1 and 2 **28**: 101; **39**: 130; **42**: 141; **48**: 143, 175; **57**: 108; **65**: 306
Henry V **49**: 219, 247, 260
Henry VIII **2**: 39, 49, 51, 58, 60, 65, 67, 71, 72, 75, 78, 81; **24**: 74, 121, 124; **41**: 146; **56**: 242; **61**: 101
Julius Caesar **7**: 161, 169, 191, 205, 218, 221, 245, 262, 264, 279, 282, 310, 324, 333, 346; **17**: 317, 318, 321, 323, 334, 350, 351, 358, 378, 382, 394, 406; **22**: 137, 280; **25**: 272, 280; **30**: 285, 297, 316, 321, 342, 374, 379; **37**: 203; **50**: 13
King John **9**: 218, 224, 260, 280; **13**: 163; **22**: 120; **37**: 132; **41**: 221, 228; **56**: 314, 325
King Lear **46**: 269; **50**: 45; **61**: 160, 172, 187, 237
Love's Labour's Lost **64**: 114, 179
Macbeth **52**: 29; **57**: 218, 228
Measure for Measure **23**: 379; **49**: 274
A Midsummer Night's Dream **29**: 243
Pericles **37**: 361; **66**: 224

The Tempest **8**: 304, 307, 315, 353, 359, 364, 401, 408; **16**: 426; **19**: 421; **29**: 339; **37**: 336; **42**: 320; **45**: 272, 280; **52**: 43; **61**: 315
Timon of Athens **27**: 223, 230; **50**: 13
Titus Andronicus **27**: 282; **48**: 264
Troilus and Cressida **3**: 536, 560, 606; **16**: 84; **59**: 225, 318

popularity
Pericles **2**: 536, 538, 546; **37**: 361
Richard III **8**: 144, 146, 154, 158, 159, 162, 181, 228; **39**: 383
The Taming of the Shrew **9**: 318, 338, 404
Venus and Adonis **10**: 410, 412, 418, 427; **25**: 328

power
Henry IV **57**: 108
Henry V **37**: 175
Measure for Measure **13**: 112; **22**: 85; **23**: 327, 330, 339, 352; **33**: 85; **65**: 100f
The Merchant of Venice **53**: 136
A Midsummer Night's Dream **42**: 46; **45**: 84; **58**: 151
Much Ado about Nothing **22**: 85; **25**: 77; **31**: 231, 245

pride and rightful self-esteem
Othello **4**: 522, 536, 541; **35**: 352

primitivism
Macbeth **20**: 206, 213; **45**: 48

primogeniture
As You Like It **5**: 66, 158; **34**: 109, 120
Titus Andronicus **50**: 13

as "problem" plays
The Comedy of Errors **34**: 251
Julius Caesar **7**: 272, 320
Measure for Measure **2**: 416, 429, 434, 474, 475, 503, 514, 519; **16**: 102; **23**: 313, 328, 351; **49**: 358, 370; **65**: 111
Troilus and Cressida **3**: 555, 566
    lack of resolution **43**: 277; **59**: 278

procreation
Sonnets **10**: 379, 385; **16**: 461
Venus and Adonis **10**: 439, 449, 466; **33**: 321, 377

Protestant aspects
Henry IV, Parts 1 and 2 **57**: 167; **66**: 256
Henry VIII **61**: 129

providential order
General Commentary **56**: 15, 25
Henry IV, Parts 1 and 2 **56**: 15
Henry V **56**: 15
King Lear **2**: 112, 116, 137, 168, 170, 174, 177, 218, 226, 241, 253; **22**: 271; **49**: 1, 73; **56**: 25
Macbeth **3**: 208, 289, 329, 336; **57**: 218
Measure for Measure **48**: 1
Richard II **56**: 15
Richard III **60**: 304, 322
Tempest **52**: 43

Psychoanalytic Interpretations of Shakespeare's Works (Volume 44: 1, 11, 18, 28, 35, 44, 57, 66, 79, 89, 93)
As You Like It **5**: 146, 158; **23**: 141, 142; **34**: 109; **48**: 42
The Comedy of Errors **66**: 1
Coriolanus **44**: 93; **64**: 40, 62,
Cymbeline **45**: 67, 75
Hamlet **1**: 119, 148, 154, 179, 202; **21**: 197, 213, 361; **25**: 209; **28**: 223; **35**: 95, 104, 134, 237; **37**: 241; **44**: 133, 152, 160, 180, 209, 219
Henry IV, Parts 1 and 2 **13**: 457; **28**: 101; **42**: 185; **44**: 44
Henry V **13**: 457; **44**: 44
Julius Caesar **45**: 10
Macbeth **3**: 219, 223, 226; **44**: 11, 284, 289, 297; **45**: 48, 58
Measure for Measure **23**: 331, 332, 333, 334, 335, 340, 355, 356, 359, 379, 395; **44**: 89; **65**: 100
Merchant of Venice **45**: 17; **66**: 135
A Midsummer Night's Dream **3**: 440, 483; **28**: 15; **29**: 225; **44**: 1; **45**: 107, 117; **58**: 167
Othello **4**: 468, 503; **35**: 265, 276, 282, 301, 317, 320, 347; **42**: 198; **44**: 57
Romeo and Juliet **5**: 513, 556; **51**: 253
The Tempest **45**: 259
Troilus and Cressida **43**: 287, 349
Twelfth Night **46**: 333; **62**: 348

psychological elements
Cymbeline **36**: 134; **44**: 28; **60**: 240; **61**: 18

public versus private principles
Julius Caesar **7**: 161, 179, 252, 262, 268, 284, 298; **13**: 252

public versus private speech
Love's Labour's Lost **2**: 356, 362, 371

public versus private worlds
As You Like It **46**: 164; **65**: 285
Coriolanus **37**: 283; **42**: 218
Romeo and Juliet **5**: 520, 550; **25**: 181; **33**: 274

as "pure" poetry
The Phoenix and Turtle **10**: 14, 31, 35; **38**: 329

Puritanism
Measure for Measure **2**: 414, 418, 434; **49**: 325
Twelfth Night **1**: 549, 553, 555, 632; **16**: 53; **25**: 47; **46**: 338; **66**: 312

Pyramus and Thisbe interlude
A Midsummer Night's Dream **50**: 74

Race (Volume 53: 1, 11, 21, 32, 45, 53, 64, 67, 77, 86, 92)
Antony and Cleopatra **53**: 67, 77
The Merchant of Venice **53**: 111, 116, 127, 136, 159, 169; **55**: 27; **66**: 165
A Midsummer Night's Dream **53**: 1, 32
Othello **4**: 370, 380, 384, 385, 392, 399, 401, 402, 408, 427, 564; **13**: 327; **16**: 293; **25**: 189, 257; **28**: 249, 330; **35**: 369;

42: 198; **53:** 1, 233, 238, 246, 255, 261, 268, 275, 289, 298, 304; **55:** 27; **66:** 317
The Rape of Lucrece **53:** 1
Sonnets **53:** 1
The Tempest **53:** 1, 21, 45, 64, 67
Titus Andronicus **53:** 86, 92

rape
Titus Andronicus **43:** 227, 255; **48:** 277
The Rape of Lucrece **59:** 189, 193, 206, 212

realism
See also **idealism versus realism**
The Merry Wives of Windsor **38:** 313
The Tempest **8:** 340, 359, 464
Troilus and Cressida **43:** 357

reality and illusion
The Tempest **8:** 287, 315, 359, 401, 435, 439, 447, 454; **22:** 302; **45:** 236, 247

reason
See also **love and reason** and **love versus reason**
Venus and Adonis **10:** 427, 439, 449, 459, 462, 466; **28:** 355; **33:** 309, 330

reason versus imagination
Antony and Cleopatra **6:** 107, 115, 142, 197, 228; **45:** 28
A Midsummer Night's Dream **3:** 381, 389, 423, 441, 466, 506; **22:** 23; **29:** 190; **45:** 96

rebellion
See also **usurpation**
Henry IV, Parts 1 and 2 **22:** 395; **28:** 101
Henry VIII **22:** 395; **56:** 230
King John **9:** 218, 254, 263, 280, 297; **66:** 271
Richard III **22:** 395

rebirth, regeneration, resurrection, or immortality
All's Well That Ends Well **7:** 90, 93, 98
Antony and Cleopatra **6:** 100, 103, 125, 131, 159, 181
Cymbeline **4:** 38, 64, 73, 93, 105, 113, 116, 129, 138, 141, 162, 170
Measure for Measure **13:** 84; **16:** 102, 114; **23:** 321, 327, 335, 340, 352; **25:** 12
Pericles **2:** 555, 564, 584, 586, 588; **36:** 205
The Tempest **8:** 302, 312, 320, 334, 348, 359, 370, 384, 401, 404, 414, 429, 439, 447, 454; **16:** 442; **22:** 302; **29:** 297; **37:** 336
The Winter's Tale **7:** 397, 414, 417, 419, 429, 436, 451, 452, 456, 480, 490, 497, 506; **25:** 339 452, 480, 490, 497, 506; **45:** 366; **60:** 40

reconciliation
As You Like It **46:** 156
All's Well That Ends Well **7:** 90, 93, 98; **51:** 33
Antony and Cleopatra **6:** 100, 103, 125, 131, 159, 181
Cymbeline **4:** 38, 64, 73, 93, 105, 113, 116, 129, 138, 141, 162, 170; **61:** 2

The Merry Wives of Windsor **5:** 343, 369, 374, 397, 402
A Midsummer Night's Dream **3:** 412, 418, 437, 459, 468, 491, 497, 502, 513; **13:** 27; **29:** 190
Romeo and Juliet **5:** 415, 419, 427, 439, 447, 480, 487, 493, 505, 533, 536, 562
The Tempest **8:** 302, 312, 320, 334, 348, 359, 370, 384, 401, 404, 414, 429, 439, 447, 454; **16:** 442; **22:** 302; **29:** 297; **37:** 336; **45:** 236

reconciliation of opposites
As You Like It **5:** 79, 88, 103, 116, 122, 138; **23:** 127, 143; **34:** 161, 172; **46:** 156

redemption
The Comedy of Errors **19:** 54; **26:** 188; **54:** 152, 189
Cymbeline **61:** 18

regicide
Macbeth **3:** 248, 275, 312; **16:** 317, 328

relation to tetralogy
Henry V **49:** 223

relationship to other Shakespearean plays
Twelfth Night **46:** 303
Henry IV, Parts 1 and 2 **42:** 99, 153; **48:** 167; **49:** 93, 186

relationship between Parts 1 and 2
Henry IV, Parts 1 and 2 **32:** 136; **39:** 100; **49:** 178

Religion and Theology (Volume 66: 249, 256, 260, 266, 271, 280, 286, 292, 300, 305, 312, 317, 326, 335)
All's Well That Ends Well **66:** 266
Hamlet **66:** 266, 305
Henry IV, Parts 1 and 2 **66:** 256
Henry V **66:** 280
King John **66:** 271
King Lear **66:** 260, 326
Macbeth **44:** 324, 341, 351, 361, 366, 373
Measure for Measure **48:** 1; **66:** 300
The Merchant of Venice **66:** 292
Othello **66:** 317
Richard III **66:** 286
Twelfth Night **66:** 312

religious, mythic, or spiritual content
See also **Christian elements**
All's Well That Ends Well **7:** 15, 45, 54, 67, 76, 98, 109, 116; **66:** 335
Antony and Cleopatra **6:** 53, 94, 111, 115, 178, 192, 224; **47:** 71; **58:** 24, 41; **60:** 179
As You Like It **60:** 231
Cymbeline **4:** 22, 29, 78, 93, 105, 108, 115, 116, 127, 134, 138, 141, 159; **28:** 373; **36:** 142, 158, 186; **47:** 219, 260, 274
Hamlet **1:** 98, 102, 130, 184, 191, 209, 212, 231, 234, 254; **21:** 361; **22:** 258; **28:** 280; **32:** 238; **35:** 134; **59:** 2; **60:** 194; **66:** 266, 305
Henry IV, Parts 1 and 2 **1:** 314, 374, 414, 421, 429, 431, 434; **32:** 103; **48:** 151; **57:** 147, 156, 167; **60:** 26; **66:** 256

Henry V **25:** 116; **32:** 126; **60:** 26
King Lear **49:** 67; **66:** 326
Macbeth **3:** 208, 269, 275, 318; **29:** 109
Measure for Measure **48:** 1
Othello **4:** 483, 517, 522, 525, 559, 573; **22:** 207; **28:** 330; **66:** 317
Pericles **2:** 559, 561, 565, 570, 580, 584, 588; **22:** 315; **25:** 365; **51:** 97
Richard III **62:** 66, 71
The Tempest **8:** 328, 390, 423, 429, 435; **45:** 211, 247; **61:** 280
Timon of Athens **1:** 505, 512, 513, 523; **20:** 493

repentance and forgiveness
Much Ado about Nothing **8:** 24, 29, 111; **55:** 228
The Two Gentlemen of Verona **6:** 450, 514, 516, 555, 564
The Winter's Tale **44:** 66

resolution
Measure for Measure **2:** 449, 475, 495, 514, 516; **16:** 102, 114; **54:** 65; **65:** 2, 14, 19, 111
The Merchant of Venice **4:** 263, 266, 300, 319, 321; **13:** 37; **51:** 1
The Two Gentlemen of Verona **6:** 435, 436, 439, 445, 449, 453, 458, 460, 462, 465, 466, 468, 471, 476, 480, 486, 494, 509, 514, 516, 519, 529, 532, 541, 549; **19:** 34; **54:** 307, 311, 338

retribution
Henry VI, Parts 1, 2, and 3 **3:** 27, 42, 51, 59, 77, 83, 92, 100, 109, 115, 119, 131, 136, 151
Julius Caesar **7:** 160, 167, 200
Macbeth **3:** 194, 208, 318; **48:** 214
Richard III **8:** 163, 170, 177, 182, 184, 193, 197, 201, 206, 210, 218, 223, 228, 243, 248, 267

revenge
Hamlet **1:** 74, 194, 209, 224, 234, 254; **16:** 246; **22:** 258; **25:** 288; **28:** 280; **35:** 152, 157, 167, 174, 212; **44:** 180, 209, 219, 229; **54:** 96; **59:** 10, 79
The Merchant of Venice **60:** 276
The Merry Wives of Windsor **5:** 349, 350, 392; **38:** 264, 307
Othello **35:** 261
Titus Andronicus **60:** 276; **62:** 258

revenge tragedy elements
Julius Caesar **7:** 316
Titus Andronicus **4:** 618, 627, 628, 636, 639, 644, 646, 664, 672, 680; **16:** 225; **27:** 275, 318

reversals
A Midsummer Night's Dream **29:** 225; **60:** 245
The Two Gentlemen of Verona **54:** 338

rhetoric
Romeo and Juliet **42:** 266; **65:** 119
Venus and Adonis **33:** 377; **51:** 335, 345, 352

rhetoric of consolation
Sonnets **42:** 375

rhetoric of politeness
Henry VIII **22:** 182; **56:** 262

rhetorical style
King Lear **16:** 301; **47:** 9

riddle motif
Pericles **22:** 315; **36:** 205, 214

rings episode
The Merchant of Venice **22:** 3; **40:** 106, 151, 156; **66:** 59, 63, 144, 158

role-playing
Julius Caesar **7:** 356; **37:** 229
The Taming of the Shrew **9:** 322, 353, 355, 360, 369, 370, 398, 401, 407, 413, 419, 424; **13:** 3; **31:** 288, 295, 315; **64:** 239, 320

as romance play
As You Like It **5:** 55, 79; **23:** 27, 28, 40, 43

romance or chivalric tradition, influence of
Much Ado about Nothing **8:** 53, 125; **51:** 15

romance or folktale elements
All's Well That Ends Well **7:** 32, 41, 43, 45, 54, 76, 104, 116, 121; **26:** 117

romance or pastoral tradition, influence of
The Tempest **8:** 336, 348, 396, 404; **37:** 336

romance versus history
Henry VIII **61:** 101

Roman citizenry, portrayal of
Julius Caesar **50:** 64, 230

romantic and courtly conventions
The Two Gentlemen of Verona **6:** 438, 460, 472, 478, 484, 486, 488, 502, 507, 509, 529, 541, 549, 560, 568; **12:** 460, 462; **40:** 354, 374; **54:** 344

romantic elements
The Comedy of Errors **1:** 13, 16, 19, 23, 25, 30, 31, 36, 39, 53; **66:** 38
Cymbeline **4:** 17, 20, 46, 68, 77, 141, 148, 172; **15:** 111; **25:** 319; **28:** 373; **61:** 34
King Lear **31:** 77, 84
The Taming of the Shrew **9:** 334, 342, 362, 375, 407

royalty
Antony and Cleopatra **6:** 94

sacrifice
Titus Andronicus **62:** 258, 265

Salic Law
Henry V **5:** 219, 252, 260; **28:** 121

as satire or parody
Love's Labour's Lost **2:** 300, 302, 303, 307, 308, 315, 321, 324, 327; **23:** 237, 252; **54:** 234
The Merry Wives of Windsor **5:** 338, 350, 360, 385; **38:** 278, 319; **47:** 354, 363

satire or parody of pastoral conventions
As You Like It **5:** 46, 55, 60, 72, 77, 79, 84, 114, 118, 128, 130, 154

satirical elements
Hamlet **59:** 79
The Phoenix and Turtle **10:** 8, 16, 17, 27, 35, 40, 45, 48
Timon of Athens **27:** 155, 235
Troilus and Cressida **3:** 539, 543, 544, 555, 558, 574; **27:** 341

Saturnalian elements
Twelfth Night **1:** 554, 571, 603, 620, 642; **16:** 53

schemes and intrigues
The Merry Wives of Windsor **5:** 334, 336, 339, 341, 343, 349, 355, 379

Scholasticism
Macbeth **52:** 23
The Phoenix and Turtle **10:** 21, 24, 31; **51:** 188; **64:** 211

School of Night, allusions to
Love's Labour's Lost **2:** 321, 327, 328

self-conscious or artificial nature of play
Cymbeline **4:** 43, 52, 56, 68, 124, 134, 138; **36:** 99

self-deception
Twelfth Night **1:** 554, 561, 591, 625; **47:** 45

self-indulgence
Twelfth Night **1:** 563, 615, 635

self-interest or expediency
Henry V **5:** 189, 193, 205, 213, 217, 233, 260, 287, 302, 304; **30:** 273; **49:** 223; **66:** 280

self-knowledge
As You Like It **5:** 32, 82, 102, 116, 122, 133, 164; **57:** 45
Much Ado about Nothing **8:** 69, 95, 100
Timon of Athens **1:** 456, 459, 462, 495, 503, 507, 515, 518, 526; **20:** 493; **27:** 166

self-love
Sonnets **10:** 372; **25:** 374; **51:** 270, 300, 304; **62:** 180
Twelfth Night **60:** 265, 270, 287

Senecan or revenge tragedy elements
Timon of Athens **27:** 235
Titus Andronicus **4:** 618, 627, 628, 636, 639, 644, 646, 664, 672, 680; **16:** 225; **27:** 275, 318; **43:** 170, 206, 227; **62:** 208

servitude
See also **freedom and servitude**
Comedy of Errors **42:** 80

setting
The Merry Wives of Windsor **47:** 375; **59:** 89, 139
Much Ado about Nothing **18:** 173, 174, 183, 184, 185, 186, 187, 188, 189, 190, 191, 192, 193, 195, 197, 199, 201, 204, 206, 207, 208, 209, 210, 254
Richard III **14:** 516, 528; **52:** 263; **62:** 104
The Two Gentlemen of Verona **12:** 463, 465, 485

sexual ambiguity and sexual deception
As You Like It **46:** 134, 142; **57:** 23, 40, 45
Twelfth Night **1:** 540, 562, 620, 621, 639, 645; **22:** 69; **34:** 311, 344; **37:** 59; **42:** 32; **62:** 319, 325
Troilus and Cressida **43:** 365

sexual anxiety
Macbeth **16:** 328; **20:** 283

sexual politics
General Commentary **55:** 68
King Lear **55:** 68
Measure for Measure **55:** 68; **65:** 61, 72, 80
The Merchant of Venice **22:** 3; **51:** 44
The Merry Wives of Windsor **19:** 101; **38:** 307; **59:** 95

Sexuality in Shakespeare (Volume 33: 1, 12, 18, 28, 39)
As You Like It **46:** 122, 127, 134, 142
All's Well That Ends Well **7:** 67, 86, 90, 93, 98, 126; **13:** 84; **19:** 113; **22:** 78; **28:** 38; **44:** 35; **49:** 46; **51:** 44; **55:** 109, 131, 143, 176
Coriolanus **9:** 112, 142, 174, 183, 189, 198; **30:** 79, 111, 125, 142
Cymbeline **4:** 170, 172; **25:** 319; **32:** 373; **47:** 245
Hamlet **55:** 56; **59:** 31, 68
King Lear **25:** 202; **31:** 133, 137, 142
Love's Labour's Lost **22:** 12; **51:** 44; **64:** 154
Measure for Measure **13:** 84; **16:** 102, 114; **23:** 321, 327, 335, 340, 352; **25:** 12; **33:** 85, 90, 112; **49:** 286, 338; **51:** 44; **65:** 28, 44, 45, 61, 100
A Midsummer Night's Dream **22:** 23, 93; **29:** 225, 243, 256, 269; **42:** 46; **45:** 107; **53:** 45; **58:** 203, 215, 220
Othello **22:** 339; **28:** 330, 344; **35:** 352, 360; **37:** 269; **44:** 57, 66; **51:** 44; **53:** 275, 310, 315
Romeo and Juliet **25:** 181; **33:** 225, 233, 241, 246, 274, 300; **51:** 227, 236
Sonnets **25:** 374; **48:** 325; **62:** 153
The Tempest **53:** 45; **61:** 288
Troilus and Cressida **22:** 58, 339; **25:** 56; **27:** 362; **43:** 365; **59:** 323, 337, 349
The Two Noble Kinsmen **58:** 338, 345, 356

Shakespeare and Classical Civilization (Volume 27: 1, 9, 15, 21, 30, 35, 39, 46, 56, 60, 67)
Antony and Cleopatra
Egyptian versus Roman values **6:** 31, 33, 43, 53, 104, 111, 115, 125, 142, 155,

159, 178, 181, 211, 219; **17:** 48; **19:** 270; **27:** 82, 121, 126; **28:** 249; **47:** 96, 103, 113, 149; **58:** 59, 71, 88, 105; **60:** 179
The Rape of Lucrece
  Roman history, relation to **10:** 84, 89, 93, 96, 98, 109, 116, 125, 135; **22:** 289; **25:** 305; **33:** 155, 190; **59:** 175
Timon of Athens **27:** 223, 230, 325
Titus Andronicus **27:** 275, 282, 293, 299, 306
  Roman elements **43:** 206, 222; **62:** 277, 284
Troilus and Cressida
  Trojan versus Greek values **3:** 541, 561, 574, 584, 590, 596, 621, 638; **27:** 370

Shakespeare's artistic growth, Richard III's contribution to
  Richard III **8:** 165, 167, 182, 193, 197, 206, 210, 228, 239, 267; **25:** 164; **39:** 305, 326, 370

Shakespeare's canon, place in
  Titus Andronicus **4:** 614, 616, 618, 619, 637, 639, 646, 659, 664, 668; **43:** 195
  Twelfth Night **1:** 543, 548, 557, 569, 575, 580, 621, 635, 638

Shakespeare's dramas, compared with
  The Phoenix and Turtle **51:** 151, 155; **64:** 217, 225
  The Rape of Lucrece **43:** 92; **59:** 159

Shakespeare's moral judgment
  Antony and Cleopatra **6:** 33, 37, 38, 41, 48, 51, 64, 76, 111, 125, 136, 140, 146, 163, 175, 189, 202, 211, 228; **13:** 368, 523; **25:** 257

Shakespeare's other plays, compared with
  King John **56:** 306, 348, 357
  The Merchant of Venice: **53:** 74
  Much Ado about Nothing **55:** 189, 209, 232, 241, 249
  The Taming of the Shrew **50:** 74; **55:** 331
  Twelfth Night **62:** 297, 308

Shakespeare's political sympathies
  Coriolanus **9:** 8, 11, 15, 17, 19, 26, 39, 52, 53, 62, 80, 92, 142; **25:** 296; **30:** 74, 79, 89, 96, 105, 133; **50:** 172
  Richard II **6:** 277, 279, 287, 347, 359, 364, 391, 393, 402
  Richard III **8:** 147, 163, 177, 193, 197, 201, 223, 228, 232, 243, 248, 267; **39:** 349; **42:** 130

Shakespeare's Representation of History
  (**Volume 56:** 2, 3, 15, 25, 47, 53, 60, 95, 196, 286)
  Henry VI **56:** 95, 110, 122, 131, 145
  Henry VIII **56:** 196, 201, 209, 220, 230
  King John **56:** 286, 296, 306, 348, 357

Shakespeare's Representation of Women
  (**Volume 31:** 1, 3, 8, 12, 16, 21, 29, 34, 35, 41, 43, 48, 53, 60, 68)
  Henry VI, Parts 1, 2, and 3 **3:** 103, 109, 126, 140, 157; **16:** 183; **39:** 196

King John **9:** 222, 303; **16:** 161; **19:** 182; **41:** 215, 221
King Lear **31:** 117, 123, 133
Love's Labour's Lost **19:** 92; **22:** 12; **23:** 215; **25:** 1
The Merry Wives of Windsor **5:** 335, 341, 343, 349, 369, 379, 390, 392, 402; **19:** 101; **38:** 307
Much Ado about Nothing **31:** 222, 231, 241, 245
Othello **19:** 253; **28:** 344
Richard III **62:** 31, 41, 52
The Taming of the Shrew **31:** 288, 300, 307, 315
The Winter's Tale **22:** 324; **36:** 311; **42:** 301; **51:** 30; **57:** 294, 305, 356; **60:** 254

Shakespeare's romances, compared with
  Henry VIII **41:** 171; **54:** 35; **56:** 273
  Pericles **54:** 35; **66:** 186
  The Two Noble Kinsmen **54:** 35

shame
  Coriolanus **42:** 243

sibling rivalry
  As You Like It **34:** 109
  Henry VI, Parts 1, 2, and 3 **22:** 193

slander or hearsay, importance of
  Coriolanus **48:** 230
  Much Ado about Nothing **8:** 58, 69, 82, 95, 104; **55:** 249

social action
  Sonnets **48:** 352; **62:** 159

social and moral corruption
  King Lear **2:** 116, 133, 174, 177, 241, 271; **22:** 227; **31:** 84, 92; **46:** 269; **61:** 160

social and political context
  All's Well That Ends Well **13:** 66; **22:** 78; **38:** 99, 109, 150, 155; **49:** 46

social aspects
  Measure for Measure **23:** 316, 375, 379, 395; **65:** 45
  The Merchant of Venice **53:** 214; **66:** 124

Social Class (**Volume 50:** 1, 13, 24, 34, 45, 51, 59, 64, 74, 86)
  General Commentary **50:** 1, 34
  Coriolanus **50:** 105, 110, 119
  Julius Caesar **50:** 189, 194, 196, 211, 230
  Timon of Athens **1:** 466, 487, 495; **25:** 198; **27:** 184, 196, 212
  The Two Noble Kinsmen **50:** 295, 305, 310

social milieu
  The Merry Wives of Windsor **18:** 75, 84; **38:** 297, 300; **59:** 132, 139, 144

social order
  As You Like It **37:** 1; **46:** 94; **57:** 2
  The Comedy of Errors **34:** 238; **54:** 155, 215
  Richard III **60:** 322
  Henry VIII **61:** 101

society
  Coriolanus **9:** 15, 17, 18, 19, 26, 33, 43, 53, 62, 65, 73, 80, 92, 106, 110, 112, 121, 144, 153, 157, 164, 180; **22:** 248; **25:** 296; **30:** 58, 67, 79, 89, 96, 105, 111, 125; **50:** 13, 105, 119, 152
  Troilus and Cressida **43:** 298

soldiers
  Henry V **49:** 194

songs, role of
  Love's Labour's Lost **2:** 303, 304, 316, 326, 335, 362, 367, 371, 375; **54:** 240

sonnet arrangement
  Sonnets **10:** 174, 176, 182, 205, 226, 230, 236, 315, 353; **28:** 363; **40:** 238; **62:** 121, 128

sonnet form
  Sonnets **10:** 255, 325, 367; **37:** 347; **40:** 284, 303; **51:** 270

sonnets, compared with
  A Lover's Complaint **48:** 336

source of tragic catastrophe
  Romeo and Juliet **5:** 418, 427, 431, 448, 458, 469, 479, 480, 485, 487, 493, 509, 522, 528, 530, 533, 542, 565, 571, 573; **33:** 210; **51:** 245

sources
  General Commentary **56:** 25
  Antony and Cleopatra **6:** 20, 39; **19:** 304; **27:** 96, 126; **28:** 249
  As You Like It **5:** 18, 32, 54, 59, 66, 84; **34:** 155; **46:** 117; **60:** 231
  The Comedy of Errors **1:** 13, 14, 16, 19, 31, 32, 39; **16:** 3; **34:** 190, 215, 258; **54:** 155, 176
  Coriolanus **60:** 205
  Cymbeline **4:** 17, 18; **13:** 401; **28:** 373; **47:** 245, 265, 277
  Hamlet **1:** 76, 81, 113, 125, 128, 130, 151, 191, 202, 224, 259; **59:** 68
  Henry IV, Parts 1 and 2 **56:** 2
  Henry V **56:** 2
  Henry VI, Parts 1, 2, and 3 **3:** 18, 21, 29, 31, 35, 39, 46, 51; **13:** 131; **16:** 217; **39:** 196; **56:** 2, 122, 131, 187
  Henry VIII **2:** 16, 17; **24:** 71, 80; **61:** 111
  Julius Caesar **7:** 149, 150, 156, 187, 200, 264, 272, 282, 284, 320; **30:** 285, 297, 326, 358
  King John **9:** 216, 222, 300; **32:** 93, 114; **41:** 234, 243, 251; **56:** 296, 357
  King Lear **2:** 94, 100, 143, 145, 170, 186; **13:** 352; **16:** 351; **28:** 301; **60:** 185; **61:** 250
  Love's Labour's Lost **16:** 17
  Macbeth **60:** 214
  Measure for Measure **2:** 388, 393, 427, 429, 437, 475; **13:** 94; **49:** 349; **60:** 281
  The Merry Wives of Windsor **5:** 332, 350, 360, 366, 385; **32:** 31; **52:** 69; **59:** 123
  A Midsummer Night's Dream **29:** 216; **60:** 259
  Much Ado about Nothing **8:** 9, 19, 53, 58, 104

Othello **28:** 330
Pericles **2:** 538, 568, 572, 575; **25:** 365; **36:** 198, 205; **51:** 118, 126
The Phoenix and Turtle **10:** 7, 9, 18, 24, 45; **38:** 326, 334, 350, 367; **51:** 138; **64:** 198, 209, 217, 225
The Rape of Lucrece **10:** 63, 64, 65, 66, 68, 74, 77, 78, 89, 98, 109, 121, 125; **25:** 305; **33:** 155, 190; **43:** 77, 92, 148; **59:** 165
Richard II **56:** 2
Richard III **52:** 263, 290; **56:** 2; **62:** 2, 31, 60, 78
   chronicles **8:** 145, 165, 193, 197, 201, 206, 210, 213, 228, 232
   Marlowe, Christopher **8:** 167, 168, 182, 201, 206, 218
   morality plays **8:** 182, 190, 201, 213, 239
   Seneca, other classical writers **8:** 165, 190, 201, 206, 228, 248; **62:** 31, 60
Romeo and Juliet **5:** 416, 419, 423, 450; **32:** 222; **33:** 210; **45:** 40; **54:** 125; **65:** 151, 190, 214
Sonnets **10:** 153, 154, 156, 158, 233, 251, 255, 293, 353; **16:** 472; **28:** 407; **42:** 375; **62:** 121, 128
The Taming of the Shrew
   Ariosto **60:** 281; **64:** 255
   folk tales **9:** 332, 390, 393; **64:** 283
   Old and New Comedy **9:** 419; **64:** 255
   Ovid **9:** 318, 370, 430
   Plautus **9:** 334, 341, 342
   shrew tradition **9:** 355; **19:** 3; **32:** 1, 56; **55:** 342; **64:** 283
   text and sources **55:** 334, 357
The Tempest **45:** 226; **61:** 326
Timon of Athens **16:** 351; **27:** 191; **52:** 301
Titus Andronicus **62:** 208, 277, 284
Troilus and Cressida **3:** 537, 539, 540, 541, 544, 549, 558, 566, 574, 587; **27:** 376, 381, 391, 400
Twelfth Night **1:** 539, 540, 603; **34:** 301, 323, 344; **46:** 291; **60:** 265, 270, 287; **62:** 308
The Two Gentlemen of Verona **6:** 436, 460, 462, 468, 476, 480, 490, 511, 547; **19:** 34; **40:** 320; **54:** 295
The Two Noble Kinsmen **19:** 394; **41:** 289, 301, 363, 385; **50:** 326, 348; **58:** 361, 371
Venus and Adonis **10:** 410, 412, 420, 424, 429, 434, 439, 451, 454, 466, 473, 480, 486, 489; **16:** 452; **25:** 305; **28:** 355; **33:** 309, 321, 330, 339, 347, 352, 357, 370, 377; **42:** 347
The Winter's Tale **60:** 254, 281

spectacle
   Love's Labour's Lost **38:** 226
   Macbeth **42:** 258
   Pericles **42:** 352
   Titus Andronicus **62:** 277

spectacle versus simple staging
   The Tempest **15:** 206, 207, 208, 210, 217, 219, 222, 223, 224, 225, 227, 228, 305, 352; **28:** 415

stage history
   As You Like It **46:** 117; **57:** 56
   Antony and Cleopatra **17:** 84, 94, 101

The Merry Wives of Windsor **18:** 66, 67, 68, 70, 71; **59:** 123

staging issues
   See also **performance issues**
   All's Well That Ends Well **19:** 113; **26:** 15, 19, 48, 52, 64, 73, 85, 92, 93, 94, 95, 97, 114, 117, 128; **54:** 30
   Antony and Cleopatra **17:** 6, 12, 84, 94, 101, 104, 110; **27:** 90; **47:** 142
   As You Like It **13:** 502; **23:** 7, 17, 19, 22, 58, 96, 97, 98, 99, 101, 110, 137; **28:** 82; **32:** 212; **57:** 56, 75
   The Comedy of Errors **26:** 182, 183, 186, 188, 190; **54:** 136; **66:** 27, 29, 30
   Coriolanus **17:** 172, 242, 248; **64:** 83, 85, 86, 87, 88, 89
   Cymbeline **15:** 6, 23, 75, 105, 111, 121, 122; **22:** 365
   Hamlet **13:** 494, 502; **21:** 11, 17, 31, 35, 41, 44, 50, 53, 78, 81, 89, 101, 112, 127, 139, 142, 145, 148, 151, 157, 160, 172, 182, 183, 202, 203, 208, 225, 232, 237, 242, 245, 249, 251, 259, 268, 270, 274, 283, 284, 301, 311, 334, 347, 355, 361, 371, 377, 379, 380, 381, 384, 386, 392, 407, 410, 416; **44:** 198
   Henry IV, Parts 1 and 2 **32:** 212; **47:** 1; **49:** 102
   Henry V **5:** 186, 189, 192, 193, 198, 205, 226, 230, 241, 281, 314; **13:** 194, 502; **14:** 293, 295, 297, 301, 310, 319, 328, 334, 336, 342; **19:** 217; **32:** 185
   Henry VI, Parts 1, 2, and 3 **24:** 21, 22, 27, 31, 32, 36, 38, 41, 45, 48, 55; **32:** 212; **56:** 154, 172, 180, 187
   Henry VIII **24:** 67, 70, 71, 75, 77, 83, 84, 85, 87, 89, 91, 101, 106, 113, 120, 127, 129, 136, 140, 146, 150, 152, 155; **28:** 184; **56:** 220, 248
   Julius Caesar **48:** 240; **50:** 186
   King John **16:** 161; **19:** 182; **24:** 171, 187, 203, 206, 211, 225, 228, 241, 245, 249; **56:** 286, 365
   King Lear **11:** 136, 137, 142, 145, 150, 151, 154, 158, 161, 165, 169; **32:** 212; **46:** 205, 218
   Love's Labour's Lost **23:** 184, 187, 191, 196, 198, 200, 201, 202, 207, 212, 215, 216, 217, 229, 230, 232, 233, 237, 252; **64:** 136, 137, 138, 140
   Macbeth **13:** 502; **20:** 12, 17, 32, 64, 65, 70, 73, 107, 113, 151, 175, 203, 206, 210, 213, 245, 279, 283, 312, 318, 324, 329, 343, 345, 350, 353, 363, 367, 374, 376, 379, 382, 387, 400, 406, 413; **22:** 365; **32:** 212
   Measure for Measure **2:** 427, 429, 437, 441, 443, 456, 460, 482, 491, 519; **23:** 283, 284, 285, 286, 287, 291, 293, 294, 298, 299, 311, 315, 327, 338, 339, 340, 342, 344, 347, 363, 372, 375, 395, 400, 405, 406, 413; **32:** 16; **65:** 38, 44, 111
   The Merchant of Venice **12:** 111, 114, 115, 117, 119, 124, 129, 131
   The Merry Wives of Windsor **18:** 74, 75, 84, 86, 90, 95
   A Midsummer Night's Dream **3:** 364, 365, 371, 372, 377; **12:** 151, 152, 154, 158, 159, 280, 284, 291, 295; **16:** 34; **19:** 21; **29:** 183, 256; **48:** 23

Much Ado about Nothing **8:** 18, 33, 41, 75, 79, 82, 108; **16:** 45; **18:** 245, 247, 249, 252, 254, 257, 261, 264; **28:** 63; **55:** 221
Othello **11:** 273, 334, 335, 339, 342, 350, 354, 359, 362
Pericles **16:** 399; **48:** 364; **51:** 99; **53:** 233, 304; **66:** 215
Richard II **13:** 494; **24:** 273, 274, 278, 279, 280, 283, 291, 295, 296, 301, 303, 304, 310, 315, 317, 320, 325, 333, 338, 346, 351, 352, 356, 364, 383, 386, 395, 402, 405, 411, 414, 419, 423, 428; **25:** 89; **58:** 241
Richard III **14:** 515, 527, 528, 537; **16:** 137; **52:** 263, 272
Romeo and Juliet **11:** 499, 505, 507, 514, 517; **13:** 243; **25:** 181; **32:** 212; **65:** 170, 175, 176, 178, 183, 184
The Taming of the Shrew **64:** 313, 317, 318, 319
The Tempest **15:** 343, 346, 352, 361, 364, 366, 368, 371, 385; **28:** 391, 415; **29:** 339; **32:** 338, 343; **42:** 332; **45:** 200; **54:** 19; **61:** 297
Timon of Athens **20:** 445, 446, 481, 491, 492, 493
Titus Andronicus **17:** 449, 452, 456, 487; **25:** 245; **32:** 212, 249
Troilus and Cressida **16:** 70; **18:** 289, 332, 371, 395, 403, 406, 412, 419, 423, 442, 447, 451; **59:** 225, 323
Twelfth Night **26:** 219, 233, 257, 337, 342, 346, 357, 359, 360, 364, 366, 371, 374; **46:** 310, 369; **54:** 19
The Two Gentlemen of Verona **12:** 457, 464; **42:** 18
The Winter's Tale **7:** 414, 425, 429, 446, 464, 480, 483, 497; **13:** 409; **15:** 518; **48:** 309

Stoicism
   Hamlet **48:** 195; **66:** 266
   Julius Caesar **50:** 249

strategic analysis
   Antony and Cleopatra **48:** 206

structure
   All's Well That Ends Well **7:** 21, 29, 32, 45, 51, 76, 81, 93, 98, 116; **22:** 78; **26:** 128; **38:** 72, 123, 142; **66:** 335f
   Antony and Cleopatra **58:** 71, 88
   As You Like It **5:** 19, 24, 25, 35, 44, 45, 46, 86, 93, 116, 138, 158; **23:** 7, 8, 9, 10, 11; **34:** 72, 78, 131, 147, 155
   The Comedy of Errors **66:** 31
   Coriolanus **9:** 8, 9, 11, 12, 13, 14, 16, 26, 33, 45, 53, 58, 72, 78, 80, 84, 92, 112, 139, 148; **25:** 263; **30:** 79, 96
   Hamlet **22:** 378; **28:** 280, 325; **35:** 82, 104, 215; **44:** 152; **59:** 2, 42
   Henry IV, Parts 1 and 2 **49:** 93; **56:** 53, 60; **57:** 181
   Henry V **5:** 186, 189, 205, 213, 230, 241, 264, 289, 310, 314; **30:** 220, 227, 234, 244
   Henry VI, Parts 1, 2, and 3 **3:** 31, 43, 46, 69, 83, 103, 109, 119, 136, 149, 154; **39:** 213; **56:** 77, 80, 85

Henry VIII **2**: 16, 25, 27, 28, 31, 36, 44, 46, 51, 56, 68, 75; **24**: 106, 112, 113, 120; **56**: 209
Julius Caesar **7**: 152, 155, 159, 160, 179, 200, 210, 238, 264, 284, 298, 316, 346; **13**: 252; **30**: 374
King John **9**: 208, 212, 222, 224, 229, 240, 244, 245, 254, 260, 263, 275, 284, 290, 292, 300; **24**: 228, 241; **41**: 260, 269, 277
King Lear **28**: 325; **32**: 308; **46**: 177
Love's Labour's Lost **22**: 378; **23**: 191, 237, 252; **38**: 163, 172
Macbeth **16**: 317; **20**: 12, 245
Measure for Measure **2**: 390, 411, 449, 456, 466, 474, 482, 490, 491; **33**: 69; **49**: 379; **65**: 2
The Merchant of Venice **4**: 201, 215, 230, 232, 243, 247, 254, 261, 263, 308, 321; **12**: 115; **28**: 63; **60**: 276
The Merry Wives of Windsor **5**: 332, 333, 334, 335, 343, 349, 355, 369, 374; **18**: 86; **22**: 378; **59**: 89, 111
A Midsummer Night's Dream **3**: 364, 368, 381, 402, 406, 427, 450, 513; **13**: 19; **22**: 378; **29**: 175; **45**: 126, 175; **58**: 186, 189
Much Ado about Nothing **8**: 9, 16, 17, 19, 28, 29, 33, 39, 48, 63, 69, 73, 75, 79, 82, 115; **31**: 178, 184, 198, 231; **55**: 189
Othello **22**: 378; **28**: 325
The Phoenix and Turtle **10**: 27, 31, 37, 45, 50; **38**: 342, 345, 357; **51**: 138, 143; **64**: 205, 209, 225
The Rape of Lucrece **10**: 84, 89, 93, 98, 135; **22**: 294; **25**: 305; **43**: 102, 141; **59**: 159
Richard II **6**: 282, 304, 317, 343, 352, 359, 364, 39; **24**: 307, 322, 325, 356, 395; **58**: 229, 241
Richard III **8**: 154, 161, 163, 167, 168, 170, 177, 184, 193, 197, 201, 206, 210, 218, 223, 228, 232, 243, 252, 262, 267; **16**: 150; **62**: 14, 18, 91
Romeo and Juliet **5**: 438, 448, 464, 469, 470, 477, 480, 496, 518, 524, 525, 528, 547, 559; **33**: 210, 246; **65**: 119, 185, 208
Sonnets **10**: 175, 176, 182, 205, 230, 260, 296, 302, 309, 315, 337, 349, 353; **40**: 238; **62**: 146
The Taming of the Shrew **9**: 318, 322, 325, 332, 334, 341, 362, 370, 390, 426; **22**: 48, 378; **31**: 269; **55**: 278, 342, 371; **64**: 244, 255
The Tempest **8**: 294, 295, 299, 320, 384, 439; **28**: 391, 415; **29**: 292, 297; **45**: 188; **65**: 264
Timon of Athens **27**: 157, 175, 235; **52**: 338, 345, 349 375
Titus Andronicus **4**: 618, 619, 624, 631, 635, 640, 644, 646, 647, 653, 656, 659, 662, 664, 668, 672; **27**: 246, 285; **60**: 276
Troilus and Cressida **3**: 536, 538, 549, 568, 569, 578, 583, 589, 611, 613; **27**: 341, 347, 354, 391
Twelfth Night **1**: 539, 542, 543, 546, 551, 553, 563, 570, 571, 590, 600, 660; **26**: 374; **34**: 281, 287; **46**: 286; **62**: 308
The Two Gentlemen of Verona **6**: 445, 450, 460, 462, 504, 526
The Two Noble Kinsmen **37**: 313; **50**: 326, 361; **58**: 322

Venus and Adonis **10**: 434, 442, 480, 486, 489; **33**: 357, 377

style
Henry VIII **41**: 158
The Phoenix and Turtle **10**: 8, 20, 24, 27, 31, 35, 45, 50; **38**: 334, 345, 357; **51**: 171, 188; **64**: 205, 225
The Rape of Lucrece **10**: 64, 65, 66, 68, 69, 70, 71, 73, 74, 77, 78, 81, 84, 98, 116, 131, 135; **43**: 113, 158
Titus Andronicus **62**: 254
Venus and Adonis **10**: 411, 412, 414, 415, 416, 418, 419, 420, 423, 424, 428, 429, 439, 442, 480, 486, 489; **16**: 452

subjectivity
Hamlet **45**: 28; **59**: 42
Sonnets **37**: 374

subplot
Twelfth Night **62**: 297, 339, 343, 348

substitution of identities
Measure for Measure **2**: 507, 511, 519; **13**: 112; **49**: 313, 325; **65**: 44

subversion or transgression
Measure for Measure **65**: 45

subversiveness
Cymbeline **22**: 302
The Tempest **22**: 302
The Winter's Tale **22**: 302

Succession (Volume **60**: 295, 304, 322, 329, 340, 346, 357)
General Commentary **60**: 346, 357
Hamlet **60**: 346
Henry IV, Parts 1 and 2 **60**: 304; **65**: 235
Henry V **60**: 304
Henry VI, Parts 1, 2, and 3 **60**: 304; **65**: 235
King John **60**: 295, 304, 329
Macbeth **60**: 340, 357
Richard II **60**: 304
Richard III **60**: 304, 322; **65**: 235
Titus Andronicus **4**: 638

supernatural grace versus evil or chaos
Measure for Measure **48**: 1

suffering
King Lear **2**: 137, 160, 188, 201, 218, 222, 226, 231, 238, 241, 249, 265; **13**: 343; **22**: 271; **25**: 218; **50**: 24
Pericles **2**: 546, 573, 578, 579; **25**: 365; **36**: 279

symbolism
The Winter's Tale **7**: 425, 429, 436, 452, 456, 469, 490, 493

textual arrangement
Henry VI, Parts 1, 2, and 3 **24**: 3, 4, 6, 12, 17, 18, 19, 20, 21, 24, 27, 42, 45; **37**: 165
Richard II **24**: 260, 261, 262, 263, 271, 273, 291, 296, 356, 390

textual issues
Henry IV, Parts 1 and 2 **22**: 114
King Lear **22**: 271; **37**: 295; **49**: 73; **61**: 262
A Midsummer Night's Dream **16**: 34; **29**: 216; **58**: 151
The Taming of the Shrew **22**: 48; **31**: 261, 276; **31**: 276; **55**: 342, 371
The Winter's Tale **19**: 441; **45**: 333; **57**: 278, 285, 356

textual problems
Henry V **5**: 187, 189, 190; **13**: 201

textual revisions
Pericles **15**: 129, 130, 132, 134, 135, 136, 138, 152, 155, 167, 181; **16**: 399; **25**: 365; **51**: 99

textual variants
Hamlet **13**: 282; **16**: 259; **21**: 11, 23, 72, 101, 127, 129, 139, 140, 142, 145, 202, 208, 259, 270, 284, 347, 361, 384; **22**: 258; **32**: 238

theatrical viability
Henry VI, Parts 1, 2, and 3 **24**: 31, 32, 34; **56**: 80, 172

theatricality
Antony and Cleopatra **47**: 96, 103, 107, 113
Macbeth **16**: 328
Measure for Measure **23**: 285, 286, 294, 372, 406; **49**: 358; **65**: 91
The Merry Wives of Windsor **47**: 325

thematic disparity
Henry VIII **2**: 25, 31, 56, 68, 75; **41**: 146

themes
Hamlet **59**: 74, 79

Time (Volume **65**: 226, 235, 248, 251, 255, 259, 264, 270, 277, 285, 290, 297, 306, 311)
As You Like It **5**: 18, 82, 112, 141; **23**: 146, 150; **34**: 102; **46**: 88, 156, 164, 169; **65**: 255, 285, 336
Antony and Cleopatra **65**: 270
Hamlet **65**: 235
Henry IV, Parts 1 and 2 **66**: 256
Macbeth **3**: 234, 246, 283, 293; **20**: 245; **57**: 218; **65**: 226, 297, 317
Othello **65**: 327
Richard II **22**: 137
Richard III **65**: 248
Sonnets **10**: 265, 302, 309, 322, 329, 337, 360, 379; **13**: 445; **40**: 292; **65**: 235, 259, 277, 345
The Tempest **8**: 401, 439, 464; **25**: 357; **29**: 278, 292; **45**: 236; **65**: 235, 264, 311
Troilus and Cressida **3**: 561, 571, 583, 584, 613, 621, 626, 634; **65**: 226, 290
Twelfth Night **37**: 78; **46**: 297; **65**: 336
The Winter's Tale **7**: 397, 425, 436, 476, 490; **19**: 366; **36**: 301, 349; **45**: 297, 329, 366, 374; **65**: 235

time and change, motif of
Henry IV, Parts 1 and 2 **1**: 372, 393, 411; **39**: 89; **48**: 143

As You Like It **46:** 156, 164, 169

time scheme
Othello **4:** 370, 384, 390, 488; **22:** 207; **35:** 310; **47:** 51

topical allusions or content
Hamlet **13:** 282
Henry V **5:** 185, 186; **13:** 201
Love's Labour's Lost **2:** 300, 303, 307, 315, 316, 317, 319, 321, 327, 328; **23:** 187, 191, 197, 203, 221, 233, 237, 252; **25:** 1; **64:** 140, 166, 179
Macbeth **13:** 361; **20:** 17, 350; **29:** 101

traditional values
Richard III **39:** 335

tragicomedy, as
Cymbeline **61:** 2, 18

tragedies of major characters
Henry VIII **2:** 16, 39, 46, 48, 49, 51, 56, 58, 68, 81; **41:** 120

tragic elements
The Comedy of Errors **1:** 16, 25, 27, 45, 50, 59; **34:** 229; **54:** 144
Cymbeline **25:** 319; **28:** 373; **36:** 129; **47:** 296
Hamlet **55:** 78
Henry V **5:** 228, 233, 267, 269, 271
Henry VI, Parts 1, 2, and 3 **60:** 33
Julius Caesar **50:** 258, 265
King John **9:** 208, 209, 244
King Lear **55:** 78; **61:** 250
Macbeth **52:** 15; **55:** 78; **57:** 189
A Midsummer Night's Dream **3:** 393, 400, 401, 410, 445, 474, 480, 491, 498, 511; **29:** 175; **45:** 169; **58:** 175, 186
Othello **55:** 78
The Rape of Lucrece **10:** 78, 80, 81, 84, 98, 109; **43:** 85, 148
Richard II **58:** 229
Romeo and Juliet **55:** 78; **65:** 151, 190
The Tempest **8:** 324, 348, 359, 370, 380, 408, 414, 439, 458, 464
Twelfth Night **1:** 557, 569, 572, 575, 580, 599, 621, 635, 638, 639, 645, 654, 656; **26:** 342

treachery
Coriolanus **30:** 89
King John **9:** 245

treason and punishment
Macbeth **13:** 361; **16:** 328
Richard II **58:** 307

trial scene
The Merchant of Venice **49:** 1, 23, 37

trickster, motif of
Cymbeline **22:** 302
The Tempest **22:** 302; **29:** 297
The Winter's Tale **22:** 302; **45:** 333

triumph over death or fate
Romeo and Juliet **5:** 421, 423, 427, 505, 509, 520, 530, 536, 565, 566; **51:** 219

Trojan War
Troilus and Cressida
as myth **43:** 293

The Troublesome Reign (anonymous), compared with
King John **41:** 205, 221, 260, 269; **48:** 132; **56:** 357

Troy
Troilus and Cressida **43:** 287

Troy passage
The Rape of Lucrece **43:** 77, 85; **59:** 206

Tudor doctrine
King John **9:** 254, 284, 297; **41:** 221; **56:** 345; **66:** 271

Tudor myth
Henry VI, Parts 1, 2, and 3 **3:** 51, 59, 77, 92, 100, 109, 115, 119, 131; **39:** 222
Richard III **8:** 163, 165, 177, 184, 193, 201, 218, 228, 232, 243, 248, 252, 267; **39:** 305, 308, 326, 387; **42:** 130

Turkish elements
Henry IV, Parts 1 and 2 **19:** 170
Henry V **19:** 170

two fathers
Henry IV, Parts 1 and 2 **14:** 86, 101, 105, 108; **39:** 89, 100; **49:** 102

tyranny
King John **9:** 218

unity
Antony and Cleopatra **6:** 20, 21, 22, 24, 25, 32, 33, 39, 43, 53, 60, 67, 111, 125, 146, 151, 165, 208, 211, 219; **13:** 374; **27:** 82, 90, 135
Cymbeline **61:** 54
Hamlet **1:** 75, 76, 87, 103, 113, 125, 128, 142, 148, 160, 184, 188, 198, 264; **16:** 259; **35:** 82, 215
Henry VI, Parts 1, 2, and 3 **39:** 177, 222
A Midsummer Night's Dream **3:** 364, 368, 381, 402, 406, 427, 450, 513; **13:** 19; **22:** 378; **29:** 175, 263

unity of double plot
The Merchant of Venice **4:** 193, 194, 201, 232; **12:** 16, 67, 80, 115; **40:** 151

unnatural ordering
Hamlet **22:** 378
Love's Labour's Lost **22:** 378
The Merry Wives of Windsor **22:** 378
A Midsummer Night's Dream **22:** 378
Othello **22:** 378

as unsuccessful play
Measure for Measure **2:** 397, 441, 474, 482; **23:** 287

usurpation
See also **rebellion**
Richard II **6:** 263, 264, 272, 287, 289, 315, 323, 331, 343, 354, 364, 381, 388, 393, 397; **24:** 383; **52:** 108, 141, 154
The Tempest **8:** 304, 370, 408, 420; **25:** 357, 382; **29:** 278, 362, 377; **37:** 336

utopia
The Tempest **45:** 280

value systems
Troilus and Cressida **3:** 578, 583, 589, 602, 613, 617; **13:** 53; **27:** 370, 396, 400; **59:** 234, 245; **59:** 287, 295, 318

Venetian politics
Othello **32:** 294

Venice, Elizabethan perceptions of
The Merchant of Venice **28:** 249; **32:** 294; **40:** 127; **66:** 123

Venus and Adonis
The Rape of Lucrece **43:** 148

Vergil, influence of
Titus Andronicus **27:** 306; **28:** 249

verisimilitude
As You Like It **5:** 18, 23, 28, 30, 32, 39, 125; **23:** 107

Verona society
Romeo and Juliet **5:** 556, 566; **13:** 235; **33:** 255; **51:** 245

Violence in Shakespeare's Works (Volume 43: 1, 12, 24, 32, 39, 61)
Hamlet **59:** 26
Henry IV, Parts 1 and 2 **25:** 109
Henry VI, Parts 1, 2, and 3 **24:** 25, 31; **37:** 157
Julius Caesar **48:** 240
Love's Labour's Lost **22:** 12
Macbeth **20:** 273, 279, 283; **45:** 58; **57:** 228, 267
Othello **22:** 12
The Rape of Lucrece **43:** 148, 158; **59:** 189, 193, 212
The Taming of the Shrew **55:** 322; **64:** 320
Titus Andronicus **13:** 225; **25:** 245; **27:** 255; **28:** 249; **32:** 249, 265; **43:** 186, 203, 227, 239, 247, 255, 262; **62:** 208, , 225, 233, 242, 254, 258, 265
Troilus and Cressida **43:** 329, 340, 351, 357, 365, 377

virginity or chastity, importance of
Much Ado about Nothing **8:** 44, 75, 95, 111, 121, 125; **31:** 222; **55:** 268

Virgo vs. Virago
King Lear **48:** 222

visual arts, relation to
Sonnets **28:** 407

visual humor
   Love's Labour's Lost **23**: 207, 217

virtue versus vice
   Antony and Cleopatra **60**: 222
   Macbeth **60**: 214

war
   Coriolanus **25**: 263; **30**: 79, 96, 125, 149
   Henry V **5**: 193, 195, 197, 198, 210, 213, 219, 230, 233, 246, 281, 293; **28**: 121, 146; **30**: 262; **32**: 126; **37**: 175, 187; **42**: 141; **49**: 194, 236, 247, 260

Wars of the Roses
   Richard III **8**: 163, 165, 177, 184, 193, 201, 218, 228, 232, 243, 248, 252, 267; **39**: 308; **62**: 71

Watteau, influence on staging
   Love's Labour's Lost **23**: 184, 186

wealth
   The Merchant of Venice **4**: 209, 261, 270, 273, 317; **12**: 80, 117; **22**: 69; **25**: 22; **28**: 249; **40**: 117, 197, 208; **45**: 17; **49**: 1; **51**: 15

wealth and social class
   Timon of Athens **1**: 466, 487, 495; **25**: 198; **27**: 184, 196, 212; **50**: 13

wheel of fortune, motif of
   Antony and Cleopatra **6**: 25, 178; **19**: 304
   Hamlet **52**: 35
   Henry VIII **2**: 27, 65, 72, 81; **61**: 144

widowhood and remarriage, themes of
   Hamlet **32**: 238

wisdom
   King Lear **37**: 213; **46**: 210
   Love's Labour's Lost **54**: 257

wit
   The Merry Wives of Windsor **5**: 335, 336, 337, 339, 343, 351
   Much Ado about Nothing **8**: 27, 29, 38, 69, 79, 91, 95; **31**: 178, 191; **55**: 228

witchcraft
   See **Magic and the Supernatural**

women, role of
   See **Shakespeare's Representation of Women**

wonder, dynamic of
   The Comedy of Errors **37**: 12

wordplay
   As You Like It **46**: 105
   Romeo and Juliet **32**: 256

written versus oral communication
   Love's Labour's Lost **2**: 359, 365; **28**: 63

youth
   The Two Gentlemen of Verona **6**: 439, 450, 464, 514, 568

youth versus age
   All's Well That Ends Well **7**: 9, 45, 58, 62, 76, 81, 86, 93, 98, 104, 116, 126; **26**: 117; **38**: 109

Shakespearean Criticism
Cumulative Topic Index, by Play

The Cumulative Topic Index, by Play identifies the principal topics of discussion in the criticism of each play and non-dramatic poem. The topics are arranged alphabetically by play. Page references indicate the beginning page number of each essay containing substantial commentary on that topic. A parenthetical reference after a play indicates which volumes discuss the play extensively.

All's Well That Ends Well (Volumes 7, 26, 38, 55)

appearance versus reality **7:** 37, 76, 93; **26:** 117
audience perspective **7:** 81, 104, 109, 116, 121
bed-trick **7:** 8, 26, 27, 29, 32, 41, 86, 93, 98, 113, 116, 126; **13:** 84; **26:** 117; **28:** 38; **38:** 65, 118; **49:** 46; **54:** 52; **55:** 109, 131, 176
Bertram
    characterization **7:** 15, 27, 29, 32, 39, 41, 43, 98, 113; **26:** 48; **26:** 117; **55:** 90
    conduct **7:** 9, 10, 12, 16, 19, 21, 51, 62, 104; **50:** 59; **55:** 143, 154
    desire **22:** 78
    transformation or redemption **7:** 10, 19, 21, 26, 29, 32, 54, 62, 81, 90, 93, 98, 109, 113, 116, 126; **13:** 84
comic elements **26:** 97, 114; **48:** 65; **55:** 148, 154, 164
conclusion **38:** 123, 132, 142; **54:** 52; **55:** 148, 154, 170
dark elements **7:** 27, 37, 39, 43, 54, 109, 113, 116; **26:** 85; **48:** 65; **50:** 59; **54:** 30; **55:** 164, 170
Decameron (Boccaccio), compared with **7:** 29, 43
desire **38:** 99, 109, 118; **55:** 122
displacement **22:** 78
education **7:** 62, 86, 90, 93, 98, 104, 116, 126
elder characters **7:** 9, 37, 39, 43, 45, 54, 62, 104
gender issues **7:** 9, 10, 67, 126; **13:** 77, 84; **19:** 113; **26:** 128; **38:** 89, 99, 118; **44:** 35; **55:** 101, 109, 122, 164
genre **48:** 65
Helena
    as agent of reconciliation, renewal, or grace **7:** 67, 76, 81, 90, 93, 98, 109, 116; **55:** 176; **66:** 335
    as dualistic or enigmatic character **7:** 15, 27, 29, 39, 54, 58, 62, 67, 76, 81, 98, 113, 126; **13:** 66; **22:** 78; **26:** 117; **54:** 30; **55:** 90, 170, 176
    as "female achiever" **19:** 113; **38:** 89; **55:** 90, 101, 109, 122, 164
    desire **38:** 96; **44:** 35; **55:** 109, 170

pursuit of Bertram **7:** 9, 12, 15, 16, 19, 21, 26, 27, 29, 32, 43, 54, 76, 116; **13:** 77; **22:** 78; **49:** 46; **55:** 90
virginity **38:** 65; **55:** 131, 176
virtue and nobility **7:** 9, 10, 12, 16, 19, 21, 27, 32, 41, 51, 58, 67, 76, 86, 126; **13:** 77; **50:** 59; **55:** 122
implausibility of plot, characters, or events **7:** 8, 45
irony, paradox, and ambiguity **7:** 27, 32, 58, 62, 67, 81, 86, 109, 116
King **38:** 150; **55:** 148
language and imagery **7:** 12, 29, 45, 104, 109, 121; **38:** 132; **48:** 65
Lavatch **26:** 64; **46:** 33, 52, 68; **55:** 143
love **7:** 12, 15, 16, 51, 58, 67, 90, 93, 116; **38:** 80; **51:** 33, 44
merit versus rank **7:** 9, 10, 19, 37, 51, 76; **38:** 155; **50:** 59
"mingled yarn" **7:** 62, 93, 109, 126; **38:** 65
morality plays, influence of **7:** 29, 41, 51, 98, 113; **13:** 66
mythic or mythological elements **60:** 169
naturalism **60:** 169
opening scene **54:** 30
Parolles
    characterization **7:** 8, 9, 43, 76, 81, 98, 109, 113, 116, 126; **22:** 78; **26:** 48, 73, 97; **26:** 117; **46:** 68; **55:** 90, 154
    exposure **7:** 9, 27, 81, 98, 109, 113, 116, 121, 126
Falstaff, compared with **7:** 8, 9, 16
reconciliation **7:** 90, 93, 98; **51:** 33
religious, mythic, or spiritual content **7:** 15, 45, 54, 67, 76, 98, 109, 116; **66:** 335
romance or folktale elements **7:** 32, 41, 43, 45, 54, 76, 104, 116, 121; **26:** 117
sexuality **7:** 67, 86, 90, 93, 98, 126; **13:** 84; **19:** 113; **22:** 78; **28:** 38; **44:** 35; **49:** 46; **51:** 44; **55:** 109, 131, 143, 176
social and political context **13:** 66; **22:** 78; **38:** 99, 109, 150, 155; **49:** 46
staging issues **19:** 113; **26:** 15, 19, 48, 52, 64, 73, 85, 92, 93, 94, 95, 97, 114, 117, 128; **54:** 30
structure **7:** 21, 29, 32, 45, 51, 76, 81, 93, 98, 116; **22:** 78; **26:** 128; **38:** 72, 123, 142; **66:** 335
youth versus age **7:** 9, 45, 58, 62, 76, 81, 86, 93, 98, 104, 116, 126; **26:** 117; **38:** 109

Antony and Cleopatra (Volumes 6, 17, 27, 47, 58)

allegorical elements **52:** 5
All for Love (John Dryden), compared with **6:** 20, 21; **17:** 12, 94, 101
ambiguity **6:** 53, 111, 161, 163, 180, 189, 208, 211, 228; **13:** 368
androgyny **13:** 530
Antony
    characterization **6:** 22, 23, 24, 31, 38, 41, 172, 181, 211; **16:** 342; **19:** 270; **22:** 217; **27:** 117; **47:** 77, 124, 142; **58:** 2, 41, 118, 134
    Cleopatra, relationship with **6:** 25, 27, 37, 39, 48, 52, 53, 62, 67, 71, 76, 85, 100, 125, 131, 133, 136, 142, 151, 161, 163, 165, 180, 192; **27:** 82; **47:** 107, 124, 165, 174
    death scene **25:** 245; **47:** 142; **58:** 41; **60:** 46
    dotage **6:** 22, 23, 38, 41, 48, 52, 62, 107, 136, 146, 175; **17:** 28
    nobility **6:** 22, 24, 33, 48, 94, 103, 136, 142, 159, 172, 202; **25:** 245
    political conduct **6:** 33, 38, 53, 107, 111, 146, 181
    public versus private personae **6:** 165; **47:** 107; **58:** 41; **65:** 270
    self-knowledge **6:** 120, 131, 175, 181, 192; **47:** 77
    as superhuman figure **6:** 37, 51, 71, 92, 94, 178, 192; **27:** 110; **47:** 71
    as tragic hero **6:** 38, 39, 52, 53, 60, 104, 120, 151, 155, 165, 178, 192, 202, 211; **22:** 217; **27:** 90
audience response **48:** 206; **58:** 88
Caesar **65:** 270
Cleopatra
    Antony, relationship with **6:** 25, 27, 37, 39, 48, 52, 53, 62, 67, 71, 76, 85, 100, 125, 131, 133, 136, 142, 151, 161, 163, 165, 180, 192; **25:** 257; **27:** 82; **47:** 107, 124, 165, 174
    characterization **47:** 77, 96, 113, 124; **58:** 24, 33, 59, 118, 134
    contradictory or inconsistent nature **6:** 23, 24, 27, 67, 76, 100, 104, 115, 136, 151, 159, 202; **17:** 94, 113; **27:** 135
    costume **17:** 94
    creativity **6:** 197; **47:** 96, 113

383

death, decay, and nature's destructiveness **6:** 23, 25, 27, 41, 43, 52, 60, 64, 76, 94, 100, 103, 120, 131, 133, 136, 140, 146, 161, 165, 180, 181, 192, 197, 208; **13:** 383; **17:** 48, 94; **25:** 245; **27:** 135; **47:** 71
death scene **60:** 46
histrionic nature **65:** 270
personal attraction of **6:** 24, 38, 40, 43, 48, 53, 76, 104, 115, 155; **17:** 113
self-knowledge **47:** 77, 96
staging issues **17:** 94, 113
as subverter of social order **6:** 146, 165; **47:** 113
suicide **58:** 33
as superhuman figure **6:** 37, 51, 71, 92, 94, 178, 192; **27:** 110; **47:** 71, 174, 192; **58:** 24
as tragic heroine **6:** 53, 120, 151, 192, 208; **27:** 144
as voluptuary or courtesan **6:** 21, 22, 25, 41, 43, 52, 53, 62, 64, 67, 76, 146, 161; **47:** 107, 174; **58:** 24
comic elements **6:** 52, 85, 104, 125, 131, 151, 192, 202, 219; **47:** 77, 124, 149, 165; **58:** 41
contemptus mundi **6:** 85, 133
dreams **45:** 28
dualisms **19:** 304; **27:** 82; **58:** 2, 71, 79, 105
Egyptian versus Roman values **6:** 31, 33, 43, 53, 104, 111, 115, 125, 142, 155, 159, 178, 181, 211, 219; **17:** 48; **19:** 270; **27:** 82, 121, 126; **28:** 249; **47:** 96, 103, 113, 149; **58:** 59, 71, 88, 105; **60:** 179
Elizabethan culture, relation to **47:** 103; **58:** 118
Enobarbus **6:** 22, 23, 27, 43, 94, 120, 142; **16:** 342; **17:** 36; **22:** 217; **27:** 135
gender issues **13:** 368; **25:** 257; **27:** 144; **47:** 174, 192; **53:** 67, 77; **58:** 59
imperialism **53:** 67, 77
irony or paradox **6:** 53, 136, 146, 151, 159, 161, 189, 192, 211, 224
Jacobean culture, relation to **58:** 79, 134
Jacobean politics, relation to **58:** 79, 134
language and imagery **6:** 21, 25, 39, 64, 80, 85, 92, 94, 100, 104, 142, 146, 155, 159, 161, 165, 189, 192, 202, 211; **13:** 374, 383; **25:** 245, 257; **27:** 96, 105, 135; **58:** 79, 88, 118
love and passion **6:** 51, 64, 71, 80, 85, 100, 115, 159, 165, 180; **25:** 257; **27:** 126; **47:** 71, 124, 174, 192; **51:** 25, 33, 44; **58:** 2, 41, 105; **60:** 179, 222
love and time **65:** 235, 270
monument scene **13:** 374; **16:** 342; **17:** 104, 110; **22:** 217; **47:** 142, 165
morality **52:** 5
moral relativism **22:** 217; **27:** 121
mythic or mythological elements **60:** 222
mythological allusions **16:** 342; **19:** 304; **27:** 110, 117; **47:** 71, 192; **60:** 179, 222
Octavius **6:** 22, 24, 31, 38, 43, 53, 62, 107, 125, 146, 178, 181, 219; **25:** 257; **58:** 33
opening scene **54:** 6
political and social disintegration **6:** 31, 43, 53, 60, 71, 80, 100, 107, 111, 146; 180, 197, 219; **22:** 217; **25:** 257; **27:** 121
race **53:** 67, 77
reason versus imagination **6:** 107, 115, 142, 197, 228; **45:** 28
reconciliation **6:** 100, 103, 125, 131, 159, 181
religious, mythic, or spiritual content **6:** 53, 94, 111, 115, 178, 192, 224; **47:** 71; **58:** 24, 41; **60:** 179
royalty **6:** 94
Seleucus episode (Act V, scene ii) **6:** 39, 41, 62, 133, 140, 151; **27:** 135; **58:** 33
Shakespeare's major tragedies, compared with **6:** 25, 53, 60, 71, 120, 181, 189, 202; **22:** 217; **47:** 77
Shakespeare's moral judgment **6:** 33, 37, 38, 41, 48, 51, 64, 76, 111, 125, 136, 140, 146, 163, 175, 189, 202, 211, 228; **13:** 368, 523; **25:** 257
sources **6:** 20, 39; **19:** 304; **27:** 96, 126; **28:** 249
stage history **17:** 84, 94, 101
staging issues **17:** 6, 12, 84, 94, 101, 104, 110; **27:** 90; **47:** 142
strategic analysis **48:** 206
structure **58:** 71, 88
theatricality and role-playing **47:** 96, 103, 107, 113
unity **6:** 20, 21, 22, 24, 25, 32, 33, 39, 43, 53, 60, 67, 111, 125, 146, 151, 165, 208, 211, 219; **13:** 374; **27:** 82, 90, 135
virtue versus vice **60:** 222
wheel of fortune, motif of **6:** 25, 178; **19:** 304

As You Like It (Volumes 5, 23, 34, 46, 57)

Appearance versus Reality **46:** 105; **57:** 35, 40
androgyny **23:** 98, 100, 122, 138, 143, 144; **34:** 172, 177; **46:** 134; **57:** 13
anti-romantic elements **34:** 72
aristocracy **34:** 120
art versus nature **5:** 128, 130, 148; **34:** 147; **57:** 35, 75
Audrey **46:** 122
autobiographical elements **5:** 25, 35, 43, 50, 55, 61
bawdy elements **46:** 122
Celia **46:** 94
characterization **5:** 19, 24, 25, 36, 39, 54, 82, 86, 116, 148; **34:** 72; **48:** 42; **65:** 336
Christian elements **5:** 39, 98, 162; **57:** 31
contradiction, paradox, and opposition **46:** 105
comic form **46:** 105; **51:** 1; **57:** 2
comic resolution **52:** 63
corruption in society **46:** 94; **57:** 35
costume **46:** 117
courtship and marriage **34:** 109, 177; **48:** 32; **51:** 44
death, decay, nature's destructiveness **46:** 169
deception, disguise, and duplicity **46:** 134; **57:** 40
desire **37:** 43; **52:** 63; **60:** 115
domestic elements **46:** 142
dramatic shortcomings or failure **5:** 19, 42, 52, 61, 65
duration of time **5:** 44, 45
Elizabethan culture, relation to **5:** 21, 59, 66, 68, 70, 158; **16:** 53; **28:** 46; **34:** 120; **37:** 1; **46:** 142; **57:** 23, 31, 64, 75
Fathers and Daughters **46:** 94
feminism **23:** 107, 108; **57:** 2, 13
Forest of Arden
as "bitter" Arcadia **5:** 98, 118, 162; **23:** 97, 98, 99, 100, 122, 139
Duke Frederick's court, contrast with **5:** 46, 102, 103, 112, 130, 156; **16:** 53; **23:** 126, 128, 129, 131, 134; **34:** 78, 102, 131; **46:** 164; **57:** 64; **65:** 255, 285
pastoral elements **5:** 18, 20, 24, 32, 35, 47, 50, 54, 55, 57, 60, 77, 128, 135, 156; **23:** 17, 20, 27, 46, 137; **34:** 78, 147; **46:** 88
as patriarchal society **5:** 168; **23:** 150; **34:** 177; **57:** 2
as source of self-knowledge **5:** 98, 102, 103, 128, 130, 135, 148, 158, 162; **23:** 17; **34:** 102; **57:** 35
as timeless, mythical world **5:** 112, 130, 141; **23:** 132; **34:** 78; **37:** 43; **46:** 88; **65:** 255
theme of play **46:** 88
gender identity **46:** 127, 134; **57:** 13, 23, 45
genre **5:** 46, 55, 79
homoerotic elements **46:** 127, 142; **57:** 23; **60:** 115
homosexuality **46:** 127, 142; **57:** 13
Hymen episode **5:** 61, 116, 130; **23:** 22, 48, 54, 109, 111, 112, 113, 115, 146, 147; **57:** 40
irony **5:** 30, 32, 154
Jaques
love-theme, relation to **5:** 103; **23:** 7, 37, 118, 128
as malcontent **5:** 59, 70, 84
melancholy **5:** 20, 28, 32, 36, 39, 43, 50, 59, 63, 68, 77, 82, 86, 135; **23:** 20, 26, 103, 104, 107, 109; **34:** 85; **46:** 88, 94
pastoral convention, relation to **5:** 61, 63, 65, 79, 93, 98, 114, 118
Seven Ages of Man speech (Act II, scene vii) **5:** 28, 52, 156; **23:** 48, 103, 105, 126, 138, 152; **46:** 88, 156, 164, 169
Shakespeare, relation to **5:** 35, 50, 154
as superficial critic **5:** 28, 30, 43, 54, 55, 63, 65, 68, 75, 77, 82, 86, 88, 98, 138; **34:** 85
justice **46:** 94
juxtaposition of opposing perspectives **5:** 86, 93, 98, 141; **16:** 53; **23:** 119; **34:** 72, 78, 131
language and imagery **5:** 19, 21, 35, 52, 75, 82, 92, 138; **23:** 15, 21, 26; **28:** 9; **34:** 131; **37:** 43; **48:** 42; **57:** 35, 56
love **5:** 24, 44, 46, 57, 79, 88, 103, 116, 122, 138, 141, 162; **28:** 46, 82; **34:** 85
Love in a Forest (Charles Johnson adaptation) **23:** 7
metadramatic elements **5:** 128, 130, 146; **34:** 130
morality **52:** 63; **57:** 13
mythological allusions **46:** 142
nature **46:** 94; **60:** 231
Neoclassical rules **5:** 19, 20
Orlando
as ideal man **5:** 32, 36, 39, 162; **34:** 161; **46:** 94
relationship with Rosalind/Ganymede **60:** 115
as younger brother **5:** 66, 158; **46:** 94
pastoral characters (Silvius, Phebe, and Corin) **23:** 37, 97, 98, 99, 108, 110, 118, 122, 138; **34:** 147; **60:** 115
pastoral convention, parodies of **5:** 54, 57, 72
pastoral convention, relation to **5:** 72, 77, 122; **34:** 161; **37:** 1
primogeniture **5:** 66, 158; **34:** 109, 120
psychoanalytic interpretation **5:** 146, 158; **23:** 141, 142; **34:** 109; **48:** 42
public versus private worlds **46:** 164; **65:** 285
reconciliation of opposites **5:** 79, 88, 103, 116, 122, 138; **23:** 127, 143; **34:** 161, 172; **46:** 156
religious, mythic, or spiritual content **60:** 231
as romance **5:** 55, 79; **23:** 27, 28, 40, 43
Rosalind **46:** 94, 122
Beatrice, compared with **5:** 26, 36, 50, 75
charm **5:** 55, 75; **23:** 17, 18, 20, 41, 89, 111
disguise, role of **5:** 75, 107, 118, 122, 128, 130, 133, 138, 141, 146, 148, 164, 168; **13:** 502; **23:** 35, 42, 106, 119, 123, 146; **34:** 130; **46:** 134
femininity **5:** 26, 36, 52, 75; **23:** 24, 29, 46, 54, 103, 108, 121, 146
as Ganymede **46:** 127, 142; **60:** 115
love-theme, relation to **5:** 79, 88, 103, 116, 122, 138, 141; **23:** 114, 115; **34:** 85, 177
rustic characters **5:** 24, 60, 72, 84; **23:** 127; **34:** 78, 161

sexual ambiguity and sexual deception **46:** 134, 142; **57:** 23, 40, 45
Sexuality in Shakespeare **46:** 122, 127, 134, 142
as satire or parody of pastoral conventions **5:** 46, 55, 60, 72, 77, 79, 84, 114, 118, 128, 130, 154
self-knowledge **5:** 32, 82, 102, 116, 122, 133, 164; **57:** 45
sibling rivalry **34:** 109
social order **37:** 1; **46:** 94; **57:** 2
sources **5:** 18, 32, 54, 59, 66, 84; **34:** 155; **46:** 117; **60:** 231
stage history **46:** 117; **57:** 56
staging issues **13:** 502; **23:** 7, 17, 19, 22, 58, 96, 97, 98, 99, 101, 110, 137; **28:** 82; **32:** 212; **57:** 56, 75
structure **5:** 19, 24, 25, 35, 44, 45, 46, 86, 93, 116, 138, 158; **23:** 7, 8, 9, 10, 11; **34:** 72, 78, 131, 147, 155
time **5:** 18, 82, 112, 141; **23:** 146, 150; **34:** 102; **46:** 88, 156, 164, 169; **65:** 255, 285, 336
Touchstone
  callousness **5:** 88
  comic and farcical elements **46:** 117
  as philosopher-fool **5:** 24, 28, 30, 32, 36, 63, 75, 98; **23:** 152; **34:** 85; **46:** 1, 14, 18, 24, 33, 52, 60, 88, 105
  relation to pastoral convention **5:** 54, 61, 63, 72, 75, 77, 79, 84, 86, 93, 98, 114, 118, 135, 138, 166; **34:** 72, 147, 161
selflessness **5:** 30, 36, 39, 76
verisimilitude **5:** 18, 23, 28, 30, 32, 39, 125; **23:** 107
wordplay **46:** 105

The Comedy of Errors (Volumes 1, 26, 34, 54, 66)

Adriana **16:** 3; **34:** 211, 220, 238; **54:** 189
adultery **34:** 215
Aemelia **66:** 1
Antipholus of Ephesus
  crisis of identity **66:** 51
  as ideal ego of Antipholus of Syracuse **66:** 17
  as Shakespeare's ego **66:** 1
Antipholus of Syracuse
  characterization **66:** 1, 17, 51
  madness **66:** 22
  search for self **66:** 1, 17
  as Shakespeare's alter ego **66:** 1
audience perception **1:** 37, 50, 56; **19:** 54; **34:** 258; **54:** 136, 144
autobiographical elements **1:** 16, 18
characterization **1:** 13, 21, 31, 34, 46, 49, 50, 55, 56; **19:** 54; **25:** 63; **34:** 194, 201, 208, 245; **54:** 144, 176
classical influence and sources **1:** 13, 14, 16, 31, 32, 43, 61; **54:** 169
comic elements **1:** 43, 46, 55, 56, 59; **26:** 183, 186, 188, 190; **34:** 190, 245; **66:** 17
composition date **1:** 18, 23, 34, 55
dramatic structure **1:** 19, 27, 40, 43, 46, 50; **26:** 186, 190; **34:** 190, 229, 233; **37:** 12; **54:** 136, 155, 189
Dromio brothers **42:** 80; **54:** 136, 152; **66:** 1
Elizabethan culture, relation to **26:** 138, 142; **34:** 201, 215, 233, 238, 258; **42:** 80; **54:** 169, 200; **66:** 22, 51
farcical elements **1:** 14, 16, 19, 23, 30, 34, 35, 46, 50, 59, 61; **19:** 54; **26:** 188, 190; **34:** 245; **54:** 136, 144, 189; **66:** 31, 38
feminist criticism **42:** 93
food, meaning of **34:** 220
gender issues **34:** 215, 220
genre **34:** 251, 258; **66:** 38
identity **34:** 201, 208, 211; **54:** 155, 169, 200

illusion **1:** 13, 14, 27, 37, 40, 45, 59, 63; **26:** 188; **34:** 194, 211; **54:** 169, 200
language and imagery **1:** 16, 25, 39, 40, 43, 57, 59; **34:** 233; **54:** 152, 162; **66:** 17, 31, 38
male/female relationships **16:** 3
marriage **34:** 251; **54:** 215
mistaken identity **1:** 13, 14, 27, 37, 40, 45, 49, 55, 57, 61, 63; **19:** 34, 54; **25:** 63; **34:** 194; **54:** 176, 162, 189, 215
Plautus's works, compared with **1:** 13, 14, 16, 53, 61; **16:** 3; **19:** 34; **54:** 162, 176; **66:** 22, 51
problem comedy **34:** 251
psychoanalytic interpretation **66:** 1
redemption **19:** 54; **26:** 188; **54:** 152, 189
romantic elements **1:** 13, 16, 19, 23, 25, 30, 31, 36, 39, 53; **66:** 38
servitude **42:** 80
social order **34:** 238; **54:** 155, 215
sources **1:** 13, 14, 16, 19, 31, 32, 39; **16:** 3; **34:** 190, 215, 258; **54:** 155, 176
staging issues **26:** 182, 183, 186, 188, 190; **54:** 136; **66:** 27, 29, 30
structure **66:** 31
supernatural, role of **1:** 27, 30; **54:** 215; **66:** 22
tragic elements **1:** 16, 25, 27, 45, 50, 59; **34:** 229; **54:** 144
wonder, dynamic of **37:** 12

Coriolanus (Volumes 9, 17, 30, 50, 64)

aggression **9:** 112, 142, 174, 183, 189, 198; **30:** 79, 111, 125, 142; **44:** 11, 79
Anthony and Cleopatra, compared with **30:** 79, 96; **50:** 105
appearance versus reality **30:** 142
Aufidius **9:** 9, 12, 17, 19, 53, 121, 148, 153, 157, 169, 180, 193; **19:** 287; **25:** 263, 296; **30:** 58, 67, 89, 96, 133; **50:** 99
body politic, metaphor of **22:** 248; **30:** 67, 96, 105, 125; **50:** 105, 110, 119, 140, 145, 152; **64:** 8
butterfly episode (Act I, scene iii) **9:** 19, 45, 62, 65, 73, 100, 125, 153, 157
capitulation scene (Act V, scene iii) **9:** 19, 26, 53, 65, 100, 117, 125, 130, 157, 164, 183
ceremonies, rites, and rituals, importance of **9:** 139, 148, 169
Christian elements **30:** 111
comic elements **9:** 8, 9, 14, 53, 80, 106
Cominius **25:** 245
Cominius's tribute (Act II, scene ii) **9:** 80, 100, 117, 125, 144, 164, 198; **25:** 296
Coriolanus
  ambition **64:** 40
  anger or passion **9:** 19, 26, 45, 80, 92, 157, 164, 177, 189; **30:** 79, 96
  as complementary figure to Aufidius **19:** 287
  death scene (Act V, scene vi) **9:** 12, 80, 100, 117, 125, 144, 164, 198; **25:** 245, 263; **50:** 110; **60:** 46
  as epic hero **9:** 130, 164, 177; **25:** 245; **50:** 119; **64:** 2
  immaturity **9:** 62, 80, 84, 110, 117, 142; **30:** 140
  inhuman attributes **9:** 65, 73, 139, 157, 164, 169, 189, 198; **25:** 263
  internal struggle **9:** 31, 43, 45, 53, 72, 117, 121, 130; **44:** 93; **64:** 62, 103
  introspection or self-knowledge, lack of **9:** 53, 80, 84, 112, 117, 130; **25:** 296; **30:** 133
  isolation or autonomy **9:** 53, 65, 142, 144, 153, 157, 164, 180, 183, 189, 198; **30:** 58, 89, 111; **50:** 128; **64:** 62
  manipulation by others **9:** 33, 45, 62, 80; **25:** 296

  modesty **9:** 8, 12, 19, 26, 53, 78, 92, 117, 121, 144, 183; **25:** 296; **30:** 79, 96, 129, 133, 149
  narcissism **30:** 111
  noble or aristocratic attributes **9:** 15, 18, 19, 26, 31, 33, 52, 53, 62, 65, 84, 92, 100, 121, 148, 157, 169; **25:** 263; **30:** 67, 74, 96; **50:** 13; **64:** 25
  pride or arrogance **9:** 8, 11, 12, 19, 26, 31, 33, 43, 45, 65, 78, 92, 121, 148, 153, 177; **30:** 58, 67, 74, 89, 96, 129
  reconciliation with society **9:** 33, 43, 45, 65, 139, 169; **25:** 296
  as socially destructive force **9:** 62, 65, 73, 78, 110, 142, 144, 153; **25:** 296
  soliloquy (Act IV, scene iv) **9:** 84, 112, 117, 130
  as tragic figure **9:** 8, 12, 13, 18, 25, 45, 52, 53, 72, 80, 92, 106, 112, 117, 130, 148, 164, 169, 177; **25:** 296; **30:** 67, 74, 79, 96, 111, 129; **37:** 283; **50:** 99; **64:** 25, 40, 79
  traitorous actions **9:** 9, 12, 19, 45, 84, 92, 148; **25:** 296; **30:** 133
  as unsympathetic character **9:** 12, 13, 62, 78, 80, 84, 112, 130, 157; **64:** 79
domestic elements **42:** 223; **50:** 145
economics **50:** 152
England and Rome, parallels between **9:** 39, 43, 106, 148, 180, 193; **25:** 296; **30:** 67, 105; **50:** 172
fable of the belly (Act I, scene i) **9:** 8, 65, 73, 80, 136, 153, 157, 164, 180, 183, 189; **25:** 296; **30:** 79, 105, 111; **50:** 13, 110, 140
fame **30:** 58
fire and water **25:** 263
flattery or dissimulation **9:** 26, 45, 92, 100, 110, 121, 130, 144, 157, 183, 193; **25:** 296
friendship **30:** 125, 142
gender issues **30:** 79, 125, 142; **44:** 93; **50:** 128
genre **9:** 42, 43, 53, 80, 106, 112, 117, 130, 164, 177; **30:** 67, 74, 79, 89, 111, 125; **50:** 99; **64:** 2, 8
honor or integrity **9:** 43, 65, 73, 92, 106, 110, 121, 144, 153, 157, 164, 177, 183, 189; **30:** 89, 96, 133; **64:** 2
identity **42:** 248; **50:** 128
irony or satire **9:** 65, 73, 80, 92, 106, 153, 157, 164, 193; **30:** 67, 89, 133
Jacobean culture, relation to **22:** 248; **64:** 25
language and imagery **9:** 8, 9, 13, 53, 64, 65, 73, 78, 84, 100, 112, 121, 136, 139, 142, 144, 153, 157, 174, 183, 193, 198; **22:** 248; **25:** 245, 263; **30:** 111, 125, 142; **37:** 283; **44:** 79; **64:** 2, 89, 94, 103
Macbeth, compared with **30:** 79
martial vs. civil law **48:** 230
Menenius **9:** 8, 9, 11, 14, 19, 26, 78, 80, 106, 148, 157; **25:** 263, 296; **30:** 67, 79, 89, 96, 111, 133
Midlands Revolt, influence of **22:** 248; **30:** 79; **50:** 140, 172; **64:** 8
naming, significance of **30:** 58, 96, 111, 125
nature, philosophy of **30:** 74
nurturing or feeding **9:** 65, 73, 136, 183, 189; **30:** 111; **44:** 79; **50:** 110
mythic or mythological elements **60:** 205
opening scene **54:** 6
paradoxical elements **9:** 73, 92, 106, 121, 153, 157, 164, 169, 193
parent-child relations **60:** 205
plebeians **9:** 8, 9, 11, 12, 15, 18, 19, 26, 33, 39, 53, 92, 125, 153, 183, 189; **25:** 296; **30:** 58, 79, 96, 111; **50:** 13, 105; **64:** 94
Plutarch and historical sources **9:** 8, 9, 13, 14, 16, 26, 39, 92, 106, 130, 142, 164; **30:** 74, 105; **50:** 99
politics **9:** 15, 17, 18, 19, 26, 33, 43, 53, 62, 65, 73, 80, 92, 106, 110, 112, 121, 144,

153, 157, 164, 180; **22:** 248; **25:** 296; **30:** 58, 67, 79, 89, 96, 105, 111, 125; **37:** 283; **42:** 223; **48:** 230; **50:** 13, 140, 172; **64:** 8, 18, 25, 79, 94
psychoanalytic interpretations **44:** 93; **64:** 40, 62
public versus private worlds **37:** 283; **42:** 223
sexuality **9:** 112, 142, 174, 183, 189, 198; **30:** 79, 111, 125, 142
shame **42:** 248
Shakespeare's political sympathies **9:** 8, 11, 15, 17, 19, 26, 39, 52, 53, 62, 80, 92, 142; **25:** 296; **30:** 74, 79, 89, 96, 105, 133; **50:** 145, 172
slander **48:** 230
society **9:** 15, 17, 18, 19, 26, 33, 43, 53, 62, 65, 73, 80, 92, 106, 110, 112, 121, 144, 153, 157, 164, 180; **22:** 248; **25:** 296; **30:** 58, 67, 79, 89, 96, 105, 111, 125; **50:** 13, 105, 119, 152
sources **60:** 205
staging issues **17:** 172, 242, 248; **64:** 83, 85, 86, 87, 88, 89
structure **9:** 8, 9, 11, 12, 13, 14, 16, 26, 33, 45, 53, 58, 72, 78, 80, 84, 92, 112, 139, 148; **25:** 263; **30:** 79, 96
treachery **30:** 89
the tribunes (Brutus and Sicinius) **9:** 9, 11, 14, 19, 33, 169, 180
Virgilia **9:** 11, 19, 26, 33, 58, 100, 121, 125; **25:** 263; **30:** 79, 96, 133; **50:** 99
Volumnia
    Coriolanus's subservience to **9:** 16, 26, 33, 53, 62, 80, 92, 100, 117, 125, 142, 177, 183; **30:** 140, 149; **44:** 79
    influence on Coriolanus **9:** 45, 62, 65, 78, 92, 100, 110, 117, 121, 125, 130, 148, 157, 183, 189, 193; **25:** 263, 296; **30:** 79, 96, 125, 133, 140, 142, 149; **44:** 93; **64:** 72
    as noble Roman matron **9:** 16, 19, 26, 31, 33; **64:** 72
    personification of Rome **9:** 125, 183; **50:** 119
war **25:** 263; **30:** 79, 96, 125, 149

Cymbeline (Volumes 4, 15, 36, 47, 61)

anachronisms **65:** 251
appearance versus reality **4:** 87, 93, 103, 162; **36:** 99; **47:** 228, 286
authorship controversy **4:** 17, 21, 35, 48, 56, 78
autobiographical elements **4:** 43, 46; **36:** 134
bawdy elements **36:** 155
Beaumont and Fletcher's romances, compared with **4:** 46, 52, 138
Belarius **4:** 48, 89, 141
British nationalism **4:** 19, 78, 89, 93, 129, 141, 159, 167; **32:** 373; **36:** 129; **45:** 67; **47:** 219, 265; **61:** 54
Cloten **4:** 20, 116, 127, 155; **22:** 302, 365; **25:** 245; **36:** 99, 125, 142, 155; **47:** 228
combat scenes **22:** 365
comic elements **4:** 35, 56, 113, 141; **15:** 111, 122; **47:** 296
Cymbeline **61:** 54
dramatic structure **4:** 17, 18, 19, 20, 21, 22, 24, 38, 43, 48, 53, 64, 68, 89, 116, 129, 141; **22:** 302, 365; **25:** 319; **36:** 115, 125; **60:** 240; **61:** 2
dreams **4:** 162, 167; **44:** 28; **45:** 67, 75
dualisms **4:** 29, 64, 73
Elizabethan dramatic conventions **4:** 53, 124
family, theme of **44:** 28
genre controversy **61:** 2
Guiderius and Arviragus **4:** 21, 22, 89, 129, 141, 148; **25:** 319; **36:** 125, 158
historical elements **47:** 260
Iachimo **25:** 245, 319; **36:** 166

Imogen **4:** 21, 22, 24, 29, 37, 45, 46, 52, 56, 78, 89, 108; **15:** 23, 32, 105, 121; **19:** 411; **25:** 245, 319; **28:** 398; **32:** 373; **36:** 129, 142, 148; **47:** 25, 205, 228, 245, 274, 277; **61:** 34, 45, 76
Imogen's reawakening (Act IV, scene ii) **4:** 37, 56, 89, 103, 108, 116, 150; **15:** 23; **25:** 245; **47:** 252
irony **4:** 64, 77, 103
language and imagery **4:** 43, 48, 61, 64, 70, 73, 93, 108; **13:** 401; **25:** 245; **28:** 373, 398; **36:** 115, 158, 166, 186; **47:** 205, 286, 296; **60:** 240
Jacobean politics **61:** 54, 76
James I **61:** 54
love ideal **61:** 34, 45
Lucretia, analogies to **36:** 148
marriage **61:** 34, 45
misperception **19:** 411; **36:** 99, 115; **47:** 228, 237, 252, 277, 286, 296
mythic or mythological elements **60:** 240
negative appraisals **4:** 20, 35, 43, 45, 48, 53, 56, 68; **15:** 32, 105, 121
pastoralism **61:** 18
patriarchy **32:** 373; **36:** 134; **47:** 237; **51:** 30
peace **61:** 54
political allegory **61:** 76
politics **61:**
Posthumus **4:** 24, 30, 53, 78, 116, 127, 141, 155, 159, 167; **15:** 89; **19:** 411; **25:** 245, 319; **36:** 142; **44:** 28; **45:** 67, 75; **47:** 25, 205, 228; **61:** 34, 45, 76
psychological elements **36:** 134; **44:** 28; **45:** 67, 75; **60:** 240; **61:** 18
reconciliation **4:** 38, 64, 73, 93, 105, 113, 116, 129, 138, 141, 162, 170; **61:** 2
redemption **61:** 18
religious, mythical, or spiritual content **4:** 22, 29, 78, 93, 105, 108, 115, 116, 127, 134, 138, 141, 159; **28:** 373; **36:** 142, 158, 186; **47:** 219, 260, 274
romantic elements **4:** 17, 20, 46, 68, 77, 141, 148, 172; **15:** 111; **25:** 319; **28:** 373; **61:** 34
self-conscious or artificial nature of play **4:** 43, 52, 56, 68, 124, 134, 138; **36:** 99
sexuality **4:** 170, 172; **25:** 319; **32:** 373; **47:** 245
Shakespeare's lyric poetry, compared with **13:** 401
sources **4:** 17, 18; **13:** 401; **28:** 373; **47:** 245, 265, 277
staging issues **15:** 6, 23, 75, 105, 111, 121, 122; **22:** 365
subversiveness **22:** 302
tragedy, as **61:** 2
tragicomedy, as **61:** 2, 18
tragic elements **25:** 319; **28:** 373; **36:** 129; **47:** 296
unity **61:** 54
trickster, motif of **22:** 302
vision scene (Act V, scene iv) **4:** 17, 21, 28, 29, 35, 38, 78, 105, 108, 134, 150, 167; **47:** 205
wager plot **4:** 18, 24, 29, 53, 78, 155; **22:** 365; **25:** 319; **47:** 205, 277

Hamlet (Volumes 1, 21, 35, 44, 59)

ambiguity **1:** 92, 160, 198, 227, 230, 234, 247, 249; **21:** 72; **35:** 241; **66:** 266
appearance versus reality **1:** 95, 116, 166, 169, 198; **35:** 82, 126, 132, 144, 238; **44:** 248; **45:** 28
aristocracy **42:** 217
audience response **28:** 325; **32:** 238; **35:** 167; **44:** 107
autobiographical elements **1:** 98, 115, 119; **13:** 487
beginning **54:** 19; **59:** 18
Calvinist implications **48:** 195; **66:** 266

classical Greek tragedies, compared with **1:** 74, 75, 130, 184, 212; **13:** 296; **22:** 339
Claudius **13:** 502; **16:** 246; **21:** 259, 347, 361, 371; **28:** 232, 290; **35:** 104, 182; **44:** 119, 241; **59:** 62
closet scene (Act III, scene iv) **16:** 259; **21:** 151, 334, 392; **35:** 204, 229; **44:** 119, 237
conflict between idealism and pragmatism **60:** 71
costume **21:** 81
death, decay, and nature's destructiveness **1:** 144, 153, 188, 198, 221, 242; **13:** 502; **28:** 280, 311; **35:** 241; **42:** 284; **60:** 71, 91, 194
dreams **45:** 28
dumbshow and play scene (Act III, scene ii) **1:** 76, 86, 134, 138, 154, 160, 207; **13:** 502; **21:** 392; **35:** 82; **44:** 241; **46:** 74; **59:** 42, 62
Elizabethan culture, relation to **1:** 76, 148, 151, 154, 160, 166, 169, 171, 176, 184, 202, 209, 254; **13:** 282, 494; **19:** 330; **21:** 407, 416; **22:** 258; **59:** 74
Elizabethan and Jacobean politics, relation to **28:** 232; **28:** 290, 311; **35:** 140
ending **54:** 96; **59:** 74; **60:** 346
feminist criticism **55:** 56; **59:** 31, 39
fencing scene (Act V, scene ii) **21:** 392; **54:** 96; **59:** 26
Fortinbras **21:** 136, 347; **28:** 290
gender issues **35:** 144; **44:** 189, 195, 198; **59:** 31, 39
genre **1:** 176, 212, 237
Gertrude **21:** 259, 347, 392; **28:** 311; **32:** 238; **35:** 182, 204, 229; **44:** 119, 160, 189, 195, 237, 248; **59:** 39, 62, 74
Ghost **1:** 75, 76, 84, 85, 128, 134, 138, 154, 171, 218, 231, 254; **16:** 246; **21:** 17, 44, 112, 151, 334, 371, 377, 392; **25:** 288; **35:** 152, 157, 174, 237; **44:** 119; **59:** 2, 10
gravedigger scene (Act V, scene i) **21:** 392; **28:** 280; **46:** 74; **60:** 71
grotesque elements **42:** 284
Hamlet
    compared to Vindice **59:** 10
    death of **60:** 46
    delay **1:** 76, 83, 88, 90, 94, 98, 102, 103, 106, 114, 115, 116, 119, 120, 148, 151, 166, 171, 179, 188, 191, 194, 198, 221, 268; **13:** 296, 502; **21:** 81; **25:** 209, 288; **28:** 223; **35:** 82, 174, 212, 215, 237; **44:** 180, 209, 219, 229; **59:** 10
    divided nature **16:** 246; **28:** 223; **32:** 288; **35:** 182, 215; **37:** 241; **59:** 2
    elocution of the character's speeches **21:** 96, 104, 112, 127, 132, 172, 177, 179, 194, 245, 254, 257
    as a fool **46:** 1, 29, 52, 74
    and identity (nature of) **59:** 18
    madness **1:** 76, 81, 83, 95, 102, 106, 128, 144, 154, 160, 234; **21:** 35, 50, 72, 81, 99, 112, 311, 339, 355, 361, 371, 377, 384; **35:** 117, 132, 134, 140, 144, 212; **44:** 107, 119, 152, 209, 219, 229; **59:** 31
    meeting with the pirates (Act IV, scene vi) **59:** 56
    melancholy **21:** 99, 112, 177, 194; **35:** 82, 95, 117; **44:** 209, 219
    as negative character **1:** 86, 92, 111, 171, 218; **21:** 386; **25:** 209; **35:** 167; **59:** 10
    reaction to his father's death **22:** 339; **35:** 104, 174; **44:** 133, 160, 180, 189
    reaction to Gertrude's marriage **1:** 74, 120, 154, 179; **16:** 259; **21:** 371; **22:** 339; **35:** 104, 117; **44:** 133, 160, 189, 195
    romantic aspects of the character **21:** 96; **44:** 198; **59:** 47

as scourge or purifying figure **1:** 144, 209, 242; **25:** 288; **35:** 157; **59:** 26, 62, 79; **66:** 305
sentimentality versus intellectuality **1:** 75, 83, 88, 91, 93, 94, 96, 102, 103, 115, 116, 120, 166, 191; **13:** 296; **21:** 35, 41, 44, 72, 81, 89, 99, 129, 132, 136, 172, 213, 225, 339, 355, 361, 371, 377, 379, 381, 386; **25:** 209; **44:** 198
soliloquies **1:** 76, 82, 83, 148, 166, 169, 176, 191; **21:** 17, 31, 44, 53, 89, 112, 268, 311, 334, 347, 361, 384, 392; **25:** 209;**28:** 223; **44:** 107, 119, 229
as a stoic at the end **54:** 96; **66:** 266
theatrical interpretations **21:** 11, 31, 78, 101, 104, 107, 160, 177, 179, 182, 183, 192, 194, 197, 202, 203, 208, 213, 225, 232, 237, 249, 253, 254, 257, 259, 274, 311, 339, 347, 355, 361, 371, 377, 380
virility **21:** 213, 301, 355; **44:** 198
Hamlet with Alterations (David Garrick adaptation) **21:** 23, 334, 347
Horatio **44:** 189
idealism versus pragmatism **16:** 246; **28:** 325
Laertes **21:** 347, 386; **28:** 290; **35:** 182; **59:** 26
language and imagery **1:** 95, 144, 153, 154, 160, 188, 198, 221, 227, 249, 259, 270; **22:** 258, 378; **28:** 311; **35:** 144, 152, 238, 241; **42:** 217; **44:** 248; **52:** 35; **59:** 42, 47, 56, 62, 74
madness **19:** 330; **35:** 104, 126, 134, 140, 144; **44:** 107, 119, 152, 209, 219, 229
marriage **22:** 339; **51:** 44
Marxist criticism **42:** 234
medieval drama **59:** 68
moral choice **52:** 35
nunnery scene (Act III, scene i) **21:** 157, 381, 410
opening scene **54:** 2, 6, 19
Ophelia **1:** 73, 76, 81, 82, 91, 96, 97, 154, 166, 169, 171, 218, 270; **13:** 268; **16:** 246; **19:** 330; **21:** 17, 41, 44, 72, 81, 101, 104, 107, 112, 136, 203, 259, 347, 381, 386, 392, 416; **28:** 232, 325; **35:** 104, 126, 140, 144, 182, 238; **44:** 189, 195, 248; **59:** 31, 39, 68
paradoxical elements **59:** 47
Petrarchan love poetry **59:** 47
Polonius **21:** 259, 334, 347, 386, 416; **35:** 182
prayer scene (Act III, scene iii) **1:** 76, 106, 160, 212, 231; **44:** 119
psychoanalytic interpretations **1:** 119, 148, 154, 179, 202; **21:** 197, 213, 361; **25:** 209; **28:** 223; **35:** 95, 104, 134, 237; **37:** 241; **44:** 133, 152, 160, 180, 209, 219
religious, mythic, or spiritual content **1:** 98, 102, 130, 184, 191, 209, 212, 231, 234, 254; **21:** 361; **22:** 258; **28:** 280; **32:** 238; **35:** 134; **59:** 2; **60:** 194; **66:** 266, 305
revenge **1:** 74, 194, 209, 224, 234, 254; **16:** 246; **22:** 258; **25:** 288; **28:** 280; **35:** 152, 157, 167, 174, 212; **44:** 180, 209, 219, 229; **54:** 96; **59:** 10, 79
Richard II, compared with **1:** 264
rites, rituals, and ceremonies, importance of **13:** 268; **28:** 232
satire **59:** 79
sexuality **55:** 56; **59:** 31, 68
sources **1:** 76, 81, 113, 125, 128, 130, 151, 191, 202, 224, 259; **59:** 68
staging issues **13:** 494, 502; **21:** 11, 17, 31, 35, 41, 44, 50, 53, 78, 81, 89, 101, 112, 127, 139, 142, 145, 148, 151, 157, 160, 172, 182, 183, 202, 203, 208, 225, 232, 237, 242, 245, 249, 251, 259, 268, 270, 274, 283, 284, 301, 311, 334, 347, 355, 361, 371, 377, 379, 380, 381, 384, 386, 392, 407, 410, 416; **44:** 198; **54:** 19

Stoicism **48:** 195; **66:** 266
structure **22:** 378; **28:** 280, 325; **35:** 82, 104, 215; **44:** 152; **59:** 2, 42
subjectivity **45:** 28; **59:** 42
succession **60:** 346
textual variants **13:** 282; **16:** 259; **21:** 11, 23, 72, 101, 127, 129, 139, 140, 142, 145, 202, 208, 259, 270, 284, 347, 361, 384; **22:** 258; **32:** 238
time **65:** 235
themes **59:** 74, 79
topical allusions or content **13:** 282
tragic elements **13:** 78
unity **1:** 75, 76, 87, 103, 113, 125, 128, 142, 148, 160, 184, 188, 198, 264; **16:** 259; **35:** 82, 215
unnatural ordering **22:** 378
violence **59:** 26
wheel of fortune, motif of **52:** 35
widowhood and remarriage, themes of **32:** 238

Henry IV, Parts 1 and 2 (Volumes 1, 14, 39, 49, 57)

adaptations of **60:** 154
ambition **57:** 94
Biblical references **57:** 147
carnival elements **28:** 203; **32:** 103
Catholic components **57:** 167
characterization **1:** 321, 328, 332, 333, 336, 344, 365, 383, 385, 389, 391, 397, 401; **19:** 195; **39:** 123, 137; **42:** 101, 164; **49:** 93; **57:** 88, 167, 181
comic elements **1:** 286, 290, 314, 327, 328, 336, 353; **19:** 195; **25:** 109; **39:** 72; **57:** 120
contractual and economic relations **13:** 213
contrasting dramatic worlds **14:** 56, 60, 61, 84, 105; **48:** 95; **49:** 162; **57:** 183
critical history **42:** 187; **48:** 167
deception, disguise, and duplicity **1:** 397, 406, 425; **42:** 101; **47:** 1, 60; **48:** 95
desire **60:** 154
divine right versus justice **49:** 116; **57:** 88, 130
Elizabethan culture, relation to **19:** 195; **48:** 117, 143, 151, 175
Elizabethan politics, relation to **22:** 395; **28:** 203; **47:** 60; **48:** 117, 143, 167, 175; **57:** 88, 94
Falstaff
  characterization **1:** 287, 298, 312, 333; **25:** 245; **28:** 203; **39:** 72, 134, 137, 143; **57:** 120, 156
  as comic figure **1:** 287, 311, 327, 344, 351, 354, 357, 410, 434; **39:** 89; **46:** 1, 48, 52; **49:** 178; **57:** 120
  as coward or rogue **1:** 285, 290, 296, 298, 306, 307, 313, 317, 323, 336, 337, 338, 342, 354, 366, 374, 391, 396, 401, 433; **14:** 7, 111, 125, 130, 133; **32:** 166
  dual personality **1:** 397, 401, 406, 434; **49:** 162
  female attributes **13:** 183; **44:** 44; **60:** 154
  Iago, compared with **1:** 341, 351
  Marxist interpretation **1:** 358, 361
  moral reformation **60:** 26
  as outlaw **49:** 133
  as parody of the historical plot **1:** 314, 354, 359; **39:** 143
  as positive character **1:** 286, 287, 290, 296, 298, 311, 312, 321, 325, 333, 344, 355, 357, 389, 401, 408, 434
  rejection by Hal **1:** 286, 287, 290, 312, 314, 317, 324, 333, 338, 344, 357, 366, 372, 374, 379, 380, 389, 414; **13:** 183; **25:** 109; **39:** 72, 89; **57:** 147; **66:** 256
  as satire of feudal society **1:** 314, 328, 361; **32:** 103
  as scapegoat **1:** 389, 414; **57:** 156

stage interpretations **14:** 4, 6, 7, 9, 15, 116, 130, 146; **47:** 1
  as subversive figure **16:** 183; **25:** 109
  as Vice figure **1:** 342, 361, 366, 374
flattery **22:** 395
gender issues **13:** 183; **25:** 151; **44:** 44; **48:** 175; **60:** 154
Hal
  audience's perspective of **49:** 153; **57:** 116
  and betrayal **49:** 123
  as the central character **1:** 286, 290, 314, 317, 326, 338, 354, 366, 374, 396; **39:** 72, 100
  compared with the fair friend of the sonnets **60:** 154
  dual personality **1:** 397, 406; **25:** 109, 151; **49:** 112, 139, 153, 162; **57:** 130
  as Everyman **1:** 342, 366, 374
  fall from humanity **1:** 379, 380, 383
  general assessment **1:** 286, 287, 289, 290, 314, 317, 326, 327, 332, 357, 397; **25:** 245; **32:** 212; **39:** 134; **57:** 116, 130; **65:** 306
  Henry's perspective of **49:** 153
  as ideal ruler **1:** 289, 309, 317, 321, 326, 337, 342, 344, 374, 389, 391, 434; **25:** 109; **39:** 123; **47:** 60; **60:** 154
  as Machiavellian ruler **47:** 60
  as negative character **1:** 312, 332, 333, 357; **32:** 212
  as outlaw **49:** 112
  preparation for rule **49:** 112; **57:** 116, 130
  reformation **57:** 160
  Richard II, compared with **1:** 332, 337; **39:** 72
  as restorer of law **49:** 133
Henry **39:** 123, 137; **49:** 139
  effectiveness as ruler **49:** 116
  guilt **49:** 112
  illegitimacy of rule **49:** 112, 133, 137
  as tragic figure **49:** 186
  as usurper **49:** 116, 137
historical content **1:** 310, 328, 365, 366, 370, 374, 380, 387, 421, 424, 427, 431; **16:** 172; **19:** 157; **25:** 151; **32:** 136; **39:** 143; **48:** 143, 167; **49:** 139; **57:** 137
historical and dramatic elements **49:** 93
historical epic, place in or relation to Shakespeare's **1:** 309, 314, 328, 374, 379, 424, 427; **48:** 167
historiography **56:** 2, 15, 25
homosexuality **60:** 154
Hostess **60:** 26
Hotspur **25:** 151; **28:** 101; **39:** 72, 134, 137; **42:** 101; **49:** 137; **60:** 154
  and prisoners of war **49:** 137
  versus Henry **49:** 137
John of Lancaster, Prince
  and betrayal **49:** 123
justice **49:** 112, 123; **57:** 137
kingship **1:** 314, 318, 337, 366, 370, 374, 379, 380, 383, 424; **16:** 172; **19:** 195; **28:** 101; **39:** 100, 116, 123, 130; **42:** 143; **48:** 143; **57:** 88, 94, 108, 137, 160; **65:** 306
language and imagery **13:** 213; **16:** 172; **25:** 245; **28:** 101; **39:** 116, 130; **42:** 155; **47:** 1; **57:** 137
Lord Chief Justice
  as keeper of law and justice **49:** 133
  as medieval allegory or morality play **1:** 323, 324, 342, 361, 366, 373, 374; **32:** 166; **39:** 89; **47:** 60
Mortimer **25:** 151
multiple endings **49:** 102
Neoclassical rules **1:** 286, 287, 290, 29
politics **28:** 101; **39:** 130; **42:** 143; **48:** 143, 175; **57:** 108; **65:** 306
power **49:** 139; **57:** 108
Protestant aspects **57:** 167; **66:** 256
providential order **56:** 15

psychoanalytic interpretations **13:** 457; **28:** 101; **42:** 187; **44:** 44
rebellion **22:** 395; **28:** 101
redemption **57:** 116
references to **22:** 114; **32:** 166; **48:** 117
relationship to other Shakespearean plays **1:** 286, 290, 309, 329, 365, 396; **28:** 101; **42:** 101, 155; **48:** 167; **49:** 93, 186
relationship of Parts 1 and 2 **32:** 136; **39:** 100; **49:** 178; **57:** 160, 181
  as autonomous works **1:** 289, 337, 338, 347, 348, 373, 387, 393, 411, 418, 424
  comparison **1:** 290, 295, 329, 348, 358, 393, 411, 419, 429, 431, 441
  unity of both parts **1:** 286, 290, 309, 314, 317, 329, 365, 373, 374, 396, 402, 404, 419
religious, mythic, or spiritual content **1:** 314, 374, 414, 421, 429, 431, 434; **32:** 103; **48:** 151; **57:** 147, 156, 167; **60:** 26; **66:** 256
sources **56:** 2
sovereignty **57:** 94
staging issues **32:** 212; **47:** 1; **49:** 102
structure **49:** 93; **56:** 53, 60; **57:** 181
succession **60:** 304; **65:** 235
textual issues **22:** 114
time and change, motif of **1:** 372, 393, 411; **39:** 89; **48:** 143; **66:** 256
Turkish elements **19:** 170
two fathers **14:** 86, 101, 105, 108; **39:** 89, 100; **49:** 102
violence **25:** 109

Henry V (Volumes 5, 14, 30, 49)

  battle of Agincourt **5:** 197, 199, 213, 246, 257, 281, 287, 289, 293, 310, 318; **19:** 217; **30:** 181
  Canterbury and churchmen **5:** 193, 203, 205, 213, 219, 225, 252, 260; **22:** 137; **30:** 215, 262; **66:** 280
  characterization **5:** 186, 189, 192, 193, 199, 219, 230, 233, 252, 276, 293; **30:** 227, 278
  Chorus, role of **5:** 186, 192, 226, 228, 230, 252, 264, 269, 281, 293; **14:** 301, 319, 336; **19:** 133; **25:** 116, 131; **30:** 163, 202, 220; **49:** 194, 200, 211, 219, 260
  class distinctions, conflict, and relations **28:** 146
  colonialism **22:** 103
  comic elements **5:** 185, 188, 191, 192, 217, 230, 233, 241, 252, 260, 276; **19:** 217; **28:** 121; **30:** 193, 202
  economic relations **13:** 213
  Elizabethan culture, relation to **5:** 210, 213, 217, 223, 257, 299, 310; **16:** 202; **19:** 133, 233; **28:** 121, 159; **30:** 215, 262; **37:** 187; **49:** 260
  English language and colonialism **22:** 103; **28:** 159
  epic elements **5:** 192, 197, 246, 257, 314; **30:** 181, 220, 237, 252
  Falstaff **5:** 185, 186, 187, 189, 192, 195, 198, 210, 226, 257, 269, 271, 276, 293, 299; **28:** 146; **46:** 48
    death of **60:** 26
  Fluellen **30:** 278; **37:** 105
  French aristocrats and the Dauphin **5:** 188, 191, 199, 205, 213, 281; **22:** 137; **28:** 121
  French language, Shakespeare's use of **5:** 186, 188, 190; **25:** 131
  gender issues **13:** 183; **28:** 121, 146, 159; **44:** 44
  Henry
    brutality and cunning **5:** 193, 203, 209, 210, 213, 219, 233, 239, 252, 260, 271, 287, 293, 302, 304; **30:** 159
    characterization in 1 and 2 Henry IV contrasted **5:** 189, 190, 241, 304, 310; **19:** 133; **25:** 131; **32:** 157
    chivalry **37:** 187
    courage **5:** 191, 195, 210, 213, 228, 246, 257, 267
    disguise **30:** 169, 259
    education **5:** 246, 267, 271, 289; **14:** 297, 328, 342; **30:** 259
    emotion, lack of **5:** 209, 212, 233, 244, 264, 267, 287, 293, 310
    as heroic figure **5:** 192, 205, 209, 223, 244, 252, 257, 260, 269, 271, 299, 304; **28:** 121, 146; **30:** 237, 244, 252; **37:** 187; **49:** 194, 200, 236, 247
    humor **5:** 189, 191, 212, 217, 239, 240, 276
    intellectual and social limitations **5:** 189, 191, 203, 209, 210, 225, 226, 230, 293; **30:** 220
    interpersonal relations **5:** 209, 233, 267, 269, 276, 287, 293, 302, 318; **19:** 133; **28:** 146
    mercy **5:** 213, 267, 289, 293
    mixture of good and bad qualities **5:** 199, 205, 209, 210, 213, 244, 260, 304, 314; **30:** 262, 273; **49:** 211
    piety **5:** 191, 199, 209, 217, 223, 239, 257, 260, 271, 289, 310, 318; **30:** 244; **32:** 126; **66:** 280
    public versus private selves **22:** 137; **30:** 169, 207
    self-doubt **5:** 281, 310
    slaughter of prisoners **5:** 189, 205, 246, 293, 318; **28:** 146
    speech **5:** 212, 230, 233, 246, 264, 276, 287, 302; **28:** 146; **30:** 163, 227
  heroism **49:** 194, 200, 211, 236
  historical content **5:** 185, 188, 190, 192, 193, 198, 246, 314; **13:** 201; **19:** 133; **25:** 131; **30:** 193, 202, 207, 215, 252; **49:** 223
  historical epic, place in or relation to Shakespeare's **5:** 195, 198, 205, 212, 225, 241, 244, 287, 304, 310; **14:** 337, 342; **30:** 215
  historiography **56:** 2, 15
  homoerotic elements **16:** 202
  Hotspur **5:** 189, 199, 228, 271, 302
  hypocrisy **5:** 203, 213, 219, 223, 233, 260, 271, 302
  imperialism **22:** 103; **28:** 159
  Irish affairs **22:** 103; **28:** 159
  irony **5:** 192, 210, 213, 219, 223, 226, 233, 252, 260, 269, 281, 299, 304; **14:** 336; **30:** 159, 193; **66:** 280
  Katherine **5:** 186, 188, 189, 190, 192, 260, 269, 299, 302; **13:** 183; **19:** 217; **30:** 278; **44:** 44
  kingship **5:** 205, 223, 225, 233, 239, 244, 257, 264, 267, 271, 287, 289, 299, 302, 304, 314, 318; **16:** 202; **22:** 137; **30:** 169, 202, 259, 273; **49:** 200; **66:** 280
  language and imagery **5:** 188, 230, 233, 241, 264, 276; **19:** 203; **25:** 131; **30:** 159, 181, 207, 234
  law and justice **49:** 223, 226, 260
  Machiavellianism **5:** 203, 225, 233, 252, 287, 304; **25:** 131; **30:** 273; **60:** 304
  MacMorris **22:** 103; **28:** 159; **30:** 278
  Marlowe's works, compared with **19:** 233
  metadramatic elements **13:** 194; **30:** 181; **49:** 200, 211
  Mistress Quickly **5:** 186, 187, 210, 276, 293; **30:** 278
  morality **5:** 195, 203, 213, 223, 225, 239, 246, 260, 271, 293
  obscenity **5:** 188, 190, 260
  order **5:** 205, 257, 264, 310, 314; **30:** 193
  patriarchy **37:** 105; **44:** 44
  politics and ideology **49:** 219, 247, 260
  providential order **56:** 15
  nationalism and patriotism **5:** 198, 205, 209, 210, 213, 219, 223, 233, 246, 252, 257, 269, 299; **19:** 133, 217; **30:** 227, 262; **49:** 219, 247
  Pistol **28:** 146
  power **37:** 175
  psychoanalytic interpretations **13:** 457; **44:** 44
  religious, mythic, or religious content **25:** 116; **32:** 126; **60:** 26
  Salic Law **5:** 219, 252, 260; **28:** 121
  self-interest or expediency **5:** 189, 193, 205, 213, 217, 233, 260, 287, 302, 304; **30:** 273; **49:** 223; **66:** 280
  soldiers **5:** 203, 239, 267, 276, 281, 287, 293, 318; **28:** 146; **30:** 169; **49:** 194
  sources **56:** 2
  staging issues **5:** 186, 189, 192, 193, 198, 205, 226, 230, 241, 281, 314; **13:** 194, 502; **14:** 293, 295, 297, 301, 310, 319, 328, 334, 336, 342; **19:** 217; **32:** 185
  structure **5:** 186, 189, 205, 213, 230, 241, 264, 289, 310, 314; **30:** 220, 227, 234, 244
  succession **60:** 304
  tetralogy, relation to **49:** 223
  textual problems **5:** 187, 189, 190; **13:** 201
  topical allusions or content **5:** 185, 186; **13:** 201
  tragic elements **5:** 228, 233, 267, 269, 271
  traitors (Scroop, Grey, and Cambridge) **16:** 202; **30:** 220, 278
    Southampton conspiracy **49:** 223
  Turkish elements **19:** 170
  violence **43:** 24
  war **5:** 193, 195, 197, 198, 210, 213, 219, 230, 233, 246, 281, 293; **28:** 121, 146; **30:** 262; **32:** 126; **37:** 175, 187; **42:** 143; **49:** 194, 236, 247, 260
  Williams **13:** 502; **16:** 183; **28:** 146; **30:** 169, 259, 278
  wooing scene (Act V, scene ii) **5:** 186, 188, 189, 191, 193, 195, 260, 276, 299, 302; **14:** 297; **28:** 121, 159; **30:** 163, 207

Henry VI, Parts 1, 2, and 3 (Volumes 3, 24, 39, 56)

  ambivalent or ironic elements **3:** 69, 151, 154; **39:** 160; **56:** 131
  authorship controversy **3:** 16, 18, 19, 20, 21, 26, 27, 29, 31, 35, 39, 41, 55, 66; **24:** 51; **56:** 77
  autobiographical elements **3:** 41, 55
  Bordeaux sequence **37:** 165
  Cade scenes **3:** 35, 67, 92, 97, 109; **16:** 183; **22:** 156; **25:** 102; **28:** 112; **37:** 97; **39:** 160, 196, 205; **50:** 45, 51; **56:** 117, 122, 131, 180
  carnival elements **22:** 156
  characterization **3:** 18, 20, 24, 25, 31, 57, 64, 73, 77, 109, 119, 151; **24:** 22, 28, 38, 42, 45, 47; **39:** 160
  class distinctions, conflict, and relations **37:** 97; **39:** 187; **50:** 45, 51; **56:** 117, 131
  dance **22:** 156
  decay of heroic ideals **3:** 119, 126; **56:** 95
  disorder and civil dissension **3:** 59, 67, 76, 92, 103, 126; **13:** 131; **16:** 183; **24:** 11, 17, 28, 31, 47; **25:** 102; **28:** 112; **39:** 154, 177, 187, 196, 205; **56:** 80, 85, 110
  Elizabethan literary and cultural influences **3:** 75, 97, 100, 119, 143; **22:** 156; **28:** 112; **37:** 97; **56:** 162, 180
  Folk rituals, elements and influence of **39:** 205
  Henry
    characterization **3:** 64, 77, 151; **39:** 160, 177; **47:** 32

source of social disorder **3:** 25, 31, 41, 115; **39:** 154, 187
as sympathetic figure **3:** 73, 143, 154; **24:** 32
historical accuracy or revisionism **3:** 18, 21, 35, 46, 51; **16:** 217; **24:** 16, 18, 25, 31, 45, 48; **56:** 85, 110, 122, 131, 145
historical epic, place in or relation to Shakespeare's **3:** 24, 59; **24:** 51; **56:** 95
historiography **56:** 2, 25
as humanistic play **3:** 83, 92, 109, 115, 119, 131, 136, 143
Humphrey **13:** 131; **56:** 187
as inferior or flawed play **3:** 20, 21, 25, 26, 35
Joan of Arc **16:** 131; **32:** 212; **60:** 33
kingship **3:** 69, 73, 77, 109, 115, 136, 143; **24:** 32; **39:** 154, 177, 187; **47:** 32
language and imagery **3:** 21, 50, 52, 55, 57, 66, 67, 71, 75, 76, 97, 105, 109, 119, 126, 131; **24:** 28; **37:** 157; **39:** 213, 222; **56:** 154, 162, 172, 180
legitimacy **3:** 89, 157; **39:** 154
Machiavellianism **22:** 193; **60:** 304
Margaret
 characterization **3:** 18, 26, 35, 51, 103, 109, 140, 157; **24:** 48
 Suffolk, relationship with **3:** 18, 24, 26, 157; **39:** 213
Marlowe's works, compared with **19:** 233
medieval literary influence **3:** 59, 67, 75, 100, 109, 136, 151; **13:** 131
molehill scene (3 Henry VI, Act III, scene ii) **3:** 75, 97, 126, 149; **56:** 154; **60:** 33
moral inheritance **3:** 89, 126
multiple perspectives of characters **3:** 69, 154; **56:** 131
nationalism and patriotism **24:** 25, 45, 47; **56:** 25, 45, 47, 80
Neoclassical rules **3:** 17, 18
patriarchal claims **16:** 131; **25:** 102
play-within-the-play, convention of **3:** 75, 149
retribution **3:** 27, 42, 51, 59, 77, 83, 92, 100, 109, 115, 119, 131, 136, 151
Richard of Gloucester
 characterization **3:** 35, 48, 57, 64, 77, 143, 151; **22:** 193; **39:** 160, 177
 as revenger **22:** 193
 soliloquy (3 Henry VI, Act III, scene ii) **3:** 17, 48
sibling rivalry **22:** 193
sources **3:** 18, 21, 29, 31, 35, 39, 46, 51; **13:** 131; **16:** 217; **39:** 196; **56:** 2, 122, 131, 187
staging issues **24:** 21, 22, 27, 31, 32, 36, 38, 41, 45, 48, 55; **32:** 212; **56:** 154, 172, 180, 187
structure **3:** 31, 43, 46, 69, 83, 103, 109, 119, 136, 149, 154; **39:** 213; **56:** 77, 80, 85
succession **60:** 304; **65:** 235
Talbot **39:** 160, 213, 222; **56:** 85, 145; **60:** 33
textual arrangement **24:** 3, 4, 6, 12, 17, 18, 19, 20, 21, 24, 27, 42, 45; **37:** 165
theatrical viability **24:** 31, 32, 34; **56:** 80, 172
tragic elements **60:** 33
Tudor myth **3:** 51, 59, 77, 92, 100, 109, 115, 119, 131; **39:** 222
Unity **39:** 177, 222
violence **24:** 25, 31; **37:** 157
women, role of **3:** 103, 109, 126, 140, 157; **16:** 183; **39:** 196; **60:** 33
York's death **13:** 131; **60:** 33

Henry VIII (Volumes 2, 24, 41, 56, 61)

ambition or pride **2:** 15, 38, 67
authorship controversy **2:** 16, 18, 19, 22, 23, 27, 28, 31, 35, 36, 42, 43, 44, 46, 48, 51, 58, 64, 68; **41:** 129, 146, 158, 171
Anne Boleyn **2:** 21, 24, 31; **41:** 180; **61:** 129
Buckingham **22:** 182; **24:** 129, 140; **37:** 109
change **2:** 27, 65, 72, 81
characterization **2:** 17, 23, 25, 32, 35, 39; **24:** 106
composition date **2:** 19, 22, 35; **24:** 129
costumes **24:** 82, 87; **28:** 184
Cranmer's prophecy **2:** 25, 31, 46, 56, 64, 68, 72; **24:** 146; **32:** 148; **41:** 120, 190; **56:** 196, 230, 248, 273; **61:** 144
Chronicle sources **61:** 111
conscience **61:** 136
Cymbeline, compared with **2:** 67, 71
discrepancy between prophetic ending and preceding action **2:** 22, 25, 31, 46, 49, 56, 60, 65, 68, 75, 81; **32:** 148; **41:** 190; **56:** 273
divine providence **61:** 144
Elizabethan dramatic conventions **24:** 155; **56:** 196, 248
Elizabethan politics, relation to **22:** 395; **24:** 115, 129, 140; **32:** 148; **56:** 201, 248
English Reformation, influence of **2:** 25, 35, 39, 51, 67; **24:** 89; **56:** 201; **61:** 92
flattery **22:** 395
English nationalism **61:** 92, 111
historical and romantic elements, combination of **2:** 46, 49, 51, 75, 76, 78; **24:** 71, 80, 146; **41:** 129, 146, 180; **56:** 196, 201
historical epic, as epilogue to Shakespeare's **2:** 22, 25, 27, 39, 51, 60, 65
historical relativity, theme of **41:** 146; **56:** 220; **61:** 111
historiography **37:** 109; **56:** 201, 209, 230; **61:** 92, 101, 111
honor **61:** 101
inconsistencies **2:** 16, 27, 28, 31, 60
ironic aspects **41:** 129; **56:** 220
Jacobean court and politics **61:** 92
Katherine
 characterization **2:** 18, 19, 23, 24, 38; **24:** 129; **37:** 109; **41:** 180; **61:** 119, 144
 feminine power **61:** 119
 Hermione, compared with **2:** 24, 51, 58, 76
 politeness strategies **22:** 182; **56:** 262
 religious discourse **22:** 182
 as tragic figure **2:** 16, 18
King Henry
 as agent of divine retribution **2:** 49
 characterization **2:** 23, 39, 51, 58, 60, 65, 66, 75; **28:** 184; **37:** 109; **56:** 242; **61:** 119, 136
 incomplete portrait **2:** 15, 16, 19, 35; **41:** 120; **56:** 209
 as realistic figure **2:** 21, 22, 23, 25, 32
 patriarchy **61:** 119
 kingship **2:** 49, 58, 60, 65, 75, 78; **24:** 113; **41:** 129, 171; **56:** 242; **61:** 92, 119
language and imagery **41:** 180, 190; **56:** 262, 273
law and justice **61:** 92
legitimacy **37:** 109; **56:** 209, 220, 230
masculine identity **61:** 129
moral intent **2:** 15, 19, 25; **24:** 140; **54:** 35; **61:** 92, 101, 144
Norfolk **22:** 182
pageantry **2:** 14, 15, 18, 51, 58; **24:** 77, 83, 84, 85, 89, 91, 106, 113, 118, 120, 126, 127, 140, 146, 150; **41:** 120, 129, 190
patience **2:** 58, 76, 78
patriarchy **61:** 129
personal motives **61:** 92
politics **2:** 39, 49, 51, 58, 60, 65, 67, 71, 72, 75, 78, 81; **24:** 74, 121, 124; **41:** 146; **56:** 242; **61:** 101
Porter **24:** 155
Prologue **54:** 35
Protestant philosophy **61:** 92, 129
romance versus history **61:** 101
rebellion **22:** 395; **56:** 230
rhetoric of politeness **22:** 182; **56:** 262
Shakespeare's romances, compared with **2:** 46, 51, 58, 66, 67, 71, 76; **41:** 171; **54:** 35; **56:** 273
social order **61:** 101
sources **2:** 16, 17; **24:** 71, 80
staging issues **24:** 67, 70, 71, 75, 77, 83, 84, 85, 87, 89, 91, 101, 106, 113, 120, 127, 129, 136, 140, 146, 150, 152, 155; **28:** 184; **56:** 220, 248
Stephen Gardiner **24:** 129
structure **2:** 16, 25, 27, 28, 31, 36, 44, 46, 51, 56, 68, 75; **24:** 106, 112, 113, 120; **56:** 209
style **41:** 158
thematic disparity **2:** 25, 31, 56, 68, 75; **41:** 146
tragedies of major characters **2:** 16, 39, 46, 48, 49, 51, 56, 58, 68, 81; **41:** 120
wheel of fortune, motif of **2:** 27, 65, 72, 81; **61:** 144
Wolsey (Cardinal Wolsey) **2:** 15, 18, 19, 23, 24, 38; **22:** 182; **24:** 80, 91, 112, 113, 129, 140; **37:** 109; **41:** 129; **56:** 248, 262; **61:** 144

Julius Caesar (Volumes 7, 17, 30, 50)

anachronisms **7:** 331; **65:** 251
Antony
 characterization **7:** 160, 179, 189, 221, 233, 284, 320, 333; **17:** 269, 271, 272, 284, 298, 306, 313, 315, 358, 398; **25:** 272; **30:** 316
 funeral oration **7:** 148, 154, 159, 204, 210, 221, 238, 259, 350; **25:** 280; **30:** 316, 333, 362
aristocratic values **16:** 231; **22:** 280; **30:** 379; **50:** 194, 196, 211
the assassination **7:** 156, 161, 179, 191, 200, 221, 264, 272, 279, 284, 350; **25:** 272; **30:** 326
audience interpretation **48:** 240
audience response **7:** 179, 238, 253, 255, 272, 316, 320, 336, 350; **19:** 321; **48:** 240
Brutus **50:** 194, 258
 arrogance **7:** 160, 169, 204, 207, 264, 277, 292, 350; **25:** 280; **30:** 351
 as chief protagonist or tragic hero **7:** 152, 159, 189, 191, 200, 204, 242, 250, 253, 264, 268, 279, 284, 298, 333; **17:** 272, 372, 387
 citizenship **25:** 272
 funeral oration **7:** 154, 155, 204, 210, 350
 motives **7:** 150, 156, 161, 179, 191, 200, 221, 227, 233, 245, 292, 303, 310, 320, 333, 350; **25:** 272; **30:** 321, 358
 nobility or idealism **7:** 150, 152, 156, 159, 161, 179, 189, 191, 200, 221, 242, 250, 253, 259, 264, 277, 303, 320; **17:** 269, 271, 273, 279, 280, 284, 306, 308, 321, 323, 324, 345, 358; **25:** 272, 280; **30:** 351, 362; **50:** 194
 political ineptitude or lack of judgment **7:** 169, 188, 200, 205, 221, 245, 252, 264, 277, 282, 310, 316, 331, 333, 343; **17:** 323, 358, 375, 380; **50:** 13
 self-knowledge or self-deception **7:** 191, 200, 221, 242, 259, 264, 268, 279, 310, 333, 336, 350; **25:** 272; **30:** 316; **60:** 46
 soliloquy (Act II, scene i) **7:** 156, 160, 161, 191, 221, 245, 250, 253, 264, 268, 279, 282, 292, 303, 343, 350; **25:** 280; **30:** 333
Caesar **50:** 189, 230, 234
 ambiguous nature **7:** 191, 233, 242, 250, 272, 298, 316, 320
 ambitious nature **50:** 234

arrogance **7:** 160, 207, 218, 253, 272, 279, 298; **25:** 280
idolatry **22:** 137
leadership qualities **7:** 161, 179, 189, 191, 200, 207, 233, 245, 253, 257, 264, 272, 279, 284, 298, 310, 333; **17:** 317, 358; **22:** 280; **30:** 316, 326; **50:** 234
 as tragic hero **7:** 152, 200, 221, 279; **17:** 321, 377, 384
 weakness **7:** 161, 167, 169, 179, 187, 188, 191, 207, 218, 221, 233, 250, 253, 298; **17:** 358; **25:** 280
Caesarism **7:** 159, 160, 161, 167, 169, 174, 191, 205, 218, 253, 310; **30:** 316, 321; **50:** 196, 234
Calphurnia
 dream **45:** 10
Casca
 as Cynic **50:** 249
 as proto-Christian **50:** 249
Cassius **7:** 156, 159, 160, 161, 169, 179, 189, 221, 233, 303, 310, 320, 333, 343; **17:** 272, 282, 284, 344, 345, 358; **25:** 272, 280; **30:** 351; **37:** 203; **60:** 46
ceremonies, rites, and rituals, importance of **7:** 150, 210, 255, 259, 268, 284, 316, 331, 339, 356; **13:** 260; **22:** 137; **30:** 374; **50:** 258, 269
construing the truth **7:** 320, 336, 343, 350; **37:** 229
Elizabethan culture, relation to **16:** 231; **30:** 342, 379; **50:** 13, 211, 269, 280
emulation or rivalry **16:** 231
Epicureanism **50:** 249
Flavius and Murellus **50:** 64
gender issues **13:** 260
historical determinism versus free will **7:** 160, 298, 316, 333, 346, 356; **13:** 252
irony or ambiguity **7:** 167, 257, 259, 262, 268, 282, 316, 320, 333, 336, 346, 350
language and imagery **7:** 148, 155, 159, 188, 204, 207, 227, 242, 250, 277, 296, 303, 324, 346, 350; **13:** 260; **17:** 347, 348, 350, 356, 358; **19:** 321; **22:** 280; **25:** 280; **30:** 333, 342; **50:** 196, 258
liberty versus tyranny **7:** 158, 179, 189, 205, 221, 253; **25:** 272
love and friendship **7:** 233, 262, 268; **25:** 272
medieval physiology **13:** 260
moral choice **7:** 179, 264, 279, 343
Octavius **30:** 316
omens **22:** 137; **45:** 10; **50:** 265, 280
opening scene **54:** 6
patricians versus plebeians **50:** 189, 196
philosophical elements **7:** 310, 324; **37:** 203
plebeians versus tribunes **50:** 230
the poets **7:** 179, 320, 350
politics **7:** 161, 169, 191, 205, 218, 221, 245, 262, 264, 279, 282, 310, 324, 333, 346; **17:** 317, 318, 321, 323, 334, 350, 351, 358, 378, 382, 394, 406; **22:** 137, 280; **25:** 272, 280; **30:** 285, 297, 316, 321, 342, 374, 379; **37:** 203; **50:** 13
as "problem play" **7:** 272, 320
psychoanalytic interpretation **45:** 10
public versus private principles **7:** 161, 179, 252, 262, 268, 284, 298; **13:** 252
quarrel scene (Act IV, scene iii) **7:** 149, 150, 152, 153, 155, 160, 169, 188, 191, 204, 268, 296, 303, 310
retribution **7:** 160, 167, 200
revenge tragedy elements **7:** 316
role-playing **7:** 356; **37:** 229
Roman citizenry, portrayal of **7:** 169, 179, 210, 221, 245, 279, 282, 310, 320, 333; **17:** 271, 279, 288, 291, 292, 298, 323, 334, 351, 367, 374, 375, 378; **22:** 280; **30:** 285, 297, 316, 321, 374, 379; **37:** 229; **50:** 230
Senecan elements **37:** 229

Shakespeare's English history plays, compared with **7:** 161, 189, 218, 221, 252; **22:** 137; **30:** 369
Shakespeare's major tragedies, compared with **7:** 161, 188, 227, 242, 264, 268
sources **7:** 149, 150, 156, 187, 200, 264, 272, 282, 284, 320; **30:** 285, 297, 326, 358
staging **48:** 240; **50:** 186
Stoicism **50:** 249
structure **7:** 152, 155, 159, 160, 179, 200, 210, 238, 264, 284, 298, 316, 346; **13:** 252; **30:** 374
tragic elements **50:** 258, 265
violence **48:** 240

King John (Volumes 9, 24, 41, 56)

ambiguity **13:** 152; **41:** 243
anti-Catholic rhetoric **22:** 120; **25:** 98; **66:** 271
Arthur **9:** 215, 216, 218, 219, 229, 240, 267, 275; **22:** 120; **25:** 98; **41:** 251, 277; **56:** 345, 357
autobiographical elements **9:** 209, 218, 245, 248, 260, 292
characterization **9:** 222, 224, 229, 240, 250, 292; **41:** 205, 215; **56:** 365
church versus state **9:** 209, 212, 222, 235, 240; **22:** 120; **66:** 271
commodity or self-interest **9:** 224, 229, 245, 260, 275, 280, 297; **19:** 182; **25:** 98; **41:** 228; **56:** 335
commodity versus honor **41:** 269
Constance **9:** 208, 210, 211, 215, 219, 220, 224, 229, 240, 251, 254; **16:** 161; **24:** 177, 184, 196
corruption in society **9:** 222, 234, 280, 297
Elizabethan politics, relation to **48:** 132; **56:** 306, 314, 325; **60:** 295, 329; **66:** 271
ethical or moral issues **9:** 212, 222, 224, 229, 235, 240, 263, 275, 280; **56:** 335
excess **9:** 251
Faulconbridge, the Bastard **41:** 205, 228, 251, 260, 277; **56:** 306, 314, 335, 348, 365
 as chorus or commentator **9:** 212, 218, 229, 248, 251, 260, 271, 284, 297, 300; **22:** 120
 as comic figure **9:** 219, 271, 297; **56:** 365
 development **9:** 216, 224, 229, 248, 263, 271, 275, 280, 297; **13:** 158, 163; **56:** 335
 as embodiment of England **9:** 222, 224, 240, 244, 248, 271
 heroic qualities **9:** 208, 245, 248, 254, 263, 271, 275; **25:** 98; **56:** 348
 political conduct **9:** 224, 240, 250, 260, 280, 297; **13:** 147, 158; **22:** 120; **56:** 314
Henry **41:** 277; **56:** 348
historical content **9:** 216, 219, 220, 222, 235, 240, 254, 284, 290, 292, 297, 300, 303; **13:** 163; **32:** 93, 114; **41:** 234, 243; **56:** 286, 296, 357; **60:** 329
John **41:** 205, 260; **56:** 325, 345
 death, decay, and nature's destructiveness **9:** 212, 215, 216, 240; **56:** 345
 decline **9:** 224, 235, 240, 263, 275
 Hubert, scene with (Act III, scene iii) **9:** 210, 212, 216, 218, 219, 280
 moral insensibility **13:** 147, 163
 negative qualities **9:** 209, 212, 218, 219, 229, 234, 235, 244, 245, 246, 250, 254, 275, 280, 297; **56:** 325
 positive qualities **9:** 209, 224, 235, 240, 244, 245, 263
kingship **9:** 235, 254, 263, 275, 297; **13:** 158; **19:** 182; **22:** 120; **56:** 314
language and imagery **9:** 212, 215, 220, 246, 251, 254, 267, 280, 284, 292, 297, 300; **13:** 147, 158; **22:** 120; **37:** 132; **48:** 132; **56:** 286

legitimacy or inheritance **9:** 224, 235, 254, 303; **13:** 147; **19:** 182; **37:** 132; **41:** 215; **56:** 325, 335; **60:** 295, 329
Machiavellianism **60:** 304
nationalism and patriotism **9:** 209, 218, 222, 224, 235, 240, 244, 275; **25:** 98; **37:** 132
Neoclassical rules **9:** 208, 209, 210, 212; **56:** 365
oppositions or dualisms **9:** 224, 240, 263, 275, 284, 290, 300
Papal Tyranny in the Reign of King John (Colley Cibber adaptation) **24:** 162, 163, 165
politics **9:** 218, 224, 260, 280; **13:** 163; **22:** 120; **37:** 132; **41:** 221, 228; **56:** 314, 325
rebellion **9:** 218, 254, 263, 280, 297; **66:** 271
Roman citizenry, portrayal of **50:** 64
Shakespeare's other history plays, compared with **9:** 218, 254; **13:** 152, 158; **25:** 98; **56:** 306, 348, 357
sources **9:** 216, 222, 300; **32:** 93, 114; **41:** 234, 243, 251; **56:** 296, 357
staging issues **16:** 161; **19:** 182; **24:** 171, 187, 203, 206, 211, 225, 228, 241, 245, 249; **56:** 286, 365
structure **9:** 208, 212, 222, 224, 229, 240, 244, 245, 254, 260, 263, 275, 284, 290, 292, 300; **24:** 228, 241; **41:** 260, 269, 277
succession **60:** 295, 304, 329
tragic elements **9:** 208, 209, 244
treachery **9:** 245
The Troublesome Reign (anonymous), compared with **9:** 216, 244, 260, 292; **22:** 120; **32:** 93; **41:** 205, 221, 260, 269; **48:** 132; **56:** 357
Tudor doctrine **9:** 254, 284, 297; **41:** 221; **56:** 345; **66:** 271
tyranny **9:** 218
women, role of **9:** 222, 303; **16:** 161; **19:** 182; **41:** 205, 221

King Lear (Volumes 2, 11, 31, 46, 61)

Albany **32:** 308
allegorical elements **16:** 311; **61:** 215
audience perception **19:** 295; **28:** 325; **61:** 176
autobiographical elements **2:** 131, 136, 149, 165
characterization **2:** 108, 125, 145, 162, 191; **16:** 311; **28:** 223; **46:** 177, 210
Christian elements **2:** 137, 170, 179, 188, 191, 197, 207, 218, 222, 226, 229, 238, 249, 265, 286; **22:** 233, 271; **25:** 218; **46:** 276; **49:** 67; **52:** 95; **60:** 75; **61:** 194, 262; **66:** 326
as Christian play **48:** 222; **66:** 260
Clarissa (Samuel Richardson), compared with **48:** 277
combat scenes **22:** 365
comic and tragic elements, combination of **2:** 108, 110, 112, 125, 156, 162, 245, 278, 284; **46:** 191
Cordelia
 attack on Britain **25:** 202
 characterization **2:** 110, 116, 125, 170; **16:** 311; **25:** 218; **28:** 223, 325; **31:** 117, 149, 155, 162; **46:** 225, 231, 242; **61:** 220, 230
 as Christ figure **2:** 116, 170, 179, 188, 222, 286
 rebelliousness **13:** 352; **25:** 202; **61:** 194
 self-knowledge **46:** 218
 on stage **11:** 158
 transcendent power **2:** 137, 207, 218, 265, 269, 273
Cornwall's servants (III.vii) **54:** 114
cruelty of daughters **2:** 101, 102, 106; **31:** 84, 123, 137, 142

death, decay, and nature's destructiveness **2**: 93, 94, 101, 104, 106, 109, 112, 116, 129, 131, 137, 143, 147, 149, 156, 160, 170, 179, 188, 197, 207, 218, 222, 226, 231, 238, 241, 245, 249, 253, 265, 269, 273; **16**: 301; **25**: 202, 218; **31**: 77, 117, 137, 142; **46**: 264
deaths of Lear and Cordelia **54**: 103, 110, 114; **60**: 2; **66**: 260
double-plot **2**: 94, 95, 100, 101, 104, 112, 116, 124, 131, 133, 156, 253, 257; **46**: 254
Dover Cliff scene **2**: 156, 229, 255, 269; **11**: 8, 151; **54**: 103
Edgar **28**: 223; **32**: 212; **32**: 308; **37**: 295; **47**: 9; **50**: 24, 45
Edgar-Edmund duel **22**: 365
Edmund **25**: 218; **28**: 223
Edmund's forged letter **16**: 372
Elizabethan culture, relation to **2**: 168, 174, 177, 183, 226, 241; **19**: 330; **22**: 227, 233, 365; **25**: 218; **46**: 276; **47**: 9; **49**: 67; **61**: 172, 176, 187, 194
ending **54**: 103, 110, 114; **60**: 46, 65, 75; **61**: 262; **66**: 260, 326
ethical and moral issues **52**: 1, 95
feminist criticism **55**: 68
Fool **2**: 108, 112, 125, 156, 162, 245, 278, 284; **11**: 17, 158, 169; **22**: 227; **25**: 202; **28**: 223; **46**: 1, 14, 18, 24, 33, 52, 191, 205, 210, 218, 225; **61**: 176
Gloucester **46**: 254; **61**: 250
Goneril **31**: 151; **46**: 231, 242; **61**: 160
grotesque or absurd elements **2**: 136, 156, 245; **13**: 343; **52**: 1
implausibility of plot, characters, or events **2**: 100, 136, 145, 278; **13**: 343
Job, compared with **2**: 226, 241, 245; **25**: 218
justice, divine vs. worldly **49**: 1, 67, 73; **61**: 230
Kent **25**: 202; **28**: 223; **32**: 212; **47**: 9; **60**: 185
language and imagery **2**: 129, 137, 161, 191, 199, 237, 257, 271; **16**: 301; **19**: 344; **22**: 233; **46**: 177; **61**: 215, 230
Lear **61**: 176
 curse on Goneril **11**: 5, 7, 12, 114, 116
 love-test and division of kingdom **2**: 100, 106, 111, 124, 131, 137, 147, 149, 151, 168, 186, 208, 216, 281; **16**: 351; **25**: 202; **31**: 84, 92, 107, 117, 149, 155; **46**: 231, 242; **61**: 194
 madness **2**: 94, 95, 98, 99, 100, 101, 102, 103, 111, 116, 120, 124, 125, 149, 156, 191, 208, 216, 281; **46**: 264
 as scapegoat **2**: 241, 253
 self-knowledge **2**: 103, 151, 188, 191, 213, 218, 222, 241, 249, 262; **25**: 218; **37**: 213; **46**: 191, 205, 225, 254, 264; **54**: 103; **60**: 65, 75; **61**: 215, 220, 250
 spiritual regeneration **60**: 65, 75
legal issues **46**: 276
love **2**: 109, 112, 131, 160, 162, 170, 179, 188, 197, 218, 222, 238, 265; **25**: 202; **31**: 77, 149, 151, 155, 162; **61**: 220, 237
madness **19**: 330
Marxist criticism **42**: 234; **55**: 16
medieval or morality drama, influence of **2**: 177, 188, 201; **25**: 218
misogyny **31**: 123
mythic or mythological elements **60**: 185
nihilistic or pessimistic vision **2**: 130, 143, 149, 156, 165, 231, 238, 245, 253; **22**: 271; **25**: 218; **28**: 325; **49**: 67; **66**: 326
opening scene **54**: 2, 6
order **56**: 25
pagan elements **25**: 218
patriarchal or monarchical order **13**: 353, 457; **16**: 351; **22**: 227, 233; **25**: 218; **31**: 84, 92, 107, 117, 123, 137, 142; **46**: 269; **61**: 172, 237
performance issues **2**: 106, 137, 154, 160; **11**: 10, 20, 27, 56, 57, 132, 136, 137, 145, 150, 154; **19**: 295, 344; **25**: 218; **61**: 187
poetic justice, question of **2**: 92, 93, 94, 101, 129, 137, 231, 245; **49**: 73
politics **46**: 269; **50**: 45; **61**: 160, 172, 187, 237
providential order **2**: 112, 116, 137, 168, 170, 174, 177, 218, 226, 241, 253; **22**: 271; **49**: 1, 73
Regan **31**: 151; **46**: 231, 242; **61**: 160
rhetorical style **16**: 301; **47**: 9
romantic elements **31**: 77, 84
sexuality **25**: 202; **31**: 133, 137, 142
sexual politics **55**: 68
social and moral corruption **2**: 116, 133, 174, 177, 241, 271; **22**: 227; **31**: 84, 92; **46**: 269; **61**: 160
sources **2**: 94, 100, 143, 145, 170, 186; **13**: 352; **16**: 351; **28**: 301; **60**: 185; **61**: 250
spiritual regeneration **54**: 103; **66**: 326
staging issues **11**: 1-178; **32**: 212; **46**: 205, 218; **54**: 103
structure **28**: 325; **32**: 308; **46**: 177
suffering **2**: 137, 160, 188, 201, 218, 222, 226, 231, 238, 241, 249, 265; **13**: 343; **22**: 271; **25**: 218; **50**: 24
Tate's adaptation **2**: 92, 93, 94, 101, 102, 104, 106, 110, 112, 116, 137; **11**: 10, 136; **25**: 218; **31**: 162
textual issues **22**: 271; **37**: 295; **49**: 73; **61**: 262
Timon of Athens, relation to **16**: 351
tragic elements **55**: 78; **61**: 250
Virgo vs. Virago **48**: 222
wisdom **37**: 213; **46**: 210

Love's Labour's Lost (Volumes 2, 23, 38, 54, 64)

Armado **23**: 207
artificial nature **2**: 315, 317, 324, 330; **23**: 207, 233; **54**: 234, 248, 257, 263
authorship controversy **2**: 299, 300; **32**: 308
Berowne **2**: 308, 324, 327; **22**: 12; **23**: 184, 187; **38**: 194; **47**: 35
characterization **2**: 303, 310, 317, 322, 328, 342; **23**: 237, 250, 252; **38**: 232; **47**: 35; **64**: 140, 166
as comedy of affectation **2**: 302, 303, 304; **23**: 191, 224, 226, 228, 233
comic resolution **2**: 335, 340; **16**: 17; **19**: 92; **38**: 209; **51**: 1; **54**: 240, 248, 274; **64**: 122, 145, 154
comic form **54**: 257, 263
conclusion **38**: 172; **54**: 240, 248, 274
dance and patterned action **2**: 308, 342; **23**: 191, 237
death, decay, and nature's destructiveness **2**: 305, 331, 344, 348; **64**: 145
desire **38**: 185, 194, 200, 209
dramatic shortcomings or failure **2**: 299, 301, 303, 322; **54**: 240, 248
Elizabeth I **38**: 239; **64**: 166, 179
Elizabethan culture, relation to **64**: 122
Elizabethan love poetry **38**: 232
ending **54**: 58; **64**: 122, 145
feminist criticism **42**: 93
genre **38**: 163
gift exchange **25**: 1; **64**: 122
grace and civility **2**: 351; **64**: 114
Holofernes **23**: 207
illusion versus reality **2**: 303, 308, 331, 340, 344, 348, 356, 359, 367, 371, 375; **23**: 230, 231
knowledge **22**: 12; **47**: 35
language and imagery **2**: 301, 302, 303, 306, 307, 308, 315, 319, 320, 330, 335, 344, 345, 348, 356, 359, 362, 365, 371, 374, 375; **19**: 92; **22**: 12, 378; **23**: 184, 187, 196, 197, 202, 207, 211, 221, 227, 231, 233, 237, 252; **28**: 9, 63; **38**: 219, 226; **54**: 225, 274; **64**: 114, 145, 192
love **2**: 312, 315, 340, 344; **22**: 12; **23**: 252; **38**: 194; **51**: 44
love vs. reason **54**: 225, 234
male domination **22**: 12
male/female relationships **54**: 284; **64**: 154
male sexual anxiety **16**: 17
marriage **2**: 335, 340; **19**: 92; **38**: 209, 232; **51**: 1, 44
metadramatic elements **2**: 356, 359, 362
Neoclassical rules **2**: 299, 300
oaths **54**: 257, 284
patriarchal order **64**: 192
Petrarchan influence **64**: 154
physical versus intellectual world **2**: 331, 348, 367
plot **54**: 225
politics **64**: 114, 179
public versus private speech **2**: 356, 362, 371
as satire or parody **2**: 300, 302, 303, 307, 308, 315, 321, 324, 327; **23**: 237, 252; **54**: 234
School of Night, allusions to **2**: 321, 327, 328
sexuality **22**: 12; **51**: 44; **64**: 154
songs, role of **2**: 303, 304, 316, 326, 335, 362, 367, 371, 375; **54**: 240
sources **16**: 17
spectacle **38**: 226
staging issues **23**: 184, 187, 191, 196, 198, 200, 201, 202, 207, 212, 215, 216, 217, 229, 230, 232, 233, 237, 252; **64**: 136, 137, 138, 140
structure **22**: 378; **23**: 191, 237, 252; **38**: 163, 172
theme
 idealism versus realism **38**: 163
topical allusions or content **2**: 300, 303, 307, 315, 316, 317, 319, 321, 327, 328; **23**: 187, 191, 197, 203, 221, 233, 237, 252; **25**: 1; **64**: 140, 166, 179
unnatural ordering **22**: 378
violence **22**: 12
visual humor **23**: 207, 217
Watteau, influence on staging **23**: 184, 186
women, role of **19**: 92; **22**: 12; **23**: 215; **25**: 1
wisdom and folly **54**: 257
written versus oral communication **2**: 359, 365; **28**: 63

Macbeth (Volumes 3, 20, 29, 44, 57)

antithetical or contradictory elements **3**: 185, 213, 271, 302; **25**: 235; **29**: 76, 127; **47**: 41
appearance versus reality **3**: 241, 248; **25**: 235
archetypal or mythic elements **16**: 317
audience response **20**: 17, 400, 406; **29**: 139, 146, 155, 165; **44**: 306
banquet scene (Act III, scene iv) **20**: 22, 32, 175
Banquo **3**: 183, 199, 208, 213, 278, 289; **20**: 279, 283, 406, 413; **25**: 235; **28**: 339
characterization **20**: 12, 318, 324, 329, 353, 363, 367, 374, 387; **28**: 339; **29**: 101, 109, 146, 155, 165; **44**: 289; **47**: 41; **57**: 267
Christian elements **3**: 194, 239, 260, 269, 275, 286, 293, 297, 318; **20**: 203, 206, 210, 256, 262, 289, 291, 294; **44**: 341, 366; **47**: 41; **57**: 236
combat scenes **22**: 365
conscience **52**: 15
dagger scene (Act III, scene i), staging of **20**: 406

Duncan **57:** 194, 236
Elizabethan politics, relation to **54:** 357
ending **54:** 84
evil **3:** 194, 208, 231, 234, 239, 241, 267, 289; **20:** 203, 206, 210, 374; **52:** 23; **57:** 267
female identity **57:** 256
feminine power, role of **57:** 242
free will versus fate **3:** 177, 183, 184, 190, 196, 198, 202, 207, 208, 213; **13:** 361; **44:** 351, 361, 366, 373; **54:** 6; **65:** 317
innocence **3:** 234, 241, 327; **57:** 267
Jacobean culture, relation to **19:** 330; **22:** 365; **57:** 218, 256; **60:** 340, 357
Lady Macbeth
 ambition **3:** 185, 219; **20:** 279, 345
 characterization **20:** 56, 60, 65, 73, 140, 148, 151, 241, 279, 283, 338, 350, 406, 413; **29:** 109, 146; **57:** 256, 263
 childlessness **3:** 219, 223
 good and evil, combined traits of **3:** 173, 191, 213; **20:** 60, 107
 inconsistencies **3:** 202; **20:** 54, 137
 influence on Macbeth **3:** 171, 185, 191, 193, 199, 262, 289, 312, 318; **13:** 502; **20:** 345; **25:** 235; **29:** 133; **57:** 263
 psychoanalytic interpretations **20:** 345; **44:** 289, 297, 324; **45:** 58
 as sympathetic figure **3:** 191, 193, 203
 language and imagery **3:** 170, 193, 213, 231, 234, 241, 245, 250, 253, 256, 263, 271, 283, 300, 302, 306, 323, 327, 338, 340, 349; **13:** 476; **16:** 317; **20:** 241, 279, 283, 367, 379, 400; **25:** 235; **28:** 339; **29:** 76, 91; **42:** 263; **44:** 366; **45:** 58; **65:** 317
laws of nature, violation of **3:** 234, 241, 280, 323; **29:** 120; **57:** 242, 263; **65:** 226
legitimacy **60:** 340
letter to Lady Macbeth **16:** 372; **20:** 345; **25:** 235
Macbeth
 ambition **44:** 284, 324; **57:** 256; **65:** 317
 characterization **20:** 20, 42, 73, 107, 113, 130, 146, 151, 241, 279, 283, 312, 338, 343, 379, 406, 413; **29:** 139, 152, 155, 165; **44:** 289; **57:** 189, 194, 236, 263, 267
 courage **3:** 172, 177, 181, 182, 183, 186, 234, 312, 333; **20:** 107; **44:** 315
 despair **65:** 297
 disposition **3:** 173, 175, 177, 182, 186; **20:** 245, 376
 imagination **3:** 196, 208, 213, 250, 312, 345; **20:** 245, 376; **44:** 351; **65:** 226
 as "inauthentic" king **3:** 245, 302, 321, 345
 inconsistencies **3:** 202
 as Machiavellian villain **3:** 280; **57:** 236
 manliness **20:** 113; **29:** 127, 133; **44:** 315; **57:** 256
 psychoanalytic interpretations **20:** 42, 73, 238, 376; **44:** 284, 289, 297, 324; **45:** 48, 58; **57:** 267
 Richard III, compared with **3:** 177, 182, 186, 345; **20:** 86, 92; **22:** 365; **44:** 269
 as Satan figure **3:** 229, 269, 275, 289, 318
 self-awareness **3:** 312, 329, 338; **16:** 317; **44:** 361; **57:** 256; **60:** 46
 as sympathetic figure **3:** 229, 306, 314, 338; **29:** 139, 152; **44:** 269, 306, 337
 as tragic hero **44:** 269, 306, 315, 324, 337; **57:** 267
Macduff **3:** 226, 231, 253, 262,; **25:** 235; **29:** 127, 133, 155; **57:** 194
Machiavellianism **52:** 29; **57:** 236
madness **19:** 330
major tragedies, relation to Shakespeare's other **3:** 171, 173, 213; **44:** 269; **57:** 189
Malcolm **25:** 235
manhood **3:** 262, 309, 333; **29:** 127, 133; **57:** 242, 263
Marxist criticism **42:** 234; **55:** 16

medieval mystery plays, relation to **44:** 341; **57:** 194
morality **52:** 15, 23, 29
moral lesson **20:** 23
murder scene (Act II, scene ii) **20:** 175
mythic or mythological elements **60:** 169, 214
naturalism **60:** 169
Neoclassical rules **3:** 170, 171, 173, 175; **20:** 17
nightmarish quality **3:** 231, 309; **20:** 210, 242; **44:** 261
nihilism **65:** 297, 317
opening scene **54:** 2, 6
politics **52:** 29; **57:** 218, 228
Porter scene (Act II, scene iii) **3:** 173, 175, 184, 190, 196, 203, 205, 225, 260, 271, 297, 300; **20:** 283; **44:** 261; **46:** 29, 78; **60:** 89
primitivism **20:** 206, 213; **45:** 48
providential order **3:** 208, 289, 329, 336; **57:** 218
psychoanalytic interpretations **3:** 219, 223, 226; **44:** 11, 284, 289, 297
regicide **16:** 317, 328; **45:** 48 248, 275, 312
religious and theological issues **44:** 324, 341, 351, 361, 366, 373
religious, mythic, or spiritual content **3:** 208, 269, 275, 318; **29:** 109
retribution **3:** 194, 208, 318; **48:** 214
Scholasticism **52:** 23
sexual anxiety **16:** 328; **20:** 283
sleepwalking scene (Act V, scene i) **3:** 191, 203, 219; **20:** 175; **44:** 261
sources **60:** 214
staging issues **13:** 502; **20:** 12, 17, 32, 64, 65, 70, 73, 107, 113, 151, 175, 203, 206, 210, 213, 245, 279, 283, 312, 318, 324, 329, 343, 345, 350, 353, 363, 367, 374, 376, 379, 382, 387, 400, 406, 413; **22:** 365; **32:** 212
structure **16:** 317; **20:** 12, 245
succession **60:** 340, 357
supernatural grace versus evil or chaos **3:** 241, 286, 323
theatricality **16:** 328
time **3:** 234, 246, 283, 293; **20:** 245; **57:** 218; **65:** 226, 297, 317
topical allusions or content **13:** 361; **20:** 17, 350; **29:** 101
tragic elements **52:** 15; **55:** 78; **57:** 189
treason and punishment **13:** 361; **16:** 328
violence **20:** 273, 279, 283; **45:** 58; **57:** 228, 267
virture versus vice **60:** 214
witches and supernaturalism **3:** 171, 172, 173, 175, 177, 182, 183, 184, 185, 194, 196, 198, 202, 207, 208, 213, 219, 229, 239; **16:** 317; **19:** 245; **20:** 92, 175, 213, 279, 283, 374, 387, 406, 413; **25:** 235; **28:** 339; **29:** 91, 101, 109, 120; **44:** 351, 373; **57:** 194, 242

***Measure for Measure* (Volumes 2, 23, 33, 49, 65)**

allegorical elements **52:** 69; **65:** 14
ambiguity **2:** 417, 420, 432, 446, 449, 452, 474, 479, 482, 486, 495, 505; **65:** 14, 19
Angelo
 anxiety **16:** 114
 authoritarian portrayal of **23:** 307; **49:** 274
 characterization **2:** 388, 390, 397, 402, 418, 427, 432, 434, 463, 484, 495, 503, 511; **13:** 84; **23:** 297; **32:** 81; **33:** 77; **49:** 274, 293, 379; **65:** 100
 hypocrisy **2:** 396, 399, 402, 406, 414, 421; **23:** 345, 358, 362
 repentance or pardon **2:** 388, 390, 397, 402, 434, 463, 511, 524

audience response **48:** 1; **60:** 12
autobiographical elements **2:** 406, 410, 414, 431, 434, 437
Barnardine **13:** 112; **65:** 30
bed-trick **13:** 84; **49:** 313; **54:** 52
characterization **2:** 388, 390, 391, 396, 406, 420, 421, 446, 466, 475, 484, 505, 516, 524; **23:** 299, 405; **33:** 77; **65:**22, 14, 38
Christian elements **2:** 391, 394, 399, 421, 437, 449, 466, 479, 491, 511, 522; **48:** 1; **49:** 325; **60:** 12; **66:** 300
Clarissa (Samuel Richardson), compared with **48:** 277
Claudio **60:** 12
comic form **2:** 456, 460, 479, 482, 491, 514, 516; **13:** 94, 104; **23:** 309, 326, 327; **49:** 349; **65:** 2
death, decay, and nature's destructiveness **2:** 394, 452, 516; **25:** 12; **49:** 370
death, motif of **60:** 12
displacement **22:** 78
Duke
 as authoritarian figure **23:** 314, 317, 347; **33:** 85; **49:** 274, 300, 358; **65:** 19, 30, 45, 80, 100
 characterization **2:** 388, 395, 402, 406, 411, 421, 429, 456, 466, 470, 498, 511; **13:** 84, 94, 104; **23:** 363, 416; **32:** 81; **42:** 1; **44:** 89; **49:** 274, 293, 300, 358; **60:** 12
 dramatic shortcomings or failure **2:** 420, 429, 441, 479, 495, 505, 514, 522
 godlike portrayal of **23:** 320; **65:** 14, 91
 noble portrayal of **23:** 301; **65:** 53
 speech on death (Act III, scene i) **2:** 390, 391, 395
 as spiritual guide **66:** 300
Elbow **22:** 85; **25:** 12
Elbow, Mistress **33:** 90
Elizabethan betrothal and marriage customs **2:** 429, 437, 443, 503; **49:** 286; **65:** 80
Elizabethan culture, relation to **2:** 394, 418, 429, 432, 437, 460, 470, 482, 503
ending **54:** 52, 65
ethical or moral issues **52:** 69; **65:** 72
feminist criticism **55:** 16, 68; **65:** 61
feminist interpretation **23:** 320
good and evil **2:** 432, 452, 524; **33:** 52, 61; **52:** 69
homosexuality **42:** 1
immortality **16:** 102
inconsistency between first and second halves **2:** 474, 475, 505, 514, 524; **49:** 349, 358
Isabella **2:** 388, 390, 395, 396, 397, 401, 402, 406, 409, 410, 411, 418, 420, 421, 432, 437, 441, 466, 475, 491, 495, 524; **16:** 114; **23:** 278, 279, 280, 281, 282, 296, 344, 357, 363, 405; **28:** 92; **33:** 77, 85; **60:** 12; **65:** 28, 53, 72, 100
judicial versus natural law **2:** 446, 507, 516, 519; **22:** 85; **33:** 58, 117; **49:** 1, 293
justice and mercy **2:** 391, 395, 399, 402, 406, 409, 411, 416, 421, 437, 443, 463, 466, 470, 491, 495, 522, 524; **22:** 85; **33:** 52, 61, 101; **49:** 1, 274, 293, 300; **65:** 14, 30, 91
language and imagery **2:** 394, 421, 431, 466, 486, 505; **13:** 112; **28:** 9; **33:** 69; **49:** 370
Lucio **13:** 104; **49:** 379; **65:** 19
Mariana **65:** 53
marriage **2:** 443, 507, 516, 519, 524, 528; **25:** 12; **33:** 61, 90; **49:** 286; **51:** 44; **65:** 80
as medieval allegory or morality play **2:** 409, 421, 443, 466, 475, 491, 505, 511, 522; **13:** 94; **60:** 12
metadramatic elements **13:** 104
misgovernment **2:** 401, 432, 511; **22:** 85
misogyny **23:** 358

moral seriousness, question of **2:** 387, 388, 396, 409, 417, 421, 452, 460, 495; **23:** 316, 321
mythic or mythological elements **60:** 281
Neoclassical rules **2:** 387, 388, 390, 394; **23:** 269
Ovid's Metamorphoses, relation to **60:** 281
politics **23:** 379; **49:** 274
power **13:** 112; **22:** 85; **23:** 327, 330, 339, 352; **33:** 85; **65:** 100
as "problem play" **2:** 416, 429, 434, 474, 475, 503, 514, 519; **16:** 102; **23:** 313, 328, 351; **49:** 358, 370; **65:** 111
providential order **48:** 1
psychoanalytic interpretations **23:** 331, 332, 333, 334, 335, 340, 355, 356, 359, 379, 395; **44:** 79; **65:** 100
Puritanism **2:** 414, 418, 434; **49:** 325
rebirth, regeneration, resurrection, or immortality **13:** 84; **16:** 102, 114; **23:** 321, 327, 335, 340, 352; **25:** 12
religious and theological issues **48:** 1; **66:** 300
religious, mythic, or spiritual content **48:** 1; **65:** 53
resolution **2:** 449, 475, 495, 514, 516; **16:** 102, 114; **54:** 65; **65:** 2, 14, 19, 111
sexuality **13:** 84; **16:** 102, 114; **23:** 321, 327, 335, 340, 352; **25:** 12; **33:** 85, 90, 112; **49:** 286, 338; **51:** 44; **65:** 28, 44, 45, 61, 100
sexual politics **55:** 68; **65:** 61, 72, 80
social aspects **23:** 316, 375, 379, 395; **49:** 338; **65:** 45
sources **2:** 388, 393, 427, 429, 437, 475; **13:** 94; **49:** 349; **52:** 69; **60:** 281
staging issues **2:** 427, 429, 437, 441, 443, 456, 460, 482, 491, 519; **23:** 283, 284, 285, 286, 287, 291, 293, 294, 298, 299, 311, 315, 327, 338, 339, 340, 342, 344, 347, 363, 372, 375, 395, 400, 405, 406, 413; **32:** 16; **65:** 38, 44, 111
structure **2:** 390, 411, 449, 456, 466, 474, 482, 490, 491; **33:** 69; **49:** 379; **65:** 2
substitution of identities **2:** 507, 511, 519; **13:** 112; **49:** 313, 325; **65:** 44
subversion or transgression **65:** 45
supernatural grace vs. evil or chaos **48:** 1
theatricality **23:** 285, 286, 294, 372, 406; **49:** 358; **65:** 91
tragic and comic elements, combination of **16:** 102; **65:** 2, 111
as unsuccessful play **2:** 397, 441, 474, 482; **23:** 287

The Merchant of Venice (Volumes 4, 12, 40, 53, 66)

Act V, relation to Acts I through IV **4:** 193, 194, 195, 196, 204, 232, 270, 273, 289, 300, 319, 321, 326, 336, 356; **66:** 135
allegorical elements **4:** 224, 250, 261, 268, 270, 273, 282, 289, 324, 336, 344, 350; **53:** 179, 187
ambiguity **66:** 91, 124
Antonio
 excessive or destructive love **4:** 279, 284, 336, 344; **12:** 54; **37:** 86
 love for Bassanio **40:** 156; **66:** 63, 78, 127, 135
 melancholy **4:** 221, 238, 279, 284, 300, 321, 328; **22:** 69; **25:** 22; **66:** 78, 127, 153
 pitiless **4:** 254
 as pivotal figure **12:** 25, 129; **66:** 91
 as representative Christian **66:** 292
 versus Shylock **53:** 187; **66:** 153, 180
 appearance versus reality **4:** 209, 261, 344; **12:** 65; **22:** 69; **66:** 59, 91
Bassanio **25:** 257; **37:** 86; **40:** 156; **66:** 63, 135
bonding **4:** 293, 317, 336; **13:** 37
casket scenes **4:** 226, 241, 308, 344; **12:** 23, 46, 47, 65, 117; **13:** 43; **22:** 3; **40:** 106; **49:** 27; **66:** 59, 63, 78, 135,
Christian elements **52:** 89
comparison to other works of Shakespeare **53:** 105
contrasting dramatic worlds **44:** 11; **66:** 78, 158
conflict between Christianity and Judaism **4:** 224, 250, 268, 289, 324, 344; **12:** 67, 70, 72, 76; **22:** 69; **25:** 257; **40:** 117, 127, 166, 181; **48:** 54, 77; **53:** 105, 159, 214; **66:** 87, 110, 126, 127, 153, 180
desire **22:** 3; **40:** 142; **45:** 17; **66:** 135
disappointment, theme of **53:** 211; **66:** 153
economics and exchange **40:** 197, 208; **53:** 116; **66:** 59, 78
Elizabethan culture, relation to **32:** 66; **40:** 117, 127, 142, 166, 181, 197, 208; **48:** 54, 77; **49:** 37; **53:** 105, 111, 127, 159, 169, 214, 224; **66:** 117, 144
ending **54:** 52, 65
feminist criticism **55:** 27
genre **4:** 191, 200, 201, 209, 215, 221, 232, 238, 247; **12:** 48, 54, 62; **54:** 65; **66:** 292
homosexuality **22:** 3, 69; **37:** 86; **40:** 142, 156, 197; **66:** 127
imperialism **53:** 116
implausibility of plot, characters, or events **4:** 191, 192, 193; **12:** 52, 56, 76, 119
irony **4:** 254, 300, 321, 331, 350; **28:** 63; **66:** 91, 158, 171
Jessica **4:** 196, 200, 228, 293, 342; **53:** 159, 211; **66:** 171
justice and mercy **4:** 213, 214, 224, 250, 261, 273, 282, 289, 336; **12:** 80, 129; **40:** 127; **49:** 1, 23, 27, 37; **66:** 180
language and imagery **4:** 241, 267, 293; **22:** 3; **25:** 257; **28:** 9, 63; **32:** 41; **40:** 106; **53:** 169; **66:** 165
Launcelot Gobbo **46:** 24, 60; **50:** 64; **53:** 187, 214; **66:** 158
law and justice **53:** 169; **66:** 180
love **4:** 221, 226, 270, 284, 312, 344; **22:** 3, 69; **25:** 257; **40:** 156; **51:** 1, 44; **66:** 63, 127
medieval homilies, influence of **4:** 224, 250, 289
morality **52:** 89
music and harmony, Lorenzo's speech on **66:** 171
mythic or mythological elements **60:** 276; **66:** 63
Ovid's Metamorphoses, relation to **60:** 276
Portia **4:** 194, 195, 196, 215, 254, 263, 336, 356; **12:** 104, 107, 114; **13:** 37; **22:** 3, 69; **25:** 22; **32:** 294; **37:** 86; **40:** 142, 156, 197, 208; **49:** 27; **66:** 63, 91, 124, 144
psychoanalytic interpretation **45:** 17; **66:** 135
race **53:** 111, 116, 127, 136, 159, 169; **55:** 27; **66:** 165
religious principles **66:** 292
resolution **4:** 263, 266, 300, 319, 321; **13:** 37; **51:** 1
revenge **60:** 276
rings episode **22:** 3; **40:** 106, 151, 156; **66:** 59, 63, 144, 158
sacrificial love **13:** 43; **22:** 69; **40:** 142
sexual politics **22:** 3; **51:** 44
Shylock
 alienation **4:** 279, 312; **40:** 175; **49:** 23, 37; **66:** 91
 ambiguity **4:** 247, 254, 315, 319, 331; **12:** 31, 35, 36, 50, 51, 52, 56, 81, 124; **40:** 175; **53:** 111; **66:** 87, 110, 117
 forced conversion **4:** 209, 252, 268, 282, 289, 321; **53:** 127; **66:** 110, 144, 180, 292
 ghettoization of **53:** 127; **66:** 78
 Jewishness **4:** 193, 194, 195, 200, 201, 213, 214, 279; **22:** 69; **25:** 257; **40:** 142, 175, 181; **66:** 87, 110, 117, 126, 292
 master-slave relationship **53:** 136
 motives in making the bond **4:** 252, 263, 266, 268; **22:** 69; **25:** 22; **66:** 59, 110
 as outsider **53:** 127, 224; **66:** 87, 144, 158, 165
 as Puritan **40:** 127, 166
 as scapegoat figure **4:** 254, 300; **40:** 166; **49:** 27
 as traditional comic villain **4:** 230, 243, 261, 263, 315; **12:** 40, 62, 124; **40:** 175; **66:** 87, 117
 as tragic figure **12:** 6, 9, 10, 16, 21, 23, 25, 40, 44, 66, 67, 81, 97; **40:** 175; **66:** 87, 117, 124, 126, 153, 180, 292
social criticism **53:** 214; **66:** 124
staging issues **12:** 111, 114, 115, 117, 119, 124, 129, 131; **66:** 123, 124
structure **4:** 201, 215, 230, 232, 243, 247, 254, 261, 263, 308, 321; **12:** 115; **28:** 63; **60:** 276
trial scene **13:** 43; **25:** 22; **40:** 106, 156; **49:** 1, 23, 27, 37
unity of double plot **4:** 193, 194, 201, 232; **12:** 16, 67, 80, 115, **40:** 151
Venetians **4:** 195, 200, 228, 254, 273, 300, 321, 331
Venice, Elizabethan perceptions of **28:** 249; **32:** 294; **40:** 127; **66:** 123
wealth **4:** 209, 261, 270, 273, 317; **12:** 80, 117; **22:** 69; **25:** 22; **28:** 249; **40:** 117, 197, 208; **45:** 17; **49:** 1; **51:** 15

The Merry Wives of Windsor (Volumes 5, 18, 38, 47, 59)

Anne Page-Fenton plot **5:** 334, 336, 343, 353, 376, 390, 395, 402; **22:** 93; **47:** 308
avarice **5:** 335, 353, 369, 376, 390, 395, 402
Caius, Doctor **47:** 354
caricature **5:** 343, 347, 348, 350, 385, 397
characterization **5:** 332, 334, 335, 337, 338, 351, 360, 363, 366, 374, 379, 392; **18:** 74, 75; **38:** 264, 273, 313, 319
class distinctions, conflict, and relations **5:** 338, 343, 346, 347, 366, 390, 395, 400, 402; **22:** 93; **28:** 69
comic and farcical elements **5:** 336, 338, 346, 350, 360, 369, 373; **18:** 74, 75, 84; **59:** 105
The Comical Gallant (John Dennis adaptation) **18:** 5, 7, 8, 9, 10
deception, disguise, and duplicity **5:** 332, 334, 336, 354, 355, 379; **22:** 93; **47:** 308, 314, 321, 325, 344
desire **38:** 286, 297, 300
Elizabethan society **47:** 331
Elizabeth's influence **5:** 333, 334, 335, 336, 339, 346, 355, 366, 402; **18:** 5, 86; **38:** 278; **47:** 344
Evans, Sir Hugh **47:** 354
Falstaff
 characterization in 1 and 2 Henry IV, compared with **5:** 333, 335, 336, 337, 339, 346, 347, 348, 350, 373, 400; **18:** 5, 7, 75, 86; **22:** 93
 diminishing powers **5:** 337, 339, 343, 347, 350, 351, 392; **28:** 373; **47:** 363
 as Herne the Hunter **38:** 256, 286; **47:** 358
 incapability of love **5:** 335, 336, 339, 346, 348; **22:** 93
 as Jack-a-Lent **47:** 363
 personification of comic principle or Vice figure **5:** 332, 338, 369, 400; **38:** 273
 recognition and repentance of follies **5:** 338, 341, 343, 348, 369, 374, 376, 397
 as scapegoat **47:** 358, 363, 375
 sensuality **5:** 339, 343, 353, 369, 392

shrewdness **5:** 332, 336, 346, 355
threat to community **5:** 343, 369, 379, 392, 395, 400; **38:** 297
as unifying force **47:** 358
vanity **5:** 332, 339
victimization **5:** 336, 338, 341, 347, 348, 353, 355, 360, 369, 373, 374, 376, 392, 397, 400; **59:** 144
as villain **47:** 358
as a woman **47:** 325
folk rituals, elements and influence of **5:** 353, 369, 376, 392, 397, 400; **38:** 256, 300
Ford, Francis **5:** 332, 334, 343, 355, 363, 374, 379, 390; **38:** 273; **47:** 321
Ford, Mistress Alice **47:** 321
genre, issues of **59:** 111
insults **47:** 331
Italian comedy, influence of **59:** 105
jealousy **5:** 334, 339, 343, 353, 355, 363; **22:** 93; **38:** 273, 307
Jonsonian humors comedy, influence of **38:** 319; **59:** 105
knighthood **5:** 338, 343, 390, 397, 402; **47:** 354
language and imagery **5:** 335, 337, 343, 347, 351, 363, 374, 379; **19:** 101; **22:** 93; **28:** 9, 69; **38:** 313, 319; **59:** 89
male discontent **5:** 392, 402
marriage **5:** 343, 369, 376, 390, 392, 400; **22:** 93; **38:** 297; **51:** 44; **59:** 95
mediation **5:** 343, 392
morality **5:** 335, 339, 347, 349, 353, 397; **59:** 132
Neoclassical rules **5:** 332, 334
Page, Anne **47:** 321
Page, Mistress Margaret **47:** 321
pastoral elements **59:** 132
play and theatricality **47:** 325
play-within-the-play, convention of **5:** 354, 355, 369, 402
realism **38:** 313
reconciliation **5:** 343, 369, 374, 397, 402
revenge **5:** 349, 350, 392; **38:** 264, 307
as satire or parody **5:** 338, 350, 360, 385; **38:** 278, 319; **47:** 354, 363
schemes and intrigues **5:** 334, 336, 339, 341, 343, 349, 355, 379
setting **47:** 375 **59:** 89, 139
sexual politics **19:** 101; **38:** 307; **59:** 95
social milieu **18:** 75, 84; **38:** 297, 300; **59:** 132, 139, 144
sources **5:** 332, 350, 360, 366, 385; **32:** 31; **59:** 123
stage history **18:** 66, 67, 68, 70, 71; **59:** 123
staging issues **18:** 74, 75, 84, 86, 90, 95
structure **5:** 332, 333, 334, 335, 343, 349, 355, 369, 374; **18:** 86; **22:** 378; **59:** 89, 111
unnatural ordering **22:** 378
wit **5:** 335, 336, 337, 339, 343, 351
women, role of **5:** 335, 341, 343, 349, 369, 379, 390, 392, 402; **19:** 101; **38:** 307

A Midsummer Night's Dream (Volumes 3, 12, 29, 45, 58)

adaptations **12:** 144, 146, 147, 153, 280, 282
ambiguity **3:** 401, 459, 486; **45:** 169
appearance, perception, and illusion **3:** 368, 411, 425, 427, 434, 447, 459, 466, 474, 477, 486, 497, 516; **19:** 21; **22:** 39; **28:** 15; **29:** 175,190; **45:** 136
Athens and the forest, contrast between **3:** 381, 427, 459, 466, 497, 502; **29:** 175
autobiographical elements **3:** 365, 371, 379, 381, 389, 391, 396, 402, 432
Bottom
 awakening speech (Act IV, scene i) **3:** 406, 412, 450, 457, 486, 516; **16:** 34; **58:** 181
 his dream **60:** 142
folly of **46:** 1, 14, 29, 60
imagination **3:** 376, 393, 406, 432, 486; **29:** 175, 190; **45:** 147
self-possession **3:** 365, 376, 395, 402, 406, 480; **45:** 158
Titania, relationship with **3:** 377, 406, 441, 445, 450, 457, 491, 497; **16:** 34; **19:** 21; **22:** 93; **29:** 216; **45:** 160; **58:** 203, 215
transformation **3:** 365, 377, 432; **13:** 27; **22:** 93; **29:** 216; **45:** 147, 160
brutal elements **3:** 445, 491, 497, 511; **12:** 259, 262, 298; **16:** 34; **19:** 21; **29:** 183, 225, 263, 269; **45:** 169
capriciousness of the young lovers **3:** 372, 395, 402, 411, 423, 437, 441, 450, 497, 498; **29:** 175, 269; **45:** 107
ceremonies, rites, and rituals, importance of **58:** 189
the changeling **58:** 162, 167
chastity **45:** 143
class distinctions, conflict, and relations **22:** 23; **25:** 36; **45:** 160; **50:** 74, 86
colonialism **53:** 32
as dream-play **3:** 365, 370, 372, 377, 389, 391; **29:** 190; **45:** 117; **58:** 181
dreams **45:** 96, 107, 117
duration of time **3:** 362, 370, 380, 386, 494; **45:** 175
Elizabethan culture, relation to **50:** 86; **58:** 220
erotic elements **3:** 445, 491, 497, 511; **12:** 259, 262, 298; **16:** 34; **19:** 21; **29:** 183, 225, 269; **58:** 194
fairies **3:** 361, 362, 372, 377, 395, 400, 423, 450, 459, 486; **12:** 287, 291, 294, 295; **19:** 21; **29:** 183, 190; **45:** 147
farcical elements **58:** 169
feminist interpretation **48:** 23
gender **53:** 1; **58:** 215
Helena **29:** 269; **58:** 194
Helena and Hermia, relationship between **60:** 142
Hermia **29:** 225, 269; **45:** 117; **58:** 194
Hippolytus, myth of **29:** 216; **45:** 84
homosexuality **60:** 142
identity **29:** 269; **58:** 215
imagination and art **3:** 365, 371, 381, 402, 412, 417, 421, 423, 434, 441, 459, 468, 506, 516, 520; **22:** 39
language and imagery **3:** 397, 401, 410, 412, 415, 432, 453, 459, 468, 494; **22:** 23, 39, 93, 378; **28:** 9; **29:** 263; **45:** 96, 126, 136, 143, 147, 169, 175; **48:** 23, 32; **58:** 181, 186, 194
the lovers **58:** 151, 169
male domination **3:** 483, 520; **13:** 19; **25:** 36; **29:** 216, 225, 243, 256, 269; **42:** 46; **45:** 84; **58:** 203, 220; **60:** 142
marriage **3:** 402, 423, 450, 483, 520; **29:** 243, 256; **45:** 136, 143; **48:** 32; **51:** 1, 30, 44; **58:** 175
metadramatic elements **3:** 427, 468, 477, 516, 520; **29:** 190, 225, 243; **50:** 86
Metamorphoses (Golding translation of Ovid) **16:** 25
mimetic desire **60:** 172, 245
Minotaur, myth of **3:** 497, 498; **29:** 216
music and dance **3:** 397, 400, 418, 513; **12:** 287, 289; **25:** 36
mythic or mythological elements **58:** 194 **60:** 172, 245, 259
Oberon **58:** 151, 162, 167, 203; **60:** 142
 as controlling force **3:** 434, 459, 477, 502; **29:** 175
Ovid, influence of **3:** 362, 427, 497, 498; **22:** 23; **29:** 175, 190, 216; **60:** 172
parent-child relations **13:** 19; **29:** 216, 225, 243
passionate or romantic love **3:** 372, 389, 395, 396, 402, 408, 411, 423, 441, 450, 480,
497, 498, 511; **29:** 175, 225, 263, 269; **45:** 126, 136; **51:** 44; **58:** 175
patriarchy **60:** 259
Pauline doctrine **3:** 457, 486, 506
Platonic elements **3:** 368, 437, 450, 497; **45:** 126
politics **29:** 243
power **42:** 46; **45:** 84; **58:** 151
psychoanalytic interpretations **3:** 440, 483; **28:** 15; **29:** 225; **44:** 1; **45:** 107, 117; **58:** 167
Puck **45:** 96, 158
Pyramus and Thisbe interlude **3:** 364, 368, 379, 381, 389, 391, 396, 408, 411, 412, 417, 425, 427, 433, 441, 447, 457, 468, 474, 511; **12:** 254; **13:** 27; **16:** 25; **22:** 23; **29:** 263; **45:** 107, 175; **50:** 74
race **53:** 1, 32
reason versus imagination **3:** 381, 389, 423, 441, 466, 506; **22:** 23; **29:** 190; **45:** 96
reconciliation **3:** 412, 418, 437, 459, 468, 491, 497, 502, 513; **13:** 27; **29:** 190
reversal **29:** 225; **60:** 245
Romeo and Juliet, compared with **3:** 396, 480
rustic characters **3:** 376, 397, 432; **12:** 291, 293; **45:** 147, 160
sexuality **22:** 23, 93; **29:** 225, 243, 256, 269; **42:** 46; **45:** 107 **53:** 32; **58:** 203, 215, 220
sources **29:** 216; **60:** 259
staging issues **3:** 364, 365, 371, 372, 377; **12:** 151, 152, 154, 158, 159, 280, 284, 291, 295; **16:** 34; **19:** 21; **29:** 183, 256; **48:** 23
structure **3:** 364, 368, 381, 402, 406, 427, 450, 513; **13:** 19; **22:** 378; **29:** 175; **45:** 126, 175; **58:** 186, 189
textual issues **16:** 34; **29:** 216; **58:** 151
Theseus **51:** 1
 characterization **3:** 363; **58:** 151, 220
 Hippolyta, relationship with **3:** 381, 412, 421, 423, 450, 468, 520; **29:** 175, 216, 243, 256; **45:** 84
 as ideal **3:** 379, 391
 "lovers, lunatics, and poets" speech (Act V, scene i) **3:** 365, 371, 379, 381, 391, 402, 411, 412, 421, 423, 441, 498, 506; **29:** 175
 as representative of institutional life **3:** 381, 403
Titania **29:** 243; **58:** 151, 162, , 167, 203
tragic elements **3:** 393, 400, 401, 410, 445, 474, 480, 491, 498, 511; **29:** 175; **45:** 169; **58:** 175, 186
as a transgressive play **60:** 142
unity **3:** 364, 368, 381, 402, 406, 427, 450, 513; **13:** 19; **22:** 378; **29:** 175, 263
unnatural ordering **22:** 378

Much Ado about Nothing (Volumes 8, 18, 31, 55)

appearance versus reality **8:** 17, 18, 48, 63, 69, 73, 75, 79, 88, 95, 115; **31:** 198, 209; **55:** 259, 268
battle of the sexes **8:** 14, 16, 19, 48, 91, 95, 111, 121, 125; **31:** 231, 245 **55:** 199
Beatrice and Benedick
 Beatrice's femininity **8:** 14, 16, 17, 24, 29, 38, 41, 91; **31:** 222, 245; **55:** 221
 Beatrice's request to "kill Claudio" (Act IV, scene i) **8:** 14, 17, 33, 41, 55, 63, 75, 79, 91, 108, 115; **18:** 119, 120, 136, 161, 245, 257; **55:** 268
 Benedick's challenge of Claudio (Act V, scene i) **8:** 48, 63, 79, 91; **31:** 231
 Claudio and Hero, compared with **8:** 19, 28, 29, 75, 82, 115; **31:** 171, 216; **55:** 189

marriage and the opposite sex, attitudes toward **8:** 9, 13, 14, 16, 19, 29, 36, 48, 63, 77, 91, 95, 115, 121; **16:** 45; **31:** 216
mutual attraction **8:** 13, 14, 19, 24, 29, 33, 41, 75
nobility **8:** 13, 19, 24, 29, 36, 39, 41, 47, 82, 91, 108
popularity **8:** 13, 38, 41, 53, 79
transformed by love **8:** 19, 29, 36, 48, 75, 91, 95, 115; **31:** 209, 216; **55:** 236
unconventionality **8:** 48, 91, 95, 108, 115, 121; **55:** 221, 249, 268
vulgarity **8:** 11, 12, 33, 38, 41, 47
wit and charm **8:** 9, 12, 13, 14, 19, 24, 27, 28, 29, 33, 36, 38, 41, 47, 55, 69, 95, 108, 115; **31:** 241; **55:** 199
Borachio and Conrade **8:** 24, 69, 82, 88, 111, 115
Christian elements **8:** 17, 19, 29, 55, 95, 104, 111, 115; **31:** 209; **55:** 228
church scene (Act IV, scene i) **8:** 13, 14, 16, 19, 33, 44, 47, 48, 58, 63, 69, 75, 79, 82, 91, 95, 100, 104, 111, 115; **18:** 120, 130, 138, 145, 146, 148, 192; **31:** 191, 198, 245; **55:** 236
Claudio
  boorish behavior **8:** 9, 24, 33, 36, 39, 44, 48, 63, 79, 82, 95, 100, 111, 115; **31:** 209
  credulity **8:** 9, 17, 19, 24, 29, 36, 41, 47, 58, 63, 75, 77, 82, 95, 100, 104, 111, 115, 121; **31:** 241; **47:** 25
  mercenary traits **8:** 24, 44, 58, 82, 91, 95
  noble qualities **8:** 17, 19, 29, 41, 44, 58, 75; **55:** 232
  reconciliation with Hero **8:** 33, 36, 39, 44, 47, 82, 95, 100, 111, 115, 121; **55:** 236
  repentance **8:** 33, 63, 82, 95, 100, 111, 115, 121; **31:** 245
  sexual insecurities **8:** 75, 100, 111, 115, 121
courtship and marriage **8:** 29, 44, 48, 95, 115, 121, 125; **31:** 191, 231; **51:** 33, 44; **55:** 209
deception, disguise, and duplicity **8:** 29, 55, 63, 69, 79, 82, 88, 108, 115; **31:** 191, 198; **55:** 236
Dogberry and the Watch **8:** 9, 12, 13, 17, 24, 28, 29, 33, 39, 48, 55, 69, 79, 82, 88, 95, 104, 108, 115; **18:** 138, 152, 205, 208, 210, 213, 231; **22:** 85; **31:** 171, 229; **46:** 60; **55:** 189, 249
Don John **8:** 9, 12, 16, 17, 19, 28, 29, 36, 39, 41, 47, 48, 55, 58, 63, 82, 104, 108, 111, 121
Don Pedro **8:** 17, 19, 48, 58, 63, 82, 111, 121
eavesdropping scenes (Act II, scene iii and Act III, scene i) **8:** 12, 13, 17, 19, 28, 29, 33, 36, 48, 55, 63, 73, 75, 82, 121; **18:** 120, 138, 208, 215, 245, 264; **31:** 171, 184; **55:** 259
egotism or narcissism **8:** 19, 24, 28, 29, 55, 69, 95, 115; **55:** 209
Elizabethan culture, relation to **8:** 23, 33, 44, 55, 58, 79, 88, 104, 111, 115; **51:** 15; **55:** 209, 241, 259
Friar **8:** 24, 29, 41, 55, 63, 79, 111; **55:** 249
genre **8:** 9, 18, 19, 28, 29, 39, 41, 44, 53, 63, 69, 73, 79, 82, 95, 100, 104; **48:** 14; **55:** 232, 268
Hero **8:** 13, 14, 16, 19, 28, 29, 44, 48, 53, 55, 82, 95, 104, 111, 115, 121; **31:** 231, 245; **47:** 25; **55:** 209
implausibility of plot, characters, or events **8:** 9, 12, 16, 19, 33, 36, 39, 44, 53, 100, 104
irony **8:** 14, 63, 79, 82; **28:** 63
justice and mercy **22:** 85
language and imagery **8:** 9, 38, 43, 46, 55, 69, 73, 88, 95, 100, 115, 125; **19:** 68; **25:** 77; **28:** 63; **31:** 178, 184, 222, 241, 245; **48:** 14; **55:** 199, 259
law versus passion for freedom **22:** 85
love **8:** 24, 55, 75, 95, 111, 115; **28:** 56; **51:** 30
Messina **8:** 19, 29, 48, 69, 82, 91, 95, 108, 111, 121, 125; **31:** 191, 209, 229, 241, 245
misgovernment **22:** 85; **55:** 241
music and dance **19:** 68; **31:** 222
"nothing," significance of **8:** 17, 18, 23, 55, 73, 95; **19:** 68; **55:** 259
performance issues **18:** 173, 174, 183, 184, 185, 186, 187, 188, 189, 190, 191, 192, 193, 195, 197, 199, 201, 204, 206, 207, 208, 209, 210, 254; **55:** 221
power **22:** 85; **25:** 77; **31:** 231, 245
repentance or forgiveness **8:** 24, 29, 111; **55:** 228
resurrection, metamorphosis, or transformation **8:** 88, 104, 111, 115; **55:** 209
romance or chivalric tradition, influence of **8:** 53, 125; **51:** 15
self-knowledge **8:** 69, 95, 100
setting **18:** 173, 174, 183, 184, 185, 186, 187, 188, 189, 190, 191, 192, 193, 195, 197, 199, 201, 204, 206, 207, 208, 209, 210, 254
slander or hearsay, importance of **8:** 58, 69, 82, 95, 104; **55:** 249
sources **8:** 9, 19, 53, 58, 104
staging issues **8:** 18, 33, 41, 75, 79, 82, 108; **16:** 45; **18:** 245, 247, 249, 252, 254, 257, 261, 264; **28:** 63; **55:** 221
structure **8:** 9, 16, 17, 19, 28, 29, 33, 39, 48, 63, 69, 73, 75, 79, 82, 115; **31:** 178, 184, 198, 231; **55:** 189
virginity or chastity, importance of **8:** 44, 75, 95, 111, 121, 125; **31:** 222; **55:** 268
wit **8:** 27, 29, 38, 69, 79, 91, 95; **31:** 178, 191; **55:** 228
works by Shakespeare or other authors, compared with **8:** 16, 19, 27, 28, 33, 38, 39, 41, 53, 69, 79, 91, 104, 108; **31:** 231; **55:** 189, 209, 232, 241, 249

Othello (Volumes 4, 11, 35, 53)

adaptations **65:** 327
autobiographical elements **4:** 440, 444; **53:** 324
Brabantio **25:** 189
Cassio **25:** 189
Clarissa (Samuel Richardson), compared with **48:** 277
consummation of marriage **22:** 207; **53:** 246, 333
contrasts and oppositions **4:** 421, 455, 457, 462, 508; **25:** 189; **53:** 268
Desdemona
  as Christ figure **4:** 506, 525, 573; **35:** 360
  culpability **4:** 408, 415, 422, 427; **13:** 313; **19:** 253, 276; **35:** 265, 352, 380
  innocence **35:** 360; **47:** 25; **53:** 310, 333
  as mother figure **22:** 339; **35:** 282; **53:** 324
  passivity **4:** 402, 406, 421, 440, 457, 470, 582, 587; **25:** 189; **35:** 380
  spiritual nature of her love **4:** 462, 530, 559
  staging issues **11:** 350, 354, 359; **13:** 327; **32:** 201
dramatic structure **4:** 370, 390, 399, 427, 488, 506, 517, 569; **22:** 207; **28:** 243; **53:** 261
Duke **25:** 189
Emilia **4:** 386, 391, 392, 415, 587; **35:** 352, 380
ending **54:** 119; **60:** 2
evil **52:** 78; **60:** 91
gender issues **32:** 294; **35:** 327; **53:** 255, 268, 310, 315, 324
handkerchief, significance of **4:** 370, 384, 385, 396, 503, 530, 562; **35:** 265, 282, 380; **53:** 333
Hercules Furens (Seneca) as source **16:** 283
Iago
  affinity with Othello **4:** 400, 427, 468, 470, 477, 500, 506; **25:** 189; **44:** 57
  as conventional dramatic villain **4:** 440, 527, 545, 582; **53:** 288
  as homosexual **4:** 503; **53:** 275
  Machiavellian elements **4:** 440, 455, 457, 517, 545; **35:** 336, 347; **65:** 327
  motives **4:** 389, 390, 397, 399, 402, 409, 423, 424, 427, 434, 451, 462, 545, 564; **13:** 304; **25:** 189; **28:** 344; **32:** 201; **35:** 265, 276, 310, 336, 347; **42:** 278; **53:** 246, 275, 324
  revenge scheme **4:** 392, 409, 424, 451; **65:** 327
  as scapegoat **4:** 506
  as victim **4:** 402, 409, 434, 451, 457, 470
idealism versus realism **4:** 457, 508, 517; **13:** 313; **25:** 189; **53:** 350
implausibility of plot, characters, or events **4:** 370, 380, 391, 442, 444; **47:** 51
jealousy **4:** 384, 488, 527; **35:** 253, 265, 282, 301, 310; **44:** 57, 66; **51:** 30
justice **35:** 247; **53:** 288, 350
language and imagery **4:** 433, 442, 445, 462, 493, 508, 517, 552, 587, 596; **13:** 304; **16:** 272; **22:** 378; **25:** 189, 257; **28:** 243, 344; **42:** 278; **47:** 51; **53:** 261
love **4:** 412, 493, 506, 512, 530, 545, 552, 569, 570, 575, 580, 591; **19:** 253; **22:** 207; **25:** 257; **28:** 243, 344; **32:** 201; **35:** 261, 317; **51:** 25, 30; **53:** 315; **54:** 119
love and reason **4:** 512, 530, 580; **19:** 253
madness **35:** 265, 276, 282
marriage **35:** 369; **51:** 44; **53:** 315
Marxist criticism **42:** 234
Measure for Measure, compared with **25:** 189
medieval dramatic conventions, influence of **4:** 440, 527, 545, 559, 582
Merchant of Venice, compared with **53:** 288, 255, 268, 298; **66:** 317
military and sexual hierarchies **16:** 272; **53:** 324
moral corruption **52:** 78
opening scene **54:** 2, 6
Othello
  affinity with Iago **4:** 400, 427, 468, 470, 477, 500, 506; **25:** 189; **35:** 276, 320, 327
  as conventional "blameless hero" **4:** 445, 486, 500; **53:** 233, 288, 298, 304
  conversion to Christianity **66:** 317
  credulity **4:** 384, 385, 388, 390, 396, 402, 434, 440, 455; **13:** 327; **32:** 302; **47:** 25, 51; **65:** 327
  Desdemona, relationship with **22:** 339; **35:** 301, 317; **37:** 269; **53:** 315
  divided nature **4:** 400, 412, 462, 470, 477, 493, 500, 580, 582, 592; **16:** 293; **19:** 276; **25:** 189; **35:** 320; **53:** 268, 289, 343
  egotism **4:** 427, 470, 477, 493, 522, 536, 541, 573, 597; **13:** 304; **35:** 247, 253
  self-destructive anger **16:** 283; **53:** 324
  self-dramatizing or self-deluding **4:** 454, 457, 477, 592; **13:** 313; **16:** 293; **35:** 317; **60:** 46
  self-knowledge **4:** 462, 470, 477, 483, 508, 522, 530, 564, 580, 591, 596; **13:** 304, 313; **16:** 283; **28:** 243; **35:** 253, 317; **53:** 233, 343
  spiritual state **4:** 483, 488, 517, 525, 527, 544, 559, 564, 573; **28:** 243; **35:** 253; **53:** 298; **60:** 46
perception **19:** 276; **25:** 189, 257; **53:** 246, 289
poetic justice, question of **4:** 370, 412, 415, 427

pride and rightful self-esteem **4:** 522, 536, 541; **35:** 352
psychoanalytic interpretations **4:** 468, 503; **35:** 265, 276, 282, 301, 317, 320, 347; **42:** 203; **44:** 57; **53:** 275, 343
racial issues **4:** 370, 380, 384, 385, 392, 399, 401, 402, 408, 427, 564; **13:** 327; **16:** 293; **25:** 189, 257; **28:** 249, 330; **35:** 369; **42:** 203; **37:** 336; **53:** 1, 233, 238, 246, 255, 261, 268, 275, 289, 298, 304; **55:** 27; **66:** 317
religious, mythic, or spiritual content **4:** 483, 517, 522, 525, 559, 573; **22:** 207; **28:** 330; **53:** 289; **66:** 317
revenge **35:** 261
Romeo and Juliet, compared with **32:** 302
sexuality **22:** 339; **28:** 330, 344; **35:** 352, 360; **37:** 269; **44:** 57, 66; **51:** 44; **53:** 275, 310, 315
sources **28:** 330
staging issues **11:** 273, 334, 335, 339, 342, 350,354, 359, 362; **53:** 233, 304
structure **22:** 378; **28:** 325
time **65:** 327
time scheme **4:** 370, 384, 390, 488; **22:** 207; **35:** 310; **47:** 51; **53:** 333
tragic elements **55:** 78
unnatural ordering **22:** 378
Venetian politics **32:** 294; **53:** 350
violence **22:** 12; **43:** 32
The Winter's Tale, compared with **35:** 310
women, role of **19:** 253; **28:** 344; **53:** 310

Pericles (Volumes 2, 15, 36, 51, 66)

archetypal structure **2:** 570, 580, 582, 584, 588; **25:** 365; **51:** 71, 79
art and nature **22:** 315; **36:** 233
audience perception **42:** 359; **48:** 364
authorship controversy **2:** 538, 540, 543, 544, 545, 546, 548, 550, 551, 553, 556, 558, 564, 565, 568, 576, 586; **15:** 132, 141, 148, 152; **16:** 391, 399; **25:** 365; **36:** 198, 244; **66:** 219, 236
autobiographical elements **2:** 551, 554, 555, 563, 581; **66:** 208,
brothel scenes (Act IV, scenes ii and vi) **2:** 548, 550, 551, 553, 554, 586, 590; **15:** 134, 145, 154, 166, 172, 177; **36:** 274; **51:** 118
Cerimon **66:** 236
composition date **2:** 537, 544
Deconstructionist interpretation of **48:** 364
Diana
as symbol of nature **22:** 315; **36:** 233; **51:** 71; **66:** 236
disguise **66:** 201
doubling of roles **15:** 150, 152, 167, 173, 180
as a dream **66:** 233
Gower chorus **2:** 548, 575; **15:** 134, 141, 143, 145, 149, 152, 177; **36:** 279; **42:** 359; **66:** 208
incest, motif of **2:** 582, 588; **22:** 315; **36:** 257, 264; **51:** 110, 97; **66:** 190, 224
as inferior or flawed play **2:** 537, 546, 553, 563, 564; **15:** 139, 143, 156, 167, 176; **36:** 198; **51:** 79; **66:** 186
innocence **36:** 226, 274
Jacobean culture, relation to **37:** 361; **51:** 110, 86; **66:** 224
language and imagery **2:** 559, 560, 565, 583; **16:** 391; **19:** 387; **22:** 315; **36:** 198, 214, 233, 244, 251, 264; **51:** 86, 99; **66:** 233
Marina **37:** 361; **51:** 118; **66:** 201
as miracle play **2:** 569, 581; **36:** 205; **51:** 97
music **66:** 236
nature as book **22:** 315; **36:** 233
oaths, importance of **19:** 387
patience **2:** 572, 573, 578, 579; **36:** 251

Pericles **66:** 201
characterization **36:** 251; **37:** 361
patience **2:** 572, 573, 578, 579
suit of Antiochus's daughter **2:** 547, 565, 578, 579; **51:** 126; **66:** 190
Ulysses, compared with **2:** 551
politics **37:** 361; **66:** 224
popularity **2:** 536, 538, 546; **37:** 361
Prologue **54:** 35
recognition scene (Act V, scene i) **15:** 138, 139, 141, 145, 161, 162, 167, 172, 175; **66:** 186
reconciliation **2:** 555, 564, 584, 586, 588; **36:** 205
religious, mythic, or spiritual content **2:** 559, 561, 565, 570, 580, 584, 588; **22:** 315; **25:** 365; **51:** 97
riddle motif **22:** 315; **36:** 205, 214
Shakespeare's other romances, relation to **2:** 547, 549, 551, 559, 564, 570, 571, 584, 585; **15:** 139; **16:** 391, 399; **36:** 226, 257; **51:** 71, 79; **54:** 35; **66:** 186
spectacle **42:** 359
sources **2:** 538, 568, 572, 575; **25:** 365; **36:** 198, 205; **51:** 118, 126
staging issues **16:** 399; **48:** 364; **51:** 99; **66:** 215
suffering **2:** 546, 573, 578, 579; **25:** 365; **36:** 279
textual revisions **15:** 129, 130, 132, 134, 135, 136, 138, 152, 155, 167, 181; **16:** 399; **25:** 365; **51:** 99
Thaisa **66:** 201

The Phoenix and Turtle (Volumes 10, 38, 51, 64)

alchemy **64:** 211
allegorical elements **10:** 7, 8, 9, 16, 17, 48; **38:** 334, 378; **51:** 138, 188; **64:** 198, 209, 211
art and nature **10:** 7, 42; **64:** 209
authenticity **10:** 7, 8, 16; **64:** 217
autobiographical elements **10:** 14, 18, 42, 48; **51:** 155; **64:** 217, 225
bird imagery **10:** 21, 27; **38:** 329, 350, 367; **51:** 145, 181, 184; **64:** 198, 205, 217
Christian elements **10:** 21, 24, 31; **38:** 326; **51:** 162, 171, 181; **64:** 211, 217, 225
complex or enigmatic nature **10:** 7, 14, 35, 42; **38:** 326, 357; **51:** 145, 162; **64:** 205, 209, 225
consciously philosophical **10:** 7, 21, 24, 31, 48; **38:** 342, 378
constancy and faithfulness **10:** 18, 20, 21, 48; **38:** 329; **64:** 209
Court of Love **10:** 9, 24, 50
Donne, John, compared with **10:** 20, 31, 35, 37, 40; **51:** 143; **64:** 225
satiric elements **10:** 8, 16, 17, 27, 35, 40, 45, 48
love **10:** 31, 37, 40, 50; **38:** 342, 345, 367; **51:** 145, 151, 155; **64:** 209, 211, 217
as metaphysical poem **10:** 7, 8, 9, 20, 31, 35, 37, 40, 45, 50; **51:** 143, 171, 184; **64:** 211, 225
Neoplatonism **10:** 7, 9, 21, 24, 40, 45, 50; **38:** 345, 350, 367, 184
as "pure" poetry **10:** 14, 31, 35; **38:** 329
Scholasticism **10:** 21, 24, 31; **51:** 188; **64:** 211
Shakespeare's dramas, compared with **10:** 9, 14, 17, 18, 20, 27, 37, 40, 42, 48; **38:** 342; **51:** 151, 155; **64:** 217, 225
sources **10:** 7, 9, 18, 24, 45; **38:** 326, 334, 350, 367; **51:** 138; **64:** 198, 209, 217, 225
structure **10:** 27, 31, 37, 45, 50; **38:** 342, 345, 357; **51:** 138, 143; **64:** 205, 225

style **10:** 8, 20, 24, 27, 31, 35, 45, 50; **38:** 334, 345, 357, 171; **51:** 188; **64:** 205, 225

The Rape of Lucrece (Volumes 10, 33, 43, 59)

allegorical elements **10:** 89, 93
Brutus **10:** 96, 106, 109, 116, 121, 125, 128, 135
Christian elements **10:** 77, 80, 89, 96, 98, 109; **59:** 165
Collatine **10:** 98, 131; **43:** 102; **59:** 180
Elizabethan culture, relation to **33:** 195; **43:** 77
feminist criticism **59:** 165, 189, 193
gender **53:** 1; **59:** 189, 193, 206
irony or paradox **10:** 93, 98, 128
language and imagery **10:** 64, 65, 66, 71, 78, 80, 89, 93, 116, 109, 125, 131; **22:** 289, 294; **25:** 305; **32:** 321; **33:** 144, 155, 179, 200; **43:** 102, 113, 141; **59:** 159,175,212
Lucrece
chastity **33:** 131, 138; **43:** 92
as example of Renaissance virtù **22:** 289; **43:** 148
heroic **10:** 84, 93, 109, 121, 128; **59:** 175, 193
patriarchal woman, model of **10:** 109, 131; **33:** 169, 200
Philomela, compared with **59:** 193
self-responsibility **10:** 89, 96, 98, 106, 125; **33:** 195; **43:** 85, 92, 158; **59:** 206
unrealistic **10:** 64, 65, 66, 121
verbose **10:** 64, 81, 116; **25:** 305; **33:** 169
as victim **22:** 294; **25:** 305; **32:** 321; **33:** 131, 195; **43:** 102, 158; **59:** 175, 180, 189, 193, 206
male/female relationships **10:** 109, 121, 131; **22:** 289; **25:** 305; **43:** 113, 141; **59:** 180,193
narrative strategies **22:** 294
patriarchy **59:** 189, 206
Petrarchan lovers, parody of **59:** 180
race **53:** 1
rape **59:** 189, 193, 206, 212
Roman history, relation to **10:** 84, 89, 93, 96, 98, 109, 116, 125, 135; **22:** 289; **25:** 305; **33:** 155, 190; **59:** 175
Shakespeare's dramas, compared with **10:** 63, 64, 65, 66, 68, 71, 73, 74, 78, 80, 81, 84, 98, 116, 121, 125; **43:** 92; **59:** 159
sources **10:** 63, 64, 65, 66, 68, 74, 77, 78, 89, 98, 109, 121, 125; **25:** 305; **33:** 155, 190; **43:** 77, 92, 148; **59:** 165
Southampton, Earl of **59:** 165
structure **10:** 84, 89, 93, 98, 135; **22:** 294; **25:** 305; **43:** 102, 141; **59:** 159
style **10:** 64, 65, 66, 68, 69, 70, 71, 73, 74, 77, 78, 81, 84, 98, 116, 131, 135; **43:** 113, 158
Tarquin **10:** 80, 93, 98, 116, 125; **22:** 294; **25:** 305; **32:** 321; **33:** 190; **43:** 102
tragic elements **10:** 78, 80, 81, 84, 98, 109; **43:** 85, 148
the Troy passage **10:** 74, 89, 98, 116, 121, 128; **22:** 289; **32:** 321; **33:** 144, 179; **43:** 77, 85; **59:** 206
Venus and Adonis, compared with **10:** 63, 66, 68, 69, 70, 73, 81; **22:** 294; **43:** 148
violence **43:** 148, 158; **59:** 189, 193, 212

Richard II (Volumes 6, 24, 39, 52, 58)

abdication scene (Act IV, scene i) **6:** 270, 307, 317, 327, 354, 359, 381, 393, 409; **13:** 172; **19:** 151; **24:** 274, 414; **52:** 141, 144

acting and dissimulation **6:** 264, 267, 307, 310, 315, 368, 393, 409; **24:** 339, 345, 346, 349, 352, 356
allegorical elements **6:** 264, 283, 323, 385
audience perception **24:** 414, 423; **39:** 295; **58:** 293
Bolingbroke
   comic elements **28:** 134
   guilt **24:** 423; **39:** 279
   language and imagery **6:** 310, 315, 331, 347, 374, 381, 397; **32:** 189; **58:** 301
   as Machiavellian figure **6:** 305, 307, 315, 331, 347, 388, 393, 397; **24:** 428
   as politician **6:** 255, 263, 264, 272, 277, 294, 364, 368, 391; **24:** 330, 333, 405, 414, 423, 428; **39:** 256; **52:** 124
   Richard, compared with **6:** 307, 315, 347, 374, 391, 393, 409; **24:** 346, 349, 351, 352, 356, 395, 419, 423, 428; **52:** 108, 124; **58:** 241
   his silence **24:** 423
   structure, compared with **39:** 235
   usurpation of crown, nature of **6:** 255, 272, 289, 307, 310, 347, 354, 359, 381, 385, 393; **13:** 172; **24:** 322, 356, 383, 419; **28:** 178; **52:** 108, 124
Bolingbroke and Richard as opposites **24:** 423
Bolingbroke-Mowbray dispute **22:** 137
Bushy, Bagot, and Greene **58:** 259
carnival elements **19:** 151; **39:** 273
censorship **24:** 260, 261, 262, 263, 386; **42:** 120; **52:** 141, 144
ceremonies, rites, and rituals, importance of **6:** 270, 294, 315, 368, 381, 397, 409, 414; **24:** 274, 356, 411, 414, 419
comic elements **24:** 262, 263, 395; **39:** 243
contractual and economic relations **13:** 213; **49:** 60
costumes **24:** 274, 278, 291, 304, 325, 356, 364, 423
deposition scene (Act III, scene iii) **24:** 298, 395, 423; **42:** 120
Elizabethan attitudes, influence of **6:** 287, 292, 294, 305, 321, 327, 364, 402, 414; **13:** 494; **24:** 325; **28:** 188; **39:** 273; **42:** 120; **52:** 141, 144; **58:** 283, 293
Elizabethan culture, relation to **58:** 267, 275
Essex Rebellion, relation to **6:** 249, 250; **24:** 356; **58:** 293
family honor, structure, and inheritance **6:** 338, 368, 388, 397, 414; **39:** 263, 279
fate **6:** 289, 294, 304, 352, 354, 385
garden scene (Act III, scene iv) **6:** 264, 283, 323, 385; **24:** 307, 356, 414
Gaunt **6:** 255, 287, 374, 388, 402, 414; **24:** 274, 322, 325, 414, 423; **39:** 263, 279
gender issues **25:** 89; **39:** 295
historical sources, compared with **6:** 252, 279, 343; **28:** 134; **39:** 235; **49:** 60; **58:** 259, 275, 283
historiography **56:** 2, 15
irony **6:** 270, 307, 364, 368, 391; **24:** 383; **28:** 188
King of Misrule **19:** 151; **39:** 273
kingship **6:** 263, 264, 272, 277, 289, 294, 327, 354, 364, 381, 388, 391, 402, 409, 414; **19:** 151, 209; **24:** 260, 289, 291, 322, 325, 333, 339, 345, 346, 349, 351, 352, 356, 395, 408, 419, 428; **28:** 134; **39:** 235, 243, 256, 273, 279, 289; **42:** 175; **58:** 275, 301
language and imagery **6:** 252, 282, 283, 294, 298, 315, 323, 331, 347, 368, 374, 381, 385, 397, 409; **13:** 213, 494; **24:** 269, 270, 298, 301, 304, 315, 325, 329, 333, 339, 356, 364, 395, 405, 408, 411, 414, 419; **28:** 134, 188; **39:** 243, 273, 289, 295; **42:** 175; **52:** 154, 157, 169, 174, 183; **58:** 253, 267, 293, 301, 307; **60:** 21

Marlowe's works, compared with **19:** 233; **24:** 307, 336; **42:** 175
medievalism and chivalry, presentation of **6:** 258, 277, 294, 327, 338, 388, 397, 414; **24:** 274, 278, 279, 280, 283; **39:** 256
mercantilism and feudalism **13:** 213
mirror scene (Act IV, scene i) **6:** 317, 327, 374, 381, 393, 409; **24:** 267, 356, 408, 414, 419, 423; **28:** 134, 178; **39:** 295
mythological elements **52:** 154, 157, 169
negative assessments **6:** 250, 252, 253, 255, 282, 307, 317, 343, 359
Northumberland **24:** 423
providential order **56:** 15
Richard
   artistic temperament **6:** 264, 267, 270, 272, 277, 292, 294, 298, 315, 331, 334, 347, 368, 374, 393, 409; **24:** 298, 301, 304, 315, 322, 390, 405, 408, 411, 414, 419; **39:** 289
   Bolingbroke, compared with **24:** 346, 349, 351, 352, 356, 419; **39:** 256; **52:** 108, 124; **58:** 275
   characterization **6:** 250, 252, 253, 254, 255, 258, 262, 263, 267, 270, 272, 282, 283, 304, 343, 347, 364, 368; **24:** 262, 263, 267, 269, 270, 271, 272, 273, 274, 278, 280, 315, 322, 325, 330, 333, 390, 395, 402, 405, 423; **28:** 134; **39:** 279, 289; **52:** 169; **58:** 229, 241, 253, 259, 267, 307
   dangerous aspects **24:** 405; **58:** 253
   death of **60:** 21
   delusion **6:** 267, 298, 334, 368, 409; **24:** 329, 336, 405
   homosexuality **24:** 405
   kingship **6:** 253, 254, 263, 272, 327, 331, 334, 338, 364, 402, 414; **24:** 278, 295, 336, 337, 339, 356, 419; **28:** 134, 178; **39:** 256, 263; **52:** 169; **58:** 241, 275
   language and imagery **58:** 301
   loss of identity **6:** 267, 338, 368, 374, 381, 388, 391, 409; **24:** 298, 414, 428
   as martyr-king **6:** 289, 307, 321; **19:** 209; **24:** 289, 291; **28:** 134
   nobility **6:** 255, 258, 259, 262, 263, 391; **24:** 260, 263, 274, 280, 289, 291, 402, 408, 411
   political acumen **6:** 263, 264, 272, 292, 310, 327, 334, 364, 368, 374, 388, 391, 397, 402, 409; **24:** 405; **39:** 256
   private versus public persona **6:** 317, 327, 364, 368, 391, 409; **24:** 428
   role-playing **24:** 419, 423; **28:** 178
   role in Gloucester's death **52:** 108, 124
   seizure of Gaunt's estate **6:** 250, 338, 388; **49:** 60
   self-dramatization **6:** 264, 267, 307, 310, 315, 317, 331, 334, 368, 393, 409; **24:** 339; **28:** 178; **60:** 21
   self-hatred **13:** 172; **24:** 383; **39:** 289
   self-knowledge **6:** 255, 267, 331, 334, 338, 352, 354, 368, 388, 391; **24:** 273, 289, 411, 414; **39:** 263, 289; **60:** 21, 46
   spiritual redemption **6:** 255, 267, 331, 334, 338, 352, 354, 368, 388, 391; **24:** 273, 289, 411, 414; **52:** 124; **60:** 21, 46
Shakespeare's other histories, compared with **6:** 255, 264, 272, 294, 304, 310, 317, 343, 354, 359; **24:** 320, 325, 330, 331, 332, 333; **28:** 178
Shakespeare's sympathies, question of **6:** 277, 279, 287, 347, 359, 364, 391, 393, 402
Sicilian Usurper (Nahum Tate adaptation) **24:** 260, 261, 262, 263, 386, 390
sources **56:** 2
staging issues **13:** 494; **24:** 273, 274, 278, 279, 280, 283, 291, 295, 296, 301, 303, 304, 310, 315, 317, 320, 325, 333, 338, 346, 351, 352, 356, 364, 383, 386, 395, 402, 405, 411, 414, 419, 423, 428; **25:** 89; **58:** 241
structure **6:** 282, 304, 317, 343, 352, 359, 364, 39; **24:** 307, 322, 325, 356, 395; **58:** 229, 241
succession **60:** 304
textual arrangement **24:** 260, 261, 262, 263, 271, 273, 291, 296, 356, 390
time **22:** 137
treason and punishment **58:** 307
tragic elements **58:** 229
usurpation **6:** 263, 264, 272, 287, 289, 315, 323, 331, 343, 354, 364, 381, 388, 393, 397; **24:** 383; **52:** 108, 141, 154
York **6:** 287, 364, 368, 388, 402, 414; **24:** 263, 320, 322, 364, 395, 414; **39:** 243, 279; **58:** 241

Richard III (Volumes 8, 14, 39, 52, 62)

allegorical elements **52:** 5; **62:** 60
ambivalence and ambiguity **44:** 11; **47:** 15
conscience **8:** 148, 152, 162, 165, 190, 197, 201, 206, 210, 228, 232, 239, 243, 252, 258; **39:** 341; **52:** 5, 196, 205
Elizabethan culture, relation to **62:** 66
Elizabethan politics, relation to **22:** 395; **25:** 141; **37:** 144; **39:** 345, 349; **42:** 132; **52:** 201, 214, 257; **62:** 2
ending **54:** 84
evil **52:** 78
family honor, structure and inheritance **8:** 177, 248, 252, 263, 267; **25:** 141; **39:** 335, 341, 349, 370
flattery **22:** 395
gender issues **25:** 141; **37:** 144; **39:** 345; **52:** 223, 239; **62:** 41
genre **8:** 181, 182, 197, 206, 218, 228, 239, 243, 252, 258; **13:** 142; **39:** 383; **52:** 239; **62:** 2, 41
ghost scene (Act V, scene iii) **8:** 152, 154, 159, 162, 163, 165, 170, 177, 193, 197, 210, 228, 239, 243, 252, 258, 267
Henry VI, relation to **8:** 159, 165, 177, 182, 193, 201, 210, 213, 218, 228, 243, 248, 252, 267; **25:** 164; **39:** 370; **62:** 41
historical accuracy **8:** 144, 145, 153, 159, 163, 165, 168, 213, 223, 228, 232; **39:** 305, 308, 326, 383
historical principles **39:** 308, 326, 387
historiography **56:** 2
language and imagery **8:** 159, 161, 165, 167, 168, 170, 177, 182, 184, 186, 193, 197, 201, 206, 218, 223, 243, 248, 252, 258, 262, 267; **16:** 150; **25:** 141, 245; **39:** 360, 370, 383; **47:** 15; **52:** 285, 290; **62:** 14, 18, 66, 71, 91, 104
Margaret **8:** 153, 154, 159, 162, 163, 170, 193, 201, 206, 210, 218, 223, 228, 243, 248, 262; **39:** 345; **62:** 2, 14, 18, 31, 52, 78
Christopher Marlowe's works, compared with **19:** 233
minor characters **8:** 154, 159, 162, 163, 168, 170, 177, 184, 186, 201, 206, 210, 218, 223, 228, 232, 239, 248, 262, 267
modernization **14:** 523
moral corruption of English society **8:** 154, 163, 165, 177, 193, 201, 218, 228, 232, 243, 248, 252, 267; **39:** 308; **52:** 78, 201
morality **52:** 5, 78
omens **62:** 14, 18
plot and incident **8:** 146, 152, 159; **25:** 164
popularity **8:** 144, 146, 154, 158, 159, 162, 181, 228; **39:** 383
providential order **60:** 304, 322
rebellion **22:** 395
religious, mythic, or spiritual content **62:** 66, 71

religious or theological elements **66:** 286
retribution **8:** 163, 170, 177, 182, 184, 193, 197, 201, 206, 210, 218, 223, 228, 243, 248, 267
Richard III
  ambition **8:** 148, 154, 165, 168, 170, 177, 182, 213, 218, 228, 232, 239, 252, 258, 267; **39:** 308, 341, 360, 370, 383; **52:** 201, 223
  attractive qualities **8:** 145, 148, 152, 154, 159, 161, 162, 165, 168, 170, 181, 182, 184, 185, 197, 201, 206, 213, 228, 243, 252, 258; **16:** 150; **39:** 370, 383; **52:** 272, 280, 285; **62:** 104
  credibility, question of **8:** 145, 147, 154, 159, 165, 193; **13:** 142
  death, decay, and nature's destructiveness **8:** 145, 148, 154, 159, 165, 168, 170, 177, 182, 197, 210, 223, 228, 232, 243, 248, 252, 258, 267
  deformity as symbol **8:** 146, 147, 148, 152, 154, 159, 161, 165, 170, 177, 184, 185, 193, 218, 248, 252, 267; **19:** 164; **62:** 110
  inversion of moral order **8:** 159, 168, 177, 182, 184, 185, 197, 201, 213, 218, 223, 232, 239, 243, 248, 252, 258, 262, 267; **39:** 360; **52:** 205, 214
  as Machiavellian villain **8:** 165, 182, 190, 201, 218, 232, 239, 243, 248; **39:** 308, 326, 360, 387; **52:** 201, 205, 257, 285; **62:** 2, 60, 78, 110
  as monster or symbol of diabolic **8:** 145, 147, 159, 162, 165, 168, 170, 177, 182, 193, 197, 201, 228, 239, 248, 258; **13:** 142; **37:** 144; **39:** 326, 349; **52:** 227, 272; **66:** 286
  other literary villains, compared with **8:** 148, 161, 162, 165, 181, 182, 206, 213, 239, 267
  role-playing, hypocrisy, and dissimulation **8:** 145, 148, 154, 159, 162, 165, 168, 170, 182, 190, 206, 213, 218, 228, 239, 243, 252, 258, 267; **25:** 141, 164, 245; **39:** 335, 341, 387; **52:** 257, 267; **62:** 78
  as scourge or instrument of God **8:** 163, 177, 193, 201, 218, 228, 248, 267; **39:** 308; **62:** 60
  as seducer **52:** 223; **62:** 91, 104
  self-esteem **52:** 196; **62:** 78
  shamelessness **52:** 196
  as Vice figure **8:** 190, 201, 213, 228, 243, 248, 252; **16:** 150; **39:** 383, 387; **52:** 223, 267; **62:** 78
Richmond **8:** 154, 158, 163, 168, 177, 182, 193, 210, 218, 223, 228, 243, 248, 252; **13:** 142; **25:** 141; **39:** 349; **52:** 214, 257, 285; **66:** 286
settings **14:** 516, 528; **52:** 263; **62:** 104
Shakespeare's artistic growth, Richard III's contribution to **8:** 165, 167, 182, 193, 197, 206, 210, 228, 239, 267; **25:** 164; **39:** 305, 326, 370
Shakespeare's political sympathies **8:** 147, 163, 177, 193, 197, 201, 223, 228, 232, 243, 248, 267; **39:** 349; **42:** 132
social order **60:** 322
sources **52:** 263, 290; **56:** 2; **62:** 2, 31, 60, 78
  chronicles **8:** 145, 165, 193, 197, 201, 206, 210, 213, 228, 232
  Marlowe, Christopher **8:** 167, 168, 182, 201, 206, 218
  morality plays **8:** 182, 190, 201, 213, 239
  Seneca, other classical writers **8:** 165, 190, 201, 206, 228, 248; **62:** 31, 60
staging issues **14:** 515, 527, 528, 537; **16:** 137; **52:** 263, 272
structure **8:** 154, 161, 163, 167, 168, 170, 177, 184, 193, 197, 201, 206, 210, 218, 223, 228, 243, 252, 262, 267; **16:** 150; **62:** 14, 18, 91

succession **60:** 304, 322; **65:** 235
time **65:** 248
The Tragical History of King Richard III (Colley Cibber adaptation), compared with **8:** 159, 161, 243
traditional values **39:** 335
Tudor myth **8:** 163, 165, 177, 184, 193, 201, 218, 228, 232, 243, 248, 252, 267; **39:** 305, 308, 326, 387; **42:** 132
Wars of the Roses **8:** 163, 165, 177, 184, 193, 201, 218, 228, 232, 243, 248, 252, 267; **39:** 308; **62:** 71
wooing scenes (Act I, scene ii and Act IV, scene iv) **8:** 145, 147, 152, 153, 154, 159, 161, 164, 170, 190, 197, 206, 213, 218, 223, 232, 239, 243, 252, 258, 267; **16:** 150; **19:** 164; **25:** 141, 164; **39:** 308, 326, 360, 387; **52:** 227, 249, 280; **62:** 31, 78, 91, 110

Romeo and Juliet **(Volumes 5, 11, 33, 51, 65)**

accident or chance **5:** 418, 444, 448, 467, 470, 487, 573
adolescence **33:** 249, 255, 257
amour-passion or Liebestod myth **5:** 484, 489, 528, 530, 542, 550, 575; **32:** 256; **51:** 195, 219, 236; **65:** 214
androgyny **13:** 530
anxiety **13:** 235; **60:** 96
balcony scene **32:** 276; **51:** 219
Caius Marius (Thomas Otway adaptation) **11:** 377, 378, 488, 495
Capulet **65:** 201
comic and tragic elements, combination of **5:** 496, 524, 528, 547, 559; **46:** 78
contradiction, paradox, and opposition **5:** 421, 427, 431, 496, 509, 513, 516, 520, 525, 528, 538; **33:** 287; **44:** 11; **54:** 125; **65:** 208
costuming **11:** 505, 509
courtly love tradition, influence of **5:** 505, 542, 575; **33:**
death **60:** 233
desire **51:** 227, 236
detention of Friar John **5:** 448, 467, 470
divine will, role of **5:** 485, 493, 505, 533, 573
double opening **54:** 6
dramatic shortcomings or failure **5:** 416, 418, 420, 426, 436, 437, 448, 464, 467, 469, 480, 487, 524, 562
Elizabethan poetics, influence of **5:** 416, 520, 522, 528, 550, 559, 575; **65:** 185
ending **54:** 125
evil **5:** 485, 493, 505
as experimental play **5:** 464, 509, 528
fate **5:** 431, 444, 464, 469, 470, 479, 480, 485, 487, 493, 509, 530, 533, 562, 565, 571, 573; **33:** 249; **54:** 125
feud **5:** 415, 419, 425, 447, 458, 464, 469, 479, 480, 493, 509, 522, 556, 565, 566, 571, 575; **25:** 181; **51:** 245; **65:** 201
Friar Lawrence
  contribution to catastrophe **5:** 437, 444, 470; **33:** 300; **51:** 253; **60:** 96
  philosophy of moderation **5:** 427, 431, 437, 438, 443, 444, 445, 458, 467, 479, 505, 538
  as Shakespeare's spokesman **5:** 427, 431, 437, 458, 467
gender issues **32:** 256; **51:** 253; **65:** 119, 142, 190
ideal love **5:** 421, 427, 431, 436, 437, 450, 463, 469, 498, 505, 575; **25:** 257; **33:** 210, 225, 272; **51:** 25, 44, 195, 203, 219
lamentation scene (Act IV, scene v) **5:** 425, 492, 538
language and imagery **5:** 420, 426, 431, 436, 437, 456, 477, 479, 489, 492, 496, 509,

520, 522, 528, 538, 542, 550, 559; **25:** 181, 245, 257; **32:** 276; **33:** 210, 272, 274, 287; **42:** 271; **51:** 203, 212, 227; **65:** 119, 159, 185, 208, 214
love and time **65:** 235
love versus fate **5:** 421, 437, 438, 443, 445, 458; **33:** 249; **54:** 125
love versus friendship **65:** 142
medieval influence **5:** 480, 505, 509, 573
Mercutio
  bawdy **5:** 463, 525, 550, 575
  death, decay, and nature's destructiveness **5:** 415, 418, 419, 547; **33:** 290
  as worldly counterpoint to Romeo **5:** 425, 464, 542; **33:** 290; **51:** 195
  myth of Psyche and Cupid **60:** 96
  relationship with Romeo **65:** 142, 151
Neoclassical rules **5:** 416, 418, 426
Nurse **5:** 419, 425, 463, 464, 575; **33:** 294
Othello, compared with **32:** 302
patriarchy **65:** 119, 190
Petrarchian poetics, influence of **5:** 416, 520, 522, 528, 550, 559, 575; **32:** 276; **51:** 212, 236
prose adaptations of Juliet's character **19:** 261
psychoanalytic interpretation **5:** 513, 556; **51:** 253
public versus private worlds **5:** 520, 550; **25:** 181; **33:** 274
reconciliation **5:** 415, 419, 427, 439, 447, 480, 487, 493, 505, 533, 536, 562
rhetoric **42:** 271; **65:** 119
rival productions **11:** 381, 382, 384, 385, 386, 487
Romeo and Juliet
  characterization **65:** 159
  death-wish **5:** 431, 489, 505, 528, 530, 538, 542, 550, 566, 571, 575; **32:** 212
  first meeting (Act I, scene v) **51:** 212
  immortality **5:** 536
  Juliet's epithalamium speech (Act III, scene ii) **5:** 431, 477, 492
  Juliet's innocence **5:** 421, 423, 450, 454; **33:** 257; **65:** 201
  maturation **5:** 437, 454, 467, 493, 498, 509, 520, 565; **33:** 249, 257; **65:** 159
  rebellion **25:** 257
  reckless passion **5:** 419, 427, 431, 438, 443, 444, 448, 467, 479, 485, 505, 533, 538, 542; **33:** 241
  Romeo's dream (Act V, scene i) **5:** 513, 536, 556; **45:** 40; **51:** 203
  Rosaline, Romeo's relationship with **5:** 419, 423, 425, 427, 438, 498, 542, 575
sexuality **25:** 181; **33:** 225, 233, 241, 246, 274, 300; **51:** 227, 236
source of tragic catastrophe **5:** 418, 427, 431, 448, 458, 469, 479, 480, 485, 487, 493, 509, 522, 528, 530, 533, 542, 550, 566, 571, 573; **33:** 210; **51:** 245
sources **5:** 416, 419, 423, 450; **32:** 222; **33:** 210; **45:** 40; **54:** 125; **65:** 151, 190, 214
staging issues **11:** 499, 505, 507, 514, 517; **13:** 243; **25:** 181; **32:** 212; **65:** 170, 175, 176, 178, 183, 184
structure **5:** 438, 448, 464, 469, 470, 477, 480, 496, 518, 524, 525, 528, 547, 559; **33:** 210, 246; **65:** 119, 185, 208
tomb scene (Act V, scene iii) **5:** 416, 419, 423; **13:** 243; **25:** 181, 245; **51:** 219; **54:** 125
tragic elements **55:** 78; **65:** 151, 190
triumph over death or fate **5:** 421, 423, 427, 505, 509, 520, 530, 536, 565, 566; **51:** 219
Verona society **5:** 556, 566; **13:** 235; **33:** 255; **51:** 245
wordplay **32:** 256

Sonnets (Volumes 10, 40, 51, 62)

    ambiguity **10:** 251, 256; **28:** 385; **40:** 221, 228, 268
    audience **51:** 316
    authenticity **10:** 153, 154, 230, 243; **48:** 325; **62:** 128
    autobiographical elements **10:** 159, 160, 166, 167, 175, 176, 182, 196, 205, 213, 215, 226, 233, 238, 240, 251, 279, 283, 302, 309, 325, 337, 377; **13:** 487; **16:** 461; **28:** 363, 385; **42:** 303; **48:** 325
    beauty **10:** 247; **51:** 288
    Christian elements **10:** 191, 256
    composition date **10:** 153, 154, 161, 166, 196, 217, 226, 270, 277; **28:** 363, 385
    Dark Lady **10:** 161, 167, 176, 216, 217, 218, 226, 240, 302, 342, 377, 394; **25:** 374; **37:** 374; **40:** 273; **48:** 346; **51:** 284, 288, 292, 321; **62:** 121
    deception, disguise, and duplicity **25:** 374; **40:** 221
    dramatic elements **10:** 155, 182, 240, 251, 283, 367
    editorial and textual issues **28:** 363; **40:** 273; **42:** 303
    Elizabeth, audience of **48:** 325
    the Friend **10:** 279, 302, 309, 379, 385, 391, 394; **51:** 284, 288, 292, 300, 304, 316, 321; **62:** 121; **65:** 259, 345
    friendship **10:** 185, 279; **28:** 380; **51:** 284
    gender issues **37:** 374; **40:** 238, 247, 254, 264, 268, 273; **53:** 1
    homoerotic elements **10:** 155, 156, 159, 161, 175, 213, 391; **16:** 461; **28:** 363, 380; **37:** 347; **40:** 254, 264, 273; **51:** 270, 284; **62:** 128
    homosexuality **60:** 105
    identities of persons **10:** 154, 155, 156, 161, 166, 167, 169, 173, 174, 175, 185, 190, 191, 196, 218, 226, 230, 233, 240; **40:** 238; **62:** 128
    Ireland, William Henry, forgeries of **48:** 325
    irony or satire **10:** 256, 293, 334, 337, 346; **51:** 300
    Italian influences **28:** 407; **62:** 121, 146
    language and imagery **10:** 247, 251, 255, 256, 290, 353, 372, 385; **13:** 445; **28:** 380, 385; **32:** 327, 352; **40:** 228, 247, 284, 292, 303; **51:** 270, 304; **62:** 153, 159, 170, 180, 196; **65:** 259, 277
    love **10:** 173, 247, 287, 290, 293, 302, 309, 322, 325, 329, 394; **28:** 380; **37:** 347; **51:** 270, 284, 288, 292; **62:** 153, 170; **65:** 277
    love versus reason **10:** 329
    A Lover's Complaint (the Rival Poet) **10:** 243, 353
        gender issues **48:** 336
        pastoral tradition, compared with **48:** 336
        sonnets, compared with **48:** 336
    lust **51:** 292; **65:** 277
    lust versus reason **51:** 288
    magic **48:** 346
    Mr. W. H. **10:** 153, 155, 161, 169, 174, 182, 190, 196, 217, 218, 377
    Montaigne's Essais, relation to **42:** 382
    mutability, theme of **42:** 382
    Neoplatonism **10:** 191, 205
    occult **48:** 346
    other sonnet writers, Shakespeare compared with **10:** 247, 260, 265, 283, 290, 293, 309, 353, 367; **28:** 380, 385, 407; **37:** 374; **40:** 247, 264, 303; **42:** 303
    pedagogy **37:** 374
    performative issues **48:** 352; **62:** 159
    poet-patron relationship **48:** 352; **62:** 128
    poetic style **10:** 153, 155, 156, 158, 159, 160, 161, 173, 175, 182, 214, 247, 251, 255, 260, 265, 283, 287, 296, 302, 315, 322, 325, 337, 346, 349, 360, 367, 385; **16:** 472; **40:** 221, 228; **51:** 270
    procreation **10:** 379, 385; **16:** 461
    race **53:** 1
    rhetoric of consolation **42:** 382
    the Rival Poet **10:** 169, 233, 334, 337, 385; **48:** 352
    self-love **10:** 372; **25:** 374; **51:** 270, 300, 304; **62:** 180
    selfishness versus self-knowledge **51:** 292
    sexuality **25:** 374; **62:** 153
    as social action **48:** 352; **62:** 159
    sonnet arrangement **10:** 174, 176, 182, 205, 226, 230, 236, 315, 353; **28:** 363; **40:** 238; **62:** 121, 128
    sonnet form **10:** 255, 325, 367; **37:** 347; **40:** 284, 303; **51:** 270
    sonnets (individual):
        3 **10:** 346
        12 **10:** 360
        15 **40:** 292
        18 **40:** 292
        20 **10:** 391; **13:** 530; **60:** 105
        21 **32:** 352
        26 **10:** 161
        30 **10:** 296
        35 **10:** 251
        49 **10:** 296
        53 **10:** 349; **32:** 327, 352
        54 **32:** 352
        55 **13:** 445
        57 **10:** 296
        59 **16:** 472
        60 **10:** 296; **16:** 472
        64 **10:** 329, 360
        65 **10:** 296; **40:** 292
        66 **10:** 315
        68 **32:** 327
        71 **10:** 167
        73 **10:** 315, 353, 360
        76 **10:** 334
        79 **32:** 352
        82 **32:** 352
        86 **32:** 352
        87 **10:** 296; **40:** 303
        93 **13:** 487
        94 **10:** 256, 296; **32:** 327
        95 **32:** 327
        98 **32:** 352
        99 **32:** 352
        104 **10:** 360
        105 **32:** 327
        107 **10:** 270, 277
        116 **10:** 329, 379; **13:** 445
        117 **10:** 337
        119 **10:** 337
        121 **10:** 346
        123 **10:** 270
        124 **10:** 265, 270, 329
        126 **10:** 161
        129 **10:** 353, 394; **22:** 12
        130 **10:** 346
        138 **10:** 296
        144 **10:** 394
        145 **10:** 358; **40:** 254
        146 **10:** 353
    sonnets (groups):
        1-17 **10:** 296, 315, 379, 385; **16:** 461; **40:** 228; **62:** 170
        1-21 **10:** 176; **40:** 268
        1-126 **10:** 161, 176, 185, 191, 196, 205, 213, 226, 236, 279, 309, 315, 372; **62:** 180, 196; **65:** 259, 345
        18-22 **10:** 315
        18-126 **10:** 379
        23-40 **10:** 315
        27-55 **10:** 176
        33-9 **10:** 329
        56-77 **10:** 176
        76-86 **10:** 315
        78-80 **10:** 334, 385
        78-101 **10:** 176
        82-6 **10:** 334
        100-12 **10:** 337
        102-26 **10:** 176
        123-25 **10:** 385
        127-52 **10:** 293, 385
        127-54 **10:** 161, 176, 185, 190, 196, 213, 226, 236, 309, 315, 342, 394
        151-52 **10:** 315
    sources **10:** 153, 154, 156, 158, 233, 251, 255, 293, 353; **16:** 472; **28:** 407; **42:** 382; **62:** 121, 146
    structure **10:** 175, 176, 182, 205, 230, 260, 296, 302, 309, 315, 337, 349, 353; **40:** 238; **62:** 146
    subjectivity **37:** 374
    time **10:** 265, 302, 309, 322, 329, 337, 360, 379; **13:** 445; **40:** 292; **65:** 235, 259, 277, 345
    visual arts, relation to **28:** 407
    voice **51:** 316
        apparent inconsistencies in **51:** 321

The Taming of the Shrew (Volumes 9, 12, 31, 55, 64)

    appearance versus reality **9:** 343, 350, 353, 365, 369, 370, 381, 390. 430; **12:** 416; **31:** 326; **55:** 278, 299, 334
    Baptista **9:** 325, 344, 345, 375, 386, 393, 413; **55:** 334
    Bianca **9:** 325, 342, 344, 345, 360, 362, 370, 375
    Bianca-Lucentio subplot **9:** 365, 370, 375, 390, 393, 401, 407, 413, 430; **16:** 13; **31:** 339; **64:** 255
    Catherine and Petruchio (David Garrick adaptation) **12:** 309, 310, 311, 416
    class distinctions, conflict, and relations **31:** 300, 351; **50:** 64, 74; **55:** 342
    deception, disguise, and duplicity **12:** 416
    Elizabethan culture, relation to **31:** 288, 295, 300, 315, 326, 345, 351; **55:** 315, 322, 334; **64:** 296, 327, 333, 343
    ending **54:** 58, 65; **64:** 244, 296, 327
    as farce **9:** 330, 337, 338, 341, 342, 365, 381, 386, 413, 426; **55:** 357; **64:** 233
    folk elements **9:** 381, 393, 404, 426
    gender issues **28:** 24; **31:** 261, 268, 276, 282, 288, 295, 300, 335, 351; **55:** 278, 299, 305, 315, 322, 357; **64:** 320, 327, 333, 343, 352
    genre **9:** 329, 334, 362, 375; **22:** 48; **31:** 261, 269, 276; **55:** 278; **64:** 239
    induction **9:** 320, 322, 332, 337, 345, 350, 362, 365, 369, 370, 381, 390, 393, 407, 419, 424, 430; **12:** 416, 427, 430, 431, 441; **19:** 34, 122; **22:** 48; **31:** 269, 315, 351; **55:** 331, 357; **64:** 244, 255, 343
    irony or satire **9:** 340, 375, 398, 407, 413; **13:** 3; **19:** 122; **55:** 278, 299, 322
    Kate
        characterization **32:** 1; **64:** 244, 296, 343, 352
        final speech (Act V, scene ii) **9:** 318, 319, 329, 330, 338, 340, 341, 345, 347, 353, 355, 360, 365, 381, 386, 401, 404, 413, 426, 430; **19:** 3; **22:** 48; **55:** 299, 331; **64:** 296
        love for Petruchio **9:** 338, 340, 353, 430; **12:** 435; **55:** 294
        portrayals of **31:** 282
        shrewishness **9:** 322, 323, 325, 332, 344, 345, 360, 365, 370, 375, 386, 393, 398, 404, 413; **64:** 283
        transformation **9:** 323, 341, 355, 370, 386, 393, 401, 404, 407, 419, 424, 426, 430; **16:** 13; **19:** 34; **22:** 48; **31:** 288, 295, 339, 351; **55:** 294, 315; **64:** 233, 244, 273, 283, 320
    Kiss Me, Kate (Cole Porter adaptation) **31:** 282

language and imagery **9:** 336, 338, 393, 401, 404, 407, 413; **22:** 378; **28:** 9; **31:** 261, 288, 300, 326, 335, 339; **32:** 56; **64:** 273, 296, 352
Lucentio **9:** 325, 342, 362, 375, 393
marriage **9:** 322, 325, 329, 332, 329, 332, 334, 341, 342, 343, 344, 345, 347, 353, 360, 362, 375, 381, 390, 398, 401, 404, 413, 426, 430; **13:** 3; **19:** 3; **28:** 24; **31:** 288; **51:** 44; **55:** 315, 331; **64:** 239, 320
metadramatic elements **9:** 350, 419, 424; **31:** 300, 315
metamorphosis or transformation **9:** 370, 430
mythic or mythological elements **60:** 281
Ovid' Metamorphoses, relation to **60:** 281
pedagogy **19:** 122
performance history **31:** 282; **55:** 357
performance issues **12:** 313, 314, 316, 317, 337, 338; **31:** 315; **55:** 357
Petruchio
  admirable qualities **9:** 320, 332, 341, 344, 345, 370, 375, 386; **55:** 294; **64:** 266
  audacity or vigor **9:** 325, 337, 355, 375, 386, 404
  characterization **32:** 1
  coarseness or brutality **9:** 325, 329, 365, 390, 393, 398, 407; **19:** 122; **64:** 283
  as lord of misrule **9:** 393; **50:** 64; **55:** 322
  love for Kate **9:** 338, 340, 343, 344, 386; **12:** 435
  portrayals of **31:** 282
  pragmatism **9:** 329, 334, 375, 398, 424; **13:** 3; **31:** 345, 351
  as rhetorician **64:** 273, 296
  taming method **9:** 320, 323, 329, 340, 341, 343, 345, 355, 369, 370, 375, 390, 398, 407, 413, 419, 424; **19:** 3, 12, 21; **31:** 269, 295, 326, 335, 339; **55:** 334; **64:** 233, 239, 266, 273, 283, 333, 352
popularity **9:** 318, 338, 404
role-playing **9:** 322, 353, 355, 360, 369, 370, 398, 401, 407, 413, 419, 424; **13:** 3; **31:** 288, 295, 315; **64:** 239, 320
romantic elements **9:** 334, 342, 362, 375, 407
Shakespeare's other plays, compared with **9:** 334, 342, 360, 393, 426, 430; **31:** 261; **50:** 74; **55:** 331
Sly **9:** 320, 322, 350, 370, 381, 390, 398, 430; **12:** 316, 335, 416, 427, 441; **16:** 13; **19:** 34, 122; **22:** 48; **37:** 31; **50:** 74; **64:** 244, 343, 352
sources **60:** 281
  Ariosto **9:** 320, 334, 341, 342, 370; **64:** 255
  folk tales **9:** 332, 390, 393; **64:** 283
  Gascoigne **9:** 370, 390
  Old and New Comedy **9:** 419; **64:** 255
  Ovid **9:** 318, 370, 430
  Plautus **9:** 334, 341, 342
  shrew tradition **9:** 355; **19:** 3; **32:** 1, 56; **55:** 342; **64:** 283
staging issues **64:** 313, 317, 318, 319
structure **9:** 318, 322, 325, 332, 334, 341, 362, 370, 390, 426; **22:** 48, 378; **31:** 269; **55:** 278, 342, 371; **64:** 244, 255
play-within-a-play **12:** 416; **22:** 48
The Taming of a Shrew (anonymous), compared with **9:** 334, 350, 426; **12:** 312; **22:** 48; **31:** 261, 276, 339; **55:** 305, 371
text and sources **55:** 334, 357
textual issues **22:** 48; **31:** 261, 276; **31:** 276; **55:** 342, 371
violence **43:** 61; **55:** 322; **64:** 320

The Tempest (Volumes 8, 15, 29, 45, 61)

allegorical elements **8:** 294, 295, 302, 307, 308, 312, 326, 328, 336, 345, 364; **42:** 327; **61:** 326

Antonio and Sebastian **8:** 295, 299, 304, 328, 370, 396, 429, 454; **13:** 440; **29:** 278, 297, 343, 362, 368, 377; **61:** 338
Ariel **8:** 289, 293, 294, 295, 297, 304, 307, 315, 320, 326, 328, 336, 340, 345, 356, 364, 420, 458; **22:** 302; **29:** 278, 297, 362, 368, 377
art versus nature **8:** 396, 404; **29:** 278, 297, 362; **61:** 356
autobiographical elements **8:** 302, 308, 312, 324, 326, 345, 348, 353, 364, 380; **61:** 272
beginning **54:** 19
Caliban **8:** 286, 287, 289, 292, 294, 295, 297, 302, 304, 307, 309, 315, 326, 328, 336, 353, 364, 370, 380, 390, 396, 401, 414, 420, 423, 429, 435, 454; **13:** 424, 440; **15:** 189, 312, 322, 374, 379; **22:** 302; **25:** 382; **28:** 249; **29:** 278, 292, 297, 343, 368, 377, 396; **32:** 367; **45:** 211, 219, 226, 259; **53:** 45, 64; **61:** 307, 356, 362
characterization **8:** 287, 289, 292, 294, 295, 308, 326, 334, 336; **28:** 415; **42:** 339; **45:** 219; **65:** 311
classical influence and sources **29:** 278, 343, 362, 368; **61:** 362
colonialism **13:** 424, 440; **15:** 228, 268, 269, 270, 271, 272, 273; **19:** 421; **25:** 357, 382; **28:** 249; **29:** 343, 368; **32:** 338, 367, 400; **42:** 327; **45:** 200, 280; **53:** 11, 21, 45, 67; **61:** 297, 307
compassion, theme of **42:** 346
conspiracy or treason **16:** 426; **19:** 357; **25:** 382; **29:** 377
dreams **45:** 236, 247, 259
education or nurturing **8:** 353, 370, 384, 396; **29:** 292, 368, 377
exposition scene (Act I, scene ii) **8:** 287, 289, 293, 299, 334
Ferdinand **8:** 328, 336, 359, 454; **19:** 357; **22:** 302; **29:** 362, 339, 377
freedom and servitude **8:** 304, 307, 312, 429; **22:** 302; **29:** 278, 368, 377; **37:** 336
gender **53:** 64, 67
Gonzalo **22:** 302; **29:** 278, 343, 362, 368
Gonzalo's commonwealth **8:** 312, 336, 370, 390, 396, 404; **19:** 357; **29:** 368; **45:** 280
good versus evil **8:** 302, 311, 315, 370, 423, 439; **29:** 278, 297; **61:** 338, 362
historical content **8:** 364, 408, 420; **16:** 426; **25:** 382; **29:** 278, 343, 368; **45:** 226; **53:** 21, 53; **61:** 297
the island **8:** 308, 315, 447; **25:** 357, 382; **29:** 278, 343
language and imagery **8:** 324, 348, 384, 390, 404, 454; **19:** 421; **29:** 278; **29:** 297, 343, 368, 377; **61:** 280, 288
love **8:** 435, 439; **29:** 297, 339, 377, 396
magic or supernatural elements **8:** 287, 293, 304, 315, 340, 356, 396, 401, 404, 408, 435, 458; **28:** 391, 415; **29:** 297, 343, 377; **45:** 272; **61:** 272, 356
the masque (Act IV, scene i) **8:** 404, 414, 423, 435, 439; **25:** 357; **28:** 391, 415; **29:** 278, 292, 339, 343, 368; **42:** 339; **45:** 188
Miranda **8:** 289, 301, 304, 328, 336, 370, 454; **19:** 357; **22:** 302; **28:** 249; **29:** 278, 297, 362, 368, 377, 396; **53:** 64
Montaigne's Essais, relation to **42:** 346
morality **52:** 43; **61:** 338
music **8:** 390, 404; **29:** 292; **37:** 321; **42:** 339; **61:** 315
nature **8:** 315, 370, 390, 408, 414; **29:** 343, 362, 368, 377; **61:** 362
Neoclassical rules **8:** 287, 292, 293, 334; **25:** 357; **29:** 292; **45:** 200

politics **8:** 304, 307, 315, 353, 359, 364, 401, 408; **16:** 426; **19:** 421; **29:** 339; **37:** 336; **42:** 327; **45:** 272, 280; **52:** 43; **61:** 315
Prospero
  characterization **8:** 312, 348, 370, 458; **16:** 442; **22:** 302; **45:** 188, 272; **61:** 307
  as God or Providence **8:** 311, 328, 364, 380, 429, 435
  magic, nature of **8:** 301, 340, 356, 396, 414, 423, 458; **25:** 382; **28:** 391; **29:** 278, 292, 368, 377, 396; **32:** 338, 343; **61:** 272
  psychoanalytic interpretation **45:** 259
  redemptive powers **8:** 302, 320, 353, 370, 390, 429, 439, 447; **29:** 297; **61:** 326, 338
  as ruler **8:** 304, 308, 309, 420, 423; **13:** 424; **22:** 302; **29:** 278, 362, 377, 396; **61:** 315
  self-control **8:** 312, 414, 420; **22:** 302; **44:** 11
  self-knowledge **16:** 442; **22:** 302; **29:** 278, 292, 362, 377, 396
  as Shakespeare or creative artist **8:** 299, 302, 308, 312, 320, 324, 353, 364, 435, 447; **61:** 280, 288
  as tragic hero **8:** 359, 370, 464; **29:** 292
providential order **52:** 43
race **53:** 11, 21, 45, 53, 64, 67
realism **8:** 340, 359, 464
reality and illusion **8:** 287, 315, 359, 401, 435, 439, 447, 454; **22:** 302; **45:** 236, 247
reconciliation **8:** 302, 312, 320, 334, 348, 359, 370, 384, 401, 404, 414, 429, 439, 447, 454; **16:** 442; **22:** 302; **29:** 297; **37:** 336; **45:** 236
religious, mythic, or spiritual content **8:** 328, 390, 423, 429, 435; **45:** 211, 247; **61:** 280
romance or pastoral tradition, influence of **8:** 336, 348, 396, 404; **37:** 336
sexuality **53:** 45; **61:** 288
Shakespeare's other plays, compared with **8:** 294, 302, 324, 326, 348, 353, 380, 401, 464; **13:** 424
spectacle versus simple staging **15:** 206, 207, 208, 210, 217, 219, 222, 223, 224, 225, 227, 228, 305, 352; **28:** 415
sources **45:** 226; **61:** 326
staging issues **15:** 343, 346, 352, 361, 364, 366, 368, 371, 385; **28:** 391, 415; **29:** 339; **32:** 338, 343; **42:** 339; **45:** 200; **54:** 19; **61:** 297
Stephano and Trinculo, comic subplot of **8:** 292, 297, 299, 304, 309, 324, 328, 353, 370; **25:** 382; **29:** 377; **46:** 14, 33
structure **8:** 294, 295, 299, 320, 384, 439; **28:** 391, 415; **29:** 292, 297; **45:** 188; **65:** 264
subversiveness **22:** 302
The Tempest; or, The Enchanted Island (William Davenant/John Dryden adaptation) **15:** 189, 190, 192, 193
The Tempest; or, The Enchanted Island (Thomas Shadwell adaptation) **15:** 195, 196, 199
time **8:** 401, 439, 464; **25:** 357; **29:** 278, 292; **45:** 236; **65:** 235, 264, 311
tragic elements **8:** 324, 348, 359, 370, 380, 408, 414, 439, 458, 464
trickster, motif of **22:** 302; **29:** 297
usurpation or rebellion **8:** 304, 370, 408, 420; **25:** 357, 382; **29:** 278, 362, 377; **37:** 336
utopia **45:** 280

Timon of Athens (Volumes 1, 20, 27, 52)

Alcibiades **25:** 198; **27:** 191

alienation **1**: 523; **27**: 161
Apemantus **1**: 453, 467, 483; **20**: 476, 493; **25**: 198; **27**: 166, 223, 235
appearance versus reality **1**: 495, 500, 515, 523; **52**: 311, 329
Athens **27**: 223, 230
authorship controversy **1**: 464, 466, 467, 469, 474, 477, 478, 480, 490, 499, 507, 518; **16**: 351; **20**: 433
autobiographical elements **1**: 462, 467, 470, 473, 474, 478, 480; **27**: 166, 175
Elizabethan culture, relation to **1**: 487, 489, 495, 500; **20**: 433; **27**: 203, 212, 230; **50**: 13; **52**: 320, 354
as inferior or flawed play **1**: 476, 481, 489, 499, 520; **20**: 433, 439, 491; **25**: 198; **27**: 157, 175; **52**: 338, 349
genre **1**: 454, 456, 459, 460, 462, 483, 492, 499, 503, 509, 511, 512, 515, 518, 525, 531; **27**: 203
King Lear, relation to **1**: 453, 459, 511; **16**: 351; **27**: 161; **37**: 222
language and imagery **1**: 488; **13**: 392; **25**: 198; **27**: 166, 184, 235; **52**: 329, 345, 354
language and philosophy **52**: 311
as medieval allegory or morality play **1**: 492, 511, 518; **27**: 155
mixture of genres **16**: 351; **25**: 198
nihilistic elements **1**: 481, 513, 529; **13**: 392; **20**: 481
pessimistic elements **1**: 462, 467, 470, 473, 478, 480; **20**: 433, 481; **27**: 155, 191
Poet and Painter **25**: 198; **52**: 320
politics **27**: 223, 230; **50**: 13
religious, mythic, or spiritual content **1**: 505, 512, 513, 523; **20**: 493
satirical elements **27**: 155, 235
self-knowledge **1**: 456, 459, 462, 495, 503, 507, 515, 518, 526; **20**: 493; **27**: 166
Senecan elements **27**: 235
Shakespeare's other tragedies, compared with **27**: 166; **52**: 296
sources **16**: 351; **27**: 191; **52**: 301
staging issues **20**: 445, 446, 481, 491, 492, 493
structure **27**: 191; **52**: 338, 345, 349
Timon
  comic traits **25**: 198
  death of **60**: 46
  as flawed hero **1**: 456, 459, 462, 472, 495, 503, 507, 515; **16**: 351; **20**: 429, 433, 476; **25**: 198; **27**: 157, 161
  misanthropy **13**: 392; **20**: 431, 464, 476, 481, 491, 492, 493; **27**: 161, 175, 184, 196; **37**: 222; **52**: 296, 301
  as noble figure **1**: 467, 473, 483, 499; **20**: 493; **27**: 212
wealth and social class **1**: 466, 487, 495; **25**: 198; **27**: 184, 196, 212; **50**: 13

Titus Andronicus (Volumes 4, 17, 27, 43, 62)

Aaron **4**: 632, 637, 650, 651, 653, 668, 672, 675; **27**: 255; **28**: 249, 330; **43**: 176; **53**: 86, 92
amputations, significance of **48**: 264
authorship controversy **4**: 613, 614, 615, 616, 617, 619, 623, 624, 625, 626, 628, 631, 632, 635, 642; **62**: 208, 254
autobiographical elements **4**: 619, 624, 625, 664
banquet scene **25**: 245; **27**: 255; **32**: 212
ceremonies, rites, and rituals, importance of **27**: 261; **32**: 265; **48**: 264; **62**: 254
characterization **4**: 613, 628, 632, 635, 640, 644, 647, 650, 675; **27**: 293; **43**: 170, 176
Christian elements **4**: 656, 680
civilization versus barbarism **4**: 653; **27**: 293; **28**: 249; **32**: 265; **62**: 265, 270

colonialism **62**: 270
Clarissa (Samuel Richardson), compared with **48**: 277
Elizabethan culture, relation to **27**: 282; **62**: 233, 270
Euripides, influence of **27**: 285
evil **53**: 86, 92
gender issues **62**: 242
language and imagery **4**: 617, 624, 635, 642, 644, 646, 659, 664, 668, 672, 675; **13**: 225; **16**: 225; **25**: 245; **27**: 246, 293, 313, 318, 325; **43**: 186, 222, 227, 239, 247, 262; **62**: 225, 254
language versus action **4**: 642, 644, 647, 664, 668; **13**: 225; **27**: 293, 313, 325; **43**: 186; **62**: 225
Lavinia **27**: 266; **28**: 249; **32**: 212; **43**: 170, 239, 247, 255, 262; **62**: 225, 233, 242
marriage as political tyranny **48**: 264
medieval literary influence **4**: 646, 650; **27**: 299
mythic or mythological elements **60**: 276
order versus disintegration **4**: 618, 647; **43**: 186, 195
Ovid, influence of **4**: 647, 659, 664, 668; **13**: 225; **27**: 246, 275, 285, 293, 299, 306; **28**: 249; **43**: 195, 203, 206
Ovid' Metamorphoses, relation to **60**: 276
patriarchy **50**: 13
political content **43**: 262
politics **27**: 282; **48**: 264
primogeniture **50**: 13
race **53**: 86, 92
rape **43**: 227, 255; **48**: 277
revenge **60**: 276
rightful succession **4**: 638
Roman elements **43**: 206, 222; **62**: 277, 284
Romans versus Goths **27**: 282; **62**: 265, 270
sacrifice **62**: 258, 265
Senecan or revenge tragedy elements **4**: 618, 627, 628, 636, 639, 644, 646, 664, 672, 680; **16**: 225; **27**: 275, 318; **43**: 170, 206, 227; **62**: 208, 258
Shakespeare's canon, place in **4**: 614, 616, 618, 619, 637, 639, 646, 659, 664, 668; **43**: 195
Shakespeare's other tragedies, compared with **16**: 225; **27**: 275, 325
sources **62**: 208, 277, 284
spectacle **62**: 277
staging issues **17**: 449, 452, 456, 487; **25**: 245; **32**: 212, 249
structure **4**: 618, 619, 624, 631, 635, 640, 644, 646, 647, 653, 656, 659, 662, 664, 668, 672; **27**: 246, 285; **60**: 276
style **62**: 254
Tamora **4**: 632, 662, 672, 675; **27**: 266; **43**: 170; **62**: 233
Titus **4**: 632, 637, 640, 644, 647, 653, 656, 662; **25**: 245; **27**: 255; **62**: 258
Vergil, influence of **27**: 306; **28**: 249
violence **13**: 225; **25**: 245; **27**: 255; **28**: 249; **32**: 249, 265; **43**: 1, 186, 203, 227, 239, 247, 255, 262; **62**: 208, 225, 233, 242, 254, 258, 265

Troilus and Cressida (Volumes 3, 18, 27, 43, 59)

Achilles and Patroclus, relationship between **60**: 105
allegorical elements **52**: 5
ambiguity **3**: 544, 568, 583, 587, 589, 599, 611, 621; **27**: 400; **43**: 365
ambivalence **43**: 340; **59**: 287
assignation scene (Act V, scene ii) **18**: 442, 451
autobiographical elements **3**: 548, 554, 557, 558, 574, 606, 630
body, role of **42**: 66; **59**: 225, 287, 306

characterization **3**: 538, 539, 540, 541, 548, 566, 571, 604, 611, 621; **27**: 381, 391; **59**: 234, 245, 251, 257, 261, 265, 272; **65**: 290
Chaucer's Criseyde, compared with **43**: 305
chivalry, decline of **16**: 84; **27**: 370, 374
communication, failure of **43**: 277
conclusion **3**: 538, 549, 558, 566, 574, 583, 594
comedy vs. tragedy **43**: 351; **59**: 278
contradictions **43**: 377; **59**: 318
costumes **18**: 289, 371, 406, 419; **59**: 323
courtly love **22**: 58; **59**: 349
Cressida
  as ambiguous figure **43**: 305
  inconsistency **3**: 538; **13**: 53; **16**: 70; **22**: 339; **27**: 362
  individual will versus social values **3**: 549, 561, 571, 590, 604, 617, 626; **13**: 53; **27**: 396; **59**: 234, 272
  infidelity **3**: 536, 537, 544, 554, 555; **18**: 277, 284, 286; **22**: 58, 339; **27**: 400; **43**: 298
  lack of punishment **3**: 536, 537
  as mother figure **22**: 339
  objectification of **43**: 329; **59**: 323; **65**: 290
  as sympathetic figure **3**: 557, 560, 604, 609; **18**: 284, 423; **22**: 58; **27**: 396, 400; **43**: 305; **59**: 234, 245
  as a Trojan **59**: 257
cynicism **43**: 298
desire **43**: 317, 329, 340; **59**: 337
disillusioned or cynical tone **3**: 544, 548, 554, 557, 558, 571, 574, 630, 642; **18**: 284, 332, 403, 406, 423; **27**: 376; **59**: 234
disorder **3**: 578, 589, 599, 604, 609; **18**: 332, 406, 412, 423; **27**: 366; **54**: 84; **55**: 48; **59**: 251; **65**: 226
double plot **3**: 569, 613
Elizabeth I
  waning power **43**: 365
Elizabethan culture, relation to **3**: 560, 574, 606; **25**: 56
ending **54**: 84; **59**: 225, 295, 306
feminist criticism **55**: 37, 48; **59**: 337
food imagery **43**: 298; **59**: 306
genre **3**: 541, 542, 549, 558, 566, 571, 574, 587, 594, 604, 630, 642; **27**: 366; **59**: 278
Greece **43**: 287
Hector
  combat with Ajax **59**: 251
  as a Trojan **59**: 257
homosexuality **60**: 105
inaction **3**: 587, 621; **27**: 347
infidelity **55**: 37, 48; **59**: 251
language and imagery **3**: 561, 569, 596, 599, 606, 624, 630, 635; **22**: 58, 339; **27**: 332, 366; **42**: 66; **59**: 287, 295, 306, 318
love and honor **3**: 555, 604; **27**: 370, 374; **59**: 251, 257, 337
love versus war **18**: 332, 371, 406, 423; **22**: 339; **27**: 376; **43**: 377; **59**: 234, 251, 257
male/female relationships **16**: 70; **22**: 339; **27**: 362; **59**: 349
marriage **22**: 339; **51**: 44
master-slave relationship **22**: 58; **59**: 265
medieval chivalry **3**: 539, 543, 544, 555, 606; **27**: 376; **59**: 349
mimetic rivalry **60**: 172
moral corruption **3**: 578, 589, 599, 604, 609; **18**: 332, 406, 412, 423; **27**: 366; **43**: 298; **54**: 84; **59**: 261, 265
morality **52**: 5; **59**: 251, 257
mythic or mythological elements **60**: 172
Neoclassical rules **3**: 537, 538; **18**: 276, 278, 281
nihilistic elements **27**: 354
Pandarus **59**: 245
patriarchy **22**: 58; **59**: 272, 337, 349

politics **3:** 536, 560, 606; **16:** 84; **59:** 225, 318
  as "problem play" **3:** 555, 566
  lack of resolution **43:** 277; **59:** 278
psychoanalytical criticism **43:** 287; **59:** 349
rape **43:** 357
satirical elements **3:** 539, 543, 544, 555, 558, 574; **27:** 341
sexuality **22:** 58, 339; **25:** 56; **27:** 362; **43:** 365; **59:** 323, 337, 349
sources **3:** 537, 539, 540, 541, 544, 549, 558, 566, 574, 587; **27:** 376, 381, 391, 400
staging issues **16:** 70; **18:** 289, 332, 371, 395, 403, 406, 412, 419, 423, 442, 447, 451; **59:** 225, 323
structure **3:** 536, 538, 549, 568, 569, 578, 583, 589, 611, 613; **27:** 341, 347, 354, 391
Thersites **13:** 53; **25:** 56; **27:** 381; **59:** 265
time **3:** 561, 571, 583, 584, 613, 621, 626, 634; **65:** 226, 290
Troilus
  contradictory behavior **3:** 596, 602, 635; **27:** 362
  Cressida, relationship with **3:** 594, 596, 606; **22:** 58; **59:** 245, 261
  integrity **3:** 617
  opposition to Ulysses **3:** 561, 584, 590
  as a Trojan **59:** 257
  as unsympathetic figure **18:** 423; **22:** 58, 339; **43:** 317; **59:** 261
  as warrior **3:** 596; **22:** 339
Troilus and Cressida, or Truth Found too late (John Dryden adaptation) **18:** 276, 277, 278, 280, 281, 283
Trojan versus Greek values **3:** 541, 561, 574, 584, 590, 596, 621, 638; **27:** 370
Trojan War
  as myth **43:** 293
Troy **43:** 287
Ulysses **59:** 245
Ulysses's speech on degree (Act I, scene iii) **3:** 549, 599, 609, 642; **27:** 396
value systems **3:** 578, 583, 589, 602, 613, 617; **13:** 53; **27:** 370, 396, 400; **59:** 234, 245, 287, 295, 318
violence **43:** 329, 351, 357, 365, 377
  through satire **43:** 293

Twelfth Night (Volumes 1, 26, 34, 46, 62)

androgyny **60:** 129
ambiguity **1:** 554, 639; **34:** 287, 316
Antonio **22:** 69; **60:** 115
appetite **1:** 563, 596, 609, 615; **52:** 57
autobiographical elements **1:** 557, 561, 599; **34:** 338
bear-baiting **19:** 42
beginning **54:** 19
characterization **1:** 539, 540, 543, 545, 550, 554, 581, 594; **26:** 257, 337, 342, 346, 364, 366, 371, 374; **34:** 281, 293, 311, 338; **46:** 286, 324
Christian elements **46:** 338; **66:** 312
comic elements **26:** 233, 257, 337, 342, 371; **51:** 1; **52:** 57
composition date **37:** 78
credibility **1:** 540, 542, 543, 554, 562, 581, 587
cross-dressing **62:** 297, 319
dark or tragic elements **46:** 310
desire **60:** 115, 129
Elizabethan culture, relation to **1:** 549, 553, 555, 563, 581, 587, 620; **16:** 53; **19:** 42, 78; **26:** 357; **28:** 1; **34:** 323, 330; **46:** 291; **51:** 15; **62:** 319, 348
ending **62:** 308
ethical or moral issues **52:** 57
fancy **1:** 543, 546
Feste
  characterization **1:** 558, 655, 658; **26:** 233, 364; **46:** 1, 14, 18, 33, 52, 60, 303, 310
  role in play **1:** 546, 551, 553, 566, 570, 571, 579, 635, 658; **46:** 297, 303, 310
  song **1:** 543, 548, 561, 563, 566, 570, 572, 603, 620, 642; **46:** 297
festive or folklore elements **46:** 338; **51:** 15
gender issues **19:** 78; **34:** 344; **37:** 59; **42:** 32; **46:** 347, 362, 369; **60:** 129; **62:** 297, 319, 325
homosexuality **22:** 69; **42:** 32; **46:** 362; **60:** 115, 129
language and imagery **1:** 570, 650, 664; **22:** 12; **28:** 9; **34:** 293; **37:** 59; **62:** 343
love **1:** 543, 546, 573, 580, 587, 595, 600, 603, 610, 660; **19:** 78; **26:** 257, 364; **34:** 270, 293, 323; **46:** 291, 333, 347, 362; **51:** 30; **52:** 57; **62:** 297
madness **1:** 554, 639, 656; **26:** 371
Malvolio
  characterization **1:** 540, 544, 545, 548, 550, 554, 558, 567, 575, 577, 615; **26:** 207, 233, 273; **46:** 286; **62:** 339, 348
  forged letter **16:** 372; **28:** 1
  punishment **1:** 539, 544, 548, 549, 554, 555, 558, 563, 577, 590, 632, 645; **46:** 291, 297, 338
  as Puritan **1:** 549, 551, 555, 558, 561, 563; **25:** 47; **66:** 312
  role in play **1:** 545, 548, 549, 553, 555, 563, 567, 575, 577, 588, 610, 615, 632, 645; **26:** 337, 374; **46:** 347; **62:** 339
music **1:** 543, 566, 596
mythic or mythological elements **60:** 265, 270, 287
Olivia **1:** 540, 543, 545; **46:** 286, 333, 369; **47:** 45; **62:** 325, 343
order **1:** 563, 596; **34:** 330; **46:** 291, 347
Orsino **46:** 286, 333; **47:** 45; **62:** 343
Ovid's Metamorphoses, relation to **60:** 265, 270, 287
philosophical elements **1:** 560, 563, 596; **34:** 301, 316; **46:** 297
plot **62:** 297, 339, 343, 348
Puritanism **1:** 549, 553, 555, 632; **16:** 53; **25:** 47; **46:** 338; **66:** 312
psychoanalytic criticism **46:** 333; **62:** 348
Saturnalian elements **1:** 554, 571, 603, 620, 642; **16:** 53
Sebastian and Antonio, relations between **60:** 129
self-deception **1:** 554, 561, 591, 625; **47:** 45
self-indulgence **1:** 563, 615, 635
self-love or narcissism **60:** 265, 270, 287
sexual ambiguity and sexual deception **1:** 540, 562, 620, 621, 639, 645; **22:** 69; **34:** 311, 344; **37:** 59; **42:** 32; **62:** 319, 325
Shakespeare's canon, place in **1:** 543, 548, 557, 569, 575, 580, 621, 635, 638
Shakespeare's other plays, relation to **34:** 270; **46:** 303; **62:** 297, 308
sources **1:** 539, 540, 603; **34:** 301, 323, 344; **46:** 291; **60:** 265, 270, 287; **62:** 308
staging issues **26:** 219, 233, 257, 337, 342, 346, 357, 359, 360, 364, 366, 371, 374; **46:** 310, 369; **54:** 19
structure **1:** 539, 542, 543, 546, 551, 553, 563, 570, 571, 590, 600, 660; **26:** 374; **34:** 281, 287; **46:** 286; **62:** 308
subplot **62:** 297, 339, 343, 348
time **37:** 78; **46:** 297
tragic elements **1:** 557, 569, 572, 575, 580, 599, 621, 635, 638, 639, 645, 654, 656; **26:** 342
Viola **26:** 308; **46:** 286, 324, 347, 369; **60:** 115, 129; **62:** 308, 319, 325; **66:** 312

The Two Gentlemen of Verona (Volumes 6, 12, 40, 54)

absurdities, inconsistencies, and shortcomings **6:** 435, 436, 437, 439, 464, 507, 541, 560; **54:** 295, 311
appearance versus reality **6:** 494, 502, 511, 519, 529, 532, 549, 560
audience versus character perceptions **6:** 499, 519, 524
authorship controversy **6:** 435, 436, 437, 438, 439, 449, 466, 476
characterization **6:** 438, 442, 445, 447, 449, 458, 462, 560; **12:** 458; **40:** 312, 327, 330, 365; **54:** 338
Christian elements **6:** 438, 494, 514, 532, 555, 564
education **6:** 490, 494, 504, 526, 532, 555, 568
Elizabethan setting **12:** 463, 485
forest **6:** 450, 456, 492, 514, 547, 555, 564, 568
genre **6:** 460, 468, 472, 516; **40:** 320
identity **6:** 494, 511, 529, 532, 547, 560, 564, 568; **19:** 34
ironic or parodic elements **6:** 447, 472, 478, 484, 502, 504, 509, 516, 529, 549; **13:** 12; **54:** 295, 307
Julia or Silvia **6:** 450, 453, 458, 476, 494, 499, 516, 519, 549, 564; **40:** 312, 327, 374; **54:** 325, 332
language and imagery **6:** 437, 438, 439, 445, 449, 490, 504, 519, 529, 541; **28:** 9; **40:** 343
Launce and Speed, comic function of **6:** 438, 439, 442, 456, 458, 460, 462, 472, 476, 478, 484, 502, 504, 507, 509, 516, 519, 549; **40:** 312, 320
love **6:** 442, 445, 456, 479, 488, 492, 494, 502, 509, 516, 519, 549; **13:** 12; **40:** 327, 335, 343, 354, 365; **51:** 30, 44
love versus friendship **6:** 439, 449, 450, 458, 460, 465, 468, 471, 476, 480; **40:** 354, 359, 365; **54:** 295, 307, 325, 344
marriage **48:** 32
mimetic rivalry **13:** 12; **40:** 335; **54:** 332
morality **6:** 438, 492, 494, 514, 532, 555, 564
Proteus **6:** 439, 450, 458, 480, 490, 511; **40:** 312, 327, 330, 335, 359; **42:** 18; **54:** 325, 332
repentance and forgiveness **6:** 450, 514, 516, 555, 564
resolution **6:** 435, 436, 439, 445, 449, 453, 458, 460, 462, 465, 466, 468, 471, 476, 480, 486, 494, 509, 514, 516, 519, 529, 532, 541, 549; **19:** 34; **54:** 307, 311, 338
reversals **54:** 338
romantic and courtly conventions **6:** 438, 460, 472, 478, 484, 486, 488, 502, 507, 509, 529, 541, 549, 560, 568; **12:** 460, 462; **40:** 354, 374; **54:** 344
setting **12:** 463, 465, 485
sources **6:** 436, 460, 462, 468, 476, 480, 490, 511, 547; **19:** 34; **40:** 320; **54:** 295
staging issues **12:** 457, 464; **42:** 18
structure **6:** 445, 450, 460, 462, 504, 526
youth **6:** 439, 450, 464, 514, 568
Valentine **54:** 325, 332

The Two Noble Kinsmen (Volumes 9, 41, 50, 58)

amorality, question of **9:** 447, 460, 492
audience response **58:** 330
authorship controversy **58:** 330
  Shakespeare not a co-author **9:** 445, 447, 455, 461
  Shakespearean portions of the text **9:** 446, 447, 448, 455, 456, 457, 460, 462, 463, 471, 479, 486; **41:** 308, 317, 355; **58:** 330

Shakespeare's part in the overall conception or design **9:** 444, 446, 448, 456, 457, 460, 480, 481, 486, 490; **37:** 313; **41:** 326; **50:** 326
ceremonies, rites, and rituals, importance of **9:** 492, 498
characterization **9:** 457, 461, 471, 474; **41:** 340, 385; **50:** 305, 326
chivalry **50:** 305, 348
class distinctions, conflict and relations **50:** 295, 305, 310
Emilia **9:** 460, 470, 471, 479, 481; **19:** 394; **41:** 372, 385; **42:** 368; **58:** 322, 338, 345, 356, 361
free will versus fate **9:** 474, 481, 486, 492, 498
friendship **9:** 448, 463, 470, 474, 479, 481, 486, 490; **19:** 394; **41:** 355, 363, 372; **42:** 368; **58:** 345, 356, 371
gender issues **42:** 368; **50:** 310
innocence to experience **9:** 481, 502; **19:** 394
irony or satire **9:** 463, 481, 486; **41:** 301; **50:** 348
the jailer's daughter **9:** 457, 460, 479, 481, 486, 502; **41:** 340; **50:** 295, 305, 310, 348, 361; **58:** 338, 371
language and imagery **9:** 445, 446, 447, 448, 456, 461, 462, 463, 469, 471, 498, 502; **41:** 289, 301, 308, 317, 326; **50:** 310; **58:** 322, 330
love **9:** 479, 481, 490, 498; **41:** 289, 355, 301, 363, 372, 385; **50:** 295, 361; **58:** 345, 356, 371
marriage **58:** 338, 345, 356
masque elements **9:** 490
Palamon and Arcite **9:** 474, 481, 490, 492, 502; **50:** 295, 305, 348, 361; **58:** 322, 338, 345, 356, 361
Prologue **54:** 35
relation to Shakespeare's other romances **54:** 35
sexuality **50:** 361; **58:** 338, 345, 356
sources **19:** 394; **41:** 289, 301, 363, 385; **50:** 326, 348; **58:** 361, 371
structure **37:** 313; **50:** 326, 361; **58:** 322

Venus and Adonis (Volumes 10, 33, 51)

Adonis **10:** 411, 420, 424, 427, 429, 434, 439, 442, 451, 454, 459, 466, 473, 489; **25:** 305, 328; **28:** 355; **33:** 309, 321, 330, 347, 352, 357, 363, 370, 377; **51:** 345, 377
allegorical elements **10:** 427, 434, 439, 449, 454, 462, 480; **28:** 355; **33:** 309, 330
ambiguity **10:** 434, 454, 459, 462, 466, 473, 480, 486, 489; **33:** 352; **51:** 368, 377, 388
beauty **10:** 420, 423, 427, 434, 454, 480; **33:** 330, 352
the boar **10:** 416, 451, 454, 466, 473; **33:** 339, 347, 370; **51:** 359, 368
comic elements **51:** 377
the courser and the jennet **10:** 418, 439, 466; **33:** 309, 339, 347, 352
death, decay, and nature's destructiveness **10:** 419, 427, 434, 451, 454, 462, 466, 473, 480, 489; **25:** 305; **33:** 309, 321, 347, 352, 363, 370
dramatic elements **10:** 459, 462, 486
domesticity **51:** 359
eroticism or sensuality **10:** 410, 411, 418, 419, 427, 428, 429, 442, 448, 454, 459, 466, 473; **25:** 305, 328; **28:** 355; **33:** 321, 339, 347, 352, 363, 370; **51:** 345, 352, 359, 368
Faerie Queene (Edmund Spenser), compared with **33:** 339
forgiveness **51:** 377

Hero and Leander (Christopher Marlowe), compared with **10:** 419, 424, 429; **33:** 309, 357; **51:** 345, 377
comic elements **10:** 429, 434, 439, 442, 459, 462, 489; **33:** 352
hunt motif **10:** 434, 451, 466, 473; **33:** 357, 370
imagery **10:** 414, 415, 416, 420, 429, 434, 449, 459, 466, 473, 480; **25:** 328; **28:** 355; **33:** 321, 339, 352, 363, 370, 377; **42:** 348; **51:** 335, 388
love versus lust **10:** 418, 420, 427, 434, 439, 448, 449, 454, 462, 466, 473, 480, 489; **25:** 305; **28:** 355; **33:** 309, 330, 339, 347, 357, 363, 370; **51:** 359
morality **10:** 411, 412, 414, 416, 418, 419, 420, 423, 427, 428, 439, 442, 448, 449, 454, 459, 466; **33:** 330
negative appraisals **10:** 410, 411, 415, 418, 419, 424, 429
Ovid, compared with **32:** 352; **42:** 348; **51:** 335, 352
pictorial elements **10:** 414, 415, 419, 420, 423, 480; **33:** 339
popularity **10:** 410, 412, 418, 427; **25:** 328
procreation **10:** 439, 449, 466; **33:** 321, 377
reason **10:** 427, 439, 449, 459, 462, 466; **28:** 355; **33:** 309, 330
rhetoric **33:** 377; **51:** 335, 345, 352
Shakespeare's plays, compared with **10:** 412, 414, 415, 434, 459, 462
Shakespeare's sonnets, compared with **33:** 377
sources **10:** 410, 412, 420, 424, 429, 434, 439, 451, 454, 466, 473, 480, 486, 489; **16:** 452; **25:** 305; **28:** 355; **33:** 309, 321, 330, 339, 347, 352, 357, 370, 377; **42:** 348; **51:** 335
structure **10:** 434, 442, 480, 486, 489; **33:** 357, 377
style **10:** 411, 412, 414, 415, 416, 418, 419, 420, 423, 424, 428, 429, 439, 442, 480, 486, 489; **16:** 452
Venus **10:** 427, 429, 434, 439, 442, 448, 449, 451, 454, 466, 473, 480, 486, 489; **16:** 452; **25:** 305, 328; **28:** 355; **33:** 309, 321, 330, 347, 352, 357, 363, 370, 377; **51:** 335, 352, 377, 388
Wat the hare **10:** 424, 451

The Winter's Tale (Volumes 7, 15, 36, 45, 57)

Antigonus
 characterization **7:** 394, 451, 464
 death scene (Act III, scene iii) **7:** 377, 414, 464, 483; **15:** 518, 532; **19:** 366
appearance versus reality **7:** 429, 446, 479; **57:** 336
art versus nature **7:** 377, 381, 397, 419, 452; **36:** 289, 318; **45:** 329; **57:** 278
audience perception, Shakespeare's manipulation of **7:** 394, 429, 456, 483, 501; **13:** 417; **19:** 401, 431, 441; **25:** 339; **45:** 374
autobiographical elements **7:** 395, 397, 410, 419
Autolycus **7:** 375, 380, 382, 387, 389, 395, 396, 414; **15:** 524; **22:** 302; **37:** 31; **45:** 333; **46:** 14, 33; **50:** 45
Christian elements **7:** 381, 387, 402, 410, 417, 419, 425, 429, 436, 452, 460, 501; **36:** 318; **60:** 40
counsel **19:** 401
court society **16:** 410; **57:** 305, 336
dramatic structure **7:** 382, 390, 396, 399, 402, 407, 414, 429, 432, 473, 479, 493, 497, 501; **15:** 528; **25:** 339; **36:** 289, 295, 362, 380; **45:** 297, 344, 358, 366; **57:** 278, 285, 347
ethnicity **37:** 306
folk drama, relation to **7:** 420, 451; **57:** 356

forgiveness or redemption **7:** 381, 389, 395, 402, 407, 436, 456, 460, 483; **36:** 318
fusion of comic, tragic, and romantic elements **7:** 390, 394, 396, 399, 410, 412, 414, 429, 436, 479, 483, 490, 501; **13:** 417; **15:** 514, 524, 532; **25:** 339; **36:** 295, 380; **45:** 295, 329; **57:** 347
grace **7:** 420, 425, 460, 493; **36:** 328
Hermione
 characterization **7:** 385, 395, 402, 412, 414, 506; **15:** 495, 532; **22:** 302, 324; **25:** 347; **32:** 388; **36:** 311; **47:** 25; **49:** 18; **57:** 319
 restoration (Act V, scene iii) **7:** 377, 379, 384, 385, 387, 389, 394, 396, 412, 425, 436, 451, 452, 456, 464, 483, 501; **15:** 411, 412, 413, 518, 528, 532; **49:** 18; **57:** 294, 367; **60:** 2, 40
 supposed death **25:** 339; **47:** 25
 trial of **49:** 18
as historical allegory **7:** 381; **15:** 528
homosexuality **48:** 309
hospitality **19:** 366
irony **7:** 419, 420
Jacobean culture, relation to **19:** 366, 401, 431; **25:** 347; **32:** 388; **37:** 306; **57:** 305, 336, 356
language and imagery **7:** 382, 384, 417, 418, 420, 425, 460, 506; **13:** 409; **19:** 431; **22:** 324; **25:** 347; **36:** 295; **42:** 308; **45:** 297, 333, 344; **50:** 45; **57:** 278, 285, 319, 347
Leontes
 characterization **19:** 431; **45:** 366
 jealousy **7:** 377, 379, 382, 383, 384, 387, 389, 394, 395, 402, 407, 412, 414, 425, 429, 432, 436, 464, 480, 483, 497; **15:** 514, 518, 532; **22:** 324; **25:** 339; **36:** 334, 344, 349; **44:** 66; **45:** 295, 297, 344, 358; **47:** 25; **57:** 294
 Othello, compared with **7:** 383, 390, 412; **15:** 514; **36:** 334; **44:** 66; **47:** 25
 repentance **7:** 381, 389, 394, 396, 402, 414, 497; **36:** 318, 362; **44:** 66; **57:** 294
love **7:** 417, 425, 469, 490; **51:** 30, 33, 44
Mamillius **7:** 394, 396, 451; **22:** 324
metadramatic elements **16:** 410
myth of Demeter and Persephone, relation to **7:** 397, 436
mythic or mythological elements **60:** 254, 281
nationalism and patriotism **32:** 388
nature **7:** 397, 418, 419, 420, 425, 432, 436, 451, 452, 473, 479; **19:** 366; **45:** 329
Neoclassical rules **7:** 376, 377, 379, 380, 383, 410; **15:** 397
Ovid's Metamorphoses, relation to **42:** 308; **57:** 319, 367; **60:** 281
Pandosto, compared with **7:** 376, 377, 390, 412, 446; **13:** 409; **25:** 347; **36:** 344, 374
Paulina **7:** 385, 412, 506; **15:** 528; **22:** 324; **25:** 339; **36:** 311; **57:** 319
Perdita
 characterization **7:** 395, 412, 414, 419, 429, 432, 452, 506; **22:** 324; **25:** 339; **36:** 328
 reunion with Leontes (Act V, scene ii) **7:** 377, 379, 381, 390, 432, 464, 480
plot **7:** 376, 377, 379, 382, 387, 390, 396, 452; **13:** 417; **15:** 518; **45:** 374; **57:** 285
rebirth, regeneration, resurrection, or immortality **7:** 397, 414, 417, 419, 429, 436, 451, 452, 456, 480, 490, 497, 506; **25:** 339, 452, 480, 490, 497, 506; **45:** 366; **60:** 40
sheep-shearing scene (Act IV, scene iv) **7:** 379, 387, 395, 396, 407, 410, 412, 419, 420, 429, 432, 436, 451, 479, 490; **16:** 410; **19:** 366; **25:** 339; **36:** 362, 374; **45:** 374

sources **60:** 254, 281
staging issues **7:** 414, 425, 429, 446, 464, 480, 483, 497; **13:** 409; **15:** 518; **48:** 309
statue scene (Act V, scene iii) **7:** 377, 379, 384, 385, 387, 389, 394, 396, 412, 425, 436, 451, 456, 464, 483, 501; **15:** 411, 412, 518, 528, 532; **25:** 339, 347; **36:** 301; **57:** 294, 367; **60:** 40
subversiveness **22:** 302

symbolism **7:** 425, 429, 436, 452, 456, 469, 490, 493
textual issues **19:** 441; **45:** 333; **57:** 278, 285, 356
Time-Chorus **7:** 377, 380, 412, 464, 476, 501; **15:** 518
time **7:** 397, 425, 436, 476, 490; **19:** 366; **36:** 301, 349; **45:** 297, 329, 366, 374; **65:** 235
trickster, motif of **22:** 302; **45:** 333

Union debate, relation to **25:** 347
violence **43:** 39
witchcraft **22:** 324
women, role of **22:** 324; **36:** 311; **42:** 308; **51:** 30; **57:** 294, 305, 319, 356; **60:** 254

ISBN 0-7876-5844-8

90000